Modern P [illegible]
Analysis

Fifth Edition

Modern Power System Analysis

Fifth Edition

D.P. Kothari

BOG Chairman, THDC Institute of Hydropower Engineering and Technology, Tehri (UK), India
Former Vice Chancellor, VIT University, Vellore, Tamil Nadu, India
Former Director-in-Charge, IIT Delhi, Delhi, India
Former Principal, VRCE, Nagpur, India

I.J. Nagrath

Adjunct Professor and Former Deputy Director
Birla Institute of Technology and Science
Pilani (Rajasthan), India

R.K. Saket

Professor
Indian Institute of Technology (Banaras Hindu University)
Varanasi (Uttar Pradesh), India

McGraw Hill Education (India) Private Limited

Published by McGraw Hill Education (India) Private Limited
Registered Office: Anjana Complex No: 5/90 A, Butt Road, St. Thomas Mount, Chennai – 600016

Modern Power System Analysis, 5e

Print Edition:
ISBN (13): 978-93-5460-096-8
ISBN (10): 93-5460-096-4

E-Book Edition:
ISBN (13): 978-93-5460-097-5
ISBN (10): 93-5460-097-2

1 2 3 4 5 6 7 8 9 7101558 26 25 24 23 22

Printed and bound in India.

Managing Director: *Lalit Singh*

Director—Product: *Tanweer Ahmad*
Head—Higher Education Portfolio: *Nikhil Wadhera*
Portfolio Manager: *Navneet Kumar*
Content Developer: *Aastha Khanna*
Lead Production Services: *Atul Gupta*
Assistant Manager—Production Services: *Suhaib Ali*

General Manager—Production: *Rajender P Ghansela*
Senior Manager—Production: *Reji Kumar*

Typeset at Transcend Content Solution, 163F Jaigirghat Road, Panchanantala, Kolkata – 700 063 and printed at

Magic International Pvt. Ltd., Plot No. 26E, Sector-31, (Industrial), Site-IV, Greater Noida 201306
Cover Image Source: xuanhuongho/Shutterstock
Cover Designer: Kapil Gupta
Visit us at: www.mheducation.co.in
Write to us at: info.india@mheducation.com
CIN: U80302TN2010PTC111532
Toll Free Number: 1800 103 5875

About the Authors

Dr. D.P. Kothari obtained his B.E. in Electrical Engineering in 1967, M.E. with specialisation in Power Systems in 1969 and Ph.D. in 1975 from Birla Institute of Technology & Science, Pilani (Rajasthan) India. From 1969 to 1977, he was involved in teaching and development of several courses at BITS Pilani. Earlier, Dr. Kothari served as Vice-Chancellor, VIT, Vellore; Director in-charge and Deputy Director (Administration) as well as Head in the Centre of Energy Studies at IIT, Delhi; and as Principal, VRCE, Nagpur, India. He was visiting professor at the Royal Melbourne Institute of Technology, Melbourne, Australia, during 1982–83 and 1989, for two years. He was also NSF Fellow at Perdue University, USA, in 1992. He also taught at Melbourne University Australia for one semester in 1989. Dr. Kothari, who is a recipient of the most Active Researcher Award, has published and presented 830 research papers in various national as well as international journals, conferences, guided 56 Ph.D. scholars and 68 M.Tech. students, and has authored 68 books in various allied areas. He has delivered several keynote addresses, more than 100 Webinars and invited lectures at both national and international conferences. He has also delivered 42 video lectures on YouTube with a maximum of 100,000 hits!

Dr. Kothari is a Fellow of the National Academy of Engineering (FNAE), Fellow of Indian National Academy of Science (FNASc), Fellow of Institution of Engineers (FIE), Fellow IEEE, Hon. Fellow ISTE and Fellow IETE. Having received 77 awards till now, his many awards include the National Khosla Award for Lifetime Achievements in Engineering (2005) from IIT, Roorkee. The University Grants Commission (UGC), Government of India, has bestowed the UGC National Swami Pranavandana Saraswati Award (2005) in the field of education for his outstanding scholarly contributions. He is also the recipient of the Lifetime Achievement Award (2009) conferred by the World Management Congress, New Delhi, for his contribution to the areas of educational planning and administration. He received Excellent Academic Award at IIT Guwahati by NPSC-2014.

He has received six Life Time Achievement awards by various agencies on 19th February, 4th March, 11th March, 18th March, 20th March and 25th March 2016, respectively. On 20th April 2016, he received 'Living Legend' Award in Chennai Conference. Recently, he received 'Malviya Award for Excellence in Power System' conferred by IIT (BHU) during the NPSC at IIT Gandhinagar on December 17, 2020. Dr. Kothari is also distinguished Emeritus Professor and adjunct professor at several institutes such as Charutar University Gujrat and Wainganga College of Engineering, Nagpur. Currently, Dr. Kothari is with S.B. Jain Institute of Management, Research and Technology, Nagpur, serving as Director Research and Professor. He is also Chairman of Board of Governors of THDC Institute of Hydropower Engineering and Technology, Tehri, India.

Wikipedia Link: http://en.wikipedia.org/wiki/D.P.Kothari

Professor I.J. Nagrath obtained his B.E. with honours in Electrical Engineering from Birla Engineering College in 1951 and M.S. from the University of Wisconsin, USA, in 1956. He was Adjunct Professor with the Department of Electrical and Electronics Engineering at Birla Institute of Technology and Science, Pilani (Rajasthan) India. He retired as a Professor of Electrical Engineering, Administrative Dean and Deputy Director of BITS Pilani (Rajasthan) in July 1999. Dr. Nagrath has co-authored several successful books, which include *Electric Machines, Power System Engineering, Modern Power System Analysis, Basic Electrical Engineering, Signals and Systems: Modelling and Analysis, and Modern Control Systems*. He has guided 10 Ph.D. scholars and 40 M.Tech. students with several research publications in prestigious national and international journals and reputed conference proceedings. His research interest includes power system engineering, electrical machines and drives, modern industrial control systems, power system reliability, and reliability evaluation of electric power components and systems.

Dr. R.K. Saket is currently a Professor with the Department of Electrical Engineering, Indian Institute of Technology (Banaras Hindu University) Varanasi (UP), India. Previously, he was a faculty member at Government Engineering College, Rewa (MP), India; Birla Institute of Technology and Science, Pilani (Rajasthan), India; Sam Higginbottom University of Agriculture, Technology and Sciences, Allahabad (UP), India, and University Institute of Technology, Rajiv Gandhi University of Technology, Bhopal (MP), India. He has provided his industrial services to Electrical Safety Division of the M.P. Electricity Board, Government of Madhya Pradesh, Ujjain Division (MP), India, as an Electrical Safety Engineer. He has more than twenty years of academic, industrial and research experience. He is the author/co-author of approximately 160 scientific articles, book chapters and research papers in indexed international journals and prestigious conference proceedings. He has supervised 12 Ph.D. research scholars and 50 M.Tech. students. He has delivered many technical talks and honoured as a resource person of the power system reliability engineering. He has delivered his academic and research lecture(s) at World Academy of Science, Engineering & Technology, Paris (France) on September 21–23, 2014; International Theravada University, Yangon (Myanmar) on December 02–04, 2014; Thammasat University, Bangkok (Thailand) on January 21–23, 2017; and Tokyo City University, Tokyo (Japan) on March 09–11, 2018. He has visited many countries including France, Nepal, Myanmar, Thailand and Japan. His research interests include reliability engineering, electrical machines and drives, power system reliability, reliability enhancement of industrial components and systems, and reliability aspects in renewable energy systems.

Prof. Saket is a Fellow of the Institution of Engineers (India), Senior Member of IEEE (USA), Member of IET (UK) and a Life Member of the Indian Society for Technical Education, New Delhi (India). He is an Associate Editor of the *IET Renewable Power Generation (UK), IET Electrical Systems in Transportation (UK)*, and *IEEE Access (USA)*. He is an Editorial Board Member of the *Journal of Electrical Systems (France)*, and *Engineering, Technology and Applied Science Research (Greece)*. He has received many awards, honours and recognitions for his academic and research contributions, including the prestigious Gandhian Young Technological Innovation Award–2018 appreciated by the Hon'ble President of India at Rashtrapati Bhavan, New Delhi, India; Design Impact Award–2018 by Padma Vibhushan Ratan Tata at Mumbai, India, and Nehru Encouragement Award–1988 and 1990 by the Hon'ble Chief Minister of M.P. State Government, Bhopal, India.

To my wife
Shobha
—D.P. Kothari

To my wife
Pushpa
—I.J. Nagrath

To my wife
Sparsh
—R.K. Saket

Contents

Content Available on the Online Learning Center

Preface to the Fifth Edition

Modern power systems have grown larger and spread over larger geographical areas with many interconnections between neighbouring systems. Optimal planning, reliability evaluation, operation and control of such large-scale systems require advanced computer-based techniques, many of which are explained in student-oriented and reader-friendly manner by means of the numerical examples throughout this book. Electric utility engineers will also be benefitted by fifth edition of the book, as it will prepare those more adequately to face the new challenges. The excellent response to the fourth edition by both students and academicians of Indian and foreign universities and also by the practising engineers has encouraged us to bring out the fifth edition to include the latest developments in the field of power system engineering. Each edition of this book has embodied many changes; however, the main objective has remained the same. The wide range of topics facilitate versatile selection of chapters and sections for completion in the semester time frame. Footnotes and references throughout the book suggest sources of further information on most of the topics presented.

Modern Power System Analysis has been written primarily (first edition: 1980, second edition: 1989, third edition 2003, fourth edition: 2011 and fifth edition: 2022) for the undergraduate students in Electrical Engineering of Indian and foreign universities. The book covers conventional topics like the line constant calculation, performance of lines etc. and the more advanced topics like load flow studies, economic load dispatch, load frequency control, power system reliability, future grid etc. Since the appearance of the fourth edition in 2011, the overall energy situation has changed considerably and this has generated great interest in nonconventional and renewable energy sources, energy conservation and management, power reforms and restructuring and distributed and dispersed generation. As a consequence, a sizable portion of the existing content had to be expanded and rewritten. Two teaching appendices power system reliability and future grid of the fourth edition have now been rewritten as full-fledged chapters, since these topics continue to be important parts of the curriculum and innovative research work. We hope that undergraduate/postgraduate students, research scholars and faculty members will welcome these aspects.

Salient Features of This Edition

- Recent developments in the area of power systems.
- Computational algorithms for various system studies.
- Current and future Indian and World energy scenario.
- Comprehensive descriptions of biggest thermal, hydroelectric, solar and wind power stations of India.
- New chapters on power system reliability and future grid, without which power system courses cannot be complete for innovative research enhancements and comprehensive analysis of modern power systems.
- A large number of new teaching appendices with latest reference materials.
- Large number of solved examples and unsolved problems with answers at the end of each chapter for practice and self-evaluation.

- A large number of multiple-choice questions with answers at the end of each chapter have been added, so that the students can prepare better for the competitive examinations.
- MATLAB and SIMULINK programs along with 18 solved examples illustrating their use in solving representative power system problems.
- An extensive bibliography to help the academicians and researchers to locate detailed information on various topics and chapters of their interest.

Chapter Organisation

The fifth edition of this book consists of 21 chapters and 14 appendices. The present edition contains all the major topics covered in the fourth edition. The highlight of this edition lies in the additions and changes that have been brought about in all the chapters and appendices, in an attempt to keep students up-to-date with their study. Therefore, chapter 1 has been enlarged and completely rewritten with incorporation of the latest energy scenario and industrial enhancements up to 2021. The main highlights of this edition are the two new chapters. Chapter 20 covers the important topic on modern aspects of future grid. This chapter describes importance and road map of the future grid. Optimisation of smart grid with integration of renewables and energy storage systems are illustrated. Information and communication technology, measurement and automation, and importance of power electronics have been described in detail in this chapter.

Chapter 21 deals with power system reliability. The historical background and comprehensive importance of reliability engineering are described in this chapter. The basic concepts of reliability, such as distribution of power components, reliability analysis of composite power system structure, failure distribution functions, generation capacity, reliability evaluation, loss of load probability, combined generation – transmission reliability aspects and distribution system reliability evaluation are described in detail in this new chapter.

The fifth edition also contains appendices that elaborate on the important concepts covered in the chapters. Thus, Appendices A to P have been retained from the fourth edition, with some minor additions to the existing content and reference materials. Appendices G and N of the fourth edition related to 'Some Aspects of Smart Grid' and 'Power System Reliability Studies', respectively, have been converted into new chapters.

In addition, the book also contains a set of enhanced pedagogical features such as summary, solved examples and problems, and multiple-choice questions that will help students in understanding and evaluating the concepts of modern power system engineering.

Online Content

Additional learning material in the form of Appendices and Answer to Problems have been provided. This material is easily accessible online. [For List of Appendices, refer to *Contents*]

Other instructor resources that can be found on https://connect.mheducation.com

- Solutions Manual
- Chapter-wise PPT

How to Use the Book?

With all the said features, this is an indispensable text for electrical engineering UG/PG students and Doctoral research scholars. AMIE, GATE, state PSC examinations, UPSC Engineering Services (IES), UPSC Civil Services (IAS, IPS, IFS etc.) and other PG entrance exams aspirants, along with practicing engineers would also find this book extremely valuable as a text/reference book. It can also be used for scoring high at the entry-level examinations for multinational companies and Indian public sectors such as BHEL, NTPC, and Power Grid.

The present fifth edition, like the earlier four, is designed for several undergraduate power system courses and for a two-semester postgraduate study. The book covers a very wide spectrum of electrical power systems studies which is normally not available in one single book. The book is so comprehensively written that at least three courses on power systems can be designed. A first-level postgraduate course may be taught from chapter 1 (selected sections), Chapters 6, 7, 8, Sections 9.6, 9.7, 11.7, Chapters 12, 13, 14, 15, 16, 17, 18, 19, 20, 21 and Appendices F, G, H, J, K, L, M and N. For undergraduate courses, a combination of chapters may be chosen depending on the syllabus of a university and type of the course.

Acknowledgements

While revising this text, we have had the benefit of valuable advice and suggestions from many academicians, research scholars, postgraduate students, practicing engineers and other readers who used the earlier editions of this book. All these individuals have influenced this edition. We express our thanks and appreciation to them. The publishers and authors gratefully acknowledge the suggestions and also express their appreciation for all those reviewers who took out time to review the book. We hope this support and response would continue in the future also. We also thank our publishers McGraw-Hill (India) Pvt. Ltd., New Delhi, our family members and well-wishers who supported us during this pandemic period and for providing all possible help so that this book could see the light of the day.

Authors' and Publisher's Note

The response received from the readers in the last four editions has been overwhelming. In keeping with the standards and the quality, it will encourage us to receive your comments, compliments and ideas on this present edition. Please write to us at *info.india@mheducation.com* by mentioning the title and the author's name along with your feedback. We welcome any constructive criticism of the book and will be grateful for an appraisal by the readers. The constructive suggestions for improvement of the book can be sent to *dpkvits@gmail.com* and *rksaket@ieee.org*. As always, we have profited by the letters and emails from users of past editions. We hope these correspondences will continue in the future.

D.P. Kothari
R.K. Saket

Preface to the Fourth Edition

Since the appearance of the third edition in 2007, a sea-change has occurred in the energy and power sectors. As a consequence, a sizable portion of the existing content had to be expanded and rewritten. A large number of teaching appendices of the third edition have now been rewritten as full-fledged chapters, since all these topics continue to be important parts of the curriculum. We hope students and teachers will welcome this.

Salient Features and New to this Edition

- Recent developments in the area of power system.
- Computational algorithms for various system studies.
- Current and future Indian/World energy scenario.
- New chapters on power system transients and HVDC, without which power system courses cannot be taught. The chapter on power system transients also deals with insulation co-ordination, lightning phenomena and neutral grounding. Without studying HVDC, electric power transmission is incomplete. Knowledge of power electronics, AC/DC conversion, working of converters actually help in understanding this vital chapter.
- A large number of new teaching appendices.
- Large number of solved examples and unsolved problems with answers at the end of each chapter for practice and self evaluation.
- A large number of multiple-choice questions with answers at the end of each chapter have been added.

MATLAB and SIMULINK programs along with 18 solved examples illustrating their use in solving representative power system problems.

Chapter Organisation

The book consists of 19 chapters and 16 appendices. The present edition contains all the major topics covered in the third edition. The highlight of this edition lies in the additions and changes that have been brought about in the following chapters and appendices, in an attempt to keep students up-to-date with their study.

Therefore, **Chapter 1** has been enlarged and completely rewritten. In addition, the influences of environmental constraints are also discussed. In **Chapters 2** and **3**, magnetic field induction and electrostatic induction have been added, respectively. In **Chapter 4**, a few sections/topics such as power transformer have been added. In **Chapter 5**, voltage control topic has been boosted by including control by midline boosters. Two appendices, K and I of the first edition on lightning phenomenon and neutral grounding, have now been brought in the main chapters as per the wishes of readers for completeness and clarity. In **Chapter 6**, load flow under power electronic control, that is, AC-DC-LF has been added. In **Chapter 7**, maintenance scheduling, power system reliability, have been included. For the first time, unit commitment has been further elaborated as an appendix to **Chapter 7**. In **Chapter 8**, AGC of restructured power system is added, keeping in line with the latest changes in the power sector. **Chapters 9** to **13** contain topics covered in the third edition with certain new contents that have been added to keep students abreast with the latest developments. In **Chapter 14**, new topics such as isolators, fuses and contractors, kilometric faults have now been included as per the review reports. In **Chapter 15**, numerical (digital) relay has now been introduced along with new trends. Large portions of **Chapters 16** to **19** have been rewritten along with new content added to the existing ones.

The fourth edition also contains appendices that elaborate on the important concepts covered in the chapters. Thus, **appendices A** to **G** have been retained from the third edition, with some minor additions to the existing content. **Appendix H** deals with 'Smart Grid' which is essential for present day smart student and teacher. **Appendix I** discusses the topic of 'Substations' including intelligent substation. **Appendix J** throws light on convergence of load flow methods which are bread and butter of any power system study. **Appendix K** deals with 'Power Quality' which is must for a power engineer. **Appendix L** discusses recent trends in power system communication without which no power system can exist. **Appendix M** deals with 'restructured power system'. Power system reliability is described in **Appendix N**. This is a prerequisite for topics like Unit Commitment (Chapter 7) and Maintenance Scheduling (**Appendix P**). A separate appendix, **Appendix O** on minimum emission generation scheduling/ emission control has also been added.

In addition, the book also contains a set of enhanced pedagogical features like, **summary**, **solved examples** and **problems**, and **multiple-choice questions** that will help students in understanding and evaluating the concepts.

How to Use the Book

With all these features, this is an indispensable text for electrical engineering UG/PG/Doctoral students. AMIE, GATE, UPSC engineering services, IAS and other PG entrance exams aspirants, along with practicing engineers would also find this book extremely valuable as a text/reference book. It can also be used for scoring high at the entry level examinations for multinationals such as BHEL, NTPC and Power Grid.

The present fourth edition, like the earlier three is designed for several undergraduate power system courses and for a two-semester postgraduate study.

A first level PG course may be taught from Chapter 1(selected sections), chapters 6, 7, 8, sections 9.6, 9.7, 11.7, chapters 12,13,14,15,16,17,18,19 and appendices F,G,H,J,K,L,M,N,O and P. For UG courses, a combination of chapters may be chosen depending on the syllabus of a university and type of the course.

Acknowledgements

While revising this text, we have had the benefit of valuable advice and suggestions from many teachers, students and other readers who used the earlier editions of this book. All these individuals have influenced this edition. We hope this support/response would continue in future also.

We are grateful to the authorities of VIT University, Vellore and Vindhya Group of Institutions, Indore, for providing all the facilities for writing the book.

The publishers and authors would like to thank and also express their appreciation for all those reviewers who took out time to review the book. Their names are given as follows.

S.N. Singh	*Indian Institute of Technology, Kanpur, Uttar Pradesh*
Hari Om Gupta	*Indian Institute of Technology, Roorkee, Uttarakhand*
K.R. Niazi	*Malviya National Institute of Technology, Jaipur, Rajasthan*
Ashwani Chandel	*National Institute of Technology, Hamirpur, Himachal Pradesh*
Ashwani Kumar	*National Institute of Technology, Kurukshetra, Haryana*
Manoj Nair	*Jai Narain College of Technology, Bhopal, Madhya Pradesh*
Sankar Mahato	*National Institute of Technology, Durgapur, West Bengal*
Ashoke Kumar Basu	*Calcutta Institute of Engineering and Management, West Bengal*
S.A. Soman	*Indian Institute of Technology, Bombay, Maharashtra*
R.P. Hasbe	*Walchand Engineering College, Sangli, Maharashtra*
M. Ammiraju	*Murthy Institute of Engineering and Technology Hyderabad, Andhra Pradesh*
G. Srinivas	*Hasvitha Institute of Engineering and Technology, Andhra Pradesh*
M.S. Raviprakasha	*Malnad College of Engineering, Hassan, Karnataka*
S. Krishna	*Indian Institute of Technology, Madras, Tamil Nadu*
Subha Puttankuttil	*National Institute of Technology, Calicut, Kerala*
Pratibha P.K.	*Rajagiri School of Engineering and Technology, Kochi, Kerala*
M.P. Selvan	*National Institute of Technology, Tiruchirapalli, Tamil Nadu*
M. Venkata Kirthiga	*National Institute of Technology, Tiruchirapalli, Tamil Nadu*
Saina Deepthi	*Rajiv Gandhi Institute of Technology, Tamil Nadu*

We also thank our publishers, i.e., Tata McGraw Hill Education Pvt. Ltd., and our families who supported us during this period and for providing all possible help so that this book could see the light of the day.

Special Note from Dr Kothari

Dr. Kothari wishes to thank his colleagues—Mr. K. Palanisamy, Mr. Dilip Debnath, Mr. B. Saravanan, Dr. Jayaprakash, GCEK, Kerala, Prof. L.D. Arya, Dr. S.C. Srivastava, Mrs. C. Rani, Mrs. Vijayapriya, Dr. Manojkumar Maharana, Dr. Meikandasivam, Dr. Subir Sen of Power Grid, Mr. K.P. Singh of NPTI, Faridabad, Dr. Shekar Kelapure GE, Mr. S. Prabhakar Karthikeyan, Mr. K. Sathishkumar, Mr. Periyaswamy, Dr. Sunil Bhat, Dr. Ram Narayan Patel, Dr. Vijay Kumar, Mrs. R. Deepa, Miss. Khushnam, Mr. Rahul, Mr. Rakesh, Miss. Shweta, Miss. Mahima, Mr. Hemendra Khedekar and

Mr. Paramasivam for their help in preparing and typing rough drafts of certain portions of the manuscript, writing MATLAB programs and solving problems using Simulink (MATLAB) and for helping in preparing the solutions of examples and unsolved problems of certain chapters.

Feedback

We welcome any constructive criticism of the book and will be grateful for an appraisal by the readers. The suggestions can be sent to *dpk0710@yahoo.com*

D.P. Kothari
I.J. Nagrath

Publisher's Note

The response received from the readers in the last four editions has been overwhelming. In keeping with the standards and the quality, it will encourage us to receive your comments/ compliments/ ideas on this present edition. Please write to us at *info.india@mheducation.com* by mentioning the title and the author's name along with your feedback. Report of any piracy related problems will be highly appreciated, both by the author and the publisher.

CHAPTER 1

Introduction

1.1 ▶ ELECTRIC POWER SYSTEM

We are in need of energy for our industrial, commercial and day-to-day activities, and we use energy in different forms. Out of all the forms of energy, electric energy is the most important one as it can be generated efficiently, transmitted easily and utilised ultimately at a very reasonable cost. The ease of transmission of electric energy gives rise to a possibility of generating electric energy in bulk at a centralised place and transmit it over a long distance to be used ultimately by a large number of users. If we generate in small scale, say for example, just to light a house, we can perhaps intuitively make the connections needed for a reasonably reliable and efficient operation. But when we have generation in bulk, transmission over a long distance and utilisation by a number of distributed users; we cannot do by intuition. We need to follow systematic methodology to have reliable, efficient, economic and safe use of electric energy. The components needed for generation, transmission and large-scale distribution of electric energy form a huge complex system termed as *Electric Power System*. Power system is the branch of Electrical Engineering where we study in depth for its design, analysis, operation, control, stability, reliability and maintenance. The power plant, power transformer, transmission lines, substations, distribution lines and distribution transformer are main components of the composite power system.

Electric power systems are a technical wonder and as per one opinion, electricity and its accessibility are the greatest engineering achievements of the 20th century, ahead of computers and airplanes. A modern society cannot exist without electricity. As will be explained in Sections 1.17 and 1.18, today's centralised (regulated) utilities will be distributed (deregulated) when already utilities (SEBs) have been forced to breakup in separate generation, transmission and distribution companies. The company provides a versatile and robust range of solutions for connecting and evacuating power from generation sources onto the grid, providing utilities with the tools needed to support the increase in demand swiftly. There is distributed generation (DG) by independent power producers (IPP), who can generate electric power by whatever means and must be allowed open access to the power grid to sell power to consumers. The breakup has been encouraged by tremendous benefits of deregulation in communication and airline industries resulting in fierce competition leading to economy and better consumer service. In India, some states are pursuing this deregulation and unbundling aggressively and some more cautiously. The aim is that the independent Transmission System Operators (TSO) wheel power for a charge from anywhere and anyone to the customer site. The TSO is an entity entrusted with transporting energy in the form of electrical power on a national or regional level using fixed infrastructure. The reliable operation is ensured by the TSOs and the financial transactions are governed by real time bidding to buy and sell power to earn profit (buying at lower prices and selling at higher prices) in the spot market. Safety and reliability are a critical issue for TSOs, since any failure on their grid or their electrical generation sources might propagate to a very large number of customers, causing personal and property damages. Natural hazards and generation/consumption imbalances are a major cause of concern. To minimise the probability of grid instability and failure, regional or national transmission system operators are interconnected to each other.

1.2 ► INDIAN POWER SECTOR

1.2.1 Historical Background

Sidrapong Hydroelectric Power Station, located at the foothills of Arya Tea Estate 12 km from Darjeeling town, is the oldest hydroelectric power plant in India commissioned on 10 November 1897. The first plant consisted of two 65 kW Crompton–Brunton single-phase, 2300 volt 83.3 Hz alternators coupled with two Gunther's turbines. Its original capacity was 2 × 65 kW, which was expanded in phases for increased demands to a total 1000 kW in 1916. In 1931, the seven old machines of the single-phase system were replaced with five 200 kW units in the new three-phase system, one of them at the Lower Power House and four at the higher Jubilee Power House. At the time of independence, total installed capacity was 1360 MW (mostly owned by private companies in cities). After the enactment of Electricity Act in 1948, barring few licenses, the entire power sector was owned by state governments and largely managed by vertically integrated State Electricity Boards (SEBs). In 1975, Central Government, through Central Public Sector Undertakings, (NTPC, etc.) also entered in the field of Generation and Transmission to supplement the efforts of cash starved State Electricity Boards. In 1989, Power Grid Corporation of India was formed to develop the transmission network and grid. In 1990, first HVDC bi-pole line was made operative. In 1990, power generation was opened to private sector. In 1998, Electricity Regulatory Commission Act was enacted for establishing Regulatory Commissions. Tariff is now obtained through competitive bidding to be adopted by the regulator. Congestion is managed by e-bidding.

In 1998, first 765 kV transmission line was erected which was initially charged at 400 kV. In 2003, Electricity Act 2003 was enacted to have open access in transmission. In 2005–06, National Electricity Plan was finalised. In 2006, a big step was taken for formulation of national grid [Fig. 1.1(a)] by way of synchronisation of NR with ER-NER-WR. The first interconnection of regional grids was established in October 1991 when the north-eastern and eastern grids were interconnected. The western grid was interconnected with these grids in March 2003. The northern grid was also interconnected in August 2006, forming a central grid that was synchronously connected and operating at one frequency. The sole remaining regional grid, the southern grid, was synchronously interconnected to the central grid on 31 December 2013 with the commissioning of the 765 kV Raichur–Solapur transmission line, establishing the national grid. In 2010–11, 800 kV HVDC bi-pole line will start operating. Challenge is evacuation of power along with generation addition and also from surplus to deficit area. India is the world's third largest producer and third largest consumer of electricity. The national electric grid in India has an installed capacity of 371.977 GW as of 31 July 2020. Renewable power plants, which also include large hydroelectric plants, constitute 35.94% of India's total installed capacity. During the 2018–19 fiscal year, the gross electricity generated by utilities in India was 1,372 TWh and the total electricity generation (utilities and non-utilities) in the country was 1,547 TWh. The gross electricity consumption in 2018–19 was 1,181 kWh per capita. In 2015–16, electric energy consumption in agriculture was recorded as being the highest (17.89%) worldwide. The per capita electricity consumption is low compared to most other countries despite India having a low electricity tariff. India has a surplus power generation capacity but lacks adequate distribution infrastructure. To address this, the Government of India launched a program called "Power for All" in 2016. The program was accomplished by December 2018 in providing the necessary infrastructure to ensure uninterrupted electricity supply to all households, industries, and commercial establishments. India's electricity sector is dominated by fossil fuels, in particular coal, which

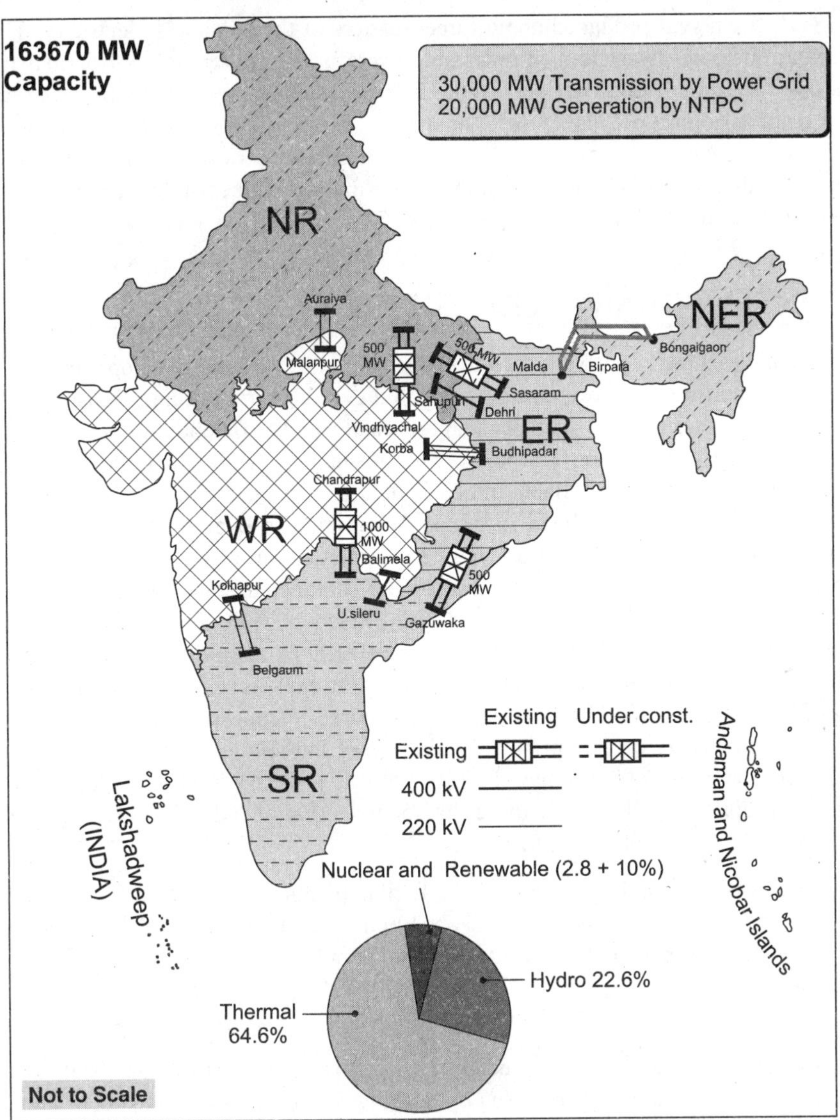

Installed transmission lines and distribution capacity (MVA) as on **31 July 2020**

Sr. No.	Capacity	Substations (MVA)	Transmission Lines (circuit km)	Circuit km/MVA Ratio
1	HVDC ± 220 kV and above	22,500	15,556	0.691
2	765 kV	197,500	36,673	0.185
3	400 kV	292,292	173,172	0.707
4	220 kV	335,696	170,748	0.592
5	220 kV and above	847,988	396,149	0.467

Fig. 1.1(a) *Development of Indian Grid*

during the 2018–19 fiscal year produced about three-quarters of the country's electricity. The government is making efforts to increase investment in renewable energy. The government's National Electricity Plan of 2018 states that the country does not need more non-renewable power plants in the utility sector until 2027, with the commissioning of 50,025 MW coal-based power plants under construction and addition of 275,000 MW total renewable power capacity after the retirement of nearly 48,000 MW old coal-fired plants. It is expected that non-fossil fuels generation contribution is likely to be around 44.7% of the total gross electricity generation by the year 2029–30.

1.3 ► A CONTEMPORARY PERSPECTIVE

Electric energy is an essential ingredient for the industrial and all-round development of any country. It is a coveted form of energy, because it can be generated centrally in bulk and transmitted economically over long distances. Furthermore, it can be adapted easily and efficiently to domestic and industrial applications, particularly for lighting purposes and mechanical work*, e.g., drives. The per capita consumption of electrical energy is a reliable indicator of a country's state of development—The per capita electricity consumption in India has been increasing continuously over the last decade because of the significant improvement in electrification of villages. Electrification of remote villages is still a priority item on the agenda of successive governments. India's per capita electricity consumption is lowest among the BRICS nations. It is also about 1/3rd the world's average per capita electricity consumption. During the 2018–19 fiscal year, the gross electricity generated by utilities in India was 1,372 TWh and the total electricity generation (utilities and non-utilities) in the country was 1,547 TWh. The gross electricity consumption in 2018–19 was 1,181 kWh per capita. Compared to some of the developed countries of the world, the per capita electricity consumption in India is very low. India's per capita consumption is 1/3rd of the world average and is just 10% of that of Australia. It is just 7.5% that of USA and 6.6% of Canada. The per capita consumption in UK also is more than 5 times that of India. The average power per capita was calculated according to the following formula.

$$\text{Electric energy per capita (in watt-hour)} = [\text{Total population electricity consumption (in kW-h/yr)} \times 1000]/\text{population}$$

$$\text{Electric power per capita (in watt)} = [\text{Total population electricity consumption (in kW-h/yr)} \times 0.114077116]/\ \text{population}$$

$$1\ \text{kW-h/yr} = 1000\ \text{Wh}/(365.25 \times 24)\text{h} = 0.11408\ \text{Watt.}$$

Conventionally, electric energy is obtained by conversion from fossil fuels (coal, oil, natural gas), nuclear and hydro sources. Heat energy released by burning fossil fuels or by fission of nuclear material is converted to electricity by first converting heat energy to the mechanical form through a thermocycle and then converting mechanical energy through generators to the electrical form. Thermocycle is basically a low efficiency process—highest efficiencies for modern large size plants range up to 40%, while smaller plants may have considerably lower efficiencies. The earth has fixed nonreplenishable resources of fossil fuels and nuclear materials, with certain countries overendowed by nature while others deficient. Hydro energy, though replenishable, is also limited in terms of power. The world's increasing power requirements can only be partially met by hydro sources. Furthermore, ecological and biological factors

* Electricity is a very inefficient agent for heating purposes, because it is generated by the low efficiency thermocycle

place a stringent limit on the use of hydro sources for power production. The USA has already developed around 50% of its hydro potential and hardly any further expansion is planned because of ecological considerations.

With the ever increasing per capita energy consumption and exponentially rising population, technologists already see the end of the earth's nonreplenishable fuel resources.† The oil crisis of the 1970s has dramatically drawn attention to this fact. In fact, we can no longer afford to use oil as a fuel for generation of electricity. In terms of bulk electric energy generation, a distinct shift is taking place across the world in favour of coal and in particular nuclear sources for generation of electricity. Also, the problems of air and thermal pollution caused by power generation have to be efficiently tackled to avoid ecological disasters. A coordinated worldwide action plan is, therefore, necessary to ensure that energy supply to humanity at large is assured for a long time and at low economic cost. Some of the factors to be considered and actions to be taken are

Curtailment of Energy Consumption The energy consumption of most developed countries has already reached a level, which this planet cannot afford. There is, in fact, a need to find ways and means of reducing this level. The developing countries, on the other hand, have to intensify their efforts to raise their level of energy production to provide basic amenities to their teeming millions. Of course, in doing so they need to constantly draw upon the experiences of the developed countries and guard against obsolete technology.

Intensification of Efforts to Develop Alternative Sources of Energy including Unconventional Sources like Solar, Tidal Energy, etc. Distant hopes are pitched on fusion energy but the scientific and technological advances have a long way to go in this regard. Fusion when harnessed could provide an inexhaustible source of energy. A breakthrough in the conversion from solar to electric energy could provide another answer to the world's steeply rising energy needs. Rewa Ultra Mega Solar is the first solar project in the country to break the grid parity barrier. It is one of the largest solar power plants in India and Asia's largest single site solar plant. It is an operational ground mounted, grid-connected photovoltaic solar park spread over an area of 1,590 acres (6.4 km2) in the Gurh tehsil of Rewa district of Madhya Pradesh. The project was commissioned with 750 MW capacity in December 2019.

Recycling of Nuclear Wastes Fast breeder reactor technology is expected to provide the answer for extending nuclear energy resources to last much longer. Nuclear waste is recyclable. Once reactor fuel (uranium or thorium) is used in a reactor, it can be treated and put into another reactor as fuel. In fact, typical reactors only extract a few percent of the energy in their fuel.

Development and Application of Antipollution Technologies In this regard, the developing countries already have the example of the developed countries whereby they can avoid going through the phases of intense pollution in their programmes of energy development. Bulk power generating stations are more easily amenable to control the pollution since centralised one-point measures can be adopted.

Electric energy today constitutes about 30% of the total annual energy consumption on a worldwide basis. This figure is expected to rise as oil supply for industrial uses becomes more stringent. Transportation

† Varying estimates have been put forth for reserves of oil, gas and coal and fissionable materials. At the projected consumption rates, oil and gases are not expected to last much beyond 50 years; several countries will face serious shortages of coal after 2200 A.D. while fissionable materials may carry us well beyond the middle of the next century. These estimates, however, cannot be regarded as highly dependable.

can be expected to go electric in a big way in the long run, when nonconventional energy resources are well developed or a breakthrough in fusion is achieved.

To understand some of the problems that the power industry faces let us briefly review some of the characteristic features of generation and transmission. Electricity, unlike water and gas, cannot be stored economically (except in very small quantities—in batteries), and the electric utility can exercise little control over the load (power demand) at any time. The power system must, therefore, be capable of matching the output from generators to the demand at any time at a specified voltage and frequency. The difficulty encountered in this task can be imagined from the fact that load variations over a day comprise three components—a steady component known as *base load*; a varying component whose daily pattern depends upon the time of day; weather, season, a popular festival, etc., and a purely randomly varying component of relatively small amplitude. Figure 1.1(b) shows a typical daily load curve. The characteristics of a daily load curve on a gross basis are indicated by *peak load*, and the time of its occurrence and *load factor* defined as

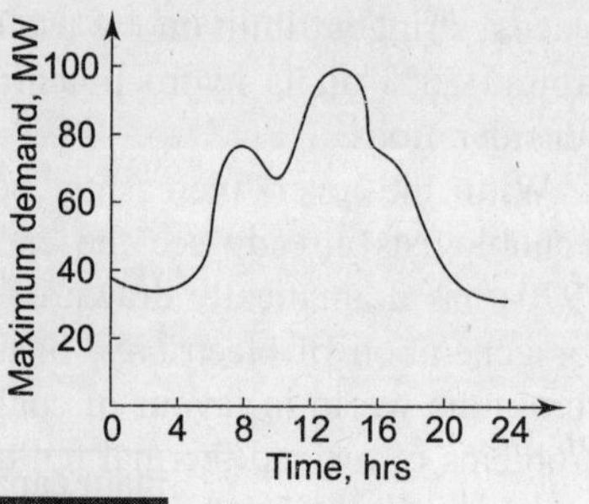

Fig. 1.1(b) *Typical daily load curve*

$$\frac{\text{average load}}{\text{maximum (peak) load}} = \text{Load Factor (less than unity)}$$

The average load determines the energy consumption over the day, while the peak load along with considerations of standby capacity determines plant capacity for meeting the load.

A high load factor helps in drawing more energy from a given installation. As individual load centres have their own characteristics, their peaks in general have a time diversity, which when utilised through transmission interconnection, greatly aids in jacking up load factors at an individual plant—excess power of a plant during light load periods is evacuated through long distance high voltage transmission lines, while a heavily loaded plant receives power.

1.3.1 Diversity Factor

This is defined as the sum of individual maximum demands on the consumers, divided by the maximum load on the system. This factor gives the time diversification of the load and is used to decide the installation of sufficient generating and transmission plant. If all the demands came at the same time, i.e., unity diversity factor, the total installed capacity required would be much more. Luckily, the factor is much higher than unity, especially for domestic loads.

A high diversity factor could be obtained by

1. Giving incentives to farmers and/or some industries to use electricity in the night or light load periods.
2. Using day-light saving as in many other countries.
3. Staggering the office timings.
4. Having different time zones in the country like USA, Australia, etc.
5. Having two-part tariff in which consumer has to pay an amount dependent on the maximum demand he makes, plus a charge for each unit of energy consumed. Sometimes consumer is charged on the basis of kVA demand instead of kW to penalise loads of low power factor.

Two other factors used frequently are

$$\textit{Plant capacity factor} = \frac{\text{Actual energy produced}}{\text{maximum possible energy that could have been produced (based on installed plant capacity)}}$$

$$= \frac{\text{Average demand}}{\text{Installed capacity}}$$

$$\textit{Plant use factor} = \frac{\text{Actual energy produced (kWh)}}{\text{plant capacity (kW)} \times \text{Time (in hours) the plant has been in operation}}$$

Tariffs The cost of electric power is normally given by the expression ($a + b \times \text{kW} + c \times \text{kWh}$) per annum, where a is a fixed charge for the utility, independent of the power output; b depends on the maximum demand on the system and hence on the interest and depreciation on the installed power station; and c depends on the units produced and therefore on the fuel charges and the wages of the station staff.

Tariff structures may be such as to influence the load curve and to improve the load factor.

Tariff should consider the pf (power factor) of the load of the consumer. If it is low, it takes more current for the same kWs and hence T and D (transmission and distribution) losses are correspondingly increased. The power station has to install either pf correcting (improvement) devices such as synchronous capacitors, SVC (Static Var Compensator) or voltage regulating equipment to maintain the voltages within allowed limits and thus total cost increases. One of the following alternatives may be used to avoid low pf:

1. To charge the consumers based on kVA rather than kW.
2. A pf penalty clause may be imposed on the consumer.
3. The consumer may be asked to use shunt capacitors for improving the power factor of his installations.

1.3.2 Availability Based Tariffs (ABT)*

ABT comprises three main components viz., capacity charge, energy charge and charges for deviation from schedule.

1. Capacity charge, towards reimbursement of the fixed cost of the plant, linked to the plant's capacity to supply MWs.
2. Energy charge, to reimburse the fuel cost for scheduled generation, and
3. Payment for deviations from schedule at a rate dependent on system conditions. The last component would be negative in case the power plant is delivering less power than scheduled. For example, if a power plant delivers 600 MW while it was scheduled to supply only 500 MW, the energy charge payment would be for the scheduled generation (500 MW) only, and the excess generation. (100 MW) would be paid for at a certain rate.

If the grid has surplus power at that time and frequency is above 50 Hz, the rate would be small. If the excess generation is at the time of generation deficit in the system (frequency below 50.0 Hz), the payment for extra generation would be at higher rate.

* The term Availability Tariff, particularly in the Indian context, stands for a rational tariff structure for power supply from generating stations, on a contracted basis. In the availability tariff mechanism, the fixed and variable cost components are treated separately. The payment of fixed cost to the generation company is linked to availability of the plant, i.e., its capability to deliver MWs on a day-by-day basis.

If frequency (f) is 49 Hz or below, the UI (unscheduled interchange) price is maximum (570 paise per unit), and the price is minimum (zero paisa), when frequency is 50.5 Hz or above [see Fig. 1.2].

- If the frequency is between 49.0 Hz and 50 Hz, then the UI prices vary linearly as, UI rate = 187–3.7f.
- If the frequency is between 50 Hz and 50.5 Hz, then the UI price is given by UI rate = 202–4.0 × f.
- Maximum value of ABT is fixed, according to the cost of generation of the costliest generating unit (diesel generating plants).

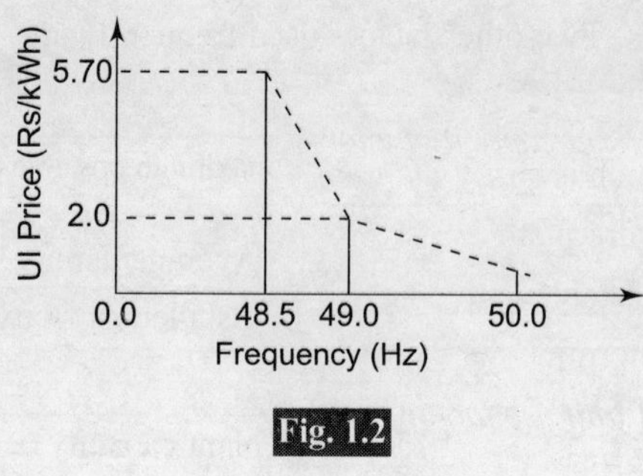

Fig. 1.2

ABT has been successfully adopted for maintaining the grid discipline and has already been implemented in Indian power system.

Example 1.1 A factory to be set up is to have a fixed load of 760 kW at 0.8 pf. The electricity board offers to supply energy at the following alternate rates:

(a) LV supply at Rs 32/kVA max demand/annum + 10 paise/kWh
(b) HV supply at Rs 30/kVA max demand/annum + 10 paise/kWh

The HV switchgear costs Rs 60/kVA and switchgear losses at full load amount to 5%. Interest and depreciation charges for the switchgear are 12% of the capital cost. If the factory is to work for 48 hours/week, determine the more economical tariff.

Solution

$$\text{Maximum demand} = \frac{760}{0.8} = 950 \text{ kVA}$$

$$\text{Loss in switchgear} = 5\%$$

$$\therefore \quad \text{Input demand} = \frac{950}{0.95} = 1000 \text{ kVA}$$

$$\text{Cost of switchgear} = 60 \times 1000 = \text{Rs } 60{,}000$$

$$\text{Annual charges on depreciation} = 0.12 \times 60{,}000 = \text{Rs } 7{,}200$$

Annual fixed charges due to maximum demand

$$\text{corresponding to tariff (b)} = 30 \times 1{,}000 = \text{Rs } 30{,}000$$

$$\text{Annual running charges due to kWh consumed} = 1000 \times 0.8 \times 48 \times 52 \times 0.10$$

$$= \text{Rs } 1{,}99{,}680$$

$$\text{Total charges/annum} = \text{Rs } 2{,}36{,}880$$

$$\text{Max. demand corresponding to tariff } (a) = 950 \text{ kVA}$$

$$\text{Annual fixed charges} = 32 \times 950 = \text{Rs } 30{,}400$$

$$\text{Annual running charges for kWh consumed} = 950 \times 0.8 \times 48 \times 52 \times 0.10$$

$$= \text{Rs } 1{,}89{,}696$$

$$\text{Total} = \text{Rs } 2{,}20{,}096$$

Therefore, tariff (a) is economical.

Example 1.2 A region has a maximum demand of 500 MW at a load factor of 50%. The load duration curve can be assumed to be a triangle. The utility has to meet this load by setting up a generating system, which is partly hydro and partly thermal. The costs are as under:

Hydro plant Rs 600 per kW per annum and operating expenses at 3p per kWh.

Thermal plant Rs 300 per kW per annum and operating expenses at 13p per kWh.

Determine the capacity of hydro plant, the energy generated annually by each, and overall generation cost per kWh.

Solution Total energy generated per year = $500 \times 1000 \times 0.5 \times 8760$

$$= 219 \times 10^7 \text{ kWh}$$

Figure 1.3 shows the load duration curve. Since the operating cost of hydro plant is low, the base load would be supplied from the hydro plant and peak load from the thermal plant.

Let the hydro capacity be P kW and the energy generated by hydro plant E kWh/year.

$$\text{Thermal capacity} = (5{,}00{,}000 - P) \text{ kW}$$

$$\text{Thermal energy} = (219 \times 10^7 - E) \text{ kWh}$$

$$\text{Annual cost of hydro plant} = 600P + 0.03E$$

$$\text{Annual cost of thermal plant} = 300\,(5{,}00{,}000 - P) + 0.13\,(219 \times 10^7 - E)$$

$$\text{Total cost } C = 600P + 0.03E + 300\,(5{,}00{,}000 - P) + 0.13\,(219 \times 10^7 - E)$$

$$\text{For minimum cost, } \frac{dC}{dP} = 0$$

$$\therefore \quad 600 + 0.03\frac{dE}{dP} - 300 - 0.13\frac{dE}{dP} = 0$$

or $$dE = 3000\,dP$$

But $$dE = dP \times t$$

$$\therefore \quad t = 3000 \text{ hours}$$

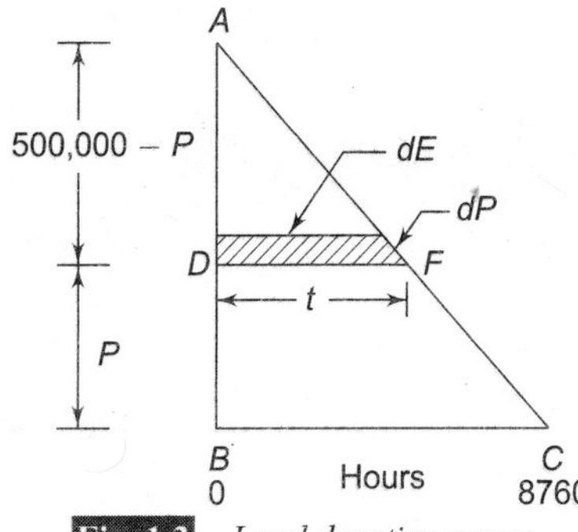

Fig. 1.3 *Load duration curve*

From $\Delta\,ADF$ and $\Delta\,ABC$,

$$\frac{5{,}00{,}000 - P}{5{,}00{,}000} = \frac{3000}{8760}$$

$$\therefore \quad P = 328, \text{ say } 330 \text{ MW}$$

$$\text{Capacity of thermal plant} = 170 \text{ MW}$$

$$\text{Energy generated by thermal plant} = \frac{170 \times 3000 \times 1000}{2}$$

$$= 255 \times 10^6 \text{ kWh}$$

$$\text{Energy generated by hydro plant} = 1935 \times 10^6 \text{ kWh}$$

$$\text{Total annual cost} = \text{Rs } 340.20 \times 10^6/\text{year}$$

$$\text{Overall generation cost} = \frac{340.20\times10^6}{219\times10^7}\times100$$

$$= 15.53 \text{ paise/kWh.}$$

Example 1.3 A generating station has a maximum demand of 25 MW, a load factor of 60%, a plant capacity factor of 50%, and a plant use factor of 72%. Find (a) the daily energy produced, (b) the reserve capacity of the plant and (c) the maximum energy that could be produced daily if the plant, while running as per schedule, were fully loaded.

Solution

$$\text{Load factor} = \frac{\text{average demand}}{\text{maximum demand}}$$

$$0.60 = \frac{\text{average demand}}{25}$$

$$\therefore \quad \text{Average demand} = 15 \text{ MW}$$

$$\text{Plant capacity factor} = \frac{\text{average demand}}{\text{installed capacity}}$$

$$0.50 = \frac{15}{\text{installed capacity}}$$

$$\therefore \quad \text{Installed capacity} = \frac{15}{0.5} = 30 \text{ MW}$$

$\therefore$ Reserve capacity of the plant = installed capacity – maximum demand

$$= 30 - 25 = 5 \text{ MW}$$

$$\text{Daily energy produced} = \text{average demand} \times 24 = 15 \times 24$$

$$= 360 \text{ MWh}$$

$$\text{Energy corresponding to installed capacity per day} = 24 \times 30 = 720 \text{ MWh}$$

$$\text{Maximum energy that could be produced} = \frac{\text{actual energy produced in a day}}{\text{plant use factor}}$$

$$= \frac{360}{0.72} = 500 \text{ MWh/day.}$$

Example 1.4 From a load duration curve, the following data are obtained: Maximum demand on the system is 20 MW. The load supplied by the two units is 14 MW and 10 MW. Unit No. 1 (base unit) works for 100% of the time, and Unit No. 2 (peak load unit) only for 45% of the time. The energy generated by Unit 1 is 1×10^8 units, and that by Unit 2 is 7.5×10^6 units. Find the load factor, plant capacity factor and plant use factor of each unit, and the load factor of the total plant.

Solution

$$\text{Annual load factor for Unit 1} = \frac{1\times10^8\times100}{14,000\times8760} = 81.54\%$$

The maximum demand on Unit 2 is 6 MW.

$$\text{Annual load factor for Unit 2} = \frac{7.5\times10^6\times100}{6000\times8760} = 14.27\%$$

$$\text{Load factor of Unit 2 for the time it takes the load} = \frac{7.5\times10^6\times100}{6000\times0.45\times8760}$$

$$= 31.71\%$$

Since no reserve is available at Unit No. 1, its capacity factor is the same as the load factor, i.e., 81.54%. Also since Unit 1 has been running throughout the year, the plant use factor equals the plant capacity factor, i.e., 81.54%.

$$\text{Annual plant capacity factor of Unit 2} = \frac{7.5\times10^6\times100}{10\times8760\times1000} = 8.56\%$$

$$\text{Plant use factor of Unit 2} = \frac{7.5\times10^6\times100}{10\times0.45\times8760\times1000} = 19.02\%$$

$$\text{The annual load factor of the total plant} = \frac{1.075\times10^8\times100}{20,000\times8760} = 61.35\%.$$

Comments The various plant factors, the capacity of base and peak load units can thus be found out from the load duration curve. The load factor of the peak load unit is much less than that of the base load unit, and thus the cost of power generation from the peak load unit is much higher than that from the base load unit.

Example 1.5 There are three consumers of electricity having different load requirements at different times. Consumer 1 has a maximum demand of 5 kW at 6 p.m. and a demand of 3 kW at 7 p.m. and a daily load factor of 20%. Consumer 2 has a maximum demand of 5 kW at 11 a.m., a load of 2 kW at 7 p.m. and an average load of 1200 W. Consumer 3 has an average load of 1 kW and his maximum demand is 3 kW at 7 p.m. Determine: (a) the diversity factor, (b) the load factor and average load of each consumer and (c) the average load and load factor of the combined load.

Solution

(a) Consumer 1	MD 5 kW at 6 p.m.	3 kW at 7 p.m.	LF 20%
Consumer 2	MD 5 kW at 11 a.m.	2 kW at 7 p.m.	Average load 1.2 kW
Consumer 3	MD 3 kW at 7 p.m.		Average load 1 kW

Maximum demand of the system is 8 kW at 7 p.m.

Sum of the individual maximum demands = 5 + 5 + 3 = 13 kW

$\therefore$ Diversity factor = 13/8 = 1.625

(b) Consumer 1, Average load $0.2 \times 5 = 1$ kW, $\quad$ LF = 20%

Consumer 2, Average load 1.2 kW, LF = $\dfrac{1.2}{5} \times 1000 = 24\%$

Consumer 3, Average load 1 kW, $\quad$ LF = $\dfrac{1}{3} \times 100 = 33.3\%$

(c) Combined average load $= 1 + 1.2 + 1 = 3.2$ kW

$\therefore$ Combined load factor = $\dfrac{3.2}{8} \times 100 = 40\%$

1.3.3 Load Forecasting

As power plant planning and construction require a gestation period of four to eight years or even longer for the present day super power stations, energy and load demand forecasting plays a crucial role in power system studies. Load forecasting is the predicting of electrical power required to meet the short term, medium term or long term demand. The forecasting helps the utility companies in their operation and management of the supply to their customers. Electrical load forecasting is an important process that can increase the efficiency and revenues for the electrical generating and distribution companies. It helps them to plan on their capacity and operations in order to reliably supply all consumers with the required energy.

This necessitates long range forecasting. While sophisticated probabilistic methods exist in literature [5, 16, 29], the simple extrapolation technique is quite adequate for long range forecasting. Since weather has a much more influence on residential than the industrial component, it may be better to prepare forecast in constituent parts to obtain total. Both power and energy forecasts are made. Multifactors involved render forecasting an involved process requiring experience and high analytical ability.

Yearly forecasts are based on previous year's loading for the period under consideration updated by factors such as general load increases, major loads and weather trends.

In short-term load forecasting, hour-by-hour predictions are made for the particular day under consideration. A minor forecast error on low side might necessitate the use of inefficient, oil-fired turbine generators or 'peaking units' which are quite costly. On the other hand, a high side forecast error would keep excessive generation in hot reserve. Accuracy of the order of 1% is desirable. A temperature difference of 2°C can vary the total load by 1%. This indicates the importance of reliable weather forecast to a good load forecast. The short term forecast problem is not a simple one as often random factors such as unexpected storms, strikes, the sudden telecast of a good TV programme can upset the predictions. Regression analysis is often used for obtaining a short term load forecast which is very important and is required before solving unit commitment and economic load despatch problems discussed in Ch. 7. Owing to the great importance of load forecasting (an important input-before solving almost all power system problems), an entire chapter has been added in this book describing the various methods of load forecasting (Ch. 16).

In India, energy demand and installed generating capacity are both increasing exponentially (so is population growth—a truly formidable combination). Power demand* has been roughly doubling every ten years as in many other countries. India is the world's third largest producer and third largest consumer of electricity. The national electric grid in India has an installed capacity of 371.977 GW as of **31 July 2020**. Renewable power plants, which also include large hydroelectric plants, constitute 35.94% of India's

* 38% of the total power required in India is for industrial consumption. Generation of electricity in India was around 830 billion kWh in 2010–2011 AD compared to less than 200 billion kWh in 1986–87.

total installed capacity.** As per the present indications, by the time we enter the 3rd decade of the 21st century it would be nearing 4,00,000 MW—a stupendous task indeed. This, in turn, would require a corresponding development in coal resources. Development of a coalmine takes a little over four years. Coal mining is the process of extracting coal from the ground. Coal is valued for its energy content and has been widely used to generate electricity.

1.4 ▶ STRUCTURE OF POWER SYSTEMS

Generating stations, transmission lines and the distribution systems are the main components of an electric power system. Generating stations and a distribution system are connected through transmission lines, which also connect one power system (grid, area) to another. A distribution system connects all the loads in a particular area to the transmission lines.

For economical and technological reasons (which will be discussed in detail in later chapters), individual power systems are organised in the form of electrically connected areas or regional grids (also called power pools). Each area or regional grid operates technically and economically independently, but these are eventually interconnected† to form a national grid (which may even form an international grid) so that each area is contractually tied to other areas in respect to certain generation and scheduling features. India is now heading for a national grid. Developments in power sector emphasise the need for accelerated implementation of National Power Grid on priority to enable scheduled/unscheduled exchange of power as well as for providing open access to encourage competition in power market. It is one of the largest operational synchronous grids in the world with 371.054 GW of installed power generation capacity as of **30 June 2020**. India's grid is connected as a wide area synchronous grid nominally running at 50 Hz.

The siting of hydro stations is determined by the natural water power sources. The choice of site for coal fired thermal stations is more flexible. The following two alternatives are possible:

1. Power stations may be built close to coal mines (called pit head stations) and electric energy is evacuated over transmission lines to the load centres.
2. Power stations may be built close to the load centres and coal is transported to them from the mines by rail road.

In practice, however, power station siting will depend upon many factors—technical, economical and environmental. As it is considerably cheaper to transport bulk electric energy over extra high voltage (EHV) transmission lines than to transport equivalent quantities of coal over rail road, the recent trends in India (as well as abroad) have been to build super (large) thermal power stations near coal mines. Bulk power can be transmitted to fairly long distances over transmission lines of 400/765 kV and above.

** Installed capacity by source in India as on **31 July 2020** comprises 13.6% hydro, 55.2% thermal, 1.8% nuclear, 10.2% wind, 9.8 solar, 6.7% gas and 2.7% biomass.

† Interconnection has the economic advantage of reducing the reserve generation capacity in each area. Under conditions of sudden increase in load or loss of generation in one area, it is immediately possible to borrow power from adjoining interconnected areas. Interconnection causes larger currents to flow on transmission lines under faulty condition with a consequent increase in capacity of circuit breakers. Also, the synchronous machines of all interconnected areas must operate stably and in a synchronised manner. The disturbance caused by a short circuit in one area must be rapidly disconnected by circuit breaker openings before it can seriously affect adjoining areas. It permits the construction of larger and more economical generating units and the transmission of large chunk of power from the generating plants to major load centres. It provides capacity savings by seasonal exchange of power between areas having opposing winter and summer requirements. It permits capacity savings from time zones and random diversity. It facilitates transmission of off-peak power. It also gives the flexibility to meet unexpected emergency loads.

However, the country's coal resources are located mainly in the eastern belt and some coal fired stations will continue to be sited in distant western and southern regions.

As nuclear stations are not constrained by the problems of fuel transport and air pollution, a greater flexibility exists in their siting, so that these stations are located close to load centres while avoiding high density pollution areas to reduce the risks, however remote, of radioactivity leakage.

In India, as of now, about 57% of electric power used is generated in thermal plants (including nuclear). 13.6% from mostly hydro stations and 29.4% come from renewables and others. Coal is the fuel for most of the steam plants, the rest depends upon oil/natural gas and nuclear fuels.

Electric power is generated at a voltage of 11 to 25 kV which then is stepped up to the transmission levels in the range of 66 to 765 kV (or higher). As the transmission capability of a line is proportional to the square of its voltage, research is continuously being carried out to raise transmission voltages. Some of the countries are already employing 765 kV. The voltages are expected to rise to 800 kV in the near future. In India, several 400 kV lines are already in operation. Several 765 kV lines have been built so far in India.

For very long distances (over 600 km), it is economical to transmit bulk power by DC transmission (see Ch. 20). It also obviates some of the technical problems associated with very long distance AC transmission. The DC voltages used are 400 kV and above, and the line is connected to the AC systems at the two ends through a transformer and converting/inverting equipment (silicon-controlled rectifiers are employed for this purpose). Several DC transmission lines have been constructed in Europe and the USA. In India, several HVDC transmission lines (bipolar) have already been commissioned and several others are being planned. Four back to back HVDC systems are in operation (for details, see Ch. 14).

The first stepdown of voltage from transmission level is at the bulk power substation, where the reduction is to a range of 33 to 132 kV, depending on the transmission line voltage. Some industries may require power at these voltage levels. This stepdown is from the transmission and grid level to subtransmission level.

The next stepdown in voltage is at the distribution substation. Normally, two distribution voltage levels are employed (see Ch. 21 of Ref. 28).

1. The primary or feeder voltage (11 kV).
2. The secondary or consumer voltage (415 V three phase/230 V single phase).

The distribution system, fed from the distribution transformer stations, supplies power to the domestic or industrial and commercial consumers.

Thus, the power system operates at various voltage levels separated by transformer. Figure 1.4 depicts schematically the structure of a power system.

Though the distribution system design, planning and operation are subjects of great importance, we are compelled, for reasons of space, to exclude them from the scope of this book.

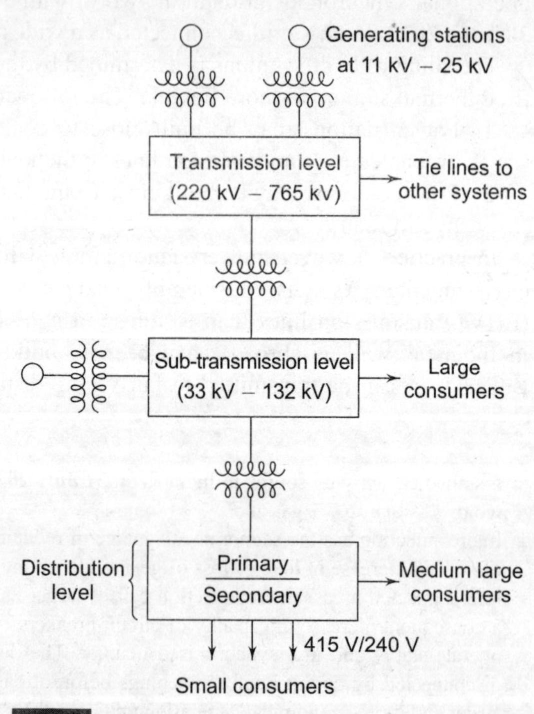

Fig. 1.4 *Schematic diagram depicting power system structure*

1.5 ▶ CONVENTIONAL SOURCES OF ELECTRIC ENERGY

Thermal (coal, oil, nuclear) and hydro generations are the main conventional sources of electric energy. The necessity to conserve fossil fuels has forced scientists and technologists across the world to search for nonconventional sources of electric energy. Some of the sources being explored are solar, wind and tidal sources. The conventional and some of the nonconventional sources and techniques of energy generation are briefly surveyed here with a stress on future trends, particularly with reference to the Indian electric energy scenario. A panoramic view of energy conversion to electrical form is presented in Fig. 1.5.

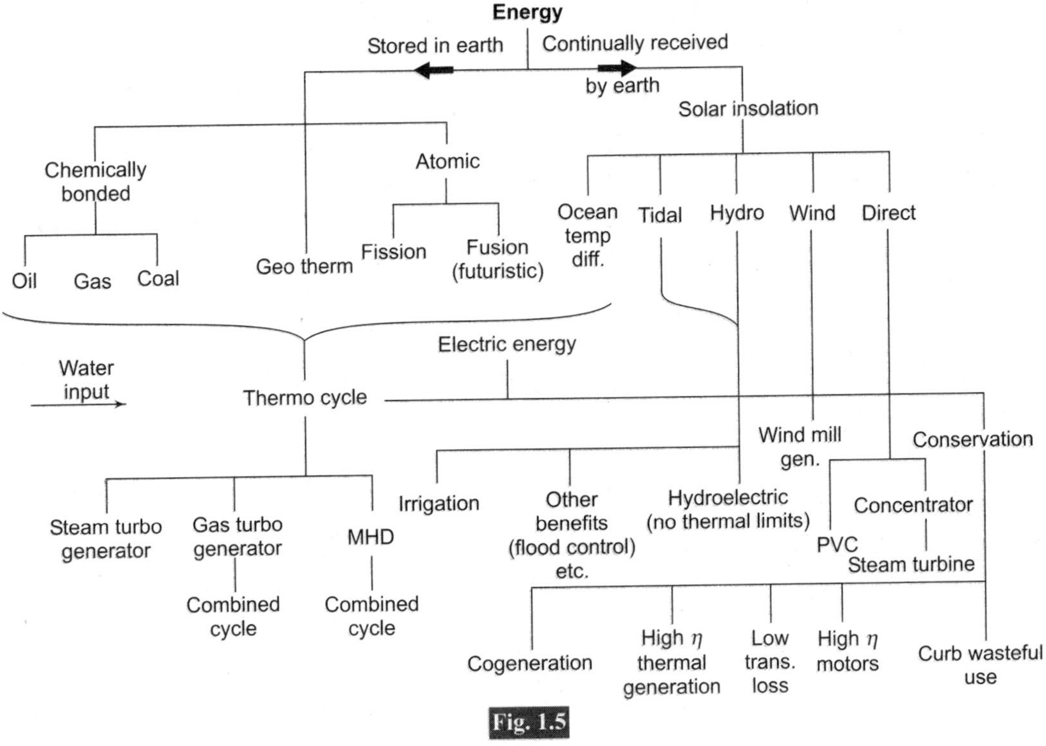

Fig. 1.5

1.5.1 Thermal Power Stations—Steam/Gas-based

The heat released during the combustion of coal, oil or gas is used in a boiler to raise steam. In India, heat generation is mostly coal based except in small sizes, because of limited indigenous production of oil. Therefore, we shall discuss only coal-fired boilers for raising steam to be used in a turbine for electric generation. Natural gas is India's most important potential alternative to coal. India is planning to use natural gas in power generation and in the industrial and residential sectors. Our heavy reliance on highly polluting coal makes development and installation of clean coal technology (cct) a high priority.

The chemical energy stored in coal is transformed into electric energy in thermal power plants. The heat released by the combustion of coal produces steam in a boiler at high pressure and temperature, which when passed through a steam turbine gives off some of its internal energy as mechanical energy. The axial-flow type of turbine is normally used with several cylinders on the same shaft. The steam turbine acts as a prime mover and drives the electric generator (alternator). A simple schematic diagram of a coal fired thermal plant is shown in Fig. 1.6(a).

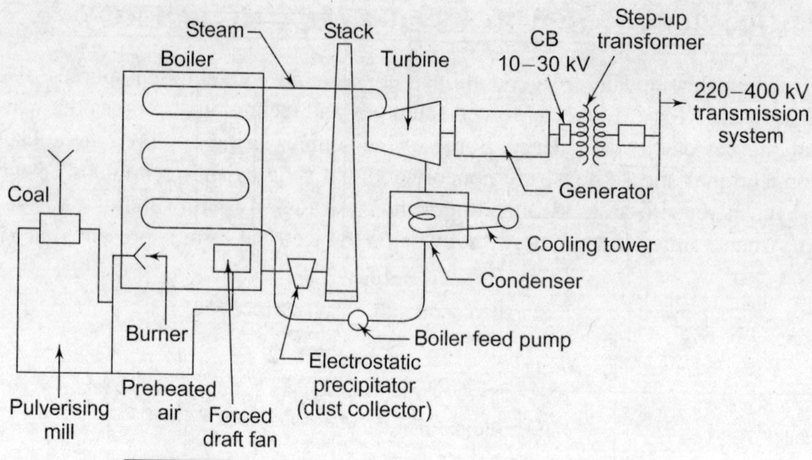

Fig. 1.6(a) *Schematic diagram of a coal fired steam plant*

The efficiency of the overall conversion process is poor and its maximum value is about 40% because of the high heat losses in the combustion gases and the large quantity of heat rejected to the condenser which has to be given off in cooling towers or into a stream/lake in the case of direct condenser cooling. The steam power station operates on the Rankine cycle, modified to include superheating, feed-water heating, and steam reheating as shown in Fig. 1.6(b). The thermal efficiency (conversion of heat to mechanical energy) can be increased by using steam at the highest possible pressure and temperature. With steam turbines of this size, additional increase in efficiency is obtained by reheating the steam after it has been partially expanded by an external heater. The reheated steam is then returned to the turbine where it is expanded through the final states of bleeding.

To take advantage of the principle of economy of scale (which applies to units of all sizes), the present trend is to go in for larger sizes of units. Larger units can be installed at much lower cost per kilowatt. They are also cheaper to operate because of higher efficiency. They require lower labour and maintenance expenditure. According to Kashkari [3], there may be a saving of as high as 15% in capital cost per kilowatt by going up from a 100 to 250 MW unit size and an additional saving in fuel cost of about 8% per kWh. Since larger units consume less fuel per kWh, they produce less air, thermal and waste pollution, and this is a significant advantage in our concern for environment. The only trouble in the case of a large unit is the tremendous shock to the system when outage of such a large capacity unit occurs. This shock can be tolerated so long as this unit size does not exceed 10% of the on-line capacity of a large grid.

In India, in 1970s the first 500 MW superthermal unit had been commissioned at Trombay. Bharat Heavy Electricals Limited (BHEL) has produced several turbogenerator sets of 500 MW capacity. Today's maximum generator unit size is (nearly 1200 MW) limited by the permissible current densities used in rotor and stator windings. Efforts are on to develop *super conducting* machines where the winding temperature will be nearing absolute zero. Extreme high current and flux densities obtained in such machines could perhaps increase unit sizes to several GWs which would result in better generating economy.

Air and thermal pollution is always present in a coal fired steam plant. The air polluting agents (consisting of particulates and gases such as NOX, CO, CO_2, SOX, etc.) are emitted via the exhaust gases and thermal pollution is due to the rejected heat transferred from the condenser to cooling water. Cooling towers are used in situations where the stream/lake cannot withstand the thermal burden without excessive temperature rise. The problem of air pollution can be minimised through scrubbers and electrostatic precipitators and by resorting to minimum emission dispatch [44]. In addition, Clean Air Act has already been passed in Indian Parliament.

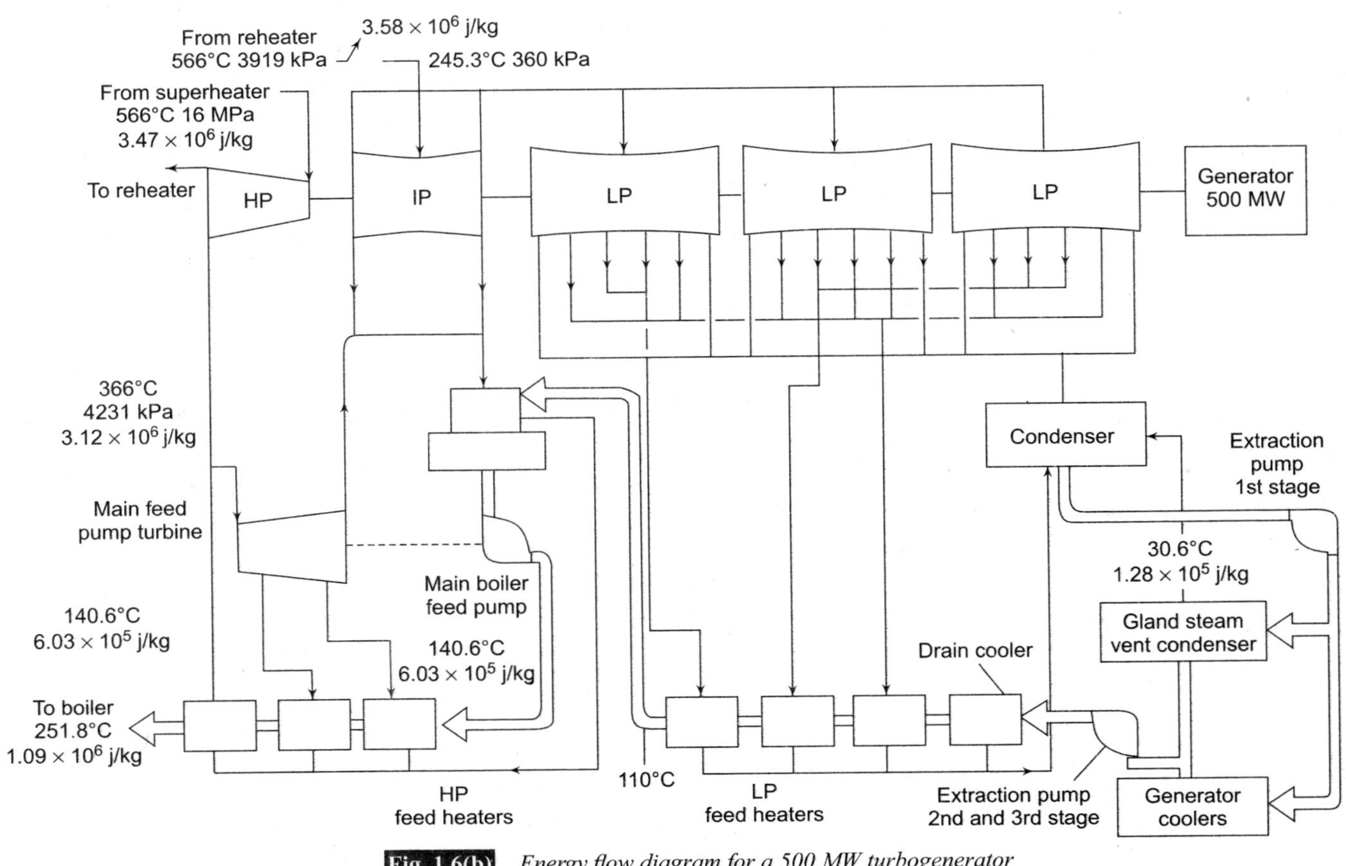

Fig. 1.6(b) *Energy flow diagram for a 500 MW turbogenerator*

An overview of 10 biggest thermal power stations in India The electricity generation capacity of thermal power plants in India is more than 65%. The thermal power generation capacity of coal-based power plants is 85% in the country. The following 10 biggest thermal power generation plants operating in India are all coal-based. Five of them are operated and owned by state-run National Thermal Power Corporation (NTPC) limited.

(1) **Vindhyachal Thermal Power Station (VTPS):** The Vindhyachal Thermal Power Station is located in the Singrauli district of Madhya Pradesh. The installed generation capacity of this power plant is 4,760 MW. The VTPS is currently a biggest thermal power station in India. It is a coal-based power generation station operated and owned by NTPC limited. The construction of this biggest power plant had started in 1982 by Government of India. This biggest power plant comprised 12 generation units (6×210 MW and 6×500 MW units). The first generating unit of this thermal power plant was commissioned in 1987 and 6th 500 MW unit was commissioned in April 2013. To increase the station's gross generation capacity from 4,260 MW to 4,760 MW, an additional 500 MW unit was commissioned in August 2015.

(2) **Mundra Thermal Power Station (MTPS):** The second biggest operating thermal power station in India is MTPS. The Mundra Thermal Power plant is located in the Kutch district of Gujarat state with 4,620 MW generation capacity. The MTPS is a coal-fired power generating station operated and owned by Adani Power group. This power station consists of 4×330 MW and 5×660 MW units. The first unit (330 MW) of MTPS was commissioned in May 2009 and the last unit (660 MW) was commissioned in March 2012. The water source of this power plant is the seawater of the Gulf of Kutch and coal used is mainly imported from Indonesia.

(3) **Mundra Ultra Mega Power Station (MUMPS):** This power station ranks the third largest thermal power plant in India with 4,000 MW generation capacity. The MUMPS is also located in the Kutch district of Gujarat. It is a coal-based power station operated and owned by a subsidiary of Tata Power group known as Coastal Gujarat Power Limited (CGPL). The MUMPS consists of five 800 MW generation capacity units. The construction of this station began in March 2009. The first unit of the MUMPS was commissioned in March 2012 and the last unit was commissioned in March 2019.

(4) **Sasan Ultra Mega Power Station (SUMPS):** The Sasan Ultra Mega Power Station has an installed capacity of 3,960 MW. The SUMPS is located in village Sasan, district Singrauli (Madhya Pradesh) in India. It is one of India's biggest power station integrated with a coal mine and operated by Reliance Power group. This coal-based power station includes 6×660 MW units and commissioned in April 2015. The SUMPS takes coal from the Moher and Moher-Amlohri coal mines and utilises water from Govind Vallabh Pant Sagar reservoir for stable operations. This power plant supplies reliable and low-cost power to approximately 420 million people across 7 states.

(5) **Tiroda Thermal Power Station (TTPS):** The Tiroda Thermal Power Station is a coal-based power generation plant located in Maharashtra with generation capacity of 3,300 MW. The TTPS is owned and operated by Adani Power and consists of 5×660 MW generating units. The first unit of the TTPS was commissioned in August 2012 and the last power generation unit was commenced operations in October 2014. This power station uses state-of-the-art supercritical technology and draws water from the Wainganga River for its reliable and stable operations.

(6) **Talcher Super Thermal Power Station (TSTPS):** The Talcher Super Thermal Power Station is a 3,000 MW coal-fired power station, which is owned and operated by NTPC. The TSTPS is located in the Angul district of Odisha with 6×500 MW power generation units. The first unit of the TSTPS was commissioned in February 1995 and the last unit started operations in February 2005. The Turbines used in this power station were manufactured by ABB and BHEL. The coal used by TSTPS is obtained from the Lingraj Block of Talcher Coal Field and water is resourced from the Samal Barrage Reservoir on the Brahmani River in Odisha.

(7) **Rihand Thermal Power Station (RTPS):** The RTPS is located at Rihandnagar under Sonebhadra district of Uttar Pradesh state. This coal-fired NTPC has an installed capacity of 3,000 MW with construction of 6 × 500 MW unit. The first and sixth units of the RTPS were commissioned in March 1988 and October 2013, respectively. The coal for RTPS is sourced from the Dudhichua mines in Madhya Pradesh and Amlori, Amloric expansion. The required water is sourced from the Rihand Reservoir built on Son River. The RTPS supplies reliable electricity to various states of the northern India including Uttar Pradesh, Delhi, Rajasthan, Punjab, Haryana, Himachal Pradesh, Jammu & Kashmir, and Chandigarh.

(8) **Sipat Thermal Power Station (STPS):** The Sipat Super Thermal Power Station with generation capacity of 2,980 MW is located at Sipat under district Bilaspur of Chhattisgarh state. The STPS ranks as the eighth-largest thermal power plant in India owned and operated by NTPC. The STPS built in two stages with six generating units consists of 3 × 660 MW supercritical units and 3 × 500 MW units. The first and last units of the plant commenced commercial operations in August 2008 and June 2012, respectively.

(9) **Chandrapur Super Thermal Power Station (CSTPS):** The Chandrapur Super Thermal Power Station with generation capacity of 2,920 MW is located in Chandrapur, Maharashtra. The CSTPS is the biggest power station operated by the Maharashtra State Power Generation Company (MSPGC). The plant is equipped with 5 × 500 MW and 2 × 210 MW units. The first and last units of CSTPS were commissioned in 1985 and 2016, respectively.

(10) **National Thermal Power Corporation Dadri (NTPC Dadri):** The National Capital Power Station (NCPS) Dadri is located in the Gautam Budh Nagar district of Uttar Pradesh state. This NCPS is owned and operated by NTPC which is located about 48 km from the Indian capital New Delhi. The NTPC Dadri ranks as the sixth largest thermal plant in India with an installed capacity of 2637 MW (1820 MW coal-based and 817 MW gas-based units). This power generation station consists of six coal-based power units (4 × 210 MW and 2 × 490 MW units) and six gas-based power units (4 × 130.19 MW gas turbines and 2 × 154.51 MW steam turbines). The first and last coal-fired units were commissioned in October 1991 and July 2010, respectively. The gas-based power generation units were commissioned between 1992 and 1997 for production of the stable and reliable electricity.

Fluidised-bed Boiler The main problem with coal in India is its high ash content (up to 40% max). To solve this, *fluidised bed combustion technology* is being developed and perfected. The fluidised-bed boiler is undergoing extensive development and is being preferred due to its lower pollutant level and better efficiency. Direct ignition of pulverised coal is being introduced but initial oil firing support is needed.

Cogeneration Considering the tremendous amount of waste heat generated in thermal power generation, it is advisable to save fuel by the simultaneous generation of electricity and steam (or hot water) for industrial use or space heating. Now called cogeneration, such systems have long been common, here and abroad. Currently, there is renewed interest in these because of the overall increase in energy efficiencies which are claimed to be as high as 65%.

Cogeneration of steam and power is highly energy efficient and is particularly suitable for chemicals, paper, textiles, food, fertiliser and petroleum refining industries. Thus, these industries can solve energy shortage problem in a big way. Further, they will not have to depend on the grid power which is not so reliable. Of course, they can sell the extra power to the government for use in deficient areas. They may also sell power to the neighbouring industries, a concept called *wheeling power*.

As per Annual Report 2016–17 of Ministry, As of December 2016, the Ministry was successful in deploying a total of 50068.37 MW capacity of grid-based renewable energy. 28700.44 MW of which was

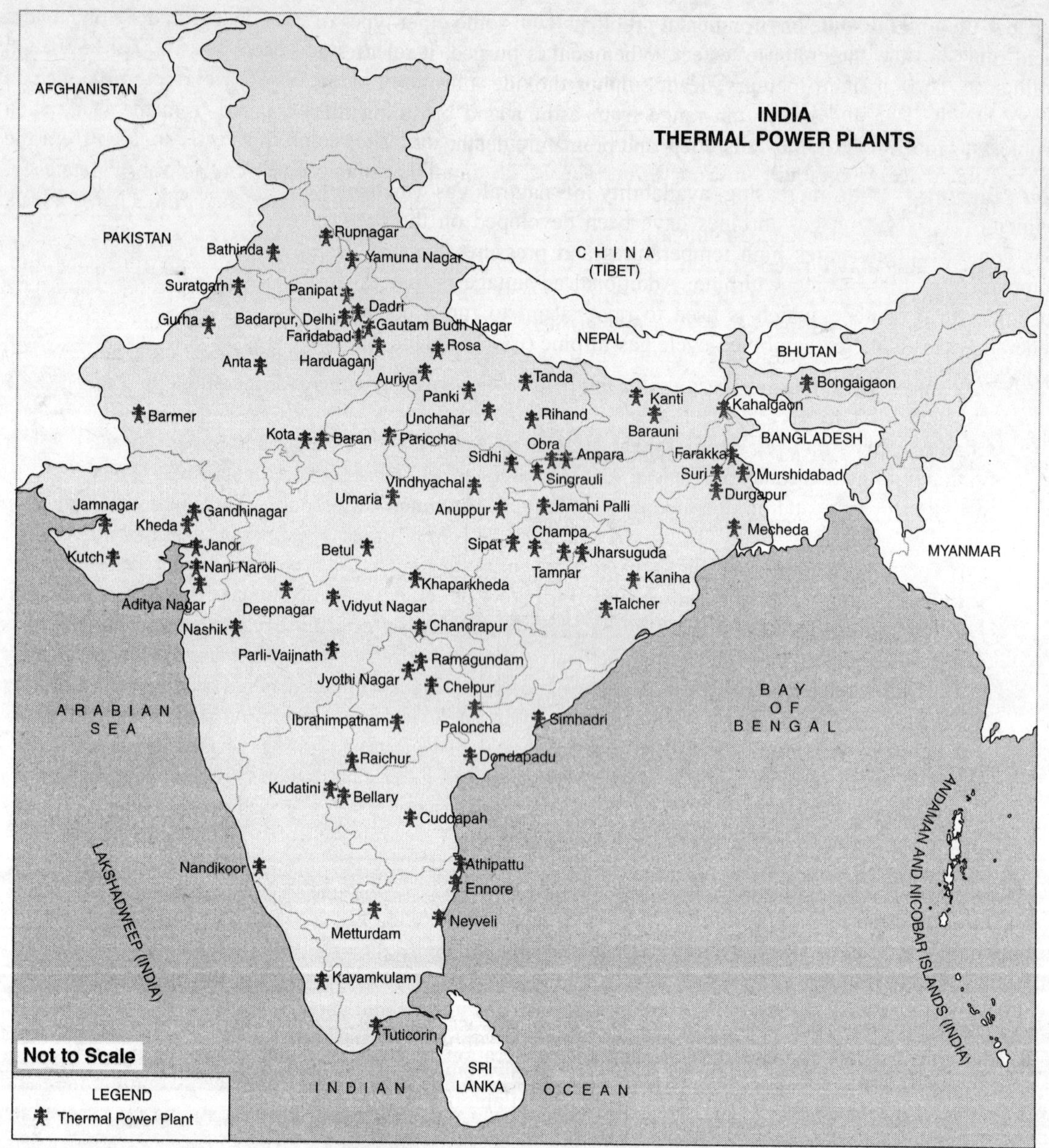

Fig. 1.6(c) *Thermal power plants in India*

from Wind power, 4333.85 MW from Small hydro Power, 7907.34 MW from Bio power, 9012.66 MW from Solar power (SPV) and the rest 114.08 MW from Waste to Power.

There are two possible ways of cogeneration of heat and electricity: (i) Topping cycle, (ii) Bottoming cycle. In the topping cycle, fuel is burnt to produce electrical or mechanical power and the waste heat from the power generation provides the process heat. In the bottoming cycle, fuel first produces process heat and the waste heat from the processes is then used to produce power.

Coal-fired plants share environmental problems with some other types of fossil-fuel plants; these include 'acid rain' and the 'greenhouse' effect. When coal is burned, it releases a number of airborne toxins and pollutants. They include mercury, lead, sulphur dioxide, nitrogen oxides, particulates and various other heavy metals. Health impacts can range from asthma and breathing difficulties to brain damage, heart problems, cancer, neurological disorders and premature death.

Gas Turbines With increasing availability of natural gas (methane) (recent finds in Bangladesh), primemovers based on gas turbines have been developed on the lines similar to those used in aircraft. Gas combustion generates high temperatures and pressures, so that the efficiency of the gas turbine is comparable to that of steam turbine. Additional advantage is that exhaust gas from the turbine still has sufficient heat content, which is used to raise steam to run a conventional steam turbine coupled to a generator. This is called combined-cycle gas-turbine (CCGT) plant. The schematic diagram of such a plant is drawn in Fig. 1.7.

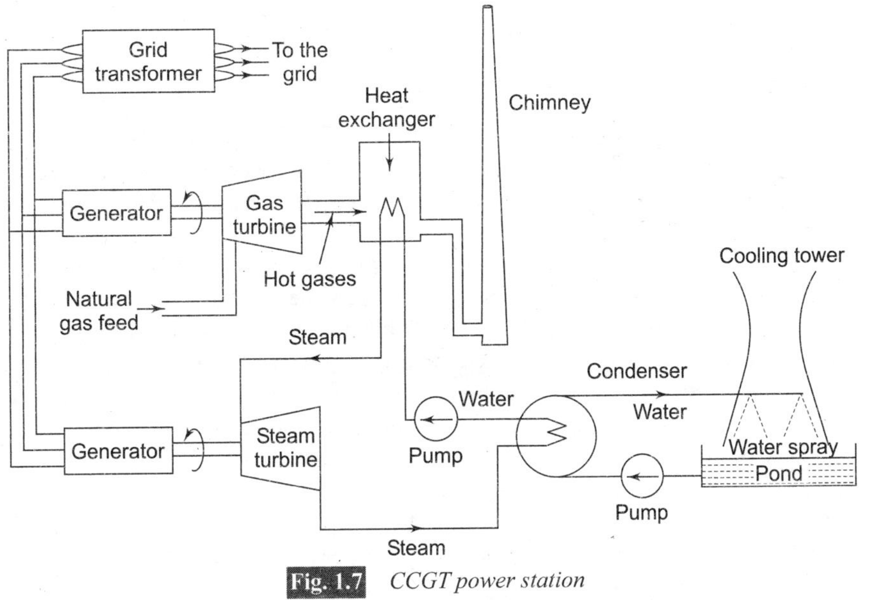

Fig. 1.7 *CCGT power station*

The CCGT plant has a fast start of 2–3 min for the gas turbine and about 20 min for the steam turbine. Local storage tanks of gas can be used in case of gas supply interruption. The unit can take up to 10% overload for short periods of time to take care of any emergency. CCGT unit produces 55% of CO_2 produced by a coal/oil-fired plant. Units are now available for a fully automated operation for 24 h or to meet the peak demands. In Delhi (India), a CCGT unit of 2 × 110 MW is installed at Pragati Power Plant. To bridge the gap between demand and supply and to have reliable supply to the Capital City, a 330 MW combined cycle Gas Turbine Power Project (GTPP) was set up on fast track basis. This plant consists of 2 × 104 MW frame 9-E Gas Turbine Units commissioned in 2002–03 and 1 × 122 MW STG unit commissioned in 2003–04. Recently, this plant consists of 4 × 104 MW Gas Turbine Units and 2 × 122 MW STG units. Gas supply has been tied up with GAIL through HBJ pipeline. The environmental friendly quality power generation through this station is pumped to 220kV sub-station of Delhi Transco Limited and the entire power is being utilised by citizen of Delhi.

There are currently many installations using gas turbines in the world with 100 MW generators. A 6 × 30 MW gas turbine station has already been put up in Delhi. A gas turbine unit can also be used as synchronous compensator to help maintain flat voltage profile in the system.

1.5.2 Nuclear Power Generation

Nuclear Reaction Considerable binding energy is released on breaking a large nucleus into smaller fragments. This process is called *fission*. Nucleus of uranium isotope ^{235}U undergoes fission when struck by a fast moving neutron. This fission is expressed in the standard nuclear reaction as

$$\underset{\substack{\uparrow \\ \text{(neutron)}}}{} {}^{235}_{92}\text{U(fissile)} + {}_0\text{n}^1 \rightarrow \underset{\substack{\text{(excited uranium} \\ \text{nucleus)}}}{{}^{236}_{92}\text{U}^*} \rightarrow \overset{\substack{\text{(Xenon)} \\ \downarrow}}{{}^{140}_{54}\text{Xe}} + \underset{\text{(Strontium)}}{{}^{94}_{38}\text{Sr}} + 2\,{}_0\text{n}^1 + \text{E (20 MeV)} \qquad (1.1)$$

Nuclear Reactor The fission of a nuclear material (Eq. (1.1)) is carried out in a nuclear reactor. A nuclear reactor is a very efficient source of energy as a small amount of fissile material produces large chunks of energy. For example, 1 g of ^{235}U releases energy at the rate of 1 MW/day, whereas 2.6 tonnes of coal produces the same power in a conventional thermal plant per day (this figure is much larger for Indian coal, which contains considerable amount of dust in it).

Uranium metal extracted from the base ore consists mainly of two isotopes ^{238}U (99.3% by weight) and ^{235}U (0.7% by weight). Of these only ^{235}U is fissile and when struck by slow moving neutrons, its nucleus splits into two fast moving neutrons and 3×10^{-11} J of kinetic energy. The fast moving neutrons hit the surrounding atoms, thus producing heat before coming to rest. The neutrons travel further, hitting more atoms and producing further fissions. The number of neutrons thus multiplies and under certain critical conditions a sustainable chain reaction results. For sustainability, the reactor core or moderator must slow down the moving neutrons to achieve a more effective splitting of the nuclei.

The energy given off in a reactor appears in the form of heat, which is removed by a gas or liquid coolant. The hot coolant is then used in a heat exchanger to raise steam. If the coolant is ordinary water, steam could be raised inside the reactor. Steam so raised runs a turbogenerator for producing electric energy.

Fuel Fuels used in reactors have some components of ^{238}U. Natural uranium is sometimes used and although the energy density is considerably less than that for pure isotope, it is still much better than fossil fuels. The uranium used at present comes from metal-rich areas, which have limited world resources ($\approx 2 \times 10^6$ tonnes). Therefore, the era of nuclear energy would be comparatively short, probably less than a century. Fortunately, it is possible to manufacture certain fissile isotopes from abundant nonfissile materials like thorium by a process of conversion in a breeder reactor (details in later portion of this section). This would assure virtually an unlimited reserve of nuclear energy.

In an advanced gas-cooled reactor (AGR), whose schematic diagram is shown in Fig. 1.8, enriched uranium dioxide fuel in pellet form, encased in stainless steel cans, is used. A number of cans form a cylindrical fuel element, which is placed in a vertical hollow housing in the core. In certain reactors fuel could be in the form of rods enclosed in stainless steel.

Moderators To slow down the neutrons, the reactor elements are placed inside a moderator, a substance whose nuclei absorb energy as fast moving neutrons collide with these but do not capture the neutrons.

Commonly used moderators are graphite (as in AGR of Fig. 1.8), light water and heavy water. It could also be beryllium and its oxide, and possibly certain organic compounds.

Coolants These remove the heat generated in the core by circulation and transfer it outside for raising steam. Common coolants are light ordinary water, heavy water, gas (CO_2) (this is used in AGR of Fig. 1.8) and also metals like sodium or sodium-potassium alloy in liquid form.

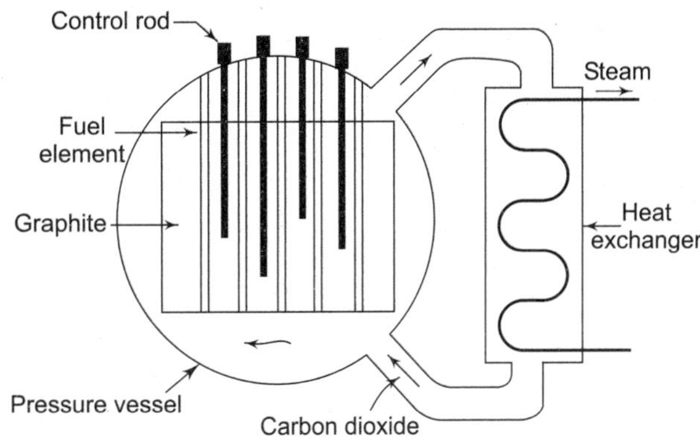

Fig. 1.8 *Schematic view of a British Magnox type nuclear reactor*

Control Materials In nuclear reactors, control is achieved by means of a neutron absorbing material. The control elements are commonly located in the core in the form of either rods or plates. The control rods are moved in to decrease the fission rate or neutron flux and moved out to increase it. The most commonly used neutron absorber is *boron.* This element has a very high melting point and a large cross-section for neutron absorption.

Other control materials are cadmium and an alloy of silver 15%, iradium 15% and cadmium 5%.

Reactor Shielding Nuclear reactors are sources of intense neutron and γ-radiation and, therefore, represent hazard to persons in the immediate vicinity of the reactor. Provisions for their health protection are made by surrounding the reactor core with a radiation shield, also called *biological shield.* It generally consists of a layer of concrete, about 1.8–2.5 m thick and capable of absorbing both γ-rays and neutrons. Part of the shield which is in immediate contact with the core heats up considerably and requires a special cooling facility to prevent it from cracking. A shield made of a 5–10 cm thick steel is located close to the core.

Power Reactor Types The primary purpose of a power reactor is the utilisation of fission energy produced in the reactor core by converting it to a useful mechanical-electrical form. The heat generated in the fission process is used to produce steam at high temperature and pressure, which runs a turbogenerator. For raising steam, a heat exchanger stage is interposed between the reactor and boiler. The choice of the heat exchange fluid (or gas) is governed by three considerations:

1. It must have a high thermal conductivity so as to carry away heat efficiently and give it up in a heat exchanger.
2. It must have a low neutron capture cross-section so as not to upset the reactor characteristics.
3. It must not be decomposed by intense radiation.

Now we shall discuss some of the reactor types which are in current use in various countries. Advanced gas reactor (AGR) has already been presented earlier for discussing the various components and processes involved in a reactor.

Boiling Water Reactor (Fig. 1.9(a)) This type of power plant is designed to allow steam to be generated directly in the reactor core. This uses light water as moderator and coolant. Therefore, no external heat exchanger is required. Enriched uranium is used as fuel.

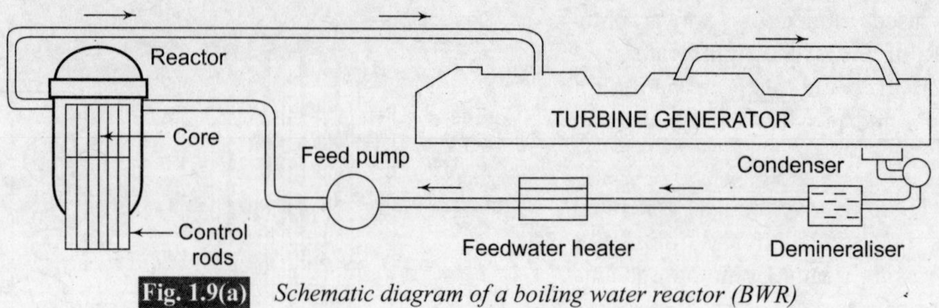

Fig. 1.9(a) *Schematic diagram of a boiling water reactor (BWR)*

The 420 MW power station, at Tarapur (India), consists of two enriched uranium reactors of the boiling water type. These reactors were built with the help of the General Electric Company of the United States and became operational on April 1, 1969.

Pressurised Water Reactor (Fig. 1.9(b)) It uses slightly enriched uranium (1.4 or 2% of U^{235}) as fuel and light water as moderator and coolant. The fuel elements are in the form of rods or plates. The core is contained in a vessel under a pressure of $(6.5 \text{ to } 13.8) \times 10^6 \text{ N/m}^2$.

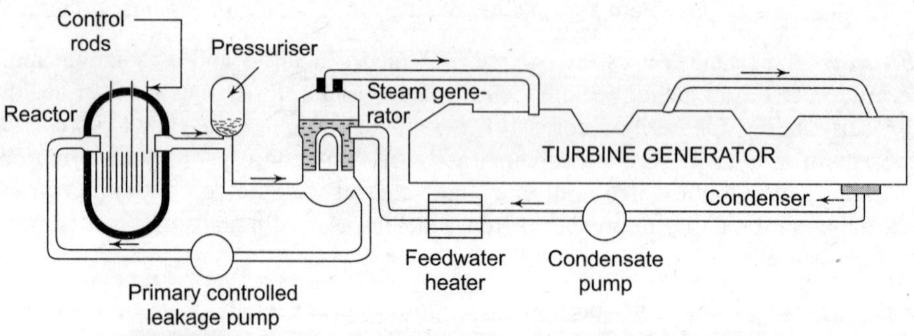

Fig. 1.9(b) *Schematic diagram of a pressured water reactor (PWR)*

The pressurised water is circulated through the reactor core from which it removes heat. This heat is transferred to a boiler through a heat exchanger for raising steam for turbogeneration as shown in Fig. 1.9(b).

Heavy Water (D_2O) Moderated Reactor (Fig. 1.10) It is of the pressurised water reactor type with heavy water as moderator and coolant instead of light water. The first prototype of this type of reactor is the Nuclear Power Demonstration Reactor (NPDR) called CANDU (Canada Deuterium Uranium) type reactor completed in 1962 at Canada.

The 430 MW power station near Kota at Rana Pratap Sagar in Rajasthan employs a heavy water mode gated reactor using natural uranium as fuel. This started feeding power in 1973. The other two reactors of this type are at Kalpakkam (470 MW), about 100 km away from Chennai, and the other at Narora in Uttar Pradesh (UP), Kakrapar in Gujarat. Several other nuclear power plants will be commissioned by 2012. It is planned to raise nuclear power generation to 20,000 MW by 2020.

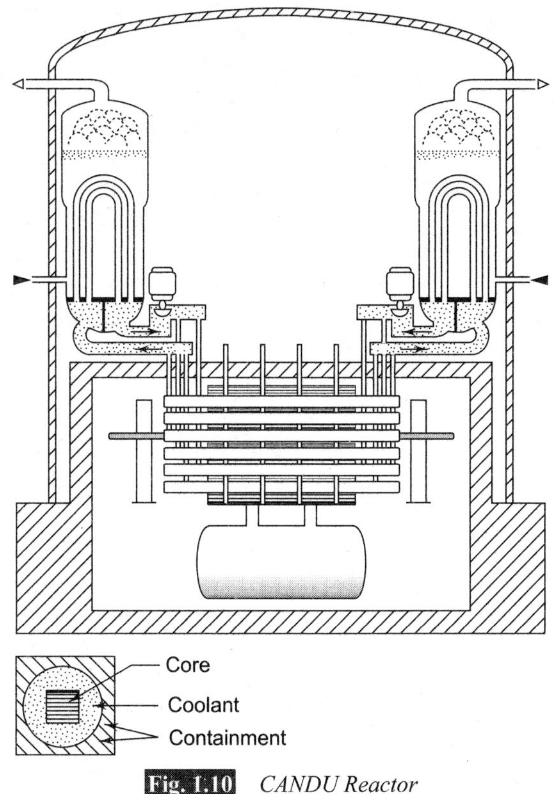

Fig. 1.10 *CANDU Reactor*

Fast Breeder Reactor (FBR) Such type of reactors are designed to produce more fissile material (Plutonium) than they consume (Thorium, U^{232}). The nuclear equations for breeding are as under.

$$ {}_0n^1 \rightarrow {}^{232}_{90}\text{Th (nonfissile)} \rightarrow {}^{233}_{90}\underset{\text{Th (22 min)}}{\overset{\beta \atop \uparrow}{}} \rightarrow {}^{233}_{91}\underset{\text{Pa (27 d)}}{\overset{\beta \atop \uparrow}{}} \rightarrow {}^{233}_{92}\text{U (fissile)} \quad (1.2)$$

Bred fuel

$$ {}_0n^1 \rightarrow {}^{238}_{92}\text{U (nonfissile)} \rightarrow {}^{239}_{92}\underset{\text{U (24 min)}}{\overset{\beta \atop \uparrow}{}} \rightarrow {}^{239}_{93}\underset{\text{Np (2.3 d)}}{\overset{\beta \atop \uparrow}{}} \rightarrow {}^{239}_{94}\text{Pu (fissile)}$$

Bred fuel
(Plutonium) (1.3)

According to the above reactions, there are two types of fast breeder reactors:

1. A blanket of ^{232}Th surrounds ^{239}Pu and is converted to ^{233}U which is fissile (Eq. (1.2)).
2. Core 20% ^{239}Pu surrounded by a blanket of 80% ^{238}U (Thorium). About three neutrons are emitted when a ^{239}Pu nucleus fissions. Of these, one is required to sustain the reaction leaving the other two to account for breeding more ^{239}Pu (Eq. 1.3).

The power density in a fast breeder reactor is considerably higher than in normal reactors. Therefore, liquid sodium which is an efficient coolant and does not moderate neutrons is used to take away heat generated in the core. Schematic diagram of an FBR reactor is shown in Fig. 1.11(a).

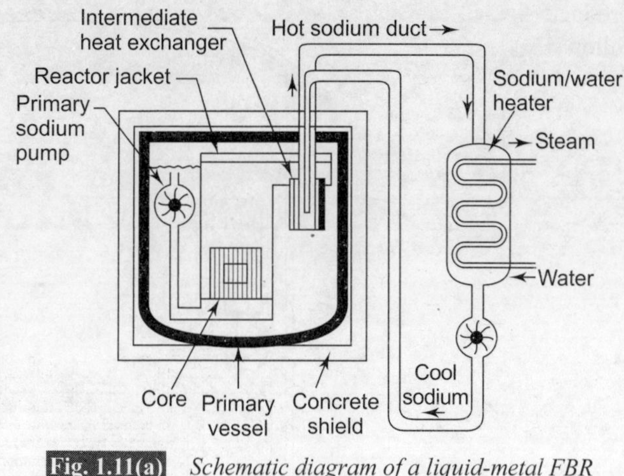

Fig. 1.11(a) *Schematic diagram of a liquid-metal FBR*

An important advantage of FBR technology, brought out through the reaction equations given above, is that it can use Thorium (as fertile material) which gets converted to ^{233}U, a fissile isotope. This holds great promise for India as we have one of the world's largest deposits of Thorium—about 450,000 tonnes in the form of sand dunes in Kerala and along the Gopalpur Chattarpur coast of Orissa.

Typical power densities (MW/m^3) in fission reactor cores are: gas cooled 0.53, high temperature gas cooled 7.75, heavy water 18.0, boiling water 29.0, pressurised water 54.75 and fast breeder reactor 760.0.

The associated merits and problems of nuclear power plants as compared to conventional thermal plants are as follows:

Merits

1. A nuclear power plant is totally free of air pollution. Nuclear fuel is greener than coal.
2. It requires very little fuel in terms of volume and weight, and therefore poses no transportation problems and may be sited, independently of nuclear fuel supplies, close to load centres. However, safety considerations require that these be normally located away from populated areas.
3. It lasts longer—over 45 years as against 30 in case of coal and 15 in case of gas turbines.

Problems

1. Nuclear reactors produce radioactive fuel waste, the disposal of which poses serious environmental hazards.
2. The rate of nuclear reaction can be lowered only by a small margin, so the load on a nuclear power plant can only be permitted to be marginally reduced below its full load value. Nuclear power stations must, therefore, be reliably connected to a power network, as tripping of the lines connecting the station can be quite serious and may require shutting down of the reactor with all its consequences.
3. Because of a relatively high capital cost as against the running cost, the nuclear plant should operate continuously as a base load station. Wherever possible, it is preferable to support such a station with a pumped storage scheme discussed later (p. 33).
4. There are risks in terms of fuel supplies and safety.

Safety and Environmental Considerations The nuclei that result from fission are called fission fragments. From the nuclear reactor there is a continuous emission of β- and γ-rays, and α-particles and fission fragments. If these fission fragments cannot be retreated as a fuel element, then these become waste products, which are highly radioactive. Some of the important waste products with their half life are as follows:

$^{3}_{1}H_2$ (Tritium) – 12.26 years

^{90}Sr (Strontium) – 28.8 years

^{137}Cs (Cesium) – 32.2 years

^{131}I (Iodine) – 8 days

^{85}Kr (Krypton) – 10.76 years

^{133}Xe (Xenon) – 5.27 days

Waste products having a long life create serious problems. These are called high level wastes, e.g., ^{90}Sr. At the moment, the wastes are concentrated in the liquid form and stored in stainless steel containers. Burying nuclear wastes deep underground currently seems to be the best long-term way to dispose them off. The location should be geologically stable, should not be earthquake prone, a type of rock that does not disintegrate in the presence of heat and radiation and not near ground water as that might become contaminated. At present over 15,000 tonnes of spent nuclear fuel is being stored on a temporary basis in the United States.

In the design and construction of reactors, great care is taken to cover every contingency. Many facilities, e.g., control system, are at least duplicated and have alternative electrical supplies. In March 1979, failure in its cooling system disabled one of the reactors of Three Mile Island in Pennsylvania and a certain amount of radioactive material escaped, although a catastrophe was narrowly avoided. Then in April 1986, a severe accident destroyed a 1000 MW reactor at Chernobyl, in erstwhile Soviet Union. Latest is at Sendai, Japan on 13th March 2011. Much radioactive material escaped into the atmosphere and was carried around the world by winds. Tens of thousands of people were evacuated from the reactor vicinity and hundreds of plant and rescue workers died as a result of exposure to radiation. The effects of radioactive exposure of population in neighbouring regions are still showing up in the form of various incurable diseases even in the next generation offsprings.

However, the health controls in the atomic power industry have, from the very outset, been much more rigorous than in any other industry.

Fusion Energy is produced in this process by combination of two light nuclei to form a single heavier one under sustained condition of extremely high temperature and high pressure for initiation. Neutron emission is not required in the process as the temperature (high) maintains the collisions of reacting nuclei.

The most promising fuels are isotopes of hydrogen known as deuterium (D) (mass 2) and tritium (T) (mass 3). The product of fusion is the helium isotope (mass 3), hydrogen, neutrons and heat. As tritium is not a naturally occurring isotope, it is produced in the reactor shield by the interaction of the fusion neutrons and the lithium isotope of mass 6. The deuterium-deuterium fusion requires higher temperature than deuterium-tritium and the latter is more likely to be used initially.

Reserves of lithium have been estimated to be roughly equal to those of fossil fuels. Deuterium, on the other hand, is contained in sea-water of a concentration of about 34 parts per million. The potential of this energy resource is therefore vast. Total nuclear power will be around 10280 MW by 2012.

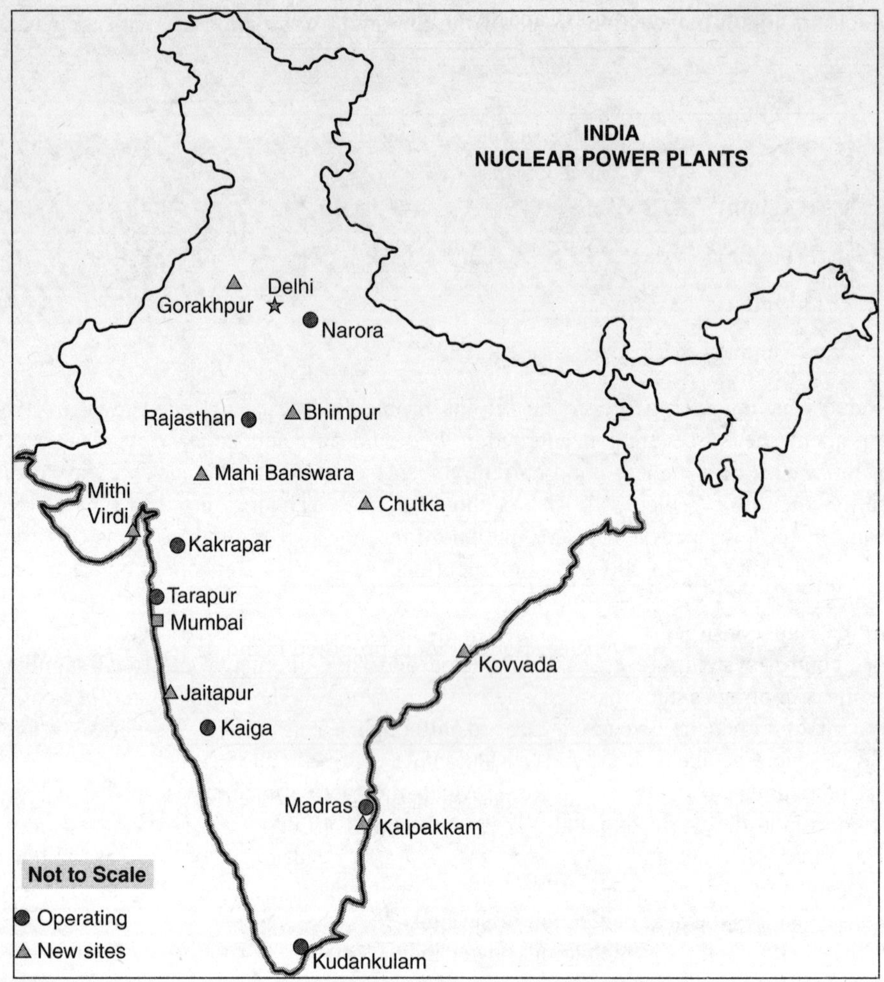

Fig. 1.11(b) *Reactors operating in India (Source: International Energy Agency, Electricity Information 2019)*

General Remarks The greatest danger in a fission reactor is in the case of loss of coolant in an accident. Even with the control rods (or plates) fully lowered quickly called *scram* operation, the fission does continue for sometime and its *after-heat* may cause vaporising and dispersal of radioactive material. This possibility does not exist in fusion process as its power density is almost 1/50th that of an FBR. The radioactive waste in fusion is the radiation damage to structural materials which would require occasional renewal. These could be recycled after 50-year period compared with centuries required for ^{90}Sr and ^{137}Cs, the fission fragments.

Intensive international research is still proceeding to develop materials and a suitable containment method, using either magnetic fields or powerful lasers to produce the high temperatures ($\approx 8 \times 10^7$ K) and pressure (above 1000 bar) to initiate a fusion reaction. It is unlikely that a successful fusion reactor will be available before 2020.

With this kind of estimated time frame for breakthrough in fusion technology, development in FBR technology and installing of power stations will continue.

Table 1.1(a) Generation Capacity of Nuclear Power in India (July 31, 2020)

Sr. No.	*Name of Nuclear Power Plant*	*State*	*Installed generation units*
1	Kaiga	Uttar Kannada (Karnataka)	4×202
2	Kakrapar	Surat (Gujarat)	2×202 2×700 (Under construction)
3	Kudankulam	Tirunelveli (Tamil Nadu)	2×932 2×1000 (Under construction)
4	Kalpakkam	Madras (Tamil Nadu)	2×205
5	Narora	Bulandshahar (UP)	2×202
6	Rawatbhata	Kota (Rajasthan)	1×90 1×187 4×202 2×700 (Under construction)
7	Tarapur	Palghar (Maharastra)	2×150 2×490

Table 1.1(b) New Nuclear Power Plants proposed in India (July 31, 2020)

Sr. No.	*Proposed Nuclear Power Plant*	*State*	*Proposed generation units*
1	Chutka	Mandla (Madhya Pradesh)	4×700
2	Bhimpur	Betul (Madhya Pradesh)	4×700
3	Gorakhpur	Fatehabad (Haryana)	4×700
4	Mahi Banswara	Banswara (Rajasthan)	4×700
5	Chhaya Mithi Virdi	Bhavnagar (Gujarat)	6×1250
6	Kovvara	Srikakulam (Andhra Pradesh)	4×1250
7	Jaitapur	Ratnagiri (Maharashtra)	6×1700

France and Canada are possibly the two countries with a fairly clean record of nuclear generation. According to Indian scientists, our heavy-water–based plants are most safe.

World scientists have to adopt a different reaction safety strategy to discover additives to automatically inhibit reaction beyond critical rather than by mechanically inserted controlled rods, which have possibilities of several primary failure events.

1.5.3 Hydro Power

The oldest and cheapest method of power generation is that of utilising the potential energy of water. The energy is obtained almost free of running cost and is completely pollution free. Of course, it involves high capital cost because of the heavy civil engineering construction works involved. Also, it requires a long gestation period of about five to eight years as compared to four to six years for steam plants. Hydroelectric stations are designed, mostly, as multipurpose projects such as river flood control, storage of drinking water, irrigation and navigation. A simple block diagram of high head hydro plant is given in Fig. 1.12. The vertical difference between the upper reservoir and the tail race pond is called the *head*.

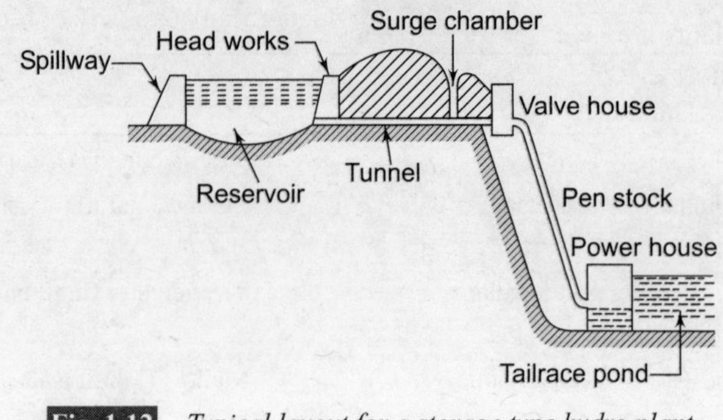

Fig. 1.12 *Typical layout for a storage type hydro plant*

Water falling through the head gains kinetic energy which then imparts energy to the blades of the hydraulic turbine. There are three main types of hydroelectric installations:

1. *High head or stored*—the storage area of reservoir fills in more than 400 hectares.
2. *Medium head or pondage*—the storage fills in 200–400 hectares.
3. *Run of river*—storage (in any) fills in less than 2 h and has a 3–15 m head.

A schematic diagram for hydroelectric schemes of Type 3 is shown in Fig. 1.13.

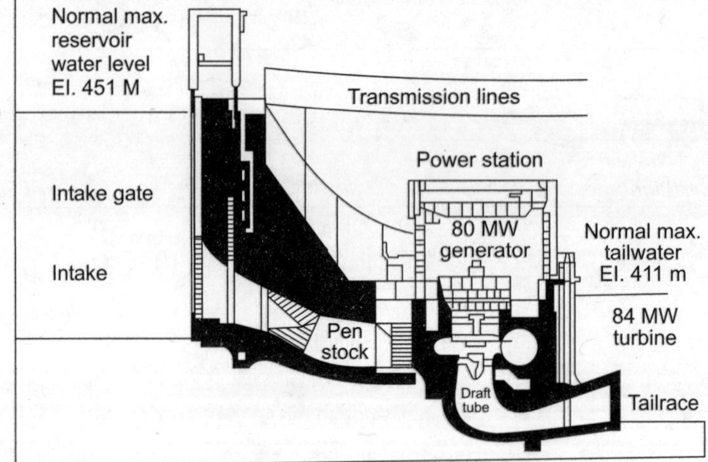

Fig. 1.13 *Run of river hydroelectric scheme—80 MW Kaplan turbine, 115.41 rpm*

There can be several of these turbines on a deep and wide river.

In India, mini and micro hydroelectric schemes have been installed on canals wherever 1 m or so head is available. Often cascaded plants are also constructed on the same water stream where the discharge of one plant becomes the inflow of a downstream plant.

For the three above identified heads of water level, the kind of turbines that are employed are as follows:

1. *Pelton*: This is used for heads of 184–1840 m and consists of a bucket wheel rotor with adjustable flow nozzles.
2. *Francis*: This is used for heads of 37–490 m and is of mixed flow type.
3. *Kaplan*: This is used for run-of-river and pondage stations with heads of up to 61 m. This type has an axial-flow rotor with variable-pitch blades.

Hydroelectric plants are capable of starting quickly—almost in 5 min. The rate of taking up load on the machines is of the order of 20 MW/min. Further, no losses are incurred at standstill. Thus, hydroelectric plants are ideal for meeting peak loads. The time from start up to the actual connection to the grid can be as short as 2 min.

The power available from a hydro plant is

$$P = g\,\rho\,WH \text{ W} \tag{1.4}$$

where W = discharge (m^3/s) through the turbine, ρ = density (1000 kg/m^3) and H = head (m), g = 9.81 m/s^2

$$\therefore \quad P = 9.81\ WH \text{ kW} \tag{1.5}$$

Problems peculiar to hydroelectric plants which inhibit expansion are

1. Silting—Bhakra dead storage has reportedly silted fully in 30 years.
2. Seepage.
3. Ecological damage to region.
4. Displacement of human habitation from areas behind the dam which will fill up and become a lake.
5. These cannot provide base load and must be used for peak shaving and energy saving in coordination with thermal plants.

Typical efficiency curves of the three types of turbines are depicted in Fig. 1.14(a). As the efficiency depends upon the head, which is continuously fluctuating, water consumption in m^3/kWh is used instead of efficiency, which is related to water head.

In certain periods when the water availability is low or when hydro-generation is not needed, it may be advantageous to run electric generators as motors from the grid, so as to act as synchronous condensers (these are overexcited). To reduce running losses, the water is pushed below the turbine runner by compressed air after closing the input valve. The runner now rotates in air and free running losses are low.

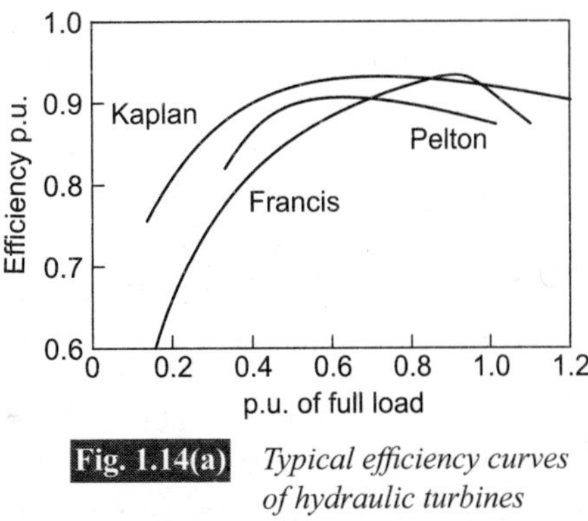

Fig. 1.14(a) *Typical efficiency curves of hydraulic turbines*

India also has a tremendous potential (5000 MW) of having large number of nano, pico, micro (< 1 MW), mini (< 1–5 MW) and small (< 15 MW) *hydel plants* in Himalayan region, North-East, HP, UP, UK, and JK which must be fully exploited to generate cheap and clean power for villages situated far away from the grid power*. At present, 394 MW capacity is under implementation.

An overview of 10 biggest hydroelectric power stations in India

(1) Tehri Hydroelectric Power Station (THPS): The THPS has the highest hydroelectric dam in India and the tenth tallest dam in the world. The historical THPS is a multi-purpose rock and earth-fill embankment dam on the Bhagirathi river at Tehri in Uttarakhand state of India. The earth-fill embankment dam has 855 feet or 260.5 meters high rock with a length of 575 meters. The generation capacity of Tehri Hydro Power Complex is 2400MW. It comprises three components for total generation capacity of 2400 MW. The components are Tehri Dam & Hydro Power Plant with 1000 MW capacity, Koteshwar Hydro Electric Project with capacity 400 MW and Tehri Pumped Storage Plant (PSP) with generation capacity of 1000 MW.

* Existing capacity (small hydro) is 36877 MW as on 2010. Total estimated potential is 15000 MW.

(2) **Koyna Hydroelectric Power Station (KHPS):** Koyna Hydroelectric Power Station is the second biggest hydroelectric power station of our country. The installed generation capacity of the project on Koyna River, Maharashtra, is 1,960 MW. The project of KHPS consists of 4 units of power generation system. The generators are connected in parallel to improve reliability in the underground powerhouses excavated deep inside the surrounding mountains of the Western Ghats. A dam foot powerhouse of KHPS also contributes for electricity generation.

(3) **Srisailam Hydroelectric Power Station (SHPS):** The dam of the Srisailam Hydroelectric Power Station is constructed across the Krishna river at Srisailam in the Kurnool district of Andhra Pradesh state in India. The SHPS is the third biggest generation capacity hydroelectric project in India with generation capacity of 1,670 MW.

(4) **Nathpa Jhakri Hydroelectric Power Station (NJHPS):** The NJHPS is a concrete gravity hydroelectric dam on the Satluj River in Himachal Pradesh of India. The comprehensive objective of the dam is to generate the hydroelectric power for customer satisfaction and industrial development. This reliable power station supplies a 1,500 MW underground power station with water energy.

(5) **Sardar Sarovar Hydroelectric Power Station (SSHPS):** Sardar Sarovar Hydroelectric Power Station has a gravity dam with 1450 MW generation capacity on the Narmada River near Navagam, Gujarat, in India. The SSHPS is the largest hydroelectric dam and a prestigious part of the Narmada Valley Project. It is a large hydraulic engineering project involving the construction of a series of large irrigation and hydroelectric multi-purpose dams on the Narmada River.

(6) **Bhakra-Nangal Hydroelectric Power Station (BNHPS):** Bhakra-Nangal Hydroelectric Power Station has a concrete gravity hydroelectric dam with 1325 MW power generation capacity across the Sutlej River. The BNHPS is located at Bilaspur, Himachal Pradesh, in India. The second largest BNHPS reservoir in India is known as the Gobind Sagar, which stores up to 9.34 billion cubic metres of water for hydroelectric power generation.

(7) **Karcham Wangtoo Hydroelectric Power Station (KWHPS):** Karcham Wangtoo Hydroelectric Power plant is a 1,000 MW power station on the Sutlej River at Kinnaur district in Himachal Pradesh state of India. The KWHPS dam is located between two villages known as Karcham and Wangtoo. This dam was constructed by Jaypee Group and sold it out to JSW Group after some time.

(8) **Indira Sagar Hydroelectric Power Station (ISHPS):** Indira Sagar is a multipurpose project of Madhya Pradesh state constructed on the Narmada River at Narmada Nagar in Khandwa district of Madhya Pradesh. In terms of the storage of water, it withholds the largest reservoir in India. The installed capacity of this multipurpose Indira Sagar Project is 1,000 MW.

(9) **Nagarjuna Sagar Hydroelectric Power Station (NSHPS):** This dam is a masonry dam with an installed capacity of 816 MW on the Krishna River at Nagarjuna Sagar. NSHPS is located in the border of Guntur and Nalgonda districts of Andhra Pradesh State of India. This dam was constructed between 1955 and 1967.

(10) **Idukki Hydroelectric Power Station (IHPS):** Idukki dam is located in Kerala state of India. It is a 168.91 meters or 554 feet tall arch hydroelectric dam. The dam is constructed with a beautiful view between the two mountains—Kuravanmala and Kurathimala. The IHPS was constructed and is owned by the Kerala State Electricity Board (KSEB). This hydroelectric dam supports to a 780 MW hydroelectric power station located in Moolamattom.

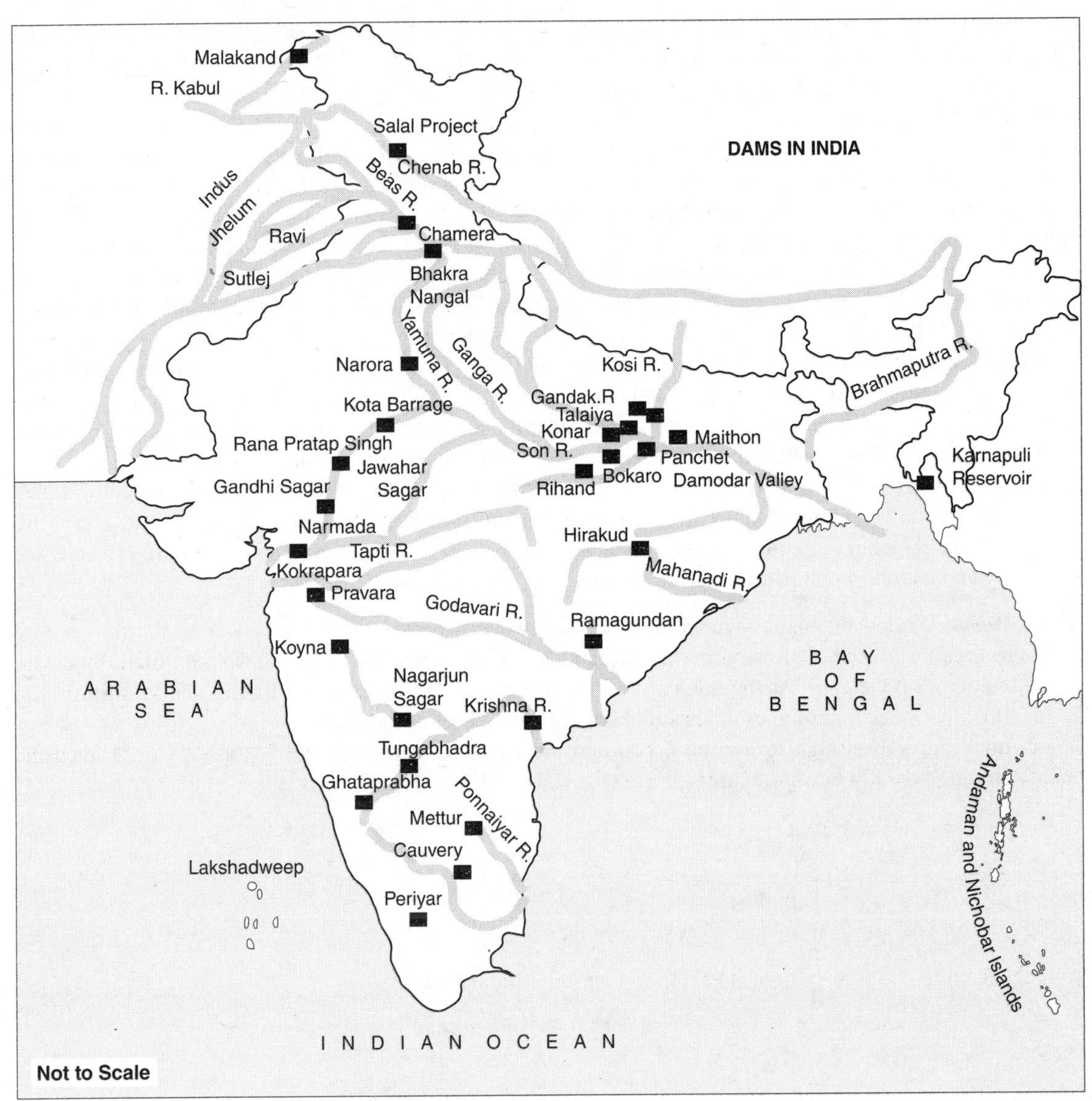

Fig. 1.14(b) *Hydroelectric Dams in India*

Pumped Storage Scheme In areas where sufficient hydrogeneration is not available, peak load may be handled by means of pumped storage. This consists of upper and lower reservoirs and reversible turbine-generator sets, which can also be used as motor-pump sets. The upper reservoir has enough storage for about 6 h of full load generation. Such a plant acts as a conventional hydroelectric plant during the peak load periods, when production costs are the highest. The turbines are driven by water from the upper reservoir in the usual manner. During the light load period, water in the lower reservoir is pumped back into the upper one so as to be ready for use in the next cycle of the peak load period. The generators in this period, change to synchronous motor action and drive the turbines which now work as pumps. The electric power is supplied to the generator sets from the general power network or an adjoining thermal plant. The overall efficiency of the generator sets is normally as high as 60–70%. The pumped storage scheme, in fact, is analogous to the charging and discharging of a battery. It has the added advantage that the synchronous machines can be used as synchronous condensers for VAR compensation of the power network, if required. In a way from the point of view of the thermal sector of the power system, the pumped storage scheme *shaves the peaks* and fills the *troughs* of the daily load-demand curve.

Some of the existing pumped storage plants are 900 MW Srisailem in AP, 80 MW of Bhiva in MS, 400 MW Kadamparai in TN. Tehri Pumped Storage Plant (PSP) comprising four reversible pump turbine units of 250 MW each, involves construction of an Underground Machine Hall on the left bank of river Bhagirathi. The 1,000MW Tehri PSP is part of the 2,400MW Tehri Hydro Power Complex being built on the river Bhagirathi, in the Indian state of Uttarakhand. The operation of Tehri PSP is based on the concept of recycling of water discharged between upper reservoir and lower reservoir. The Tehri Dam reservoir shall function as the upper reservoir and Koteshwar reservoir as the lower balancing reservoir. The Sardar Sarovar Dam is a concrete gravity dam on the Narmada river in Kevadiya near Navagam, Gujarat in India. Four Indian states, Gujarat, Madhya Pradesh, Maharashtra and Rajasthan, receive water and electricity supplied from the dam. The main power plant houses 6 × 200 MW Francis pump-turbines to generate electricity and include a pumped storage capability.

Tidal Power Along the shores with high tides and when a basin exists, the power in the tide can be hydroelectrically utilised. This requires a long and low dam across the basin. Two sets of turbines are located underneath the dam. As the tide comes in, water flows into the basin operating one set of turbines. At low tide, the water flows out of the basin operating another set of turbine.

Let tidal range from high to low be h (m) and area of water stored in the basin be A (m^2), then the energy stored in the full basin is expressed as

$$E = \rho g A \int_0^h x\,dx \tag{1.6}$$

$$= \frac{1}{2}\rho g h^2 A$$

Average power, $P = \frac{1}{2}\rho g h^2 A/(T/2)$; T = period of tidal cycle

= 14 h 44 min, normally

$$= \rho g h^2 A/T$$

A few places which have been surveyed in the world as sites for tidal power are as follows:

Passanaquoddy Bay (N. America)	5.5 m, 262 km^2, 1,800 MW
San Jose (S. America)	10.7 m, 777 km^2, 19,900 MW
Sever (UK)	9.8 m, 70 km^2, 8,000 MW

A tidal power station has been constructed on the La Rance estuary in northern France where the tidal height range is 9.2 m and the tidal flow is estimated to be 18,000 m^3/sec.

Major sites in India where preliminary investigations have been carried out are Bhavnagar, Navalakhi (Kutch), Diamond Harbour and Ganga Sagar. The potential areas are in the Gulf of Khambhat, Gulf of Kutch and southern regions in Gujarat, Palk Bay-Mannar Channel in Tamil Nadu, and Hoogly river, South Haldia and Sunderbans in West Bengal. According to the study, the Gulf of Kambhat and Gulf of Kutch near Gujarat have an estimated potential of 7,000 MW and 1,200 MW, respectively, with Sunderbans having a potential of 100 MW. According to the estimates of the Indian government, the country has a potential of 8,000 MW of tidal energy. This includes about 7,000 MW in the Gulf of Cambay in Gujarat, 1,200 MW in the Gulf of Kutch and 100 MW in the Gangetic delta in the Sunderbans region of West Bengal.

India's first Tidal Power Project is being developed by WBREDA at Durgaduani Creek in the Sunderbans delta. High tide water is stored in a reservoir and released at low tide, thus creating water flows which drive turbines that generate electricity. The total cost for 50 MW project in Gujarat is Rs 750 crores and will be ready by 2013.

The basin in Kandla in Gujarat has been estimated to have a capacity of 600 MW. The total potential of Indian coast is around 9000 MW. India has a vast coastline of 7517 kms, which does not compare favourably with the sites in the American continent stated above. The technical and economic difficulties still prevail.

1.6 ▶ MAGNETOHYDRODYNAMIC (MHD) GENERATION

In thermal generation of electric energy, the heat released by the fuel is converted to rotational mechanical energy by means of a thermocycle. The mechanical energy is then used to rotate the electric generator. Thus, two stages of energy conversion are involved in which the heat to mechanical energy conversion has an inherently low efficiency. Also, the rotating machine has its associated losses and maintenance problems. In MHD, technology electric energy is directly generated by the hot gases produced by the combustion of fuel without the need for mechanical moving parts.

In an MHD generator, electrically conducting gas at a very high temperature is passed in a strong magnetic field, thereby generating electricity. High temperature is needed to ionise the gas, so that it has good electrical conductivity. The conducting gas is obtained by burning a fuel and injecting a seeding material such as potassium carbonate in the products of combustion. The principle of MHD power generation is illustrated in Fig. 1.15. Electrically conducting gas as it flows is equivalent to electric current flowing in an imaginary conductor at 90° to the magnetic field. The result is induction of emf across an anode and cathode with current flowing through the load. About 50% efficiency can be achieved, if the MHD generator is operated in tandem with a conventional steam plant.

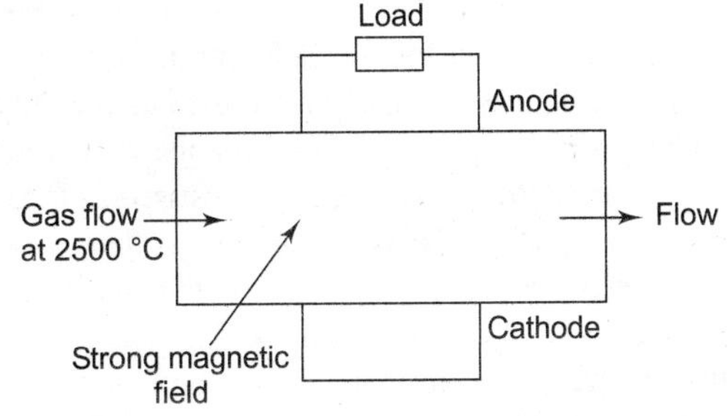

Fig. 1.15 *The principle of MHD power generation*

Although the technological feasibility of MHD generation has been established, its economic feasibility is yet to be demonstrated. In fact with the development of CCGT systems, which are being installed in many countries, MHD development has been put on the shelf.

1.7 ▶ GEOTHERMAL ENERGY

The outer crust of earth contains a very large reserve of energy as sensible heat. It is estimated to be one to two orders of magnitude larger than all the energy recoverable from uranium (by fission) and thorium (by breeder reactor assuming 60–70% efficiency). Fusion as and when it becomes technologically practical would represent a large energy resource than geothermal energy.

Geothermal energy is present over the entire extent of earth's surface except that it is nearer to the surface in volcanic areas. Heat transfer from the earth's interior is by three primary means:

1. Direct heat conduction,
2. Rapid injection of ballistic magma along natural rifts penetrating deep into earth's mantle, and
3. Bubble like magma that buoys upwards towards the surface.

Rift geothermal areas in sedimentary rock basins undergo repeated injection of magma, though in small amount. Over a long period of time, these processes cause massive amounts of hot water to accumulate. Examples are the Imperiod Valley of Africa. The weight of the overburden in these sedimentary basins compresses the trapped water giving rise to a geopressurised geothermal resource. These high pressures serve to increase the productivity of hot-water wells, which may be natural or drilled.

Pressure released in the hot wells causes boiling and the steam and water mixture rise upwards. This mixture is passed through steam separators, which then is used to drive low-pressure steam turbines. Corrosive effects of this wet steam, because of mineral particles in it, have been tackled by advanced metallurgy. The capital cost of these plants is 40 to 60% less than that of fossil fuel and nuclear plants, because no boiler or nuclear reactor is needed to generate steam.

Geothermal plants have proved useful for base-load power plants. These kind of plants are primarily entering the market where modest sized plants are needed with low capital cost, short construction period and life-long fuel (i.e., geothermal heat). The geothermal energy installed capacity is experimental in India; however, the potential capacity is more than 10,000 MW. Geothermal Atlas of India, prepared by the Geological Survey of India (GSI), gives information/data for more than 300 geothermal potential sites. Following are the six most promising geothermal energy sites in India−Tattapani in Chhattisgarh, Puga in Jammu & Kashmir, Cambay Graben in Gujarat, Manikaran in Himachal Pradesh, Surajkund in Jharkhand and Chhumathang in Jammu & Kashmir.

High air-quality standards are easily attained by geothermal plants at a minimal cost such that they have an edge over clean coal-fuelled plants. Considerable research and development effort is being devoted towards geothermal plants siting, designing, fabricating, installation and operation. Efforts are also on to tap the heat potential of volcanic regions and from hot volcanic rock.

No worth mentioning effort is being made in India at present. In India, feasibility studies of a 1 MW station at Peggy valley in Ladakh are being carried out. Another geothermal field has been located at Chumantang. There are a number of hot springs in India, but the total exploitable energy potential seems to be very little.

The present installed geothermal plant capacity in the world is about 10715 MW and the total estimated capacity is immense, provided volcanic 'regions' heat can be utilised. Since the pressure and temperatures are low, the efficiency is even less than that of the conventional fossil-fuelled plants, but the capital costs are less and the fuel is available free of cost.

1.8 ▶ ENVIRONMENTAL ASPECTS OF ELECTRIC ENERGY GENERATION

As far as environmental and health risks involved in nuclear plants of various kinds are concerned, these have already been discussed at length in Section 1.7. Equally, the problems related to large hydroelectric plants have been dwelled upon in Section 1.5. Therefore, we shall now focus our attention on fossil-fuel plants including gas-based plants.

Conversion of one form of energy or another to electrical form has unwanted side effects and the pollutants generated in the process have to be disposed off. The reader may refer to Fig. 1.16, which brings out all the

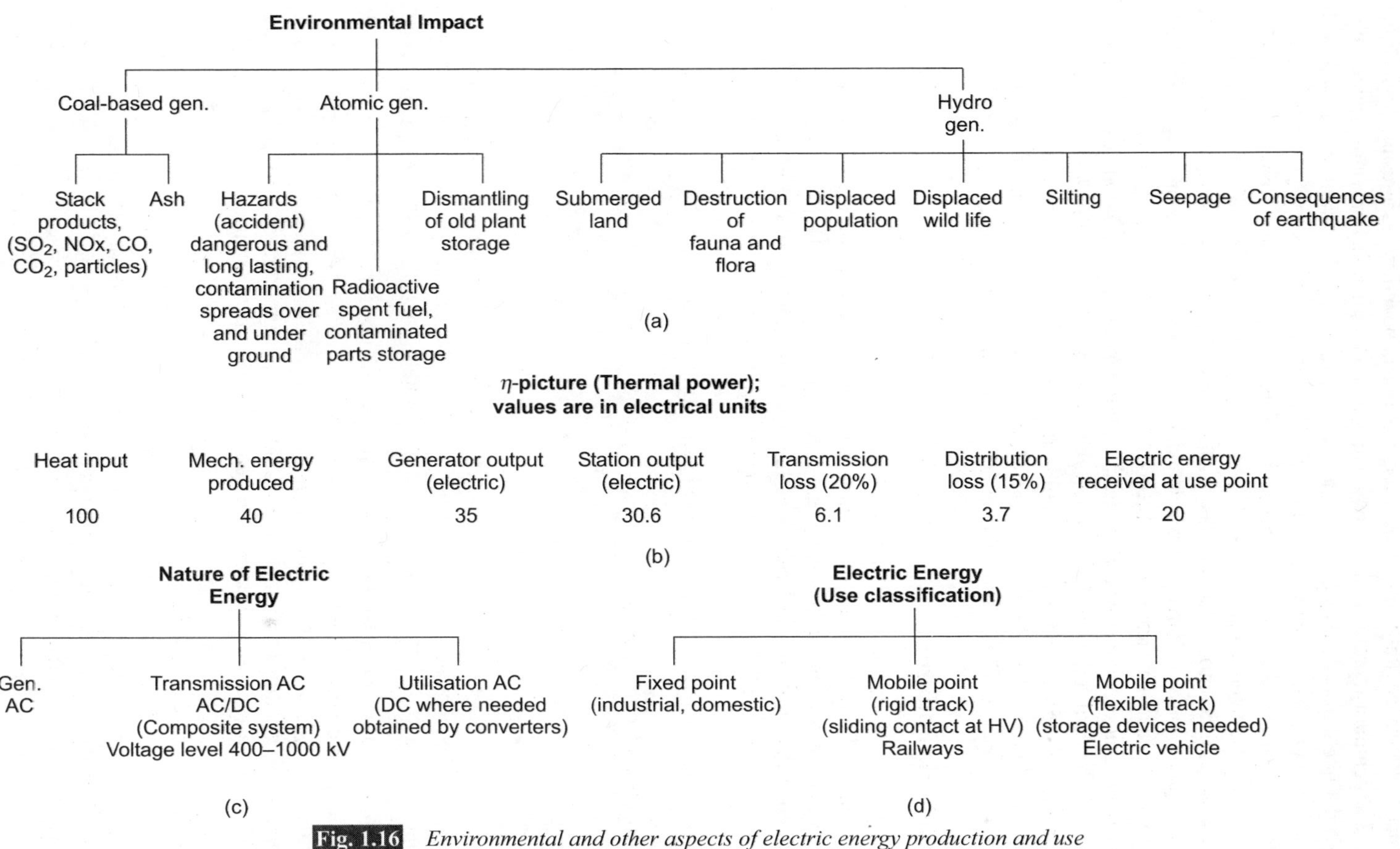

Fig. 1.16 *Environmental and other aspects of electric energy production and use*

associated problems at a glance. Pollutants know no geographical boundary; as a result of which the pollution issue has become a nightmarish problem and strong national and international pressure groups have sprung up and are having a definite impact on the development of energy resources. Governmental awareness has created increasing legislation at national and international levels. The power engineers have to be fully conversant with these in their professional practice and in the survey and planning of large power projects. Lengthy, time consuming procedures at government level, PIL (public interest litigation) and demonstrative protests have delayed several projects in several countries. This has led to favouring of small size projects and redevelopment of existing sites. But with the yawning gap in electric demand and production, our country has to move forward for several large thermal, hydro and nuclear power projects.

Emphasis is being laid on conservation issues, curtailment of transmission losses, theft, subsidised power supplies and above all on *sustainable development* with *appropriate technology* wherever feasible. It has to be particularly assured that no irreversible damage is caused to the environment which would affect the living conditions of the future generations. Irreversible damages like ozone layer holes and global warming caused by increase in CO_2 in the atmosphere are already showing up.

1.8.1 Atmospheric Pollution

We shall treat here only pollution as caused by thermal plants using coal as feed-stock. The fossil fuel-based generating plants form the backbone of power generation in our country and also round the globe as other options (like nuclear and even hydro) have even stronger hazards associated with them. Also, it should be understood that pollution in large cities like Delhi is caused more by vehicular traffic and their emission. In Delhi of course, Inderprastha and Badarpur power stations contribute their share in certain areas.

Problematic pollutants in emission of coal-based generating plants are

1. SO_2
2. NO_x, nitrogen oxides
3. CO
4. CO_2
5. Certain hydrocarbons
6. Particulates

Although the account that follows will be general, it needs to be mentioned here that Indian coal has a comparatively low sulphur content but a very high ash content, which in some coals may be as high as 53%.

A brief account of various pollutants, their likely impact and methods of abatements are presented below.

Oxides of Sulphur (SO_2) Most of the sulphur present in the fossil fuel is oxidised to SO_2 in the combustion chamber before being emitted by the chimney. In atmosphere it gets further oxidised to H_2SO_4 and metallic sulphates, which are the major source of concern as these can cause acid rain, impaired visibility and damage to buildings and vegetation. Sulphate concentrations of 9–10 $\mu g/m^3$ of air, aggravate asthma, lung and heart disease. It may also be noted that although sulphur does not accumulate in air, it does so in soil.

Sulphur emission can be controlled by

1. Use of fuel with less than 1% sulphur; generally not a feasible solution,
2. Use of chemical reaction to remove sulphur in the form of sulphuric acid from combustion products by limestone scrubbers or fluidised bed combustion, and
3. Removing sulphur from the coal by gasification or floatation processes.

It has been noticed that the byproduct sulphur could off-set the cost of sulphur recovery plant.

Oxides of Nitrogen (NO_x) Of these Nitrogen oxide, NO_2 is a major concern as a pollutant. It is soluble in water and can have adverse effects on human health as it enters the lungs on inhaling and after combining with moisture converts to nitrous and nitric acids, which damage the lungs. At levels of 25–100 parts per million, NO_x can cause acute bronchitis and pneumonia.

Emission of NO_x can be controlled by fitting advanced technology burners which can assure more complete combustion, thereby reducing these oxides from being emitted by the stack. These can also be removed from the combustion products by absorption process by certain solvents going on to the stack.

Oxides of Carbon (CO, CO_2) CO is a very toxic pollutant, but it gets converted to CO_2 in the open atmosphere (if available) surrounding the plant. On the other hand, CO_2 has been identified as a major cause of global warming. It is not yet a serious problem in developing countries.

Hydrocarbons During the oxidation process in combustion chamber, certain light weight hydrocarbons may be formed. The compounds are a major source of photo-chemical reaction that add to the depletion of ozone layer.

Particulates (Fly ash) Dust content is particularly high in the Indian coal. Particulates come out of the stack in the form of fly ash. It comprises fine particles of carbon, ash and other inert materials. In high concentrations, these can cause poor visibility and respiratory diseases.

Concentration of pollutants can be reduced by the dispersal over a wider area by use of high stacks. Precipitators can be used to remove particles as the flue gases rise up the stack. If in the stack a vertical wire is strung in the middle and charged to a high negative potential, it emits electrons. These electrons are captured by the gas molecules thereby becoming negative ions. These ions accelerate towards the walls, get neutralised on hitting the walls and the particles drop down the walls. Precipitators have a high efficiency, up to 99% for large particles, but they have a poor performance for particles of size less than 0.1 μm in diameter. The efficiency of precipitators is high with reasonable sulphur content in flue gases but drops for low sulphur content coals; 99% for 3% sulphur and 83% for 0.5% sulphur.

Fabric filters in the form of bag houses also have been employed and are located before the flue gases enter the stack.

1.8.2 Thermal Pollution

Steam from low-pressure turbine has to be liquefied in a *condenser* and reduced to lowest possible temperature to maximise the thermodynamic efficiency. The best efficiency of steam cycle practically achievable is about 40%. It means that 60% of the heat in steam at the end of cycle must be removed. This is achieved by two methods:

1. Once Through Circulation through condenser cooling tubes of sea or river water where available. This raises the temperature of water in these two sources and threatens sea and river life around in sea and downstream in river. These are serious environmental objections and many times cannot be overruled and also, there may be legislation against it.

2. Cooling Towers Cool water is circulated around the condenser tube to remove heat from the exhaust steam in order to condense it. The circulating water gets hot in the process. It is pumped to the cooling towers and is sprayed through nozzles into a rising volume of air. Some of the water evaporates providing cooling. The latent heat of water is 2×10^6 J/kg and cooling can occur fast. But this has the disadvantage of raising the humidity to high (undesirable) levels in the surrounding areas. Of course, the water evaporated must be made up in the system by adding fresh water from the source. These cooling towers are known as *wet towers*.

Closed cooling towers where condensate flows through tubes and air is blown on these tubes avoids the humidity problem but at much higher cost. In India, only wet towers are being used.

1.8.3 Electromagnetic Radiation from Overhead Lines

Biological effects of electromagnetic radiation from power lines and even cables in close proximity of buildings have recently attracted attention and have also caused some concern. Power frequency (50/60 Hz) and even their harmonics are not considered harmful. Investigations carried out in certain advanced countries have so far proved inconclusive. The electrical and electronics engineers, while being aware of this controversy, must know that many other environmental agents are moving around that can cause far greater harm to human health than does electromagnetic radiation.

As a piece of information, it may be quoted that directly under an overhead line of 400 kV, the electric field strength is 11000 V/m and magnetic flux density (depending on current) may as much as 40 μT. Electric field strength in the range of 10,000–15,000 V/m is considered safe.

1.8.4 Visual and Audible Impacts

These environmental problems are caused by the following factors:

1. Right of way acquires land underneath. At present it is not a serious problem in India, but in future the problem will show up. This is futuristic.
2. Lines converging at a large substation mar the beauty of the landscape around. Underground cables as an alternative are too expensive a proposition except in congested city areas.
3. Radio frequency interference (RFI) has to be taken into account and countered by various means.
4. The phenomenon of *corona* (a sort of electric discharge around the high tension line) produces a hissing noise which is audible when habitation is in close proximity. At the towers, great attention must be paid to tightness of joints, avoidance of sharp edges and use of earth screen shielding to limit audible noise to acceptable levels. (For details, see Ch.19 of Ref. 28.)
5. Workers inside a power plant are subjected to various kinds of noise (particularly near the turbines) and vibration of floor. To reduce this noise to a tolerable level, foundations and vibration filters have to be designed properly and simulation studies carried out. The workers must be given regular medical examinations and sound medical advice.

1.9 ▶ RENEWABLE ENERGY RESOURCES

In the account that has preceded, we have concentrated mostly on those energy resources which are nonreplenishable as brought out in Fig. 1.5 (left side). These are mainly coal, oil, gas and nuclear fission. Apart from the fact that these cannot last for long, considering the galloping rate at which electricity use is rising, they have serious environmental impacts and hazards associated with electric power generation as brought out in Fig. 1.16(a). This has led to a concerted international effort in research and development of renewable energy resources. They offer viable options to address the energy security issues. India has one of the highest potentials for the effective use of renewables. Special emphasis has been laid on the generation of grid quality power from them.

A major source of renewable energy is solar radiation being cyclically received by most land area of the globe. Its various manifestations presented in Fig. 1.5 (right side) are as follows:

1. Direct use;
2. Winds on land area of globe;

3. Potential energy of rain and snow at high altitudes, i.e., hydro energy, and
4. Biofuel.

Gravitational pull of moon on earth

1. Tidal energy;
2. Wave energy.

Geothermal It is considered renewable because the resource is unlimited.

All the above resources, other than geothermal, pass through the environment as *energy current or flow*. Together, these energy flows are called *energy flux*. The earth's habitable surface is crossed by or accessible to an average energy flux of about 500 W/m^2. If this flux can be harnessed at just about 4% efficiency, a 10 m × 10 m surface would contribute 2 kW of power using suitable methods. Assume that an average suburban person consumes 2 kW and a population density of 500 persons/km^2. At 2 kW per person, the total energy demand of 1000 kW/km^2 could be met by using just 5% of land area for energy production. This could provide a fairly satisfactory standard of living across the globe. Realistically, it is not that promising, as harnessing renewable energy is not an easy task and ridden with technological problems whose economic solutions are yet to be found. To further complicate matters, the renewable energy flux is far from uniformally distributed round the globe.

On account of the environmental impact of harnessing hydro energy and the limitation of harnessing tidal energy, these have been treated in Section 1.5. Geothermal energy has also been considered along with thermal generation in Section 1.7.

We shall now study solar energy and wind energy, the methods of harnessing these and the difficulties encountered. We shall also touch up biofuel.

Wave Energy The energy content of sea waves is very high. In India, with several hundreds of kilometres of coastline, a vast source of energy is available. The power in the wave is proportional to the square of the amplitude and to the period of the motion. Therefore, the long period (~10 s), large amplitude (~2 m) waves are of considerable interest for power generation, with energy fluxes commonly averaging between 50 and 70 kW/m width of oncoming wave. Though the engineering problems associated with wave-power are formidable, the amount of energy that can be harnessed is large and the development work is in progress. Sea wave power estimated potential is 20,000 MW.

Ocean Thermal Energy Conversion (OTEC) The ocean is the world's largest solar collector. Temperature difference of 20°C between warm, solar absorbing surface water and cooler 'bottom' water can occur. This can provide a continually replenished store of thermal energy which is in principle available for conversion to other energy forms. OTEC refers to the conversion of some of this thermal energy into work and thence into electricity. Estimated potential of ocean thermal power in India is 50,000 MW.

A proposed plant using sea temperature difference would be situated 25 km east of Miami (USA), where the temperature difference is 17.5°C.

1.10 ► SOLAR ENERGY AND ITS UTILISATION

Solar energy is a free source which is not only naturally renewable but is also environment friendly and thus, helps in lessening the greenhouse effects. As shall be seen in the account that follows, it can only supplement to a (very) limited extent the burgeoning need for energy across the globe. In India, with a deficient grid power and large number of sunny days across the country, solar energy as a supplement is particularly attractive.

1.10.1 The Sun and Solar Energy

The sun is a spherical mass of hot gases, with a diameter of about 1.39×10^9 m and at an average distance of 1.5×10^{11} m from the earth. Energy is being continuously produced in the sun through various nuclear fusion reactions, the most important one being where four protons combine to form a helium nucleus.

$$H_2 + H_2 \rightarrow He + 15 \text{ MeV}$$

The mass lost in the process is converted into energy. These reactions occur in the innermost core of the sun, where the temperature is estimated to be $(8\text{–}40) \times 10^6$ K. The various layers of differing temperatures and densities emit and absorb different wavelengths making the solar spectrum quite composite. However, the sun essentially acts as a black body having a 5800 K temperature. The spectral distribution of solar radiation at the earth's mean distance is shown in Fig. 1.17.

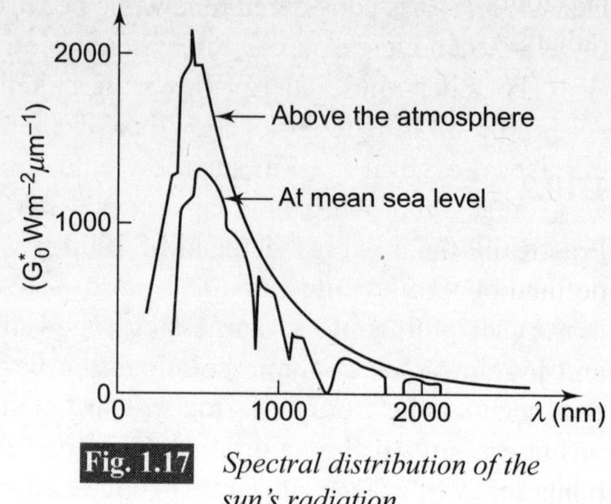

Fig. 1.17 *Spectral distribution of the sun's radiation*

The solar constant is the radiant flux density incident on a plane normal to the sun's rays at a distance of 1.49×10^8 km from the sun and is given by the area under the curve in Fig. 1.17. It has a value of

$$G_o^* = 1367 \text{ W/m}^2$$

The received flux density varies by ±1.5% during the day's course due to variations in the sun's output, and by about ±4% over the year due to the earth's elliptic orbit. The solar spectrum can be divided into three main regions:

1. Ultraviolet region ($\lambda < 400$ µm) 9%;
2. Visible region (400 nm $< \lambda <$ 700 nm) 45%; and
3. Infrared region ($\lambda > 700$ nm) 46%.

The radiation in the wavelengths above 2500 nm are negligible.

The earth's atmosphere absorbs various components of the radiation to different levels. The short wave UV and X-ray regions are almost completely absorbed by oxygen and nitrogen gases and ions; the ozone absorbs UV rays. The atmosphere unaffected by dust or clouds acts as an open window for the visible region. Up to 20% of the IR (Infrared) radiation is absorbed by the water vapour and CO_2. The carbon dioxide concentration in the atmosphere is about 0.03% by volume and is beginning to rise with pollutants being let off into the atmosphere. The water vapour concentration can vary greatly (up to 4% by volume). Dust, water droplets and other molecules scatter the sun's radiation.

The sun's radiation at the earth's surface is composed of two components: *beam radiation* and *diffuse radiation*. Beam or direct radiation consists of radiation along the line connecting the sun and the receiver as shown in Fig. 1.18(a). Diffuse radiation is the radiation scattered by the atmosphere without any unique direction as in Fig. 1.18(b). There is also a reflected component due to terrestrial surface. Total radiation is shown in Fig. 1.18(c).

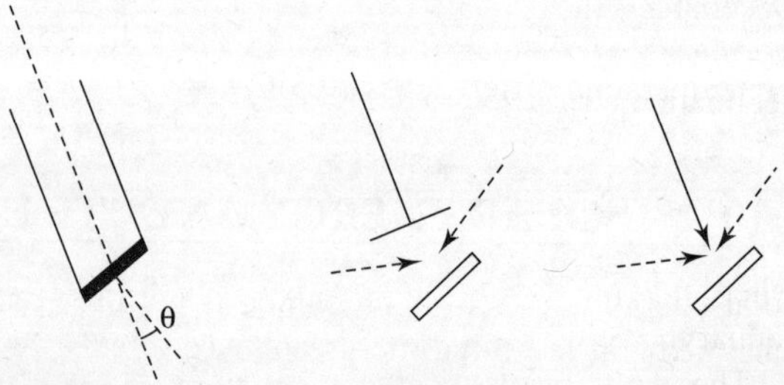

θ

(a) Beam component G_{bc} (b) Diffuse G_{dc} (c) Total G_{tc}

Fig. 1.18 *Components of solar radiation reaching earth*

It easily follows from these figures that [21]

$$G_{bc} = G^*_b \cos \theta \tag{1.7}$$

For a horizontal surface, the relation becomes

$$G_{bh} = G^*_b \cos \theta_z \tag{1.8}$$

Here, θ_z (called the Zenith angle) is the angle of incidence of beam component of solar radiation for a horizontal surface. θ is shown in Fig. 1.18(a). G^*_b is intensity of beam component of normally incident solar radiation on a surface. Adding the beam of the diffuse components, we get

$$G = G_{tc} = G_{bc} + G_{dc} \tag{1.9}$$

1.10.2 Variation of Insolation

Practically the earth is a sphere of radius 6400 km which rotates once in 24 h about its own axis. The axis defined by the North and South poles is shown in Fig. 1.19.

Any point P on the earth's surface is determined by its latitude ϕ and longitude ψ. The latitude is positive in the northern hemisphere, and negative in the southern hemisphere. The longitude is measured positive eastward from Greenwich, England. The vertical North-South plane through P is called *Local Meridional Plane*. Solar noon at P and all places of the same longitude is defined, when the sun is included in the meridional plane. However, clocks do not necessarily show solar time as they are set to civil time common to time zones spanning 15° of longitude. Also, the true interval between two successive solar noons is not exactly 24 h due to the elliptic orbit of the earth. The hour angle ω is the angle by which the earth has rotated since the solar noon.

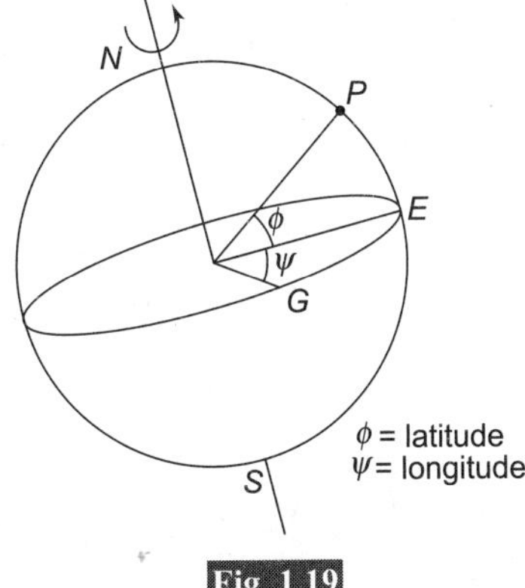

Fig. 1.19

$$\omega = 15°/\text{h} \times (T_{\text{solar}} - 12\text{ h}) \tag{1.10}$$

or

$$\omega = 15°\text{ h} \times (T_{\text{zone}} - 12\text{ h}) + (\psi - \psi_{\text{zone}}) \tag{1.11}$$

where T_{solar} is the solar time and T_{zone} is the zone time.

The earth revolves around the sun in an elliptic orbit in 365 days with its axis inclined at angle $\delta_0 = 23.5°$ to the normal to the plane of revolution around the sun.

The *declination* δ is defined as the angle between the equatorial plane and the sun's direction. It varies from +23.5° to –23.5° from 21st June to 21st December—the *summer and winter solstices in the Northern Hemisphere*. It is zero on the *equinoxes*. The declination can be expressed as

$$\delta = \delta_0 \sin \left(\frac{360°(284 + n)}{365} \right) \tag{1.12}$$

where n is the day of the year counted from the 1st of January.

The daily insolation is the total energy received from the sun per unit area in one day. The variation of daily insolation with latitude and season is shown in Fig. 1.20.

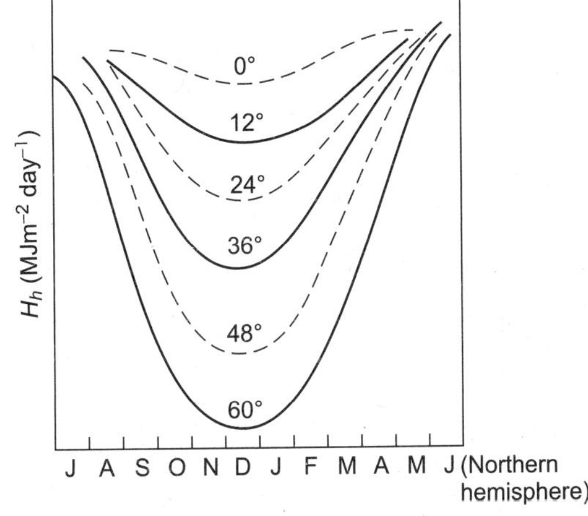

Fig. 1.20 Variation in daily insolation

The variation arises due to three main factors:

1. Variation in the length of the day;
2. Orientation of the receiving surface due to the earth's declination; and
3. Variation in atmospheric absorption.

1.10.3 Geometry of the Collector and Solar Beam

For a tilted collector surface as in Fig. 1.21, the following angles are defined. Slope β is the angle between the collector surface and the horizontal surface. *Azimuth angle* γ is the deviation of the projection of the normal to the collector surface on a horizontal plane. In the northern hemisphere for a south facing surface or horizontal surface, $\lambda = 0$. λ is positive for surface facing West of South, and negative for surfaces facing East of South. The general relation between various angles can be shown to be

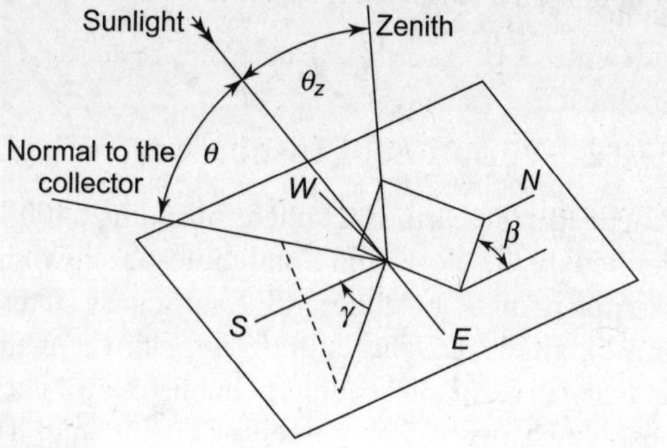

Fig. 1.21 *Geometry of the collector and solar beam*

$$\cos\theta = (A - B)\sin\delta + [C\sin\omega + (D + E)\cos\omega]\cos\delta \quad (1.13)$$

where

$$A = \sin\phi\cos\beta$$

$$B = \cos\phi\sin\beta\cos\gamma$$

$$C = \sin\beta\sin\gamma$$

$$D = \cos\phi\cos\beta$$

$$E = \sin\phi\sin\beta\cos\gamma$$

ω = hour angle given by the equation

For a horizontal plane, $\gamma = \beta = 0$; giving

$$\cos\theta = \sin\phi\sin\delta + \cos\phi\cos\omega\cos\delta \quad (1.14)$$

If the collector's slope equals the latitude, i.e., $\beta = \phi$, it will face the solar beam directly at noon. In this case,

$$\cos\theta = \cos\omega\cos\delta \quad (1.15)$$

1.10.4 Optimum Orientation of the Collectors

The insolation received at the collector's plane is the sum of beam and diffuse components, i.e.,

$$H_c = \int (G_b^* \cos\theta + G_d)\,dt \quad (1.16)$$

To maximise the energy collected, cos θ should be as close to 1 as possible. This is achieved by continuous *tracking*, always maintaining cos θ as 1 by letting the collector directly face the solar beam. By mounting the array on a two-axis tracker, upto 40% more energy, as compared to a fixed slope collector, can be collected. But this increases complexity and results in higher capital operation and maintenance costs. Single-axis tracking is less complex, but yields a smaller gain. However, as cos $\theta \approx 1$ for $\theta < 30°$, for most applications the collector can be kept with $\beta = \phi$ and $\gamma = 0°$. The specific tracking method to be adopted will depend on the energy demand variation. Tracking is particularly important in systems that operate under concentrated sunlight.

1.10.5 Applications of Solar Energy

Solar energy finds many applications, some of these being water heating, solar drying, desalination, industrial process heating and passive/active heating of buildings. However, because of the well-known advantages of electrical power, the methods of converting solar radiation into electricity have attracted the greatest attention. There are two essential ways of converting solar energy into electricity.

1. *Solar thermomechanical systems:* Here, the solar radiation is used to heat a working fluid which runs turbines.
2. *Solar photovoltaics:* Solar photovoltaics (SPV) convert radiant energy directly into an electric current.

In both of these systems, collecting systems are used to receive the radiant energy. These are described below.

Flat-plate Collectors These are used in low efficiency photovoltaics and low medium temperature thermal systems. In thermomechanical system, the flat-plate collector acts as a heat exchanger; transferring the radiant energy to a working fluid. The advantages of flat-plate collectors over concentrators are as follows:

1. Absorb the diffuse, direct and reflected components of the radiation;
2. Comparatively easy to fabricate and is cheaper; and
3. Since these are usually fixed in tilt and orientation, tracking is not required—this makes them maintenance free, except for surface cleaning.

For a solar-thermal flat-plate collector the components are as follows:

1. A flat metallic plate painted black to absorb radiation;
2. Channels attached to the plate where a working fluid removes the thermal energy; and
3. Thermal insolation at the back and sides of the collector, and a glass cover to minimise thermal losses.

Flat-plate collectors are popular in water heating systems.

Concentrating Collectors They are used in high temperature solar thermal systems and some high efficiency photovoltaics. There are various methods of classifying solar concentrators. They may be classified as refracting or reflecting, imaging or non-imaging, and on the basis of the type of reflecting surface as parabolic, spherical or flat. High temperatures are obtained by using central tower receivers and *heliostats*.

1.10.6 Solar Thermomechanical Systems

In solar thermomechanical systems, solar energy is converted to thermal energy of a working fluid. This thermal energy gets converted into shaft work by a turbine which runs generators. Heat engines (turbine) are based on the Rankine cycle, Sterling cycle or the Brayton cycle. Usually a fossil fuel heat source is also present as standby.

A schematic flow diagram for a solar power plant operating on Rankine cycle is shown in Fig. 1.22. The maximum theoretical *thermal efficiency*, the ratio of useful work done to the heat supplied, is expressed for the Carnot cycle in terms of the temperature of the reservoirs with which it is exchanging heat.

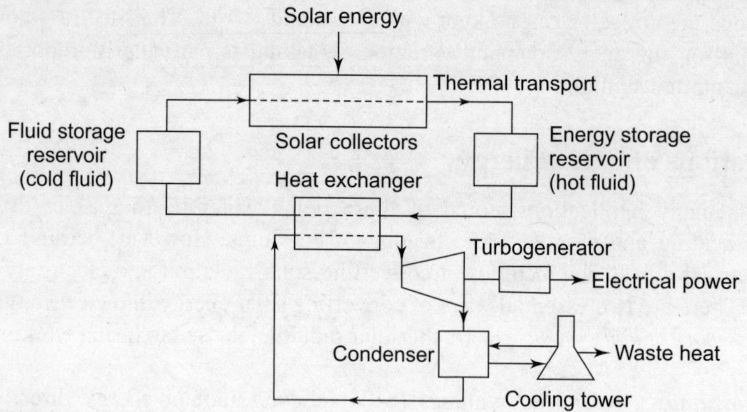

Fig. 1.22 *Schematic diagram of a solar power plant operating on the Rankine cycle*

$$\eta = 1 - \frac{T_L}{T_H} \tag{1.17}$$

where,

η = thermal efficiency of the Carnot cycle

T_L = absolute temperature (°C + 273) of the sink

T_H = absolute temperature of the source

For a solar energy system collecting heat at 121°C, the maximum thermal efficiency of any heat engine using this heat and rejecting heat to atmosphere at a low temperature of 10°C is

$$\eta = 1 - \frac{273 + 10}{273 + 121} = 0.282 \text{ or } 28.2\%$$

The efficiency of a real engine will be considerably less.

For obtaining efficiencies close to those of fossil fuel based stations, T_H must be raised to the same order of value. This is achieved by installing an array of mirrors, called heliostats, tracking the sun. One proposed scheme is shown in Fig. 1.23 for major generation of electricity with reflectors (with concentration factor of 30 or more) concentrating the sun's rays on to a single boiler for raising steam. A collector area of 1 km^2 would raise 100 MW of electrical power. The cost of such a scheme at present is prohibitive.

A less attractive alternative to this scheme (because of the lower temperatures) is the use of many individual absorbers tracking the sun unidirectionally, the thermal energy being transferred by a fluid (water or liquid sodium) to a central boiler.

Solar-thermal electric systems have certain inherent disadvantages of a serious nature. These are as follows:

1. Low efficiency. Raising efficiency to acceptable value brings in prohibitive costs.
2. The efficiency of the collecting system decreases as its temperature increases, but the efficiency of the heat engine increases with temperature.
3. All solar-thermal schemes essentially require storage because of the fluctuating nature of the sun's energy, although it has been proposed that the schemes be used as pure fuel savers.
4. In general, mechanical systems need great maintenance.
5. For a reliable system, fossil fuel backup may be needed.

Because of these factors considerable research effort is being devoted to solar photovoltaics as a viable alternative.

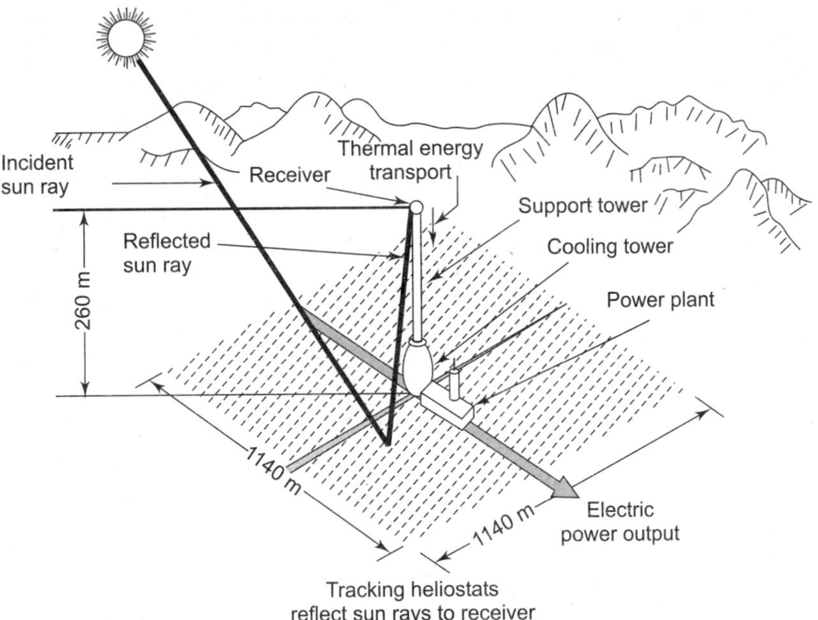

Fig. 1.23 *Proposed scheme for a large central solar-thermal electric generation*

1.10.7 Direct Conversion of Sunlight into Electricity

Photovoltaic (PV) or solar cell is a semiconductor device that converts sunlight directly into electricity. Initially PV cells had very limited use, e.g., in supplying electricity to satellites in space or for meeting energy requirements of defence personnel stationed at remote areas. However, with a gradual reduction in the cost of PV cells, current international price is now between 5 and 10$ per peak-watt and its use has been increasing steadily. It is projected that by the year 2015 or so, its share in power generation may be around 10–15%.

A PV cell can be classified–

1. in terms of materials: noncrystalline silicon, polycrystalline silicon, amorphous silicon, gallium arsenide, cadmium telluride, cadmium sulphide, idium arsenide, etc.
2. in terms of technology for fabrication single crystal bonds (or cylinders), ribbon growth, thin-film, etc.

Some of the important characteristics of various types of PV cells, measured at normal temperature (25°C) and under illumination level of 100 mW/cm^2, are listed in Table 1.1(c).

Table 1.1(c)

PV cell	*ff**	*Short-circuit current density (Isc) (mA/cm^2)*	*Open-circuit voltage (V_{oc}) (V)*	*Conversion efficiency (%)*
Monocrystalline silicon	0.85	20–22	0.5–0.6	13–14
Polycrystalline silicon	0.85	18–20	0.5–0.6	9–12
Amorphous silicon		13–14	2.2–2.4	5–6
Gallium arsenide	0.87	–	–	20–25

* *ff* is fill-factor which is defined later.

Basic Structure of PV Cell The basic structure of a typical PV cell is shown in Fig. 1.24(a) and (b). Various layers from top to bottom and their functions are as follows:

1. Top layer is a glass cover, transparency 90–95%. Its purpose is to protect the cell from dust, moisture, etc.
2. The next is a transparent adhesive layer which holds the glass cover.
3. Underneath the adhesive is an antireflection coating (ARC) to reduce the reflected sunlight to below 5%.

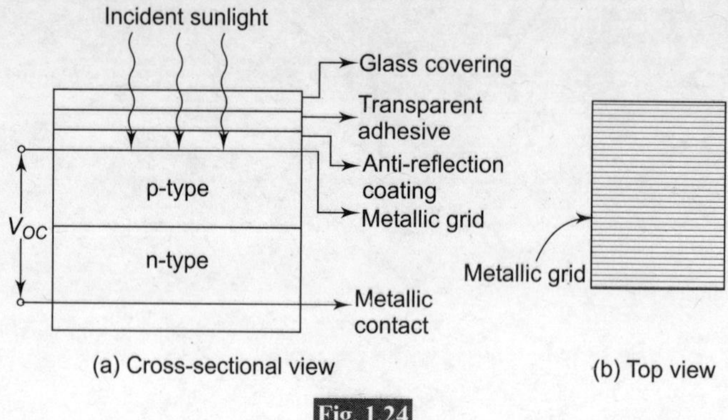

Fig. 1.24

4. Then follows a metallic grid (aluminium or silver) (Fig. 1.24(b)) which collects the charge carriers, generated by the cell under incidence of sunlight, for circulating to outside load.
5. Under the lower side of the metallic grid lies a p-layer followed by n-layer forming a pn-junction at their interface. The thickness of the top p-layer is so chosen that enough photons cross the junction to reach the lower n-layer.
6. Then follows another metallic grid in contact with the lower n-layer. This forms the second terminal of the cell.

Operation and Circuit Model The incidence of photons (sunlight) causes the generation of electron-hole pairs in both p and n-layers. Photons generated minority carriers (electrons in p-layer and holes in n-layer) freely cross the junction. This increases the minority carrier flow manifolds. Its major component is the light generated current I_G (when load is connected across the cell terminals). There is also the thermally generated small reverse saturation current I_s (minority carrier flow in same direction as I_G), also called *dark current* as it flows even in absence of light. I_G flows in opposite direction to I_D, the forward diode current of the junction. The cell feeds current I_L to load with a terminal voltage V.

The above operation suggests the circuit model of a PV cell as drawn in Fig. 1.25. The following Eq. (1.19) can be written from the circuit model and the well-known expression for

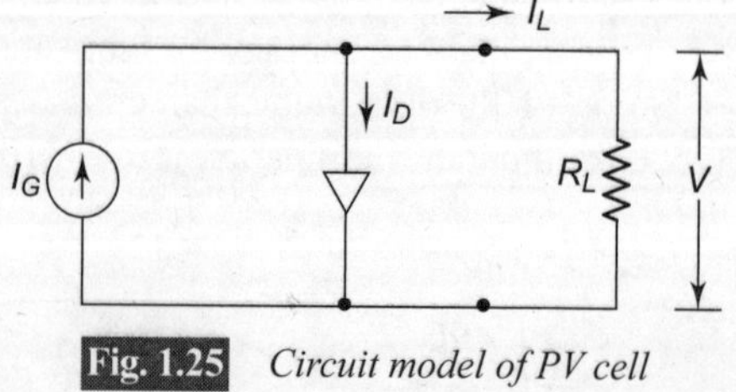

Fig. 1.25 *Circuit model of PV cell*

$$I_D = I_s\,(e^{\lambda V} - 1);\ \lambda = \frac{e}{kT} \tag{1.18}$$

where,

k = Boltzmann constant,

e = electronic charge and

T = cell temperature in degree K.

Load current $I_L = I_G - I_D$

$$= I_G - I_s\,(e^{\lambda V} - 1) \tag{1.19}$$

From this equation, it easily follows that

$$V_{OC}\,(I_L = 0) = \frac{1}{\lambda}\ \ln\left(\frac{I_G}{I_s} + 1\right) \tag{1.20}$$

and $$I_{SC}\,(V = 0) = I_G \tag{1.21}$$

Solar radiation generated current I_G is dependent on the intensity of light. The I–V characteristics of the cell are drawn in Fig. 1.26(a) for various values of intensity of solar radiation. One typical I–V characteristic of the cell is drawn in Fig. 1.26(b). Each point on this curve belongs to a particular power output. The point Q indicated on the curve pertains to the maximum power output at which the cell should be operated. At this point,

$$P_{\max} = V_{P\max}\, I_{P\max} \tag{1.22}$$

The *fill-factor* (ff) of a cell is defined as

$$ff = \frac{P_{\max}}{I_{SC}V_{SC}} \tag{1.23}$$

The cell efficiency is given as

$$\eta = \frac{P_{\text{out}}}{P_{\text{in}}} \tag{1.24}$$

where P_{out} is the power delivered to load and P_{in} is the solar power incident on the cell.

Effect of Temperature on Solar Cell Efficiency As the temperature increases, the diffusion of electrons and holes in the length of Si (or GaAs) increases causing an increase in the dark current and a decrease in V_{OC}. The overall effect causes a reduction in the efficiency of solar cell as the temperature increases. The practical efficiency of Si solar cell is about 12% and that of GaAs solar cell is 25% at the normal temperature of 300 K. With each degree rise in temperature, the efficiency decreases by a factor of 0.0042%.

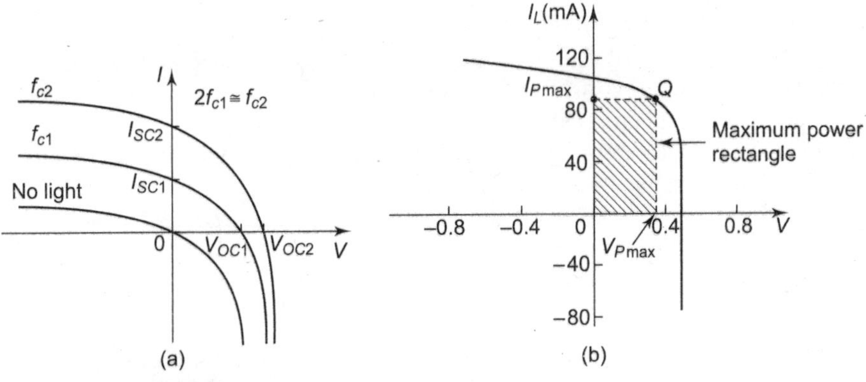

Fig. 1.26 *I–V (current–voltage) characteristics of a PV cell*

Spectral Response It is seen from the spectral response curves of Fig. 1.27 that the Selenium cell response curve nearly matches that of the eye. Because of this fact Se cell has a widespread application in photographic equipment such as exposure meters and automatic exposure diaphragm. Silicon response also overlaps the visible spectrum but has its peak at the 0.8 μm (8000 Å) wavelength, which is in the infrared region. In general, silicon has a higher conversion efficiency and greater stability and is less subject to fatigue. It is therefore widely used for present day commercial solar cells.

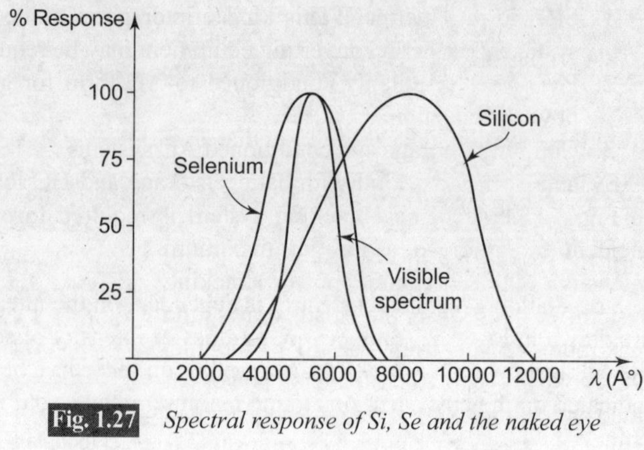

Fig. 1.27 *Spectral response of Si, Se and the naked eye*

1.10.8 Prevalent Technologies for Fabricating Silicon PV Cell

The most commonly used methods of manufacturing silicon PV cell from purified silicon feedstock are as follows:

1. Single crystal silicon with a uniform chemical structure.
2. Polycrystalline silicon-series of crystalline structures within a PV cell.
3. Amorphous silicon with a random atomic chemical structure.

The technological details of these three types of methods for manufacturing PV cells is not within the scope of this book. In general as the atomic structure becomes more random, less energy input and manufacturing complexity is required. However, more uniform structure means increased current collection and increased efficiency. Most PV power uses flat-plate modules of cut and polished wafer like cells of crystalline silicon, which are now about 12% conversion efficient.

Thin-film Technologies There are two main reasons why thin film offers promise of significant cost reduction. These are as follows:

1. Thin-film cells use only a few microns of direct material, instead of tens of mills used by crystalline, polycrystalline or *ribbon silicon modules*.
2. Construction of monolithic thin-film modules can be done at the same time that the cells are formatted, thus eliminating most of the cost of module fabrication. These two aspects of thin-film technology are further explained below.
   (a) Cadmium telluride can absorb 99% of the sun's energy in less than 0.5 μm thickness as opposed to the 8 mill requirement for crystalline silicon.
   (b) In conventional technologies, cells cut into individual parts are then circuited back together as discrete elements. Monolithic interconnection during cell fabrication eliminates labour and in addition produces a superior looking product because of its uniform finish.

1.10.9 Bulk Energy Conversion by SPV (Solar Photovoltaic) Cells

Bulk SPV power is feasible in bright, clear areas with sun most days of the year such that incident solar energy is about 2600 kWh/m^2 annually.

SPV cell produces DC power which is maximum at a particular point on its *I–V* characteristics (which changes with sunlight received). There are three ways in which this power can be used:

1. Storage in batteries – This kind of storage is limited in capacity and is therefore meant for small systems. Further reconverting equipment may be required for end use in AC form.
2. PV power is suitably conditioned to AC form for grid interactive use. This is the case with bulk power production.
3. Combined storage and conditioned AC systems.

System of the first kind with battery storage and DC load is drawn in conceptual block diagram form in Fig. 1.28. Mechanical tracking system is required to orient the SPV module at an angle 90° to the incident radiation so as to get maximum intensity. The maximum power tracking system ensures that the load draws the maximum power from the SPV module. DC voltage regulator delivers power at rated voltage despite variation in generated voltage and power. The charge controller is meant to protect the battery bank from both overcharging as well as deep discharging.

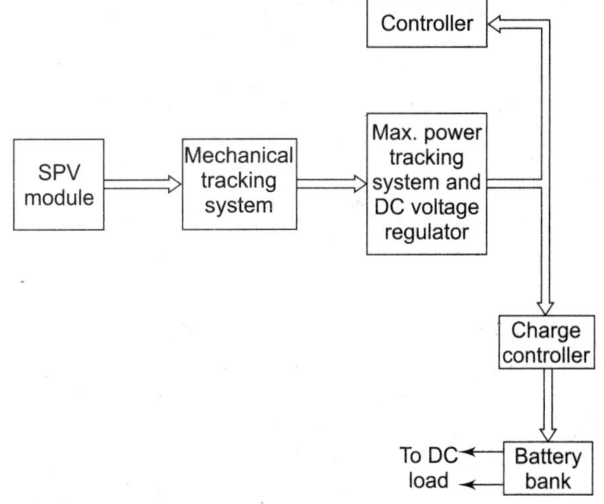

Fig. 1.28 *SPV system for feeding DC load with battery storage*

A grid interactive SPV system for domestic use is shown in the form of conceptual blocks in Fig. 1.29. Solar cells are connected in series–parallel and the voltage after conversion to AC form by solid state devices is not compatible with grid voltage (400 V at distribution load). This scheme, therefore, differs from that of Fig. 1.22 as the DC voltage has to be raised by the method of DC/DC high frequency chopping with an intervening inductor for raising the voltage. For grid interaction, a converter–inverter is required so that power can flow either way depending upon the amount of solar power availability during the day. A battery via converter–inverter feeds the domestic load at night (or on a cloudy day) if the grid outage occurs.

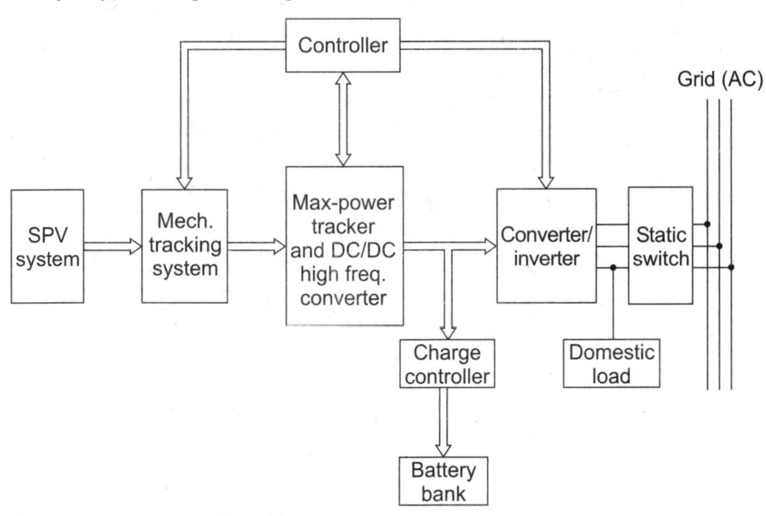

Fig. 1.29 *Grid interactive SPV system*

The process of conversion and reconversion with solid state devices like SCR (Silicon Controlled Rectifier) is called *power conditioning*. Such systems are already being used in cities in Japan, and are now available in India. For bulk solar power systems, the basic scheme will be similar except that it would directly feed power into the grid and no power need flow the other way. As and when a breakthrough in SPV technology and sharp reduction in cost is achieved, domestic and bulk power systems will become a common place. However, the intensity of solar insolation being low (1367 W/m^2), use of solar power requires considerable land area coverage (with shade underneath, all times, a different kind of pollution). The best estimate is that solar power will meet only 5–10% of the total electric energy need.

Total energy potential in India is 8×10^{15} kWh/yr. Upto 31.12.2010, 6,40,000 solar cookers, 55×10^4 m^2 solar thermal collector area, 47 MW of SPV power, 270 community lights, 5,38,718 solar lanterns (PV domestic lighting units), 640 TV (solar), 54,795 PV street lights and 7002 solar PV water pumps were installed. Village power plants (stand-alone) of 1.5 MW capacity and 1.1 MW of grid connected power plants were in operation. As per one estimate [2], solar power will overtake wind in 2040 and would become the world's overall largest source of electricity by 2050. 5000 MW grid-interactive solar power could be feasible by 2032 (MNES Annual Report 2005–06). Solar water heating systems are increasingly becoming more popular for homes, hostels, hotels and industrial and domestic purposes. Research has shown that the Gallium Arsenide (GaAs) based PV cell with multijunction device could give maximum efficiency of nearly 30% and Carbon Nano Tube (CNT) based PV cell may give upto 50% efficiency. The detailed information about five largest solar power plants in India is illustrated below.

An overview of five largest solar power plants in India (30.04.2020) The solar power production capacity of India has third position in Asia and fourth rank in the world. The solar power plants currently account for about 38% of its total capacity of renewable energy. The National Solar Mission of India was launched in 2010. During this initial moment, a solar power generation plant with 10 MW capacity was installed. The objective of this mission was to generate a 20 GW power before the end of the 2020 decade. However, due to significant activity within the solar power sector over the following years, India has raised its target by several notches and now aims to achieve 100 GW of solar power capacity by 2022. Some of the biggest solar power plants of India are found in the states of Rajasthan, Karnataka, Andhra Pradesh, Madhya Pradesh and Tamil Nadu.

(1) **Bhadla Solar Park (Generation capacity 2,250 MW):** Bhadla Solar Park claimed to be the biggest solar power plant in the world. The Bhadla Solar Park is located in Bhadla village of Jodhpur district in Rajasthan, India. The fully operational power plant is installed with a generation capacity of nearly 2,250 MW in 14,000 acres of land.

(2) **Shakti Sthala Solar Power Project (Generation capacity 2,050 MW):** Shakti Sthala Solar Power Project is the largest fully operational solar park until the end of 2019. SSSPP is now the second-largest solar power plant in India after Rajasthan's Bhadla. The generation capacity of SSSPP is 2,050 MW. This solar power plant is located in Pavagada taluk at Tumakuru district of Karnataka.

(3) **Ultra-Mega Solar Park (Generation capacity 1,000 MW):** Ultra-Mega Solar Park is situated in Orvakal, Kurnool district of Andhra Pradesh state. This state is another leading Indian state in terms of solar power generation plants. The generation capacity of UMSP is 1,000 MW. Ultra Mega Solar Park spans in an area of more than 5,932 acres and is the third-largest solar power plant in India at a single location.

(4) **Rewa Solar Power Project (Generation capacity 750 MW):** Rewa Ultra Mega Solar is the first solar project in the country to break the grid parity barrier. The RSPP is one of the largest solar power generation plants in India and largest single site solar plant in Asia. The generation capacity of RSPP is 750 MW. This solar power project is spread over an area of 1,590 acres. RSPP is constructed and operated by Rewa Ultra Mega Solar Ltd. This plant is developed by Mahindra

Renewables, Solengeri Power and ACME Solar Holdings. The RSPP is one of the major power suppliers to the Delhi Metro.

(5) Kamuthi Solar Power Plant (Generation capacity 648 MW): The Kamuthi Solar Power Plant is located in Ramanathapuram district of the southern state of Tamil Nadu. It is the fifth-largest solar power plant in India. The KSPP is connected to a 400 kV substation of the Tamil Nadu Transmission Corporation. The solar panels of KSPP are cleaned daily by a self-charged robotic system.

1.11 ▶ WIND POWER

A growing concern for the environmental degradation has led to the world's interest in renewable energy resources. Wind is commercially and operationally the most viable renewable energy resource. Wind power generation capacity in India has significantly increased in recent years. As of 29 February 2020 the total installed wind power capacity was 37.669 GW, the fourth largest installed wind power capacity in the world. Wind power capacity is mainly spread across the Southern, Western and Northern regions.

Worldwide, five nations—Germany, USA, China, Spain and India—account for 73% of the world's installed wind energy capacity. The total worldwide wind power installed capacity is 1,57,899 MW. Kinetic energy available in the wind is converted to electrical energy by using rotor, gearbox and generator. The wind turns the blades of a windmill-like machine. The rotating blades turn the shaft to which they are attached. The turning shaft typically can either power a pump or turn a generator, producing electricity. Larger blades capture more wind. As the diameter of the circle formed by the blades doubles, the power increases four times.

Wind is air set in motion by the small amount of insolation reaching the upper atmosphere of earth. Nature generates about 1.67×10^5 kWh of wind energy annually over land area of earth and 10 times this figure over the entire globe. Wind contains kinetic energy which can easily be converted to electrical energy. Wind energy has been used in wind mills for centuries. In 1980s, wind energy use received a fillip with availability of excellent wind sites and rising cost of conventionally generated electrical power. Later in 1990s, interest in wind generated electrical power to displace conventional power, received further enhancement in order to reduce air pollution levels in the atmosphere. Wind is a clean power generating agent as it causes no pollution.

Power density in moving air is given by

$$P_W = KV^3 \text{ W/m}^2; \text{ [Here } K = 1.3687 \times 10^{-2}] \tag{1.25}$$

or

$$P_W = 0.5\, \rho\, AV^3 \text{ W}$$

where ρ = air density (1201 g/m^3 at *NTP*)

V = wind speed in km/h, mean air velocity (m/s)

A = Swept area (m^2)

Theoretically a fraction 16/27 = 0.5926 of the power in the wind is recoverable. This is called *Gilbert's limit* or *Betz coefficient*. Aerodynamical efficiency for converting wind energy to mechanical energy can be reasonably assumed to be 70%. So the mechanical energy available at the rotating shaft is limited to 40% or at the most 45% of wind energy.

Wind Characteristics

1. Wind speed increases roughly as the 1/7th power of height. Typical tower heights are about 20–30 m.
2. *Energy-pattern factor*: It is the ratio of actual energy in varying wind to energy calculated from the cube of mean wind speed. This factor is always greater than unity which means that energy estimates based on mean (hourly) speed are pessimistic.

Utilisation Aspects There are three broad categories of utilisation of wind energy:

1. Isolated continuous duty systems which need suitable energy storage and reconversion systems.
2. Fuel-supplement systems in conjunction with power grid or isolated conventional generating units.
3. Small rural systems which can use energy when wind is available.

Category 2 is the most predominant in use as it saves fuel and is fast growing particularly in energy deficient grids. Category 3 has application in developing countries with large isolated rural areas.

Aeroturbine Types and Characteristics Modern horizontal-axis aeroturbines (wind turbines) have a sophisticated blade design. They are installed on towers 20–30 m high to utilise somewhat high wind speed and also permit land use underneath. Cross-section view of a typical horizontal-axis wind turbine is shown in Fig. 1.30.

Tip Speed, also called *specific speed*, is by far the single most important parameter to be considered. It is defined as

$$\text{Tip speed} = \frac{\text{Peripheral speed}}{\text{wind speed}}$$

This ratio ranges from 2 to 10. Ratios less than 4 require rotor with several blades and have lower rotational speed whereas higher ratios (4 to 10) require fewer blades and have higher rotational speeds. Higher tip speed rotors have lower efficiency because of higher frictional loss. Typical blade diameters are about 20 m and rotor speeds 100–150 rpm.

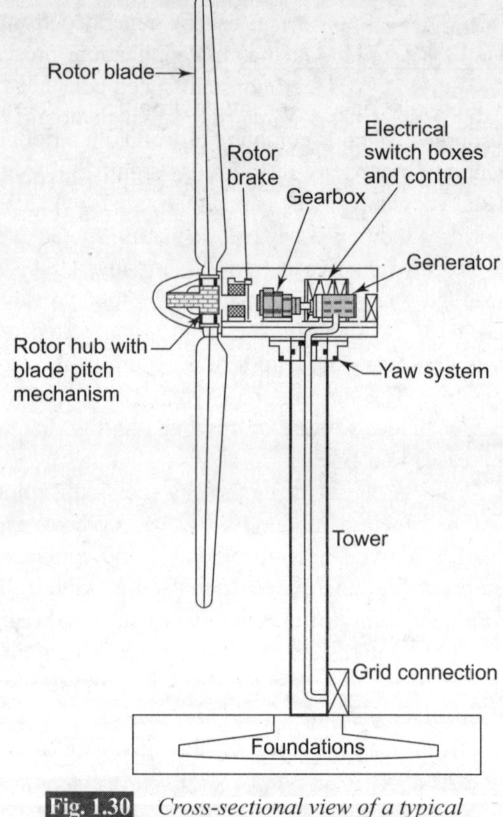

Fig. 1.30 *Cross-sectional view of a typical horizontal-axis aeroturbine*

Power Coefficient C_p is defined as the fraction of wind power at the rotor shaft. It is dependent on (i) tip speed ratio and (ii) pitch angle of blades. Rather than designing for C_p (max), these factors are determined by economics.

Blade Arrangements For harnessing large power, two to three blade configurations are used. Two blade arrangement is cost effective but prone to vibrations, which disappear with three blades. No unique answer on this issue has been arrived as yet. Modern machines have metal blades based on aircraft technology. Glass reinforced plastic has also been used successfully.

Vertical-axis Wind Turbines (VAWTs) Vertical-axis aeroturbines accept the wind from any direction and have the added advantage that the generator is located on ground. As a result the weight on tower is considerably reduced. The technology of these turbines has reached the stage where their efficiencies are comparable with those of horizontal-axis machines.

A number of vertical-axis designs have been developed and tested. We shall discuss here the one that is now commercially available—the Darrieus. The Darrieus rotor has two or more curved airfoil blades, held together at the top and the bottom. These are so positioned that they respond to wind from any direction. Physically, it resembles the lower portion of an egg beater. The rotors are nonself-starting and operate at blade tip ratios of 6 to 8. These have efficiencies around 35–40%.

Wind to Electric Energy Conversion The choice of electrical system for an aeroturbine is guided by three factors:

1. *Type of electrical output*–DC, variable-frequency AC, constant-frequency AC.
2. *Aeroturbine rotational speed*–constant speed with variable blade pitch, nearly constant speed with simpler pitch-changing mechanism or variable speed with fixed pitch blades.
3. *Utilisation of electrical energy output*–in conjunction with battery or other form of storage, or interconnection with power grid.

Large scale electrical energy generated from wind is expected to be fed to the power grid to displace fuel generated kWh. For this application, present economics and technological developments are heavily weighted in favour of constant-speed constant-frequency (CSCF) system with alternator as the generating unit. It must be reminded here that to obtain high efficiencies, the blade pitch varying mechanism and controls have to be installed.

Wind turbines of electrical rating of 100 kW and above normally are of constant-speed type and are coupled to synchronous generators (conventional type). The turbine rated at less than 100 kW is coupled to fairly constant speed induction generators connected to grid and so operating at constant frequency drawing their excitation VARs from the grid or capacitor compensators.

The present scenario related to electricity generation has been inclined towards renewable energy sources, including wind energy, biomass energy, solar energy, etc. Wind energy is proven to be a better source of renewable energy due to its round the clock availability. Wind energy can be generated using a wind turbine or several wind turbines called Wind Farm (WF) or wind power station. Several drawbacks include larger area requirement, installation problems and uncertainty in output power have been observed for the WF. But these drawbacks have been outperformed by the WF ability to produce green energy for 24 hours, years of operational life, and no intermediate energy conversion process. The strategy involved in wind power production is known as wind energy conversion system (WECS) in which the wind power is converted to mechanical power and mechanical power is then converted to electrical power as seen in Fig. 1.31(b). The related equations have been described in eqs. 1.25(a) and 1.25(b).

$$P_{\text{mech}} = \frac{1}{2} \times \rho \times V_{\text{wind}^3} \times C_p \tag{1.25a}$$

$$P_{\text{WTG}} = \begin{cases} 0; 0 \le V \le V_{\text{cin}} \text{ (or) } V \ge V_{\text{count}} \\ P_{\text{WTG,rated}} \times \left(\dfrac{V - V_{\text{cin}}}{V_{\text{rated}} - V_{\text{cin}}} \right); \; V_{\text{cin}} \le V \le V_{\text{rated}} \\ P_{\text{WTG,rated}}; V_{\text{rated}} \le V \le V_{\text{count}} \end{cases} \tag{1.25b}$$

The five different configurations of wind turbine generator are used which consist of squirrel cage induction machine (SCIM), permanent magnet synchronous machine (PMSM), wound rotor induction machine (WRIM) and doubly-fed induction machine (DFIM). Brief discussions on Doubly-Fed Induction Generator (DFIG) and Self-Excited Induction Generator (SEIG) are illustrated in following sections.

Doubly-Fed Induction Generator (DFIG) Wind power is the best renewable energy source which has been extensively developed in recent decades. Wind energy has several advantages such as no pollution, comparatively low capital cost involved and the short gestation period. The simple induction generators have a few disadvantages such as reactive power utilisation along with unfettered voltage profile throughout changeable rotor speed. These troubles can solve using the execution of DFIG along with power electronic converter. The power captured by the wind turbines is converted into electrical power by the induction generator and it is transmitted to the grid by both the stator as well as rotor windings. The control system generates the control signals to control the active power, reactive power as well as currents, the injected frequency compensation to the rotor windings and lastly the DC voltage control of the common coupling link capacitor.

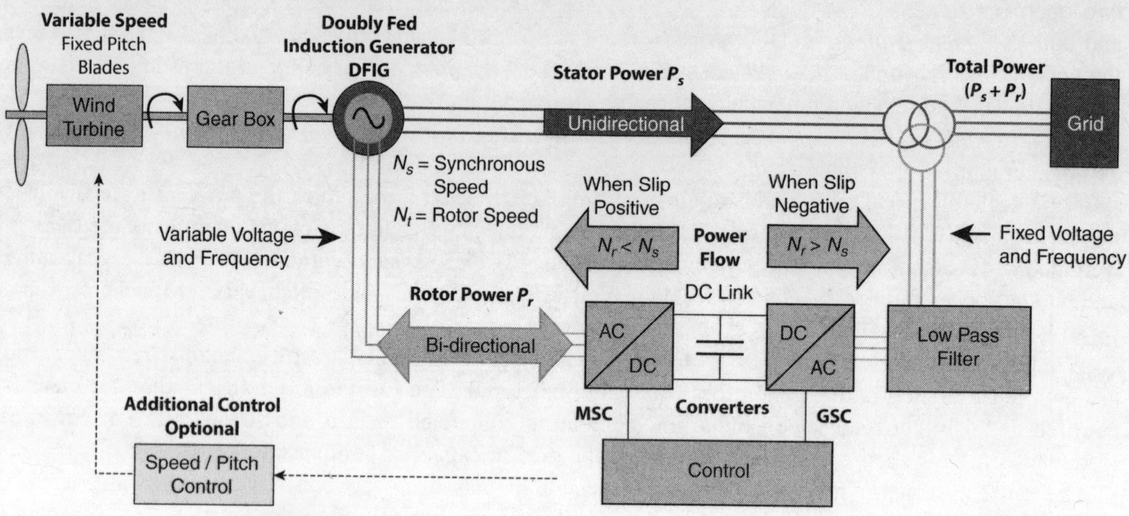

Fig. 1.31(a) *DFIG typical installation diagram as a wind generator*

The DFIG is basically a wound rotor induction machine. It can operate in super-synchronous and sub-synchronous manner as shown in Fig. 1.31(a). The benefits of the DFIG as compared with fixed speed generators are to improve power quality, reduce fluctuations and mechanical stress also excellent power imprisons. The function of the DFIG associated with the grid is facilitated through rotor as well as network side converter. However, inverter related to rotor side to give a fundamental frequency to sustain stator frequency at an invariable stage, even though in mechanical power variations.

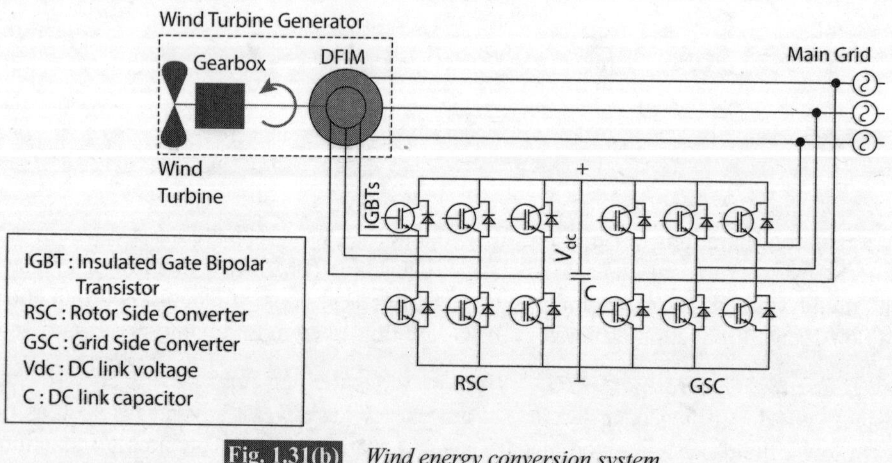

Fig. 1.31(b) *Wind energy conversion system*

DFIG is in nature a wound rotor induction generator, and the rotor circuit is usually controlled by power electric devices to allow variable speed operation. DFIG stator winding directly associates to grid by a power transformer and DFIG's power is normally ranged from a few kilowatts to several megawatts. DFIGs have two operating modes; in (i) mode $N_r > N_s$, s is –ve, then generator operates in super-synchronous mode and both stators, as well as rotor windings, convey power to the grid. While in (ii) mode $N_r < N_s$, s is +ve the generator in sub-synchronous mode and stator winding provides power to both the grid as well as rotor winding. The WECS with aerodynamic and electrical power control arrangements is shown in Fig. 1.31(c).

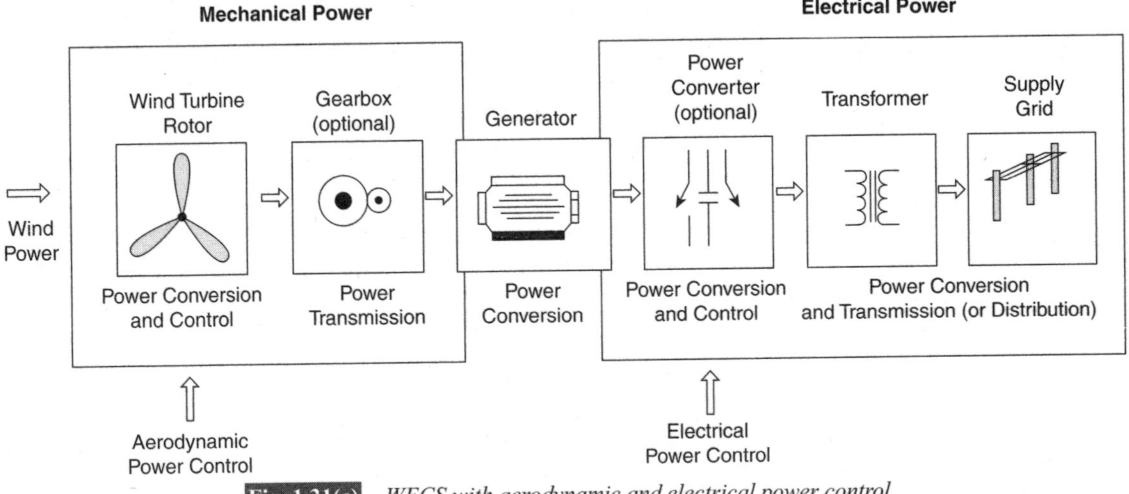

Fig. 1.31(c) *WECS with aerodynamic and electrical power control*

The advantages and disadvantages of generators used in WECS are given in following Table 1.2(a).

Table 1.2(a) Advantages and disadvantages of WECS generators details

Type	*Advantages*	*Disadvantages*
Induction Generator	(i) Full speed range (ii) No brushes (iii) Active and reactive power control (iv) Proven technology	(i) Full scale power converter (ii) Need gearbox
Synchronous Generator	(i) Full speed range (ii) Possible to avoid gearbox (iii) Active and reactive power control	(i) Small converter for field (ii) Fully scale power converter
Permanent Magnet Synchronous Generator	(i) Full speed range (ii) Brushless (iii) No power converter for field (iv) Possible to avoid gearbox (v) Active and reactive power control	(i) Fully scale power converter (ii) Multi pole generator (iii) Permanent magnets High cost (iv) Demagnetisation possibility
Doubly-Fed Induction Generator	(i) Sub-synchronous and super synchronous operation is possible (ii) Inexpensive PWM inverter (iii) Active and reactive power control	(i) Need slip rings (ii) Direct connect to grid is Somewhat difficult (iii) Need gearbox

Self-Excited Induction Generator (SEIG) The growing power demand and exploration of renewable energy sources have been the subject of considerable attention of scientists, technocrats, researchers and academicians in recent decade of the 21st century. The increasing concern of green house gas emission, environmental degradation, the crises of draining fossil fuel and depletion of conventional energy sources have motivated the world for utilising renewable energy sources to generate electricity. Induction Generator has been found to be very suitable for renewable energy conversion. Wound rotor induction generator is suitable for grid connected applications. The stator of a WRIG is directly connected to the utility, and the rotor is also connected to the utility through the power conversion system. The generated voltage and frequency of the SEIG depend on turbine speed, machine parameters, excitation capacitor and nature of loads. The external reactive supply from the power grid or externally connected capacitor banks is provided to excide the standalone generator as shown in Fig. 1.31(d). The rotating magnetic field of the stator winding produces magnetic field in the rotor and finally induces current in the winding. If rotor speed is slower than the rate of change of the rotating flux, the machine acts as an induction motor. Similarly, if the rotor rotates faster, the machine produces power at synchronous frequency and it acts as a generator. The generating machine draws magnetising current from the grid, if power grid is available in the site. In case of unavailability of the power grid, the magnetising flux is established by externally connected capacitor bank in the standalone induction generator. The reactive power requirement, poor power factor, poor voltage and frequency regulation are the main disadvantages of standalone induction generators. Therefore, the application of the SEIG is dependent on the methodologies to be adopted to overcome the capability to handle dynamic loading, its poor voltage and frequency regulation and its performance under unbalanced conditions.

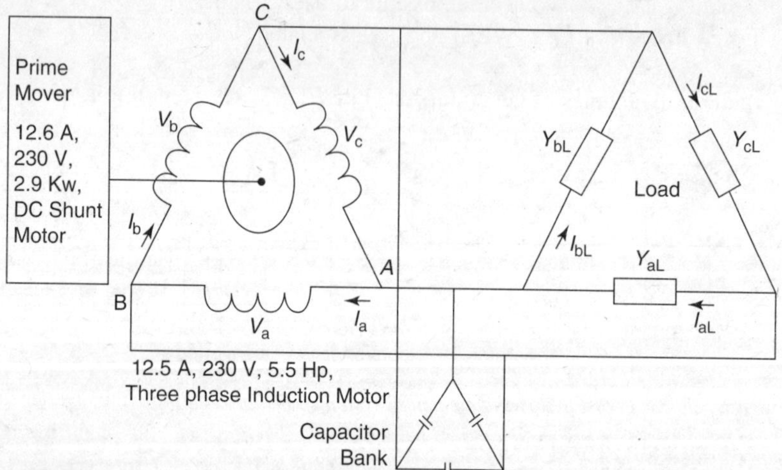

Fig. 1.31(d) *Experimental arrangement of three-phase SEIG with load impedance*

The process of voltage build-up and self-excitation process in an induction generator is very much similar to dc generator. In case of a grid-connected mode, the induction generator draws reactive power from the grid. For an isolated mode, there must be a suitable capacitor bank connected across the generator terminals for voltage build up process. This phenomenon is known as capacitive self-excitation process and the induction generator is called self-excited induction generator (SEIG). For self-excitation process, suitable value of residual magnetism must be present in the rotor of the machine. In the absence of the proper value of residual magnetism, the voltage build up process fails. Therefore, it is desirable to maintain a high level of residual magnetism for self excitation process of the machine. During starting of the induction generator, a small voltage is produced by the residual magnetism in the rotor circuit. This small voltage produces current in the capacitor bank. This current increases the voltage gradually until the fully voltage built up process completes. The no-load terminal voltage of the SEIG is the intersection of the magnetisation curve with capacitor load line. The magnetisation curve of the induction generator is obtained by running the machine as a motor at no load and measuring the armature current as a function of terminal voltage. The external capacitor must be able to supply the magnetising current during this process to achieve the required voltage level across the SEIG terminals. The phenomenon of self-excitation in induction machine can be examined by no load test in laboratory. The no load magnetisation curve is useful to calculate the capacitor range required for excitation in SEIG. Installed wind power capacity and generation in India from financial year 2010–2011 to 2019–2020 is illustrated in Table 1.2(b).

Table 1.2(b) Installed wind power capacity and generation in India from financial year 2010–2011 to 2019–2020

Financial year	*2010–11*	*2011–12*	*2012–13*	*2013–14*	*2014–15*	*2015–16*	*2016–17*	*2017–18*	*2018–19*	*2019–20*
Installed capacity (MW)	16,084	18,421	20,150	22,465	23,447	26,777	32,280	34,046	35,626	37,669
Generation (GWh)	–	–	–	–	28,214	28,604	46,011	52,666	62,036	64,485

With the advent of power switching technology (high power diodes and thyristors) and chip-based associated control circuitry, it has now become possible to use variable-speed constant-frequency (VSCF) systems. VSCF wind electrical systems (WES) and its associated *power conditioning* system operates is shown in Fig. 1.31(e).

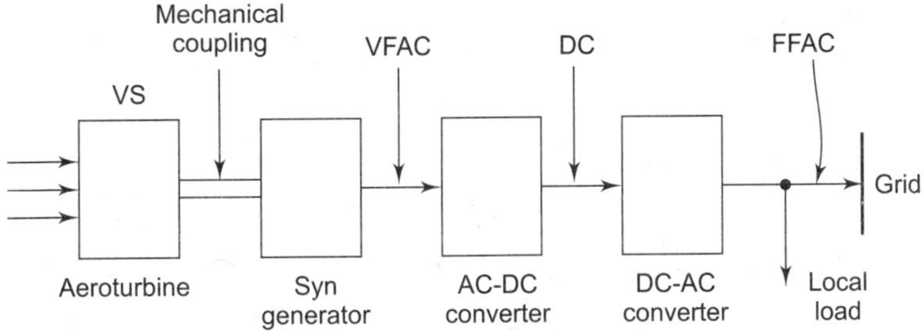

Fig. 1.31(e) *Block schematic of VSCF wind electrical system; VF (variable frequency), FF (fixed frequency)*

Various advantages of this kind of VSCF WES are

1. No complex pitch changing mechanism is needed;
2. Aeroturbine always operates at maximum efficiency point (constant tip-speed ratio);
3. Extra energy in the high wind speed region of the speed-duration curve can be extracted; and
4. Significant reduction in aerodynamic stresses, which are associated with constant-speed operation.

1.11.1 Operation and Control of Wind Electrical Systems (WES)

To understand the operation and control of WES, let us first consider a typical wind duration curve of Fig. 1.32(a). Any point on this curve gives the number of hours in a year for which the wind speed is higher than the value corresponding to this point.

Sensors sense the wind direction and the *yaw control* (Fig. 1.30) orients the rotor to face the wind in case of horizontal-axis machines. With reference to the wind duration curve of Fig. 1.32(a) it is seen that the wind turbine begins to deliver power at the *cut-in-speed* V_C and the plant must be shut down for wind speed at the maximum safe limit called the *furling speed* V_F. Between these two limits, mechanical power output of the turbine is determined by the power coefficient C_p. The electrical power output is determined therefrom, by the coefficients η_m and η_g of the mechanical drive and the electrical generator, respectively.

In CSCF WES, the conventional synchronous generator locks into the grid and maintains a constant speed irrespective of wind speed. A suitable controller senses the generating/motoring mode of operation and makes the needed pitch adjustments and other changes for a smooth operation.

As the generator output reaches the rated value, the electrical load is held constant even though the wind speed may increase beyond this value. This extra energy in the wind is allowed to be lost as indicated in Fig. 1.32(b). This is also the case for an induction generator whose speed remains substantially constant.

With VSCF system, suitable output controls can be installed to maintain a constant tip speed ratio so as to keep C_p at its near maximum value. This results in somewhat more power output throughout the operating range compared to the CSCF system as shown in Fig. 1.32(b). Also, there is no need to install sophisticated pitch control systems. The extra cost entailed in the power conditioning system gets more or less balanced against the cost of extra energy output. Considerable development effort is therefore being applied to CSCF system for large rating WES. These systems are yet to be proved in the field.

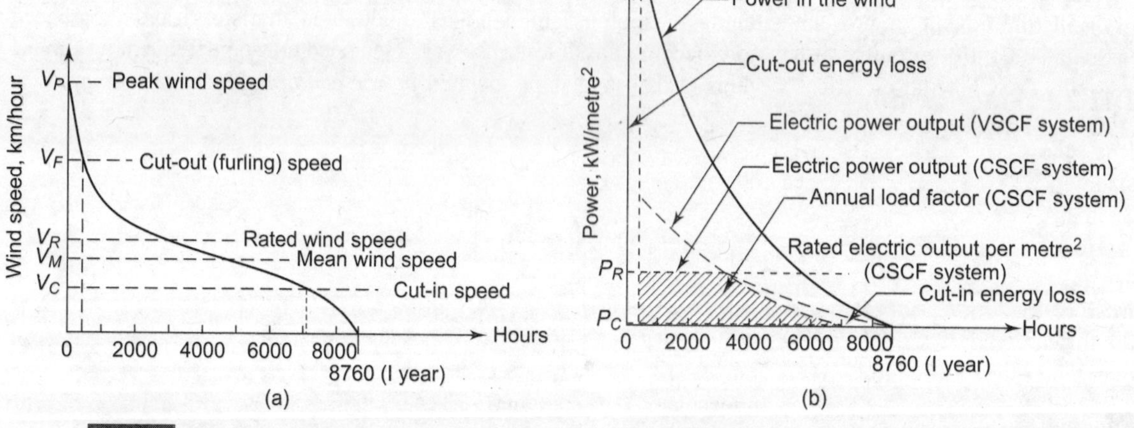

Fig. 1.32 *(a) Typical wind-speed-duration curve (b) Power-duration curve of wind-driven generator*

For CSCF WES, the operating curve shown shaded in Fig. 1.32(b) is redrawn in Fig. 1.33 with speed axis reversed for clarity. The aerogenerator starts to generate power at wind speed V_C, the cut-in speed. The aerogenerator produces rated power at speed V_R. At higher wind speeds, the aerogenerator speed is held constant by changing the pitch of blades (part of wind energy is being lost during this part of operation). The aerogenerator must be cut-out at V_F, the furling speed.

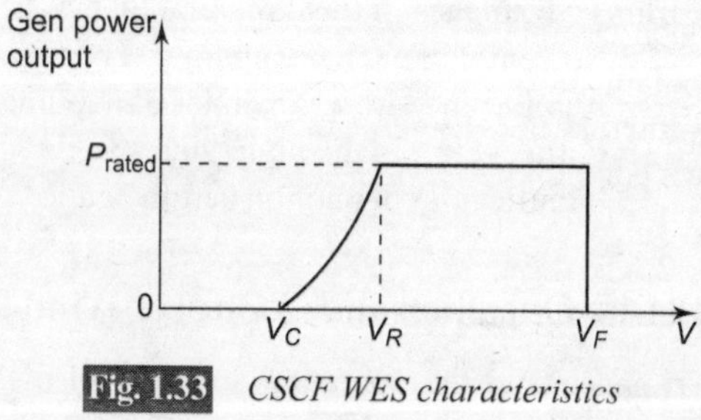

Fig. 1.33 *CSCF WES characteristics*

Typical wind turbine rotors of 20 m diameter rotate at 100–500 rpm and are geared upto about 750 rpm to drive an eight-pole induction generator excited from 400 V, 3-phase, 50 Hz rural distribution system.

Consider as an example, an area with mean wind speed of 10 km/h. Power output of 300 MW is to be produced using aeroturbines of 20 m blade diameter. Let us calculate the number of aeroturbines required.

Power in the wind is given by the relationship,

$$P_W = KV^2/\text{m}^2 \text{ kW}$$

$$V = \text{wind speed in km/h}$$

$$K = 1.368 \times 10^{-2}$$

For the aeroturbine,

$$P_{\text{aero}} (\text{mech}) = 1.368 \times 10^{-2} \times (10)^2 \pi \left(\frac{20}{2}\right)^2$$

$$= 4290 \text{ kW}$$

$$P_{\text{gen}} (\text{elect}) = 4290 \times 0.4 = 1716 \text{ kW}$$

$$\approx 1.7 \text{ MW}$$

Number of aeroturbines needed

$$= \frac{300}{1.7} = 177$$

These aerogenerators will be installed in a *wind farm* with suitable X, Y spacing so that the air turbulence of one aeroturbine on the exit side and also sideways does not affect the successive turbine.

1.11.2 Wind Farm

It is seen from the example given above that to contribute significant power to the grid, several standard size wind turbines have to be employed at a site where there is a vast enough wind field, flat or in a valley. Such an arrangement is called a wind farm.

How closely can the individual wind turbines be located to each other in a wind farm? The operation of a wind turbine causes an air turbulence on its back as well as sides; the region of turbulence is called the *wake* of the turbine. Optimal location of wind turbines is such that no turbines are located in the wake of the forward and side turbines. Any turbine that lies in the wake of another has its power output reduced and over a period of time, fatigue damage caused by stresses generated can occur specially for the yaw drive.

Spacing Rule A wind turbine has to be aligned perpendicular to the direction of wind. Where wind is unidirectional all day (which is rare), the spacing between turbines of a row (side ways) is $2D$ to $3D$, D being the diameter of the rotor. Inter row spacing is about $10D$. Normally, wind is not unidirectional; in which case a uniform spacing of $5D$ to $7D$ is recommended. A computer software 'Micropositioning' is available for this purpose.

Internal transformers and cabling will connect the aerogenerator to the grid. Each turbine will have its own control circuitry. Grid connection requires a certain sophisticated protection scheme whose purpose is

1. To isolate the wind farm in case of any internal fault in the electrical system, and
2. To disconnect the wind farm if there is a fault on any section of utility network (grid).

Brief information about top 5 largest wind farms and windmill parks of India is illustrated below.

An overview of 5 Largest Windmill Parks and Wind Farms in India

(1) **Muppandal Windfarm Kanyakumari (Tamil Nadu):** Muppandal is a small village in Kanyakumari district of Tamil Nadu state. This village is one of the most important sites of wind

farm in this state. MWK uses wind from the Arabian Sea to produce renewable energy. The total generation capacity of MWK is 1500 MW. This is the largest generation capacity of WECS in India.

(2) Jaisalmer Wind Park (Rajasthan): Jaisalmer Wind Park is the largest operational onshore wind farm in India. The JWP is located at Amarsagar in Jaisalmer district of Rajasthan. The installation capacity of JWP is 1,064 MW. This generation capacity of JWP makes it one of the largest wind farms in the world and largest of its kind in India.

(3) Brahmanvel Wind Farm Dhule (Maharashtra): This WECS project located at Brahmanvel in Dhule district of Maharashtra has 32 wind turbines. Many more Wind Farms are constructed in Maharashtra state such as Andhra Lake Wind Farm, Wind Power Facility Sangli and Ratnagiri Wind Farm.

(4) Damanjodi Wind Farm (Odisha): The coastal area of Odisha state has higher potential for wind energy conversion system. Damanjodi Wind Farm (DWF) is one of the largest wind power plants in the state. The DWF has 99 MW wind power project in Orissa by Suzlon at Damanjodi in Koraput district of Odisha.

(5) Tuppadahalli Wind Farm (Karnataka): Tuppadahalli Wind Park is located in the state of Karnataka. TWF is located about 55 km from Chitradurga and 260 km from Bangalore. The installed 56.1 MW wind power project produces 140 GWh of clean energy per annum. The coastal area of Karnataka is rich for installation of the wind farms compared with other states of India.

Other WECS facilities in India are available at Dhalgaon wind farm of Sangli, Vankusawade wind park of Satara, and Vaspet wind farm of Maharashtra, and Beluguppa wind park, and Anantapur wind park in Andhra Pradesh.

1.12 ▶ BIOFUELS

We shall explain the biofuels and their utilisation with the help of Fig. 1.34 and explanation of certain terms.

Biomass It is the material of all the plants and animals. The organic carbon part of this material reacts with oxygen in combustion and in the natural metabolic processes. The end product of these processes is mainly CO_2 and heat as shown in Fig. 1.34.

Biofuels The biomass can be transformed by chemical and biological processes into intermediate products like methane gas, ethanol liquid or charcoal solid.

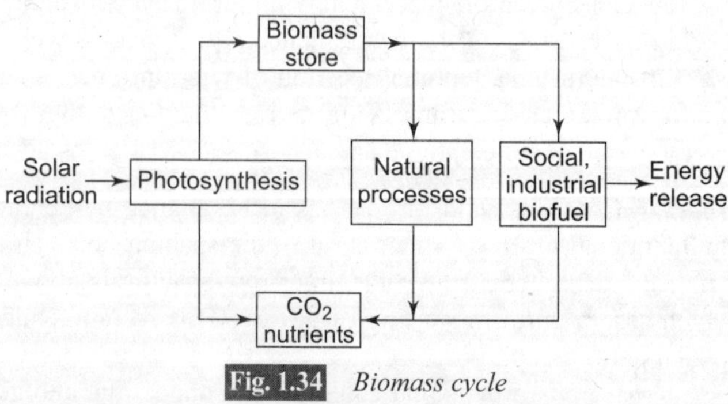

Fig. 1.34 *Biomass cycle*

Agro Industries The use of biofuels when linked carefully to natural ecological cycles (Fig. 1.34) may be nonpolluting. Such systems are called agro industries. The well established of these industries are the sugarcane and forest product industries.

Biofuels can be used to produce electricity in two ways:

1. By burning in a furnace to raise steam to drive turbines; or
2. By allowing fermentation in landfill sites or in special anaerobic tanks, both of which produce methane gas which can be used as fuel for household stoves and in spark ignition engines or gas

turbines. The CO_2 produced in this process must be recycled by cultivating next crop or planting trees as CO_2 is absorbed by photosynthesis by plants.

Biofuels have a potential to meet about 5% of the electricity requirements of an industrialised country by exploiting all forms of these household and industrial wastes, sewerage, sledge (for digestion) and agricultural waste (cow dung, chicken litter, straw, sugarcane, etc.).

1.13 ▶ GENERATING RESERVE, RELIABILITY AND CERTAIN FACTORS

Electric loads present a highly fluctuating picture and is not easily amenable to statistics and probability; moreover it is a nonstationary process as its statistics are changing with time. It is, therefore, best to interpret generation and loads in terms of certain overall factors without any direct link to probability. Some of the important factors in use and their significance are presented below.

Reserve Generating Capacity Modern generating plants are stressed to limits of temperature and pressure to reduce the overall power costs. Therefore, extra generation capacity must be installed to meet the need of scheduled *downtimes* for preventive maintenance. This reserve capacity also takes care of forced equipment outages and the possibility of the actual load exceeding the forecast, while additional generating stations are in completion phase.

The amount of reserve capacity to be provided is a subjective judgement and somewhat related to the past experience. Inadequate reserve means load outages at times and excessive reserve adds to generation costs.

Reliability It is measured by the ability of power systems to serve all power demands without failure over long periods of times. Various quantitative methods have been devised for estimation of reliability. From the point of view of generation of power, reliability is added to the system by providing *spinning reserve*. In certain stations of the system, some machines are kept on line but are kept only partially loaded to meet almost instantaneously any contingency of loss of a generator feeding the load. The amount of spinning reserve is also based on generator outage statistics and subjective judgement. Reliability is considerably increased by system interconnection or grid formation and also transmission line redundancy. A cost has to be borne for a reliable system.

Availability (operational) It is the percentage of the time a unit is available to produce power whether needed by the system or not. It is indeed a measure of overall unit reliability.

Capacity Factor It is defined as

$$\text{Annual capacity factor} = \frac{\text{actual annual generation (MWh)}}{\text{maximum rating (MW)} \times 8760 \text{ h}}$$

It is always lower than operational availability because of the need to provide spinning reserve and variations in hourly load.

Maximum Load The average load over half hour of maximum output.

Annual Load Factor

$$\text{Annual LF} = \frac{\text{Total annual load (MWh)}}{\text{annual peak load (MW)} \times 8760 \text{ h}}$$

LF varies with the type of load, being poor for lighting load (about 12%), and high for industrial load (80–90%).

Diversity Factor It is already introduced earlier in Section 1.3. It is defined again as

$$\text{DF} = \frac{\sum \text{individual maximum demand of consumers}}{\text{maximum load on the system}}$$

This factor is more than unity. It is high for domestic load. It can be made high by adjustment of timing and kind operation in each shift in industry by providing incentives.

Diversity factor also has same meaning at HV buses where loads are fed to different time zones in a large country. Although India uses one civil time, there is half an hour of diversity between the eastern and western region.

Consider four loads which are constant at $L_{\max}$ for 6 h duration and zero for rest of the time. Now we calculate LF and DF for two imaginary cases.

Case 1 Loads occur one after another around 24 h of day. Then,

$$\text{LF} = \frac{L_{\max} \times 24}{L_{\max} \times 24} = 1; \text{DF} = 4$$

Case 2 All the loads occur at the same time. Then the total load is 4 $L_{\max}$ (the capacity of supply point). Then,

$$\text{LF} = \frac{4L_{\max} \times 6}{4L_{\max} \times 24} = 0.25; \text{DF} = 1$$

Local Variations For computational purpose, the yearly data can be plotted in the form of a *load-duration* curve as shown in Fig. 1.35.

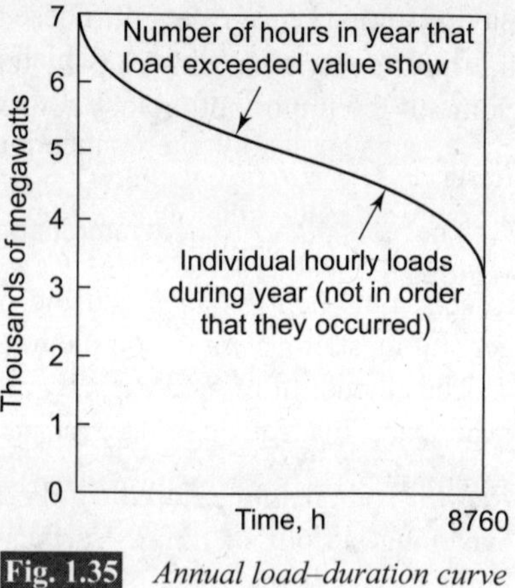

Fig. 1.35 *Annual load–duration curve*

1.13.1 Generating Capacity Mix

For economically meeting the cyclically varying load, the generating capacity can be divided into three basic types (all types may not be available in a small power system):

1. Base-load capacity;
2. Intermediate-load-range capacity; and
3. Peaking capacity.

Base-load capacity runs at full rating continuously round the year (except for preventive maintenance when such capacity kept in spare is brought in). These are large units, which exploit the *economy of scale*, with all the fuel-economising features built in (see Fig. 1.6(b)).

Nuclear units have very high capital cost and very low fuel cost and thus are base-load units. Also, not much underloading is permitted in these units.

For large hydroelectric dams, throughout the year, the basin is more or less full. Thus, hydro unit could serve the base load purpose.

Intermediate-load-range capacity is employed to pick up the load when it rises above the base value. As this capacity does not run round the year, these units may be less efficient than base units.

Peaking capacity is run to take up the peak load of the day and the season. Since their annual output is not very high, high efficiency like in base-load unit is not a necessity. Gas turbines, small hydro units and pumped storage units are most suitable for peaking load as these are *quick start*.

These aspects of the three types of capacity are tabulated in Table 1.2(c).

Table 1.2(c)

Designation capacity	*Capital cost*	*Fuel cost*	*Typical annual LF%*
Base load	High	Low	65–75
Intermediate load	Intermediate	Intermediate	30–40
Peaking load	Low	High	5–15

Interconnection and Pooling As our country is moving towards national grid formation and more private power generating companies are coming up, which can feed power in the grid, certain inherent saving and advantages result. These are as follows:

1. *Economy interchange*, which is permitted by low fuel cost stations near the coal bearing regions.
2. Each pool region needs less reserve capacity (both standby and spinning) as the reserve capacity gets pooled by interconnection.
3. *Diversity interchange* between various regions make the countrywise LF higher.

The above mentioned interchanges are possible only when strong power transporting lines link the regions into a grid.

1.13.2 Load Management

The procedure to modify the shape of load curve so that the load factor (LF) is raised for operational economy have been mentioned earlier here and there. These procedures and methods are as follows:

1. Offering tariff incentives in light load periods to fill in the troughs;
2. Peaking shaving by
   (a) pumped storage (hydro), and
   (b) CCGT use at peak load.
3. In advanced countries, radio-controlled means (Ripple control) are employed to cut-off comfort conditioning at the peak load hour and then to switch them on.

As mentioned earlier by various 'load management' schemes, it is possible to shift demand away from peak hours. Remote timer controlled on/off switches help achieve adjustment of electric use by a consumer. Most of the potential for load control lies in the domestic sector. Power companies are now planning the introduction of system-wide load management schemes.

Future power systems would include a transmission mix of AC and DC. Future controllers would be more and more microprocessor based, which can be modified or upgraded without requiring hardware changes, and without bringing the entire system down. While one controller is in action, the duplicate controller is there as a 'hot standby' in case of sudden need.

It is by now clear that HVDC transmission is already a reliable, efficient and cost-effective alternative to HVAC for many applications. Currently, a great deal of effort is being devoted to further research and development in solid state technology. This gives hope that HVDC converters and multiterminal DC (MTDC) systems will play an even greater role in the power systems of the 21st century.

1.14 ▶ ENERGY STORAGE

Because of tremendous difficulties in storage of electricity, it has to be constantly generated, transmitted and utilised. Large scale storage of energy, which can be quickly converted to electrical form, can help fast changing loads. This would help to ease operation and make the overall system economical as large capacity need not be kept on line to take up short duration load surges. The options available are as follows:

1. Pumped storage (see Section 1.5.3);
2. Compressed air storage;
3. Heat storage;
4. Hydrogen gas storage;
5. Batteries; and
6. Fly wheels, superconducting coils; of doubtful promise.

Most important of these is the pumped storage which has been dealt at length in Section 1.5.3.

1.14.1 Compressed Air Storage

Compressed air can be stored in natural underground caverns or old mines. The energy stored equals the volume of air multiplied by pressure. At the time of need this air can be mixed with gas fuel to run a gas turbine as shown in Fig. 1.36. Gas fuel combustion efficiency is thereby doubled compared to normal operation. A disadvantage of the scheme is that much of the energy used in compressing air appears in the form of heat and gets wasted; temperature of air is 450°C at 20 bar pressure.

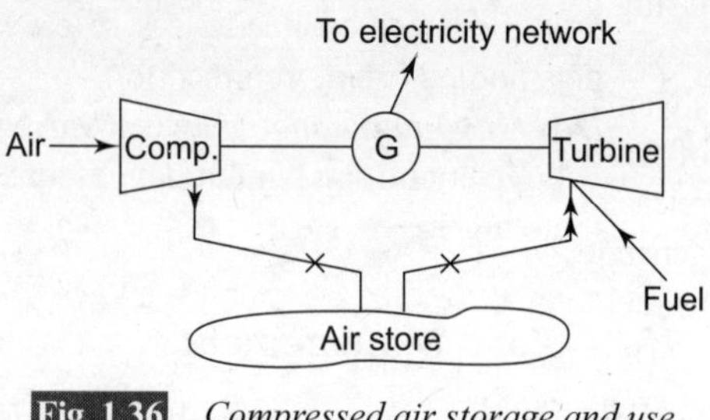

Fig. 1.36 *Compressed air storage and use*

1.14.2 Heat Storage

No large scale storage of heat has been found to be feasible. Water with good specific and latent heat has been suggested. Liquid sodium is another candidate. (It is used in FBRs for heat transfer). In a generating station, boilers can be kept ready on full steam for the turbine to pick up fast rising load. Boiler steam when not in use can heat feed-water for boilers in the station.

1.14.3 Secondary Batteries

These have possible use in local fluctuating loads, electric vehicles and as backup for wind and solar power (see Fig. 1.28). Considerable research and development effort is being devoted by international laboratories for secondary batteries. The present status is shown in Table 1.3.

Table 1.3

Battery	*Energy density*	*Operating temperature (where high)*	*Remarks*
Lead–acid cell (popular)	15 Wh/kg (low)	–	–
Nickel–Cadmium cell	40 Wh/kg	–	–
Sodium–sulphur cell	200 Wh/kg	300°C	Sodium electrolyte, liquid electrodes

A 3 MW battery storage plant has been installed in Berlin for frequency control in emergencies.

1.14.4 Hydrogen Energy Systems

Hydrogen can be used as a medium for energy transmission and storage. Transmission of natural gas via a network is well established. India is setting up a national gas grid; Hazira–Jagdishpur pipeline is one link of the grid being developed. The energy transmission capacity of a gas pipeline is high compared to electric energy transmission via HV lines.

$$\text{Calorific value (cv) of hydrogen gas} = 12 \times 10^6 \text{ J m}^{-3} \text{ (ATP)}$$

$$\text{Power transmitted} = \text{flow rate (volume)} \times \text{cv (at working pressure)}$$

For long gas pipelines, pressure drop is compensated by booster compressor stations.

A typical gas system: Pipe of internal diameter = 0.914 m

Pressure = 68 atm

Gas velocity = 7 m/s

Power transferred = 12 GW (gigawatts)

Using gas, electric power can be generated by CCGT near the load centres.

A 1 m diameter pipe carrying hydrogen gas is equivalent to 4–400 kV, 3-phase transmission lines. The major advantage that hydrogen gas has is that it can be stored. The disadvantage being it is produced by electrolysis of water. An alternative method, under development, is to use heat from a nuclear station to 'crack' water for releasing hydrogen at a temperature of about 3000°C. Solar energy is also being used for water splitting to generate hydrogen which can be converted back to electricity by means of fuel cells. Also, the use of hydrogen as fuel for aircraft and automobiles could encourage its large scale production, storage and distribution.

Hydrogen may prove to be a wonder element. It is nonpolluting, safe and sustainable. It is most lauded alternative transportation fuel after biofuels. However, system efficiency, system cost and safety related aspects are yet to be addressed for H_2 based technology. A fuel cell run car is available in US and Japan. An H_2 and fuel cell facility is available at Solar Energy Centre, Gurgaon. Today, its price is Rs 150/W. Alcohol mixed petrol is tried successfully in some countries such as Brazil. Class I cities generate 27×10^6 tonnes of municipal waste, 4400×10^3 m^3 of sewage per year. This can be converted to energy. Estimated potential from urban, municipal and industrial waste to energy is 25,000 MW or 50 million units/year of grid power. With the largest cattle population in the world of some 262 million, India holds tremendous potential for biogas development. India has 68.35 million hectares of wasteland (poor/semidesert), ideal for Jatropha plantation for production of *biodiesel*. It is nontoxic, 100% natural and biodegradable supplement for diesel.

India has total offshore gas hydrate resources of 1894 trillion m^3, which is 1900 times the country's current gas reserves. Even if 1% of the estimated gas hydrate reserves is tapped, our energy requirement for the coming decades can be met.

World-over hydrogen is produced from

steam reformation of natural gas	(48%)
partial oxidation of oil	(30%)
gasification of coal	(18%)
electrolysis of water	(4%)

In India, about 2.8 MMT produced annually (fertiliser industry, petroleum refineries) for captive consumption. About 0.4 MMT by-product hydrogen is available from chlor-alkali industries. It is used in automobiles and power generation using IC engines and fuel cells. H_2 is also produced through renewable energy sources and can be stored in many ways such as hydrides, carbon nano-tubes and nano-fibres.

1.14.5 Fuel Cell

A fuel cell converts chemical energy to electrical form by electrochemical reaction with no intermediate combustion cycle. One electrode is continuously supplied with fuel (H_2) and the other with an oxidant (usually oxygen). A simple form of a fuel cell is shown in Fig. 1.37 where the fuel is hydrogen, which diffuses through a porous metal (nickel) electrode. This electrode has a catalyst deposited around the pores, which aids the absorption of H_2 on its surface. In this process, hydrogen ions react with hydroxyl ions in the electrolyte to form water ($2H_2 + O_2 \rightarrow 2H_2O$). The cell has a theoretical emf of 1.2 V at 25°C. Other fuels are CO (1.33 V) and methanol (1.21 V) both at 25°C. Conversion efficiencies of practical cell are about 80%. The major use of the cell is in conjunction with hydrogen-oxygen system.

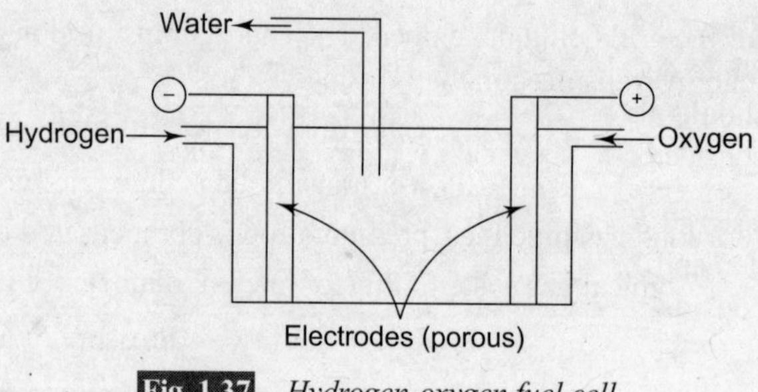

Fig. 1.37 *Hydrogen-oxygen fuel cell*

Intense R&D effort is on for various types of cells for power generation. Most successful of these is the phosphoric cell, which uses methane as fuel and operates at about 200–300°C. It has been constructed to produce 200 kW of electric power plus 200 kW heat energy with an overall efficiency of 80%. Higher temperatures give still higher efficiency. The main reason why fuel cells are not in wide use is its high cost. Global electricity generating capacity from fuel cells has grown from just 75 MW in 2001 to 15,000 MW in 2010. R&D projects on PAFC, PEMFC, DMFC, DEFC and SOFC are supported by MNRE, and other funding agencies and organisations such as NTPC, IITs, BHEL, CECRI, Karaikudi. PEMFC is considered suitable for use in automobiles and also for decentralised power generation (few kW). Other FCs for higher scale (MW scale) are also available. Fuel cell based 3 kW UPS is also developed. Fuel cell-battery hybrid electric vehicle is also available.

1.15 ▶ ENERGY CONSERVATION

We shall restrict our discussion only to energy conservation associated with generation, transmission, distribution and utilisation of electric energy. Some of the issues have been touched upon in previous sections. Various important conservation methods have been brought on the right most side of Fig. 1.5.

1.15.1 Generation

Ideal heat engine has Carnot cycle efficiency. To bring the practical efficiency as close to Carnot as possible, Rankine cycle is used by heating steam to the highest temperature (and pressure) permitted by economically feasible boiler and piping materials. This is done by *superheating* steam in upper part of the boiler. Other steps that are taken to improve the overall efficiency of the turbine set as brought out in Fig. 1.6(b) are as follows:

1. LP steam from IP and HP turbines is reheated in the boiler before feeding it to LP turbines.
2. Some of the LP steam from IP turbine and also LP turbine is used to heat feedwater to boiler.
3. Hot water from generator cooler heated by LP steam from LP turbines constitutes a part of feedwater to boiler.
4. Cooled water from cooling towers is circulated through condenser tubes to reduce the condenser pressure to the lowest possible value. This lowers the back pressure of LP ends of LP turbines.
5. Heating feedwater by the heat stored in flue gases from the combustion chamber forms the first stage of feedwater heating process.

Cogeneration Process steam is used for generation before or after. For details see Section 1.3.

CCGT Gas turbine combined with steam turbine is employed for peak load shaving. This is more efficient than normal steam turbine and has a quick automated start and shut down. It improves the load factor of the steam station. For details refer to Section 1.3.

T and D (*transmission and distribution*) *Loss* Losses in transmission and distribution should be kept low while designing these lines. Of course, this has to be matched against the cost factor. In any case, this loss should not exceed 20%. For transporting large chunks of power over long distances, HVDC option must be considered as this method has lower transmission loss; see Ch. 20 of Ref. 28.

Energy Storage It can play an important role where there is time or rate mismatch between supply and demand of energy. This has been discussed in Section 1.14. Pumped storage (hydro) scheme has been considered in Section 1.5.3.

1.15.2 Industry

In India, corporate sector is required by law, to include in their annual report, the measures taken for energy conservation.

Steps for energy conservation:

1. Keep an energy audit. This will put a finger on the places and items where there is wasteful use.
2. Use of energy efficient electric drives. No oversize motors as these would run at low power factor and efficiency.
3. Use of regenerative braking particularly the motors which require frequent start/stop operation. In regeneration, energy stored in mechanically moving parts of the machinery being driven and the rotor of the motor is fed back electrically to the mains.
4. Use of high efficiency motors.

1.15.3 Building—Industrial, Commercial and Domestic

Heating Electric space heating is out of question. Space heating in areas, where needed, is done by steam boiler and piping. Electric geysers are commonly used for heating water for bath in severe winter. Its thermostat should be set at the lowest acceptable temperature. In India where most areas have large number of sunny days, hot water for bath and kitchen by solar water heaters is becoming common for commercial buildings, hostels and even hospitals. For cloudy days in winter, some electric support system may be necessary for essential use.

Cooling Chilled water system saves electricity for space cooling. Air conditioning for offices and individual rooms in houses should be set at temperature of 27°C and 60% relative humidity. In dry areas and in hot weather a contrivance called 'water cooler' is quite common now. The humidity and temperature are both uncontrolled except manual switching ON/OFF. In large cities in Northern India, all these appliances plus refrigerators constitute more load than lighting. At present, there is no other natural alternative to cool high rise buildings.

Lighting Buildings should be designed to bring in natural light but in summer heat access has to be almost eliminated. A combination of fluorescent tube and electric lamp gives acceptable and efficient lighting for homes and even offices. In commercial buildings and street lighting, energy efficient devices as CFL (Compact Fluorescent Lamp) should be used. Their initial high cost is made up by the reduced electricity bill.

There is a lot of wasteful use of lighting prevalent in commercial buildings where the lights are kept 'on' even when not needed or the room(s) is not being used. As in corporate sector commercial buildings, energy audit must be made a requirement in educational institutions and other users where large areas are lighted. Public has to be educated that 20 units of electricity at user end, require 100 units of heat input at generation end.

In India where vast regions are deficient in electric supply and are subjected to long hours of power (load) shedding (mostly random), the use of small diesel/petrol generators and inverters are very common in commercial and domestic use. These are highly wasteful energy devices for the following reasons:

1. Small diesel/petrol engines (1–2 kVA) are highly inefficient. So it is a national waste. Further, these cause serious noise pollution.
2. Inverters are storage battery based. When the line power is ON, they draw a heavy charging current over and above the normal load. When a large number of consumers use these inverters, power load is considerably increased when the power is ON. This in fact adds to line outage. Further, pollution is caused inside the house by battery fumes.

This situation needs to be rectified speedily. By proper planned maintenance, the downtime of existing large stations can be cut down. Further, HVAC and transmission lines must be installed to evacuate the excess power available in Eastern region of the country. Power Grid Corporation has already been set up for this purpose. These actions will also improve the load factor of most power stations, which would indirectly contribute to energy conservation.

Losses There is now a movement towards estimating and monitoring AT&C (Aggregate Technical and Commercial) loss in the country. GOI has adopted AT&C as a measure of commercial efficiency in all distribution reform programmes.

1.16 ▶ GROWTH OF POWER SYSTEMS IN INDIA

India is fairly rich in natural resources like coal and lignite; while some oil reserves have been discovered so far, intense exploration is being undertaken in various regions of the country. India has immense water power resources also of which only around 25% have so far been utilised, i.e., only 25,000 MW has so far been commissioned up to the end of 9th plan. As per a recent report of the CEA (Central Electricity Authority), the total potential of hydro power is 84,044 MW at 60% load factor. As regards nuclear power, India is deficient in uranium, but has rich deposits of thorium which can be utilised at a future date in fast breeder reactors. Since independence, the country has made tremendous progress in the development of electric energy. Today, it has the largest system among the developing countries.

When India attained independence, the installed capacity was as low as 1360 MW in the early stages of the growth of power system, the major portion of generation was through thermal stations, but due to economical reasons, hydro development received attention in areas like Kerala, Tamil Nadu, Uttar Pradesh and Punjab.

In the beginning of the First Five Year Plan (1951–56), the total installed capacity was around 2300 MW (560 MW hydro, 1004 MW thermal, 149 MW through oil stations and 587 MW through nonutilities). For transporting this power to the load centres, transmission lines of upto 110 kV voltage level were constructed.

The emphasis during the Second Plan (1956–61) was on the development of basic and heavy industries and thus there was a need to step up power generation. The total installed capacity which was around 3420 MW at the end of the First Five Year Plan became 5700 MW at the end of the Second Five Year Plan in 1962, the introduction of 230 kV transmission voltage came up in Tamil Nadu and Punjab. During this Plan, totally about 1009 circuit kilometres were energised. In 1965–66, the total installed capacity was increased to 10,170 MW. During the Third Five Year Plan (1961–66) transmission growth took place very rapidly, with a nine-fold expansion in voltage level below 66 kV. Emphasis was on rural electrification. A significant development in this phase was the emergence of an inter-state grid system. The country was divided into five regions, each with a regional electricity board, to promote integrated operation of the constituent power systems. Figure 1.38(a) shows these five regions of the country with projected energy requirement and peak load in the year 2011–12 [19].

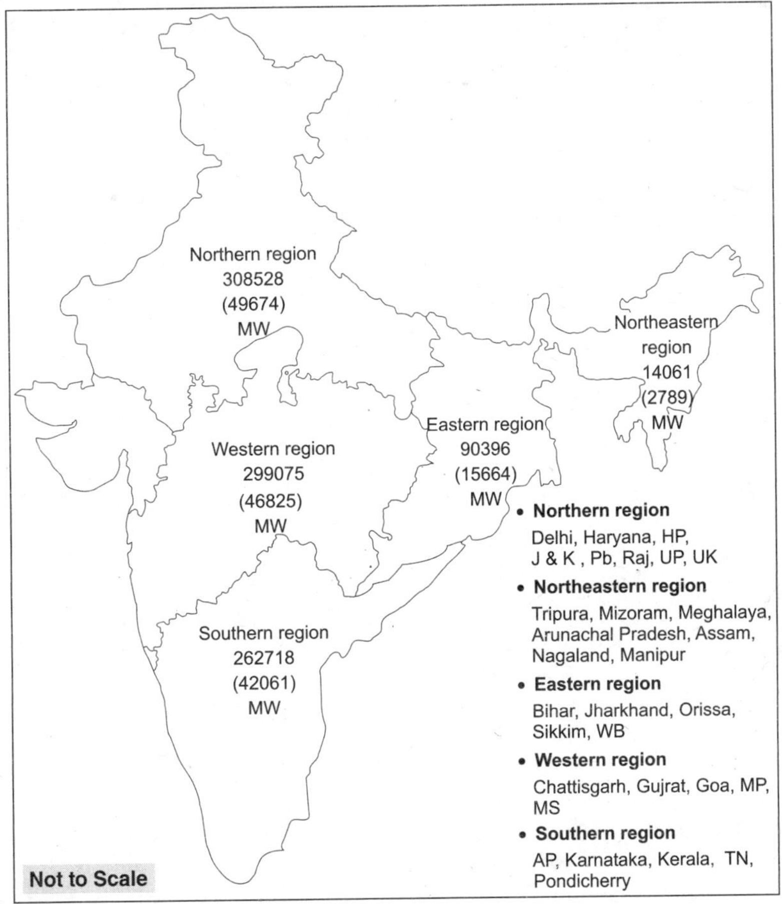

Fig. 1.38(a) *Map of India showing five regional projected energy requirement in MkWh and peak load in MW for year 2011–12*

During the Fourth Five Year Plan, India started generating nuclear power. At the Tarapur Nuclear Plant, 2 × 210 MW units were commissioned in April-May 1969. This station uses two boiling water reactors of American design. By August 1972, the first unit of 220 MW of the Rajasthan Atomic Power Project, Kota (Rajasthan), was added to the nuclear generating capability. The total generating capacity at Kota is 430 MW with nuclear reactors of Canadian design which use natural uranium as fuel and heavy water as a moderator and coolant. The third nuclear power station of 2 × 235 MW has been commissioned at Kalpakkam (Tamil Nadu). This is the first nuclear station to be completely designed, engineered and constructed by Indian scientists and engineers. A reactor research centre has been set up near the Madras Atomic Power Station to carry out study in fast breeder reactor technology. The fourth nuclear power plant has been set up at Narora in Uttar Pradesh. It has two units of 235 MW each. The fifth is in Kaiga in Karnataka and sixth in Gujarat near Surat, Kakrapar (440 MW). Several other nuclear power plants was commissioned by 2012.

The growth of generating capacity in India on March 31, 2019 is given in Table 1.4.

Table 1.4 Growth of installed capacity in India in MW (March 31, 2019)

Installed capacity as on	*Thermal (MW)*					*Renewables (MW)*				
	Coal	*Gas*	*Diesel*	*Sub-total Thermal*	*Nuclear*	*Hydro*	*Wind and Solar*	*Sub-total Renewable*	*Total MW*	*% Growth (On Yearly Basis)*
31-Dec-1947	756	–	98	854	–	508	–	508	1,362	–
31-Dec-1950	1,004	–	149	1,153	–	560	–	560	1,713	8.59%
31-Mar-1956	1,597	–	228	1,825	–	1,061	–	1,061	2,886	13.04%
31-Mar-1961	2,436	–	300	2,736	–	1,917	–	1,917	4,653	12.25%
31-Mar-1966	4,417	137	352	4,903	–	4,124	–	4,124	9,027	18.80%
31-Mar-1974	8,652	165	241	9,058	640	6,966	–	6,966	16,664	10.58%
31-Mar-1979	14,875	168	164	15,207	640	10,833	–	10,833	26,680	12.02%
31-Mar-1985	26,311	542	177	27,030	1,095	14,460	–	14,460	42,585	9.94%
31-Mar-1990	41,236	2,343	165	43,764	1,565	18,307	–	18,307	63,636	9.89%
31-Mar-1997	54,154	6,562	294	61,010	2,225	21,658	902	22,560	85,795	4.94%
31-Mar-2002	62,131	11,163	1,135	74,429	2,720	26,269	1,628	27,897	105,046	4.49%
31-Mar-2007	71,121	13,692	1,202	86,015	3,900	34,654	7,760	42,414	132,329	5.19%
31-Mar-2012	112,022	18,381	1,200	131,603	4,780	38,990	24,503	63,493	199,877	9.00%
31-Mar-2017	192,163	25,329	838	218,330	6,780	44,478	57,260	101,138	326,841	10.31%
31-Mar-2018	197,171	24,897	838	222,906	6,780	45,293	69,022	114,315	344,002	5.25%
31-Mar-2019	200,704	24,937	637	226,279	6,780	45,399	77,641	123,040	356,100	3.52%

Pattern of utilisation of electrical energy in 2009–10 was domestic 28.5%, commercial 8.6%, irrigation 20.7%, industry 34.7% and others 7.5%. It was expected to remain more or less same in 2011–12.

To be self-sufficient in power, BHEL has plants spread out all over the country and these turn out an entire range of power equipment, viz., turbo sets, hydro sets, turbines for nuclear plants, high pressure boilers, power transformers, switch gears, etc. Each plant specialises in a range of equipment. BHEL's first 500 MW turbo-generator was commissioned at Singrauli. Today BHEL is considered one of the major power plant equipment manufacturers in the world. Figure 1.38(b) shows main powergrid lines as on 2010.

1.17 ▶ DEREGULATION

For over one hundred years, the electric power industry worldwide operated as a *regulated* industry. In any area there was only one company or government agency (mostly state-owned) that produced, transmitted, distributed and sold electric power and services. Deregulation as a concept came in early 1990s. It brought in changes designed to encourage competition.

Restructuring involves disassembly of the power industry and reassembly into another form or functional organisation. *Privatisation* started sale by a government of its state-owned electric utility assets, and operating economy, to private companies. In some cases, deregulation was driven by privatisation needs.

The state wants to sell its electric utility investment and change the rules (deregulation) to make the electric industry more palatable for potential investors, thus raising the price it could expect from the sale. *Open access* is nothing but a common way for a government to encourage competition in the electric industry and tackle monopoly. The consumer is assured of good quality power supply at competitive price.

The structure for deregulation is evolved in terms of Genco (Generation Company), Transco (Transmission Company) and ISO (Independent System Operator). It is expected that the optimal bidding will help Genco to maximise its payoffs. The consumers are given choice to buy energy from different retail energy suppliers who in turn buy the energy from Genco in a power market (independent power producer, IPP).

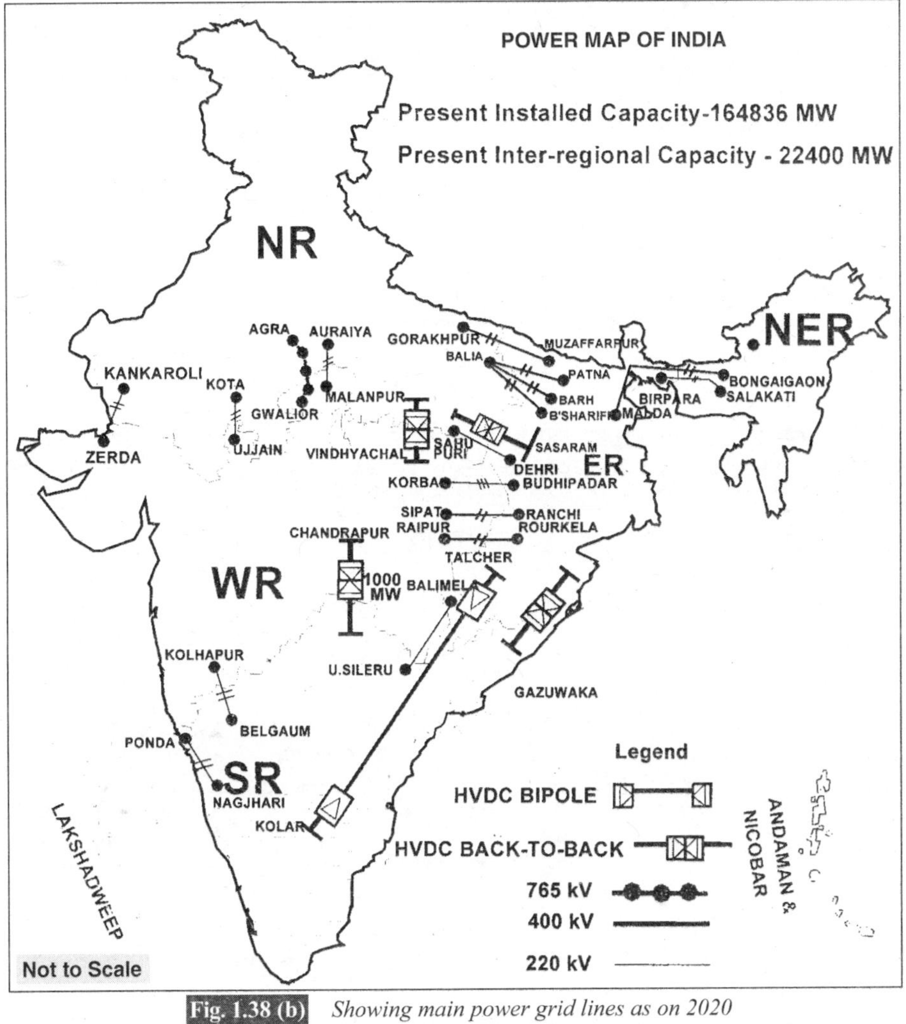

Fig. 1.38 (b) *Showing main power grid lines as on 2020*

The restructuring of the electricity supply industry that normally accompanies the introduction of competition provides a fertile ground for the growth of embedded generation, i.e., generation that is connected to the distribution system rather than to the transmission system.

The earliest reforms in power industries were initiated in Chile. They were followed by England, the USA, etc. Now India has also implemented the restructuring. Lot of research is needed to clearly understand the power system operation under deregulation. The focus of research is now shifting towards finding the optimal bidding methods which take into account local optimal dispatch, revenue adequacy and market uncertainties.

India had enacted the Electricity Regulatory Commissions Act, 1998 and the Electricity (Laws) Amendment Act, 1998. These laws enabled setting up of Central Electricity Regulatory Commission (CERC) at central level and State Electricity Regulatory Commissions (SERC) at state level. The main purpose of CERC is to promote efficiency, economy and competition in bulk electricity supply. Every state has completed the process of restructuring the power sector in their respective states.

Four important terms connected with deregulated power systems are defined below:

1. ***Open Access*** Open access is the nondiscriminatory provision for the use of transmission lines or distribution system or associated facilities with such lines or system by any licensee or consumer or a person engaged in generation in accordance with the regulations specified by the Appropriate Commission. It will promote competition and, in turn, lead to availability of cheaper power.

2. ***Wheeling*** Wheeling is the operation whereby the distribution system and associated facilities of a transmission or distribution licensee are used by another person for the conveyance of electricity on payment of charges to be determined by the Appropriate Commission.

3. ***Energy Banking*** Energy banking is a process under which the Captive Power Plant (CPP) or a co-generator supplies power to the grid not with the intention of selling it to either a third party or to a licensee, but with the intention of exercising his eligibility to draw back this power from the grid at a prescribed time during next financial year, after deduction of banking charges.

4. ***Unbundling/Corporatisation*** Many state electricity boards have either been unbundled or corporatised. Distribution business is privatised in some states such as Delhi and Orissa.

1.18 ▶ DISTRIBUTED AND DISPERSED GENERATION

Distributed Generation (DG) entails using many small generators of 2–50 MW output, installed at various strategic points throughout the area, so that each provides power to a small number of consumers nearby. These may be solar, mini/micro hydel or wind turbine units, highly efficient gas turbines, small combined cycle plants, micro-turbines since these are the most economical choices.

Dispersed generation refers to use of still smaller generating units, of less than 500 kW output and often sized to serve individual homes or businesses. Micro gas turbines, fuel cells, diesel, and small wind and solar PV generators make up this category. The beauty is these are modular and relocatable power generating technologies.

Dispersed generation has been used for decades as an emergency backup power source. Most of these units are used only for reliability reinforcement. Nowadays inverters are being increasingly used in domestic sector as an emergency supply during black outs. The distributed/dispersed generators can be stand alone/autonomous or grid connected depending upon the requirement.

At the time of writing this (2011) there still is and will probably always be some economy of scale favouring large generators. But the margin of economy decreased considerably in last 10 years [23]. Even if the power itself costs a bit more than central station power, there is no need of transmission lines, and perhaps a reduced need for distribution equipment as well. Another major advantage of dispersed generation is its modularity, portability and relocatability. Dispersed generators also include two new types of fossil fuel units—fuel cells and microgas turbines.

The main challenge today is to upgrade the existing technologies and to promote development, demonstration, scaling up and commercialisation of new and emerging technologies for widespread adaptation. In the rural sector main thrust areas are biomass briquetting, biomass-based cogeneration, etc. In solar PV (Photovoltaic), large size solar cells/modules based on crystalline silicon thin films need to be developed. Solar cells efficiency is to be improved to 20% to be of use at commercial level. Other areas are development of high efficiency inverters. Urban and industrial wastes are used for various energy applications including power generation which was around 79 MW in 2010.

However, recently there has been a considerable revival in connecting generation to the distribution network and this has come to be known as *embedded* or dispersed generation. The term 'embedded generation' comes from the concept of generation embedded in the distribution network while 'dispersed generation' is used to distinguish it from central generation. The two terms can be used interchangeably.

There are already 35 million improved chulhas. If growing energy needs in the rural areas are met by decentralised and hybrid energy systems (distributed/dispersed generation), this can stem growing migration of rural population to urban areas in search of better living conditions. Thus, India will be able to achieve a smooth transition from fossil fuel economy to sustainable renewable-energy based economy and bring 'Energy for all' and 'Energy for ever' era for equitable, environment-friendly, and sustainable development.

1.19 ▶ POWER SYSTEM ENGINEERS AND POWER SYSTEM STUDIES

The power system engineer of the second decade of the twenty-first century has to face a variety of challenging tasks, which he can meet only by keeping abreast of the recent scientific advances and the latest techniques. On the planning side, he or she has to make decisions on how much electricity to generate—where, when, and by using what fuel. He has to be involved in construction tasks of great magnitude both in generation and transmission. He has to solve the problems of planning and coordinated operation of a vast and complex power network, so as to achieve a high degree of economy and reliability. In a country like India, he has to additionally face the perennial problem of power shortages and to evolve strategies for energy conservation and load management.

For planning the operation, improvement and expansion of a power system, a power system engineer needs load flow studies, short circuit studies, and stability studies. He has to know the principles of economic load despatch and load frequency control. All these problems are dealt within the next few chapters after some basic concepts in the theory of transmission lines are discussed. The solutions to these problems and the enormous contribution made by digital computers to solve the planning and operational problems of power systems are also investigated.

1.20 ▶ USE OF COMPUTERS AND MICROPROCESSORS

The first methods for solving various power system problems were AC and DC network analysers developed in early 1930s. AC analysers were used for load flow and stability studies whereas DC were preferred for short-circuit studies.

Analogue computers were developed in 1940s and were used in conjunction with AC network analyser to solve various problems for off-line studies. In 1950s, many analogue devices were developed to control the on-line functions such as generation control, frequency and tie-line control.

The 1950s also saw the advent of digital computers which were first used to solve a load flow problem in 1956. Power system studies by computers gave greater flexibility, accuracy, speed and economy. Till 1970s, there was a widespread use of computers in system analysis. With the entry of micro-processors in the arena, now, besides main frame computers, mini, micro and personal computers are all increasingly being used to carry out various power system studies and solve power system problems for off-line and on-line applications.

Off-line applications include research, routine evaluation of system performance and data assimilation and retrieval. It is mainly used for planning and analysing some new aspects of the system. On-line and real time applications include data-logging and the monitoring of the system state.

A large central computer is used in central load despatch centres for economic and secure control of large integrated systems. Microprocessors and computers installed in generating stations control various local processes such as starting up of a generator from the cold state, etc. Table 1.5 depicts the time scale of various hierarchical control problems to be solved by computers/microprocessors. Some of these problems are tackled in this book.

Table 1.5

Time scale	*Control problems*
Milliseconds	Relaying and system voltage control and excitation control
2 s–5 min	AGC (Automatic generation control)
10 min–few hours	ED (Economic despatch)
– do–	Security analysis
few hours–1 week	UC (Unit commitment)
1 month–6 months	Maintenance scheduling
1 year–10 years	System planning (modification/extension)

1.21 ▶ PROBLEMS FACING INDIAN POWER INDUSTRY AND ITS CHOICES

The electricity requirements of India have grown tremendously and the demand has been running ahead of supply. Electricity generation and transmission processes in India are very inefficient in comparison with those of some developed countries. As per one estimate, in India generating capacity is utilised on an average for 3600 hours out of 8760 hours in a year, while in Japan it is used for 5100 hours. If the utilisation factor could be increased, it should be possible to avoid power cuts. The transmission loss in 2007–08 on a national basis was 23.68% consisting of both technical losses in transmission lines and transformers, and also nontechnical losses caused by energy thefts and meters not being read correctly. It should be possible to achieve considerable saving by reducing this loss to 15% by the end of the Eleventh Five Year Plan by using well-known ways and means and by adopting sound commercial practices. Further, every attempt should be made to improve system load factors by flattening the load curve by giving proper tariff incentives and taking other administrative measures. As per the Central Electricity Authority's (CEA) seventeenth annual power survey of India report, the all India load factor up to 2006–07 was of the order of 78%. In future it is likely to be 71%. By 2009, 4.96 lakhs of villages (86%) have been electrified and 117 lakh of pumpsets have been energised.

Assuming a very modest average annual energy growth of 5%, India's electrical energy requirement in the year 2011 will be enormously high. A difficult and challenging task of planning, engineering and constructing new power stations is imminent to meet this situation. The government has built several super thermal stations such as at Singrauli (Uttar Pradesh), Farakka (West Bengal), Korba (Madhya Pradesh), Ramagundam (Andhra Pradesh), and Neyveli (Tamil Nadu), and Chandrapur (Maharashtra) all in coal mining areas, each with a capacity in the range of 2000 MW*. Many more super thermal plants would be built in future. Intensive work must be conducted on boiler furnaces to burn coal with high ash content. National Thermal Power Corporation (NTPC) is in charge of these large scale generation projects.

Hydro power will continue to remain cheaper than the other types for the next decade. As mentioned earlier, India has so far developed only around 41.4% of its estimated total hydro potential of 89,000 MW. The utilisation of this perennial source of energy would involve massive investments in dams, channels and generation–transmission system. The Central Electricity Authority, the Planning Commission and the Ministry of Power are coordinating to work out a perspective plan to develop all hydroelectric sources by the end of this century to be executed by the National Hydro Power Corporation (NHPC). NTPC has also started recently the development of hydro and nuclear power plants.

Nuclear energy assumes special significance in energy planning in India. Because of limited coal reserves and its poor quality, India has no choice but to keep going on with its nuclear energy plans. According to the Atomic Energy Commission, India's nuclear power generation will increase to 15,000 MW by year 2015. Everything seems to be set for a take off in nuclear power production using the country's thorium reserves in breeder reactors.

In India, concerted efforts to develop solar energy and other nonconventional sources of energy need to be emphasised, so that the growing demand can be met and depleting fossil fuel resources may be conserved. To meet the energy requirement, it is expected that the coal production will have to be increased to more than 507 million tonnes in 2010–11 as compared to 450 million tonnes in 2004–05.

A number of 400 kV lines are operating successfully since 1980s as mentioned already. This was the first step in working towards a national grid. There is a need in future to go in for even higher voltages (800 kV). It is expected that by the year 2011–12, 5400 circuit km of 800 kV lines and 48,000 circuit km of 400 kV lines would be in operation. Also, lines may be series and shunt compensated to carry huge blocks of power with greater stability. There is a need for constructing HVDC (High Voltage DC) links in the country since DC lines can carry considerably more power at the same voltage and require fewer conductors. A 400 kV Singrauli–Vindhyachal of 500 MW capacity first HVDC back-to-back scheme has been commissioned by NPTC (National Power Transmission Corporation) followed by first point-to-point bulk EHVDC transmission of 1500 MW at $\pm$ 500 kV over a distance of 915 km from Rihand to Delhi. Power Grid recently commissioned on 14 February 2003 a 2000 MW Talcher–Kolar ±500 kV HVDC bipole transmission system thus enabling excess power from East to flow to South. 7000 ckt km of $\pm$500 kV HVDC line was expected by 2011–12.

At the time of writing, the whole energy scenario is so clouded with uncertainty that it would be unwise to try any quantitative predictions for the future. However, certain trends that will decide the future developments of electric power industry are clear.

Generally, unit size will go further up from 500 MW. A higher voltage (1200 kV) will come eventually at the transmission level. There is little chance for six-phase transmission becoming popular though there are few such lines in USA. More of HVDC lines will come in operation. As population has already touched the 1000 million mark in India, we may see a trend to go toward underground transmission in urban areas.

Public sector investment in power has increased from Rs 2600 million in the First Plan to Rs 2,42,330 million in the Seventh Plan (1985–90). Shortfall in the Sixth Plan has been around 26%. There have been serious power shortages and generation and availability of power in turn have lagged too much from the industrial, agricultural and domestic requirements. Huge amounts of funds (of the order of Rs 18,93,200 million) will be required if we have to achieve power surplus position by the time we reach the terminal year to the XI Plan (2011–12). Otherwise, achieving a target of 975 billion units of electric power will remain an utopian dream.

Power grid is planning creation of transmission highways to conserve Right-of-way. Strong national grid is being developed in phased manner. In 2001, the interregional capacity was 5000 MW. By 2011–12, it was expected to be 50,000 MW. Huge investment is planned to the tune of US $20 billion in the coming decade. Present figures for HVDC is 3136 circuit km, 800 kV is 950 circuit km, 400 kV is 45,500 circuit km and

* NTPC has also built seven gas-based combined cycle power stations such as Anta and Auraiya.

220/132 kV is 2,15,000 circuit km. First 1200 kV line is expected to be operational by 2015–16. Target upto March 2012 is 7850 ckm for 765 kV, 7432 ckm for HVDC ±500 kV, 12500 ckm for 400 kV; 150000 ckm for 230/220 kV and total transmission lines will be 290282 ckm. State-of-the art technologies which are being used in India currently are HVDC bipole, HVDC back-to-back, SVC (Static Var Compensator), FACTs (Flexible AC Transmissions) devices, etc. Improved O and M (Operation and Maintenance) technologies which are being used today are hotline maintenance, emergency restoration system, thermovision scanning, etc. 24 hours of supply of good-quality power would help small industries in rural areas. It will also facilitate delivery of modern health care, education and application of information and communication technologies.

Because of power shortages, many of the industries, particularly power-intensive ones, have installed their own captive power plants.* Currently 20% of electricity generated in India comes from the captive power plants and this is bound to go up in the future. Consortium of industrial consumers should be encouraged to put up coal-based captive plants. Import should be liberalised to support this activity. Now alternative fuels are increasingly being used for surface transportation. Battery operated vehicles (electric cars) are being used.

With the ever increasing complexity and growth of power networks and their economic and integrated operation, several central/regional automatic load despatch centres with real time computer control have been established. In very near future, it is envisaged that using SCADA (Supervisory Control and Data Acquisition) etc., will be possible to achieve nationwide on-line monitoring and real time control of power system. It may also be pointed out that this book will also help in training and preparing the large number of professionals trained in computer aided power system operation and control that would be required to handle vast expansion planned in power system in the coming decades.

1.22 ▶ SUMMARY

This chapter describes the basic aspects related to electric power systems including historical background of Indian power sectors. The modern growth of power systems in India with comprehensive overview of the thermal, hydro, nuclear, wind and solar power plants is described in detail.

ANNEXURE 1.1

1. The Indian Electricity Rules; [25]
   The Indian Electricity Act, 1910 deals with the provisions relating to supply and use of electrical energy and the rights and obligations of persons licensed under Part II of that Act to supply energy. Under Section 36A of the Act, a Board called the Central Electricity Board is constituted to exercise the powers conferred by Section 37. In exercise of the powers conferred under that section, the Central Electricity Board framed the Indian Electricity Rules, 1956 for the whole or any part of the territories to which the Act extends, to regulate the generation, transmission, supply and use of energy, and generally to carry out the purposes and objects of the Act.

ANNEXURE 1.2

The Central Electricity Authority (CEA) of India is an organisation originally constituted under Section 3(1) of the repealed Electricity (Supply) Act, 1948. The CEA is substituted by Section 70 of the

* Captive diesel plants (and small diesel sets for commercial and domestic uses) are very uneconomical from a national point of view. Apart from being lower efficiency plants they use diesel which should be conserved for transportation sector.

Electricity Act, 2003. It was established as a part-time body in 1951 and made a full-time body in 1975. The functions and duties of CEA are delineated under Section 73 of the Electricity Act, 2003. Annual exercise of assessment and finalisation of the generation targets and the planned maintenance schedules of the generating units are available online in CEA home page. Although the generation performance of the various stations and their outages for planned and unscheduled outages are regularly monitored in CEA. The gross generations program from conventional sources like thermal, hydro and nuclear stations of 25 MW and above are available online in CEA site.

The Ministry of New and Renewable Energy (MNRE) is a ministry of the Government of India that is mainly responsible for research and development, in intellectual property protection, and international cooperation, promotion, and coordination in renewable energy sources such as wind power, small hydro, biogas, and solar power. The aim of the renewable energy ministry is to develop and deploy the new and renewable energy for supplementing the energy requirements of India. The annual, monthly and daily data records are available online in MNRE website. The readers are suggested to make regular visits of CEA and MNRE sites to get updated information about the power growth in modern India.

Additional Solved Examples

Example 1.6 If the average flow during the period of interest is 575 m^3/s and head is 100 m, find the power that can be developed per cubic meter per second if the efficiency of the hydraulic turbine and electric generator together is 90%.

Solution

$$P = 9.81\, \eta \rho\, W H \times 10^{-6} \text{ MW}$$

$$= 9.81 \times 0.9 \times 1000 \times 575 \times 100 \times 10^{-6} \text{ MW}$$

$$= 9.81 \times 0.9 \times 5.75 = 508 \text{ MW}$$

Example 1.7 How much power can be extracted from a 5 m/s wind striking a wind mill whose blades have a radius of 3 m? Assume that the efficiency of the turbine is 40%.

Solution

$$\text{Power} = \frac{1}{2} C_p \rho A V^3$$

$C_p = 0.4 =$ power coefficient gives the maximum amount of wind power that can be converted into mechanical power by wind turbine

$$A = \pi r^2 = 3.14 \times 3^2 = 28.26 \text{ m}^2$$

$$V = 5 \text{ m/s} \quad \rho = 1.24 \text{ kg/m}^2$$

$$\therefore \quad \text{Power} = \frac{1}{2} \times 0.4 \times 1.24 \times 28.26 \times 5^3 \times 10^{-3} = 0.876 \text{ kW}$$

Example 1.8 A wind generator whose power curve is shown in Fig. 1.39 has a blade diameter of 10 m. Find the net efficiency of the Wind Energy Converting System at a wind speed of 5 m/s.

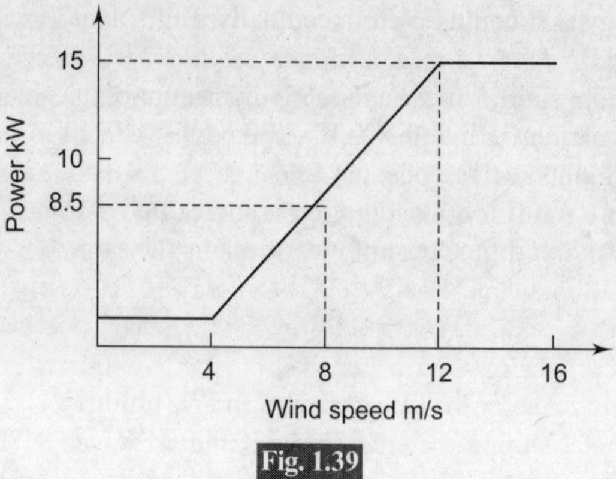

Fig. 1.39

Solution

$$A = \pi r^2 = 3.14 \times 5^2$$

$$V = 8 \text{ m/s}$$

$$\rho = 1.24 \text{ kg/m}^3$$

$$P = 1/2\, \rho' AV^3$$

$$P_{input} = 1/2 \times 1.24 \times 3.14 \times 5^2 \times 8^3 \times 10^{-3} = 24.9 \text{ kW}$$

8 m/s wind velocity

$$P = 8.5 \text{ kW}$$

$$\eta = 8.5/24.9 \times 100 = 34.14\%$$

Example 1.9 Calculate the maximum power by a solar cell at an intensity of 200 W/m^2. Given V_{OC} = 0.24 V, I_{SC} = – 9 mA, V_{max} = 0.14 V and I_{max} = – 6 mA. Also calculate the cell efficiency if the area is 4 cm^2.

Solution Solar cell maximum power

$$P_{max} = I_{max} V_{max}$$

$$P_{max} \text{ (output)} = -6 \times 10^{-3} \times 0.14 = -0.84 \text{ mW}$$

$$= -0.84 \times 10^{-3} \text{ W}$$

$$P_{input} = \text{Intensity} \times \text{area}$$

$$= 200 \times 4 \times 10^{-4} \text{ W}$$

$$\text{cell } \eta = \frac{0.84 \times 10^{-3}}{200 \times 4 \times 10^{-4}} \times 100 = 1.05\%$$

Problems

1.1 Maximum demand of a generating station is 200 MW, a load factor is 70%. The plant capacity factor and plant use factor are 50% and 70%, respectively. Determine

(a) daily energy produced

(b) installed capacity of plant

(c) the reserve capacity of plant

(d) maximum energy that can be produced daily if the plant is running all the time

(e) the minimum energy that could be produced daily if the plant is running at full load
(f) utilisation factor

1.2 Load factor of a consumer is 40% and the monthly consumption is 500 kWh. If the rate of electricity is Rs 200 per kW of maximum demand plus Rs 2.00 per kWh. Find
(a) the monthly bill and the average cost per kWh.
(b) the overall cost per kWh if the consumption is increased by 20% with the same load factor.
(c) the overall cost per kWh if the consumption remains the same except the load factor.

Multiple Choice Questions

1.1 Total installed generating capacity in India today (2011) is around
(a) 100,000 MW (b) 175,000 MW
(c) 50,000 MW (d) 200,000 MW

1.2 Load factor is defined as
(a) $\frac{\text{peak load}}{\text{average load}}$ (b) $\frac{\text{maximum load}}{\text{minimum load}}$
(c) $\frac{\text{average load}}{\text{peak load}}$ (d) $\frac{\text{peak load}}{\text{rated load}}$

1.3 Diversity factor is always
(a) 1 (b) 0
(c) greater than 1 (d) ∞

1.4 Nuclear power station is normally used for
(a) Peak load (b) Base load
(c) Average load (d) Any load

1.5 Theoretical power in a wind system is given by
(a) $P = 0.5\ \text{A}v^3$ W (b) $P = 0.5\ \rho \text{A}v^2$ W
(c) $P = 0.5\ \rho \text{A}v$ W (d) $P = 0.5\ \rho \text{A}v^3$ W

1.6 Electric power can be produced by solar energy
(a) By solar-thermal route (b) Photovoltaic route
(c) Both (a) and (b) (d) Cannot be generated

1.7 Fuel cell
(a) Converts chemical energy into electric energy
(b) Mechanical energy into electric energy
(c) Solar energy into electrical energy
(d) Wind energy into electrical energy

1.8 Hydrogen can be used as a medium for
(a) Energy transmission (b) For energy storage
(c) Both (a) and (b) (d) For electrolysis

1.9 First nuclear power plant in India was started at
(a) Kota (b) Tarapur
(c) Kalpakkam (d) Narora

1.10 Geothermal power plant was first started in
(a) New Zealand (b) Pakistan
(c) India (d) Italy

1.11 Low grade fuels have
(a) Low ash content (b) Low calorific value
(c) Low carbon content (d) Low moisture content

1.12 Which variety of coal has lowest calorific value?
(a) Lignite (b) Steam coal
(c) Bituminous coal (d) Anthracite

1.13 Betz law finds application in
(a) Wind mills (b) MHD
(c) Solar (d) Geothermal

1.14 Which plant can never have 100% load factor?
(a) Hydro (b) Nuclear
(c) Peak (d) Base load plant

1.15 During load shedding
(a) System voltage is reduced (b) System frequency is reduced
(c) System power factor is changed (d) Some loads are switched off

1.16 The oldest hydroelectric power plant in India is
(a) Nagarjunasagar Hydro Electric Power plant
(b) Sidrapong Hydroelectric Power Station
(c) Sardar Sarovar Hydro Electric Power plant
(d) Tehri Hydro Electric Power plant

1.17 The southern grid was synchronously interconnected to the central grid for establishment of the national grid on 31 December 2013 with the commissioning of the 765 kV transmission line. The name of the high voltage transmission line is
(a) Raichur–Solapur transmission line
(b) Kalapakkam– Rameshwaram transmission line
(c) Kudankulam–Ananthpur transmission line
(d) Tarapur–Kolhapur transmission line

1.18 The largest Ultra Mega Solar power plant in India and Asia's largest single site solar plant is located in the following place.
(a) Bengaluru (Karnataka) (b) Allahabad (UP)
(c) Rewa (MP) (d) Jamnagar (Gujarat)

1.19 India is the world's third largest producer and third largest consumer of electricity. The national electric grid in India has an installed capacity as of 31 July 2020.
(a) 294.173 GW (b) 421.845 GW
(c) 257.579 GW (d) 371.977 GW

1.20 A 330 MW combined cycle Gas Turbine Power Project was set up on fast track basis at New Delhi. What is the name of the power plant?
(a) Swadeshi Power Plant (b) Pragati Power Plant
(c) Aatmanirbhar Power Plant (d) Make in India Power Plant

1.21 The name of the highest dam in India and the tenth tallest dam in the world is:
(a) Koyna Hydroelectric Dam (b) Sardar Sarovar Dam
(c) Tehri Hydroelectric Dam (d) Bhakra-Nangal Dam

1.22 Consider the following pairs of nuclear power plants and states of India.

Name of nuclear power plants		Name of states
1. Kakrapar	:	Gujarat
2. Kalpakkam	:	Karnataka
3. Rawatbhata	:	Rajasthan

Which of the pairs given above are correctly matched?

(a) 1 and 2 only (b) 2 and 3 only

(c) 1 and 3 only (d) 1, 2 and 3

1.23 Consider the following pairs of nuclear power plants and places of India.

Name of nuclear power plants		Name of places
1. Chhaya Mithi Virdi	:	Bhavnagar (Gujarat)
2. Chutka	:	Mandla (Madhya Pradesh)
3. Gorakhpur	:	Fatehabad (Haryana)

Which of the pairs given above are correctly matched?

(a) 1 and 2 only (b) 2 and 3 only

(c) 1 and 3 only (d) 1, 2 and 3

1.24 Consider the following pairs of power generating hydroelectric dams and rivers of India.

Name of hydroelectric dams		Name of rivers
1. Nathpa Jhakri	:	Satluj
2. Sardar Sarovar	:	Narmada
3. Bhakra-Nangal	:	Satluj

Which of the pairs given above are correctly matched?

(a) 1 and 2 only (b) 2 and 3 only

(c) 1 and 3 only (d) 1, 2 and 3

1.25 Consider the following pairs of thermal power plants and states of India.

Name of thermal power plants		Name of states
1. Vindhyachal Thermal Power Station	:	Madhya Pradesh
2. Sasan Ultra Mega Thermal Power Plant	:	Madhya Pradesh
3. Rihand Thermal Power Station	:	Uttar Pradesh

Which of the pairs given above are correctly matched?

(a) 1 and 2 only (b) 2 and 3 only

(c) 1 and 3 only (d) 1, 2 and 3

1.26 Consider the following pairs of wind power plants and places/states of India.

Name of wind power plants		Name of states
1. Brahmanvel Wind Farm	:	Dhule, Maharashtra
2. Damanjodi Wind Farm	:	Koraput, Odisha
3. Tuppadahalli Wind Farm	:	Kanyakumari, Tamil Nadu

Which of the pairs given above are correctly matched?

(a) 1 and 2 only (b) 2 and 3 only

(c) 1 and 3 only (d) 1, 2 and 3

1.27 The DFIG is operating in super-synchronous mode ($Nr > Ns$) with negative slip. The following statement is correct for DFIG operation.

(a) The stator winding will provide power to the grid.

(b) The rotor winding will provide power to the grid.

(c) The stator as well as rotor windings will provide power to the grid.

(d) The grid will provide power to stator winding of the DFIG.

1.28 The DFIG is operating in sub-synchronous mode ($Nr < Ns$) with positive slip. The following statement is correct for DFIG operation:

(a) The stator winding provides power to the grid.

(b) Stator winding provides power to both the grid as well as rotor winding.

(c) The stator as well as rotor windings provides power to the grid.

(d) The stator winding provides power to rotor winging.

1.29 The Doubly-Fed Induction Generator used in Wind Energy Conversion System is
 (a) a wound rotor induction machine
 (b) a slip ring induction machine
 (c) a synchronous type induction generator
 (d) a permanent speed induction generator

1.30 The standalone induction generator used in wind energy conversion system is called:
 (a) Doubly fed induction generator
 (b) Synchronous generator
 (c) Three-phase alternator
 (d) Self-excited induction generator

References

Books

1. D.P. Kothari and I.J. Nagrath, *Electric Machines*, Tata McGraw-Hill, New Delhi, 4th edn, 2010.
2. D.P. Kothari, R. Ranjan, and K.C. Singhal, *Renewable Energy Sources and Technology*, 2nd edn, PHI, 2011.
3. C. Kashkari, *Energy Resources, Demand and Conservation with Special Reference to India*, Tata McGraw-Hill, New Delhi, 1975.
4. T.C. Kandpal and H.P. Garg, *Financial Evaluation of Renewable Technologies,* Macmillan India Ltd, New Delhi, 2003.
5. R.L. Sullivan, *Power System Planning*, McGraw-Hill, New York, 1977.
6. B.G.A. Skrotzki and W.A. Vopat, *Power Station Engineering and Economy*, McGraw-Hill, New York, 1960.
7. T.H. Car, *Electric Power Stations*, vols I and II, Chapman and Hall, London, 1944.
8. Central Electricity Generating Board, *Modern Power Station Practice*, 2nd edn, Pergamon, 1976.
9. E.W. Golding, *The Generation of Electricity by Wind Power*, Chapman and Hall, London, 1976.
10. M.M. El-Wanil, *Powerplant Technology*, McGraw-Hill, New York, 1984.
11. D.J. Bennet, *The Elements of Nuclear Power*, Longman, 1972.
12. J. Casazza and F. Delea, *Understanding Electric Power Systems: An Overview of the Technology and Marketplace*, IEEE Press and Wiley Interscience, 2003.
13. M.J. Steinberg and T.H. Smith, *Economy-loading of Power Plants and Electric Systems*, Wiley, New York, 1943.
14. Power System Planning and Operations: Future Problems and Research Needs, *EPRI EL-377-SR*, February 1977.
15. J.W. Twidell and A.D. Weir, *Renewable Energy Resources*, Tailor & Francis, London, 2nd edn, 2006.
16. A.K. Mahalanabis, D.P. Kothari, and S.I. Ahson, *Computer Aided Power System Analysis and Control*, Tata McGraw-Hill, New Delhi, 1988.
17. R. Noyes (Ed.), *Cogeneration of Steam and Electric Power*, Noyes Dali Corp., USA, 1978.
18. H.M. Rustebakke (Ed.), *Electric Utility Systems and Practices*, 4th edn, Wiley, New York, Aug. 1983.
19. CEA 12, *Annual Survey of Power Report*, Aug 1985; 14th Report, March 1991; 16th Electric Power Survey of India, Sept. 2000, 17th Electric Power Survey of India, May 2007.
20. D.P. Kothari and D.K. Sharma (Eds), *Energy Engineering: Theory and Practice*, S Chand, 2000.
21. D.P. Kothari and I.J. Nagrath, *Basic Electrical Engineering*, Tata McGraw-Hill, New Delhi, 3rd edn, 2002 (Ch. 15).
22. L.A. Wehenkel, *Automatic Learning Techniques in Power Systems*, Kluwer, Norwell, MA: 1997.

23. L. Philipson and H. Lee Willis, *Understanding Electric Utilities and Deregulation*, Marcel Dekker Inc, NY, 1999.
24. M.M. Singhe, *Economics of Power Systems Reliability and Planning*, John Hopkins University Press, 1980.
25. *The Indian Electricity Rules*, 1956, Commercial Law Publishers, Delhi, 2005.
26. J. Nick *et al.*, *Embedded Generation*, IEE, UK, 2000.
27. M. Ned, *First Course on Power Systems*, MNPER, Minneapolis, 2006.
28. D.P. Kothari and I.J. Nagrath, *Power System Engineering*, Tata McGraw-Hill, New Delhi, 2nd edition, 2008.

Papers

29. H. Goyal, M. Handmandlu and D.P. Kothari, "A Novel Modelling Technique For ALFC of Small Hydro Power Plants", *Int Journal of Modelling and Simulation*, volume: 27, issue: 2, 2007.
30. M. Rizwan, M. Jamil, and D.P. Kothari, "Performance Evaluation of Solar Irradiance Models: A Comparative Study", *International Journal on Electronics and Electrical Engineering*, volume: 1, issue: 1, pp: 141–151, 2009.
31. A. Ranjan, S. Prabhakar Karthikeyan, A. Ahuja, K. Palanisamy, I. Jacob Raglend, and D.P. Kothari, "Impact of Reactive Power in Power Evacuation from Wind Turbines", Presented at APPEEC-09, Wuhan University China and published in the *Journal of Electromagnetic Analysis and Applications*, volume: 1, pp: 15–23, 2009.
32. M. Rizwan, M. Jamil, and D.P. Kothari, "Solar Energy Estimation using REST Model for PV-ECS Based Distributed Power Generating System", *Solar Energy Materials and Solar Cells*, volume: 94, pp: 1324–1328, 2010.
33. K.L. Chandrasekar and D.P. Kothari, "Three Gorges Dam—Stochastic Perspective for the project planning issues", *Management Dynamics*, volume: 9, issue: 1, pp: 71–81, 2009.
34. S. Umashankar, D.P. Kothari, and P. Mangayarkarasi, "Wind Turbine Modelling of a Fully-fed Induction Machine", Wind Power (Book Chapter), Intech Publications, Croatia, pp: 93–112, 2010.
35. Om Prakash Bharti, Kumari Sarita, Aanchal Singh S. Vardhan, Akanksha Singh S. Vardhan, and R.K. Saket, "Controller Design for DFIG-based WT Using Gravitational Search Algorithm for Wind Power Generation", *IET Renewable Power Generation (UK)*, volume: 15, issue: 9, pp: 1956–1967, 2021.
36. P. Jayaprakash, B. Singh, D.P. Kothari, A. Chandra, and K. Al-Haddad, "Control of Reduced-Rating Dynamic Voltage Restorer with a Battery Energy Storage System", *IEEE Transactions on Industry Applications*, volume: 50, issue: 2, pp: 1295–1303, 2013.
37. S. Kumar, R.K. Saket, and D.P. Kothari, "Hydropower and Floods", *Flood Handbook, Taylor and Francis (USA)*, volume: 3, pp: 1–30, 2020.
38. S. Kumar, R.K. Saket, Dharmendra Kumar Dheer, Jens Bo Holm-Nielsen, and P. Sanjeevikumar, "Reliability Enhancement of Electrical Power System Including Impacts of Renewable Energy Sources: A Comprehensive Review", *IET Generation, Transmission & Distribution*, volume: 14, issue: 10, pp: 1799–1815, 2020.
39. S. Upadhyay, D.P. Kothari, and U. Shanker, "Renewable Energy Technologies for Cooking: Transforming Rural Lives", *IEEE Technology and Society Magazine*, volume: 32, issue: 3, 65–72, 2013.
40. O.P. Bharti, R.K. Saket, and S.K. Nagar, "Reliability Assessment and Performance Analysis of DFIG Based WT for Wind Energy Conversion System", *International Journal of Reliability and Safety,* volume: 13, issue: 4, pp: 235–266, 2019.
41. B. Saravanan, S. Das, S. Sikri, and D.P. Kothari, "A Solution to the Unit Commitment Problem—A Review", *Frontiers in Energy*, volume: 7, issue: 2, pp: 223–236, 2013.
42. D.P. Kothari, Energy Problems Facing the Third World, *Seminar to the Bio-Physics Workshop*, 8 Oct 1986, Trieste, Italy.

43. D.P. Kothari, *Energy System Planning and Energy Conservation, Presented at XXIV National Convention of IIIE*, New Delhi, Feb 1982.
44. D.P. Kothari, *et al.*, Minimisation of Air Pollution due to Thermal Plants, *JIE* (India), volume: 57, issue: 65, Feb 1977.
45. D.P. Kothari and J. Nanda, Power Supply Scenario in India "Retrospects and Prospects", Proc. NPC Cong., *on Captive Power Generation,* New Delhi, Mar 1986.
46. O.P. Bharti, R.K. Saket, and S.K. Nagar, "Controller Design for Doubly Fed Induction Generator Using Particle Swarm Optimization Technique", Renewable Energy, volume: 114, Part B, pp: 1394–1406, 2017.
47. D.P. Kothari, Mini and Micro Hydropower Systems in India, invited chapter in the book, *Energy Resources and Technology*, Scientific Publishers, pp: 147–158, 1992.
48. M. Rizwan, M. Jamil, S. Kirmani, and D.P. Kothari, "Fuzzy Logic Based Modeling and Estimation of Global Solar Energy Using Meteorological Parameters", *Energy*, volume: 70, pp: 685–691, 2014.
49. R. Choudhary and R.K. Saket, "A Critical Review on the Self-Excitation Process and Steady State Analysis of an SEIG Driven by Wind Turbine", *Renewable and Sustainable Energy Reviews*, volume: 47, pp: 344–353, 2015.
50. T.S. Shikha Bhatti and D.P. Kothari, "Wind as an Eco-friendly Energy Source to meet the Electricity Needs of SAARC Region", *Proc. Int. Conf. (ICME 2001)*, BUET, Dhaka, Bangladesh, pp: 11–16, Dec 2001.
51. R.C. Bansal, D.P. Kothari, and T.S. Bhatti, "On Some of the Design Aspects of Wind Energy Conversion Systems", *Int. J. Energy Conversion and Management*, volume: 43, pp: 2175–2187, 16 Nov. 2002.
52. D.P. Kothari and A. Arora, Fuel Cells in Transportation-Beyond Batteries, *Proc. Nat. Conf. on Transportation Systems*, IIT Delhi, pp: 173–176, April 2002.
53. A. Saxena and D.P. Kothari, *et al.*, "*Analysis of Multimedia and Hypermedia for Computer Simulation and Growth*", EJEISA, UK, volume: 3, pp: 14–28, 1 Sept 2001.
54. R.C. Bansal, T.S. Bhatti, and D.P. Kothari, "A Bibliographical Survey on Induction Generators for Application of Nonconventional Energy Systems", *IEEE Trans. on Energy Conversions*, volume: 18, pp: 433–439, Sept 2003.
55. M. Kolhe, J.C. Joshi, and D.P. Kothari, "LOLP of stand-alone solar PV system", *Int. Journal of Energy Technology and Policy.*, volume: 1, issue: 3, pp: 315–323, 2003.
56. T.S. Shikha Bhatti and D.P. Kothari, Vertical Axis Wind Rotor with Concentration by Convergent Nozzles, *Wind Engg*, volume: 27, issue: 6, pp: 555–559, 2003.
57. T.S. Shikha Bhatti and D.P. Kothari, On Some Aspects of Technological Development of Wind Turbines, *Energy Engg*, volume: 129, issue: 3, pp: 69–80, Dec 2003.
58. T.S. Shikha Bhatti and D.P. Kothari, "Wind Energy Conversion Systems as a Distributed Source of Generation", *Energy Engg*, volume: 129, issue: 3, pp: 81–95, Dec 2003.
59. T.S. Shikha Bhatti and D.P. Kothari, "Indian Scenario of Wind Energy: Problems and Solutions", *Energy Sources*, volume: 26, issue: 9, pp: 811–819, July 2004.
60. M. Kolhe, J.C. Joshi, and D.P. Kothari, "Performance Analysis of a Directly Coupled PV Water Pumping Systems", *IEEE Trans., on Energy Conversion*, volume: 19, issue: 3, pp: 613–618, Sept 2004.
61. T.S. Shikha Bhatti and D.P. Kothari, "The Power Coefficient of Windmills in Ideal Conditions", *Int J of Global Energy Issues*, volume: 21, issue: 3, pp: 236–242, 2004.
62. R.C. Bansal, T.S. Bhatti, and D.P. Kothari, "Automatic Reactive Power Control of Isolated Wind-Diesel Hybrid Power Systems for Variable Wind Speed/Slip", *Electric Power Components and Systems*, volume: 32, pp: 901–912, 2004.

63. T.S. Shikha Bhatti and D.P. Kothari, "Wind Energy in India: Shifting Paradigms and Challenges Ahead", *Energy Engg*, volume: 130, issue: 3, pp: 67–80, Dec 2004.
64. T.S. Shikha Bhatti and D.P. Kothari, "New Horizons for Offshore. Wind Energy: Shifting Paradigms and Challenges", *Energy Sources*, volume: 27, issue: 4, pp: 349–360, March 2005.
65. T.S. Shikha Bhatti and D.P. Kothari, "Development of Vertical and Horizontal Axis Wind Turbines: A Review," *Int J of Wind Engg*, volume: 29, issue: 3, pp: 287–300, May 2005.
66. T.S. Shikha Bhatti and D.P. Kothari, "A Review of Wind Resource Assessment Technology", *Energy Engg*, volume: 132, issue: 1, pp: 8–14, April 2006.
67. S.C. Kaushik, S. Ramesh, and D.P. Kothari, "Energy Conservation Studies in Buildings," *Presented at PCRA Conf*, New Delhi, May 19, 2005.
68. H. Goyal, T.S. Bhatti, and D.P. Kothari, "A Novel Technique proposed for automatic control of small Hydro Power Plants," *Special Issue of International Journal of Global Energy Issues*, volume: 24, pp: 29–46, 2005.
69. R.C. Bansal T.S. Bhatti, D.P. Kothari, and S. Bhat, "Reactive Power Control of Wind-diesel-microhydro Power Systems Using Matlab/Simulink", *International Journal of Global Energy Issues*, volume: 24, issue: 1, pp: 86–99, 2005.
70. H. Goyal, M. Hanmandlu, and D.P. Kothari, "A New Optimal Flow Control Approach for Automatic Control of Small Hydro Power Plants", *JIE (I)*, volume: 87, pp: 1–5, May 2006.
71. L. Varshney and R.K. Saket, "Reliability Evaluation of SEIG Rotor Core Magnetization with Minimum Capacitive Excitation for Unregulated Renewable Energy Applications in Remote Areas", *Ain Shams Engineering Journal*, volume: 5, issue: 3, pp: 751–757, 2014.
72. R.K. Saket, "Design Aspects and Probabilistic Approach for Generation Reliability Evaluation of MWW Based Micro-hydro Power Plant", *Renewable and Sustainable Energy Reviews*, volume: 28, pp: 917–929, 2013.
73. R.C. Bansal, Ahmed F. Zobaa, and R.K. Saket, "Some Issues Related to Power Generation Using Wind Energy Conversion System: An Overview", *International Journal of Emerging Electric Power System*, volume: 3, issue: 2, pp: 01–19, 2005.
74. L.D. Arya, S.C. Choube, and R.K. Saket, "Generation System Adequacy Evaluation Using Probability Theory", *Journal of the Institution of Engineers (India), Series B*, volume: 81, pp: 170–174, 2001.
75. L.D. Arya, S.C. Choube, and R.K. Saket, "Composite System Reliability Evaluation Based on Static Voltage Stability Limit", *Journal of the Institution of Engineers (India), Series B*, volume: 80, pp: 133–140, 2000.
76. S. Mishra, C.K. Panigrahi, and D.P. Kothari, "Design and Simulation of a Solar–Wind–Biogas Hybrid System Architecture Using HOMER in India", *International Journal of Ambient Energy*, volume: 37, issue: 2, pp: 184–191, 2016.
77. A.J. Siddiqui, S.K. Bharadwaj, D.P. Kothari, and B. Deshmukh, "Current Developments in Renewable Energy Resources-Based Hybrid Energy System: A Review", *International Journal of Energy Technology and Policy*, volume: 12, issue: 4, pp: 333–356, 2016.
78. N. Narang, J.S. Dhillon, and D.P. Kothari, "Multi-Objective Short-Term Hydrothermal Generation Scheduling Using Predator–Prey Optimization", *Electric Power Components and Systems*, volume: 40, issue: 15, pp: 1708–1730, 2012.
79. M. Rizwan, M. Jamil, and D.P. Kothari, "Generalized Neural Network Approach for Global Solar Energy Estimation in India", *IEEE Transactions on Sustainable Energy*, volume: 3, issue: 3, pp: 576–584, 2012.
80. R.C. Bansal, T.S. Bhatti, and D.P. Kothari, "A Novel Mathematical Modelling of Induction Generator for Reactive Power Control of Isolated Hybrid Power Systems", *International Journal of Modelling & Simulation*, volume: 24, issue: 1, pp: 1–7, 2011.

CHAPTER 2

Inductance and Resistance of Transmission Lines

2.1 ▶ INTRODUCTION

The four parameters which affect the performance of a transmission line as an element of a power system are inductance, capacitance, resistance and conductance. Shunt conductance, which is normally due to leakage over line insulators, is almost always neglected in overhead transmission lines. This chapter deals with the series line parameters, i.e., inductance and resistance. These parameters are uniformly distributed along the line and they together form the series impedance of the line.

Inductance is by far the most dominant line parameter from a power system engineer's viewpoint. As we shall see in later chapters, it is the inductive reactance which limits the transmission capacity of a line.

2.2 ▶ DEFINITION OF INDUCTANCE

Voltage induced in a circuit is given by

$$e = \frac{\mathrm{d}\psi}{\mathrm{d}t} \text{ V} \tag{2.1}$$

where ψ represents the flux linkages of the circuit in weber-turns (Wb-T). This can be written in the form

$$e = \frac{\mathrm{d}\psi}{\mathrm{d}i} \cdot \frac{\mathrm{d}i}{\mathrm{d}t} = L\frac{\mathrm{d}i}{\mathrm{d}t} \text{ V} \tag{2.2}$$

where $L = \frac{\mathrm{d}\psi}{\mathrm{d}i}$ is defined as the inductance of the circuit in henry, which in general may be a function of i. In a linear magnetic circuit, i.e., a circuit with constant permeability, flux linkages vary linearly with current such that the inductance is constant given by

$$L = \frac{\psi}{i} \text{ H}$$

or,

$$\psi = Li \text{ Wb-T} \tag{2.3}$$

If the current is alternating, the above equation can be written as

$$\lambda = LI \tag{2.4}$$

where λ and I are the rms values of flux linkages and current respectively. These are of course in phase.

Replacing $\frac{\mathrm{d}}{\mathrm{d}t}$ in Eq. (2.1) by $j\omega$, we get the steady-state AC voltage drop due to alternating flux linkages as

$$V = j\omega LI = j\omega\lambda \text{ V} \tag{2.5}$$

On similar lines, the mutual inductance between two circuits is defined as the flux linkages of one circuit due to current in another, i.e.,

$$M_{12} = \frac{\lambda_{12}}{I_2} \text{ H} \tag{2.6}$$

The voltage drop in circuit 1 due to current in circuit 2 is

$$V_1 = j\omega M_{12} I_2 = j\omega\lambda_{12} \text{ V} \tag{2.7}$$

The concept of mutual inductance is required while considering the coupling between parallel lines and the influence of power lines on telephone lines.

2.3 ▶ FLUX LINKAGES OF AN ISOLATED CURRENT-CARRYING CONDUCTOR

Transmission lines are composed of parallel conductors which, for all practical purposes, can be considered as infinitely long. Let us first develop expressions for flux linkages of a long isolated current-carrying cylindrical conductor with return path lying at infinity. This system forms a single-turn circuit, flux linking which is in the form of circular lines concentric to the conductor. The total flux can be divided into two parts, that which is internal to the conductor and the flux external to the conductor. Such a division is helpful as the internal flux progressively links a smaller amount of current as we proceed inwards, towards the centre of the conductor, while the external flux always links the total current inside the conductor.

2.3.1 Flux Linkages due to Internal Flux

Figure 2.1 shows the cross-sectional view of a long cylindrical conductor carrying current I.

The mmf round a concentric closed circular path of radius y internal to the conductor as shown in the figure is

$$\oint H_y \cdot \mathrm{d}s I_y \text{ (Ampere's law)} \tag{2.8}$$

where,

H_y = magnetic field intensity (AT/m)

I_y = current enclosed (A)

By symmetry, H_y is constant and is in the direction of ds all along the circular path. Therefore, from Eq. (2.8), we have

$$2\pi y H_y = I_y \tag{2.9}$$

Assuming uniform current density*

$$I_y = \left(\frac{\pi y^2}{\pi r^2}\right) I = \left(\frac{y^2}{r^2}\right) I \tag{2.10}$$

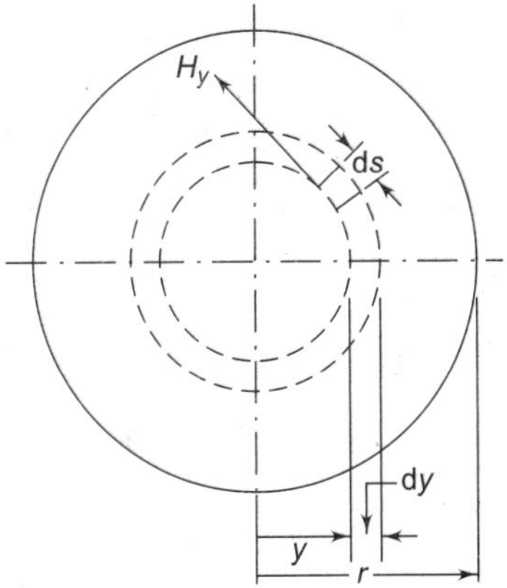

Fig. 2.1 *Flux linkages due to internal flux (cross-sectional view)*

From Eqs (2.9) and (2.10), we obtain

$$H_y = \frac{yI}{2\pi r^2} \text{ AT/m} \tag{2.11}$$

* For power frequency of 50 Hz, it is quite reasonable to assume uniform current density. The effect of non-uniform current density is considered later in this chapter while treating resistance.

The flux density B_y, y metres from the centre of the conductors, is

$$B_y = \mu H_y = \frac{\mu y I}{2\pi r^2} \text{ Wb/m}^2 \tag{2.12}$$

where μ is the permeability of the conductor.

Consider now an infinitesimal tubular element of thickness dy and length 1m. The flux in the tubular element $d\phi = B_y$ dy webers links the fractional turn ($I_y/I = y^2/r^2$) resulting in flux linkages of

$$d\lambda = \left(\frac{y^2}{r^2}\right) d\phi = \left(\frac{y^2}{r^2}\right)\frac{\mu y I}{2\pi r^2} dy \text{ Wb-T/m} \tag{2.13}$$

Integrating, we get the total internal flux linkages as

$$\lambda_{int} = \int_0^r \frac{\mu I}{2\pi r^4} y^3 dy = \frac{\mu I}{8\pi} \text{ Wb-T/m} \tag{2.14}$$

For a relative permeability $\mu_r = 1$ (nonmagnetic conductor), $\mu = 4\pi \times 10^{-7}$ H/m; therefore,

$$\lambda_{int} = \frac{I}{2} \times 10^{-7} \text{ Wb-T/m} \tag{2.15}$$

and

$$L_{int} = \frac{1}{2} \times 10^{-7} \text{ H/m} \tag{2.16}$$

2.3.2 Flux Linkages due to Flux between Two Points External to Conductor

Figure 2.2 shows two points P_1 and P_2 at distances D_1 and D_2 from a conductor which carries a current of I amperes. As the conductor is far removed from the return current path, the magnetic field external to the conductor is concentric circles around the conductor and therefore all the flux between P_1 and P_2 lines within the concentric cylindrical surfaces are passing through P_1 and P_2.

Magnetic field intensity at distance y from the conductor is

$$H_y = \frac{I}{2\pi y} \text{ AT/m}$$

The flux $d\phi$ contained in the tubular element of thickness dy is

$$d\phi = \frac{\mu I}{2\pi y} dy \text{ Wb/m length of conductor}$$

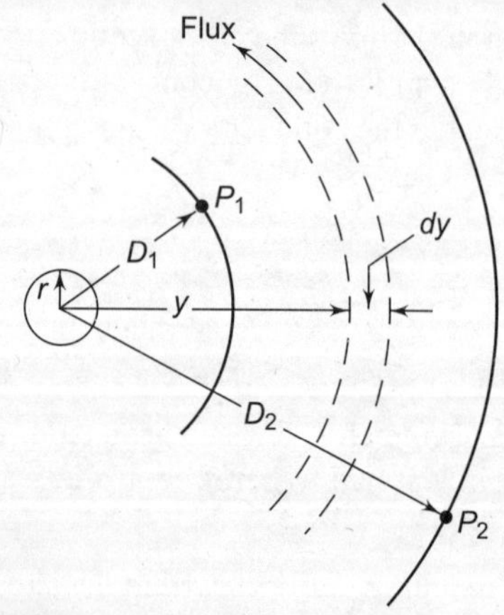

Fig. 2.2 *Flux linkages due to flux between external points P_1, P_2*

The flux $d\phi$ being external to the conductor, links all the current in the conductor which together with the return conductor at infinity forms a single return, such that its flux linkages are given by

$$d\lambda = 1 \times d\phi = \frac{\mu I}{2\pi y} dy$$

Therefore, the total flux linkages of the conductor due to flux between points P_1 and P_2 is

$$\lambda_{12} = \int_{D_1}^{D_2} \frac{\mu I}{2\pi y} dy = \frac{\mu}{2\pi} I \ln \frac{D_2}{D_1} \text{ Wb-T/m}$$

where ln stands for natural logarithm*.

Since $\mu_r = 1$, $\mu = 4\pi \times 10^{-7}$

$$\therefore \quad \lambda_{12} = 2 \times 10^{-7} I \ln \frac{D_2}{D_1} \text{ Wb-T/m} \tag{2.17}$$

The inductance of the conductor contributed by the flux included between points P_1 and P_2 is then

$$L_{12} = 2 \times 10^{-7} \ln \frac{D_2}{D_1} \text{ H/m} \tag{2.18}$$

or

$$L_{12} = 0.461 \log \frac{D_2}{D_1} \text{ mH/km} \tag{2.19}$$

2.3.3 Flux Linkages due to Flux upto an External Point

Let the external point be at distance D from the centre of the conductor. Flux linkages of the conductor due to external flux (from the surface of the conductor upto the external point) is obtained from Eq. (2.17) by substituting $D_1 = r$ and $D_2 = D$, i.e.,

$$\lambda_{ext} = 2 \times 10^{-7} I \ln \frac{D}{r} \tag{2.20}$$

Total flux linkages of the conductor due to internal and external flux are

$$\lambda = \lambda_{int} + \lambda_{ext}$$

$$= \frac{I}{2} \times 10^{-7} + 2 \times 10^{-7} I \ln \frac{D}{r}$$

$$= 2 \times 10^{-7} I \left(\frac{1}{4} + \ln \frac{D}{r} \right)$$

$$= 2 \times 10^{-7} I \ln \frac{D}{re^{-1/4}}$$

Let,

$$r' = re^{-1/4} = 0.7788r$$

$$\therefore \quad \lambda = 2 \times 10^{-7} I \ln \frac{D}{r'} \text{ Wb-T/m} \tag{2.21a}$$

Inductance of the conductor due to flux upto an external point is therefore

$$L = 2 \times 10^{-7} \ln \frac{D}{r'} \text{ H/m} \tag{2.21b}$$

Here r' can be regarded as the radius of a fictitious conductor with no internal inductance but the same total inductance as the actual conductor.

* Throughout the book ln denotes natural logarithm (base e), while log denotes logarithm to base 10.

2.4 ▶ INDUCTANCE OF A SINGLE-PHASE TWO-WIRE LINE

Consider a simple two-wire line composed of solid round conductors carrying currents I_1 and I_2 as shown in Fig. 2.3. In a single-phase line,

$$I_1 + I_2 = 0$$

or

$$I_2 = -I_1$$

It is important to note that the effect of earth's presence on magnetic field geometry* is insignificant. This is so because the relative permeability of earth is about the same as that of air and its electrical conductivity is relatively small.

To start with, let us consider the flux linkages of the circuit caused by current in conductor 1 only. We make three observations in regard to these flux linkages:

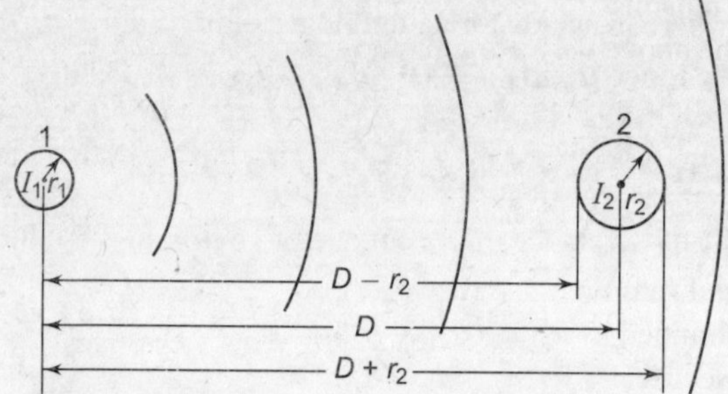

Fig. 2.3 *Single-phase two-wire line and the magnetic field due to current in conductor 1 only*

1. External flux from r_1 to $(D - r_2)$ links all the current I_1 in conductor 1.
2. External flux from $(D - r_2)$ to $(D + r_2)$ links a current whose magnitude progressively reduces from I_1 to zero along this distance, because of the effect of negative current flowing in conductor 2.
3. Flux beyond $(D + r_2)$ links a net current of zero.

For calculating the total inductance due to current in conductor 1, a simplifying assumption will now be made. If D is much greater than r_1 and r_2 (which is normally the case for overhead lines), it can be assumed that the flux from $(D - r_2)$ to the centre of conductor 2 links all the current I_1 and the flux from the centre of conductor 2 to $(D + r_2)$ links zero current**.

Based on the above assumption, the flux linkages of the circuit caused by current in conductor 1 as per Eq. (2.21a) are

$$\lambda_1 = 2 \times 10^{-7} I_1 \ln \frac{D}{r'_1} \tag{2.22a}$$

The inductance of the conductor due to current in conductor 1 only is then

$$L_1 = 2 \times 10^{-7} \ln \frac{D}{r'_1} \tag{2.22b}$$

Similarly, the inductance of the circuit due to current in conductor 2 is

$$L_2 = 2 \times 10^{-7} \ln \frac{D}{r'_2} \tag{2.23}$$

Using the superposition theorem, the flux linkages and likewise the inductances of the circuit caused by current in each conductor considered separately may be added to obtain the total circuit inductance. Therefore, for the complete circuit

$$L = L_1 + L_2 = 4 \times 10^{-7} \ln \frac{D}{\sqrt{r'_1 r'_2}} \text{ H/m} \tag{2.24}$$

---

* The electric field geometry will, however, be very much affected as we shall see later while dealing with capacitance.

** Kimbark [10] has shown that the results based on this assumption are fairly accurate even when D is not much larger than r_1 and r_2.

If $r_1' = r_2' = r'$; then

$$L = 4 \times 10^{-7} \ln D/r' \text{ H/m} \tag{2.25a}$$

$$L = 0.921 \log D/r' \text{ mH/km} \tag{2.25b}$$

Transmission lines are infinitely long compared to D in practical situations and therefore the end effects in the above derivation have been neglected.

2.5 ▶ CONDUCTOR TYPES

So far we have considered transmission lines consisting of single solid cylindrical conductors for forward and return paths. To provide the necessary flexibility for stringing, conductors used in practice are always stranded except for very small cross-sectional areas. Stranded conductors are composed of strands of wire, electrically in parallel, with alternate layers spiralled in opposite direction to prevent unwinding. The total number of strands (N) in concentrically stranded cables with total annular space filled with strands of uniform diameter (d) is given by

$$N = 3x^2 - 3x + 1 \tag{2.26a}$$

where x is the number of layers wherein the single central strand is counted as the first layer. The overall diameter (D) of a stranded conductor is

$$D = (2x - 1)d \tag{2.26b}$$

Aluminium is now the most commonly employed conductor material. It has the advantages of being cheaper and lighter than copper though with less conductivity and tensile strength. Low density and low conductivity result in larger overall conductor diameter, which offers another incidental advantage in high voltage lines. Increased diameter results in reduced electrical stress at conductor surface for a given voltage so that the line is *corona free*. Aluminium-alloy conductors have higher tensile strength than the ordinary electrical conductor grade of aluminium. ACSR consists of a central core of steel strands surrounded by layers of aluminium strands. Aluminium conductor alloy reinforced (ACAR) has a central core of higher strength aluminium surrounded by layers of electrical-conductor-grade aluminium. Figure 2.4 shows the cross-sectional view of an ACSR conductor with 24 strands of aluminium and 7 strands of steel.

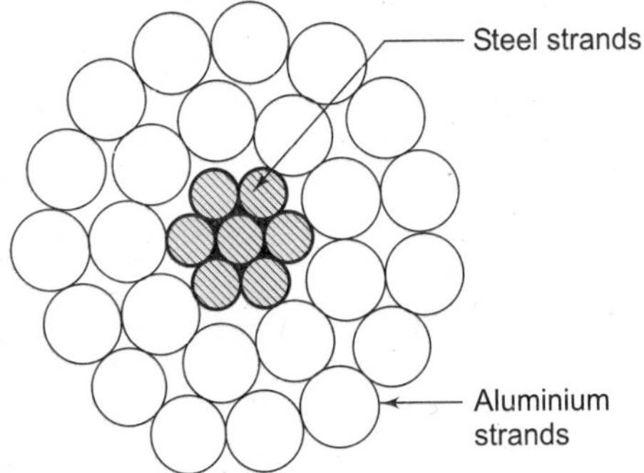

Fig. 2.4 *Cross-sectional view of ACSR-7 steel strands, 24 aluminium strands*

In extra high voltage (EHV) transmission line, *expanded* ACSR conductors are used. These are provided with paper or hessian between various layers of strands so as to increase the overall conductor diameter in an attempt to reduce electrical stress at conductor surface and prevent corona. The most effective way of constructing *corona-free* EHV lines (Ch.19) is to provide several conductors per phase in suitable geometrical configuration. These are known as *bundled conductors* and are a common practice now for EHV lines.

Table 2.1 ACSR Conductor Characteristic (Aluminium Conductor Steel Reinforced)

Sl. No.	*Name*	*Overall Dia (mm)*	*DC Resistance (ohms/km)*	*Current Capacity (Amp) 75 deg. C*
1.	Mole	4.50	2.78	70
2.	Squirrel	6.33	1.394	107

(*Contd.*)

Table 2.1 (Contd.)

Sl. No.	*Name*	*Overall Dia (mm)*	*DC Resistance (ohms/km)*	*Current Capacity (Amp) 75 deg. C*
3.	Weasel	7.77	0.9291	138
4.	Rabbit	10.05	0.5524	190
5.	Racoon	12.27	0.3712	244
6.	Dog	14.15	0.2792	291
7.	Wolf	18.13	0.1871	405
8.	Lynx	19.53	0.161	445
9.	Panther	21.00	0.139	487
10.	Zebra	28.62	0.06869	737
11.	Dear	29.89	0.06854	756
12.	Moose	31.77	0.05596	836
13.	Bersimis	35.04	0.04242	998

Note: For more technical particulars of ACSR 'Panther', 'Zebra' and 'Moose' conductors, the reader may refer to http://www.upptdcl.org/tech_info/table_14I.html

2.6 ▸ FLUX LINKAGES OF ONE CONDUCTOR IN GROUP

As shown in Fig. 2.5, consider a group of n parallel round conductors carrying phasor currents I_1, I_2,..., I_n whose sum equals zero. Distances of these conductors from a remote point P are indicated as D_1, D_2,..., D_n. Let us obtain an expression for the total flux linkages of the ith conductor of the group considering flux upto the point P only.

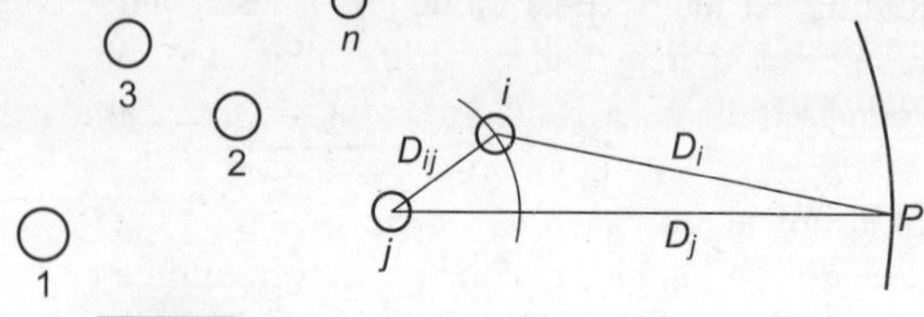

Fig. 2.5 *Arbitrary group of n parallel round conductors carrying currents*

The flux linkages of ith conductor due to its own current I_i (self linkages) are given by [see Eq. (2.21)]

$$\lambda_{ii} = 2 \times 10^{-7} I_i \ln \frac{D_i}{r'_i} \text{ Wb-T/m} \tag{2.27}$$

The flux linkages of conductor i due to current in conductor j [refer to Eq. (2.17)] are

$$\lambda_{ij} = 2 \times 10^{-7} I_j \ln \frac{D_j}{D_{ij}} \text{ Wb-T/m} \tag{2.28}$$

where D_{ij} is the distance of ith conductor from jth conductor carrying current I_j. From Eq. (2.27) and by repeated use of Eq. (2.28), the total flux linkages of conductor i due to flux upto point P are

$$\lambda_i = \lambda_{i1} + \lambda_{i2} + \cdots + \lambda_{ii} + \cdots + \lambda_{in} = 2 \times 10^{-7} \left(I_1 \ln \frac{D_1}{D_{i1}} + I_2 \ln \frac{D_2}{D_{i2}} + \cdots + I_i \ln \frac{D_i}{r'_i} + \cdots + I_n \ln \frac{D_n}{D_{in}} \right)$$

The above equation can be reorganised as

$$\lambda_i = 2 \times 10^{-7} \left[\left(I_1 \ln \frac{1}{D_{i1}} + I_2 \ln \frac{1}{D_{i2}} + \cdots + I_i \ln \frac{1}{r'_i} + \cdots + I_n \ln \frac{1}{D_{in}} \right) + (I_1 \ln D_1 + I_2 \ln D_2 + \cdots \right.$$
$$\left. + I_i \ln D_i + \cdots + I_n \ln D_n) \right] \tag{2.29}$$

But, $I_n = -(I + I_2 + \cdots + I_{n-1})$.

Substituting for I_n in the second term of Eq. (2.29) and simplifying, we have

$$\lambda_i = 2\times 10^{-7}\left[\left(I_1 \ln\frac{1}{D_{i1}} + I_2 \ln\frac{1}{D_{i2}} + \cdots + I_i \ln\frac{1}{r_i'} + \cdots + I_n \ln\frac{1}{D_{in}}\right)\right.$$
$$\left.+\left(I_1 \ln\frac{D_1}{D_n} + I_2 \ln\frac{D_2}{D_n} + \cdots + I_i \ln\frac{D_i}{D_n} \cdots + I_{n-1} \ln\frac{D_{n-1}}{D_n}\right)\right]$$

In order to account for total flux linkages of conductor i, let the point P now recede to infinity. The terms such as $\ln D_1/D_n$, etc., approach $\ln 1 = 0$. Also for the sake of symmetry, denoting r'_i as D_{ii}, we have

$$\lambda_i = 2\times 10^{-7}\left(I_1 \ln\frac{1}{D_{i1}} + I_2 \ln\frac{1}{D_{i2}} + \cdots I_2 \ln\frac{1}{D_{ii}} + \cdots + I_n \ln\frac{1}{D_{in}}\right)\text{Wb-T/m} \quad (2.30)$$

2.7 ▶ INDUCTANCE OF COMPOSITE CONDUCTOR LINES

We are now ready to study the inductance of transmission lines composed of composite conductors. Figure 2.6 shows such a single-phase line comprising composite conductors A and B with A having n parallel filaments and B having m' parallel filaments. Though the inductance of each filament will be somewhat different (their resistances will be equal if conductor diameters are chosen to be uniform), it is sufficiently accurate to assume that the current is equally divided among the filaments of each composite conductor. Thus, each filament of A is taken to carry a current I/n, while each filament of conductor B carries the return current of $-I/m'$.

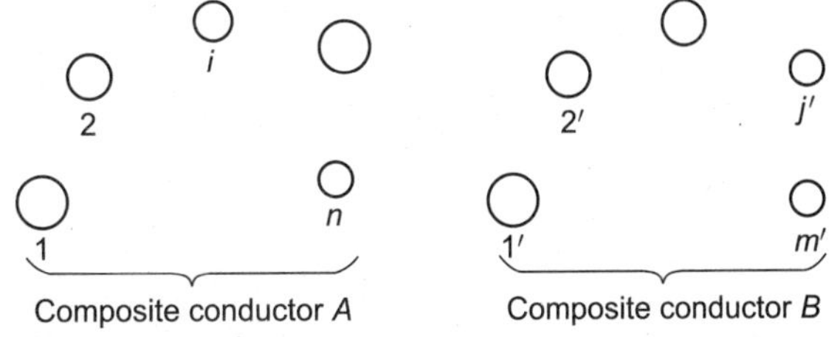

Fig. 2.6 *Single-phase line consisting of two composite conductors*

Applying Eq. (2.30) to filament i of conductor A, we obtain its flux linkages as

$$\lambda_i = 2\times10^{-7}\frac{I}{n}\left(\ln\frac{1}{D_{i1}} + \ln\frac{1}{D_{i2}} + \cdots + \ln\frac{1}{D_{ii}} + \cdots + \ln\frac{1}{D_{in}}\right) - 2\times10^{-7}\frac{I}{m'}\left(\ln\frac{1}{D_{i1'}} + \ln\frac{1}{D_{i2'}} + \cdots + \ln\frac{1}{D_{im'}}\right)$$

$$= 2\times 10^{-7} I \ln\frac{(D_{i1'}D_{i2'}\ldots D_{im'})^{1/m'}}{(D_{i1}D_{i2}\ldots D_{ii}\ldots D_{in})^{1/n}} \text{ Wb-T/m}$$

The inductance of filament i is then

$$L_i = \frac{\lambda_i}{I/n} = 2n\times10^{-7}\ln\frac{(D_{i1'}\ldots D_{ij'}\ldots D_{im'})^{1/m'}}{(D_{i1}\ldots D_{ii}\ldots D_{in})^{1/n}} \text{ H/m} \quad (2.31)$$

The average inductance of the filaments of composite conductor A is

$$L_{\text{avg}} = \frac{L_1 + L_2 + L_3 + \cdots + L_n}{n}$$

Since conductor A is composed of n filaments electrically in parallel, its inductance is

$$L_A = \frac{L_{\text{avg}}}{n} = \frac{L_1 + L_2 + \cdots + L_n}{n^2} \quad (2.32)$$

Using the expression for filament inductance from Eq. (2.31) in Eq. (2.32), we obtain

$$L_A = 2 \times 10^{-7} \ln \frac{[(D_{11'} \ldots D_{1j'} \ldots D_{1m'}) \ldots (D_{i1'} \ldots D_{ij'} \ldots D_{im'}) \cdots (D_{nl'} \ldots D_{nj'} \ldots D_{nm'})]^{1/m'n}}{[(D_{1l} \ldots D_{1j} \ldots D_{1n}) \ldots (D_{il} \ldots D_{ii} \ldots D_{in}) \cdots (D_{n1} \ldots D_{ni} \ldots D_{nn})]^{1/n^2}} \text{ H/m} \quad (2.33)$$

The numerator of the argument of the logarithm in Eq. (2.33) is the $m'n$th root of the $m'n$ terms, which are the products of all possible mutual distances from the n filaments of conductor A to m' filaments of conductor B. It is called mutual *geometric mean distance* (mutual GMD) between conductors A and B and is abbreviated as D_m. Similarly, the denominator of the argument of the logarithm in Eq. (2.33) is the n^2th root of n^2 product terms (n sets of n product terms each). Each set of n product term pertains to a filament and consists of $r'(D_{ii})$ for that filament and $(n - 1)$ distances from that filament to every other filament in conductor A. The denominator is defined as the *self geometric mean distance* (self GMD) of conductor A, and is abbreviated as D_{sA}. Sometimes, self GMD is also called *geometric mean radius* (GMR).

In terms of the above symbols, we can write Eq. (2.33) as

$$L_A = 2 \times 10^{-7} \ln \frac{D_m}{D_{sA}} \text{ H/m} \quad (2.34a)$$

$$= 0.461 \log \frac{D_m}{D_{sA}} \text{ mH/km} \quad (2.34b)$$

Note the similarity of the above relation with Eq. (2.22b), which gives the inductance of one conductor of a single-phase line for the special case of two solid, round conductors. In Eq. (2.22b), r_1' is the self GMD of a single conductor and D is the mutual GMD of two single conductors.

The inductance of the composite conductor B is determined in a similar manner, and the total inductance of the line is

$$L = L_A + L_B$$

Example 2.1 A conductor is composed of seven identical copper strands, each having a radius r, as shown in Fig. 2.7. Find the self GMD of the conductor.

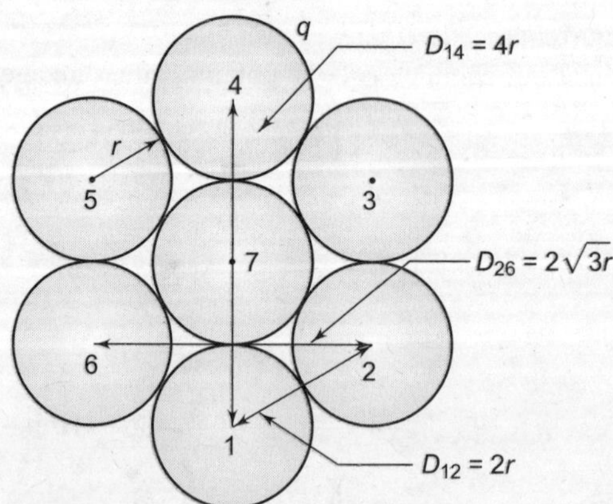

Fig. 2.7 *Cross-section of a seven-strand conductor*

Solution The self GMD of the seven strand conductor is the 49th root of the 49 distances. Thus,

$$D_s = ((r')^7 (D^2_{12} D^2_{26} D_{14} D_{17})^6 (2r)^6)^{1/49}$$

Substituting the values of various distances,

$$D_s = ((0.7788r)^7 (2^2r^2 \times 3 \times 2^2r^2 \times 2^2r \times 2r \times 2r)^6)^{1/49}$$

or

$$D_s = \frac{2r(3(0.7788))^{1/7}}{6^{1/49}} = 2.177r.$$

Example 2.2 The outside diameter of the single layer of aluminium strands of an ACSR conductor shown in Fig. 2.8 is 5.04 cm. The diameter of each strand is 1.68 cm. Determine the 50 Hz reactance at 1 m spacing; neglect the effect of the central strand of steel and advance reasons for the same.

Solution The conductivity of steel being much poorer than that of aluminium and the internal inductance of steel strands being μ-times that of aluminium strands, the current conducted by the central strands of steel can be assumed to be zero.

Diameter of steel strand = 5.04 – 2 × 1.68 = 1.68 cm

Thus, all strands are of the same diameter, say d. For the arrangement of strands as given in Fig. 2.8(a),

$$D_{12} = D_{16} = d$$

$$D_{13} = D_{15} = \sqrt{3}d$$

$$D_{14} = 2d$$

$$D_s = \left(\left[\left(\frac{d'}{2}\right) d^2 (\sqrt{3}\,d)^2 (\sqrt{2}\,d)\right]^6\right)^{1/36}$$

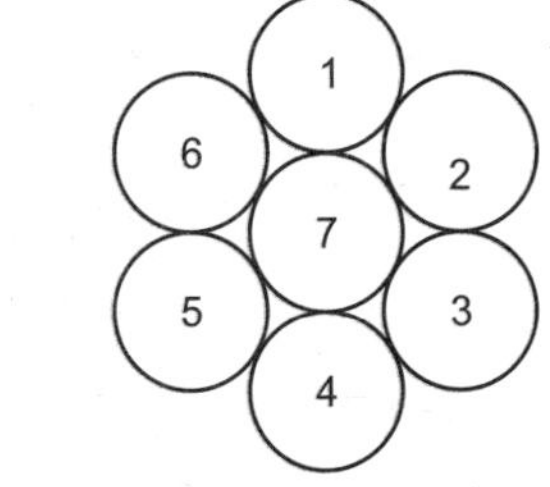

(a) Cross-section of ACSR conductor

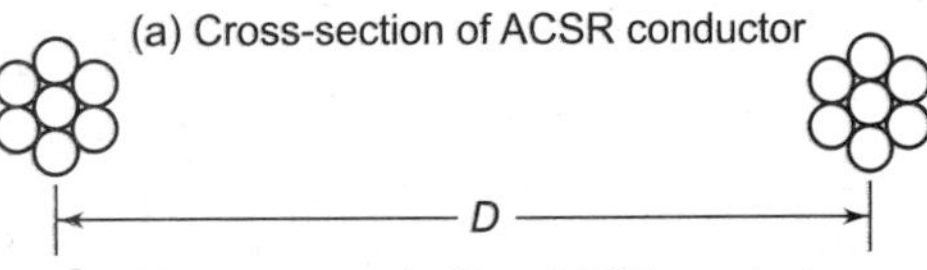

(b) Line composed of two ACSR conductors

Fig. 2.8

Substituting $d' = 0.7788d$ and simplifying

$$D_s = 1.155d = 1.155 \times 1.68 = 1.93 \text{ cm}$$

$$D_m \simeq D \quad \text{since} \quad D \gg d$$

Now, the inductance of each conductor is

$$L = 0.461 \log \frac{100}{1.93} = 0.789 \text{ mH/km}$$

$$\text{Loop inductance} = 2 \times 0.789 = 1.578 \text{ mH/km}$$

$$\text{Loop reactance} = 1.578 \times 314 \times 10^{-3} = 0.495 \text{ ohms/km.}$$

Example 2.3 The arrangement of conductors of a single-phase transmission line is shown in Fig. 2.9, wherein the forward circuit is composed of three solid wires 2.5 mm in radius and the return circuit of two wires of radius 5 mm placed symmetrically with respect to the forward circuit. Find the inductance of each side of the line and that of the complete line.

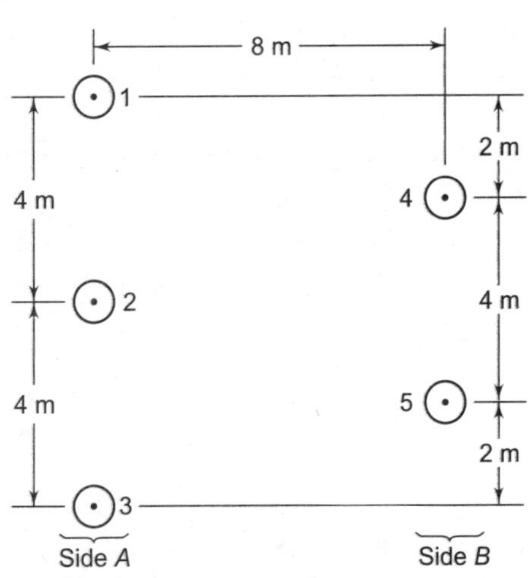

Fig. 2.9 *Arrangement of conductors for Example 2.3*

Solution The mutual GMD between sides A and B is

$$D_m = ((D_{14}D_{15})(D_{24}D_{25})(D_{34}D_{35}))^{1/6}$$

From the figure it is obvious that

$$D_{14} = D_{24} = D_{25} = D_{35} = \sqrt{68}\ \text{m}$$
$$D_{15} = D_{34} = 10\ \text{m}$$
$$D_m = (68^2 \times 100)^{1/6} = 8.8\ \text{m}$$

The self GMD for side A is

$$D_{sA} = ((D_{11}D_{12}D_{13})(D_{21}D_{22}D_{23})(D_{31}D_{32}D_{33}))^{1/9}$$

Here,

$$D_{11} = D_{22} = D_{33} = 2.5 \times 10^{-3} \times 0.7788\ \text{m}$$

Substituting the values of various interdistances and self distances in D_{sA}, we get

$$D_{sA} = ((2.5 \times 10^{-3} \times 0.7788)^3 \times 4^4 \times 8^2)^{1/9}$$
$$= 0.367\ \text{m}$$

Similarly,

$$D_{sB} = ((5 \times 10^{-3} \times 0.7788)^2 \times 4^2)^{1/4}$$
$$= 0.125\ \text{m}$$

Substituting the values of D_m, D_{sA} and D_{sB} in Eq. (2.25b), we get the various inductances as

$$L_A = 0.461 \log \frac{8.8}{0.367} = 0.635\ \text{mH/km}$$

$$L_B = 0.461 \log \frac{8.8}{0.125} = 0.85\ \text{mH/km}$$

$$L = L_A + L_B = 1.485\ \text{mH/km}$$

If the conductors in this problem are each composed of seven identical strands as in Example 2.1, the problem can be solved by writing the conductor self distances as

$$D_{ii} = 2.177 r_i$$

where r_i is the strand radius.

2.8 ▶ INDUCTANCE OF THREE-PHASE LINES

2.8.1 Inductance with Equilateral Spacing

In previous sections, we have considered inductance evaluation of only single-phase lines. The equations we have derived are quite easily adapted in this section to calculate the inductance of three-phase lines. Figure 2.10(a) shows the conductors of a three-phase line spaced at the corners of an equilateral triangle.

If we assume that there is no neutral wire, or if we assume balanced three-phase phasor currents, $I_a + I_b + I_c = 0$. Equation (2.30) determines the flux linkages of conductor 'a' as follows:

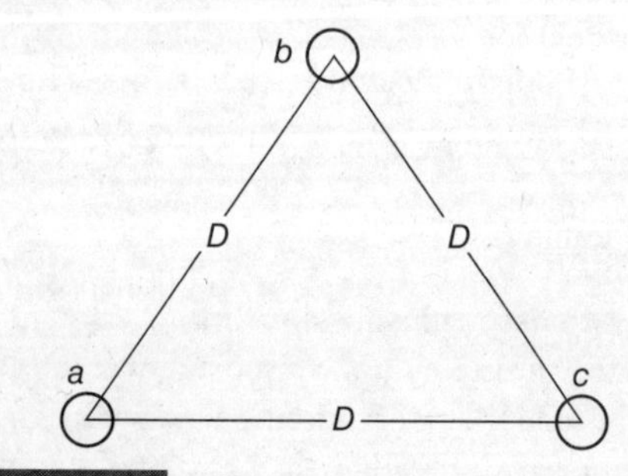

Fig. 2.10(a) *Cross-sectional view of the equilaterally spaced conductors of a three-phase line*

$$\psi_a = 2 \times 10^{-7} \left(I_a\, ln\frac{1}{D_s} + I_b\, ln\frac{1}{D} + I_c\, ln\frac{1}{D} \right) \quad \text{Wbt/m} \tag{2.35a}$$

Since $I_a = -(I_b + I_c)$, equation (2.35a) becomes

$$\psi_a = 2\times10^{-7}\left(I_a\, In\frac{1}{D_s} - I_a\, In\frac{1}{D}\right) = 2\times10^{-7} I_a\, In\frac{D}{D_s} \quad \text{Wbt/m} \tag{2.35b}$$

and

$$L_a = 2\times10^{-7}\, In\frac{D}{D_s} \quad \text{H/m} \tag{2.35c}$$

Equation (2.35c) is the same in form as we have derived the equations (2.22b) and (2.23) for a single-phase line except that D_s replaces r'. Because of symmetry, the inductances of conductors b and c are the same as the inductance of conductor a. Since each phase consists of only one conductor, equation (2.35c) gives the inductance per phase of the three-phase line.

2.8.2 Inductance with Unsymmetrical Spacing

So far we have considered only single-phase lines. The basic equations developed can, however, be easily adapted to the calculation of the inductance of three-phase lines. Figure 2.10(b) shows the conductors of a three-phase line with unsymmetrical spacing.

Assume that there is no neutral wire, so that

$$I_a + I_b + I_c = 0$$

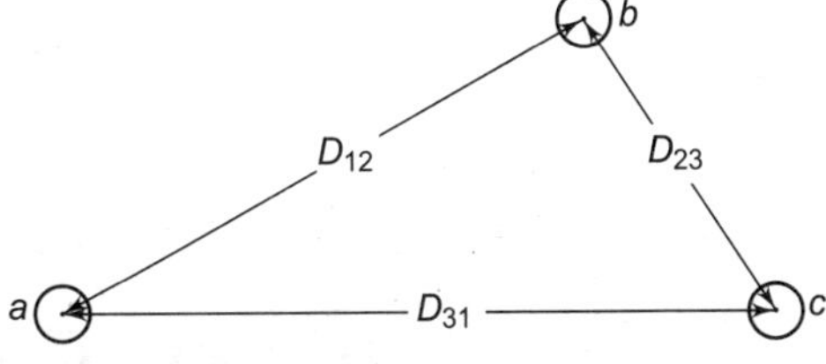

Fig. 2.10(b) *Cross-sectional view of a three-phase line with unsymmetrical spacing*

Unsymmetrical spacing causes the flux linkages and therefore the inductance of each phase to be different resulting in unbalanced receiving-end voltages even when sending-end voltages and line currents are balanced. Also, voltages will be induced in adjacent communication lines even when line currents are balanced. This problem is tackled by exchanging the positions of the conductors at regular intervals along the line such that each conductor occupies the original position of every other conductor over an equal distance. Such an exchange of conductor positions is called *transposition*. A complete transposition cycle is shown in Fig. 2.11. This arrangement causes each conductor to have the same average inductance over the transposition cycle. Over the length of one transposition cycle, the total flux linkages and net voltage induced in a nearby telephone line are therefore zero.

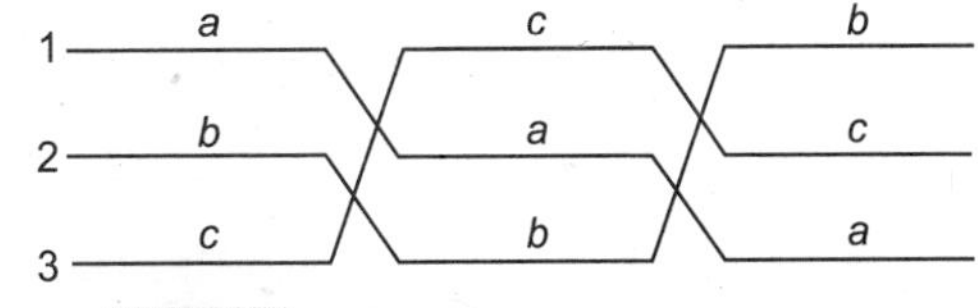

Fig. 2.11 *A complete transposition cycle*

To find the average inductance of each conductor of a transposed line, the flux linkages of the conductor are found for each position it occupies in the transposed cycle. Applying Eq. (2.30) to conductor a of Fig. 2.11, for Section 1 of the transposition cycle wherein a is in position 1, b is in position 2 and c is in position 3, we get

$$\lambda_{a1} = 2\times10^{-7}\left(I_a \ln\frac{1}{r_a'} + I_b \ln\frac{1}{D_{12}} + I_c \ln\frac{1}{D_{31}}\right) \text{ Wb-T/m}$$

For the second section,

$$\lambda_{a2} = 2\times10^{-7}\left(I_a \ln\frac{1}{r_a'} + I_b \ln\frac{1}{D_{23}} + I_c \ln\frac{1}{D_{12}}\right) \text{ Wb-T/m}$$

For the third section,

$$\lambda_{a3} = 2 \times 10^{-7} \left(I_a \ln \frac{1}{r_a'} + I_b \ln \frac{1}{D_{13}} + I_c \ln \frac{1}{D_{23}} \right) \text{ Wb-T/m}$$

Average flux linkages of conductor a are

$$\lambda_a = \frac{\lambda_{a1} + \lambda_{a2} + \lambda_{a3}}{3} = 2 \times 10^{-7} \left(I_a \ln \frac{1}{r_a'} + I_b \ln \frac{1}{(D_{12}D_{23}D_{31})^{1/3}} + I_c \ln \frac{1}{(D_{12}D_{23}D_{31})^{1/3}} \right)$$

But, $I_b + I_c = -I_a$; hence

$$\lambda_a = 2 \times 10^{-7} I_a \ln \frac{(D_{12}D_{23}D_{31})^{1/3}}{r_a'}.$$

Let,

$$D_{eq} = (D_{12}D_{23}D_{31})^{1/3} = \text{equivalent equilateral spacing}$$

Then,

$$L_a = 2 \times 10^{-7} \ln \frac{D_{eq}}{r_a'} = 2 \times 10^{-7} \ln \frac{D_{eq}}{r_a'} \text{ H/m} \tag{2.36}$$

This is the same relation as Eq. (2.34a) where $D_m = D_{eq}$, the mutual GMD between the three-phase conductors. If $r_a = r_b = r_c$, we have

$$L_a = L_b = L_c$$

It is not the present practice to transpose the power lines at regular intervals. However, an interchange in the position of the conductors is made at switching stations to balance the inductance of the phases. For all practical purposes, the dissymmetry can be neglected and the inductance of an untransposed line can be taken equal to that of a transposed line.

If the spacing is equilateral, then

$$D_{eq} = D$$

and

$$L_a = 2 \times 10^{-7} \ln \frac{D}{r_a'} \text{ H/m} \tag{2.37}$$

If $r_a = r_b = r_c$, it follows from Eq. (2.37) that

$$L_a = L_b = L_c$$

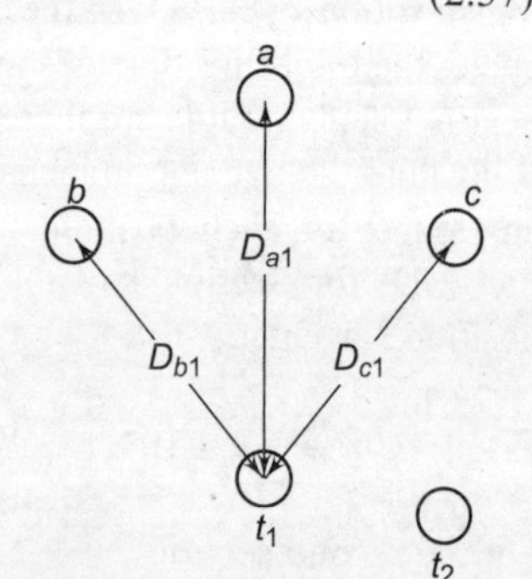

Fig. 2.12 *Effect of transposition on induced voltage of a telephone line*

Example 2.4 Show that over the length of one transposition cycle of a power line, the total flux linkages of a nearby telephone line are zero, for balanced three-phase currents.

Solution Referring to Fig. 2.12, the flux linkages of the conductor t_1 of the telephone line are

$$\lambda_{t1} = 2 \times 10^{-7} \left(I_a \ln \frac{1}{D_{a1}} + I_b \ln \frac{1}{D_{b1}} + I_c \ln \frac{1}{D_{c1}} \right) \text{ Wb-T/m} \tag{2.38}$$

Similarly,

$$\lambda_{t2} = 2 \times 10^{-7} \left(I_a \ln \frac{1}{D_{a2}} + I_b \ln \frac{1}{D_{b2}} + I_c \ln \frac{1}{D_{c2}} \right) \text{Wb-T/m} \tag{2.39}$$

The net flux linkages of the telephone line are

$$\lambda_t = \lambda_{t1} - \lambda_{t2} = 2 \times 10^{-7} \left(I_a \ln \frac{D_{a2}}{D_{a1}} + I_b \ln \frac{D_{b2}}{D_{b1}} + I_c \ln \frac{D_{c2}}{D_{c1}} \right) \text{Wb-T/m} \tag{2.40}$$

The emf induced in the telephone line loop is

$$E_t = 2\pi f \lambda_t \text{ V/m}$$

Under balanced load conditions, λ_t is not very large because there is a cancellation to a great extent of the flux linkages due to I_a, I_b and I_c. Such cancellation does not take place with harmonic currents which are multiples of three and are therefore in phase. Consequently, these frequencies, if present, may be very troublesome.

If the power line is fully transposed with respect to the telephone line

$$\lambda_{t1} = \frac{\lambda_{t1}(\text{I}) + \lambda_{t1}(\text{II}) + \lambda_{t1}(\text{III})}{3}$$

where $\lambda_{t1}(\text{I})$, $\lambda_{t1}(\text{II})$ and $\lambda_{t1}(\text{III})$ are the flux linkages of the telephone line t_1 in the three transposition sections of the power line.

Writing for $\lambda_{t1}(\text{I})$, $\lambda_{t2}(\text{II})$ and $\lambda_{t3}(\text{III})$ by repeated use of Eq. (2.38), we have

$$\lambda_{t1} = 2 \times 10^{-7} (I_a + I_b + I_c) \ln \frac{1}{(D_{a1} D_{b1} D_{c1})^{1/3}}$$

Similarly,

$$\lambda_{t2} = \frac{\lambda_{t2}(\text{I}) + \lambda_{t2}(\text{II}) + \lambda_{t2}(\text{III})}{3}$$

$$= 2 \times 10^{-7} (I_a + I_b + I_c) \ln \frac{1}{(D_{a2} D_{b2} D_{c2})^{1/3}}$$

$$\therefore \quad \lambda_t = 2 \times 10^{-7} (I_a + I_b + I_c) \ln \frac{(D_{a2} D_{b2} D_{c2})^{1/3}}{(D_{a1} D_{b2} D_{c3})^{1/3}} \tag{2.41}$$

If $I_a + I_b + I_c = 0$, $\lambda_t = 0$, i.e., voltage induced in the telephone loop is zero over one transposition cycle of the power line.

It may be noted here that the condition $I_a + I_b + I_c = 0$ is not satisfied for—

1. power frequency L-G (line-to-ground fault) currents, where

$$I_a + I_b + I_c = 3I_0$$

2. third and multiple of third harmonic currents under healthy condition, where,

$$I_a(3) + I_b(3) + I_c(3) = 3I(3)$$

$$\therefore \quad E_t(3) = 6\pi f \lambda_t(3)$$

The harmonic line currents are troublesome in two ways:

1. Induced emf is proportional to thc frequency.
2. Higher frequencies come within the audible range.

Thus, there is a need to avoid the presence of such harmonic currents on power line from considerations of the performance of nearby telephone lines.

It has been shown above that voltage induced in a telephone line running parallel to a power line is reduced to zero, if the power line is transposed and provided, it carries balanced currents. It was also shown that power line transposition is ineffective in reducing the induced telephone line voltage when power line currents are unbalanced or when they contain third harmonics. Power line transposition apart from being ineffective introduces mechanical and insulation problems. It is, therefore, easier to eliminate induced voltages by transposing the telephone line instead. In fact, the reader can easily verify that even when the power line currents are unbalanced or when they contain harmonics, the voltage induced over complete transposition cycle (called a *barrel*) of a telephone line is zero. Some induced voltage will always be present on a telephone line running parallel to a power line because in actual practice transposition is never completely symmetrical. Therefore, when the lines run parallel over a considerable length, it is a good practice to transpose both power and telephone lines. The two transposition cycles are staggered and the telephone line is transposed over shorter lengths compared to the power line.

Example 2.5 A three-phase, 50 Hz, 15 km long line has four No. 4/0 wires (1 cm dia) spaced horizontally 1.5 m apart in a plane. The wires in order are carrying currents I_a, I_b and I_c, and the fourth wire, which is a neutral, carries zero current. The currents are:

$$I_a = -30 + j50 \text{ A}$$
$$I_b = -25 + j55 \text{ A}$$
$$I_c = 55 - j105 \text{ A}$$

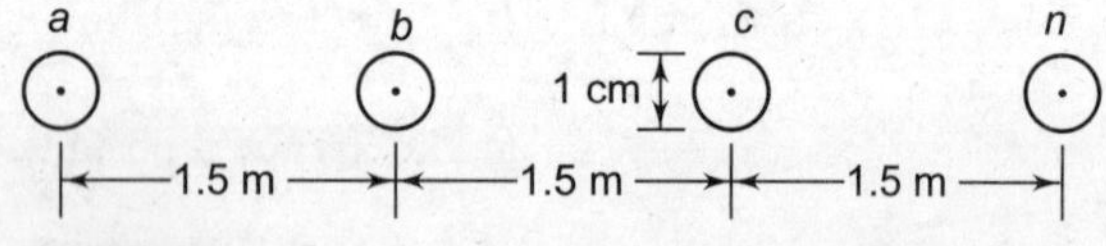

Fig. 2.13 *Arrangement of conductors for Example 2.5*

The line is untransposed.

(a) From the fundamental consideration, find the flux linkages of the neutral. Also, find the voltage induced in the neutral wire.

(b) Find the voltage drop in each of the three-phase wires.

Solution

(a) From Fig. 2.13,

$$D_{an} = 4.5 \text{ m}, D_{bn} = 3 \text{ m}, D_{cn} = 1.5 \text{ m}$$

Flux linkages of the neutral wire n are

$$\lambda_n = 2 \times 10^{-7} \left(I_a \ln \frac{1}{D_{an}} + I_b \ln \frac{1}{D_{bn}} + I_c \ln \frac{1}{D_{cn}} \right) \text{ Wb-T/m}$$

Substituting the values of D_{an}, D_{bn} and D_{cn}, and simplifying, we get

$$\lambda_n = -2 \times 10^{-7} (1.51 I_a + 1.1 I_b + 0.405 I_c) \text{ Wb-T/m}$$

Since $I_c = -(I_a + I_b)$ (this is easily checked from the given values),

$$\lambda_n = -2 \times 10^{-7}(1.105 I_a + 0.695 I_b) \text{ Wb-T/m}$$

The voltage induced in the neutral wire is then

$$V_n = j\omega\lambda_n \times 15 \times 10^3 \text{ V}$$
$$= -j314 \times 15 \times 10^3 \times 2 \times 10^{-7}(1.105 I_a + 0.695 I_b) \text{ V}$$

or,
$$V_n = -j0.942\,(1.105\, I_a + 0.695\, I_b) \text{ V}$$

Substituting the values of I_a and I_b, and simplifying,

$$V_n = 0.942 \times 106 = 100 \text{ V.}$$

(b) From Eq. (2.30), the flux linkages of the conductor a are

$$\lambda_a = 2 \times 10^{-7} \left(I_a \ln \frac{1}{r_a'} + I_b \ln \frac{1}{D} + I_c \ln \frac{1}{2D} \right) \text{ Wb-T/m}$$

The voltage drop/metre in phase a can be written as

$$\Delta V_a = 2 \times 10^{-7} j\omega \left(I_a \ln \frac{1}{r_a'} + I_b \ln \frac{1}{D} + I_c \ln \frac{1}{2D} \right) \text{ V/m}$$

Since $I_c = -(I_a + I_b)$, and further since $r_a = r_b = r_c = r$, the expression for ΔV_a can be written in simplified form

$$\Delta V_a = 2 \times 10^{-7} j\omega \left(I_a \ln \frac{2D}{r'} + I_b \ln 2 \right) \quad \text{V/m}$$

Similarly, voltage drop/metre of phases b and c can be written as

$$\Delta V_b = 2 \times 10^{-7} j\omega I_b \ln \frac{D}{r'}$$

$$\Delta V_c = 2 \times 10^{-7} j\omega \left(I_b \ln 2 + I_c \ln \frac{2D}{r'} \right)$$

Using matrix notation, we can present the result in compact form

$$\begin{bmatrix} \Delta V_a \\ \Delta V_b \\ \Delta V_c \end{bmatrix} = 2 \times 10^{-7} j\omega \begin{bmatrix} \ln 2D/r' & \ln 2 & 0 \\ 0 & \ln D/r' & 0 \\ 0 & \ln 2 & \ln 2D/r' \end{bmatrix} \begin{bmatrix} I_a \\ I_b \\ I_c \end{bmatrix}$$

The voltage drop of phase a is calculated below

$$\Delta V_a = j2 \times 10^{-7} \times 314 \times 15 \times 10^3 \left(\ln \frac{300}{0.39} (-30 + j50) + 0.693(-25 + j55) \right)$$

$$= -(348.6 + j204) \text{ V}$$

Example 2.6 A single-phase 50 Hz power line is supported on a horizontal cross-arm. The spacing between the conductors is 3 m. A telephone line is supported symmetrically below the power line as shown in Fig. 2.14. Find the mutual inductance between the two circuits and the voltage induced per kilometre in the telephone line if the current in the power line is 100 A. Assume the telephone line current to be zero (see Section 2.13).

Solution Flux linkages of conductor T_1

$$\lambda_{t1} = 2 \times 10^{-7} \left(I \ln \frac{1}{D_1} - I \ln \frac{1}{D_2} \right) = 2 \times 10^{-7} I \ln \frac{D_2}{D_1}$$

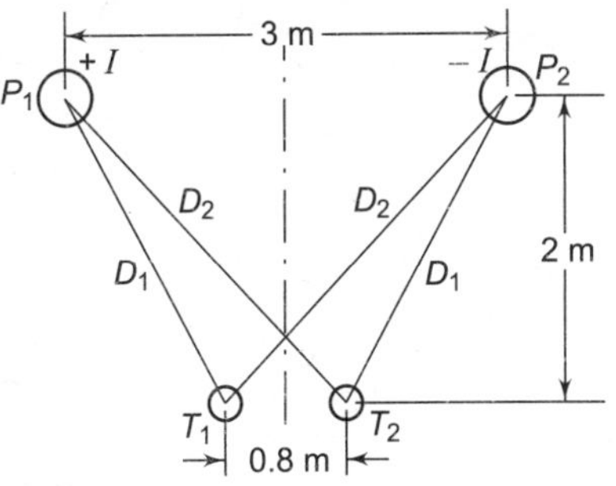

Fig. 2.14 *Power and telephone lines for Example 2.6*

Flux linkages of conductor T_2

$$\lambda_{t2} = 2 \times 10^{-7} I \ln \frac{D_1}{D_2}$$

Total flux linkage of the telephone circuit

$$\lambda_t = \lambda_{t1} - \lambda_{t2} = 4 \times 10^{-7} I \ln \frac{D_2}{D_1}$$

$$M_{pt} = 4 \times 10^{-7} \ln \frac{D_2}{D_1} \quad \text{H/m}$$

$$= 0.921 \log \frac{D_2}{D_1} \quad \text{mH/km}$$

$$D_1 = (1.1^2 + 2^2)^{1/2} = (5.21)^{1/2}$$

$$D_2 = (1.9^2 + 2^2)^{1/2} = (7.61)^{1/2}$$

$$M_{pt} = 0.921 \log \left(\frac{761}{521}\right)^{1/2} = 0.0758 \quad \text{mH/km}$$

Voltage induced in the telephone circuit $V_t = j\,\omega M_{pt} I$

$$|V_t| = 314 \times 0.0758 \times 10^{-3} \times 100 = 2.379 \quad \text{V/km.}$$

2.9 ▶ DOUBLE-CIRCUIT THREE-PHASE LINES

It is common practice to build double-circuit three-phase lines so as to increase transmission reliability at somewhat enhanced cost. From the point of view of power transfer from one end of the line to the other (see Section 12.3), it is desirable to build the two lines with as low an inductance/phase as possible. In order to achieve this, self GMD (D_s) should be made high and mutual GMD (D_m) should be made low. Therefore, the individual conductors of a phase should be kept as far apart as possible (for high self GMD), while the distance between phases be kept as low as permissible (for low mutual GMD).

Figure 2.15 shows the three sections of the transposition cycle of two parallel circuit three-phase lines with vertical spacing (it is a very commonly used configuration).

It may be noted here that conductors a and a' in parallel compose phase a and similarly b and b' compose phase b and c and c' compose phase c. In order to achieve high D_s, the conductors of two phases are placed diametrically opposite to each other and those of the third phase are horizontally opposite to each other. (The reader can try other configurations to verify that these will lead to low D_s). Applying the method of GMD, the equivalent equilateral spacing is

$$D_{eq} = (D_{ab} D_{bc} D_{ca})^{1/3} \tag{2.42}$$

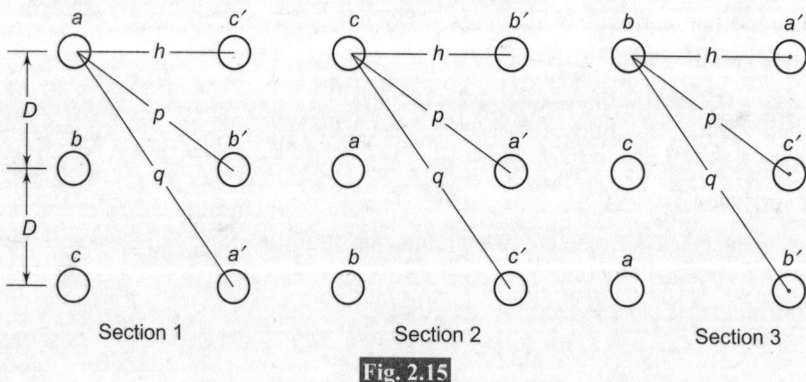

Fig. 2.15

where, D_{ab} = mutual GMD between phases a and b in Section 1 of the transposition cycle
$= (DpDp)^{1/4} = (Dp)^{1/2}$

D_{bc} = mutual GMD between phases b and c in Section 1 of the transposition cycle
$= (Dp)^{1/2}$

D_{ca} = mutual GMD between phases c and a in Section 1 of the transposition cycle
$= (2Dh)^{1/2}$

Hence, $$D_{eq} = 2^{1/6}D^{1/2}p^{1/3}h^{1/6} \tag{2.43}$$

It may be noted here that D_{eq} remains the same in each section of the transposition cycle, as the conductors of each parallel circuit rotate cyclically, so do D_{ab}, D_{bc} and D_{ca}. The reader is advised to verify this for Sections 2 and 3 of the transposition cycle in Fig. 2.15.

Self GMD in Section 1 of phase a (i.e., conductors a and a') is

$$D_{sa} = (r'qr'q)^{1/4} = (r'q)^{1/2}$$

Self GMD of phases b and c in Section 1 are respectively

$$D_{sb} = (r'hr'h)^{1/4} = (r'h)^{1/2}$$
$$D_{sc} = (r'qr'q)^{1/4} = (r'q)^{1/2}$$

$\therefore$ Equivalent self GMD, $D_s = (D_{sa}D_{sb}D_{sc})^{1/3}$

$$= (r')^{1/2}q^{1/3}h^{1/6} \tag{2.44}$$

Because of the cyclic rotation of conductors of each parallel circuit over the transposition cycle, D_s also remains the same in each transposition section. The reader should verify this for Sections 2 and 3 in Fig. 2.15.

The inductance per phase is

$$L = 2 \times 10^{-7} \ln \frac{D_{eq}}{D_s}$$

$$= 2 \times 10^{-7} \ln \frac{2^{1/6}D^{1/2}p^{1/3}h^{1/6}}{(r')^{1/2}q^{1/3}h^{1/6}}$$

$$= 2 \times 10^{-7} \ln \left(2^{1/6} \left(\frac{D}{r'}\right)^{1/2} \left(\frac{p}{q}\right)^{1/3} \right) \text{ H/phase/m} \tag{2.45}$$

The self inductance of each circuit is given by

$$L_s = 2 \times 10^{-7} \ln \frac{(2)^{1/3} D}{r'}$$

Equation (2.45) can now be written as

$$L = \frac{1}{2}\left[2\times10^{-7} \ln \frac{(2)^{1/3} D}{r'} + 2\times10^{-7} \ln \left(\frac{p}{q}\right)^{2/3} \right] \tag{2.46}$$

$$= \frac{1}{2}(L_s + M)$$

where M is the mutual inductance between the two circuits, i.e.,

$$M = 2 \times 10^{-7} \ln \left(\frac{p}{q}\right)^{2/3}$$

This is a well-known result for the two coupled circuits connected in parallel (at similar polarity ends).

If $h \gg D, \left(\dfrac{p}{q}\right) \to 1$ and $M \to 0$, i.e., the mutual impedance between the circuits becomes zero. Under this condition,

$$L = 1 \times 10^{-7} \ln \frac{3\sqrt{2}\, D}{r'} \tag{2.47}$$

The GMD method, though applied above to a particular configuration of a double circuit, is valid for any configuration as long as the circuits are electrically parallel.

While the GMD method is valid for fully transposed lines, it is commonly applied for untransposed lines and is quite accurate for practical purposes.

2.10 ▶ BUNDLED CONDUCTORS

It is economical to transmit large chunks of power over long distances by employing EHV lines. However, the line voltages that can be used are severely limited by the phenomenon of *corona*. Corona, in fact, is the result of ionisation of the atmosphere when a certain field intensity (about 3,000 kV/m at NTP) is reached. Corona discharge causes communication interference and associated power loss which can be severe in bad weather conditions. Critical line voltage for formation of corona can be raised considerably by the use of bundled conductors—a group of two or more conductors per phase. This increase in critical corona voltage is dependent on the number of conductors in the group, the clearance between them and the distance between the groups forming the separate phases*. Reichman [11] has shown that the spacing of conductors in a bundle affects voltage gradient and the optimum spacing is of the order of 8–10 times the conductors diameter, irrespective of the number of conductors in the bundle.

Further, because of increased self GMD** line, inductance is reduced considerably with the incidental advantage of increased transmission capacity of the line.

Since the voltage gradient is reduced by using bundled conductors, the radio interference is also reduced. Finally, we know that surge impedance of a line is given by $\sqrt{L/C}$, where L is the inductance and C the capacitance per unit length of the line. Since by bundling, the self GMD is increased, the inductance is reduced and capacitance increased, as a result the surge impedance is reduced. This in turn means that the maximum power that can be transmitted is increased. Therefore, for large power transmission at higher voltages, bundled conductors should be used. The overall advantages of bundled conductors are summarised as these reduce reactance, voltage gradient, corona loss, radio interference, and surge impedance. The calculation of GMR is exactly the same as that of a stranded conductor. Each conductor of a two-conductor bundle, for instance, is treated as one strand of a two-strand conductor. If we let D_s^b indicate the GMR of a bundled conductor and D_s the GMR of the individual conductors composing the bundle, we find the following relations referring to configuration of bundled conductors of Fig. 2.16.

(a) For a two-strand bundle

$$D_s^b = \sqrt[4]{(D_s \times d)^2} = \sqrt{D_s \times d} \tag{2.48a}$$

* The bundle usually comprises two, three or four conductors arranged in configurations illustrated in Fig. 2.16. The current will not divide equally among them.

** The more the number of conductors in a bundle, the more is the self GMD.

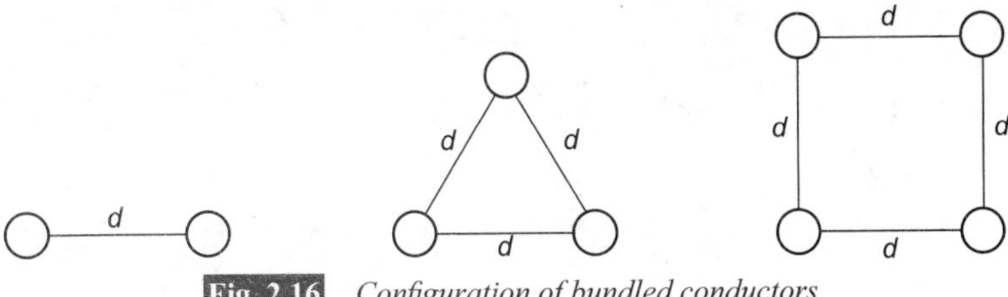

Fig. 2.16 *Configuration of bundled conductors*

(b) For a three-strand bundle

$$D_s^b = \sqrt[9]{(D_s \times d \times d)^3} = \sqrt[3]{D_s \times d^2} \tag{2.48b}$$

(c) For a four-strand bundle

$$D_s^b = \sqrt[16]{\left(D_s \times d \times d \times d \times 2^{1/2}\right)^4} = 1.09\sqrt[4]{D_s \times d^3} \tag{2.48c}$$

Example 2.7 Find the inductive reactance in ohms per kilometer at 50 Hz of a three-phase bundled conductor line with two conductors per phase as shown in Fig. 2.17. All the conductors are ACSR with radii of 1.725 cm.

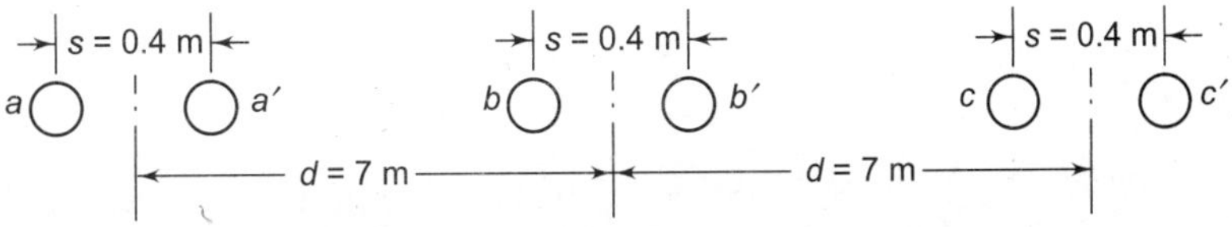

s = 0.4 m   s = 0.4 m   s = 0.4 m
a a′   b b′   c c′
d = 7 m   d = 7 m

Fig. 2.17 *Bundled conductor three-phase line*

Solution Even though the power lines are not normally transposed (except when they enter and leave a switching station), it is sufficiently accurate to assume complete transposition (of the bundles as well as of the conductors within the bundle) so that the method of GMD can be applied.

The mutual GMD between bundles of phases a and b

$$D_{ab} = (d\,(d+s)\,(d-s)\,d)^{1/4}$$

Mutual GMD between bundles of phases b and c

$$D_{bc} = D_{ab} \text{ (by symmetry)}$$

Mutual GMD between bundles of phases c and a

$$D_{ca} = (2d\,(2d+s)\,(2d-s)2d)^{1/4}$$

$$\begin{aligned} D_{eq} &= (D_{ab}D_{bc}D_{ca})^{1/3} \\ &= (4d^6(d+s)^2(d-s)^2(2d+s)(2d-s))^{1/12} \\ &= (4(7)^6(7.4)^2(6.6)^2(14.4)(13.6))^{1/12} \\ &= 8.81 \text{ m} \end{aligned}$$

$$\begin{aligned} D_s &= (r'sr's)^{1/4} = (r's)^{1/2} = (0.7788 \times 1.725 \times 10^{-2} \times 0.4)^{1/2} \\ &= 0.073 \text{ m} \end{aligned}$$

Inductive reactance per phase

$$X_L = 314 \times 0.461 \times 10^{-3} \log \frac{8.81}{0.073}$$
$$= 0.301 \text{ ohm/km}$$

In most cases, it is sufficiently accurate to use the centre to centre distances between bundles rather than mutual GMD between bundles for computing D_{eq}. With this approximation, we have for the example in hand

$$D_{eq} = (7 \times 7 \times 14)^{1/3} = 8.82 \text{ m}$$

$$X_L = 314 \times 0.461 \times 10^{-3} \log \frac{8.82}{0.073}$$
$$= 0.301 \text{ ohm/km}$$

Thus, the approximate method yields almost the same reactance value as the exact method. It is instructive to compare the inductive reactance of a bundled conductor line with an equivalent (on heuristic basis) single conductor line. For the example in hand, the equivalent line will have $d = 7$ m and conductor diameter (for same total cross-sectional area) as $\sqrt{2} \times 1.725$ cm.

$$X_L = 314 \times 0.461 \times 10^{-3} \log \frac{(7 \times 7 \times 14)^{1/3}}{0.7788 \times \sqrt{2} \times 1.725 \times 10^{-3}}$$
$$= 0.531 \text{ ohm/km}$$

This is 76.41% higher than the corresponding value for a bundled conductor line. As already pointed out, lower reactance of a bundled conductor line increases its transmission capacity.

2.11 ▶ RESISTANCE

Though the contribution of line resistance to series line impedance can be neglected in most cases, it is the main source of line power loss. Thus while considering transmission line economy, the presence of line resistance must be considered.

The effective AC resistance is given by

$$R = \frac{\text{average power loss in conductor in watts}}{I^2} \text{ ohms} \tag{2.49a}$$

where I is the rms current in the conductor in amperes. Ohmic or DC resistance is given by the formula

$$R_O = \frac{\rho l}{A} \text{ ohms} \tag{2.49b}$$

where,
ρ = resistivity of the conductor, ohm-m
l = length, m
A = cross-sectional area, m^2

The effective resistance given by Eq. (2.49a) is equal to the DC resistance of the conductor given by Eq. (2.49b) only if the current distribution is uniform throughout the conductor.

For small changes in temperature, the resistance increases with temperature in accordance with the relationship

$$R_t = R(1 + \alpha_0 t) \tag{2.50}$$

where,
R = resistance at temperature 0°C
α_0 = temperature coefficient of the conductor at 0°C

Equation (2.50) can be used to find the resistance R_{t2} at a temperature t_2, if resistance R_{t1} at temperature t_1 is known

$$\frac{R_{t2}}{R_{t1}} = \frac{1/\alpha_0 + t_2}{1/\alpha_0 + t_1} \tag{2.51}$$

2.12 ▶ SKIN EFFECT AND PROXIMITY EFFECT

The distribution of current throughout the cross-section of a conductor is uniform only when DC is passing through it. On the contrary when AC is flowing through a conductor, the current is non-uniformly distributed over the cross-section in a manner that the current density is higher at the surface of the conductor compared to the current density at its centre. This effect becomes more pronounced as frequency is increased. This phenomenon is called *skin effect*. It causes larger power loss for a given rms AC than the loss when the same value of DC is flowing through the conductor. Consequently, the effective conductor resistance is more for AC than for DC. A qualitative explanation of the phenomenon is given below.

Imagine a solid round conductor (a round shape is considered for convenience only) to be composed of annular filaments of equal cross-sectional area. The flux linking the filaments progressively decreases as we move towards the outer filaments for the simple reason that the flux inside a filament does not link it. The inductive reactance of the imaginary filaments therefore decreases outwards with the result that the outer filaments conduct more AC than the inner filaments (filaments being parallel). With the increase of frequency the non-uniformity of inductive reactance of the filaments becomes more pronounced, so also the non-uniformity of current distribution. For large solid conductors, the skin effect is quite significant even at 50 Hz. The analytical study of skin effect requires the use of Bessel's functions and is beyond the scope of this book.

Apart from the skin effect, non-uniformity of current distribution is also caused by *proximity effect*. Consider a two-wire line as shown in Fig. 2.18. Each line conductor can be divided into sections of equal cross-sectional area (say three sections). Pairs *aa′*, *bb′* and *cc′* can form three loops in parallel. The flux linking loop *aa′* (and therefore its inductance) is the least and it increases somewhat for loops *bb′* and *cc′*. Thus, the density of AC flowing through the conductors is highest at the inner edges (*aa′*) of the conductors and is the least at the outer edges (*cc′*). This type of non-uniform AC current distribution becomes more pronounced as the distance between conductors is reduced. Like skin effect, the non-uniformity of current distribution caused by proximity effect also increases the effective conductor resistance. For normal spacing of overhead lines, this effect is always of negligible order. However, for underground cables where conductors are located close to each other, proximity effect causes an appreciable increase in effective conductor resistance.

Fig. 2.18

Both skin and proximity effects depend upon conductor size, frequency, distance between conductors and permeability of conductor material.

2.13 ▶ MAGNETIC FIELD INDUCTION

Transmission lines are used to transmit the bulk amount of power at higher voltages. These lines establish electromagnetic and electrostatic fields of sufficient magnitude in the neighbouring vicinity. These fields induce currents and voltages in the objects that lie in the vicinity of these fields and have a considerable length parallel to the line, i.e., telephone lines, pipe lines etc. (see Example 2.6).

It is a common practice to run the communication lines in parallel or along the same route as the power lines. The induced currents, voltages in the communication lines cause interference with communication service, e.g., damage to apparatus, hazard to person, etc. In the past, researchers have shown that these fields adversely affect the blood composition, growth, immune system and neural functions.

The presence of harmonics and multiple of third harmonics is dangerous for the communication circuits.

2.14 ▶ SUMMARY

This chapter has dealt with two important series parameters of transmission lines namely resistance and inductance. Use of bundled conductors, magnetic field induction have also been discussed.

Additional Solved Example

Example 2.8 The arrangement of single-phase transmission line conductors is shown in following Fig. 2.19. One circuit is composed of three solid 0.25 cm radius wires and return circuit is composed of two 0.5 cm radius wires. Find the inductance due to the current in each side of the line and the inductance of the complete line in henrys per meter and in millihenrys per mile.

Solution The mutual GMD between conductors of sides X and Y

$$D_m = \sqrt[6]{D_{ad}\, D_{ae}\, D_{bd}\, D_{be}\, D_{cd}\, D_{ce}}$$

$$D_{ad} = D_{be} = 10m$$

$$D_{ae} = D_{bd} = D_{ce} = \sqrt{5^2 + 10^2} = \sqrt{25+100} = \sqrt{125} = 11.1803$$

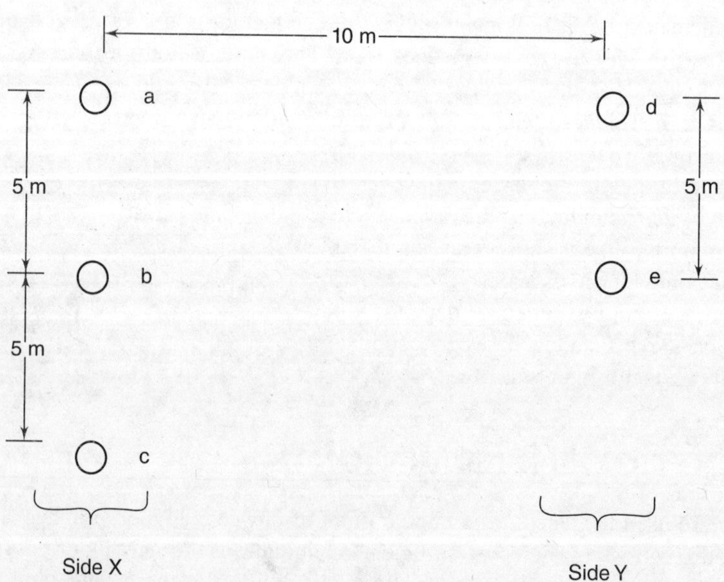

Fig. 2.19 *Arrangement of single-phase transmission line conductors*

$$D_{cd} = \sqrt{10^2 + 10^2} = \sqrt{200} = 14.1422$$

$$D_m = \sqrt[6]{10^2 \times 14.1422 \times (11.1803)^3} = 11.2024 \text{ m}$$

The GMR of conductors for side X

$$D_s = \sqrt[9]{D_{aa}\, D_{ab}\, D_{ac}\, D_{ba}\, D_{bb}\, D_{bc}\, D_{ca}\, D_{cb}\, D_{cc}}$$

$$= \sqrt[9]{\left(0.25 \times 0.7788 \times 10^{-2}\right)^3 \times 5^4 \times 10^2} = 0.4259\, m$$

The GMR of conductors for side Y

$$D_s = \sqrt[4]{D_{dd}\, D_{de}\, D_{ee}\, D_{ed}}$$

$$D_s = \sqrt[4]{(0.5 \times 0.7788 \times 10^{-2})^2 \times 5^2} = 0.1395\, m$$

The inductance due to the current in X side of the line

$$L_x = 2 \times 10^{-7}\, In \frac{11.2024}{0.4259} = 6.5393 \times 10^{-7}\, H/m$$

The inductance due to the current in Y side of the line

$$L_y = 2 \times 10^{-7}\, In \frac{11.2024}{0.1395} = 8.77163 \times 10^{-7}\, H/m$$

The inductance of the complete line in henrys per meter

$$L = L_x + L_y = 15.31093 \times 10^{-7}\, H/m$$

The inductance of the complete line in millihenrys per mile

$$L = 15.31093 \times 10^{-7} \times 1609 \times 10^3 = 2.46353\, mH/mi$$

Problems

2.1 Derive the formula for the internal inductance in H/m of a hollow conductor having inside radius r_1 and outside radius r_2 and also determine the expression for the inductance in H/m of a single-phase line consisting of the hollow conductors described above with conductors spaced a distance D apart.

2.2 Calculate the 50 Hz inductive reactance at 1 m spacing in ohms/km of a cable consisting of 12 equal strands around a nonconducting core. The diameter of each strand is 0.25 cm and the outside diameter of the cable is 1.25 cm.

2.3 A concentric cable consists of two thin-walled tubes of mean radii r and R respectively, derive an expression for the inductance of the cable per unit length.

2.4 A single-phase 50 Hz circuit comprises two single-core lead-sheathed cables laid side by side; if the centres of the cables are 0.5 m apart and each sheath has a mean diameter of 7.5 cm, estimate the longitudinal voltage induced per km of sheath when the circuit carries a current of 800 A.

2.5 Two long parallel conductors carry currents of $+I$ and $-I$. What is the magnetic field intensity at a point P, shown in Fig. P-2.5?

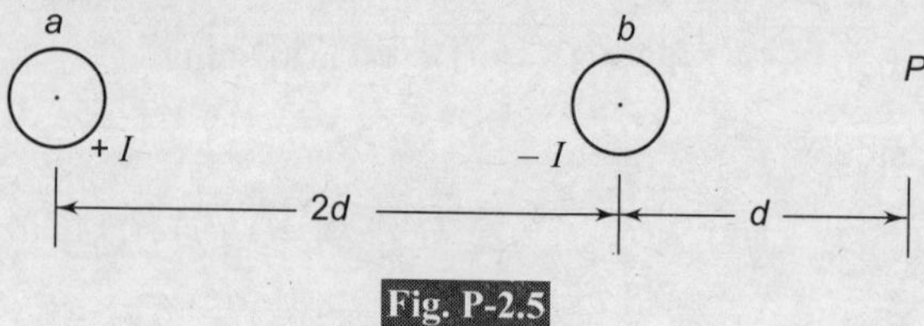

Fig. P-2.5

2.6 Two three-phase lines connected in parallel have self-reactances of X_1 and X_2. If the mutual reactance between them is X_{12}, what is the effective reactance between the two ends of the line?

2.7 A single-phase 50 Hz power line is supported on a horizontal cross-arm. The spacing between conductors is 2.5 m. A telephone line is also supported on a horizontal cross-arm in the same horizontal plane as the power line. The conductors of the telephone line are of solid copper spaced 0.6 m between centres. The distance between the nearest conductors of the two lines is 20 m. Find the mutual inductance between the circuits and the voltage per kilometre induced in the telephone line for 150 A current flowing over the power line.

2.8 A telephone line runs parallel to an untransposed three-phase transmission line, as shown in Fig. P-2.8. The power line carries balanced current of 400 A per phase. Find the mutual inductance between the circuits and calculate the 50 Hz voltage induced in the telephone line per km.

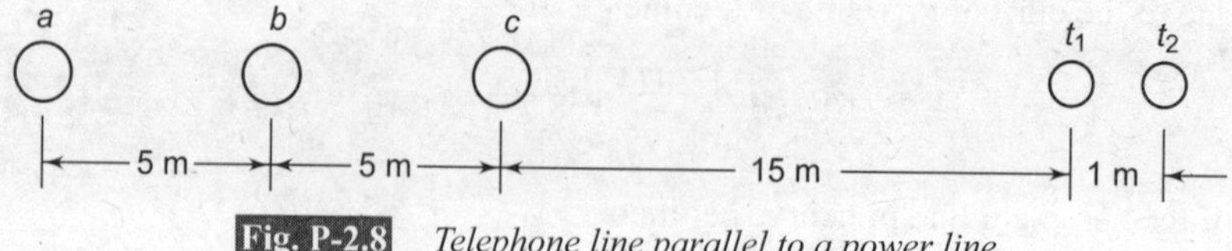

Fig. P-2.8 *Telephone line parallel to a power line*

2.9 A 500 kV line has a bundling arrangement of two conductors per phase as shown in Fig. P-2.9.

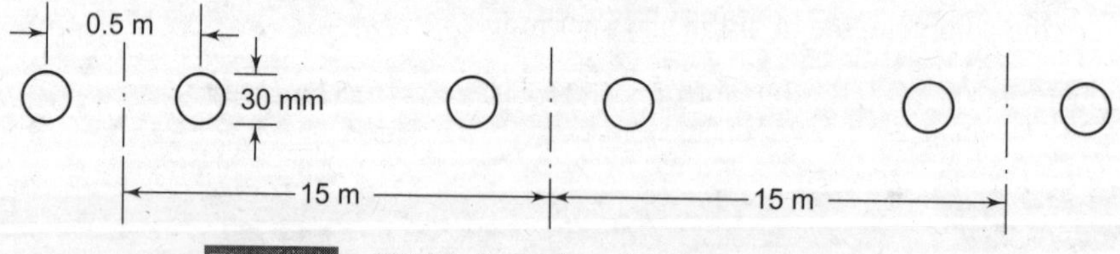

Fig. P-2.9 *500 kV, three-phase bundled conductor line*

Compute the reactance per phase of this line at 50 Hz. Each conductor carries 50% of the phase current. Assume full transposition.

2.10 An overhead line 50 kms in length is to be constructed of conductors 2.56 cm in diameter, for single-phase transmission. The line reactance must not exceed 31.4 ohms. Find the maximum permissible spacing.

2.11 In Fig. P-2.11 which depicts two three-phase circuits on a steel tower, there is symmetry in both the horizontal and vertical centre lines. Let each three-phase circuit be transposed by replacing a by b and then by c, so that the reactances of the three phases are equal and the GMD method of reactance calculations can be used. Each circuit remains on its own

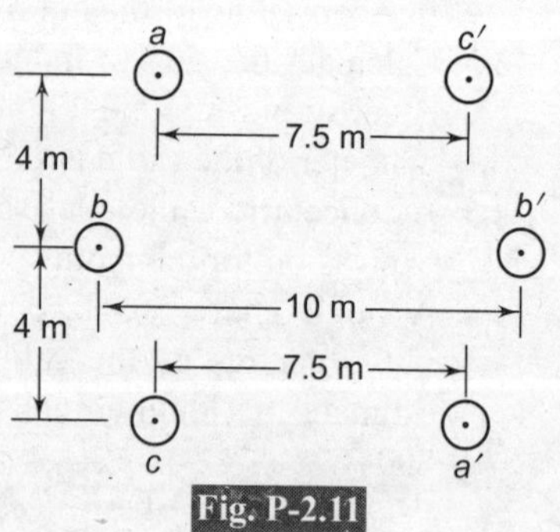

Fig. P-2.11

side of the tower. Let the self GMD of a single conductor be 1 cm. Conductors a and a' and other corresponding phase conductors are connected in parallel. Find the reactance per phase of the system.

2.12 A double-circuit three-phase line is shown in Fig. P-2.12. The conductors $a, a'; b, b'$ and c, c' belong to the same phase respectively. The radius of each conductor is 1.5 cm. Find the inductance of the double-circuit line in mH/km/phase.

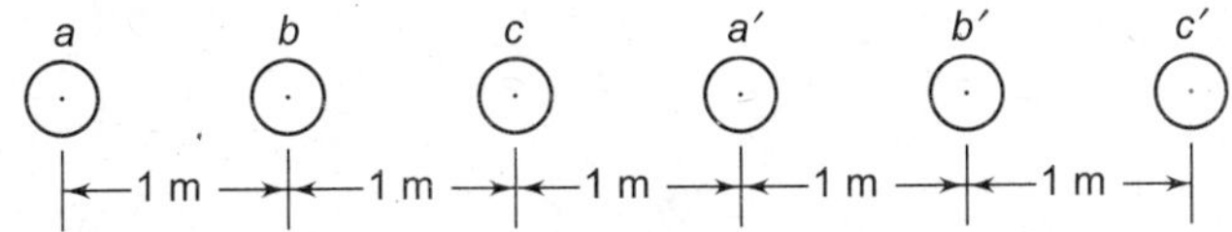

Fig. P-2.12 *Arrangement of conductors for a double-circuit three-phase line*

2.13 A three-phase line with equilateral spacing of 3 m is to be rebuilt with horizontal spacing ($D_{13} = D_{12} = D_{22}$). The conductors are to be fully transposed. Find the spacing between adjacent conductors such that the new line has the same inductance as the original line.

2.14 Find the self GMD of three arrangements of bundled conductors shown in Fig. 2.16 in terms of the total cross-sectional area A of conductors (same in each case) and the distance d between them.

Multiple Choice Questions

2.1 Bundled conductors in EHV transmission lines results to
(a) Reduce inductance (b) Increase capacitance
(c) Increase inductance (d) Increase resistance

2.2 The internal flux linkage due to internal flux of a conductor is
(a) $I \times 10^{-7}$ Wb-T/m (b) $\frac{I}{4} \times 10^{-7}$ Wb-T/m
(c) $\frac{I}{2} \times 10^{-7}$ Wb-T/m (d) $\frac{1}{2} \times 10^{-7}$ Wb-T/m

2.3 A conductor of radius 'r' will have the fictitious radius 'r' for the inductance calculation
(a) $r' = 2r$ (b) $r' = r$ (c) $r' = 0.7788\, r$ (d) $r' = \frac{r}{0.7788}$

2.4 Aluminium is now most commonly employed conductor material in transmission lines than copper because
(a) It is more conductive (b) Its tensile strength is more
(c) Costlier (d) It is cheaper and lighter

2.5 A conductor is composed of seven identical copper strands each having a radius r, the self GMD of the conductor will be
(a) r (b) $3.177\, r$ (c) $2.177\, r$ (d) none of the above

2.6 The 'skin effect' shows that
(a) The distribution of AC current is uniform through the cross-section of the conductor
(b) Current density is more at the centre of the conductor
(c) Current density is lower at the surface of the conductor
(d) Current density is highest at the surface of the conductor

2.7 Apart from the 'skin effect' the non-uniformity of the current distribution is also caused by
(a) Faraday's effect (b) Bundled conductor (c) Proximity effect (d) Ferranti effect

2.8 The total number of strands (N) in concentrically stranded cable with total annular space filled with strands of uniform diameter is given by (if x is the number of layers wherein the single central strand is counted as the first layer).
(a) $N = 3x^2 + 3x + 1$ (b) $N = 3x^2 - 2x + 1$ (c) $N = 3x^2 - 6x + 1$ (d) $N = 3x^2 - 3x + 1$

2.9 Which of the following is correct:
1. Bundle conductors reduce the corona loss.
2. Bundle conductor increases the inductance and reduces the capacitance.
3. Corona loss causes radio interference in adjoining telephone lines

(a) 1 (b) 1 and 2 (c) 2 (d) 1 and 3

2.10 Bundle conductors are used in transmission lines, the effective capacitance and inductance will respectively
(a) Decrease and increase (b) Increase and decrease
(c) Remain same and increase (d) Decrease and remain same

2.11 Transmission lines are transposed to
(a) Reduce Ferranti effect
(b) Reduce skin effect
(c) Reduce transmission loss
(d) Reduce interference with neighbouring communication lines

2.12 In a transmission line, the distributed constants are
(a) Resistance, inductance (b) Resistance, capacitance
(c) Resistance, inductance, capacitance (d) None of the above

2.13 Skin effect is more pronounced at
(a) High frequency (b) Low frequency (c) Cut-off frequency (d) Half power frequency

2.14 As frequency increases the flux inside the conductor will
(a) Increase (b) Decrease (c) be constant (d) Vanish

2.15 Self GMD is
(a) More than GMR (b) Less than GMR (c) Both are same (d) None of the above

2.16 GMR of a solid conductor is
(a) 0.707 r (b) 0.909 r (c) 0.505 r (d) 0.717 r

2.17 The skin effect of conductor will increase when
(a) Diameter decrease (b) Resistivity decrease
(c) Frequency decrease (d) All of the above

2.18 The fact that a current density is higher at the surface when compared to centre is known as
(a) Skin effect (b) Corona (c) Proximity effect (d) All of the above

2.19 The inductance of single-phase two-wire line is given by
(a) $4 \times 10^{-7} \ln D/r'$ H/m (b) $0.4 \times 10^{-7} \ln D/r'$ H/m
(c) $4 \times 10^{-7} \ln r'/D$ H/m (d) $0.4 \times 10^{-7} \ln r'/D$ H/m

2.20 ACSR means
(a) Aluminium core steel reinforced (b) Aluminium conductor steel reinforced
(c) Aluminium copper steel reinforced (d) All conductor steel reinfroced

2.21 If the diameter of the conductor is increased
(a) The inductance is increased (b) The inductance is decreased
(c) The resistance is decreased (d) No change in inductance and resistance

2.22 If the self GMD of the conductor is 2.77r, then what is the GMR of the same conductor
(a) 2.77 r (b) 1.385 r (c) 5.54 r (d) (2.77 + 1) r

2.23 The specification of ACSR conductor which having 7 strands of steel and 24 strands of aluminium is
(a) 24/7 (b) 7/24 (c) 7/13 (d) 31/7

2.24 The non-uniformity of current distribution is caused by
(a) Skin effect only (b) Proximity effect (c) Both (a) and (b) (d) Neither (a) nor (b)
(e) Neither (a) or (b)

2.25 Due to proximity effect, the increase in conductor resistance is not negligible in
(a) Underground cable (b) Overhead transmission line
(c) Communication line (d) All of the above

2.26 For a single-phase two-wire line the diameter 1.213 cm and spacing them is 1.25 m at 50 Hz. The loop inductance is
(a) 22.3×10^{-7} H/m (b) 11.15×10^{-7} H/m
(c) 22.3×10^{-4} H/m (d) 11.15×10^{-4} H/m

2.27 Bundled conductors are used for EHV transmission lines primarily for reducing the
(a) Corona loss (b) Surge impedance of the line
(c) Voltage drop across the line (d) I^2R losses

2.28 Expanded ACSR are conductors composed of
(a) Larger diameter individual strands for a given cross-section of the aluminium strands
(b) Larger diameter of the central steel strands for a given overall diameter of the conductor
(c) Larger diameter of the aluminium strands only for a given overall diameter of the conductor
(d) A filler between the inner steel and the outer aluminium strands to increase the overall diameter of the conductor

2.29 Hollow conductors are used in transmission lines to
(a) Reduce weight of copper (b) Improve stability
(c) Reduce corona (d) Increase power transmission capacity

2.30 The inductance of single-phase two-wire power transmission line per kilometer gets doubled when the
(a) Distance between the wires is doubled
(b) Distance between the wires is increased fourfold
(c) Distance between the wires is increased as square of original distance
(d) Radius of the wire is doubled

2.31 Which of the following statements regarding corona are true?
1. It causes radio interference
2. It attenuates lightning surges
3. It amplifies switching surges
4. It causes power loss
5. It is more prevalent in the middle conductor of a transmission line employing a flat conductor configuration

Select the correct answer using the codes given below
(a) 1, 3 and 5 (b) 2, 3 and 4 (c) 1, 2, 4 and 5 (d) 2, 3, 4 and 5

2.32 Corona loss is less when the shape of the conductor is
(a) Circular (b) Flat (c) Oval (d) Independent of shape

2.33 Corona loss increases with
(a) Increase in supply frequency and conductor size
(b) Increase in supply frequency but reduction in conductor size
(c) Decrease in supply frequency and conductor size
(d) Decrease in supply frequency but increase in conductor size

2.34 The corona loss on a particular system at 50 Hz is 1 kW/phase per km. The corona loss on the same system with supply frequency 25 Hz will be
(a) 0.137 kW/phase/km (b) 0.485 kW/phase/km
(c) 0.667 kw/phase/km (d) 0.926 kw/phase/km

2.35 The inductance per km per phase of a single circuit 460 kV line using two-bundle conductors per phase with diameter of each conductor = 5 cm is
(a) 0.829 mH/km/phase (b) 0.582 mH/km/phase
(c) 0.096 mH/km/phase (d) 0.906 mH/km/phase

References

Books

1. *Electrical Transmission and Distribution Book*, Westinghouse Electric and Manufacturing Co., East Pittsburgh, Pennsylvania, 1964.
2. H. Waddicor, *Principles of Electric Power Transmission*, 5th edn, Chapman and Hall, London, 1964.
3. D.P. Kothari and I.J. Nagrath, *Electric Machines*, 4th edn, Tata McGraw-Hill, New Delhi, 2010.
4. W.D. Stevenson, *Elements of Power System Analysis*, 4th edn, McGraw-Hill, New York, 1982.
5. *EHV Transmission Line Reference Book*, Edison Electric Institute, 1968.
6. The Aluminium Association, *Aluminium Electrical Conductor Handbook*, New York, 1971.
7. L.F. Woodruff, *Principles of Electric Power Transmission*, Wiley, New York, 1947.
8. C.A. Gross, *Power System Analysis*, Wiley, New York, 1979.
9. B.M. Weedy and B.J. Cory, *Electric Power Systems*, 4th edn, Wiley, New York, 1998.
10. E.W. Kimbark, *Electrical Transmission of Power and Signals*, Wiley, New York, 1949.

Papers

11. J. Reichman, "Bundled Conductor Voltage Gradient Calculations", *AIEE Trans.*, pt III, 78, 598, 1959.
12. IEEE Society, "IEEE Guide for the Parameter Measurement of AC Transmission Lines", *IEEE Standard 1870-2019*, pp: 1–99, 2019.
13. IEEE Society, "IEEE Approved Draft Guide for the Parameter Measurement of AC Transmission Lines", *IEEE P1870/D7*, pp: 1–90, 2018.
14. Q. Hu, L. Shu, X. Jiang, C. Sun, S. Zhang, and Y. Shang, "Effects of Air Pressure and Humidity on the Corona Onset Voltage of Bundle Conductors", *IET Generation, Transmission & Distribution*, volume: 5, issue: 6, pp: 621–629, 2011.
15. Wang-ling He, Jun-jia He, Bao-quan Wan, Yu-chao Chen, Chun-ming Pei, Jian-gong Zhang, and Jin Zhang, "Radio Interference Excitation Function of Conductor Bundles based on Cage Test Results and Comparison with Long-Term Data", *IET Science, Measurement & Technology*, volume: 9, issue: 5, pp: 621–627, 2015.
16. Alberto De Conti and Fernando H. Silveira, "Modelling of Power Transmission Line Components", in *Lightning Interaction with Power Systems*, volume: 1: Fundamentals and Modelling, pp: 345–380, 2020.
17. K.F. Goddard, A.A. Roy, and J.K. Sykulski, "Inductance and Resistance Calculations for Isolated Conductors", *IEE Proceedings – Science, Measurement and Technology*, volume: 152, issue: 1, pp: 7–14, 2005.
18. K.F. Goddard, A.A. Roy, and J.K. Sykulski, "Inductance and Resistance Calculations for a Pair of Rectangular Conductors", *IEE Proceedings – Science, Measurement and Technology*, volume: 152, issue: 2, pp: 73–78, 2005.
19. C. Xiao and Z. Hu, "Live Line Measuring the Impedance Parameters of Transmission Lines Based on Interference Sources", *International Conference on Energy and Environment Technology, Guilin, Guangxi*, pp: 160–163, 2009.
20. Z. Hu, J. Fan, M. Chen, and Z. Xu, "New Method of Live Line Measuring the Parameters of T-Connection Transmission Lines with Mutual Inductance", *2009 IEEE Power & Energy Society General Meeting, Calgary, AB*, pp: 1–5, 2009.

CHAPTER 3 Capacitance of Transmission Lines

3.1 ▶ INTRODUCTION

The capacitance together with conductance forms the shunt admittance of a transmission line. As mentioned earlier, the conductance is the result of leakage over the surface of insulators and is of negligible order. When an alternating voltage is applied to the line, the line capacitance draws a leading sinusoidal current called the *charging current* which is drawn even when the line is open circuited at the far end. The line capacitance being proportional to its length, the charging current is negligible for lines less than 100 km long. For longer lines, the capacitance becomes increasingly important and has to be accounted for.

3.2 ▶ ELECTRIC FIELD OF A LONG STRAIGHT CONDUCTOR

Imagine an infinitely long straight conductor far removed from other conductors (including earth) carrying a uniform charge of q coulomb/metre length. By symmetry, the equipotential surfaces will be concentric cylinders, while the lines of electrostatic stress will be radial. The electric field intensity at a distance y from the axis of the conductor is

$$\varepsilon = \frac{q}{2\pi k y} \text{ V/m}$$

where k is the permittivity* of the medium.

As shown in Fig. 3.1, consider two points P_1 and P_2 located at distances D_1 and D_2 respectively from the conductor axis. The potential difference V_{12} (between P_1 and P_2) is given by

$$V_{12} = \oint \varepsilon \, \mathrm{d}y = \oint \frac{q}{2\pi k y} \mathrm{d}y \text{ V}$$

As the potential difference is independent of the path, we choose the path of integration as P_1PP_2 shown in thick line. Since the path PP_2 lies along an equipotential, V_{12} is obtained simply by integrating along P_1P, i.e.,

$$V_{12} = \int_{D_1}^{D_2} \frac{q}{2\pi k y} \mathrm{d}y = \frac{q}{2\pi k} \ln \frac{D_2}{D_1} \; V \qquad (3.1)$$

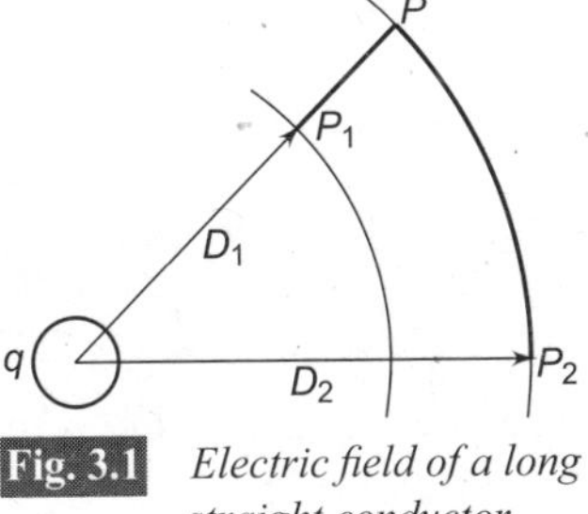

Fig. 3.1 *Electric field of a long straight conductor*

3.3 ▶ POTENTIAL DIFFERENCE BETWEEN TWO CONDUCTORS OF A GROUP OF PARALLEL CONDUCTORS

Figure 3.2 shows a group of parallel charged conductors. It is assumed that the conductors are far removed from the ground and are sufficiently removed from each other, i.e., the conductor radii are much smaller than

* In SI units, the permittivity of free space is $k_0 = 8.85 \times 10^{-12}$ F/m. Relative permittivity for air is $k_r = k/k_0 = 1$.

the distances between them. The spacing commonly used in overhead power transmission lines always meets these assumptions. Further, these assumptions imply that the charge on each conductor remains uniformly distributed around its periphery and length. The potential difference between any two conductors of the group can then be obtained by adding the contributions of the individual charged conductors by repeated application of Eq. (3.1). So, the potential difference between conductors a and b (voltage drop from a to b) is

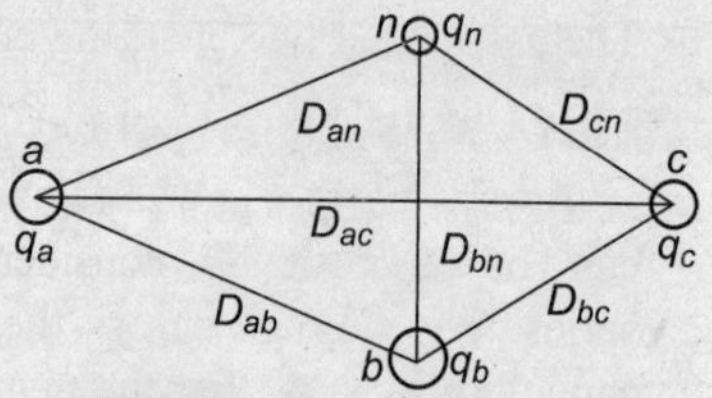

Fig. 3.2 *A group of parallel charged conductors*

$$V_{ab} = \frac{1}{2\pi k}\left(q_a \ln \frac{D_{ab}}{r_a} + q_b \ln \frac{r_b}{D_{ba}} + q_c \ln \frac{D_{cb}}{D_{ca}} + \ldots q_n \ln \frac{D_{nb}}{D_{na}} \right) \text{V} \tag{3.2}$$

Each term in Eq. (3.2) is the potential drop from a to b caused by charge on one of the conductors of the group. Expressions on similar lines could be written for voltage drop between any two conductors of the group.

If the charges vary sinusoidally, so do the voltages (this is the case for AC transmission line), the expression of Eq. (3.2) still applies with charges/metre length and voltages regarded as phasor quantities. Equation (3.2) is thus valid for instantaneous quantities and for sinusoidal quantities as well, wherein all charges and voltages are phasors.

3.4 ▶ CAPACITANCE OF A TWO-WIRE LINE

Consider a two-wire line shown in Fig. 3.3 excited from a single-phase source. The line develops equal and opposite sinusoidal charges on the two conductors which can be represented as phasors q_a and q_b so that $q_a = -q_b$.

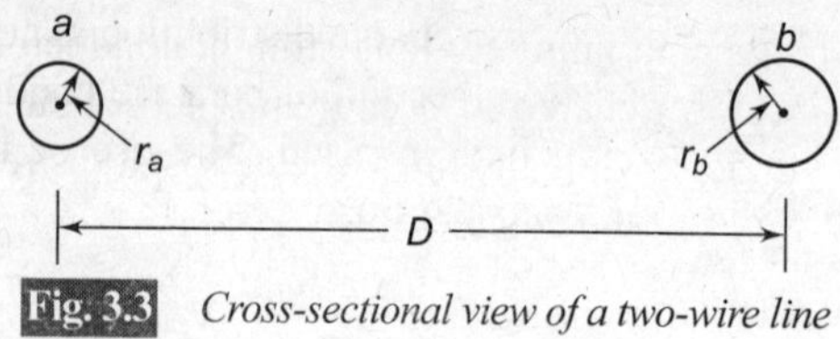

Fig. 3.3 *Cross-sectional view of a two-wire line*

The potential difference V_{ab} can be written in terms of the contributions made by q_a and q_b by use of Eq. (3.2) with associated assumptions (i.e., D/r is large and ground is far away). Thus,

$$V_{ab} = \frac{1}{2\pi k}\left(q_a \ln \frac{D}{r_a} + q_b \ln \frac{r_b}{D} \right) \tag{3.3}$$

Since $q_a = -q_b$, we have

$$V_{ab} = \frac{q_a}{2\pi k} \ln \frac{D^2}{r_a r_b}$$

The line capacitance C_{ab} is then

$$C_{ab} = \frac{q_a}{V_{ab}} = \frac{\pi k}{\ln (D/(r_a r_b)^{1/2})} \text{ F/m length of line} \tag{3.4a}$$

or

$$C_{ab} = \frac{0.0121}{\log (D/(r_a r_b)^{1/2})} \ \mu\text{F/km} \tag{3.4b}$$

If $r_a = r_b = r$,

$$C_{ab} = \frac{0.0121}{\log (D/r)} \ \mu\text{F/km} \tag{3.4c}$$

The associated line charging current is

$$I_c = j\omega C_{ab} V_{ab} \text{ A/km} \tag{3.5}$$

As shown in Figs 3.4(a) and (b), the line-to-line capacitance can be equivalently considered as two equal capacitances in series. The voltage across the lines divides equally between the capacitances such that the neutral point n is at the ground potential. The capacitance of each line to neutral is then given by

$$C_n = C_{an} = C_{bn} = 2C_{ab}$$

$$= \frac{0.0242}{\log(D/r)} \ \mu\text{F/km} \tag{3.6}$$

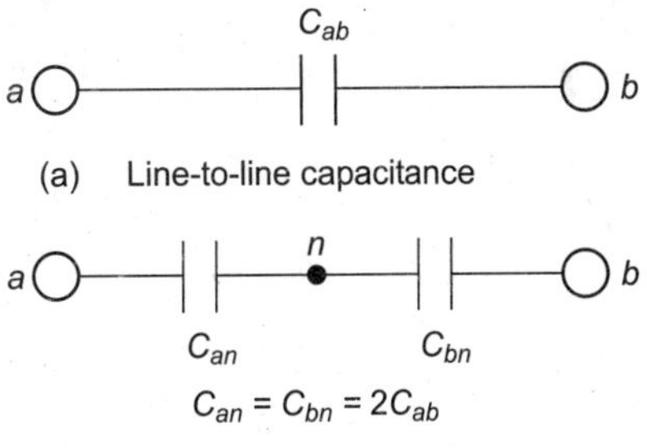

C_{ab}

a b

(a) Line-to-line capacitance

a n b

C_{an} C_{bn}

$C_{an} = C_{bn} = 2C_{ab}$

(b) Line-to-neutral capacitance

Fig. 3.4

The assumptions inherent in the above derivation are:

1. The charge on the surface of each conductor is assumed to be uniformly distributed, but this is strictly not correct.
   If non-uniformity of charge distribution is taken into account, then

$$C_n = \frac{0.0242}{\log\left(\frac{D}{2r} + \left(\frac{D^2}{4r^2} - 1\right)^{1/2}\right)} \ \mu\text{F/km} \tag{3.7}$$

   If $D/2r \gg 1$, the above expression reduces to that of Eq. (3.6) and the error caused by the assumption of uniform charge distribution is negligible.
2. The cross-section of both the conductors is assumed to be circular, while in actual practice stranded conductors are used. The use of the radius of the circumscribing circle for a stranded conductor causes insignificant error.

3.5 ▶ CAPACITANCE OF A THREE-PHASE LINE WITH EQUILATERAL SPACING

Figure 3.5 shows a three-phase line composed of three identical conductors of radius r placed in equilateral configuration.

Using Eq. (3.2), we can write the expressions for V_{ab} and V_{ac} as

$$V_{ab} = \frac{1}{2\pi k}\left(q_a \ln\frac{D}{r} + q_b \ln\frac{r}{D} + q_c \ln\frac{D}{D}\right) \tag{3.8}$$

$$V_{ac} = \frac{1}{2\pi k}\left(q_a \ln\frac{D}{r} + q_b \ln\frac{D}{D} + q_c \ln\frac{r}{D}\right) \tag{3.9}$$

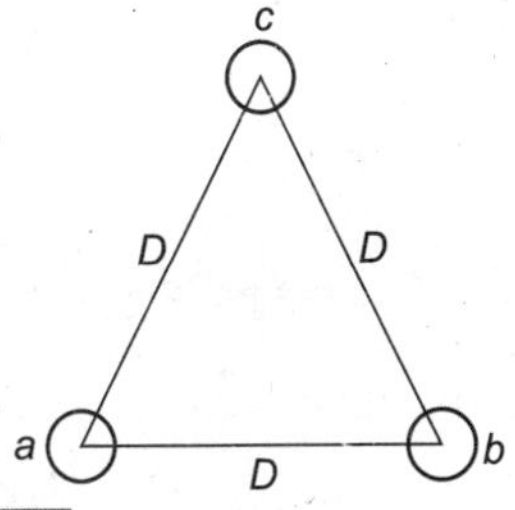

c

D D

a b

D

Fig. 3.5 *Cross-section of a three-phase line with equilateral spacing*

Adding Eqs (3.8) and (3.9), we get

$$V_{ab} + V_{ac} = \frac{1}{2\pi k}\left[2q_a \ln\frac{D}{r} + (q_b + q_c)\ln\frac{r}{D}\right] \tag{3.10}$$

Since there are no other charges in the vicinity, the sum of charges on the three conductors is zero. Thus $q_b + q_c = -q_a$, which when substituted in Eq. (3.10) yields

$$V_{ab} + V_{ac} = \frac{3q_a}{2\pi k} \ln\frac{D}{r} \tag{3.11}$$

With balanced three-phase voltages applied to the line, it follows from the phasor diagram of Fig. 3.6 that

$$V_{ab} + V_{ac} = 3V_{an} \tag{3.12}$$

Substituting for $(V_{ab} + V_{ac})$ from Eq. (3.12) in Eq. (3.11), we get

$$V_{an} = \frac{q_a}{2\pi k} \ln \frac{D}{r} \tag{3.13}$$

The capacitance of line to neutral immediately follows as

$$C_n = \frac{q_a}{V_{an}} = \frac{2\pi k}{\ln (D/r)} \tag{3.14a}$$

For air medium ($k_r = 1$),

$$C_n = \frac{0.0242}{\log (D/r)} \ \mu\text{F/km} \tag{3.14b}$$

The line charging current of phase a is

$$I_a \text{ (line charging)} = j\omega C_n V_{an} \tag{3.15}$$

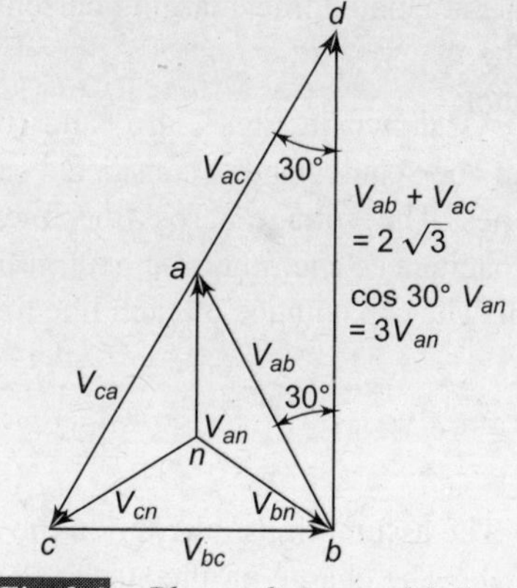

Fig. 3.6 *Phasor diagram of balanced three-phase voltages*

3.6 ▶ CAPACITANCE OF A THREE-PHASE LINE WITH UNSYMMETRICAL SPACING

Figure 3.7 shows the three identical conductors of radius r of a three-phase line with unsymmetrical spacing. It is assumed that the line is fully transposed. As the conductors are rotated cyclically in the three sections of the transposition cycle, correspondingly three expressions can be written for V_{ab}. These expressions are:

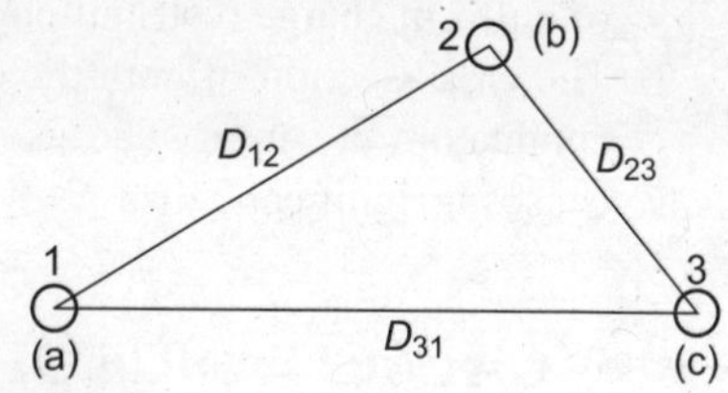

Fig. 3.7 *Cross-section of a three-phase line with asymmetrical spacing (fully transposed)*

For the first section of the transposition cycle

$$V_{ab} = \frac{1}{2\pi k}\left(q_{a1} \ln \frac{D_{12}}{r} + q_{b1} \ln \frac{r}{D_{12}} + q_{c1} \ln \frac{D_{23}}{D_{31}} \right) \tag{3.16a}$$

For the second section of the transposition cycle

$$V_{ab} = \frac{1}{2\pi k}\left(q_{a2} \ln \frac{D_{23}}{r} + q_{b2} \ln \frac{r}{D_{23}} + q_{c2} \ln \frac{D_{31}}{D_{12}} \right) \tag{3.16b}$$

For the third section of the transposition cycle

$$V_{ab} = \frac{1}{2\pi k}\left(q_{a3} \ln \frac{D_{31}}{r} + q_{b3} \ln \frac{r}{D_{31}} + q_{c3} \ln \frac{D_{12}}{D_{23}} \right) \tag{3.16c}$$

If the voltage drop along the line is neglected, V_{ab} is the same in each transposition cycle. On similar lines, three such equations can be written for $V_{bc} = V_{ab} \angle -120°$. Three more equations can be written equating to zero the summation of all line charges in each section of the transposition cycle. From these nine (independent) equations, it is possible to determine the nine unknown charges. The rigorous solution though possible is too involved.

With the usual spacing of conductors, sufficient accuracy is obtained by assuming

$$q_{a1} = q_{a2} = q_{a3} = q_a\,;\, q_{b1} = q_{b2} = q_{b3} = q_b;\, q_{c1} = q_{c2} = q_{c3} = q_c \tag{3.17}$$

This assumption of equal charges/unit length of a line in the three sections of the transposition cycle requires, on the other hand, three different values of V_{ab} designated as V_{ab1}, V_{ab2} and V_{ab3} in the three sections. The solution can be considerably simplified by taking V_{ab} as the average of these three voltages, i.e.,

$$V_{ab}\,(\text{avg}) = \frac{1}{3}(V_{ab1} + V_{ab2} + V_{ab3})$$

or,

$$V_{ab} = \frac{1}{6\pi k}\left[q_a \ln\left(\frac{D_{12}D_{23}D_{31}}{r^3}\right) + q_b \ln\left(\frac{r^3}{D_{12}D_{23}D_{31}}\right) + q_c \ln\left(\frac{D_{12}D_{23}D_{31}}{D_{12}D_{23}D_{31}}\right)\right]$$

$$= \frac{1}{2\pi k}\left(q_a \ln \frac{D_{eq}}{r} + q_b \ln \frac{r}{D_{eq}}\right) \tag{3.18}$$

where $D_{eq} = (D_{12}D_{23}D_{31})^{1/3}$

Similarly,

$$V_{ac} = \frac{1}{2\pi k}\left(q_a \ln \frac{D_{eq}}{r} + q_c \ln \frac{r}{D_{eq}}\right) \tag{3.19}$$

Adding Eqs (3.18) and (3.19), we get

$$V_{ab} + V_{ac} = \frac{1}{2\pi k}\left(q_a \ln \frac{D_{eq}}{r} + (q_b + q_c) \ln \frac{r}{D_{eq}}\right) \tag{3.20}$$

As per Eq. (3.12) for balanced three-phase voltages

$$V_{ab} + V_{ac} = 3V_{an}$$

and also $(q_b + q_c) = -q_a$

Use of these relationships in Eq. (3.20) leads to

$$V_{an} = \frac{q_a}{2\pi k} \ln \frac{D_{eq}}{r} \tag{3.21}$$

The capacitance of line to neutral of the transposed line is then given by

$$C_n = \frac{q_a}{V_{an}} = \frac{2\pi k}{\ln (D_{eq}/r)} \text{ F/m to neutral} \tag{3.22a}$$

For air medium ($k_r = 1$)

$$C_n = \frac{0.0242}{\log (D_{eq}/r)} \ \mu\text{F/km to neutral} \tag{3.22b}$$

It is obvious that for equilateral spacing $D_{eq} = D$, the above (approximate) formula gives the exact result presented earlier.

The line charging current for a three-phase line in phasor form is

$$I_a \text{ (line charging)} = j\omega C_n V_{an} \text{ A/km} \tag{3.23}$$

3.7 ▶ EFFECT OF EARTH ON TRANSMISSION LINE CAPACITANCE

So far, in calculating the capacitance of transmission lines, the presence of earth was ignored. The effect of earth on capacitance can be conveniently taken into account by the method of images.

3.7.1 Method of Images

The electric field of transmission line conductors must conform to the presence of the earth below. The earth for this purpose may be assumed to be a perfectly conducting horizontal sheet of infinite extent which therefore acts like an equipotential surface.

The electric field of two long, parallel conductors charged $+q$ and $-q$ per unit is such that it has a zero potential plane midway between the conductors as shown in Fig. 3.8. If a conducting sheet of infinite dimensions is placed at the zero potential plane, the electric field remains undisturbed. Further, if the conductor carrying charge $-q$ is now removed, the electric field above the conducting sheet stays intact, while that below it vanishes. Using these well-known results in reverse, we may equivalently replace the presence of ground below a charged conductor by a fictitious conductor having equal and opposite charge and located as far below the surface of ground as the overhead conductor above it—such a fictitious conductor is the *mirror image* of the overhead conductor. This method of creating the same electric field as in the presence of earth is known as the *method of images* originally suggested by Lord Kelvin.

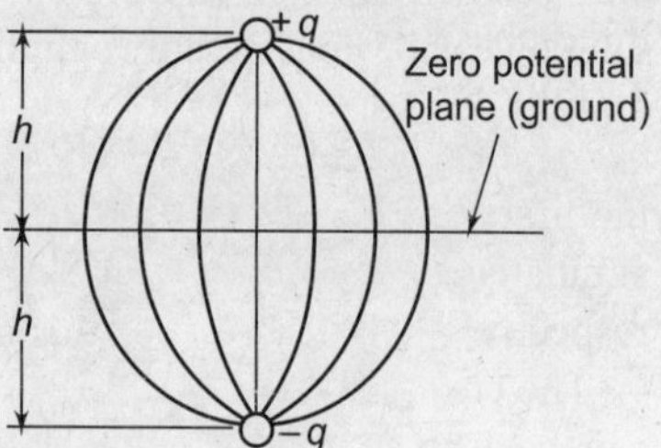

Fig. 3.8 *Electric field of two long, parallel, oppositely charged conductors*

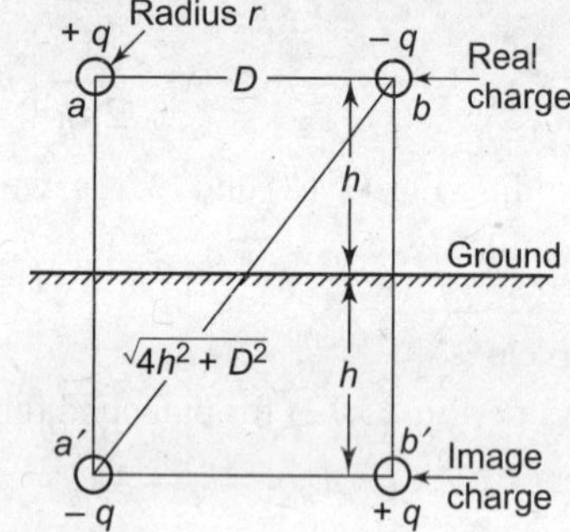

Fig. 3.9 *Single-phase transmission line with images*

Capacitance of a Single-Phase Line Consider a single-phase line shown in Fig. 3.9. It is required to calculate its capacitance taking the presence of earth into account by the method of images described above. The equation for the voltage drop V_{ab} as determined by the two charged conductors a and b, and their images a' and b' can be written as follows:

$$V_{ab} = \frac{1}{2\pi k}\left[q_a \ln\frac{D}{r} + q_b \ln\frac{r}{D} + q_{a'} \ln\frac{(4h^2+D^2)^{1/2}}{2h} + q_{b'} \ln\frac{2h}{(4h^2+D^2)^{1/2}}\right] \tag{3.24}$$

Substituting the values of different charges and simplifying, we get

$$V_{ab} = \frac{q}{\pi k}\ln\frac{2hD}{r(4h^2+D^2)^{1/2}} \tag{3.25}$$

It immediately follows that

$$C_{ab} = \frac{\pi k}{\ln\dfrac{D}{r(1+(D^2/4h^2))^{1/2}}} \text{ F/m line-to-line} \tag{3.26a}$$

and

$$C_n = \frac{2\pi k}{\ln\dfrac{D}{r(1+(D^2/4h^2))^{1/2}}} \text{ F/m to neutral} \tag{3.26b}$$

It is observed from the above equation that the presence of earth modifies the radius r to $r(1 + (D^2/4h^2))^{1/2}$. For h large compared to D (this is the case normally), the effect of earth on line capacitance is of negligible order.

Capacitance of a Three-Phase Line The method of images can similarly be applied for the calculation of capacitance of a three-phase line, shown in Fig. 3.10. The line is considered to be fully transposed. The conductors *a, b* and *c* carry the charges q_a, q_b and q_c and occupy positions 1, 2 and 3, respectively, in the first section of the transposition cycle. The effect of earth is simulated by image conductors with charges $-q_a$, $-q_b$ and $-q_c$ respectively, as shown.

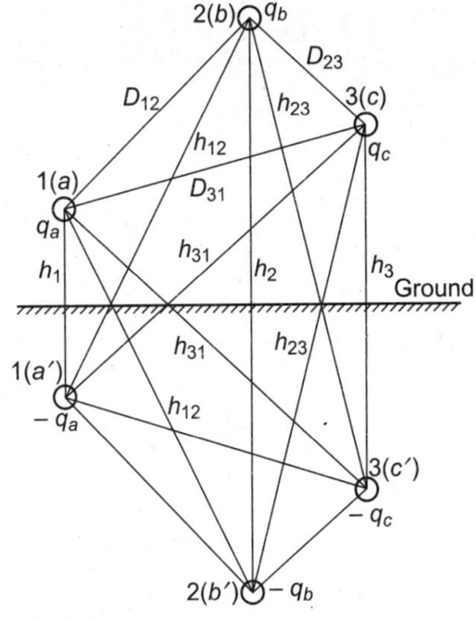

Fig. 3.10 *Three-phase line with images*

The equations for the three sections of the transposition cycle can be written for the voltage drop V_{ab} as determined by the three charged conductors and their images. With conductor *a* in position 1, *b* in position 2 and *c* in position 3,

$$V_{ab} = \frac{1}{2\pi k}\left[q_a\left(\ln\frac{D_{12}}{r} - \ln\frac{h_{12}}{h_1}\right) + q_b\left(\ln\frac{r}{D_{12}} - \ln\frac{h_2}{h_{12}}\right) + q_c\left(\ln\frac{D_{23}}{D_{31}} - \ln\frac{h_{23}}{h_{31}}\right)\right] \tag{3.27}$$

Similar equations for V_{ab} can be written for the second and third sections of the transposition cycle. If the fairly accurate assumption of constant charge per unit length of the conductor throughout the transmission cycle is made, the average value of V_{ab} for the three sections of the cycle is given by

$$V_{ab} = \frac{1}{2\pi k}\left[q_a\left(\ln\frac{D_{eq}}{r} - \ln\frac{(h_{12}h_{23}h_{31})^{1/3}}{(h_1h_2h_3)^{1/3}}\right) + q_b\left(\ln\frac{r}{D_{eq}} - \ln\frac{(h_1h_2h_3)^{1/3}}{(h_{12}h_{23}h_{31})^{1/3}}\right)\right] \tag{3.28}$$

where $D_{eq} = (D_{12}D_{23}D_{31})^{1/3}$.

The equation for the average value of the phasor V_{ac} is found in a similar manner. Proceeding on the lines of Section 3.6 and using $V_{ab} + V_{ac} = 3V_{an}$ and $q_a + q_b + q_c = 0$, we ultimately obtain the following expression for the capacitance to neutral.

$$C_n = \frac{2\pi k}{\ln\dfrac{D_{eq}}{r} - \ln\left(\dfrac{(h_{12}h_{23}h_{31})^{1/3}}{(h_1h_2h_3)^{1/3}}\right)} \text{ F/m to neutral} \tag{3.29a}$$

or,

$$C_n = \frac{0.0242}{\log\dfrac{D_{eq}}{r} - \log\dfrac{(h_{12}h_{23}h_{31})^{1/3}}{(h_1h_2h_3)^{1/3}}} \ \mu\text{F/km to neutral} \tag{3.29b}$$

Comparing Eqs (3.22a) and (3.29a), it is evident that the effect of earth is to increase the capacitance of a line. If the conductors are high above earth compared to the distances among them, the effect of earth on the capacitance of three-phase lines can be neglected.

Example 3.1 Calculate the capacitance to neutral/km of a single-phase line composed of No. 2 single strand conductors (radius = 0.328 cm) spaced 3 m apart and 7.5 m above the ground. Compare the results obtained by Eqs (3.6), (3.7) and (3.26b).

Solution

1. Neglecting the presence of earth [Eq. (3.6)]

$$C_n = \frac{0.0242}{\log \dfrac{D}{r}} \ \mu\text{F/km}$$

$$= \frac{0.0242}{\log \dfrac{300}{0.328}} = 0.00817 \ \mu\text{F/km}$$

By the rigorous relationship [(Eq. (3.7)]

$$C_n = \frac{0.0242}{\log\left(\dfrac{D}{2r} + \left(\dfrac{D^2}{4r^2} - 1\right)^{1/2}\right)} \ \mu\text{F/km}$$

Since $\dfrac{D}{r} = 915$, the effect of non-uniformity of charge distribution is almost negligible.

$\therefore \quad C_n = 0.00817 \ \mu\text{F/km}.$

2. Considering the effect of earth and neglecting non-uniformity of charge distribution [Eq. (3.26b)]

$$C_n = \frac{0.0242}{\log \dfrac{D}{r(1+(D^2/4h^2))^{1/2}}}$$

$$\frac{D}{r\sqrt{1.04}} = \frac{300}{0.328\sqrt{1.04}} = 897$$

$$C_n = \frac{0.0242}{2.953} = 0.0082 \ \mu\text{F/km}$$

Note: The presence of earth increases the capacitance by approximately 3 parts in 800.

Example 3.2 A three-phase 50 Hz transmission line has flat horizontal spacing with 3.5 m between adjacent conductors. The conductors are No. 2/0 hard-drawn seven-strand copper (outside conductor diameter = 1.05 cm). The voltage of the line is 110 kV. Find the capacitance to neutral and the charging current per kilometre of line.

Solution

$$D_{eq} = (3.5 \times 3.5 \times 7)^{1/3} = 4.4 \text{ m}$$

$$C_n = \frac{0.0242}{\log (D_{eq}/r)} = \frac{0.0242}{\log (440/0.525)}$$

$$= 0.00826 \ \mu\text{F/km}$$

$$X_n = \frac{1}{\omega C_n} = \frac{10^6}{314 \times 0.00826}$$

$$= 0.384 \times 10^6 \ \Omega\text{/km to neutral}$$

$$\text{Charging current} = \frac{V_n}{X_n} = \frac{(110/\sqrt{3}) \times 1000}{0.384 \times 10^6}$$

$$= 0.17 \text{ A/km}$$

Example 3.3 The six conductors of a double-circuit three-phase line having an overall radius of 0.865 $\times 10^{-2}$ m are arranged as shown in Fig. 3.11. Find the capacitive reactance to neutral and charging current per kilometre per conductor at 110 kV, 50 Hz.

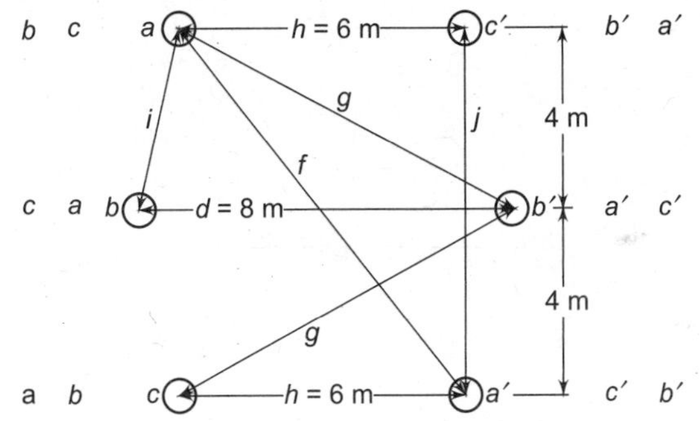

Fig. 3.11 *Cross-section of a double-circuit three-phase line*

Solution As in Section 3.6, assume that the charge per conductor on each phase is equal in all the three sections of the transposition cycle. For Section I of the transposition cycle,

$$V_{ab}(\text{I}) = \frac{1}{2\pi k}\left[q_a\left(\ln\frac{i}{r}+\ln\frac{g}{f}\right)+q_b\left(\ln\frac{r}{i}+\ln\frac{d}{g}\right)+q_c\left(\ln\frac{i}{j}+\ln\frac{g}{h}\right)\right] \tag{3.30}$$

For Section II of the transposition cycle,

$$V_{ab}(\text{II}) = \frac{1}{2\pi k}\left[q_a\left(\ln\frac{i}{r}+\ln\frac{g}{d}\right)+q_b\left(\ln\frac{r}{i}+\ln\frac{f}{g}\right)+q_c\left(\ln\frac{j}{i}+\ln\frac{h}{g}\right)\right] \tag{3.31}$$

For Section III of the transposition cycle,

$$V_{ab}(\text{III}) = \frac{1}{2\pi k}\left[q_a\left(\ln\frac{j}{r}+\ln\frac{h}{f}\right)+q_b\left(\ln\frac{r}{j}+\ln\frac{f}{h}\right)+q_c\left(\ln\frac{i}{j}+\ln\frac{g}{g}\right)\right] \tag{3.32}$$

Average value of V_{ab} over the transposition cycle is given by

$$V_{ab}(\text{avg}) = \frac{1}{6\pi k}\left[q_a\ln\left(\frac{ig\ ig\ jh}{rf\ rd\ rf}\right)+q_b\ln\left(\frac{rd\ rf\ rf}{ig\ ig\ jh}\right)\right]$$

$$= \frac{1}{2\pi k}(q_a-q_b)\ln\left(\frac{i^2g^2jh}{r^3f^2d}\right)^{1/3} \tag{3.33}$$

Similarly,

$$V_{ac}(\text{avg}) = \frac{1}{2\pi k}(q_a-q_c)\ln\left(\frac{i^2g^2jh}{r^3f^2d}\right)^{1/3} \tag{3.34}$$

Now,

$$V_{ab}+V_{ac} = 3V_{an} = \frac{1}{2\pi k}(2q_a-q_b-q_c)\ln\left(\frac{i^2g^2jh}{r^3f^2d}\right)^{1/3} \tag{3.35}$$

$$3V_{an} = \frac{3q_a}{2\pi k}\ln\left(\frac{i^2g^2jh}{r^3f^2d}\right)^{1/3}$$

Capacitance to neutral per conductor $= \dfrac{2\pi k}{\ln\left(\dfrac{i^2 g^2 jh}{r^3 f^2 d}\right)^{1/3}}$ (3.36)

Total capacitance to neutral for two conductors in parallel

$$C_n = \frac{4\pi k}{\ln\left(\dfrac{i^2 g^2 jh}{r^3 f^2 d}\right)^{1/3}} \text{ F/m} \tag{3.37}$$

Now, $h = 6$ m; $d = 8$ m; $j = 8$ m. Referring to Fig. 3.12, we can write

$$i = \left[\left(\frac{j}{2}\right)^2 + \left(\frac{d-h}{2}\right)^2\right]^{1/2} = \sqrt{17} \text{ m}$$

$$f = (j^2 + h^2)^{1/2} = 10 \text{ m}$$

$$g = (7^2 + 4^2)^{1/2} = \sqrt{65} \text{ m}$$

Conductor radius (overall) $= 0.865 \times 10^{-2}$ m

Substituting the values for various distances, we have

$$C_n = \frac{4\pi \times 1 \times 8.85 \times 10^{-12} \times 10^6 \times 1000}{\ln\left[\dfrac{17 \times 65 \times 8 \times 6}{100 \times 8}\left(\dfrac{100}{0.865}\right)^3\right]^{1/3}} \ \mu\text{F/km}$$

$$= 0.0181 \ \mu\text{F/km}$$

$$\omega C_n = 314 \times 0.0181 \times 10^{-6}$$

$$= 5.68 \times 10^{-6} \ \Omega/\text{km}$$

$$\text{Charging current/phase} = \frac{110 \times 1000}{\sqrt{3}} \times 5.68 \times 10^{-6}$$

$$= 0.361 \text{ A/km}$$

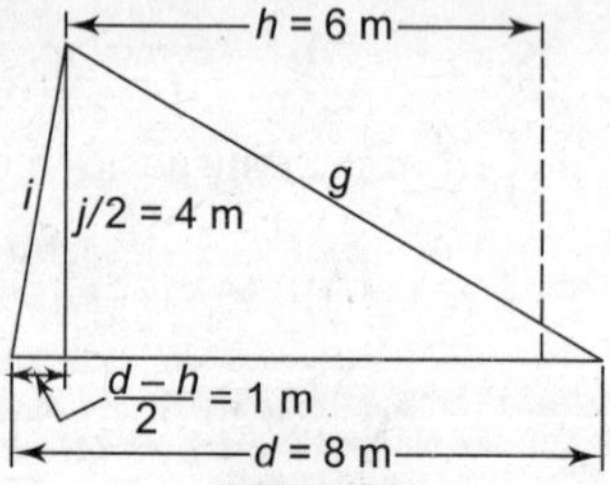

$\therefore$ Charging current/conductor $= \dfrac{0.361}{2} = 0.1805$ A/km

Fig. 3.12

Example 3.4 Derive from the first principles the capacitance per km to neutral of a three-phase overhead transmission line with unsymmetrical spacing of conductors, assuming proper transposition.

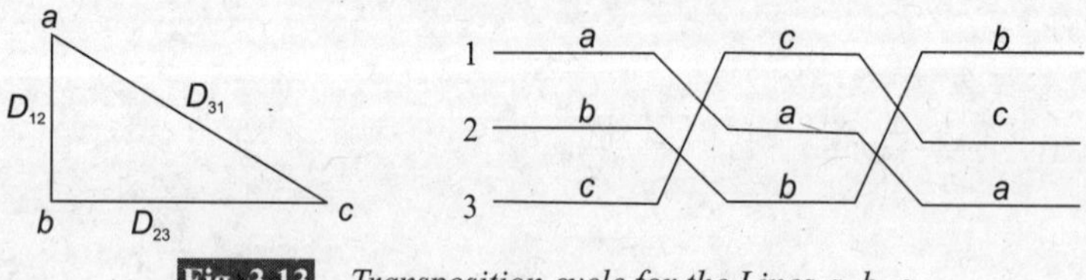

Fig. 3.13 *Transposition cycle for the Lines a, b, c*

Solution It is assumed that the charge per unit length of the conductor remains the same in different positions of the transposition cycle. With this assumption, q_a, q_b, q_c have the same magnitude but 120° appart in phase.

$$q_a = q_a \angle 0° \ ; \ q_b = q_a \angle 120° \ ; \ q_c = q_a \angle 120°$$

Referring to the above figure, the potential difference between 'a' and 'b' when 'a' is in position 1, 'b' in 2 and 'c' in 3.

$$(V_{ab})_1 = \frac{1}{2\pi\varepsilon}\left[q_a \ln\frac{D_{12}}{r} + q_b \ln\frac{r}{D_{12}} + q_c \ln\frac{D_{23}}{D_{31}}\right] \tag{3.38}$$

When 'a' in position 2, 'b' in 3 and 'c' in 1,

$$(V_{ab})_2 = \frac{1}{2\pi\varepsilon}\left[q_a \ln\frac{D_{23}}{r} + q_b \ln\frac{r}{D_{23}} + q_c \ln\frac{D_{31}}{D_{12}}\right] \tag{3.39}$$

When 'a' in position 3, 'b' in 1 and 'c' in 2,

$$(V_{ab})_3 = \frac{1}{2\pi\varepsilon}\left[q_a \ln\frac{D_{31}}{r} + q_b \ln\frac{r}{D_{31}} + q_c \ln\frac{D_{12}}{D_{23}}\right] \tag{3.40}$$

The average value of potential difference between conductors 'a' and 'b' in three positions of the transposition cycle,

$$V_{ab} = \frac{1}{3}\left[(V_{ab})_1 + (V_{ab})_2 + (V_{ab})_3\right]$$

$$V_{ab} = \frac{1}{3}\times\frac{1}{2\pi\in}\left[q_a \ln\frac{D_{12}D_{23}D_{31}}{r^3} + q_b \ln\frac{r^3}{D_{12}D_{23}D_{31}} + q_c \ln\frac{D_{12}D_{23}D_{31}}{D_{12}D_{23}D_{31}}\right]$$

$$= \frac{1}{6\pi\varepsilon}\left[q_a \ln\frac{D_m^3}{r^3} + q_b \ln\frac{r^3}{D_m^3}\right] = \frac{1}{2\pi\varepsilon}\left[q_a \ln\frac{D_m}{r} + q_b \ln\frac{r}{D_m}\right] \tag{3.41}$$

where $D_m = (D_{12}\ D_{23}\ D_{31})^{1/3}$ is the mutual geometric mean distance between the phases.

Similarly, the average potential difference between 'a' and 'c'

$$V_{ac} = \frac{1}{2\pi\varepsilon}\left[q_a \ln\frac{D_m}{r} + q_c \ln\frac{r}{D_m}\right] \tag{3.42}$$

But, $\quad V_{ab} + V_{ac} = 3V_{an}$.

Adding Eqs (3.41) and (3.42)

$$3V_{an} = \frac{1}{2\pi\varepsilon}\left[2q_a \ln\frac{D_m}{r} + (q_b + q_c)\ln\frac{r}{D_m}\right]$$

Since, $q_n + q_b + q_c = 0$ in a three-phase three-wire system,

$$3V_{an} = \frac{1}{2\pi\varepsilon}\left[2q_a \ln\frac{D_m}{r} + (-q_a)\ln\frac{r}{D_m}\right]$$

or,
$$3V_{an} = \frac{1}{2\pi\varepsilon}\left[2q_a \ln\frac{D_m}{r} - q_a \ln\frac{r}{D_m}\right]$$

or,
$$3V_{an} = \frac{1}{2\pi\varepsilon}\left[2q_a \ln\frac{D_m}{r} + q_a \ln\frac{D_m}{r}\right] = \frac{3q_a}{2\pi\varepsilon}\ln\frac{D_m}{r}$$

or,
$$3V_{an} = \frac{q_a}{2\pi\varepsilon}\ln\frac{D_m}{r}.$$

The capacitance of line to neutral is thus,

$$C_n = \frac{q_n}{V_{an}} = \frac{2\pi\varepsilon}{\ln\dfrac{D_m}{r}} \text{ F/m} = \frac{2\pi\varepsilon}{10^{-3}\ln\dfrac{D_m}{r}} \text{ F/km.}$$

Example 3.5 A three-phase, 50 Hz, 110 kV, transmission line has flat horizontal spacing with 3.5 m between adjacent conductors. The conductor diameter is 1.05 cm.

Find the capacitance to neutral and the charging current per km of line. Assume full transposition.

Solution The equivalent spacing,

$$D_{eq} = (3.5 \times 3.5 \times 7)^{1/3} = 4.5 \text{ m}$$

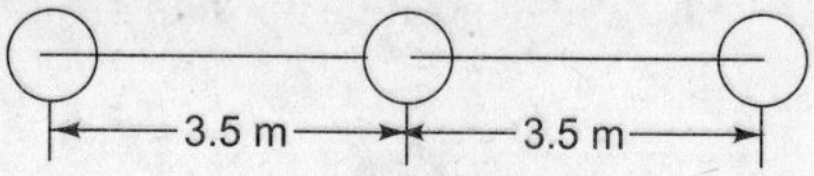

Fig. 3.14

Radius of conductor,

$$r = \frac{1}{2} \times 1.05 \times 10^{-2} = 5.23 \times 10^{-3} \text{ m}$$

Capacitance to neutral, $C_n = \dfrac{2\pi\varepsilon}{\ln\dfrac{D_m}{r}}$

where, ε = absolute permittivity = $\varepsilon_0\varepsilon_r$

ε_0 = permittivity of space = 8.854×10^{12} F/m

ε_r = relative permittivity = 1 (for aid)

D_m = mutual geometric main distance between the phases

$= D_{eq} = 4.5$ m

$$C_n = \frac{2\pi\varepsilon_0\varepsilon_r}{\ln\dfrac{D_m}{r}} = \frac{2\pi \times 8.854 \times 10^{-12}}{\ln\dfrac{4.5}{5.23 \times 10^{-3}}} = 8.26 \times 10^{-12} \text{ F/m}$$

$= 8.26 \times 10^{9}$ F/km $= 8.26 \times 10^{3}$ μF/km

Capacitive reactance to neutral,

$$X_c = \frac{1}{2\pi f C_n} = \frac{1}{2\pi \times 50 \times 8.26 \times 10^{-9}} = \Omega\text{/km}$$

$= 3.853 \times 10^5$ |/km

$$\text{Charging current, } I_c = \frac{V_m}{X_c} = \frac{110 \times 10^3/\sqrt{3}}{3.853 \times 10^5} = 0.1648 \text{ A/km}$$

$$\text{Reactive volt amperes generated by the line} = \frac{(V_L)^2}{X_C} = \frac{(110 \times 10^3)^2}{3.853 \times 10^5} = 31399 \text{ VAR} = 31.399 \text{ kVAR.}$$

3.8 ▶ METHOD OF GMD (MODIFIED)

A comparison of various expressions for inductance and capacitance of transmission lines [e.g., Eqs (2.22b) and (3.6)] brings out the fact that the two are similar except that in inductance expressions we have to use the fictitious conductor radius $r' = 0.7788r$, while in the expressions for capacitance actual conductor radius r is used. This fact suggests that the method of GMD (Geometric Mean Distance) would be applicable in the calculations for capacitance as well provided it is modified by using the outer conductor radius for finding D_s, the self geometric mean distance.

Example 3.3 can be conveniently solved as under by using the modified GMD method.

For the first section of the transposition cycle, mutual GMD is

$$D_{ab} = ((ig)\,(ig))^{1/4} = (ig)^{1/2}$$

$$D_{bc} = (ig)^{1/2}$$

$$D_{ca} = (jh)^{1/2}$$

$$\therefore \quad D_{eq} = (D_{ab}D_{bc}D_{ca})^{1/3} = [(i^2g^2jh)^{1/3}]^{1/2}$$

In the first section of the transposition cycle, self GMD is

$$D_{sa} = (rf\,rf)^{1/4} = (rf)^{1/2}$$

$$D_{sb} = (rd)^{1/2}$$

$$D_{sc} = (rf)^{1/2}$$

$$D_s = (D_{sa}D_{sb}D_{sc})^{1/3} = [(r^3f^2d)^{1/3}]^{1/2}$$

Now,

$$C_n = \frac{2\pi k}{\ln \dfrac{D_{eq}}{D_s}} = \frac{2\pi k}{\ln\left[\left(\dfrac{i^2g^2jh}{r^3f^2d}\right)^{1/3}\right]^{1/2}}$$

$$= \frac{4\pi k}{\ln\left(\dfrac{i^2g^2jh}{r^3f^2d}\right)^{1/3}} \text{ F/m}$$

This result obviously checks with the fundamentally derived expression in Example 3.3.

3.9 ▶ BUNDLED CONDUCTORS

A bundled conductor line is shown in Fig. 3.15. The conductors of any one bundle are in parallel, and it is assumed that the charge per bundle divides equally among the conductors of the bundle as $D_{12} >> d$. Also, $D_{12} - d \approx D_{12} + d \approx D_{12}$ for the same reason. The results obtained with these assumptions are fairly accurate for usual spacings. Thus, if the charge on phase a is q_a, the conductors a and a' have a charge of $q_a/2$ each; similarly the charge is equally divided for phases b and c.

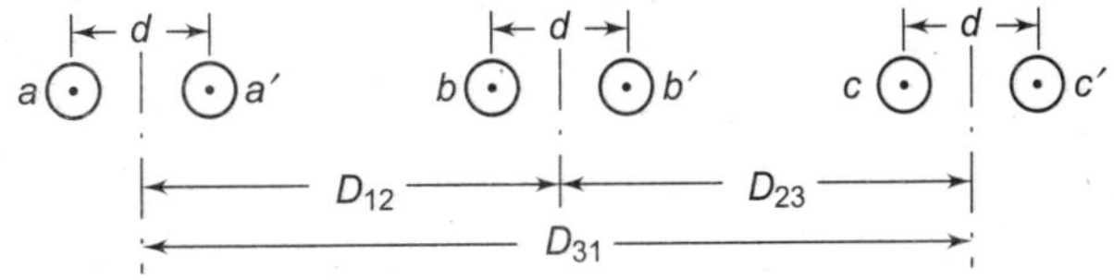

Fig. 3.15 *Cross-section of a bundled conductor three-phase transmission line*

Now, writing an equation for the voltage from conductor a to conductor b, we get

$$V_{ab} = \frac{1}{2\pi k}\left[0.5q_a\left(\ln\frac{D_{12}}{r} + \ln\frac{D_{12}}{d}\right) + 0.5q_b\left(\ln\frac{r}{D_{12}} + \ln\frac{d}{D_{12}}\right) + 0.5q_c\left(\ln\frac{D_{23}}{D_{31}} + \ln\frac{D_{23}}{D_{31}}\right)\right] \tag{3.43}$$

or,

$$V_{ab} = \frac{1}{2\pi k}\left(q_a \ln\frac{D_{12}}{\sqrt{rd}} + q_b \ln\frac{\sqrt{rd}}{D_{12}} + q_c \ln\frac{D_{23}}{D_{31}}\right) \tag{3.44}$$

Considering the line to be transposed and proceeding in the usual manner, the final result will be

$$C_n = \frac{0.0242}{\log(D_{eq}/\sqrt{rd})} \ \mu\text{F/km to neutral} \tag{3.45}$$

where $$D_{eq} = (D_{12}D_{23}D_{31})^{1/3}.$$

It is obvious from Eq. (2.42) that the method of modified GMD is equally valid in this case (as it should be).

3.10 ▶ ELECTROSTATIC INDUCTION

Transmission lines as mentioned in Ch. 2, establish both magnetic and electric fields. The electric field also affects the objects that lie in the proximity of the line. Electric fields, related to the voltage of the line, are the main cause of induction to vehicles, buildings and objects of comparable size. The human body is affected adversely by the electric discharges. It has been observed that the current densities in human bodies induced by electric fields are much higher than those induced by magnetic fields.

3.11 ▶ SUMMARY

In this chapter, the main shunt parameter of transmission namely capacitance has been thoroughly discussed including the effect of earth and bundled conductors and electrostatic induction is finally dealt with.

Problems

3.1 Derive an expression for the charge (complex) value per metre length of conductor a of an untransposed three-phase line shown in Fig. P-3.1. The applied voltage is balanced three-phase, 50 Hz. Take the voltage of phase a as reference phasor. All conductors have the same radii. Also find the charging current of phase a. Neglect the effect of ground.

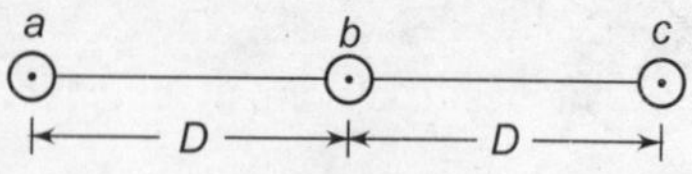

a b c
D D

Fig. P-3.1

3.2 A three-phase double-circuit line is shown in Fig. P-3.2. The diameter of each conductor is 2.0 cm. The line is transposed and carries balanced load. Find the capacitance per phase to neutral of the line.

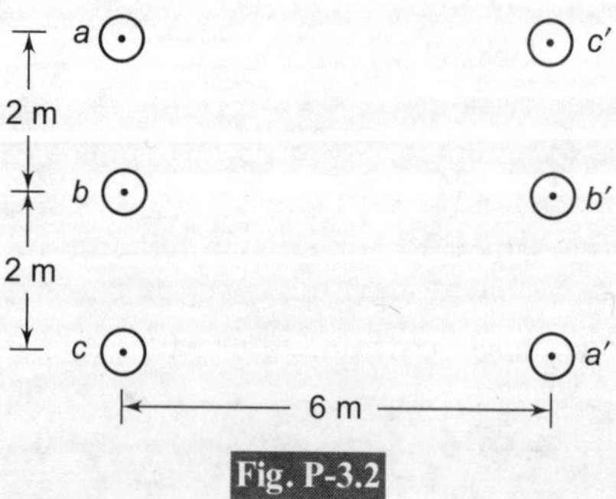

Fig. P-3.2

3.3 A three-phase, 50 Hz overhead line has regularly transposed conductors equilaterally spaced 4 m apart. The capacitance of such a line is 0.01 μF/km. Recalculate the capacitance per kilometre to neutral when the conductors are in the same horizontal plane with successive spacing of 4 m and are regularly transposed.

3.4 Consider the 500 kV, three-phase bundled conductor line as shown in Fig. P-2.9. Find the capacitive reactance to neutral in ohms/km at 50 Hz.

3.5 A three-phase transmission line has flat, horizontal spacing with 2 m between adjacent conductors. The radius of each conductor is 0.25 cm. At a certain instant the charges on the centre conductor and on one of the outside conductors are identical and voltage drop between these identically charged conductors is 775 V. Neglect the effect of ground, and find the value of the identical charge in coulomb/km at the instant specified.

3.6 Find the 50 Hz susceptance to neutral per kilometre of a double-circuit three phase line with transposition as shown in Fig. P-3.6. Given $D = 7$ m and radius of each of the six conductors is 1.38 cm.

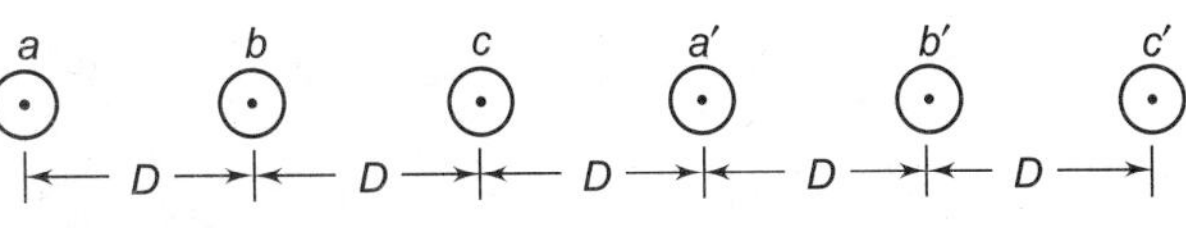

Fig. P-3.6 *Double circuit three-phase line with flat spacing*

3.7 A single conductor power cable has a conductor of No. 2 solid copper (radius = 0.328 cm). Paper insulation separating the conductor from the concentric lead sheath has a thickness of 2.5 mm and a relative permittivity of 3.8. The thickness of the lead sheath is 2 mm. Find the capacitive reactance per kilometre between the inner conductor and the lead sheath.

3.8 Find the capacitance of phase to neutral per kilometre of a three-phase line having conductors of 2 cm diameter placed at the corners of a triangle with sides 5 m, 6 m and 7 m respectively. Assume that the line is fully transposed and carries balanced load.

3.9 Derive an expression for the capacitance per metre length between two long parallel conductors, each of radius, r, with axes separated by a distance D, where $D \gg r$, the insulating medium being air. Calculate the maximum potential difference permissible between the conductors, if the electric field strength between them is not to exceed 25 kV/cm, r being 0.3 cm and $D = 35$ cm.

Multiple Choice Questions

3.1 The presence of earth in case of overhead lines
(a) Increases capacitance (b) Decreases capacitance
(c) Increases inductance (d) Decreases inductance

3.2 The term self GMD is used to calculate
(a) Capacitance (b) Inductance
(c) Both inductance and capacitance (d) Resistance

3.3 The presence of ground causes the line capacitance to
(a) Increase by about 12% (b) Decrease by about 12%
(c) Increase by about 0.2% (d) None of the above

3.4 If we increase the spacing between the phase conductors, the line capacitance
(a) Decreases (b) Increases (c) Remains the same (d) Not affected

3.5 If we increase the length of transmission line, the charging current
(a) Decreases (b) Increases (c) Remains the same (d) Not affected

3.6 When an alternating voltage is applied to the line, the line capacitance draws a
(a) Leading sinusoidal current (b) Lagging sinusoidal current
(c) A current in phase with voltage (d) None of the above

3.7 The capacitance becomes increasingly important for
(a) Short transmission lines (b) Medium transmission lines
(c) Both (a) and (b) (d) Long transmission lines

3.8 An infinitely long straight conductor carries a uniform charge of q coulomb per metre length. If k is permittivity of the medium wherein two points are located at distance D_1 and D_2 respectively from the conductor axis. The potential difference V_{12} (between the two points) is given by

(a) $V_{12} = \dfrac{q}{\pi k} \ln D_2/D_1$ (b) $V_{12} = \dfrac{q}{2\pi k} \ln \dfrac{D_1}{D_2}$

(c) $V_{12} = \dfrac{q}{2\pi k} \ln \dfrac{D_2}{D_1}$ (d) $V_{12} = \dfrac{q}{2\pi k} \log_{10} D_2/D_1$

3.9 Consider a two-wire line shown in figure excited from a single-phase source.

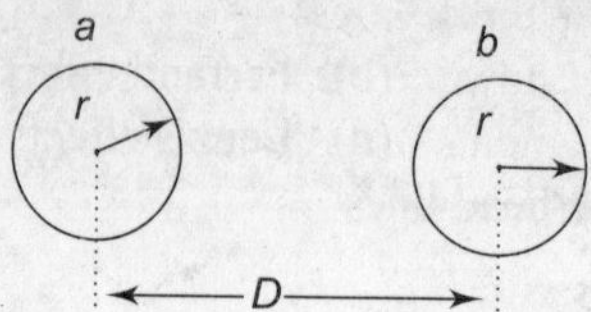

The line capacitance C_{ab} is given by

(a) $C_{ab} = \dfrac{0.0121}{\log(r/D)}$ μF/km (b) $C_{ab} = \dfrac{0.0121}{\log(D/r)}$ μF/km

(c) $C_{ab} = 0.0121 \log(D/r)$ μF/km (d) $C_{ab} = \dfrac{0.0121}{\log(D/r)}$ F/km

3.10 The method of images originally suggested by Lord Kelvin is used in
(a) Calculation of inductance (b) Calculation of resistance
(c) Effect of earth on line capacitance (d) None of the above

3.11 For a transmission line of length not more than 80 km, it is convenient to lump the capacitance at
(a) Receiving end (b) Sending end
(c) Midpoint (d) Anywhere along the line

3.12 At the no load conditions, the current is detected in the transmission line. This can be attributed due to
(a) corona effect (b) proximity effect
(c) capacitance effect (d) back flow through earth

3.13 Use of additional shunt capacitor can be made for increasing the capability of the line as it will
(a) increase phase shift (b) reduce surge impedance
(c) increase the angle α (d) all of the mentioned

3.14 To increase the transmission capability of a high voltage long line
(a) resistance can be increased (b) resistance can be decreased
(c) shunt admittance can be reduced (d) series reactance can be reduced

3.15 Skin effect
(a) Reduces the effective resistance but increases the effective internal reactance.
(b) Increases the effective resistance but reduces the effective internal reactance
(c) Reduces the effective resistance and effective internal reactance
(d) Increases the effective resistance and effective internal reactance

3.16 Transposition of transmission line is done to
(a) Reduce corona (b) Balance line voltage drop
(c) Reduced skin effect (d) Reduce line loss

3.17 Increase in frequency of transmission line causes
(a) No change in line resistance (b) Increases in line resistance
(c) Decreases in line resistance (d) Decreases in line series reactance

3.18 The main objective of the transposition of transmission line is to reduce the
(a) Line losses
(b) Capacitive effect
(c) Disturbance to nearby communication circuits
(d) Effect of surge voltages induced on the line

3.19 The conductor carries more current on the surface in comparison to its core. This phenomenon is called the
(a) Skin effect (b) Ferranti effect
(c) Corona (d) Lenz's effect

3.20 The presence of earth in case of overhead lines
(a) Increases the capacitance
(b) Increases the inductance
(c) Decreases the capacitance and increases the inductance
(d) Does not affect any of the line constants

3.21 Skin effect in transmission line is due to
(a) Supply frequency
(b) Self-inductance of conductor
(c) High sensitivity of material in the centre
(d) Both (a) and (b)

3.22 If the effect of earth is taken into account, then the capacitance of line to ground
(a) Decreases (b) Increases
(c) Remains unaltered (d) Becomes infinite

3.23 In a transmission line the distributed constants are
(a) Resistance and shunt conductance only
(b) Resistance and inductance only
(c) Resistance, inductance and capacitance only
(d) Resistance, inductance, capacitance and shunt conductance.

3.24 The presence of earth in case of overhead lines
(a) Increases the capacitance (b) Increases the inductance
(c) Decreases the capacitance (d) Decreases the inductance

3.25 A three-phase 50 Hz transmission line has a capacitance of line to neutral $C_n = 0.01$ μF/km. The voltage of the line is 100 kV. The charging current per kilometre of line is

(a) $\frac{314}{\sqrt{3}}$ A/km (b) $\frac{314}{\sqrt{3}\times 10^3}$ A/km

(c) $\frac{\sqrt{3}\times 10^3}{314}$ A/km (d) $\sqrt{3}\times 10^3$ A/km

References

Books

1. W.D. Stevenson, *Elements of Power System Analysis*, 4th edn, McGraw-Hill, New York, 1982.
2. H. Cotton and H. Barber, *The Transmission and Distribution of Electrical Energy*, 3rd edn, Hodder and Stoughton, 1970.
3. A.T. Starr, *Generation, Transmission and Utilisation of Electric Power*, Pitman, 1962.

Papers

4. J.E. Parton and A. Wright, "Electric Stresses Associated with Bundle Conductors", *International Journal of Electrical Engineering Education,* volume: 3, p: 357, 1965.
5. R.A. Stevens and D.M. German, "The Capacitance and Inductance of Overhead Transmission Lines", *International Journal of Electrical Engineering & Education,* volume: 2, p: 71, 1964.
6. H.E. Green, "A Simplified Derivation of the Capacitance of a Two-Wire Transmission Line", *IEEE Transactions on Microwave Theory and Techniques*, volume: 47, issue: 3, pp. 365–366, 1999.
7. Mohamed Saih, Hicham Rouijaa, Abdelilah Ghammaz, "Computation of Multi-Conductor Transmission Line Capacitance Using Method of Moment", *Proceedings of 2014 Mediterranean Microwave Symposium, Marrakech*, pp: 1–6, 2014.
8. M.T. Correia de Barros, "Identification of the Capacitance Coefficients of Multiphase Transmission Lines Exhibiting Corona under Transient Conditions", *IEEE Transactions on Power Delivery*, volume: 10, issue: 3, pp: 1642–1648, 1995.
9. "IEEE Guide for the Parameter Measurement of AC Transmission Lines", *IEEE Standard* 1870–2019, pp: 1–99, 2019.
10. Zhiwei Mi, Feng Ji, Lu Gao, Chang Lin, Linyu Hou, and Gang Liu, "Capacitance Calculation of Overhead Transmission Line Based on Moment Method", *2019 4th IEEE Workshop on the Electronic Grid (eGRID), Xiamen, China*, pp: 1–5, 2019.
11. Sarhan M. Musa and Matthew N.O. Sadiku, "Application of the Finite Element Method in Calculating the Capacitance and Inductance of Multiconductor Transmission Lines", *IEEE SoutheastCon 2008, Huntsville, AL*, pp: 300–304, 2008.
12. D.F. Williams and R.B. Marks, "Transmission Line Capacitance Measurement", *IEEE Microwave and Guided Wave Letters*, volume: 1, issue: 9, pp: 243–245, 1991.
13. Putu Agus Aditya Pramana, Aristo Adi Kusuma, and Buyung Sofiarto Munir, "Evaluation of Transmission Line Parameter for Non-horizontal Earth Contour", *IEEE International Conference on Smart Green Technology in Electrical and Information Systems, Bali*, pp: 144–148, 2016.
14. "IEEE Approved Draft Guide for the Parameter Measurement of AC Transmission Lines", *IEEE P1870/D7, October 2018*, volume: 1, issue: 1, pp: 1–90, 2019.
15. D.F. Williams and R.B. Marks, "Transmission Line Capacitance Measurement", *IEEE Microwave and Guided Wave Letters*, volume: 1, issue: 9, pp: 243–245, 1991.
16. A.E. Ruehli and P.A. Brennan, "Efficient Capacitance Calculations for Three-Dimensional Multi-conductor Systems", *IEEE Transactions on Microwave Theory and Techniques*, volume: 21, issue: 2, pp: 76–82, 1973.
17. M.J. Degerstrom, B.K. Gilbert, and E.S. Daniel, "Accurate Resistance, Inductance, Capacitance and Conductance (RLCG) from Uniform Transmission Line Measurements", *IEEE-EPEP Conference on Electrical Performance of Electronic Packaging, San Jose, CA*, pp: 77–80, 2008.
18. B.N. Das, S. Das, and D. Parida, "Capacitance of Transmission Line of Parallel Cylinders with Variable Radial Width", *IEEE Transactions on Electromagnetic Compatibility*, volume: 40, issue: 4, pp: 325–330, 1998.
19. H.E. Green, J.D. Cashman, and W.J. Getsinger, "A Comparison of Two Recently Proposed Formulas for End Capacitance in Open Circuited, Two Wire Transmission Lines [and reply]", *IEEE Transactions on Microwave Theory and Techniques*, volume: 42, issue: 5, pp: 921–922, 1994.
20. S. Gajare, A.K. Pradhan, and V. Terzija, "A Method for Accurate Parameter Estimation of Series Compensated Transmission Lines Using Synchronized Data", *2018 IEEE Power & Energy Society General Meeting (PESGM), Portland, OR*, pp: 1–1, 2018.

CHAPTER

4

Representation of Power System Components

4.1 ▶ INTRODUCTION

A complete diagram of a power system representing all the three phases becomes too complicated for a system of practical size, so much so that it may no longer convey the information it is intended to convey. It is much more practical to represent a power system by means of simple symbols for each component resulting in what is called *a one-line diagram.*

Per unit system leads to great simplification of three-phase networks involving transformers. An impedance diagram drawn on a per unit basis does not require ideal transformers to be included in it.

An important element of a power system is the synchronous machine, which greatly influences the system behaviour during both steady state and transient conditions. The synchronous machine model in steady state is presented in this chapter. The transient model of the machine will be presented in Ch. 9.

4.2 ▶ SINGLE-PHASE REPRESENTATION OF BALANCED THREE-PHASE NETWORKS

The solution of a three-phase network under balanced conditions is easily carried out by solving the single-phase network corresponding to the reference phase. Figure 4.1 shows a simple, balanced three-phase network. The generator and load neutrals are therefore at the same potential, so that $I_n = 0$. Thus, the neutral impedance Z_n does not affect network behaviour. For the reference phase a

$$E_a = (Z_G + Z_L)I_a \tag{4.1}$$

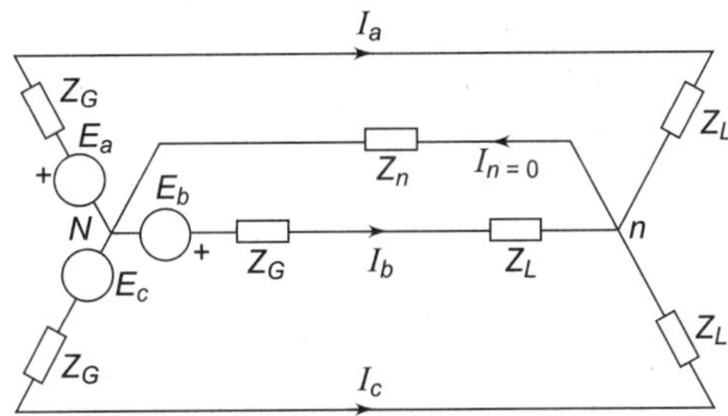

Fig. 4.1 *Balanced three-phase network*

The currents and voltages in the other phases have the same magnitude but are progressively shifted in phase by 120°. Equation (4.1) corresponds to the single-phase network of Fig. 4.2 whose solution completely determines the solution of the three-phase network.

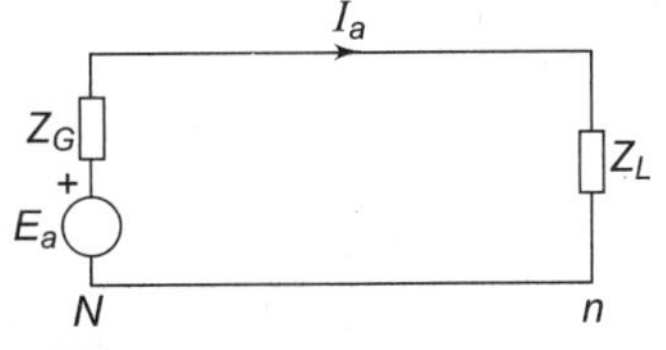

Fig. 4.2 *Single-phase equivalent of a balanced three-phase network of Fig. 4.1*

Consider now the case where a three-phase transformer forms part of a three-phase system. If the transformer is *Y*/*Y* connected as shown in Fig. 4.3(a), in the single-phase equivalent of the three-phase circuit it can be obviously represented by a single-phase transformer [as in Fig. 4.3(b)] with primary and secondary pertaining to phase a of the three-phase transformer.

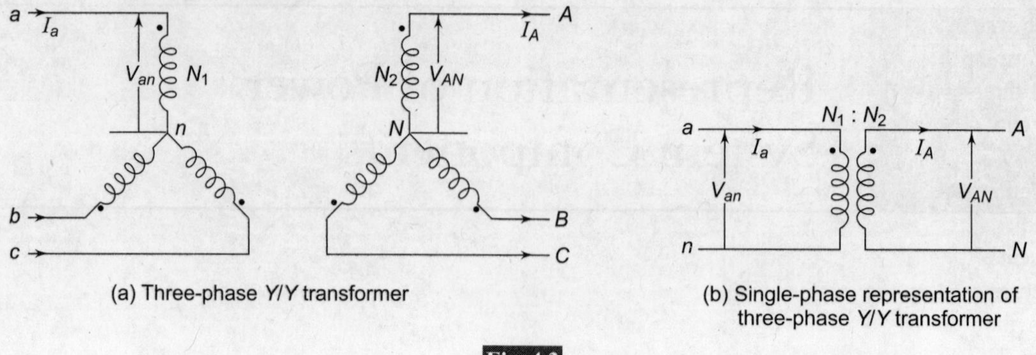

(a) Three-phase *Y*/*Y* transformer

(b) Single-phase representation of three-phase *Y*/*Y* transformer

Fig. 4.3

If the transformer is *Y*/Δ connected as in Fig. 4.4(a), the delta side has to be replaced by an equivalent star connection as shown dotted so as to obtain the single-phase equivalent of Fig. 4.4(b). An important fact has, however, to be observed here. On the delta side, the voltage to neutral V_{AN} and line current I_A have a certain phase angle shift* from the star side values V_{an} and I_a (90º for the phase labelling shown). In the single-phase equivalent, (V_{AN}, I_A) are respectively in phase with (V_{an}, I_a). Since both phase voltage and line current shift through the same phase angle from star to delta side, the transformer per phase impedance and power flow are preserved in the single-phase equivalent. In most analytical studies, we are merely interested in the magnitude of voltages and currents so that the single-phase equivalent of Fig. 4.4(b) is an acceptable proposition. Wherever proper phase angles of currents and voltages are needed, correction can be easily applied after obtaining the solution through a single-phase transformer equivalent.

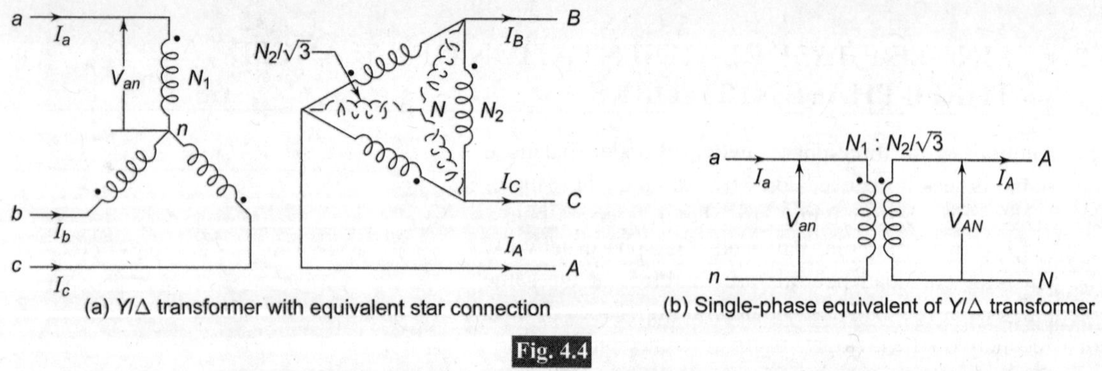

(a) *Y*/Δ transformer with equivalent star connection

(b) Single-phase equivalent of *Y*/Δ transformer

Fig. 4.4

It may be noted here that irrespective of the type of connection, the transformation ratio of the single-phase equivalent of a three-phase transformer is the same as the line-to-line transformation ratio.

4.3 ► THE ONE-LINE DIAGRAM AND THE IMPEDANCE OR REACTANCE DIAGRAM

A one-line diagram of a power system shows the main connections and arrangements of components. Any particular component may or may not be shown depending on the information required in a system study, e.g., circuit breakers need not be shown in a load flow study but are a must for a protection study.

* See Section 10.3.

Power system networks are represented by one-line diagrams using suitable symbols for generators, motors, transformers and loads. It is a convenient practical way of network representation rather than drawing the actual three-phase diagram which may indeed be quite cumbersome and confusing for a practical size power network. Generator and transformer connections—star, delta and neutral grounding are indicated by symbols drawn by the side of the representation of these elements. Circuit breakers are represented as rectangular blocks. Figure 4.5 shows the one-line diagram of a simple power system. The reactance data of the elements are given below.

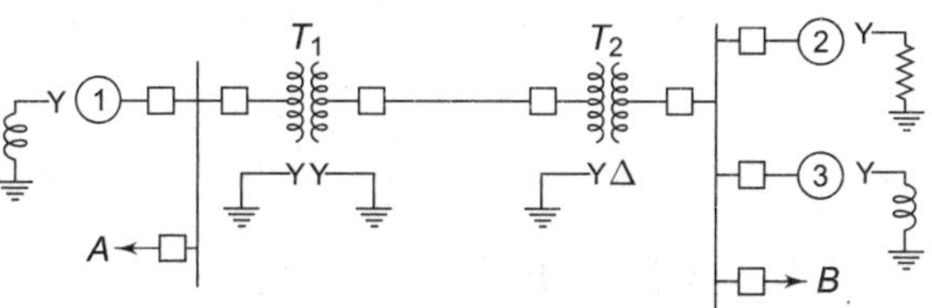

Fig. 4.5 *One-line representation of a simple power system*

Generator No. 1	30 MVA,	10.5 kV,	$X'' = 1.6$ ohms
Generator No. 2	15 MVA,	6.6 kV,	$X'' = 1.2$ ohms
Generator No. 3	25 MVA,	6.6 kV,	$X'' = 0.56$ ohms
Transformer T_1	15 MVA, (3 phase)	33/11 kV,	$X = 15.2$ ohms per phase on high tension side
Transformer T_2	15 MVA, (3 phase)	33/6.2 kV,	$X = 16$ ohms per phase on high tension side
Transmission line 20.5 ohms/phase			
Load A	40 MW,	11 kV,	0.9 lagging power factor
Load B	40 MW,	6.6 kV,	0.85 lagging power factor

Note: Generators are specified in three-phase MVA, line-to-line voltage and per phase reactance (equivalent star). Transformers are specified in three-phase MVA, line-to-line transformation ratio and per phase (equivalent star) impedance on one side. Loads are specified in three-phase MW, line-to-line voltage and power factor.

The impedance diagram on single-phase basis for use under balanced operating conditions can be easily drawn from the one-line diagram. For the system of Fig. 4.5, the impedance diagram is drawn in Fig. 4.6. Single-phase transformer equivalents are shown as ideal transformers with transformer impedances indicated on the appropriate side. Magnetising reactances of the transformers have been neglected. This is a fairly good approximation for most power system studies. The generators are represented as voltage sources with series resistance and inductive reactance (synchronous machine model will be discussed in Section 4.6). The transmission line is represented by a π-model (to be discussed in Ch. 5). Loads are assumed to be passive (not involving rotating machines) and are represented by resistance and inductive reactance in series. Neutral grounding impedances do not appear in the diagram as balanced conditions are assumed.

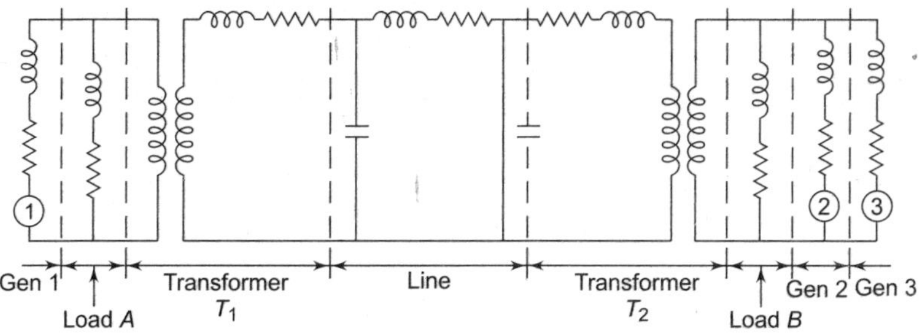

Fig. 4.6 *Impedance diagram of the power system of Fig. 4.5*

Three voltage levels (6.6, 11 and 33 kV) are present in this system. The analysis would proceed by transforming all voltages and impedances to any selected voltage level, say that of the transmission line (33 kV). The voltages of generators are transformed in the ratio of transformation and all impedances by the square of ratio of transformation. This is a very cumbersome procedure for a large network with several voltage levels. The per unit method discussed in the next section is the most convenient for power system analysis and will be used throughout this book.

4.4 ▶ PER UNIT (PU) SYSTEM

It is usual to express voltage, current, voltamperes and impedance of an electrical circuit in per unit (or percentage) of base or reference values of these quantities. The per unit* value of any quantity is defined as:

$$\frac{\text{the actual value in any units}}{\text{the base or reference value in the same units}}$$

The per unit method is particularly convenient in power systems as the various sections of a power system are connected through transformers and have different voltage levels.

Consider first a single-phase system. Let,

$$\text{Base voltamperes} = (\text{VA})_B$$

$$\text{Base voltage} = V_B \text{ V}$$

Then,

$$\text{Base current } I_B = \frac{(\text{VA})_B}{V_B} \text{ A} \tag{4.2a}$$

$$\text{Base impedance } Z_B = \frac{V_B}{I_B} = \frac{V_B^2}{(\text{VA})_B} \text{ ohms} \tag{4.2b}$$

If the actual impedance is Z (ohms), its per unit value is given by

$$Z(\text{pu}) = \frac{Z}{Z_B} = \frac{Z(\text{ohms}) \times (\text{VA})_B}{V_B^2} \tag{4.3}$$

For a power system, practical choice of base values are:

$$\text{Base megavoltamperes} = (\text{MVA})_B$$

or,

$$\text{Base kilovoltamperes} = (\text{kVA})_B$$

$$\text{Base kilovolts} = (\text{kV})_B$$

$$\text{Base current } I_B = \frac{1000 \times (\text{MVA})_B}{(\text{kV})_B} = \frac{(\text{kVA})_B}{(\text{kV})_B} \text{ A} \tag{4.4}$$

$$\text{Base impedance } Z_B = \frac{1000 \times (\text{kV})_B}{I_B}$$

$$= \frac{(\text{kV})_B^2}{(\text{MVA})_B} = \frac{1000 \times (\text{kV})_B^2}{(\text{kVA})_B} \text{ ohms} \tag{4.5}$$

$$\text{Per unit impedance } Z(\text{pu}) = \frac{Z(\text{ohms}) \times (\text{MVA})_B}{(\text{kV})_B^2} \tag{4.6}$$

$$= \frac{Z(\text{ohms}) \times (\text{kVA})_B}{(\text{kV})_B^2 \times 1000}$$

---

* Per cent value = per unit value × 100.
Per cent value is not convenient for use as the factor of 100 has to be carried in computations.

In a three-phase system rather than obtaining the per unit values using per phase base quantities, the per unit values can be obtained directly by using three-phase base quantities. Let,

$$\text{Three-phase base megavoltamperes} = (\text{MVA})_B$$

$$\text{Line-to-line base kilovolts} = (\text{kV})_B$$

Assuming star connection (equivalent star can always be found),

$$\text{Base current } I_B = \frac{1000 \times (\text{MVA})_B}{\sqrt{3}(\text{kV})_B} \text{ A} \tag{4.7}$$

$$\text{Base impedance } Z_B = \frac{1000 \times (\text{kV})_B}{\sqrt{3}\, I_B} \text{ ohms}$$

$$= \frac{(\text{kV})_B^2}{(\text{MVA})_B} = \frac{1000 \times (\text{kV})_B^2}{(\text{kVA})_B} \text{ ohms} \tag{4.8}$$

$$\text{Per unit impedance } Z\,(\text{pu}) = \frac{Z(\text{ohms}) \times (\text{MVA})_B}{(\text{kV})_B^2} \tag{4.9}$$

$$= \frac{Z(\text{ohms}) \times (\text{kVA})_B}{(\text{kV})_B^2 \times 1{,}000}$$

When MVA base is changed from $(\text{MVA})_{B,\text{ old}}$ to $(\text{MVA})_{B,\text{ new}}$, and kV base is changed from $(\text{kV})_{B,\text{ old}}$, to $(\text{kV})_{B,\text{ new}}$, the new per unit impedance from Eq. (4.9) is given by

$$Z\,(\text{pu})_{\text{new}} = Z(\text{pu})_{\text{old}} \times \frac{(\text{MVA})_{B,\text{ new}}}{(\text{MVA})_{B,\text{ old}}} \times \frac{(\text{kV})_{B,\text{old}}^2}{(\text{kV})_{B,\text{new}}^2} \tag{4.10}$$

4.4.1 Per Unit Representation of a Transformer

It has been said in Sec. 4.2 that a three-phase transformer forming part of a three-phase system can be represented by a single-phase transformer in obtaining per phase solution of the system. The delta connected winding of the transformer is replaced by an equivalent star so that the transformation ratio of the equivalent single-phase transformer is always the line-to-line voltage ratio of the three-phase transformer.

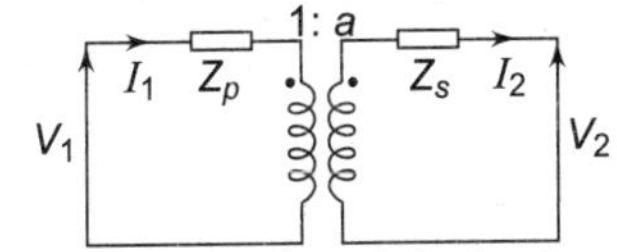

(a) Representation of single-phase transformer (magnetizing impedance neglected)

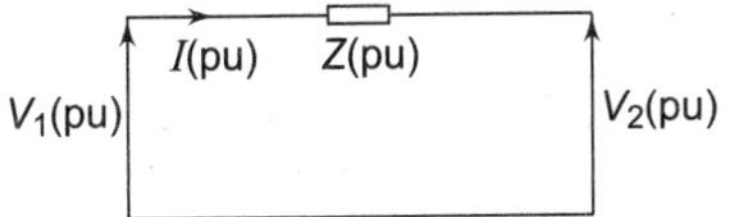

(b) Per unit equivalent circuit of single-phase transformer

Fig. 4.7

Figure 4.7(a) represents a single-phase transformer in terms of primary and secondary leakage reactances Z_p and Z_s and an ideal transformer of ratio 1:a. The magnetising impedance is neglected. Let us choose a voltampere base of $(\text{VA})_B$ and voltage bases on the two sides of the transformer in the ratio of transformation, i.e.

$$\frac{V_{1B}}{V_{2B}} = \frac{1}{a} \tag{4.11a}$$

Therefore,

$$\frac{V_{1B}}{V_{2B}} = a \text{ (as } (\text{VA})_B \text{ is common)} \tag{4.11b}$$

$$Z_{1B} = \frac{V_{1B}}{I_{1B}},\ Z_{2B} = \frac{V_{2B}}{I_{2B}} \tag{4.11c}$$

From Fig. 4.7(a), we can write

$$V_2 = (V_1 - I_1 Z_p)\, a - I_2 Z_s \tag{4.12}$$

We shall convert Eq. (4.12) into per unit form

$$V_2(\text{pu})V_{2B} = [V_1(\text{pu})V_{1B} - I_1(\text{pu})I_{1B}Z_p(\text{pu})Z_{1B}]$$
$$a - I_2(\text{pu})I_{2B}Z_s(\text{pu})Z_{2B}$$

Dividing by V_{2B} throughout and using base relations (4.11a, b, c), we get

$$V_2(\text{pu}) = V_1(\text{pu}) - I_1(\text{pu})Z_p(\text{pu}) - I_2(\text{pu})Z_s(\text{pu}) \tag{4.13}$$

Now,
$$\frac{I_1}{I_2} = \frac{I_{1B}}{I_{2B}} = a$$

or,
$$\frac{I_1}{I_{1B}} = \frac{I_2}{I_{2B}}$$

∴
$$I_1(\text{pu}) = I_2(\text{pu}) = I\,(\text{pu})$$

Equation (4.13) can therefore be written as

$$V_2(\text{pu}) = V_1(\text{pu}) - I(\text{pu})Z(\text{pu}) \tag{4.14}$$

where,

$$Z(\text{pu}) = Z_p(\text{pu}) + Z_s(\text{pu})$$

Equation (4.14) can be represented by the simple equivalent circuit of Fig. 4.7(b) which does not require an ideal transformer. Considerable simplification has therefore been achieved by the per unit method with a common voltampere base and voltage bases on the two sides in the ratio of transformation.

Z(pu) can be determined directly from the equivalent impedance on primary or secondary side of a transformer by using the appropriate impedance base.

On primary side:

$$Z_1 = Z_p + Z_s/a^2$$

$$Z_1(\text{pu}) = \frac{Z_1}{Z_{1B}} = \frac{Z_p}{Z_{1B}} + \frac{Z_s}{Z_{1B}} \times \frac{1}{a^2}$$

But,

$$a^2 Z_{1B} = Z_{2B}$$

∴
$$Z_1(\text{pu}) = Z_p(\text{pu}) + Z_s(\text{pu}) = Z(\text{pu}) \tag{4.15}$$

On secondary side:

$$Z_2 = Z_S + a^2 Z_p$$

$$Z_2(\text{pu}) = \frac{Z_2}{Z_{2B}} = \frac{Z_s}{Z_{2B}} + a^2\frac{Z_p}{Z_{2B}}$$

or,
$$Z_2(\text{pu}) = Z_s(\text{pu}) + Z_p(\text{pu}) = Z(\text{pu}) \tag{4.16}$$

Thus, the per unit impedance of a transformer is the same whether computed from primary or secondary side so long as the voltage bases on the two sides are in the ratio of transformation (equivalent per phase ratio of a three-phase transformer which is the same as the ratio of line-to-line voltage rating).

The pu transformer impedance of a three-phase transformer is conveniently obtained by direct use of three-phase MVA base and line-to-line kV base in relation (4.9). Any other impedance on either side of a transformer is converted to pu value just like Z_p or Z_s.

4.4.2 Per Unit Impedance Diagram of a Power System

From a one-line diagram of a power system, we can directly draw the impedance diagram by following the steps given below:

1. Choose an appropriate common MVA (or kVA) base for the system.
2. Consider the system to be divided into a number of sections by the transformers. Choose an appropriate kV base in one of the sections. Calculate kV bases of other sections in the ratio of transformation.
3. Calculate per unit values of voltages and impedances in each section and connect them up as per the topology of the one-line diagram. The result is the single-phase per unit impedance diagram.

The above steps are illustrated by the following examples.

Example 4.1 Obtain the per unit impedance (reactance) diagram of the power system of Fig. 4.5.

Solution The per phase impedance diagram of the power system of Fig. 4.5 has been drawn in Fig. 4.6. We shall make some further simplifying assumptions.

1. Line capacitance and resistance are neglected so that it is represented as a series reactance only.
2. We shall assume that the impedance diagram is meant for short circuit studies. Current drawn by static loads under short circuit conditions can be neglected. Loads A and B are therefore ignored.

Let us convert all reactances to per unit form. Choose a common three-phase MVA base of 30 and a voltage base of 33 kV line-to-line on the transmission line. Then the voltage base in the circuit of generator 1 is 11 kV line-to-line and that in the circuits of generators 2 and 3 is 6.2 kV.

The per unit reactances of various components are calculated below:

$$\text{Transmission line: } \frac{20.5\times 30}{(33)^2} = 0.564$$

$$\text{Transformer } T_1\text{: } \frac{15.2\times 30}{(33)^2} = 0.418$$

$$\text{Transformer } T_2\text{: } \frac{16\times 30}{(33)^2} = 0.44$$

$$\text{Generator 1: } \frac{1.6\times 30}{(11)^2} = 0.396$$

$$\text{Generator 2: } \frac{1.2\times 30}{(6.2)^2} = 0.939$$

$$\text{Generator 3: } \frac{0.56\times 30}{(6.2)^2} = 0.437$$

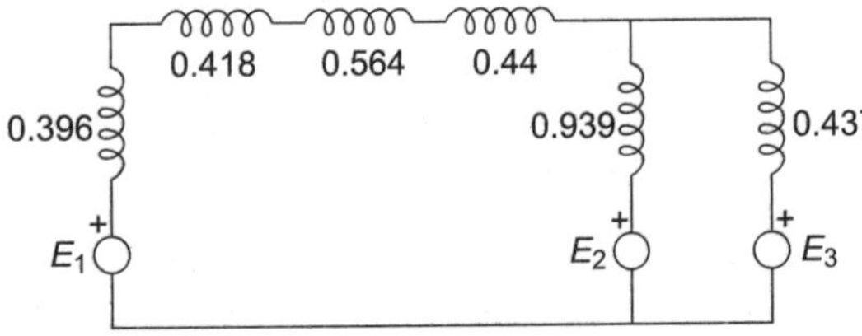

Fig. 4.8(a) *Reactance diagram of the system of Fig. 4.5 (loads neglected)*

The reactance diagram of the system is shown in Fig. 4.8(a).

E_1, E_2 and E_3 are per unit values of voltages to which the generators are excited. Quite often in a short circuit study, these will be taken as $1 \angle 0°$ pu (no load condition).

Example 4.2 The reactance data of generators and transformers are usually specified in pu (or per cent) values, based on equipment ratings rather than in actual ohmic values as given in Example 4.1; while the transmission line impedances may be given in actual values. Let us resolve Example 4.1 by assuming the following pu values of reactances:

Transformer T_1:	0.209
Transformer T_2:	0.220
Generator G_1:	0.435
Generator G_2:	0.413
Generator G_3:	0.3214

Solution With a base MVA of 30, base voltage of 11 kV in the circuit of generator 1 and base voltage of 6.2 kV in the circuit of generators 2 and 3 as used in Example 4.1, we now calculate the pu values of the reactances of transformers and generators as per relation (4.10):

Transformer T_1: $$0.209 \times \frac{30}{15} = 0.418$$

Transformer T_2: $$0.22 \times \frac{30}{15} = 0.44$$

Generator 1: $$0.435 \times \frac{(10.5)^2}{(11)^2} = 0.396$$

Generator 2: $$0.413 \times \frac{30}{15} \times \frac{(6.6)^2}{(6.2)^2} = 0.936$$

Generator 3: $$0.3214 \times \frac{30}{25} \times \frac{(6.6)^2}{(6.2)^2} = 0.437$$

Obviously these values are the same as obtained already in Example 4.1.

Example 4.3 The one-line diagram of a power system is shown in Fig. 4.8(b). The generator supplies a number of synchronous motors over a 64 km transmission line having transformers at both ends as shown on the one-line diagram. The generator, transformers and motors are rated as follows:

Generator : 300 MVA, 20 kV, $X'' = 20\%$

Motor M_1 : Rated input = 200 MVA, 13.2 kV, $X'' = 20\%$. The neutral of motor M_1 is grounded through reactance

Motor M_2 : Rated input = 100 MVA, 13.2 kV, $X'' = 20\%$. The neutral of the motor M_2 is not connected to ground as an unusual condition

Transformer T_1 : 350 MVA, 230/20 kV with leakage reactance of 10%

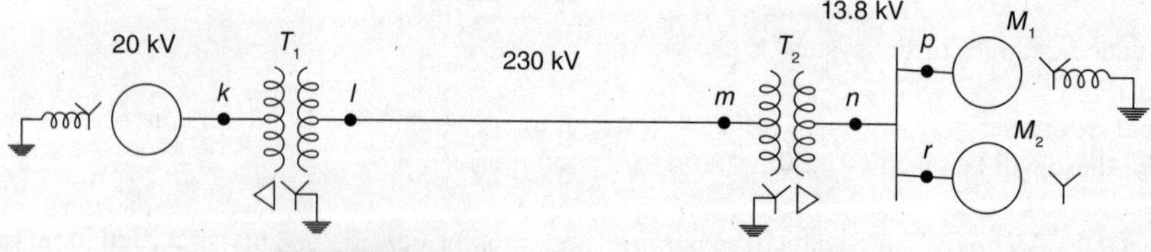

Fig. 4.8(b) *One line diagram of the system of example 4.3*

Transformer T_2 : Composed of three single-phase transformers, each rated 100 MVA, 127/13.2 kV with leakage reactance of 10%

The Series reactance of the transmission line is 0.5 ohm/km. Draw the reactance diagram with all reactance marked in per unit. Select the generator rating as base in the generator circuit.

Solution The transformer T_2 is composed of three single-phase transformers with 100 MVA individual power ratings. The three-phase rating of transformer T_2 is 3 × 100 = 300 kVA and its line-to-line voltage ratio is

$$\sqrt{3}\times\frac{127}{13.2}=\frac{220}{13.2}\text{ kV}$$

A base of 300 MVA, 20 kV in the generator circuit requires a 300 MVA base in all parts of the system and the following voltage bases:

In the transmission line: 230 kV (since T_1 is rated 230/20 kV)

$$\text{In the motor circuit: } 230\frac{13.2}{220}=13.8\text{ kV}$$

The reactance of the transformers converted to the proper base are

$$\text{Transformer } T_1: \quad X=0.1\times\frac{300}{350}=0.0857\text{ per unit}$$

$$\text{Transformer } T_2: \quad X=0.1\times\left(\frac{13.2}{13.2}\right)^2=0.0915\text{ per unit}$$

The base impedance of the transmission line is

$$\frac{(230)^2}{300}=176.3\ \Omega$$

The reactance of the line is

$$\frac{0.5\times 64}{176.3}=0.1815\text{ per unit}$$

$$\text{Reactance of motor } M_1=0.2\left(\frac{300}{200}\right)\left(\frac{13.2}{13.8}\right)^2=0.2745\text{ per unit}$$

$$\text{Reactance of motor } M_2=0.2\left(\frac{300}{100}\right)\left(\frac{13.2}{13.8}\right)^2=0.5490\text{ per unit}$$

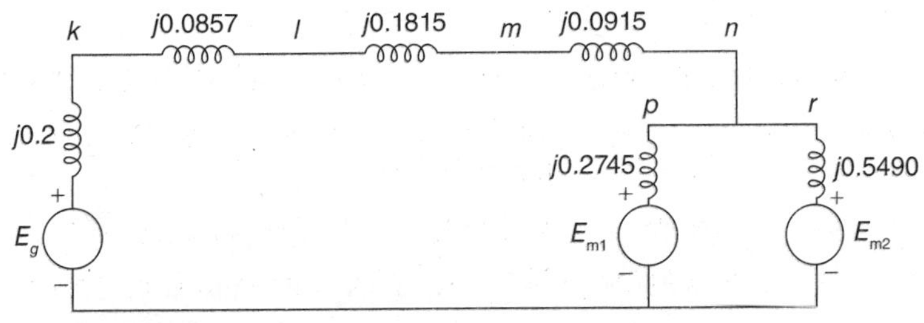

Fig. 4.8(c) *Reactance diagram of the system of Fig. 4.8(b)*

Example 4.4 If the motors M_1 and M_2 of Example 4.3 have inputs of 120 and 60 MW respectively at 13.2 kV, and both operate at unity power factor, find the voltage at the terminals of the generator and the voltage regulation of the line.

Solution Both the motors take 180 MW together, or

$$\frac{180}{300} = 0.6 \text{ per unit}$$

Therefore, with V and I at the motors in per unit,

$$|V| \times |I| = 0.6 \text{ per unit}$$

With phase-a voltage at the motor terminals as reference, we have

$$V = \frac{13.2}{13.8} = 0.9565\angle 0° \text{ per unit}$$

$$I = \frac{0.6}{0.9565} = 0.6273\angle 0° \text{ per unit}$$

Phase-a per unit voltage at other points of Fig. 4.8(c) are

At m: $V = 0.9565 + 0.6273(j0.0915)$

$0.9565 + j0.0574 = 0.9582\angle 3.434°$ per unit

At l: $V = 0.9565 + 0.6273(j0.0915 + j0.1815)$

$0.9565 + j0.1713 = 0.9717\angle 10.154°$ per unit

At k: $V = 0.9565 + 0.6273(j0.0915 + j0.1815 + j0.0857)$

$0.9565 + j0.2250 = 0.9826\angle 13.237°$ per unit

The voltage regulation of the line is

$$\text{Percent regulation} = \frac{0.9826 - 0.9582}{0.9582} \times 100 = 2.55\%$$

And the magnitude of the voltage at the generator terminal is

$$0.9826 \times 20 = 19.652 \text{ kV}$$

If it is desired to show the phase shifts due to the $Y - \Delta$ transformers, the angles of the phase-a voltages at m and l should be increased by 30°. Then the angle of the phase-a current in the line should also be increased by 30° from 0°.

Example 4.5 The one-line diagram of a power system is shown in Fig. 4.8(d). The generator is connected to the motors through a transmission line and transformers as shown in the one-line diagram. The generator, transformers and motors are rated as follows:

Generator : 100 MVA, 33 kV, 3-phase, sub-transient reactance = 15%

Motor M_1 : Rated input = 30 MVA, 30 kV, sub-transient reactance = 20%

Motor M_2 : Rated input = 20 MVA, 30 kV, sub-transient reactance = 20%

Motor M_3 : Rated input = 50 MVA, 30 kV, sub-transient reactance = 20%

Transformers T_1 and T_2 : 110 MVA, 32 kV/110 kV ($\Delta - Y$ connections) with leakage reactance of 8%

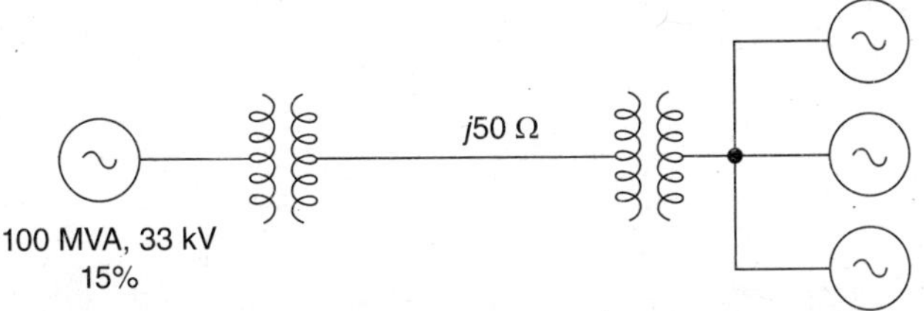

Fig. 4.8(d) *One line diagram of the system of example 4.5*

The transmission line has a reactance of 50 Ω. Selecting the generator rating as the base quantities in the generator circuit, determine the base quantities in other parts of the power system and evaluate the corresponding pu values.

Solution Considering the base values as 100 MVA and 33 kV in the generator circuit, the pu reactance of generator will be 15%. The base value of voltage in the transmission line will be

$$33 \times \frac{110}{32} = 113.43 \text{ kV}$$

The voltage in the motor circuit will be

$$113.43 \times \frac{32}{110} = 33 \text{ kV}$$

The reactance of the transformer is 8% corresponding to 110 MVA, 32 kV. Therefore, corresponding to 100 MVA and 33 kV, the per unit reactance will be

$$0.08 \times \frac{100}{110} \times \left(\frac{32}{33}\right)^2 = 0.0684 \text{ pu}$$

$$\text{The impedance value of transmission line} = \frac{50 \times 100}{(113.43)^2} = 0.3886 \text{ pu}$$

$$\text{The reactance value of motor } M_1 = 0.2 \times \frac{100}{30} \times \left(\frac{30}{33}\right)^2 = 0.551 \text{ pu}$$

$$\text{The reactance value of motor } M_2 = 0.2 \times \frac{100}{20} \times \left(\frac{30}{33}\right)^2 = 0.826 \text{ pu}$$

$$\text{The reactance value of motor } M_3 = 0.2 \times \frac{100}{50} \times \left(\frac{30}{33}\right)^2 = 0.3305 \text{ pu}$$

The reactance diagram of the power system is shown in Fig. 4.8(e).

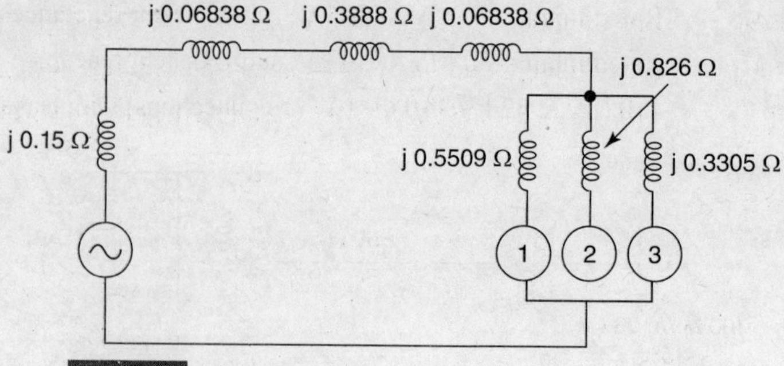

Fig. 4.8(e) *Reactance diagram of the system of Fig. 4.8(d)*

4.5 ▶ COMPLEX POWER

Consider a single-phase load fed from a source as in Fig. 4.9. Let,

$$V = |V| \angle \delta$$
$$I = |I| \angle (\delta - \theta)$$

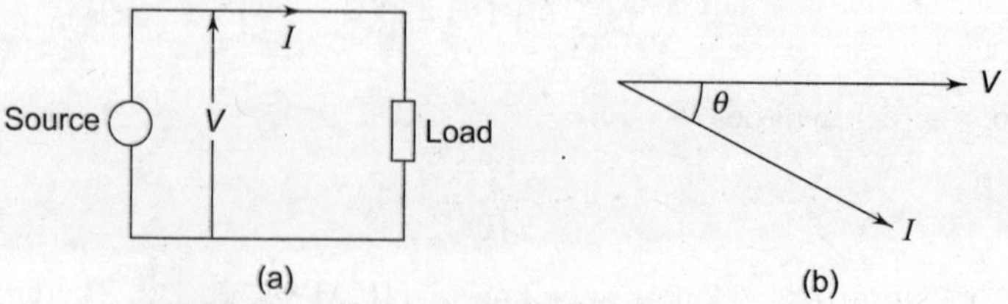

(a) (b)

Fig. 4.9 *Complex power flow in a single-phase load*

When θ is positive, the current lags behind voltage. This is a convenient choice of sign of θ in power systems where loads have mostly lagging power factors.

Complex power flow in the direction of current indicated is given by

$$S = VI^*$$
$$= |V|\,|I| \angle \theta$$
$$= |V|\,|I| \cos \theta + j|V|\,|I| \sin \theta = P + jQ \tag{4.17}$$

or,

$$|S| = (P^2 + Q^2)^{1/2}$$

Here,

S = complex power (VA, kVA, MVA)

$|S|$ = apparent power (VA, kVA, MVA); it signifies rating of equipments (generators, transformers)

$P = |V|\,|I| \cos \theta$ = real (active) power (watts, kW, MW)

$Q = |V|\,|I| \sin \theta$ = reactive power

= voltamperes reactive (VAR)

= kilovoltamperes reactive (kVAR)

= megavoltamperes reactive (MVAR)

It immediately follows from Eq. (4.17) that Q, the reactive power, is positive for lagging current (lagging power factor load) and negative for leading current (leading power factor load). With the direction of current indicated in Fig. 4.9, $S = P + jQ$ is supplied by the source and is absorbed by the load.

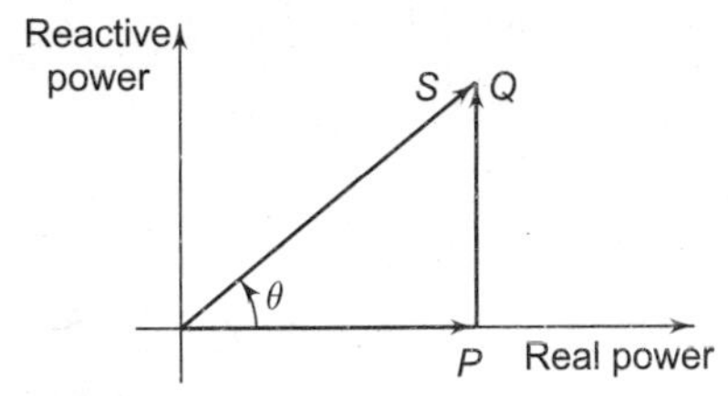

Fig. 4.10 *Phasor representation of complex power (lagging pf load)*

Equation (4.17) can be represented by the phasor diagram of Fig. 4.10, where

$$\theta = \tan^{-1} \frac{Q}{P} = \text{positive for lagging current} \quad (4.18)$$

$= \text{negative for leading current}$

If two (or more) loads are in parallel as in Fig. 4.11

$$\begin{aligned} S &= VI^* = V(I_1^* + I_2^*) \\ &= VI_1^* + VI_2^* \\ &= S_1 + S_2 = (P_1 + P_2) + j(Q_1 + Q_2) \end{aligned} \quad (4.19)$$

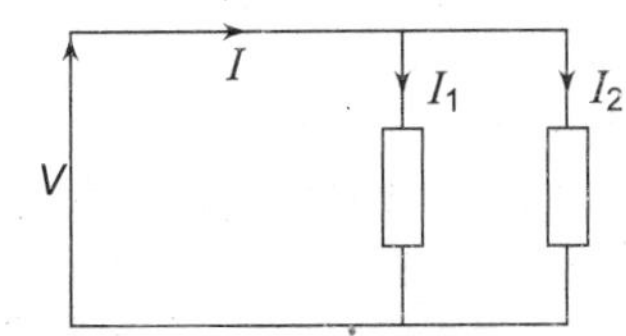

Fig. 4.11 *Two loads in parallel*

As per Eq. (4.19), Kirchhoff's current law applies to complex power (also applies separately to real and reactive powers).

In a series RL load carrying current I,

$$V = I(R + jX_L)$$

$$S = VI^* = I^2R + jI^2X_L$$

$\therefore$ $P = I^2R$ = active power absorbed by load

$Q = I^2X_L$ = reactive power absorbed by load

In case of a series RC load carrying current I,

$$P = I^2R$$

$Q = -I^2X_C$ (reactive power absorbed is negative)

Consider now a balanced three-phase load represented in the form of an equivalent star as shown in Fig. 4.12. The three-phase complex power fed into load is given by

$$S = 3V_PI_L^* = 3\,|V_P| \angle\delta_P I_L^* = \sqrt{3}\,|V_L| \angle\delta_P I_L^* \quad (4.20)$$

If

$$I_L = |I_L| \angle (\delta_P - \theta)$$

then,

$$\begin{aligned} S &= \sqrt{3}\,|V_L|\,|I_L| \angle\theta \\ &= \sqrt{3}\,|V_L|\,|I_L| \cos\theta + j\sqrt{3}\,|V_L|\,|I_L| \sin\theta = P + jQ \end{aligned} \quad (4.21)$$

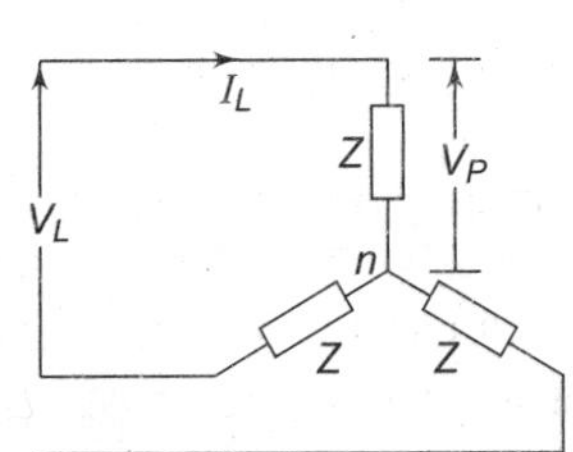

Fig. 4.12 *Complex power fed to three-phase load*

Here,

$$|S| = \sqrt{3}\,|V_L|\,|I_L|$$

$$P = \sqrt{3}\,|V_L|\,|I_L| \cos\theta$$

$$Q = \sqrt{3}\,|V_L|\,|I_L| \sin\theta$$

where,

θ = power factor angle

If V_L, the line voltage, is expressed in kV; and I_L, the line current in amperes, S is in kVA; and if the line current is in kiloamperes, S is in MVA.

In terms of load impedance Z,

$$I_L = \frac{V_P}{Z} = \frac{|V_L| \angle\delta_P}{\sqrt{3}Z}$$

Substituting for I_L in Eq. (4.20)

$$S = \frac{|V_L|^2}{Z^*} \tag{4.22a}$$

If V_L is in kV, S is now given in MVA. Load impedance Z if required can be calculated from

$$Z = \frac{|V_L|^2}{S^*} = \frac{|V_L|^2}{P - jQ} \tag{4.22b}$$

4.6 ▶ STEADY-STATE MODEL OF SYNCHRONOUS MACHINE

The synchronous machine is the most important element of a power system. It converts mechanical power into electrical form and feeds it into the power network or, in the case of a motor, it draws electrical power from the network and converts it into the mechanical form. The machine excitation which is controllable determines the flow of VARs into or out of the machine. Books on electrical machines [1, 2, 4] may be consulted for a detailed account of the synchronous machine. We shall present here a simplified circuit model of the machine which with suitable modifications wherever necessary (under transient conditions) will be adopted throughout this book.

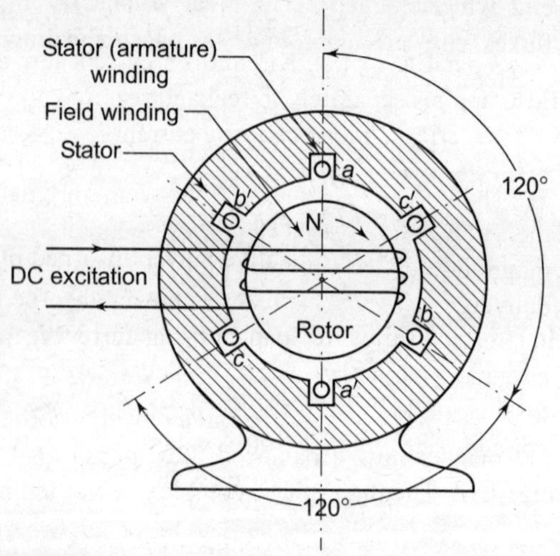

Fig. 4.13 *Schematic diagram of a round rotor synchronous generator*

Figure 4.13 shows the schematic cross-sectional diagram of a three-phase synchronous generator (alternator) having a two-pole structure. The stator has a balanced three-phase winding—*aa*′, *bb*′ and *cc*′. The winding shown is a concentrated one, while the winding in an actual machine is distributed across the stator periphery. The rotor shown is a cylindrical* one (round rotor or nonsalient pole rotor) with rotor winding excited by the DC source. The rotor winding is so arranged on rotor periphery that the field excitation produces nearly sinusoidally distributed flux/pole (ϕ_f) in the air gap. As the rotor rotates, three-phase emfs are produced in stator winding. Since the machine is a balanced one and balanced loading will be considered, it can be modelled on per phase basis for the reference phase *a*.

In a machine with more than two poles, the above defined structure repeats electrically for every pair of poles. The frequency of induced emf is given by

$$f = \frac{NP}{120} \text{ Hz}$$

where,

N = rotor speed (synchronous speed) in rpm

P = number of poles

* High-speed turbo-generators have cylindrical rotors and low-speed hydro-generators have salient pole rotors.

On no load the voltage E_f induced in the reference phase a lags 90° behind ϕ_f which produces it and is proportional to ϕ_f if the magnetic circuit is assumed to be unsaturated. This phasor relationship is indicated in Fig. 4.14. Obviously the terminal voltage $V_t = E_f$.

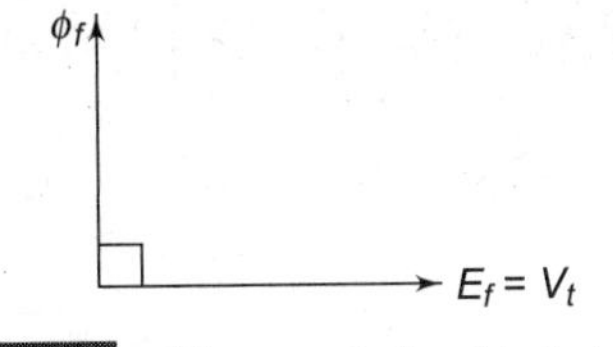

Fig. 4.14 *Phasor relationship between ϕ_f and E_f*

As balanced steady load is drawn from the three-phase stator winding, the stator currents produce synchronously rotating flux ϕ_a/pole (in the direction of rotation of the rotor). This flux, called *armature reaction* flux, is therefore stationary with respect to field flux ϕ_f. It intuitively follows that ϕ_a is in phase with phase a current I_a which causes it. Since the magnetic circuit has been assumed to be unsaturated, the superposition principle is applicable so that the resultant air gap flux is given by the phasor sum

$$\phi_r = \phi_f + \phi_a \tag{4.23}$$

Further assuming that the armature leakage reactance and resistance are negligible, ϕ_r induces the armature emf which equals the terminal voltage V_t. Phasor diagram under loaded (balanced) conditions showing fluxes, currents and voltages as phasors is drawn in Fig. 4.15.

Here,

θ = power factor angle

δ = angle by which E_f leads V_t called *load angle* or *torque angle*

We shall see in Section 5.10 that δ mainly determines the power delivered by the generator and the magnitude of E_f (i.e., excitation) determines the VARs delivered by it.

Because of the assumed linearity of the magnetic circuit, voltage phasors E_f, E_a and V_t are proportional to flux phasors ϕ_f, ϕ_a and ϕ_r, respectively; further, voltage phasors lag 90° behind flux phasors. It therefore easily follows from Fig. 4.15 that phasor $AB = -E_a$ is proportional to ϕ_a (and therefore I_a) and is 90° leading ϕ_a (or I_a). With the direction of phasor AB indicated on the diagram

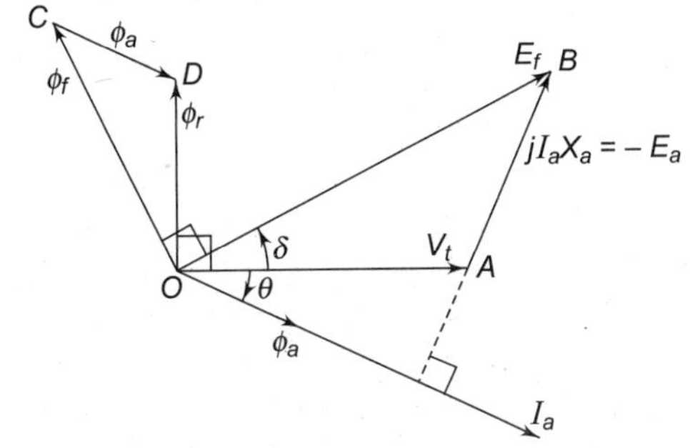

Fig. 4.15 *Phasor diagram of synchronous generator*

$$AB = jI_aX_a$$

where X_a is the constant of proportionality.

In terms of the above definition of X_a, we can directly write the following expression for voltages without the need of invoking flux phasors.

$$V_t = E_f - jI_aX_a \tag{4.24}$$

where,

E_f = voltage induced by field flux ϕ_f alone

= no load emf

The circuit model of Eq. (4.24) is drawn in Fig. 4.16 wherein X_a is interpreted as inductive reactance which accounts for the effect of armature reaction thereby avoiding the need of resorting to addition of fluxes [Eq. (4.23)].

The circuit of Fig. 4.16 can be easily modified to include the effect of armature leakage reactance and resistance (these are series effects) to give the complete circuit model of the synchronous generator as in Fig. 4.17. The total reactance $(X_a + X_l) = X_s$ is called the *synchronous reactance* of the machine. Equation (4.24) now becomes

$$V_t = E_f - jI_aX_s - I_aR_a \tag{4.25}$$

This model of the synchronous machine can be further modified to account for the effect of magnetic saturation where the principle of superposition does not hold.

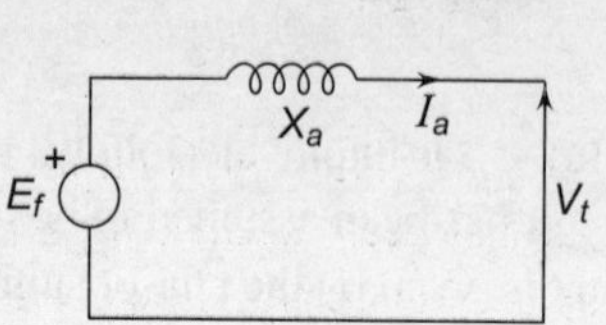

Fig. 4.16 *Circuit model of round rotor synchronous generator (resistance and leakage reactance neglected)*

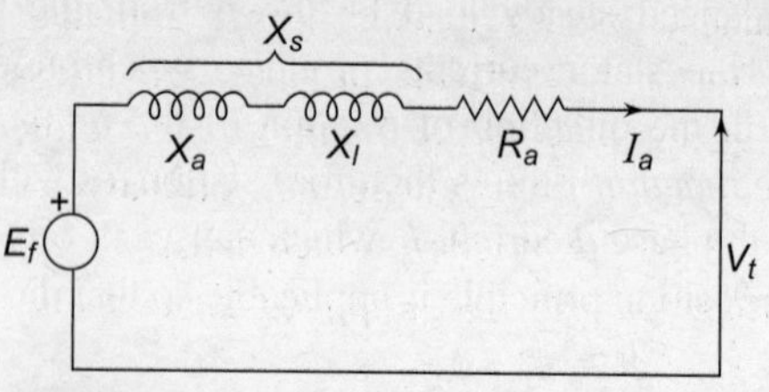

Fig. 4.17 *Circuit model of round rotor synchronous generator*

Armature resistance R_a is invariably neglected in power system studies. Therefore, in the place of the circuit model of Fig. 4.17, the simplified circuit model of Fig. 4.18 will be used throughout this book. The corresponding phasor diagram is given in Fig. 4.19. The field-induced emf E_f leads the terminal voltage by the torque (load) angle δ. This, in fact, is the condition for active power to flow out of the generator. The magnitude of power delivered depends upon sin δ.

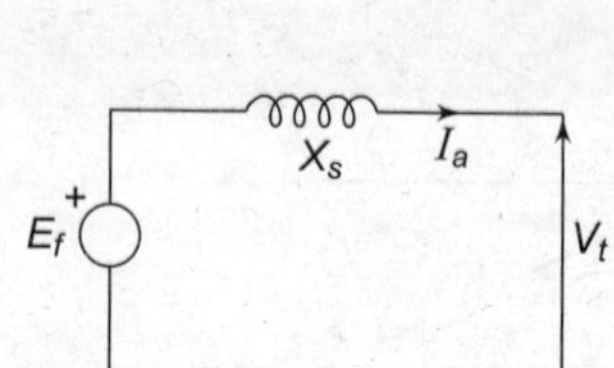

Fig. 4.18 *Simplified circuit model of round rotor synchronous generator*

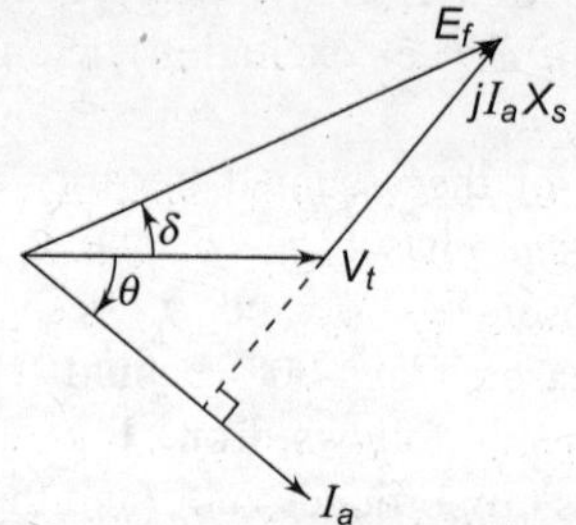

Fig. 4.19 *Phasor diagram of synchronous generator*

In the motoring operation of a synchronous machine, the current I_a reverses as shown in Fig. 4.20, so that Eq. (4.25) modifies to

$$E_f = V_t - jI_aX_s \tag{4.26}$$

which is represented by the phasor diagram of Fig. 4.21. It may be noted that V_t now leads E_f by δ. This in fact is the condition for power to flow into motor terminals.

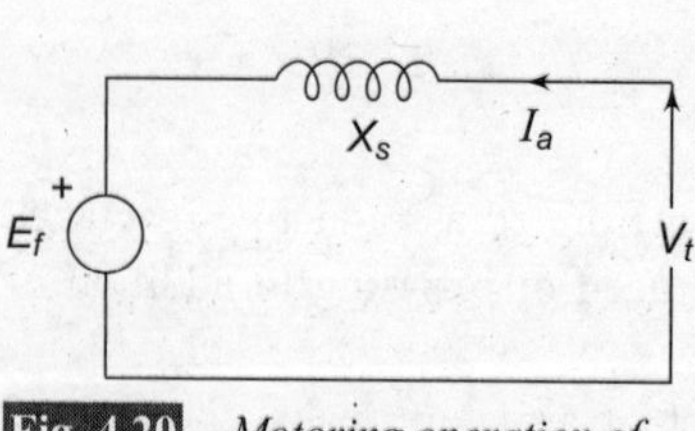

Fig. 4.20 *Motoring operation of synchronous machine*

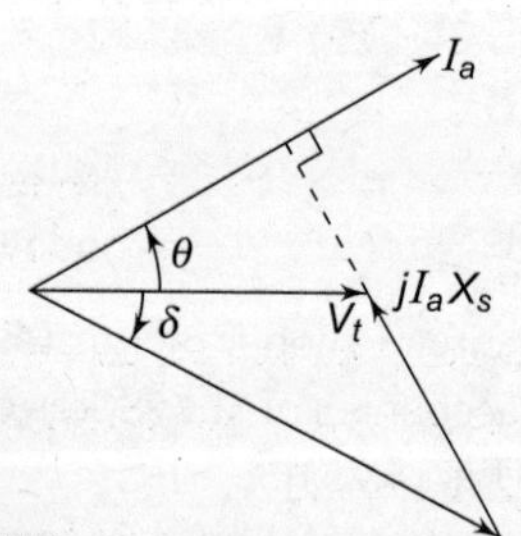

Fig. 4.21 *Phasor diagram of motoring operation*

The flow of reactive power and terminal voltage of a synchronous machine is mainly controlled by means of its excitation. This is discussed in detail in Section 5.10. Voltage and reactive power flow are often automatically regulated by voltage regulators (see Section 8.6) acting on the field circuits of generators and by automatic tap changing devices on transformers.

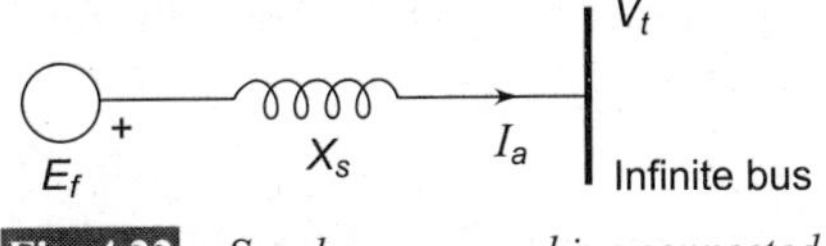

Fig. 4.22 *Synchronous machine connected to infinite bus*

Normally, a synchronous generator operates in parallel with other generators connected to the power system. For simplicity of operation, we shall consider a generator connected to an *infinite bus* as shown in Fig. 4.22. As infinite bus means a large system whose voltage and frequency remain constant independent of the power exchange between the synchronous machine and the bus, and independent of the excitation of the synchronous machine.

Consider now a synchronous generator feeding constant active power into an infinite bus bar. As the machine excitation is varied, armature current I_a and its angle θ, i.e., power factor, change in such a manner as to keep

$$|V_t|\,|I_a| \cos \theta = \text{constant} = \text{active power output}$$

It means that since $|V_t|$ is fixed, the projection $|I_a| \cos \theta$ of the phasor I_a on V_t remains constant, while the excitation is varied. Phasor diagrams corresponding to high, medium and low excitations are presented in Fig. 4.23. The phasor diagram of Fig. 4.23(b) corresponds to the unity power factor case. It is obvious from the phasor diagram that for this excitation

$$|E_f| \cos \delta = |V_t|$$

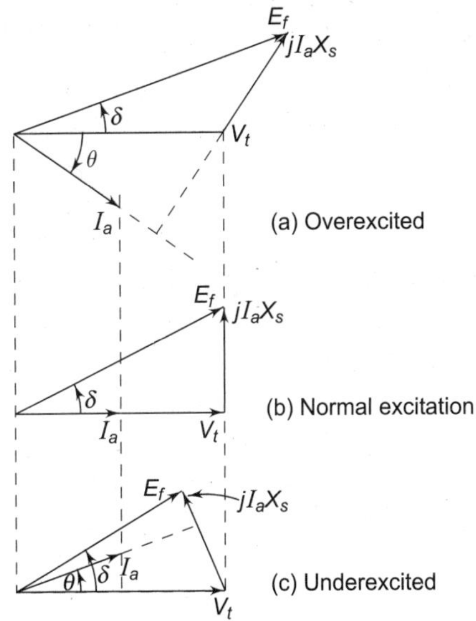

Fig. 4.23 *Phasor diagrams of synchronous generator feeding constant power as excitation is varied*

This is defined as *normal excitation*. For the *overexcited* case (Fig. 4.23(a)), i.e., $|E_f| \cos \delta > |V_t|$, I_a lags behind V_t so that the generator feeds positive reactive power into the bus (or draws negative reactive power from the bus). For the *underexcited* case (Fig. 4.23(c)), i.e., $|E_f| \cos \delta < |V_t|$, I_a leads V_t so that the generator feeds negative reactive power into the bus (or draws positive reactive power from the bus).

Figure 4.24 shows the overexcited and underexcited cases of synchronous motor (connected to infinite bus) with constant power drawn from the infinite bus. In the overexcited case, I_a leads V_t, i.e., the motor draws negative reactive power (or supplies positive reactive power); while in the underexcited case I_a lags V_t, i.e., the motor draws positive reactive power (or supplies negative reactive power).

From the above discussion, we can draw the general conclusion that a synchronous machine (generating or motoring) while operating at constant power supplies positive reactive power into the bus bar (or draws negative reactive power from the bus bar) when overexcited. An underexcited machine, on the other hand, feeds negative reactive power into the bus bar (or draws positive reactive power from the bus bar).

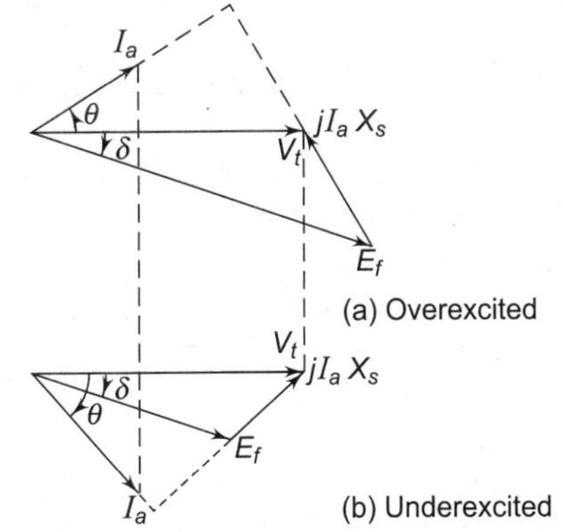

Fig. 4.24 *Phasor diagrams of synchronous motor drawing constant power as excitation is varied*

Consider now the power delivered by a synchronous generator to an infinite bus. From Fig. 4.19 this power is

$$P = |V_t|\,|I_a| \cos \theta$$

The above expression can be written in a more useful form from the phasor geometry. From Fig. 4.19

$$\frac{|E_f|}{\sin (90^\circ + \theta)} = \frac{|I_a| X_s}{\sin \delta}$$

or,

$$|I_a| \cos \theta = \frac{|E_f|}{X_s} \sin \delta \tag{4.27}$$

$$\therefore \quad P = \frac{|E_f||V_t|}{X_s} \sin \delta \tag{4.28}$$

The plot of P versus δ, shown in Fig. 4.25, is called the *power angle curve*. The maximum power that can be delivered occurs at $\delta = 90°$ and is given by

$$P_{\max} = \frac{|E_f||V_t|}{X_s} \tag{4.29}$$

For $P > P_{\max}$ or for $\delta > 90°$, the generator will have stability problem. This problem (the stability) will be discussed at length in Ch. 12.

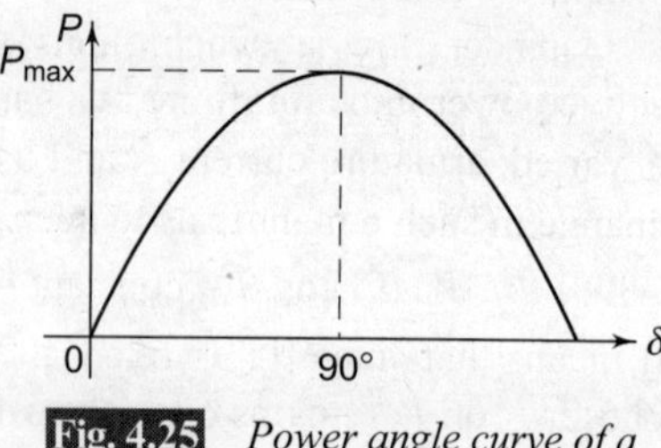

Fig. 4.25 *Power angle curve of a synchronous generator*

4.6.1 Power Factor and Power Control

While Figs 4.23 and 4.24 illustrate how a synchronous machine power factor changes with excitation for fixed power exchange, these do not give us a clue regarding the quantitative values of $|I_a|$ and δ. This can easily be accomplished by recognising from Eq. (4.27) that

$$|E_f| \sin \delta = |I_a| X_s \cos \theta$$

$$= \frac{PX_s}{|V_t|} = \text{constant (for constant exchange of power to infinite bus bar)} \tag{4.30}$$

Figure 4.26 shows the phasor diagram for a generator delivering constant power to infinite bus but with varying excitation. As $|E_f| \sin \delta$ remains constant, the tip of phasor E_f moves along a line parallel to V_t as excitation is varied. The direction of phasor I_a is always 90° lagging jI_aX_s and its magnitude is obtained from $(|I_a|X_s)/X_s$. Figure 4.27 shows the case of limiting excitation with $\delta = 90°$. For excitation lower than this value, the generator becomes unstable.

Similar phasor diagrams can be drawn for synchronous motor as well for constant input power (or constant load if copper and iron losses are neglected and mechanical loss is combined with load).

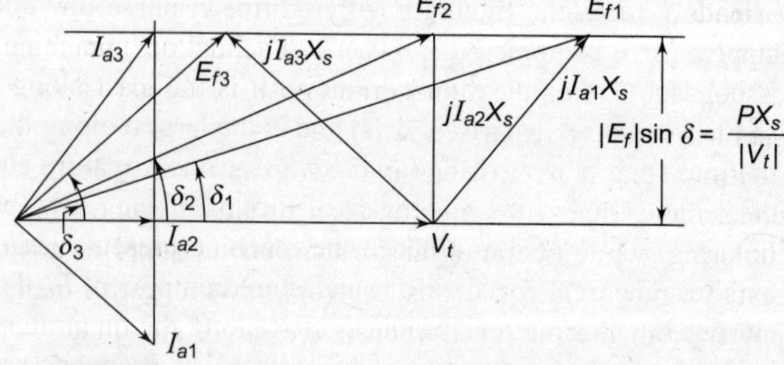

Fig. 4.26 *Effect of varying excitation of generator delivering constant power to infinite bus bar*

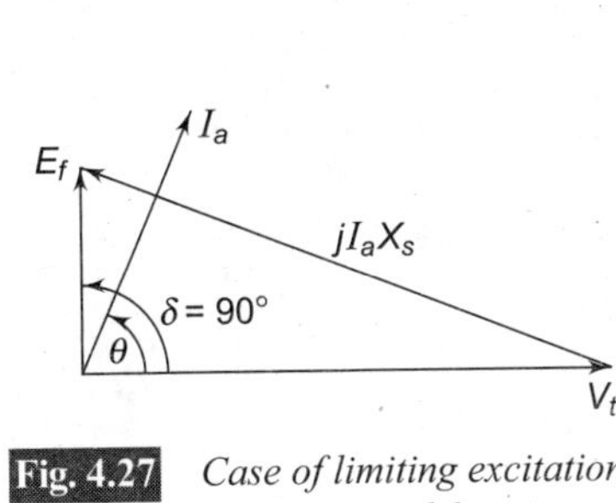

Fig. 4.27 *Case of limiting excitation of generator delivering constant power to infinite bus bar*

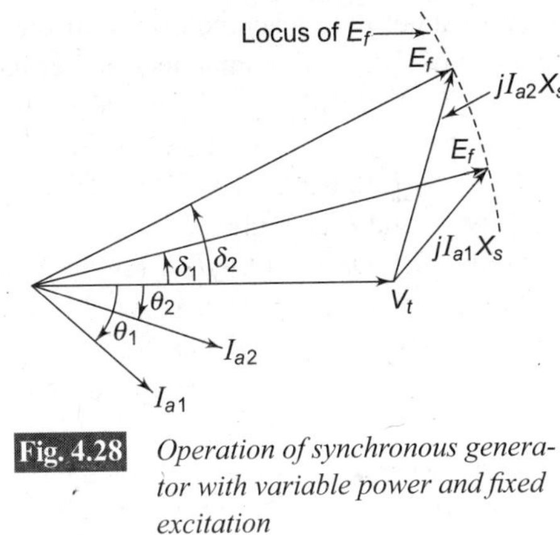

Fig. 4.28 *Operation of synchronous generator with variable power and fixed excitation*

Another important operating condition is variable power and fixed excitation. In this case $|V_t|$ and $|E_f|$ are fixed, while δ and active power vary in accordance with Eq. (4.28). The corresponding phasor diagram for two values of δ is shown in Fig. 4.28. It is seen from this diagram that as δ increases, current magnitude increases and power factor improves. It will be shown in Section 5.10 that as δ changes, there is no significant change in the flow of reactive power.

4.6.2 Salient Pole Synchronous Generator

A salient pole synchronous machine, as shown in Fig. 4.29, is distinguished from a round rotor machine by constructional features of field poles which project with a large interpolar air gap. This type of construction is commonly employed in machines coupled to hydroelectric turbines which are inherently slow-speed ones so that the synchronous machine has multiple pole pairs as different from machines coupled to high-speed steam turbines (3,000/1,500 rpm) which have a two- or four-pole structure. Salient pole machine analysis is made through the *two-reaction theory* outlined below.

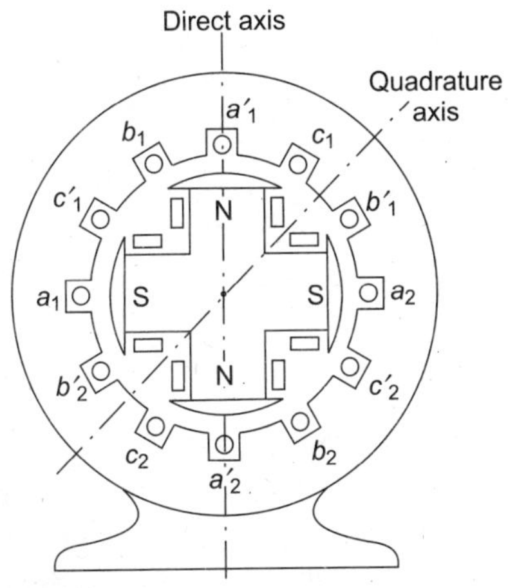

Fig. 4.29 *Salient pole synchronous machine (4-pole structure)*

In a round rotor machine, armature current in phase with field-induced emf E_f or in quadrature (at 90°) to E_f, produces the same flux linkages per ampere as the air gap is uniform so that the armature reaction reactance offered to in-phase or quadrature current is the same ($X_a + X_l = X_s$). In a salient pole machine, air gap is non-uniform along rotor periphery. It is the least along the axis of main poles (called *direct axis*) and is the largest along the axis of the interpolar region (called *quadrature axis*). Armature current in quadrature with E_f produces flux along the direct axis and the reluctance of flux path being low (because of small air gap), it produces larger flux linkages per ampere and hence the machine presents larger armature reaction reactance X_d (called direct axis reactance) to the flow of quadrature component I_d of armature current I_a. On the other hand, armature current in phase with E_f produces flux along the quadrature axis and the reluctance of the flux path being high (because of large interpolar air gap), it produces smaller flux linkages per ampere and hence the machine presents smaller armature reaction reactance X_q (quadrature axis reactance < X_d) to the flow of in-phase component I_q of armature current I_a.

Since a salient pole machine offers different reactances to the flow of I_d and I_q components of armature current I_a, a circuit model cannot be drawn. The phasor diagram of a salient pole generator is shown in Fig. 4.30. It can be easily drawn by following the steps given below:

1. Draw V_t and I_a at angle θ.
2. Draw $I_a R_a$. Draw $CQ = jI_a X_d (\perp \text{ to } I_a)$.
3. Make $|CP| = |I_a| X_q$ and draw the line OP which gives the direction of E_f phasor.
4. Draw a $\perp$ from Q to the extended line OP such that $OA = E_f$.

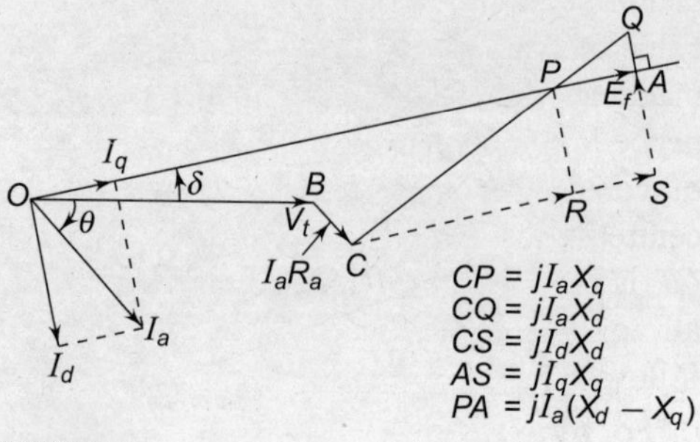

Fig. 4.30 *Phasor diagram of salient pole synchronous generator*

It can be shown by the above theory that the power output of a salient pole generator is given by

$$P = \frac{|V_t||E_f|}{X_d} \sin \delta + \frac{|V_t|^2 (X_d - X_q)}{2 X_d X_q} \sin 2\delta \tag{4.31}$$

The first term is the same as for a round rotor machine with $X_s = X_d$ and constitutes the major part in power transfer. The second term is quite small (about 10–20%) compared to the first term and is known as *reluctance power.*

P versus δ is plotted in Fig. 4.31. It is noticed that the maximum power output occurs at $\delta < 90°$ (about 70°). Further $\frac{dP}{d\delta}$ (change in power per unit change in power angle for small changes in power angle), called the *synchronising power coefficient*, in the operating region ($\delta < 70°$) is larger in a salient pole machine than in a round rotor machine.

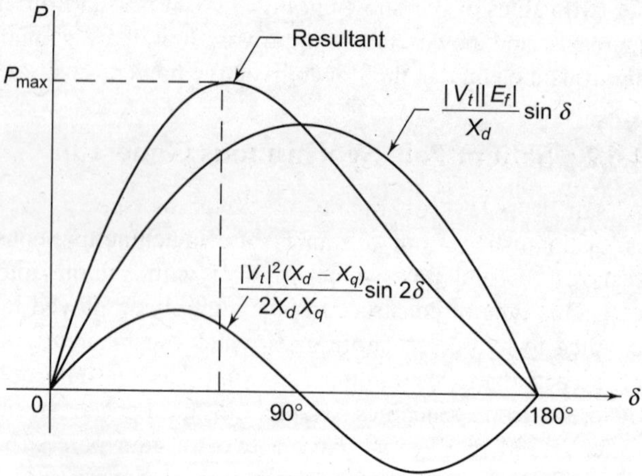

Fig. 4.31 *Power angle curve for salient pole generator*

In this book, we shall neglect the effect of saliency and take

$$X_s = X_d$$

in all types of power system studies considered.

During a machine transient, the direct axis reactance changes with time acquiring the following distinct values during the complete transient.

X''_d = subtransient direct axis reactance

X'_d = transient direct axis reactance

X_d = steady state direct axis reactance

The significance and use of these three values of direct axis reactance will be elaborated in Ch. 9.

4.6.3 Operating Chart of a Synchronous Generator

While selecting a large generator, besides rated MVA and power factor, the greatest allowable stator and rotor currents must also be considered as they influence mechanical stresses and temperature rise. Such limiting parameters in the operation are brought out by means of an *operating chart* or *performance chart.*

For simplicity of analysis, the saturation effects, saliency and resistance are ignored and an unsaturated value of synchronous reactance is considered. Consider Fig. 4.32, the phasor diagram of a cylindrical rotor machine. The locus of constant $|I_a|X_s,|I_a|$ and hence MVA is a circle centred at M. The locus of constant $|E_f|$ (excitation) is also a circle centred at O. As MP is proportional to MVA, QP is proportional to MVAR and MQ to MW, all to the same scale which is obtained as follows.

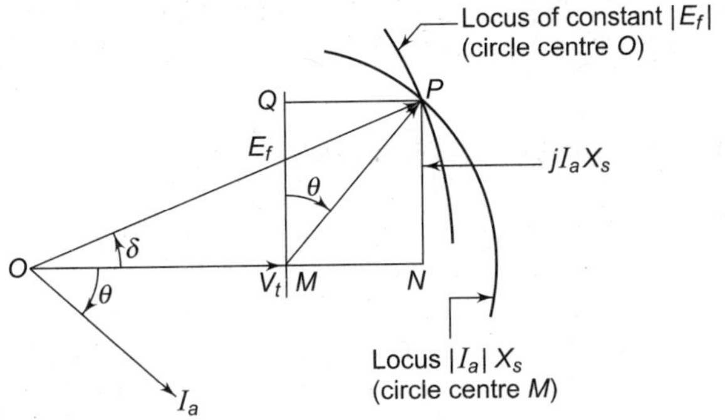

Fig. 4.32 *Phasor diagram of synchronous generator*

For zero excitation, i.e., $|E_f| = 0$

$$-jI_aX_s = V_t$$

or,

$$I_a = jV_t/X_s$$

i.e., $|I_a| = |V_t|/X_s$ leading at 90° to OM which corresponds to VARs/phase.

Consider now the chart shown in Fig. 4.33 which is drawn for a synchronous machine having $X_s = 1.43$ pu. For zero excitation, the current is 1.0/1.43 = 0.7 pu, so that the length MO corresponds to reactive power of 0.7 pu, fixing both active and reactive power scales.

With centre at O, a number of semicircles are drawn with radii equal to different pu MVA loadings. Circles of per unit excitation are drawn from centre M with 1.0 pu excitation corresponding to the fixed terminal voltage OM. Lines may also be drawn from O corresponding to various power factors but for clarity only 0.85 pf lagging line is shown. The operational limits are fixed as follows.

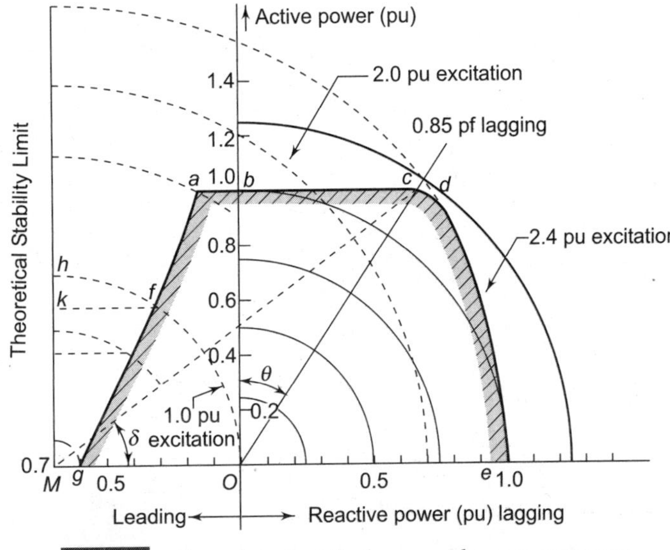

Fig. 4.33 *Operating chart for large synchronous generator*

Taking 1.0 per unit active power as the maximum allowable power, a horizontal limit-line abc is drawn through b at 1.0 pu. It is assumed that the machine is rated to give 1.0 pu unit active power at power factor 0.85 lagging and this fixes point c. Limitation of the stator current to the corresponding value requires the limit-line to become a circular arc cd about centre O. At point d the rotor heating becomes more important and the arc de is fixed by the maximum excitation current allowable, in this case assumed to be $|E_f| = 2.40$ pu (i.e., 2.4 times $|V_t|$). The remaining limit is decided by loss of synchronism at leading power factors. The theoretical limit is the line perpendicular to MO at M (i.e., $\delta = 90°$), but in practice a safety margin is brought into permit a further small increase in load before instability. In Fig. 4.33, a 0.1 pu margin is employed and is shown by the curve afg which is drawn in the following way.

Consider a point h on the theoretical limit on the $|E_f| = 1.0$ pu excitations arc, the power Mh is reduced by 0.1 pu to Mk; the operating point must, however, still be on the same $|E_f|$ arc and k is projected to f

which is the required point on the desired limiting curve. This is repeated for other excitations giving the curve *afg*. The complete working area, shown shaded, is *gfabcde*. A working point placed within this area at once defines the MVA, MW, MVAR, current, power factor and excitation. The load angle δ can be measured as shown in the figure.

4.7 ▶ POWER TRANSFORMER

Transformers are essential elements in any power system. They allow the relatively low voltages from generators to be raised to a very high level for efficient power transmission. At the load end, the transformers reduce the voltage to values suitable for various categories of loads. The detailed coverage on power transformer (Fig. 4.34) is given in Ch. 3 of Ref. 1. Single-phase equivalents and one-line diagram of three-phase transformers are given in Section 4.2. Any standard textbook on Electric Machines, such as Ref. 1, gives detailed treatment on transformer performance such as regulation, efficiency; autotransformers and three-winding transformers voltage and phase angle control of transformers is given in Ch. 6.

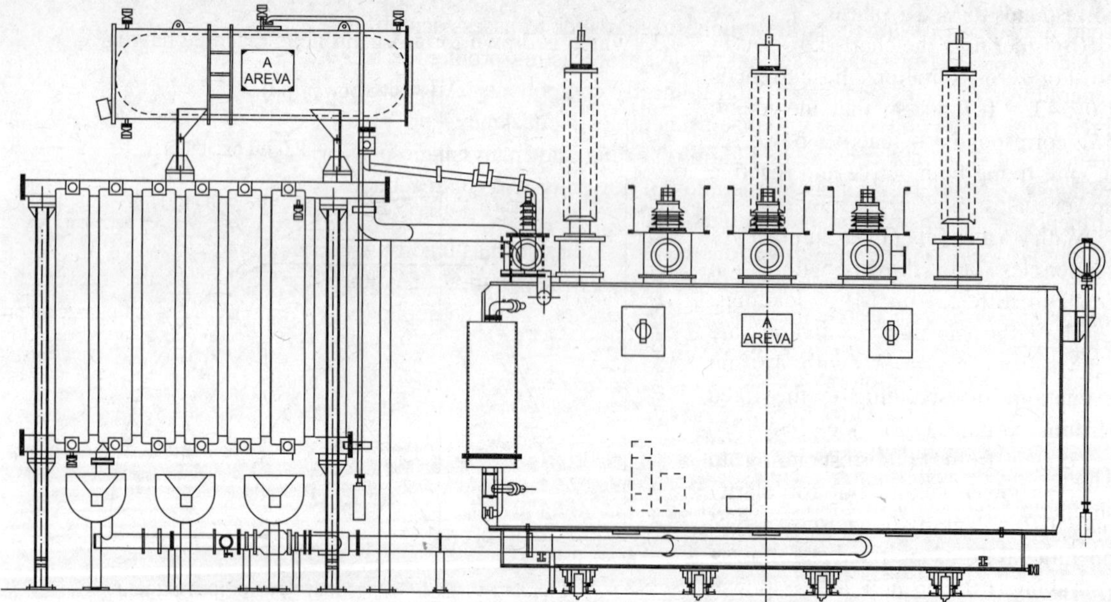

2 × 370 MVA, 20/230 kV, Generator Transformer for Reliance Energy, A/c. Haryana Power Development Corporation

Fig. 4.34 *Largest generator transformer manufactured in India*

4.8 ▶ TRANSMISSION OF ELECTRIC POWER

The purpose of an overhead transmission network is to transfer electric energy from power stations to the distribution system which finally supplies the load. Line parameters (R, L, G and C) have already been discussed in Chs. 2 and 3. Characteristics and performance of power transmission lines are dealt with in full details in the next chapter. How power flows in a grid is the subject matter of Ch. 6. Economic operation and how optimally transmit power over lines is explained in Ch. 7. Loud frequency control and voltage control are discussed in Ch. 8. Chapters 9–11 deal with faults on lines etc. Stable operation is discussed in Ch. 12. Where overhead lines cannot be used for power transmission, power is transmitted using underground cables (Ch. 16 of Ref. 6).

4.9 ▶ SYSTEM PROTECTION

Besides generators, transformers, lines and cables, other devices are required for the satisfactory operation and protection of a power system. Some of the protective devices directly connected to the circuits are called switchgear. They include instrument transformers, circuit breakers, disconnect switches, fuses and lightning arresters. These devices are required to de-energise either for normal operation or on occurrence of faults. The necessary control equipment and protective relays are kept in switchboard in control houses. These aspects are covered in Chs. 14 and 15 of Ref. 6.

4.10 ▶ REPRESENTATION OF LOADS

Load drawn by consumers is the toughest parameter to assess scientifically. The magnitude of the load, in fact, changes continuously so that the load forecasting problem is truly a statistical one. The loads are generally composed of industrial and domestic components. An industrial load consists mainly of large three-phase induction motors with sufficient load constancy and predictable duty cycle, whereas the domestic load mainly consists of lighting, heating and many single-phase devices used in a random way by householders. The design and operation of power systems both economically and electrically are greatly influenced by the nature and magnitude of loads.

In representation of loads for various system studies such as load flow and stability studies, it is essential to know the variation of real and reactive power with variation of voltage. Normally in such studies, the load is of composite nature with both industrial and domestic components. A typical composition of load at a bus may be

Induction motors	55 – 75%
Synchronous motors	5 – 15%
Lighting and heating	20 – 30%

Though it is always better to consider the P – V and Q – V characteristics of each of these loads for simulation, the analytic treatment would be very cumbersome and complicated. In most of the analytical work, one of the following three ways of load representation is used.

Constant Power Representation This is used in load flow studies. Both the specified MW and MVAR are taken to be constant.

Constant Current Representation Here the load current is given by Eq. (4.17), i.e.,

$$I = \frac{P - jQ}{V^*} = |I| \angle (\delta - \theta)$$

where $V = |V| \angle\delta$ and $\theta = \tan^{-1} Q/P$ is the power factor angle. It is known as constant current representation because the magnitude of current is regarded as constant in the study.

Constant Impedance Representation This is quite often used in stability studies. The load specified in MW and MVAR at nominal voltage is used to compute the load impedance (Eq. (4.22b)). Thus,

$$Z = \frac{V}{I} = \frac{VV^*}{P - jQ} = \frac{|V|^2}{P - jQ} = \frac{1}{Y}$$

which then is regarded as constant throughout the study.

4.11 ▶ SUMMARY

In this chapter, representation of various power system components have been described including loads, transformer and synchronous machine.

Problems

4.1 Figure P-4.1 shows the schematic diagram of a radial transmission system. The ratings and reactances of the various components are shown therein. A load of 60 MW at 0.9 power factor lagging is tapped from the 66 kV substation which is to be maintained at 60 kV. Calculate the terminal voltage of the synchronous machine. Represent the transmission line and the transformers by series reactances only.

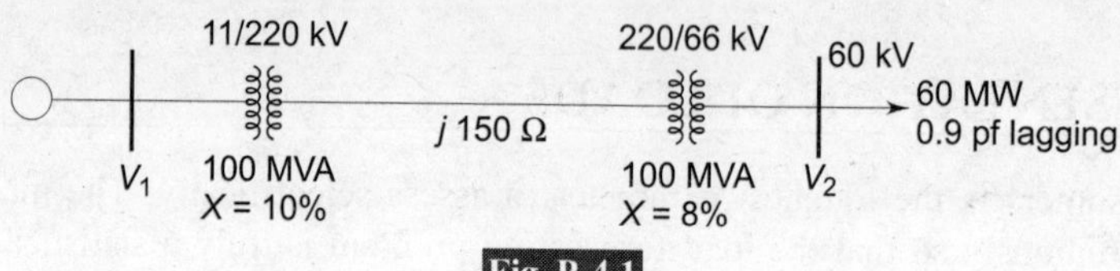

Fig. P-4.1

4.2 Draw the pu impedance diagram for the power system shown in Fig. P-4.2. Neglect resistance, and use a base of 100 MVA, 220 kV in 50 Ω line. The ratings of the generator, motor and transformers are

Generator	40 MVA,	25 kV,	$X'' = 20\%$
Motor	50 MVA,	11 kV,	$X'' = 30\%$
Y–Y transformer,	40 MVA,	33 Y–220 Y kV,	$X = 15\%$
Y–Δ transformer,	30 MVA,	11 Δ–220 Y kV,	$X = 15\%$

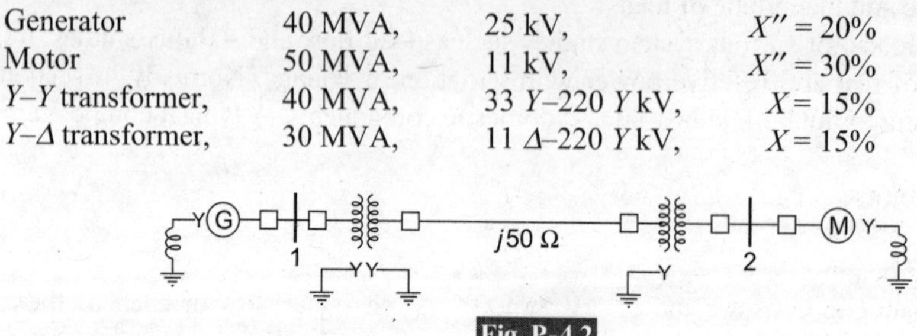

Fig. P-4.2

4.3 The one-line diagram of an unloaded power system is shown in Fig. P-4.3. The reactances of the two sections of transmission line are shown on the diagram. The generators and transformers are rated as follows:

Generator 1:	25 MVA,	13.8 kV,	$X'' = 0.25$ per unit
Generator 2:	30 MVA,	18 kV,	$X'' = 0.25$ per unit
Generator 3:	30 MVA,	20 kV,	$X'' = 0.25$ per unit
Transformer T_1:	25 MVA,	220Y/13.8Δ kV,	$X = 10\%$
Transformer T_2:	Single-phase units each rated 10 MVA, 127/18 kV, $X = 8\%$		
Transformer T_3:	30 MVA,	220Y/22Y kV,	$X = 12\%$

Draw the impedance diagram with all reactances marked in per unit and with letters to indicate points corresponding to the one-line diagram. Choose a base of 50 MVA, 13.8 kV in the circuit of generator 1.

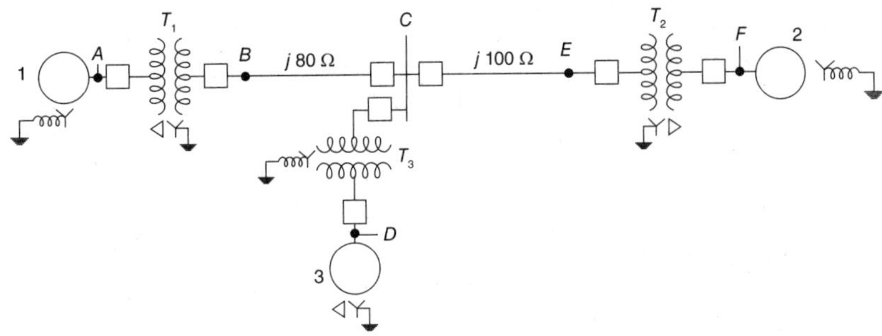

Fig. P-4.3

4.4 Draw the impedance diagram for the power system shown in Fig. P-4.4 and mark the impedances in per unit. Neglect resistance, and use a base of 50 MVA, 138 kV in the 40Ω line. The ratings of the generators, motors and transformers are

Generator 1:	25 MVA,	18 kV,	$X'' = 15\%$
Generator 2:	25 MVA,	18 kV,	$X'' = 15\%$
Synchronous motor 3:	30 MVA,	13.8 kV,	$X'' = 18\%$
Three-phase $Y - Y$ transformers:	25 MVA,	$138Y/20Y$ kV,	$X = 10\%$
Three-phase Y–Δ transformers:	20 MVA,	$138Y/13.8\Delta$ kV,	$X = 12\%$

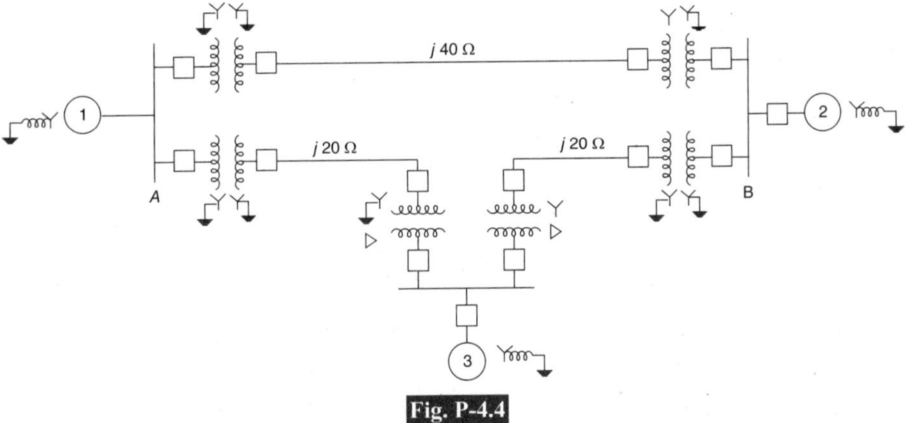

Fig. P-4.4

Multiple Choice Questions

4.1 The per unit value of any quantity is defined as

(a) (The actual value in any units) × (The base value in the same units)

(b) $\dfrac{\text{The actual value in any units}}{\text{The base value in same units}}$

(c) $\dfrac{\text{The base value in any units}}{\text{The actual value in same units}}$

(d) $\dfrac{1}{\text{The base value in same units}}$

4.2 The per unit impedance Z(pu) is given by

(a) $\dfrac{Z(\text{ohms}) \times (\text{kVA})_\text{B}}{(\text{kV})_\text{B}^2}$ (b) $\dfrac{Z(\text{ohms}) \times (\text{MVA})_\text{B}}{(\text{kV})_\text{B}^2}$

(c) $\dfrac{Z(\text{ohms}) \times (\text{MVA})_\text{B}}{(\text{kV})_\text{B}^2 \times 100}$ (d) $\dfrac{Z(\text{ohms}) \times (\text{MVA})_\text{B} \times 100}{(\text{kV})_\text{B}^2}$

4.3 Which of the following is correct

(a) $Z(\text{pu})\text{new} = Z(\text{pu})\text{old} \times \dfrac{(\text{MVA})_\text{B,old}}{(\text{MVA})_\text{B,new}} \times \dfrac{(\text{kV})_\text{B,old}^2}{(\text{kV})_\text{B,new}^2}$

(b) $Z(\text{pu})\text{new} = Z(\text{pu})\text{old} \times \dfrac{(\text{MVA})_\text{B,old}}{(\text{MVA})_\text{B,new}} \times \dfrac{(\text{kV})_\text{B,new}^2}{(\text{kV})_\text{B,old}^2}$

(c) $Z(\text{pu})\text{new} = Z(\text{pu})\text{old} \times \dfrac{(\text{MVA})_\text{B,new}}{(\text{MVA})_\text{B,old}} \times \dfrac{(\text{kV})_\text{B,old}^2}{(\text{kV})_\text{B,new}^2}$

(d) $Z(\text{pu})\text{new} = Z(\text{pu})\text{old} \times \dfrac{(\text{MVA})_\text{B,new}}{(\text{MVA})_\text{B,old}} \times \dfrac{(\text{kV})_\text{B,new}^2}{(\text{kV})_\text{B,old}^2}$

4.4 If the transformer winding resistances and reactances are expressed in pu value, then

(a) $R_1(\text{pu}) = R_2(\text{pu})$ and $X_1(\text{pu}) \neq X_2(\text{pu})$ (b) $R_1(\text{pu}) \neq R_2(\text{pu})$ and $X_1(\text{pu}) = X_2(\text{pu})$

(c) $R_1(\text{pu}) = \dfrac{1}{2}\, R_2(\text{pu})$ and $X_1(\text{pu}) = \dfrac{1}{2}\, X_2(\text{pu})$ (d) $R_1(\text{pu}) = R_2(\text{pu})$ and $X_1(\text{pu}) = X_2(\text{pu})$

4.5 If X_a is the armature reactance of a synchronous machine and X_l is the leakage reactance of the same machine, then synchronous reactance X_s is

(a) $X_s = \dfrac{1}{2}\, X_a$ (b) $X_s = \dfrac{1}{2}\,(X_a - X_l)$ (c) $X_s = X_a + X_l$ (d) $X_s < X_a$

4.6 An Infinite bus in power system is

(a) A small system whose voltage varies with the power exchange between the synchronous machine and bus.

(b) A large system whose voltage and frequency vary with the power exchange between the synchronous machine and bus.

(c) A large system whose voltage and frequency remain constant independent of the power exchange between the synchronous machine and the bus.

(d) A large system with infinite voltage.

4.7 The per unit impedance of a circuit element is 0.30. If the base kV and base MVA are halved, then the new value of the per unit impedance of the circuit element will be

(a) 0.30 (b) 0.60 (c) 0.0030 (d) 0.0060

4.8 The power delivered by a synchronous generator to an infinite bus is given by

(a) $P = \dfrac{|V_t||E_f|}{R_a} \sin\delta$ (b) $P = \dfrac{|V_t||E_f|^2}{X_s} \sin\delta$

(c) $P = \dfrac{|V_t||E_f|}{X_s} \sin\delta$ (d) $P = \dfrac{|V_t||E_f|}{X_s} \cos\delta$

4.9 A synchronous machine is
(a) A single excited machine (b) A doubly excited machine
(c) Made to run at a speed less than N_s (d) Generally a lagging power factor machine

4.10 The per unit value of a 2 ohm resistor at 100 MVA base and 10 kV base voltage is
(a) 4 pu (b) 2 pu (c) $\frac{1}{2}$ pu (d) 0.2 pu

4.11 The regulation of a line at full/load 0.8 pf lagging is 11.
A long line under no load conditions, for a good voltage profile needs
(a) Shunt resistance at receiving-end (b) Shunt reactors at the receiving-end
(c) Shunt capacitors at receiving-end (d) All of the above

4.12 For a 500 Hz frequency excitation, a 100 km long power line will be modelled as
(a) Short line (b) Medium line (c) Long line (d) None of the above

4.13 In a power system, the 3-phase fault MVA is always higher than the LG fault MVA at a bus.
(a) True (b) False

4.14 The charging current of a 400 kV line is more than that of a 220 kV line of the same length
(a) True (b) False

4.15 If in a line, resistance and reactance are found to be equal and regulation is zero, then load will have
(a) upf (b) zero pf (c) 0.707 leading pf (d) 0.707 lagging pf

4.16 A three-phase transformer has a nameplate rating of 30 MVA, 230Y/69Y kV with a leakage reactance of 10% and the transformer connection is *Y–Y*. Choosing a base of 30 MVA and 230 kV on high voltage side, the transformer reactance referred to the high voltage side will be
(a) 176.33 Ω (b) 17.67 Ω (c) 158.7 Ω (d) 15.87 Ω

4.17 The per unit impedance of a circuit element is 0.30. If the base kV and base MVA are halved, then the new value of the per unit impedance of the circuit element will be
(a) 0.30 (b) 0.60 (c) 0.0030 (d) 0.0060

4.18 The angular moment of 10 MVA generator is 0.2. Find the new value of angular moment for 20 MVA base.
(a) 0.2 pu (b) 0.1 pu (c) 0.25 pu (d) 0.4 pu

4.19 A three-phase transformer has a nameplate rating of 30 MVA, 230Y/69Y kV with a leakage reactance of 10% and the transformer connection is *Y–Y*. Choosing a base of 30 MVA and 230 kV on high voltage side, the reactance of transformer in per units is
(a) 0.1 (b) 0.3 (c) 0.03 (d) 1.5

4.20 The per unit value of a 2 ohm resistor at 100 MVA and 10 kV base voltage is
(a) 4 pu (b) 2 pu (c) 0.5 pu (d) 0.2 pu

4.21 Advantage(s) of per unit system as compared to absolute system.
(a) only one equation is required
(b) calculation time is less
(c) memory required is less
(d) all of the above

4.22 A transmission line has $(2 + j4)$ Ω impedance, 100 MVA and base voltage is 10 KV. Find the per unit impedance value of transmission line.
(a) $(2 + j4)$ pu (b) $(1 + j2)$ pu (c) $(4 + j8)$ pu (d) $(0.5 + j1)$ pu

4.23 A generator has a rating of 10 MVA, 5 kV has a reactance of 0.02 pu. Find the reactance at new base values of 50 MVA, 10 kV?
(a) 0.02 (b) 0.025 (c) 0.05 (d) 0.25

4.24 A 10 MVA generator has reactance of 0.2 pu. Find the new reactance value for 50 MVA base.
(a) 5 pu (b) 0.2 pu (c) 0.25 pu (d) 1 pu

4.25 A 20 MVA generator has inertia constant of 0.5 pu. Find new value for 50 MVA base.
(a) 0.5 pu (b) 0.1 pu (c) 0.2 pu (d) 0.4 pu

4.26 Three generators rated 100 MVA, 11 kV have an impedance of 0.15 pu each. If in the same plant, these generators are being replaced by a single equivalent generator, the effective impedance of equivalent generator will be
(a) 0.15 pu (b) 0.45 pu (c) 0.05 pu (d) 0.25 pu

4.27 What will be the per unit impedance of a synchronous motor having a rating of 100 kVA, 13.2 kV and having a reactance of 75 Ω/phase?
(a) 0.043 pu (b) 0.057 pu (c) 0.036 pu (d) 0.298 pu

4.28 What is infinite bus in power system?
(a) A large system with infinite voltage
(b) A large system in which the voltage and frequency vary
(c) A large system whose voltage and frequency remain constant throughout
(d) Both (a) and (b)

4.29 Which among these is the major advantage of per unit computations?
(a) Per unit impedance of transformers is the same referred to either side of it.
(b) For simulating steady state and transient models in the computer this method is very useful.
(c) Manufactures usually specify the impedance of an apparatus in per unit system.
(d) All of these

4.30 What is the simplified diagram called, after omitting all resistances, static loads, capacitance of the transmission lines and magnetising circuit of the transformer?
(a) Single line diagram (b) Resistance diagram
(c) Reactance diagram (d) Both (a) and (b)

4.31 A transmission line has 0.2 pu impedance on a base of 132 kV, 100 MVA. On a base of 220 kV, 50 MVA, it will have a pu impedance of
(a) $0.2\times\frac{50}{100}\times\left(\frac{220}{132}\right)^2$ (b) $0.2\times\frac{100}{50}\times\left(\frac{132}{220}\right)^2$
(c) $0.2\times\frac{50}{100}\times\left(\frac{132}{100}\right)^2$ (d) $0.2\times\frac{100}{50}\times\left(\frac{220}{132}\right)^2$

4.32 A generator is connected through a 20 MVA, 13.8/138 kV step up transformer, to a transmission line. At the receiving end of the line, a load is supplied through a step down transformer of 10 MVA, 138/69 kV rating. A 0.72 pu load, evaluated, on load side transformer ratings as base values of 10 MVA and 69 kV in load circuit, the value of the load (in per unit) in generator circuit will be
(a) 36 (b) 1.44 (c) 0.72 (d) 0.18

4.33 A new generator having $E_g = 1.4\angle 30°$ [equivalent to $(1.212 + j0.70)$ pu] and synchronous reactance 'X_s' of 1.0 pu on the system base is to be connected to a bus having voltage V_t in the existing power system. This existing power system can be represented by Thevenin's voltage $E_{th} = 0.9\angle 0°$ pu in series with Thevenin's impedance $Z_{th} = 0.25\angle 90°$ pu. The magnitude of the voltage, V_t, of the system in pu will be
(a) 0.990 (b) 0.973 (c) 0.963 (d) 0.900

4.34 A 75 MVA, 10 kV synchronous generator has $X_d = 0.4$ p.u. The X_d value (in pu) is a base of 100 MVA, 11 kV is
(a) 0.578 (b) 0.279 (c) 0.412 (d) 0.44

4.35 Three generators rated 100 MVA, 11 kV have an impedance of 0.15 pu each. If in the same plant, these generators are being replaced by a single equivalent generator, the effective impedance of equivalent generator will be

(a) 0.05 pu (b) 0.15 pu (c) 0.25 pu (d) 0.45 pu

4.36 The per-unit impedance of a circuit element of 0.15. If the base kV and base MVA are halved, then the new value of the per-unit impedance of the circuit element will be

(a) 0.075 (b) 0.15 (c) 0.30 (d) 0.60

4.37 The per-unit impedance of an alternator corresponding to base values 13.2 kV and 30 MVA is 0.2 pu. The pu value of the impedance for base values 13.8 kV and 50 MVA in pu will be

(a) 0.131 (b) 0.226 (c) 0.305 (d) 0.364

4.38 Single line diagram of which of the following power system is possible?

(a) Power system with LLG fault
(b) Power system with LG fault
(c) Power system with LL fault
(d) Balanced power system

4.39 Reactance diagram contains which of the following?

(a) Resistance of Alternator
(b) Resistance of transformer winding
(c) Induction motor's equivalent circuit
(d) Inductive reactance of transmission lines

4.40 Which of the following is not neglected during formation of reactance diagram from impedance diagram?

(a) Resistance of various power system components
(b) Static loads
(c) Shunt component of transformers
(d) Reactance of alternators

References

Books

1. D.P. Kothari and I.J. Nagrath, *Electric Machines*, 5th edition 2017, Tata McGraw-Hill, New Delhi.
2. E. Van Mablekos, *Electric Machine Theory for Power Engineers*, Harper and Raw, New York, 1980.
3. V. DelToro, *Electric Machines and Power Systems*, Prentice-Hall, Englewood Cliffs, NJ, 1985.
4. D.P. Kothari and I.J. Nagrath, *Theory and Problems of Electric Machines*, 2nd edn, Tata McGraw-Hill, New Delhi, 2002.
5. N. Mohan, *First Course on Power Systems*, MNPERE, Minneapolis, 2006.
6. D.P. Kothari and I.J. Nagrath, *Power System Engineering*, 3rd edition 2019, Tata McGraw-Hill, New Delhi.

Papers

7. IEEE Committee Report, "The Effect of Frequency and Voltage on Power System Load", Presented at IEEE Winter Power Meeting, New York, 1966.
8. "IEEE Standard Definitions of Basic per Unit Quantities for Alternating-Current Rotating Machines", in *IEEE Standard 86-1975 (Revision of IEEE Standard 86-1961)*, volume: 01, issue: 01, pp: 1–10, 1975.
9. I. Kasikci, M. Darwish, and P. Mehta, "Analytical Load Model for Power System Components", *Proceedings of the IEEE 1999 International Conference on Power Electronics and Drive Systems. PEDS'99 (Cat. No.99TH8475), Hong Kong*, volume: 02, pp: 673–676, 1999.

10. "IEEE Recommended Practice for Determining the Electric Power Station Ground Potential Rise and Induced Voltage from a Power Fault", in *ANSI/IEEE Standard 367-1987*, volume: 01, issue: 01, pp: 1–165, 1988.
11. T.R. Specht, "Transformer Reactance Calculation by Reactive Power", *IEEE Transactions on Power Apparatus and Systems*, volume: PAS-99, issue: 02, pp: 738–746, 1980.
12. M.B. Reed and R.M. Roberge, "Generalization of the Normalization (Per-Unit) Technique", *IEEE Transactions on Power Apparatus and Systems*, volume: PAS-88, issue: 11, pp: 1665–1672, 1969.
13. "IEEE Draft Guide for Synchronous Generator Modeling Practices and Parameter Verification with Applications in Power System Stability Analyses", *IEEE P1110/D06, December 2018*, volume: 01, issue: 01, pp: 1–91, 2019.
14. "IEEE Guide for Synchronous Generator Modeling Practices and Parameter Verification with Applications in Power System Stability Analyses", *IEEE Std 1110-2019 (Revision of IEEE Std 1110-2002)* , volume: 01, issue: 01, pp: 1–92, 2020.
15. A.B. Birchfield and T.J. Overbye, "Techniques for Drawing Geographic One-Line Diagrams: Substation Spacing and Line Routing", *IEEE Transactions on Power Systems*, volume: 33, issue: 6, pp: 7269–7276, 2018.
16. I. Lendák, A. Vidács, and A. Erdeljan, "Electric Power System One-Line Diagram Generation with Branch and Bound Algorithm", 2012 *IEEE International Energy Conference and Exhibition (ENERGYCON), Florence*, pp: 947–951, 2012.
17. U. Corbellini, "Power Systems Single Line Diagrams Standardization Proposal For An International Horizontal Standard", 2014 *AEIT Annual Conference—From Research to Industry: The Need for a More Effective Technology Transfer (AEIT), Trieste*, pp: 1–6, 2014.
18. R.K. Saket, R.C. Bansal and Col. Gurmit Singh, "Power Systems Component Modelling and Reliability Evaluation of Generation Capacity", *International Journal of Reliability and Safety*, volume: 03, issue: 04, pp: 427–441, 2009.

CHAPTER 5

Characteristics and Performance of Power Transmission Lines

5.1 ▶ INTRODUCTION

This chapter deals primarily with the characteristics and performance of transmission lines. A problem of major importance in power systems is the flow of load over transmission lines such that the voltage at various nodes is maintained within specified limits. While this general interconnected system problem will be dealt with in Ch. 6, attention is presently focussed on performance of a single transmission line so as to give the reader a clear understanding of the principle involved.

Transmission lines are normally operated with a balanced three-phase load; the analysis can therefore proceed on a per phase basis. A transmission line on a per phase basis can be regarded as a two-port network, wherein the sending-end voltage V_S and current I_S are related to the receiving-end voltage V_R and current I_R through *ABCD* constants* as

$$\begin{bmatrix} V_S \\ I_S \end{bmatrix} = \begin{bmatrix} A & B \\ C & D \end{bmatrix} \begin{bmatrix} V_R \\ I_R \end{bmatrix} \tag{5.1}$$

Also the following identity holds for *ABCD* constants:

$$AD - BC = 1 \tag{5.2}$$

These constants can be determined easily for short- and medium-length lines by suitable approximations lumping the line impedance and shunt admittance. For long lines exact analysis has to be carried out by considering the distribution of resistance, inductance and capacitance parameters and the *ABCD* constants of the line are determined therefrom.

Equations for power flow on a line and receiving- and sending-end circle diagrams will also be developed in this chapter so that various types of end conditions can be handled.

The following nomenclature has been adopted in this chapter:

z = series impedance/unit length/phase
y = shunt admittance/unit length/phase to neutral
r = resistance/unit length/phase
L = inductance/unit length/phase
C = capacitance/unit length/phase to neutral
l = transmission line length
$Z = zl$ = total series impedance/phase
$Y = yl$ = total shunt admittance/phase to neutral

Subscript S stands for a sending-end quantity.
Subscript R stands for a receiving-end quantity.

---

* Refer to Appendix A.

5.2 ▶ SHORT TRANSMISSION LINE

For short lines of length 100 km or less, the total 50 Hz shunt admittance* ($j\omega Cl$) is small enough to be negligible resulting in the simple equivalent circuit of Fig. 5.1.

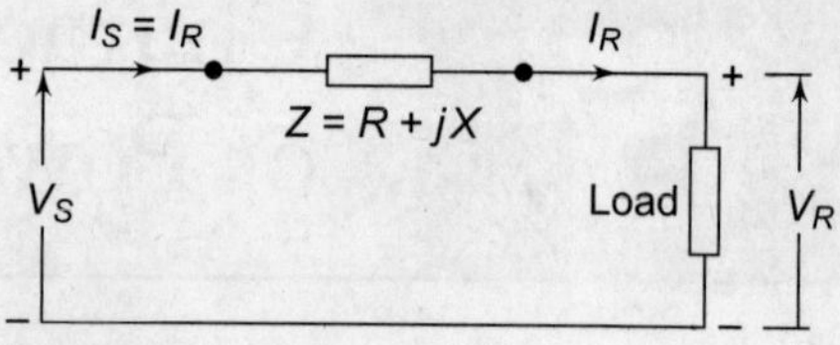

This being a simple series circuit, the relationship between sending-end and receiving-end voltages and currents can be immediately written as:

$$\begin{bmatrix} V_S \\ I_S \end{bmatrix} = \begin{bmatrix} 1 & Z \\ 0 & 1 \end{bmatrix} \begin{bmatrix} V_R \\ I_R \end{bmatrix} \quad (5.3)$$

Fig. 5.1 *Equivalent circuit of a short line*

The phasor diagram for the short line is shown in Fig. 5.2, for the lagging current case. From this figure we can write,

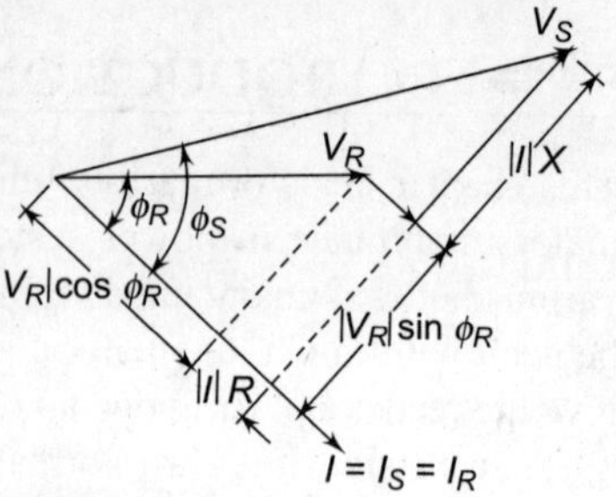

$$|V_S| = [(|V_R| \cos \phi_R + |I|R)^2 + (|V_R| \sin \phi_R + |I|X)^2]^{1/2}$$

$$|V_S| = [|V_R|^2 + |I|^2 (R^2 + X^2) + 2|V_R|\,|I|\,(R \cos \phi_R + X \sin \phi_R)]^{1/2} \quad (5.4)$$

$$= |V_R| \left[1 + \frac{2|I|R}{|V_R|} \cos \phi_R + \frac{2|I|X}{|V_R|} \sin \phi_R + \frac{|I|^2 (R^2 + X^2)}{|V_R|^2} \right]^{1/2}$$

Fig. 5.2 *Phasor diagram of a short line for lagging current*

The last term is usually of negligible order.

$$\therefore \qquad |V_S| \simeq |V_R| \left[1 + \frac{2|I|R}{|V_R|} \cos \phi_R + \frac{2|I|X}{|V_R|} \sin \phi_R \right]^{1/2}$$

Expanding binomially and retaining first order terms, we get

$$|V_S| \simeq |V_R| \left[1 + \frac{|I|R}{|V_R|} \cos \phi_R + \frac{|I|X}{|V_R|} \sin \phi_R \right]$$

or

$$|V_S| \simeq |V_R| + |I| (R \cos \phi_R + X \sin \phi_R) \quad (5.5)$$

The above equation is quite accurate for the normal load range.

5.2.1 Voltage Regulation

Voltage regulation of a transmission line is defined as the rise in voltage at the receiving end, expressed as percentage of full load voltage, when full load at a specified power factor is thrown off, i.e.,

$$\text{Per cent regulation} = \frac{|V_{R0}| - |V_{RL}|}{|V_{RL}|} \times 100 \quad (5.6)$$

where

$|V_{R0}|$ = magnitude of no-load receiving-end voltage

$|V_{RL}|$ = magnitude of full load receiving-end voltage (at a specified power factor).

* For overhead transmission lines, shunt admittance is mainly capacitive susceptance ($j\omega\ Cl$) as the line conductance (also called *leakance*) is always negligible.

For short line, $|V_{R0}| = |V_S|, |V_{RL}| = |V_R|$

$\therefore$ Per cent regulation $= \dfrac{|V_S| - |V_R|}{|V_R|}$

$$= \frac{|I| R \cos\phi_R + |I| X \sin\phi_R}{|V_R|} \times 100 \quad (5.7)$$

In the above derivation, ϕ_R has been considered positive for a lagging load. It will be negative for a leading load.

$$\text{Per cent regulation} = \frac{|I| R \cos\phi_R - |I| X \sin\phi_R}{|V_R|} \times 100 \quad (5.8)$$

Voltage regulation becomes negative (i.e., load voltage is more than no load voltage), when in Eq. (5.8)

$$X \sin \phi_R > R \cos \phi_R, \text{ or } \tan \phi_R \text{ (leading)} > \frac{R}{X}$$

It also follows from Eq. (5.8) that for zero voltage regulation

$$\tan \phi_R = \frac{R}{X} = \cot \theta$$

i.e., $$\phi_R \text{ (leading)} = \frac{\pi}{2} - \theta \quad (5.9)$$

where θ is the angle of the transmission line impedance. This is, however, an approximate condition. The exact condition for zero regulation is determined as follows.

Figure 5.3 shows the phasor diagram under conditions of zero voltage regulation, i.e.,

$$|V_S| = |V_R|$$

or $$OC = OA$$

$$\sin \angle AOD = \frac{AD}{OA} = \frac{AC/2}{|V_R|} = \frac{|I||Z|}{2|V_R|}$$

or $$\angle AOD = \sin^{-1}\frac{|I||Z|}{2|V_R|}$$

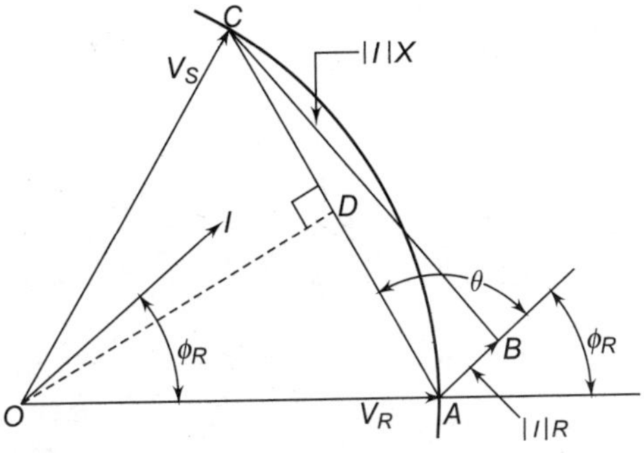

Fig. 5.3 *Phasor diagram under zero regulation condition*

It follows from the geometry of angles at A, that for zero voltage regulation,

$$\phi_R \text{ (leading)} = \left(\frac{\pi}{2} - \theta + \sin^{-1}\frac{|I||Z|}{2|V_R|}\right) \quad (5.10)$$

From the above discussion, it is seen that the voltage regulation of a line is heavily dependent upon load power factor. Voltage regulation improves (decreases) as the power factor of a lagging load is increased and it becomes zero at a leading power factor given by Eq. (5.10).

Example 5.1 A single-phase 50 Hz generator supplies an inductive load of 5,000 kW at a power factor of 0.707 lagging by means of an overhead transmission line 20 km long. The line resistance and inductance are 0.0195 ohm and 0.63 mH per km. The voltage at the receiving end is required to be kept constant at 10 kV.

Find (a) the sending-end voltage and voltage regulation of the line; (b) the value of the capacitors to be placed in parallel with the load such that the regulation is reduced to 50% of that obtained in part (a); and (c) compare the transmission efficiency in parts (a) and (b).

Solution The line constants are

$$R = 0.0195 \times 20 = 0.39\ \Omega$$

$$X = 314 \times 0.63 \times 10^{-3} \times 20 = 3.96\ \Omega$$

(a) This is the case of a short line with $I = I_R = I_S$ given by

$$|I| = \frac{5{,}000}{10 \times 0.707} = 707\ \text{A}$$

From Eq. (5.5),

$$|V_S| \simeq |V_R| + |I|\,(R \cos \phi_R + X \sin \phi_R)$$

$$= 10{,}000 + 707(0.39 \times 0.707 + 3.96 \times 0.707)\ \text{V}$$

$$= 12.175\ \text{kV}$$

Voltage regulation $= \dfrac{12.175 - 10}{10} \times 100 = 21.75\%.$

(b) Voltage regulation desired $= \dfrac{21.75}{2} = 10.9\%$

$$\therefore \quad \frac{|V_S| - 10}{10} = 0.109$$

or

$$\text{new value of } |V_S| = 11.09\ \text{kV}$$

Figure 5.4 shows the equivalent circuit of the line with a capacitive reactance placed in parallel with the load.

Assuming $\cos \phi_R$ now to be the power factor of load and capacitive reactance taken together, we can write

$$(11.09 - 10) \times 10^3 = |I_R|\,(R \cos \phi_R + X \sin \phi_R) \qquad \text{(i)}$$

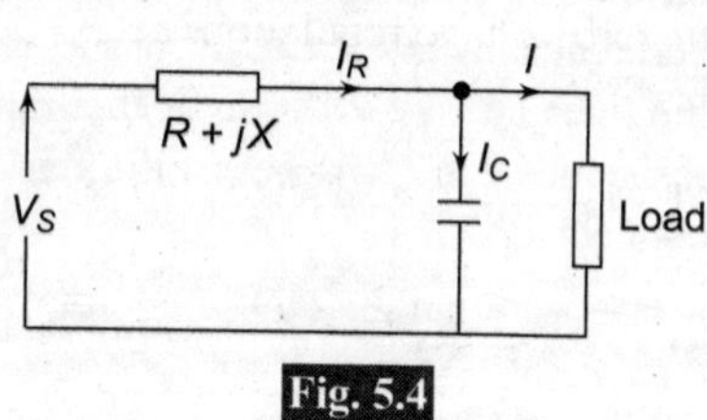

Fig. 5.4

Since the capacitance does not draw any real power, we have

$$|I_R| = \frac{5{,}000}{10 \times \cos \phi_R} \qquad \text{(ii)}$$

Solving Eqs (i) and (ii), we get

$$\cos \phi_R = 0.911 \text{ lagging}$$

and

$$|I_R| = 549\ \text{A}$$

Now,

$$I_C = I_R - I$$

$$= 549(0.911 - j0.412) - 707(0.707 - j0.707)$$

$$= 0.29 + j273.7$$

Note that the real part of 0.29 appears due to the approximation in (i). Ignoring it, we have

$$I_C = j273.7\ \text{A}$$

$$\therefore \qquad X_C = \frac{1}{314 \times C} = \left|\frac{V_R}{I_C}\right| = \frac{10 \times 1000}{273.7}$$

or

$$C = 87 \ \mu\text{F}$$

(c) Efficiency of transmission

$$\eta = \frac{\text{output}}{\text{output} + \text{loss}}$$

Case (a)

$$\eta = \frac{5,000}{5,000 + (707)^2 \times 0.39 \times 10^{-3}} = 96.2\%$$

Case (b)

$$\eta = \frac{5,000}{5,000 + (549)^2 \times 0.39 \times 10^{-3}} = 97.7\%$$

It is to be noted that by placing a capacitor in parallel with the load, the receiving-end power factor improves (from 0.707 lag to 0.911 lag), the line current reduces (from 707 A to 549 A), the line voltage regulation decreases (one half the previous value) and the transmission efficiency improves (from 96.2 to 97.7%). Adding capacitors in parallel with load is a powerful method of improving the performance of a transmission system and will be discussed further towards the end of this chapter.

Example 5.2 A substation as shown in Fig. 5.5 receives 5 MVA at 6 kV, 0.85 lagging power factor on the low voltage side of a transformer from a power station through a cable having per phase resistance and reactance of 8 and 2.5 ohms, respectively. Identical 6.6/33 kV transformers are installed at each end of the line. The 6.6 kV side of the transformers is delta connected while the 33 kV side is star connected. The resistance and reactance of the star connected windings are 0.5 and 3.75 ohms, respectively and for the delta connected windings are 0.06 and 0.36 ohms. What is the voltage at the bus at the power station end?

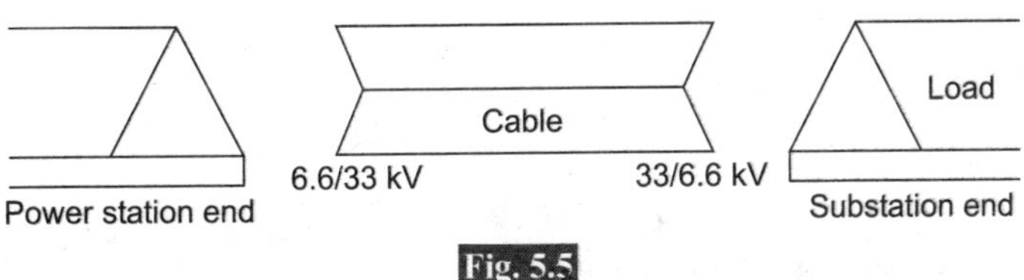

Fig. 5.5

Solution It is convenient here to employ the per unit method. Let us choose,

$$\text{Base MVA} = 5$$

$$\text{Base kV} = 6.6 \text{ on low voltage side}$$

$$= 33 \text{ on high voltage side}$$

$$\text{Cable impedance} = (8 + j2.5) \ \Omega/\text{phase}$$

$$= \frac{(8 + j2.5) \times 5}{(33)^2} = (0.037 + j0.0115) \text{ pu}$$

Equivalent star impedance of 6.6 kV winding of the transformer

$$= \frac{1}{3}(0.06 + j0.36) = (0.02 + j0.12) \ \Omega/\text{phase}$$

Per unit transformer impedance,

$$Z_T = \frac{(0.02 + j0.12) \times 5}{(6.6)^2} + \frac{(0.5 + j3.75) \times 5}{(33)^2}$$

$$= (0.0046 + j0.030) \text{ pu}$$

$$\text{Total series impedance} = (0.037 + j0.0115) + 2(0.0046 + j0.030)$$

$$= (0.046 + j0.072) \text{ pu}$$

Given:

$$\text{Load MVA} = 1 \text{ pu}$$

$$\text{Load voltage} = \frac{6}{6.6} = 0.91 \text{ pu}$$

$$\therefore \quad \text{Load current} = \frac{1}{0.91} = 1.1 \text{ pu}$$

Using Eq. (5.5), we get

$$|V_S| = 0.91 + 1.1(0.046 \times 0.85 + 0.072 \times 0.527)$$

$$= 0.995 \text{ pu}$$

$$= 0.995 \times 6.6 = 6.57 \text{ kV (line-to-line)}$$

Example 5.3 Input to a single-phase short line shown in Fig. 5.6 is 2,000 kW at 0.8 lagging power factor. The line has a series impedance of (0.4 + j0.4) ohms. If the load voltage is 3 kV, find the load and receiving-end power factor. Also find the supply voltage.

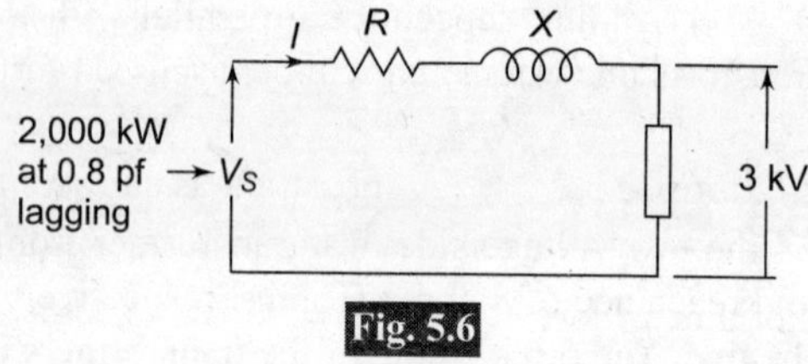

Fig. 5.6

Solution It is a problem with mixed-end conditions—load voltage and input power are specified. The exact solution is outlined below.

Sending-end active/reactive power = receiving-end active/reactive power + active/reactive line losses

For active power,

$$|V_S|\,|I| \cos \phi_S = |V_R|\,|I| \cos \phi_R + |I|^2 R \tag{i}$$

For reactive power,

$$|V_S|\,|I| \sin \phi_S = |V_R|\,|I| \sin \phi_R + |I|^2 X \tag{ii}$$

Squaring (i) and (ii), adding and simplifying, we get

$$|V_S|^2\,|I|^2 = |V_R|^2\,|I|^2 + 2|V_R|\,|I|^2\,(|I|R \cos \phi_R + |I|X \sin \phi_R) + |I|^4\,(R^2 + X^2) \tag{iii}$$

Note: This, in fact, is the same as Eq. (5.4) if $|I|^2$ is cancelled throughout. For the numerical values given

$$|Z|^2 = (R^2 + X^2) = 0.32$$

$$|V_S|\,|I| = \frac{2{,}000 \times 10^3}{0.8} = 2{,}500 \times 10^3$$

$$|V_S|\,|I| \cos \phi_S = 2{,}000 \times 10^3$$

$$|V_S|\,|I| \sin \phi_S = 2{,}500 \times 10^3 \times 0.6 = 1{,}500 \times 10^3$$

From Eqs (i) and (ii), we get

$$|I| \cos \phi_R = \frac{2{,}000 \times 10^3 - 0.4\,|I|^2}{3{,}000} \tag{iv}$$

$$|I| \sin \phi_R = \frac{1{,}500 \times 10^3 - 0.4|I|^2}{3{,}000} \quad \text{(v)}$$

Substituting all the known values in Eq. (iii), we have

$$(2{,}500 \times 10^3)^2 = (3{,}000)^2 |I|^2 + 2 \times 3{,}000 |I|^2 \left[0.4 \times \frac{2{,}000 \times 10^3 - 0.4|I|^2}{3{,}000} + 0.4 \times \frac{1{,}500 \times 10^3 - 0.4|I|^2}{3{,}000}\right] + 0.32 |I|^4$$

Simplifying, we get

$$0.32 |I|^4 - 11.8 \times 10^6 |I|^2 + 6.25 \times 10^{12} = 0$$

which upon solution yields

$$|I| = 725 \text{ A}$$

Substituting for $|I|$ in Eq. (iv), we get

$$\cos \phi_R = 0.82$$

$$\therefore \quad \text{Load } P_R = |V_R|\,|I| \cos \phi_R = 3{,}000 \times 725 \times 0.82$$

$$= 1{,}790 \text{ kW}$$

Now,

$$|V_S| = |I| \cos \phi_S = 2{,}000$$

$$\therefore \quad |V_S| = \frac{2{,}000}{725 \times 0.8} = 3.44 \text{ kV}$$

5.3 ▶ MEDIUM TRANSMISSION LINE

For lines more than 100 km long, charging currents due to shunt admittance cannot be neglected. For lines in range 100 km to 250 km length, it is sufficiently accurate to lump all the line admittance at the receiving end, resulting in the equivalent diagram shown in Fig. 5.7.

Starting from fundamental circuit equations, it is fairly straightforward to write the transmission line equations in the *ABCD* constant form given below:

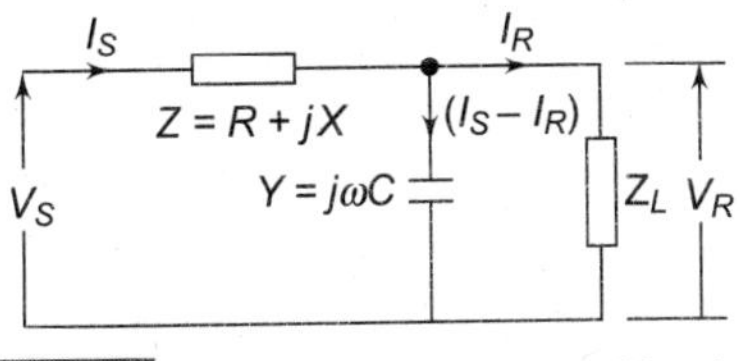

Fig. 5.7 *Medium line, localised load-end capacitance*

$$\begin{bmatrix} V_S \\ I_S \end{bmatrix} = \begin{bmatrix} 1 + YZ & Z \\ Y & 1 \end{bmatrix} \begin{bmatrix} V_R \\ I_R \end{bmatrix} \quad (5.11)$$

5.3.1 Nominal-*T* Representation

If all the shunt capacitance is lumped at the middle of the line, it leads to the nominal-*T* circuit shown in Fig. 5.8.

For the nominal-*T* circuit, the following circuit equations can be written:

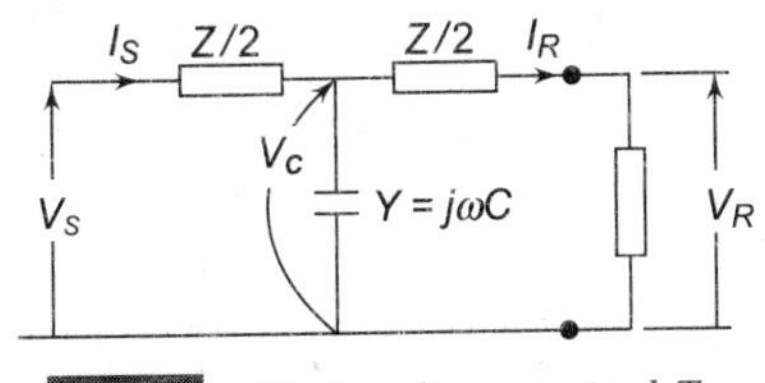

Fig. 5.8 *Medium line, nominal-T representation*

$$V_C = V_R + I_R(Z/2)$$

$$I_S = I_R + V_C Y$$

$$= I_R + YV_R + I_R(Z/2)Y$$

$$V_S = V_C + I_S(Z/2)$$

Substituting for V_C and I_S in the last equation, we get

$$V_S = V_R + I_R(Z/2) + (Z/2)\left[I_R\left(1+\frac{ZY}{2}\right)+YV_R\right]$$

$$= V_R\left(1+\frac{ZY}{2}\right)+I_R\,Z\left(1+\frac{YZ}{4}\right)$$

Rearranging the results, we get the following equations:

$$\begin{bmatrix}V_S\\ I_S\end{bmatrix}=\begin{bmatrix}\left(1+\frac{1}{2}ZY\right) & Z\left(1+\frac{1}{4}YZ\right)\\ Y & \left(1+\frac{1}{2}YZ\right)\end{bmatrix}\begin{bmatrix}V_R\\ I_R\end{bmatrix} \tag{5.12}$$

5.3.2 Nominal-π Representation

In this method, the total line capacitance is divided into two equal parts which are lumped at the sending- and receiving ends, resulting in the nominal-π representation as shown in Fig. 5.9.

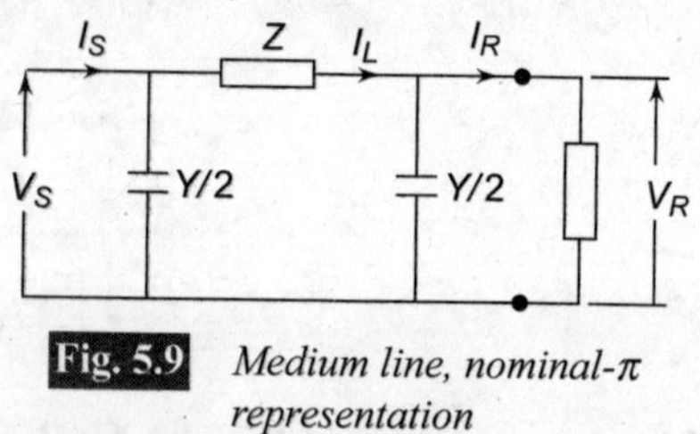

Fig. 5.9 *Medium line, nominal-π representation*

From Fig. 5.9, we have

$$I_S = I_R + \frac{1}{2}V_RY + \frac{1}{2}V_SY$$

$$V_S = V_R + \left(I_R + \frac{1}{2}V_RY\right)Z = V_R\left(1+\frac{1}{2}YZ\right)+I_RZ$$

$$\therefore\quad I_S = I_R + \frac{1}{2}V_RY + \frac{1}{2}Y\left[V_R\left(1+\frac{1}{2}YZ\right)+I_RZ\right]$$

$$= V_RY\left(1+\frac{1}{4}YZ\right)+I_R\left(1+\frac{1}{2}YZ\right)$$

Finally, we have

$$\begin{bmatrix}V_S\\ I_S\end{bmatrix}=\begin{bmatrix}\left(1+\frac{1}{2}YZ\right) & Z\\ Y\left(1+\frac{1}{4}YZ\right) & \left(1+\frac{1}{2}YZ\right)\end{bmatrix}\begin{bmatrix}V_R\\ I_R\end{bmatrix} \tag{5.13}$$

It should be noted that nominal-T and nominal-π with the above constants are not equivalent to each other. The reader should verify this fact by applying star-delta transformation to either one.

Example 5.4 Using the nominal-π method, find the sending-end voltage and voltage regulation of a 250 km, three-phase, 50 Hz, transmission line delivering 25 MVA at 0.8 lagging power factor to a balanced load at 132 kV. The line conductors are spaced equilaterally 3 m apart. The conductor resistance is 0.11 ohm/km and its effective diameter is 1.6 cm. Neglect leakance.

Solution Now,

$$L = 0.461\log\frac{D}{r'} = 0.461\log\frac{300}{0.7788\times0.8} = 1.24\ \text{mH/km}$$

$$C = \frac{0.0242}{\log D/r} = \frac{0.0242}{\log \dfrac{300}{0.8}} = 0.0094 \ \mu\text{F/km}$$

$$R = 0.11 \times 250 = 27.5 \ \Omega$$

$$X = 2\pi f L = 2\pi \times 50 \times 1.24 \times 10^{-3} \times 250 = 97.4 \ \Omega$$

$$Z = R + jX = 27.5 + j97.4 = 101.2 \ \angle 74.2^\circ \ \Omega$$

$$Y = j\omega Cl = 314 \times 0.0094 \times 10^{-6} \times 250 \ \angle 90^\circ$$

$$= 7.38 \times 10^{-4} \ \angle 90^\circ \ \mho$$

$$I_R = \frac{25 \times 1,000}{\sqrt{3} \times 132} \angle -36.9^\circ = 109.3 \ \angle -36.9^\circ \text{ A}$$

$$V_R \text{(per phase)} = (132/(\sqrt{3}) \ \angle 0^\circ = 76.2 \ \angle 0^\circ \text{ kV}$$

$$V_S = \left(1 + \frac{1}{2} YZ\right) V_R + ZI_R$$

$$= \left(1 + \frac{1}{2} \times 7.38 \times 10^{-4} \angle 90^\circ \times 101.2 \angle 74.2^\circ\right) \times 76.2$$

$$+ 101.2 \ \angle 74.2^\circ \times 109.3 \times 10^{-3} \ \angle -36.9^\circ$$

$$= 76.2 + 2.85 < 164.2^\circ + 11.06 < 37.3^\circ$$

$$= 82.26 + j7.48 = 82.6 < 5.2^\circ$$

$$\therefore \qquad |V_S| \text{ (line)} = 82.6 \times \sqrt{3} = 143 \text{ kV}$$

$$1 + \frac{1}{2} YZ = 1 + 0.0374 \ \angle 164.2^\circ = 0.964 + j0.01$$

$$|V_{R0}| \text{ (line no load)} = \frac{143}{\left|1 + \dfrac{1}{2} YZ\right|} = \frac{143}{0.964} = 148.3 \text{ kV}$$

$$\therefore \quad \text{Voltage regulation} = \frac{148.3 - 132}{132} \times 100 = 12.3\%$$

5.4 ▶ THE LONG TRANSMISSION LINE—RIGOROUS SOLUTION

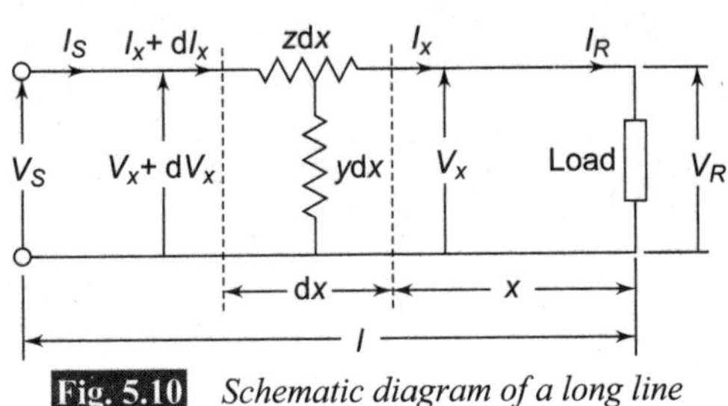

Fig. 5.10 *Schematic diagram of a long line*

For lines over 250 km, the fact that the parameters of a line are not lumped but distributed uniformly throughout its length must be considered.

Figure 5.10 shows one phase and the neutral return (of zero impedance) of a transmission line. Let dx be an elemental section of the line at a distance x from the receiving end having a series impedance z dx and a shunt admittance y dx. The rise in voltage* to neutral over the elemental section in the direction of increasing x is dV_x. We can write the following differential relationships across the elemental section:

* Here V_x is the complex expression of the rms voltage, whose magnitude and phase vary with distance along the line.

$$dV_x = I_x z\, dx \quad \text{or} \quad \frac{dV_x}{dx} = zI_x \tag{5.14}$$

$$dI_x = V_x y\, dx \quad \text{or} \quad \frac{dI_x}{dx} = yV_x \tag{5.15}$$

It may be noticed that the kind of connection (e.g., T or π) assumed for the elemental section does not affect these first order differential relations.

Differentiating Eq. (5.14) with respect to x, we obtain

$$\frac{d^2V_x}{dx^2} = \frac{dI_x}{dx} z$$

Substituting the value of $\frac{dI_x}{dx}$ from Eq. (5.15), we get

$$\frac{d^2 V_x}{dx^2} = yzV_x \tag{5.16}$$

This is a linear differential equation whose general solution can be written as follows:

$$V_x = C_1 e^{\gamma x} + C_2 e^{-\gamma x} \tag{5.17}$$

where

$$\gamma = \sqrt{yz} \tag{5.18}$$

and C_1 and C_2 are arbitrary constants to be evaluated.

Differentiating Eq. (5.17) with respect to x,

$$\frac{dV_x}{dx} = C_1 \gamma e^{\gamma x} - C_2 \gamma e^{-\gamma x} = zI_x$$

$$\therefore \quad I_x = \frac{C_1}{Z_c} e^{\gamma x} - \frac{C_2}{Z_c} e^{-\gamma x} \tag{5.19}$$

where

$$Z_c = \left(\frac{z}{y}\right)^{1/2} \tag{5.20}$$

The constants C_1 and C_2 may be evaluated by using the end conditions, i.e., when $x = 0$, $V_x = V_R$ and $I_x = I_R$. Substituting these values in Eqs (5.17) and (5.19) gives

$$V_R = C_1 + C_2$$

$$I_R = \frac{1}{Z_c} (C_1 - C_2)$$

which upon solving yields

$$C_1 = \frac{1}{2}(V_R + Z_c I_R)$$

$$C_2 = \frac{1}{2}(V_R - Z_c I_R)$$

With C_1 and C_2 as determined above, Eqs (5.17) and (5.19) yield the solution for V_x and I_x as

$$V_x = \left(\frac{V_R + Z_c I_R}{2}\right) e^{\gamma x} + \left(\frac{V_R - Z_c I_R}{2}\right) e^{-\gamma x} \tag{5.21}$$

$$I_x = \left(\frac{V_R/Z_c + I_R}{2}\right)e^{\gamma x} - \left(\frac{V_R/Z_c - I_R}{2}\right)e^{-\gamma x}$$

Here Z_c is called the *characteristic impedance* of the line and γ is called the *propagation constant.*

Knowing V_R, I_R and the parameters of the line, using Eq. (5.21) complex number rms values of V_x and I_x at any distance x along the line can be easily found out.

A more convenient form of expression for voltage and current is obtained by introducing hyperbolic functions. Rearranging Eq. (5.21), we get

$$V_x = V_R\left(\frac{e^{\gamma x} + e^{-\gamma x}}{2}\right) + I_R Z_c\left(\frac{e^{\gamma x} - e^{-\gamma x}}{2}\right)$$

$$I_x = V_R\frac{1}{Z_c}\left(\frac{e^{\gamma x} - e^{-\gamma x}}{2}\right) + I_R\left(\frac{e^{\gamma x} + e^{-\gamma x}}{2}\right)$$

These can be rewritten after introducing hyperbolic functions, as

$$V_x = V_R \cosh \gamma x + I_R Z_c \sinh \gamma x \tag{5.22}$$

$$I_x = I_R \cosh \gamma x + V_R \frac{1}{Z_c} \sinh \gamma x$$

when $x = l$, $V_x = V_S$, $I_x = I_S$

$$\therefore \quad \begin{bmatrix} V_S \\ I_S \end{bmatrix} = \begin{bmatrix} \cosh \gamma l & Z_c \sinh \gamma l \\ \frac{1}{Z_c}\sinh \gamma l & \cosh \gamma l \end{bmatrix}\begin{bmatrix} V_R \\ I_R \end{bmatrix} \tag{5.23}$$

Here,

$$A = D = \cosh \gamma l$$
$$B = Z_c \sinh \gamma l \tag{5.24}$$
$$C = \frac{1}{Z_c}\sinh \gamma l$$

In case $[V_S\, I_S]$ is known, $[V_R\, I_R]$ can be easily found by inverting Eq. (5.23). Thus,

$$\begin{bmatrix} V_R \\ I_R \end{bmatrix} = \begin{bmatrix} D & -B \\ -C & A \end{bmatrix}\begin{bmatrix} V_S \\ I_S \end{bmatrix} \tag{5.25}$$

5.4.1 Evaluation of ABCD Constants

The *ABCD* constants of a long line can be evaluated from the results given in Eq. (5.24). It must be noted that $\gamma = \sqrt{yz}$ is in general a complex number and can be expressed as

$$\gamma = \alpha + j\beta \tag{5.26}$$

The hyperbolic function of complex numbers involved in evaluating *ABCD* constants can be computed by any one of the three methods given below:

Method 1

$$\cosh(\alpha l + j\beta l) = \cosh \alpha l \cos \beta l + j \sinh \alpha l \sin \beta l$$
$$\sinh(\alpha l + j\beta l) = \sinh \alpha l \cos \beta l + j \cosh \alpha l \sin \beta l \tag{5.27}$$

Note that sinh, cosh, sin and cos of real numbers as in Eq. (5.27) can be looked up in standard tables.

Method 2

$$\cosh \gamma l = 1 + \frac{\gamma^2 l^2}{2!} + \frac{\gamma^4 l^4}{4!} + \ldots \approx \left(1 + \frac{YZ}{2}\right)$$
$$\sinh \gamma l = \gamma l + \frac{\gamma^3 l^3}{3!} + \frac{\gamma^5 l^5}{5!} + \ldots \approx \sqrt{YZ}\left(1 + \frac{YZ}{6}\right) \tag{5.28a}$$

This series converges rapidly for values of γl usually encountered for power lines and can be conveniently approximated as above. The corresponding expressions for *ABCD* constants are

$$A = D \approx 1 + \frac{YZ}{2}$$
$$B \approx Z\left(1 + \frac{YZ}{6}\right) \tag{5.28b}$$
$$C \approx Y\left(1 + \frac{YZ}{6}\right)$$

The above approximation is computationally convenient and quite accurate for lines up to 400/500 km.

Method 3

$$\cosh(\alpha l + j\beta l) = \frac{e^{\alpha l}e^{j\beta l} + e^{-\alpha l}e^{-j\beta l}}{2} = \frac{1}{2}(e^{\alpha l}\angle\beta l + e^{-\alpha l}\angle -\beta l)$$
$$\sinh(\alpha l + j\beta l) = \frac{e^{\alpha l}e^{j\beta l} - e^{-\alpha l}e^{-j\beta l}}{2} = \frac{1}{2}(e^{\alpha l}\angle\beta l - e^{-\alpha l}\angle -\beta l) \tag{5.29}$$

5.5 ▶ THE EQUIVALENT CIRCUIT OF A LONG LINE

So far as the end conditions are concerned, the exact equivalent circuit of a transmission line can be established in the form of a *T*- or π-network.

The parameters of the equivalent network are easily obtained by comparing the performance equations of a π-network and a transmission line in terms of end quantities.

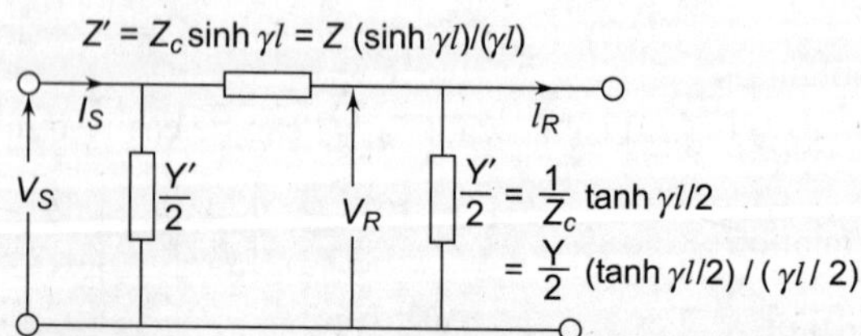

Fig. 5.11 *Equivalent-π network of a transmission line*

For a π-network shown in Fig. 5.11 [refer to Eq. (5.13)].

$$\begin{bmatrix} V_S \\ I_S \end{bmatrix} = \begin{bmatrix} \left(1 + \frac{1}{2}Y'Z'\right) & Z' \\ Y'\left(1 + \frac{1}{4}Y'Z'\right) & \left(1 + \frac{1}{2}Y'Z'\right) \end{bmatrix} \begin{bmatrix} V_R \\ I_R \end{bmatrix} \tag{5.30}$$

According to exact solution of a long line [refer to Eq. (5.23)].

$$\begin{bmatrix} V_S \\ I_S \end{bmatrix} = \begin{bmatrix} \cosh \gamma l & Z_c \sinh \gamma l \\ \frac{1}{Z_c}\sinh \gamma l & \cosh \gamma l \end{bmatrix} \begin{bmatrix} V_R \\ I_R \end{bmatrix} \tag{5.31}$$

For exact equivalence, we must have

$$Z' = Z_c \sinh \gamma l \tag{5.32}$$

$$1 + \frac{1}{2} Y'Z' = \cosh \gamma l \tag{5.33}$$

From Eq. (5.32)

$$Z' = \sqrt{\frac{z}{y}} \sinh \gamma l = zl \frac{\sinh \gamma l}{l\sqrt{yz}} = Z\left(\frac{\sinh \gamma l}{\gamma l}\right) \tag{5.34}$$

Thus, $\dfrac{\sinh \gamma l}{\gamma l}$ is the factor by which the series impedance of the nominal-π must be multiplied to obtain the Z' parameter of the equivalent-π.

Substituting Z' from Eq. (5.32) in Eq. (5.33), we get

$$1 + \frac{1}{2} Y'Z_c \sinh \gamma l = \cosh \gamma l$$

$$\therefore \quad \frac{1}{2} Y' = \frac{1}{Z_c}\left(\frac{\cosh \gamma l - 1}{\sinh \gamma l}\right)$$

$$= \frac{1}{Z_c} \tanh \frac{\gamma l}{2} = \sqrt{\frac{y}{z}} \tanh \frac{\gamma l}{2}$$

$$= \frac{yl}{2}\left(\frac{\tanh \gamma l/2}{\gamma l/2}\right)$$

or

$$\frac{1}{2} Y' = \frac{Y}{2}\left(\frac{\tanh \gamma l/2}{\gamma l/2}\right) \tag{5.35}$$

Thus, $\left(\dfrac{\tanh \gamma l/2}{\gamma l/2}\right)$ is the factor by which the shunt admittance arm of the nominal-π must be multiplied to obtain the shunt parameter ($Y'/2$) of the equivalent-π.

Note that $Y'\left(1 + \frac{1}{4} Y'Z'\right) = \frac{1}{Z_c} \sinh \gamma l$ is a consistent equation in terms of the above values of Y' and Z'.

For a line of medium length, $\dfrac{\tanh \gamma l/2}{\gamma l/2} \simeq 1$ and $\dfrac{\sinh \gamma l}{\gamma l} \simeq 1$ so that the equivalent-π network reduces to that of nominal-π. The equivalent-T network is shown in Fig. 5.12.

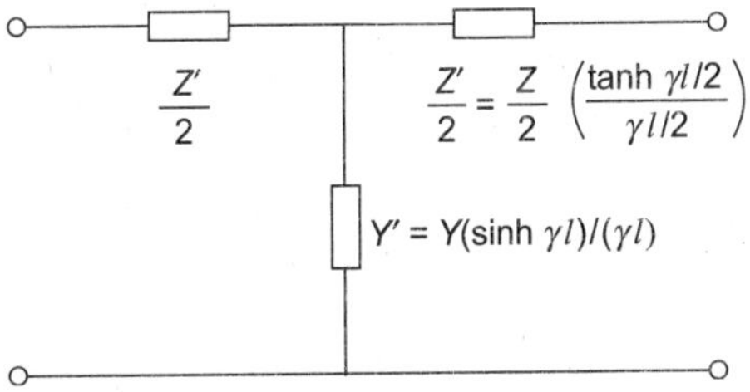

Fig. 5.12 *Equivalent-T network of a transmission line*

Equivalent-T network parameters of a transmission line are obtained on similar lines.

As we shall see in Ch. 6, equivalent-π (or nominal-π) network is easily adopted to load flow studies and is, therefore, universally employed.

Example 5.5 A 50 Hz transmission line 300 km long has a total series impedance of $40 + j125$ ohms and a total shunt admittance of 10^{-3} mho. The receiving-end load is 50 MW at 220 kV with 0.8 lagging power factor. Find the sending-end voltage, current, power and power factor using

(a) Short line approximation,
(b) Nominal-π method,
(c) Exact transmission line equation [Eq. (5.27)],
(d) Approximation [Eq. (5.28b)].
Compare the results and comment.

Solution

$$Z = 40 + j125 = 131.2 \angle 72.3^\circ\ \Omega$$
$$Y = 10^{-3} \angle 90^\circ\ \Omega$$

The receiving-end load is 50 MW at 220 kV, 0.8 pf lagging.

$$\therefore \quad I_R = \frac{50}{\sqrt{3} \times 220 \times 0.8} \angle -36.9^\circ = 0.164 \angle -36.9^\circ \text{ kA}$$

$$V_R = \frac{220}{\sqrt{3}} \angle 0^\circ = 127 \angle 0^\circ \text{ kV}$$

(a) Short line approximation:
From Eq. (5.3),

$$V_S = 127 + 0.164 \angle -36.9^\circ \times 131.2 \angle 72.3^\circ$$
$$= 145 \angle 4.9^\circ$$
$$|V_S|_{\text{line}} = 251.2 \text{ kV}$$
$$I_S = I_R = 0.164 \angle -36.9^\circ \text{ kA}$$
$$\text{Sending-end power factor} = \cos(4.9^\circ + 36.9^\circ = 41.8^\circ)$$
$$= 0.745 \text{ lagging}$$
$$\text{Sending-end power} = \sqrt{3} \times 251.2 \times 0.164 \times 0.745$$
$$= 53.2 \text{ MW}$$

(b) Nominal-π method:

$$A = D = 1 + \frac{1}{2} YZ = 1 + \frac{1}{2} \times 10^{-3} \angle 90^\circ \times 131.2 \angle 72.3^\circ$$
$$= 1 + 0.0656 \angle 162.3^\circ = 0.938 \angle 1.2^\circ$$
$$B = Z = 131.2 \angle 72.3^\circ$$
$$C = Y\left(1 + \frac{1}{4} YZ\right) = Y + \frac{1}{4} Y^2 Z$$
$$= 0.001 \angle 90^\circ + \frac{1}{4} \times 10^{-6} \angle 180^\circ \times 131.2 \angle 72.3^\circ$$
$$= 0.001 \angle 90^\circ$$
$$V_S = 0.938 \angle 1.2^\circ \times 127 + 131.2 \angle 72.3^\circ \times 0.164 \angle -36.9^\circ$$
$$= 119.1 \angle 1.2^\circ + 21.5 \angle 35.4^\circ = 137.4 \angle 6.2^\circ$$
$$|V_S|_{\text{line}} = 238 \text{ kV}$$
$$I_S = 0.001 \angle 90^\circ \times 127 + 0.938 \angle 1.2^\circ \times 0.164 \angle -36.9^\circ$$
$$= 0.127 \angle 90^\circ + 0.154 \angle -35.7^\circ = 0.13 \angle 16.5^\circ$$
$$\text{Sending-end pf} = \cos(16.5^\circ - 6.2^\circ) = 0.984 \text{ leading}$$
$$\text{Sending-end power} = \sqrt{3} \times 238 \times 0.13 \times 0.984$$
$$= 52.7 \text{ MW}$$

(c) Exact transmission line equations (Eq. 5.29).

$$\gamma l = \alpha l + j\beta l = \sqrt{YZ}$$
$$= \sqrt{10^{-3}\angle 90^\circ \times 131.2 \angle 72.3^\circ}$$
$$= 0.0554 + j0.3577$$
$$= 0.362 \angle 81.2^\circ$$

$$\cosh(\alpha l + j\beta l) = \frac{1}{2}(e^{\alpha l} \angle \beta l + e^{-\alpha l} \angle -\beta l)$$

$$\beta l = 0.3577 \text{ (radians)} = \angle 20.49^\circ$$
$$e^{0.0554} \angle(20.49^\circ) = 1.057 \angle 20.49^\circ = 0.99 + j0.37$$
$$e^{-0.0554} \angle -20.49^\circ = 0.946 \angle -20.49^\circ = 0.886 - j0.331$$

$\therefore$
$$\cosh \gamma l = 0.938 + j0.02 = 0.938 \angle 1.2^\circ$$
$$\sinh \gamma l = 0.052 + j0.35 = 0.354 \angle 81.5^\circ$$

$$Z_c = \sqrt{\frac{Z}{Y}} = \sqrt{\frac{131.2 \angle 72.3^\circ}{10^{-3}\angle 90^\circ}} = 362.21 \angle -8.85^\circ$$

$$A = D = \cosh \gamma l = 0.938 \angle 1.2^\circ$$
$$B = Z_c \sinh \gamma l = 362.21 \angle -8.85^\circ \times 0.354 \angle 81.5^\circ$$
$$= 128.2 \angle 72.65^\circ$$

Now,

$$V_S = 0.938 \angle 1.2^\circ \times 127 \angle 0^\circ + 128.2 \angle 72.65^\circ \times 0.164 \angle -36.9^\circ$$
$$= 119.13 \angle 1.2^\circ + 21.03 \angle 35.75^\circ$$
$$= 136.97 \angle 6.2^\circ \text{ kV}$$
$$|V_S|_{\text{line}} = 237.23 \text{ kV}$$

$$C = \frac{1}{Z_c} \sinh \gamma l = \frac{1}{362.21\angle -8.85^\circ} \times 0.354 \angle 81.5^\circ$$
$$= 9.77 \times 10^{-4} \angle 90.4^\circ$$

$$I_S = 9.77 \times 10^{-4} \angle 90.4^\circ \times 127 + 0.938\angle 1.2^\circ \times 0.164 \angle -36.9^\circ$$
$$= 0.124 \angle 90.4^\circ + 0.154 \angle -35.7^\circ$$
$$= 0.1286 \angle 15.3^\circ \text{ kA}$$

$$\text{Sending-end pf} = \cos(15.3^\circ - 6.2^\circ = 9.1^\circ) = 0.987 \text{ leading}$$

$$\text{Sending-end power} = \sqrt{3} \times 237.23 \times 0.1286 \times 0.987$$
$$= 52.15 \text{ MW}$$

(d) Approximation (5.28b):

$$A = D = 1 + \frac{1}{2} YZ$$
$$= 0.938 \angle 1.2^\circ \text{ (already calculated in part (b))}$$

$$B = Z\left(1 + \frac{YZ}{6}\right) = Z + \frac{1}{6} YZ^2$$

$$= 131.2 \angle 72.3^\circ + \frac{1}{6} \times 10^{-3} \angle 90^\circ \times (131.2)^2 \angle 144.6^\circ$$

$$= 131.2 \angle 72.3^\circ + 2.87 \angle -125.4^\circ$$

$$= 128.5 \angle 72.7^\circ$$

$$C = Y\left(1+\frac{YZ}{6}\right) = 0.001 \angle 90^\circ + \frac{1}{6} \times 10^{-6} \angle 180^\circ \times 131.2 \angle 72.3^\circ$$

$$= 0.001 \angle 90^\circ$$

$$V_S = 0.938 \angle 1.2^\circ \times 127 \angle 0^\circ + 128.5 \angle 72.7^\circ \times 0.164 \angle -36.9^\circ$$

$$= 119.13 \angle 1.2^\circ + 21.07 \angle 35.8^\circ = 136.2 + j14.82$$

$$= 137 \angle 6.2^\circ \text{ kV}$$

$$|V_S|_{\text{line}} = 237.3 \text{ kV}$$

$$I_S = 0.13 \angle 16.5^\circ \text{ (same as calculated in part (b))}$$

$$\text{Sending-end pf} = \cos(16.5^\circ - 6.2^\circ = 10.3^\circ) = 0.984 \text{ leading}$$

$$\text{Sending-end power} = \sqrt{3} \times 237.3 \times 0.13 \times 0.984$$

$$= 52.58 \text{ MW}$$

The results are tabulated as:

	Short line approximation	*Nominal-π*	*Exact*	*Approximation (5.28b)*
$\lvert V_s\rvert_{\text{line}}$	251.2 kV	238 kV	237.23 kV	237.3 kV
I_s	0.164 ∠–36.9° kA	0.13 ∠16.5° kA	0.1286 ∠15.3° kA	0.13 ∠16.5° kA
pf_s	0.745 lagging	0.984 leading	0.987 leading	0.984 leading
P_s	53.2 MW	52.7 MW	52.15 MW	52.58 MW

Comments We find from the above example that the results obtained by the nominal-π method and the approximation (5.28b) are practically the same and are very close to those obtained by exact calculations (part (c)). On the other hand, the results obtained by the short line approximation are in considerable error. Therefore, for a line of this length (about 300 km), it is sufficiently accurate to use the nominal-π (or approximation (5.28b)) which results in considerable saving in computational effort.

5.6 ► INTERPRETATION OF THE LONG LINE EQUATIONS

As already said in Eq. (5.26), γ is a complex number which can be expressed as

$$\gamma = \alpha + j\beta$$

The real part α is called the *attenuation constant* and the imaginary part β is called the *phase constant*. Now V_x of Eq. (5.21) can be written as

$$V_x = \left|\frac{V_R + Z_c I_R}{2}\right| e^{\alpha x} e^{j(\beta x + \phi_1)} + \left|\frac{V_R - Z_c I_R}{2}\right| e^{-\alpha x} e^{-j(\beta x - \phi_2)}$$

where

$$\phi_1 = \angle(V_R + I_R Z_c)$$

$$\phi_2 = \angle(V_R - I_R Z_c) \tag{5.36}$$

The instantaneous voltage $v_x(t)$ can be written from Eq. (5.36) as

$$v_x(t) = \text{Re}\left[\sqrt{2}\left|\frac{V_R + Z_c I_R}{2}\right| e^{\alpha x} e^{j(\omega t + \beta x + \phi_1)} + \sqrt{2}\left|\frac{V_R - Z_c I_R}{2}\right| e^{-\alpha x} e^{j(\omega t - \beta x + \phi_2)}\right] \quad (5.37)$$

The instantaneous voltage consists of two terms each of which is a function of two variables—time and distance. Thus, they represent two travelling waves, i.e.,

$$v_x = v_{x_1} + v_{x_2} \quad (5.38)$$

Now,

$$v_{x_1} = \sqrt{2}\left|\frac{V_R + Z_c I_R}{2}\right| e^{\alpha x} \cos(\omega t + \beta x + \phi_1) \quad (5.39)$$

At any instant of time t, v_{x_1} is sinusoidally distributed along the distance from the receiving-end with amplitude increasing exponentially with distance, as shown in Fig. 5.13 ($\alpha > 0$ for a line having resistance).

After time Δt, the distribution advances in distance phase by $(\omega \Delta t/\beta)$. Thus, this wave is travelling towards the receiving end and is the *incident wave*. Line losses cause its amplitude to decrease exponentially in going from the sending- to the receiving end.

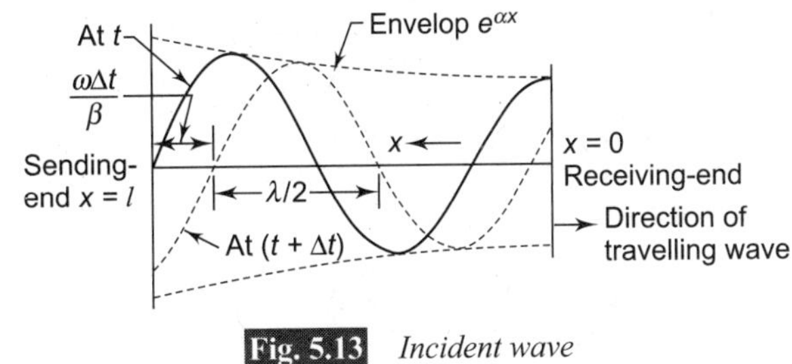

Fig. 5.13 *Incident wave*

Now,

$$v_{x_2} = \sqrt{2}\left|\frac{V_R - Z_c I_R}{2}\right| e^{-\alpha x} \cos(\omega t - \beta x + \phi_2) \quad (5.40)$$

After time Δt the voltage distribution retards in distance phase by $(\omega \Delta t/\beta)$. This is the *reflected wave* travelling from the receiving-end to the sending end with amplitude decreasing exponentially in going from the receiving end to the sending end, as shown in Fig. 5.14.

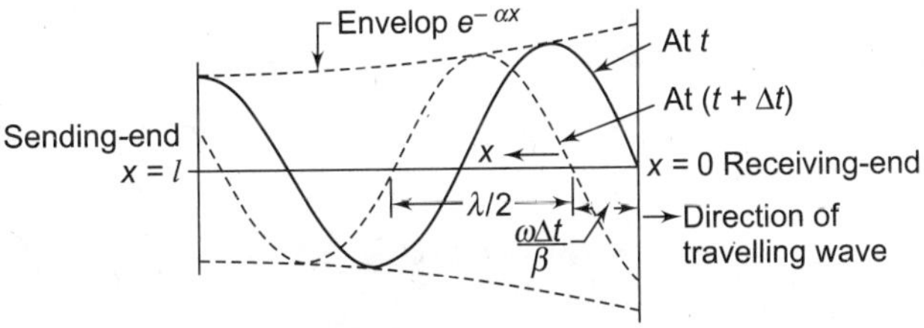

Fig. 5.14 *Reflected wave*

At any point along the line, the voltage is the sum of incident and reflected voltage waves present at the point [Eq. (5.38)]. The same is true of current waves. Expressions for incident and reflected current waves can be similarly written down by proceeding from Eq. (5.21). If Z_c is pure resistance, current waves can be simply obtained from voltage waves by dividing by Z_c.

If the load impedance $Z_L = \dfrac{V_R}{I_R} = Z_c$, i.e., the line is terminated in its characteristic impedance, the reflected voltage wave is zero ($V_R - Z_c I_R = 0$).

A line terminated in its characteristic impedance is called the *infinite line*. The incident wave under this condition cannot distinguish between a termination and an infinite continuation of the line.

Power system engineers normally call Z_c the *surge impedance*. It has a value of about 400 ohms for an overhead line and its phase angle normally varies from 0° to –15°. For underground cables, Z_c is roughly one-tenth of the value for overhead lines. The term surge impedance is, however, used in connection with surges (due to lightning or switching) or transmission lines, where the line loss can be neglected such that

$$Z_c = Z_s = \left(\frac{j\omega L}{-j\omega C}\right)^{1/2} = \left(\frac{L}{C}\right)^{1/2}, \text{ a pure resistance}$$

Surge Impedance Loading (SIL) of a transmission line is defined as the power delivered by a line to purely resistive load equal in value to the surge impedance of the line. Thus, for a line having 400 ohms surge impedance,

$$\text{SIL} = \sqrt{3}\frac{|V_R|}{\sqrt{3}\times 400}\,|V_R| \times 1000 \text{ kW}$$

$$= 2.5\,|V_R|^2 \text{ kW} \tag{5.41}$$

where $|V_R|$ is the line-to-line receiving-end voltage in kV. Sometimes, it is found convenient to express line loading in per unit of SIL, i.e., as the ratio of the power transmitted to surge impedance loading.

At any time the voltage and current vary harmonically along the line with respect to x, the space coordinate. A complete voltage or current cycle along the line corresponds to a change of 2π rad in the angular argument βx. The corresponding line length is defined as the *wavelength*.

If β is expressed in rad/m,

$$\lambda = 2\pi/\beta \text{ m} \tag{5.42}$$

Now, for a typical power transmission line

$$g \text{ (shunt conductance/unit length)} \simeq 0$$

$$r << \omega L$$

$$\therefore \quad \gamma = (yz)^{1/2} = (j\omega C(r + j\omega L))^{1/2}$$

$$= j\omega (LC)^{1/2}\left(1 - j\frac{r}{\omega L}\right)^{1/2}$$

or

$$\gamma = \alpha + j\beta \simeq j\omega (LC)^{1/2}\left(1 - j\frac{r}{2\omega L}\right)$$

$$\therefore \quad \alpha = \frac{r}{2}\left(\frac{C}{L}\right)^{1/2} \tag{5.43}$$

$$\beta \simeq \omega (LC)^{1/2} \tag{5.44}$$

Now, time for a phase change of 2π is $(1/f)$ sec., where $f = \omega/2\pi$ is the frequency in cycles/s. During this time the wave travels a distance equal to λ, i.e., one wavelength.

$$\therefore \quad \text{Velocity of propagation of wave, } v = \frac{\lambda}{1/f} = f\lambda \text{ m/s} \tag{5.45}$$

which is a well-known result.

For a lossless transmission line ($R = 0$, $G = 0$),

$$\gamma = (yz)^{1/2} = j\omega (LC)^{1/2}$$

such that $\alpha = 0$, $\beta = \omega (LC)^{1/2}$

$$\therefore \quad \lambda = \frac{2\pi}{\beta} = \frac{2\pi}{\omega (LC)^{1/2}} = \frac{1}{f(LC)^{1/2}} \text{ m} \tag{5.46}$$

and

$$v = f\lambda = 1/(LC)^{1/2} \text{ m/s} \tag{5.47}$$

For a single-phase transmission line

$$L = \frac{\mu_0}{2\pi} \ln \frac{D}{r'}$$

$$C = \frac{2\pi k_0}{\ln D/r}$$

$$\therefore \quad v = \frac{1}{\left(\dfrac{\mu_0}{2\pi} \ln \dfrac{D}{r'} \dfrac{2\pi k_0}{\ln D/r}\right)^{1/2}}$$

Since r and r' are quite close to each other, when log is taken, it is sufficiently accurate to assume that $\ln \dfrac{D}{r'} \simeq \ln D/r$.

$$\therefore \quad v \simeq \frac{1}{(\mu_0 k_0)^{1/2}} = \text{velocity of light} \tag{5.48}$$

The actual velocity of the propagation of wave along the line would be somewhat less than the velocity of light.

Wavelength of a 50 Hz power transmission is approximately given by

$$\lambda \simeq \frac{3 \times 10^8}{50} = 6{,}000 \text{ km}$$

Practical transmission lines are much shorter than this (usually several hundred kilometres). **It needs to be pointed out here that the waves drawn in Figs 5.13 and 5.14 are for illustration only and do not pertain to a real power transmission line.**

Example 5.6 A three-phase 50 Hz transmission line is 400 km long. The voltage at the sending end is 220 kV. The line parameters are $r = 0.125$ ohm/km, $x = 0.4$ ohm/km and $y = 2.8 \times 10^{-6}$ ohm/km.

Find the following:

(a) The sending-end current and receiving-end voltage when there is no-load on the line.
(b) The maximum permissible line length if the rceiving-end no-load voltage is not to exceed 235 kV.
(c) For part (a), the maximum permissible line frequency, if the no-load voltage is not to exceed 250 kV.

Solution The total line parameters are

$$R = 0.125 \times 400 = 50.0 \ \Omega$$
$$X = 0.4 \times 400 = 160.0 \ \Omega$$
$$Y = 2.8 \times 10^{-6} \times 400 \angle 90^\circ = 1.12 \times 10^{-3} \angle 90^\circ \ \Omega$$
$$Z = R + jX = (50.0 + j160.0) = 168.0 \angle 72.6^\circ \ \Omega$$
$$YZ = 1.12 \times 10^{-3} \angle 90^\circ \times 168 \angle 72.6^\circ$$
$$= 0.188 \angle 162.6^\circ$$

(a) At no-load

$$V_S = AV_R; \ I_S = CV_R$$

A and C are computed as follows:

$$A \simeq 1 + \frac{1}{2} YZ = 1 + \frac{1}{2} \times 0.188 \angle 162.6^\circ$$
$$= 0.91 + j0.028$$

$$|A| = 0.91$$

$$C = Y(1 + YZ/6) = 1.12 \times 10^{-3} \angle 90^\circ \left(1 + \frac{0.188}{6} \angle 162.6^\circ\right)$$

$$= 1.09 \times 10^{-3} \angle 90.55^\circ$$

Now,

$$|V_R|_{\text{line}} = \frac{220}{|A|} = \frac{220}{0.91} = 242 \text{ kV}$$

$$|I_S| = |C|\,|V_R| = 1.09 \times 10^{-3} \times \frac{242}{\sqrt{3}} \times 10^3 = 152 \text{ A}$$

It is to be noted that under no-load conditions, the receiving-end voltage (242 kV) is more than the sending-end voltage. This phenomenon is known as the Ferranti effect and is discussed at length in Section 5.7.

(b) Maximum permissible no-load receiving-end voltage = 235 kV.

$$|A| = \left|\frac{V_S}{V_R}\right| = \frac{220}{235} = 0.936$$

Now,

$$A \approx 1 + \frac{1}{2} YZ$$

$$= 1 + \frac{1}{2} l^2 \times j2.8 \times 10^{-6} \times (0.125 + j0.4)$$

$$= (1 - 0.56 \times 10^{-6} l^2) + j0.175 \times 10^{-6} l^2$$

Since the imaginary part will be less than $\frac{1}{10}$th of the real part, $|A|$ can be approximated as

$$|A| = 1 - 0.56 \times 10^{-6} l^2 = 0.936$$

$$\therefore \quad l^2 = \frac{1 - 0.936}{0.56 \times 10^{-6}}$$

or $\quad l = 338$ km

(c) $$|A| = \frac{220}{250} = 0.88$$

$$A \simeq 1 + \frac{1}{2} \times j1.12 \times 10^{-3} \times \frac{f}{50}\left(50 + j160 \times \frac{f}{50}\right)$$

Neglecting the imaginary part, we can write

$$|A| = 1 - \frac{1}{2} \times 1.12 \times 10^{-3} \times 160 \times \frac{f^2}{(50)^2} = 0.88$$

Simplifying, we obtain the maximum permissible frequency as

$$f = 57.9 \text{ Hz}$$

Example 5.7 If in Example 5.6 the line is open-circuited with a receiving-end voltage of 220 kV, find the rms value and phase angle of the following:

(a) The incident and reflected voltages to neutral at the receiving end.
(b) The incident and reflected voltages to neutral at 200 km from the receiving end.
(c) The resultant voltage at 200 km from the receiving end.

Note: Use the receiving-end line to neutral voltage as reference.

Solution From Example 5.6, we have the following line parameters:

$$r = 0.125\ \Omega/\text{km};\ x = 0.4\ \Omega/\text{km};\ y = j2.8 \times 10^{-6}\ \Omega/\text{km}$$

$$\therefore \quad z = (0.125 + j0.4)\ \Omega/\text{km} = 0.42\ \angle 72.6^\circ\ \Omega/\text{km}$$

$$\gamma = (yz)^{1/2} = (2.8 \times 10^{-6} \times 0.42\ \angle(90^\circ + 72.6^\circ))^{1/2}$$

$$= 1.08 \times 10^{-3}\ \angle 81.3^\circ$$

$$= (0.163 + j1.068) \times 10^{-3} = \alpha + j\beta$$

$$\therefore \quad \alpha = 0.163 \times 10^{-3};\ \beta = 1.068 \times 10^{-3}$$

(a) At the receiving end;
For open circuit $I_R = 0$

$$\text{Incident voltage} = \frac{V_R + Z_c I_R}{2} = \frac{V_R}{2}$$

$$= \frac{220/\sqrt{3}}{2} = 63.51\ \angle 0^\circ\ \text{kV (to neutral)}$$

$$\text{Reflected voltage} = \frac{V_R - Z_c I_R}{2} = \frac{V_R}{2}$$

$$= 63.51\ \angle 0^\circ\ \text{kV (to neutral)}$$

(b) At 200 km from the receiving end:

$$\text{Incident voltage} = \left.\frac{V_R}{2} e^{\alpha x} e^{j\beta x}\right|_{x = 200\ \text{km}}$$

$$= 63.51 \exp(0.163 \times 10^{-3} \times 200) \times \exp(j1.068 \times 10^{-3} \times 200)$$

$$= 65.62\ \angle 12.2^\circ\ \text{kV (to neutral)}$$

$$\text{Reflected voltage} = \left.\frac{V_R}{2} e^{-\alpha x} e^{-j\beta x}\right|_{x = 200\ \text{km}}$$

$$= 63.51\ e^{-0.0326}\ e^{-j0.2135}$$

$$= 61.47\ \angle -12.2^\circ\ \text{kV (to neutral)}$$

(c) Resultant voltage at 200 km from the receiving end

$$= 65.62\ \angle 12.2^\circ + 61.47\ \angle -12.2^\circ$$

$$= 124.2 + j0.877 = 124.2\ \angle 0.4^\circ$$

Resultant line-to-line voltage at 200 km

$$= 124.2 \times \sqrt{3} = 215.1\ \text{kV}$$

5.7 ▶ FERRANTI EFFECT

As has been illustrated in Example 5.6, the effect of the line capacitance is to cause the no-load receiving-end voltage to be more than the sending-end voltage. The effect becomes more pronounced as the line length increases. This phenomenon is known as the *Ferranti effect*. A general explanation of this effect is advanced below:

Substituting $x = l$ and $I_R = 0$ (no-load) in Eq. (5.21), we have

$$V_S = \frac{V_R}{2} e^{\alpha l} e^{j\beta l} + \frac{V_R}{2} e^{-\alpha l} e^{-j\beta l} \tag{5.49}$$

The above equation shows that at $l = 0$, the incident (E_{i0}) and reflected (E_{r0}) voltage waves are both equal to $V_R/2$. With reference to Fig. 5.15, as l increases, the incident voltage wave increases exponentially in magnitude $\left(\frac{V_R}{2} e^{\alpha l}\right)$ and turns through a positive angle βl (represented by phasor OB); while the reflected voltage wave decreases in magnitude exponentially $\left(\frac{V_R}{2} e^{-\alpha l}\right)$ and turns through a negative angle βl (represented by phasor OC). It is apparent from the geometry of this figure that the resultant phasor voltage V_S (OF) is such that $|V_R| > |V_S|$.

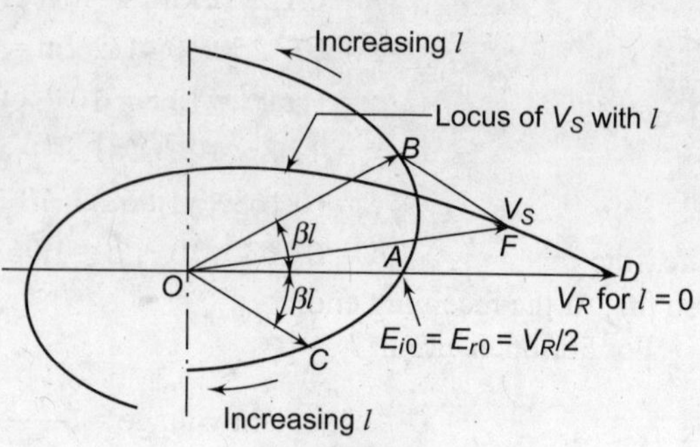

Fig. 5.15

A simple explanation of the Ferranti effect on an approximate basis can be advanced by lumping the inductance and capacitance parameters of the line. As shown in Fig. 5.16, the capacitance is lumped at the receiving end of the line.

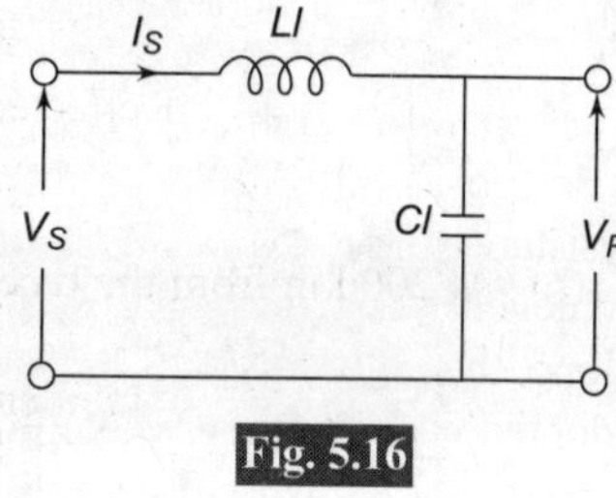

Fig. 5.16

Here,

$$I_S = \frac{V_S}{\left(\frac{1}{j\omega Cl} + j\omega Ll\right)}$$

Since C is small compared to L, ωLl can be neglected in comparison to $1/\omega Cl$. Thus,

$$I_S \simeq jV_S\omega Cl$$

Now,

$$V_R = V_S - I_S(j\omega Ll) = V_S + V_S\omega^2 CLl^2$$

$$= V_S(1 + \omega^2 CLl^2) \tag{5.50}$$

Magnitude of voltage rise $= |V_S|\omega^2 CLl^2$

$$= |V_S|\frac{\omega^2 l^2}{v^2} \tag{5.51}$$

where $v = 1/\sqrt{LC}$ is the velocity of propagation of the electromagnetic wave along the line, which is nearly equal to the velocity of light.

5.8 ▶ TUNED POWER LINES

Equation (5.23) characterises the performance of a long line. For an overhead line shunt conductance G is always negligible and it is sufficiently accurate to neglect line resistance R as well. With this approximation

$$\gamma = \sqrt{yz} = j\omega\sqrt{LC}$$

$$\cosh \gamma l = \cosh j\omega l\sqrt{LC} = \cos \omega l\sqrt{LC}$$

$$\sinh \gamma l = \sinh j\omega l\sqrt{LC} = j \sin \omega l\sqrt{LC}$$

Hence Eq. (5.23) simplifies to

$$\begin{bmatrix} V_S \\ I_S \end{bmatrix} = \begin{bmatrix} \cos \omega l\sqrt{LC} & jZ_c \sin \omega l\sqrt{LC} \\ \dfrac{j}{Z_c} \sin \omega l\sqrt{LC} & \cos \omega l\sqrt{LC} \end{bmatrix} \begin{bmatrix} V_R \\ I_R \end{bmatrix} \tag{5.52}$$

Now, if $\omega l\sqrt{LC} = n\pi;\ n = 1, 2, 3, \ldots$

$$|V_S| = |V_R|$$

$$|I_S| = |I_R|$$

i.e., the receiving-end voltage and current are numerically equal to the corresponding sending-end values, so that there is no voltage drop on load. Such a line is called a *tuned line*.

For 50 Hz, the length of line for tuning is

$$l = \frac{n\pi}{2\pi f\sqrt{LC}}$$

Since $1/\sqrt{LC} \simeq v$, the velocity of light

$$l = \frac{1}{2}(n\lambda) = \frac{1}{2}\lambda, \lambda, \frac{3}{2}\lambda, \ldots \tag{5.53}$$

$$= 3{,}000 \text{ km}, 6{,}000 \text{ km}, \ldots$$

It is too long a distance of transmission from the point of view of cost and efficiency (note that line resistance was neglected in the above analysis). For a given line, length and frequency tuning can be achieved by increasing L or C, i.e., by adding series inductances or shunt capacitances at several places along the line length. The method is impractical and uneconomical for power frequency lines and is adopted for telephony where higher frequencies are employed.

A method of tuning power lines which is being presently experimented with, uses series capacitors to cancel the effect of the line inductance and shunt inductors to neutralise line capacitance. A long line is divided into several sections which are individually tuned. However, so far the practical method of improving line regulation and power transfer capacity is to add series capacitors to reduce line inductance; shunt capacitors under heavy load conditions; and shunt inductors under light or no-load conditions.

5.9 ▶ POWER FLOW THROUGH A TRANSMISSION LINE

So far the transmission line performance equation was presented in the form of voltage and current relationships between sending and receiving ends. Since loads are more often expressed in terms of real (watts/kW) and reactive (VARs/kVAR) power, it is convenient to deal with transmission line equations in the form of sending- and receiving-end complex power and voltages. While the problem of flow of power in a general network will be treated in the next chapter, the principles involved are illustrated here through a single transmission line (2-node/2-bus system) as shown in Fig. 5.17.

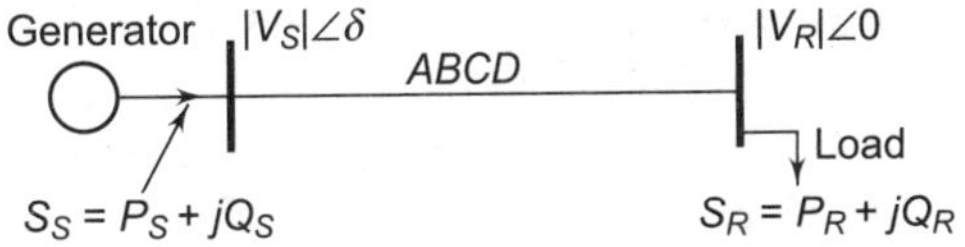

Fig. 5.17 *A two-bus system*

Let us take receiving-end voltage as a reference phasor ($V_R = |V_R| \angle 0°$) and let the sending-end voltage lead it by an angle δ ($V_S = |V_S| \angle \delta$). The angle δ is known as the torque angle whose significance has been explained in Ch. 4 and will further be taken up in Ch. 12 while dealing with the problem of stability.

The complex power leaving the receiving end and entering the sending end of thc transmission line can be expressed as (on per phase basis)

$$S_R = P_R + jQ_R = V_R I_R^* \tag{5.54}$$

$$S_S = P_S + jQ_S = V_S I_S^* \tag{5.55}$$

Receiving- and sending-end currents can, however, be expressed in terms of receiving- and sending-end voltages [by rearranging Eq. (5.1)] as

$$I_R = \frac{1}{B} V_S - \frac{A}{B} V_R \tag{5.56}$$

$$I_S = \frac{D}{B} V_S - \frac{1}{B} V_R \tag{5.57}$$

Let A, B, D, the transmission line constants, be written as

$$A = |A| \angle\alpha,\ B = |B| \angle\beta,\ D = |D| \angle\alpha \text{ (since } A = D)$$

Therefore, we can write

$$I_R = \left|\frac{1}{B}\right| |V_S| \angle(\delta - \beta) - \left|\frac{A}{B}\right| |V_R| \angle(\alpha - \beta)$$

$$I_S = \left|\frac{D}{B}\right| |V_S| \angle(\alpha + \delta - \beta) - \left|\frac{1}{B}\right| |V_R| \angle -\beta$$

Substituting for I_R in Eq. (5.54), we get

$$S_R = |V_R| \angle 0 \left[\left|\frac{1}{B}\right| |V_S| \angle(\beta - \delta) - \left|\frac{A}{B}\right| |V_R| \angle(\beta - \alpha)\right]$$

$$= \frac{|V_S||V_R|}{|B|} \angle(\beta - \delta) - \left|\frac{A}{B}\right| |V_R|^2 \angle(\beta - \alpha) \tag{5.58}$$

Similarly,

$$S_S = \left|\frac{D}{B}\right| |V_S|^2 \angle(\beta - \alpha) - \frac{|V_S||V_R|}{|B|} \angle(\beta + \delta) \tag{5.59}$$

In the above equations, S_R and S_S are per phase complex voltamperes, while V_R and V_S are expressed in per phase volts. If V_R and V_S are expressed in kV line, then the three-phase receiving-end complex power is given by

$$S_R \text{(three-phase VA)} = 3\left\{\frac{|V_S||V_R| \times 10^6}{\sqrt{3} \times \sqrt{3}\,|B|} \angle(\beta - \delta) - \left|\frac{A}{B}\right| \frac{|V_R|^2 \times 10^6}{3} \angle(\beta - \alpha)\right\}$$

$$S_R \text{(three-phase MVA)} = \frac{|V_S||V_R|}{|B|} \angle(\beta - \delta) - 3\left|\frac{A}{B}\right| |V_R|^2 \angle(\beta - \alpha) \tag{5.60}$$

This indeed is same as Eq. (5.58). The same result holds for S_S. Thus, we see that Eqs (5.58) and (5.59) give the three-phase MVA if V_S and V_R are expressed in kV line.

If Eq. (5.58) is expressed in real and imaginary parts, we can write the real and reactive powers at the receiving end as

$$P_R = \frac{|V_S||V_R|}{|B|} \cos(\beta - \delta) - \left|\frac{A}{B}\right| |V_R|^2 \cos(\beta - \alpha) \tag{5.61}$$

$$Q_R = \frac{|V_S||V_R|}{|B|} \sin(\beta - \delta) - \left|\frac{A}{B}\right| |V_R|^2 \sin(\beta - \alpha) \tag{5.62}$$

Similarly, the real and reactive powers at sending-end are

$$P_S = \left|\frac{D}{B}\right| |V_S|^2 \cos(\beta - \alpha) - \frac{|V_S||V_R|}{|B|} \cos(\beta + \delta) \tag{5.63}$$

$$Q_S = \left|\frac{D}{B}\right| |V_S|^2 \sin(\beta - \alpha) - \frac{|V_S||V_R|}{|B|} \sin(\beta + \delta) \tag{5.64}$$

It is easy to see from Eq. (5.61) that the received power P_R will be maximum at

$$\delta = \beta$$

such that

$$P_R(\max) = \frac{|V_S||V_R|}{|B|} - \frac{|A||V_R|^2}{|B|} \cos(\beta - \alpha) \tag{5.65}$$

The corresponding Q_R (at max P_R) is

$$Q_R = -\frac{|A||V_R|^2}{|B|} \sin(\beta - \alpha)$$

Thus, the load must draw this much leading MVAR in order to receive the maximum real power.

Consider now the special case of a short line with a series impedance Z. Now,

$$A = D = 1 \angle 0;\ B = Z = |Z| \angle \theta$$

Substituting these in Eqs (5.61) to (5.64), we get the simplified results for the short line as

$$P_R = \frac{|V_S||V_R|}{|Z|} \cos(\theta - \delta) - \frac{|V_R|^2}{|Z|} \cos\theta \tag{5.66}$$

$$Q_R = \frac{|V_S||V_R|}{|Z|} \sin(\theta - \delta) - \frac{|V_R|^2}{|Z|} \sin\theta \tag{5.67}$$

for the receiving end and for the sending end

$$P_S = \frac{|V_S|^2}{|Z|} \cos\theta - \frac{|V_S||V_R|}{|Z|} \cos(\theta + \delta) \tag{5.68}$$

$$Q_S = \frac{|V_S|^2}{|Z|} \sin\theta - \frac{|V_S||V_R|}{|Z|} \sin(\theta + \delta) \tag{5.69}$$

The above short line equation will also apply for a long line when the line is replaced by its equivalent-π (or nominal-π) and the shunt admittances are lumped with the receiving-end load and sending-end generation. In fact, this technique is always used in the load flow problem to be treated in the next chapter.

From Eq. (5.66), the maximum receiving-end power is received, when $\delta = \theta$, so that

$$P_R(\max) = \frac{|V_S||V_R|}{|Z|} - \frac{|V_R|^2}{|Z|} \cos\theta$$

Now, $\quad \cos\theta = R/|Z|$,

$$\therefore \quad P_R(\max) = \frac{|V_S||V_R|}{|Z|} - \frac{|V_R|^2}{|Z|^2} R \tag{5.70}$$

Normally the resistance of a transmission line is small compared to its reactance (since it is necessary to maintain a high efficiency of transmission), so that $\theta = \tan^{-1} X/R \simeq 90°$; where $Z = R + jX$. The receiving-end Eqs (5.66) and (5.67) can then be approximated as

$$P_R = \frac{|V_S||V_R|}{X} \sin\delta \tag{5.71}$$

$$Q_R = \frac{|V_S||V_R|}{X} \cos\delta - \frac{|V_R|^2}{X} \tag{5.72}$$

Equation (5.72) can be further simplified by assuming cos $\delta \simeq 1$, since δ is normally small*. Thus,

$$Q_R = \frac{|V_R|}{X}(|V_S| - |V_R|) \tag{5.73}$$

Let $|V_S| - |V_R| = |\Delta V|$, the magnitude of voltage drop across the transmission line.

$$\therefore \quad Q_R = \frac{|V_R|}{X}|\Delta V| \tag{5.74}$$

Several important conclusions that easily follow from Eqs (5.71) to (5.74) are enumerated below:

1. For $R \simeq 0$ (which is a valid approximation for a transmission line) the real power transferred to the receiving end is proportional to sin δ ($\simeq \delta$ for small values of δ), while the reactive power is proportional to the magnitude of the voltage drop across the line.
2. The real power received is maximum for $\delta = 90^\circ$ and has a value $|V_S||V_R|/X$. Of course, δ is restricted to values well below 90° from considerations of stability to be discussed in Ch. 12.
3. Maximum real power transferred for a given line (fixed X) can be increased by raising its voltage level. It is from this consideration that voltage levels are being progressively pushed up to transmit larger chunks of power over longer distances warranted by large size generating stations.

   For very long lines, voltage level cannot be raised beyond the limits placed by present-day high voltage technology. To increase power transmitted in such cases, the only choice is to reduce the line reactance. This is accomplished by adding series capacitors in the line. This idea will be pursued further in Ch. 12. Series capacitors would of course increase the severity of line over voltages under switching conditions.
4. The VARs (lagging reactive power) delivered by a line is proportional to the line voltage drop and is independent of δ. Therefore, in a transmission system if the VARs demand of the load is large, the voltage profile at that point tends to sag rather sharply. To maintain a desired voltage profile, the VARs demand of the load must be met locally by employing positive VAR generators (condensers). This will be discussed at length in Section 5.10.

A somewhat more accurate yet approximate result expressing line voltage drop in terms of active and reactive powers can be written directly from Eq. (5.5), i.e.,

$$|\Delta V| = |I_R|\, R \cos \phi + |I_R|\, X \sin \phi$$

$$= \frac{|V_R||I_R|R \cos \phi + |V_R||I_R|X \sin \phi}{|V_R|}$$

$$= \frac{RP_R + XQ_R}{|V_R|} \tag{5.75}$$

This result reduces to that of Eq. (5.74) if $R = 0$.

Example 5.8 An interconnector cable links generating stations 1 and 2 as shown in Fig. 5.18. The desired voltage profile is flat, i.e., $|V_1| = |V_2| = 1$ pu. The total demands at the two buses are

$$S_{D1} = 15 + j5 \text{ pu}$$

$$S_{D2} = 25 + j15 \text{ pu}$$

The station loads are equalised by the flow of power in the cable. Estimate the torque angle and the station power factors: (a) for cable $Z = 0 + j0.05$ pu, and (b) for cable $Z = 0.005 + j0.05$ pu. It is given that generator G_1 can generate a maximum of 20.0 pu real power.

---

* Small δ is necessary from considerations of system stability which will be discussed at length in Ch. 12.

Solution The powers at the various points in the fundamental (two-bus) system are defined in Fig. 5.18(a).

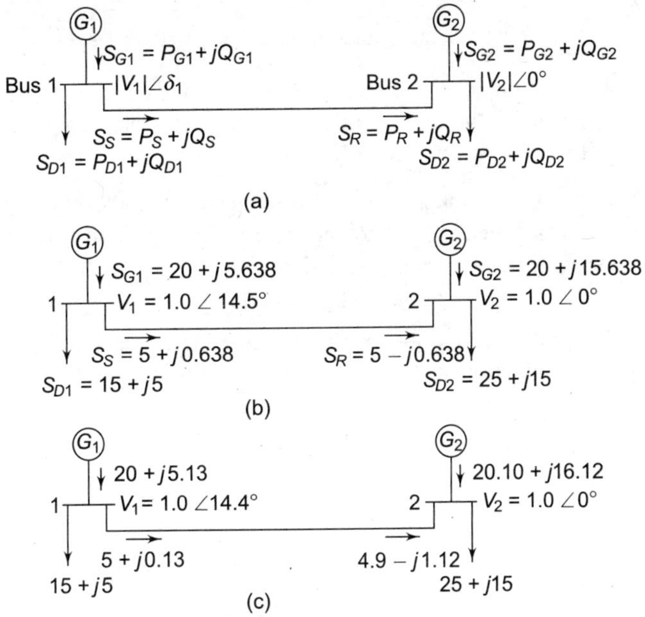

Case (a) Cable impedance = $j0.05$ pu. Since cable resistance is zero, there is no real power loss in the cable. Hence

$$P_{G1} + P_{G2} = P_{D1} + P_{D2} = 40 \text{ pu}$$

For equalisation of station loads,

$$P_{G1} = P_{G2} = 20 \text{ pu}$$

Equalisation means that $P_S = P_R = 5$ MW

The voltage of bus 2 is taken as reference, i.e., $V_2\ \angle 0°$ and voltage of bus 1 is $V_1\ \angle \delta_1$. Further, for flat voltage profile $|V_1| = |V_2| = 1$.

Real power flow from bus 1 to bus 2 is obtained from Eq. (5.58) by recognising that since $R = 0$, $\theta = 90°$.

Hence,

$$P_S = P_R = \frac{|V_1||V_2|}{X} \sin \delta_1$$

$$5 = \frac{1 \times 1}{0.05} \sin \delta_1$$

Fig. 5.18 *Two-bus system*

or $\delta_1 = 14.5°$

$\therefore$ $V_1 = 1\ \angle 14.5°$

From Eq. (5.69)

$$Q_S = \frac{|V_1|^2}{X} - \frac{|V_1||V_2|}{X} \cos \delta_1$$

$$= \frac{1}{0.05} - \frac{1}{0.05} \times 0.968 = 0.638 \text{ pu}$$

From Eq. (5.67)

$$Q_R = \frac{|V_1||V_2|}{X} \cos\ \delta_1 - \frac{|V_1|^2}{X} = -\ Q_S = -\ 0.638 \text{ pu}$$

Reactive power loss* in the cable is

$$Q_L = Q_S - Q_R = 2Q_S = 1.276 \text{ pu}$$

$$\text{Total load on station 1} = (15 + j5) + (5 + j0.638)$$

$$= 20 + j5.638$$

$$\text{Power factor at station 1} = \cos \left(\tan^{-1} \frac{5.638}{20} \right) = 0.963 \text{ lagging}$$

$$\text{Total load on station 2} = (25 + j15) - (5 - j0.638)$$

$$= 20 + j15.638$$

* Reactive power loss can also be computed as $|I|^2X = \dfrac{5^2 + (0.638)^2}{1} \times 0.05 = 1.27$ pu.

$$\text{Power factor at station 2} = \cos\left(\tan^{-1}\frac{15.638}{20}\right) = 0.788 \text{ lagging}$$

The station loads, load demands and line flows are shown in Fig. 5.18(b). It may be noted that to maintain a flat voltage profile, the generators are required to supply reactive powers $Q_{G1} = 5.638$ and Q_{G2}=15.638, respectively.

Case (b) Cable impedance = $0.005 + j0.05 = 0.0502 \angle 84.3°$ pu. In this case the cable resistance causes real power loss which is not known a priori. The real load flow is thus not obvious as was in the case of $R = 0$. We specify the generation at station 1 as

$$P_{G1} = 20 \text{ pu}$$

The consideration for fixing this generation is economic as we shall see in Ch. 7.

The generation at station 2 will be 20 pu plus the cable loss. The unknown variables in the problem are

$$P_{G2}, \delta_1, Q_{G1}, Q_{G2}$$

Let us now examine as to how many system equations can be formed.

From Eqs (5.68) and (5.69),

$$P_{G1} - P_{D1} = P_S = \frac{|V_1|^2}{|Z|}\cos\theta - \frac{|V_1||V_2|}{|Z|}\cos(\theta + \delta_1)$$

$$5 = \frac{1}{0.0502}\cos 84.3° - \frac{1}{0.0502}\cos(84.3° + \delta_1) \qquad \text{(i)}$$

$$Q_{G1} - Q_{D1} = Q_S = \frac{|V_1|^2}{|Z|}\sin\theta - \frac{|V_1||V_2|}{|Z|}\cos(\theta + \delta_1)$$

$$Q_{G1} - 5 = \frac{1}{0.0502}\sin 84.3° - \frac{1}{0.0502}\sin(84.3° + \delta_1) \qquad \text{(ii)}$$

From Eqs (5.66) and (5.67),

$$P_{D2} - P_{G2} = P_R = \frac{|V_1||V_2|}{|Z|}\cos(\theta - \delta_1) - \frac{|V_1|^2}{|Z|}\cos\theta$$

$$25 - P_{G2} = \frac{1}{0.0502}\cos(84.3° - \delta_1) - \frac{1}{0.0502}\cos 84.3° \qquad \text{(iii)}$$

$$Q_{D2} - Q_{G2} = Q_R = \frac{|V_1||V_2|}{|Z|}\sin(\theta - \delta_1) - \frac{|V_1|^2}{|Z|}\sin\theta$$

$$15 - Q_{G2} = \frac{1}{0.0502}\sin(84.3° - \delta_1) - \frac{1}{0.0502}\sin 84.3° \qquad \text{(iv)}$$

Thus, we have four equations, Eqs (i) to (iv), in four unknowns P_{G2}, δ_1, Q_{G1}, Q_{G2}. Even though these are nonlinear algebraic equations, solution is possible in this case. Solving Eq. (i) for δ_1, we have

$$\delta_1 = 14.4°$$

Substituting δ_1 in Eqs (ii), (iii) and (iv), we get

$$Q_{G1} = 5.13,\ Q_{G2} = 16.12,\ P_{G2} = 20.10$$

The flow of real and reactive powers for this case is shown in Fig. 5.18(c).

It may be noted that the real power loss of 0.1 pu is supplied by $G_2(P_{G2} = 20.10)$.

The problem presented above is a two-bus load flow problem. Explicit solution is always possible in a two-bus case. The reader should try the case when

$$Q_{G2} = j10 \text{ and } |V_2| = ?$$

The general load flow problem will be taken up in Ch. 6. It will be seen that explicit solution is not possible in the general case and iterative techniques have to be resorted to.

Example 5.9 A 275 kV transmission line has the following line constants:

$$A = 0.85\ \angle 5°;\ B = 200\ \angle 75°$$

(a) Determine the power at unity power factor that can be received if the voltage profile at each end is to be maintained at 275 kV.
(b) What type and rating of compensation equipment would be required if the load is 150 MW at unity power factor with the same voltage profile as in part (a)?
(c) With the load as in part (b), what would be the receiving-end voltage if the compensation equipment is not installed?

Solution

(a) Given $|V_S| = |V_R| = 275$ kV; $\alpha = 5°$, $\beta = 75°$. Since the power is received at unity power factor

$$Q_R = 0$$

Substituting these values in Eq. (5.62), we can write

$$0 = \frac{275 \times 275}{200} \sin(75° - \delta) - \frac{0.85}{200} \times (275)^2 \sin(75° - 5°)$$

$$0 = 378 \sin(75° - \delta) - 302$$

which gives

$$\delta = 22°$$

From Eq. (5.61),

$$P_R = \frac{275 \times 275}{200} \cos(75° - 22°) - \frac{0.85}{200} \times (275)^2 \cos 70°$$

$$= 227.6 - 109.9 = 117.7 \text{ MW}$$

(b) Now, $|V_S| = |V_R| = 275$ kV
Power demanded by load = 150 MW at UPF

$\therefore \quad P_D = P_R = 150$ MW; $Q_D = 0$

From Eq. (5.61),

$$150 = \frac{275 \times 275}{200} \cos(75° - \delta) - \frac{0.85}{200} \times (275)^2 \cos 70°$$

$$150 = 378 \cos(75° - \delta) - 110$$

or

$$\delta = 28.46°$$

From Eq. (5.62),

$$Q_R = \frac{275 \times 275}{200} \sin(75° - 28.46°) - \frac{0.85}{200} \times (275)^2 \sin 70°$$

$$= 274.46 - 302 = -27.56 \text{ MVAR}$$

Thus, in order to maintain 275 kV at a receiving end, $Q_R = -27.56$ MVAR must be drawn along with the real power of $P_R = 150$ MW. The load being 150 MW at unity power factor, i.e., $Q_D = 0$, compensation equipment must be installed at the receiving end. With reference to Fig. 5.19, we have

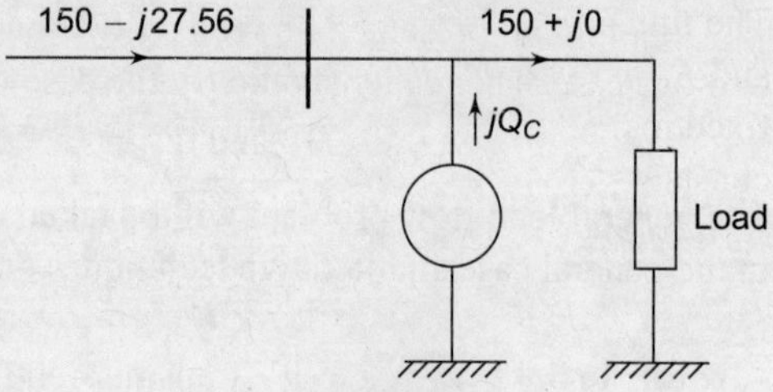

$$-27.56 + Q_C = 0$$

or $$Q_C = +27.56 \text{ MVAR}$$

Fig. 5.19

i.e., the compensation equipment must feed positive VARs into the line. See Subsection 5.10 for a more detailed explanation.

(c) Since no compensation equipment is provided

$$P_R = 150 \text{ MW}, Q_R = 0$$

Now,

$$|V_S| = 275 \text{ kV}, |V_R| = ?$$

Substituting this data in Eqs (5.61) and (5.62), we have

$$150 = \frac{275|V_R|}{200} \cos(75^\circ - \delta) - \frac{0.85}{200}|V_R|^2 \cos 70^\circ \qquad \text{(i)}$$

$$0 = \frac{275|V_R|}{200} \sin(75^\circ - \delta) - \frac{0.85}{200}|V_R|^2 \sin 70^\circ \qquad \text{(ii)}$$

From Eq. (ii), we get

$$\sin(75^\circ - \delta) = 0.0029|V_R|$$

$$\therefore \quad \cos(75^\circ - \delta) = (1 - (0.0029)^2|V_R|^2)^{1/2}$$

Substituting in Eq. (i), we obtain

$$150 = 1.375\,|V_R|\,(1 - (0.0029)^2\,|V_R|^2)^{1/2} - 0.00145|V_R|^2$$

Solving the quadratic and retaining the higher value of $|V_R|$, we obtain

$$|V_R| = 244.9 \text{ kV}$$

Note: The second and lower value solution of $|V_R|$, though feasible, is impractical as it corresponds to abnormally low voltage and efficiency.

It is to be observed from the results of this problem that larger power can be transmitted over a line with a fixed voltage profile by installing compensation equipment at the receiving-end capable of feeding positive VARs into the line.

5.9.1 Circle Diagrams

It has been shown above that the flow of active and reactive power over a transmission line can be handled computationally. It will now be shown that the locus of complex sending- and receiving-end power is a circle. Since circles are convenient to draw, the circle diagrams are a useful aid to visualise the load flow problem over a single transmission line.

The expressions for complex number receiving- and sending-end powers are reproduced below from Eqs (5.58) and (5.59),

$$S_R = -\left|\frac{A}{B}\right| |V_R|^2 \angle(\beta - \alpha) + \frac{|V_S||V_R|}{|B|} \angle(\beta - \delta) \qquad (5.58)$$

$$S_S = \left|\frac{D}{B}\right| |V_R|^2 \angle(\beta - \alpha) - \frac{|V_S||V_R|}{|B|} \angle(\beta + \delta) \qquad (5.59)$$

The units for S_R and S_S are MVA (three-phase) with voltages in kV line. As per the above equations, S_R and S_S are each composed of two phasor components—one a constant phasor and the other a phasor of fixed magnitude but variable angle. The loci for S_R and S_S would, therefore, be circles drawn from the tip of constant phasors as centres.

It follows from Eq. (5.58) that the centre of receiving-end circle is located at the tip of the phasor

$$-\left|\frac{A}{B}\right| |V_R|^2 \angle(\beta-\alpha) \tag{5.76}$$

in polar coordinates or in terms of rectangular coordinates.

Horizontal coordinate of the centre

$$= -\left|\frac{A}{B}\right| |V_R|^2 \cos(\beta-\alpha) \text{ MW} \tag{5.77}$$

Vertical coordinate of the centre

$$= -\left|\frac{A}{B}\right| |V_R|^2 \sin(\beta-\alpha) \text{ MVAR}$$

The radius of the receiving-end circle is

$$\frac{|V_S||V_R|}{|B|} \text{ MVA} \tag{5.78}$$

The receiving-end circle diagram is drawn in Fig. 5.20. The centre is located by drawing OC_R at an angle $(\beta-\alpha)$ in the positive direction from the negative MW-axis. From the centre C_R the receiving-end circle is drawn with the radius $|V_S|\,|V_R|/|B|$. The operating point M is located on the circle by means of the received real power P_R. The corresponding Q_R (or θ_R) can be immediately read from the circle diagram. The torque angle δ can be read in accordance with the positive direction indicated from the reference line.

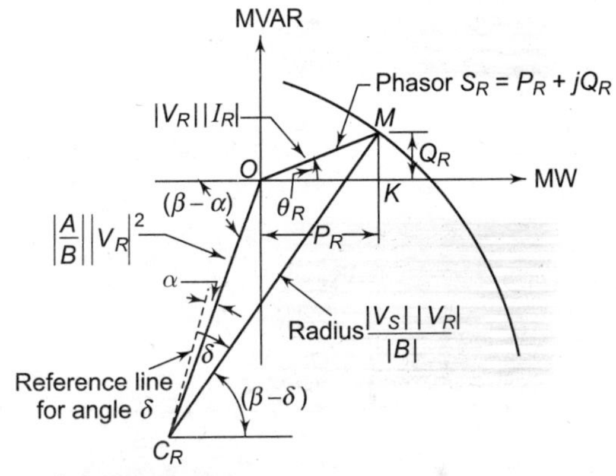

Fig. 5.20 *Receiving-end circle diagram*

For constant $|V_R|$, the centre C_R remains fixed and concentric circles result for varying $|V_S|$. However, for the case of constant $|V_S|$ and varying $|V_R|$ the centres of circles move along the line OC_R and have radii in accordance to $|V_S|\,|V_R|/|B|$.

Similarly, it follows from Eq. (5.59) that the centre of the sending-end circle is located at the tip of the phasor

$$\left|\frac{D}{B}\right| |V_S|^2 \angle(\beta-\alpha) \tag{5.79}$$

in the polar coordinates or in terms of rectangular coordinates.

Horizontal coordinate of the centre

$$= \left|\frac{D}{B}\right| |V_S|^2 \cos(\beta-\alpha) \text{ MW} \tag{5.80}$$

Vertical coordinate of the centre

$$= \left|\frac{D}{B}\right| |V_S|^2 \sin(\beta-\alpha) \text{ MVAR}$$

The radius of the sending-end circle is

$$\frac{|V_S||V_R|}{|B|} \tag{5.81}$$

The sending-end circle diagram is shown in Fig. 5.21. The centre is located by drawing OC_S at angle $(\beta - \alpha)$ from the positive MW axis. From the centre the sending-end circle is drawn with a radius $\frac{|V_S||V_R|}{|B|}$ (same as in the case of receiving end). The operating point N is located by measuring the torque angle δ (as read from the receiving-end circle diagram) in the direction indicated from the reference line.

For constant $|V_S|$ the centre C_S remains fixed and concentric circles result for varying $|V_R|$. However, if $|V_R|$ is fixed and $|V_S|$ varies, the centres of the circles move along the line OC_S and have radii in accordance to $|V_S|\,|V_R|/|B|$.

For the case of a short line with a series impedance $|Z| \angle\theta$, the simplified circle diagrams can be easily drawn by recognising

$$|A| = |D| = 1,\ \alpha = 0$$
$$|B| = |Z|, \quad \beta = \theta$$

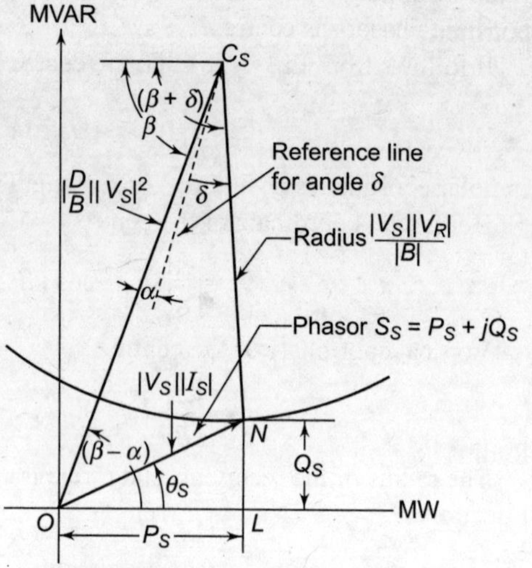

Fig. 5.21 *Sending-end circle diagram*

The corresponding receiving- and sending-end circle diagrams have been drawn in Figs 5.22 and 5.23.

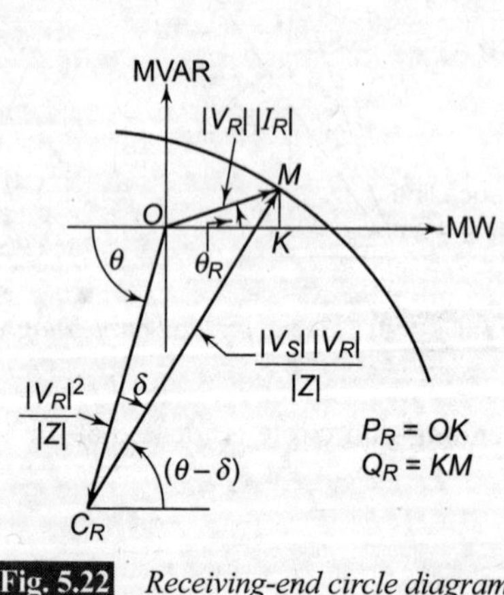

Fig. 5.22 *Receiving-end circle diagram for a short line*

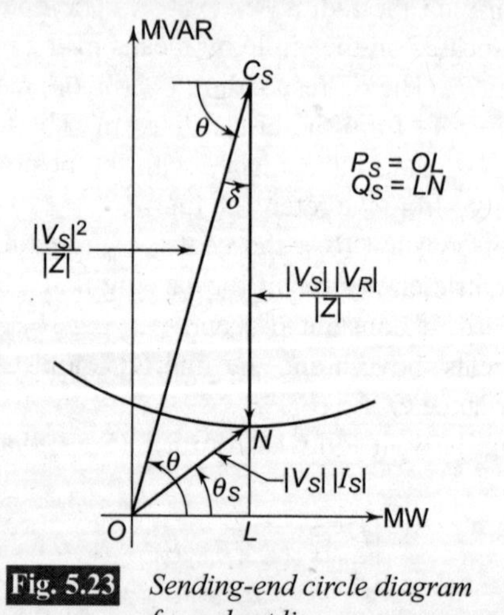

Fig. 5.23 *Sending-end circle diagram for a short line*

The use of circle diagrams is illustrated by means of the two examples given below:

Example 5.10 A 50 Hz, three-phase, 275 kV, 400 km transmission line has the following parameters:

Resistance = 0.035 Ω/km per phase

Inductance = 1.1 mH/km per phase

Capacitance = 0.012 μF/km per phase

If the line is supplied at 275 kV, determine the MVA rating of a shunt reactor having negligible losses that would be required to maintain 275 kV at the receiving-end when the line is delivering no load. Use nominal-π method.

Solution

$$R = 0.035 \times 400 = 14\ \Omega$$
$$X = 314 \times 1.1 \times 10^{-3} \times 400 = 138.2\ \Omega$$
$$Z = 14 + j138 = 138.7\ \angle 84.2^\circ\ \Omega$$
$$Y = 314 \times 0.012 \times 10^{-6} \times 400\ \angle 90^\circ = 1.507 \times 10^{-3}\ \angle 90^\circ\ \mho$$
$$A = \left(1 + \frac{1}{2}YZ\right) = 1 + \frac{1}{2} \times 1.507 \times 10^{-3} \times 138.7\ \angle 174.2^\circ$$
$$= (0.896 + j0.0106) = 0.896\ \angle 0.7^\circ$$
$$B = Z = 138.7\ \angle 84.2^\circ$$
$$|V_S| = 275\ \text{kV},\ |V_R| = 275\ \text{kV}$$

$$\text{Radius of receiving end circle} = \frac{|V_S||V_R|}{|B|} = \frac{275 \times 275}{138.7} = 545.2\ \text{MVA}$$

Location of the centre of receiving end circle,

$$\left|\frac{A}{B}\right| |V_R|^2 = \frac{275 \times 275 \times 0.896}{138.7} = 488.5\ \text{MVA}$$
$$\angle(\beta - \alpha) = 84.2^\circ - 0.7^\circ = 83.5^\circ$$

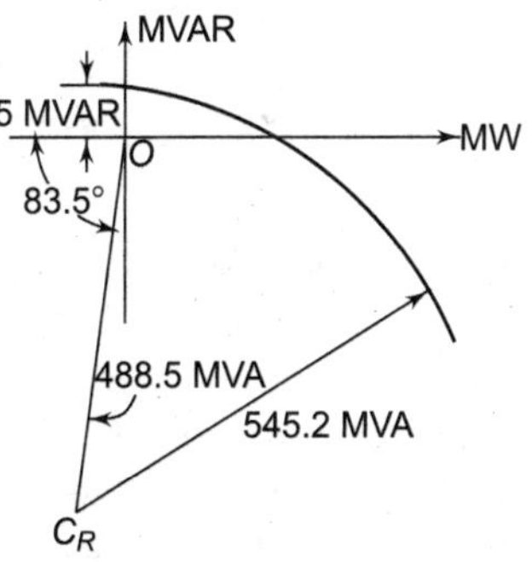

Fig. 5.24 *Circle diagram for Example 5.10*

From the circle diagram of Fig. 5.24, +55 MVAR must be drawn from the receiving end of the line in order to maintain a voltage of 275 kV. Thus, rating of shunt reactor needed = 55 MVA.

Example 5.11 A 275 kV, three-phase line has the following line parameters:

$$A = 0.93\ \angle 1.5^\circ,\ B = 115\ \angle 77^\circ$$

If the receiving end voltage is 275 kV, determine:

(a) The sending end voltage required if a load of 250 MW at 0.85 lagging pf is being delivered at the receiving end.

(b) The maximum power that can be delivered if the sending end voltage is held at 295 kV.

(c) The additional MVA that has to be provided at the receiving end when delivering 400 MVA at 0.8 lagging pf, the supply voltage being maintained at 295 kV.

Solution In Fig. 5.25 the centre of the receiving-end circle is located at

$$\left|\frac{A}{B}\right| |V_R|^2 = \frac{275 \times 275 \times 0.93}{115} = 611.6\ \text{MVA}$$
$$\cos^{-1} 0.85 = 31.8^\circ$$
$$\angle(\beta - \alpha) = 77^\circ - 1.5^\circ = 75.5^\circ$$

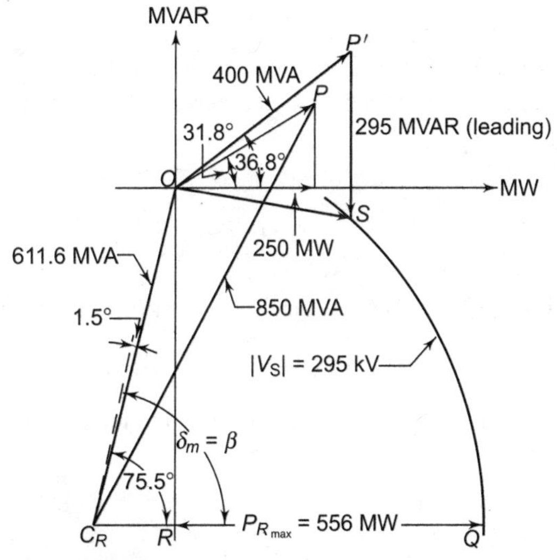

Fig. 5.25 *Circle diagram for Example 5.11*

(a) Locate OP corresponding to the receiving-end load of 250 MW at 0.85 lagging pf (+ 31.8°). Then,

$$C_R P = 850 = \frac{|V_S||V_R|}{|B|} = \frac{275|V_S|}{115}$$

$$\therefore \quad |V_S| = 355.5 \text{ kV}$$

(b) Given $\quad |V_S| = 295$ kV

$$\text{Radius of circle diagram} = \frac{295 \times 275}{115} = 705.4 \text{ MVA}$$

Drawing the receiving-end circle (see Fig. 5.25) and the line $C_R Q$ parallel to the MW-axis, we read

$$P_{R\,\max} = RQ = 556 \text{ MW}$$

(c) Locate OP' corresponding to 400 MVA at 0.8 lagging pf (+ 36.8°). Draw $P'S$ parallel to MVAR-axis to cut the circle drawn in part (b) at S. For the specified voltage profile, the line load should be OS. Therefore, additional MVA to be drawn from the line is

$$P'S = 295 \text{ MVAR or } 295 \text{ MVA leading}$$

5.10 ► METHODS OF VOLTAGE CONTROL

Practically all equipment used in power system is rated for a certain voltage with a permissible band of voltage variations. Voltage at various buses must, therefore, be controlled within a specified regulation figure. This article will discuss the two methods by means of which voltage at a bus can be controlled.

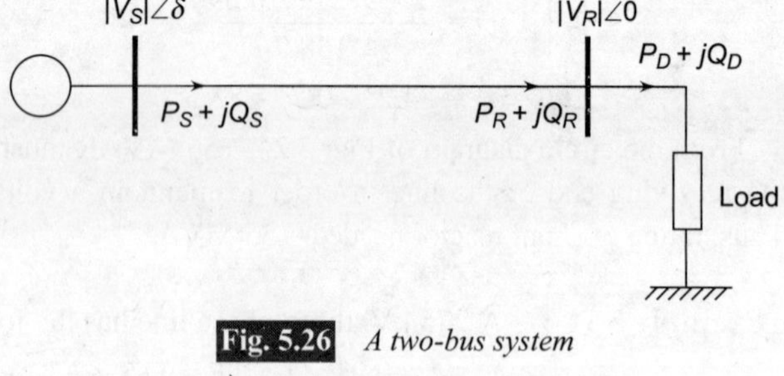

Fig. 5.26 *A two-bus system*

Consider the two-bus system shown in Fig. 5.26 (already exemplified in Section 5.9). For the sake of simplicity, let the line be characterised by a series reactance (i.e., it has negligible resistance). Further, since the torque angle δ is small under practical conditions, real and reactive powers delivered by the line for fixed sending-end voltage $|V_S|$ and a specified receiving-end voltage $|V_R^s|$ can be written as below from Eqs (5.71) and (5.73).

$$P_R = \frac{|V_S||V_R^s|}{X} \sin \delta \tag{5.82}$$

$$Q_R^s = \frac{|V_R^s|}{X}(|V_S| - |V_R^s|) \tag{5.83}$$

Equation (5.83) upon quadratic solution* can also be written as

$$|V_R^s| = \frac{1}{2}|V_S| + \frac{1}{2}|V_S|(1 - 4XQ_R^s/|V_S|^2)^{1/2} \tag{5.84}$$

Since the real power demanded by the load must be delivered by the line,

$$P_R = P_D$$

Varying real power demand P_D is met by consequent changes in the torque angle δ.

---

* Negative sign in the quadratic solution is rejected because otherwise the solution would not match the specified receiving-end voltage which is only slightly less than the sending-end voltage (the difference is less than 12%).

It is, however, to be noted that the received reactive power of the line must remain fixed at Q_R^s as given by Eq. (5.83) for fixed $|V_S|$ and specified $|V_R^s|$. The line would, therefore, operate with specified receiving-end voltage for only one value of Q_D given by

$$Q_D = Q_R^s$$

Practical loads are generally lagging in nature and are such that the VAR demand Q_D may exceed Q_R^s. It easily follows from Eq. (5.83) that for $Q_D > Q_R^s$ the receiving-end voltage must change from the specified value $|V_R^s|$ to some value $|V_R|$ to meet the demanded VARs. Thus,

$$Q_D = Q_R = \frac{|V_R|}{X}(|V_S| - |V_R|) \text{ for } (Q_D > Q_R^s)$$

The modified $|V_R|$ is then given by

$$|V_R| = \frac{1}{2}|V_S| + \frac{1}{2}|V_S|(1 - 4XQ_R/|V_S|^2)^{1/2} \tag{5.85}$$

Comparison of Eqs (5.84) and (5.85) reveals that for $Q_D = Q_R = Q_R^s$, the receiving-end voltage is $|V_R^s|$, but for $Q_D = Q_R > Q_R^s$,

$$|V_R| < |V_R^s|$$

Thus, a VAR demand larger than Q_R^s is met by a consequent fall in receiving-end voltage from the specified value. Similarly, if the VAR demand is less than Q_R^s, it follows that

$$|V_R| > |V_R^s|$$

Indeed, under light load conditions, the charging capacitance of the line may cause the VAR demand to become negative resulting in the receiving-end voltage exceeding the sending-end voltage (this is the Ferranti effect already illustrated in Subsection 5.7).

In order to regulate the line voltage under varying demands of VARs, the two methods discussed below are employed.

5.10.1 Reactive Power Injection

It follows from the above discussion that in order to keep the receiving-end voltage at a specified value $|V_R^s|$, a fixed amount of VARs (Q_R^s) must be drawn from the line.* To accomplish this under conditions of a varying VAR demand Q_D, a local VAR generator (controlled reactive source/compensating equipment) must be used as shown in Fig. 5.27. The VAR balance equation at the receiving-end is now

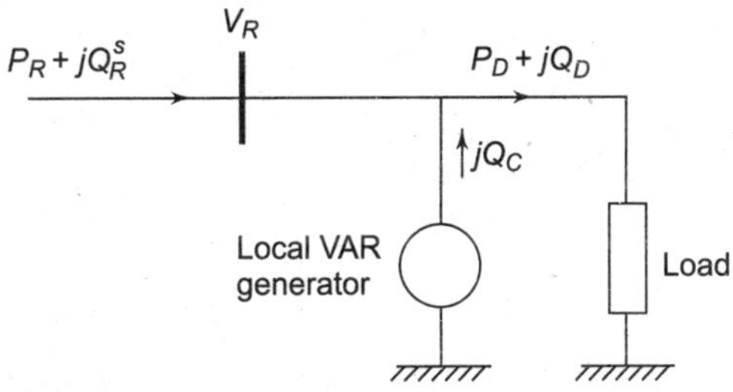

Fig. 5.27 *Use of local VAR generator at the load bus*

$$Q_R^s + Q_C = Q_D$$

Fluctuations in Q_D are absorbed by the *local VAR generator* Q_C such that the VARs drawn from the line remain fixed at Q_R^s. The receiving-end voltage would thus remain fixed at $|V_R^s|$ (this of course assumed a fixed sending-end voltage $|V_S|$). Local VAR compensation can, in fact, be made automatic by using the signal from the VAR meter installed at the receiving end of the line.

* Of course, since $|V_R^S|$ is specified within a band, Q_R^S may vary within a corresponding band.

Two types of VAR generators are employed in practice—*static type* and *rotating type*. These are discussed below:

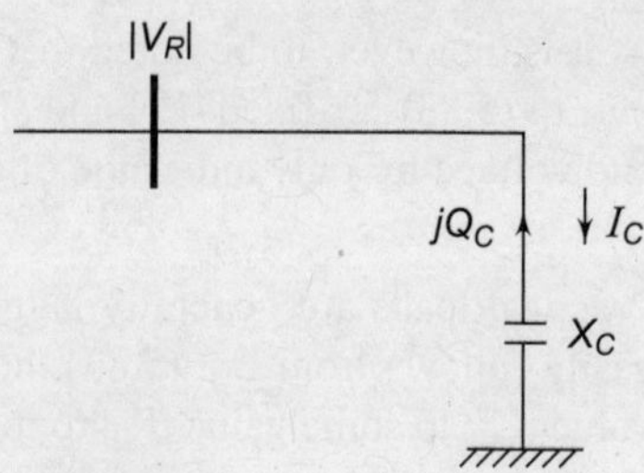

Fig. 5.28 *Static capacitor bank*

Static VAR generator It is nothing but a bank of three-phase static capacitors and/or inductors. With reference to Fig. 5.28, if $|V_R|$ is in line kV, and X_C is the per phase capacitive reactance of the capacitor bank on an equivalent star basis, the expression for the VARs fed into the line can be derived as under.

$$I_C = j\frac{|V_R|}{\sqrt{3}X_C} \text{ kA}$$

$$jQ_C(\text{three-phase}) = 3\frac{|V_R|}{\sqrt{3}}(-I^*_C)$$

$$= j3 \times \frac{|V_R|}{\sqrt{3}} \times \frac{|V_R|}{\sqrt{3}X_C} \text{ MVA}$$

$$\therefore \quad Q_C(\text{three-phase}) = \frac{|V_R|^2}{X_C} \text{ MVAR} \tag{5.86}$$

If inductors are employed instead, VARs fed into the line are

$$Q_L(\text{three-phase}) = -\frac{|V_R|^2}{X_L} \text{ MVAR} \tag{5.87}$$

Under heavy load conditions, when positive VARs are needed, capacitor banks are employed; while under light load conditions, when negative VARs are needed, inductor banks are switched on.

The following observations can be made for static VAR generators:

1. Capacitor and inductor banks can be switched on in steps. However, stepless (smooth) VAR control can now be achieved using SCR (Silicon Controlled Rectifier) circuitry.
2. Since Q_C is proportional to the square of terminal voltage, for a given capacitor bank, their effectiveness tends to decrease as the voltage sags under full load conditions.
3. If the system voltage contains appreciable harmonics, the fifth being the most troublesome, the capacitors may be overloaded considerably.
4. Capacitors act as short circuit when switched 'on'.
5. There is a possibility of series resonance with the line inductance particularly at harmonic frequencies.

Rotating VAR generator It is nothing but a synchronous motor running at no-load and having excitation adjustable over a wide range. It feeds positive VARs into the line under overexcited conditions and feeds negative VARs when underexcited. A machine thus running is called a *synchronous condenser*.

Figure 5.29 shows a synchronous motor connected to the receiving-end bus bars and running at no load. Since the motor draws negligible real power from the bus bars, E_G and V_R are nearly in phase. X_S is the synchronous reactance of the motor which is assumed to have negligible resistance. If $|E_G|$ and $|V_R|$ are in line kV, we have

$$I_C = \frac{(|V_R| - |E_G|)\angle 0°}{\sqrt{3} \times jX_S} \text{ kA}$$

|VR|
jQC
IC
XS
Adjustable excitation
EG

Fig. 5.29 *Rotating VAR generation*

$$jQ_C = 3\frac{|V_R|\angle 0°}{\sqrt{3}}(-I_C^*)$$

$$= 3\frac{|V_R|}{\sqrt{3}}\left(-\frac{|V_R|-|E_G|}{-jX_S\sqrt{3}}\right)$$

$$= j|V_R|(|E_G| - |V_R|)/X_S \text{ MVA}$$

$$\therefore \qquad Q_C = |V_R|(|E_G| - |V_R|)/X_S \text{ MVAR} \qquad (5.88)$$

It immediately follows from the above relationship that the machine feeds positive VARs into the line when $|E_G| > |V_R|$ (overexcited case) and injects negative VARs if $|E_G| < |V_R|$ (underexcited case). VARs are easily and continuously adjustable by adjusting machine excitation which controls $|E_G|$.

In contrast to static VAR generators, the following observations are made in respect of rotating VAR generators.

1. These can provide both positive and negative VARs which are continuously adjustable.
2. VAR injection at a given excitation is less sensitive to changes in bus voltage. As $|V_R|$ decreases and $(|E_G| - |V_R|)$ increases with consequent smaller reduction in Q_C compared to the case of static capacitors.

From the observations made above in respect of static and rotating VAR generators, it seems that rotating VAR generators would be preferred. However, economic considerations, installation and maintenance problems limit their practical use to such buses in the system where a large amount of VAR injection is needed.

5.10.2 Control by Transformers

The VAR injection method discussed above lacks the flexibility and economy of voltage control by transformer tap changing. The transformer tap changing is obviously limited to a narrow range of voltage control. If the voltage correction needed exceeds this range, tap changing is used in conjunction with the VAR injection method.

Receiving-end voltage which tends to sag owing to VARs demanded by the load, can be raised by simultaneously changing the taps of sending- and receiving-end transformers. Such tap changes must be made 'on-load' and can be done either manually or automatically, the transformer being called a tap changing under load (TCUL) transformer.

Consider the operation of a transmission line with a tap changing transformer at each end as shown in Fig. 5.30. Let t_S and t_R be the fractions of the nominal transformation ratios, i.e., the tap ratio/nominal ratio. For example, a transformer with nominal ratio 3.3 kV/11 kV when tapped to give 12 kV with 3.3 kV input has $t_S = 12/11 = 1.09$.

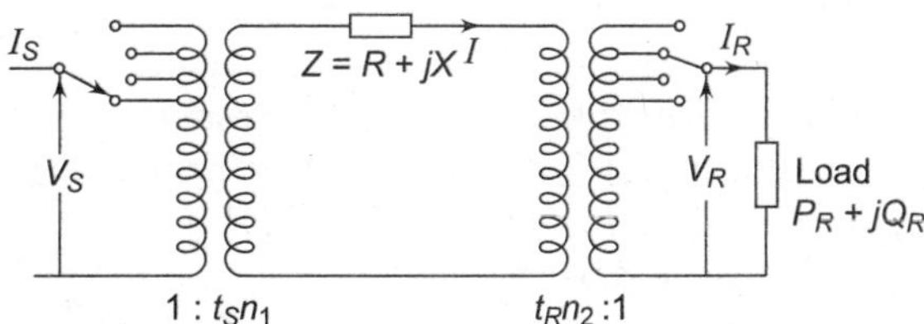

Fig. 5.30 *Transmission line with tap changing transformer at each end*

With reference to Fig. 5.30, let the impedances of the transformer be lumped in Z along with the line impedance. To compensate for voltage in the line and transformers, let the transformer taps be set at off nominal values, t_S and t_R. With reference to the circuit shown, we have

$$t_S n_1 V_S = t_R n_2 V_R + IZ \qquad (5.89)$$

From Eq. (5.75) the voltage drop referred to the high voltage side is given by

$$|\Delta V| = \frac{RP_R + XQ_R}{t_R n_2 |V_R|} \qquad (5.90)$$

Now, $\quad |\Delta V| = t_S n_1 |V_S| - t_R n_2 |V_R|$

$$\therefore \quad t_S n_1 |V_S| = t_R n_2 |V_R| + \frac{RP_R + XQ_R}{t_R n_2 |V_R|} \tag{5.91}$$

In order that the voltage on the HV side of the two transformers be of the same order and the tap setting of each transformer be the minimum, we choose

$$t_S t_R = 1 \tag{5.92}$$

Substituting $t_R = 1/t_S$ in Eq. (5.91) and reorganising, we obtain

$$t_S^2 \left(1 - \frac{RP_R + XQ_R}{n_1 n_2 |V_S||V_R|}\right) = \frac{n_2 |V_R|}{n_1 |V_S|} \tag{5.93}$$

For complete voltage drop compensation, the right-hand side of Eq. (5.93) should be unity.

It is obvious from Fig. 5.30 that $t_S > 1$ and $t_R < 1$ for voltage drop compensation. Equation (5.90) indicates that t_R tends to increase* the voltage $|\Delta V|$ which is to be compensated. Thus, merely tap setting as a method of voltage drop compensation would give rise to excessively large tap setting if compensation exceeds certain limits. Thus, if the tap setting dictated by Eq. (5.93) to achieve a desired receiving-end voltage exceeds the normal tap setting range (usually not more than $\pm$ 20%), it would be necessary to simultaneously inject VARs at the receiving end in order to maintain the desired voltage level.

5.10.3 Control by Mid-Line Boosters

It may be desirable on technical or economic grounds to increase the voltage at an intermediate point in a line rather than at the ends as with tap-changing transformers. Boosters are generally used in distribution feeders where the cost of tap-changing transformers is not warranted. Fig. 5.31 shows the connection of in-phase booster transformer.

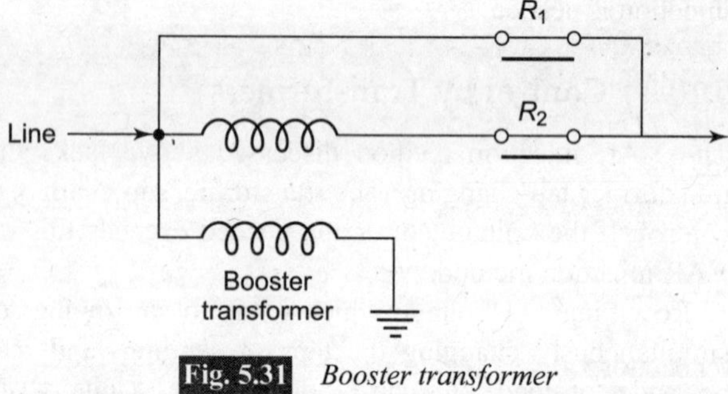

Fig. 5.31 *Booster transformer*

The booster can be pressed into the circuit by closure of relay R_2 and the opening of relay R_1 and vice versa.

Owing to increasing voltages and line lengths, and also the greater use of cables, the light-load reactive problem for an interconnected system becomes significant, specially with latest generators of limited VAR absorption capability. At peak load, transmission systems are required to increase their VAR generation, and as the load reduces during light load period, they need to reduce the generated VARs by the following methods listed in order of economic viability:

1. switch out shunt capacitors,
2. switch in shunt reactors,
3. run hydro plant on maximum VAR absorption,
4. switch out one cable in a double-circuit link,
5. tap-stagger transformers,
6. run base load generators at maximum VAR absorption.

---

* This is so because $t_R < 1$ increases the line current I and hence voltage drop.

5.10.4 Compensation of Transmission Lines

The performance of long EHV AC transmission systems can be improved by reactive compensation of series or shunt (parallel) type. Series capacitors and shunt reactors are used to reduce artificially the series reactance and shunt susceptance of lines and thus they act as the line compensators. Compensation of lines results in improving the system stability (Ch. 12) and voltage control, in increasing the efficiency of power transmission, facilitating line energisation and reducing temporary and transient overvoltages.

Series capacitor compensation reduces the series impedance of the line which causes voltage drop and is the most important factor in finding the maximum power transmission capability of a line (Eq. 5.70). *A, C* and *D* constants are functions of *Z* and therefore are also affected by change in the value of *Z*, but these changes are small in comparison to the change in *B* as $B = Z$ for the nominal-π and equals $Z\,(\sinh \gamma l/\gamma l)$ for the equivalent-π.

The voltage drop ΔV due to series compensation is given by

$$\Delta V \approx IR \cos \phi_r + I(X_L - X_C) \sin \phi_r \tag{5.94}$$

Here X_C is the capacitive reactance of the series capacitor bank per phase and X_L is the total inductive reactance of the line/phase. In practice, X_C may be so selected that the factor $(X_L - X_C) \sin \phi_r$ becomes negative and equals (in magnitude) $R \cos \phi_r$ so that ΔV becomes zero. The ratio X_C/X_L is called 'compensation factor' and when expressed as a percentage is known as the 'percentage compensation'.

The extent of effect of compensation depends on the number, location and circuit arrangements of series capacitor and shunt reactor stations. While planning long-distance lines, besides the average degree of compensation required, it is required to find out the most appropriate location of the reactors and capacitor banks, the optimum connection scheme and the number of intermediate stations. For finding the operating conditions along the line, the *ABCD* constants of the portions of line on each side of the capacitor bank, and *ABCD* constants of the bank may be first found out and then equivalent constants of the series combination of line-capacitor-line can then be arrived at by using the formulae given in Appendix B.

In India, in states like UP, series compensation is quite important since super thermal plants are located (east) several hundred kilometres from load centres (west) and large chunks of power must be transmitted over long distances. Series capacitors also help in balancing the voltage drop of two parallel lines.

When series compensation is used, there are chances of sustained overvoltage to the ground at the series capacitor terminals. This overvoltage can be the power limiting criterion at high degree of compensation. A spark gap with a high speed contactor is used to protect the capacitors under overvoltage conditions.

Under light load or no-load conditions, charging current should be kept less than the rated full-load current of the line. The charging current is approximately given by $B_C|V|$ where B_C is the total capacitive susceptance of the line and $|V|$ is the rated voltage to neutral. If the total inductive susceptance is B_L due to several inductors connected (shunt compensation) from line to neutral at appropriate places along the line, then the charging current would be

$$I_{\text{chg}} = (B_C - B_L)\,|V| = B_C|\,V\,|\left(1 - \frac{B_L}{B_C}\right) \tag{5.95}$$

Reduction of the charging current is by the factor of $(1 - B_L/B_C)$ and B_L/B_C is the shunt compensation factor. Shunt compensation at no-load also keeps the receiving-end voltage within limits which would otherwise be quite high because of the Ferranti effect. Thus, reactors should be introduced as load is removed for proper voltage control.

As mentioned earlier, the shunt capacitors are used across an inductive load so as to provide part of the reactive VARs required by the load to keep the voltage within desirable limits. Similarly, the shunt reactors are kept across capacitive loads or in light load conditions, as discussed above, to absorb some of the leading VARs for achieving voltage control. Capacitors are connected either directly to a bus or through tertiary winding of the main transformer and are placed along the line to minimise losses and the voltage drop.

It may be noted that for the same voltage boost, the reactive power capacity of a shunt capacitor is greater than that of a series capacitor. The shunt capacitor improves the pf of the load while the series capacitor has hardly any impact on the pf. Series capacitors are more effective for long lines for improvement of system stability.

Thus, we see that in both series and shunt compensation of long transmission lines it is possible to transmit large amounts of power efficiently with a flat voltage profile. Proper type of compensation should be provided in proper quantity at appropriate places to achieve the desired voltage control. The reader is encouraged to read the details about the Static Var Systems (SVS) in Refs [7, 8, 16].

Example 5.12 Figure 5.32 represents the π-equivalent of a power line with the series and shunt admittance branches. Find the values of P_1, P_2, Q_1 and Q_2 at different values of the power angle.

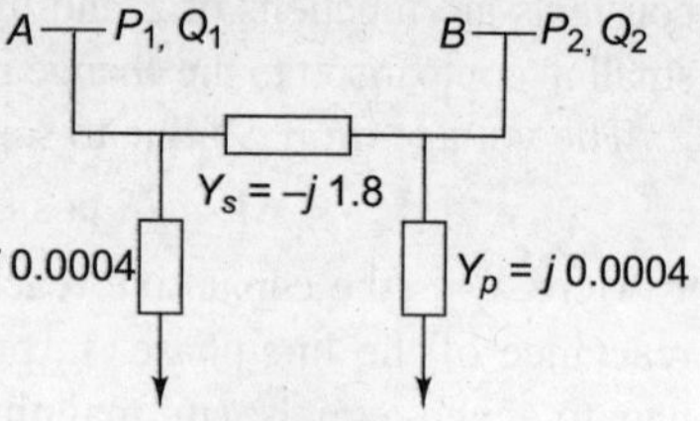

A — P_1, Q_1 B — P_2, Q_2

$Y_s = -j\,1.8$

$Y_p = j\,0.0004$ $Y_p = j\,0.0004$

Fig. 5.32

Solution Here in Figure 5.32,

$$Y_{AA}\angle\theta_2 = Y_S + Y_P = -j1.8 + j0.0004 = -j\,1.7996$$
$$= 1.7996\angle{-90°}$$
$$Y_{AB}\angle\theta_1 = -Y_S = j1.8 = 1.8\angle 90°$$
$$\theta_{AB} = \angle 90° - \theta_1 = 90° - 90° = 0°$$
$$\theta_{AA} = 90° - \theta_2 = 90° - (-90°) = 90° + 90° = 180°$$

Since the circuit is symmetrical,

$$Y_{BB} = Y_{AA} \text{ and } Y_{AB} = Y_{BA}$$
$$\theta_{BB} = \theta_{AA} \text{ and } \theta_{AB} = \theta_{BA}$$
$$Y_{AA} = Y_{BB} = 1.7996,\ E_A = E_B = 1.00$$
$$Y_{AB} = Y_{BA} = 1.8$$
$$\theta_{AA} = \theta_{BB} = 180°$$
$$\theta_{AB} = \theta_{BA} = 0°$$

Therefore,

$$P_1 = E^2_A Y_{AA} \sin\theta_{AA} + E_A E_B Y_{AB} \sin(\delta_{AB} - \theta_{AB})$$
$$= 1.7996 \sin 180° + 1.8 \sin(\delta_{AB} - 0°)$$
$$= 1.8 \sin\delta_{AB}$$
$$P_2 = -E^2_B Y_{BB} \sin\theta_{BB} + E_A E_B Y_{AB} \sin(\delta_{AB} + \theta_{AB})$$
$$= -1.7996 \sin 180° + 1.8 \sin(\delta_{AB} + 0°)$$
$$= 1.8 \sin\delta_{AB}$$
$$Q_1 = E^2_A Y_{AA} \cos\theta_{AA} + E_A E_B Y_{AB} \cos(\delta_{AB} - \theta_{AB})$$
$$= 1.7996 \cos 180° - 1.8 \cos(\delta_{AB} - 0°)$$
$$= 1.7996 - 1.8 \cos\delta_{AB}$$
$$Q_2 = -E^2_B Y_{BB} \cos\theta_{BB} + E_A E_B Y_{AB} \cos(\delta_{AB} + \theta_{AB})$$
$$= 1.7996 \cos 180° + 1.8 \cos(\delta_{AB} + 0°)$$
$$= 1.7996 + 1.8 \cos\delta_{AB}$$

where P_1 and P_2 are the real powers and Q_1 and Q_2 are the reactive powers at both the ends. E_A and E_B are the voltages operating at angles δ_1 and δ_2, respectively.

Y_{AA} and Y_{AB} are the short-circuit driving point admittance and transfer admittance with their angles θ_{AA} and θ_{BB}, respectively.

The values of P_1, P_2, Q_1 and Q_2 for different power analysis of Example 5.12 are given below. Values of P_1, P_2, Q_1 and Q_2 for different values of power angle.

δ_{AB}	$P_2 = P_1$	Q_1	$Q_2 = -Q_1$
0	0.0000	–3.5996	3.5996
10	0.3125	–3.5722	3.5722
20	0.6156	–3.4910	3.4910
30	0.900	–3.3584	3.3584
40	1.1570	–3.1784	3.1784
50	1.3788	–2.9566	2.9566
60	1.5588	–2.6996	2.6996
70	1.6914	–2.4152	2.4152
80	1.7726	–2.1121	2.1121
90	1.8000	–1.7996	1.7996
110	1.6914	–1.1839	1.1839
130	1.3788	–0.6425	0.6425
150	0.9000	–0.2407	0.2407
170	0.3125	–0.0269	0.0269
180	0.0000	–0.0004	0.0004
200	–0.6156	–0.1081	0.1081
220	–1.1570	–0.4207	0.4207
240	–1.5588	–0.8996	0.8996
260	–1.7726	–1.4870	1.4870
280	–1.7726	–2.1121	2.1121
300	–1.5588	–2.6996	2.6996
320	–1.1570	–3.1784	3.1784
340	–0.6156	–3.4910	3.4910
360	0.0000	–3.5996	3.5996

Example 5.13 Repeat Example 5.12 for another equivalent π-section of a line shown in Figure 5.33.

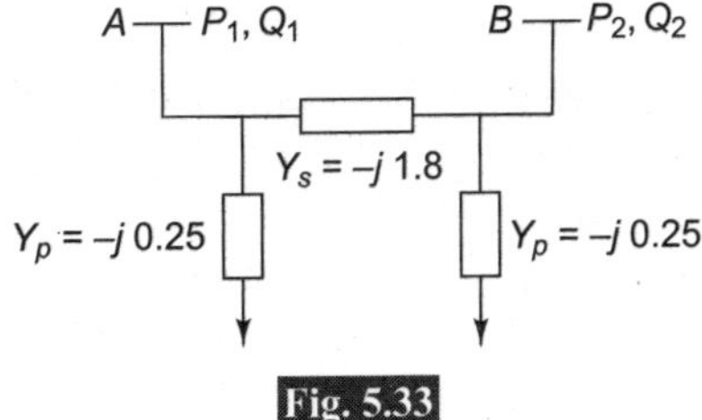

Fig. 5.33

Solution

$$Y_{AA} \angle\theta_2 = Y_S + Y_P = -j1.8 - j0.25$$
$$= -j2.05 = 2.05 \angle -\angle 90° \text{ p.u}$$
$$Y_{AB} \angle\theta_1 = -Y_S = j1.8 = 1.8 \angle 90° \text{ p.u}$$
$$\theta_{AB} = \angle 90° - \theta_1 = 90° - 90° = 0°$$
$$\theta_{AA} = 90° - \theta_2 = 90° - (-90°) = 90° + 90° = 180°$$

Since the circuit is symmetrical,

$$Y_{BB} = Y_{AA} \text{ and } Y_{AB} = Y_{BA}$$

$$\theta_{BB} = \theta_{AA} \text{ and } \theta_{AB} = \theta_{BA}$$
$$Y_{AA} = Y_{BB} = 2.05$$
$$Y_{AB} = Y_{BA} = 1.8$$
$$\theta_{AA} = \theta_{BB} = 180°$$
$$\theta_{AB} = \theta_{BA} = 0°$$

Therefore,
$$P_1 = E^2_A Y_{AA} \sin \theta_{AA} + E_A E_B Y_{AB} \sin(\delta_{AB} - \theta_{AB})$$
$$= 2.05 \sin 180° + 1.8 \sin(\delta_{AB} - 0°)$$
$$= 1.8 \sin \delta_{AB}$$
$$P_2 = -E^2_B Y_{BB} \sin \theta_{BB} = E_A E_B Y_{AB} \sin(\delta_{AB} + \theta_{AB})$$
$$= -2.05 \sin 180° + 1.8 \sin(\delta_{AB} + 0°)$$
$$= 1.8 \sin \delta_{AB}$$
$$Q_1 = E^2_A Y_{AA} \cos \theta_{AA} + E_A E_B Y_{AB} \cos(\delta_{AB} - \theta_{AB})$$
$$= 2.05 \cos 180° + 1.8 \cos(\delta_{AB} - 0°)$$
$$= -2.05 - 1.8 \cos \delta_{AB}$$
$$Q_2 = -E^2_B Y_{BB} \cos \theta_{BB} + E_A E_B Y_{AB} \cos(\delta_{AB} + \theta_{AB})$$
$$= -2.05 \cos 180° + 1.8 \cos(\delta_{AB} + 0°)$$
$$= 2.05 + 1.8 \cos \delta_{AB}$$

The values of P_1, P_2, Q_1 and Q_2 for different values of power angle are given below:

δ_{AB}	$P_2 = P_1$	Q_1	$Q_2 = -Q_1$
0	0.0000	–3.8500	3.8500
10	0.3125	–3.8226	3.8226
20	0.6156	–3.7414	3.7414
30	0.9000	–3.6088	3.6088
40	1.1570	–3.4288	3.4288
50	1.3788	–3.2070	3.2070
60	1.5588	–2.9500	2.9500
70	1.6914	–2.6652	2.6652
80	1.7726	–2.3625	2.3625
90	1.8000	–2.0500	2.0500
110	1.6914	–1.4343	1.4343
130	1.3788	–0.8929	0.8929
150	0.9000	–0.4919	0.4919
170	0.3125	–0.2773	–0.2773
180	0.0000	–0.2500	0.2500
200	–0.6156	–0.3585	0.3585
220	–1.1570	–0.6711	0.6711
240	–1.5588	–1.1500	1.1500
260	–1.7726	–1.7374	1.7374
280	–1.7726	–2.3625	2.3625
300	–1.5588	–2.9500	2.9500
320	–1.1570	–3.4288	3.4288
340	–0.6156	–3.7414	3.7414
360	0.000	–3.8500	3.8500

Example 5.14 There are four sets of double circuit EHV lines of 400 kV capacity, having a line reactance of 50 ohms per phase for each line and carrying a line current of 1000 amperes. Find how much additional series reactive loss will occur for outage of a single set of line. Assume that the load remains the same.

Solution When all the lines are in service, the series reactive loss (I^2x) is

$$4 \text{ lines } *3 \text{ phase}* (1000 \text{ A})^2 *50 \text{ ohms} = 600 \text{ MVAR}$$

When one line is out of service, its load is to be catered by the remaining three lines. Hence, line current at each 400 kV EHV line is now 1333 A. The new series reactive loss is

$$3 \text{ lines } *3 \text{ phase}* (1333 \text{ A})^2 *50 \text{ ohms} = 800 \text{ MVAR}$$

Hence, a single line outage increases the series reactive loss by 33.33%. The effect is voltage drop at the load terminal which further increases the series reactive loss. The reactive power generation is dropped and the situation may be cumulative leading to voltage collapse. Local reactive power reserve is very much necessary to keep the system voltage at or near the nominal value.

5.11 ▶ SUMMARY

In this chapter modelling, characteristics and performance of power transmission lines have been dealt with in considerable details. This is a prerequisite for future chapters and further studies in power systems.

Problems

5.1 A three-phase voltage of 11 kV is applied to a line having $R = 10\ \Omega$ and $X = 12\ \Omega$ per conductor. At the end of the line is a balanced load of P kW at a leading power factor. At what value of P is the voltage regulation zero when the power factor of the load is (a) 0.707, (b) 0.85?

5.2 A long line with $A = D = 0.9\ \angle 1.5°$ and $B = 150\ \angle 65°\ \Omega$ has at the load end a transformer having a series impedance $Z_T = 100\ \angle 67°\ \Omega$. The load voltage and current are V_L and I_L. Obtain expressions for V_S and I_S in form of

$$\begin{bmatrix} V_S \\ I_S \end{bmatrix} = \begin{bmatrix} A' & B' \\ C' & D' \end{bmatrix} \begin{bmatrix} V_L \\ I_L \end{bmatrix}$$

and evaluate these constants.

5.3 A three-phase overhead line 200 km long has resistance = 0.16 Ω/km and conductor diameter of 2 cm with spacing 4 m, 5 m and 6 m transposed. *Find*: (a) the *ABCD* constants using Eq. (5.28b), (b) the V_S, I_S, pf_S, P_S when the line is delivering full load of 50 MW at 132 kV and 0.8 lagging pf, (c) efficiency of transmission, and (d) the receiving-end voltage regulation.

5.4 A short 230 kV transmission line with a reactance of 18 Ω/phase supplies a load at 0.85 lagging power factor. For a line current of 1,000 A the receiving- and sending-end voltages are to be maintained at 230 kV. Calculate (a) rating of synchronous capacitor required, (b) the load current, (c) the load MVA. Power drawn by the synchronous capacitor may be neglected.

5.5 A 40 MVA generating station is connected to a three-phase line having

$$Z = 300\ \angle 75°\ \Omega \quad Y = 0.0025\ \angle 90°\ \mho.$$

The power at the generating station is 40 MVA at unity power factor at a voltage of 120 kV. There is a load of 10 MW at unity power factor at the mid point of the line. Calculate the voltage and load at the distant end of the line. Use nominal-T circuit for the line.

5.6 The generalised circuit constants of a transmission line are

$$A = 0.93 + j0.016$$
$$B = 20 + j140$$

The load at the receiving end is 60 MVA, 50 Hz, 0.8 power factor lagging. The voltage at the supply end is 220 kV. Calculate the load voltage.

5.7 Find the incident and reflected currents for the line of Problem 5.3 at the receiving end and 200 km from the receiving end.

5.8 If the line of Problem 5.6 is 200 km long and delivers 50 MW at 220 kV and 0.8 power factor lagging, determine the sending-end voltage, current, power factor and power. Compute the efficiency of transmission, characteristic impedance, wavelength and velocity of propagation.

5.9 For Example 5.7, find the parameters of the equivalent-π circuit for the line.

5.10 An interconnector cable having a reactance of 6 Ω links generating stations 1 and 2 as shown in Fig. 5.18(a). The desired voltage profile is $|V_1| = |V_2| = 22$ kV. The loads at the two-bus bars are 40 MW at 0.8 lagging power factor and 20 MW at 0.6 lagging power factor, respectively. The station loads are equalised by the flow of power in the cable. Estimate the torque angle and the station power factors.

5.11 A 50 Hz, three-phase, 275 kV, 400 km transmission line has the following parameters (per phase):

Resistance = 0.035 Ω/km
Inductance = 1 mH/km
Capacitance = 0.01 μF/km

If the line is supplied at 275 kV, determine the MVA rating of a shunt reactor having negligible losses that would be required to maintain 275 kV at the receiving end, when the line is delivering no-load. Use nominal-π method.

5.12 A three-phase feeder having a resistance of 3 Ω and a reactance of 10 Ω supplies a load of 2.0 MW at 0.85 lagging power factor. The receiving-end voltage is maintained at 11 kV by means of a static condenser drawing 2.1 MVAR from the line. Calculate the sending end voltage and power factor. What is the voltage regulation and efficiency of the feeder?

5.13 A three-phase overhead line has resistance and reactance of 5 and 20 Ω, respectively. The load at the receiving end is 30 MW, 0.85 power factor lagging at 33 kV. Find the voltage at the sending end. What will be the kVAR rating of the compensating equipment inserted at the receiving end so as to maintain a voltage of 33 kV at each end? Find also the maximum load that can be transmitted.

5.14 Construct a receiving-end power circle diagram for the line of Example 5.7. Locate the point corresponding to the load of 50 MW at 220 kV with 0.8 lagging power factor. Draw the circle passing through the load point. Measure the radius and determine therefrom $|V_S|$. Also draw the sending-end circle and determine therefrom the sending-end power and power factor.

5.15 A three-phase overhead line has resistance and reactance per phase of 5 and 25 Ω, respectively. The load at the receiving end is 15 MW, 33 kV, 0.8 power factor lagging. Find the capacity of the compensation equipment needed to deliver this load with a sending-end voltage of 33 kV.

Calculate the extra load of 0.8 lagging power factor which can be delivered with the compensating equipment (of capacity as calculated above) installed, if the receiving-end voltage is permitted to drop to 28 kV.

Multiple Choice Questions

5.1 As the frequency of the system is increased, the charging MVAR
(a) Increases (b) Decreases (c) Remains the same (d) None of the above

5.2 The receiving-end voltage for a long line under no load condition is
(a) Less than the sending-end voltage (b) More than the sending-end voltage
(c) Equal to the sending-end voltage (d) Any of the above

5.3 For a given receiving-end voltage in a long transmission line, the sending-end voltage is more than the actual value calculated by
(a) Nominal-π method (b) Nominal-T method
(c) Load end capacitance method (d) None of the above

5.4 A short line with R/X ratio 1, the zero regulation is obtained when the power factor of the load is
(a) 0.5 (b) unity (c) 0 leading (d) 0.707 leading

5.5 If the line is loaded with the surge impedance; the receiving-end voltage is
(a) Less than the sending-end voltage (b) Equal to the sending-end voltage
(c) Greater than the sending-end voltage (d) None of these

5.6 The transfer of reactive power over a line mainly depends upon
(a) V_r (b) V_s (c) $|V_s| - |V_r|$ (d) Power angle

5.7 With 100% series compensation of lines
(a) Low transient voltage (b) High transient current
(c) The current is series resonant at power frequency (d) Both (b) and (c)

5.8 The line constants of a transmission line are
(a) Lumped (b) Non-uniformly distributed
(c) Uniformly distributed (d) None of the above

5.9 Surge impedance of 400 Ω means
(a) Line can be theoretically loaded upto 400 Ω (b) Line can be practically loaded upto 400 Ω
(c) Open circuit impedance of 400 Ω (d) Short circuit impedance of 400 Ω

5.10 The main objectives of electrical power transmission system is/are
(a) Transmission system must be more efficient with minimum line losses
(b) Voltage regulation of the transmission line must be zero or minimum
(c) Only 1 is correct
(d) Both 1 and 2 are correct

5.11 Compared with a solid conductor of the same radius, corona appears on a stranded conductor at a lower voltage, because stranding
(a) Assists ionisation
(b) Makes the current flow spirally about the axis of the conductor
(c) Produces oblique sections to a plane perpendicular to the axis of the conductor
(d) Produces surfaces of smaller radius

5.12 Advantages of higher transmission voltage is/are
(a) Power transfer capability of the transmission line is increased
(b) Transmission line losses are reduced
(c) Area of cross section and volume of the conductor are reduced
(d) all of the above

5.13 Power transmission lines are transposed to
(a) Reduce copper loss
(b) Reduce skin effect
(c) Prevent interference with neighbouring telephone lines
(d) Prevent short-circuit between any two lines

5.14 Maximum power transfer capability of transmission lines can be improved by
(a) Parallel transmission lines (b) Using series capacitance
(c) Using bundled conductors (d) all of the above

5.15 A single-phase transmission line of impedance $(0 + j0.8)$ ohm supplies a resistive load of 500 A at 300 V. The sending-end power factor of system is
(a) Unity (b) 0.8 lagging
(c) 0.8 leading (d) 0.6 lagging

5.16 Ferranti effect will not occur in which of the following transmission lines?
(a) Long transmission lines (b) Short transmission lines
(c) Medium transmission lines (d) all of the above

5.17 The presence of earth in case of overhead lines
(a) Increase inductance (b) Increase capacitance
(c) Decrease inductance (d) Decrease capacitance

5.18 Which of the following methods is/are used for reactive or voltage compensation?
(a) Shunt capacitor (b) Series capacitor
(c) Generation excitation control (d) all of the above

5.19 The charging current in a transmission line increases due to corona effect because corona increases
(a) Line current (b) Effective line voltage
(c) Power loss in lines (d) The effective conductor diameter

5.20 Ferranti effect in power transmission system can be compensated by the following:
(a) Shunt capacitor (b) Shunt reactor
(c) Series capacitor (d) Both 1 and 2

5.21 In a short transmission line, if resistance and inductive reactance are found to be equal and regulation appears to be zero, then the load will
(a) Have unity power factor (b) Have zero power factor
(d) Be 0.707 lagging (c) Be 0.707 leading

5.22 The stability of a transmission line can be improved by
(a) Shunt capacitor (b) Series capacitor
(c) Shunt reactor (d) Both 1 and 2

5.23 Which of the following are the advantages of interconnected operation of power systems?
(a) Less reserve capacity requirement (b) More reliability
(c) High power factor (d) Reduction in short-circuit level

5.24 Which of the following methods is used for changing power factor from leading to lagging?
(a) Shunt capacitor (b) Series capacitor
(c) Shunt reactor (d) Any of the above

5.25 When bundle conductors are used in place of single conductors, the effective inductance and capacitance will respectively
(a) Increase and decrease (b) Decrease and increase
(c) Decrease and remain unaffected (d) remain unaffected and increase

5.26 Which lines are transposed to reduce the radio interference?
(a) Power transmission lines only
(b) Telecommunication lines only
(c) Both power and telecommunication lines
(d) Either 1 or 2

5.27 For a transmission line with negligible losses and a given receiving-end voltage, the lagging reactive power (VAR) delivered at the receiving-end is directly proportional to the
(a) Square of the line voltage drop
(b) Line voltage drop
(c) Line inductive reactance
(d) Line capacitive reactance

5.28 In which of the following configurations power transferability of transmission line is higher?
(a) Triangular configuration
(b) Horizontal configuration
(c) Same in both configurations
(d) None of the above

5.29 A 3-phase line having negligible resistance and 22 ohm inductive reactance per phase operates with 110 kV sending-end voltage and 100 kV receiving-end voltage. The maximum power that this line can transmit is
(a) $500\sqrt{3}$ MW
(b) 500 MW
(c) 1500 MW
(d) $1500/\sqrt{3}$ MW

5.30 Proximity effect is more in case of
(a) Power cables
(b) Power transformers
(c) Over head lines
(d) Neutral lines

5.31 When there is interference in an overhead communication line running parallel and in close proximity to an overhead power line, the voltage induced in the communication line in the longitudinal and lateral directions by the power line are due to
(a) Magnetic induction and electric induction, respectively
(b) Electric induction and magnetic induction, respectively
(c) Both magnetic induction and electric induction
(d) Magnetic induction only

5.32 Proximity effect in power transmission systems depends on
(a) Frequency
(b) Distance between the conductors
(c) Relative permeability
(d) all of the above

5.33 The good effect and advantages of corona on overhead transmission lines are to
(a) Increase the line-carrying capacity due to conducting ionised air envelop around the conductor
(b) Increase the power factor due to corona loss
(c) Reduce the radio interference from the conductor
(d) Reduce the steepness of surge fronts

5.34 Skin effect in electrical power transmission system is more in case of
(a) Communication lines
(b) Power lines
(c) Transformers
(d) Induction generators

5.35 The inductance per unit length of an overhead line due to internal flux linkages
(a) Depends on the size of the conductor
(b) is independent of the size of conductor and constant
(c) Depends on the current through the conductor
(d) Depends on distance between conductors

5.36 Power transmission lines in electrical power systems are transposed to reduce
(a) Ferranti effect
(b) Skin effect
(c) Proximity effect
(d) Interference with neighbouring communication lines

5.37 The skin effect of conductor will increase when
(a) Diameter decreases
(b) Resistivity decreases
(c) Frequency decreases
(d) Voltage increases

5.38 If the diameter of the conductor is increased
(a) the inductance increases
(b) the inductance decreases
(c) the resistance increases
(d) no change in inductance and resistance

5.39 Three-phase transmission line conductors were arranged in horizontal spacing, with 'd' as the distance between adjacent conductors. If these conductors are rearranged to form an equilateral triangle with sides equal 'd', then the
(a) Capacitance and the inductance will increase
(b) Capacitance will increase and the inductance will decrease
(c) Capacitance and the inductance will remain the same
(d) Capacitance will decrease and the inductance will increase

5.40 Which one of the following statements is not correct for the use of bundled conductors in power transmission lines?
(a) Control of voltage gradient
(b) Reduction in corona loss
(c) Reduction in radio interference
(d) Increase in interference with communication lines

References

Books

1. *Transmission Line Reference Book—345 kV and Above*, 2nd edn, Electric Power Research Institute, Palo Alto, CA, 1982.
2. J. McCombe and F.J. Haigh, *Overhead-line Practice*, Macdonald, London, 1966.
3. W.D. Stevenson, *Elements of Power System Analysis*, 4th edn, McGraw-Hill, New York, 1982.
4. J. Arrillaga, High Voltage Direct Current Transmission, *IEE Power Engineering Series 6*, Peter Peregrinus Ltd., London, 1983.
5. E.W. Kimbark, *Direct Current Transmission*, volume: 1, Wiley, New York, 1971.
6. E. Uhlmann, *Power Transmission by Direct Current*, Springer-Verlag, Berlin, 1975.
7. T.J.E. Miller, *Reactive Power Control in Electric Systems*, Wiley, New York, 1982.
8. R.M. Mathur (Ed.), *Static Compensators for Reactive Power Control*, Context Pub., Winnipeg, 1984.
9. M.V. Desphande, *Electrical Power System Design*, Tata McGraw-Hill, New Delhi, 1984.

Papers

10. R.D. Dunlop, R. Gautam, and D.P. Marchenko, "Analytical Development of Loadability Characteristics for EHV and UHV Transmission Lines", *IEEE Trans.*, PAS, volume: 98, p: 606, 1979.
11. "EHV Transmission", (Special Issue), *IEEE Trans.*, PAS-85, volume: 6, June 1966.
12. R.D. Goodrich, "A Universal Power Circle Diagram", *AIEE Trans*., volume: 70, p: 70, 2042.
13. C.S. Indulkar, Parmod Kumar, and D.P. Kothari, "Sensitivity Analysis of a Multiconductor Transmission Line", *Proc. IEEE*, volume: 70, p: 299, March 1982.
14. C.S. Indulkar, Parmod Kumar, and D.P. Kothari, "Some Studies on Carrier Propagation in Overhead Transmission Lines", *IEEE Trans.*, PAS-4, volume: 102, p: 942, 1983.
15. P.R. Bijwe, D.P. Kothari, J. Nanda, and K.S. Lingamurthy, "Optimal Voltage Control Using Constant Sensitivity Matrix", *Electric Power System Research*, volume: 3, p: 195, 1986.

16. D.P. Kothari, *et al.*, "Microprocessors Controlled Static VAR Systems", *Proc. Int. Conf. Modelling and Simulation*, Gorakhpur, volume: 2, p: 139, Dec. 1985.
17. "IEEE Guide for the Parameter Measurement of AC Transmission Lines", *IEEE Standard 1870-2019*, pp: 1–99, 2019.
18. C. Dufour and H. Le-Huy, "Highly Accurate Modeling of Frequency-Dependent Balanced Transmission Lines", *IEEE Transactions on Power Delivery*, volume: 15, issue: 2, pp: 610–615, 2000.
19. M. Zunec, I. Ticar, and F. Jakl, "Determination of Current and Temperature Distribution in Overhead Conductors by Using Electromagnetic-Field Analysis Tools", *IEEE Transactions on Power Delivery*, volume: 21, issue: 3, pp: 1524–1529, 2006.
20. A.R. Djordjevic, A.G. Zajic, D.V. Tosic, and Truc Hoang, "A Note on the Modeling Of Transmission-Line Losses", *IEEE Transactions on Microwave Theory and Techniques*, volume: 51, issue: 2, pp: 483–486, 2003.
21. "IEEE Approved Draft Guide for the Parameter Measurement of AC Transmission Lines", *IEEE P1870/D7, October 2018*, pp: 1–90, 2019.
22. A. Wehenkel, A. Mukhopadhyay, J.-Y.L. Boudec, and M. Paolone, "Parameter Estimation of Three-Phase Untransposed Short Transmission Lines from Synchrophasor Measurements", *IEEE Transactions on Instrumentation and Measurement*, volume: 69, issue: 9, pp: 6143–6154, 2020.
23. L.D. Arya, S.C. Choube, and R.K. Saket, "Composite System Reliability Evaluation Based on Static Voltage Stability Limit", *Journal of the Institution of Engineers (India): Series B*, volume: 80, pp: 133–140, 2000
24. D.C. Agouridis, "Thermal Noise of Transmission Lines: A Generalized Solution", *IEEE Transactions on Instrumentation and Measurement*, volume: IM-36, issue: 1, pp: 132–134, 1987.
25. S. Kurokawa, R.S. Daltin, A.J. Prado, and J. Pissolato, "An Alternative Modal Representation of a Symmetrical Nontransposed Three-Phase Transmission Line", *IEEE Transactions on Power Systems*, volume: 22, issue: 1, pp: 500–501, 2007.
26. J.A.B. Faria and R. Araneo, "Computation, Properties, and Realizability of the Characteristic Immittance Matrices of Nonuniform Multiconductor Transmission Lines", *IEEE Transactions on Power Delivery*, volume: 33, issue: 4, pp: 1885–1894, 2018.
27. R. Dias, A. Lima, C. Portela, and M. Aredes, "Extra Long-Distance Bulk Power Transmission", *IEEE Transactions on Power Delivery,* volume 26: issue 3, pp: 1440–1448, 2011.
28. R.K. Saket, R.C. Bansal, and Col. Gurmit Singh, "Power Systems Component Modelling and Reliability Evaluation of Generation Capacity", *International Journal of Reliability and Safety*, volume: 03, issue: 04, pp: 427–441, 2009.
29. H. Rahman and B.H. Khan, "Power Upgrading of Transmission Line by Combining AC–DC Transmission", *IEEE Transactions on Power Systems*, volume: 22, issue: 1, pp: 459–466, 2007.
30. D. Debnath, A. De, A. Chakrabarti, and D.P. Kothari, "Studies on the Impact of Capacitor Bank Switching on Grid Connected Transformers", *International Journal of Electrical Power & Energy Systems*, volume: 43, issue: 1, pp: 126–130, 2012.

CHAPTER

6 Load Flow Studies

6.1 ▶ INTRODUCTION

With the background of the previous chapters, we are now ready to study the operational features and electrical performance of a composite power system. The symmetrical steady state is, in fact, the most important mode of operation of a power system. Three major problems encountered in this mode of operation are listed below in their hierarchical order.

1. Load flow problem
2. Optimal load scheduling problem
3. Systems control problem

This chapter is devoted to the load flow problem, while the other two problems will be treated in later chapters.

Load flow study in power system parlance is the steady-state solution of the power system network. The power system is modelled by an electric network and solved for the steady-state powers and voltages at various buses. The direct analysis of the circuit is not possible, as the loads are given in terms of complex powers rather than impedances, and the generators behave more like power sources than voltage sources. The main information obtained from the load flow study comprises magnitudes and phase angles of load bus voltages, reactive powers and voltage phase angles at generator buses, real and reactive power flow on transmission lines together with power at the reference bus, other variables being specified. This information is essential for the continuous monitoring of the current state of the system and for analysing the effectiveness of the alternative plans for the future, such as adding new generator sites, meeting increased load demand and locating new transmission sites.

In load flow analysis, we are mainly interested in voltages at various buses and power injection into the transmission system. Figure 6.1 shows the one-line diagram of a power system having five buses.

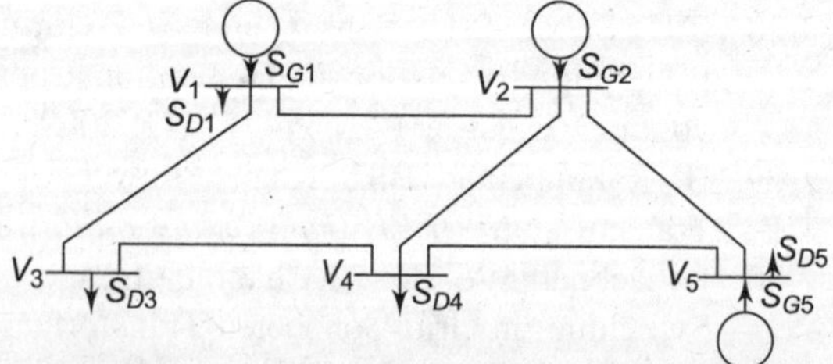

Fig. 6.1 *One-line diagram of a five-bus system*

Here S_{Gs} and S_{Ds} represent the complex powers injected by generators and complex powers drawn by the loads and Vs represent the complex voltages at the various buses. Thus, there results a net injection of power into the transmission system. In a practical system, there may be thousands of buses and transmission links. We shall concentrate mainly on the transmission system with the generators and loads modelled by the complex powers. The transmission system may be a primary transmission system, which transmits bulk power from the generators to the bulk power substation, or a subtransmission system which transmits power from substations or some old generators to the distribution substations. The transmission system is to be designed in such a manner that the power system operation is reliable and economic, and no difficulties are encountered in its operation. The likely difficulties are, one or more transmission lines becoming overloaded, generator(s) becoming overloaded, or the stability margin for a transmission link being too small, etc. Also, there may be emergencies, such as the loss of one or more transmission links, shut-down of generators, etc., which gives rise to overloading of some generators and transmission links. In system operation and planning, the voltages and powers are kept within certain limits and alternative plans are developed for easy and reliable operation. At the same time, it is also necessary to consider the economy of operation with respect to fuel costs to generate all the power needed. It may happen that each of the objectives mentioned above gives conflicting results. Usually, a compromise has to be made with such results so that the system is reliable to operate in an emergency, and at the same time, is economical in operation.

The power system network of today is highly complicated consisting of hundreds of buses and transmission links. Thus, the load flow study involves extensive calculations. Before the advent of digital computers, the AC calculating board was the only means of carrying out load flow studies. These studies were, therefore, tedious and time consuming. With the availability of fast and large sized digital computers, all kinds of power system studies, including load flow study can now be carried out conveniently. In fact, some of the advanced level sophisticated studies, which were almost impossible to carry out on the AC calculating board, have now become possible. The AC calculating board has been rendered obsolete.

6.2 ▶ NETWORK MODEL FORMULATION

Consider an *i*th bus of an '*n*' bus power system as shown in Fig. 6.2.

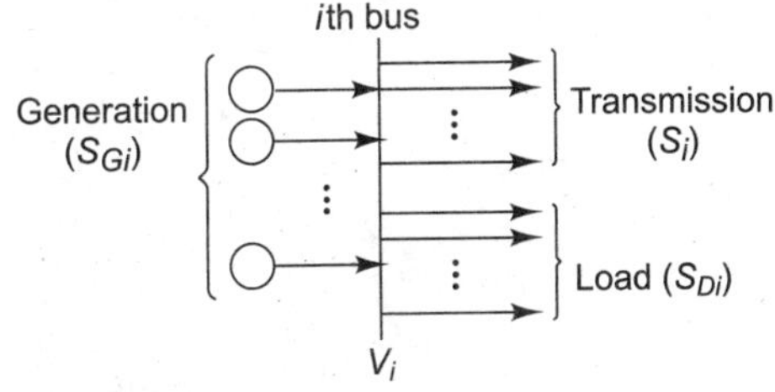

Fig. 6.2 *ith bus in general connected to generators, loads and transmission lines*

It is convenient to work with power at each bus injected into the transmission system, called the 'Bus Power'. The *i*th bus power is defined as

$$S_i = S_{Gi} - S_{Di}$$

The complex 'Bus Power' S_i can also be visualised by splitting a bus as shown in Fig. 6.3.

Writing the complex powers in terms of real and reactive powers, we have

$$S_{Gi} = P_{Gi} + jQ_{Gi}$$
$$S_{Di} = P_{Di} + jQ_{Di} \qquad (6.1a)$$
$$S_i = P_i + jQ_i$$

where $i = 1, ..., n$

Also,

$$S_i = S_{Gi} - S_{Di}$$
$$= (P_{Gi} - P_{Di}) + j(Q_{Gi} - Q_{Di}) \qquad (6.1b)$$

where $i = 1, ..., n$

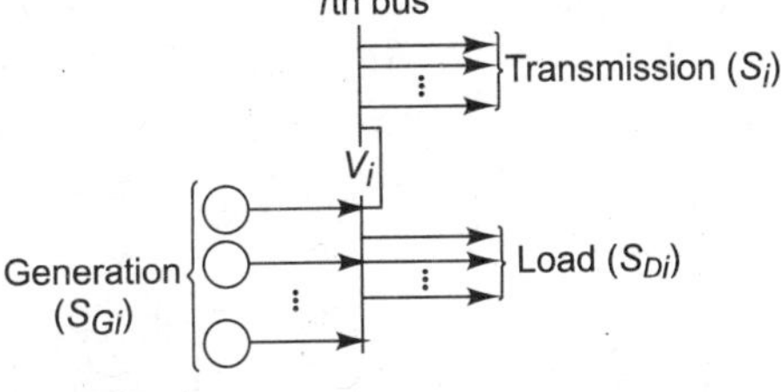

Fig. 6.3 *ith bus split to visualise S_i which is the injected complex bus power*

The 'Bus Current' at the *i*th bus is defined as

$$I_i = I_{Gi} - I_{Di}$$

Thus, the 'Bus Current' I_i can also be visualised by splitting a bus as shown in Fig. 6.4.

We next develop the relation between bus currents and bus voltages under the following assumptions:

1. That there is no mutual coupling between the transmission lines, and
2. That there is an absence of regulating transformers.

Later on, we consider their presence and show that these modify the current–voltage relationship.

Let y_{ik} $(i \neq k)$ be the total admittance connected between the ith and kth buses and y_{i0} be the admittance between ith bus and the ground.

This is usually due to the capacitance present between transmission lines and the ground. The admittance y_{i0} can be realised when the transmission lines connected to the ith bus are replaced by their π-equivalent circuits. Thus, each transmission line will present an admittance between the bus and the ground. The total admittance (y_{i0}) is the sum of the admittances due to all the transmission lines connected to the bus.

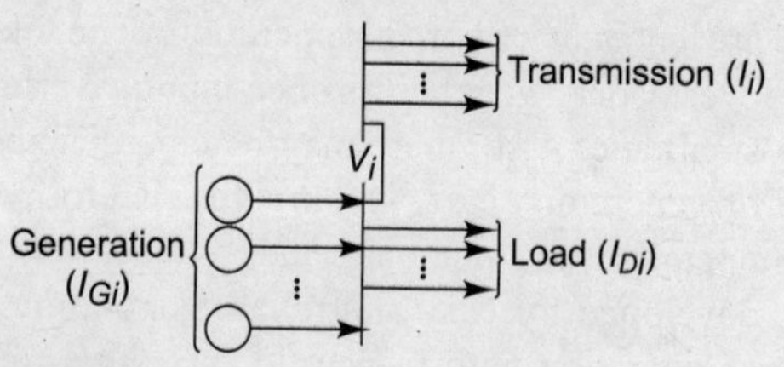

Fig. 6.4 *Visualising Bus Current I_i at the ith bus injected into the transmission system*

Also y_{ik} $(i \neq k) = 0$, if there is no transmission line between the ith and the kth bus.

By applying KCL at the ith bus, we get

$$I_i = y_{i0}V_i + y_{i1}(V_i - V_1) + y_{i2}(V_i - V_2) + \cdots + y_{i,\,i-1}(V_i - V_{i-1}) + y_{i,\,i+1}(V_i - V_{i+1}) + \cdots + y_{in}(V_i - V_n)$$

or $$I_i = -y_{i1}V_1 - y_{i2}V_2 - y_{i3}V_3 - \cdots - y_{i,\,i-1}V_{i-1} + (y_{i0} + y_{i1} + \cdots + y_{i,\,i-1} + y_{i,\,i+1} + \cdots + y_{in})V_i - y_{i,\,i+1}V_{i+1} - \cdots - y_{in}V_n \quad (6.2a)$$

Thus, in general,

$$I_i = Y_{i1}V_1 + Y_{i2}V_2 + \cdots + Y_{ii}V_i + \cdots + Y_{in}V_n$$

$$= \sum_{k=1}^{n}(Y_{ik}V_k) \quad (6.2b)$$

where $i = 1, \ldots, n$

where

$$Y_{ik}\,(i \neq k) = \frac{I_i}{V_k} \text{ (all } V = 0 \text{ except } V_k) \quad (6.3)$$

= Short circuit transfer admittance between ith and kth bus

and $$Y_{ii} = \frac{I_i}{V_i} \text{ (all } V = 0 \text{ except } V_i) \quad (6.4)$$

= Short circuit driving point admittance or self-admittance at the ith bus

From Eqs. (6.2a) and (6.3)

$$Y_{ik}\,(i \neq k) = -y_{ki} = \text{Negative of the total admittance connected between } i\text{th and } k\text{th bus} \quad (6.5a)$$

(Y_{ik} $(i \neq k) = 0$ if there is no transmission line between ith and kth bus)

From Eqs. (6.2a) and (6.4)

$$Y_{ii} = y_{i0} + y_{i1} + y_{i2} + \cdots + y_{i,\,i-1} + y_{i,\,i+1} + \cdots + y_{in} \quad (6.5b)$$

= Sum of the admittances directly connected to ith bus

Writing Eq. (6.2b) for all the n buses, we can write its matrix form as

$$I_{BUS} = Y_{BUS}V_{BUS} \quad (6.6)$$

where I_{BUS} is $n \times 1$ column vector of bus currents
V_{BUS} is $n \times 1$ column vector of bus voltages
Y_{BUS} is $n \times n$ matrix of admittances given as

$$\boldsymbol{Y}_{\text{BUS}} = \begin{bmatrix} Y_{11} & Y_{12} & \dots & Y_{1n} \\ Y_{21} & Y_{22} & \dots & Y_{2n} \\ \vdots & \vdots & & \vdots \\ Y_{n1} & Y_{n2} & \dots & Y_{nn} \end{bmatrix}_{n\times n}$$

It follows that

1. The diagonal element of $\boldsymbol{Y}_{\text{BUS}}$ is given by Eq. (6.5b) and is the self-admittance. The off-diagonal element of $\boldsymbol{Y}_{\text{BUS}}$ is given by Eq. (6.5a) and is the transfer admittance.
2. $\boldsymbol{Y}_{\text{BUS}}$ is $n \times n$ matrix where n is the number of buses.
3. $\boldsymbol{Y}_{\text{BUS}}$ is a symmetric matrix ($Y_{ik} = Y_{ki}$ (for $k \neq i$)) if the regulating transformers are not involved. So only $\dfrac{n\times n - n}{2} + n = \dfrac{n(n+1)}{2}$ terms are to be stored for an n-bus system.
4. $Y_{ik}(i \neq k) = 0$ if ith and kth buses are not connected.

Since in a power network each bus is connected only to a few other buses (two or three), the $\boldsymbol{Y}_{\text{BUS}}$ of a large network is very sparse, i.e., it has a large number of zero elements.

Equation (6.6) can also be written in the form

$$\boldsymbol{V}_{\text{BUS}} = \boldsymbol{Z}_{\text{BUS}}\,\boldsymbol{I}_{\text{BUS}} \tag{6.7}$$

where $\quad \boldsymbol{Z}_{\text{BUS}}$ (Bus Impedance Matrix) $= \boldsymbol{Y}_{\text{BUS}}^{-1}$ (6.8)

$$\boldsymbol{Z}_{\text{BUS}} = \begin{bmatrix} Z_{11} & Z_{12} & \dots & Z_{1n} \\ Z_{21} & Z_{22} & \dots & Z_{2n} \\ \vdots & \vdots & & \vdots \\ Z_{n1} & Z_{n2} & \dots & Z_{nn} \end{bmatrix}_{n\times n \text{ for } n \text{ bus system}}$$

1. The diagonal elements are short circuit driving point impedances, and the off-diagonal elements are short circuit transfer impedances.
2. Symmetric $\boldsymbol{Y}_{\text{BUS}}$ yields symmetric $\boldsymbol{Z}_{\text{BUS}}$.
3. $\boldsymbol{Z}_{\text{BUS}}$ is a full-matrix, i.e., zero elements in $\boldsymbol{Y}_{\text{BUS}}$ become nonzero elements in the corresponding $\boldsymbol{Z}_{\text{BUS}}$.

$\boldsymbol{Y}_{\text{BUS}}$ is often used in solving load flow problems. It has gained widespread application owing to its simplicity in data preparation, and the ease with which it can be formed and modified for network changes. One of its greatest advantages is its sparsity, as it heavily reduces computer memory and time requirements.

The formation of a bus impedance matrix requires either matrix inversion or use of involved algorithms. $\boldsymbol{Z}_{\text{BUS}}$ is, however, most useful for short circuit studies and will be elaborated in the relevant chapter.

Note: 1. Tinney and Associates at Bonnevile Power Authority were the first to exploit the sparsity feature of $\boldsymbol{Y}_{\text{BUS}}$ in greatly reducing numerical computations and in minimising memory requirements.

2. In more sophisticated load flow studies of large power systems, it has been shown that a certain ordering of buses (nodes) produces faster convergence and solution. This ordering is known as optimal ordering.
3. $\boldsymbol{Y}_{\text{BUS}}/\boldsymbol{Z}_{\text{BUS}}$ constitute models of the passive portions of the power network.

Example 6.1 Figure 6.5(a) shows the one-line diagram of a four-bus system, which is replaced by its equivalent circuit in Fig. 6.5(b), where the equivalent power source at each bus is represented by a shaded circle. The equivalent power source at the ith bus injects currents I_i into the bus. The structure of the power system is such that all the sources are always connected to a common ground node. The transmission lines are replaced by their nominal-π equivalent. Figure 6.5(b) is redrawn in Fig. 6.5(c), after lumping the shunt admittances at the buses. The line admittance between nodes i and k is depicted by y_{ik}. Also, $y_{ik} = y_{ki}$. Further, the mutual admittances between the lines are assumed to be zero. In Fig. 6.5(c), there are five nodes, viz., the ground node zero and the nodes corresponding to the four buses. Applying KCL at nodes 1, 2, 3 and 4, respectively, we get four equations as follows:

$$I_1 = y_{10}\,V_1 + y_{12}\,(V_1 - V_2) + y_{13}\,(V_1 - V_3)$$
$$I_2 = y_{20}\,V_2 + y_{12}\,(V_2 - V_1) + y_{23}\,(V_2 - V_3) + y_{24}\,(V_2 - V_4)$$
$$I_3 = y_{30}\,V_3 + y_{13}\,(V_3 - V_1) + y_{23}\,(V_3 - V_2) + y_{34}\,(V_3 - V_4)$$
$$I_4 = y_{40}\,V_4 + y_{24}\,(V_4 - V_2) + y_{34}\,(V_4 - V_3)$$

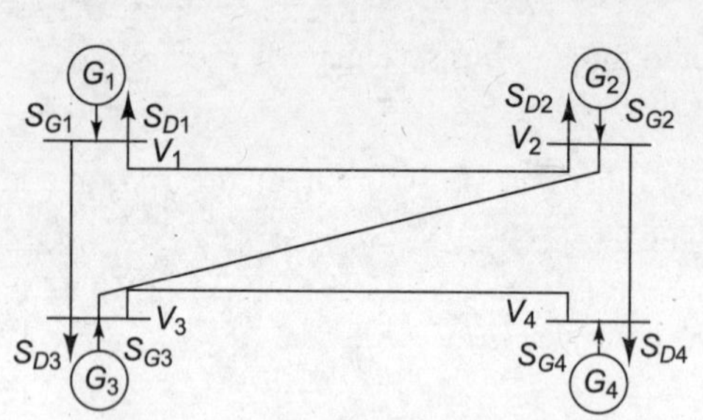

(a) One-line diagram of a four-bus system

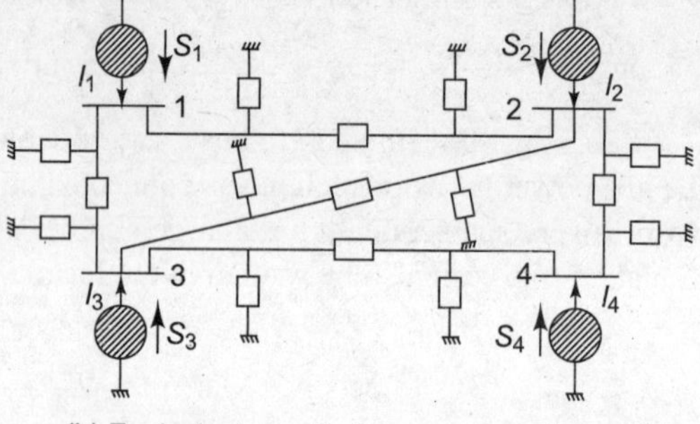

(b) Equivalent circuit of the power system of (a)

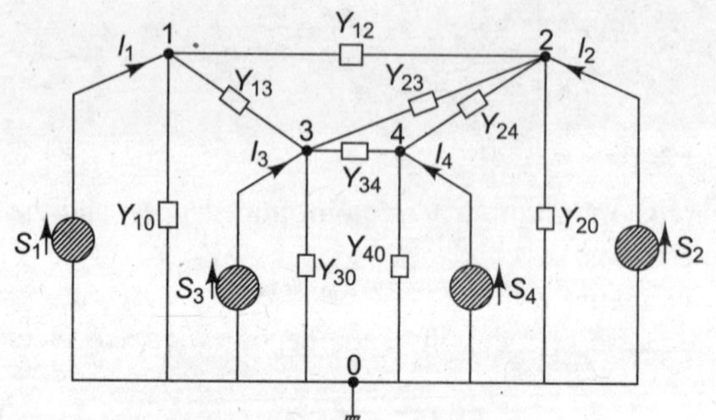

(c) Reduced circuit diagram of the power system

Fig. 6.5 (a)-(c) *Sample four-bus system*

Rearranging and writing in matrix form, we get

$$\begin{bmatrix} I_1 \\ I_2 \\ I_3 \\ I_4 \end{bmatrix} = \begin{bmatrix} (y_{10} + y_{12} + y_{13}) & -y_{12} & -y_{13} & 0 \\ -y_{12} & (y_{20} + y_{12} + y_{23} + y_{24}) & -y_{23} & -y_{24} \\ -y_{13} & -y_{23} & (y_{30} + y_{13} + y_{23} + y_{34}) & -y_{34} \\ 0 & -y_{24} & -y_{34} + y_{34}) & (y_{40} + y_{24} \end{bmatrix} \begin{bmatrix} V_1 \\ V_2 \\ V_3 \\ V_4 \end{bmatrix}$$

Writing in the standard form, we get

$$\begin{bmatrix} I_1 \\ I_2 \\ I_3 \\ I_4 \end{bmatrix} = \begin{bmatrix} Y_{11} & Y_{12} & Y_{13} & Y_{14} \\ Y_{21} & Y_{22} & Y_{23} & Y_{24} \\ Y_{31} & Y_{32} & Y_{33} & Y_{34} \\ Y_{41} & Y_{42} & Y_{43} & Y_{44} \end{bmatrix} \begin{bmatrix} V_1 \\ V_2 \\ V_3 \\ V_4 \end{bmatrix}$$

or

$$I_{BUS} = Y_{BUS} V_{BUS}$$

where
$$Y_{BUS} = \begin{bmatrix} Y_{11} & Y_{12} & Y_{13} & Y_{14} \\ Y_{21} & Y_{22} & Y_{23} & Y_{24} \\ Y_{31} & Y_{32} & Y_{33} & Y_{34} \\ Y_{41} & Y_{42} & Y_{43} & Y_{44} \end{bmatrix}$$

As already concluded in Eqs. 6.5(a) and (b), we observe that the diagonal elements of $\boldsymbol{Y}_{BUS}$ are self-admittances, and are given by

$$Y_{11} = y_{10} + y_{12} + y_{13}$$
$$Y_{22} = y_{20} + y_{12} + y_{23} + y_{24}$$
$$Y_{33} = y_{30} + y_{13} + y_{23} + y_{34}, \text{ and}$$
$$Y_{44} = y_{40} + y_{24} + y_{34}$$

The off-diagonal elements of $\boldsymbol{Y}_{BUS}$ are transfer admittances, and are given by

$$Y_{12} = Y_{21} = -y_{12}$$
$$Y_{13} = Y_{31} = -y_{13}$$
$$Y_{14} = Y_{41} = 0$$
$$Y_{23} = Y_{32} = -y_{23}$$
$$Y_{24} = Y_{42} = -y_{24}$$
$$Y_{34} = Y_{43} = -y_{34}$$

6.2.1 Algorithm for the Formation of Y_{BUS} Matrix

Assuming no Mutual Coupling between Transmission Lines Initially all the elements of $\boldsymbol{Y}_{BUS}$ are set to zero. Addition of an element of admittance y between buses i and j affects four entries in $\boldsymbol{Y}_{BUS}$, viz., Y_{ii}, Y_{ij}, Y_{ji}, Y_{jj}, as follows:

$$\begin{aligned} Y_{ii\text{ new}} &= Y_{ii\text{ old}} + y \\ Y_{ij\text{ new}} &= Y_{ij\text{ old}} - y \\ Y_{ji\text{ new}} &= Y_{ji\text{ old}} - y \\ Y_{jj\text{ new}} &= Y_{jj\text{ old}} + y \end{aligned} \tag{6.9a}$$

Addition of an element of admittance y from bus i to ground will only affect Y_{ii}, i.e.,

$$Y_{ii\text{ new}} = Y_{ii\text{ old}} + y \tag{6.9b}$$

Example 6.2 Consider the sample four-bus system in Fig. 6.5. Initially, set all the elements of $\boldsymbol{Y}_{BUS}$ to zero.

1. Addition of y_{10} affects only Y_{11}

$$Y_{11\text{ new}} = Y_{11\text{ old}} + y_{10} = 0 + y_{10} = y_{10}$$

2. Addition of y_{12} affects Y_{11}, Y_{12}, Y_{21}, Y_{22}

$$Y_{11\text{ new}} = Y_{11\text{ old}} + y_{12} = y_{10} + y_{12}$$
$$Y_{12\text{ new}} = Y_{12\text{ old}} - y_{12} = 0 - y_{12} = -y_{12} \tag{i}$$
$$Y_{21\text{ new}} = Y_{21\text{ old}} - y_{12} = 0 - y_{12} = -y_{12} \tag{ii}$$
$$Y_{22\text{ new}} = Y_{22\text{ old}} - y_{12} = 0 + y_{12}$$

3. Addition of y_{13} affects $Y_{11}, Y_{13}, Y_{31}, Y_{33}$

$$Y_{11\,\text{new}} = Y_{11\,\text{old}} + y_{13} = y_{10} + y_{12} + y_{13} \quad \text{(iii)}$$
$$Y_{13\,\text{new}} = Y_{13\,\text{old}} - y_{13} = 0 - y_{13} = -y_{13} \quad \text{(iv)}$$
$$Y_{31\,\text{new}} = Y_{31\,\text{old}} - y_{13} = 0 - y_{13} = -y_{13} \quad \text{(v)}$$
$$Y_{33\,\text{new}} = Y_{33\,\text{old}} + y_{13} = 0 + y_{13} = y_{13}$$

4. Addition of y_{20} affects only Y_{22}

$$Y_{22\,\text{new}} = Y_{22\,\text{old}} + y_{20} = y_{12} + y_{20}$$

5. Addition of y_{23} affects $Y_{22}, Y_{23}, Y_{32}, Y_{33}$

$$Y_{22\,\text{new}} = Y_{22\,\text{old}} + y_{23} = (y_{20} + y_{12}) + y_{23} = y_{20} + y_{12} + y_{23}$$
$$Y_{23\,\text{new}} = Y_{23\,\text{old}} - y_{23} = 0 - y_{23} = -y_{23} \quad \text{(vi)}$$
$$Y_{32\,\text{new}} = Y_{32\,\text{old}} - y_{23} = 0 - y_{23} = -y_{23} \quad \text{(vii)}$$
$$Y_{33\,\text{new}} = Y_{33\,\text{old}} + y_{23} = y_{13} + y_{23}$$

6. Addition of y_{24} affects $Y_{22}, Y_{24}, Y_{42}, Y_{44}$

$$Y_{22\,\text{new}} = Y_{22\,\text{old}} + y_{24} = (y_{20} + y_{12} + y_{23}) + y_{24} \quad \text{(viii)}$$
$$= y_{20} + y_{12} + y_{23} + y_{24}$$
$$Y_{24\,\text{new}} = Y_{24\,\text{old}} - y_{24} = 0 - y_{24} = -y_{24} \quad \text{(ix)}$$
$$Y_{42\,\text{new}} = Y_{42\,\text{old}} - y_{24} = 0 - y_{24} = -y_{24} \quad \text{(x)}$$
$$Y_{44\,\text{new}} = Y_{44\,\text{old}} + y_{24} = 0 + y_{24} = y_{24}$$

7. Addition of y_{30} affects only Y_{33}

$$Y_{33\,\text{new}} = Y_{33\,\text{old}} + y_{30} = (y_{13} + y_{23}) + y_{30} + y_{13} + y_{23}$$

8. Addition of y_{34} affects $Y_{33}, Y_{34}, Y_{43}, Y_{44}$

$$Y_{33\,\text{new}} = Y_{33\,\text{old}} + y_{34} = (y_{30} + y_{13} + y_{23}) + y_{34} \quad \text{(xi)}$$
$$= y_{30} + y_{13} + y_{23} + y_{34}$$
$$Y_{34\,\text{new}} = Y_{34\,\text{old}} - y_{34} = 0 - y_{34} = -y_{34} \quad \text{(xii)}$$
$$Y_{43\,\text{new}} = Y_{43\,\text{old}} - y_{34} = 0 - y_{34} = -y_{34} \quad \text{(xiii)}$$
$$Y_{44\,\text{new}} = Y_{44\,\text{old}} + y_{34} = y_{24} + y_{34}$$

9. Addition of y_{40} affects only Y_{44}

$$Y_{44\,\text{new}} = Y_{44\,\text{old}} + y_{40} = (y_{24} + y_{34}) + y_{40} = y_{40} + y_{24} + y_{34} \quad \text{(xiv)}$$

The final values of the elements of the bus admittance matrix are given by appropriate equation from Eqs. (i) through (xiv).

Further
$$Y_{14} = Y_{41} = 0$$

Assuming Mutual Coupling between Transmission Lines The equivalent circuit of mutually coupled transmission lines is shown in Fig. 6.6. Shunt elements are omitted for simplicity; this effect can be included in a straight forward manner as seen in Example 6.1. The mutual impedance between the transmission lines is z_m, and the series impedances are z_{s1} and z_{s2}. From Fig. 6.6, we have

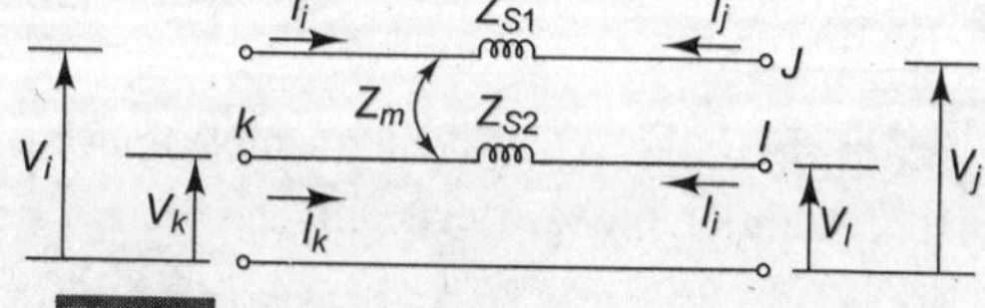

Fig. 6.6 *Mutually coupled transmission lines*

$$V_i = z_{s1} I_i + z_m I_k + V_j$$
$$V_k = z_{s2} I_k + z_m I_i + V_l$$

or

$$\begin{bmatrix} V_i \\ V_k \end{bmatrix} - \begin{bmatrix} V_j \\ V_l \end{bmatrix} = \begin{bmatrix} z_{s1} & z_m \\ z_m & z_{s2} \end{bmatrix} \begin{bmatrix} I_i \\ I_k \end{bmatrix}$$

or

$$\begin{bmatrix} I_i \\ I_k \end{bmatrix} = \begin{bmatrix} y_{s1} & y_m \\ y_m & y_{s2} \end{bmatrix} \begin{bmatrix} V_i - V_j \\ V_k - V_l \end{bmatrix} \tag{6.10a}$$

Similarly, we have

$$\begin{bmatrix} I_j \\ I_l \end{bmatrix} = \begin{bmatrix} y_{s1} & y_m \\ y_m & y_{s2} \end{bmatrix} \begin{bmatrix} V_j - V_i \\ V_l - V_k \end{bmatrix} \tag{6.10b}$$

where

$$\begin{bmatrix} y_{s1} & y_m \\ y_m & y_{s2} \end{bmatrix} = \begin{bmatrix} z_{s1} & z_m \\ z_m & z_{s2} \end{bmatrix}^{-1}$$

From Eqs. 6.10(a) and (b), the elements of $\boldsymbol{Y}_{\text{BUS}}$ become

$$\left\{\begin{array}{l} Y_{ii\,\text{new}} = Y_{ii\,\text{old}} + y_{s1} \\ Y_{jj\,\text{new}} = Y_{jj\,\text{old}} + y_{s1} \\ Y_{kk\,\text{new}} = Y_{kk\,\text{old}} + y_{s2} \\ Y_{ll\,\text{new}} = Y_{ll\,\text{old}} + y_{s2} \end{array}\right\} \tag{6.11a}$$

$$\left\{\begin{array}{l} Y_{ij\,\text{new}} = Y_{ji\,\text{new}} = Y_{ij\,\text{old}} - y_{s1} \\ Y_{kl\,\text{new}} = Y_{lk\,\text{new}} = Y_{kl\,\text{old}} - y_{s2} \end{array}\right\} \tag{6.11b}$$

$$\left\{\begin{array}{l} Y_{ik\,\text{new}} = Y_{ki\,\text{new}} = Y_{ik\,\text{old}} + y_m \\ Y_{jl\,\text{new}} = Y_{lj\,\text{new}} = Y_{jl\,\text{old}} + y_m \end{array}\right\} \tag{6.11c}$$

$$\left\{\begin{array}{l} Y_{il\,\text{new}} = Y_{li\,\text{new}} = Y_{il\,\text{old}} - y_m \\ Y_{jk\,\text{new}} = Y_{kj\,\text{new}} = Y_{jk\,\text{old}} - y_m \end{array}\right\} \tag{6.11d}$$

Example 6.3 Figure 6.7 shows the one-line diagram of a simple four-bus system. Table 6.1 gives the line impedances identified by the buses on which these terminate. The shunt admittance at all the buses is assumed to be negligible.

(a) Find $\boldsymbol{Y}_{\text{BUS}}$, assuming that the line shown dotted is not connected.

(b) What modifications need to be carried out in $\boldsymbol{Y}_{\text{BUS}}$ if the line shown dotted is connected?

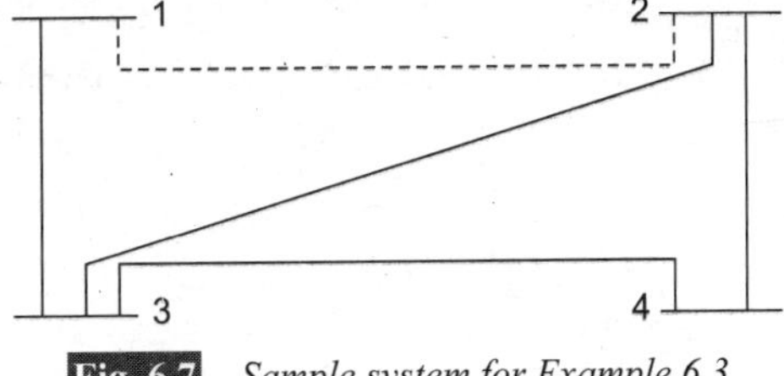

Fig. 6.7 *Sample system for Example 6.3*

Solution (a) From Table 6.1, Table 6.2 is obtained from which $\boldsymbol{Y}_{\text{BUS}}$ for the system can be written as

Table 6.1

Line, bus to bus	*R, pu*	*X, pu*
1–2	0.05	0.15
1–3	0.10	0.30
2–3	0.15	0.45
2–4	0.10	0.30
3–4	0.05	0.15

Table 6.2

Line	*G, pu*	*B, pu*
1–2	2.000	– 6.0
1–3	1.000	– 3.0
2–3	0.666	– 2.0
2–4	1.000	– 3.0
3–4	2.000	– 6.0

$$\boldsymbol{Y}_{\text{BUS}} = \begin{bmatrix} Y_{11} & Y_{12} & Y_{13} & Y_{14} \\ Y_{21} & Y_{22} & Y_{23} & Y_{24} \\ Y_{31} & Y_{32} & Y_{33} & Y_{34} \\ Y_{41} & Y_{42} & Y_{43} & Y_{44} \end{bmatrix} \tag{i}$$

$$\boldsymbol{Y}_{\text{BUS}} = \begin{bmatrix} y_{13} & 0 & -y_{13} & 0 \\ 0 & (y_{23}+y_{24}) & -y_{23} & -y_{24} \\ -y_{13} & -y_{23} & (y_{31}+y_{32}+y_{34}) & -y_{34} \\ 0 & -y_{24} & -y_{34} & (y_{43}+y_{42}) \end{bmatrix} \tag{ii}$$

$$\boldsymbol{Y}_{\text{BUS}} = \begin{bmatrix} 1-j3 & 0 & -1+j3 & 0 \\ 0 & 1.666-j5 & -0.666+j2 & -1+j3 \\ -1+j3 & -0.666+j2 & 3.666-j11 & -2+j6 \\ 0 & -1+j3 & -2+j6 & 3-j9 \end{bmatrix} \tag{iii}$$

(b) The following elements of $\boldsymbol{Y}_{\text{BUS}}$ of part (a) are modified when a line is added between buses 1 and 2.

$$\begin{aligned} Y_{11\text{ new}} &= Y_{11\text{ old}} + (2-j6) = 3-j9 \\ Y_{12\text{ new}} &= Y_{12\text{ old}} - (2-j6) = -2+j6 = Y_{21\text{ new}} \\ Y_{22\text{ new}} &= Y_{22\text{ old}} + (2-j6) = 3.666-j11 \end{aligned} \tag{iv}$$

Modified $\boldsymbol{Y}_{\text{BUS}}$ is written as

$$\boldsymbol{Y}_{\text{BUS}} = \begin{bmatrix} 3-j9 & -2+j6 & -1+j3 & 0 \\ -2+j6 & 3.666-j11 & -0.666+j2 & -1+j3 \\ -1+j3 & -0.666+j2 & 3.666-j11 & -2+j6 \\ 0 & -1+j3 & -2+j6 & 3-j9 \end{bmatrix} \tag{v}$$

6.3 ▶ FORMATION OF Y_{BUS} BY SINGULAR TRANSFORMATION

The matrix pair Y_{BUS} and Z_{BUS} form the network models for load flow studies. The Y_{BUS} can be alternatively assembled by the use of singular transformation given by a graph theoretical approach. This approach is of great theoretical and practical significance, and is therefore discussed here. To start with, the graph theory is briefly reviewed.

6.3.1 Graph

To describe the geometrical features of a network, it is replaced by single line segments called *elements*, whose terminals are called *nodes*. The resulting figure is called the *graph* of the given network. A *linear graph* depicts the geometrical interconnection of the elements of a network. A *connected graph* is one in which there is at least one path between every pair of nodes. If each element of a connected graph is assigned a direction*, it is called an *oriented graph*.

Power networks are so structured that out of the m total number of nodes, one node (normally described by 0) is always at ground potential and the remaining $n = m - 1$ nodes are the buses at which the source power is injected. Figure 6.8 shows the oriented linear graph of the power network of Fig. 6.5(c). Here the overall line admittance between any two buses (nodes in the corresponding graph) are represented by a single line element. Also, each source and the shunt admittance connected across it are represented by a single line element. In fact, this combination represents the most general network element, and is described under the subheading Primitive Network.

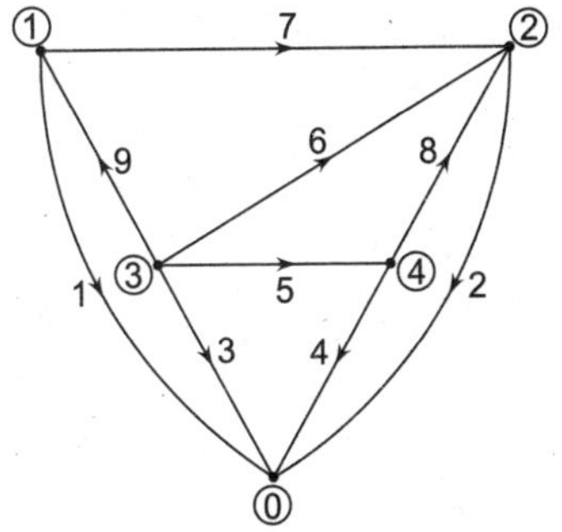

Fig. 6.8 *Oriented linear graph of the circuit in Fig. 6.5(c)*

A connected subgraph containing all the nodes of a graph but having no closed paths is called a *tree*. The elements of a tree are called *branches* or *tree branches*. The number of branches b that form a tree is given by

$$b = m - 1 = n \text{ (number of buses)} \tag{6.12}$$

Those elements of the graph that are not included in the tree are called *links* or *link branches*, and they form a subgraph, not necessarily connected, called *co-tree*. The number of links l of a connected graph with e elements is

$$l = e - b = e - m + 1 \tag{6.13}$$

There may be more than one possible trees (and therefore, co-trees) of a graph.

A tree and the corresponding co-tree of the graph of Fig. 6.8 are shown in Fig. 6.9. The reader should try and find some other tree and co-tree pairs.

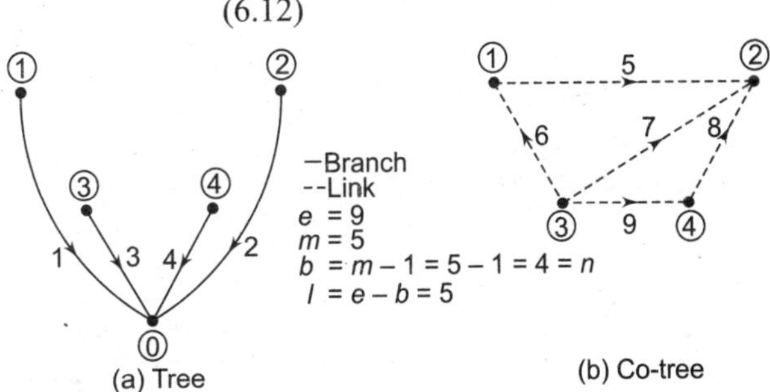

Fig. 6.9 *Tree and co-tree of the oriented connected graph of Fig. 6.6*

If a link is added to the tree, the corresponding graph contains one closed path called a basic loop. Thus, a graph has as many basic loops as the number of links. A loop is distinguished from a basic loop, as it can

* For convenience, direction is so assigned as to coincide with the assumed positive direction of the element current.

be any loop in the original graph. Therefore, the number of loops is greater than, or at the most equal to, the number of basic loops in a graph.

6.3.2 Primitive Network

A network element may in general contain active and passive components. Figure 6.10 shows a general network element, connected between nodes r and s, with its alternative impedance and admittance form. The impedance form is a voltage source e_{rs} in series with an impedance z_{rs}, while the admittance form is a current source j_{rs} in parallel with an admittance y_{rs}. The element current is i_{rs}, and the element voltage is $v_{rs} = E_r - E_s$, where E_r and E_s are the voltages of the element nodes r and s, respectively.

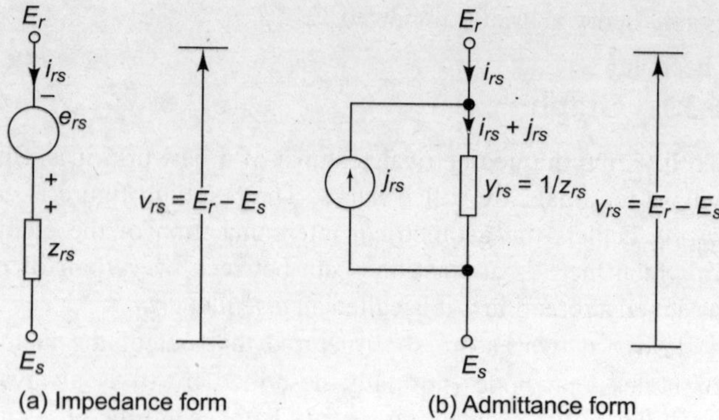

Fig. 6.10 *Representation of a network element*

It may be remembered here that for steady-state AC performance, all element variables (v_{rs}, E_r, E_s, i_{rs}, j_{rs}) are phasors, and the element parameters (z_{rs}, y_{rs}) are complex numbers. The voltage relation for Fig. 6.10 can be written as

$$v_{rs} + e_{rs} = z_{rs}\, i_{rs} \tag{6.14}$$

Similarly, the current relation for Fig. 6.10 can be written as

$$i_{rs} + j_{rs} = y_{rs}\, v_{rs} \tag{6.15}$$

The forms of Fig. 6.10(a) and (b) are equivalent, wherein the parallel source current in admittance form is related to the series voltage in impedance form by

$$j_{rs} = y_{rs}\, e_{rs}$$

Also,

$$y_{rs} = 1/z_{rs}$$

A set of unconnected elements is defined as a primitive network. The performance equations of a primitive network are given by

In impedance form,

$$\boldsymbol{V} + \boldsymbol{E} = \boldsymbol{ZI} \tag{6.16}$$

In admittance form,

$$\boldsymbol{I} + \boldsymbol{J} = \boldsymbol{YV} \tag{6.17}$$

Here $\boldsymbol{V}$ and $\boldsymbol{I}$ are the element voltage and current vectors, respectively, and $\boldsymbol{J}$ and $\boldsymbol{E}$ are the source vectors. $\boldsymbol{Z}$ and $\boldsymbol{Y}$ are referred to as the primitive impedance and admittance matrices, respectively. These are related as $\boldsymbol{Z} = \boldsymbol{Y}^{-1}$. If there is no mutual coupling between elements, $\boldsymbol{Z}$ and $\boldsymbol{Y}$ are diagonal matrices, where the diagonal entries are the impedances/admittances of the network elements and are reciprocal.

6.3.3 Network Variables in Bus Frame of Reference

The linear network graph helps in the systematic assembly of a network model. The main problem in deriving mathematical models for large and complex power network is to select a minimum or zero redundancy (linearly independent) set of current or voltage variables, which is sufficient to give the information about all element voltages and currents. One set of such variables is the b tree voltages. By topological reasoning, these variables constitute a nonredundant set. The knowledge of b tree voltages allows us to compute all element voltages, and therefore, all bus currents assuming all element admittances being known.

Consider a tree graph shown in Fig. 6.9(a) where the ground node is chosen as the reference node. This is the most appropriate tree choice for the power network. With this choice, the b tree branch voltages become identical with the bus voltages as the tree branches are incidental to the ground node.

6.3.4 Bus Incidence Matrix

For the specific system of Fig. 6.8, we obtain the following relations between the nine element voltages and the four bus (i.e., tree branch) voltages V_1, V_2, V_3 and V_4.

$$\begin{aligned}
V_{b1} &= V_1 \\
V_{b2} &= V_2 \\
V_{b3} &= V_3 \\
V_{b4} &= V_4 \\
V_{l5} &= V_1 - V_2 \\
V_{l6} &= V_1 - V_3 \\
V_{l7} &= V_2 - V_3 \\
V_{l8} &= V_2 - V_4 \\
V_{l9} &= V_3 - V_4
\end{aligned} \tag{6.18}$$

or, in matrix form

$$V = A V_{\text{BUS}} \tag{6.19}$$

where V is the vector of element voltages of order $e \times 1$ (e = number of elements), V_{BUS} is the vector of bus voltages of order $b \times 1$ (b = number of branches = number of buses = n) and A is the bus incidence matrix of order $e \times b$ given by

e↓ \ Bus→	1	2	3	4
1	1	0	0	0
2	0	1	0	0
3	0	0	1	0
4	0	0	0	1
5	1	−1	0	0
6	1	0	−1	0
7	0	1	−1	0
8	0	1	0	−1
9	0	0	1	−1

(Elements \ Buses; rows 1–4: Branches; rows 5–9: links)

$$= \begin{bmatrix} A_b \\ \hline A_l \end{bmatrix} = \begin{bmatrix} I \\ \hline A_l \end{bmatrix} \tag{6.20}$$

This matrix is rectangular, and therefore, singular. Its elements a_{ik} are found as per the following rules:

a_{ik} = 1 if ith element is incident to and oriented away from the kth node (bus)

= – 1 if ith element is incident to but oriented towards the kth node

= 0 if the ith element is not incident to the kth node

Substituting Eq. (6.19) into (6.17), we get

$$I + J = YAV_{BUS} \tag{6.21}$$

Premultiplying by A^T,

$$A^T I + A^T J = A^T YAV_{BUS} \tag{6.22}$$

each component of the n-dimensional vector $A^T I$ is the algebraic sum of the element currents leaving nodes 1, 2, ..., n(n = number of buses). Therefore, the application of KCL must result in

$$A^T I = 0 \tag{6.23}$$

Similarly, each component of the vector $A^T J$ can be recognised as the algebraic sum of all source currents injected into nodes 1, 2, ..., n. These components are therefore the bus currents. Hence, we can write

$$A^T J = I_{BUS} \tag{6.24}$$

Equation (6.22) then is simplified to

$$I_{BUS} = (A^T YA)\, V_{BUS} \tag{6.25}$$

Thus, following an alternative systematic approach, we obtain the same nodal current equation as Eq. (6.6). The bus admittance matrix can then be obtained from the singular transformation of the primitive Y matrix, i.e.,

$$Y_{BUS} = A^T YA \tag{6.26}$$

A computer programme can be developed to write the bus incidence matrix A from the interconnected data of the directed elements of the power system. Standard matrix transpose and multiplication subroutines can then be used to compute Y_{BUS} from Eq. (6.26).

Example 6.4 Find the Y_{BUS} using singular transformation for the system of Fig. 6.5(c) whose graph is shown in Fig. 6.8.

Solution As there is no mutual coupling between any two lines, the primitive Y matrix is diagonal and given by the following.

Elements	1	2	3	4	5	6	7	8	9
1	y_{10}								0
2		y_{20}							
3			y_{30}						
4				y_{40}					
Y = 5					y_{12}				
6						y_{13}			
7							y_{23}		
8								y_{24}	
9	0								y_{34}

Using A from Eq. (6.20), we get

$$YA = \begin{bmatrix} y_{10} & 0 & 0 & 0 \\ 0 & y_{20} & 0 & 0 \\ 0 & 0 & y_{30} & 0 \\ 0 & 0 & 0 & y_{40} \\ y_{12} & -y_{12} & 0 & 0 \\ y_{13} & 0 & -y_{13} & 0 \\ 0 & -y_{23} & y_{23} & 0 \\ 0 & y_{24} & 0 & -y_{24} \\ 0 & 0 & y_{34} & -y_{34} \end{bmatrix}$$

Finally,

$$Y_{BUS} = A^T YA = \begin{bmatrix} (y_{10} + y_{12} + y_{13}) & -y_{12} & -y_{13} & 0 \\ -y_{12} & (y_{20} + y_{12} + y_{23} + y_{24}) & -y_{23} & -y_{24} \\ -y_{13} & -y_{23} & (y_{30} + y_{13} + y_{23} + y_{34}) & -y_{34} \\ 0 & -y_{24} & -y_{34} & (y_{40} + y_{24} + y_{34}) \end{bmatrix}$$

The elements of this matrix, of course, agree with those previously calculated in Example 6.1.

If there is mutual coupling between elements i and j of the network, the primitive $\boldsymbol{Y}$ matrix will not be diagonal. Thus, the element corresponding to the ith row and jth column (also, jth row and ith column) will be equal to the mutual admittance between the elements i and j. Thus, $\boldsymbol{Y}_{\text{BUS}}$ is also modified as given by Eq. (6.26).

6.4 ▶ LOAD FLOW PROBLEM

The complex power injected by the source into the ith bus of a power system is

$$S_i = P_i + jQ_i = V_i I_i^*, \; i = 1, 2, ..., n$$

Since it is convenient to work with I_i instead of I_i^*, we take the complex conjugate of the above equation,

$$P_i - jQ_i = V_i^* I_i, \; i = 1, 2, ..., n$$

Substituting $I_i = \left(\sum_{k=1}^{n} (Y_{ik}V_k)\right)$ from Eq. (6.2b) in the above equation, we have

$$P_i - jQ_i = V_i^* \left(\sum_{k=1}^{n} (Y_{ik}V_k)\right), \quad i = 1, 2, ..., n$$

Equating real and imaginary parts, we get

$$P_i \text{ (Real power)} = \text{Real}\left(V_i^*\left(\sum_{k=1}^{n} (Y_{ik}V_k)\right)\right) \tag{6.27a}$$

$$Q_i \text{ (Reactive power)} = -\text{Imaginary}\left(V_i^*\left(\sum_{k=1}^{n} (Y_{ik}V_k)\right)\right) \tag{6.27b}$$

Let

$$V_i = |V_i| e^{j\delta_i}, \; V_k = |V_k| e^{j\delta_k}$$

$$Y_{ik} = |Y_{ik}| e^{j\theta_{ik}}$$

then,

$$P_i \text{ (Real power)} = |V_i| \sum_{k=1}^{n} |V_k||Y_{ik}| \cos(\theta_{ik} + \delta_k - \delta_i) \tag{6.28a}$$

$$Q_i \text{ (Reactive power)} = -|V_i| \sum_{k=1}^{n} |V_k||Y_{ik}| \sin(\theta_{ik} + \delta_k - \delta_i) \tag{6.28b}$$

$$(i = 1, 2, ..., n)$$

Equations 6.28(a) and (b) are called power flow equations. There are n real and n reactive power flow equations giving a total of $2n$ power flow equations.

At each bus, there are four variables, viz., $|V_i|$, δ_i, P_i and Q_i, giving a total of $4n$ variables (for n buses). If at every bus two variables are specified (thus specifying a total of $2n$ variables), the remaining two variables at every bus (a total of $2n$ remaining variables) can be found by solving the $2n$ power flow Eqs. 6.28(a) and (b). When a physical system is considered, specifying variables at every bus depends on what devices are connected to that bus. In general, there are four possibilities giving rise to four types of buses as follows.

6.4.1 Slack Bus/Swing Bus/Reference Bus

This bus is distinguished from the remaining types by the fact that real and reactive powers at this bus are not specified. Instead, voltage magnitude (normally set equal to 1 pu) and voltage phase angle (normally set equal to zero) are specified. Usually, there is only one bus of this type in a given power system. The need of such a bus for a load flow study is explained in the example that follows. The slack bus is numbered 1, for convenience.

6.4.2 PQ Bus/Load Bus

At this type of bus, the net powers P_i and Q_i are known (P_{Di} and Q_{Di} are known from load forecasting and P_{Gi} and Q_{Gi} are specified). The unknowns are $|V_i|$ and δ_i. A pure load bus (no generating facility at the bus, i.e., $P_{Gi} = Q_{Gi} = 0$) is a PQ bus. PQ buses are the most common, comprising almost 80% of all the buses in a given power system.

6.4.3 PV Bus/Generator Bus

This bus has always a generator connected to it. Thus, P_{Gi} and $|V_i|$ are specified. Hence, the net power P_i is known (as P_{Di} is known from load forecasting). Hence, the knowns are P_i and $|V_i|$ and unknowns are Q_i and δ_i. PV buses comprise about 10% of all the buses in a power system.

6.4.4 Voltage Controlled Bus

Frequently the PV bus and the voltage controlled bus are grouped together. But they have physical differences and slightly different calculation strategies. The voltage controlled bus has also voltage control capabilities, and uses a tap-adjustable transformer and/or a static var compensator instead of a generator. Hence, $P_{Gi} = Q_{Gi} = 0$ at these buses. Thus, $P_i = -P_{Di}$, $Q_i = -Q_{Di}$ and $|V_i|$ are known at these buses and the unknown is δ_i.

Example 6.5 This example will also demonstrate the need of a slack bus. Consider a simple four-bus system [Fig. 6.5(a)] out of which two buses are PQ buses, one is PV bus, and the remaining one is a slack bus. The buses are numbered as shown in Table 6.3 [Refer Fig. 6.5(c)].

Table 6.3

No.	*Bus Type*	*Known*	*Unknown*
1.	Slack Bus	$\|V_1\|, \delta_1$	P_1, Q_1
2.	PQ Bus	P_2, Q_2	$\|V_2\|, \delta_2$
3.	PQ Bus	P_3, Q_3	$\|V_3\|, \delta_3$
4.	PV Bus	$P_4, \|V_4\|$	Q_4, δ_4

$$\text{Total Real Power Loss, } P_L = \Sigma P_i = P_1 + P_2 + P_3 + P_4$$
$$= P_1 + K_1$$

where $K_1 = P_2 + P_3 + P_4$ (known).

$$\text{Total Reactive Power Loss, } Q_L = \Sigma Q_i = Q_1 + Q_2 + Q_3 + Q_4$$
$$= Q_1 + Q_4 + K_2$$

where $K_2 = Q_2 + Q_3$ (known).

Since P_L and Q_L are not known prior to load flow solution, the real and reactive powers (P_i and Q_i) cannot be fixed at all the buses. In the above example, P_1, Q_1 and Q_4 cannot be fixed prior to load flow solution. After the load flow solution is complete, the total real and reactive powers, $P_L = \sum_i P_i$ and $Q_L = \sum_i Q_i$ become known and the slack bus has to supply excess real power $P_1 = P_L - K_1$, and excess reactive power $Q_1 = Q_L - Q_4 - K_2$. This is why a slack bus is needed in load flow solution.

Thus, after a load flow solution is complete, real power at the slack bus (P_1) is known, and hence the real power generation P_{G1} (as P_{D1} is known from load forecasting) is known. As V_1 is already specified for a slack bus, the slack bus must be a generator bus. It is required that the variations in real and reactive powers at the slack bus be a small percentage of its generating capacity. So, the bus connected to the largest generating station is normally selected as the slack bus.

Equations 6.28(a) and (b) which are written below for convenience are referred to as Static Load Flow Equations (SLFE).

$$P_i \text{ (Real power)} = |V_i| \sum_{k=1}^{n} (|V_k|\,|Y_{ik}| \cos(\theta_{ik} + \delta_k - \delta_i)) \tag{6.28a}$$

$$Q_i \text{ (Reactive power)} = -|V_i| \sum_{k=1}^{n} (|V_k|\,|Y_{ik}| \sin(\theta_{ik} + \delta_k - \delta_i))$$

where $\quad i = 1, 2, \ldots, n$ (6.28b)

By transposing all the variables on one side, these equations can be written in the vector form

$$\boldsymbol{f}(\boldsymbol{x}, \boldsymbol{y}) = \boldsymbol{0} \tag{6.29}$$

where $\boldsymbol{f}$ = vector function of dimension $2n \times 1$

$\boldsymbol{x}$ = vector of dependent or state variables of dimension $2n \times 1$ ($2n$ independent variables specified *a priori*)

$\boldsymbol{y}$ = vector of independent variables of dimension $2n \times 1$ ($2n$ unspecified variables)

Some of the independent variables in $\boldsymbol{x}$ can be used to manipulate some of the state variables. These adjustable independent variables are called control variables. The remaining independent variables which are fixed are called fixed parameters. Vector $\boldsymbol{x}$ can then be partitioned into a vector $\boldsymbol{u}$ of control variables and a vector $\boldsymbol{p}$ of fixed parameters,

$$\boldsymbol{x} = \begin{bmatrix} \boldsymbol{u} \\ \boldsymbol{p} \end{bmatrix} \tag{6.30}$$

Control variables may be voltage magnitude on PV bus, P_{Gi} at buses with controllable power, etc. Fixed parameters are those which are uncontrollable.

For SLFE solution to have practical significance, all the state and control variables must be within specified practical limits. These limits are dictated by specifications of power system hardware and operating constraints, and are described below:

1. Voltage magnitude $|V_i|$ must satisfy the inequality

   $$|V_i|_{\min} \le |V_i| \le |V_i|_{\max} \tag{6.31a}$$

   This limit arises due to the fact that the power system equipment is designed to operate at fixed voltages with allowable variations of ±(5–10)% of rated values.
2. Certain of the δ_is (state variables) must satisfy

   $$|\delta_i - \delta_k| \le |\delta_i - \delta_k|_{\max} \tag{6.31b}$$

This constraint limits the maximum permissible power angle of transmission line connecting buses i and k and is imposed by considerations of stability.

3. Owing to physical limitations of P and/or Q generation sources, P_{Gi} and Q_{Gi} are constrained as follows:

$$P_{Gi,\,\min} \le P_{Gi} \le P_{Gi,\,\max}$$
$$Q_{Gi,\,\min} \le Q_{Gi} \le Q_{Gi,\,\max} \tag{6.31c}$$

Also, we have

$$\sum_i P_{Gi} = \sum_i (P_{Di}) + P_L \tag{6.32a}$$

$$\sum_i Q_{Gi} = \sum_i (Q_{Di}) + Q_L \tag{6.32b}$$

where P_L and Q_L are system real and reactive power losses.

The load flow problem can now be fully defined as follows:

Assume a certain nominal bus load configuration. Specify $P_{Gi} + jQ_{Gi}$ at all PQ buses (this specifies $P_i + jQ_i$ at these buses, specify P_{Gi} (this specifies P_i) and $|V_i|$ at all PV buses; and specify $|V_1|$ and δ_1 (= 0) at the slack bus. Thus, all the $2n$ variables of vector $\boldsymbol{x}$ are specified. Thus, $2n$ SLFE, which are nonlinear algebraic equations,* can be solved (iteratively) to determine the values of the $2n$ variables of the vector $\boldsymbol{y}$, comprising voltages and angles at the PQ buses; reactive powers and angles at the PV buses; and active and reactive powers at the slack bus.

The next logical step is to compute the line flows.

From the above definition, we can state two versions of the load flow problem. In both the cases, bus 1 is assumed as the slack bus.

Case I We assume all the remaining buses are PQ buses. We have
Given $V_1, S_2, S_3, \ldots, S_n$
Find $S_1, V_2, V_3, \ldots, V_n$

Case II We assume both PV and PQ buses. We number the buses so that buses 2, 3, ... m are PQ buses and $m + 1, \ldots, n$ are PV buses.
Thus,
Given $V_1, S_2, \ldots, S_m, (P_{m+1}, |V_{m+1}|), \ldots, (P_n, |V_n|)$
Find $S_1, V_2, \ldots, V_m, (Q_{m+1}, \delta_{m+1}), \ldots, (Q_n, \delta_n)$

Since the load flow equations are essentially nonlinear, they have to be solved through iterative numerical techniques. At the cost of solution accuracy, it is possible to linearise load flow equations by making suitable assumptions and approximations so that fast and explicit solutions become possible. Such techniques have value, particularly for planning studies where load flow solutions have to be carried out repeatedly but a high degree of accuracy is not needed. An approximate load flow solution is dealt in Example 6.6.

Once a load flow problem is formulated, it can be seen that there exists a range of every independent variable in the vector $\boldsymbol{x}$ for which there is no solution, or there are multiple solutions. For visualising this problem, we consider a simple two-bus system in Example 6.6.

Example 6.6 In Fig. 6.11, bus 1 is the reference bus with $V_1 = 1\angle 0°$ and bus 2 is PQ bus. We are to find S_1 and V_2.

---

* It is because cosine and sine functions are involved in real and reactive power Eqs. 6.28(a) and (b).

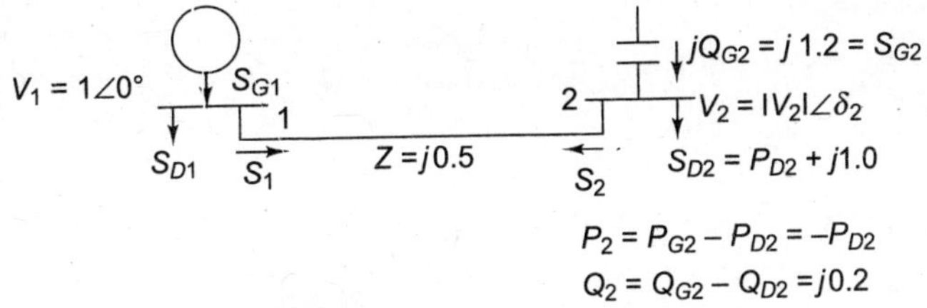

$$P_2 = P_{G2} - P_{D2} = -P_{D2}$$
$$Q_2 = Q_{G2} - Q_{D2} = j0.2$$

Fig. 6.11 *A simple two-bus system*

Solution The complex power injected at the bus 2, S_2 is given by

$$S_2 = S_{G2} - S_{D2} = -P_{D2} + j0.2 \quad \text{(i)}$$

Also from Section 5.9 of Ch. 5, we have

$$S_2 = S_{21}$$

$$= \frac{|V_2|^2}{|Z|}\angle\theta - \frac{|V_2||V_1|}{Z}\angle(\theta + \delta_2 - \delta_1) \quad \text{(ii)}$$

where $Z = |Z|\angle\theta = 0.5\angle 90°$ (iii)

$$\delta_1 = 0° \text{ as } V_1 = |V_1|\angle\delta_1 = 1\angle 0°$$

From (i), (ii) and (iii), we get

$$-P_{D2} + j0.2 = j2|V_2|^2 - 2|V_2|\cos(\theta + \delta_2) - j2|V_2|\sin(\theta + \delta_2)$$

Equating the real and the imaginary parts on both sides, we get

$$P_{D2} = 2|V_2|\cos(\theta + \delta_2)$$
$$0.2 = 2|V_2|^2 - 2|V_2|\sin(\theta + \delta_2)$$

or we get

$$\cos(\theta + \delta_2) = \frac{P_{D2}}{2|V_2|} \quad \text{(iv)}$$

$$\sin(\theta + \delta_2) = \frac{2|V_2|^2 - 0.2}{2|V_2|} = \frac{|V_2|^2 - 0.1}{|V_2|} \quad \text{(v)}$$

Squaring and adding, we get

$$1 = \frac{P_{D2}^2}{4|V_2|^2} + \frac{(|V_2|^2 - 0.1)^2}{|V_2|^2}$$

or

$$4|V_2|^4 - 4.8|V_2|^2 + (P_{D2}^2 + 0.04) = 0$$

or

$$|V_2|^2 = \frac{4.8 \pm \sqrt{4.8^2 - 16(P_{D2}^2 + 0.04)}}{8}$$

Thus, if $16(P_{D2}^2 + 0.04) > (4.8)^2$ or $P_{D2} > 1.183$, there are no real solutions. If $P_{D2} = 1.183$, $|V_2| = 0.775$, the solution is unique. If $P_{D2} < 1.183$, there are two real solutions, and hence the solution is non-unique. Let $P_{D2} = 0.5$; then $|V_2| = 0.253$ and 1.066 pu.

Thus, there may be no solution, or at least no unique solution, depending on the given data. In most cases having non-unique solutions, the practical solution is the one with voltage closest to 1 pu. Thus, with $P_{D2} = 0.5$, the desired solution is $|V_2| = 1.066$, and the angle δ_2 is given by Eq. (iv) as

$$\cos(\theta + \delta_2) = \cos(90 + \delta_2) = -\sin\delta_2 = \frac{P_{D2}}{2|V_2|}$$

or

$$\sin\delta_2 = -\frac{P_{D2}}{2|V_2|} = \frac{0.5}{2 \times 1.066} = -0.2345$$

or

$$\delta_2 = -13.56^\circ$$

Also,

$$S_1 = -S_2 = P_{D2} - j0.2 = 0.5 - j0.2$$

The solution of a load flow problem becomes simple when only two buses are present. But, in a normal power system, there are large number of buses and the solution becomes quite complex, tedious and time consuming. Hence, there is no choice but to use iterative methods. The most commonly used iterative methods are the Gauss–Siedel, the Newton–Raphson and fast-decoupled load flow methods.

6.4.5 An Approximate Load Flow Solution

Let us make the following assumptions and approximations in the load flow Eqs. 6.28(a) and (b):

1. Line resistances, being small, are neglected (shunt conductance of overhead lines is always negligible), i.e., P_L, the active power loss of the system is zero. Thus, in Eqs. 6.28(a) and (b), $\theta_{ik} = 90^\circ$ and $\theta_{ii} = -90^\circ$.
2. $(\delta_i - \delta_k)$ is small $[< (\pi/6)]$, so that $\sin(\delta_i - \delta_k) \simeq (\delta_i - \delta_k)$. This is justified from considerations of stability (see Ch. 12).
3. All buses other than the slack bus (numbered as 1) are PV buses, i.e., voltage magnitudes at all the buses, including the slack bus, are specified.

Equations 6.28(a) and (b) then reduce to

$$P_i = |V_i| \sum_{k=1}^{n} |V_k||Y_{ik}|(\delta_i - \delta_k)\; i = 2, 3, \ldots, n \tag{6.33}$$

$$Q_i = -|V_i| \sum_{\substack{k=1 \\ k \neq i}}^{n} (|V_k||Y_{ik}|\cos(\delta_i - \delta_k)) + |V_i|^2 |Y_{ii}|, i = 1, 2, \ldots, n \tag{6.34}$$

Since $|V_i|$s are specified, Eq. (6.33) represents a set of linear algebraic equations in δ_is, which are $(n - 1)$ in number as δ_1 is specified at the slack bus ($\delta_1 = 0$). The nth equation corresponding to the slack bus ($n = 1$) is redundant as the real power injected at this bus is now fully specified as $P_1 = \Sigma P_{Di} - \Sigma P_{Gi}$; ($P_L = 0$). Equation (6.33) can be solved explicitly (non-iteratively) for $\delta_2, \delta_3, \ldots, \delta_n$, which, when substituted in Eq. (6.34), yields Q_is, the reactive power bus injections. It may be noted that the assumptions made have decoupled Eqs. (6.33) and (6.34), so that these need not be solved simultaneously but can be solved sequentially. Solution of Eq. (6.34) follows immediately upon simultaneous solution of Eq. (6.33). Since the solution is non-iterative and the dimension is reduced to $(n - 1)$ from $2n$, it is computationally highly economical.

Example 6.7 Consider the four-bus sample system of Fig. 6.12, wherein line reactances are indicated in pu. Line resistances are considered negligible. The magnitudes of all four-bus voltages are specified to be 1.0 pu. The bus powers are specified in Table 6.4.

Solution Figure 6.12 indicates bus injections for the data specified in Table 6.4. As bus voltages are specified, all the buses must have controllable Q sources. It is also obvious from the data that buses 3 and 4 only have Q sources. Further, since the system is assumed lossless, the real power generation at bus 1 is known *a priori* to be $P_{G1} = P_{D1} + P_{D2} + P_{D3} + P_{D4} - P_{G2} = 2.0$ pu. Therefore, we have 7 unknowns instead of $2 \times 4 = 8$.

In the present problem, the unknown state and control variables are δ_2, δ_3, δ_4, Q_{G1}, Q_{G2}, Q_{G3} and Q_{G4}.

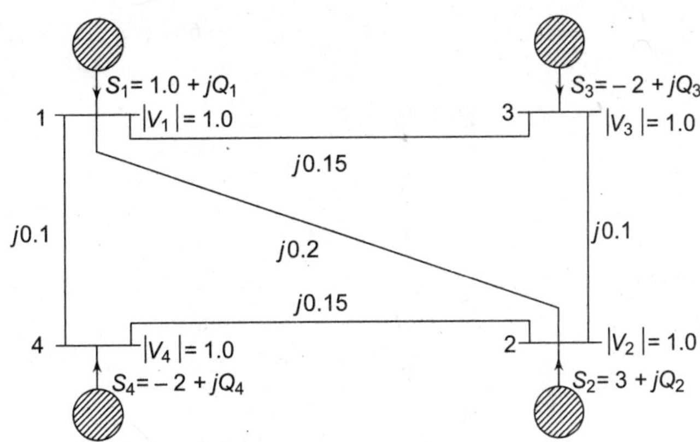

Fig. 6.12 *Four-bus lossless sample system*

Table 6.4

Bus	*Real Demand*	*Reactive Demand*	*Real Generation*	*Reactive Generation*
1.	$P_{D1} = 1.0$	$Q_{D1} = 0.5$	$P_{G1} = ?$	Q_{G1} (unspecified)
2.	$P_{D2} = 1.0$	$Q_{D2} = 0.4$	$P_{G2} = 4.0$	Q_{G2} (unspecified)
3.	$P_{D3} = 2.0$	$Q_{D3} = 1.0$	$P_{G3} = 0.0$	Q_{G3} (unspecified)
4.	$P_{D4} = 2.0$	$Q_{D4} = 1.0$	$P_{G4} = 0.0$	Q_{G4} (unspecified)

Though the real losses are zero, the presence of the reactive losses requires that the total reactive generation must be more than the total reactive demand (2.9 pu)

From the data given, $\boldsymbol{Y}_{\text{BUS}}$ can be written as follows:

$$\boldsymbol{Y}_{\text{BUS}} = \begin{array}{c} \\ 1 \\ 2 \\ 3 \\ 4 \end{array} \begin{array}{c} \begin{array}{cccc} 1 & 2 & 3 & 4 \end{array} \\ \begin{bmatrix} -j21.667 & j5.000 & j6.667 & j10.000 \\ j5.000 & -j21.667 & j10.000 & j6.667 \\ j6.667 & j10.000 & -j16.667 & j0.000 \\ j10.000 & j6.667 & j0.000 & -j16.667 \end{bmatrix} \end{array} \quad \text{(i)}$$

Using the above $\boldsymbol{Y}_{\text{BUS}}$ and bus powers as shown in Fig. 6.12, approximate load flow Eq. (6.33) is expressed as (all voltage magnitudes are equal to 1.0 pu)

$$P_2 = 3 = 5(\delta_2 - \delta_1) + 10(\delta_2 - \delta_3) + 6.667(\delta_2 - \delta_4) \quad \text{(ii)}$$

$$P_3 = -2 = 6.667\,(\delta_3 - \delta_1) + 10(\delta_3 - \delta_2) \quad \text{(iii)}$$

$$P_4 = -2 = 10(\delta_4 - \delta_1) + 6.667(\delta_4 - \delta_2) \quad \text{(iv)}$$

Taking bus 1 as a reference bus, i.e., $\delta_1 = 0$, and solving (ii), (iii) and (iv), we get

$$\begin{aligned} \delta_2 &= -0.077 \text{ rad} = 4.41^\circ \\ \delta_3 &= -0.074 \text{ rad} = -4.23^\circ \\ \delta_4 &= -0.089 \text{ rad} = -5.11^\circ \end{aligned} \quad \text{(v)}$$

Substituting δs in Eq. (6.34), we have

$$Q_1 = -5 \cos 4.41^\circ - 6.667 \cos 4.23^\circ - 10 \cos 5.11^\circ + 21.667$$

$$Q_2 = -5 \cos 4.41^\circ - 10 \cos 8.64^\circ - 6.667 \cos 9.52^\circ + 21.667$$

$$Q_3 = -6.667 \cos 4.23^\circ - 10 \cos 8.64^\circ + 16.667$$

$$Q_4 = -10 \cos 5.11° - 6.667 \cos 9.52° + 16.667$$

or

$$\begin{aligned} Q_1 &= 0.07 \text{ pu} \\ Q_2 &= 0.22 \text{ pu} \\ Q_3 &= 0.132 \text{ pu} \\ Q_4 &= 0.132 \text{ pu} \end{aligned} \qquad \text{(vi)}$$

Reactive power generations at the four buses are

$$\begin{aligned} Q_{G1} &= Q_1 + 0.5 = 0.57 \text{ pu} \\ Q_{G2} &= Q_2 + 0.4 = 0.62 \text{ pu} \\ Q_{G3} &= Q_3 + 1.0 = 1.132 \text{ pu} \\ Q_{G4} &= Q_4 + 1.0 = 1.132 \text{ pu} \end{aligned} \qquad \text{(vii)}$$

Reactive line losses are

$$\begin{aligned} Q_L &= \sum_{i=1}^{4} Q_{Gi} - \sum_{i=1}^{4} Q_{Di} \\ &= 3.454 - 2.9 = 0.554 \text{ pu} \end{aligned} \qquad \text{(viii)}$$

Now, let us find the line flows. Equation (5.68) can be written in the form ($|Z| = X$, $\theta = 90°$)

$$P_{ik} = -P_{ki} = \frac{|V_i||V_k|}{X_{ik}} \sin (\delta_1 - \delta_k)$$

where P_{ik} is the real power flow from bus i to bus k.

$$\begin{aligned} P_{13} &= -P_{31} = \frac{1}{0.15} \sin (\delta_1 - \delta_3) = \sin 4.23°/0.15 = 0.492 \text{ pu} \\ P_{12} &= -P_{21} = \frac{1}{0.2} \sin (\delta_1 - \delta_2) = -\sin 4.41°/0.02 = -0.385 \text{ pu} \\ P_{14} &= -P_{41} = \frac{1}{0.1} \sin (\delta_1 - \delta_4) = \sin 5.11°/0.1 = 0.891 \text{ pu} \end{aligned} \qquad \text{(ix)}$$

Real power flows on other lines can be similarly calculated. For reactive power flow, Eq. (5.69) can be written in the general form ($Z = X$, $\theta = 90°$)

$$Q_{ik} = \frac{|V_i|^2}{X_{ik}} - \frac{|V_i||V_k|}{X_{ik}} \cos (\delta_i - \delta_k)$$

where Q_{ik} is the reactive power flow from bus i to bus k.

$$\begin{aligned} Q_{12} &= Q_{21} = \frac{1}{0.2} - \frac{1}{0.2} \cos (\delta_1 - \delta_2) = 0.015 \text{ pu} \\ Q_{13} &= Q_{31} = \frac{1}{0.15} - \frac{1}{0.15} \cos (\delta_1 - \delta_3) = 0.018 \text{ pu} \\ Q_{14} &= Q_{41} = \frac{1}{0.15} - \frac{1}{0.15} \cos (\delta_1 - \delta_4) = 0.04 \text{ pu} \end{aligned} \qquad \text{(x)}$$

Reactive power flows on other lines can similarly be calculated. Generations and load demands at all the buses and all the line flows are indicated in Fig. 6.13.

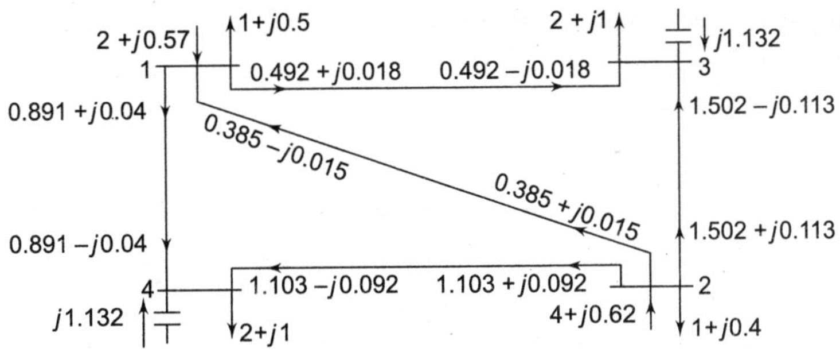

Fig. 6.13 *Load flow solution for the four bus system*

6.5 ▶ GAUSS–SIEDEL METHOD

The Gauss–Siedel (GS) method is an iterative algorithm for solving a set of nonlinear algebraic equations. We consider a system of n equations in n unknowns $x_1, \ldots, x_n$. We rewrite these n equations in the form:

$$x_i = f_i(x_1, \ldots, x_n),\ i = 1, \ldots, n$$

To find the solution, we assume initial values for $x_1, \ldots, x_n$, based on guidance from practical experience in a physical situation. Let the initial values be $x^0_1, \ldots, x^0_n$. Then, we get the first approximate solution by substituting these initial values in the above n equations as follows:

$$x_1^1 = f_1\left(x_1^0, x_2^0 \ldots, x_n^0\right)$$

$$\vdots$$

$$x_i^1 = f_i\left(x_1^1, x_2^1, \ldots, x_{i-1}^1, x_i^0, \ldots, x_n^0\right)$$

$$\vdots$$

$$x_n^1 = f_n\left(x_1^1, x_2^1, \ldots, x_{n-1}^1, x_n^0\right)$$

This completes one iteration. In general, we get the kth approximate solution in the kth iteration as follows:

$$x_i^k = f_i(x_1^k, \ldots, x_{i-1}^k, x_i^{k-1}, x_{i+1}^{k-1}, \ldots, x_n^{k-1}),\quad i = 1, 2, \ldots, n$$

We note that the value of x_i for the kth iteration is obtained by substituting $x_1^k, x_2^k, \ldots, x_{i-1}^k$ (obtained in kth iteration) and $x_i^{k-1}, \ldots, x_n^{k-1}$ (obtained in $(k-1)$th iteration) in the equation $x_i = f_i$. If $|x_i^k - x_i^{k-1}| < \varepsilon$ (a very small number), for all i values, then the solution is said to converge. The iterative process is repeated till the solution converges within prescribed accuracy. The convergence is quite sensitive to the starting values assumed. Fortunately, in a load flow study, a starting vector close to the final solution can be easily identified with previous experience.

To solve a load flow problem by GS method, we consider two cases depending on the type of buses present. In the first case, we assume all the buses other than the slack bus are PQ buses. In the second case, we assume the presence of both PQ and PV buses, other than the slack bus. Later on we also include the presence of voltage controlled bus, whose voltage is controlled by a regulating transformer.

Case I The slack bus is numbered one, and the remaining $(n-1)$ buses are PQ buses $(i = 2, \ldots, n)$. With slack bus voltage assumed, the remaining $(n-1)$ bus voltages are found through iterative process as follows:

where α is a real number called the acceleration factor. A suitable value of α for any system can be obtained by trial load flow studies. A generally recommended value is $\alpha = 1.6$. A wrong choice of α may indeed slow down convergence or even cause the method to diverge.

This concludes the load flow analysis for PQ buses only. Next, we consider the presence of PV buses (see Example 6.9).

Case II Here we consider $(m - 1)$ PQ buses, $(n - m)$ PV buses and the slack bus.

Given $V_1, (P_2, Q_2), \ldots, (P_m, Q_m), (P_{m+1}, |V_{m+1}|), \ldots, (P_n, |V_n|)$

To find $S_1, V_2, \ldots, V_m, (Q_{m+1}, \delta_{m+1}), \ldots, (Q_n, \delta_n)$.

Algorithm (Case II) We first repeat the iteration for PQ buses as in Case I, then continue the iteration for PV buses. At the PV buses, P and $|V|$ are specified and Q and δ are unknowns to be determined. Therefore, the values of Q and δ are to be updated in every GS iteration through appropriate bus equations. This is accomplished in the following steps:

1. From Eq. (6.27b),

$$Q_i = -\operatorname{Im}\left\{V_i^* \sum_{k=1}^{n} Y_{ik} V_k\right\}, \quad i = m+1, \ldots, n$$

The revised value of Q_i is obtained from the above equation by substituting most updated values of voltages on the right-hand side. For the $(r + 1)$th iteration we can write,

$$Q_i^{(r+1)} = -\operatorname{Im}\left\{\left(V_i^{(r)}\right)^* \sum_{k=1}^{i-1} Y_{ik} V_k^{(r+1)} + \left(V_i^{(r)}\right)^* \sum_{k=i}^{n} Y_{ik} V_k^{(r)}\right\}, \quad i = m+1, \ldots, n \tag{6.46}$$

2. The revised value of δ_i is obtained from Eq. (6.41) immediately after step 1.

$$\delta_i^{(r+1)} = \angle V_i^{(r+1)} = \text{Angle}\left[\frac{A_i^{(r+1)}}{\left(V_i^{(r)}\right)^*} - \sum_{k=1}^{i-1} B_{ik} V_k^{(r+1)} - \sum_{k=i+1}^{n} B_{ik} V_k^{(r)}\right] \tag{6.47}$$

where

$$A_i^{(r+1)} = \frac{P_i - jQ_i^{(r+1)}}{Y_{ii}}, \quad i = m+1, \ldots, n \tag{6.48}$$

Physical limitations of Q generation require that Q demand at any bus must be in the range $Q_{\min}$ to $Q_{\max}$. If at any stage during iteration, Q at any bus goes outside these limits, it is fixed at $Q_{\min}$ or $Q_{\max}$ as the case may be, and the bus voltage specification is dropped, i.e., the bus is now treated like a PQ bus. Thus, Step 1 above branches out to Step 3 as follows:

3. If $Q_i^{(r+1)} \le Q_{i,\min}$, we set $Q_i^{(r+1)} = Q_{i,\min}$ or if $Q_i^{(r+1)} \ge Q_{i,\max}$, we set $Q_i^{(r+1)} = Q_{i,\max}$, and treat the bus i as a PQ bus. We compute $A_i^{(r+1)}$ and $V_i^{(r+1)}$ from Eqs. (6.48) and (6.41), respectively.

Now, all the computational steps are summarised in the detailed flow chart of Fig. 6.15. It is assumed that out of n buses, the first is slack bus, then $2, 3, \ldots, m$ are PQ buses, and the remaining, $m + 1, \ldots, n$ are PV buses.

Case III We consider here the presence of voltage controlled buses in addition to PQ and PV buses other than the slack bus. This case will be dealt in Example 6.9.

Example 6.8 For the sample system of Fig. 6.7, the generators are connected at all the four buses, while loads are at buses 2 and 3. Values of real and reactive powers are listed in Table 6.5. All buses other than the slack are PQ type.

Assuming a flat voltage start, find the voltages and bus angles at the three buses at the end of the first GS iteration.

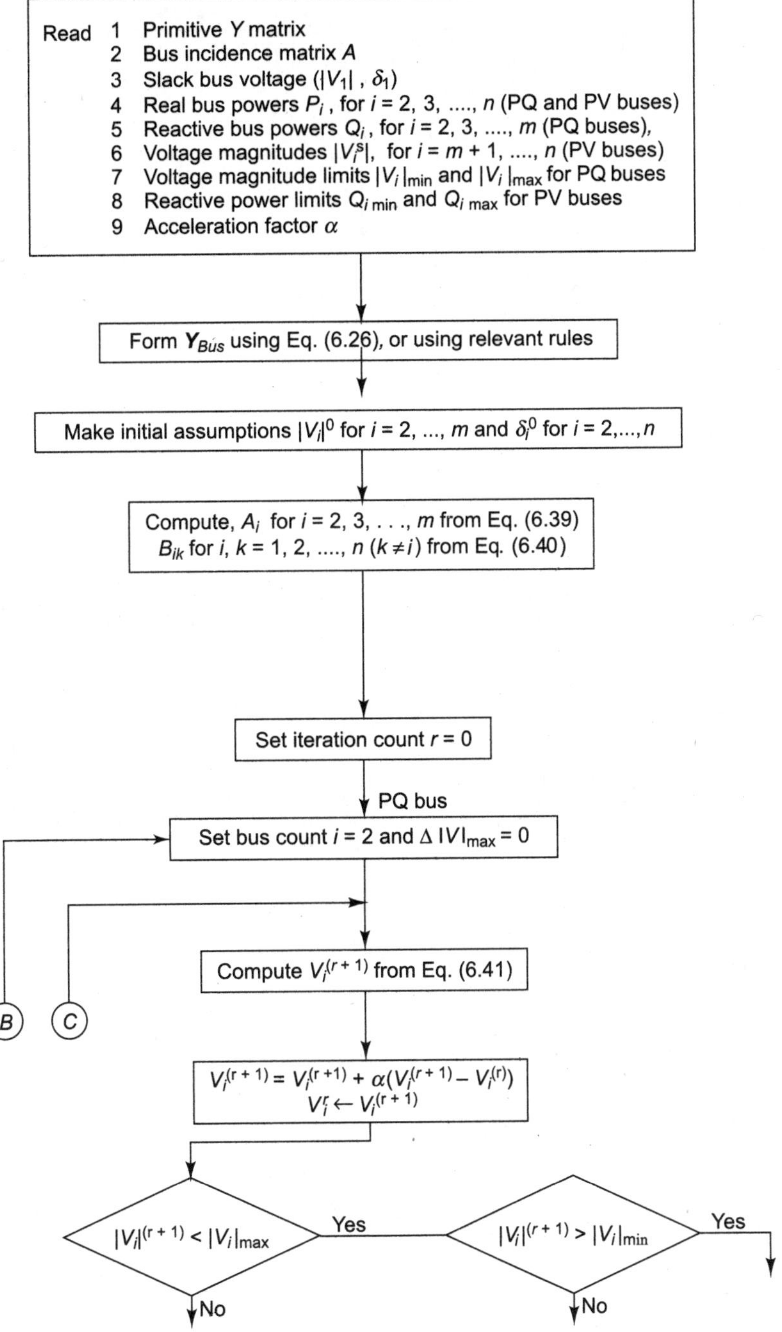

Read 1 Primitive Y matrix
2 Bus incidence matrix A
3 Slack bus voltage ($|V_1|$, δ_1)
4 Real bus powers P_i, for i = 2, 3, ..., n (PQ and PV buses)
5 Reactive bus powers Q_i, for i = 2, 3, ..., m (PQ buses),
6 Voltage magnitudes $|V_i^s|$, for $i = m + 1$, ..., n (PV buses)
7 Voltage magnitude limits $|V_i|_{min}$ and $|V_i|_{max}$ for PQ buses
8 Reactive power limits $Q_{i\,min}$ and $Q_{i\,max}$ for PV buses
9 Acceleration factor α
Form $\mathbf{Y}_{Bus}$ using Eq. (6.26), or using relevant rules
Make initial assumptions $|V_i|^0$ for i = 2, ..., m and δ_i^0 for i = 2,...,n
Compute, A_i for i = 2, 3, . . ., m from Eq. (6.39)
B_{ik} for i, k = 1, 2, ..., n ($k \neq i$) from Eq. (6.40)
Set iteration count $r = 0$
PQ bus
Set bus count $i = 2$ and $\Delta |V|_{max} = 0$
Compute $V_i^{(r+1)}$ from Eq. (6.41)
B
C
$V_i^{(r+1)} = V_i^{(r+1)} + \alpha(V_i^{(r+1)} - V_i^{(r)})$
$V_i^r \leftarrow V_i^{(r+1)}$
$|V_i|^{(r+1)} < |V_i|_{max}$
Yes
$|V_i|^{(r+1)} > |V_i|_{min}$
Yes
No
No

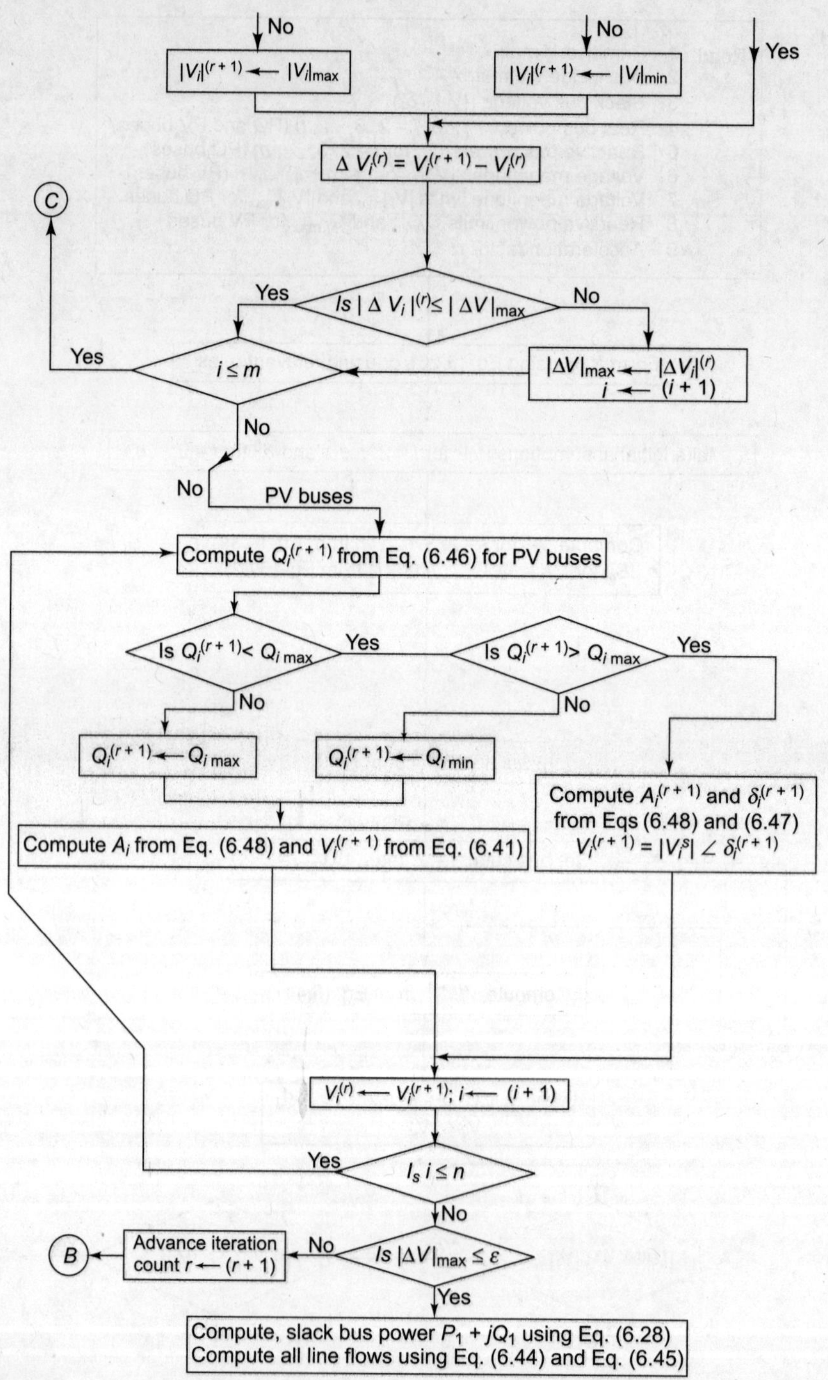

Fig. 6.15 *Flow chart for load flow solution by the Gauss–Siedel iterative method using* $\mathbf{Y}_{BUS}$

Solution

Table 6.5 Input data

Bus	P_i, *pu*	Q_i, *pu*	V_i, *pu*	*Remarks*
1	–	–	$1.04 \angle 0°$	Slack bus
2	0.5	– 0.2	–	PQ bus
3	– 1.0	0.5	–	PQ bus
4	0.3	– 0.1	–	PQ bus

$$= \frac{2.991 - j9.253}{3 - j9} = 1.025 - j0.0093 \text{ pu}$$

The Y_{BUS} for the sample system has been calculated earlier in Example 6.3(b) (i.e., the dotted line is assumed to be connected). In order to approach the accuracy of a digital computer, the computations given below have been performed on an electronic calculator.

Bus voltages at the end of the first iteration are calculated using Eq. (6.41).

$$V_2^1 = \frac{1}{Y_{22}}\left[\frac{P_2 - jQ_2}{\left(V_2^0\right)^*} - Y_{21}V_1 - Y_{23}V_3^0 - Y_{24}V_4^0\right]$$

$$= \frac{1}{Y_{22}}\left[\frac{0.5 + j0.2}{1 - j0} - 1.04\,(-2 + j6) - (-0.666 + j2) - (-1 + j3)\right]$$

$$= \frac{4.246 - j11.04}{3.666 - j11} = 1.019 + j0.046 \text{ pu}$$

$$V_3^1 = \frac{1}{Y_{33}}\left[\frac{P_3 - jQ_3}{\left(V_3^0\right)^*} - Y_{31}V_1 - Y_{32}V_2^1 - Y_{34}V_4^0\right]$$

$$= \frac{1}{Y_{33}}\left[\frac{-1 - j0.5}{1 - j0} - 1.04(-1 + j3) - (-0.666 + j2)(1.019 + j0.046) - (-2 + j6)\right]$$

$$= \frac{2.81 - j11.627}{3.666 - j11} = 1.028 - j0.087 \text{ pu}$$

$$V_4^1 = \frac{1}{Y_{44}}\left[\frac{P_4 - jQ_4}{\left(V_4^0\right)^*} - Y_{41}V_1 - Y_{42}V_2^1 - Y_{43}V_3^1\right]$$

$$= \frac{1}{Y_{44}}\left[\frac{0.3 + j0.1}{1 - j0} - (-1 + j3)(1.019 + j0.046) - (-2 + j6)(1.028 - j0.087)\right]$$

Example 6.9 In Example 6.8, let bus 2 be a PV bus now with $|V_2| = 1.04$ pu. Once again assuming a flat voltage start, find Q_2, δ_2, V_3, V_4 at the end of the first GS iteration.

Given $0.2 \le Q_2 \le 1$ pu

Solution From Eq. (6.46), we get (*Note:* $\delta_2^0 = 0$, i.e., $V_2^0 = 1.04 + j0$)

$$Q_2^1 = -\text{Im}\,((V_2^0)^*\, Y_{21}\, V_1 + (V_2^0)^*\, (Y_{22}\, V_2^0 + Y_{23}\, V_3^0 + Y_{24}\, V_4^0))$$

$$= -\text{Im}\,(1.04\,(-2 + j6)\,1.04 + 1.04\,((3.666 - j11)1.04 + (-0.666 + j2) + (-1 + j3)))$$

$$= -\text{Im}\,(-0.0693 - j0.2097) = 0.2079 \text{ pu}$$

From Eq. (6.47),

$$\delta_2^1 = \angle \frac{1}{Y_{22}} \left[\frac{P_2 - jQ_2^1}{\left(V_2^0\right)*} - Y_{21}\, V_1 - Y_{23}\, V_3^0 - Y_{24}\, V_4^0 \right]$$

$$= \angle \frac{1}{Y_{22}} \left[\frac{0.5 - j0.2079}{1.04 - j0} - (-2 + j6)(1.04 + j0) - (-0.666 + j2)(1 + j0) - (-1 + j3)(1 + j0) \right]$$

$$= \angle \left[\frac{4.2267 - j11.439}{3.666 - j11} \right] = \angle (1.0512 + j0.0339)$$

$$= 1.84658° = 0.032 \text{ red}$$

$$V_2^1 = 1.04\,(\cos \delta_2^1 + j \sin \delta_2^1)$$

$$= 1.04\,(0.99948 + j0.0322)$$

$$= 1.03946 + j0.03351$$

$$V_3^1 = \frac{1}{Y_{33}} \left[\frac{P_3 - jQ_3}{\left(V_3^0\right)*} - Y_{31}\, V_1 - Y_{32}\, V_2^1 - Y_{34}\, V_4^0 \right]$$

$$= \frac{1}{Y_{33}} \left[\frac{-1 - j0.5}{1 - j0} - (-1 + j3)1.04 - (-0.66 + j2)(1.03946 + j0.03351) - (-2 + j6) \right]$$

$$= \frac{2.7992 - j11.6766}{3.666 - j11} = 1.0317 - j0.08937$$

$$V_4^1 = \frac{1}{Y_{44}} \left[\frac{P_4 - jQ_4}{\left(V_4^0\right)*} - Y_{41}\, V_1 - Y_{42}\, V_2^1 - Y_{43}\, V_3^1 \right]$$

$$= \frac{1}{Y_{44}} \left[\frac{0.3 + j0.1}{1 - j0} - (-1 + j3)(1.0394 + j0.0335) - (-2 + j6)(1.0317 - j0.08937) \right]$$

$$= \frac{2.9671 - j8.9962}{3 - j9} = 0.9985 - j0.0031$$

Now, suppose the permissible limits on Q_2 (reactive power injection) are revised as follows:

$$0.25 \le Q_2 \le 1.0 \text{ pu}$$

It is clear that other data remaining the same, the calculated Q_2 (= 0.2079) is now less than the $Q_{2\,\min}$. Hence, Q_2 is set equal to $Q_{2\,\min}$ i.e.,

$$Q_2 = 0.25 \text{ pu}$$

Bus 2, therefore, becomes a PQ bus from a PV bus. Therefore, $|V_2|$ can no longer remain fixed at 1.04 pu. The value of V_2 at the end of the first iteration is calculated as follows. (*Note:* $V_2^0 = 1 + j0$ by virtue of a flat start).

$$V_2^1 = \frac{1}{Y_{22}}\left[\frac{P_2 - jQ_2}{(V_2^0)^*} - Y_{21}V_1 - Y_{23}V_3^0 - Y_{24}V_4^0\right]$$

$$= \frac{1}{Y_{22}}\left[\frac{0.5 - j0.25}{1 - j0} - (-2 + j6)1.04 - (-0.666 + j2) - (-1 + j3)\right]$$

$$= \frac{4.246 - j11.49}{3.666 - j11} = 1.0559 + j0.0341$$

$$V_3^1 = \frac{1}{Y_{33}}\left[\frac{P_3 - jQ_3}{(V_3^0)^*} - Y_{31}V_1 - Y_{32}V_2^1 - Y_{34}V_4^0\right]$$

$$= \frac{1}{Y_{33}}\left[\frac{-1 - j0.5}{1 - j0} - (-1 + j3)1.04 - (-0.666 + j2)(1.0559 + j0.0341) - (-2 + j6)\right]$$

$$= \frac{2.8112 - j11.709}{3.666 - j11} = 1.0347 - j0.0893 \text{ pu}$$

$$V_4^1 = \frac{1}{Y_{44}}\left[\frac{P_4 - jQ_4}{(V_4^0)^*} - Y_{41}V_1 - Y_{42} - V_2^1 - Y_{43}V_3^1\right]$$

$$= \frac{1}{Y_{44}}\left[\frac{0.3 + j0.1}{1 - j0} - (-1 + j3)(1.0509 + j0.0341) - (-2 + j6)(1.0347 - j0.0893)\right]$$

$$= \frac{4.0630 - j9.4204}{3 - j9} = 1.0775 + j0.0923 \text{ pu}$$

6.6 ▶ NEWTON–RAPHSON METHOD

The Newton–Raphson (NR) method is a powerful method of solving nonlinear algebraic equations. It works faster, and is sure to converge in most cases as compared to the Gauss–Siedel (GS) method. (For its convergence properties see Appendix L, *available online*). It is indeed the practical method of load flow solution of large power networks. Its only drawback is the large requirement of computer memory, which can be overcome through a compact storage scheme. Convergence can be considerably speeded up by performing the first iteration through the GS method, and using the values so obtained for solving the NR iterations.

We consider a set of n nonlinear algebraic equations

$$f_i(x_1, x_2, ..., x_n) = 0 \qquad \text{where } i = 1, 2, ..., n \tag{6.49}$$

We assume initial values of unknowns as $x_1^0, x_2^0, \ldots, x_n^0$. Let $\Delta x_1^0, \Delta x_2^0, \ldots, \Delta x_n^0$ be the corrections to be found out, which on being added to the initial values, give the actual solution. Therefore,

$$f_i(x_1^0 + \Delta x_1^0, \ldots, x_n^0 + \Delta x_n^0) = 0; \qquad i = 1, 2, ..., n \tag{6.50}$$

Expanding these equations around the initial values by Taylor series, we have

$$f_i^0(x_1^0, ..., x_n^0) + \left[\left(\frac{\partial f_i}{\partial x_1}\right)^0 \Delta x_1^0 + \cdots + \left(\frac{\partial f_i}{\partial x_n}\right)^0 \Delta x_n^0\right] + \text{higher order terms} = 0 \tag{6.51}$$

where $\left(\frac{\partial f_i}{\partial x_1}\right)^0, \ldots, \left(\frac{\partial f_i}{\partial x_n}\right)^0$ are the derivatives of f_i wrt $x_1, x_2, ..., x_n$ evaluated at $x_0^1, ..., x_n^0$.

Neglecting the higher order terms, Eq. (6.51) can be written in matrix form as

$$\begin{bmatrix} f_1^0 \\ \vdots \\ f_n^0 \end{bmatrix} + \begin{bmatrix} \left(\dfrac{\partial f_1}{\partial x_1}\right)^0 & \cdots & \left(\dfrac{\partial f_1}{\partial x_n}\right)^0 \\ \vdots & & \vdots \\ \left(\dfrac{\partial f_n}{\partial x_1}\right)^0 & \cdots & \left(\dfrac{\partial f_n}{\partial x_n}\right)^0 \end{bmatrix} \begin{bmatrix} \Delta x_1^0 \\ \vdots \\ \Delta x_n^0 \end{bmatrix} \cong \begin{bmatrix} 0 \\ \vdots \\ 0 \end{bmatrix} \tag{6.52}$$

or in vector matrix form

$$\boldsymbol{f}^0 + \boldsymbol{J}^0 \Delta \boldsymbol{x}^0 = 0 \tag{6.53}$$

where $\boldsymbol{J}^0$ is the Jacobian matrix evaluated at $\boldsymbol{x}^0$.

In compact notation,

$$\boldsymbol{J}^0 = \left(\frac{\delta \boldsymbol{f}(\boldsymbol{x})}{\partial \boldsymbol{x}}\right)^0 \tag{6.54}$$

In Eq. (6.53), $\Delta \boldsymbol{x}^0$ is the vector of approximate correction. This can be written in the form

$$\Delta \boldsymbol{x}^0 = (-\boldsymbol{J}^0)^{-1} \boldsymbol{f}^0 \tag{6.55}$$

Thus, $\Delta \boldsymbol{x}^0$ can be evaluated by calculating the inverse of $\boldsymbol{J}^0$. But, in practice, we do not evaluate the inverse matrix, as it is computationally expensive and not really needed. Also, the inverse has to be found for every iteration. We write Eq. (6.53) in the form

$$\boldsymbol{J}^0 \Delta \boldsymbol{x}^0 \cong -\boldsymbol{f}^0 \tag{6.56}$$

These, being a set of linear algebraic equations, can be solved for $\Delta \boldsymbol{x}^0$ efficiently by triangularisation and back substitution. Updated values of $\boldsymbol{x}$ are then

$$\boldsymbol{x}^1 = \boldsymbol{x}^0 + \Delta \boldsymbol{x}^0$$

In general, for the $(r + 1)$th iteration

$$(\boldsymbol{J}(\boldsymbol{x}^r))\, \Delta \boldsymbol{x}^r = -\boldsymbol{f}(\boldsymbol{x}^r)$$

or

$$(-\boldsymbol{J}(\boldsymbol{x}^r))\, \Delta \boldsymbol{x}^r = \boldsymbol{f}(\boldsymbol{x}^r) \tag{6.57}$$

or

$$(-\boldsymbol{J}^r)\, \Delta \boldsymbol{x}^r = \boldsymbol{f}^r$$

and

$$\boldsymbol{x}^{(r+1)} = \boldsymbol{x}^r + \Delta \boldsymbol{x}^r \tag{6.58}$$

Iterations are continued till Eq. (6.49) is satisfied to any desired accuracy, i.e.,

$$|f_i(\boldsymbol{x}^r)| < \varepsilon \text{ (a specified value)}, \quad i = 1, 2, \ldots, n$$

Thus, each iteration involves the evaluation of $\boldsymbol{f}(\boldsymbol{x}^r)$, $\boldsymbol{J}(\boldsymbol{x}^r)$ and the correction $\Delta \boldsymbol{x}^r$. Therefore, time taken for each iteration by NR method is more compared to the GS method, but the method converges in only a few iterations and the total computation time is much less than by the GS method.

6.6.1 NR Algorithm for Load Flow Solution

We first consider the presence of PQ buses only apart from a slack bus. From Eq. (6.28), for an ith bus,

$$P_i = \sum_{k=1}^{n} |V_i||V_k||Y_{ik}| \cos(\theta_{ik} + \delta_k - \delta_i) = P_i(|V|, \delta) \tag{6.59a}$$

$$Q_i = -\sum_{k=1}^{n} |V_i||V_k||Y_{ik}| \sin(\theta_{ik} + \delta_k - \delta_i) = Q_i(|V|, \delta) \tag{6.59b}$$

i.e., both real and reactive powers are functions of $(|V|, \delta)$, where

$$|V| = (|V_1|, ..., |V_n|^T) \; \delta = (\delta_1, ..., \delta_n)^T$$

We write

$$P_i(|V|, \delta) = P_i(x)$$

$$Q_i(|V|, \delta) = Q_i(x)$$

where

$$x = \begin{bmatrix} \delta \\ \hline |V| \end{bmatrix}$$

Let P_i (scheduled) and Q_i (scheduled) be the scheduled powers at the load buses. In the course of iteration x should tend to that value which makes

$$P_i - P_i(x) = 0 \text{ and } Q_i - Q_i(x) = 0 \tag{6.60a}$$

Writing Eq. 6.60(a) for all load buses, we get its matrix form

$$f(x) = \begin{bmatrix} P(\text{scheduled}) - P(x) \\ Q(\text{scheduled}) - Q(x) \end{bmatrix} = \begin{bmatrix} \Delta P(x) \\ \Delta Q(x) \end{bmatrix} \cong 0 \tag{6.60b}$$

At the slack bus (bus number 1), P_1 and Q_1 are unspecified. Therefore, the values $P_1(x)$ and $Q_1(x)$ do not enter into Eq. 6.60(a), and hence 6.60(b). Thus, x is a $2(n-1)$ vector ($n-1$ load buses), with each element function of $(n-1)$ variables given by the vector $x = \begin{bmatrix} \delta \\ |V| \end{bmatrix}$

From Eq. (6.57), we can write

$$f(x) = \begin{bmatrix} \Delta P(x) \\ \Delta Q(x) \end{bmatrix} = \begin{bmatrix} -J_{11}(x) & -J_{12}(x) \\ -J_{21}(x) & -J_{22}(x) \end{bmatrix} \begin{bmatrix} \Delta\delta \\ \Delta|V| \end{bmatrix} \tag{6.61a}$$

where $\Delta\delta = (\Delta\delta_2, .., \Delta\delta_n)^T$

$$\Delta|V| = (\Delta|V_2|, ..., \Delta|V_n|)^T$$

$$J(x) = \begin{bmatrix} -J_{11}(x) & -J_{12}(x) \\ -J_{21}(x) & -J_{22}(x) \end{bmatrix} \tag{6.61b}$$

$J(x)$ is the Jacobian matrix, each J_{11}, J_{12}, J_{21}, J_{22} are $(n-1) \times (n-1)$ matrices. It follows from Eq. (6.52) and Eq. (6.60b) that

$$\begin{aligned} -J_{11}(x) &= \frac{\partial P(x)}{\partial \delta} \\ -J_{12}(x) &= \frac{\partial P(x)}{\partial |V|} \\ -J_{21}(x) &= \frac{\partial Q(x)}{\partial \delta} \\ -J_{22}(x) &= \frac{\partial Q(x)}{\partial |V|} \end{aligned} \tag{6.62}$$

The elements of $-J_{11}, -J_{12}, -J_{21}, -J_{22}$ are $\dfrac{\partial P_i(x)}{\partial \delta_k}, \dfrac{\partial P_i(x)}{\partial |V_k|}, \dfrac{\partial Q_i(x)}{\partial \delta_k}, \dfrac{\partial Q_i(x)}{\partial |V_k|}$, where $i = 2, ..., n$; $k = 2, ..., n$.

From Eqs. 6.59(a) and (b), we have

$$\frac{\partial P_i(x)}{\partial \delta_k} = -|V_i||V_k||Y_{ik}|\sin(\theta_{ik}+\delta_k-\delta_i) \quad (i \neq k)$$

$$= \sum_{\substack{k=1 \\ k\neq i}}^{n} |V_i||V_k||Y_{ik}|\sin(\theta_{ik}+\delta_k-\delta_i)) \quad (i = k) \tag{6.63a}$$

$$\frac{\partial P_i(x)}{\delta |V_k|} = |V_i||Y_{ik}|\cos(\theta_{ik}+\delta_k-\delta_i) \quad (i \neq k) \tag{6.63b}$$

$$= 2|V_i||Y_{ii}|\cos\theta_{ii} + \sum_{\substack{k=1 \\ k\neq i}}^{n} (|V_k||Y_{ik}|\cos(\theta_{ik}+\delta_k-\delta_i)) \quad (i = k)$$

$$\frac{\partial Q_i(x)}{\partial \delta_k} = |V_i||Y_{ik}||V_k|\cos(\theta_{ik}+\delta_k-\delta_i) \quad (i \neq k)$$

$$= -\sum_{\substack{k=1 \\ k\neq i}}^{n} (|V_i||V_k||Y_{ik}|\cos(\theta_{ik}+\delta_k-\delta_i)) \quad (i = k) \tag{6.63c}$$

$$\frac{\partial Q_i(x)}{\partial |V_k|} = |V_i||Y_{ik}|\sin(\theta_{ik}+\delta_k-\delta_i) \quad (i \neq k)$$

$$= 2|V_i||Y_{ii}|\sin\theta_{ii} + \sum_{\substack{k=1 \\ k\neq i}}^{n} (|V_k||Y_{ik}|\sin(\theta_{ik}+\delta_k-\delta_i)) \quad (i = k) \tag{6.63d}$$

An important observation can be made with respect to the elements of Jacobian matrix. If there is no connection between ith and kth bus, then $Y_{ik} = 0$, and from Eq. (6.63), the elements of the Jacobian matrix corresponding to ith and kth buses are zero. Hence, like $\boldsymbol{Y}_{\text{BUS}}$ matrix, the Jacobian matrix is also sparse. There are computational techniques to take advantage of this sparsity in the computer solution.

The Jacobian matrix in Eq. (6.61) is rearranged for obtaining the approximate correction vectors and can be written as

$$\begin{array}{c} i\text{th} \\ \text{PQ} \\ \text{bus} \end{array}\left\{\begin{bmatrix} \vdots \\ \Delta P_i \\ \Delta Q_i \\ \vdots \end{bmatrix}\right. = \begin{array}{c} i\text{th} \\ \text{bus} \end{array}\overset{m\text{th bus}}{\begin{bmatrix} & \cdots & & \\ & H_{im} & N_{im} & \\ & J_{im} & L_{im} & \\ & \cdots & & \end{bmatrix}} \begin{bmatrix} \vdots \\ \Delta\delta_m \\ \Delta|V_m| \\ \vdots \end{bmatrix} \begin{array}{c} m\text{th} \\ \text{PQ} \\ \text{bus} \end{array} \tag{6.64a}$$

$i = 2, \ldots, n$ and $m = 2, \ldots, n$, where

$$H_{im} = \frac{\partial P_i}{\partial \delta_m}$$

$$N_{im} = \frac{\partial P_i}{\partial |V_m|} \tag{6.64b}$$

$$J_{im} = \frac{\partial Q_i}{\partial \delta_m}$$

$$L_{im} = \frac{\partial Q_i}{\partial |V_m|} \tag{6.64c}$$

It is to be immediately observed that the Jacobian elements corresponding to the ith bus residuals and mth bus corrections are a 2×2 matrix enclosed in the box in Eq. (6.64), where i and m are both PQ buses.

Consider now the presence of PV buses. Since Q_i is not specified and $|V_i|$ is fixed for a PV bus, ΔQ_i does not enter on the LHS of Eq. (6.64), and $\Delta |V_i|$ (= 0) does not enter on the RHS of Eq. (6.64). Let ith and mth buses be PQ buses and jth and kth buses be PV buses. Then, we have

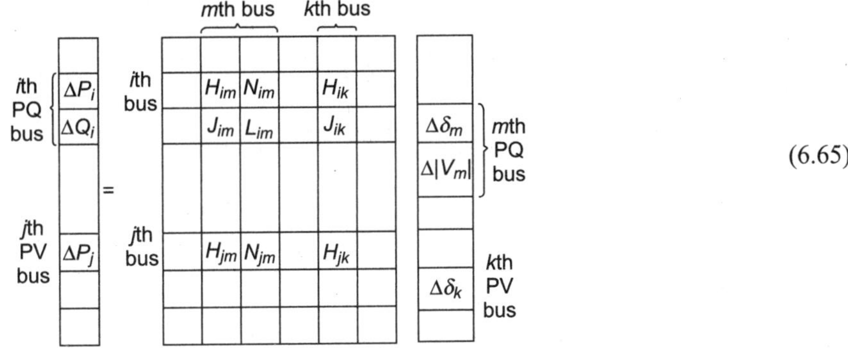

(6.65)

It is convenient for numerical solution to normalise the voltage corrections as $\Delta |V_m| / |V_m|$, as a consequence of which, the corresponding Jacobian elements become

$$N_{im} = \frac{\partial P_i}{\partial |V_m|} |V_m|$$

$$L_{im} = \frac{\partial Q_i}{\partial |V_m|} |V_m| \tag{6.66}$$

Expressions for elements of the Jacobian (in normalised form) of load flow Eq. (6.60b) are derived in Appendix D and are given below:

Case 1 $(m \neq i)$

$$H_{im} = L_{im} = a_m f_i - b_m e_i$$
$$N_{im} = -J_{im} = a_m e_i + b_m f_i \tag{6.67}$$

where $Y_{im} = G_{im} + JB_{im}$

$$V_i = e_i + jf_i$$
$$a_m + jb_m = (G_{im} + jB_{im})(e_m + jf_m)$$

Case 2 $m = i$

$$H_{ii} = -Q_i - B_{ii}|V_i|^2$$
$$N_{ii} = P_i + G_{ii}|V_i|^2 \tag{6.68}$$
$$J_{ii} = P_i - G_{ii}|V_i|^2$$
$$L_{ii} = Q_i - B_{ii}|V_i|^2$$

If buses i and m are not connected, $Y_{im} = 0$ $(G_{im} = B_{im} = 0)$.
Hence from Eq. (6.67), we can, write

$$H_{im} = H_{mi} = 0$$
$$N_{im} = N_{mi} = 0$$
$$J_{im} = J_{mi} = 0 \tag{6.69}$$
$$L_{im} = L_{mi} = 0$$

Thus, the Jacobian is as sparse as the $\boldsymbol{Y}_{\text{BUS}}$ matrix.

Formation of Eq. (6.65) of the NR method is best illustrated by a problem. Figure 6.16 shows a five-bus power network with bus types indicated therein. The matrix equation for determining vector of corrections from the vector of residuals follows very soon.

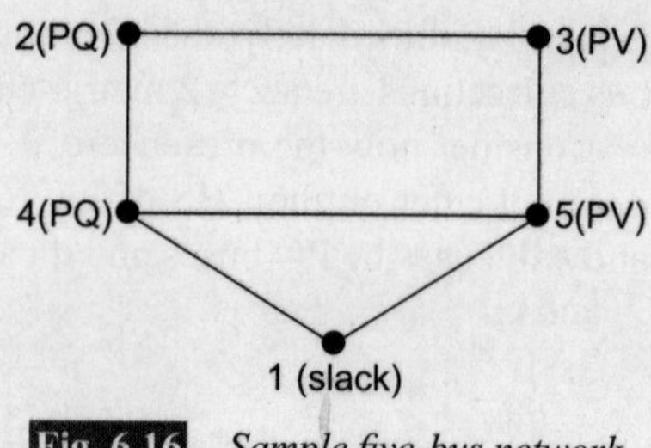

Fig. 6.16 *Sample five-bus network*

Corresponding to a particular vector of variables $(\delta_2, |V_2|, \delta_3, \delta_4, \Delta Q_2, |V_4|, \delta_5)^T$, the vector of residuals is $(\Delta P_2, \Delta Q_2, \Delta P_3, \Delta P_4, \Delta Q_4, \Delta P_5)^T$ and the Jacobian (6×6 in this example) are computed.

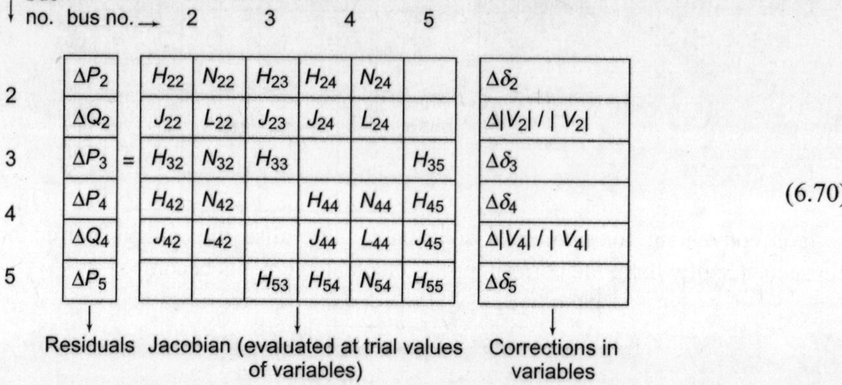

$$
\begin{bmatrix} \Delta P_2 \\ \Delta Q_2 \\ \Delta P_3 \\ \Delta P_4 \\ \Delta Q_4 \\ \Delta P_5 \end{bmatrix}
=
\begin{bmatrix}
H_{22} & N_{22} & H_{23} & H_{24} & N_{24} & \\
J_{22} & L_{22} & J_{23} & J_{24} & L_{24} & \\
H_{32} & N_{32} & H_{33} & & & H_{35} \\
H_{42} & N_{42} & & H_{44} & N_{44} & H_{45} \\
J_{42} & L_{42} & & J_{44} & L_{44} & J_{45} \\
 & & H_{53} & H_{54} & N_{54} & H_{55}
\end{bmatrix}
\begin{bmatrix} \Delta\delta_2 \\ \Delta|V_2|/|V_2| \\ \Delta\delta_3 \\ \Delta\delta_4 \\ \Delta|V_4|/|V_4| \\ \Delta\delta_5 \end{bmatrix}
\tag{6.70}
$$

Equation 6.70 is then solved by triangularisation and back substitution procedure to obtain the vector of corrections $(\Delta\delta_2, \Delta|V_2|/|V_2|, \Delta\delta_3, \Delta\delta_4, \Delta|V_4|/|V_4|, \Delta\delta_5)^T$. Corrections are then added to update the vector of variables.

6.6.2 Iterative Algorithm

The iterative algorithm for the solution of the load flow problem by the NR method is as follows:

1. With the voltage and angle at the slack bus fixed at $V_1 \angle\delta_1$ $(= 1 \angle 0^\circ)$, we assume $|V|, \angle\delta$ at all PQ buses and δ at all PV buses. In the absence of any information, flat voltage start is recommended.
2. In the rth iteration, we have (see Eqs. 6.28(a) and (b))

$$P_i^r = \sum_{k=1}^{n} |V_i|^r |V_k|^r |Y_{ik}| \cos(\theta_{ik} + \delta_k^r - \delta_i^r) \tag{6.71a}$$

$$Q_i^r = -\sum_{k=1}^{n} |V_i|^r |V_k|^r |Y_{ik}| \sin(\theta_{ik} + \delta_k^r - \delta_i^r) \tag{6.71b}$$

Let
$$e_i^r = |V_i|^r \cos\delta_i^r, f_i^r = |V_i|^r \sin\delta_i^r \tag{6.72}$$
$$G_{ik} = |Y_{ik}| \cos\theta_{ik}, B_{ik} = |Y_{ik}| \sin\theta_{ik} \tag{6.73}$$

Using Eqs. (6.72) and (6.73) in Eqs. 6.71(a) and (b), we have

$$P_i^r = \sum_{k=1}^{n} (e_i^r(e_k^r G_{ik} - f_k^r B_{ik}) + f_i^r(f_k^r G_{ik} + e_k^r B_{ik})) \tag{6.74a}$$

$$Q_i^r = \sum_{k=1}^{n} (f_i^r(e_k^r G_{ik} - f_k^r B_{ik}) - e_i^r(f_k^r G_{ik} + e_k^r B_{ik})), \; i = 2, \ldots, n \tag{6.74b}$$

We next compute

$$\Delta P_i^r = P_i\,(\text{scheduled}) - P_i^r \quad \text{for PV and PQ buses} \tag{6.75a}$$

$$\Delta Q_i^r = Q_i\,(\text{scheduled}) - Q_i^r \quad \text{for PQ buses} \tag{6.75b}$$

If all values of ΔP_i^r and ΔQ_i^r are less than the prescribed tolerance, we stop the iteration, calculate P_1 and Q_1 and print the entire solution, including line flows.

3. If the convergence criterion is not satisfied, we evaluate the Jacobian elements using Eqs. (6.67) and (6.68).
4. We solve Eq. (6.65) for correction of voltage magnitudes $\Delta |V|^r$ and angle $\Delta\delta^r$.
5. Next we update voltage magnitudes and angles,

$$|V|^{(r+1)} = |V|^r + |\Delta V|^r$$

$$\delta^{(r+1)} = \delta^r + \Delta\delta^r$$

Then we return to step 2.

It is to be noted that

1. In step 2, if there are limits on the controllable Q sources at PV buses, Q is computed each time using Eq. (6.74b), and if it violates the limits, it is made equal to the limiting value and the corresponding PV bus is made PQ bus in that iteration. If in subsequent computation, Q comes with the prescribed limits, the bus is switched back to a PV bus. Thus, if $|Q_i|^r \geq Q_{i\,\max}$, then we let $|Q_i| = Q_{i\,\max}$ and we have from Eq. (6.65)

$$\Delta Q_i^r = Q_i - Q_i^r = \sum_{k=2}^{m} (J_{ik}^r \Delta\delta_k^r + L_{ik}^r \Delta |V_k|^r) + \sum_{k=m+1}^{n} J_{ik}^r \Delta\delta_k^r \tag{6.76}$$

In the RHS of Eq. (6.76), all $\Delta\delta_k$s and $\Delta|V_k|$s are known except $\Delta|V_i|^r \cdot J_{ik}$s and L_{ik}s are calculated from Eqs. (6.67) and (6.68).

Hence, from Eq. (6.76)

$$\Delta|V_i|^r = \frac{1}{L_{ii}^r}\left[\Delta Q_i^r - \sum_{\substack{k=2\\k\neq i}}^{n} (J_{ik}\Delta\delta_k^r + L_{ik}^r \Delta|V_k|^r) - \sum_{\substack{k=m+1\\k\neq i}}^{n} (J_{ik}^r\Delta\delta_k^r) - J_{ii}^r\Delta\delta_i^r\right] \tag{6.77}$$

After computing $\Delta|V_i|^r$, the new value of $|V_i|$ (scheduled) for the PV bus (now a PQ bus due to violation of the limits on Q_i^r) is

$$|V_i| = |V_i|\,(\text{scheduled}) + \Delta|V_i|^r \tag{6.78}$$

With this scheduled value of $|V_i|$, the bus is restored to PV bus, and the next iteration is continued. The above procedure is repeated till Q_i^r lies within its limits.

2. Similarly, if there are voltage limits on a PQ bus, and if any of these limits is violated, the corresponding PQ bus is made a PV bus in that iteration with voltage fixed at the limiting value.

The detailed flow chart for load flow solution by NR method is given in Fig. 6.18.

Example 6.10 Consider the three-bus system of Fig. 6.17. Each of the three lines has a series impedance of $0.02 + j0.08$ pu and a total shunt admittance of $j0.02$ pu. The specified quantities at the buses are tabulated below:

Bus	Real load demand P_D	Reactive load demand Q_D	Real power generation P_G	Reactive power generation Q_G	Voltage specification
1	2.0	1.0	Unspecified	Unspecified	$V_1 = 1.04 + j0$ (Slack bus)
2	0.0	0.0	0.5	1.0	Unspecified (PQ bus)
3	1.5	0.6	0.0	Q_{G3} = ?	$V_3 = 1.04$ (PV bus)

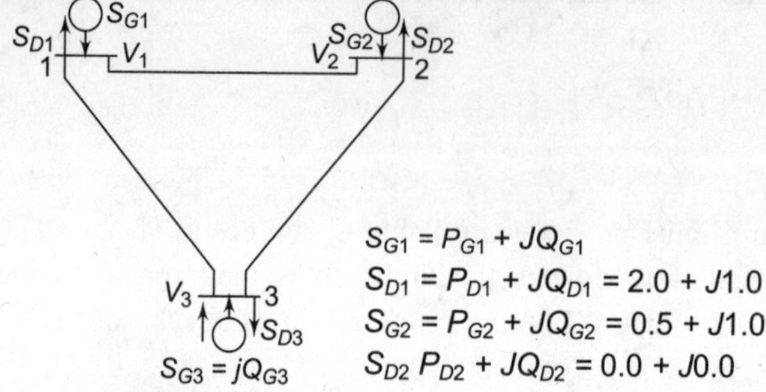

Fig. 6.17 *Three-bus system for Example 6.9*

Controllable reactive power source is available at bus 3 with the constraint,

$$0 \le Q_{G3} \le 1.5 \text{ pu}$$

Find the load flow solution using the NR method. Use a tolerance of 0.01 for power mismatch.

Solution Using the nominal-π model for transmission lines, $\boldsymbol{Y}_{\text{BUS}}$ for the given system is obtained as follows. For each line

$$y_{\text{series}} = \frac{1}{0.02 + J\,0.08} = 2.941 - j11.764 = 12.13 \angle -75.96°$$

Each off-diagonal term = – 2.941 + j11.764

Each self term = $2((2.941 - j11.764) + j0.01)$

$= 5.882 - j23.528 = 24.23 \angle -75.95°$

$$\boldsymbol{Y}_{\text{BUS}} = \begin{bmatrix} 24.23\angle-75.95° & 12.13\angle104.04° & 12.13\angle104.04° \\ 12.13\angle104.04° & 24.23\angle-75.95° & 12.13\angle104.04° \\ 12.13\angle104.04° & 12.13\angle104.04° & 24.23\angle-75.95° \end{bmatrix}$$

To start iteration, choose $V_2^0 = 1 + j0$ and $\delta_3^0 = 0$.

From Eqs. 6.28(a) and (b)

$P_2 = [|V_2||V_1||Y_{21}|\cos(\theta_{21} + \delta_1 - \delta_2) + |V_2|^2|Y_{22}|\cos\theta_{22} + |V_2||V_3||Y_{23}|\cos(\theta_{23} + \delta_3 - \delta_2)]$

$P_3 = [|V_3||V_1||Y_{31}|\cos(\theta_{31} + \delta_1 - \delta_3) + |V_3||V_2||Y_{32}|\cos(\theta_{32} + \delta_2 - \delta_3) + |V_3|^2|Y_{33}|\cos\theta_{33}]$

$Q_2 = [-|V_2||V_1||Y_{21}|\sin(\theta_{21} + \delta_1 - \delta_2) - |V_2|^2|Y_{22}|\sin\theta_{22} - |V_2||V_3||Y_{23}|\sin(\theta_{23} + \delta_3 - \delta_2)]$

Substituting given and assumed values of different quantities, we get the values of powers as

$$P_2^0 = -0.23 \text{ pu}$$
$$P_3^0 = 0.12 \text{ pu}$$
$$Q_2^0 = -0.96 \text{ pu}$$

Power residuals as per Eq. (6.60b) are

$$\Delta P_2^0 = P_2 \text{ (specified)} - P_2^0 \text{ (calculated)} = 0.5 - (-0.23) = 0.73$$

$$\Delta P_3^0 = -1.5 - (0.12) = -1.62$$

$$\Delta Q_2^0 = 1 - (-0.96) = 1.96$$

The changes in variables at the end of the first iteration are obtained as follows:

$$\begin{bmatrix} \Delta P_2 \\ \Delta P_3 \\ \Delta Q_2 \end{bmatrix} = \begin{bmatrix} \partial P_2/\partial \delta_2 & \partial P_2/\partial \delta_3 & \partial P_2/\partial |V_2| \\ \partial P_3/\partial \delta_2 & \partial P_3/\partial \delta_3 & \partial P_3/\partial |V_2| \\ \partial Q_2/\partial \delta_2 & \partial Q_2/\partial \delta_3 & \partial Q_2/\partial |V_2| \end{bmatrix} = \begin{bmatrix} \Delta \delta_2 \\ \Delta \delta_3 \\ \Delta |V_2| \end{bmatrix}$$

Jacobian elements can be evaluated by differentiating the expressions given above for P_2, P_3, Q_2 with respect to δ_2, δ_3 and $|V_2|$ and substituting the given and assumed values at the start of iteration. The changes in variables are obtained as

$$\begin{bmatrix} \Delta \delta_2^1 \\ \Delta \delta_3^1 \\ \Delta |V_2|^1 \end{bmatrix} = \begin{bmatrix} 24.47 & -12.23 & 5.64 \\ -12.23 & 24.95 & -3.05 \\ -6.11 & 3.05 & 22.54 \end{bmatrix}^{-1} \begin{bmatrix} 0.73 \\ -1.62 \\ 1.96 \end{bmatrix} = \begin{bmatrix} -0.0230 \\ -0.0654 \\ 0.0890 \end{bmatrix}$$

$$\begin{bmatrix} \delta_2^1 \\ \delta_3^1 \\ |V_2|^1 \end{bmatrix} = \begin{bmatrix} \delta_2^0 \\ \delta_3^0 \\ |V_2|^0 \end{bmatrix} + \begin{bmatrix} \Delta \delta_2^1 \\ \Delta \delta_3^1 \\ \Delta |V_2|^1 \end{bmatrix} = \begin{bmatrix} 0 \\ 0 \\ 1 \end{bmatrix} + \begin{bmatrix} -0.0230 \\ -0.0654 \\ +0.0890 \end{bmatrix} = \begin{bmatrix} -0.0230 \\ -0.0654 \\ 1.0890 \end{bmatrix}$$

We can now calculate, using Eq. (6.28b),

$$Q_3^1 = 0.4677$$

$$Q_{G3}^1 = Q_3^1 + Q_{D3} = 0.4677 + 0.6 = 1.0677$$

which is within limits.

If the same problem is solved using a digital computer, the solution converges in three iterations. The final results are given below:

$$V_2 = 1.081 \angle -0.024 \text{ rad}$$

$$V_3 = 1.04 \angle -0.0655 \text{ rad}$$

$$Q_{G3} = -0.15 + 0.6 = 0.45 \text{ (within limits)}$$

$$S_1 = 1.031 + j(-0.791)$$

$$S_2 = 0.5 + j1.00$$

$$S_3 = -1.5 - j0.15$$

Transmission loss = 0.031 pu

Line Flows The following matrix shows the real part of line flows.

$$\begin{bmatrix} 0.0 & 0.191312E00 & 0.839861E00 \\ -0.184229E00 & 0.0 & 0.684697E00 \\ -0.826213E00 & -0.673847E00 & 0.0 \end{bmatrix}$$

The following matrix shows the imaginary part of line flows.

$$\begin{bmatrix} 0.0 & -0.599464E00 & -0.191782E00 \\ -0.605274E00 & 0.0 & 0.396045E00 \\ 0.224742E00 & -0.375165E00 & 0.0 \end{bmatrix}$$

6.6.3 Rectangular Power-Mismatch Version

Equation (6.60) represents a set of independent equations

$$\Delta P_i(|V|, \delta) = 0 \quad (i = 2, ..., n;\ n = \text{number of buses})$$

$$\Delta Q_i(|V|, \delta) = 0 \quad (i = 2, ..., m;\ m - 1 = \text{number of PQ buses})$$

each a function of $|V| = (|V_2|, ..., |V_m|$ and

$$\delta = (\delta_2, ..., \delta_n)^T$$

Thus, this involves the solution of a total of $(m + n - 2)$ independent equations in $(m + n - 2)$ variables $|V_i| \to (m - 1)$ and $\delta_i \to (n - 1)$. In rectangular power-mismatch version, the variables used are e_i and f_i $(1 = 2, ..., n)$ giving a total of $2(n - 1)$ variables. Here, in addition to the independent power difference equations, we also have the independent voltage difference equations $(|V_i|^2 - (e_i^2 + f_i^2)) = 0$ for PV buses, thus giving a total of $2(n - 1)$ independent equations in $2(n - 1)$ variables. Thus, the number of equations and variables in rectangular power mismatch version is greater than for Eq. (6.60), by the number of PV buses. With sparsity programming, this increase in order is hardly of any significance. Indeed, each iteration is marginally faster than for Eq. (6.60) since there are no time consuming sine and cosine terms. It may, however, be noted that even the polar version avoids these, as far as possible, by using rectangular arithmetic in constructing Eqs. (6.67) and (6.68). The rectangular version seems to be slightly less reliable, but faster in convergence than the polar version.

Thus, we have the following independent equations:

$$P_i(\text{specified}) - \sum_{k=1}^{n} (e_i(e_k G_{ik} - f_i B_{ik}) + f_i(f_k G_{ik} + e_k B_{ik})) = 0 \tag{6.79a}$$

$i = 2, ..., n$ for both PQ and PV buses

$$Q_i(\text{specified}) - \sum_{k=1}^{n} (f_i(e_k G_{ik} - f_i B_{ik}) - e_i(f_k G_{ik} + e_k B_{ik})) = 0 \tag{6.79b}$$

$i = 2, ..., m$ for each PQ buses

and also

$$(|V_i|(\text{specified}))^2 - (e_i^2 + f_i^2) = 0 \tag{6.79c}$$

$i = m + 1, ..., n$ for each PV buses

or

$$P_i - P_i(\boldsymbol{e}, \boldsymbol{f}) = 0 \quad \text{(for both PQ and PV buses)} \tag{6.79d}$$

$$Q_i - Q_i(\boldsymbol{e}, \boldsymbol{f}) = 0 \quad \text{(for each PQ buses)} \tag{6.79e}$$

$$|V_i|^2 - (e_i^2 + f_i^2) = 0 \quad \text{(for each PV buses)} \tag{6.79f}$$

where $\boldsymbol{e} = (e_2, ..., e_n)^T$ and $\boldsymbol{f} = (f_2, ..., f_n)^T$.

In general, $(e_i^2 + f_i^2)$ is also a function of $(\boldsymbol{e}, \boldsymbol{f})$. Using the NR method, the linearised equations in the rth iteration of the iterative process can be written as

$$\begin{bmatrix} \Delta \boldsymbol{P} \\ \Delta \boldsymbol{Q} \\ \Delta |\boldsymbol{V}|^2 \end{bmatrix}^{(r)} = \begin{bmatrix} \boldsymbol{J}_1 & \boldsymbol{J}_2 \\ \boldsymbol{J}_3 & \boldsymbol{J}_4 \\ \boldsymbol{J}_5 & \boldsymbol{J}_6 \end{bmatrix}^{(r)} \begin{bmatrix} \Delta \boldsymbol{e} \\ \Delta \boldsymbol{f} \end{bmatrix}^{(r)} \tag{6.80}$$

where

For $i \neq j$

$$\begin{aligned} J_{1,ij} &= -J_{4,ij} = G_{ij} e_i f_i \\ J_{2,ij} &= J_{3,ij} = -B_{ij} e_i + G_{ij} f_i \\ J_{5,ij} &= J_{6,ij} = 0 \end{aligned} \tag{6.81a}$$

Read
1 Primitive Y matrix, Bus incidence matrix A
2. Slack bus voltage ($|V_1|$, δ_1) or (e_1, f_1)
3. Real bus powers P_i, for $i = 2, \ldots, n$ (PQ and PV buses)
4. Reactive bus powers Q_i, for $i = 2, \ldots m$ (PQ buses)
5. Voltage magnitudes $|V_i^s|$ for $i = (m+1), \ldots, n$ (PV buses)
6. Reactive power limits $Q_{i\min}$ and $Q_{i\max}$ for PV buses
7. Voltage magnitude limits $|V_i|_{\min}$ and $|V_i|_{\max}$ for PQ buses

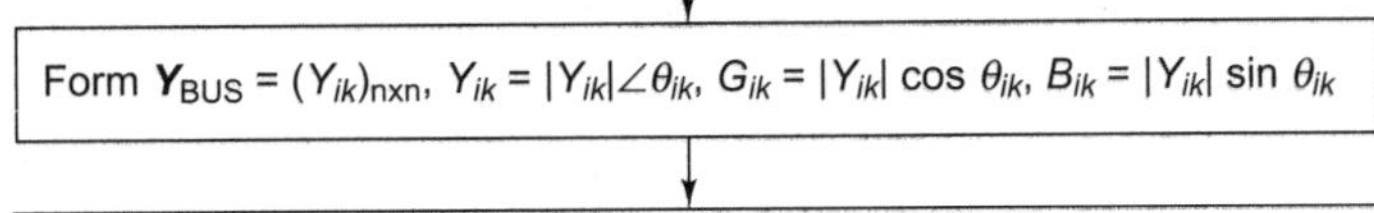

Make initial assumptions:
$|V_i|^0$ for $i = 2, \ldots, M$; δ_i^0 for $i = 2, \ldots, n$
$e_i^0 = |V_i|^0 \cos\delta_i^0$; $f_i^0 = |V_i|^0 \sin\delta_i^0$ for $i = 2, \ldots, n$
$e_i^0 = |V_i|^0 \cos\delta_i^0$; $f_i^0 = |V_i|^0 \sin\delta_i^0$ for $i = (m+1), \ldots, n$

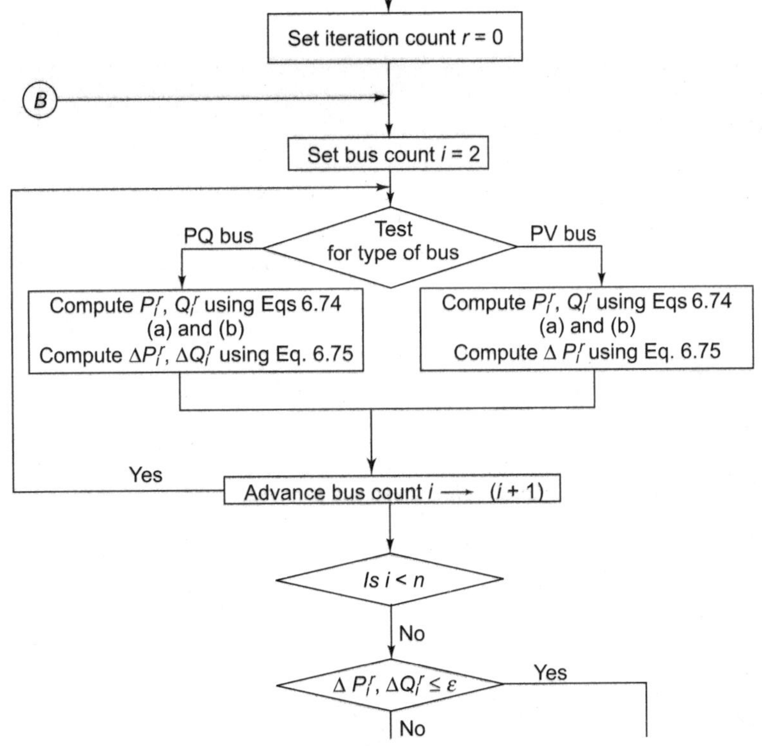

Fig. 6.18 (Contd.)

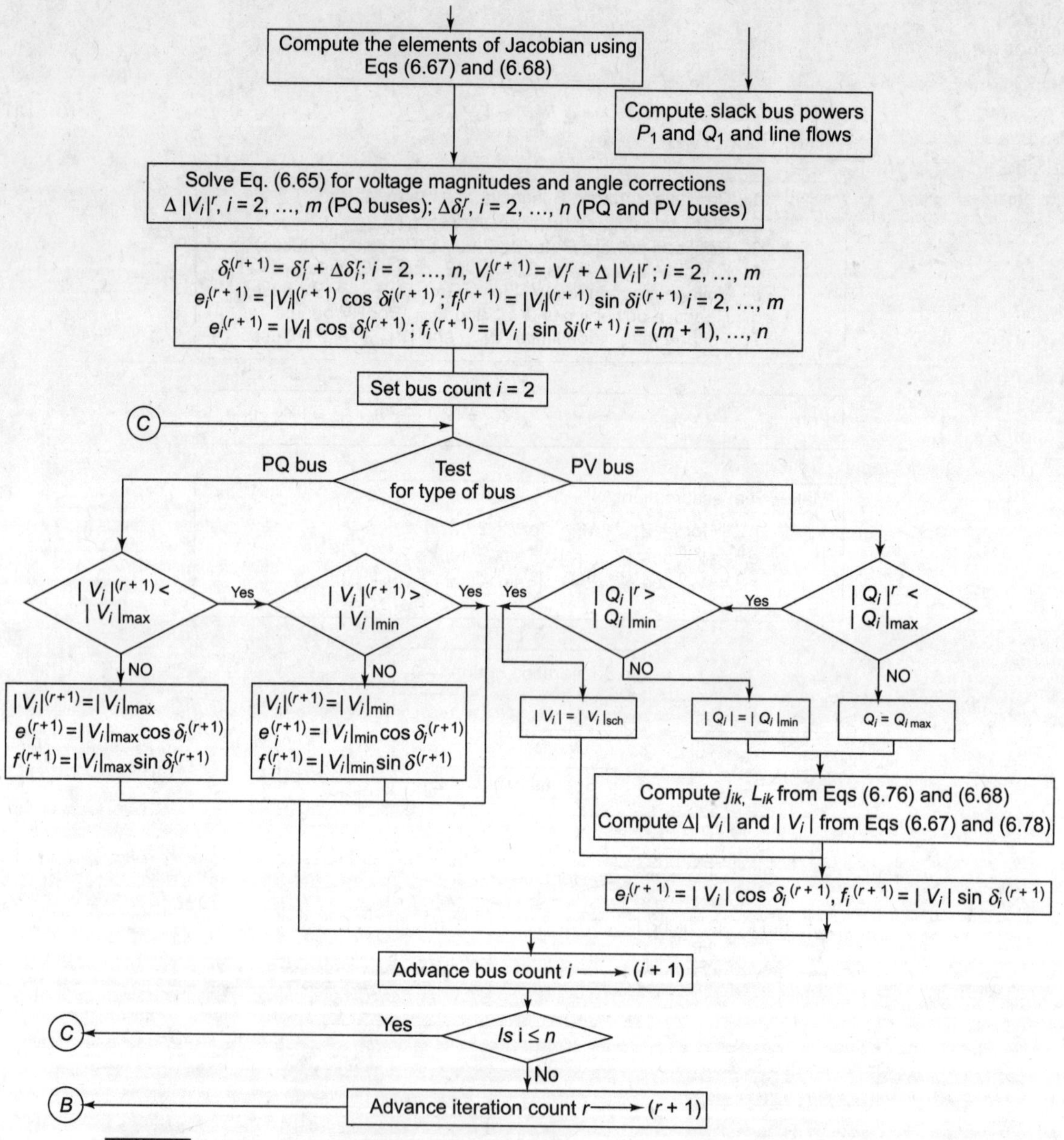

Fig. 6.18 *Flow chart for load flow solution by Newton–Raphson iterative method using* $\mathbf{Y}_{BUS}$

For $i = j$

$$
\begin{aligned}
J_{1,ii} &= a_i + G_{ii}e_i + B_{ii}f_i \\
J_{4,ii} &= a_i - G_{ii}e_i - B_{ii}f_i \\
J_{2,ii} &= b_i - B_{ii}e_i + G_{ii}f_i \\
J_{3,ii} &= b_i - B_{ii}e_i + G_{ii}f_i \\
J_{5,ii} &= 2e_i, J_{6,ii} = 2f_i
\end{aligned}
\tag{6.81b}
$$

a_i and b_i are the components of the current flowing into node i, i.e., for the rth iteration

$$I^r_i = a^r_i + jb^r_i = \sum_{k=1}^{n} (G_{ik} + jB_{ik})(e^r_k + jf^r_k) \tag{6.82}$$

Steps in solution procedure are similar to the polar coordinates case, except that the initial estimates of real and imaginary parts of the voltage at the PQ buses are made, and the corrections required are obtained in each iteration, using

$$\begin{bmatrix} \Delta e^{(r)} \\ \Delta f^{(r)} \end{bmatrix} = \begin{bmatrix} J_1^{(r)} & J_2^{(r)} \\ J_3^{(r)} & J_4^{(r)} \\ J_5^{(r)} & J_6^{(r)} \end{bmatrix}^{(-1)} \begin{bmatrix} \Delta P^{(r)} \\ \Delta Q^{(r)} \\ \Delta |V|^{2(r)} \end{bmatrix} \tag{6.83}$$

The corrections are then applied to e and f and the calculations are repeated till convergence is achieved. A detailed flow chart describing the procedure for load flow analysis using rectangular power-mismatch version by NR method is given in Fig. 6.19.

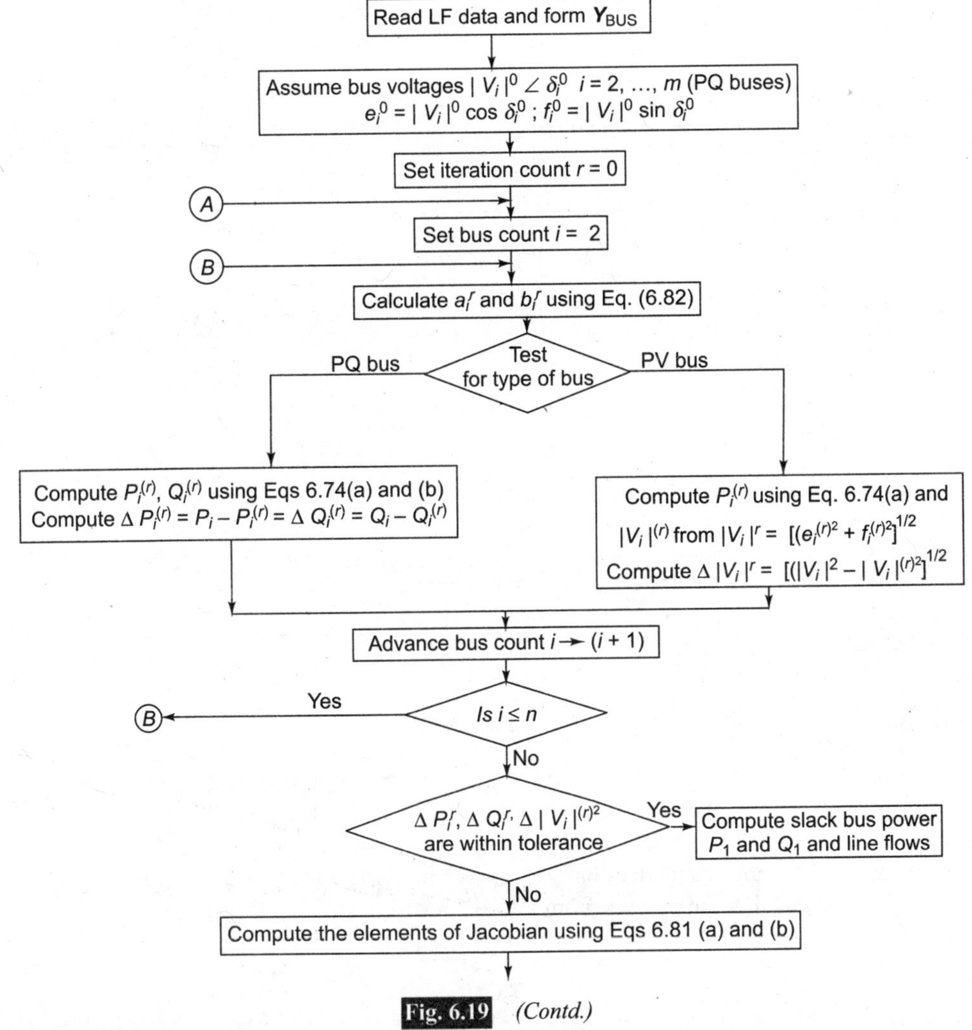

Fig. 6.19 *(Contd.)*

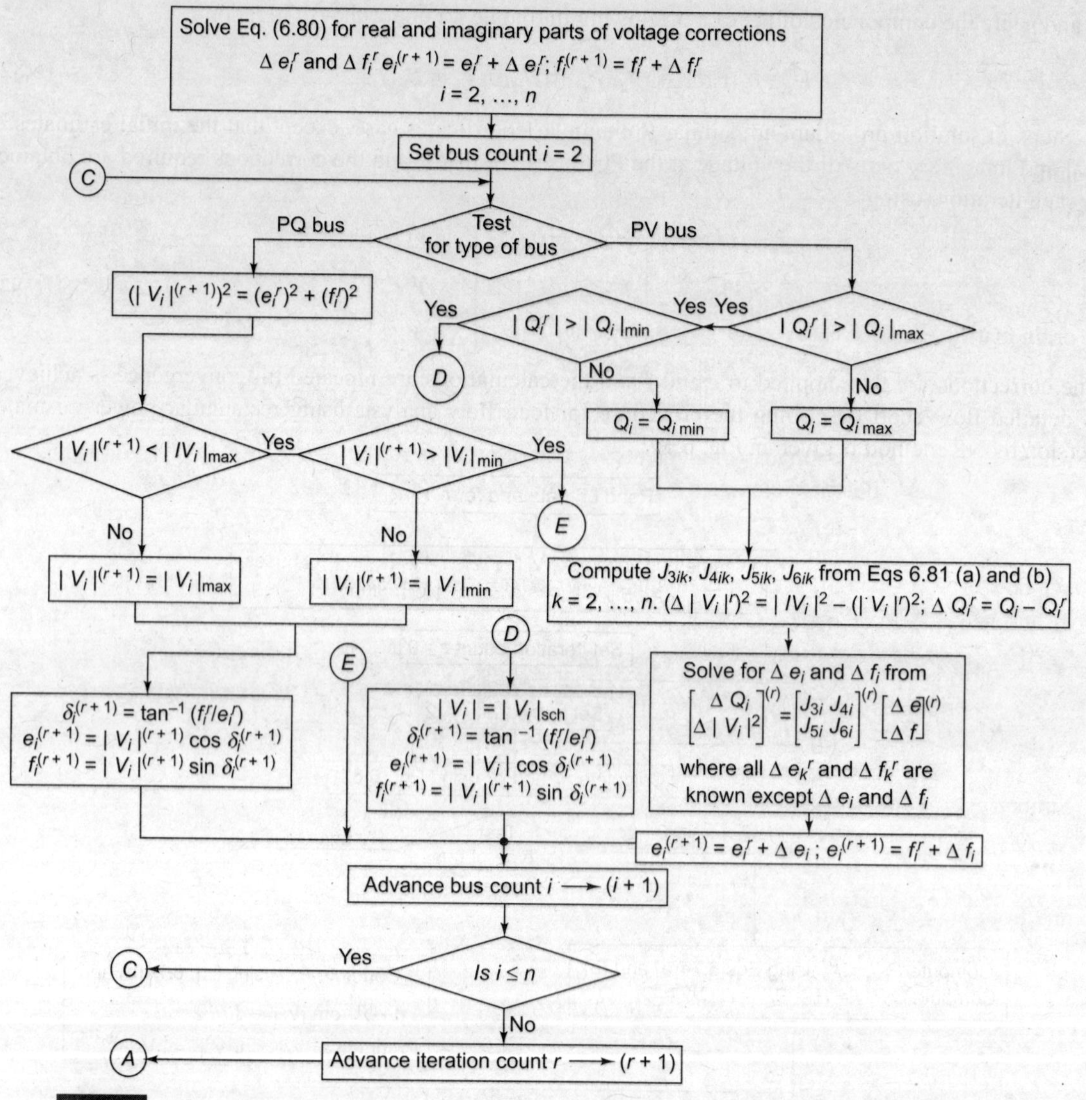

Fig. 6.19 *Flow chart of load flow analysis using rectangular power mismatch version by NR method*

6.7 ▶ DECOUPLED LOAD FLOW STUDIES

An important characteristic of any practical power transmission system operating in steady state is that the change in real power from the specified value at a bus is more dependent on the changes in voltage angles at various buses than the changes in voltage magnitudes, and the change in reactive power from the specified value at a bus is more dependent on the changes in voltage magnitudes at various buses than the changes in voltage angles. This can be seen from Eq. (6.65) by considering the values of Jacobian elements as follows:

After normalising the voltage corrections in Eq. (6.65), we get

$$\Delta P_i = \sum_{k=2}^{n} (H_{ik}\,\Delta\delta_k) + \sum_{k=2}^{m} (N_{ik}\Delta\,|V_k|/|V_k|) \tag{6.84a}$$

for both PQ and PV buses

and

$$\Delta Q_i = \sum_{k=2}^{n} (J_{ik}\,\Delta\delta_k) + \sum_{k=2}^{m} (L_{ik}\Delta\,|V_k|/|V_k|) \tag{6.84b}$$

for PQ buses

or, in matrix form

$$\begin{bmatrix} \Delta \boldsymbol{P} \\ \Delta \boldsymbol{Q} \end{bmatrix} = \begin{bmatrix} \boldsymbol{H} & \boldsymbol{N} \\ \boldsymbol{J} & \boldsymbol{L} \end{bmatrix} \begin{bmatrix} \Delta\delta \\ \Delta|\boldsymbol{V}|/|\boldsymbol{V}| \end{bmatrix} \tag{6.85}$$

where $\boldsymbol{H}$ is a square matrix of elements H_{ik} and of order $(n-1)$,
$\boldsymbol{N}$ is a matrix of elements N_{ik} and of order $(n-1)\times(m-1)$,
$\boldsymbol{J}$ is a matrix of elements J_{ik} and of order $(m-1)\times(n-1)$,
$\boldsymbol{L}$ is a square matrix of elements L_{ik} and of order $(m-1)$.

We now proceed to show that the elements N_{ik}, J_{ik} are small compared with the elements H_{ik}, L_{ik}. From Eq. (6.67)

$$\begin{aligned} H_{ik} = L_{ik} &= a_k f_i - b_k e_i \\ &= (G_{ik}e_k - B_{ik}f_k)f_i - (B_{ik}e_k + G_{ik}f_k)e_i \\ &= G_{ik}(e_k f_i - e_i f_k) - B_{ik}(f_i f_k + e_i e_k) \\ &= |V_i|\,|V_k|\,(G_{ik}\sin(\delta_i - \delta_k) - B_{ik}\cos(\delta_i - \delta_k)) \end{aligned} \tag{6.86a}$$

Similarly,

$$\begin{aligned} N_{ik} = -J_{ik} &= a_k e_i - b_k f_i \\ &= |V_i|\,|V_k|\,(G_{ik}\cos(\delta_i - \delta_k) + B_{ik}\sin(\delta_i - \delta_k)) \end{aligned} \tag{6.86b}$$

and from Eq. (6.68), and also from Eqs 6.28(a) and (b)

$$\begin{aligned} H_{ii} &= -Q_i - B_{ii}|V_i|^2 \\ &= -B_{ii}|V_i|^2 + \sum_{k=1}^{n} (|V_i|\,|V_k|\,|Y_{ik}|\sin(\theta_{ik} + \delta_k - \delta_i)) \\ &= -B_{ii}|V_i|^2 + \sum_{k=1}^{n} (|V_i|\,|V_k|\,(-G_{ik}\sin(\delta_i - \delta_k) + B_{ik}\cos(\delta_i - \delta_k))) \end{aligned} \tag{6.86c}$$

Similarly,

$$\begin{aligned} N_{ii} &= P_i + G_{ii}|V_i|^2 \\ &= G_{ii}|V_i|^2 + \sum_{k=1}^{n} (|V_i|\,|V_k|\,(G_{ik}\cos(\delta_i - \delta_k) + B_{ik}\sin(\delta_i - \delta_k))) \end{aligned} \tag{6.86d}$$

$$\begin{aligned} J_{ii} &= P_i - G_{ii}|V_i|^2 \\ &= -G_{ii}|V_i|^2 + \sum_{k=1}^{n} (|V_i|\,|V_k|\,(G_{ik}\cos(\delta_i - \delta_k) + B_{ik}\sin(\delta_i - \delta_k))) \end{aligned} \tag{6.86e}$$

$$L_{ii} = Q_i - B_{ii}|V_i|^2$$

$$= -B_{ii} | V_i|^2 + \sum_{k=1}^{n} (| V_i | | V_k | (G_{ik} \sin (\delta_i - \delta_k) - B_{ik} \cos (\delta_i - \delta_k))) \tag{6.86f}$$

where $\quad Y_{ik} = G_{ik} + jB_{ik} + | Y_{ik} | \angle\theta_{ik}$.

Since transmission lines are mostly reactive, the conductances, Gs are very small compared to the susceptances, Bs. Also, under normal operating conditions, the angle $(\delta_i - \delta_k)$ is small (typically less than 10°). Utilising these characteristics of the transmission system in Eqs. 6.86(a) to (f), we find that the elements Ns and Js are small compared to the elements Hs and Ls, and hence are neglected. Thus, Eqs. 6.84(a) and (b) become

$$\Delta P_i = \sum_{k=2}^{n} H_{ik} \Delta\delta_k \qquad i = 2, ..., n \tag{6.87a}$$

$$\Delta Q_i = \sum_{k=2}^{m} L_{ik} \frac{\Delta|V_k|}{|V_k|} \qquad i = 2, ..., n \tag{6.87b}$$

Thus, there is a fairly good decoupling between the equations for active power and reactive power. This decoupling feature can be used in simplifying the NR algorithm for load flow analysis.

6.7.1 Decoupled Newton Method

On neglecting the elements of N and J matrix, Eq. (6.85) reduces to

$$\begin{bmatrix} \Delta \boldsymbol{P} \\ \Delta \boldsymbol{Q} \end{bmatrix} = \begin{bmatrix} \boldsymbol{H} & \boldsymbol{0} \\ \boldsymbol{0} & \boldsymbol{L} \end{bmatrix} \begin{bmatrix} \Delta\delta \\ \dfrac{\Delta|\boldsymbol{V}|}{|\boldsymbol{V}|} \end{bmatrix} \tag{6.88}$$

or

$$[\Delta \boldsymbol{P}] = [\boldsymbol{H}] [\Delta\delta] \tag{6.89a}$$

$$[\Delta \boldsymbol{Q}] = [\boldsymbol{L}] [\Delta | \boldsymbol{V}|/| \boldsymbol{V}|] \tag{6.89b}$$

Equations 6.89(a) and (b) can be constructed and solved simultaneously with each other at each iteration, updating the $(\boldsymbol{H})$ and $(\boldsymbol{L})$ matrices in each iteration using Eqs. 6.86(a), (c) and (f). A better approach is to conduct each iteration by first solving Eq. (6.89a) for $\Delta\delta$, and use the updated δ in constructing and then solving Eq. (6.89b) for $\Delta | \boldsymbol{V}|$. This will result in Eqs. 6.84 (a)–(f) faster convergence than in the simultaneous mode.

The main advantage of the Decoupled Load Flow (DLF) as compared to the NR method is its reduced memory requirements in storing the Jacobian elements. Storage of the Jacobian and matrix triangularisation is saved by a factor 4, that is an overall saving of 30–40 per cent on the formal Newton load flow. Computation time per iteration is less than the Newton method. However, the DLF takes more number of iterations to converge because of the approximation made.

6.7.2 Fast Decoupled Load Flow (FDLF)

The Jacobian of the decoupled Newton load flow can be made constant in value, based on physically justifiable assumptions. Hence, the triangularisation has to be done only once per solution. The Fast Decoupled Load Flow (FDLF) was developed by B. Stott in 1974 [20] in the process of further simplifications and assumptions. The assumptions which are valid in normal power system operation are made as follows:

$$\cos \delta_{ik} \cong 1 \tag{6.90}$$

$$\sin \delta_{ik} \cong 0 \tag{6.91}$$

$$G_{ij} \sin \delta_{ik} << B_{ik}; \text{ and}$$
$$Q_i << B_{ii} | V_i |^2$$

With these assumptions, the entries of the [*H*] and [*L*] submatrices become considerably simplified, and are given by

$$H_{ik} = L_{ik} = -| V_i | | V_k | B_{ik} \qquad i \neq k \tag{6.92a}$$
$$H_{ii} = L_{ii} = -B_{ii} | V_i |^2 \qquad i = k \tag{6.92b}$$

Matrices [*H*] and [*L*] are square matrices with dimensions (n – 1) and (m – 1), respectively, (m – 1 = number of PQ buses, and n – 1 = number of PQ and PV buses).

Equations 6.87(a) and (b) can now be written as (after substituting the values of H_{ik}, L_{ik}, H_{ii}, L_{ii} from Eqs. 6.92(a) and (b)

$$\frac{\Delta P_i}{|V_i|} = -\sum_{k=2}^{n} | V_k | B_{ik} \Delta\delta_k \qquad i = 2, ..., n \tag{6.93a}$$

$$\frac{\Delta Q_i}{|V_i|} = -\sum_{k=2}^{n} B_{ik} \Delta | V_k | \qquad i = 2, ..., m \tag{6.93b}$$

Setting $| V_k | = 1$ pu on the RHS of Eq. 6.93(a), we get

$$\frac{\Delta P_i}{|V_i|} = \sum_{k=2}^{n} [-B_{ik}] \Delta\delta_k \qquad i = 2, ..., n$$

$$\frac{\Delta Q_i}{|V_i|} = \sum_{k=2}^{n} [-B_{ik}] \Delta | V_k | \qquad i = 2, ..., m$$

or in matrix form, after writing for all i's, we get

$$\left[\frac{\Delta \boldsymbol{P}}{|\boldsymbol{V}|}\right]_{(n-1)\times 1} = [\boldsymbol{B}']_{(n-1)\times(n-1)} [\Delta\delta]_{(n-1)\times 1} \tag{6.94a}$$

$$\left[\frac{\Delta \boldsymbol{Q}}{|\boldsymbol{V}|}\right]_{(m-1)\times 1} = [\boldsymbol{B}'']_{(m-1)\times(m-1)} [\Delta | \boldsymbol{V} |]_{(m-1)\times 1} \tag{6.94b}$$

where $\boldsymbol{B}'$ and $\boldsymbol{B}''$ are matrices of elements $-B_{ik}$ ($i = 2, ..., n$ and $k = 2, ..., n$) and $-B_{ik}$ ($i = 2, ..., m$ and $k = 2, ..., n$)

Further simplification of the FDLF algorithm is achieved by

1. Omitting the elements of [*B′*] that predominantly affect reactive power flows, i.e., shunt reactances and transformer off-nominal in-phase taps.
2. Omitting from [*B″*] the angle shifting effect of phase shifter (that which predominantly affects real power flow).
3. Ignoring the series resistance in calculating the elements of [*B′*], which then becomes the DC approximation of the power flow matrix.

After these simplifications, Eqs. 6.94(a) and (b) are rewritten as

$$[\Delta \boldsymbol{P} / | \boldsymbol{V} |] = [\boldsymbol{B}'] [\Delta\delta] \tag{6.95a}$$
$$[\Delta \boldsymbol{Q} / | \boldsymbol{V} |] = [\boldsymbol{B}''] [\Delta | \boldsymbol{V} |] \tag{6.95b}$$

In Eqs. 6.95(a) and (b), both (*B′*) and (*B″*) are real, sparse and have the structures of [*H*] and [*L*], respectively. Since they contain only admittances, they are constant and need to be triangularised (or inverted) only once at the beginning of load flow analysis. If the phase shifters are not present, both [*B′*] and [*B″*] are always symmetrical, and their constant sparse upper triangular factors are calculated and stored only once at the beginning of the solution.

Equations 6.95(a) and (b) are solved alternatively, always employing the most recent voltage values. One iteration implies one solution for [$\Delta\delta$], to update [δ], and then one solution for [$\Delta |V|$], to update [$|V|$] to be called $1-\delta$ and $1-V$ iteration. Separate convergence tests are applied for the real and reactive power mismatches as follows:

$$\max [\Delta \boldsymbol{P}] \leq \varepsilon_P; \text{ and } \max [\Delta \boldsymbol{Q}] \leq \varepsilon_Q$$

where ε_P and ε_Q are the tolerances.

In FDLF method usually two to five iterations are required for practical accuracies. The method is more reliable than the formal NR method. The speed for iterations is about five times that of the formal NR method or about two-thirds that of the GS method. Storage requirements are about 60 per cent of the formal NR method, but slightly more than the DLF method.

A flow chart giving FDLF algorithm is presented in Fig. 6.20.

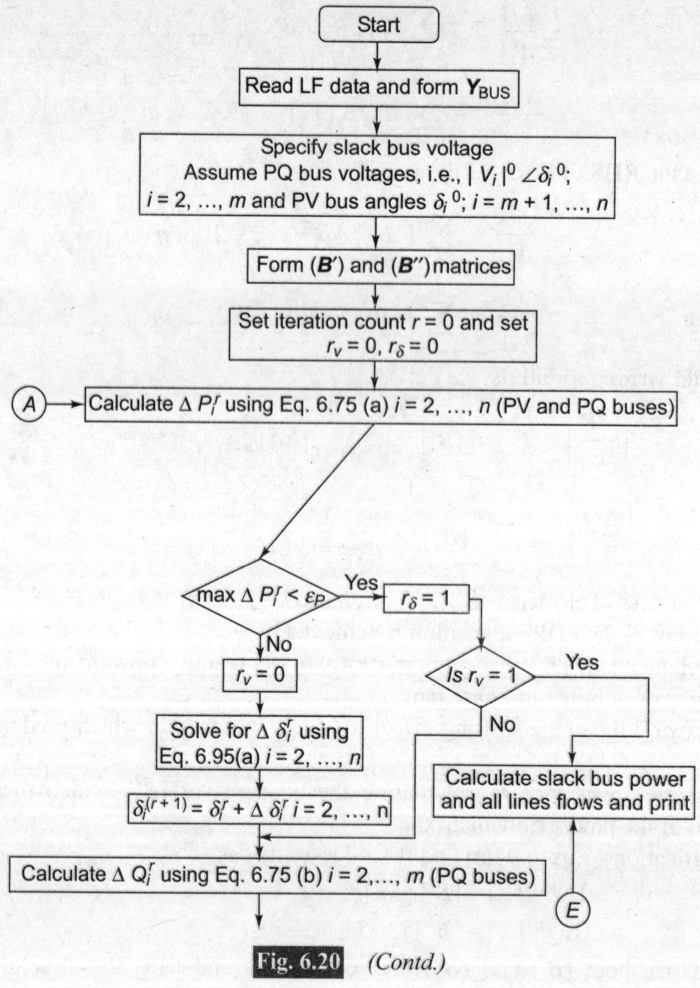

Fig. 6.20 *(Contd.)*

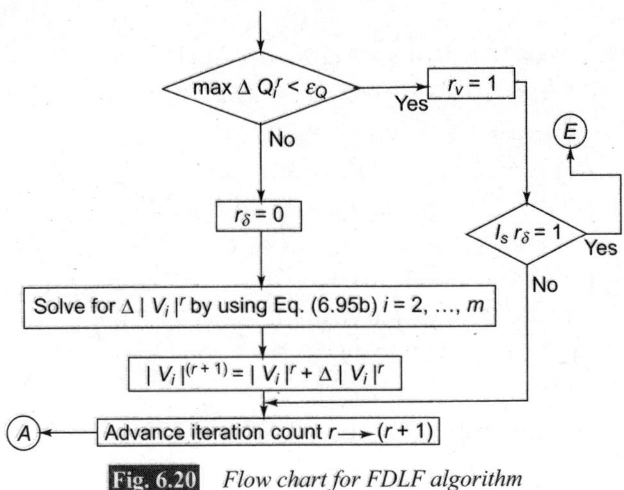

Fig. 6.20 *Flow chart for FDLF algorithm*

Example 6.11 Consider the three-bus system of Example 6.10 (Fig. 6.17). Use (a) Decoupled NR method and (b) FDLF method to obtain one iteration of the load flow solution.

Solution

(a) *Decoupled NR method*: The equations to be solved are 6.89(a) and (b). Substituting relevant values in Eqs. 6.86(a), (c) and (f), we have

$$H_{22}^{(0)} = 0.96 + 23.508 = 24.47$$

$$H_{23}^{(0)} = H_{32}^{(0)} = 1.04(-B_{23}) = -1.04 \times 11.764 = -12.23$$

$$\begin{aligned} H_{33}^{(0)} &= -Q_3 - B_{33}\,(1.04)^2 \\ &= (-B_{31}\,|\,V_3\,|^2 - B_{32}\,|\,V_3\,|^2 - B_{33}\,|\,V_3\,|^2) - B_{33}\,(1.04)^2 \\ &= -11.764 \times (1.04)^2 - 11.764 \times 1.04 + (1.04)^2 \times 2 \times 23.508 \\ &= 25.89 \end{aligned}$$

$$L_{22}^{(0)} = Q_2 - B_{22} = 1 + 23.508 = 24.508$$

$$\begin{bmatrix} \Delta P_2 \\ \Delta P_3 \end{bmatrix}^{(0)} = \begin{bmatrix} H_{22} & H_{23} \\ H_{32} & H_{33} \end{bmatrix}^{(0)} \begin{bmatrix} \Delta\delta_2 \\ \Delta\delta_3 \end{bmatrix}^{(0)} \tag{i}$$

and

$$[\Delta Q_2]^{(0)} = [L_{22}]^{(0)} \left[\frac{\Delta |V_2|}{|V_2|} \right]^{(0)}$$

From Example 6.10,

$$\Delta P_2^{(0)} = 0.73$$

$$\Delta P_3^{(0)} = -1.62$$

Therefore,

$$\begin{bmatrix} 0.73 \\ -1.62 \end{bmatrix} = \begin{bmatrix} 24.47 & -12.23 \\ -12.23 & 25.89 \end{bmatrix} \begin{bmatrix} \Delta\delta_2^{(0)} \\ \Delta\delta_3^{(0)} \end{bmatrix}$$

$$[\Delta Q_2^{(0)}] = [24.51] \left[\frac{\Delta |V_2|^{(1)}}{|V_2|^{(1)}} \right] \tag{ii}$$

Solving Eq. (i), we get

$$\Delta\delta_2^{(0)} = -0.0082 - 0.0401 = -0.002 \text{ rad} = -0.115°$$

$$\Delta\delta_3^{(0)} = -0.018 - 0.08 = -0.062 \text{ rad} = -3.55°$$

$$\delta_2^{(1)} = \delta_2^{(0)} + \Delta\delta_2^{(0)} = 0 - 0.155° = -0.115°$$

$$\delta_3^{(0)} = \delta_3^{(0)} + \Delta\delta_3^{(0)} = 0 - 3.55° = -3.55°$$

$$Q_2^{(0)} = [-|V_2||V_1||Y_{21}|\sin(\theta_{21} + \delta_1 - \delta_2^{(1)}) - |V_2|^2|Y_{22}|\sin\theta_{22} - |V_2||V_3||Y_{23}|\sin(\theta_{23} + \delta_2^{(1)} - \delta_3^{(1)})]$$

$$Q_2^{(0)} = (-1.04 \times 12.13 \sin(104.04° + 0° - 0.115°) - 24.23 \sin(-75.95°) - 1.04 \times 12.13 \sin(104.04° + 0.115° - 3.55°))$$

$$= -12.24 + 23.505 - 12.39$$

$$\therefore \quad Q_2^{(0)} = -1.125$$

$$\therefore \quad \Delta Q_2^{(0)} = Q_2\,(\text{specified}) - Q_2{}^0 = 1 - (-1.125) = 2.125$$

Substituting in Eq. (ii),

$$(2.115) = (24.51)\left[\frac{\Delta|V_2^0|}{|V_2^{(0)}|}\right]$$

$$\therefore \quad \Delta|V_2^{(0)}| = 0.086$$

or

$$|V_2^{(1)}| = |V_2^{(0)}| + \Delta|V_2^{(0)}|$$

$$= 1.086 \text{ pu}$$

$Q_3^{(0)}$ can be similarly calculated using Eq. (6.28).

(b) *FDLF Method:* The matrix equations for the solution of load flow by FDLF method are [see Eqs. 6.95(a) and (b)]

$$\begin{bmatrix} \dfrac{\Delta P_2^{(0)}}{|V_2^{(0)}|} \\ \dfrac{\Delta P_3^{(0)}}{|V_3^{(0)}|} \end{bmatrix} = \begin{bmatrix} -B_{22} & -B_{23} \\ -B_{23} & -B_{33} \end{bmatrix} \begin{bmatrix} \Delta\delta_2^{(0)} \\ \Delta\delta_3^{(0)} \end{bmatrix} \tag{iii}$$

and

$$\left[\frac{\Delta Q_2^{(0)}}{|V_2^{(0)}|}\right] = [-B_{22}]\,[\Delta|V_2^{(0)}|] \tag{iv}$$

$$\begin{bmatrix} \dfrac{0.73}{1} = 0.73 \\ \dfrac{-1.62}{1.04} = -1.557 \end{bmatrix} = \begin{bmatrix} 23.508 & -11.764 \\ -11.764 & 23.508 \end{bmatrix} \begin{bmatrix} \Delta\delta_2^{(0)} \\ \Delta\delta_3^{(0)} \end{bmatrix} \tag{v}$$

Solving Eq. (v), we get

$$\Delta\delta_2^{(0)} = -0.003 \text{ rad}$$

$$\Delta\delta_3^{(0)} = -0.068 \text{ rad}$$

$$\delta_2^{(1)} = 0 - 0.003 = -0.003 \text{ rad}$$

$$\delta_3^{(1)} = 0 - 0.068 = -0.008 \text{ rad}$$

From Eq. (iv), we have

$$(2.125) = (23.508)\ (\Delta\,|\,V_2^{(1)}\,|)$$
$$\Delta\,|\,V_2^{(0)}| = 0.09$$
$$|\,V_2^{(1)}\,| = |\,V_2^{(0)}\,| + \Delta\,|\,V_2^{(0)}\,|$$
$$= 1 + 0.09$$
$$|\,V_2^{(1)}| = 1.09$$

Now, Q_3 can be calculated.

These values are used to compute bus power mismatches for the next iteration. Using the values of $(\Delta \boldsymbol{P}/|\,V|)$ and $(\Delta \boldsymbol{Q}/|\,V|)$, the above equations are solved alternatively, with the most recent values, till the solution converges within the specified limits.

6.8 ▶ COMPARISON OF LOAD FLOW METHODS

In this section, GS and NR methods are compared when both use $\boldsymbol{Y}_{\text{BUS}}$ as the network model. It is experienced that the GS method works well when programmed using rectangular co-ordinates, whereas the NR method requires more memory when rectangular coordinates are used. Hence, polar coordinates are preferred for the NR method. However, to avoid time consuming sine and cosine terms in the Jacobian elements in the polar version of NR method, the elements of the Jacobian are calculated by the rectangular version. The rectangular version is faster in convergence, but slightly less reliable than the polar version.

The GS method requires the smallest number of arithmetic operations to complete an iteration. This is because of the sparsity of the network matrix and the simplicity of the solution techniques. Consequently, this method requires less time per iteration. With the NR method, the power differences and elements of the Jacobian are to be computed per iteration and triangularisation has also to be done per iteration, so that the time taken per iteration is considerably longer. For the typical large systems, the time per iteration in the NR method is roughly equivalent to 7 times that of the GS method [19]. The time per iteration in both these methods increases almost directly as the number of buses of the network.

The rate of convergence of the GS method is slow (linear convergence characteristic), requiring a considerably greater number of iterations to obtain a solution than the NR method. Due to quadratic convergence of bus voltages, in the NR method, high accuracy is obtained only in a few iterations. In addition, the number of iterations for the GS method increases directly as the number of buses of the network, whereas the number of iterations for the NR method remains practically constant, independent of the system size. The NR method needs 3 to 5 iterations to reach an acceptable solution for a large system. In the GS and other methods, convergence is affected by the choice of the slack bus and the presence of series capacitor, but the sensitivity of the NR method is minimal to these factors which cause poor convergence. Therefore, for large systems, the NR method is faster and more accurate (near exact solution) than the GS or any other known method. In fact, it works for any size and kind of problem and is able to solve a wider variety of ill-conditioned problems [22]. The NR method is also more reliable than the GS method.

The chief advantage of the GS method is the ease of programming and most efficient utilisation of core memory. It is, however, restricted in use to small size systems because of its doubtful convergence and longer time needed for solution of large power networks. The programming logic of NR method is complex and it has the disadvantage of requiring a large computer memory, even when a compact storage scheme is used for the Jacobian and admittance matrices. The NR method can be made even faster by adopting the scheme of optimally renumbered buses. The method is best suited for optimal load flow studies (Ch. 7) because of its high accuracy which is restricted only by round off errors.

Thus, the NR method is decidedly more suitable than the GS method for all but very small systems.

The reliability of decoupled Newton method is comparable to the formal Newton method for ill-conditioned problems. But, the decoupled method is simple and computationally efficient than the formal Newton method. Also, the storage of Jacobian elements and triangularisation is saved by a factor of 4 in the decoupled method and computation time per iteration is less than the Newton method. However, the convergence characteristics of the decoupled method are geometric compared to the quadratic convergence of the Newton method. Thus, for high accuracies, more iterations are required by the decoupled Newton method.

For FDLF method, the convergence is geometric; 2 to 5 iterations are normally required for practical accuracies. This is due to the fact that the elements of $[B']$ and $[B'']$ are fixed approximations to the tangents of the defining functions $\Delta P/|V|$ and $\Delta Q/|V|$, and are not sensitive to any humps in the defining functions. If $\Delta P/|V|$ and $\Delta Q/|V|$ are calculated efficiently, then the speed for iterations of the FDLF is nearly five times that of the formal NR or about two-thirds that of the GS method. Storage requirements are around 60 per cent of the formal NR method, but slightly more than the decoupled NR method.

Because of high accuracies obtained in only a few iterations, the NR method is important for the use of load flow in short-circuit and stability studies. The method can be readily extended to include tap-changing transformers, variable constraints on bus voltages, optimal real and reactive power scheduling. Network modifications can be easily made. The FDLF can be employed in optimisation studies, and is specially used for obtaining information of both real and reactive power for multiple load flow studies, as in contingency evaluation for system security assessment and enhancement analysis.

Note: When a series of load flow calculations are performed, the final values of bus voltages in each case are normally used as the initial voltages of the next case. This reduces the number of iterations, particularly when there are minor changes in system conditions.

The comparison of Load Flow Methods is summarised in Table 6.6

Table 6.6 Comparison of Load Flow Methods

Sl. No.	*Parameter of Comparison*	*Gauss Siedel*	*Newton Raphson*	*Fast Decoupled Load Flow*
1.	Coordinates	Works well with Rectangular Coordinates	Polar coordinates preferred as rectangular coordinates occupies more memory	Polar coordinates
2.	Arithmetic operations	Least in number to completer one iteration	Elements of Jacobian to be calculated in each iteration	Less than Newton Raphson
3.	Time	Requires less time per iteration, but increases with in number of buses	Time/iteration is 7 times of Gauss Siedal and increases with increase in number of buses	Less time when compared to Newton Raphson and Gauss Siedal
4.	Convergence	Linear convergence	Quadratic convergence	Geometric convergence
5.	No. of iterations	Larger number, increases with increase in buses	Very less (3 to 5 only) for large systems and is practically constant	Only 2 to 5 iterations for practical accuracies
6.	Slack bus selection	Choice of slack bus affects convergence adversely	Sensitivity to this is minimal	Moderate
7.	Accuracy	Less accurate	More accurate	Moderate

(Contd.)

Table 6.6 (Contd.)

Sl. No.	Parameter of Comparison	Gauss Siedel	Newton Raphson	Fast Decoupled Load Flow
8.	Memory	Less memory because of sparsity of matrix	Large memory even with compact storage scheme	Only 60% of memory when compared to NR
9.	Usage/application	Small size systems	Large systems, ill-conditioned problems, optimal load flow studies	Optimisation studies, multiple load flow studies, contingency evaluation for security assessment and enhancement
10.	Programming Logic	Easy	Very difficult	Moderate
11.	Reliability	Reliable only for small systems	Reliable even for large systems	More reliable than NR method

6.9 ▶ CONTROL OF VOLTAGE PROFILE

6.9.1 Control by Generators

Control of voltage at the receiving bus in the fundamental two-bus system was discussed in Section 5.10. Though the same general conclusions hold for an interconnected system, it is important to discuss this problem in greater detail.

At a bus with generation, voltage can be conveniently controlled by adjusting generator excitation. This is illustrated by means of Fig. 6.21, where the equivalent generator at the ith bus is modelled by a synchronous reactance (resistance is assumed negligible) and voltage behind synchronous reactance.

| E_{Gi} | $\angle\delta_{Gi}$ $\quad jX_{Gi}$ $\quad P_{Gi} + jQ_{Gi}$ $\quad P_i + jQ_i$ $\quad P_{Di} + jQ_{Di}$ $\quad$ Power system

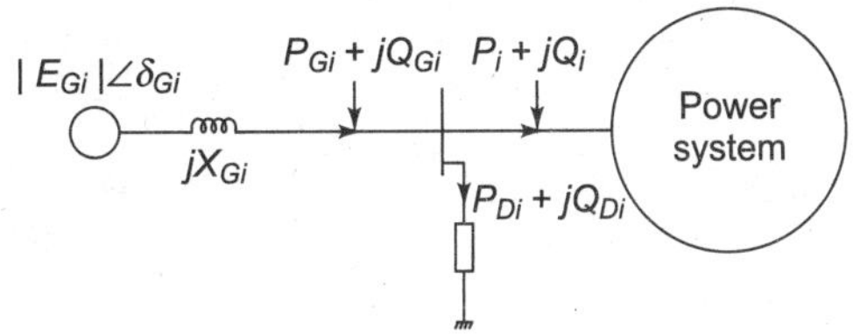

Fig. 6.21 *Voltage control by adjusting generator excitation*

It immediately follows upon application of Eqs. (5.71) and (5.73) that

$$P_{Gi} = \frac{|V_i||E_{Gi}|}{X_{Gi}} \sin(\delta_{Gi} - \delta_i) \tag{6.96a}$$

$$Q_{Gi} = \frac{|V_i|}{X_{Gi}} (-|V_i| + |E_{Gi}|) \tag{6.96b}$$

With $(P_{Gi} + jQ_{Gi})$ and $|V_i| \angle\delta_i$ given by the load flow solution, these values can be achieved at the bus by adjusting generator excitation to give $|E_{Gi}|$ as required by Eq. (6.96b), and by adjusting the governor setting so that the power input to generator from turbine is P_{Gi} plus losses, resulting in load angle of $(\delta_{Gi} - \delta_i)$ corresponding to Eq. 6.96(a). If Q_{Gi} demand exceeds the capacity of generators, VAR generators (synchronous or static capacitor) have to be used to modify the local demand.

6.9.2 Control by VAR Generators (Synchronous or Static Capacitors)

It follows from above that to control the voltage profile of an interconnected system, buses with generators are usually made PV (i.e., voltage control) buses. Load flow solution then gives the voltage levels at the load buses. If some of the load bus voltages work out to be less than the specified lower voltage limit, it is indicative of the fact that the reactive power flow capacity of transmission lines for specified voltage limits cannot meet the reactive load demand (reactive line flow from bus i to bus k is proportional to $|\Delta V| = |V_i| - |V_k|$. This situation can be remedied by installing VAR generators at some of the load buses. These buses in the load flow analysis are then regarded as PV buses with the resulting solution giving the requisite values of VAR (jQ_C) injection at these buses.

The fact that positive VAR injection at any bus of an interconnected system would help to raise the voltage at the bus is easily demonstrated as follows:

Figure 6.22(a) shows the Thevenin equivalent circuit of the power system as seen from the ith bus. Obviously, $E_{th} = V_i$. If now jQ_C from the VAR generator is injected into this bus as shown in Fig. 6.22(b), we have from Eq. (5.73)

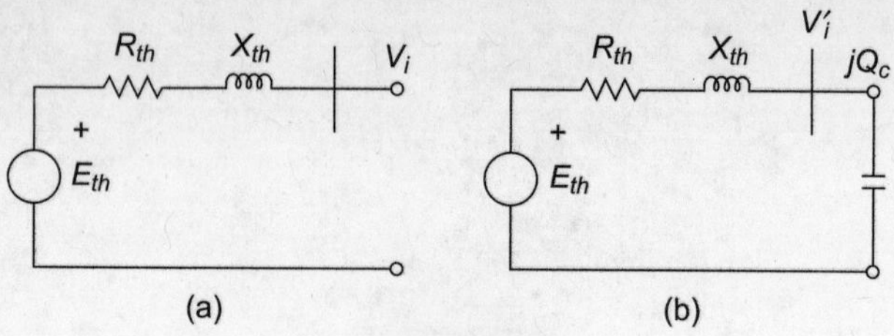

R_{th} X_{th} V_i E_{th} (a)

R_{th} X_{th} V_i' jQ_c E_{th} (b)

Fig. 6.22

$$|\Delta V| = |E_{th}| - |V_i'| = -\frac{X_{th}}{|V_i'|} Q_C$$

or

$$|V_i'| = |E_{th}| + \left[\frac{X_{th}}{|V_i'|}\right] Q_C = |V_i| + \left[\frac{X_{th}}{|V_i'|}\right] Q_C$$

Since we are considering a voltage rise of a few per cent, $|V_i'|$ can be further approximated as

$$|V_i'| \cong |V_i| + \left[\frac{X_{th}}{|V_i|}\right] Q_C \tag{6.97}$$

Thus, the VAR injection of $+jQ_C$ causes the voltage at the ith bus to rise approximately by $(X_{th}/|V_i|)Q_C$. The voltage at other load buses will also rise owing to this injection to a varying, but smaller, extent.

6.9.3 Control by Transformers

Transformers provide a convenient means of controlling real power, and reactive power flow along a transmission line. As has already been clarified, real power is controlled by means of shifting the phase of voltage, and reactive power, by changing its magnitude. Voltage magnitude can be changed by transformers provided with tap changing under load (TCUL) gear. Transformers specially designed to adjust voltage magnitude or phase angle through small values are called regulating transformers.

Figure 6.23 shows a regulating transformer for control of voltage magnitude, which is achieved by adding in-phase boosting voltage in the line.

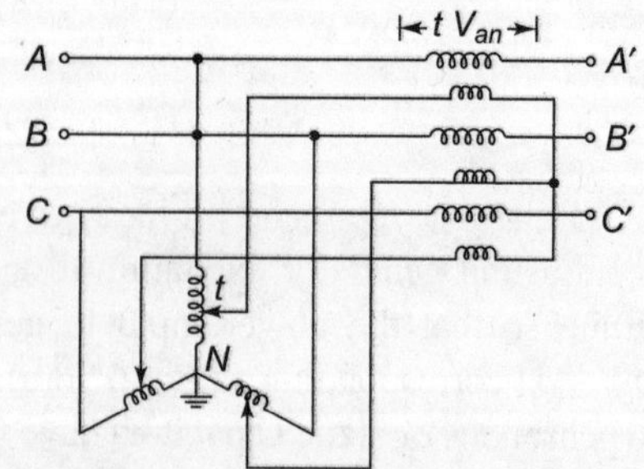

Fig. 6.23 *Regulating transformer for control of voltage magnitude*

Figure 6.24(a) shows a regulating transformer which shifts voltage phase angle with no appreciable change in its magnitude. This is achieved by adding a voltage in series with the line at 90° phase angle to the corresponding line to neutral voltage as illustrated by means of phasor diagram of Fig. 6.24(b). Here

$$V'_{an} = (V_{an} + tV_{bc}) = (1 - j\sqrt{3}t)V_{an} = aV_{an} \tag{6.98}$$

where

$$a = (1 - j\sqrt{3}t) \simeq 1\angle - \tan^{-1}\sqrt{3}\,t$$

since t is small.

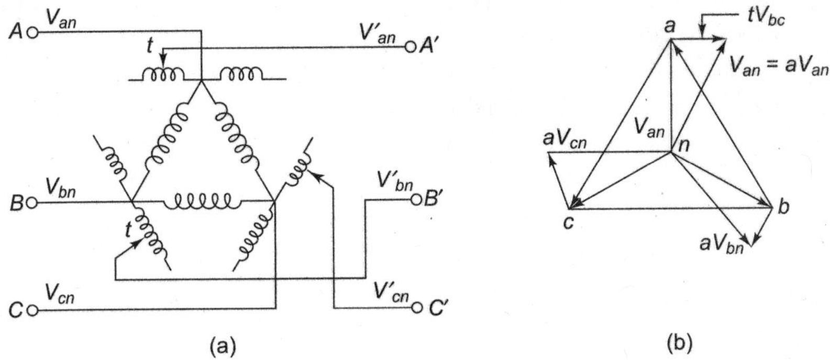

Fig. 6.24 *Regulating transformer for control and voltage phase angle*

The presence of regulating transformers in lines modifies the Y_{BUS} matrix, thereby modifying the load flow solution. Consider a line, connecting two buses, having a regulating transformer with off-nominal turns (tap) ratio a included at one end as shown in Fig. 6.25(a). It is quite accurate to neglect the small impedance of the regulating transformer, i.e., it is regarded as an ideal device. Figure 6.25(b) gives the corresponding circuit representation with line represented by a series admittance.

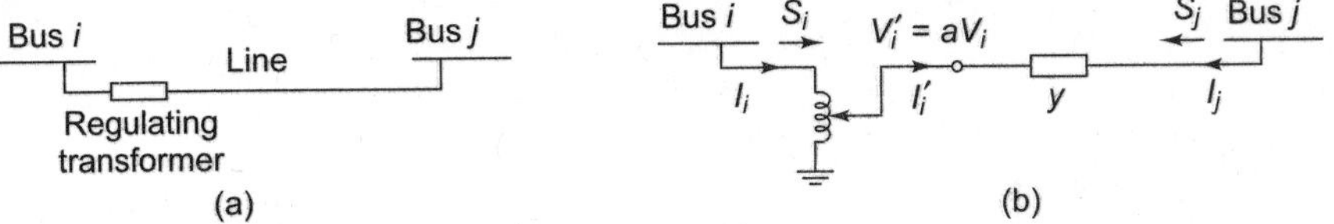

Fig. 6.25 *Line with regulating transformer and its circuit representation*

Since the transformer is assumed to be ideal, the complex power output from it equals complex power input,

i.e.,

$$S_i = V_i I_i^* = V_i' I_i'^*$$

or

$$V_i I_i^* = aV_i I_i'^*$$

or

$$I_i = a^* I_i' \tag{6.99}$$

For the transmission line

$$I_i' = y(aV_i - V_j)$$

or

$$I_i = a^* I_i' = |a|^2 yV_i - a^* yV_j \tag{6.100a}$$

Also,

$$I_j = y(V_j - aV_i) = -ayV_i + yV_j \tag{6.100b}$$

Equations 6.100(a) and (b) cannot be represented by a bilateral network. The $\boldsymbol{Y}$ matrix representation can be written down as follows from Eqs. 6.100(a) and (b).

$$\boldsymbol{Y} = \begin{matrix} & i & j \\ i & a^2 y & -a^* y \\ j & -ay & y \end{matrix} \tag{6.101}$$

where y is the series admittance of the line. The entries of $\boldsymbol{Y}$ matrix of Eq. (6.101) would then be used in writing the $\boldsymbol{Y}_{\text{BUS}}$ matrix of the complete power network.

Equations 6.100(a) and (b) can also be written as

$$\begin{aligned} I_i &= a^*y(V_i - V_j) - a^*yV_i + |a|^2 yV_i \\ &= a^*(a-1)yV_i + a^*y(V_i - V_j) \end{aligned} \tag{6.102a}$$

and

$$\begin{aligned} I_j &= ay(V_j - V_i) - ayV_j + yV_j \\ &= y(1 - ay)V_j + ay(V_j - V_i) \end{aligned} \tag{6.102b}$$

The above equations for I_i and I_j cannot be represented by the π-network because

$$y_{ij} = \left. \frac{I_i}{V_j} \right|_{V_i = 0, V_j \neq 0} = -a^*y$$

$$y_{ji} = \left. \frac{I_j}{V_i} \right|_{V_j = 0, V_i \neq 0} = -ay$$

i.e., because $y_{ij} \neq y_{ji}$.

For a voltage regulating transformer a is real i.e., $a^* = a$; therefore, Eqs. 102(a) and (b) become

$$I_i = a(a-1)yV_i + ay(V_i - V_j)$$
$$I_j = (1-a)y\,V_j + ay(V_j - V_i)$$

which can be represented by the π-network of Fig. 6.26. Here we note that $y_{ij} = y_{ji} = -ay$.

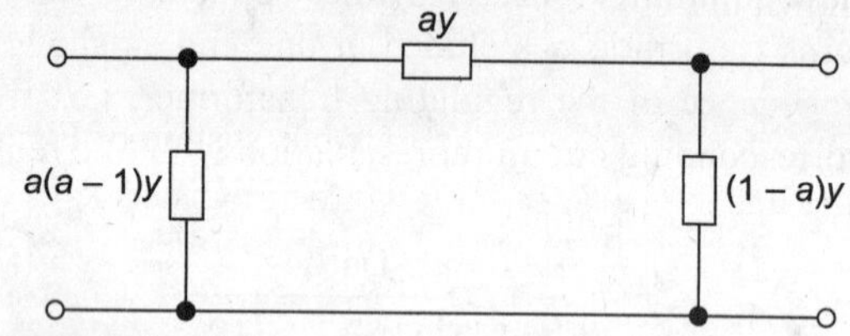

Fig. 6.26 *Circuit representation of a line with off-nominal tap-setting or voltage regulating transformer*

In Fig. 6.27(a), the line shown in Fig. 6.25 is represented by a π-network with shunt admittances y_0 at each end. Also, a is real, i.e., $a^* = a$.

From Fig. 6.27(a)

$$\begin{aligned} I_i &= a^* I_i' = aI_i' = a(aV_i y_0 + y(aV_i - V_j)) \\ &= a^2(y + y_0)V_i - ay\,V_j \\ &= a^2 y_0 V_i + a(a-1)y\,V_i + ay\,(V_i - V_j) \end{aligned}$$

Similarly,

$$I_j = y_0 V_j + (1-a)yV_j + ay(V_j - V_i)$$

which can be represented by the π-network of Fig. 6.27(b), where additional shunt admittances $a_2 y_0$ appear at bus j and y_0 at bus i.

The above derivations also apply for a transformer with off-nominal tap-setting $a = (kV)_{\text{base}}/(kV)_{\text{tap}}$, a real value.

With off-nominal tap setting transformers at each end of the line as shown in Fig. 6.28, we have

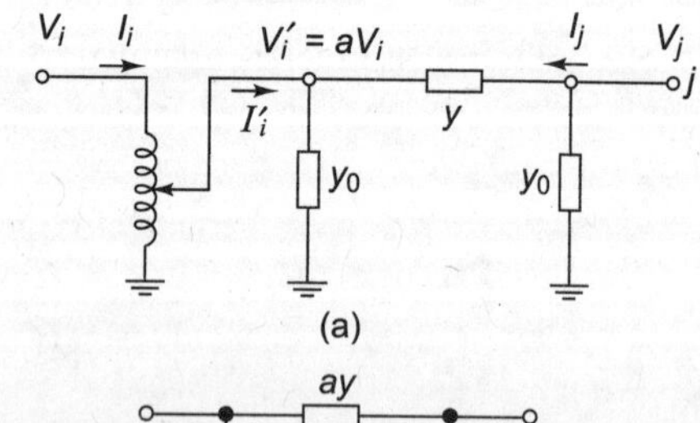

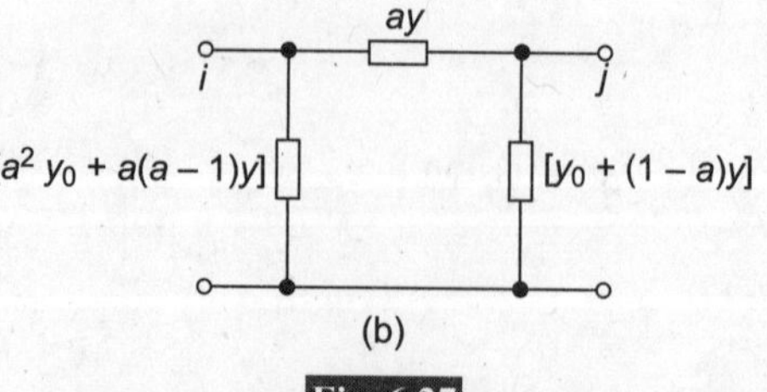

Fig. 6.27

$$\begin{bmatrix} I_i' \\ I_j' \end{bmatrix} = \begin{bmatrix} y & -y \\ -y & y \end{bmatrix} \begin{bmatrix} V_i' \\ V_j' \end{bmatrix} \quad \text{(i)}$$

$$\begin{bmatrix} V_i' \\ V_j' \end{bmatrix} = \begin{bmatrix} a_i & 0 \\ 0 & a_j \end{bmatrix} \begin{bmatrix} V_i \\ V_j \end{bmatrix}; \begin{bmatrix} I_i' \\ I_j' \end{bmatrix} = \begin{bmatrix} 1/a_i^* & 0 \\ 0 & 1/a_j^* \end{bmatrix} \begin{bmatrix} I_i \\ I_j \end{bmatrix} \quad \text{(ii)}$$

Substituting (ii) in (i) and solving, we get

$$\begin{bmatrix} I_i \\ I_j \end{bmatrix} = \begin{bmatrix} |a_i|^2 y & -a_i^* a_j y \\ -a_i a_j^* y & |a_j|^2 y \end{bmatrix} \begin{bmatrix} V_i \\ V_j \end{bmatrix} \quad \text{(iii)}$$

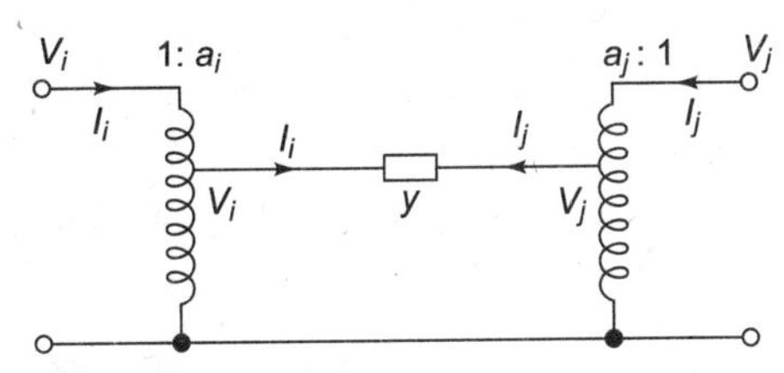

Fig. 6.28 *Off-nominal transformers at both line ends (a_i, a_j are complex)*

Thus,

$$\boldsymbol{Y} = \begin{bmatrix} |a_i|^2 y & -a_i^* a_j y \\ -a_i a_j^* y & |a_j|^2 y \end{bmatrix}$$

Note: When a_i, a_j are real

$$\boldsymbol{Y} = \begin{bmatrix} a_i^2 y & -a_i a_j y \\ -a_i a_j y & a_j^2 y \end{bmatrix}$$

and the π-equivalent circuit of Fig. 6.28 can now be drawn as shown in Fig. 6.29.

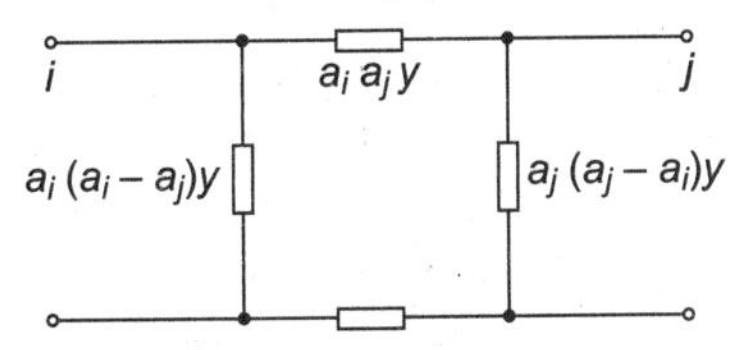

Fig. 6.29 *π-equivalent of Fig. 6.28 with a_i and a_j real*

Example 6.12 The four-bus system of Fig. 6.7 is now modified to include a regulating transformer in the line 3–4 near bus 3. Find the modified $\boldsymbol{Y}_{\text{BUS}}$ of the system for

1. $V_3/V_3' = 1.04$ or $a = 1/1.04$
2. $V_3/V_3' = e^{j3°}$ or $a = e^{-j3°}$ $\quad |a| = 1; a = V_3'/V_3$

Solution

1. With regulating transformer in line 3–4, the elements of the corresponding submatrix in Eq. (v) of Example 6.3 are modified as under.

$$\begin{array}{c} \\ 3 \\ 4 \end{array}\begin{array}{c} \begin{array}{cc} 3 & 4 \end{array} \\ \begin{bmatrix} (Y_{33}\text{ (old)} - y_{34} + a^2 y_{34}) & (y_{34}\text{(old)} + y_{34} - a y_{34}) \\ (Y_{43}\text{ (old)} + y_{34} - a y_{34}) & (y_{44}\text{ (old)}) \end{bmatrix} \end{array}$$

$$\begin{array}{c} \\ 3 \\ 4 \end{array}\begin{array}{c} \begin{array}{cc} 3 & 4 \end{array} \\ \begin{bmatrix} (3.666 - j11) - (2 - j6) + \dfrac{1}{(1.04)^2}(2 - j6) & (-2 + j6) + (2 - j6) - \dfrac{1}{(1.04)}(2 - j6) \\ (-2 + j6) + (2 - j6) - \dfrac{1}{(1.04)}(2 - j6) & (3 - j9) \end{bmatrix} \end{array}$$

$$\begin{array}{c} \\ 3 \\ 4 \end{array}\begin{array}{c} \begin{array}{cc} 3 & 4 \end{array} \\ \begin{bmatrix} (3.516 - j10.547) & (-2.3113 + j5.8871) \\ (-1.683 + j6.0965) & (3 - j9) \end{bmatrix} \end{array}$$

The old values of Y_{33}, Y_{34}, Y_{43}, Y_{44} are given in Example 6.3.

2. Modified submatrix in Eq. (v) of Example 6.3 is

$$\begin{matrix}3\\4\end{matrix}\begin{bmatrix}(Y_{33}\,(\text{old}) - y_{34} + |a|^2\, y_{34}) & (Y_{34}(\text{old}) + y_{34} - a^* y_{34})\\ (Y_{43}\,(\text{old}) + y_{34} - ay_{34}) & (Y_{44}\,(\text{old}))\end{bmatrix}$$

It follows from Eq. (6.101)

$$\begin{matrix}3\\4\end{matrix}\overset{\qquad\qquad 3 \qquad\qquad\qquad\qquad\qquad\qquad 4}{\begin{bmatrix}(3.666 - j11) - (2 - j6) + 1(2 - j6) & (-2 + j6) + (2 - j6) - \varepsilon^{-j3^\circ}(2 - j6)\\ (-2 + j6) + (2 - j6) - \varepsilon^{j3^\circ}(2 - j6) & (3 - j9)\end{bmatrix}}$$

$$\begin{matrix}3\\4\end{matrix}\begin{bmatrix}3.666 - j11 & -2.3113 + j5.8871\\ -1.683 + j6.0965 & 3 - j9\end{bmatrix}$$

Voltage Controlled Buses Consider a regulating transformer between ith and jth buses with the voltage at the ith bus to be controlled. From Eqs. 6.100(a) and (b), it follows that

$$I_i = |a|^2\, yV_i - a^*\, yV_j \tag{6.100a}$$

$$I_j = -ayV_i + yV_j \tag{6.100b}$$

where y is the series admittance of the line and 'a' is the complex transformer turns ratio given by

$$a = |a| \angle\alpha \tag{6.100c}$$

where $|a|$ is the turns ratio and α is the phase shift. In a regulating transformer these two parameters are independently adjustable over small ranges, such as

$$(1 - K) \le |a| \le (1 + K) \quad K << 1 \quad (\text{typically } K \le 0.1) \tag{6.103a}$$

$$-\beta^\circ \le \alpha \le \beta^\circ \qquad (\text{typically } \beta \le 10^\circ) \tag{6.103b}$$

Both variables are physically adjustable in fixed steps of $\Delta|a|$ and $\Delta\alpha$, where $\Delta|a| << |a|$ and $\Delta\alpha << \alpha$ (typically $\Delta|a| \le 0.05$ and $\Delta\alpha \le 2.5°$).

Let $|V_i|_{\text{spec}}$ be the voltage specified at the ith voltage controlled bus. Since $P_{Gi} = Q_{Gi} = 0$ for a voltage controlled bus, Q_i is specified in addition to P_i and $|V_i|$. In the rth iteration, $|V_i|^{(r+1)}$ is evaluated using Eq. (6.37) (for GS method) or Eq. (6.76) (for NR method). If

$$|V_i^{(r+1)}| - |V_i|_{\text{spec}} < \frac{\Delta|a|}{2}\,|V_i|_{\text{spec}} \tag{6.104}$$

then $|V_i^{(r+1)} \equiv V_i|_{\text{spec}}$, so that $|V_i|$ is kept at $|V_i|^{(r+1)}$. Otherwise, $|a|$ is increased (if $|V_i|^{(r+1)}$ is high) or decreased (if $|V_i|^{(r+1)}$ is low) in steps of $\Delta|a|$ till Eq. (6.104) is satisfied.

The power flow across the line (assuming lossless transformer) is given by

$$P_{ij} = \text{Re}\,(V_i I_i^*) = \text{Re}\,(V_i^*\, I_i) \tag{6.105a}$$

Substituting Eq. 6.100(a) in Eq. 6.105(a), we get

$$P_{ij} \cong \text{Re}\,(V_i\,(|a|^2\, y^*\, V_i^* - ay^*\, V_j^*))$$

$$= \text{Re}\,(|a|^2\,|y|\,|V_i|^2 \angle -\theta - |a|\,|y|\,|V_i|\,|V_j| \angle(\delta_i - \delta_j + \alpha - \theta))$$

or

$$P_{ij} \cong |a|^2\,|y|\,|V_i|^2 \cos\theta - |a|\,|y|\,|V_i|\,|V_j| \cos\,(\delta_i - \delta_j + \alpha - \theta) \tag{6.105b}$$

where $\quad y = |y| \angle\theta.$

Next, we estimate the change ΔP_{ij} due to the change $\Delta\alpha$. We have from Eq. 6.105(b)

$$\frac{\partial P_{ij}}{\partial \alpha} = |a||y||V_i||V_j|\sin(\delta_i - \delta_j + \alpha - \theta) \tag{6.106}$$

And we approximate

$$\Delta P_{ij} = \frac{\partial P_{ij}}{\partial \alpha}\Delta\alpha \tag{6.107}$$

If

$$|P_{ij} - P_{ij,\,\text{spec}}| \le \Delta P_{ij}/2 \tag{6.108}$$

where $P_{ij,\ \text{spec}}$ is the specified value, then α is not changed. Otherwise, α is increased (causing more real power flow) or decreased (decreasing real power flow) depending on whether P_{ij} is low or high.

After updating the values of $|a|$ and α above, the corresponding elements in the $\boldsymbol{Y}_{\text{BUS}}$ also change and have to be updated for the next iteration. We have, therefore,

$$\begin{aligned} Y_{ii\text{ new}} &= Y_{ii\text{old}} - y_{ii\text{old}} + y_{ii\text{ new}} \\ Y_{ij\text{ new}} &= Y_{ij\text{ old}} + y_{ij\text{ old}} - y_{ij\text{ new}} \\ Y_{ji\text{ new}} &= Y_{ji\text{ old}} + y_{ji\text{ old}} - y_{ji\text{ new}} \\ Y_{jj\text{ new}} &= Y_{jj\text{ old}} - y_{jj\text{ old}} + y_{jj\text{ new}} \end{aligned} \tag{6.109}$$

where y_{ii}, y_{ij}, y_{ji} and y_{jj} are given by Eqs. 6.100(a) and (b). By substituting the corresponding 'old' and 'new' values of $a = |a|\angle\alpha$, we get 'old' and 'new' values of y_{ii}, y_{ij}, y_{ji}, y_{jj}. From Eqs. 6.100(a) and (b),

$$\begin{aligned} y_{ii} &= I_i/V_i\,|\,(V_j = 0,\ V_i \ne 0) = |a|^2 y \\ y_{ij} &= I_i/V_j\,|\,(V_i = 0,\ V_j \ne 0) = -a^* y \\ y_{jj} &= I_j/V_i\,|\,(V_j = 0,\ V_i \ne 0) = -\,ay \\ y_j &= I_j/V_j\,|\,(V_i = 0,\ V_j \ne 0) = y \end{aligned} \tag{6.110}$$

6.10 ▶LOAD FLOW UNDER POWER ELECTRONIC CONTROL

Note: This section is to be read after studying Ch. 20 on HVDC transmission. The recent availability of HV power electronic switching has made it possible to develop HVDC transmission (Ch. 20) and FACTS technologies (Ch. 15 of Ref. 14). In fact, the original purpose of the former was a return to DC transmission for large distances, most of the schemes actually in use are back-to-back (interconnection of asynchronous power systems).

The FACTS technology is primarily used to enhance the controllability of the synchronous transmission system thereby improving the stability limits. In this section we will briefly describe how to incorporate these two power electronic, technologies in conventional load flow solutions wherever feasible.

It is preferable to use original full NR method described earlier to incorporate FACTS devices in the load flow solution to have better convergence.

Some FACTS devices pose no special problem, as their steady-state behaviour is properly represented by the standard load flow specifications. This is so with static VAR compensation (TCR or STATCON type). This can be specified by a zero active power and constant voltage magnitude, like the conventional synchronous condensers. Chapter 5 of Ref. 13 describes in detail the incorporation of FACTS devices in LF solution. Static tap changing, phase-shifting, TCSC and UPFC are considered.

6.10.1 AC-DC Load Flow

A combined AC-DC power system with 3 buses and 4 terminals is drawn in Fig. 6.30 to bring into clarity to the procedures that follow. The label terminal (term) is given to those buses in which there is DC connection via a transformer and converter (T and C).

At any converter terminal the complex power flows are indicated in Fig. 6.31; this is the more general form of Fig. 6.3 for AC system. From this figure the power balance equations at the terminal are

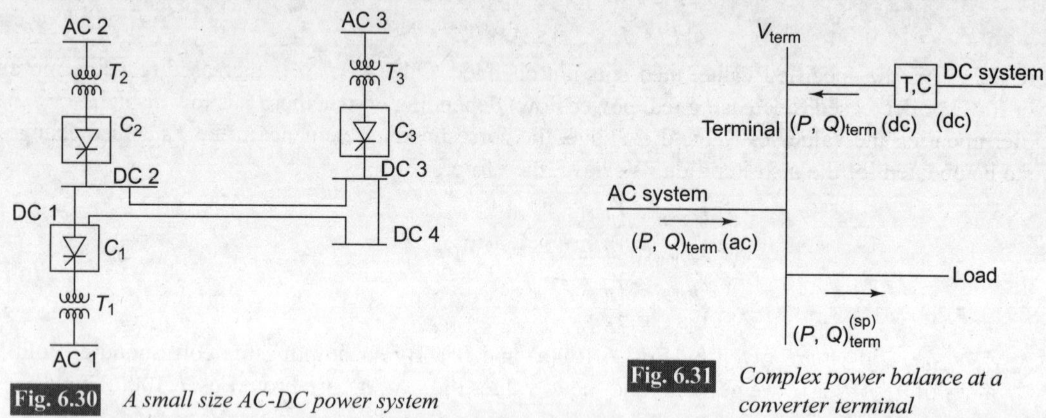

Fig. 6.30 *A small size AC-DC power system*

Fig. 6.31 *Complex power balance at a converter terminal*

$$P_{\text{term}}^{\text{sp}} - P_{\text{term}}\,(\text{ac}) - P_{\text{term}}\,(\text{dc}) = 0 \tag{6.111}$$

$$Q_{\text{term}}^{\text{sp}} - Q_{\text{term}}\,(\text{ac}) - Q_{\text{term}}\,(\text{dc}) = 0 \tag{6.112}$$

where

1. $(P, Q)_{\text{term}}$ (ac) are injected powers (real, reactive) which are functions of AC system variables (V, δ).
2. $(P, Q)_{\text{term}}$ (dc) are injected power from the DC system which are functions of DC system variables.
3. $(P, Q)_{\text{term}}^{\text{sp}}$ is the AC system load at the terminal

$(P, Q)_{\text{term}}$ (dc) are dependent on

$$P_{\text{term}}(\text{dc}) = f_p(V_{\text{term}}, x) \tag{6.113}$$

$$Q_{\text{term}}(\text{dc}) = f_q(V_{\text{term}}, x) \tag{6.114}$$

where x is a vector dc variables (converter settings).

The operating state of an AC–DC system are

$$[V, \delta, x]^T$$

where, V is vector of ac voltage magnitude
δ is vector ac system angles
x is vector of dc variables

We shall use NR formulations.

The equations derived from the specified AC system conditions may be summarised as

$$\begin{bmatrix} \Delta \bar{P}(\bar{V}, \bar{\delta}) \\ \Delta \bar{P}_{\text{term}}\,(\bar{V}, \bar{\delta}, \bar{x}) \\ \Delta \bar{Q}(\bar{V}, \bar{\delta}) \\ \Delta \bar{Q}_{\text{term}}\,(\bar{V}, \bar{\delta}, \bar{x}) \end{bmatrix} = 0 \tag{6.115}$$

where the mismatches at the converter terminal bus bars are indicated separately.

A further set of independent equations are derived from DC system conditions. These are designated as

$$\bar{R}(V_{\text{term}}, \bar{x})_k = 0 \tag{6.116}$$

for $k = 1$, no. of converters present.

The general AC–DC load flow problem may be summarised as the solution of [Ch. 6, Ref. 11]

$$\begin{bmatrix} \Delta \bar{P}(\bar{V}, \bar{\delta}) \\ \Delta \bar{P}_{\text{term}}(\bar{V}, \bar{\delta}, \bar{x}) \\ \Delta \bar{Q}(\bar{V}, \bar{\delta}) \\ \Delta \bar{Q}_{\text{term}}(\bar{V}, \bar{\delta}, \bar{x}) \\ \bar{R}(V_{\text{term}}, \bar{x}) \end{bmatrix} = 0 \tag{6.117}$$

The DC system equations (6.113), (6.114) and (6.116) are made independent of the AC system angles δ by selecting a separate angle reference for the DC system variable as defined in Fig. 6.32. This improves the algorithmic performance by effectively decoupling the angle dependence of AC and DC systems.

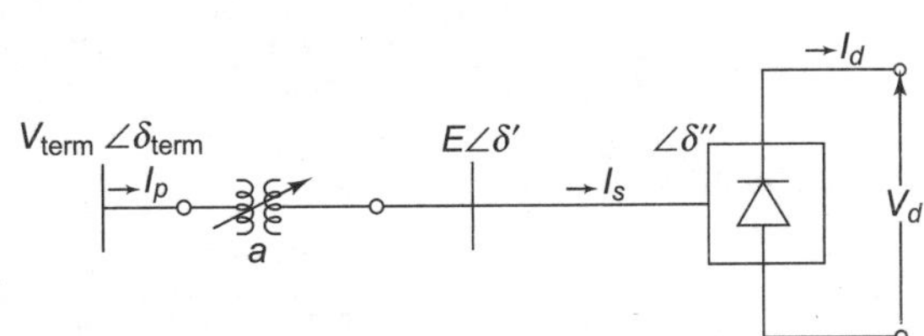

Fig. 6.32 *Basic DC converter (angles refer to AC system reference)*

6.10.2 Converter Model

Under balanced conditions, similar converter bridges, attached to the same AC terminal bus, will operate identically regardless of the transformer connection. They can, therefore, be replaced by an equivalent single bridge for the purpose of single-phase load flow analysis.

Two independent variables are sufficient to model a DC converter, operating under balanced conditions, from a known terminal voltage source.

The following set of variables allow simple relationships for all the normal control strategies

$$[\bar{x}] = [V_d, I_d, a, \cos \alpha, \phi]^T$$

variable ϕ is included to ensure a simple expression for Q_{dc}.

Here,

a = transformer off-nominal tap ratio

$V_{\text{term}} \angle \phi$ converter terminal bus nodal voltage (phase angle referred to the converter reference)

$E \angle \psi$ fundamental frequency component of the voltage waveform at the converter transformer secondary.

α = firing delay angle

V_d = average DC voltage

I_d = converter direct current

Figure 6.33 shows an equivalent circuit for the converter.

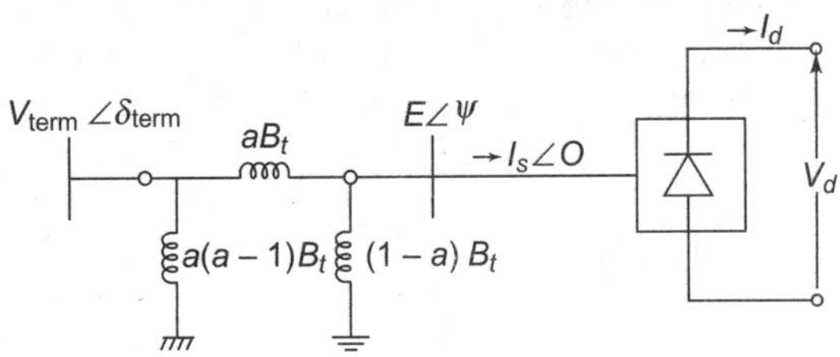

Fig. 6.33 *Single-phase equivalent circuit for basic converter (angles refer to DC reference)*

6.10.3 Solution Technique

The solution to a single converter connected to AC busbar is given below:

Unified Solution The unified solution gives recognition to the interdependence of AC and DC system equations and simultaneously solves the complete system. Referring to Eq. (6.117) the standard Newton–Raphson Algorithm involves repeat solution of the matrix equations

$$\begin{bmatrix} \Delta \bar{P}(\bar{V}, \delta) \\ \Delta \bar{P}_{\text{term}}(\bar{V}, \delta, \bar{x}) \\ \Delta \bar{Q}(\bar{V}, \delta) \\ \Delta \bar{Q}_{\text{term}}(\bar{V}, \delta, \bar{x}) \\ \bar{R}(V_{\text{term}}, \bar{x}) \end{bmatrix} = [J] \begin{bmatrix} \Delta \bar{\delta} \\ \Delta \delta_{\text{term}} \\ \Delta \bar{V} \\ \Delta V_{\text{term}} \\ \Delta \bar{x} \end{bmatrix} \tag{6.118}$$

where J is the usual Jacobian.

$$\Delta P_{\text{term}} = P^{\text{sp}}_{\text{term}} - P_{\text{term}}(\text{ac}) - P_{\text{term}}(\text{dc}) \tag{6.119}$$

$$\Delta Q_{\text{term}} = Q^{\text{sp}}_{\text{term}} - Q_{\text{term}}(\text{ac}) - Q_{\text{term}}(\text{dc}) \tag{6.120}$$

and

$$P_{\text{term}}(\text{dc}) = f(V_{\text{term}}, \bar{x}) \tag{6.121}$$

$$Q_{\text{term}}(\text{dc}) = f(V_{\text{term}}, \bar{x}) \tag{6.122}$$

Applying the AC fast decoupled assumptions to all Jacobian elements related to the AC system equations, yields

$$\begin{bmatrix} \Delta \bar{P}/\bar{V} \\ \Delta P_{\text{term}}/V_{\text{term}} \\ \Delta \bar{Q}/\bar{V} \\ \Delta Q_{\text{term}}/\bar{V}_{\text{term}} \\ \bar{R} \end{bmatrix} = [O, B', B'', A] \begin{bmatrix} \Delta \bar{\delta} \\ \Delta \delta_{\text{term}} \\ \Delta \bar{V} \\ \Delta V_{\text{term}} \\ \Delta x \end{bmatrix} \tag{6.123}$$

where all matrix elements are zero unless otherwise indicated. The matrices $[\boldsymbol{B'}]$ and $[\boldsymbol{B''}]$ are the usual single-phase fast decoupled Jacobians and are constant in value. The other matrices $[A]$ indicated vary at each iteration in the solution process.

In the above formulation, the DC variable x are coupled to both the real and reactive power AC mismatches. However Eq. (6.123) may be separated to enable a block successive iteration scheme to be used.

The DC mismatches and variables can be appended to the two fast decoupled AC, equations in which case the following equation results.

$$\begin{bmatrix} \Delta \bar{P}/\bar{V} \\ \Delta P_{\text{term}}/V_{\text{term}} \\ \bar{R} \end{bmatrix} = \begin{bmatrix} B' & \\ & AA' \\ & A \end{bmatrix} \begin{bmatrix} \Delta \delta \\ \Delta \delta_{\text{term}} \\ \Delta x \end{bmatrix} \tag{6.124}$$

$$\begin{bmatrix} \Delta \bar{Q}/\bar{V} \\ \Delta Q_{\text{term}}/V_{\text{term}} \\ \bar{R} \end{bmatrix} = \begin{bmatrix} B'' & & \\ & B''_{ii} & AA'' \\ & BB'' & A \end{bmatrix} \begin{bmatrix} \Delta \bar{V} \\ \Delta V_{\text{term}} \\ \Delta \bar{x} \end{bmatrix} \tag{6.125}$$

The algorithm may be further simplified by recognising the following physical characteristics of the AC and DC systems:

1. The coupling between DC variables and the AC terminal voltage is strong.
2. There is no coupling between DC mismatches and AC system angles.
3. Under all Practical Control Strategies, the DC power is well constrained and this implies that the changes in DC variables $\bar{x}$ do not greatly affect the real power mismatches at the terminals.

These features justify the removal of the DC equations from Eqs. (6.124) and (6.125) to yield a $[P, Q_{dc}]$ block successive iteration scheme, represented by the following two equations:

$$\left[\Delta\bar{P}/\bar{V}\right] = [B']\left[\Delta\bar{\delta}\right] \tag{6.126}$$

$$\begin{bmatrix} \Delta\bar{Q}/\bar{V} \\ \Delta Q_{\text{term}}/V_{\text{term}} \\ \bar{R} \end{bmatrix} = \begin{array}{|c|c|c|} \hline B'' & & \\ \cline{2-3} & B''_{ii} & AA'' \\ \hline & BB'' & A \\ \hline \end{array} \begin{bmatrix} \Delta\bar{V} \\ \Delta V_{\text{term}} \\ \Delta\bar{x} \end{bmatrix} \tag{6.127}$$

6.10.4 Sequential Method

The sequential method results from a further simplification of the unified method, i.e., the AC system equations are solved with the DC system modelled simply as real and reactive power injections at the appropriate terminal bus. For a DC solution, the AC system is modelled as a constant voltage at the converter AC terminal bus.

The following equations are solved iteratively till convergence:

$$[\Delta\bar{P}/\bar{V}] = [B']\,[\Delta\delta] \tag{6.128}$$

$$[\Delta\bar{Q}/\bar{V}] = [B'']\,[\Delta\bar{V}] \tag{6.129}$$

$$[\bar{R}] = [A][\Delta\bar{x}] \tag{6.130}$$

6.11 ▶SUMMARY

In this chapter, perhaps the most important power system study, viz., load flow has been introduced and discussed in detail. Important methods available have been briefly described. It is almost impossible to say which one of the existing methods is the best, because the behaviour of different load flow methods is dictated by the types and sizes of the problems to be solved, as well as the precise details of implementation. Choice of a particular method in any given situation is normally a compromise between the various criteria of goodness of the load flow methods. It would not be incorrect to say that among the existing methods, no single method meets all the desirable requirements of an ideal load flow method, viz., high speed, low storage, reliability for ill-conditioned problems, versatility in handling various adjustments and simplicity in programming. Fortunately, not all the desirable features of a load flow method are needed in all situations.

In spite of a large number of load flow methods available, it is easy to see that only the NR and FDLF load flow methods are the most important ones for general purpose load flow analysis. The FDLF method is clearly superior to the NR method from the point of view of speed as well as storage. Yet, the NR method is still in use because of its high versatility, accuracy and reliability and, as such, is being widely used for a variety of system optimisation calculations. It gives sensitivity analysis and can be used in modern dynamic-response and outage-assessment calculations. Of course, newer methods would continue to be developed which would either reduce the computation requirements for large systems, or would be more amenable to on-line implementation. Finally, load flow under power electronic control (FACTS/ HVDC) is described.

Additional Examples

Example 6.13 Consider the two-bus system of Fig. 6.34. The line has a series impedance of 0.01 + j0.05 pu, and a total shunt admittance of j0.01 pu. The specified quantities at the two buses are given in the table as follows:

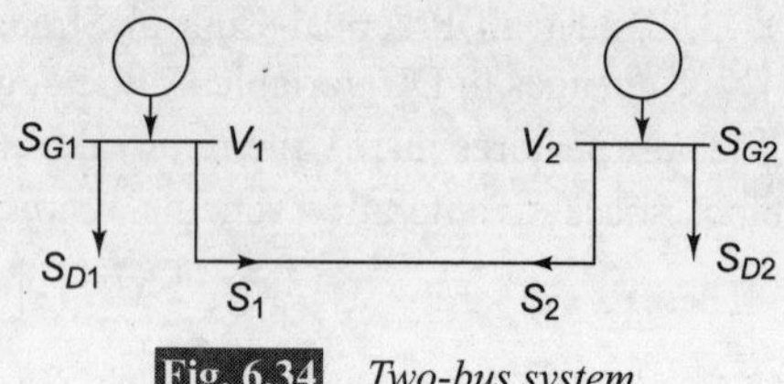

Fig. 6.34 Two-bus system

Bus i	Type	V_i pu	δ_i	Injected powers	
				P_i pu	Q_i, pu
1.	Slack bus	1	0°	—	—
2.	PQ bus	?	?	P_2	Q_2

Determine the range of P_2 and Q_2 for which the solution of $|V_2|$ exists.

Solution Using the nominal-π model for the transmission line, Y_{BUS} is obtained as follows: For the line,

$$y_{series} = \frac{1}{0.01 + j0.05} = 3.846 - j19.231 = 19.61 \angle -78.69° \text{ pu}$$

Therefore, in the Y_{BUS} matrix

Each off-diagonal term = $-3.846 + j19.231$ pu

$= 19.61 \angle 101.31°$ pu

Each self term = $(3.846 - j19.231) + (j0.005))$

$= 3.846 - j19.226$ pu

$= 19.61\angle - 78.69°$

Therefore,

$$Y_{BUS} = \begin{bmatrix} 19.61\angle -78.69° & 19.61\angle 101.31° \\ 19.61\angle 101.31° & 19.61\angle -78.69° \end{bmatrix}$$

The real and reactive powers at bus 2 are

$$P_2 = |V_2||V_1||Y_{21}|\cos(\theta_{21} + \delta_1 - \delta_2) + |V_2|^2 |Y_{22}| \cos\theta_{22}$$
$$Q_2 = |V_2||V_1||Y_{21}|\sin(\theta_{21} + \delta_1 - \delta_2) - |V_2|^2 |Y_{22}| \sin\theta_{22}$$

Substituting the value of $V_1 = 1 \angle 0°$, we get

$$\cos(\theta_{21} - \delta_2) = \frac{1}{|V_2||Y_{21}|}(P_2 - |V_2|^2 |Y_{22}| \cos\theta_{22}) \quad \text{(i)}$$

$$\sin(\theta_{21} - \delta_2) = \frac{-1}{|V_2||Y_{21}|}(Q_2 + |V_2|^2 |Y_{22}| \sin\theta_{22}) \quad \text{(ii)}$$

Squaring and adding,

$$1 = \frac{1}{|V_2|^2 |Y_{21}|^2}\left(P_2^2 + Q_2^2 + |V_2|^4 |Y_{22}|^2 + 2|Y_{22}||V_2|^2 (Q_2 \sin\theta_{22} - P_2 \cos\theta_{22})\right)$$

or

$$|Y_{22}|^2 V_2^4 + (2|Y_{22}|(Q_2 \sin\theta_{22} - P_2 \cos\theta_{22}) - |Y_{21}|^2)|V_2|^2 + (P_2^2 + Q_2^2) = 0$$

Substituting the values of $|Y_{21}|$ and $Y_{22} = |Y_{22}|\angle\theta_{22}$,

$$(384.55)|V_2|^4 + (-38.45Q_2 - 7.692P_2) - 384.55)|V_2|^2 + (P_2^2 + Q_2^2) = 0$$

or

$$|V_2|^2 = \frac{(38.45Q_2 + 7.692P_2 + 384.55) \pm \sqrt{(38.45Q_2 + 7.692P_2 + 384.55)^2 - 1538.2(P_2^2 + Q_2^2)}}{769.1} \quad \text{(iii)}$$

Therefore, real values of $|V_2|$ exist for

$$(38.45Q_2 + 7.692P_2 + 384.55)^2 \geq 1538.2(P_2^2 + Q_2^2)$$

which on simplifying yields

$$(0.196P_2 + 0.98Q_2 + 9.805)^2 \geq (P_2^2 + Q_2^2)$$

or

$$(-0.962)P_2^2 + (0.384Q_2 + 3.844)P_2 - (0.0296Q_2^2 - 19.22Q_2 - 96.138) \geq 0$$

or

$$P_2 \geq \frac{-(0.384Q_2 + 3.844) \pm \sqrt{(0.384Q_2 + 3.844)^2 - (0.1524Q_2^2 - 73.96Q_2 - 370)}}{-1.924} \quad \text{(iv)}$$

For real values of $|V_2|$, we must therefore have

$$(0.384Q_2 + 3.844)^2 \geq (0.1524\,Q_2^2 - 73.96Q_2 - 370)$$

or

$$(-4.94 \times 10^{-3})Q_2^2 + (76.91)Q_2 + 384.78 \geq 0$$

or

$$Q_2 \geq \frac{-76.91 \pm \sqrt{(76.91^2 + 4 \times 4.94 \times 384.78 \times 10^{-3})}}{-9.88 \times 10^{-3}} \quad \text{(v)}$$

$$= \frac{-76.91 \pm 76.959}{-9.88 \times 10^{-3}}$$

or

$$Q_2 \geq -4.96,\ 15.574 \times 10^3 \text{ pu}$$

Hence,

$$Q_2 \geq -4.96$$

Taking

(a) $Q_2 = -2$ pu; From (iv),

$$P_2 \geq \frac{-3.078 \pm 15.196}{-1.924} = -6.3,\ 9.5 \text{ pu}$$

or

$$P_2 \geq -6.3 \text{ pu}$$

(b) $Q_2 = 0$ pu: From (iv),

$$P_2 \geq \frac{-3.844 \pm 19.616}{-1.924} = -8.198,\ 12.193 \text{ pu}$$

or

$$P_2 \geq -8.198 \text{ pu}$$

(c) $Q_2 = 2$ pu: From (iv),

$$P_2 \geq \frac{-4.612 \pm 23.21}{-1.924} = -9.67,\ 14.46 \text{ pu}$$

or

$$P_2 \geq -9.67 \text{ pu}$$

Example 6.14 Consider a three-bus system. The specifications at various buses are given in the table. Each line impedance $z_L = j0.25$ pu. Neglect shunt admittances of all lines.

Bus i	Type	$\|V_i\|$ pu	δ_i	Injected powers	
				P_i pu	Q_i, pu
1.	Slack bus	1	0	—	—
2.	PQ bus	?	?	–0.5	–0.4
3.	PV bus	0.9	?	0.5	—

Find $|V_2|$, δ_2 and δ_3, by using small-angle approximation. Is the approximation reasonable?

Solution Series line admittance is

$$y_L = 1/z_L = -j4.0 \text{ pu}$$

$$\therefore \quad \mathbf{Y}_{\text{BUS}} = \begin{bmatrix} -j8.0 & j4.0 & j4.0 \\ j4.0 & -j8.0 & j4.0 \\ j4.0 & j4.0 & -j8.0 \end{bmatrix}$$

Now,

$$S_2^* = P_2 - jQ_2 = V_2^* \sum_{k=1}^{3} Y_{2k} V_k \tag{i}$$

$$S_3^* = P_3 - jQ_3 = V_3^* \sum_{k=1}^{3} Y_{3k} V_k \tag{ii}$$

We have

$$V_2^* V_k = |V_2||V_k|\varepsilon^{j(\delta_k - \delta_2)} = |V_2||V_k|(\cos(\delta_k - \delta_2) + j\sin(\delta_k - \delta_2))$$
$$\cong |V_2||V_k|(1 + j(\delta_k - \delta_2)) = |V_2||V_k|(1 + j\delta_{k2})$$

and similarly,

$$V_3^* V_k \cong |V_3||V_k|(1 + j(\delta_k - \delta_3)) = |V_3||V_k|(1 + j\delta_{k3})$$

Substituting in (i) and (ii),

$$P_2 - jQ_2 = |V_2|(Y_{21}|V_1|(1 + j\delta_{12}) + Y_{22}|V_2| + Y_{23}|V_3|(1 + j\delta_{32}))$$
$$= |V_2|(Y_{21}|V_1|(1 - j\delta_2) + Y_{22}|V_2| + Y_{23}|V_3|(1 + j(\delta_3 - \delta_2))) \tag{iii}$$

Similarly,

$$P_3 - jQ_3 = |V_3|(Y_{31}|V_1|(1 - j\delta_3) + Y_{32}|V_2|(1 + j(\delta_2 - \delta_3)) + Y_{33}|V_3|) \tag{iv}$$

Substituting various values in (iii) and (iv),

$$-0.5 + j0.4 = |V_2|(j4.0(1 - j\delta_2) - j8.0|V_2| + j4.0(0.9)(1 + j\delta_{32})) \tag{v}$$

$$0.5 - jQ_3 = 0.9(j4.0(1 - j\delta_3) + j4.0\,|V_2|\,(1 + j\delta_{23}) - j8.0(0.9)) \tag{vi}$$

Equating the imaginary part of (v),

$$0.4 = 4.0\,|V_2| - 8.0\,|V_2|^2 + 3.6\,|V_2|$$

or
$$8.0\,|V_2|^2 - 7.6\,|V_2| + 0.4 = 0$$

or

$$|V_2| = \frac{7.6 \pm \sqrt{(7.6^2 - 12.8)}}{16.0} = \frac{7.6 \pm 6.7}{16} = 0.894,\ 0.056 \text{ pu}$$

$$|V_2| = 0.894 \text{ pu}$$

Equating the real parts of (v) and (vi), we get

$$-0.5 = 0.894\,(4\delta_2 - 4(0.9)\,(\delta_3 - \delta_2))$$

$$0.5 = 0.9\,(4\delta_3 - 4(0.894)\,(\delta_2 - \delta_3))$$

or
$$6.7944\delta_2 - 3.2184\delta_3 = -0.5$$

$$-3.2184\delta_2 + 6.8184\delta_3 = 0.5$$

or

$$\delta_2 = \frac{-0.5(6.8184) + 0.5(3.2184)}{6.7944(6.8184) - 3.2184(3.2184)} = -0.05 \text{ rad}$$

or

$$\delta_3 = \frac{6.7944(0.5) + 3.2184(-0.5)}{6.7944(6.8184) - 3.2184(3.2184)} = 0.05 \text{ rad}$$

or

$$\delta_2 = -0.05 \text{ rad} = -2.85 \text{ deg}$$

$$\delta_3 = 0.05 \text{ rad} = 2.85 \text{ deg}$$

The approximation is reasonable, since

$$\delta_{12},\ \delta_{23},\ \delta_{31} < 10°$$

so that
$$\cos\,\delta_{ij} \cong 1,$$

and
$$\sin\,\delta_{ij} \cong \delta_{ij} \text{ rad}$$

Example 6.15 Consider the three-bus system of Fig. 6.35. Assume negligible shunt admittances of the lines. Each line admittance is $-j10$ pu. 'a' is the complex turns ratio of the regulating transformer, RT, i.e.,

$$a = |a| \angle \alpha$$

(a) Determine $\boldsymbol{Y}_{\text{BUS}}$ for $a = 1.05\angle{-2.5°} = 1.049 - j0.046$.

(b) Determine the changes in real and reactive power flows ΔP_{23} and ΔQ_{23} when 'a' changes from $1\angle 0°$ to $1\angle{-2.5°}$.

(c) Repeat (b) when 'a' changes from $1\angle 0°$ to $1.05\angle 0°$. Given $|V_2| = 1.05$ pu, $|V_3| = 0.95$ pu, $\delta_2 = -3°$, $\delta_3 = +2°$, without the regulating transformer RT.

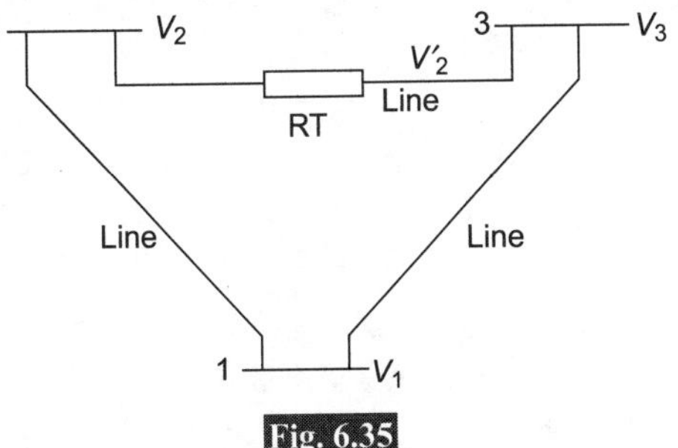

Fig. 6.35

Solution Using Eqs. (6.9) and (6.101), we get

(a)

$$
Y_{BUS} = \begin{array}{c|c|c|c}
 & 1 & 2 & 3 \\
\hline
1 & -j20 & j10 & j10 \\
2 & j10 & -j10 + |a|^2(-j10) & -a^*(-j10) \\
3 & j10 & -a(-j10) & -j20
\end{array}
$$

$$
= \begin{bmatrix} -j20 & j10 & j10 \\ j10 & -j21.025 & -0.46 + j10.49 \\ j10 & 0.46 + j10.49 & -j20 \end{bmatrix}
$$

(b) We have the complex line flow from bus 2 to 3 given by

$$S_{23}^* = P_{23} - jQ_{23}$$

$$= V_2^* I_{23}$$

$$= V_2^* (|a|^2 y_L V_2 - a^* y_L V_3) \text{ from Eq. (6.100a)}$$

$$= (|V_2|^2 |a|^2 |y_L| \angle\theta_L - |V_2||V_3||a||y_L| \angle(\theta_L + \delta_3 - \delta_2 - \alpha))$$

Equating the real and imaginary parts, we have

$$P_{23} = |y_L||V_2|(|a||V_2| \cos\theta_L - |V_3| \cos(\theta_L + \delta_3 - \delta_2 - \alpha)) \quad \text{(i)}$$

$$Q_{23} = -|a||y_L||V_2|(|a||V_2| \sin\theta_L - |V_3| \sin(\theta_L + \delta_3 - \delta_2 - \alpha)) \quad \text{(ii)}$$

When $a = 1\angle 0°$,

$$P_{23} = 10(1.05)(0 - 0.95 \cos(90° + 2° + 3° - 0°)) = 0.8694 \text{ pu}$$

$$Q_{23} = -10(1.05)(1.05 - 0.95 \sin(90° + 2° + 3° - 0°)) = -1.088 \text{ pu}$$

when a is changed to $1\angle{-2.5°}$

$$P_{23} = 10(1.05)(0 - 0.95 \cos(90° + 2° + 3° + 2.5°)) = 1.302 \text{ pu}$$

$$Q_{23} = -10(1.05)(1.05 - 0.95 \sin(90° + 2° + 3° + 2.5°)) = -1.135 \text{ pu}$$

$$\Delta P_{23} = (1.302 - 0.8694) \text{ pu} = 0.4326 \text{ pu}$$

$$\Delta Q_{23} = (-1.135 - (-1.088)) \text{ pu} = 0.047 \text{ pu}$$

Thus, the increase in real power flow is almost 10 times that of the increase in reactive power flow. Therefore, the phase shifts vary real power flow predominantly.

(c) When a is changed to $1.05\angle 0°$

$$P_{23} = (1.05)(10)(1.05)(0 - 0.95 \cos(90 + 2° + 3°)) = 0.9128 \text{ pu}$$

$$Q_{23} = -(1.05)(10)(1.05)((1.05)^2 - 0.95 \sin(90 + 2° + 3°)) = -1.7212 \text{ pu}$$

$$\Delta P_{23} = 0.9128 - 0.8694 = 0.0434 \text{ pu}$$

$$\Delta Q_{23} = -1.7212 - (-1.135) = -0.5862 \text{ pu}$$

Hence, the increase in reactive power is almost 14 times that of the increase in real power flow. Therefore, the change in voltage magnitudes affects mainly reactive power flow.

Problems

6.1 For the power system shown in Fig. P-6.1, obtain the bus incidence matrix A. Take ground as reference. Is this matrix unique? Explain.

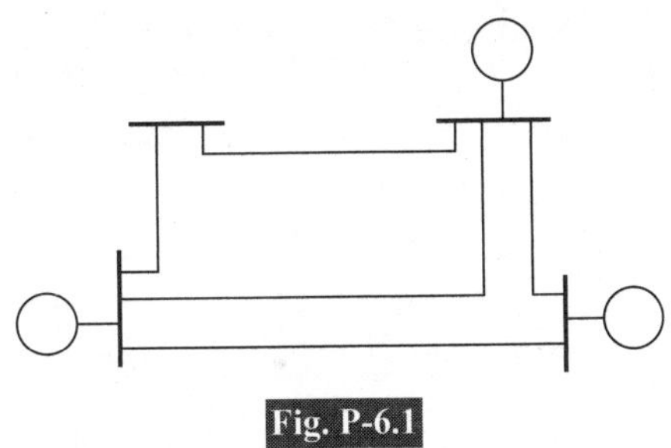

Fig. P-6.1

6.2 For the network shown in Fig. P-6.2, obtain the complex bus bar voltage at bus 2 at the end of the first iteration. Use the GS method. Line impedances shown in Fig. P-6.2 are in pu.

Given Bus 1 is slack bus with $V_1 = 1.0 \angle 0^\circ$

$P_2 + jQ_2 = -5.96 + j1.46$

$|V_3| = 1.02$

Assume $V_3^0 = 1.02\angle 0^\circ$ and $V_2^0 = 1\angle 0^\circ$

1 2 3

0.04 + *j*0.06 0.02 + *j*0.03

Fig. P-6.2

6.3 For the system of Fig. P-6.3, find the voltage at the receiving bus at the end of the first iteration. Load is 2 + *j*0.8 pu. Voltage at the sending end (slack) is 1 + *j*0 pu. Line admittance is 1.0 – *j*4.0 pu. Transformer reactance is *j*0.4 pu. Off-nominal turns ratio is 1/1.04. Use the GS technique. Assume $V_R = 1\angle 0^\circ$.

Load

Fig. P-6.3

6.4 (a) Find the bus incidence matrix ***A*** for the four-bus system in Fig. P-6.4. Take ground as a reference.

(b) Find the primitive admittance matrix for the system. It is given that all the lines are characterised by a series impedance of 0.1 + *j*0.7 Ω/km and a shunt admittance of *j*0.35 × 10^{-5} Ω/km. Lines are rated at 220 kV.

(c) Find the bus admittance matrix for the system. Use the values 220 kV and 100 MVA. Express all impedances and admittances in per unit.

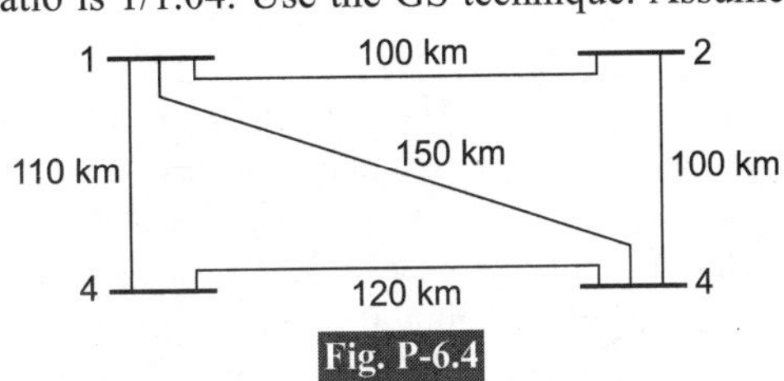

Fig. P-6.4

6.5 Consider the three-bus system of Fig. P-6.5. The pu line reactances are indicated on the figure; the line resistances are negligible. The magnitude of all the three-bus voltages are specified to be 1.0 pu. The bus powers are specified in the following table below:

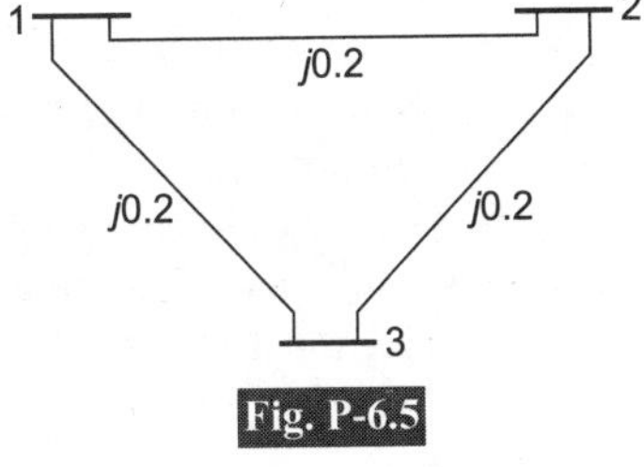

Fig. P-6.5

Bus	*Real demand*	*Reactive demand*	*Real generation*	*Reactive generation*
1.	$P_{D1} = 1.0$	$Q_{D1} = 0.6$	$P_{G1} = ?$	Q_{G1} (unspecified)
2.	$P_{D2} = 0$	$Q_{D2} = 0.0$	$P_{G2} = 1.4$	Q_{G2} (unspecified)
3.	$P_{D3} = 1.0$	$Q_{D3} = 1.0$	$P_{G3} = 0$	Q_{G3} (unspecified)

Carry out the complete approximate load flow solution. Mark generations, load demands and line flows on the one-line diagram.

6.6 (a) Repeat Problem 6.5 with bus voltage specifications changed as below:

$$|V_1| = 1.00 \text{ pu}$$
$$|V_2| = 1.04 \text{ pu}$$
$$|V_3| = 0.96 \text{ pu}$$

Your results should show that no significant change occurs in real power flows, but the reactive flows change appreciably as Q is sensitive to voltage.

(b) Resolve Problem 6.5 assuming that the real generation is scheduled as follows:

$$P_{G1} = 1.0 \text{ pu}, P_{G2} = 1.0 \text{ pu}, P_{G3} = 0$$

The real demand remains unchanged and the desired voltage profile is flat, i.e., $|V_1| = |V_2| = |V_3| = 1.0$ pu. In this case the results will show that the reactive flows are essentially unchanged, but the real flows are changed.

6.7 Consider the three-bus system of Problem 6.5. As shown in Fig. P-6.7 where a regulating transformer (RT) is now introduced in the line 1–2 near bus 1. Other system data remain as that of Problem 6.5. Consider two cases:

(i) RT is a magnitude regulator with a ratio = $V_1/V_1' = 0.99$,

(ii) RT is a phase angle regulator having a ratio = $V_1/V_1' = e^{j3°}$

(a) Find out the modified $\boldsymbol{Y}_{\text{BUS}}$ matrix.

(b) Solve the load flow equations in cases (i) and (ii). Compare the load flow picture with one in Problem 6.5. The reader should verify that in case (i) only the reactive flow will change; whereas in case (ii) the changes will occur in the real power flow.

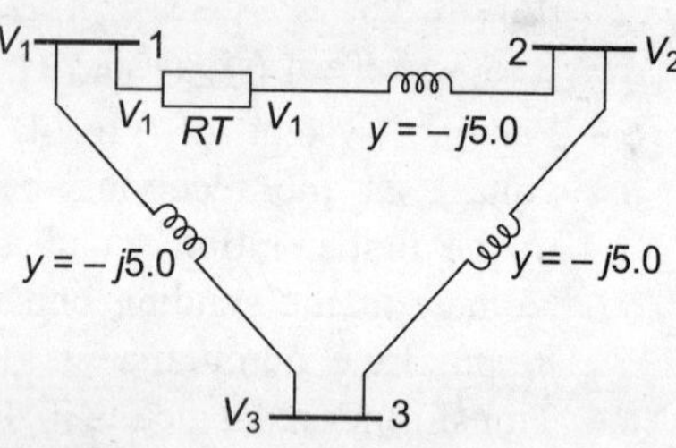

Fig. P-6.7 *Three-bus sample system containing a regulating transformer*

6.8 Calculate V_3 for the system of Fig. P-6.7 for the first iteration, using the data of Example 6.3. Start the algorithm with calculations at bus 3 rather than at bus 2.

6.9 For the sample system of Example 6.3 with bus 1 as slack, use the following methods to obtain a load flow solution.

(a) Gauss–Seidel using $\boldsymbol{Y}_{\text{BUS}}$, with acceleration factor of 1.6 and tolerances of 0.0001 for the real and imaginary components of voltage.

(b) Newton–Raphson using $\boldsymbol{Y}_{\text{BUS}}$, with tolerances of 0.01 pu for changes in the real and reactive bus powers.

Note: This problem requires the use of the digital computer.

6.10 Perform a load flow study for the system of Problem 6.4. The bus power and voltage specifications are given in Table P-6.10.

Table P-6.10

Bus	*Bus power, pu*		*Voltage magnitude, pu*	*Bus type*
	Real	*Reactive*		
1	Unspecified	Unspecified	1.02	Slack
2	0.95	Unspecified	1.01	PV
3	– 2.0	– 1.0	Unspecified	PQ
4	– 1.0	– 0.2	Unspecified	PQ

Compute the unspecified bus voltages, all bus powers and all line powers. Assume unlimited Q sources. Use the NR method.

Multiple Choice Questions

6.1 For load flow solutions, what are the quantities specified at load bus are
(a) P and $|V|$ (b) P and Q (c) P and δ (d) Q and $|V|$

6.2 Load Flow study is carried out for
(a) Load frequency control (b) System planning
(c) Stability studies (d) Fault calculations

6.3 In the solution of load flow equation, Newton-Raphson (NR) method is superior to the Gauss-Seidel (GS) method, because the
(a) Convergence characteristic of the NR methods are not affected by selection of slack bus.
(b) Number of iterations required is not independent of the size of system in the NR method.
(c) Time taken to perform one iteration in the NR method is less when compared to the time taken in the GS method.
(d) Number of iteration required in the NR method is more than compared to that in the GS method.

6.4 At slack bus, which one of the following combinations of variables is specified?
(a) $|V|, \delta$ (b) P, Q (c) P, $|V|$ (d) Q, $|V|$

6.5 Normally Z_{Bus} matrix is a
(a) Null matrix (b) Sparse matrix (c) Full matrix (d) Unity matrix

6.6 In loadflow analysis, the load at bus is represented as
(a) A voltage dependent impedance at bus.
(b) Constant real and reactive powers drawn from bus.
(c) A constant impedance connected at bus.
(d) A constant current drawn from the bus.

6.7 In Gauss-Seidel method of power flow problem, the number of iterations may be reduced if the correction in voltage at each bus is multiplied by
(a) Gauss constant (b) Acceleration constant
(c) Blocking factor (d) Deceleration constant

6.8 In load flow studies PV bus is treated as PQ bus when
(a) Phase angle becomes high (b) Reactive power goes beyond limit
(c) Voltage at the bus becomes high (d) Any of the above

6.9 In a power system the maximum number of buses are
(a) PV buses (b) Slack buses (c) PQ buses (d) Any of the above

6.10 For accurate load flow calculations on large power systems, the best method is
(a) NR method (b) GS method (c) Decoupled method (d) FDLR

6.11 Which among the following quantities are to be determined in voltage controlled bus?
(a) P and Q (b) Q and |V| (c) |V| and δ (d) Q and δ

6.12 In load flow studies of a power system, a voltage control bus is specified by
(a) Real power and reactive power (b) Reactive power and voltage magnitude
(c) Voltage and voltage phase angle (d) Real power and voltage magnitude

6.13 What percentage of buses in the power system are generator buses?
(a) 5% (b) 25% (c) 70% (d) 10%

6.14 In power system, if a voltage controlled bus is treated as a load bus then which one of the following limits would be violated?
(a) Voltage
(b) Active power
(c) Reactive power
(d) Phase angle

6.15 Which among the following quantities are specified at the generator bus?
(a) P and Q
(b) P and |V|
(c) Q and |V|
(d) P and δ

6.16 In a load flow analysis of a power system, the load connected to a bus is represented as
(a) Constant current drawn from the bus
(b) Constant impedance connected to the bus
(c) Voltage and frequency dependent sources to the bus
(d) Constant real and reactive power drawn from the bus

6.17 The voltage of a particular bus can be controlled by controlling the
(a) Active power of the bus
(b) Reactive power of the bus
(c) Phase angle
(d) All of the above

6.18 A power system network contains 100 buses in which 10 are the voltage control buses, 5 are fixed shunt capacitor buses, 20 are the reactive power support buses and 6 are the generator buses. Find the size of the Jacobian matrix.
(a) 162×162
(b) 163×163
(c) 164×164
(d) 165×165

6.19 Which of the following is/are advantages of N-R method?
(a) Number of iterations is less
(b) Applicable for large power system network
(c) Convergence is not affected by the choice of slack bus
(d) All of the above

6.20 Which of the following is/are disadvantages of N-R method?
(a) Time taken for each iteration is larger, if size of the Jacobian matrix is larger
(b) Computer memory required is larger
(c) Computer programming is difficult
(d) All of the above

6.21 The advantages of Gauss-Siedel method for load flow studies is/are
(a) Calculation time for each iteration is less
(b) Number of iterations is less
(c) Applicable for large power system network
(d) All of the above

6.22 The disadvantages of Gauss-Siedel method for load flow studies is/are
(a) More number of iterations are required
(b) The choice of slack bus affects the convergence
(c) It is not applicable for the large power system networks
(d) All of the above

6.23 The size of the Y bus matrix for n bus composite power system is
(a) $(n-1) \times (n-1)$
(b) $(n+1) \times (n+1)$
(c) $n \times n$
(d) $(n-2) \times (n-2)$

6.24 A power system contains 50 buses in which 10 are the voltage control buses, and 6 are the generator buses. What will be the size of the Jacobian matrix?
(a) 82×82
(b) 83×83
(c) 84×84
(d) 66×66

6.25 In a composite power system, n = total number of buses, and m = total number of PV buses. The size of the Jacobian matrix will be

(a) $(2n - m - 1) \times (2n - m - 1)$ (b) $(2n - m + 1) \times (2n - m + 1)$
(c) $(2n - m - 2) \times (2n - m - 2)$ (d) $(2n - m + 2) \times (2n - m + 2)$

References

Books

1. A.K. Mahalanabis, D.P. Kothari and S.I. Ahson, *Computer Aided Power System Analysis and Control*, Tata McGraw-Hill, New Delhi, 1988.
2. B.M. Weedy and B.J. Cory, *Electrical Power Systems*, 4th edn, Wiley, New York, 1998.
3. C.A. Gross, *Power System Analysis*, 2nd edn, Wiley, New York, 1986.
4. M.J.H. Sterling, *Power System Control, IEE*, England, 1978.
5. O.I. Elgerd, *Electric Energy System Theory: An Introduction*, 2nd edn, McGraw-Hill, New York, 1982.
6. G.W. Stagg and A.H. El-Abiad, *Computer Methods in Power System Analysis*, McGraw-Hill, New York, 1968.
7. D.J. Rose and R.A. Willough (Eds), *Sparse Matrices and Their Applications*, Plenum, New York, 1972.
8. G.T. Heydt, *Computer Analysis Methods for Power Systems*, Stars in a Circle Publications, 1996.
9. H.E. Brown, *Solution of Large Networks by Matrix Methods*, Wiley, New York, 1975.
10. U.G. Knight, *Power System Engineering and Mathematics*, Pergamon Press, New York, 1972.
11. Arrillaga, C.P. Arnold and B.J. Harker, *Computer Modelling of Electrical Power Systems*, John Wiley, 1983.
12. H.H. Happ, *Diakoptics and Networks,* Academic Press, New York, 1971.
13. J.C. Arrillaga and N.R. Watson, *Computer Modelling of Electrical Power Systems*, 2nd edn, Wiley, New York, 2001.
14. D.P. Kothari and I.J. Nagrath, *Modern Power System Analysis*, 3rd edn, New York, 2006.
15. A.R. Bergen, *Power System Analysis*, Prentice-Hall, Englewood Cliffs, N J, 1986.
16. J. Arrillaga and C.P. Arnold, *Computer Analysis of Power Systems*, Wiley, New York, 1990.
17. K.R. Padiyar, *HVDC Power Transmission Systems*, Wiley, Eastern New Delhi, 1990.

Papers

18. B.R. Prusty and D. Jena, “A Sensitivity Matrix-Based Temperature-Augmented Probabilistic Load Flow Study”, *IEEE Trans. on Industry Applications*, volume: 53, issue: 3, pp: 2506–2516, 2017.
19. M.A. Laughton, “Decomposition Techniques in Power System Network Load Flow Analysis Using the Nodal Impedance Matrix”, *Proc. IEE*, volume: 115, p: 539, 1968.
20. B. Stott, “Decoupled Newton Load Flow”, *IEEE Trans.*, PAS, volume: 91, p: 1955, 1972.
21. B. Stott, “Review of Load-Flow Calculation Method”, *Proc. IEEE*, volume: 916, July 1974.
22. B. Stott, and O. Alsac, “Fast Decoupled Load Flow”, *IEEE Trans.*, PAS, volume: 93, p: 859, 1974.
23. D. Kumari, S.K. Chattopadhyay, and A. Verma, “Improvement of Power Flow Capability by Using an Alternative Power Flow Controller”, *IEEE Transactions on Power Delivery*, volume: 35, issue: 5, pp: 2353–2362, 2020.
24. W.F. Tinney and C.E. Hart, “Power Flow Solution by Newton’s Method”, *IEEE Trans.*, PAS, volume: 86, issue: 11, p: 1449, November 1967.

25. Z. Hu and X. Wang, "Efficient Computation of Maximum Loading Point by Load Flow Method with Optimal Multiplier", *IEEE Transactions on Power Systems*, volume: 23, issue: 2, pp: 804–806, 2008.
26. P.G. Murthy, D.L. Shenoy, J. Nanda and D.P. Kothari, "Performance of Typical Power Flow Algorithms with Reference to Indian Power Systems", *Proc. II Symp. Power Plant Dynamics and Control*, Hyderabad, volume: 219, pp: 14–16, Feb. 1979.
27. M. Pereira and L.C. Zanetta, "A Current Based Model for Load Flow Studies with UPFC", *IEEE Transactions on Power Systems*, volume: 28, issue: 2, pp: 677–682, May 2013.
28. N. Sato and W.F. Tinney, "Techniques for Exploiting Sparsity of Network Admittance Matrix", *IEEE Trans.,* PAS, volume: 82, issue: 44, December 1963.
29. M.S. Sachdev and T.K.P. Medicherla, "A Second Order Load Flow Technique", *IEEE Trans*., PAS, volume: 96, p: 189, Jan./Feb. 1977.
30. S. Iwamoto and Y. Tamura, "A Fast Load Flow Method Retaining Non-linearity", *IEEE Trans*., PAS, volume: 97, p: 1586, Sept./Oct. 1978.
31. H. Ambriz-Perez, E. Acha, and C.R. Fuerte-Esquivel, "Advanced SVC Models for Newton-Raphson Load Flow and Newton Optimal Power Flow Studies", *IEEE Transactions on Power Systems*, volume: 15, issue: 1, pp: 129–136, 2000.
32. S. Iwamoto and Y. Tamura, "A Load Flow Calculation Method for Ill-Conditioned Power Systems", *IEEE Trans.,* PAS, volume: 100, p: 1736, April 1981.
33. M. Bazrafshan and N. Gatsis, "Convergence of the Z-Bus Method for Three-Phase Distribution Load-Flow with ZIP Loads", *IEEE Transactions on Power Systems*, volume: 33, issue: 1, pp: 153–165, 2018.
34. J.F. Dopazo, O.A. Kiltin and A.M. Sarson, "Stochastic Load Flows", *IEEE Trans.,* PAS, volume: 94, p: 299, 1975.
35. J. Nanda, D.P. Kothari and S.C. Srivastava, "Some Important Observations on FDLF Algorithm", *Proc. IEEE*, pp: 732–739, May 1987.
36. J. Nanda, P.R. Bijwe, D.P. Kothari and D.L. Shenoy, "Second Order Decoupled Load Flow", *Electric Machines and Power Systems*, volume: 12, issue: 5, pp: 301–312, 1987.
37. J. Nanda, D.P. Kothari and S.C. Srivastava, "A Novel Second Order Fast Decoupled Load Flow Method in Polar Coordinates", *Electric Machines and Power Systems*, volume: 14, issue: 5, pp: 339–351, 1989.
38. D. Das, H.S. Nagi and D.P. Kothari, "A Novel Method for Solving Radial Distribution Networks", *Proc. IEE*, ptc, volume: 141, issue: 4, pp: 291–298, July 1994.
39. D. Das, D.P. Kothari and A. Kalam, "A Simple and Efficient Method for Load Flow Solution of Radial Distribution Networks", *Int. J. EPES*, pp: 335–346, 1995.
40. C.R. Fuerte-Esquivel and E. Acha, "A Newton-Type Algorithm for the Control of Power Flow in Electrical Power Networks", *IEEE Transactions on Power Systems*, volume: 12, issue: 4, pp: 1474–1480, 1997.
41. H.T. Zhang, W. Sun, Y. Li, D. Fu, and Y. Yuan, "A Fast Optimal Power Flow Algorithm Using Powerball Method", *IEEE Transactions on Industrial Informatics*, volume: 16, issue: 11, pp: 6993–7003, 2020.
42. A.C. Zambroni De Souza, C.B. Rosa Junior, B.I. Lima Lopes, R.C. Leme, and O.A.S. Carpinteiro, "Non-Iterative Load-Flow Method as a Tool for Voltage Stability Studies", in *IET Generation, Transmission & Distribution*, volume: 1, issue: 3, pp: 499–505, 2007.

43. R.S. Salgado and A.F. Zeitune, "Power Flow Solutions Through Tensor Methods", *IET Generation, Transmission & Distribution*, volume: 3, issue: 5, pp: 413–424, 2009.
44. R.K. Saket, R.C. Bansal, and Col. Gurmit Singh, "Reliability Evaluation of Power System Considering Voltage Stability and Continuation Power Flow", *Journal of Electrical Systems, Engineering and Scientific Research Groups, France*, volume: 3, issue 2, pp: 48–60, June 2007.
45. R. Thirumalaivasan, N. Prabhu, M. Janaki, and D.P. Kothari, "Analysis of Subsynchronous Resonance with Generalized Unified Power Flow Controller", *International Journal of Electrical Power & Energy Systems, Elsevier*, volume: 53, pp: 623–631, 2013.

CHAPTER 7

Optimal System Operation

7.1 ▶ INTRODUCTION

The optimal system operation, in general, involves the consideration of economy of operation, system security, emissions at certain fossil-fuel plants, optimal releases of water at hydro generation, etc. All these considerations may make for conflicting requirements and usually a compromise has to be made for optimal system operation. In this chapter, we consider the economy of operation only, also called the *economic dispatch problem*.

The main aim in the economic dispatch problem is to minimise the total cost of generating real power (production cost) at various stations while satisfying the loads and the losses in the transmission links. For simplicity, we consider the presence of thermal plants only in the beginning. In the later part of this chapter, we will consider the presence of hydro plants which operate in conjunction with thermal plants. While there is negligible operating cost at a hydro plant, there is a limitation of availability of water over a period of time which must be used to save maximum fuel at the thermal plants.

In the load flow problem as detailed in Ch. 6, two variables are specified at each bus and the solution is then obtained for the remaining variables. The specified variables are real and reactive powers at PQ buses, real powers and voltage magnitudes at PV buses, and voltage magnitude and angle at the slack bus. The additional variables to be specified for load flow solution are the tap settings of regulating transformers. If the specified variables are allowed to vary in a region constrained by practical considerations (upper and lower limits on active and reactive generations, bus voltage limits, and range of transformer tap settings), there results an infinite number of load flow solutions, each pertaining to one set of values of specified variables. The 'best' choice in some sense of the values of specified variables leads to the 'best' load flow solution. Economy of operation is naturally predominant in determining the best choice, though there are other factors that should be given consideration. While an experienced operator could make a good guess of the best values of specified variables in a small system guided by past experience, the best solution would elude him in a modern complex system without the aid of powerful analytical tools. This chapter is devoted to the study of analytical methods of arriving at the best (optimal) operating strategies in power systems. Additionally, the optimal operating strategy must meet the minimum standards of reliability or, in other words, the continuity of supply.

To start with the economic factor in power system operation, we will focus our attention on allocation of real power at generator buses. This problem can be partitioned into two sub-problems, viz. optimum allocation (commitment) of generators (units) at each generating station at various station load levels (including load sharing among committed generators), and optimum allocation of generation to each station for various system load levels. The first problem in power system parlance is called the 'unit commitment' (UC) problem and the second is called the 'load scheduling' (LS) problem. One must first solve the UC problem before proceeding with the LS problem.

Throughout this chapter, we shall concern ourselves with an existing installation, so that the economic considerations are that of operating (running) cost and not the capital outlay.

7.2 ▶ OPTIMAL OPERATION OF GENERATORS ON A BUS BAR

Before we tackle the unit commitment problem, we shall consider the optimal operation of generators on a bus bar.

7.2.1 Generator Operating Cost

The total generator operating cost includes *fuel, labour, and maintenance costs*. For simplicity, fuel cost is the only one considered to be variable. The fuel cost is meaningful in case of thermal and nuclear stations, but for hydro stations, where the energy storage is 'apparently free', the operating cost as such is not *meaningful*. A suitable meaning will be attached to the cost of hydro stored energy in Section 7.7. Presently we shall concentrate on fuel fired stations.

The input–output curve of a generating unit specifies the *input energy rate* $F_i(P_{Gi})$ (MKcal/h) or cost of fuel used per hour $C_i(P_{Gi})$ (Rs/h) as a function of the generator power output P_{Gi}. The input–output curve can be determined *experimentally*. A typical input–output curve is shown in Fig. 7.1 and is concave upwards. It is convenient to express the input–output curves in terms of input energy rate (MKcal/h) rather than fuel-cost per hour (Rs/h) because fuel-cost can change monthly or daily in comparison with the fuel energy used per hour or input energy rate at a given output power (generating unit efficiency). In Fig. 7.1, $(\text{MW})_{\text{min}}$ is the minimum loading limit below which it is *uneconomical* (or may be *technically infeasible*) to operate the unit and $(\text{MW})_{\text{max}}$ is the maximum output limit. The curve has *discontinuities at steam valve openings* which have not been indicated in the figure.

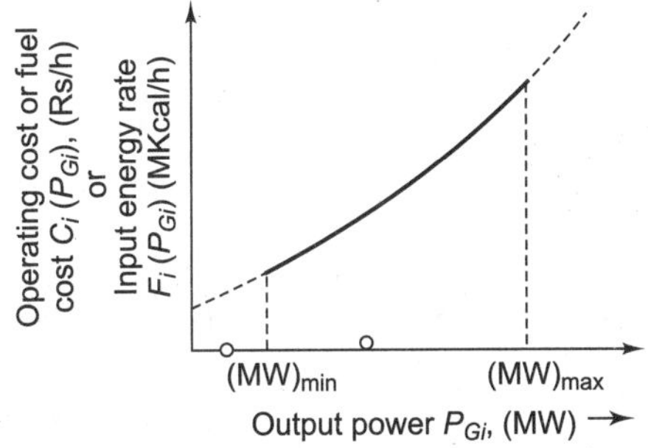

Fig. 7.1 *Input–output curve of a generating unit*

We next consider the heat-rate curve $H_i(P_{Gi})$ which is the heat energy (obtained by combustion of fuel) in (MKcal) needed to generate one unit of electric energy (MWh). Figure 7.2 shows the approximate shape of the heat rate curve, which can be determined experimentally. The generating unit efficiency can be defined as the ratio of electric energy output generated to fuel energy input. Thus, the generating unit is most efficient at the minimum heat-rate which corresponds to a particular P_{Gi}. The heat-rate (and hence efficiency) varies with the output power P_{Gi} and the curve indicates the increase in the heat-rate (or drop in efficiency) at low and high power limits. Typical peak efficiency heat-rates of modern fuel fired plants are around 2.5 MKcal/MWh giving a peak efficiency of $\dfrac{3600 \times 100}{2.5 \times 4.2 \times 1000}$ = 34%. Since all input fuel energy is not converted to electric energy output, the heat-rate indicated in Fig. 7.2 can be further reduced at all points if the conversion from input fuel energy to output electric energy is 100%. For 100% conversion, the heat rate is approximately 0.859 MKcal/MWh (1 MKcal = 1.164 MWh is the equivalent of heat).

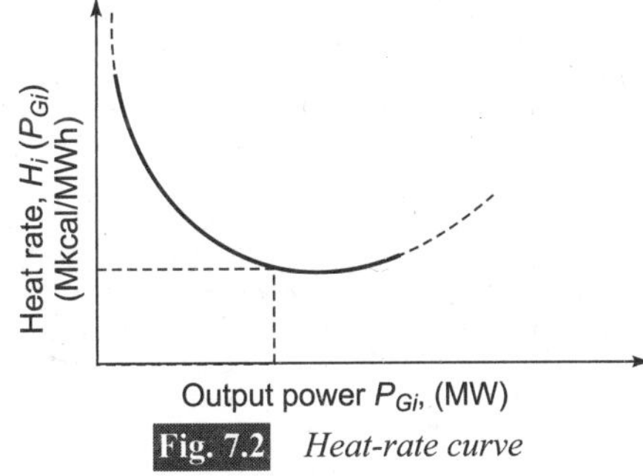

Fig. 7.2 *Heat-rate curve*

The input–output curve can be obtained from the heat-rate curve as

$$F_i(P_{Gi}) = P_{Gi}\, H_i(P_{Gi}) \quad \text{(MK cal/h)} \tag{7.1}$$

where $H_i(P_{Gi})$ is the heat-rate in MKcal/MWh. The graph of $F_i(P_{Gi})$ is the input–output curve (Fig. 7.1). Let the cost of the fuel be K Rs/MKcal. Then the input fuel-cost, $C_i(P_{Gi})$ is

$$C_i(P_{Gi}) = KF_i(P_{Gi}) = KP_{Gi}H_i(P_{Gi}) \quad \text{(Rs/h)} \tag{7.2}$$

The heat-rate curve (Fig. 7.2) may be approximated in the form,

$$H_i(P_{Gi}) = (a_i'/P_{Gi}) + b_i' + c_i' P_{Gi} \text{ (MKcal/MWh)} \tag{7.3}$$

with all coefficients positive. From Eqs. (7.1) and (7.3), we get a quadratic expression for input energy rate $F_i(P_{Gi})$ with positive coefficients in the form

$$F_i(P_{Gi}) = a_i' + b_i'P_{Gi} + c_i' P_{Gi}^2 \quad \text{(MKcal/h)} \tag{7.4}$$

From Eqs. (7.2) and (7.4), we also get a quadratic expression for fuel-cost $C_i(P_{Gi})$ with positive coefficient in the form

$$\begin{aligned} C_i(P_{Gi}) &= Ka_i' + Kb_i'P_{Gi} + Kc_i'P_{Gi}^2 \\ &= a_i + b_iP_{Gi} + c_iP_{Gi}^2 \quad \text{(Rs/h)} \end{aligned} \tag{7.5}$$

The slope of the fuel-cost curve, i.e., dC_i/dP_{Gi}, is called the incremental fuel cost (*IC*), and is expressed in Rs/MWh. A typical plot of the incremental fuel cost versus power output is shown in Fig. 7.3. From Eq. (7.5), the incremental fuel cost is

$$(IC)_i = dC_i/dP_{Gi} = b_i + 2c_i P_{Gi} \quad \text{(Rs/MWh)} \tag{7.6}$$

i.e., a linear relationship. The linearity of Eq. (7.6) arises because of the quadratic approximation for $C_i(P_{Gi})$ of Eq. (7.5). Figure 7.3 shows the actual and the linear approximation for the incremental cost curve.

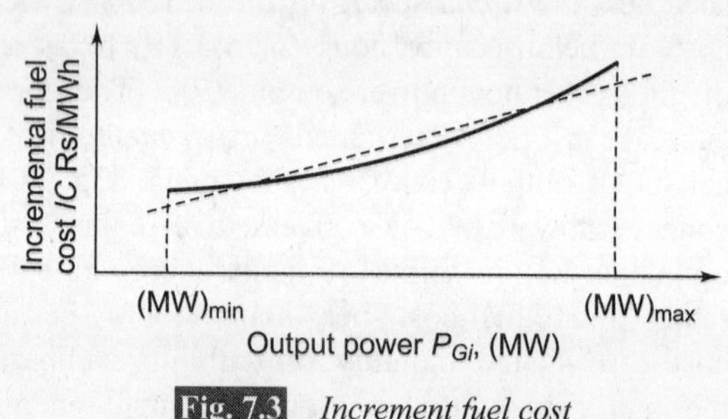

Fig. 7.3 *Increment fuel cost*

The fuel-cost curve and the incremental cost curve may have a number of discontinuities, as shown in Figs. 7.4(a) and (b). The discontinuities occur when the output power has to be extended by using additional boilers, steam condensers or other equipment. Discontinuities also appear if the cost represents the operation of an entire power station, so that cost has discontinuities on paralleling of generators.

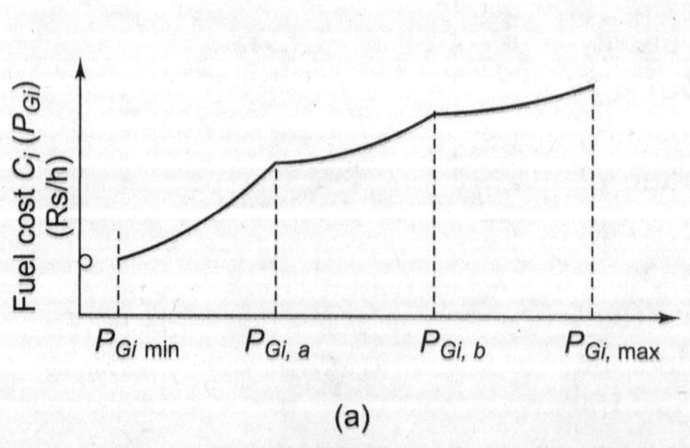

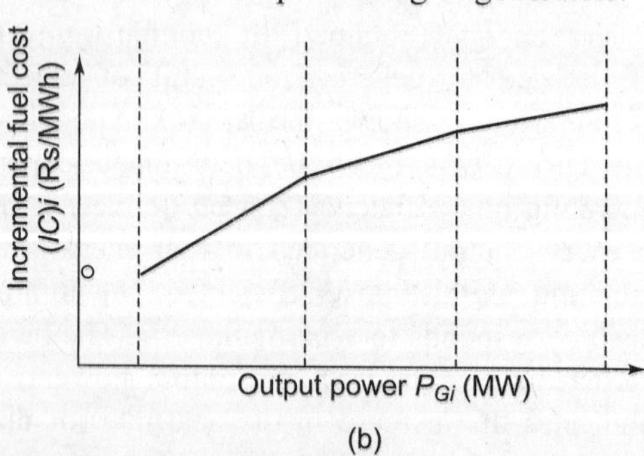

Fig. 7.4 *Cost and incremental cost curves with discontinuities*

Within the continuity range, the incremental fuel cost may be expressed by a number of short line segments (piecewise linearisation). Alternatively, we can fit a polynomial of suitable degree to represent the *IC* curve in the inverse form as

$$P_{Gi} = \alpha_i + \beta_i(IC)_i + \gamma_i(IC)_i^2 + \dots \text{ MW} \tag{7.7}$$

Example 7.1 The heat rate of a 100 MW fuel-fired generator is

10 MKcal/MWh at 25% of rating
9 MKcal/MWh at 40% of rating
10 MKcal/MWh at 100% of rating

and the cost of the fuel is Rs 2 per MKcal. Find

(a) $C(P_G)$ in the form of Eq. (7.4);
(b) the fuel input rate (heat rate) and fuel cost when 25%, 50% and 100% loaded;
(c) the incremental cost in Rs/MWh;
(d) the approximate cost and the cost using the quadratic approximation in Rs/h to deliver 101 MW.

Solution

(a) The expression for the heat rate $H(P_G)$, which leads to the expression given by Eq. (7.4), is given by Eq. (7.5) as

$$H_i(P_G) = (a'/P_G) + b' + c'P_G \quad \text{MKcal/MWh}$$

Substituting the measured values of $H(P_G)$ at different ratings, we get

$$(a'/25) + b' + c'25 = 10$$
$$(a'/40) + b' + c'40 = 9$$
$$(a'/100) + b' + c'100 = 8$$

Solving for the three unknown coefficients, a', b' and c', we get $a' = 1000/9$, $b' = 40/9$ and $c' = 2/45$. Thus

$$H(P_G) = (111.11/P_G) + 4.44 + 0.0444\, P_G \quad \text{MKcal/MWh}$$

Multiplying by P_G, we get the fuel input rate $F(P_G)$ in MKcal/h and multiplying by the cost of fuel per MKcal (Rs 2) we get fuel cost $C(P_G)$ as

$$F(P_G) = 111.11 + 4.44\, P_G + 0.0444\, P_G^2 \text{ MKcal/h}$$
$$C(P_G) = 222.22 + 8.889P_G + 0.0889P^2{}_G \text{ Rs/h.}$$

(b) At 25% rating, $P_G = 25$ MW and

$$F(25) = 250.00 \text{ MKcal/h}$$
$$C(25) = 250.00 \times 2 = 500.00 \text{ Rs/h}$$

Similarly at 40% and 100% rating,

$$F(40) = 360.00 \text{ MKcal/h}$$
$$C(40) = 720.00 \text{ Rs/h}$$
$$F(100) = 1000.00 \text{ MKcal/h}$$
$$C(100) = 2000.00 \text{ Rs/h}$$

(c) The incremental cost is

$$IC = \mathrm{d}C(P_G)/\mathrm{d}P_G = 8.889 + 0.1778P_G \quad \text{Rs/MWh.}$$

(d) At 100% rating (i.e., 100 MW)

$$IC = 8.889 + 0.1778 \times 100 = 26.667 \quad \text{Rs/MWh}$$

Approximate cost at 101 MW is

$$C(100) + IC(100) \times \Delta P_G = 2000 + 26.667 \times 1 = 2026.67 \quad \text{Rs/h}$$

where $\Delta P_G = 101 - 100 = 1$ MW

Cost, using the quadratic approximation, is

$$C(101) = 222.22 + 8.889(101) + 0.0889(101)$$
$$= 2026.75 \text{ Rs/h.}$$

Thus, the cost calculated approximately is very close to the cost calculated by using quadratic approximation, for a small change in output power ($\Delta P_G = 1$ MW) from 100 MW.

We also note that in Eq. (7.3), if the coefficient c' is negligible, then the heat-rate may be further approximated by

$$H_i(P_{Gi}) = (a_i'/P_{Gi}) + b_i' \quad \text{(MKcal/MWh)} \tag{7.8}$$

The shape of the heat-rate curve given by Eq. (7.8) is that of rectangular hyperbola as shown in Fig. 7.5. For large values of P_{Gi}, the input energy rate $H_i(P_{Gi}) \approx b_i$ a constant. From Eqs. (7.1), (7.2) and (7.8), we get linear approximations for the input energy rate $F_i(P_{Gi})$ and fuel cost $C_i(P_{Gi})$ in the form:

$$F_i(P_{Gi}) = a_i' + b_i'P_{Gi} \quad \text{(MKcal/h)} \tag{7.9a}$$

$$C_i(P_{Gi}) = a_i + b_iP_{Gi} \quad \text{(Rs/h)} \tag{7.9b}$$

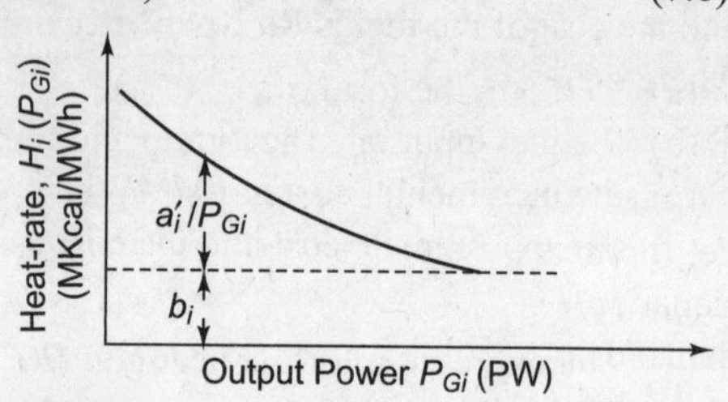

Fig. 7.5 *Heat-rate curve which gives a linear input–output curve*

Optimal Operation Let us assume that it is known *a priori* which generators are to run to meet a particular load demand on the station. This is, given a station with k generators committed and the active power load P_D given, the real power generation P_{Gi} for each generator has to be allocated so as to minimise the total cost.

$$C = \sum_{i=1}^{k} C_i(P_{Gi}) \quad \text{(Rs/h)} \tag{7.10}$$

subject to the inequality constraint

$$P_{Gi\,\min} \le P_{Gi} \le P_{Gi\,\max}; \quad i = 1, 2, ..., k \tag{7.11}$$

where $P_{Gi\,\min}$ and $P_{Gi\,\max}$ are the lower and upper real power generation limits of the ith generator. Obviously,

$$\sum_{i=1}^{k} P_{Gi\max} \ge P_D \tag{7.12a}$$

Considerations of spinning reserve, to be explained later in this chapter, require that

$$\sum_{i=1}^{k} P_{Gi\max} > P_D \tag{7.12b}$$

In Eq. (7.10), it is assumed that the cost C is largely dependent on the real power generation P_{Gi} and is insensitive to reactive power generation Q_{Gi}.

Since $C_i(P_{Gi})$ is nonlinear, and C_i is independent of P_{Gj} $(j \ne i)$, this is a separable nonlinear programming problem.

We assume that the inequality constraint of Eq. 7.12(a) is not effective, and

$$\sum_{i=1}^{k} P_{Gi} = P_D \quad \text{or} \quad \left(\sum_{i=1}^{k} P_{Gi}\right) - P_D = 0 \tag{7.13}$$

Also, for the time being we do not consider the effect of generator power limits given by Eq. (7.11).

The problem can then be solved by the method of Lagrange multipliers, which is used for minimising (or maximising) a function with side conditions in the form of equality constraints. Using this method, we define an augmented cost function (Lagrangian) as

$$\overline{C} = C - \lambda\left(\sum_{i=1}^{k} P_{Gi} - P_D\right) \tag{7.14}$$

where λ is the Lagrangian multiplier.

Minimisation is achieved by the condition

$$\frac{\partial \bar{C}}{\partial P_{Gi}} = 0$$

or

$$dC_i/dP_{Gi} = \lambda, \quad i = 1, 2, \ldots, k \tag{7.15}$$

where dC_i/dP_{Gi} is the incremental cost of the ith generator (units: Rs/MWh). Equation (7.15) can be written as

$$dC_1/dP_{G1} = dC_2/dP_{G2} = \ldots = dC_k/dP_{Gk} = \lambda \tag{7.16}$$

i.e., optimal loading of generators corresponds to the equal incremental cost point of all the generators. Equation (7.16), called the *coordination equation* numbering k is solved simultaneously with the load demand Eq. 7.13, to yield a solution for the Lagrange multiplier λ and the optimal generation of k generators. This is illustrated by means of Example 7.2 at the end of this section.

We now establish the procedure for determining λ in Eq. (7.16). If the cost curves are quadratic, then the problem reduces to the linear case. In general, the incremental cost curves may not be linear and λ can be determined by an iterative process. Computer solution for optimal loading of generators can be obtained iteratively by considering the incremental cost curves of Fig. 7.6 as follows:

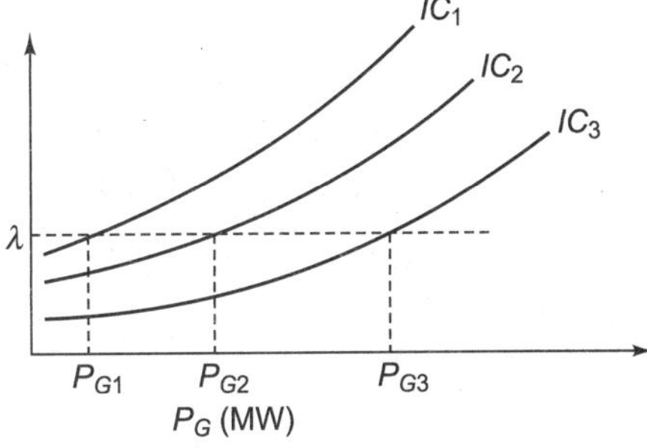

Fig. 7.6 *Incremental cost curves*

1. Choose a trial value of λ, i.e. $IC = (IC)°$.
2. Solve for P_{Gi} ($i = 1, 2, \ldots, k$) from Eq. (7.9).
3. If $\left| \sum_i P_{Gi} - P_D \right| < \varepsilon$ (a specified value), the optimal solution is reached. Otherwise,
4. Increment (IC) by $\Delta(IC)$, if $\left(\sum_i P_{Gi} - P_D \right) < 0$, or decrement (IC) by $\Delta(IC)$ if $\left(\sum_i P_{Gi} - P_D \right) > 0$ and repeat from step 2. This is possible because P_{Gi} is monotonically increasing function of (IC).

Consider now the effect of the generator limits given by the inequality constraint of Eq. (7.11). As IC is increased or decreased in the iterative process, if a particular generator loading P_{Gj} reaches the limit $P_{Gj\,\min}$ or $P_{Gj\,\max}$, its loading from then on is held fixed at this value and the balanced load is shared between the remaining generators on equal incremental cost basis. The fact that this operation is optimal can be shown by the Kuhn-Tucker theory (see Appendix I, *available online*).

Example 7.2 Incremental fuel costs in rupees per MWh for a plant consisting of two units are:

$$dC_1/dP_{G1} = 0.20P_{G1} + 40 \tag{i}$$

$$dC_2/dP_{G2} = 0.40P_{G2} + 30 \tag{ii}$$

and the generator limits are as follows:

$$30 \text{ MW} \le P_{G1} \le 175 \text{ MW}$$

$$20 \text{ MW} \le P_{G2} \le 125 \text{ MW}$$

Assume that both units are operating at all times. How will the load be shared between the two units as the system load varies over the full range of the load values? What are the corresponding values of the plant incremental costs?

Solution Figure 7.7 gives the incremental cost curves of the two units. At the lower end, $P_{G1\,min}$ (30 MW) > $P_{G2\,min}$ (20 MW) so that P_{G1} is fixed at 30 MW and P_{G2} at 20 MW (i.e., $P_D = 30 + 20 = 50$ MW). For $38 \le \lambda \le 46$, $\lambda_1 < \lambda_2$ (min), and therefore as the plant load increases beyond 50 MW, the load increments are placed on unit 2 till both units have $\lambda = 46$ ($P_D = 30 + 40 = 70$ MW). Load sharing beyond this point is carried out on equal-λ basis till unit 1 reaches its upper limit of 175 MW. Beyond this $\lambda_2 > \lambda_1$ (max) = 75 and further load increments are carried by unit 2 till it reaches its upper limit of 125 MW ($P_D = 175 + 125 = 300$ MW).

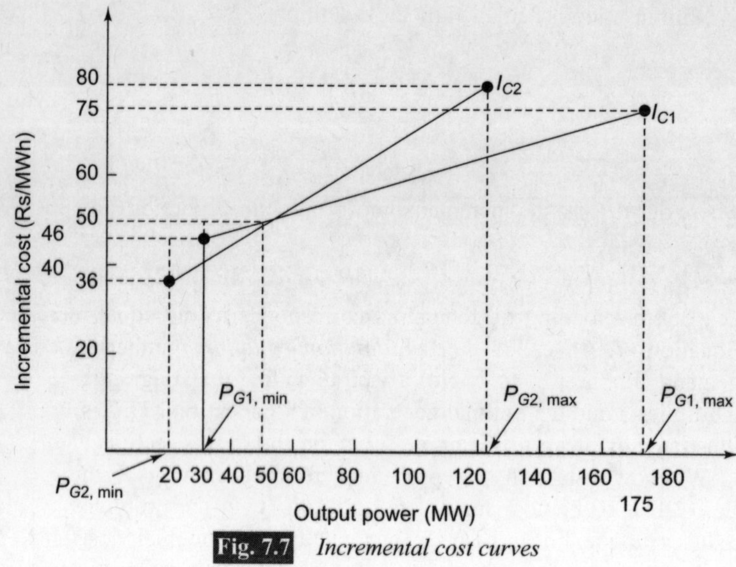

Fig. 7.7 *Incremental cost curves*

For $38 \le \lambda \le 46$,

$$\lambda = 0.40P_{G2} + 30 = 0.40(P_D - 30) + 30$$
$$= 0.40P_D + 18 \tag{iii}$$

The corresponding load range is

$$50 \le P \le 70 \text{ MW}$$

For $46 \le \lambda \le 75$,

$$\lambda = 0.20P_{Gi} + 40 = 0.40P_{G2} + 30;\ P_D = P_{G1} + P_{G2}$$

or

$$\lambda = (1/3)\,(0.40P_D + 110) \tag{iv}$$

The corresponding load range is

$$70 \le P \le 287.5 \text{ MW}$$

For $75 \le \lambda \le 80$

$$\lambda = 0.40P_{G2} + 30 = 0.40(P_D - 175) + 30$$
$$= 0.40P_D - 40 \tag{v}$$

The corresponding load range is

$$287.5 \le P_D \le 300 \text{ MW}$$

Thus,

$$\lambda = 0.40P_D + 18 \quad \text{(Rs/MWh)} \qquad (50 \le P_D \le 70) \tag{vi}$$
$$\lambda = (4/30)P_D + (110/3) \quad \text{(Rs/MWh)} \qquad (70 < P_D \le 287.5) \tag{vii}$$
$$\lambda = 0.40P_D - 40 \quad \text{(Rs/MWh)} \qquad (287.5 < P_D \le 300) \tag{viii}$$

Figure 7.8 shows the plot of the plant λ versus plant output.

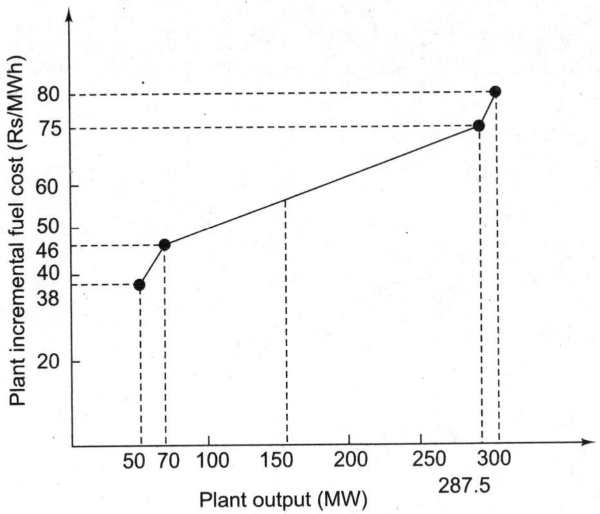

Fig. 7.8 *Plant incremental fuel cost curve as found in Example 7.2.*

Unit outputs for various plant outputs computed on above lines are given in Table 7.1 and are plotted in Fig. 7.9. Optimum load sharing for any plant can be directly read from this figure.

Table 7.1

Plant Rs/MWh	*Unit 1 P_{G1}, MW*	*Unit 2 P_{G2}, MW*	*Plant output $P_D = (P_{G1} + P_{G2})$, MW*
38	30	20	50
40	30	25	55
46	30	40	70
48	40	45	85
50	50	50	100
60	100	75	175
75	175	112.5	287.5
80	175	125	300

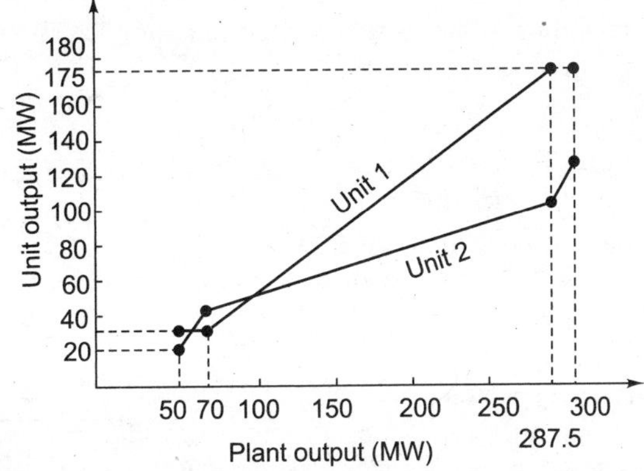

Fig. 7.9 *Output of each unit versus plant output for Example 7.2*

Example 7.3 For the plant described in Example 7.2, find the saving in fuel cost in rupees per hour for the optimal scheduling of a total load of 175 MW as compared to equal distribution of the same load between the two units.

Solution Example 7.2 reveals that for a total load of 175 MW unit 1 should take up a load of 100 MW and unit 2 should supply 75 MW. For equal distribution, each unit supplies 87.5 MW. The costs of generation for each unit are

$$C_1 = \int (\mathrm{d}C_1 / \mathrm{d}P_{G1})\mathrm{d}P_{G1} = \int IC_1 \, \mathrm{d}P_{G1}$$
$$= \int (0.20P_{G1} + 40.0)\,\mathrm{d}P_{G1}$$
$$= 0.10P_{G1}^2 + 40.0P_{G1} + k_1 \quad \text{Rs/h}$$

and

$$C_2 = \int (\mathrm{d}C_2 / \mathrm{d}P_{G1})\mathrm{d}P_{G2} = \int IC_2 \, \mathrm{d}P_{G2}$$
$$= \int (0.40P_{G2} + 30.0)\,\mathrm{d}P_{G2}$$
$$= 0.20P_{G2}^2 + 30.0P_{G2} + k_2 \quad \text{Rs/h}$$

where k_1 and k_2 are constants.

The increase in cost for unit 1 is

$$C_1(87.5) - C_1(100) = (0.10 \times 87.5^2 + 40.0 \times 87.5 + k_1) - (0.10 \times 100^2 + 40.0 \times 100 + k_1)$$
$$= -734.375 \text{ Rs/h}$$

and the increase in cost for unit 2 is

$$C_2(87.5) - C_2(75) = (0.20 \times 87.5^2 + 30.0 \times 87.5 + k_2) - (0.20 \times 75^2 + 30.0 \times 75 + k_2)$$
$$= 1891.25 \text{ Rs/h}$$

Net saving caused by optimum scheduling is

$$-734.735 + 1891.25 = 1156.875 \quad \text{Rs/h}$$

Total yearly saving assuming continuous operation

$$= \text{Rs } 10134225.00$$

This saving justifies the need for optimal load sharing and the devices to be installed for controlling the unit loadings automatically.

Example 7.4 Let the two units of the system studied in Example 7.2 have the following cost curves:

$$C_1 = 0.1\, P_{G1}^2 + 40\, P_{G1} + 120 \text{ Rs/h} \quad \text{(i)}$$
$$C_2 = 0.2\, P_{G2}^2 + 30\, P_{G2} + 100 \text{ Rs/h} \quad \text{(ii)}$$

Let us assume a daily load cycle as given in Fig. 7.10. Also assume that a cost of Rs 400 is incurred in taking either unit off the line and returning it to service after 12 hours. Consider the 24 hour period from 6 a.m. one morning to 6 a.m. the next morning. Now we want to find out whether it would be more economical to keep both the units in service for this 24-hour period or to remove one of the units from service for the 12 hours of light load.

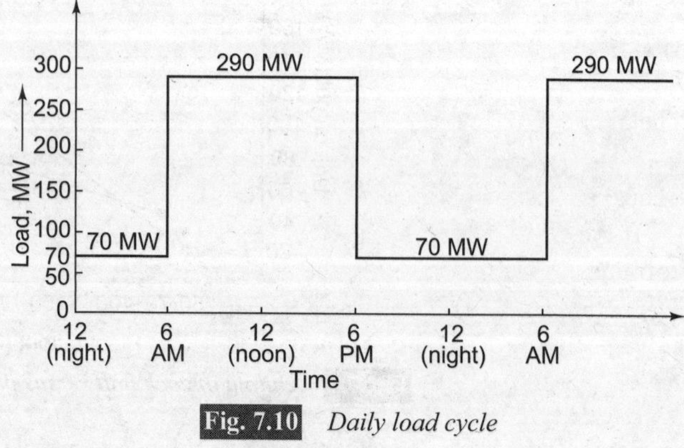

Fig. 7.10 *Daily load cycle*

Solution For the twelve-hour period when the load is 290 MW, referring to Example 7.2, we get the optimum schedule as

$$P_{G1} = 175 \text{ MW}, P_{G2} = 290 - 175 = 115 \text{ MW}$$

Total fuel cost for this period is

$$[0.1 \times 175^2 + 40 \times 175 + 120 + 0.2 \times 115^2 + 30 \times 115 + 100] \times 12 = \text{Rs } 1,96,530$$

If both units operate in the light load period (70 MW from 6 p.m. to 6 a.m.) also, then from Table 7.1 of Example 7.2, we get the optimum schedule as

$$P_{G1} = 30 \text{ MW}, P_{G2} = 40 \text{ MW}$$

Total fuel cost for this period is then

$$(0.1 \times 30^2 + 40 \times 30 + 120 + 0.2 \times 40^2 + 30 \times 40 + 100) \times 12 = \text{Rs } 36,360$$

Thus, the total fuel cost when both the units are operating throughout the 24-hour period is Rs. 2,32,890.

If only one of the units is run during the light load period, it is easily verified from Eqs. (i) and (ii) (Example 7.4) that it is economical to run unit 2 and to put off unit 1. Then the total fuel cost during this period will be

$$(0.2 \times 70^2 + 30 \times 70 + 100) \times 12 = \text{Rs } 38,160$$

Therefore total fuel cost for this case $= 1,96,530 + 38,160$

$= \text{Rs } 2,34,690$

Total operating cost for this case will be the total fuel cost plus the start-up cost of unit 1, i.e.,

$$2,34,690 + 400 = \text{Rs } 2,35,090$$

Comparing this with the earlier case, it is clear that it is economical to run both the units.

It is seen that even if the start-up cost is neglected, it is economical to run both the units.

Now consider the case when the output load is 55 MW from 6 p.m. to 6 a.m. instead of 70 MW as in the earlier case. If both units operate in this light load period, then from Table 7.1 (Example 7.2), we get the optimum schedule as

$$P_{G1} = 30 \text{ MW}, P_{G2} = 25 \text{ MW}$$

Total fuel cost for this period is

$$(0.1 \times 30^2 + 40 \times 30 + 120 + 0.2 \times 25^2 + 30 \times 25 + 100) \times 12 = \text{Rs } 28,620$$

Thus, the total fuel cost when both the units are operating throughout the 24 hours period is

$$\text{Rs } (1,96,530 + 28,620) = \text{Rs } 2,25,150$$

If only one of the units is run during the light load period again it is economical to run unit 2 and to put off unit 1. The total fuel cost during this period will be

$$(0.2 \times 55^2 + 30 \times 55 + 100) \times 12 = \text{Rs } 28,260$$

Therefore, total fuel cost for this case $= 1,96,530 + 28,260$

$= \text{Rs } 2,24,790.$

Total operating cost for this case is

$$2,24,790 + 400 = \text{Rs } 2,25,190$$

Thus, it is clear that it is economical to run both the units.

If the start-up cost is Rs 300, then it is economical to run only unit 2 in the light load period and to put off unit 1.

Physical Significance of λ For incremental changes in power generation it follows from Eq. (7.10) that

$$\Delta C = \sum_{i=1}^{k} (\partial C / \partial P_{Gi})^0 \Delta P_{Gi}$$

At the optimal operating point

$$(\partial C/\partial P_{Gi}) = (\mathrm{d}C/\mathrm{d}P_{Gi}) = (IC_i)^0 = \lambda$$

Therefore,

$$\Delta C = \lambda \sum_{i=1}^{k} \Delta P_{Gi}$$

Now,

$$\sum_{i=1}^{k} P_{Gi} = P_D$$

or

$$\sum_{i=1}^{k} \Delta P_{Gi} = \Delta P_D$$

Hence,

$$\Delta C = \lambda \Delta P_D \quad \text{or} \quad \lambda = \Delta C/\Delta P_D$$

It means that λ is the incremental cost for unit incremental change in load demand.

7.3 ► OPTIMAL UNIT COMMITMENT (UC)

As is evident, it is not economical to run all the units available all the time. To determine the units of a plant that should operate for a particular load is the problem of unit commitment (UC). This problem is of importance for thermal plants as for other types of generation such as hydro, the operating cost and start-up times are negligible so that their on–off status is not important.

A simple but sub-optimal approach to the problem is to impose priority ordering, wherein the most efficient unit is loaded first to be followed by the less efficient units in order as the load increases.

A straightforward but highly time-consuming way of finding the most economical combination of units to meet a particular load demand is to try all possible combinations of units that can supply this load; to divide the load optimally among the units of each combination by use of the coordination equations, so as to find the most economical operating cost of the combination; then, to determine the combination which has the least operating cost among all these. Considerable computational saving can be achieved by using branch and bound or a dynamic programming method for comparing the economics of combinations, as certain combinations need not be tried at all.

7.3.1 Dynamic Programming Method

In a practical problem, the UC table is to be arrived at for the complete load cycle. If the load is assumed to increase in small but finite size steps, dynamic programming (DP) can be used to advantage for computing the UC table, wherein it is not necessary to solve the coordination equations; while at the same time the unit combinations to be tried are much reduced in number. For these reasons, only the DP approach will be advanced here.

The total number of units available, their individual cost characteristics and the load cycle on the station are assumed to be known *a priori*. Further, it shall be assumed that the load on each unit or combination of units changes in suitably small but uniform steps of size ΔMW (e.g., 1 MW).

Starting arbitrarily with any two units, the most economical combination is determined for all the discrete load levels of the combined output of the two units. At each load level, the most economic answer may be to run either unit or both units with a certain load sharing between the two. The most economical cost curve in discrete form for the two units thus obtained, can be viewed as the cost curve of a single equivalent unit. The third unit is now added and the procedure repeated to find the cost curve of the three combined units. It may be noted that in this procedure the operating combinations of third and first, also third and second are not required to be worked out resulting in considerable saving in computational effort. The process is repeated, till all available units are exhausted. The advantage of this approach is that having obtained the optimal way of loading k units, it is quite easy to determine the optimal manner of loading $(k + 1)$ units.

Let a cost function $F_N(x)$ be defined as follows:

$F_N(x)$ = the minimum cost in Rs/hr of generating x MW by N units,

$f_N(y)$ = cost of generating y MW by the Nth unit

$F_{N-1}(x - y)$ = the minimum cost of generating $(x - y)$ MW by the remaining $(N - 1)$ units

Now the application of DP results in the following recursive relation:

$$F_N(x) = \min_y \{f_N(y) + F_{N-1}(x - y)\} \tag{7.17}$$

Using the above recursive relation, we can easily determine the combination of units, yielding minimum operating costs for loads ranging in convenient steps from the minimum permissible load of the smallest unit to the sum of the capacities of all available units. In this process, the total minimum operating cost and the load shared by each unit of the optimal combination are automatically determined for each load level.

The use of DP for solving the UC problem is best illustrated by means of an example. Consider a sample system having four thermal generating units with parameters listed in Table 7.2. It is required to determine the most economical units to be committed for a load of 9 MW. Let the load changes be in steps of 1 MW.

Now,

$$F_1(x) = f_1(x)$$

$$\therefore \quad F_1(9) = f_1(9) = \frac{1}{2} a_1 P^2_{G1} + b_1 P_{G1}$$

$$= 0.385 \times 9^2 + 23.5 \times 9 = \text{Rs } 242.685/\text{h}$$

Table 7.2 Generating unit parameters for the sample system

Unit No.	Capacity (MW)		Cost curve parameters (d = 0)	
	Min	Max	a (Rs/MW^2)	b (Rs/MW)
1	1.0	12.0	0.77	23.5
2	1.0	12.0	1.60	26.5
3	1.0	12.0	2.00	30.0
4	1.0	12.0	2.50	32.0

From the recursive relation (7.17), computation is made for $F_2(0), F_2(1), F_2(2), ..., F_2(9)$. Of these

$$F_2(9) = \min \{[f_2(0) + F_1(9)], [f_2(1) + F_1(8)],$$
$$[f_2(2) + F_1(7)], [f_2(3) + F_1(6)], [f_2(4) + F_1(5)],$$
$$[f_2(5) + F_1(4)], [f_2(6) + F_1(3)], [f_2(7) + F_1(2)],$$
$$[f_2(8) + F_1(1)], [f_2(9) + F_1(0)]\}$$

On computing term-by-term and comparing, we get

$$F_2(9) = [f_2(2) + F_1(7)] = \text{Rs } 239.565/\text{h}$$

Similarly, we can calculate $F_2(8), F_2(7), ..., F_2(1), F_2(0)$.

Using the recursive relation (7.17), we now compute $F_3(0), F_3(1), ..., F_3(9)$. Of these

$$F_3(9) = \min \{[f_3(0) + F_2(9)], [f_3(1) + F_2(8)], ..., [f_3(9) + F_2(0)]\}$$
$$= [f_3(0) + F_2(9)] = \text{Rs } 239.565/\text{h}$$

Proceeding similarly, we get

$$F_4(9) = [f_4(0) + F_3(9)] = \text{Rs } 239.565/\text{h}$$

Examination of $F_1(9)$, $F_2(9)$, $F_3(9)$ and $F_4(9)$ leads to the conclusion that optimum units to be committed for a 9 MW load are 1 and 2 sharing the load as 7 MW and 2 MW, respectively with a minimum operating cost of Rs 239.565/h.

It must be pointed out here that the optimal UC table is independent of the numbering of units, which could be completely arbitrary. To verify, the reader may solve the above problem once again by choosing a different unit numbering scheme.

If a higher accuracy is desired, the step size could be reduced (e.g., $\frac{1}{2}$ MW), with a considerable increase in computation time and required storage capacity.

The effect of step size could be altogether eliminated, if the branch and bound technique [24] is employed. The answer to the above problem using branch and bound technique is the same in terms of units to be committed, i.e., units 1 and 2, but with a load sharing of 7.34 MW and 1.66 MW, respectively and a total operating cost of Rs 239.2175/h.

In fact, the best scheme is to restrict the use of the DP method to obtain the UC table for various discrete load levels; while the load sharing among committed units is then decided by use of the coordination equation (7.15).

For the example under consideration, the UC table is prepared in steps of 1 MW. By combining the load range over which the unit commitment does not change, the overall result can be telescoped in the form of Table 7.3.

Table 7.3 Status* of units for minimum operating cost (Unit commitment table for the sample system)

Load range	*Unit number*			
	1	*2*	*3*	*4*
1–5	1	0	0	0
6–13	1	1	0	0
14–18	1	1	1	0
19–48	1	1	1	1

*1 = unit running; 0 = unit not running.

The UC table is prepared, once and for all, for a given set of units. As the load cycle on the station changes, it would only mean changes in starting and stopping of units with the basic UC table remaining unchanged.

Using the UC table and increasing load in steps, the most economical station operating cost is calculated for the complete range of station capacity by using the coordination equations. The result is the overall station cost characteristic in the form of a set of data points. A quadratic equation (or higher order equation, if necessary) can then be fitted to this data for later use in economic load sharing among generating stations.

Latest developments in UC are given in Annexure 7.1.

7.4 ▶ RELIABILITY CONSIDERATIONS

With the increasing dependence of industry, agriculture and day-to-day household comfort upon the continuity of electric supply, the reliability of power systems has assumed great importance. Every electric utility is normally under obligation to provide to its consumers a certain degree of continuity and quality of service (e.g., voltage and frequency in a specified range). Therefore, economy and reliability (security) must be properly coordinated in arriving at the operational unit commitment decision. In this section, we will see how the purely economic UC decision must be modified through considerations of reliability.

In order to meet the load demand under contingency of failure (forced outage) of a generator or its derating caused by a minor defect, *static reserve capacity* is always provided at a generating station so that the total installed capacity exceeds the yearly peak load by a certain margin. This is a planning problem and is beyond the scope of this book.

In arriving at the economic UC decision at any particular time, the constraint taken into account is merely the fact that the total capacity on line is at least equal to the load. The margin, if any, between the capacity of units committed and load is incidental. If under actual operation, one or more of the units were to fail perchance (random outage), it may not be possible to meet the load requirements. To start a spare (standby) thermal unit* and to bring it on steam to take up the load will take several hours (2–8 hours), so that the load cannot be met for intolerably long periods of time. Therefore, to meet contingencies, the capacity of units on line (running) must have a definite margin over the load requirements at all times. This margin which is known as the *spinning reserve* ensures continuity by meeting the load demand up to a certain extent of probable loss of generation capacity. While rules of thumb have been used, based on past experience to determine the system's spinning reserve at any time, Patton's analytical approach to this problem is the most promising.

Since the probability of unit outage increases with operating time and since a unit which is to provide the spinning reserve at a particular time has to be started several hours ahead, the problem of security of supply has to be treated in totality over a period of one day. Furthermore, the loads are never known with complete certainty. Also, the spinning reserve has to be provided at suitable generating stations of the system and not necessarily at every generating station. This indeed is a complex problem. A simplified treatment of the problem is presented below:

A unit during its useful life span undergoes alternate periods of operation and repair as shown in Fig. 7.11. The lengths of individual operating and repair periods are a random phenomenon with operating periods being much longer than repair periods. When a unit has been operating for a long time, the random phenomenon can be described by the following parameters.

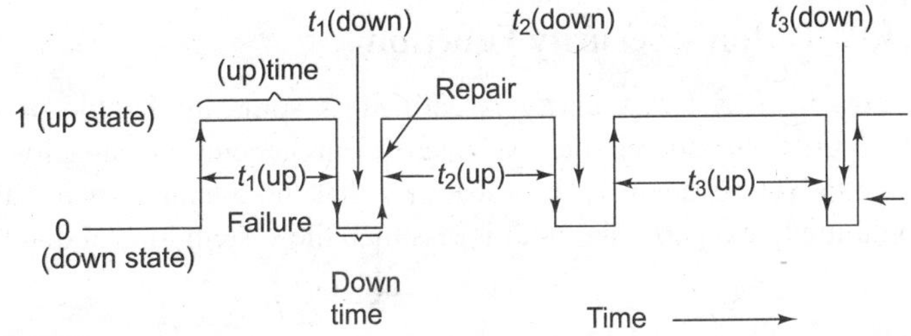

Fig. 7.11 *Random unit performance record neglecting scheduled outages*

Mean time to failure (mean 'up' time),

$$\overline{T}(\text{up}) = \frac{\sum_j t_j(\text{up})}{\text{No. of cycles}} \tag{7.18}$$

Mean time to repair (mean 'down' time),

$$\overline{T}(\text{down}) = \frac{\sum_j t_j(\text{down})}{\text{No. of cycles}} \tag{7.19}$$

$$\text{Mean cycle time} = \overline{T}(\text{up}) + \overline{T}(\text{down})$$

* If hydro generation is available in the system, it could be brought on line in a matter of minutes to take up the load.

Inverse of these times can be defined as rates [1], i.e.,

$$\text{Failure rate, } \lambda = 1/\overline{T}\,(\text{up}) \qquad (\text{failures/year})$$

$$\text{Repair rate, } \mu = 1/\overline{T}\,(\text{down}) \quad (\text{repairs/year})$$

Failure and repair rates are to be estimated from the past data of units (or other similar units elsewhere) by use of Eqs. (7.18) and (7.19). Sound engineering judgement must be exercised in arriving at these estimates. The failure rates are affected by preventive maintenance and the repair rates are sensitive to size, composition and skill of repair teams.

By ratio definition of probability, we can write the probability of a unit being in 'up' or 'down' states at any time as

$$p\,(\text{up}) = \frac{\overline{T}\,(\text{up})}{\overline{T}\,(\text{up}) + \overline{T}\,(\text{down})} = \frac{\mu}{\mu + \lambda} \tag{7.20}$$

$$p\,(\text{down}) = \frac{\overline{T}\,(\text{down})}{\overline{T}\,(\text{up}) + \overline{T}\,(\text{down})} = \frac{\lambda}{\mu + \lambda} \tag{7.21}$$

Obviously,

$$p\,(\text{up}) + p\,(\text{down}) = 1$$

p (up) and p (down) in Eqs. (7.20) and (7.21) are also termed as *availability* and *unavailability*, respectively.

When k units are operating, the system state changes because of random outages. Failure of a unit can be regarded as an event independent of the state of other units. If a particular system state i is defined as X_i units in 'down' state and Y_i in 'up' state ($k = X_i + Y_i$), the probability of the system being in this state is

$$p_i = \underset{j \in Y_i}{\pi}\, p_j\,(\text{up}) \underset{l \in X_i}{\pi}\, p_l\,(\text{down}) \tag{7.22}$$

7.4.1 Patton's Security Function

A breach of system security is defined as some intolerable or undesirable condition. The only breach of security considered here is insufficient generation capacity. The Patton's security function, which quantitatively estimates the probability that the available generation capacity (sum of capacities of units committed) at a particular hour is less than the system load at that time, is defined as [19]

$$S = \sum p_i r_i \tag{7.23}$$

where

p_i = probability of system being in state i [see Eq. (7.22)]

r_i = probability that system state i causes breach of system security.

When system load is deterministic (i.e., known with complete certainty), $r_i = 1$ if available capacity is less than load and 0 otherwise. S indeed, is a quantitative estimate of system insecurity.

Though theoretically Eq. (7.23) must be summed over all possible system states (this in fact can be very large), from a practical point of view the sum needs to be carried out over states reflecting a relatively small number of units on forced outage, e.g., states with more than two units out may be neglected as the probability of their occurrence will be too low.

7.4.2 Security Constrained Optimal Unit Commitment

Once the units to be committed at a particular load level are known from purely economic considerations, the security function S is computed as per Eq. (7.23). This figure should not exceed a certain maximum tolerable insecurity level (MTIL). MTIL for a given system is a management decision which is guided by past experience. If the value of S exceeds MTIL, the economic unit commitment schedule is modified by bringing in the next most economical unit as per the UC table. S is then recalculated and checked. The process is continued till $S \leq$ MTIL. As the economic UC table has some inherent spinning reserve, rarely more than one iteration is found to be necessary.

For illustration, reconsider the four unit example of Section 7.3. Let the daily load curve for the system be as indicated in Fig. 7.12. The economically optimal UC for this load curve is immediately obtained by use of the previously prepared UC table (see Table 7.3) and is given in Table 7.4.

Table 7.4 Economically optimal UC table for the sample system for the load curve of Fig. 7.12

Period	*Unit number*			
	1	*2*	*3*	*4*
A	1	1	1	1
B	1	1	1	0
C	1	1	0	0
D	1	1	1	0
E	1	0	0	0
F	1	1	0	0

Let us now check if the above optimal UC table is secure in every period of the load curve.

For the minimum load of 5 MW (period E of Fig. 7.12) according to optimal UC Table 7.4., only unit 1 is to be operated. Assuming identical failure rate λ of 1/year and repair rate μ of 99/year for all the four units, let us check if the system is secure for the period E. Further assume the system MTIL to be 0.005. Unit 1 can be only in two possible states—operating or on forced outage. Therefore,

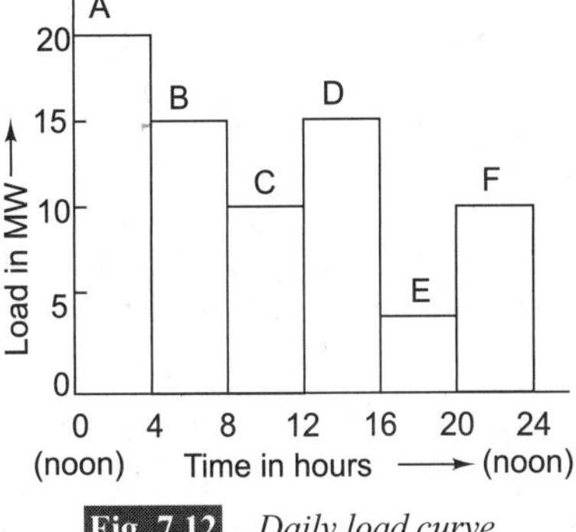

Fig. 7.12 *Daily load curve*

$$S = \sum_{i=1}^{2} p_i r_i = p_1 r_1 + p_2 r_2$$

where

$$p_1 = p(\text{up}) = \frac{\mu}{\mu + \lambda} = 0.99,\ r_1 = 0\ \text{(unit 1 = 12 MW > 5 MW)}$$

$$p_2 = p(\text{down}) = \frac{\lambda}{\mu + \lambda} = 0.01,\ r_2 = 1\ \text{(with unit 1 down, load demand cannot be met)}$$

Hence,

$$S = 0.99 \times 0 + 0.01 \times 1 = 0.01 > 0.005\ \text{(MTIL)}$$

Thus, unit 1 alone supplying 5 MW load fails to satisfy the prescribed security criterion. In order to obtain optimal and yet secure UC, it is necessary to run the next most economical unit, i.e., unit 2 (Table 7.3) along with unit 1.

With both units 1 and 2 operating, security function is contributed only by the state when both the units are on forced outage. The states with both units operating or either one failed can meet the load demand of 5 MW and so do not contribute to the security function. Therefore,

$$S = p\ (\text{down}) \times p\ (\text{down}) \times 1 = 0.0001$$

This combination (units 1 and 2 both committed) does meet the prescribed MTIL of 0.005, i.e., $S <$ MTIL.

Proceeding similarly and checking security functions for periods A, B, C, D and F, we obtain the optimal and secure UC table given in Table 7.5 for the sample system for the load curve given in Fig. 7.12.

Table 7.5 Optimal and secure UC table

Period	Unit number			
	1	2	3	4
A	1	1	1	1
B	1	1	1	0
C	1	1	0	0
D	1	1	1	0
E	1	1*	0	0
F	1	1	0	0

* Unit was started due to security considerations.

7.4.3 Start-up Considerations

The UC table as obtained above is secure and economically optimal over each individual period of the load curve. Such a table may require that certain units have to be started and stopped more than once. Therefore, start-up cost must be taken into consideration from the point of view of overall economy. For example, unit 3 has to be stopped and restarted twice during the cycle. We must, therefore, examine whether or not it will be more economical to avoid one restarting by continuing to run the unit in period C.

Case a When unit 3 is not operating in period C.

Total fuel cost for periods B, C and D as obtained by most economic load sharing are as under (detailed computation is avoided)

= 1,690.756 + 1,075.356 + 1,690.756 = Rs 4,456.868

Start-up cost of unit 3 = Rs 50.000 (say)

Total operating cost = Rs 4,506.868

Case b When all three units are running in period C, i.e., unit 3 is not stopped at the end of period B.

Total operating costs = 1,690.756 + 1,081.704 + 1,690.756

= Rs 4,463.216 (start-up cost = 0)

Clearly, Case b results in overall economy. Therefore, the optimal and secure UC table for this load cycle is modified as shown in Table 7.6, with due consideration to the overall cost.

Table 7.6 Overall optimal and secure UC table

Period	Unit number			
	1	2	3	4
A	1	1	1	1
B	1	1	1	0
C	1	1	1*	0
D	1	1	1	0
E	1	1	0	0
F	1	1	0	0

*Unit was started due to start-up considerations.

7.5 ▶ OPTIMAL GENERATION SCHEDULING

From the unit commitment table of a given plant, the fuel cost curve of the plant can be determined in the form of a polynomial of suitable degree by the method of least squares fit. If the transmission losses are neglected, the total system load can be optimally divided among the various generating plants using the equal incremental cost criterion of Eq. (7.15). It is, however, unrealistic to neglect transmission losses particularly when long distance transmission of power is involved.

A modern electric utility serves over a vast area of relatively low load density. The transmission losses may vary from 5 to 15% of the total load, and therefore, it is essential to account for losses while developing an economic load dispatch policy. It is obvious that when losses are present, we can no longer use the simple 'equal incremental cost' criterion. To illustrate the point, consider a simple system in which all the generators at each bus are identical. Equal incremental cost criterion would dictate that the total load should be shared equally by all the generators. But, considering line losses, it will be cheaper to draw more power from the generators which are closer to the loads.

In this section, we shall investigate how the load should be shared among various plants, when line losses are accounted for. The objective is to minimise the overall cost of generation.

$$C = \sum_{i=1}^{m} C_i(P_{Gi}) \tag{7.24}$$

at any time under equality constraint of meeting the load demand with the transmission losses, i.e.,

$$\sum_{i=1}^{m} P_{Gi} - \sum_{i=1}^{n} P_{Di} - P_L = 0 \quad \text{or} \quad \sum_{i=1}^{m} P_{Gi} - P_D - P_L = 0 \tag{7.25}$$

where

m = total number of generating plants

n = total number of buses

P_{Gi} = generation of ith plant

$P_D = \sum_{i=1}^{n} P_{Di}$ = sum of load demand at all buses (system load demand)

P_L = total system transmission loss

To solve the problem, we write the Lagrangian of cost as

$$\overline{C} = \sum_{i=1}^{m} C_i(P_{Gi}) - \lambda \left| \sum_{i=1}^{m} P_{Gi} - P_D - P_L \right| \quad \text{(Rs/h)} \tag{7.26}$$

From Eq. (7.25), it follows that, for a given real load P_{Di} at all buses, the system loss P_L is a function of active power generation at each plant. It will be shown later in this section that, if the power factor of load at each bus is assumed to remain constant, the system loss P_L can be shown to be a function of active power generation at each plant, i.e.,

$$P_L = P_L(P_{G1}, P_{G2}, ..., P_{Gm}) \tag{7.27}$$

Thus, in the optimisation problem posed above, P_{Gi}(i = 1, 2, ..., m) are the only control variables.

For optimum real power dispatch,

$$\partial\overline{C}/\partial P_{Gi} = \mathrm{d}C_i/\mathrm{d}P_{Gi} - \lambda + \lambda \partial P_L/\partial P_{Gi} = 0, \quad i = 1, 2, ..., m \tag{7.28}$$

Rearranging Eq. (7.28) and recognising that changing the output of only one plant can affect the cost at only that plant, we have

$$\frac{\mathrm{d}C_i/\mathrm{d}P_{Gi}}{(1 - \partial P_L/\partial P_{Gi})} = \lambda \quad \text{or} \quad (IC)_i L_i = \lambda, \quad i = 1, 2, ..., m \tag{7.29}$$

where

$$L_i = 1/(1 - \partial P_L/\partial P_{Gi}) \tag{7.30}$$

is called the *penalty factor* of the *i*th plant.

The Lagrangian multiplier λ has the units of rupees per megawatt-hour. Equation (7.29) implies that minimum fuel cost is obtained, when the incremental fuel cost of each plant multiplied by its penalty factor is the same for all the plants. The $(m + 1)$ variables $(P_{G1}, P_{G2}, ..., P_{Gm}, \lambda)$ can be obtained from m optimal dispatch equations (7.29) together with the power balance Eq. (7.25). From Eq. (7.29) it follows that higher the penalty factor for a given plant, lower the incremental cost at which that plant is operated.

The partial derivative $\partial P_L/\partial P_{Gi}$ is referred to as the incremental transmission loss $(\text{ITL})_i$, associated with the *i*th generating plant. Equation (7.29) can also be written in the alternative form

$$(IC)_i = \lambda[1 - (\text{ITL})_i]; \quad i = 1, 2, ..., m \tag{7.31}$$

This equation is referred to as the *exact coordination equation*.

Thus, it is clear that to solve the optimum load scheduling problem, it is necessary to compute ITL for each plant, and therefore, we must determine the functional dependence of transmission loss on real powers of generating plants. There are several methods, approximate and exact, for developing a transmission loss model. A full treatment of these is beyond the scope of this book.

Thus, optimum generator allocation considering line losses is obtained by operating all generators such that the product $IC_i \times L_i = \lambda$ for every generator. If the generator limits are taken into account, then all generators which are not at, or beyond, their limits are operated such that $IC_i \times L_i = \lambda$ for each of them. The generators which are at, or beyond, their limits are operated at their limits as in the lossless case.

The physical significance of λ in the case of losses can be shown to be the same as was in the lossless case. From Eq. (7.24),

$$\Delta C = \sum_{i=1}^{m} (\partial C/\partial P_{Gi})^0 \Delta P_{Gi} = \sum_{i=1}^{m} (IC_i)^0 \Delta P_{Gi} \tag{7.32}$$

But from Eq. (7.29),

$$(IC_i)^0 = \lambda(1 - (\partial P_L/\partial P_{Gi})^0) \tag{7.33}$$

Substituting Eq. (7.33) in Eq. (7.32), we get

$$\Delta C = \lambda \sum_{i=1}^{m} (1 - (\partial P_L/\partial P_{Gi})^0) \Delta P_{Gi}$$

or

$$\Delta C = \lambda \left[\sum_{i=1}^{m} \Delta P_{Gi} - \sum_{i=1}^{m} (\partial P_L/\partial P_{Gi}) \Delta P_{Gi} \right] \tag{7.34}$$

We have, from Eq. (7.27)

$$P_L = P_L(P_{G1}, P_{G2}, ..., P_{Gm})$$

Then

$$\Delta P_L = \sum_{i=1}^{m} (\partial P_L/\partial P_{Gi}) \Delta P_{Gi} \tag{7.35}$$

From Eqs. (7.34) and (7.35), we get

$$\Delta C = \lambda \left[\sum_{i=1}^{m} \Delta P_{Gi} - \Delta P_L \right] \tag{7.36}$$

Now,

$$\sum_{i=1}^{m} P_{Gi} - P_L = P_D$$

$$\therefore \qquad \sum_{i=1}^{m} \Delta P_{Gi} - \Delta P_L = \Delta P_D \tag{7.37}$$

Substituting Eq. (7.37) in Eq. (7.36),

$$\Delta C = \lambda \Delta P_D \tag{7.38}$$

Thus, λ has the same significance as in the lossless case, that is, λ represents the increment in cost (Rs/h) to the increment in load demand (MW).

7.5.1 Representation of Transmission Loss by *B*-Coefficients

One of the most important, simple but approximate methods of expressing transmission loss as a function of generator powers is through *B*-coefficients. This method uses the fact that under normal operating condition the transmission loss is quadratic in the injected bus real powers. The general form of the loss formula (derived later in this section) using *B*-coefficients is

$$P_L = \sum_{i=1}^{m} \sum_{j=1}^{m} P_i B_{ij} P_j \tag{7.39}$$

where

P_i, P_j = real power injection at i, jth buses,

B_{ij} = loss coefficients which are constants under certain assumed operating conditions,

m = number of generator buses.

If P_G s are in megawatts, B_{ij} are in reciprocal of megawatts. Computations, of course, may be carried out per unit*. Also, $B_{ij} = B_{ji}$.

Equation (7.39) for transmission loss may be written in the matrix form as

$$P_L = P^T BP \tag{7.40}$$

We obtain the incremental cost as

$$dC_i/dP_{Gi} = b_i + 2c_iP_{Gi} \quad \text{Rs/MWh}$$

Substituting dC_i/dP_{Gi} and $\partial P_L/\partial P_{Gi}$ from Eq. (7.39) in the coordination Eq. (7.28), we have

$$b_i + 2c_i P_{Gi} + \lambda \sum_{j=1}^{m} 2B_{ij}P_j = \lambda \tag{7.41}$$

or

$$b_i + 2c_iP_{Gi} + 2\lambda B_{ii}P_i + \lambda \sum_{\substack{j=1 \\ j \neq i}}^{m} 2B_{ij}P_j = \lambda \tag{7.42}$$

Substituting $P_{Gi} = P_i + P_{Di}$ and collecting all terms of P_i, we have

$$2(c_i + \lambda B_{ii})P_i = -\lambda \sum_{\substack{j=1 \\ j \neq i}}^{m} 2B_{ij}P_j - b_i + \lambda - 2c_iP_{Di} \tag{7.43}$$

* B (in pu) = B (in MW^{-1}) × Base MVA.

or
$$P_i = \frac{1 - \frac{b_i}{\lambda} + 2\frac{c_i}{\lambda} P_{Di} - \sum_{\substack{j=1 \\ j \neq i}}^{m} 2B_{ij}P_j}{2\left(\frac{c_i}{\lambda} + B_{ii}\right)}, \quad i = 1, 2, ..., m \tag{7.44}$$

For any particular value of λ, Eq. (7.44) can be solved iteratively by assuming initial values of P_i (a convenient choice is $P_i = 0$, $i = 1, 2, ..., m$). Iterations are stopped when P_i s converge within a specified accuracy.

Equation (7.44) along with the power balance equation (7.25) for a particular load demand $P_D (= P_{D1} + P_{D2} + ... + P_{Dn})$ are solved iteratively on the following lines:

1. Initially choose $\lambda = \lambda_0$.
2. Assume $P_i = 0$; $i = 1, 2, ..., m$.
3. Solve Eq. (7.44) iteratively for P_is.
4. Calculate P_L using Eq. (7.39).
5. Check if power balance Eq. (7.25) is satisfied, i.e.,
$$\left| \sum_{i=1}^{m} P_i - P_L \right| < \varepsilon \text{ (a specified value)}$$
If yes, stop. Otherwise go to step 6.
6. Increase λ by $\Delta\lambda$ (a suitable step size); if
$$\left(\sum_{i=1}^{m} P_i - P_L \right) < 0$$
or decrease λ by $\Delta\lambda$ (a suitable step size); if
$$\left(\sum_{i=1}^{m} P_i - P_L \right) > 0.$$
7. Repeat from step 3.

Note: After every step of an iteration if some P_is are such that the corresponding real power generation P_{Gi} $(= P_{Di} + P_i)$ is at its limit or not within its limits, then P_{Gi} is kept at its limit so that $P_i (= P_{Gi} - P_{Di})$ becomes constant for the next step of an iteration. This value is kept fixed till P_{Gi} falls within its limits.

Example 7.5 A two-bus system is shown in Fig. 7.13. If 100 MW is transmitted from plant 1 to the load, a transmission loss of 10 MW is incurred. Find the required generation for each plant and the power received by the load when the system λ is Rs 25/MWh.

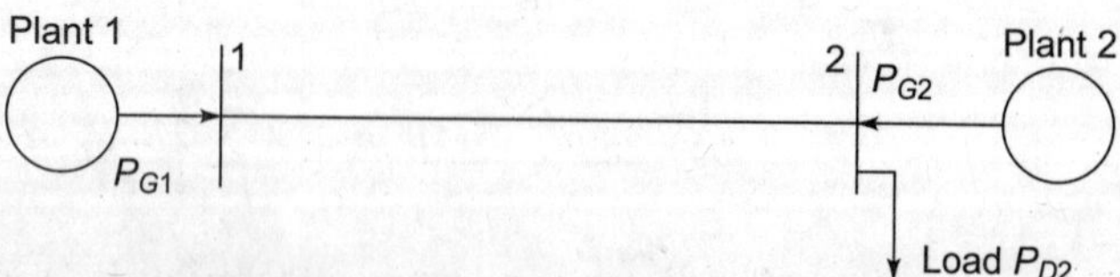

Fig. 7.13 *A two-bus system for Example 7.5*

The incremental fuel costs of the two plants are given below:

$$dC_1/dP_{G1} = 0.02P_{G1} + 16.00 \quad \text{Rs/MWh}$$
$$dC_2/dP_{G2} = 0.04P_{G2} + 20.00 \quad \text{Rs/MWh}$$

Solution Since the load is at bus 2 alone, P_2 will not have any effect on P_L. Therefore,

$$B_{22} = 0 \text{ and } B_{12} = 0 = B_{21}$$

Hence,

$$P_L = B_{11}P_1^2.$$

Since $P_{D1} = 0, P_{G1} = P_1$

For $P_{G1} = 100\text{ MW}, P_L = 10\text{ MW},$

i.e.,

$$10 = B_{11}(100)^2 \text{ or } B_{11} = 0.001\ (\text{MW})^{-1}$$

Equation (7.28) for plant 1 becomes $(\partial P_L/\partial P_{Gi} = \partial P_L/\partial P_i)$

$$0.02P_{G1} + 16.00 = \lambda(1 - \partial P_L/\partial P_1)$$

$$= \lambda(1 - 2B_{11}P_1) = \lambda(1 - 2B_{11}P_{G1}) \quad \text{(i)}$$

and for plant 2 becomes

$$0.04P_{G2} + 20.00 = \lambda(1 - \partial P_L/\partial P_2)$$

$$= \lambda(1 - 0) = \lambda \quad \text{(ii)}$$

Substituting the value of B_{11} and $\lambda = 25$, we get

$$P_{G1} = 128.57\text{ MW}$$

$$P_{G2} = 125.00\text{ MW}$$

The transmission power loss is

$$P_L = B_{11}P_1^2 = 0.001 \times (128.57)^2 = 16.53\quad\text{MW}$$

and the load is

$$P_{D2} = P_{G1} + P_{G2} - P_L = 128.57 + 125 - 16.53$$

$$= 237.04\ \text{MW}$$

Example 7.6 Consider the system of Example 7.5 with a load of 237.04 MW at bus 2. Find the optimum load distribution between the two plants (1) when losses are included but not coordinated, and (2) when losses are also coordinated. Also, find the savings in rupees per hour when losses are coordinated.

Solution

Case a If the transmission loss is not coordinated, the optimum schedules are obtained by equating the incremental fuel costs at the two plants. Thus,

$$0.02P_{G1} + 16.00 = 0.04P_{G2} + 20.00 \quad \text{(i)}$$

From the power balance equation we have

$$P_{G1} + P_{G2} = 0.001P_1^2 + 237.04 = 0.001P_{G1}^2 + 237.04 \quad \text{(ii)}$$

Solving Eqs. (i) and (ii) for P_{G1} and P_{G2}, we get

$$P_{G1} = 275.18\text{ MW and } P_{G2} = 37.59\ \text{MW}$$

Case b This case is already solved in Example 7.5. Optimum plant generations with loss coordination are

$$P_{G1} = 128.57\text{ MW}; P_{G2} = 125\text{ MW}$$

Loss coordination causes the load on plant 1 to reduce from 275.18 MW to 128.57 MW. Therefore, saving of fuel cost at plant 1 due to loss coordination is

$$\int_{128.57}^{275.18} (0.02P_{G1} + 16)\,dP_{G1} = 0.01P_{G1}^2 + 16P_{G1}\Big|_{128.57}^{275.18}$$

$$= \text{Rs } 2{,}937.69/\text{h}$$

At plant 2 the load increases from 37.59 MW to 125 MW due to loss coordination. The saving at plant 2 is

$$\int_{125}^{37.59} (0.04P_{G2} + 20)\,dP_{G2} = 0.02P_{G2}^2 + 20P_{G2}\Big|_{125}^{37.59}$$

$$= -\text{ Rs } 2{,}032.43/\text{h}$$

The net saving achieved by coordinating losses while scheduling the received load of 237.04 MW is

$$2{,}937.69 - 2{,}032.43 = \text{Rs } 905.26/\text{h}.$$

7.5.2 Derivation of Transmission Loss Formula

An accurate method of obtaining a general formula for transmission loss has been given by Kron [4]. This, however, is quite complicated. The aim of this article is to give a simpler derivation by making certain assumptions.

Figure 7.14(c) depicts the case of two generating plants connected to an arbitrary number of loads through a transmission network. One line within the network is designated as branch p.

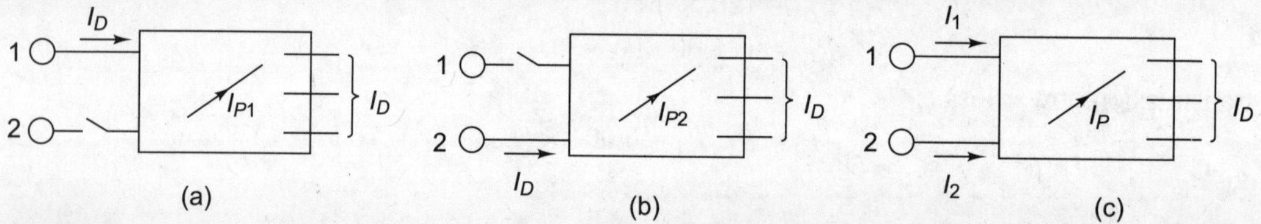

Fig. 7.14 *Schematic diagram showing two plants connected through a power network to a number of loads*

Imagine that the total load current I_D is supplied by plant 1 only, as in Fig. 7.14(a). Let the current in line p be I_{p1}. Define

$$M_{p1} = \frac{I_{p1}}{I_D} \tag{7.45}$$

Similarly, with plant 2 alone supplying the total load current Fig. 7.14(b) , we can define

$$M_{p2} = \frac{I_{p2}}{I_D} \tag{7.46}$$

M_{p1} and M_{p2} are called *current distribution factors*. The values of current distribution factors depend upon the impedances of the lines and their interconnection, and are independent of the current I_D.

When both generators 1 and 2 are supplying current into the network as in Fig. 7.14(c), applying the principle of superposition the current in the line p can be expressed as

$$I_p = M_{p1}I_1 + M_{p2}I_2 \tag{7.47}$$

where I_1 and I_2 are the currents injected at plants 1 and 2, respectively.

At this stage, let us make certain simplifying assumptions outlined below:

1. All load currents have the same phase angle with respect to a common reference. To understand the implication of this assumption, consider the load current at the ith bus. It can be written as

$$|I_{Di}| \angle (\delta_i - \phi_i) = |I_{Di}| \angle \theta_i$$

where δ_i is the phase angle of the bus voltage and ϕ_i is the lagging phase angle of the load. Since δ_i and ϕ_i vary only through a narrow range at various buses, it is reasonable to assume that θ_i is the same for all load currents at all times.

2. Ratio X/R is the same for all network branches.

These two assumptions lead us to the conclusion that I_{p1} and I_D [Fig. 7.14(a)] have the same phase angle and so have I_{p2} and I_D [Fig. 7.14(b)], such that the current distribution factors M_{p1} and M_{p2} are real rather than complex.

Let

$$I_1 = |I_1| \angle\sigma_1 \quad \text{and} \quad I_2 = |I_2| \angle\sigma_2$$

where σ_1 and σ_2 are phase angles of I_1 and I_2, respectively with respect to the common reference.

From Eq. (7.47), we can write

$$|I_p|^2 = (M_{p1}|I_1| \cos\delta_1 + M_{p2}|I_2|\cos\delta_2)^2 + (M_{p1}|I_1|\sin\delta_1 + M_{p2}|I_2|\sin\delta_2)^2 \tag{7.48}$$

Expanding and simplifying the above equation, we get

$$|I_p|^2 = M^2_{p1}|I_1|^2 + M^2_{p2}|I_2|^2 + 2M_{p1}M_{p2}|I_1||I_2|\cos(\delta_1 - \delta_2) \tag{7.49}$$

Now,

$$|I_1| = \frac{P_1}{\sqrt{3}\,|V_1|\cos\phi_1};\ |I_2| = \frac{P_2}{\sqrt{3}\,|V_2|\cos\phi_2} \tag{7.50}$$

where P_1 and P_2 are the three-phase real power injected at plants 1 and 2 at power factors of $\cos\phi_1$, and $\cos\phi_2$, and V_1 and V_2 are the bus voltages at the plants.

If R_p is the resistance of branch p, the total transmission loss is given by*

$$P_L = \sum_p 3|I_p|^2 R_p$$

Substituting for $|I_p|^2$ from Eq. (7.49), and $|I_1|$ and $|I_2|$ from Eq. (7.50), we obtain

$$P_L = \frac{P_1^2}{|V_1|^2(\cos\phi_1)^2}\sum_p M_{p1}^2 R_p + \frac{2P_1P_2\cos(\sigma_1-\sigma_2)}{|V_1||V_2|\cos\phi_1\cos\phi_2}\sum_p M_{p1}M_{p2}R_p + \frac{P_2^2}{|V_2|^2(\cos\phi_2)^2}\sum_p M_{p2}^2 R_p \tag{7.51}$$

Equation (7.51) can be recognised as

$$P_L = P_1^2B_{11} + 2P_1P_2B_{12} + P_2^2B_{22}$$

where

$$\begin{aligned}
B_{11} &= \frac{1}{|V_1|^2(\cos\phi_1)^2}\sum_p M_{p1}^2R_p \\
B_{12} &= \frac{\cos(\sigma_1-\sigma_2)}{|V_1||V_2|\cos\phi_1\cos\phi_2}\sum_p M_{p1}M_{p2}R_p \\
B_{22} &= \frac{1}{|V_2|^2(\cos\phi_2)^2}\sum_p M_{p2}^2R_p
\end{aligned} \tag{7.52}$$

The terms B_{11}, B_{12} and B_{22} are called *loss coefficients* or *B-coefficients*. If voltages are line to line kV with resistances in ohms, the units of *B*-coefficients are in MW^{-1}. Further, with P_1 and P_2 expressed in MW, P_L will also be in MW.

---

* The general expression for the power system with k plants is expressed as

$$P_L = \frac{P_1^2}{|V_1|^2(\cos\phi_1)^2}\sum_p M_{p1}^2R_p + \ldots + \frac{P_k^2}{|V_k|^2(\cos\phi_k)^2}\sum_p M_{pk}^2R_p + 2\sum_{\substack{m,n=1\\m\neq n}}^{k}\left\{\frac{P_mP_n\cos(\sigma_m-\sigma_n)}{|V_m||V_n|\cos\phi_m\cos\phi_n}\sum_p M_{pm}M_{pn}R_p\right\}$$

It can be recognised as

$$P_L = P_1^2B_{11} + \ldots + P_k^2B_{kk} + 2\sum_{\substack{m,n=1\\m\neq n}}^{k} P_mB_{mn}P_n$$

The above results can be extended to the general case of k plants with transmission loss expressed as

$$P_L = \sum_{m=1}^{k} \sum_{n=1}^{k} P_m B_{mn} P_n \tag{7.53}$$

where

$$B_{mn} = \frac{\cos(\sigma_m - \sigma_n)}{|V_m||V_n|\cos\phi_m \cos\phi_n} \sum_p M_{pm} M_{pn} R_p \tag{7.54}$$

The following assumptions including those mentioned already are necessary, if B-coefficients are to be treated as constants as total load and load sharing between plants vary. These assumptions are

1. All load currents maintain a constant ratio to the total current.
2. Voltage magnitudes at all plants remain constant.
3. Ratio of reactive to real power, i.e., power factor at each plant remains constant.
4. Voltage phase angles at plant buses remain fixed. This is equivalent to assuming that the plant currents maintain constant phase angle with respect to the common reference, since source power factors are assumed constant as per assumption 3 above.

In spite of the number of assumptions made, it is fortunate that treating B-coefficients as constants yields reasonably accurate results, when the coefficients are calculated for some average operating conditions. Major system changes require recalculation of the coefficients.

Losses as a function of plant outputs can be expressed by other methods*, but the simplicity of loss equations is the chief advantage of the B-coefficients method.

Accounting for transmission losses results in considerable operating economy. Furthermore, this consideration is equally important in future system planning and, in particular, with regard to the location of plants and building of new transmission lines.

Example 7.7 Figure 7.15 shows a system having two plants 1 and 2 connected to buses 1 and 2, respectively. There are two loads and a network of four branches. The reference bus with a voltage of $1.0 \angle 0°$ pu is shown on the diagram. The branch currents and impedances are

$I_a = 2 - j0.5$ pu $\qquad I_c = 1 - j0.25$ pu

$I_b = 1.6 - j0.4$ pu $\qquad I_d = 3.6 - j0.9$ pu

$Z_a = 0.015 + j0.06$ pu $\qquad Z_c = 0.01 + j0.04$ pu

$Z_b = 0.015 + j0.06$ pu $\qquad Z_d = 0.01 + j0.04$ pu

Calculate the loss formula coefficients of the system in pu and in reciprocal megawatts, if the base is 100 MVA.

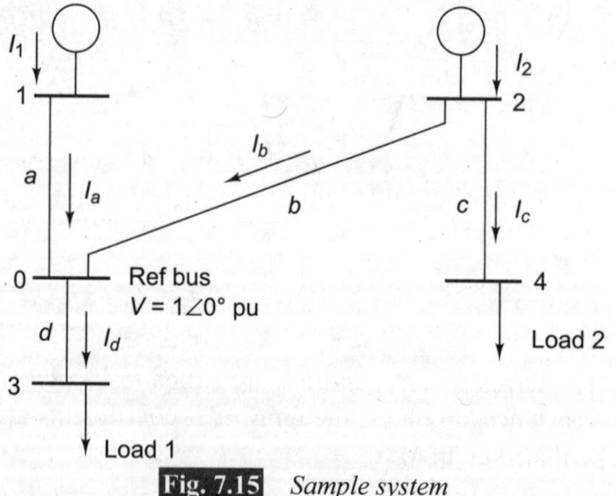

Fig. 7.15 *Sample system*

Solution As all load currents maintain a constant ratio to the total current, we have

$$\frac{I_d}{I_c + I_d} = \frac{3.6 - j0.9}{4.6 - j1.15} = 0.7826$$

$$\frac{I_c}{I_c + I_d} = \frac{1 - j0.25}{4.6 - j1.15} = 0.2174$$

* For more accurate methods and exact expression for $\partial P_L / \partial P_{Gi}$, references [16, 17] may be consulted.

$$\therefore \quad M_{a1} = 1,\ M_{b1} = -0.2174,\ M_{c1} = 0.2174,\ M_{d1} = 0.7826$$
$$M_{a2} = 0,\ M_{b2} = 0.7826,\ M_{c2} = 0.2174,\ M_{d2} = 0.7826$$

Since the source currents are known, the voltages at the source buses can be calculated. However, in a practical size network a load flow study has to be made to find power factors at the buses, bus voltages and phase angles.

The bus voltages at the plants are

$$V_1 = 1.0 + (2 - j0.5)\,(0.015 + j0.06)$$
$$= 1.06 + j0.1125 = 1.066\ \angle 6.05^\circ \text{ pu}$$
$$V_2 = 1 + (1.6 - j0.4)\,(0.015 + j0.06)$$
$$= 1.048 + j0.09 = 1.051 \angle 4.9^\circ \text{ pu}$$

The current phase angles at the plants are ($I_1 = I_a$, $I_2 = I_b + I_c$).

$$\sigma_1 = \tan^{-1}\frac{-0.5}{2} = -14^\circ;\quad \sigma_2 = \tan^{-1}\frac{-0.65}{2.6} = -14^\circ;$$

$$\cos(\sigma_2 - \sigma_1) = \cos 0^\circ = 1$$

The plant power factors are

$$pf_1 = \cos(6.05^\circ + 14^\circ) = 0.9393$$
$$pf_2 = \cos(4.9^\circ + 14^\circ) = 0.946$$

The loss coefficients are [Eq. (7.42)]

$$B_{11} = \frac{0.015\times 1^2 + 0.015\times(0.2174)^2 + 0.01\times(0.2174)^2 + 0.01\times(0.7826)^2}{(1.066)^2\times(0.9393)^2}$$
$$= 0.02224 \text{ pu}$$

$$B_{22} = \frac{0.015\times(0.7826)^2 + 0.01\times(0.2174)^2 + 0.01\times(0.7826)^2}{(1.051)^2\times(0.946)^2}$$
$$= 0.01597 \text{ pu}$$

$$B_{12} = \frac{(-0.2174)(0.7826)(0.015) + 0.01\times(0.2174)^2 + 0.01\times(0.7826)^2}{1.066\times 1.051\times 0.9393\times 0.946}$$
$$= 0.00406 \text{ pu}$$

For a base of 100 MVA, these loss coefficients must be divided by 100 to obtain their values in units of reciprocal megawatts, i.e.,

$$B_{11} = \frac{0.02224}{100} = 0.02224\times 10^{-2}\ \ \text{MW}^{-1}$$

$$B_{22} = \frac{0.01597}{100} = 0.01597\times 10^{-2}\ \ \text{MW}^{-1}$$

$$B_{12} = \frac{0.00406}{100} = 0.00406\times 10^{-2}\ \ \text{MW}^{-1}$$

7.5.3 Representation of Transmission Loss by Power Flow Equations

Earlier, the transmission loss (and hence penalty factors and incremental transmission losses) was expressed in terms of B-coefficients. The transmission loss (and hence penalty factors and incremental transmission losses) can also be expressed in terms of power flow equations. The transmission loss in terms of power injection at various buses is

$$P_L = \sum_{i=1}^{n} P_i = \sum_{i=1}^{m} P_{Gi} - \sum_{i=1}^{n} P_{Di} \tag{7.55}$$

The incremental transmission loss for the ith generating unit is

$$\partial P_L / \partial P_{Gi} = \partial P_L / \partial P_i \quad i = 1, 2, ..., m$$

where

n = total number of buses

m = number of generator buses supplying real power

From Ch. 6, the real power injection P_i is

$$P_i = \sum_{j=1}^{n} |V_i||V_j|[G_{ij} \cos(\delta_i - \delta_j) + B_{ij} \sin(\delta_i - \delta_j)] \tag{7.56}$$

where

$Y_{ij} = G_{ij} + jB_{ij}$ = element of bus admittance matrix

$|V_i|$s = voltage magnitudes at various buses

δ_is = voltage angles at various buses

δ_1 = voltage angle at the slack bus = 0

Equation (7.56) shows that for a given voltage magnitude distribution, P_i (and hence P_L from Eq. (7.55)) depends on the bus voltage angles. From Eq. (7.55), we have

$$\partial P_L/\partial \delta_k = \partial P_1/\partial \delta_k + \partial P_2/\partial \delta_k + \ldots + \partial P_m/\partial \delta_k + \cdots + \partial P_n/\partial \delta_k \tag{7.57}$$
$$k = 2, ..., n$$

Also, since $P_L = P_L(P_1, P_2, ..., P_m)$ and each $P_i (i = 1, 2, ..., m)$ is dependent on the voltage angles, we have by the rule of differentiation,

$$\partial P_L/\partial \delta_k = (\partial P_L/\partial P_1)(\partial P_1/\partial \delta_k) + (\partial P_L/\partial P_2)(\partial P_2/\partial \delta_k) + \cdots + (\partial P_L)/\partial P_m)(\partial P_m/\partial \delta_k)$$

or

$$\partial P_L/\partial \delta_k = (\partial P_L/\partial P_1)(\partial P_1/\partial \delta_k) + (\partial P_L/\partial P_2)(\partial P_2/\partial \delta_k) + \cdots + (\partial P_L/\partial P_m)(\partial P_m/\partial \delta_k)$$
$$k = 2, ..., n \tag{7.58}$$

since $\partial P_L/\partial P_{Gi} = \partial P_L/\partial P_i$ for a given load P_{Di}.

Subtracting Eq. (7.58) from Eq. (7.57), we get

$$(1 - \partial P_L/\partial P_{G1})(\partial P_1/\partial \delta_k) + (1 - \partial P_L/\partial P_{G2})(\partial P_2/\partial \delta_k) + \cdots + (1 - \partial P_L/\partial P_{Gm})(\partial P_m/\partial \delta_k) + (\partial P_m/\partial \delta_k) + \cdots$$
$$+ (\partial P_n/\partial \delta_k) = 0 \tag{7.59}$$
$$k = 2, ..., n$$

In Eqs. (7.57), (7.58) and (7.59), $k \neq 1$ because for a slack bus $\delta_1 = 0$ = constant.

Equation (7.59) can be written in matrix form as

$$\begin{bmatrix} \partial P_1/\partial \delta_2 \ldots \partial P_m/\partial \delta_2 \ldots \partial P_n/\partial \delta_2 \\ \partial P_1/\partial \delta_3 \ldots \partial P_m/\partial \delta_3 \ldots \partial P_n/\partial \delta_3 \\ \cdot \quad \cdot \quad \cdot \\ \cdot \quad \cdot \quad \cdot \\ \cdot \quad \cdot \quad \cdot \\ \partial P_1/\partial \delta_n \ldots \partial P_m/\partial \delta_n \ldots \partial P_n/\partial \delta_n \end{bmatrix}_{(n-1)\times n} \begin{bmatrix} (1 - \partial P_L/\partial P_{G1}) \\ \cdot \\ \cdot \\ \cdot \\ (1 - \partial P_L/\partial P_{Gm}) \\ \cdot \\ \cdot \\ \cdot \\ 1 \end{bmatrix}_{n\times 1} = 0 \tag{7.60}$$

An expression for $\partial P_i/\partial P_k$ ($i \neq k$ and $i = k$) can be written from Eq. (7.56) as follows:

$$\partial P_i/\partial \delta_k (i \neq k) = |V_i||V_k|[G_{ik} \sin(\delta_i - \delta_k) - B_{ik} \cos(\delta_i - \delta_k)] \tag{7.61a}$$

and $$\partial P_i/\partial \delta_i = \sum_{\substack{j=1\\ j\neq i}}^{n} |V_i||V_j|\,[-G_{ij}\sin(\delta_i-\delta_j) - B_{ij}\cos(\delta_i-\delta_j)] \tag{7.61b}$$

Equation (7.60) can be simplified if we assume that the incremental transmission loss for the slack bus is negligible, i.e., $\partial P_L/\partial P_{G1} = 0$. Thus, Eq. (7.60) reduces to

$$\begin{bmatrix} \partial P_2/\partial\delta_2 \ldots \partial P_n/\partial\delta_2 \\ \cdot \quad\quad \cdot \\ \cdot \quad\quad \cdot \\ \cdot \quad\quad \cdot \\ \partial P_1/\partial\delta_n \ldots \partial P_n/\partial\delta_n \end{bmatrix}_{(n-1)\times(n-1)} \begin{bmatrix} (1-\partial P_L/\partial P_{G2}) \\ \cdot \\ \cdot \\ \cdot \\ (1-\partial P_L/\partial P_{Gm}) \\ 1 \\ \cdot \\ \cdot \\ \cdot \\ 1 \end{bmatrix}_{(n-1)\times 1} = -\begin{bmatrix} \partial P_1/\partial\delta_2 \\ \cdot \\ \cdot \\ \cdot \\ \partial P_1/\partial\delta_n \end{bmatrix}_{(n-1)\times 1} \tag{7.62}$$

or $$\begin{bmatrix} (1-\partial P_L/\partial P_{G2}) \\ 1 \\ \cdot \\ \cdot \\ (1-\partial P_L/\partial P_{Gm}) \\ 1 \\ \cdot \\ \cdot \\ 1 \end{bmatrix}_{(n-1)\times 1} = -\begin{bmatrix} \partial P_2/\partial\delta_2 \ldots \partial P_n/\partial\delta_2 \\ \cdot \quad\quad \cdot \\ \cdot \quad\quad \cdot \\ \cdot \quad\quad \cdot \\ \partial P_2/\partial\delta_n \ldots \partial P_n/\partial\delta_n \end{bmatrix}^{-1}_{(n-1)\times(n-1)} \begin{bmatrix} \partial P_1/\partial\delta_2 \\ \cdot \\ \cdot \\ \cdot \\ \partial P_1/\partial\delta_n \end{bmatrix}_{(n-1)\times 1} \tag{7.63}$$

The values of $\partial P_i/\partial \delta_j$ ($i = 1, ..., n$; $j = 2, ..., n$) can be calculated using Eqs. 7.61(a) and (b). The various values of $|V_i|$, δ_i in Eqs. 7.61(a) and (b) can be obtained from load flow solution.

7.6 ▶ OPTIMAL LOAD FLOW SOLUTION

The problem of optimal real power dispatch has been treated in the earlier section. This section presents the *more general problem of real and reactive power flow so as to minimise the instantaneous operating costs.*

Method 1 In the first method, we solve the optimal load flow problem using Eq. (7.63). The algorithm for this problem is as follows (no generator limits):

1. The real loads at various buses are specified, P_{Di} (i = 1, 2, ..., n). Assume initial values for real generation, P^0_{Gi} (i = 2, ..., m) at the generator buses. From these we calculate the injected powers $P_i = P_{Gi} - P_{Di}$ (i = 2, 3, ..., n).
2. With the part of the load flow data available in step 1 and with remaining load flow data, the load flow solution is obtained, giving the voltage angles δ_is (i = 2, ..., n) and voltage magnitudes at the PQ buses.
3. The slack bus power P_1 is calculated using Eq. (7.56) and then $P_{G1} = P_1 + P_{D1}$.

4. Using Eq. 7.61(a), $\partial P_i/\partial \delta_k$ $(i \neq k)$ for $i = 1, 2, ..., n$ and $k = 2, ..., n$ are calculated.
   Using Eq. 7.61(b), $\delta P_i/\partial \delta_i$ for $i = 1, 2, ..., n$ are calculated.
   Equation (7.63) is then solved for $(1 - \partial P_L/\partial P_{Gi})$, $i = 2, ..., m$.
5. Taking reciprocals we have $L_i = 1/(1 - \partial P_L/\partial P_{Gi})$, $i = 2, ..., m$. Also, we note that $L_1 = 1$.
6. Knowing P_{Gi}; $i = 1, 2, ..., m$, we calculate IC_i using $IC_i = b_i + 2c_iP_{Gi}$.
7. Next, we calculate the product $L_i \times IC_i$, $i = 1, 2, ..., m$. If all are equal, we have the optimal generator allocation considering losses.

If one or more of the products $L_i \times IC_i$ are not equal, then we need to change P_{Gi} $(i = 2, 3, ..., m)$ taking $L_1 \times IC_1$ as the reference. If $L_i \times IC_i$ $(i = 2, ..., m)$ is too low (high) compared to $L_1 \times IC_1$, then P_{Gi} should be increased (decreased) by ΔP_{Gi}. The change ΔP_{Gi} can be chosen to be proportional to $(L_i \times IC_i - L_1 \times IC_1)$.

After obtaining a new set of P_{Gi} $(i = 2, ..., m)$ the iteration is repeated from step 1.

Note: As P_{Gi} is changed during the iteration process, if one or more P_{Gi} reaches its limit, then the value of P_{Gi} is fixed at this value. The iteration is repeated for the remaining generator buses. If, at any iteration it is required to change P_{Gi} (which was earlier fixed at its limit) so that it falls within its limit, then from next iteration P_{Gi} is let free.

The flow chart for the optimal load flow solution is shown in Fig. 7.16.

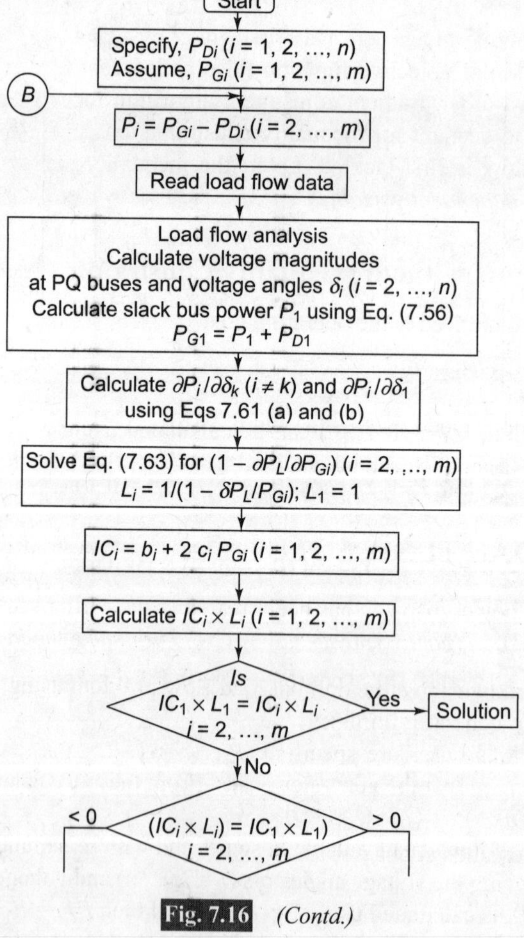

Fig. 7.16 *(Contd.)*

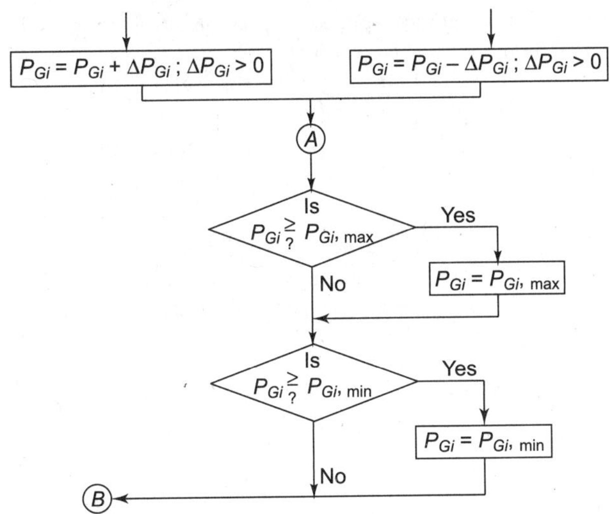

Fig. 7.16 *Flowchart for optimal load flow solution (method 1)*

Method 2 The solution technique given here was first given by *Dommel* and *Trinney* [34]. It is a *static optimisation problem* with a scalar objective function (also called cost function). It is based on load flow solution by NR method, a first-order gradient adjustment algorithm for minimising the objective function and use of penalty functions to account for inequality constraints on dependent variables. The problem of unconstrained optimal load flow is first tackled. Later, the inequality constraints are introduced, first on *control variables* and then on *dependent variables*.

7.6.1 Optimal Power Flow without Inequality Constraints

The objective function to be minimised is the operating cost

$$C = \sum_i C_i(P_{Gi})$$

subject to the load flow equations [see Eqs. 6.28(a) and 6.28(b)]

$$P_i + \sum_{j=1}^{n} |V_i||V_j||Y_{ij}| \cos(\theta_{ij} + \delta_j - \delta_i) = 0 \text{ for each PQ bus} \tag{7.64}$$

$$Q_i + \sum_{j=1}^{n} |V_i||V_j||Y_{ij}| \sin(\theta_{ij} + \delta_j - \delta_i) = 0 \text{ for each PQ bus} \tag{7.65}$$

and

$$P_i - \sum_{j=1}^{n} |V_i||V_j||Y_{ij}| \cos(\theta_{ij} + \delta_j - \delta_i) = 0 \text{ for each PV bus} \tag{7.66}$$

It is to be noted that at the ith bus

$$\begin{aligned} P_i &= P_{Gi} - P_{Di} \\ Q_i &= Q_{Gi} - Q_{Di} \end{aligned} \tag{7.67}$$

where P_{Di} and Q_{Di} are load demands at bus i.

Equations (7.64), (7.65) and (7.66) can be expressed in vector form

$$f(x, y) = \begin{bmatrix} \left\{ \begin{matrix} \text{Eq. (7.64)} \\ \text{Eq. (7.65)} \end{matrix} \right\} & \text{for each PQ bus} \\ \text{Eq. (7.66)} & \text{for each PV bus} \end{bmatrix} \tag{7.68}$$

where the vector of dependent variables is

$$x = \begin{bmatrix} \left\{ \begin{matrix} |V_i| \\ \delta_i \end{matrix} \right\} & \text{for each PQ bus} \\ \delta_i & \text{for each PV bus} \end{bmatrix} \tag{7.69a}$$

and the vector of independent variables is

$$y = \begin{bmatrix} \left\{ \begin{matrix} |V_1| \\ \delta_1 \end{matrix} \right\} & \text{for slack bus} \\ \left\{ \begin{matrix} P_i \\ Q_i \end{matrix} \right\} & \text{for each PQ bus} \\ \left\{ \begin{matrix} P_i \\ |V_i| \end{matrix} \right\} & \text{for each PV bus} \end{bmatrix} = \begin{bmatrix} u \\ p \end{bmatrix} \tag{7.69b}$$

In the above formulation, *the objective function must include the slack bus power.*

The vector of independent variables y can be partitioned into two parts—a vector u of control variables which are to be varied to achieve optimum value of objective function and a vector p *of fixed* or *disturbance* or *uncontrollable parameters*. Control parameters* may be voltage magnitudes on PV buses, P_{Gi} at buses with controllable power, etc.

The optimisation problem** can now be restated as

$$\min_{u} C(x, u) \tag{7.70}$$

subject to equality constraints

$$f(x, u, p) = 0 \tag{7.71}$$

To solve the optimisation problem, define the Lagrangian function as

$$\mathcal{L}(x, u, p) = C(x, u) + \lambda^T f(x, u, p) \tag{7.72}$$

where λ is the vector of Lagrange multipliers of same dimension as $f(x, u, p)$.

The necessary conditions to minimise the unconstrained Lagrangian function are (see Appendix G, *available online*, for differentiation of matrix functions).

$$\frac{\partial \mathcal{L}}{\partial x} = \frac{\partial C}{\partial x} + \left[\frac{\partial f}{\partial x}\right]^T \lambda = 0 \tag{7.73}$$

$$\frac{\partial \mathcal{L}}{\partial u} = \frac{\partial C}{\partial u} + \left[\frac{\partial f}{\partial u}\right]^T \lambda = 0 \tag{7.74}$$

---

* Slack bus voltage and regulating transformer tap setting may be employed as additional control variables. Dopazo *et al.* [25] use Q_{Gi} as control variable on buses with reactive power control.

** If the system real power loss is to be minimised, the objective function is

$$C = P_1(|V|, \delta)$$

Since in this case the net injected real powers are fixed, the minimisation of the real injected power P_1 at the slack bus is equivalent to minimisation of total system loss. This is known as *optimal reactive power flow problem.*

$$\frac{\partial \mathcal{L}}{\partial \lambda} = \boldsymbol{f}(\boldsymbol{x}, \boldsymbol{u}, \boldsymbol{p}) = 0 \tag{7.75}$$

Equation (7.75) is obviously the same as the equality constraints. The expressions for $\frac{\partial C}{\partial \boldsymbol{x}}$ and $\frac{\partial \boldsymbol{f}}{\partial \boldsymbol{u}}$ as needed in Eqs. (7.73) and (7.74) are rather involved*. It may, however, be observed by comparison with Eq. (6.52) that $\frac{\partial \boldsymbol{f}}{\partial \boldsymbol{x}}$ = Jacobian matrix [same as employed in the NR method of load flow solution; the expressions for the elements of Jacobian are given in Eqs. (6.67) and (6.68).

Equations (7.73), (7.74) and (7.75) are *nonlinear algebraic equations* and can only be solved *iteratively*. A simple yet efficient iteration scheme, that can be employed, is the *steepest descent method* (also called *gradient method*). The basic technique is to adjust the *control vector* $\boldsymbol{u}$, so as to move from one feasible solution point (a set of values of $\boldsymbol{x}$ which satisfies Eq. (7.75) for given $\boldsymbol{u}$ and $\boldsymbol{p}$; it indeed is the load flow solution) in the direction of steepest descent (negative gradient) to a new feasible solution point *with a lower value of objective function*. By repeating these moves in the direction of the negative gradient, *the minimum will finally be reached.*

The computational procedure for the gradient method with relevant details is given below:

Step 1 Make an initial guess for $\boldsymbol{u}$, the control variables.

Step 2 Find a feasible load flow solution from Eq. (7.75) by the NR iterative method. The method successively improves the solution $\boldsymbol{x}$ as follows:

$$\boldsymbol{x}^{(r+1)} = \boldsymbol{x}^{(r)} + \Delta \boldsymbol{x}$$

where $\Delta \boldsymbol{x}$ is obtained by solving the set of linear equations (6.57) reproduced below:

$$\left[\frac{\partial \boldsymbol{f}}{\partial \boldsymbol{x}}(\boldsymbol{x}^{(r)}, \boldsymbol{y})\right] \Delta \boldsymbol{x} = -\boldsymbol{f}(\boldsymbol{x}^{(r)}, \boldsymbol{y})$$

or

$$\Delta \boldsymbol{x} = -(\boldsymbol{J}^{(r)})^{-1} \boldsymbol{f}(\boldsymbol{x}^{(r)}, \boldsymbol{y})$$

The end results of step 2 are a feasible solution of $\boldsymbol{x}$ and the Jacobian matrix.

Step 3 Solve Eq. (7.73) for

$$\lambda = -\left[\left(\frac{\partial \boldsymbol{f}}{\partial \boldsymbol{x}}\right)^T\right]^{-1} \frac{\partial C}{\partial \boldsymbol{x}} \tag{7.76}$$

Step 4 Insert λ from Eq. (7.76) into Eq. (7.74), and compute the gradient

$$\nabla \mathcal{L} = \frac{\partial C}{\partial \boldsymbol{u}} + \left[\frac{\partial \boldsymbol{f}}{\partial \boldsymbol{u}}\right]^T \lambda \tag{7.77}$$

It may be noted that for computing the gradient, the Jacobian $\boldsymbol{J} = \frac{\partial \boldsymbol{f}}{\partial \boldsymbol{x}}$ is already known from the load flow solution (step 2 above).

Step 5 If $\nabla \mathcal{L}$ equals zero within prescribed tolerance, the minimum has been reached. Otherwise,

Step 6 Find a new set of control variables

$$\boldsymbol{u}_{\text{new}} = \boldsymbol{u}_{\text{old}} + \Delta \boldsymbol{u} \tag{7.78}$$

* The original paper of Dommel and Trinney [35] may be consulted for details.

where

$$\Delta \boldsymbol{u} = -\alpha \Delta \mathcal{L} \tag{7.79}$$

Here $\Delta \boldsymbol{u}$ is a step in the negative direction of the gradient. The step size is adjusted by the *positive scalar* α.

Steps 1 through 5 are straightforward and pose no computational problems. Step 6 is the critical part of the algorithm, where the *choice of* α is very important. Too small a value of α guarantees the convergence but *slows down the rate of convergence; too high a value causes oscillations around the minimum.* Several methods are available for optimum choice of step size.

7.6.2 Inequality Constraints on Control Variables

Though in the earlier discussion, the control variables are assumed to be unconstrained, the permissible values are, in fact, always constrained,

$$\boldsymbol{u}_{\min} \le \boldsymbol{u} \le \boldsymbol{u}_{\max}$$

e.g.,

$$P_{Gi,\min} \le P_{Gi} \le P_{Gi\max} \tag{7.80}$$

These inequality constraints on control variables can be easily handled. If the correction Δu_i in Eq. (7.78) causes u_i to exceed one of the limits, u_i is set equal to the corresponding limit, i.e.,

$$u_{i,\text{new}} = \begin{cases} u_{i,\max} & \text{if } u_{i,\text{old}} + \Delta u_i > u_{i,\max} \\ u_{i,\min} & \text{if } u_{i,\text{old}} + \Delta u_i < u_{i,\min} \\ u_{i,\text{old}} + \Delta u_i & \text{otherwise} \end{cases} \tag{7.81}$$

After a control variable reaches any of the limits, its component in the gradient should continue to be computed in later iterations, as the variable may come within limits at some later stage.

In accordance with the Kuhn-Tucker theorem (see Appendix I, *available online*), the necessary conditions for minimisation of $\mathcal{L}$ under constraint (7.80) are

$$\left.\begin{aligned} \frac{\partial \mathcal{L}}{\partial u_i} &= 0 \quad \text{if } u_{i,\min} < u_i < u_{i,\max} \\ \frac{\partial \mathcal{L}}{\partial u_i} &\le 0 \quad \text{if } u_i = u_{i,\max} \\ \frac{\partial \mathcal{L}}{\partial u_i} &\ge 0 \quad \mathrm{u_i} = u_{i,\min} \end{aligned}\right\} \tag{7.82}$$

Therefore, now, in step 5 of the computational algorithm, the gradient vector has to satisfy the optimality condition (7.82).

7.6.3 Inequality Constraints on Dependent Variables

Often, the upper and lower limits on dependent variables are specified as

$$\boldsymbol{x}_{\min} \le \boldsymbol{x} \le \boldsymbol{x}_{\max}$$

e.g.,

$$|V|_{\min} \le |V| \le |V|_{\max} \text{ on a PQ bus} \tag{7.83}$$

Such inequality constraints can be conveniently handled by the *penalty function method.* The objective function is augmented by penalties for inequality constraint violations. This forces the solution to lie sufficiently close to the constraint limits, when these limits are violated. The penalty function method is valid in this case, because these constraints are seldom *rigid limits* in the strict sense, but are in fact, *soft limits* (e.g., $|V| \leq 1.0$ on a PQ bus really means V should not exceed 1.0 too much and $|V| = 1.01$ may still be permissible).

The penalty method calls for augmentation of the objective function so that the new objective function becomes

$$C' = C(\boldsymbol{x}, \boldsymbol{u}) + \sum_j Wj \tag{7.84}$$

where the penalty $\boldsymbol{W}_j$ is introduced for each violated inequality constraint. A suitable penalty function is defined as

$$\boldsymbol{W}_j = \begin{cases} \gamma_j (x_j - x_{j,\max})^2; & \text{whenever } x_j > x_{j,\max} \\ \gamma_j (x_j - x_{j,\min})^2; & \text{whenever } x_j < x_{j,\min} \end{cases} \tag{7.85}$$

where γ_j is a real positive number which controls degree of penalty and is called the *penalty factor*.

A plot of the proposed penalty function is shown in Fig. 7.17, which clearly indicates how the rigid limits are replaced by soft limits.

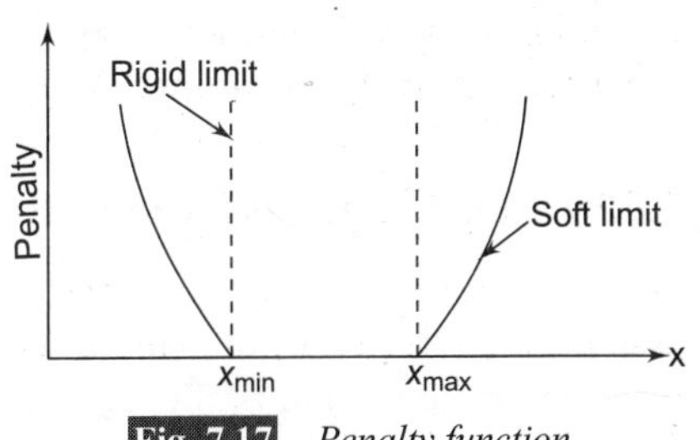

Fig. 7.17 *Penalty function*

The necessary conditions (7.73) and (7.74) would now be modified as given below, while the conditions (7.75), i.e., load flow equations, remain unchanged.

$$\frac{\partial \mathcal{L}}{\partial \boldsymbol{x}} = \frac{\partial C}{\partial \boldsymbol{x}} + \sum_j \frac{\partial \boldsymbol{W}_j}{\partial \boldsymbol{x}} + \left[\frac{\partial \boldsymbol{f}}{\partial \boldsymbol{x}}\right]^T \lambda = 0 \qquad 7.86)$$

$$\frac{\partial \mathcal{L}}{\partial \boldsymbol{u}} = \frac{\partial C}{\partial \boldsymbol{u}} + \sum_j \frac{\partial \boldsymbol{W}_j}{\partial \boldsymbol{u}} + \left[\frac{\partial \boldsymbol{f}}{\partial \boldsymbol{u}}\right]^T \lambda = 0 \tag{7.87}$$

The vector $\frac{\partial \boldsymbol{W}_j}{\partial \boldsymbol{x}}$ obtained from Eq. (7.85) would contain only one nonzero term corresponding to the dependent variable x_j; while $\frac{\partial \boldsymbol{W}_j}{\partial \boldsymbol{u}} = 0$ as the penalty functions on dependent variables are independent of the control variables.

By choosing a higher value for γ_j, the penalty function can be made steeper so that the solution lies closer to the rigid limits; the convergence, however, will become poorer. A good scheme is to start with a low value of γ_j and to increase it during the optimisation process, if the solution exceeds a certain tolerance limit.

This section has shown that the NR method of load flow can be extended to yield the optimal load flow solution that is feasible with respect to all relevant inequality constraints. These solutions are often required for system planning and operation.

7.7 ▶ OPTIMAL SCHEDULING OF HYDROTHERMAL SYSTEM

The previous sections have dealt with the problem of optimal scheduling of a power system with thermal plants only. Optimal operating policy in this case can be completely determined at any instant without reference to operation at other times. This, indeed, is the static *optimisation problem.* Operation of a system having both hydro and thermal plants is, however, far more complex as hydro plants have negligible operating cost, but are required to operate under constraints of the water available for hydro generation in a given period of time. The problem thus belongs to the realm of *dynamic optimisation.* The problem of minimising the operating cost of a hydrothermal system can be viewed as one of minimising the fuel cost of thermal plants under the constraint of water availability (storage and inflow) for hydro generation over a given period of operation.

For the sake of simplicity and understanding, the problem formulation and solution techniques are illustrated through a simplified hydrothermal system of Fig. 7.18. This system consists of one hydro and one thermal plant supplying power to a centralised load and is referred to as a *fundamental system.*

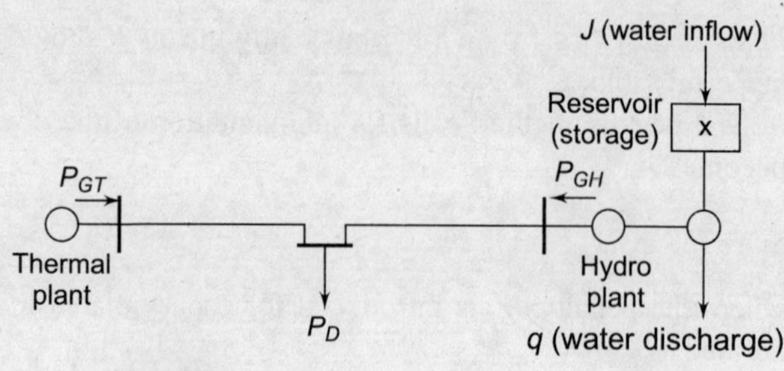

Fig. 7.18 *Fundamental hydrothermal system*

Optimisation will be carried out with real power generation as control variable, with transmission loss accounted for by the loss formula of Eq. (7.39).

7.7.1 Mathematical Formulation

For a certain period of operation T (one year, one month or one day, depending upon the requirement), it is assumed that (i) storage of hydro reservoir at the beginning and the end of the period are specified, and (ii) water inflow to reservoir (after accounting for irrigation use) and load demand on the system are known as functions of time with complete certainty (deterministic case). The problem is to determine $q(t)$, the water discharge (rate) so as to minimise the cost of thermal generation,

$$C_T = \int_0^T C'(P_{GT}(t))\,dt \tag{7.88}$$

under the following constraints:

1. Meeting the load demand

$$P_{GT}(t) + P_{GH}(t) - P_L(t) - P_D(t) = 0; \quad t \in [0,T] \tag{7.89}$$

This is called the *power balance equation.*

2. Water availability

$$X'(T) - X'(0) - \int_0^T J(t)\,dt + \int_0^T q(t)dt = 0 \tag{7.90}$$

where $J(t)$ is the water inflow (rate), $X'(t)$ water storage, and $X'(0)$, $X'(T)$ are specified water storages at the beginning and at the end of the optimisation interval.

3. The hydro generation $P_{GH}(t)$ is a function of hydro discharge and water storage (or head), i.e.,

$$P_{GH}(t) = f(X'(t), q(t)) \tag{7.91}$$

The problem can be handled conveniently by discretisation. The optimisation interval T is subdivided into M subintervals each of time length ΔT. Over each subinterval it is assumed that all the variables remain fixed in value. The problem is now posed as

$$\min_{q^m (m=1,2,\ldots,M)} \Delta T \sum_{m=1}^{M} C'\left(P_{GT}^m\right) = \min_{q^m (m=1,2,\ldots,M)} \sum_{m=1}^{M} C\left(P_{GT}^m\right) \tag{7.92}$$

under the following constraints:

1. Power balance equation

$$P_{GT}^m + P_{GH}^m - P_L^m - P_D^m = 0 \tag{7.93}$$

where

$$P_{GT}^m = \text{thermal generation in the } m\text{th interval}$$
$$P_{GH}^m = \text{hydro generation in the } m\text{th interval}$$
$$P_L^m = \text{transmission loss in the } m\text{th interval}$$
$$= B_{TT}(P_{GT}^m)^2 + 2B_{TH}\,P_{GT}^m\,P_{GH}^m + B_{HH}(P_{GH}^m)^2$$
$$P_D^m = \text{load demand in the } m\text{th interval}$$

2. Water continuity equation

$$X'^m - X'^{(m-1)} - J^m\,\Delta T + q^m\,\Delta T = 0$$

where

$$X'^m = \text{water storage at the end of the } m\text{th interval}$$
$$J^m = \text{water inflow (rate) in the } m\text{th interval}$$
$$q^m = \text{water discharge (rate) in the } m\text{th interval}$$

The above equation can be written as

$$X^m - X^{m-1} - J^m + q^m = 0, \quad m = 1, 2, ..., M \tag{7.94}$$

where $X^m = X'^m/\Delta T$ = storage in discharge units.

In Eq. (7.94), X^0 and X^M are the specified storages at the beginning and end of the optimisation interval.

3. Hydro generation in any subinterval can be expressed* as

$$P_{GH}^m = h_0\{1 + 0.5e\,(X^m + X^{m-1})\}\,(q^m - \rho) \tag{7.95}$$

where

$$h_0 = 9.81 \times 10^{-3} h_0'$$
h_0' = basic water head (head corresponding to dead storage)
e = water head correction factor to account for head variation with storage
ρ = non-effective discharge (water discharge needed to run hydro generator at no load).

In the above problem formulation, it is convenient to choose water discharges in all subintervals except one as independent variables, while hydro generations, thermal generations and water storages in all subintervals are treated as dependent variables. The fact, that water discharge in one of the subintervals is a dependent variable, is shown below.

---

* $P_{GH}^m = 9.81 \times 10^{-3}\,h_{av}^m\,(q^m - \rho)$ MW

where

$(q^m - \rho)$ = effective discharge in m^3/s
h_{av}^m = average head in the mth interval

Now,

$$h_{av}^m = h_0' + \frac{\Delta T(X^m + X^{m-1})}{2A}$$

where

A = area of cross-section of the reservoir at the given storage
h_0' = basic water head (head corresponding to dead storage)
$h_{av}^m = h_0'\{1 + 0.5e(X^m + X^{m-1})\}$

where

$$e = \frac{\Delta T}{A h_0'}; \text{ } e \text{ is tabulated for various storage values}$$

Now,

$$P_{GH}^m = h_0\,\{1 + 0.5e(X^m + X^{m-1})\}\,(q^m - \rho)$$

where

$$h_0 = 9.81 \times 10^{-3} h_0'$$

Adding Eq. (7.94) for m = 1, 2, ..., M leads to the following equation, known as *water availability equation*:

$$X^M - X^0 - \sum_m J^m + \sum_m q^m = 0 \tag{7.96}$$

Because of this equation, only (M – 1) qs can be specified independently and the remaining one can then be determined from this equation and is, therefore, a dependent variable. For convenience, q^1 is chosen as a dependent variable, for which we can write

$$q^1 = X^0 - X^M + \sum_m J^m - \sum_{m=2}^{M} q^m \tag{7.97}$$

Solution Technique The problem is solved here using non-linear programming technique in conjunction with the first-order gradient method. The Lagrangian $\mathcal{L}$ is formulated by augmenting the cost function of Eq. (7.92) with equality constraints of Eqs. (7.93)–(7.95) through Lagrange multipliers (dual variables) λ_1^m, λ_2^m and λ_3^m. Thus,

$$\mathcal{L} = \sum_m [C(P_{GT}^m) - \lambda_1^m (P_{GT}^m + P_{GH}^m - P^m{}_L - P_D^m) + \lambda_2^m (X^m - X^{m-1} - J^m + q^m)$$
$$+ \lambda_3^m \{P_{GH}^m - h_0 (1 + 0.5e(X^m + X^{m-1})) \times (q^m - \rho)\}] \tag{7.98}$$

The dual variables are obtained by equating to zero the partial derivatives of the Lagrangian with respect to the dependent variables yielding the following equations:

$$\frac{\partial \mathcal{L}}{\partial P_{GT}^m} = \frac{dC(P_{GT}^m)}{dP_{GT}^m} - \lambda_1^m \left(1 - \frac{\partial P_L^m}{\partial P_{GT}^m}\right) = 0 \tag{7.99}$$

[The reader may compare this equation with Eq. (7.29)]

$$\frac{\partial \mathcal{L}}{\partial P_{GH}^m} = \lambda_3^m - \lambda_1^m \left(1 - \frac{\partial P_L^m}{\partial P_{GH}^m}\right) = 0 \tag{7.100}$$

$$\left(\frac{\partial \mathcal{L}}{\partial X^m}\right)_{\substack{m \neq M \\ \neq 0}} = \lambda_2^m - \lambda_2^{m+1} - \lambda_3^m \{0.5h_0 e(q^m - \rho)\} - \lambda_3^{m+1} \{0.5h_0\, e\, (q^{m+1} - \rho)\} = 0 \tag{7.101}$$

and using Eq. (7.94) in Eq. (7.98), we get

$$\left(\frac{\partial \mathcal{L}}{\partial q^1}\right) = \lambda_2^1 - \lambda_3^1 h_0 \{1 + 0.5e\,(2X^0 + J^1 - 2q^1 + \rho)\} = 0 \tag{7.102}$$

The dual variables for any subinterval may be obtained as follows:

1. Obtain λ_1^m from Eq. (7.99).
2. Obtain λ_3^m from Eq. (7.100).
3. Obtain λ_2^1 from Eq. (7.102) and other values of λ_2^m ($m \neq 1$) from Eq. (7.101).

The gradient vector is given by the partial derivatives of the Lagrangian with respect to the independent variables. Thus,

$$\left(\frac{\partial \mathcal{L}}{\partial q^m}\right)_{m \neq 1} = \lambda_2^m - \lambda_3^m h_0 \{1 + 0.5e\,(2X^{m-1} + J^m - 2q^m + \rho)\} \tag{7.103}$$

For optimality, the gradient vector should be zero if there are no inequality constraints on the control variables.

Algorithm

1. Assume an initial set of independent variables $q^m (m \neq 1)$ for all subintervals except the first.
2. Obtain the values of dependent variables X^m, P_{GH}^m, P_{GT}^m, q^1 using Eqs. (7.93), (7.94), (7.95) and (7.97).
3. Obtain the dual variables λ_1^m, λ_3^m, λ_2^m $(m \neq 1)$ and λ_2^1 using Eqs. (7.99)–(7.102).
4. Obtain the gradient vector using Eq. (7.103) and check if all its elements are equal to zero within a specified accuracy. If so, optimum is reached. If not, go to step 5.
5. Obtain new values of control variables using the first-order gradient method, i.e.,

$$q^m_{\text{new}} = q^m_{\text{old}} - \alpha \left(\frac{\partial \mathcal{L}}{\partial q^m} \right); \; m \neq 1 \tag{7.104}$$

where α is a positive scalar. Repeat from step 2.

In the solution technique presented above, if some of the control variables (water discharges) cross the upper or lower bounds, these are made equal to their respective bounded values. For these control variables, step 4 above is checked in accordance with the Kuhn–Tucker conditions (7.82) given in Section 7.6.

The inequality constraints on the dependent variables are treated conveniently by augmenting the cost function with penalty functions as discussed in Section 7.6.

The method outlined above is quite general and can be directly extended to a system having multi-hydro and multi-thermal plants. The method, however, has the disadvantage of large memory requirement, since the independent variables, dependent variables and gradients need to be stored simultaneously. A modified technique known as decomposition [18] overcomes this difficulty. In this technique optimisation is carried out over each subinterval and the complete cycle of iteration is repeated, if the water availability equation does not check at the end of the cycle.

Example 7.8 Consider the fundamental hydrothermal system shown in Fig. 7.18. The objective is to find the optimal generation schedule for a typical day, wherein load varies in three steps of eight hours each as 7 MW, 10 MW and 5 MW, respectively. There is no water inflow into the reservoir of the hydro plant. The initial water storage in the reservoir is 100 m^3/s and the final water storage should be 60m^3/s, i.e., the total water available for hydro generation during the day is 40 m^3/s.

Solution Basic head is 20 m. Water head correction factor e is given to be 0.005. Assume for simplicity that the reservoir is rectangular so that e does not change with water storage. Let the non-effective water discharge be assumed as 2 m^3/s. Incremental fuel cost of the thermal plant is

$$\frac{dC}{dP_{GT}} = 1.0 P_{GT} + 25.0 \quad \text{Rs/h}$$

Further, transmission losses may be neglected.

The above problem has been specially constructed (rather oversimplified) to illustrate the optimal hydrothermal scheduling algorithm, which is otherwise computationally involved and the solution has to be worked on the digital computer. Steps of one complete iteration will be given here.

Since there are three subintervals, the control variables are q^2 and q^3. Let us assume their initial values to be

$$q^2 = 15 \text{ m}^3/\text{s}$$
$$q^3 = 15 \text{ m}^3/\text{s}$$

The value of water discharge in the first subinterval can be immediately found out using Eq. (7.97), i.e.,

$$q^1 = 100 - 60 - (15 + 15) = 10 \text{ m}^3/\text{s}$$

It is given that $X^0 = 100$ m^3/s and $X^3 = 60$ m^3/s.

From Eq. (7.94),

$$X^1 = X^0 + J^1 - q^1 = 90 \quad \text{m}^3/\text{s}$$
$$X^2 = X^1 + J^2 - q^2 = 75 \quad \text{m}^3/\text{s}$$

The values of hydro generations in the subintervals can be obtained using Eq. (7.95) as follows:

$$P_{GH}^1 = 9.81 \times 10^{-3} \times 20\ \{1 + 0.5 \times 0.005\ (X^1 + X^0)\}\ \{q^1 - \rho)$$
$$= 0.1962\ \{1 + 25 \times 10^{-4} \times 190\} \times 8$$
$$= 2.315 \text{ MW}$$
$$P_{GH}^2 = 0.1962\ \{1 + 25 \times 10^{-4} \times 165\} \times 13$$
$$= 3.602 \text{ MW}$$
$$P_{GH}^3 = 0.1962\ \{1 + 25 \times 10^{-4} \times 135\} \times 13$$
$$= 3.411 \text{ MW}$$

The thermal generations in the three intervals are then

$$P_{GT}^1 = P_D^1 - P_{GH}^1 = 7 - 2.315 \quad = 4.685 \text{ MW}$$
$$P_{GT}^2 = P_D^2 - P_{GH}^2 = 10 - 3.602 = 6.398 \text{ MW}$$
$$P_{GT}^3 = P_D^3 - P_{GH}^3 = 5 - 3.411 \quad = 1.589 \text{ MW}$$

From Eq. (7.99), we have values of λ_1^m as

$$\frac{\mathrm{d}C(P_{\mathrm{GT}}^m)}{\mathrm{d}P_{\mathrm{GT}}^m} = \lambda_1^m$$

or

$$\lambda_1^m = P_{GT}^m + 25$$

Calculating λ_1 for all the three subintervals, we have

$$\begin{bmatrix} \lambda_1^1 \\ \lambda_1^2 \\ \lambda_1^3 \end{bmatrix} = \begin{bmatrix} 29.685 \\ 31.398 \\ 26.589 \end{bmatrix}$$

Also from Eq. (7.100), we can write

$$\begin{bmatrix} \lambda_3^1 \\ \lambda_3^2 \\ \lambda_3^3 \end{bmatrix} = \begin{bmatrix} \lambda_1^1 \\ \lambda_1^2 \\ \lambda_1^3 \end{bmatrix} = \begin{bmatrix} 29.685 \\ 31.398 \\ 26.589 \end{bmatrix} \quad \text{for the lossless case}$$

From Eq. (7.102),

$$\lambda_2^1 = \lambda_3^1 h_0\ \{1 + 0.5e\ (2X^0 + J^1 - 2q^1 + \rho)\}$$
$$= 29.685 \times 0.1962\ \{1 + 25 \times 10^{-4}\ (200 - 20 + 2)\}$$
$$= 8.474$$

From Eq. (7.101) for $m = 1$ and 2, we have

$$\lambda_2^1 - \lambda_2^2 - \lambda_3^1\ \{0.5h_0 e\ (q^1 - \rho)\} - \lambda_3^2\ \{0.5h_0 e\ (q^2 - \rho)\} = 0$$
$$\lambda_2^2 - \lambda_2^3 - \lambda_3^2\ \{0.5\ h_0 e\ (q^2 - \rho)\} - \lambda_3^3\ \{0.5h_0 e\ (q^3 - \rho)\} = 0$$

Substituting various values, we get

$$\lambda_2^2 = 8.474 - 29.685\ \{0.5 \times 0.1962 \times 0.005 \times 8\} - 31.398\ \{0.5 \times 0.1962 \times 0.005 \times 13\}$$
$$= 8.1574$$
$$\lambda_2^3 = 8.1574 - 31.398\ (0.5 \times 0.1962 \times 0.005 \times 13) - 26.589\ (0.5 \times 0.1962 \times 0.005 \times 13) = 7.7877$$

Using Eq. (7.103), the gradient vector is

$$\left(\frac{\partial \mathcal{L}}{\partial q^2}\right) = \lambda_2^2 - \lambda_3^2 h_0\ \{1 + 0.5 \times 0.005\ (2 \times 90 - 2 \times 15 + 2)\}$$
$$= 8.1574 - 31.398 \times 0.1962\ \{1 + 25 \times 10^{-4} \times 152\}$$
$$= -0.3437$$

$$\left(\frac{\partial \mathcal{L}}{\partial q^3}\right) = \lambda_2^3 - \lambda_3^3 h_0 \ \{1 + 0.5e\ (2X^2 + J^3 - 2q^3 + \rho)\}$$
$$= 7.7877 - 26.589 \times 0.1962\ \{1 + 25 \times 10^{-4} \times 122\}$$
$$= 0.9799$$

If the tolerance for gradient vector is 0.1, then optimal conditions are not yet satisfied, since the gradient vector is not zero, i.e., (≤ 0.1); hence the second iteration will have to be carried out starting with the following new values of the control variables obtained from Eq. (7.104).

$$\begin{bmatrix} q^2_{\text{new}} \\ q^3_{\text{new}} \end{bmatrix} = \begin{bmatrix} q^2_{\text{old}} \\ q^3_{\text{old}} \end{bmatrix} - \alpha \begin{bmatrix} \dfrac{\partial \mathcal{L}}{\partial q^2} \\ \dfrac{\partial \mathcal{L}}{\partial q^3} \end{bmatrix}$$

Let us take $\alpha = 0.5$, then

$$\begin{bmatrix} q^2_{\text{new}} \\ q^3_{\text{new}} \end{bmatrix} = \begin{bmatrix} 15 \\ 15 \end{bmatrix} - 0.5 \begin{bmatrix} -0.3437 \\ 0.9799 \end{bmatrix} = \begin{bmatrix} 15.172 \\ 14.510 \end{bmatrix}$$

and from Eq. (7.97)

$$q^1_{\text{new}} = 100 - 60 - (15.172 + 14.510) = 10.318 \text{ m}^3/\text{s}$$

The above computation brings us to the starting point of the next iteration. Iterations are carried out till the gradient vector becomes zero within specified tolerance.

7.8 ▶ POWER SYSTEM SECURITY

7.8.1 Introduction

So far we have been primarily concerned with the economical operation of a power system. An equally important factor in the operation of a power system is the desire to maintain system security. System security involves practices suitably designed to keep the system operating when components fail. Besides economising on fuel cost, the power system should be operationally 'secure'. An operationally 'secure' power system is one with low probability of blackout or equipment damage. All these aspects require security constrained power system optimisation (SCO).

Since security and economy are normally conflicting requirements, it is inappropriate to treat them separately. The final aim of economy is the security function of the utility-company. The energy management system is to operate the system at minimum cost, with the guaranteed alleviation of emergency conditions. The emergency condition will depend on severity of violations of operating limits (branch flows and bus voltage limits). The most severe violations result from contingencies. An important part of security study, therefore, moves around the power system's ability to withstand the effects of contingencies. A particular system state is said to be secure only with reference to one or more specific contingency cases, and a given set of quantities monitored for violation.

Most of the security related functions deal with static 'snapshots' of the power system. They have to be executed at intervals compatible with the rate-of-change of system state. This quasi-static approach is, to a large extent, the only practical approach at present, since dynamic analysis and optimisation are considerably more difficult and computationally more time consuming.

System security can be said to comprise three major functions that are carried out in an energy control centre: (i) system monitoring, (ii) contingency analysis and (iii) corrective action analysis.

System monitoring supplies the power system operators with pertinent up-to-date information on the conditions of the power system. Telemetry systems measure and transmit the data. Voltages, currents, current flows, and the status of circuit breakers and switches in every substation in a transmission network are monitored. Further, other critical and important information such as frequency, generator outputs and transformer tap positions can also be telemetered. Digital computers in a control centre then process the telemetered data and place them in a data base form and inform the operators in case of an overload or out-of-limit voltage. Important data are also displayed on big monitors. Alarms/warnings may be given if required.

State estimation [11, 13] is normally used in such systems to combine telemetered data to give the best estimate (in a statistical sense) of the current system condition or 'state'. Such systems often work with supervisory control systems to help operators control circuit breakers and operate switches and taps remotely. These systems together are called SCADA (supervisory control and data acquisition) systems.

The second major security function is contingency analysis. Modern operation computers have contingency analysis programmes stored in them. These model possible system troubles (outages) before they occur. They study outage events and alert the operators to any potential overloads or serious voltage violations. For example, the simplest form of contingency analysis can be put together with a standard LF program such as studied in Ch. 6, along with procedures to set up the load flow data for each outage to be studied by the LF program. This allows the system operators to locate defensive operating states where no single contingency event will generate overloads and/or voltage violations. This analysis thus evolves operating constraints which may be employed in the ED and UC program. Thus, contingency analysis carries out emergency identification and 'what if' simulations.

The third major security function, corrective action analysis, permits the operator to change the operation of the power system if a contingency analysis program predicts a serious problem in the event of the occurrence of a certain outage. Thus, this provides preventive and post-contingency control. A simple example of corrective action is the shifting of generation from one unit to another. This may result in change in power flows and thus can change loading on overloaded lines.

These three functions together consist of a very complex set of tools that can help in the secure operation of a power system.

7.8.2 System State Classification

A formal classification of power system security levels was first suggested by DyLiacco [68] and further clarified by Fink and Carlsen [69] in order to define relevant EMS functions. Stott *et al.* [70] have recently presented a more practical static security level diagram (see Fig. 7.19) by incorporating 'correctively secure' (level 2) and 'correctable emergency' (level 4) security levels. In the figure, the arrowed lines represent involuntary transitions between levels 1 to 5 due to contingencies. The removal of violations from level 4 normally requires EMS-directed 'corrective rescheduling' or 'remedial action', bringing the system to level 3, from where it can return to either level 1 or 2 by further EMS-directed 'preventive rescheduling' depending upon the desired operational security objectives.

Levels 1 and 2 represent normal power system operation. Level 1 has the ideal security but is much too conservative and costly. The power system survives any of the credible contingencies without relying on any post-contingency corrective action. Level 2 is more economical, but depends on post-contingency corrective rescheduling to alleviate violations without loss of load, within a specified period of time. Post-contingency operating limits might be different from their pre-contingency values.

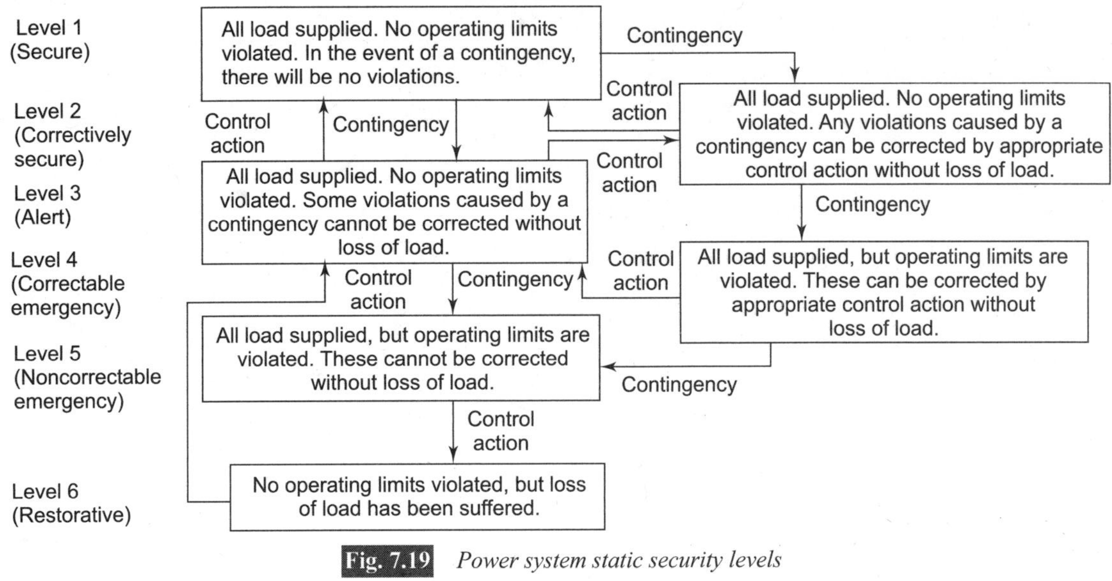

Fig. 7.19 *Power system static security levels*

7.8.3 Security Analysis

System security can be broken down into two major functions that are carried out in an operations control centre: (i) security assessment and (ii) security control. The former gives the security level of the system operating state. The latter determines the appropriate security constrained scheduling required to optimally attain the target security level.

The security functions in an EMS can be executed in 'real time' and 'study' modes. Real time application functions have a particular need for computing speed and reliability.

The static security level of a power system is characterised by the presence or otherwise of emergency operating conditions (limit violations) in its actual (pre-contingency) or potential (post-contingency) operating states. System security assessment is the process by which any such violations are detected.

System assessment involves two functions: (i) system monitoring and (ii) contingency analysis. System monitoring provides the operator of the power system with pertinent up-to-date information on the current conditions of the power system. In its simplest form, this just detects violations in the actual system operating state. Contingency analysis is much more demanding and normally performed in three distinct states, i.e., contingency definition, selection and evaluation. Contingency definition gives the list of contingencies to be processed whose probability of occurrence is high. This list, which is usually large, is in terms of network changes, i.e., branch and/or injection outages. These contingencies are ranked in rough order of severity employing contingency selection algorithms to shorten the list. Limited accuracy results are required, and therefore an approximate (linear) system model is utilised for speed. Contingency evaluation is then performed (using AC power flow) on the successive individual cases in decreasing order of severity. The evaluation process is continued up to the point where no post-contingency violations are encountered. Hence, the purpose of contingency analysis is to identify the list of contingencies that, if they occur, would create violations in system operating states. They are ranked in order of severity.

The second major security function, security control, allows operating personnel to change the power system operation in the event that a contingency analysis program predicts a serious problem should a certain outage occur. Normally, the security control is achieved through SCO program.

7.8.4 Modelling for Contingency Analysis

The power system limits of most interest in contingency analysis are those on line flows and bus voltages. Since these are soft limits, limited-accuracy models and solutions are justified. The most fundamental approximate load-flow model is the NR model discussed in Ch. 6.

$$\begin{bmatrix} \Delta P \\ \Delta Q \end{bmatrix} = [J] \begin{bmatrix} \Delta \delta \\ \Delta |V| \end{bmatrix} \tag{7.105}$$

The DC load flow model in its incremental version is normally preferred.

$$[\Delta P] = [B'] \, [\Delta \delta] \tag{7.106}$$

This model assumes voltages to remain constant after contingencies. However, this is not true for weak systems. The utility has to prespecify whether it wants to monitor post-contingency 'steady state' conditions immediately after the outage (system intertial response) or after the automatic controls* (governor, AGC, ED) have responded. Depending upon this decision, different participation factors are used to allocate the MW generation among the remaining units. The reactive problem tends to be more nonlinear and voltages are strongly influenced by active power flows. The model often used is

$$[\Delta Q/| V |] = [B''] \, [\Delta \, | V |] \tag{7.107}$$

7.8.5 Contingency Selection

There are two main approaches:

Direct methods These involve screening and direct ranking of contingency cases. They monitor the appropriate post-contingent quantities (flows, voltages). The severity measure is often a performance index.

Indirect methods These give the values of the contingency case severity indices for ranking, without calculating the monitored contingent quantities directly (e.g., use of sensitivity factors).

Simulation of line outage is more complex than a generator outage, since line outage results in a change in system configurations. The inverse matrix modification lemma (IMML) or 'compensation' method is used throughout the contingency analysis field [70]. The IMML helps in calculating the effects of network changes due to contingencies, without reconstructing and refactorising or inverting the base case network matrix. It is also possible to achieve computational economy by getting only local solutions by calculating the inverse elements in the vicinity of the contingencies. The question is how far one should go. Some form of sensitivity analysis may be used.

The problem of studying hundreds of possible outages becomes very difficult to solve if it is desired to present the results quickly so that corrective actions can be taken. One of the simplest ways of obtaining a quick calculation of possible overloads is to use network sensitivity factors. These factors show the approximate change in line flows for changes in generation on the network configuration and are derived from the DC load flow [10,13]. They are of two types:

1. Generation shift distribution factors
2. Line outage distribution factors

Reference [10] and Ch. 13 of Ref. 13 give a good account of the way they are used and derived.

In a practical situation when a contingency causing emergency occurs, control action to alleviate limit violations is always taken, if such a capability exists and a protective system (Ch. 15) permits time to do so.

* See Ch. 8 for details about these controls.

The security control function (which is normally achieved by SCO) responds to each insecure contingency case (as obtained by contingency analysis), usually in decreasing order of severity by

1. Rescheduling the pre-contingency operating state to alleviate the emergency resulting from the contingency, and/or
2. Developing a post-contingency control strategy that will eliminate the emergency, or
3. Taking no action, on the basis that post-contingency emergency is small and/or probability of its occurrence is very low.

A specific security control function, then, is designed to

1. Operate in real time or study mode
2. Schedule active or reactive power controls or both
3. Achieve a defined security level
4. Minimise a defined operational objective.

Only a small proportion of work on optional power flow (OPF) has taken into account the security constraints. The most successful applications have been to the security constrained MW dispatch OPF sub-problem. The contingency-constrained voltage/var rescheduling problem, as of the writing of this text, still remains to be solved to a satisfactory degree.

The total number of contingency constraints imposed on SCO is enormous. The SCO or contingency constrained OPF problem is solved with or without first optimising with respect to the base case (precontingency) constraints. The general procedure adopted is as follows:

1. Contingency analysis is done and cases with violations or near violations are identified.
2. The SCO problem is solved.
3. The rescheduling in step (i) might have created new violations, and therefore step (i) should be repeated till no violations exist.

Hence, SCO represents a potentially massive additional computing effort. An excellent comprehensive overview of various available methods is presented by Stott *et al.* [62].

There is still great potential for further improvement in power system security control. Better problem formulations, theory, computer solution methods and implementation techniques are required.

7.9 ▶ MAINTENANCE SCHEDULING (MS)

Maintenance scheduling of generating units is a problem of great importance in both planning and designing power systems and also in operation management. High reliability requirement of power system operation has made the generator maintenance scheduling problem very important. The intricacy of this problem arises when system size relating the total number of units grows. Also the low available reserve margin and unavoidable peak demands in modern power systems render the maintenance scheduling task much more complex. The risk of systems supply being not sufficient may be increased during the scheduled maintenance outages. Furthermore, there will be an increase in overall system cost comprising maintenance and production cost that needs to be kept to the acceptable value.

Maintenance Scheduling problem is characterised by its conflicting multi-objective nature of several incommensurable criteria like economy and reliability. MS is treated as a constrained optimisation problem.

On the whole a desirable maintenance schedule is expected to achieve the following goals:

1. Increase the reliability and economic benefits of power system,
2. Extend generator lifetime,
3. Reduce and (or) postpone installations of highly capital intensive new units.

It is a long term form of UC problem discussed earlier (see Section 7.3). Hence, Dynamic Programming can be applied successfully to solve MSP [29, 50, 55, 49, 39]. The main objective is to maintain the prescribed capacity margins at all times or failing this, to minimise the risk of energy interruption to the customer, while minimising production cost. System maintenance includes inspection, preventive maintenance and overhaul [7].

7.10 ▶ POWER-SYSTEM RELIABILITY

In Section 7.4 we considered reliability as specific to unit commitment. Here we shall examine the power system reliability as a whole. System reliability is the probability that the system will perform its intended function adequately for a specified interval of time (useful life span) under specified operating conditions.

Figure 7.20 shows a bath-tub curve which is divided into three different regions in the entire life of a component/device/system. The initial period is known as de-bugging/burn-in period/period of infant mortality during which failures may be high due to errors in design or manufacture. The region shows decreasing λ (failure or hazard rate). Then comes the useful life span. Here the failure is due to chance failures. It is more or less constant. The assumption of course in system is well maintained. The last region is the wear out period (old age).

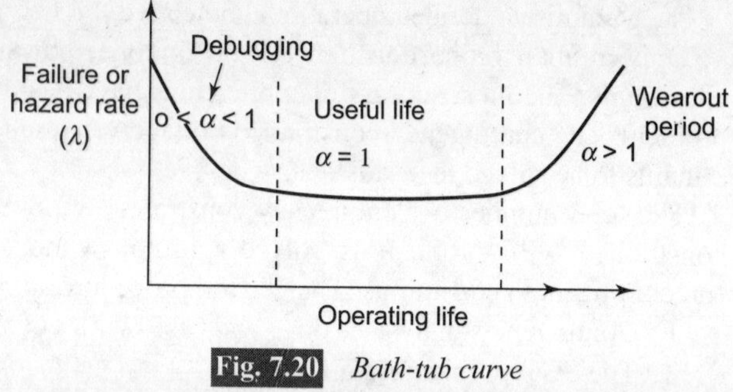

Fig. 7.20 *Bath-tub curve*

Each region can be expressed by a probability distribution function

$$\lambda(t) = Kt^{\alpha-1} \quad \text{for } t > 0 \tag{7.108}$$

K and α are constants.

7.10.1 Outage

An outage refers to that state of component/device (say a transformer) in which it is unavailable to carry out its intended function due to some event directly linked with it such an outage may or may not cause an outage of the full system (power system) or interruption of supply depending on system and degree of redundancy built in the system. An outage may be a forced outage (emergency) or a scheduled outage (maintenance). Upon forced outage of a component, it is taken out of service immediately either automatically or through a protection scheme switching operations. Outage may also be there by malfunctioning of an equipment or human error. During scheduled outage component is preplanned to be taken out of service at selected time, normally for the sake if preventive maintenance (Section 7.19) or overhaul or repair. A scheduled outage if necessary, may be postponed. A momentary outage (short duration) is caused by the reclosing breaker to clear a temporary fault. The outages (forced) in T and D systems may be there due to lightning, wind, vehicle accident, tree contact etc.

7.10.2 Continuous Markov Process

The state space method can be used for reliability evaluation. System is represented by its states and the possible transition between states.

A set of random variables with the variables ordered in a given sequence is called stochastic process. The values assumed by the variables form the state space. In power system studies, the state space is discrete but the probability index is continuous. This special class of stochastic processes is known as Markov process. A Markov process with discrete index is known as Markov chain.

Figure 7.21 shows the state space diagram of a single repairable component whose failure and repair rates are characterised by exponential distributions. Let

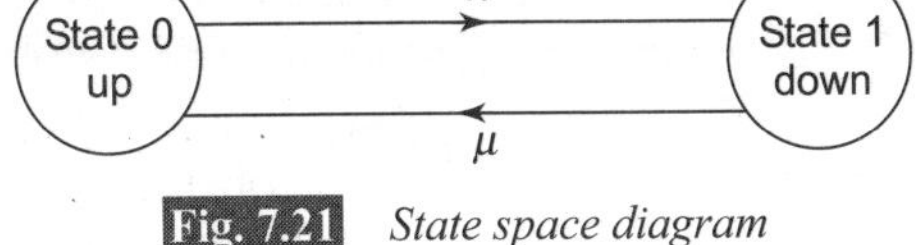

Fig. 7.21 *State space diagram*

$P_0(t)$ = prob. that the component is in state 0 at time t

$P_1(t)$ = prob. that the component is in state 1 at time t.

If the process starts from 0, i.e., the system is in state 0 at time 0, $P_0(0) = 1$ and $P_1(0) = 0$. It can then be shown that [1, 2, 8, 13];

$$\text{Reliability} = R(t) = P_0(t) = \frac{\mu}{\lambda + \mu} + \frac{\lambda\, e^{-(\lambda+\mu)t}}{\lambda + \mu} \tag{7.109}$$

$$P_1(t) = \frac{\lambda}{\lambda + \mu} + \frac{\lambda\, e^{-(\lambda+\mu)t}}{\lambda + \mu} \tag{7.110}$$

when $t \to \infty$, the probabilities are known as limiting state probabilities given by Eqs. (7.20) and (7.21).

Planning of Generating Capacity – Loss of Load Probability (LOLP) The outages of generating units may be ignored if they do not result in load-shedding i.e., loss of load. But if this results in insufficient generating capacity resulting in inability to supply the load fully. There is a need to evaluate the loss of load probability from the outage probability. For this we require:

1. List of generating units with their FOR (forced outage rate).
2. List of forecasted daily peak loads for a period of one year (see Ch. 16 of Ref. 13).

If an outage O_k has the probability P_k and if due to outage, the peak load cannot be supplied for r_k days, the probability of loss of load is $O_k\, r_k$ days. Summing up all such probabilities of the loss of load due to all probable capacity outages, the system loss of load probability

$$\text{LOLP} = \sum_k O_k r_k \quad \text{days/year} \tag{7.111}$$

Frequency and Duration of a State The forced outage rate O_k of a unit does not indicate anything about the duration of an outage stage or the frequency of encountering that state.

The frequency f_2 of encountering an outage state can be found out as

$$f_2 = \frac{1}{T} = Q\mu \tag{7.112}$$

Similarly, frequency f_1 of encountering the up state can be found out as

$$f_1 = \frac{1}{T} = R\lambda \tag{7.113}$$

T = mean cycle time

R = reliability of the unit = p(up)

Q = unreliability of the unit = p(down)

7.10.3 Reliability Planning

The ultimate goal in power system reliability analysis is the evaluation of the total system so that overall reliability measures can be achieved. However, this is too ambitious and tough task due to large number of components and complex interconnections. Hence, it is advisable to calculate reliability indices separately for the generation, transmission and distribution systems. An additional advantage is easy identification of the weakest links and components and remedial measures can be taken for reliability improvement through the use of better components and provision of redundancy. In generation subsystem it means making available additional generation capacity. In transmission subsystem it means that stronger ties should exist between plants and load centres. This extra transmission capacity can be used to avoid overloading during normal operating conditions. Redundancy in distribution subsystem means duplication of some important components and employment of better bus schemes. Avoidance of imperfect switching devices is a must as they mainly cause unreliable operation.

Example 7.9 A radial system consists of a transformer and a distributor 0.5 km long.

Given: $\lambda_{tr} = 0.6$

failures/year and $\lambda_{\text{distributor}} = 8$ failures per km per year; $\mu_{tr} = 5$ hours, $\mu_{\text{dist}} = 4$ hours.

Find: (i) λ_{system}, (ii) down time per outage, (iii) total outage time per year

Solution

(i) Failure rate = $0.6 + 8 \times 0.5 = 4.6$ outages/year

(ii) Down time = $\dfrac{0.6 \times 5 + 8 \times 4}{4.6} = 7.6$ hours/outage

(iii) Total outage time = $4.6 \times 7.6 = 34.96$ hours/year

7.10.4 Interconnected Systems

The adequacy of the generating capacity in a power system is generally improved by interconnecting the system to another power system. Each interconnected system can then operate at a given risk level with a lower reserve than would be needed otherwise. This is possible due to diversity in the probabilistic occurrence of load and capacity outages in the different systems. There are several probabilistic methods available which provide a quantitative reliability assessment of interconnected system generation capabilities. The loss of load expectation (LOLE) approach is the most widely used technique [13]. Ref. 13 also shows evaluation techniques by considering a hypothetical example. It also discusses how the effect of load forecast uncertainty can be considered.

7.10.5 Composite Generation and Transmission Systems

One of the most important elements in power system planning is to find out how much generation is needed to satisfy the given load requirements. A second equally important element in the planning process is the development of a suitable transmission network to provide the energy generated to the customer load points. The transmission network can be divided into the two general areas of bulk transmission and distribution facilities.

Distribution system design (Ch. 21) is normally a separate and independent process. The overall problem of assessing the adequacy of the generation and bulk power transmission systems to provide a dependable and suitable supply at the terminal load stations is called a composite system reliability evaluation.

Reliability concepts can be applied to power system network of Fig. 6.17 (three-bus system). The conditional probability approach can be employed to develop the expression [13] for the probability of load point failure.

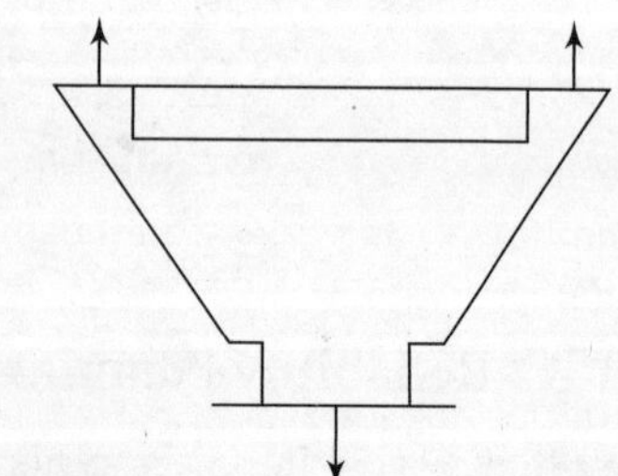

Fig. 7.22 *One possible configuration of Fig. 6.17*

The probability of inadequate transmission capability in each configuration of Fig. 6.17 can be found after performing a load flow study on each configuration, say as shown in Fig. 7.22, using the appropriate load model.

If line overload is to be considered, then a DC load flow may be used, but if voltage is also to be included as a load point criterion, then AC load flow has to be used.

The evaluation of a composite system in a practical configuration including both generation and bulk transmission is a very complex problem. The data may be deterministic or stochastic. In view of the environmental, ecological, societal and economic constraints faced by electric companies, it is expected that the reliability evaluation will receive greater attention in future.

Quantitative assessment of each subsystem or hierarchical level to be done separately and combined appropriately to give indices of relevant systems or subsets of systems. The quantitative indices so arrived at are used in the managerial decision making process at that hierarchical level in order to find out the most appropriate expansion and reinforcement schemes, operating policies and maintenance strategies. Quantitative reliability evaluation does not remove the decision-making process from the engineer or manager but only enhances the quality of the decision by adding quantitative measures to the decision process. With deregulation and privatisation, these decisions are now left to individual private power producers in response to market forces. The values of LOLP and VOLL (value of lost load) embedded in the pool (energy trading) pricing mechanism are intended to be indicators that decide the installation of additional generation.

7.11 ▶ UNIT COMMITMENT

There are many factors involved in the successful operation of electric power system. The system is expected to have power instantaneously and continuously available to meet customer's demands. In order to meet the demands, it is necessary to commit adequate generating units. The economical operation of power system calls for interaction of the major control functions such as load forecasting, unit commitment, economic dispatch, security analysis, etc. An overall solution to these set of problems must result in a continuous and reliable supply of electricity while maintaining the optimal cost of production and operation for the system while meeting the demand.

Economic factors influenced by actions of operating personnel include the loading of generating equipment, particularly of thermal plants, where unit efficiencies and fuel costs are major factors in the cost of power production. The proper operation of hydro plants can also affect generation cost, where at times of the year the availability of water is high and at other times must be conserved. Purchase power availability, cost and the scheduling of overhaul of generating unit all affect operating costs. The system operators can have considerable control over these factors.

7.11.1 An Overview

One of the most important problems in operational scheduling of electric power generation is the unit commitment. It involves determining the start-up and shut-down (ON/OFF) schedules of generating units to be used to meet forecasted demand over a short-term (24–168 hours) period. The objective is to minimise total production cost to meet system demand and reserve requirements while observing a large set of operating constraints. The unit commitment problem (UCP) is a complex mathematical optimisation problem having both integer and continuous variables.

The recent trend of installing large size thermal units (660 MW and above), complexity of power network and more concern about environment pollution has further created a need for finding better approaches for determination of economic-emission unit commitment schedule. Proper scheduling ensures that better use is made of available capacity.

Prior to solving the economic dispatch problem, unit commitment problem should be solved because only those units which were allocated to generating duties by the unit commitment solution can be considered for power generation.

Traditionally, in a vertically integrated utility environment, a utility system operator, who had the knowledge of system components, constraints and operating costs of generating units, made decisions on unit commitment for minimising the utility's generation cost. The security constrained unit commitment (SCUC) determines generating unit schedules in a utility for minimising the operating cost and satisfying the prevailing constraints, such as load balance, system spinning reserve, ramp rate limits, fuel constraints, multiple emission requirements as well as minimum up and down time limits over a set of time periods. The SCUC ensures system transmission and voltage security including the occurrences of $n - 1$ transmission contingencies. Three elements are included in the SCUC paradigm: supplying load, maximising security and minimising cost. Satisfying load is a hard constraint and an obligation for SCUC. Maximising security could often be satisfied by supplying sufficient spinning reserve at less congested regions, which could easily be accessible by loads. Cost minimisation is realised by committing less expensive units while satisfying the corresponding constraints and dispatching the committed units economically.

In the restructured deregulated environment, electric power system has now moved from vertically integrated to horizontally integrated utilities. The market share the features of decentralised competitive bidding in auction markets for energy and reserves and some degree of nondiscriminatory pricing as well as access to transmission. In some deregulated markets, the ISO commits generating units in the same way as system operators did in the vertically integrated structure using the SCUC. Suppliers submit their bids to supply the forecasted daily demand. The ISO uses the bid-in costs submitted by GENCOs for each generating unit to minimise the cost of operation, determine which units will be dispatched in how many hours and calculate the corresponding market clearing prices (MCP) while the system security is retained. The ISO also obtains information from TRANSCOs via the open access same time information system (OASIS) on transmission capability and availability.

In some other deregulated markets, the unit commitment is the responsibility of the individual GENCOs in order to maximise their own profit. GENCOs decision is associated with financial risks. This unit commitment has different objective than that of SCUC and is referred to as price-based unit commitment (PBUC) to emphasise the importance of price signal. In this case, satisfying load is no longer an obligation and the objective would be to maximise the profit. In this paradigm, the signal that would enforce a unit's ON/OFF status would be the price, including the fuel purchase price, energy sale price, ancillary service sale price, etc. GENCOs submit single-part bids to the ISO for minimising the risk of not knowing the number of hours that they would be dispatched or MCPs that would be paid on during dispatched hours. The ISO uses GENCOs' single-part bids, aggregates them and determines the MCP. Here, the ISOs objective is to maintain the system security. In the SCUC, demand forecast advised the system operators of the amount of power to be generated. However, in the PBUC, bilateral contracts will make part of the system demand known *a priori* and the remaining is forecasted.

7.11.2 Constraints of Unit Commitment Problem

The objective of UCP is to minimise the total production cost over the scheduling horizon. The total production cost consists of fuel cost, start-up cost and shut-down cost. Fuel cost is calculated by using heat rate and fuel price information. Start-up cost is expressed as a function of the number of hours the unit has been down (exponential when cooling and linear when banking). The shut-down cost is given by fixed amount for each unit shut down.

Further, UCP is a practical problem and must take into account a large number of practical constraints. These constraints are system, device/operational and environmental type. Again, these are broadly categorised as equality and inequality constraints.

Equality constraint is described by the system power balance (demand plus loss and export) also known as demand constraint i.e.,

$$\overset{N}{\Sigma} P_i = P_D$$

where P_D = Load demand

N = Number of units committed at a particular hour

Inequality constraints are

- Minimum up-time and down-time.
- Unit generation capability (upper/lower) limits.
- Ramp rate limits.
- System reserve requirement.
- Plant crew constraint.
- Unit status restrictions (must-run, fixed-MW, unavailable/available).

The most nonlinear constraints are the unit's minimum up-time and down-time restriction. A unit is to be started up only if it will run for a minimum number of continuous hours. By contrast, minimum down-time is the number of hours a unit must be off-line before it can be brought on-line again. Violation of down-time constraint may be alleviated by banking the unit.

The upper and lower limits of generation on the generating units force them to operate within their boundaries of operation.

The rate of increasing or decreasing electrical output from the unit is restricted by the ramp rate limit.

System reserve requirement pertains to supply the load throughout the scheduling period with certain degree of reliability even during outage of some committed units.

Plant crew constraint pertains to the number of units that can be started at the same time in a particular plant due to the limited personnel (crew) available.

For multi-area unit commitment, the system constraint must be modified to take into account the interchange schedules and the tie-line limitations.

7.11.3 Optimisation Techniques

The UCP belongs to the class of complex combinational optimisation problem. They ranged from simple to complicated methods. The method adopted by different entities depends on their mix of units and operating constraints. Several mathematical programming techniques have been proposed to solve this time-dependent problem. Recent mathematical developments and advances in computing technologies have made the problem to be readily solvable. Major available methods for unit commitment can be grouped as below:

1. Deterministic techniques
2. Meta-heuristic techniques
3. Hydrothermal coordination

Deterministic approaches include priority list, inter/mixed-integer programming method, dynamic and linear programming, branch-and-bound method, decomposition technique, ant colony system and Lagrangian relaxation.

Meta-heuristic approaches include expert system, fuzzy logic, artificial neural networks, genetic algorithm, evolutionary programming, simulated annealing, tabu search and memetic algorithm (hybrid technique).

Large scale UCP can also be solved using 'equivalencing' like method comprising three steps: aggregation, solution and disaggregation.

7.11.4 Hydrothermal Coordination

The problem of short-term hydro scheduling is to determine the optimum hourly generation production of hydro units, water flows through generating stations, reservoir releases and storage levels. The objective is to maximise the energy production from hydro resources.

In a hydrothermal system, short-term hydro scheduling is to done as part of hydrothermal coordination. The hydrothermal coordination problem requires the solution for the thermal unit commitments and generation dispatch as well as the hydro schedules. The objective here is to minimise the thermal production cost subject to meeting the load and other generation requirements. Most of the methods for solving the hydrothermal coordination problem are based on decomposition methods involving the unit commitment and hydro scheduling subproblems. The coordination procedure depends on the decomposition method used like heuristic decomposition, combined Lagrangian relaxation and network flow programming, genetic algorithm, etc.

7.11.5 Unit Commitment in Deregulated Market

In the deregulated markets, the UCP requires a formulation similar to the PBUC that includes the electricity market in the model. The main difficulty under deregulation is that the spot price of electricity is no longer pre-determined but set by open competition. This hourly spot prices have shown evidence of being highly volatile. The volatility of the spot prices is accounted for using a probabilistic technique to develop unit commitment schedules for continually changing loads in an interconnected power system configuration for a specified period. The SCUC programme optimises the scheduled generation and price-sensitive load while satisfying generation, reserve requirements, transmission constraints and generator operating constraints such as minimum up and down times.

Discussion Priority list (PL) method of solving UCP is the simplest and fastest but achieves sub-optimal solution. Dynamic Programming (DP) techniques, essentially based on PLs are flexible but the computation time suffers from the 'curse of dimensionality', which leads to more mathematical complexity and increase in computation time. Lagrangian relaxation (LR) methods are now among the most widely used approaches for solving UCP. The LR method provides a faster solution but it suffers from numerical convergence and existence of duality gap. Augmented LR resolves the duality gap by incorporating a penalty function with different sorts of system constraints. The integer and mixed integer methods adopt linear programming to solve and check for an integer solution. These methods fail when number of units increases because they require a large memory and suffer from great computational delay. Branch-and-bound method employs a linear function to represent fuel cost and start-up cost and obtains a lower and upper bounds. The deficiency of this method is the exponential growth in the execution time for systems of a practical size. Any colony system approach is similar to ants finding the shortest path to its destination. Ants can smell pheromone and when choosing their path, they tend to choose paths marked by strong pheromone concentrations to find their way back to the food by their nest mates.

Expert system (ES) is an intelligent technique that uses theoretical and practical knowledge inference procedures to solve the UCP. Fuzzy logic (FL) method allows a qualitative description of the behaviour of a system, the systems' characteristics and response without the need for exact mathematical formulation. Artificial neural network (ANN) has become among the most widely used tools for solving many optimisation problems. ANN parameters are estimated based on a database holding typical load curves and corresponding unit commitment optimal schedules. ANN respond to changes in operating conditions when presented with sufficient facts, even though they are trained off-line. Genetic algorithm (GA) is a general-purpose stochastic and parallel search method based on the mechanism of natural selection and natural genetics. It has the potential of obtaining near-global minimum and the capability of obtaining the solution within short time and the constraints can be easily included.

Evolutionary programmings (EP) are quite similar to the gas with the main difference being in representing and encoding of the candidates, type of alterations to create new solutions and mechanism of selecting new 'parents'. The EP has the advantages of good convergence and a significant speedup over traditional GA's and can obtain high quality solutions. The 'curse of dimensionality' is surmounted and the computational burden is almost linear with the problem scale. Simulated annealing (SA) is a powerful, general-purpose stochastic optimisation technique which can theoretically converge asymptotically to a global optimum solution. Tabu search (TS) is also a stochastic general-purpose optimisation technique that has been successfully applied to number of combinatorial optimisation problems. TS is a meta-heuristic method that iteratively explores a solution neighbourhood by incorporating adaptive memory and responsive exploration.

The hybrid methods can accommodate more complicated constraints and are claimed to have better quality solutions. Combined use of LR and MA methods provide the best result for the UCP.

7.12 ▶ OTHER ASPECTS OF UCP

Other important aspects of UCP are as under:

1. Multi-area unit commitment
2. Emission constrained unit commitment
3. Multi-objective unit commitment schedule
4. Profit-based unit commitment
5. Unit commitment with wind penetration

7.12.1 Multi-area Constraints

Many utilities and power pools have limits on power flow between different areas/regions over tie lines. Each area/region has its own pattern of load variation and generation characteristics. They also have separate spinning reserve constraints. The techniques should select the units in each area in such a way that reserve requirements and transmission constraints will be satisfied. The techniques available to handle the multi-area constraints are based on commitment utilisation factor (CUF) in conjunction with average full-load cost (AFLC) to determine the near optimal multi-area priority commitment order which is unified approach, efficient and easy to implement.

Extension of the sequential UC method that resembles 'bidding' can also be used to multi-area system employing dc power flow model to represent the inter-area transmission network. The dc power flow network model is more accurate than linear power flow model. The physical flow in transmission network is governed by the Kirchoff's current law (KCL) and Kirchoff's voltage law (KVL) which is taken care in dc model. In contrast, linear power flow model considers only the KCL. Probabilistic technique to develop a reliability constrained multi-area UC may also be used which is based on 'two risk concept'. This is useful for interconnected system with continually changing load and considering unit forced outages.

7.12.2 Emission Constraint

Generation of electricity from fossil fuel releases several pollutants, such as Sulphur Oxides (SO_2), Oxides of Nitrogen (NO_x), Carbon Dioxides (CO_2), particulate matters, etc. into the atmosphere. Reducing atmospheric pollution will be one of the major challenges for utilities with special emphasis to Kyoto Protocol. One of the economic way of reducing SO_2 emission is to switch from high sulphur to low-sulphur fuels using a fast unit commitment and dispatch heuristic. Another approach is to solve the combined planning-operation optimisation problem (i.e., minimise long run production costs including the cost of SO_2 control and emission) over a time horizon of interest using a fast UC and dispatch heuristic.

7.12.3 Multi-objective Unit Commitment

In contrast to existing UC solution, this method treats economy, security, emission and reliability as competing objectives for optimal UC solution. An operator's preference in finding a compromised solution may be required in such an environment where most of these objectives are conflicting and improvement of one objective may degrade the performance of another.

A fast and efficient approach that integrates a fuzzy expert system with pattern recognition techniques for optimum generation scheduling and evaluating security transfer limits in an inter-connected system has been established. The use of fuzzy logic in expert system reduces dimensionality of the input data while improving the results by taking into account operator's preferences. Constraints related to the security have been incorporated using a pattern data base for different system scenarios.

7.12.4 Profit Based Unit Commitment

Deregulation in power sector increases the efficiency of electricity production, offer lower prices, higher quality, a secure and a more reliable product. Generating company wishes to maximise a profit as a participant in the deregulated power and reserve markets. UC schedule depends on the market price. More number of units are committed when the market price is higher, more power is generated and participated in the deregulated market to get maximum profit. A UC algorithm that maximises profit will play an essential role in developing successful bidding strategies for the competitive generator. Profit Based Unit Commitment (PBUC) problem refers to optimising generation resources in order to maximise the GENCOs profit. In PBUC, satisfying load is no longer an obligation and the objective would be to maximise the profit and security would be unbundled from energy and priced as an ancillary services. Hybrid Lagrangian Relaxation (LR) technique is used for solving PBUC problem. The basic idea is to relax the coupling constraints (coupling either units, time periods or both) into objective function by using Lagrangian Multipliers. The relaxed problem is then decomposed into subproblems for each unit. In this process, dynamic programming (DP) is used to search the optimal commitment for each unit and Lagrangian multipliers are then updated based on the violation of coupling constraints using sub-gradient method or genetic algorithm.

Further, in the new emission-constrained competitive environment, a GENCO with thermal generation facility faces the optimal trade-off problem of how to make the present profit by the management of the energy available in fossil fuels for power generation without excessive emission. Since maximising profit and minimising emission are conflicting objectives, a multiobjective (MO) approach is used to obtain compromise solutions, also known by nondominated or Pareto-optimal solutions. A trade-off curve between profit and emission in a way to aid decision-makers concerning emission allowance trading is obtained through MO approach.

7.12.5 Unit Commitment with Wind Penetration

The rapid development of new efficient, reliable and economical wind turbines has enabled huge penetration of wind energy in the power system. India has an installed wind energy capacity of 8000 MW (Dec 2009). This represents about 8% of installed capacity in the country. The installation of huge wind farms might further increase the penetration level. With the ever-increasing wind installations and intermittent nature of the wind, it is essential to investigate the impact of huge wind penetration on the power system operation. The huge variation in wind penetration levels over the planning period makes the scheduling of the generators a challenging task. For optimal scheduling and utilisation of generators, the amount of wind in feed should be estimated with a certain level of accuracy. Moreover, the unpredictable nature of the wind requires additional power reserves for operating the wind integrated power system. The scheduled system reserve therefore has to support the generator outages and also support the unpredictable nature of the wind generation. Unit commitment for a wind integrated power system, therefore, takes into consideration the stochastic nature of both the wind generation and load.

In a general sense, the addition of wind power to a conventional generating system is always beneficial in terms of decreasing the unit commitment risk and increasing the peak load carrying capability. The actual benefits, however, are highly variable and difficult to quantify. The load carrying capability benefit is a complex phenomenon and depends on the initial wind speed, the time of the day and year, the site wind regime, the wind capacity and the size and types of the conventional units, etc. It may be necessary therefore to examine these effects for specific conditions and apply a series of approximate models applicable to specific time periods.

The major issue in developing the UC problem formulation is the modelling of the uncertainties, i.e., wind generation and load. Wind generation forecast is carried out by an ANN tool for all Wind Energy Conversion (WEC) system as a single quantity. This approach reduces the overall forecast error and also eliminates the dependency on the individual WECs. The wind generation and load are considered as two independent random processes. The sampling of these random processes results in scenarios representing the future realisations of the uncertainties. These scenarios are generated using the forecasted data, mean and standard deviation of the forecast error at every time stage. The scenarios lie within a certain probabilistic confidence interval defined by the forecasting tool. The stochastic UC problem is solved by stochastic programming approach. The aim of this optimisation process is to determine a robust UC schedule common to all scenarios and to minimise the expectation of the daily operating, costs over all possible set of scenarios. One of such stochastic approaches is adaptive particle swarm optimisation (APSO). Particle swarm optimisation (PSO) is a population-based global searching algorithm. In the process, the operator has an optimal UC schedule to plan the day-ahead operation of the power system irrespective of the actual realisation of wind generation and load uncertainties.

Security-constrained unit commitment (SCUC) algorithm is also available which takes into account the intermittency and volatility of wind power generation. The UC problem is solved in the master problem with the forecasted intermittent wind power generation. Next, possible scenarios are simulated for representing the wind power volatility. The initial dispatch is checked in the subproblem and generation redispatch is considered for satisfying the hourly volatility of wind power in simulated scenarios. If the redispatch fails to mitigate violations, benders cuts are created and added to the master problem to revise the commitment solution. The iterative process between the commitment problem and the feasibility check subproblem will continue until simulated wind power scenarios can be accommodated by redispatch.

7.13 ▶ MINIMUM EMISSION GENERATION SCHEDULING

Earlier the economy was considered to be the sole criterion in the operation of a power system. But in the context of increasing public awareness of the environmental situation and the plea for clean air, equal attention has now been focused on minimum emission dispatch. Thermal power stations are major causes of atmospheric pollution. The rising awareness regarding the environmental aspects of this pollution has necessitated a shift from the purely economic approach to economic-emission approach [19]. Power industry is the prime target of attack from ecological and pollution control agencies. The combustion of fossil fuels gives rise to particulate material and gaseous pollutants apart from the discharge of heat to water courses. The gaseous pollutants such as oxides of carbon (CO_X), oxides of sulphur (SO_X) and oxides of nitrogen (NO_X) cause detrimental effect on human beings. In the past the main concern was the effect of this pollution on human health only, but now attention has been focused on its other aspects also such as, contribution of CO_2 to enhance global warming and the role of SO_2 and NO_X in acid deposition. Emission of pollutants can be reduced automatically either by controlling unit loading or by using special post-combustion cleaning systems, such as, electrostatic precipitators, stack gas scrubbers to arrest pollutants or by switching to cleaner fuels with low emission potentials. Post-combustion removal systems require time for engineering design, construction and testing before they can be brought on line. Fuel switching, in which low emission potential fuel oil replaces the high emission potential coal, is extremely costly and also supplies are uncertain. Thus, there is a sheer need for optimum operating strategy, which can ensure minimum pollution level at minimum operating cost.

Thermal power stations are a major cause of atmospheric pollution because of the high concentration of pollutants that they cause. The emission curves for a thermal plant can be directly related to the cost curve through the emission rate per megajoule (1 Btu = 1055.06 J), which is a constant factor for a given type or grade of fuel, thus yielding quadratic NO_X, SO_2 and CO_2 emission curves in terms of active power generation. The aim is to optimise the gaseous pollutant emissions of thermal plant. The gaseous pollutant emission objective can be defined as

$$E = \sum_{i=1}^{N_G} (a_i P_{Gi}^2 + b_i P_{Gi} + c_i) \text{ Kg/h} \tag{1}$$

where a_i, b_i and c_i are the gaseous emission coefficients of ith generator, N_G is number of committed generators and P_{Gi} is real power generation by ith thermal unit.

More accurately, the gaseous pollutant emission objective can be defined as

$$E = \sum_{i=1}^{N_G} (a_i P_{Gi}^2 + b_i P_{Gi} + c_i + d_i e^{e_i P_{Gi}}) \text{ Kg/h} \tag{2}$$

where a_i, b_i, c_i, d_i are the gaseous emission coefficients of ith generator, N_G is number of committed generators and P_{Gi} is real power generation by ith thermal unit.

The total power generation must meet the total demand and power loss in transmission lines of the power system. To ensure a real and reactive power balance, the following equality constraints are imposed.

$$\sum_{i=1}^{N_G} P_{Gi} = \sum_{i=1}^{Nb} P_{Di} + P_L \tag{3}$$

where Nb are the number of buses in the system, P_{Gi} is the real and reactive powers of ith generator, respectively. P_{Di} is real demand at ith bus and P_L are real power losses in the transmission lines.

The inequality constraints are imposed on generator output are:

$$P_{Gi}^{\min} \le P_{Gi} \le P_{Gi}^{\max} \; (i = 1, 2, ..., N_G) \tag{4}$$

where, $P_{Gi}^{\min}$ and $P_{Gi}^{\max}$ are the minimum and maximum values of real power output of ith unit, respectively.

Till now, some work has been done for the minimisation of pollution level, but still much progress is possible in the area of economic-emission dispatch. A computer program is developed for on-line steam unit dispatch for minimisation of NO_X emission from a fossil steam boiler with application of the incremental loading technique and Newton-Raphson method to obtain convergence. A method for achieving controlled emission dispatch employing constant environmental restrictions at minimum operating cost and minimum pollution dispatch by applying Kuhn-Tucker conditions have described in modern research contributions.

Two nonlinear programming solution procedures are implemented for economic dispatch treating the system pollutants as an additional constraint to the problem. An interactive search method based on golden section search technique to solve the economic-emission load dispatch problem has been suggested and exhibited a computer-oriented technique for thermal power generation scheduling, which resulted in minimum NO_X emission.

A computational approach employing an improved complex box method to find minimum emission dispatch and a goal programming technique to solve the economic emission load dispatch problem for thermal generating units running with natural gas and oil have been recommended by authors in research articles. The increase in public awareness of the environmental protection and passage of Clean Air Act Amendments of 1990 has forced the utilities to modify their design or operational strategies to reduce pollution and atmospheric emissions of thermal power plants. Industrial NO_X emission is the primary cause of high ozone levels, and SO_2 emissions forming sulfates in the atmosphere, are the main reason of fine particulate problems. Consequently, the control of NO_X and SO_2 emissions in power plants has drawn greater attention over the past two decades.

Minimum NO_X emission optimal power flow scheduling by employing Newton's method and Powell's penalty function approach has been adopted for a hydro-thermal power system. Results indicated that NO_X emissions are influenced by bus voltage lower limits, reactive power generation and the hydro unit water conversion factor.

A real-time economic dispatch with line flow and emission constraints using quadratic programming is recommended with formulation of the problem related to a quadratic objective function based on the units' cost curves in quadratic or piecewise-quadratic forms. The operation constraints have been modelled as linear equality/inequality equations, resulting in a typical quadratic programming problem.

Presently, the role of multi-objective optimisation techniques for the solution of power systems' load dispatch problems is increasing day by day. Solution techniques directed to multi-criteria optimisation have experienced a remarkable change in the past years and currently represent an effective approach for solving multi-objective decision-making problems. The surrogate worth trade-off method and utility approach have been utilised to solve MOP having operating cost and emission of gaseous pollutants as objectives.

A discussion is presented on reduction in specific CO_2 emissions, industry efforts to promote use of natural gas, expanded nuclear generation and research and development works on improving efficiency of fossil plants and feasibility of HVDC interconnected power systems for environmental protection, development of hydropower, and specific possible developments in Siberia and Russia to the year 2030.

Two-stage problems of unit commitment and economic dispatch were solved by considering various constraints such as OPF constraints, transmission capacity constraints, fuel and various regulated emission requirements, spinning and operating reserve requirements, power balance, unit ramping rates, generation limits, minimum up and down times. The algorithm extends the Benders decomposition to include network, fuel and emission constraints into long-term scheduler considering the effect of generation and transmission outages.

7.14 ▶ SUMMARY

This chapter deals with economic operation of pure thermal system and hydrothermal system. Unit commitment and maintenance scheduling problems are discussed in considerable detail for pure thermal system using dynamic programming technique. A very important topic of power system optimal operation including economic dispatch, unit commitment, maintenance, reliability is fully and thoroughly discussed along with illustrative examples and computational algorithms. Power system reliability and power system security are the important topics introduced so that interested reader can do further study using existing literature. Approximate solutions with loss coefficients and exact method for optimal load flow solution have also been discussed.

Problems

7.1 Consider the following incremental cost curves in Rs/MWh for a plant having 2 units.

$$\frac{dC_1}{dP_{G1}} = 0.20\, P_{G1} + 40$$

$$\frac{dC_2}{dP_{G2}} = 0.25\, P_{G2} + 30$$

Calculate the extra cost incurred in Rs/h, if a load of 220 MW is scheduled as $P_{G1} = P_{G2} = 110$ MW.

7.2 A constant load of 300 MW is supplied by two 200 MW generators, 1 and 2, for which the respective incremental fuel costs are

$$\frac{dC_1}{dP_{G1}} = 0.1\, P_{G1} + 20$$

$$\frac{dC_2}{dP_{G2}} = 0.12\, P_{G2} + 15$$

with powers P_G in MW and costs C in Rs/h. Determine (a) the most economical division of load between the generators, and (b) the saving in Rs/day thereby obtained compared to equal load sharing between machines.

7.3 Figure P-7.3 shows the incremental fuel cost curves of generators A and B. How would a load (i) more than $2P_G$, (ii) equal to $2P_G$, and (iii) less than $2P_G$ be shared between A and B if both generators are running?

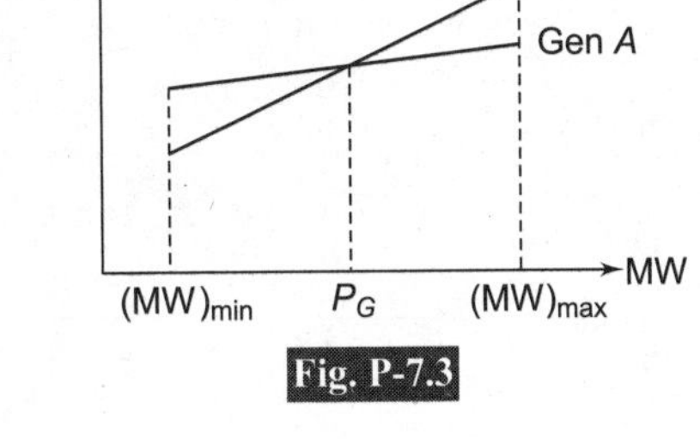

Fig. P-7.3

7.4 Consider the following three IC curves

$$P_{G1} = -100 + 50\,(IC)_1 - 2\,(IC)_1^2$$
$$P_{G2} = -150 + 60\,(IC)_2 - 2.5\,(IC)_2^2$$
$$P_{G3} = -80 + 40\,(IC)_3 - 1.8\,(IC)_3^2$$

where ICs are in Rs/MWh and P_Gs are in MW.

The total load at a certain hour of the day is 400 MW. Neglect transmission loss and develop a computer programme for optimum generation scheduling within an accuracy of ± 0.05 MW. (**Note:** This problem also has a direct solution.)

Note: All P_Gs must be real positive.

7.5 For a certain generating unit of a thermal power plant, the fuel input in millions of kilocalories per hour can be expressed as a function of power output P_G in megawatts by the equation

$$0.0001P_G^3 + 0.03P_G^2 + 12.0P_G + 150$$

Find the expression for incremental fuel cost in rupees per megawatt hour as a function of power output in megawatts. Also find a good linear approximation to the incremental fuel cost as a function of P_G.

Given: Fuel cost is Rs 2/million kilocalories.

7.6 For the system of Example 7.4, the system λ is Rs 26/MWh. Assume further the fuel costs at no load to be Rs 250 and Rs 350 per h, respectively for plants 1 and 2.

(a) For this value of system λ, what are the values of P_{G1}, P_{G2} and received load for optimum operation.

(b) For the above value of received load, what are the optimum values of P_{G1} and P_{G2}, if system losses are accounted for but not coordinated.

(c) Total fuel costs in Rs/h for parts (a) and (b).

7.7 Figure P-7.7 shows a system having two plants 1 and 2 connected to buses 1 and 2, respectively. There are two loads and a network of three branches. The bus 1 is the reference bus with voltage of $1.0\angle 0°$ pu. The branch currents and impedances are

$$I_a = 2 - j0.5 \text{ pu}$$
$$I_b = 1.6 - j0.4 \text{ pu}$$
$$I_c = 1.8 - j0.45 \text{ pu}$$
$$Z_a = 0.06 + j0.24 \text{ pu}$$
$$Z_b = 0.03 - j0.12 \text{ pu}$$
$$Z_c = 0.03 - j0.12 \text{ pu}$$

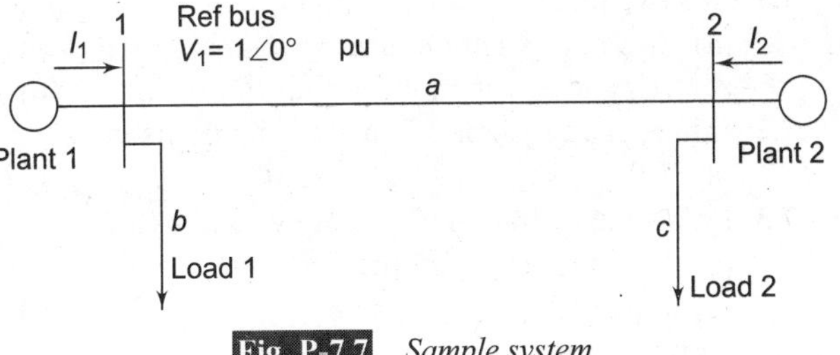

Fig. P-7.7 *Sample system*

Calculate the loss formula coefficients of the system in per unit and in reciprocal megawatts, if the base is 100 MVA.

7.8 For the power plant of the illustrative example used in Section 7.3, obtain the economically optimum unit commitment for the daily load cycle given in Fig. P-7.8. Correct the schedule to meet security requirements.

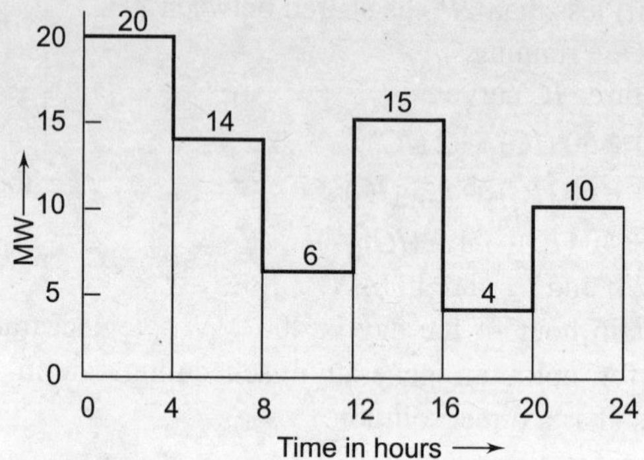

Fig. P-7.8 *Daily load curve for Problem P-7.8*

7.9 Repeat Example 7.3 with a load of 220 MW from 6 a.m. to 6 p.m. and 40 MW from 6 p.m. to 6 a.m.

7.10 For the system of Problem 7.7

$$IC_1 = 0.1\,P_{G1} + 20.0 \text{ Rs/MWh}$$
$$IC_2 = 0.2\,P_{G2} + 30.0 \text{ Rs/MWh}$$

Using λ = Rs 40/MWh, find the values of real power generation P_{G1} and P_{G2} at the buses 1 and 2.

[Ans. P_{G1} = 168.495 MW, P_{G2} = 46.96 MW]

7.11 Reformulate the optimal hydrothermal scheduling problem considering the inequality constraints on the thermal generation and water storage employing penalty functions. Find out the necessary equations and gradient vector to solve the problem.

Multiple Choice Questions

7.1 In a two plant system, the load is connected to plant no 2. The loss co-efficients
(a) B_{11}, B_{12}, B_{22} are nonzero
(b) B_{11} is nonzero but B_{12} and B_{22} are zero
(c) B_{11} and B_{12} are nonzero but B_{22} is zero
(d) B_{11} and B_{22} are nonzero but B_{12} is zero

7.2 If the penalty factor of a plant is unity, its incremental transmission loss is
(a) 1.0
(b) –1.0
(c) Zero
(d) None of the above

7.3 Economic operation of power system is carried out on the basis of
(a) Equal incremental fuel cost
(b) Equal area criterion
(c) Equal fuel cost criterion
(d) All units sharing equal power

7.4 Unit Commitment is
(a) A must before we solve economic operation problem
(b) A short term problem of maintenance scheduling
(c) More meaningful for thermal units
(d) All above

7.5 For short term planning problem losses can be found out

(a) By using approximate loss formula (b) By load flow studies
(c) By carrying out stability studies (d) Can be ignored

7.6 For long term hydrothermal problem

(a) Head variation can be ignored
(b) Transmission loss cannot be ignored
(c) Unit commitment should be taken into account
(d) All of the above

7.7 For economic operation, the generator with highest positive incremental transmission loss will operate at

(a) The highest positive incremental cost of production
(b) The highest negative incremental cost of production
(c) The lowest positive incremental cost of production
(d) The lowest negative incremental cost of production

7.8 A two-bus system has loss co-efficient as

(a) $B_{11} = 0.03$ $B_{22} = 0.05$ $B_{12} = 0.001$ $B_{21} = -0.001$
(b) $B_{11} = 0.03$ $B_{22} = 0.005$ $B_{12} = -0.001$ $B_{21} = -0.001$
(c) $B_{11} = 0.02$ $B_{22} = 0.04$ $B_{12} = -0.01$ $B_{21} = 0.001$
(d) $B_{11} = 0.02$ $B_{22} = 0.05$ $B_{12} = 0.01$ $B_{21} = 0.015$

7.9 Incremental fuel cost in rupees per MWh for a plant consisting of two units are

$$\frac{dC_1}{dP_{G1}} = 0.20\, P_{G1} + 40.0$$

$$\frac{dC_2}{dP_{G2}} = 0.25\, P_{G2} + 30.0$$

where P_{G1} and P_{G2} (in MW) are power generated by both the units for a total demand of 250 MW the load shared by the two units are

(a) $P_{G1} = \frac{350}{3}$ MW and $P_{G2} = \frac{400}{3}$ MW (b) $P_{G1} = 100$ MW and $P_{G2} = 250$ MW
(c) $P_{G1} = 125$ MW and $P_{G2} = 125$ MW (d) $P_{G1} = 150$ MW and $P_{G2} = 100$ MW

7.10 Two plants generate power as given below.
$P_{G1} = 50$ MW and $P_{G2} = 100$ MW, respectively. If the loss co-efficients of the two plants are given as $B_{11} = 0.002$, $B_{22} = 0.0015$, $B_{12} = -0.0011$. The power lost will be

(a) 20 MW (b) 15 MW (c) 18 MW (d) 22 MW

7.11 A lossless power system is supplying a load of 250 MW. Two generators G_1 and G_2 are working in the system with cost curves C_1 and C_2, respectively. The curves are defined as follows:
$C_1 = P_{G1} + 0.055\, P^2_{G1}$
$C_2 = 3\, P_{G2} + 0.03\, P^2_{G2}$
Where P_{G1} and P_{G2} are the MW injections from generators G_1 and G_2, respectively. The minimum cost dispatch in the system will be

(a) $P_{G1} = 125$ MW and $P_{G2} = 125$ MW
(b) $P_{G1} = 150$ MW and $P_{G2} = 100$ MW
(c) $P_{G1} = 120$ MW and $P_{G2} = 130$ MW
(d) $P_{G1} = 100$ MW and $P_{G2} = 150$ MW

7.12 The load is connected to plant number-II in a two-plant system. The loss coefficients of the plants are
(a) B_{11}, B_{22} are non-zero, $B_{12} = 0$
(b) B_{11}, B_{22}, B_{12} are non-zeros
(c) B_{11} is non zero, $B_{22} = B_{12} = 0$
(d) B_{11}, B_{12} are non-zero, $B_{22} = 0$

7.13 The incremental cost characteristics of a plant having two units are described by the following relations:
$IC_1 = 0.1\ P_{G1} + 8.0$ Rs./MWh
$IC_2 = 0.15\ P_{G2} + 3.0$ Rs./MWh
The optimum sharing of the total load 100 MW is

	P_{G1}	P_{G2}
(a)	45 MW	55 MW
(b)	50 MW	50 MW
(c)	60 MW	40 MW
(d)	40 MW	60 MW

7.14 Two generators with ratings of 150 MW and 250 MW are working in parallel. For incremental cost of generators $C_1 = 0.2\ P_{G1} + 60$, and $C_2 = 0.3\ P_{G2} + 40$, the load sharing of each generator for a load of 200 MW is
(a) P1 = 100 MW, P2 = 100 MW
(b) P1 = 60 MW, P2 = 140 MW
(c) $P_1 = 120$ MW, $P_2 = 80$ MW
(d) $P_1 = 80$ MW, $P_2 = 120$ MW

7.15 The transmission loss for a two-plant system in terms of the power generations and B_{mn} coefficients is
(a) $P_1^2 B_{11} - 2P_1P_2B_{12} + P_2^2 B_{22}$
(b) $P_1^2 B_{11} + 2P_1P_2B_{12} + P_2^2 B_{22}$
(c) $P_2^2 B_{11} + 2P_1P_2B_{12} + P_1^2 B_{22}$
(d) $P_1^2 B_{11} + P_1P_2B_{12} + P_2^2 B_{22}$

7.16 The cost function of a 50 MW generator with generator loading P_i is given by the following equation:
$F(P_i) = 225 + 53\ P_i + 0.02\ P^2$
When 100% loading is applied, the incremental fuel cost (IFC) of generator will be
(a) Rs. 45 per MWh
(b) Rs. 55 per MW
(c) Rs. 55 per MWh
(d) Rs. 45 per MW

7.17 The unit of incremental cost is
(a) Rs. / MVARhr
(b) Rs. / MWhr
(c) Rs. / MVAhr
(d) Rs. / MWyear

7.18 The power generated by two plants are: $P_1 = 50$ MW, $P_2 = 40$ MW. If the loss coefficients are $B_{11} = 0.001$, $B_{22} = 0.0025$ and $B_{12} = -0.0005$, then power loss will be
(a) 4.5 MW (b) 5.5 MW (c) 6.5 MW (d) 3.5 MW

7.19 The economics of power plant is greatly influenced by the following factor:
(a) Load factor (b) Diversity factor (c) Both 1 and 2 (d) Neither 1 nor 2

7.20 A load centre is at an equidistant from the two thermal generating stations G_1 and G_2. The fuel cost characteristics of the generating stations are given by following relations:
$F_1 = a + bP_1 + cP^2{}_1$
$F_2 = a + b\ P_2 + 2cP^2{}_2$
Where P_1 and P_2 are the generation in MW of G_1 and G_2, respectively, the P_1 and P_2 for most economic generation to meet 300 MW of load are
(a) $P_1 = 100$, $P_2 = 200$
(b) $P_1 = 150$, $P_2 = 150$
(c) $P_1 = 200$, $P_2 = 100$
(d) $P_1 = 175$, $P_2 = 125$

References

Books

1. R. Billinton, *Power System Reliability Evaluation*, Gordon and Breach, New York, 1970.
2. R. Billinton, R.J. Ringlee, and A.J. Wood, *Power System Reliability Calculations*, The MIT Press, Boston, Mass, 1973.
3. G.L. Kusic, *Computer Aided Power System Analysis*, Prentice-Hall, Englewood Cliffs, New Jersey, 1986.
4. L.K. Kirchmayer, *Economic Operation of Power Systems*, Wiley, New York, 1958.
5. L.K. Kirchmayer, *Economic Control of Interconnected Systems*, Wiley, New York, 1959.
6. U.G. Knight, *Power Systems Engineering and Mathematics*, Pergamon Press, New York, 1972.
7. C. Singh, and R. Billinton, *System Reliability, Modelling and Evaluation*, Hutchinson, London, 1977.
8. R.L. Sullivan, *Power System Planning*, McGraw-Hill, New York, 1977.
9. A.J. Wood and B.F. Wollenberg, *Power Generation, Operation and Control*, 2nd edn, Wiley, New York, 1996.
10. A.K. Mahalanabis, D.P. Kothari, and S.I. Ahson, *Computer Aided Power System Analysis and Control*, Tata McGraw-Hill, New Delhi, 1988.
11. A.R. Bergen, *Power System Analysis*, Prentice-Hall, Englewood Cliffs, New Jersey, 1986.
12. R. Billinton and R.N. Allan, *Reliability Evaluation of Power System*, Plenum Press, New York, 1984.
13. D.P. Kothari and I.J. Nagrath, *Power System Engineering,* 2nd edn, Tata McGraw-Hill, New Delhi, 2008.
14. H. Khatib, "Economics of Power Systems Reliability", *Technicopy* Ltd., Stonehouse, Glasgow, UK 1978.
15. K. Warwick, A.E. Kwue, and R. Aggarwal (Eds), *AI Techniques in Power Systems*, *IEE*, UK, 1997.
16. J.A. Momoh, *Electric Power System Applications of Optimization*, Marcel Dekker, Inc, NY, 2001.
17. S. Yong-Hua (Ed.), *Modern Optimization Techniques in Power Systems*, Kluwer Academic Publishers, London, 1999.
18. A.S. Debs, *Modern Power Systems Control and Operation,* KAP, New York, 1988.
19. D.P. Kothari and J.S. Dhillon, *Power System Optimization,* PHI, New Delhi, 2004.
20. R. Ramkumar, *Engineering Reliability Fundamentals and Applications,* Prentice-Hall, NJ, 1993.

Papers

21. W.S. Meyer and V.D. Albertson, "Improved Loss Formula Computation by Optimally Ordered Elimination Techniques", *IEEE Trans.,* PAS, volume: 90, p: 716, 1971.
22. E.F. Hill and W.D. Stevenson, Jr., "A New Method of Determining Loss Coefficients", *IEEE Trans.,* PAS, volume: 87, p: 1548, July 1968.
23. S.K. Agarwal and I.J. Nagrath, "Optimal Scheduling of Hydrothermal Systems", *Proc. IEEE*, volume: 199, p: 169, 1972
24. A.K. Ayub and A.D. Patton, "Optimal Thermal Generating Unit Commitment", *IEEE Trans.*, PAS, volume: 90, p: 1752, July–Aug 1971.
25. J.F. Dopazo, *et al.*, "An Optimization Technique for Real and Reactive Power Allocation", *Proc. IEEE*, p: 1877, Nov. 1967.
26. H.H. Happ, "Optimal Power Dispatch—A Comprehensive Survey", *IEEE Trans.,* PAS, volume: 96, p: 841, 1977.
27. D.C. Harker, "A Primer on Loss Formula", *AIEE Trans.,* pt. III, volume: 77, p: 1434, 1958.

28. IEEE Committee Report, "Economy-Security Functions in Power System Operations", *IEEE Special Publication 75 CHO 969.6 PWR*, New York, 1975.
29. D.P. Kothari, "Optimal Hydrothermal Scheduling and Unit Commitment", Ph D Thesis, BITS, Pilani, 1975.
30. D.P. Kothari and I.J. Nagrath, "Security Constrained Economic Thermal Generating Unit Commitment", *JIE* (India), volume: 59, p: 156, Dec. 1978.
31. I.J. Nagrath and D.P. Kothari, "Optimal Stochastic Scheduling of Cascaded Hydro-thermal Systems", *JIE* (India), volume: 56, p: 264, June 1976.
32. T.W. Berrie, *Power System Economics*, *IEE*, London, 1983.
33. T.W. Berrie, *Electricity, Economics and Planning*, *IEE*, London, 1992.
34. J. Peschen, *et al.*, "Optimal Control of Reactive Power Flow", *IEEE Trans.*, PAS, volume: 87, p: 40, 1968.
35. H.W. Dommel and W.F. Trinney, "Optimal Power Flow Solution", *IEEE Trans.*, PAS, volume: 87, p: 1866, October 1968.
36. A.M. Sasson and H.M. Merrill, "Some Applications of Optimization Techniques to Power System Problems", *Proc. IEEE*, volume: 62, p: 959, July 1974.
37. F. Wu, *et al.*, "A Two-Stage Approach to Solving Optimal Power Flows", *Proc. 1979 PICA Conf.*, pp. 126–136.
38. J. Nanda, P.R. Bijwe, and D.P. Kothari, "Application of Progressive Optimality Algorithm to Optimal Hydrothermal Scheduling Considering Deterministic and Stochastic Data", *Int. J Elect. Power and Energy Syst.*, volume: 8, p: 61, Jan. 1986.
39. D.P. Kothari, S.K. Maheshwari, and K.G. Sharma, "Minimization of Air Pollution due to Thermal Plants", *Journal of Institution of Engineers (India)*, volume: 57, issue: 2, pp: 65–68, 1977.
40. D.P. Kothari and R.K. Gupta, Optimal Stochastic Load Flow Studies, *JIE* (India), p: 34, August 1978.
41. "Description and Bibliography of Major Economy-Security Functions—Part I, II, and III", IEEE Committee Report, *IEEE Trans.*, PAS, volume: 100, pp: 211–235, Jan. 1981.
42. P.R. Bijwe, D.P. Kothari, J. Nanda, and K.S. Lingamurthy, "Optimal Voltage Control using Constant Sensitivity Matrix", *Electric Power System Research*, volume: II, issue: 3, pp: 195–203, Dec. 1986.
43. J. Nanda, D.P. Kothari, and K.S. Lingamurthy, "Economic Emission Load Dispatch through Goal Programming Techniques", *IEEE Trans., on Energy Conversion*, volume: 3, issue: 1, pp: 26–32, March 1988.
44. J. Nanda, D.P. Kothari, and S.C. Srivastava, "A New Optimal Power Dispatch Algorithm using Fletcher's QP Method", *Proc. IEE,* pte, volume: 136, issue: 3, pp: 153–161, May 1989.
45. J.S. Dhillon, S.C. Parti, and D.P. Kothari, "Stochastic Economic Emission Load Dispatch", *Int. J. of Electric Power System Research,* volume: 26, issue: 3, pp: 179–183, 1993.
46. J.S. Dhillon, S.C. Parti, and D.P. Kothari, "Multiobjective Optimal Thermal Power Dispatch", *Int. J. of EPES,* volume: 16, issue: 6, pp: 383–389, Dec. 1994.
47. D.P. Kothari and A. Ahmad, "An Expert System Approach to the Unit Commitment Problem", *"Energy Conversion and Management",* volume: 36, issue: 4, pp: 257–261, April 1995.
48. S. Sen, D.P. Kothari, and F.A. Talukdar, "Environment Friendly Thermal Power Dispatch—An Approach", *Int. J. of Energy Sources,* volume: 19, issue: 4, pp: 397–408, May 1997.
49. D.P. Kothari and A. Ahmad, "Fuzzy Dynamic Programming Based Optimal Generator Maintenance Scheduling Incorporating Load Forecasting", in *Advances in Intelligent Systems,* edited by FC Morabito, IOS Press, Ohmsha, pp: 233–240, 1997.
50. A. Ahmad and D.P. Kothari, "A Review of Recent Advances in Generator Maintenance Scheduling", *Electric Machines and Power Systems,* volume: 26, issue: 4, pp: 373–387, 1998.

51. S. Sen and D.P. Kothari, "Evaluation of Benefit of Inter-Area Energy Exchange of Indian Power System Based on Multi-Area Unit Commitment Approach", *Int. J of EMPS,* volume: 26, issue: 8, pp: 801–813, Oct. 1998.
52. Sen, S. and D.P. Kothari, "Optimal Thermal Generating Unit Commitment-A Review", *Int. J. EPES,* volume: 20, issue: 7, pp: 443–451, Oct. 1998.
53. P.S. Kulkarni, A.G. Kothari, and D.P. Kothari, "Combined Economic and Emission Dispatch using Improved BPNN", *Int. J. of EMPS,* volume: 28, issue: 1, pp: 31–43, Jan. 2000.
54. L.D. Arya, S.C. Choube, and D.P. Kothari, "Economic Despatch Accounting Line Flow Constraints using Functional Link Network", *Int. J. of Electrical Machine & Power Systems,* volume: 28, issue: 1, pp: 55–69, 2000.
55. A. Ahmad and D.P. Kothari, "A Practical Model for Generator Maintenance Scheduling with Transmission Constraints", *Int. J. of EMPS,* volume: 28, issue: 6, pp: 501–514, June 2000.
56. J.S. Dhillon and D.P. Kothari, "The Surrogate Worth Trade off Approach for Multiobjective Thermal Power Dispatch Problem". *EPSR,* volume: 56, issue: 2, pp: 103–110, Nov. 2000.
57. S. Sen and D.P. Kothari, "Large Scale Thermal Generating Unit Commitment: A New Model", in *The Next Generation of Electric Power Unit Commitment Models,* edited by BF Hobbs *et al.*, KAP, Boston, 2001, pp: 211–225.
58. J.S. Dhillon, S.C. Parti, and D.P. Kothari, "Fuzzy Decision Making in Multi-objective Long-term Scheduling of Hydrothermal System", *Int. J. of EPES,* volume: 23, issue: 1, pp: 19–29, Jan. 2001.
59. Y.S. Brar, J.S. Dhillon, and D.P. Kothari, "Multiobjective Load Dispatch by Fuzzy Logic based Searching Weightage Pattern", *Electric Power Systems Research*, volume: 63, pp: 149–160, 2002.
60. J.S. Dhillon, S.C. Parti, and D.P. Kothari, "Fuzzy Decision-making in Stochastic Multiobjective Short-term Hydrothermal Scheduling", *IEE Proc. GTD*, volume: 149, issue: 2, pp: 191–200, March 2002.
61. J. Nanda, D.P. Kothari, and K.S. Lingamurthy, "A New Approach to Economic and Minimum Emission Dispatch", *Journal of Indian Institute of Science*, volume: 67, issue: 4, pp: 249–256, 1987.
62. J. Nanda, D.P. Kothari, and K.S. Lingamurthy, "Economic Emission Load Dispatch Through Goal Programming Techniques", *IEEE Transactions on Energy Conversion*, volume: 3, issue: 1, pp: 26–32, 1988.
63. S.K. Bath, J.S. Dhillon, and D.P. Kothari, "Stochastic Multiobjective Generation Dispatch", *Int. J. of Electric Power Component and Systems*, volume: 32, pp: 1083–1103, 2004.
64. S.K. Bath, J.S. Dhillon, and D.P. Kothari, "Fuzzy Satisfying Multiobjective Generation Scheduling by Weightage Pattern Search Methods", *EPSR*, volume: 69, pp: 311–320, 2004.
65. S.K. Bath, J.S. Dhillon, and D.P. Kothari, "Stochastic Multiobjective Generation Dispatch by Search Methods", *AJIT,* volume: 4, issue: 9, pp: 823–831, 2005.
66. S.K. Bath, J.S. Dhillon, and D.P. Kothari, "Stochastic Multiobjective Generation Allocation using Pattern Search Method", *Proc. IEE GTD,* volume: 153, issue: 4, pp: 476–484, July 2006.
67. J. Dhillon, J.S. Dhillon, and D.P. Kothari, "Interactive Search based Stochastic Multiobjective Thermal Power Dispatch", *Asian Journal of Inf. Tech.,* volume: 6, issue: 3, pp: 314–322, 2007.
68. T.E. DyLiacco, "The Adaptive Reliability Control Systems", *IEEE Trans., on PAS*, volume: PAS-86, issue: 3, pp: 517–531, May 1967.
69. N.J. Singh, J.S. Dhillon, and D.P. Kothari, "Surrogate Worth Trade-Off Method for Multi-Objective Thermal Power Load Dispatch", *Energy*, volume: 138, pp: 1112–1123, 2017.
70. B. Stott, O. Alsac, and A.J. Monticelli, "Security Analysis and Optimization", *Proc. IEEE*, volume: 75, issue: 12, pp: 1623–1644, Dec. 1987.

71. L.D. Arya, "Security Constrained Power System Optimization", *Ph D Thesis*, IIT Delhi, 1990.
72. J. Nanda, D.P. Kothari, and S.C. Srivastava, "A New Optimal Power Dispatch, Algorithm using Fletcher's Quadratic Programming Method", *IEE Proc. C*, volume: 136, pt, issue: 3, pp: 153–161, May 1989.
73. J.S. Dhillon, S.C. Parti, and D.P. Kothari, "Stochastic Economic Emission Load Dispatch", *Int. J. Electric Power System Research,* volume: 26, issue: 3, 1993, pp: 179–183, 1993.
74. P.R. Bijwe, D.P. Kothari, and L.D. Arya, "Alleviation of Line Overloads and Voltage Violations by Corrective Rescheduling", *IEE Proc. C.* volume: 140, issue: 4, pp: 249–255, July 1993.
75. Y.S. Brar J.S. Dhillon, and D.P. Kothari, "Interactive Fuzzy Satisfying Multiobjective Generation Scheduling based on Genetic Weightage Pattern Search", *JIE,* volume: 86, pp: 312–318, March 2006.
76. T. Jayabarathi, V. Ramesh, D.P. Kothari, K. Pavan, and M. Thumbi, "Hybrid Differential Evolution Technique for the Economic Dispatch Problems", *Journal of Electrical Engineering and Technology*, volume: 3, issue: 4, pp: 476–483, 2008.
77. J. Nanda, L. Hari, and M.L. Kothari, "Economic Emission Load Dispatch with Line Flow Constraints Using a Classical Technique", *IEE Proceedings—Generation, Transmission and Distribution*, volume: 141, issue: 1, pp: 1–10, 1994.
78. J.S. Dhillon, J.S. Dhillon, and D.P. Kothari, "Economic-emission load dispatch using binary successive approximation-based evolutionary search", *IET Generation, Transmission and Distribution*, volume: 3, issue: 1, pp: 1–16, 2009.
79. S. Prabhakar Karthikeyan, K. Palanisamy, C. Rani, I. Jacob Raglend, and D.P. Kothari, "Security Constrained Unit Commitment Problem with Operational, Power Flow and Environmental Constraints", *WSEAS Transactions on Power Systems*, volume: 4, issues: 2, pp: 53–66, February 2009.
80. P. Karthikeyan, K. Palanisamy, I. Jacob Raglend, and D.P. Kothari, "Security Constrained UCP with Operational and Power Flow Constraints", *International Journal of Recent Trends in Engineering*, volume: 1, issues: 3, pp: 106–114, May 2009.
81. J. Raglend, S. Prabhakar Karthikeyan, K. Palanisamy, and D.P. Kothari, "Security and Emission Constrained Unit Commitment Problem with Peak Load Variations", *Emerging Journal on Electrical Science and Technology*, volume: 1, issues: 1, pp: 62–78, Nov. 2008–Jan. 2009.
82. L.D. Arya, L.S. Titare, and D.P. Kothari, "Improved Particle Swarm Optimization (PSO) Applied to Reactive Power Reserve Maximization", *International Journal of Electrical Power and Energy Systems*, volume: 32, issues: 6, pp: 368–374, June 2010.
83. B. Saravanan, C. Rani, S. Prabhakar Karthikeyan, I. Jacob Raglend, and D.P. Kothari, "Profit based Unit Commitment Problem with fuel and emission constraints using LR-EP Approach", *Emerging Journal on Engineering Science and Technology*, volume: 3, issues: 5, June 09–August 2009.
84. K.S. Swarup and S. Yamashiro, "Unit Commitment Solutions Methodology using genetic algorithm", *IEEE Trans on Power System*, volume: 17, p: 87, 2002.
85. N.J. Singh, J.S. Dhillon, and D.P. Kothari, "Synergic Predator-Prey Optimization for Economic Thermal Power Dispatch Problem", *Applied Soft Computing*, volume: 43, pp: 298–311, 2016.
86. L.D. Arya, S.C. Choube, and D.P. Kothari, "Emission Constrained Secure Economic Dispatch", *International Journal of Electric Power and Energy Systems*, volume: 19, issue: 5, pp: 279–285, 1997.
87. J.S. Dhillon and D.P. Kothari, "The Surrogate worth Trade-off Approach for Multi-Objective Thermal Power Dispatch Problem", *Electric Power Systems Research*, volume: 56, pp: 103–110, 2000.

88. P.K. Hota, R. Chakrabarti, and P.K. Chattopadhyay, "A Simulated Annealing-based Goal-Attainment Method for Economic Emission Load Dispatch with Non-smooth Fuel Cost and Emission Level Functions", *Electric Machines and Power Systems*, volume: 28, pp: 1037–1051, 2000.
89. P.K. Hota, R. Chakrabarti, and P.K. Chattopadhyay, "Economic Emission Load Dispatch Through an Interactive Fuzzy Satisfying Method", *Electric Power Systems Research,* volume: 54, pp: 151–157, 2000.
90. N.J. Singh, J.S. Dhillon, and D.P. Kothari, "Multiobjective Thermal Power Load Dispatch Using Adaptive Predator–Prey Optimization", *Applied Soft Computing*, volume: 66, pp: 370–383, 2018.
91. N.J. Singh, J.S. Dhillon, and D.P. Kothari, "Non-interactive Approach to Solve Multi-Objective Thermal Power Dispatch Problem Using Composite Search Algorithm", *Applied Soft Computing,* volume: 65, pp: 644–658, 2018.
92. N.J. Singh, J.S. Dhillon, and D.P. Kothari, "Multi-objective Thermal Power Load Dispatch Using Chaotic Differential Evolutionary Algorithm And Powell's Method", *Soft Computing, Springer Berlin Heidelberg*, volume: 22, issue: 7, pp: 2159–2174, 2018.

CHAPTER 8

Automatic Generation and Voltage Control

8.1 ▶ INTRODUCTION

Power system operation considered so far was under conditions of steady load. However, both active and reactive power demands are never steady and they continually change with the rising or falling trend. Steam input to turbo-generators (or water input to hydro-generators) must, therefore, be continuously regulated to match the active power demand, failing which the machine speed will vary with consequent change in frequency which may be highly undesirable* (maximum permissible change in power frequency is ±0.5 Hz). Also the excitation of generators must be continuously regulated to match the reactive power demand with reactive generation, otherwise the voltages at various system buses may go beyond the prescribed limits. In modern large interconnected systems, manual regulation is not feasible and therefore automatic generation and voltage regulation equipment is installed on each generator. Figure 8.1 gives the schematic diagram of load frequency and excitation voltage regulators of a turbo-generator. The controllers are set for a particular operating condition and they take care of small changes in load demand without frequency and voltage exceeding the prescribed limits. With the passage of time, as the change in load demand becomes large, the controllers must be reset either manually or automatically.

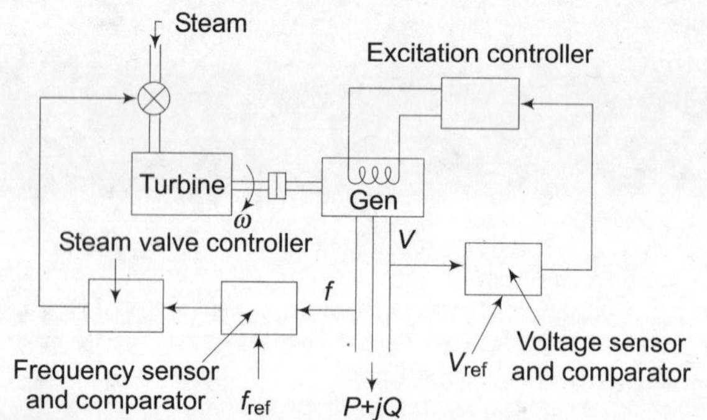

Fig. 8.1 *Schematic diagram of load frequency and excitation voltage regulators of a turbo-generator*

It has been shown in previous chapters that for small changes active power is dependent on internal machine angle δ and is independent of bus voltage; while bus voltage is dependent on machine excitation (therefore on reactive generation Q) and is independent of machine angle δ. Change in angle δ is caused by momentary change in generator speed. Therefore, load frequency and excitation voltage controls are non-interactive for small changes and can be modelled and analysed independently. Furthermore, excitation voltage control is fast acting in which the major time constant encountered is that of the generator field; while the power frequency control is slow acting with major time constant contributed by the turbine and generator moment of inertia—this time constant is much larger than that of the generator field. Thus, the transients in excitation voltage control vanish much faster and do not affect the dynamics of power frequency control.

* Change in frequency causes change in speed of the consumers' plant affecting production processes. Further, it is necessary to maintain network frequency constant so that the power stations run satisfactorily in parallel, the various motors operating on the system run at the desired speed, correct time is obtained from synchronous clocks in the system, and the entertaining devices function properly.

Changes in load demand can be identified as: (i) slow varying changes in mean demand, and (ii) fast random variations around the mean. The regulators must be designed to be insensitive to fast random changes, otherwise the system will be prone to hunting, resulting in excessive wear and tear of rotating machines and control equipment.

8.2 ▶ LOAD FREQUENCY CONTROL (SINGLE AREA CASE)

Let us consider the problem of controlling the power output of the generators of a closely knit electric area so as to maintain the scheduled frequency. All the generators in such an area constitute a *coherent* group so that all the generators speed up and slow down together maintaining their relative power angles. Such an area is defined as a *control area*. The boundaries of a control area will generally coincide with that of an individual electricity board.

To understand the load frequency control problem, let us consider a single turbo-generator system supplying an isolated load.

8.2.1 Turbine Speed Governing System

Figure 8.2 shows schematically the speed governing system of a steam turbine. The system consists of the following components:

1. *Fly ball speed governor:* This is the heart of the system which senses the change in speed (frequency). As the speed increases the fly balls move outwards and the point *B* on linkage mechanism moves downwards. The reverse happens when the speed decreases.
2. *Hydraulic amplifier:* It comprises a pilot valve and main piston arrangement. Low power level pilot valve movement is converted into high power level piston valve movement. This is necessary in order to open or close the steam valve against high pressure steam.
3. *Linkage mechanism: ABC* is a rigid link pivoted at *B* and *CDE* is another rigid link pivoted at *D*. This link mechanism provides a movement to the control valve in proportion to change in speed. It also provides a feedback from the steam valve movement (link 4).
4. *Speed changer:* It provides a steady state power output setting for the turbine. Its downward movement opens the upper pilot valve so that more steam is admitted to the turbine under steady conditions (hence more steady power output). The reverse happens for upward movement of speed changer.

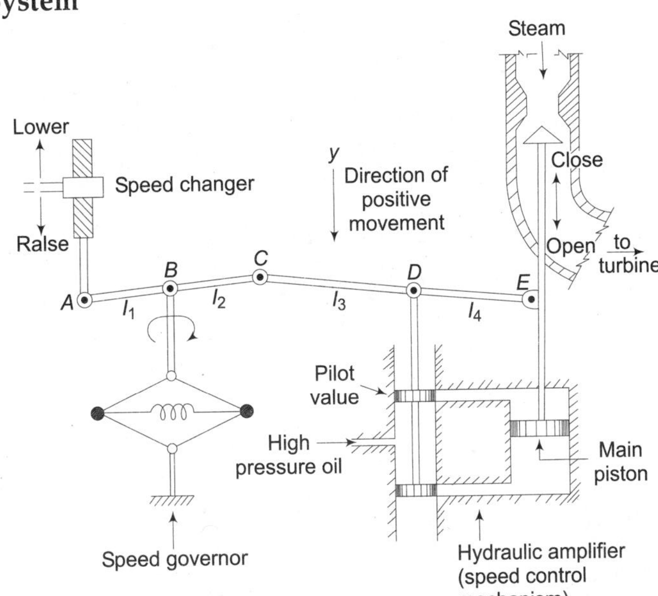

Fig. 8.2 *Turbine speed governing system (Reprinted with permission of McGraw-Hill Book Co, New York, from Olle I. Elgerd: Electric Energy System Theory: An Introduction, 1971, p 322.)*

8.2.2 Model of Speed Governing System

Assume that the system is initially operating under steady conditions—the linkage mechanism stationary and pilot valve closed, steam valve opened by a definite magnitude, turbine running at constant speed with turbine power output balancing the generator load. Let the operating conditions be characterised by

f^0 = system frequency (speed)

P_G^0 = generator output = turbine output (neglecting generator loss)

y_E^0 = steam valve setting

We shall obtain a linear incremental model around these operating conditions.

Let the point A on the linkage mechanism be moved downwards by a small amount Δy_A. It is a command which causes the turbine power output to change and can therefore be written as

$$\Delta y_A = k_C \Delta P_C \tag{8.1}$$

where ΔP_C is the commanded increase in power.

The command signal ΔP_C (i.e., Δy_E) sets into motion a sequence of events—the pilot valve moves upwards, high pressure oil flows on to the top of the main piston moving it downwards; the steam valve opening consequently increases, the turbine generator speed increases, i.e., the frequency goes up. Let us model these events mathematically.

Two factors contribute to the movement of C:

1. Δy_A contributes $-\left(\frac{l_2}{l_1}\right) \Delta y_A$ or $-k_1 \Delta y_A$ (i.e., upwards) of $-k_1 k_C \Delta P_C$.
2. Increase in frequency Δf causes the fly balls to move outwards so that B moves downwards by a proportional amount $k'_2\, \Delta f$. The consequent movement of C with A remaining fixed at Δy_A is $+\left(\frac{l_1 + l_2}{l_1}\right) k'_2 \Delta f = + k_2 \Delta f$ (i.e., downwards).

The net movement of C is therefore

$$\Delta y_C = -k_1 k_C \Delta P_C + k_2 \Delta f \tag{8.2}$$

The movement of D, Δy_D, is the amount by which the pilot valve opens. It is contributed by Δy_C and Δy_E and can be written as

$$\Delta y_D = \left(\frac{l_4}{l_3 + l_4}\right) \Delta y_C + \left(\frac{l_3}{l_3 + l_4}\right) \Delta y_E$$

$$= k_3 \Delta y_C + k_4 \Delta y_E \tag{8.3}$$

The movement Δy_D depending upon its sign opens one of the ports of the pilot valve admitting high pressure oil into the cylinder thereby moving the main piston and opening the steam valve by Δy_E. Certain justifiable simplifying assumptions, which can be made at this stage, are

1. Inertial reaction forces of main piston and steam valve are negligible compared to the forces exerted on the piston by high pressure oil.
2. Because of (i) above, the rate of oil admitted to the cylinder is proportional to port opening Δy_D.

The volume of oil admitted to the cylinder is thus proportional to the time integral of Δy_D. The movement Δy_E is obtained by dividing the oil volume by the area of the cross-section of the piston. Thus,

$$\Delta y_E = k_5 \int_0^k (-\Delta y_D)\, dt \tag{8.4}$$

It can be verified from the schematic diagram that a positive movement Δy_D causes negative (upward) movement Δy_E accounting for the negative sign used in Eq. (8.4).

Taking the Laplace transform of Eqs. (8.2), (8.3) and (8.4), we get

$$\Delta Y_C(s) = -k_1 k_C \Delta P_C(s) + k_2 \Delta F(s) \tag{8.5}$$

$$\Delta Y_D(s) = k_3 \Delta Y_C(s) + k_4 \Delta Y_E(s) \tag{8.6}$$

$$\Delta y_E(s) = -k_5 \frac{1}{s} \Delta Y_D(s) \tag{8.7}$$

Eliminating $\Delta Y_C(s)$ and $\Delta Y_D(s)$, we can write

$$\Delta Y_E(s) = \frac{k_1 k_3 k_C \Delta P_C(s) - k_2 k_3 \Delta F(s)}{\left(k_4 + \dfrac{s}{k_5}\right)}$$

$$= \left[\Delta P_C(s) - \frac{1}{R}\Delta F(s)\right] \times \left(\frac{K_{sg}}{1 + T_{sg}s}\right) \tag{8.8}$$

where

$$R = \frac{k_1 k_C}{k_2} = \text{speed regulation of the governor}$$

$$K_{sg} = \frac{k_1 k_3 k_C}{k_4} = \text{gain of speed governor}$$

$$T_{sg} = \frac{1}{k_4 k_5} = \text{time constant of speed governor}$$

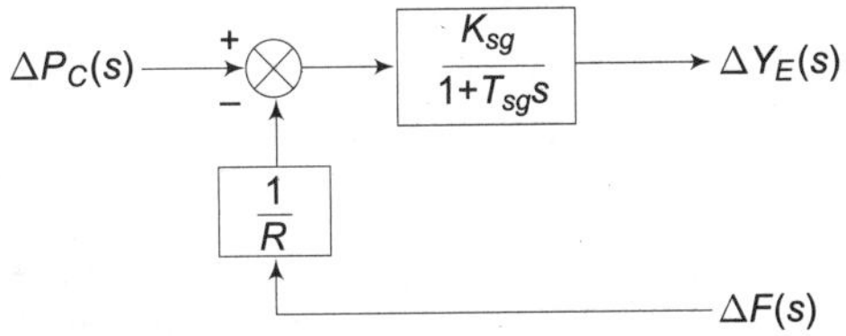

Fig. 8.3 *Block diagram representation of speed governor system*

Equation (8.8) is represented in the form of a block diagram in Fig. 8.3.

The speed governing system of a hydro-turbine is more involved. An additional feedback loop provides temporary droop compensation to prevent instability. This is necessitated by the large inertia of the penstock gate which regulates the rate of water input to the turbine. Modelling of a hydro-turbine regulating system is beyond the scope of this book.

8.2.3 Turbine Model

Let us now relate the dynamic response of a steam turbine in terms of changes in power output to changes in steam valve opening Δy_E. Figure 8.4(a) shows a two-stage steam turbine with a reheat unit. The dynamic response is largely influenced by two factors, (i) entrained steam between the inlet steam valve and first stage of the turbine, (ii) the storage action in the reheater which causes the output of the low pressure stage to lag behind that of the high pressure stage. Thus, the turbine transfer function is characterised by two time constants. For ease of analysis, it will be assumed here that the turbine can be modelled to have a single equivalent time constant. Figure 8.4(b) shows the transfer function model of a steam turbine. Typically, the time constant T_t lies in the range 0.2 to 2.5 s.

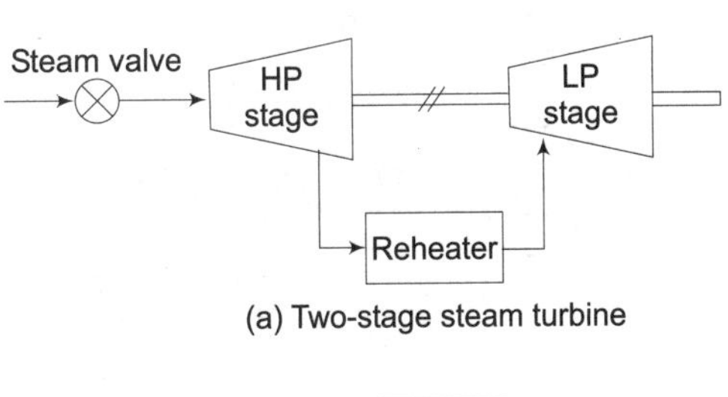

(a) Two-stage steam turbine

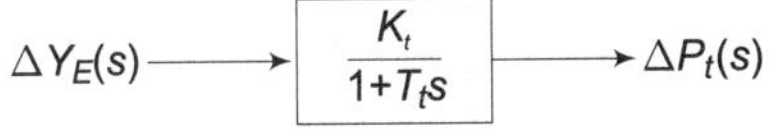

(b) Turbine transfer function model

Fig. 8.4

8.2.4 Generator Load Model

The increment in power input to the generator-load system is

$$\Delta P_G - \Delta P_D$$

where $\Delta P_G = \Delta P_t$, incremental turbine power output (assuming generator incremental loss to be negligible) and ΔP_D is the load increment.

This increment in power input to the system is accounted for in two ways:

1. Rate of increase of stored kinetic energy in the generator rotor. At scheduled frequency (f^0), the stored energy is

$$W_{ke}^0 = H \times P_r \text{ kWs (kilojoules)}$$

where P_r is the kW rating of the turbo-generator and H is defined as its inertia constant.

The kinetic energy being proportional to square of speed (frequency), the kinetic energy at a frequency of $(f^0 + \Delta f)$ is given by

$$W_{ke} = W_{ke}^0 \left(\frac{f^0 + \Delta f}{f^0} \right)^2$$

$$\simeq HP_r \left(1 + \frac{2\Delta f}{f^0} \right) \tag{8.9}$$

Rate of change of kinetic energy is therefore

$$\frac{\mathrm{d}}{\mathrm{d}t}(W_{ke}) = \frac{2HP_r}{f^0} \frac{\mathrm{d}}{\mathrm{d}t}(\Delta f) \tag{8.10}$$

2. As the frequency changes, the motor load changes being sensitive to speed, the rate of change of load with respect to frequency, i.e., $\partial P_D / \partial f$ can be regarded as nearly constant for small changes in frequency Δf and can be expressed as

$$(\partial P_D / \partial f)\, \Delta f = B\, \Delta f \tag{8.11}$$

where the constant B can be determined empirically. B is positive for a predominantly motor load.

Writing the power balance equation, we have

$$\Delta P_G - \Delta P_D = \frac{2HP_r}{f^0} \frac{\mathrm{d}}{\mathrm{d}t}(\Delta f) + B\, \Delta f$$

Dividing throughout by P_r and rearranging, we get

$$\Delta P_G(\text{pu}) - \Delta P_D(\text{pu}) = \frac{2H}{f^0} \frac{\mathrm{d}}{\mathrm{d}t}(\Delta f) + B(\text{pu})\, \Delta f \tag{8.12}$$

Taking the Laplace transform, we can write $\Delta F(s)$ as

$$\Delta F(s) = \frac{\Delta P_G(s) - \Delta P_D(s)}{B + \frac{2H}{f^0}(s)}$$

$$= [\Delta P_G(s) - \Delta P_D(s)] \times \left(\frac{K_{ps}}{1 + T_{ps} s} \right) \tag{8.13}$$

where

$$T_{ps} = \frac{2H}{Bf^0} = \text{power system time constant}$$

$$K_{ps} = \frac{1}{B} = \text{power system gain}$$

Equation (8.13) can be represented in block diagram form as shown in Fig. 8.5.

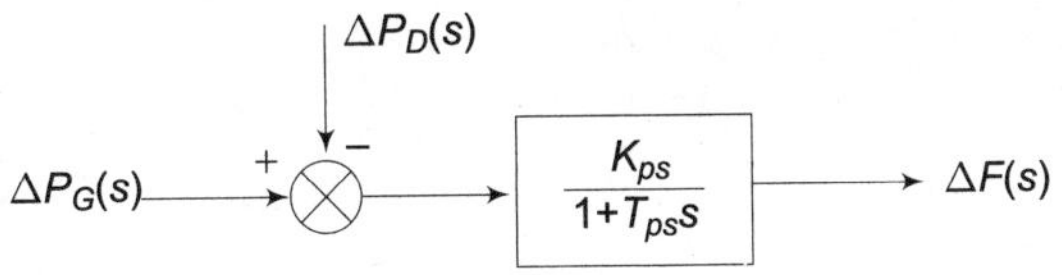

Fig. 8.5 *Block diagram representation of generator-load model*

8.2.5 Complete Block Diagram Representation of Load Frequency Control of an Isolated Power System

A complete block diagram representation of an isolated power system comprising turbine, generator, governor and load is easily obtained by combining the block diagrams of individual components, i.e., by combining Figs. 8.3, 8.4 and 8.5. The complete block diagram with feedback loop is shown in Fig. 8.6.

8.2.6 Steady State Analysis

The model of Fig. 8.6 shows that there are two important incremental inputs to the load frequency control system – ΔP_C, the change in speed changer setting; and ΔP_D, the change in load demand. Let us consider a simple situation in which the speed changer has a fixed setting (i.e., $\Delta P_C = 0$) and the load demand changes. This is known as *free governor operation*. For such an operation, the steady change in system frequency for a sudden change in load demand by an amount ΔP_D, i.e., $\Delta P_D(s) = \Delta P_D/s$ is obtained as follows:

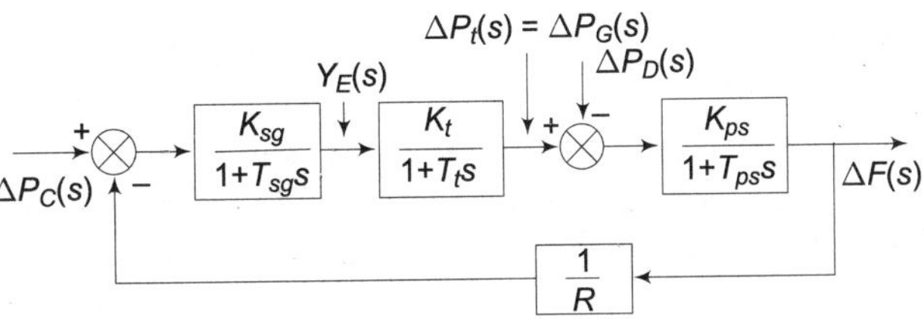

Fig. 8.6 *Block diagram model of load frequency control (isolated power system)*

$$\Delta F(s)\Big|_{\Delta P_C(s)=0} = -\frac{K_{ps}}{(1+T_{ps}s) + \dfrac{K_{sg}K_tK_{ps}/R}{(1+T_{sg}s)(1+T_ts)}} \times \frac{\Delta P_D}{s} \tag{8.14}$$

$$\Delta f\Big|_{\substack{\text{steady state}\\ \Delta P_C = 0}} = s\,\Delta F(s)\Big|_{\substack{s\to 0\\ \Delta P_C(s)=0}}$$

$$= -\left(\frac{K_{ps}}{1+(K_{sg}K_tK_{ps}/R)}\right)\Delta P_D \tag{8.15}$$

While the gain K_t is fixed for the turbine and K_{ps} is fixed for the power system, K_{sg}, the speed governor gain is easily adjustable by changing lengths of various links. Let it be assumed for simplicity that K_{sg} is so adjusted that

$$K_{sg}K_t \simeq 1$$

It is also recognised that $K_{ps} = 1/B$, where $B = \dfrac{\partial P_D}{\partial f} / P_r$ (in pu MW/unit change in frequency). Now,

$$\Delta f = -\left(\frac{1}{B+(1/R)}\right)\Delta P_D \tag{8.16}$$

The above equation gives the steady state changes in frequency caused by changes in load demand. Speed regulation R is naturally so adjusted that changes in frequency are small (of the order of 5% from no load to full load). Therefore, the linear incremental relation (8.16) can be applied from no load to full load. With this understanding, Fig. 8.7 shows the linear relationship between frequency and load for free governor operation with speed changer set to give a scheduled frequency of 100% at full load. The 'droop' or slope of this relationship is $-\left(\dfrac{1}{B+(1/R)}\right)$.

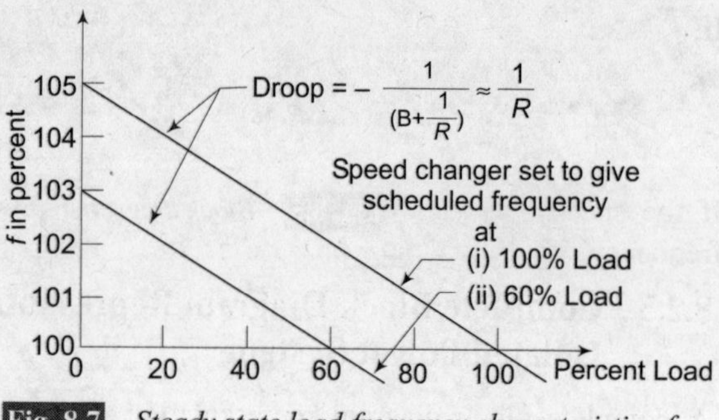

Fig. 8.7 *Steady state load-frequency characteristic of a speed governor system*

Power system parameter B is generally much smaller* than $1/R$ (a typical value is $B = 0.01$ pu MW/Hz and $1/R = 1/3$) so that B can be neglected in comparison. Equation (8.16) then simplifies to

$$\Delta f = -R(\Delta P_D) \tag{8.17}$$

The droop of the load frequency curve is thus mainly determined by R, the speed governor regulation.

It is also observed from the above that increase in load demand (ΔP_D) is met under steady conditions partly by increased generation (ΔP_G) due to opening of the steam valve and partly by decreased load demand due to drop in system frequency. From the block diagram of Fig. 8.6 (with $K_{sg}K_t \approx 1$)

$$\Delta P_G = -\frac{1}{R}\Delta f = \left(\frac{1}{BR+1}\right)\Delta P_D$$

$$\text{Decrease in system load} = B\Delta f = \left(\frac{BR}{BR+1}\right)\Delta P_D$$

Of course, the condition of decrease in system load is much less than the increase in generation. For typical values of B and R quoted earlier,

$$\Delta P_{GI} = 0.971\ \Delta P_D$$

$$\text{Decrease in system load} = 0.029\ \Delta P_D$$

Consider now the steady effect of changing speed changer setting $\left(\Delta P_C(s) = \dfrac{\Delta P_C}{s}\right)$ with load demand remaining fixed (i.e., $\Delta P_D = 0$). The steady state change in frequency is obtained as follows:

$$\Delta F(s)\Big|_{\Delta P_D(s)=0} = \frac{K_{sg}K_tK_{ps}}{(1+T_{sg}s)(1+T_ts)(1+T_{ps}s)+K_{sg}K_tK_{ps}/R} \times \frac{\Delta P_C}{s} \tag{8.18}$$

$$\Delta f\Big|_{\substack{\text{steady state}\\ \Delta P_D=0}} = \left(\frac{K_{sg}K_tK_{ps}}{1+K_{sg}K_tK_{ps}/R}\right)\Delta P_C \tag{8.19}$$

---

* For a 250 MW machine with an operating load of 125 MW, let the change in load be 1% for 1% change in frequency (scheduled frequency = 50 Hz). Then,

$$\frac{\partial P_D}{\partial f} = \frac{1.25}{0.5} = 2.5 \text{ MW/Hz}$$

$$B = \left(\frac{\partial P_D}{\partial f}\right)\Big/ P_r = \frac{2.5}{250} = 0.01 \text{ pu MW/Hz}$$

If,

$$K_{sg}K_t \approx 1$$

$$\Delta f = \left(\frac{1}{B + 1/R}\right)\Delta P_C \tag{8.20}$$

If the speed changer setting is changed by ΔP_C while the load demand changes by ΔP_D, the steady frequency change is obtained by superposition, i.e.,

$$\Delta f = \left(\frac{1}{B + 1/R}\right)(\Delta P_C - \Delta P_D) \tag{8.21}$$

According to Eq. (8.21) the frequency change caused by load demand can be compensated by changing the setting of the speed changer, i.e.,

$$\Delta P_C = \Delta P_D, \text{ for } \Delta f = 0$$

Figure 8.7 depicts two load frequency plots—one to give scheduled frequency at 100% rated load and the other to give the same frequency at 60% rated load.

Example 8.1 A 100 MVA synchronous generator operates on full load at a frequency of 50 Hz. The load is suddenly reduced to 50 MW. Due to time lag in governor system, the steam valve begins to close after 0.4 s. Determine the change in frequency that occurs in this time.
Given: $H = 5$ kWs/kVA of generator capacity.

Solution Kinetic energy stored in rotating parts of generator and turbine

$$= 5 \times 100 \times 1000 = 5 \times 10^5 \text{ kWs}$$

Excess power input to generator before the steam valve begins to close
Excess energy input to rotating parts in 0.4 s

$$= 50 \text{ MW} = 50 \times 1000 \times 0.4 = 20{,}000 \text{ kWs}$$

Stored kinetic energy $\propto$ (frequency)^2

$\therefore$ Frequency at the end of 0.4 s

$$= 50 \times \left(\frac{500{,}000 + 20{,}000}{500{,}000}\right)^{1/2} = 51 \text{ Hz}$$

Example 8.2 Two generators rated 200 MW and 400 MW are operating in parallel. The droop characteristics of their governors are 4% and 5%, respectively from no load to full load. Assuming that the generators are operating at 50 Hz at no load, how would a load of 600 MW be shared between them? What will be the system frequency at this load? Assume free governor operation.

Repeat the problem if both governors have a droop of 4%.

Solution Since the generators are in parallel, they will operate at the same frequency at steady load.
Let load on generator 1 (200 MW) $= x$ MW
and
load on generator 2 (400 MW) $= (600 - x)$ MW
Reduction in frequency $= \Delta f$
Now,

$$\frac{\Delta f}{x} = \frac{0.04 \times 50}{200} \tag{i}$$

$$\frac{\Delta f}{600 - x} = \frac{0.05 \times 50}{400} \tag{ii}$$

Equating Δf in (i) and (ii), we get

$$x = 231 \text{ MW (load on generator 1)}$$
$$600 - x = 369 \text{ MW (load on generator 2)}$$

$$\text{System frequency} = 50 - \frac{0.04 \times 50}{200} \times 231 = 47.69 \text{ Hz}$$

It is observed here that due to difference in droop characteristics of governors, generator 1 gets overloaded while generator 2 is underloaded.

It easily follows from above that if both governors have a droop of 4%, they will share the load as 200 MW and 400 MW, respectively, i.e., they are loaded corresponding to their ratings. This indeed is desirable from operational considerations.

8.2.7 Dynamic Response

To obtain the dynamic response giving the change in frequency as function of the time for a step change in load, we must obtain the Laplace inverse of Eq. (8.14). The characteristic equation being of third order, dynamic response can only be obtained for a specific numerical case. However, the characteristic equation can be approximated as first order by examining the relative magnitudes of the time constants involved. Typical values of the time constants of load frequency control system are related as

$$T_{sg} < T_t \ll T_{ps}$$

Typically* $T_{sg} = 0.4$ s, $T_t = 0.5$ s and $T_{ps} = 20$ s.

Letting $T_{sg} = T_t = 0$ (and $K_{sg} K_t \cong 1$), the block diagram of Fig. 8.6 is reduced to that of Fig. 8.8, from which we can write

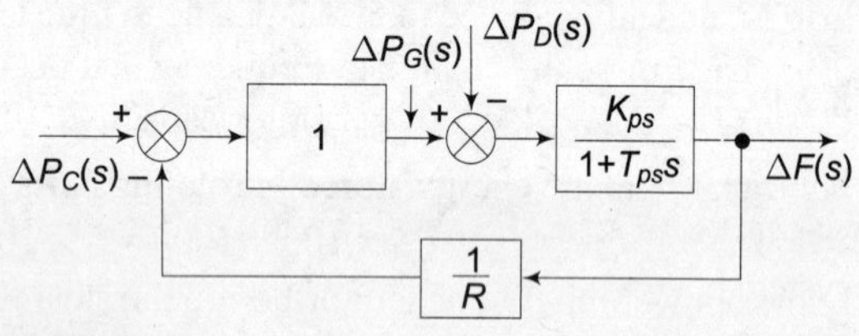

Fig. 8.8 *First-order approximate block diagram of load frequency control of an isolated area*

$$\Delta F(s)\Big|_{\Delta P_C(s)=0} = -\frac{K_{ps}}{(1 + K_{ps}/R) + T_{ps}s} \times \frac{\Delta P_D}{s}$$

$$= -\frac{K_{ps}/T_{ps}}{s\left[s + \dfrac{R + K_{ps}}{RT_{ps}}\right]} \times \Delta P_D$$

$$\Delta f(t) = -\frac{RK_{ps}}{R + K_{ps}}\left\{1 - \exp\left[-\frac{t}{T_{ps}}\left(\frac{R}{R + K_{ps}}\right)\right]\right\}\Delta P_D \tag{8.22}$$

Taking $R = 3$, $K_{ps} = 1/B = 100$, $T_{ps} = 20$, $\Delta P_D = 0.01$ pu

$$\Delta f(t) = -0.029\,(1 - e^{-1.717t}) \tag{8.23a}$$

$$\Delta f\big|_{\text{steady state}} = -0.029 \text{ Hz} \tag{8.23b}$$

The plot of change in frequency versus time for first-order approximation given above and the exact response are shown in Fig. 8.9. First-order approximation is obviously a poor approximation.

* For a 250 MW machine quoted earlier, inertia constant $H = 5$ kWs/kVA

$$T_{ps} = \frac{2H}{Bf^0} = \frac{2 \times 5}{0.01 \times 50} = 20 \text{ s}$$

8.2.8 Control Area Concept

So far we have considered the simplified case of a single turbo-generator supplying an isolated load. Consider now a practical system with a number of generating stations and loads. It is possible to divide an extended power system (say, national grid) into subareas (may be, State Electricity Boards) in which the generators are tightly coupled together so as to form a *coherent* group, i.e., all the generators respond in *unison* to changes in load or speed changer settings. Such a coherent area is called a *control area* in which the frequency is assumed to be the same throughout in static as well as dynamic conditions. For purposes of developing a suitable control strategy, a control area can be reduced to a single speed governor, turbo-generator and load system. All the control strategies discussed so far are, therefore, applicable to an independent control area.

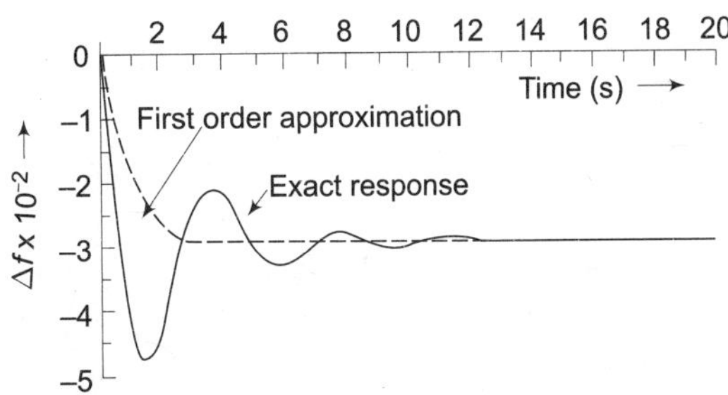

Fig. 8.9 *Dynamic response of change in frequency for a step change in load ($\Delta P_D = 0.01$ pu, $T_{sg} = 0.4$ s, $T_t = 0.5$ s, $T_{ps} = 20$ s, $K_{ps} = 100$, $R = 3$)*

8.2.9 Proportional Plus Integral Control

It is seen from the above discussion that with the speed governing system installed on each machine, the steady load frequency characteristic for a given speed changer setting has considerable droop, e.g., for the system being used for the illustration above, the steady state drop in frequency will be 2.9 Hz [see Eq. 8.23(b)] from no load to full load (1 pu load). System frequency specifications are rather stringent and, therefore, so much change in frequency cannot be tolerated. In fact, it is expected that the steady change in frequency will be zero. While steady state frequency can be brought back to the scheduled value by adjusting speed changer setting, the system could undergo intolerable dynamic frequency changes with changes in load. It leads to the natural suggestion that the speed changer setting be adjusted automatically by monitoring the frequency changes. For this purpose, a signal from Δf is fed through an integrator to the speed changer resulting in the block diagram configuration shown in Fig. 8.10. The system now modifies to a proportional plus integral controller, which, as is well known from control theory, gives zero steady state error, i.e., $\Delta f|_{\text{steady state}} = 0$.

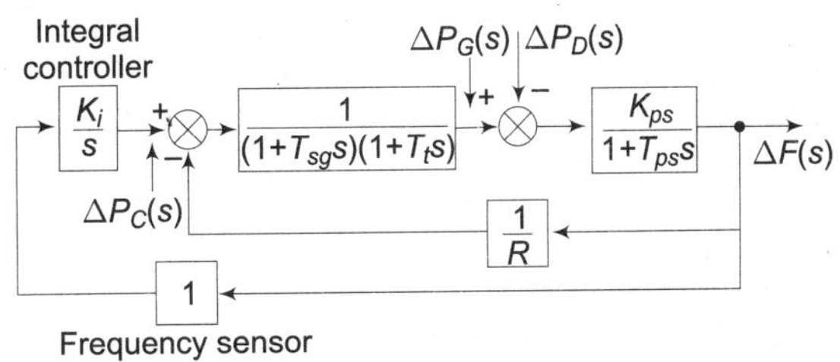

Fig. 8.10 *Proportional plus integral load frequency control*

The signal $\Delta P_C(s)$ generated by the integral control must be of opposite sign to $\Delta F(s)$ which accounts for negative sign in the block for integral controller. Now,

$$\Delta F(s) = -\frac{K_{ps}}{(1 + T_{ps}s) + \left(\frac{1}{R} + \frac{K_i}{s}\right) \times \frac{K_{ps}}{(1 + T_{sg}s)(1 + T_t s)}} \times \frac{\Delta P_D}{s}$$

$$= -\frac{RK_{ps}s(1 + T_{sg}s)(1 + T_t s)}{s(1 + T_{sg}s)(1 + T_t s)(1 + T_{ps}s)R + K_{ps}(K_i R + s)} \times \frac{\Delta P_D}{s} \quad (8.24)$$

Obviously,

$$\Delta f|_{\text{steady state}} = \lim_{s\to 0} s\ \Delta F(s) = 0 \tag{8.25}$$

In contrast to Eq. (8.16), we find that the steady state change in frequency has been reduced to zero by the addition of the integral controller. This can be argued out physically as well. Δf reaches steady state (a constant value) only when $\Delta P_C = \Delta P_D$ = constant. Because of the integrating action of the controller, this is only possible if $\Delta f = 0$.

In central load frequency control of a given control area, the change (error) in frequency is known as *Area Control Error* (ACE). The additional signal feedback in the modified control scheme presented above is the integral of ACE.

In the above scheme ACE being zero under steady conditions*, a logical design criterion is the minimisation of $\int$ACE dt for a step disturbance. This integral is indeed the *time error* of a synchronous electric clock run from the power supply. In fact, modern power systems keep track of integrated time error all the time. A corrective action (manual adjustment of ΔP_C, the speed changer setting) is taken by a large (preassigned) station in the area as soon as the time error exceeds a prescribed value.

The dynamics of the proportional plus integral controller can be studied numerically only, the system being of fourth order—the order of the system has increased by one with the addition of the integral loop. The dynamic response of the proportional plus integral controller with $K_i = 0.09$ for a step load disturbance of 0.01 pu obtained through digital computer are plotted in Fig. 8.11. For the sake of comparison, the dynamic response without integral control action is also plotted on the same figure.

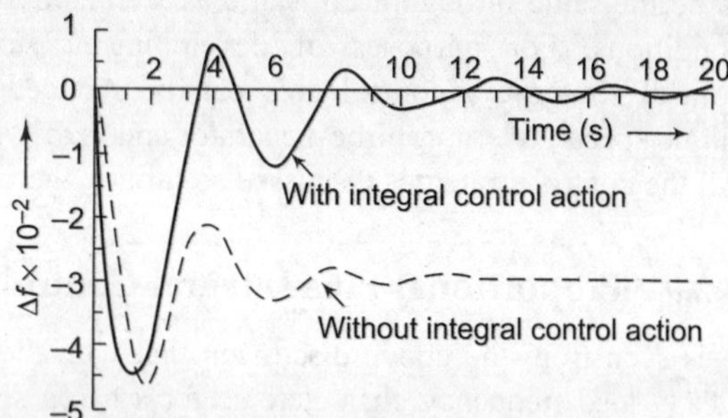

Fig. 8.11 *Dynamic response of load frequency controller with and without integral control action ($\Delta P_D = 0.01$ pu, $T_{sg} = 0.4$ s, $T_t = 0.5$ s, $T_{ps} = 20$ s, $K_{ps} = 100$, $R = 3$, $K_i = 0.09$)*

8.3 ▶ LOAD FREQUENCY CONTROL AND ECONOMIC DESPATCH CONTROL

Load frequency control with integral controller achieves zero steady state frequency error and a fast dynamic response, but it exercises no control over the relative loadings of various generating stations (i.e., *economic despatch*) of the control area. For example, if a sudden small increase in load (say, 1%) occurs in the control area, the load frequency control changes the speed changer settings of the governors of all generating units of the area so that, together, these units match the load and the frequency returns to the scheduled value (this action takes place in a few seconds). However, in the process of this change the loadings of various generating units change in a manner independent of economic loading considerations. In fact, some units in the process may even get overloaded. Some control over loading of individual units can be exercised by adjusting the gain factors (K_i) included in the signal representing integral of the area control error as fed to individual units. However, this is not satisfactory.

A satisfactory solution is achieved by using independent controls for load frequency and economic despatch. While the load frequency controller is a fast acting control (a few seconds), and regulates the

* Such a control is known as *isochronous control*, but it has its time (integral of frequency) error though steady frequency error is zero.

system around an operating point; the economic despatch controller is a slow acting control, which adjusts the speed changer setting every minute (or half a minute) in accordance with a command signal generated by the central economic despatch computer. Figure 8.12 gives the schematic diagram of both these controls for two typical units of a control area. The signal to change the speed changer setting is constructed in accordance with economic despatch error, [P_G (desired) – P_G (actual)], suitably modified by the signal representing integral ACE at that instant of time. The signal P_G (desired) is computed by the central economic despatch computer (CEDC) and is transmitted to the local economic despatch controller (EDC) installed at each station. The system, thus, operates with economic despatch error only for very short periods of time before it is readjusted.

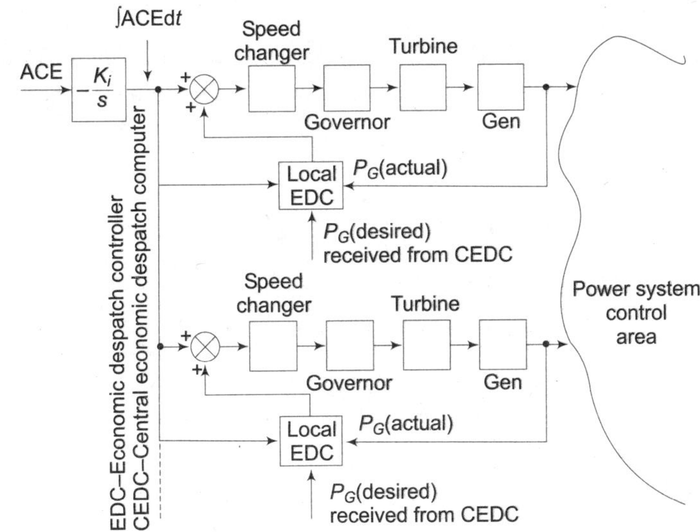

Fig. 8.12 *Control area load frequency and economic despatch control (Reprinted (with modification) with permission of McGraw Hill Book Company, New York from Olle I. Elgerd: Electric Energy Systems Theory: An Introduction, 1971, p. 345.)*

8.4 ▶ TWO-AREA LOAD FREQUENCY CONTROL

An extended power system can be divided into a number of load frequency control areas interconnected by means of tie lines. Without loss of generality, we shall consider a two-area case connected by a single tie line as illustrated in Fig. 8.13.

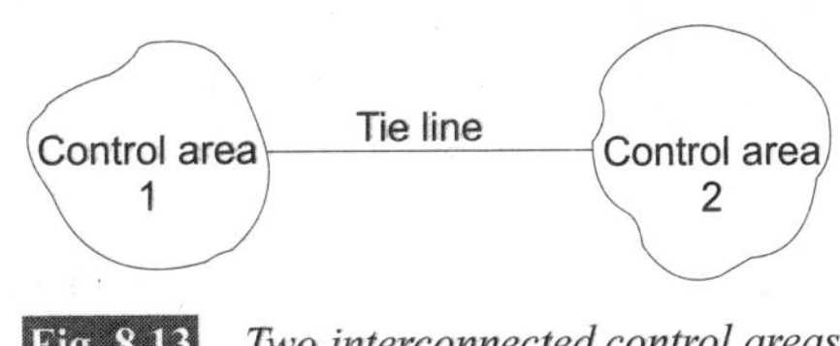

Fig. 8.13 *Two interconnected control areas (single tie line)*

The control objective now is to regulate the frequency of each area and to simultaneously regulate the tie line power as per inter-area power contracts. As in the case of frequency, proportional plus integral controller will be installed so as to give zero steady state error in tie line power flow as compared to the contracted power.

It is conveniently assumed that each control area can be represented by an equivalent turbine, generator and governor system. Symbols used with suffix 1 refer to area 1 and those with suffix 2 refer to area 2.

In an isolated control area case the incremental power ($\Delta P_G - \Delta P_D$) was accounted for by the rate of increase of stored kinetic energy and increase in area load caused by increase in frequency. Since a tie line transports power in or out of an area, this fact must be accounted for in the incremental power balance equation of each area.

Power transported out of area 1 is given by

$$P_{\text{tie, 1}} = \frac{|V_1||V_2|}{X_{12}} \sin\left(\delta_1^0 - \delta_2^0\right) \tag{8.26}$$

where

$$\delta_1^0, \delta_2^0 = \text{power angles of equivalent machines of the two areas.}$$

For incremental changes in δ_1 and δ_2, the incremental tie line power can be expressed as

$$\Delta P_{\text{tie},1}(\text{pu}) = T_{12}(\Delta\delta_1 - \Delta\delta_2) \tag{8.27}$$

where

$$T_{12} = \frac{|V_1||V_2|}{P_{r1}X_{12}}\cos\left(\delta_1^0 - \delta_2^0\right) = \text{synchronising coefficient}$$

Since incremental power angles are integrals of incremental frequencies, we can write Eq. (8.27) as

$$\Delta P_{\text{tie},1} = 2\pi T_{12}\left(\int \Delta f_1 \, dt - \int \Delta f_1 \, dt\right) \tag{8.28}$$

where Δf_1 and Δf_2 are incremental frequency changes of areas 1 and 2, respectively.

Similarly the incremental tie line power out of area 2 is given by

$$\Delta P_{\text{tie},2} = 2\pi T_{21}\left(\int \Delta f_1 \, dt - \int \Delta f_2 \, dt\right) \tag{8.29}$$

where

$$T_{21} = \frac{|V_2||V_1|}{P_{r2}X_{21}}\cos\left(\delta_2^0 - \delta_1^0\right) = \left(\frac{P_{r1}}{P_{r2}}\right)T_{12} = a_{12}T_{12} \tag{8.30}$$

With reference to Eq. (8.12), the incremental power balance equation for area 1 can be written as

$$\Delta P_{G1} - \Delta P_{D1} = \frac{2H_1}{f_1^0}\frac{d}{dt}(\Delta f_1) + B_1\Delta f_1 + \Delta P_{\text{tie},1} \tag{8.31}$$

It may be noted that all quantities other than frequency are in per unit in Eq. (8.31).

Taking the Laplace transform of Eq. (8.31) and reorganising, we get

$$\Delta F_1(s) = [\Delta P_{G1}(s) - \Delta P_{D1}(s) - \Delta P_{\text{tie},1}(s)] \times \frac{K_{ps1}}{1 + T_{ps1}s} \tag{8.32}$$

where as defined earlier [see Eq. (8.13)],

$$K_{ps1} = 1/B_1$$
$$T_{ps1} = 2H_1/B_1 f^0 \tag{8.33}$$

Compared to Eq. (8.13) of the isolated control area case, the only change is the appearance of the signal $\Delta P_{\text{tie},1}(s)$ as shown in Fig. 8.14.

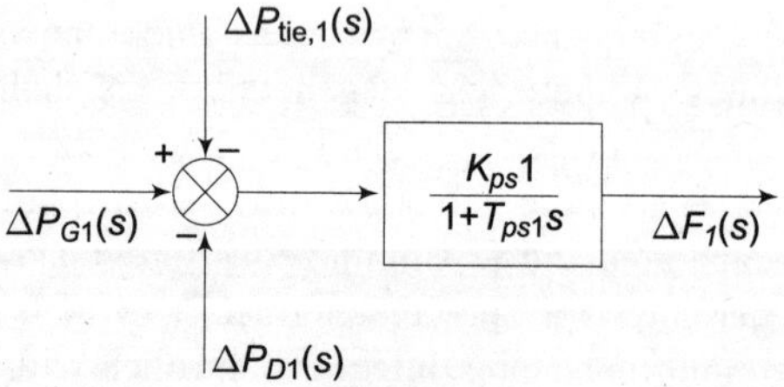

Fig. 8.14

Taking the Laplace transform of Eq. (8.28), the signal $\Delta P_{\text{tie},1}(s)$ is obtained as

$$\Delta P_{\text{tie},1}(s) = \frac{2\pi T_{12}}{s}[\Delta F_1(s) - \Delta F_2(s)] \tag{8.34}$$

The corresponding block diagram is shown in Fig. 8.15.

For the control area 2, $\Delta P_{\text{tie},2}(s)$ is given by [Eq. (8.29)]

$$\Delta P_{\text{tie},2}(s) = \frac{-2\pi a_{12}T_{12}}{s}[\Delta F_1(s) - \Delta F_2(s)] \tag{8.35}$$

which is also indicated by the block diagram of Fig. 8.15.

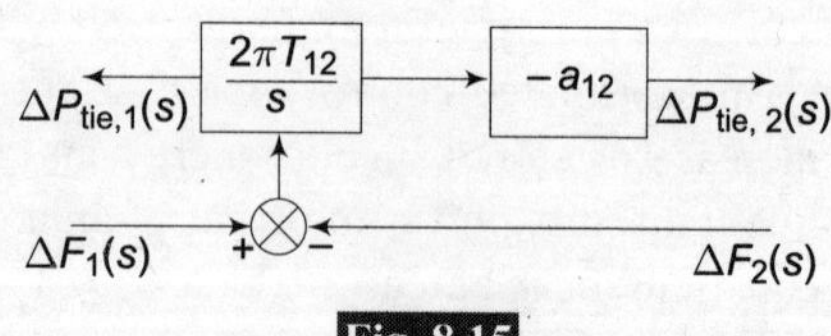

Fig. 8.15

Let us now turn our attention to ACE (area control error) in the presence of a tie line. In the case of an isolated control area, ACE is the change in area frequency which when used in integral control loop forced the steady state frequency error to zero. In order that the steady state tie line power error in a two-area control be made zero another integral control loop (one for each area) must be introduced to integrate the incremental tie line power signal and feed it back to the speed changer. This is accomplished by a single integrating block by redefining ACE as a linear combination of incremental frequency and tie line power. Thus, for control area 1,

$$\mathrm{ACE}_1 = \Delta P_{\mathrm{tie},\,1} + b_1 \Delta f_1 \tag{8.36}$$

where the constant b_1 is called area *frequency bias*.

Equation (8.36) can be expressed in the Laplace transform as

$$\mathrm{ACE}_1(s) = \Delta P_{\mathrm{tie},\,1}(s) + b_1 \Delta F_1(s) \tag{8.37}$$

Similarly, for the control area 2, ACE_2 is expressed as

$$\mathrm{ACE}_2(s) = \Delta P_{\mathrm{tie},\,2}(s) + b_2 \Delta F_2(s) \tag{8.38}$$

Combining the basic block diagrams of the two control areas corresponding to Fig. 8.6, with $\Delta P_{C1}(s)$ and $\Delta P_{C2}(s)$ generated by integrals of respective ACEs (obtained through signals representing changes in tie line power and local frequency bias) and employing the block diagrams of Figs. 8.14 to 8.15, we easily obtain the composite block diagram of Fig. 8.16.

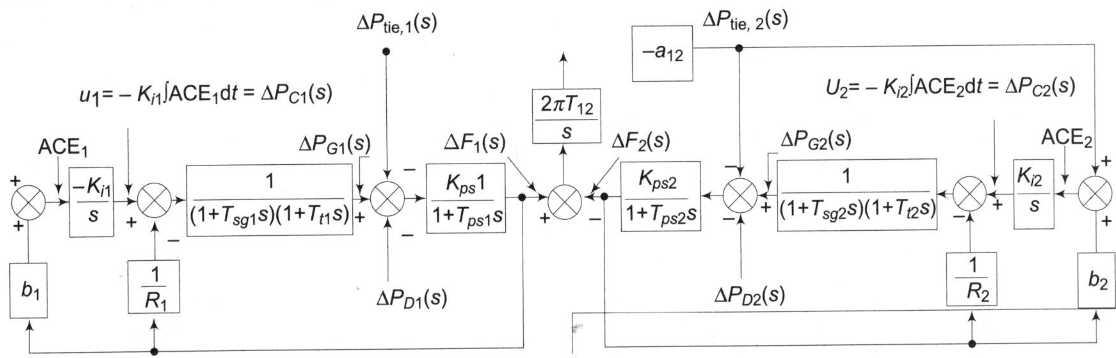

Fig. 8.16 *Composite block diagram of two-area load frequency control (feedback loops provided with integral of respective area control errors)*

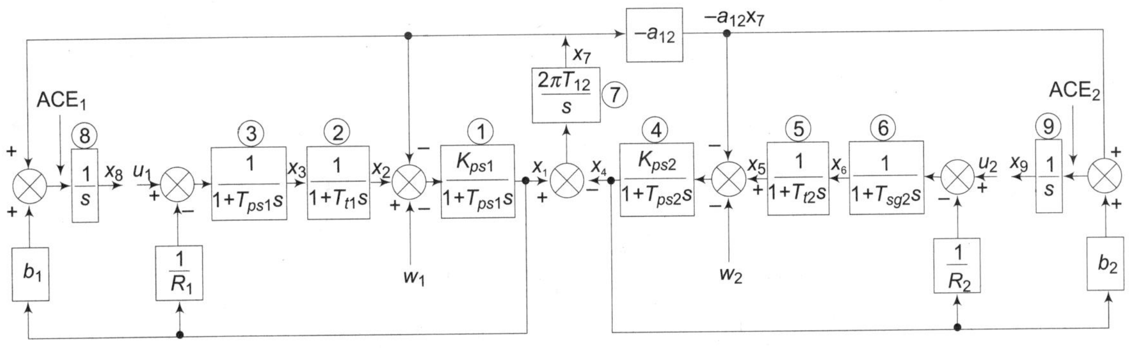

Fig. 8.17 *State space model of two-area system*

Let the step changes in loads ΔP_{D1} and ΔP_{D2} be simultaneously applied in control areas 1 and 2, respectively. When steady conditions are reached, the output signals of all integrating blocks will become constant and in order for this to be so, their input signals must become zero. We have, therefore, from Fig. 8.16,

$$\Delta P_{\text{tie, 1}} + b_1 \Delta f_1 = 0 \left(\text{input of integrating block} - \frac{K_{i1}}{s} \right) \tag{8.39a}$$

$$\Delta P_{\text{tie, 2}} + b_2 \Delta f_2 = 0 \left(\text{input of integrating block} - \frac{K_{i2}}{s} \right) \tag{8.39b}$$

$$\Delta f_1 - \Delta f_2 = 0 \left(\text{input of integrating block} - \frac{2\pi T_{12}}{s} \right) \tag{8.40}$$

From Eqs. (8.28) and (8.29)

$$\frac{\Delta P_{\text{tie,1}}}{\Delta P_{\text{tie,2}}} = -\frac{T_{12}}{T_{21}} = -\frac{1}{a_{12}} = \text{constant} \tag{8.41}$$

Hence, Eqs. (8.39) – (8.41) are simultaneously satisfied only for

$$\Delta P_{\text{tie, 1}} = \Delta P_{\text{tie, 2}} = 0 \tag{8.42}$$

and

$$\Delta f_1 = \Delta f_2 = 0$$

Thus, under steady condition, change in the tie line power and frequency of each area is zero. This has been achieved by integration of ACEs in the feedback loops of each area.

Dynamic response is difficult to obtain by the transfer function approach (as used in the single area case) because of the complexity of blocks and multi-input (ΔP_{D1}, ΔP_{D2}) and multi-output ($\Delta P_{\text{tie, 1}}$, $\Delta P_{\text{tie, 2}}$, Δf_1, Δf_2) situation. A more organised and more conveniently carried out analysis is through the state space approach (a time domain approach). Formulation of the state space model for the two-area system will be illustrated in Section 8.5.

The results of the two-area system (ΔP_{tie}, change in tie line power and Δf, change in frequency) obtained through digital computer study are shown in the form of a dotted line in Figs. 8.18 and 8.19. The two areas are assumed to be identical with system parameters given by

$$T_{sg} = 0.4 \text{ s}, T_t = 0.5 \text{ s}, T_{ps} = 20 \text{ s}$$

$$K_{ps} = 100, R = 3, b = 0.425, K_i = 0.09, 2\pi T_{12} = 0.05$$

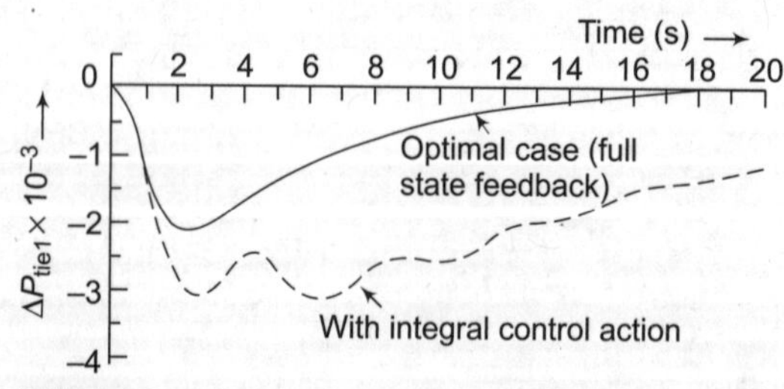

Fig. 8.18 *Change in tie line power due to step load (0.01 pu) change in area 1*

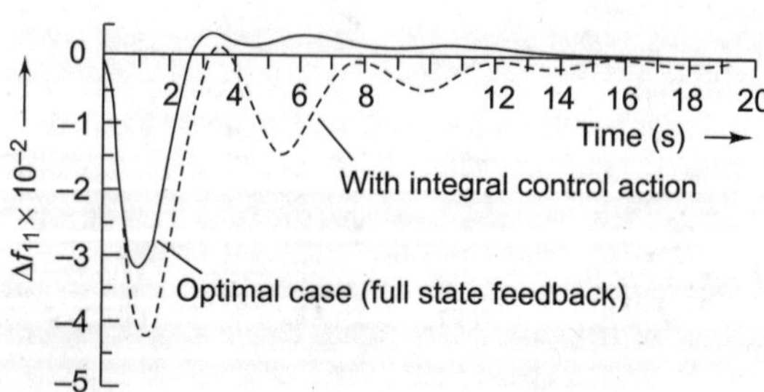

Fig. 8.19 *Change in frequency of area 1 due to step load (0.01 pu) change in area 1*

8.5 ▶ OPTIMAL (TWO-AREA) LOAD FREQUENCY CONTROL

Modern control theory is applied in this section to design an optimal load frequency controller for a two-area system. In accordance with modern control terminology, ΔP_{C1} and ΔP_{C2} will be referred to as control inputs u_1 and u_2. In the conventional approach, u_1 and u_2 were provided by the integral of ACEs. In modern control theory approach, u_1 and u_2 will be created by a linear combination of all the system states (full state feedback). For formulating the state variable model for this purpose, the conventional feedback loops are opened and each time constant is represented by a separate block as shown in Fig. 8.17. State variables are defined as the outputs of all blocks having either an integrator or a time constant. We immediately notice that the system has nine state variables.

Before presenting the optimal design, we must formulate the state model. This is achieved below by writing the differential equations describing each individual block of Fig. 8.17 in terms of state variables (note that differential equations are written by replacing s by d/dt).

Comparing Figs. 8.16 and 8.17,

$$x_1 = \Delta f_1 \qquad x_4 = \Delta f_2 \qquad x_8 = \int \text{ACE}_1 dt$$
$$x_2 = \Delta P_{G1} \qquad x_5 = \Delta P_{G2} \qquad x_9 = \int \text{ACE}_2\, dt$$
$$u_1 = \Delta P_{C1} \qquad u_2 = \Delta P_{C2}$$
$$w_1 = \Delta P_{D1} \qquad w_2 = \Delta P_{D2}$$

For block **1**

$$x_1 + T_{ps1}\dot{x}_1 = K_{ps1}(x_2 - x_7 - w_1)$$

or

$$\dot{x}_1 = -\frac{1}{T_{ps1}}x_1 + \frac{K_{ps1}}{T_{ps1}}x_2 - \frac{K_{ps1}}{T_{ps1}}x_7 - \frac{K_{ps1}}{T_{ps1}}w_1 \tag{8.43}$$

For block **2**

$$x_2 + T_{t1}\dot{x}_2 = x_3$$

or

$$\dot{x}_2 = -\frac{1}{T_{t1}}x_2 + \frac{1}{T_{t1}}x_3 \tag{8.44}$$

For block **3**

$$x_3 + T_{sg1}\dot{x}_3 = -\frac{1}{R_1}x_1 + u_1$$

or

$$\dot{x}_3 = -\frac{1}{R_1 T_{sg1}}x_1 - \frac{1}{T_{sg1}}x_3 + \frac{1}{T_{sg1}}u_1 \tag{8.45}$$

For block **4**

$$x_4 + T_{ps2}\dot{x}_4 = K_{ps2}(x_5 + a_{12}x_7 - w_2)$$

or

$$\dot{x}_4 = -\frac{1}{T_{ps2}}x_4 + \frac{K_{ps2}}{T_{ps2}}x_5 + \frac{a_{12}K_{ps2}}{T_{ps2}}x_7 - \frac{K_{ps2}}{T_{ps2}}w_2 \tag{8.46}$$

For block **5**

$$x_5 + T_{t2}\dot{x}_5 = x_6$$

or

$$\dot{x}_5 = -\frac{1}{T_{t2}}x_5 + \frac{1}{T_{t2}}x_6 \tag{8.47}$$

For block **6**

$$x_6 + T_{sg2}\dot{x}_6 = -\frac{1}{R_2}x_4 + u_2$$

or

$$\dot{x}_6 = -\frac{1}{R_2 T_{sg2}}x_4 - \frac{1}{T_{sg2}}x_6 + \frac{1}{T_{sg2}}u_2 \tag{8.48}$$

For block **7**

$$\dot{x}_7 = 2\pi T_{12}x_1 - 2\pi T_{12}x_4 \tag{8.49}$$

For block **8**

$$\dot{x}_8 = b_1x_1 + x_7 \tag{8.50}$$

For block **9**

$$\dot{x}_9 = b_2x_4 - a_{12}x_7 \tag{8.51}$$

The nine equations (8.43) to (8.51) can be organised in the following vector matrix form:

$$\dot{\boldsymbol{x}} = \boldsymbol{A}\boldsymbol{x} + \boldsymbol{B}\boldsymbol{u} + \boldsymbol{F}\boldsymbol{w} \tag{8.52}$$

where

$\boldsymbol{x} = [x_1\ \ x_2\ \ ...\ x_9]^T$ = state vector
$\boldsymbol{u} = [u_1\ \ u_2]^T$ = control vector
$\boldsymbol{w} = [w_1\ \ w_2]^T$ = disturbance vector

while the matrices $\boldsymbol{A}$, $\boldsymbol{B}$ and $\boldsymbol{F}$ are defined below:

$$\boldsymbol{A} = \begin{array}{c} \\ 1 \\ 2 \\ 3 \\ 4 \\ 5 \\ 6 \\ 7 \\ 8 \\ 9 \end{array}
\begin{array}{c}
\begin{array}{ccccccccc} 1 & 2 & 3 & 4 & 5 & 6 & 7 & 8 & 9 \end{array} \\
\left[\begin{array}{ccccccccc}
-\dfrac{1}{T_{ps1}} & \dfrac{K_{ps1}}{T_{ps1}} & 0 & 0 & 0 & 0 & -\dfrac{K_{ps1}}{T_{ps1}} & 0 & 0 \\
0 & -\dfrac{1}{T_{t1}} & \dfrac{1}{T_{t1}} & 0 & 0 & 0 & 0 & 0 & 0 \\
\dfrac{1}{R_1T_{sg1}} & 0 & -\dfrac{1}{T_{sg1}} & 0 & 0 & 0 & 0 & 0 & 0 \\
0 & 0 & 0 & -\dfrac{1}{T_{ps2}} & \dfrac{K_{ps2}}{T_{ps2}} & 0 & \dfrac{a_{12}K_{ps2}}{T_{ps2}} & 0 & 0 \\
0 & 0 & 0 & 0 & -\dfrac{1}{T_{t2}} & \dfrac{1}{T_{t2}} & 0 & 0 & 0 \\
0 & 0 & 0 & -\dfrac{1}{R_2T_{sg2}} & 0 & -\dfrac{1}{T_{sg2}} & 0 & 0 & 0 \\
2\pi T_{12} & 0 & 0 & -2\pi T_{12} & 0 & 0 & 0 & 0 & 0 \\
b_1 & 0 & 0 & 0 & 0 & 0 & 1 & 0 & 0 \\
0 & 0 & 0 & b_2 & 0 & 0 & -a_{12} & 0 & 0
\end{array}\right]
\end{array}$$

$$\boldsymbol{B}^T = \begin{bmatrix} 0 & 0 & \dfrac{1}{T_{sg1}} & 0 & 0 & 0 & 0 & 0 & 0 \\ 0 & 0 & 0 & 0 & 0 & \dfrac{1}{T_{sg2}} & 0 & 0 & 0 \end{bmatrix}$$

$$\boldsymbol{F}^T = \begin{bmatrix} -\dfrac{K_{ps1}}{T_{ps1}} & 0 & 0 & 0 & 0 & 0 & 0 & 0 & 0 \\ 0 & 0 & 0 & -\dfrac{K_{ps2}}{T_{ps2}} & 0 & 0 & 0 & 0 & 0 \end{bmatrix}$$

In the conventional control scheme of Fig. 8.16, the control inputs u_1 and u_2 are constructed as under from the state variables x_8 and x_9 only.

$$u_1 = -K_{i1}x_8 = -K_{i1} \int \text{ACE}_1 \text{d}t$$

$$u_2 = -K_{i2}x_9 = -K_{i2} \int \text{ACE}_2 \text{d}t$$

In the optimal control scheme the control inputs u_1 and u_2 are generated by means of feedbacks from all the nine states with feedback constants to be determined in accordance with an optimality criterion.

Examination of Eq. (8.52) reveals that our model is not in the standard form employed in optimal control theory. The standard form is

$$\dot{\boldsymbol{x}} = \boldsymbol{Ax} + \boldsymbol{Bu}$$

which does not contain the disturbance term $\boldsymbol{Fw}$ present in Eq. (8.52). Furthermore, a constant disturbance vector $\boldsymbol{w}$ would drive some of the system states and the control vector $\boldsymbol{u}$ to constant steady values; while the cost function employed in optimal control requires that the system state and control vectors have zero steady state values for the cost function to have a minimum.

For a constant disturbance vector $\boldsymbol{w}$, the steady state is reached when

$$\dot{\boldsymbol{x}} = 0$$

in Eq. (8.52); which then gives

$$0 = \boldsymbol{Ax}_{ss} + \boldsymbol{Bu}_{ss} + \boldsymbol{Fw} \tag{8.53}$$

Defining $\boldsymbol{x}$ and $\boldsymbol{u}$ as the sum of transient and steady state terms, we can write

$$\boldsymbol{x} = \boldsymbol{x}' + \boldsymbol{x}_{ss} \tag{8.54}$$

$$\boldsymbol{u} = \boldsymbol{u}' + \boldsymbol{u}_{ss} \tag{8.55}$$

Substituting $\boldsymbol{x}$ and $\boldsymbol{u}$ from Eqs. (8.54) and (8.55) in Eq. (8.52), we have

$$\dot{\boldsymbol{x}}' = \boldsymbol{A}(\boldsymbol{x}' + \boldsymbol{x}_{ss}) + \boldsymbol{B}(\boldsymbol{u}' + \boldsymbol{u}_{ss}) + \boldsymbol{Fw}$$

By virtue of relationship (8.53), we get

$$\dot{\boldsymbol{x}}' = \boldsymbol{Ax}' + \boldsymbol{Bu}' \tag{8.56}$$

This represents system model in terms of excursion of state and control vectors from their respective steady state values.

For full state feedback, the control vector $\boldsymbol{u}$ is constructed by a linear combination of all states, i.e.,

$$\boldsymbol{u} = -\boldsymbol{Kx} \tag{8.57a}$$

where $\boldsymbol{K}$ is the feedback matrix.

Now,

$$\boldsymbol{u}' + \boldsymbol{u}_{ss} = -\boldsymbol{K}(\boldsymbol{x}' + \boldsymbol{x}_{ss})$$

For a stable system both $\boldsymbol{x}'$ and $\boldsymbol{u}'$ go to zero, therefore

$$\boldsymbol{u}_{ss} = -\boldsymbol{Kx}_{ss}$$

Hence,

$$\boldsymbol{u}' = -\boldsymbol{Kx}' \tag{8.57b}$$

Examination of Fig. 8.17 easily reveals the steady state values of state and control variables for constant values of disturbance inputs w_1 and w_2. These are

$$\begin{aligned} x_{1ss} &= x_{4ss} = x_{7ss} = 0 \\ x_{2ss} &= x_{3ss} = w_1 \\ u_{1ss} &= w_1 \\ x_{5ss} &= x_{6ss} = w_2 \\ u_{2ss} &= w_2 \\ x_{8ss} &= \text{constant} \\ x_{9ss} &= \text{constant} \end{aligned} \tag{8.58}$$

The values of x_{8ss} and x_{9ss} depend upon the feedback constants and can be determined from the following steady state equations:

$$u_{1ss} = k_{11}x_{1ss} + \cdots + k_{18}x_{8ss} + k_{19}x_{9ss} = w_1$$
$$u_{2ss} = k_{21}x_{1ss} + \cdots + k_{28}x_{8ss} + k_{29}x_{9ss} = w_2 \tag{8.59}$$

The feedback matrix $\boldsymbol{K}$ in Eq. 8.57(b) is to be determined so that a certain performance index (PI) is minimised in transferring the system from an arbitrary initial state $x'(0)$ to origin in infinite time (i.e., $x'(\infty) = 0$). A convenient PI has the quadratic form

$$\mathbf{PI} = \frac{1}{2}\int_0^{\infty} (\boldsymbol{x}'^T \boldsymbol{Q}\boldsymbol{x}' + \boldsymbol{u}'^T \boldsymbol{R}\boldsymbol{u}')\, dt \tag{8.60}$$

The matrices $\boldsymbol{Q}$ and $\boldsymbol{R}$ are defined for the problem in hand through the following design considerations:

1. Excursions of ACEs about the steady values $(x'_7 + b_1x'_1;\ -a_{12}x'_7 + b_2x'_4)$ are minimised. The steady values of ACEs are of course zero.
2. Excursions of $\int$ACE dt about the steady values (x'_8, x'_9) are minimised. The steady values of $\int$ACE dt are, of course, constants.
3. Excursions of the control vector (u'_1, u'_2) about the steady value are minimised. The steady value of the control vector is, of course, a constant. This minimisation is intended to indirectly limit the control effort within the physical capability of components. For example, the steam valve cannot be opened more than a certain value without causing the boiler pressure to drop severely.

With the above reasoning, we can write the PI as

$$\mathbf{PI} = \frac{1}{2}\int_0^{\infty} [(x'_7 + b_1x'_1)^2 + (-a_{12}x'_7 + b_2x'_4)^2 + (x'^2_8 + x'^2_9) + k(u'^2_1 + u'^2_2)]\, dt \tag{8.61}$$

From the PI of Eq. (8.61), $\boldsymbol{Q}$ and $\boldsymbol{R}$ can be recognised as

$$\boldsymbol{Q} = \begin{bmatrix} b_1^2 & 0 & 0 & 0 & 0 & 0 & b_1 & 0 & 0 \\ 0 & 0 & 0 & 0 & 0 & 0 & 0 & 0 & 0 \\ 0 & 0 & 0 & 0 & 0 & 0 & 0 & 0 & 0 \\ 0 & 0 & 0 & b_2^2 & 0 & 0 & -a_{12}b_2 & 0 & 0 \\ 0 & 0 & 0 & 0 & 0 & 0 & 0 & 0 & 0 \\ 0 & 0 & 0 & 0 & 0 & 0 & 0 & 0 & 0 \\ b_1 & 0 & 0 & -a_{12}b_2 & 0 & 0 & (1+a_{12}^2) & 0 & 0 \\ 0 & 0 & 0 & 0 & 0 & 0 & 0 & 1 & 0 \\ 0 & 0 & 0 & 0 & 0 & 0 & 0 & 0 & 1 \end{bmatrix}$$

= symmetric matrix

$\boldsymbol{R} = k\boldsymbol{I}$ = symmetric matrix

Determination of the feedback matrix $\boldsymbol{K}$ which minimises the above PI is the standard *optimal regulator problem*. $\boldsymbol{K}$ is obtained from solution of the *reduced matrix Riccati equation** given below.

$$\boldsymbol{A}^T\boldsymbol{S} + \boldsymbol{S}\boldsymbol{A} - \boldsymbol{S}\boldsymbol{B}\boldsymbol{R}^{-1}\boldsymbol{B}^T\boldsymbol{S} + \boldsymbol{Q} = 0 \tag{8.62}$$
$$\boldsymbol{K} = \boldsymbol{R}^{-1}\boldsymbol{B}^T\boldsymbol{S} \tag{8.63}$$

The acceptable solution of $\boldsymbol{K}$ is that for which the system remains stable. Substituting Eq. 8.57(b) in Eq. (8.56), the system dynamics with feedback is defined by

$$\dot{\boldsymbol{x}}' = (\boldsymbol{A} - \boldsymbol{B}\boldsymbol{K})\boldsymbol{x}' \tag{8.64}$$

For stability all the eigenvalues of the matrix $(\boldsymbol{A} - \boldsymbol{B}\boldsymbol{K})$ should have negative real parts.

* a set of linear algebraic equations.

For illustration we consider two identical control areas with the following system parameters:

$$T_{sg} = 0.4 \text{ s}; T_t = 0.5 \text{ s}; T_{ps} = 20 \text{ s}$$
$$\boldsymbol{R} = 3; \boldsymbol{K}_{ps} = 1/B = 100$$
$$b = 0.425; \boldsymbol{K}_i = 0.09; a_{12} = 1; 2\pi T_{12} = 0.05$$

Computer solution for the feedback matrix $\boldsymbol{K}$ is presented below, while the system dynamic response is plotted in Figs. 8.18 and 8.19. These figures also give for comparison the dynamic response for the case of integral control action only. The improvement in performance achieved by the optimal controller is evident from these figures.

$$\boldsymbol{K} = \begin{bmatrix} 0.5286 & 1.1419 & 0.6813 & -0.0046 & -0.0211 & -0.0100 & -0.7437 & 0.9999 & 0.0000 \\ -0.0046 & -0.0211 & -0.0100 & 0.5286 & 1.1419 & 0.6813 & 0.7437 & 0.0000 & 0.9999 \end{bmatrix}$$

As the control areas extend over vast geographical regions, there are two ways of obtaining full state information in each area for control purposes.

1. Transport the state information of the distant area over communication channels. This is, of course, expensive.
2. Generate all the states locally (including the distant states) by means of 'observer' or 'Kalman filter' by processing the local output signal. An 'observer', being itself a high-order system, renders the overall system highly complex and may, in fact, result in impairing system stability and dynamic response which is meant to be improved through optimal control.

Because of the above mentioned difficulties encountered in implementation of an optimal control load frequency scheme, it is preferable to use a sub-optimal scheme employing only local states of the area. The design of such structurally constrained optimal control schemes is beyond the scope of this book. The conventional control scheme of Fig. 8.16 is, in fact, the local output feedback scheme in which feedback signal derived from changes in local frequency and tie line power is employed in each area.

8.6 ▶ AUTOMATIC VOLTAGE CONTROL

Figure 8.20 gives the schematic diagram of an automatic voltage regulator of a generator. It basically consists of a main exciter which excites the alternator field to control the output voltage. The exciter field is automatically controlled through error $e = V_{\text{Ref}} - V_T$, suitably amplified through voltage and power amplifiers. It is a type-0 system which requires a constant error e for a specified voltage at generator terminals. The block diagram of the system is given in Fig. 8.21. The function of important components and their transfer function are given below:

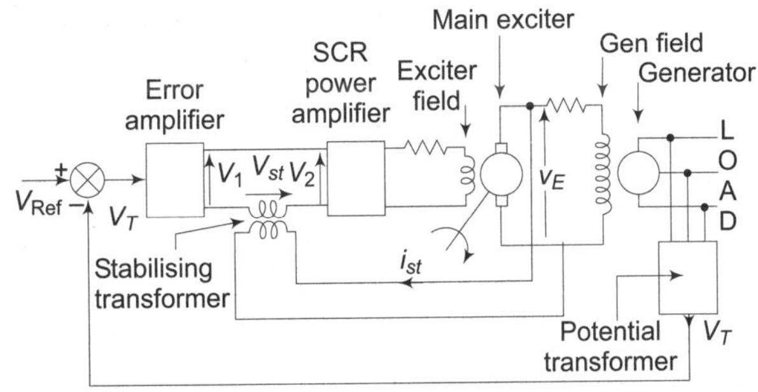

Fig. 8.20 *Schematic diagram of alternator voltage regulator scheme*

1. *Potential transformer* It gives a sample of terminal voltage V_T.

2. *Differencing device* It gives the actuating error

$$e = V_{\text{Ref}} - V_T$$

The error initiates the corrective action of adjusting the alternator excitation. Error waveform is suppressed carrier modulated, the carrier frequency being the system frequency of 50 Hz.

3. *Error amplifier* It demodulates and amplifies the error signal. Its gain is K_a.

4. *SCR power amplifier and exciter field* It provides the necessary power amplification to the signal for controlling the exciter field. Assuming the amplifier time constant to be small enough to be neglected, the overall transfer function of these two is

$$\frac{K_e}{1+T_{ef}s}$$

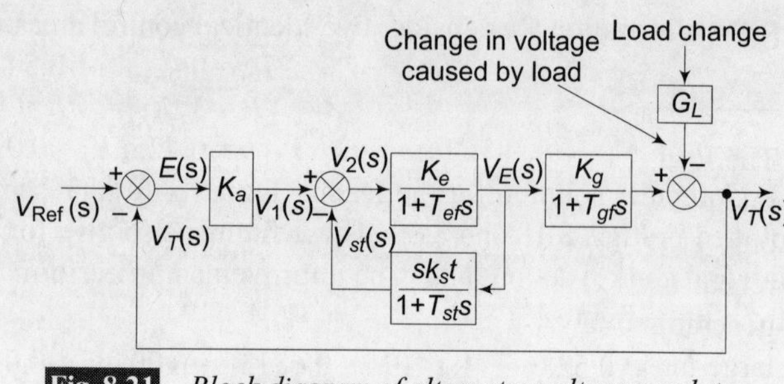

Fig. 8.21 *Block diagram of alternator voltage regulator scheme*

where T_{ef} is the exciter field time constant.

5. *Alternator* Its field is excited by the main exciter voltage V_E. Under no load it produces a voltage proportional to field current. The no load transfer function is

$$\frac{K_g}{1+T_{gf}s}$$

where

$$T_{gf} = \text{generator field time constant.}$$

The load causes a voltage drop which is a complex function of direct and quadrature axis currents. The effect is only schematically represented by block G_L. The exact load model of the alternator is beyond the scope of this book.

6. *Stabilising transformer* T_{ef} and T_{gf} are large enough time constants to impair the systems dynamic response. It is well known that the dynamic response of a control system can be improved by the internal derivative feedback loop. The derivative feedback in this system is provided by means of a stabilising transformer excited by the exciter output voltage V_E. The output of the stabilising transformer is fed negatively at the input terminals of the SCR power amplifier. The transfer function of the stabilising transformer is derived below.

Since the secondary is connected at the input terminals of an amplifier, it can be assumed to draw zero current. Now,

$$V_E = R_1 i_{st} + L_1 \frac{di_{st}}{dt}$$

$$V_{st} = M \frac{di_{st}}{dt}$$

Taking the Laplace transform, we get

$$\frac{V_{st}(s)}{V_E(s)} = \frac{sM}{R_1 + sL_1} = \frac{sM/R_1}{1+T_{st}s}$$

$$= \frac{sK_{st}}{1+T_{st}s}$$

Accurate state variable models of loaded alternator around an operating point are available in literature using which optimal voltage regulation schemes can be devised. This is, of course, beyond the scope of this book.

8.7 ▶ LOAD FREQUENCY CONTROL WITH GENERATION RATE CONSTRAINTS (GRCS)

The load frequency control problem discussed so far does not consider the effect of the restrictions on the rate of change of power generation. In power systems having steam plants, power generation can change only at a specified maximum rate. The generation rate (from safety considerations of the equipment) for reheat units is quite low. Most of the reheat units have a generation rate around 3%/min. Some have a generation rate between 5 and 10%/min. If these constraints are not considered, system is likely to chase large momentary disturbances. This results in undue wear and tear of the controller. Several methods have been proposed to consider the effect of GRCs for the design of automatic generation controllers. When GRC is considered, the system dynamic model becomes nonlinear and linear control techniques cannot be applied for the optimisation of the controller setting.

If the generation rates denoted by P_{Gi} are included in the state vector, the system order will be altered. Instead of augmenting them, while solving the state equations, it may be verified at each step if the GRCs are violated. Another way of considering GRCs for both areas is to add limiters to the governors [9, 18] as shown in Fig. 8.22, i.e., the maximum rate of valve opening or closing speed is restricted by the limiters. Here, $T_{sg}\, g_{\max}$ is the power rate limit imposed by valve or gate control. In this model

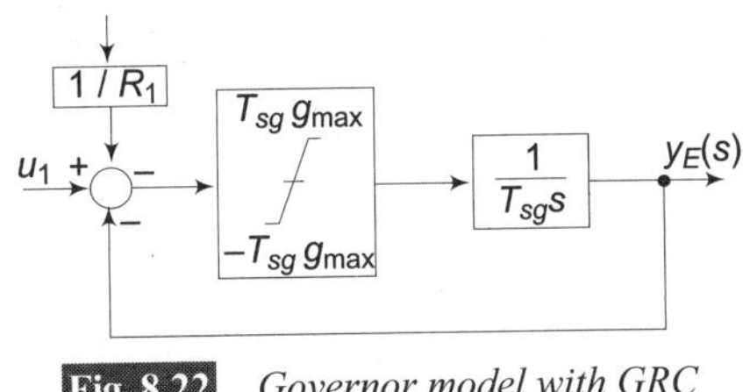

Fig. 8.22 Governor model with GRC

$$|\Delta \dot{Y}_E| < g_{\max} \tag{8.65}$$

The banded values imposed by the limiters are selected to restrict the generation rate by 10% per minute.

The GRCs result in larger deviations in ACEs as the rate at which generation can change in the area is constrained by the limits imposed. Therefore, the duration for which the power needs to be imported increases considerably as compared to the case where generation rate is not constrained. With GRCs, R should be selected with care so as to give the best dynamic response. In hydro-thermal system, the generation rate in the hydro area normally remains below the safe limit and therefore GRCs for all the hydro plants can be ignored.

8.8 ▶ SPEED GOVERNOR DEAD-BAND AND ITS EFFECT ON AGC

The effect of the speed governor dead-band is that for a given position of the governor control valves, an increase/decrease in speed can occur before the position of the valve changes. The governor dead-band can materially affect the system response. In AGC studies, the dead-band effect indeed can be significant, since relatively small signals are under considerations.

The speed governor characteristic, though nonlinear, has been approximated by linear characteristics in earlier analysis. Further, there is another nonlinearity introduced by the dead-band in the governor operation. Mechanical friction and backlash and also valve overlaps in hydraulic relays cause the governor dead-band. Due to this, though the input signal increases, the speed governor may not immediately react until the input reaches a particular value. Similar action takes place when the input signal decreases. Thus, the governor dead-band is defined as the total magnitude of sustained speed change within which there is no change in valve position. The limiting value of dead-band is specified as 0.06%. It was shown by Concordia *et al.* [19] that one of the effects of governor dead-band is to increase the apparent steady-state speed regulation R.

The effect of the dead-band may be included in the speed governor control loop block diagram as shown in Fig. 8.23. Considering the worst case for the dead-band, (i.e., the system starts responding after the whole dead-band is traversed) and examining the dead-band block in Fig. 8.23, the following set of equations completely define the behaviour of the dead-band [19].

$$\begin{aligned} y^{(r+1)} &= x^{(r)} \text{ if } x^{(r+1)} - x^{r} \leq \text{dead-band} \\ &= x^{(r+1)} - \text{dead-band; if } x^{(r+1)} - x^{(r)} > 0 \\ &= x^{(r+1)}; \text{ if } x^{r+1} - x^{r} < 0 \end{aligned} \quad (8.66)$$

(r is the step in the computation)

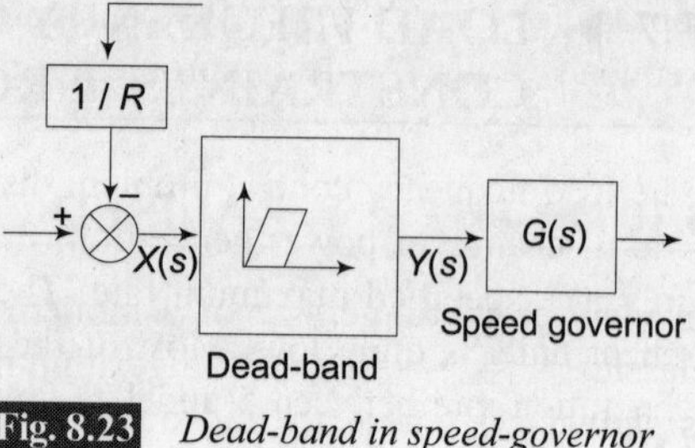

Fig. 8.23 *Dead-band in speed-governor control loop*

Reference [20] considers the effect of governor dead-band nonlinearity by using the describing function approach [11] and including the linearised equations in the state space model.

The presence of governor dead-band makes the dynamic response oscillatory. It has been seen [19] that the governor dead-band does not influence the selection of integral controller gain settings in the presence of GRCs. In the presence of GRC and dead band even for small load perturbation, the system becomes highly nonlinear and hence the optimisation problem becomes rather complex.

8.9 ▶ DIGITAL LF CONTROLLERS

In recent years, increasingly more attention is being paid to the question of digital implementation of the automatic generation control algorithms. This is mainly due to the facts that digital control turns out to be more accurate and reliable, compact in size, less sensitive to noise and drift and more flexible. It may also be implemented in a time shared fashion by using the computer systems in load despatch centre, if so desired. The ACE, a signal which is used for AGC is available in the discrete form, i.e., there occurs sampling operation between the system and the controller. Unlike the continuous-time system, the control vector in the discrete mode is constrained to remain constant between the sampling instants. The digital control process is inherently a discontinuous process and the designer has thus to resort to the discrete-time analysis for optimisation of the AGC strategies.

8.9.1 Discrete-Time Control Model

The continuous-time dynamic system is described by a set of linear differential equations

$$\dot{\boldsymbol{x}} = \boldsymbol{A}\boldsymbol{x} + \boldsymbol{B}\boldsymbol{u} + \boldsymbol{\Gamma}\boldsymbol{p} \quad (8.67)$$

where $\boldsymbol{x}$, $\boldsymbol{u}$, $\boldsymbol{p}$ are state, control and disturbance vectors, respectively and $\boldsymbol{A}$, $\boldsymbol{B}$ and Γ are constant matrices associated with the above vectors.

The discrete-time behaviour of the continuous-time system is modelled by the system of first order linear difference equations:

$$\boldsymbol{x}(k+1) = \phi\boldsymbol{x}(k) + \Psi\boldsymbol{u}(k) + \gamma\boldsymbol{p}(k) \quad (8.68)$$

where $\boldsymbol{x}(k)$, $\boldsymbol{u}(k)$ and $\boldsymbol{p}(k)$ are the state, control and disturbance vectors and are specified at $t = k$T, $k = 0, 1, 2, \ldots$ etc., and T is the sampling period. ϕ, ψ and γ are the state, control and disturbance transition matrices and they are evaluated using the following relations:

$$\phi = \boldsymbol{e}^{AT}$$
$$\psi = (\boldsymbol{e}^{AT} - I)\,\boldsymbol{A}^{-1}\boldsymbol{B}$$
$$\gamma = (\boldsymbol{e}^{AT} - I)\,\boldsymbol{A}^{-1}\Gamma$$

where $\boldsymbol{A}$, $\boldsymbol{B}$ and Γ are the constant matrices associated with $\boldsymbol{x}$, $\boldsymbol{u}$ and $\boldsymbol{p}$ vectors in the corresponding continuous-time dynamic system. The matrix $\boldsymbol{e}^{AT}$ can be evaluated using various well-documented approaches like Sylvestor's expansion theorem, series expansion technique etc. The optimal digital load frequency controller design problem is discussed in detail in Ref. [7].

8.10 ▶ DECENTRALISED CONTROL

In view of the large size of a modern power system, it is virtually impossible to implement either the classical or the modern LFC algorithm in a centralised manner. In Fig. 8.24, a decentralised control scheme is shown $\boldsymbol{x}_1$ is used to find out the vector $\boldsymbol{u}_1$ while $\boldsymbol{x}_2$ alone is employed to find out $\boldsymbol{u}_2$. Thus,

$$\boldsymbol{x} = (\boldsymbol{x}_1\ \boldsymbol{x}_2)^T$$
$$\boldsymbol{u}_1 = -\boldsymbol{k}_1\ \boldsymbol{x}_1$$
$$\boldsymbol{u}_2 = -\boldsymbol{k}_2\ \boldsymbol{x}_2$$

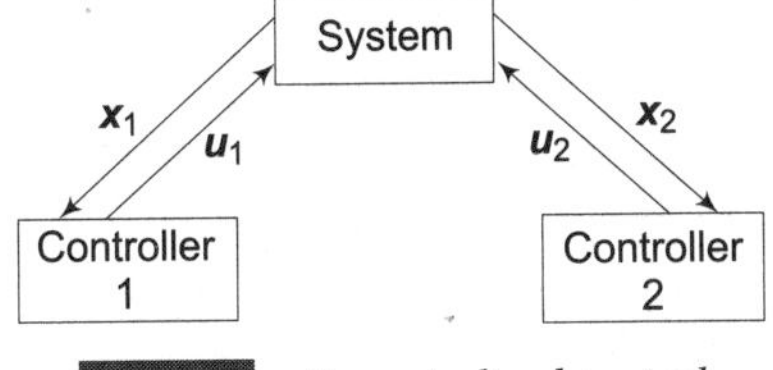

Fig. 8.24 *Decentralised control*

A systematic design of the decentralised tie-line bias control solution has been shown possible using the modal control principle. Decentralised or hierarchical implementation of the optimal LFC algorithms seems to have been studied more widely for the stochastic case since the real load disturbances are truly stochastic. A simple approach is discussed in Ref. [7].

It may be noted that other techniques of model simplification are available in the literature on alternative tools to decentralised control. These include the method of 'aggregation', 'singular perturbation', 'moment matching' and other techniques [9] for finding lower-order models of a given large scale system.

8.11 ▶ DISCRETE INTEGRAL CONTROLLER FOR AGC

An interconnected power system normally consists of combination of several areas (e.g., NREB has 08 states). This facilitates smooth operation and better control. It is a normal practice to sample system data (frequency and tie line power) and transfer information over data links to the dispatch centre. These signals are updated every few seconds.

Power system along with the controller is shown in Fig. 8.25.

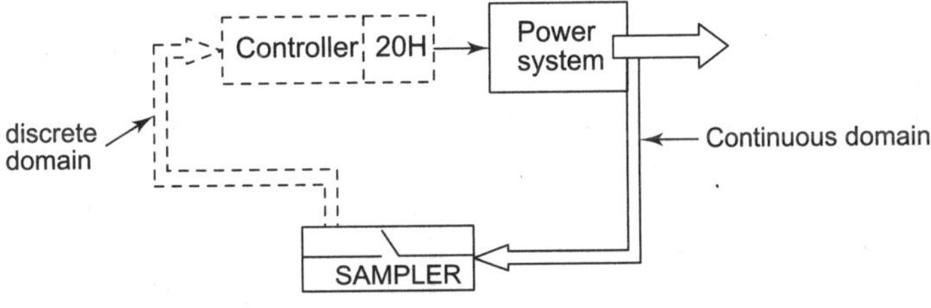

Fig. 8.25 *Power system and representation of a controller*

The controller is in the discrete domain though the power system is in the analogue or continuous-time domain. Discretisation of the model for simulation studies must be carried out as per the Shannon's sampling theorem otherwise it would result in an error, proportional to the amount of aliasing.

A mixed system of Fig. 8.25 may be analysed by modelling the entire system. The system output will be sampled at the normal sampling rate. If the sampling time $T = 1$ s, the controller output will be updated every second. Control input to the power system, therefore, is held constant for 1 s between consecutive samples.

The control law in continuous mode is given as

$$u_i(t) = -k_{Ii} \int \text{ACE}_i\,(t)\,\text{d}t \tag{8.69}$$

The discrete version of Eq. (8.69) may be written as

$$u_i(kT) = u_i[(k-1)T] - k_{Ii}T\,\text{ACE}_i(kT) \tag{8.70}$$

where k is a sampling count.

8.12 ▶ AGC IN A RESTRUCTURED POWER SYSTEM

In a restructured power system, the engineering aspects of planning and operation have to be reformulated though main concepts and ideas do not change. The electric power system currently is largely in the hands of vertically integrated utilities (VIU) Ref. [7] which own generation transmission-distribution systems that supply power to the customer at regulated rates. The electric power can be bought and sold between VIUs along the tie lines.

As explained in Ch. 1, the major change that has taken place is the emergence of IPPs (independent power producers) that can sell power to VIUs. Figure 8.26 shows the deregulated utility structure. GEN will compete in a free market to sell electricity (Electricity Bill 2003) they produce. The retail customer will continue to buy from local distribution company (DISCO). The entities that will wheel this power between GENCOs and DISCOs have been called TRANSCOs.

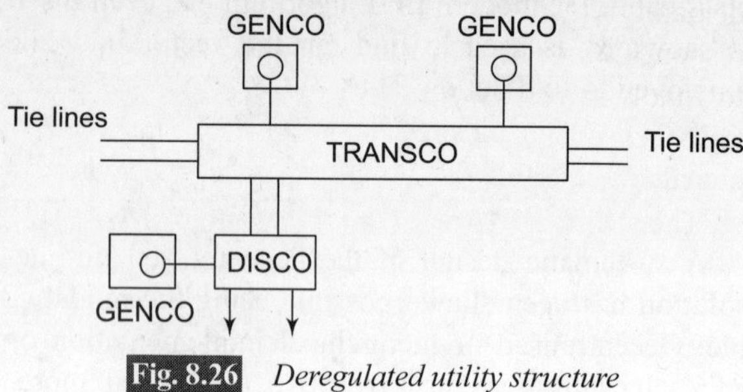

Fig. 8.26 *Deregulated utility structure*

A particular DISCO has the freedom to have a contract with any GENCO (may be in another control area) for transaction of power. All the transactions have to be cleared through an impartial entity called an 'independent system operator' (ISO). The ISO has to control a number of 'ancillary services'. AGC is one such service.

In the restructured environment, GENCOs sell power to various DISCOs at competitive prices. DISCO participation matrix (DPM) is used for easy visualisation of contracts. Figure 8.27 shows a restructured two-area power system. Each area having one GENCO and one DISCO.

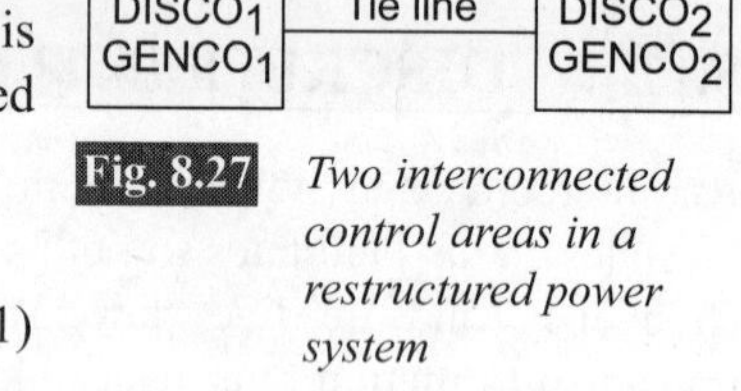

Fig. 8.27 *Two interconnected control areas in a restructured power system*

$$\text{DPM} = \begin{matrix} \\ \text{GENCO}_1 \\ \text{GENCO}_2 \end{matrix} \begin{bmatrix} \text{DISCO}_1 & \text{DISCO}_2 \\ cpf_{11} & cpf_{12} \\ cpf_{21} & cpf_{22} \end{bmatrix} \tag{8.71}$$

ijth entry in Eq. (8.71) corresponds to the fraction of the total load power contracted by DISCO$_j$ from a GENCO$_i$. Notice $cpf_{11} + cpf_{12} = 1$ DPM shows the participation of a DISCO in a contract with a GENCO, and hence the name 'DISCO participation matrix'. In Eq. (8.71), cpf_{ij} refers to 'contract participation factor'.

$$\text{In general } \sum_i cpf_{ij} = 1.0 \tag{8.72}$$

8.12.1 Block Diagram Representation

Figure 8.16 shows block diagram representation of two-area system for conventional AGC. Refs [27, 12] may be referred to for the complete analysis of AGC in a Restructured Power System.

Whenever a load demanded by a DISCO in an area changes, it is reflected as a local load in the area. This corresponds to the local load ΔP_{D1} and should appear in the deregulated AGC system block diagram at the point of input to the power system block. Since normally there are several GENCOs in each area, ACE signal has to be distributed between them in proportion to their participation in AGC. These coefficients that distribute ACE to several GENCOs are called 'ACE participation factors'.

$$\sum_{i=1}^{\text{NGENCO}_j} \alpha'_{ji} = 1.0 \tag{8.73}$$

where α'_{ji} = participation factor of ith GENCO in jth area

NGENCO_j = Number of GENCOs in jth area

Unlike the conventional AGC system, a DISCO prefers a particular GENCO for load power. As these demands should be incorporated in the dynamic models of the system, turbine and governor units must respond corresponding to this power demand. Therefore, for a specific set of GENCOs which is supposed to follow the load demanded by a DISCO, information signals must flow from a DISCO to a particular GENCO specifying corresponding demands as specified by *cpf*s and the pu MW load of a DISCO. These signals carry information as to which GENCO has to follow a load demanded by which DISCO.

The scheduled steady state power flow on the tie-line can be given as

$\Delta P_{\text{tie12}}^{\text{scheduled}}$ = (Demand of DISCOs in area 2 from GENCOs in area 1) – (Demand of DISCOs in area 1 from GENCOs in area 2)

i.e. $\Delta P_{\text{tie12}}^{\text{scheduled}} = cpf_{12}\,\Delta P_{L2} - cpf_{21}\,\Delta P_{L1}$ for the system of Fig. 8.27. (8.74)

The tie-line power error at any time is defined as

$$\Delta P_{\text{tie12}}^{\text{error}} = \Delta P_{\text{tie12}}^{\text{actual}} - \Delta P_{\text{tie12}}^{\text{scheduled}} \tag{8.75}$$

When steady state is reached, $\Delta P_{\text{tie12}}^{\text{error}}$ vanishes. However, this error signal is used to generate the respective ACE signals as in the conventional system scenario:

$$\text{ACE}_1 = B_1\,\Delta F_1 + \Delta P_{\text{tie12}}^{\text{error}} \tag{8.76}$$

$$\text{ACE}_2 = B_2\,\Delta F_2 + a_{12}\,\Delta P_{\text{tie12}}^{\text{error}} \tag{8.77}$$

For a two-area power system (Refer Fig. 8.27), contracted power supplied by ith GENCO is given as

$$\Delta P_i = \sum_{j=1}^{\text{NDISCO}=2} cpf_{ij}\,\Delta P_{Lj} \tag{8.78}$$

As an example, the block diagram representation of a two-area AGC system in a deregulated environment is shown in Fig. 8.28(a) and its simplified version is described in Fig. 8.28(b). In Fig. 8.28(b), for $i = 1$,

$$\Delta P_1 = cpf_{11}\,\Delta P_{L1} + cpf_{12}\,\Delta P_{L2} \tag{8.79}$$

Similarly, the expression for ΔP_2 can be obtained from Eq. (8.78). In Fig. 8.28(b), ΔP_{uc1} and ΔP_{uc2} are uncontracted power demand, if any.

Also note that $\Delta P_{L1,\,LOC} = \Delta P_{L1}$ and $\Delta P_{L2,\,LOC} = \Delta P_{L2}$.

In this AGC scheme implementation, contracted load is fed forward through the DPM matrix to GENCO set points. The actual loads affect system dynamics via the input $\Delta P_{L,\,LOC}$ to the blocks of the power system. The difference between actual and contracted load demands may result in a frequency deviation that will drive AGC to redispatch GENCOs according to ACE participation factors. It is to be noted that AGC scheme does not require measurement of actual loads. The inputs $\Delta P_{L1,\,LOC}$ and $\Delta P_{L2,\,LOC}$ in the block diagram of Fig. 8.28(a) and (b) are part of the power system model, not part of AGC.

8.12.2 State SPACE Model of the Two-Area Power System in Deregulated Environment

The state space model of the closed loop system of Fig. 8.28(b) is given as

$$\dot{\boldsymbol{x}} = \boldsymbol{Ax} + \boldsymbol{Bu} + \boldsymbol{\Gamma P} + \boldsymbol{\gamma P} \tag{8.80}$$

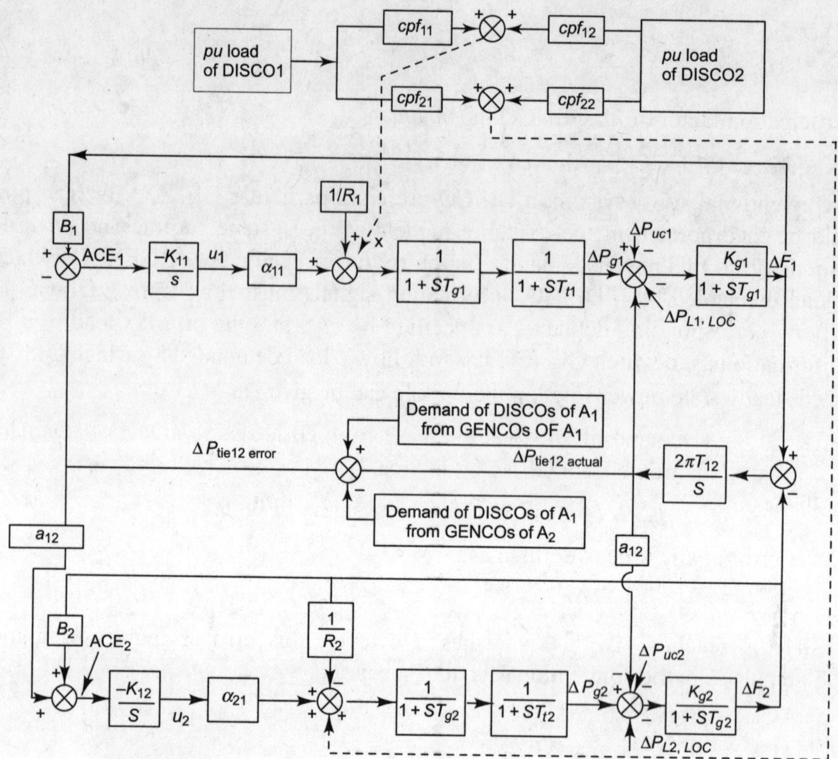

Fig. 8.28 (a) *Block diagram of two area deregulated power system*

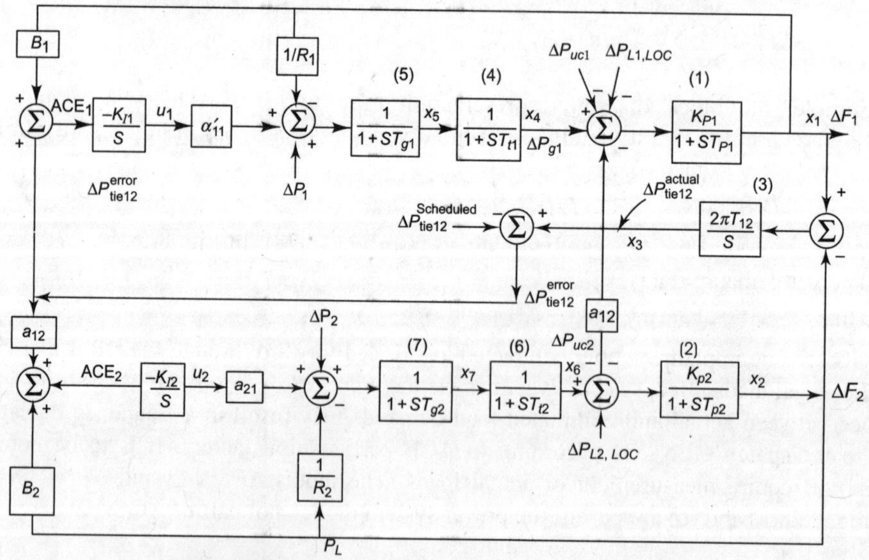

Fig. 8.28 (b) *Simplified representation of Fig. 8.28(a)*

For determining the matrices $\boldsymbol{A}$, $\boldsymbol{B}$, Γ and γ, the following equations are obtained from Fig. 8.28(b):

Block **1** $$x_1 = (-\Delta P_{uc1} - \Delta P_{L1,LOC} - x_3 + x_4)\left(\frac{K_{P1}}{1+ST_{P1}}\right)$$

or $$\dot{x}_1 = -\frac{x_1}{T_{P1}} - \frac{K_{P1}}{T_{P1}}x_3 + \frac{K_{P1}}{T_{P1}}x_4\ (\Delta P_{uc1} + \Delta P_{L1,LOC})\ \frac{K_{P1}}{T_{P1}} \tag{8.81}$$

Block **2** $$\dot{x}_2 = -\frac{x_2}{T_{P2}} - a_{12}x_3\ \frac{K_{P2}}{T_{P2}} + \frac{K_{P2}}{T_{P2}}x_6\ \ (\Delta P_{uc2} + \Delta P_{L2,LOC})\ \frac{K_{P2}}{T_{P2}} \tag{8.82}$$

Block **3** $$\dot{x}_3 = 2\pi\, T_{12}\,(x_1 - x_2) \tag{8.83}$$

Block **4** $$\dot{x}_4 = (x_5 - x_4)\ \frac{1}{T_{t1}} \tag{8.84}$$

Block **5** $$\dot{x}_5 = -\frac{x_1}{T_{g1}R_1} - \frac{x_5}{T_{g1}} + (u_1 a'_{11} + \Delta P_1)\frac{1}{T_{g1}} \tag{8.85}$$

Block **6** $$\dot{x}_6 = \frac{x_7}{T_{t2}} - \frac{x_6}{T_{t2}} \tag{8.86}$$

Block **7** $$\dot{x}_7 = \frac{x_2}{R_{2T_{g2}}} - \frac{x_7}{T_{g2}}\ \ (\alpha'_2, u_2 + \Delta P_2)\ \frac{1}{T_{g2}} \tag{8.87}$$

The order of matrices $\boldsymbol{A}$, $\boldsymbol{B}$, Γ and γ for this case will be 11×11, 11×2, 11×2 and 11×2, respectively. The structure of these matrices can be obtained from the differential equations (8.81)–(8.87) as

$$\boldsymbol{A} = \begin{bmatrix} -\dfrac{1}{T_{P1}} & 0 & -\dfrac{K_{P1}}{T_{P1}} & \dfrac{K_{P1}}{T_{P1}} & 0 & 0 & 0 \\ 0 & -\dfrac{1}{T_{P2}} & -a_{12}\dfrac{K_{P2}}{T_{P2}} & 0 & 0 & \dfrac{K_{P2}}{T_{P2}} & 0 \\ 2\pi T_{12} & -2\pi T_{12} & 0 & 0 & 0 & 0 & 0 \\ 0 & 0 & 0 & -\dfrac{1}{T_{t1}} & \dfrac{1}{T_{t1}} & 0 & 0 \\ -\dfrac{1}{R_1 T_{g1}} & 0 & 0 & 0 & -\dfrac{1}{T_{g1}} & 0 & 0 \\ 0 & 0 & 0 & 0 & 0 & -\dfrac{1}{T_{t2}} & \dfrac{1}{T_{t2}} \\ 0 & -\dfrac{1}{R_2 T_{g2}} & 0 & 0 & 0 & 0 & \dfrac{1}{T_{g2}} \end{bmatrix}$$

$$\mathbf{B} = \begin{bmatrix} 0 & 0 \\ 0 & 0 \\ 0 & 0 \\ 0 & 0 \\ -\frac{a'_{11}}{T_{g1}} & 0 \\ 0 & 0 \\ 0 & -\frac{a'_{21}}{T_{g2}} \end{bmatrix}, \Gamma = \begin{bmatrix} -\frac{K_{P1}}{T_{P1}} & 0 \\ 0 & \frac{K_{P2}}{T_{P2}} \\ 0 & 0 \\ 0 & 0 \\ \frac{cpf_{11}}{T_{g1}} & \frac{cpf_{12}}{T_{g1}} \\ 0 & 0 \\ \frac{cpf_{21}}{T_{g2}} & \frac{cpf_{22}}{T_{g2}} \end{bmatrix}, \gamma = \begin{bmatrix} -\frac{K_{P1}}{T_{P1}} & 0 \\ 0 & -\frac{K_{P2}}{T_{P2}} \\ 0 & 0 \\ 0 & 0 \\ 0 & 0 \\ 0 & 0 \\ 0 & 0 \end{bmatrix}$$

The structure of vectors U, P, p and x are as follows:

$$U = \begin{bmatrix} u_1 \\ u_2 \end{bmatrix}, P = \begin{bmatrix} \Delta P_{L1} \\ \Delta P_{L2} \end{bmatrix}, p = \begin{bmatrix} \Delta P_{uc1} \\ \Delta P_{uc2} \end{bmatrix}$$

$$X = [x_1, x_2\, x_3\, x_4\, x_5\, x_6\, x_7]^T$$

The integral control law for area-1 and area-2 are given as

$$U_1 = -K_{i1} \int \text{ACE}_1\, dt$$

and

$$U_2 = -K_{i2} \int \text{ACE}_2\, dt$$

where K_{i1} and K_{i2} are the integral gain settings of area 1 and area 2, respectively. Further analysis will be exactly as the nonregulated conventional power system.

Additional Solved Examples

Example 8.3 A 100 MW generator is operating in an infinite network. The regulation parameter R is 3 percent. By how much will the turbine power increase if the frequency drops by 0.2 Hz with reference unchanged? System frequency is 50 Hz.

Solution Turbine power will increase 100 MW for a 0.03 pu or 1.5 Hz drop in frequency.
Thus, we have regulation parameter

$$R = \frac{1.5}{100} = 0.015 \text{ Hz/MW}$$

For a frequency change of $\Delta f = -0.2$ Hz, the turbine power will experience a static change of

$$\Delta \rho_t = -\frac{1}{0.015} \times (-0.2) = 13.33 \text{ MW}$$

Example 8.4 Two generators of the ratings 40 MW and 400 MW, respectively, are supplying power to a system. The frequency is 50 Hz and each generator is half loaded. The system load increases by 110 MW and as a result the frequency drops to 49.5 Hz. What must be the individual regulations if the two generators should increase their turbine powers in proportion to their ratings?

Solution Two generators would pick up 10 MW and 100 MW, respectively.

(a) Regulation for smaller unit $(R_1) = \frac{-0.5}{10} = 0.05$ Hz/MW

(b) Regulation for larger unit $(R_2) = \dfrac{-0.5}{100} = 0.005$ Hz/MW

If we express the regulation in per unit Hertz per unit MW, then

$$R_1 = R_2 = 0.04 \text{ pu or } 4\%$$

Example 8.5 Determine K_{ps} and T_{ps} and B, the primary automatic load frequency control parameters for a control area having the following data.

Total rated area capacity = 1000 MW

Inertia constant $H = 5$ KWs/KVA

Regulation $R = 2$ Hz/pu MW (all generators)

and normal operating load = 500 MW at 50 Hz. Assume the change in load 1% for 1% change in frequency.

Solution

$$B = \left(\frac{\partial P_D}{\partial f}\right) \Big/ P_{\text{rated}}$$

$$B = \left(\frac{5}{0.5}\right) \Big/ 1000 = 0.01 \text{ Pu MW/Hz}$$

Now,

$$T_{ps} = \frac{2H}{Bf^\circ} = \frac{2\times 5}{0.01\times 50} = 20 \text{ s}$$

$$k_{ps} = \frac{1}{B} = 100 \text{ Hz/pu MW}$$

Example 8.6 Find the static frequency drop for the 1000 MW system described in previous example (Example 3) following a one percent load increase.

Solution

$$\Delta f = -\left(\frac{1}{B + \frac{1}{R}}\right) \Delta P_D$$

$$= -\left(\frac{1}{0.01 + \frac{1}{2}}\right)(0.01)$$

$$= -0.0196 \text{ Hz}$$

or 0.039 percent of normal frequency.

Example 8.7 A 1000 MW control area (1) is interconnected with a 5000 MW control area (2). The 1000 MW area has the system parameters given below

$$R = 2 \text{ Hz/pu MW}$$

$$B = 0.01 \text{ pu MW/Hz}$$

and increase in load, $\Delta P_{D1} = 0.01$ pu MW.

Area 2 has the same parameters R and B but in terms of the 5000 MW base. Find the static frequency drop.

Solution Choose 1000 MW as base power.
The parameter B on 5000 MW base

$$B_2 = 5B_1 = 5 \times 0.01 = 0.05 \text{ pu MW/Hz}$$

The parameter R on 5000 MW base

$$R_2 = \frac{1}{5}R_1 = 0.4 \text{ Hz/pu MW}$$

Now the static deviations in frequency.

$$\Delta f_0 = -\frac{\Delta P_{D_1} + \Delta P_{D_2}}{\left(B_1 + \frac{1}{R_1}\right) + \left(B_2 + \frac{1}{R_2}\right)} \quad (\Delta P_{D2} = 0)$$

$$= \frac{-0.01}{\left(0.01 + \frac{1}{2}\right) + \left(0.05 + \frac{1}{0.4}\right)}$$

$$= \frac{-0.01}{(0.51) + (2.55)} = -0.00326 \text{ Hz}$$

8.13 ▶ SUMMARY

In this chapter AGC is introduced along with automatic voltage control for both conventional and deregulated power systems. Two-area LFC and optimal controllers are also dealt with.

Problems

8.1 Two generators rated 200 MW and 400 MW are operating in parallel. The droop characteristics of their governors are 4% and 5%, respectively, from no load to full load. The speed changers are so set that the generators operate at 50 Hz sharing the full load of 600 MW in the ratio of their ratings. If the load reduces to 400 MW, how will it be shared among the generators and what will the system frequency be? Assume free governor operation.

The speed changers of the governors are reset so that the load of 400 MW is shared among the generators at 50 Hz in the ratio of their ratings. What are the no load frequencies of the generators?

8.2 Consider the block diagram model of load frequency control given in Fig. 8.6. Make the following approximation.

$$(1 + T_{sg}s)(1 + T_t s) \simeq 1 + (T_{sg} + T_t)s = 1 + T_{eq}s$$

Solve for $\Delta f(t)$ with parameters given below. Given $\Delta P_D = 0.01$ pu

$$T_{eq} = 0.4 + 0.5 = 0.9 \text{ s}; \; T_{ps} = 20 \text{ s}$$

$$K_{sg}K_t = 1; \; K_{ps} = 100; \; R = 3$$

Compare with the exact response given in Fig. 8.9.

8.3 For the load frequency control with proportional plus integral controller as shown in Fig. 8.10, obtain an expression for the steady state error in cycles, i.e., $\lim_{t\to\infty} \int_0^t \Delta f(t)\, dt$; for a unit step ΔP_D. What is the corresponding time error in seconds (with respect to 50 Hz)? Comment on the dependence of error in cycles upon the integral controller gain K_i.

$$\left[\textit{Hint}: \mathcal{L}\int_0^t \Delta f(t)\, dt = \frac{\Delta F(s)}{s}; \; \lim_{t\to\infty} \int_0^t \Delta f(t)\, dt = \lim_{s\to 0} s \times \frac{\Delta F(s)}{s} = \lim_{s\to 0} \Delta F(s) \right]$$

8.4 For the two-area load frequency control of Fig. 8.16 assume that integral controller blocks are replaced by gain blocks, i.e., ACE_1 and ACE_2 are fed to the respective speed changers through gains $-K_{i1}$ and $-K_{i2}$. Derive an expression for the steady values of change in frequency and tie line power for simultaneously applied unit step load disturbance inputs in the two areas.

8.5 For the two-area load frequency control employing integral of area control error in each area (Fig. 8.16), obtain an expression for $\Delta P_{\text{tie}}(s)$ for unit step disturbance in one of the areas. Assume both areas to be identical. Comment upon the stability of the system for parameter values given below:

$$T_{sg} = 0.4 \text{ s}; T_t = 0.5 \text{ s}; T_{ps} = 20 \text{ s}$$
$$K_{ps} = 100; R = 3; K_i = 1; b = 0.425$$
$$a_{12} = 1; 2\pi T_{12} = 0.05$$

[*Hint*: Apply Routh's stability criterion to the characteristic equation of the system.]

Multiple Choice Questions

8.1 Permissible change in power frequency is
(a) ± 0.5 Hz (b) ± 1 Hz (c) ± 5 Hz (d) ± 10 Hz

8.2 The main advantage of a digital controller used in power system is
(a) More accurate and reliable
(b) Compact in size and more flexible
(c) Less sensitive to noise and drift
(d) All of the above

8.3 In which of the following frequency control method tie line may be overloaded?
(a) Flat frequency control
(b) Flat tie line control
(c) Parallel frequency
(d) All of the above

8.4 A 250 MW, 50 Hz turbine-generator set has a speed regulation of 5% based on its own rating. If the generator frequency decreases from 50 Hz to a steady state value of 49.70 Hz with the speed changer setting unchanged. The increase in the turbine power output is
(a) 35 MW (b) 30 MW (c) 25 MW (d) 45 MW

8.5 The maximum efficiency of modern coal fired steam raising thermal power plants is restricted to a low value about 35%, mainly because of
(a) Low alternator efficiency
(b) High energy loss in boilers
(c) High energy loss in condenser
(d) Low steam turbine mechanical efficiency

8.6 Which of the following is correct?
(a) $K_{sg} \times K_T$ is nearly equal to 1
(b) $K_{sg} \times K_T$ nearly equal to 0
(c) $K_{sg} \times K_T$ equal to ∞
(d) $K_{sg} \times K_T$ any value

8.7 Most of the Reheat units have a Generation Rate around
(a) 3% (b) 10% (c) 0% (d) ∞

8.8 A 100 MW generator is operating in an infinite network at 50 Hz frequency. The regulation parameter R is 3%. If the frequency drops by 0.2 Hz with unchanged reference, the turbine power will increase
(a) 13.33 MW (b) 15.55 MW (c) 14.44 MW (d) 12.22 MW

8.9 In central AGC of a given control area, the change in (error) in frequency
(a) Area control error
(b) Volume control error
(c) Nonlinear control error
(d) Optimal control error

8.10 Laplace transform of a impulse function is
(a) Zero (b) One (c) ∞ (d) Undefined

8.11 The main objective(s) of the power system is/are
(a) Cost of electrical energy per KWh is to be minimum.
(b) Reliable power has to be available.
(c) Flexible power has to be available.
(d) All of the above.

8.12 For K_{sg} = Gain of speed governor, and T_{sg} = Time constant of speed governor, the model equation of speed governor system is
(a) $K_{sg}/(1 - T_{sg}s)$ (b) $T_{sg}K_{sg}/(1 + T_{sg}s)$
(c) $K_{sg}/(1 + T_{sg}s)$ (d) $K_{sg}/T_{sg}s$

8.13 In power system operation, the governor dead bad cause due to
(a) Mechanical friction (b) Backlash
(c) Valve overlaps in hydraulic relays (d) All of the above

8.14 The economical dispatch controller has
(a) Fast response (b) Very Fast response
(c) Slow response (d) None of the above

8.15 In order to have lower cost of power generation
(a) the load factor and diversity factor should be low
(b) the load factor should be low but diversity factor should be high
(c) the load factor should be high but diversity factor should be low
(d) The load factor and diversity factor should be high

8.16 Load frequency and economic dispatch controller are working
(a) Together with (b) Sequential
(c) Independently (d) None of the above

8.17 Cheapest plant in operation and maintenance is
(a) Steam power (b) Hydroelectric
(c) Diesel power (d) Nuclear

8.18 Decentralised control system is used for larger power system because
(a) Centralised system is not possible
(b) Modern LFC algorithm is difficult to implement in centralised manner
(c) Centralised control is more inefficient than decentralised control
(d) All of the above

8.19 The value of the neutral current in a three-phase system for perfectly balanced loads is
(a) one-third of maximum value (b) one-third of minimum value
(c) two-thirds of maximum value (d) exactly zero

8.20 The function of speed changer in power system is
(a) Steady state power output of turbine (b) Change the speed of governor
(c) Limit the speed of governor (d) All of the above

8.21 The increase in speed results in fly ball speed governor in power system
(a) Fly ball moves inwards (b) Fly ball moves outwards
(c) Fly ball remains in the same position (d) None of the above

8.22 The load frequency control is achieved by properly matching the individual machines
(a) Reactive powers (b) Generator ratings
(c) Generated voltages (d) Turbine inputs

8.23 In generation system, the turbine speed governing system consists of
(a) Fly ball speed governor (b) Hydraulic amplifier and linkage mechanism
(c) Speed changer (d) All of the above

8.24 Two alternators rated 200 MW and 400 MW are operating a parallel with their governor droop characteristics are respectively 4% and 5% from no-load to full load. At no-load the system frequency is 50 Hz. When supplying a load of 600 MW, the system frequency will be
(a) 49.8 Hz (b) 47.7 Hz (c) 49.4 Hz (d) 51.2 Hz

8.25 The time constant of turbine lies between
(a) 0 to 1 sec (b) 1 to 2 sec
(c) 0.2 to 2.5 sec (d) Depends on turbine design

8.26 Which of the following statements is true related to power system?
(a) At higher voltage, cost of transmission is increased
(b) At higher voltage, cost of transmission is reduced
(c) Efficiency decreased
(d) All of the above

8.27 A 250 MW, 50 Hz turbine generator set has a speed regulation of 5 percent based on its own rating. If the generator frequency decreases from 50 Hz to a steady state value of 49.7 Hz with the speed changer setting unchanged. The increase in the turbine power output will be
(a) 35 MW (b) 32 MW (c) 25 MW (d) 30 MW

8.28 The electrostatic precipitators in thermal power plants are used for
(a) Remove moisture from the Cole (b) Control flow rate
(c) Removal of ash from flue gas (d) All of the above

8.29 The equation of area control error (ACE) is
(a) $ACE = \Delta P_{tie} - b \cdot \Delta f$
(b) $ACE = \Delta P_{tie} + 1/b \cdot \Delta f$
(c) $ACE = \Delta P_{tie} - 1/b \cdot \Delta f$
(d) $ACE = \Delta P_{tie} + b \cdot \Delta f$

8.30 The main advantage of hydroelectric power station over thermal power station is
(a) The initial cost of hydroelectric power station is low
(b) Hydroelectric power station can supply the power throughout the year
(c) Hydroelectric station can be constructed at the place where the energy is required
(d) The operation cost of hydroelectric power station is low

References

Books

1. O.I. Elgerd, *Electric Energy System Theory: An Introduction*, 2nd edn, McGraw-Hill, New York, 1982.
2. B.M. Weedy and B.J. Cory, *Electric Power Systems*, 4th edn, Wiley, New York, 1998.
3. N. Cohn, *Control of Generation and Power Flow on Interconnected Systems*, Wiley, New York, 1971.
4. A.J. Wood and B.F. Woolenberg, *Power Generation, Operation and Control*, 2nd edn, Wiley, New York, 1994.
5. I.J. Nagrath and M. Gopal, *Control Systems Engineering*, 3rd edn, New Age, New Delhi, 2001.
6. E. Handschin (Ed.), *Real Time Control of Electric Power Systems*, Elsevier, New York, 1972.
7. A.K. Mahalanabis, D.P. Kothari, and S.I. Ahson, *Computer Aided Power System Analysis and Control*, Tata McGraw-Hill, New Delhi, 1988.
8. L.K. Kirchmayer, *Economic Control of Interconnected Systems*, Wiley, New York, 1959.
9. M. Jamshidi, *Large Scale Systems: Modelling and Control*, North Holland, New York, 1983.

10. M.G. Singh and A. Titli, *Systems Decomposition, Optimization and Control*, Pergamon Press, Oxford, 1978.
11. D.D. Siljak, *Non-Linear Systems: The Parameter Analysis and Design*, Wiley, New York, 1969.
12. D. Das, *Electrical Power Systems*, New Age Int. Pub., New Delhi, 2006.

Papers

13. O.I. Elgerd and C.E. Fosha, "The Megawatt Frequency Control Problem: A New Approach Via Optimal Control Theory", *IEEE Trans.*, PAS, volume: 89, issue: 4, p. 556, April 1970.
14. T.S. Bhatti, C.S. Indulkar, and D.P. Kothari, "Parameter Optimization of Power Systems for Stochastic Load Demands", *Proc. IFAC*, Bangalore, December 1986.
15. M.L. Kothari, P.S. Satsangi, and J. Nanda, "Sampled-Data Automatic Generation Control of Interconnected Reheat Thermal Systems Considering Generation Rate Constraints", *IEEE Trans.*, PAS, volume: 100, p: 2334, May 1981.
16. J. Nanda, M.L. Kothari, and P.S. Satsangi, "Automatic Generation Control of an Interconnected Hydro-thermal System in Continuous and Discrete Modes Considering Generation Rate Constraints", *IEE Proc.*, pt D, volume: 130, issue: 1, p: 17, January 1983.
17. IEEE Committee Report, "Dynamic Models for Steam and Hydro-turbines in Power System Studies", *IEEE Trans.*, PAS, volume: 92, p: 1904, Nov./Dec. 1973.
18. T. Hiyama, "Optimization of Discrete-type Load Frequency Regulators Considering Generation-Rate Constraints", *Proc. IEE*, volume: 129, pt C, p: 285, Nov. 1982.
19. C. Concordia, L.K. Kirchmayer, and E.A. Szyonanski, "Effect of Speed Governor Dead-band on Tie Line Power and Frequency Control Performance", *AIEE Trans.*, volume: 76, p: 429, Aug. 1957.
20. J. Nanda, M.L. Kothari, and P.S. Satsangi, "Automatic Control of Reheat Thermal System Considering Generation Rate Constraint and Governor Dead-band", *JIE* (India), volume: 63, p: 245, June 1983.
21. S.C. Tripathy, G.S. Hope, and O.P. Malik, "Optimisation of Load-frequency Control Parameters for Power Systems with Reheat Steam Turbines and Governor Dead-band Nonlinearity", *Proc. IEE*, volume: 129, pt C, issue: 1, p: 10, January 1982.
22. M.L. Kothari, J. Nanda, D.P. Kothari, and D. Das, "Discrete-mode AGC of a Two Area Reheat Thermal System with New Area Control Error", *IEEE Trans., on Power System*, volume: 4, issue: 2, p: 730, May 1989.
23. D. Das, J. Nanda, M.L. Kothari, and D.P. Kothari, "AGC of a Hydrothermal System with New ACE considering GRC", *Int. J. Electric Machines and Power System*, volume: 18, issue: 5, p: 461, 1990.
24. D. Das, M.L. Kothari, D.P. Kothari, and J. Nanda, "Variable Structure Control Strategy to AGC of an Interconnected Reheat Thermal System", *Proc. IEE*, volume: 138, pt D, p: 579, Nov. 1991.
25. Jalleli, Van Slycik *et al.*, "*Understanding Automatic Generation Control*", Paper no. 91 MW 229–5 PWRS, Presented at IEEE Winter Power Meeting, 1991.
26. N.L. Kothari, J. Nanda, D.P. Kothari, and D. Das, "Discrete Mode AGC of a Two Area Reheat Thermal System with a NACE considering GRC", *JIE* (I) volume: 72, pp: 297–303, Feb. 1992.
27. B.H. Bakken and Q.S. Grande, "AGC in a Deregulated Power System", *IEEE Trans., on Power Systems,* volume: 13, issue: 4, pp: 1401–1406, Nov. 1998.
28. P. Kumar Ibraheem and D.P. Kothari, "AGC Philosophies: A Review", *IEEE Trans., on Power Systems,* pp: 346–357, Feb. 2005.
29. M. Kaur, J.S. Dhillon, and D.P. Kothari, "Crisscross Differential Evolution Algorithm for Constrained Hydrothermal Scheduling", *Applied Soft Computing*, pp: 106–393, 2020.
30. T.G. Hlalele, R.M. Naidoo, R.C. Bansal, and J. Zhang, "Multi-objective Stochastic Economic Dispatch with Maximal Renewable Penetration Under Renewable Obligation", *Applied Energy*, volume: 270, pp: 115–120, 2020.

31. P.R. Baldivieso Monasterios and P. Trodden, "Low-Complexity Distributed Predictive Automatic Generation Control with Guaranteed Properties", *IEEE Transactions on Smart Grid*, volume: 8, issue: 6, pp: 3045–3054, 2017.
32. T.G. Hlalele, J. Zhang, R.M. Naidoo, and R.C. Bansal, "Multi-Objective Economic Dispatch with Residential Demand Response Programme under Renewable Obligation", *Energy*, pp: 119–473, 2020.
33. N.J. Singh, J.S. Dhillon, and D.P. Kothari, "Multiobjective Thermal Power Load Dispatch Using Adaptive Predator–Prey Optimization", *Applied Soft Computing*, volume: 66, pp: 370–383, 2018.
34. R. Patel, C. Li, L. Meegahapola, B. McGrath, and X. Yu, "Enhancing Optimal Automatic Generation Control in a Multi-Area Power System with Diverse Energy Resources", *IEEE Transactions on Power Systems*, volume: 34, issue: 5, pp: 3465–3475, 2019.
35. N.J. Singh, J.S. Dhillon, and D.P. Kothari, "Non-interactive Approach to Solve Multi-Objective Thermal Power Dispatch Problem Using Composite Search Algorithm", *Applied Soft Computing*, volume: 65, pp: 644–658, 2018.
36. T.G. Hlalele, R.M. Naidoo, J. Zhang, and R.C. Bansal, "Dynamic Economic Dispatch with Maximal Renewable Penetration Under Renewable Obligation", *IEEE Access*, volume: 8, 38794–38808, 2020.
37. D.J. Shiltz, S. Baros, M. Cvetković, and A.M. Annaswamy, "Integration of Automatic Generation Control and Demand Response via a Dynamic Regulation Market Mechanism", *IEEE Transactions on Control Systems Technology*, volume: 27, issue: 2, pp: 631–646, 2019.
38. A. Panwar, G. Sharma, and R.C. Bansal, "Optimal AGC Design for a Hybrid Power System Using Hybrid Bacteria Foraging Optimization Algorithm", *Electric Power Components and Systems*, volume: 47, issue: 11–12, pp: 955–965, 2019.
39. N.J. Singh, J.S. Dhillon, and D.P. Kothari, "Multi-Objective Thermal Power Load Dispatch Using Chaotic Differential Evolutionary Algorithm and Powell's Method", *Soft Computing*, volume: 22, issue: 7, pp: 2159–2174, 2018.
40. J.W. Simpson-Porco, "On Area Control Errors, Area Injection Errors, and Textbook Automatic Generation Control," *IEEE Transactions on Power Systems*, volume: 36, issue: 1, pp: 557–560, January 2021.
41. A. Ameli, A. Hooshyar, E.F. El-Saadany, and A.M. Youssef, "Attack Detection and Identification for Automatic Generation Control Systems", *IEEE Transactions on Power Systems*, volume: 33, issue: 5, pp: 4760–4774, 2018.
42. N.J. Singh, J.S. Dhillon, and D.P. Kothari, "Surrogate Worth Trade-Off Method for Multi-Objective Thermal Power Load Dispatch", *Energy*, volume: 138, pp: 1112–1123, 2017.
43. D. Apostolopoulou, A.D. Domínguez-García, and P.W. Sauer, "An Assessment of the Impact of Uncertainty on Automatic Generation Control Systems", *IEEE Transactions on Power Systems*, volume: 31, issue: 4, pp: 2657–2665, 2016.
44. N.J. Singh, J.S. Dhillon, and D.P. Kothari, "Synergic Predator-Prey Optimization for Economic Thermal Power Dispatch Problem", *Applied Soft Computing*, volume: 43, pp: 298–311, 2016.
45. J. Zhang and A.D. Domínguez-García, "On the Impact of Measurement Errors on Power System Automatic Generation Control", *IEEE Transactions on Smart Grid*, volume: 9, issue: 3, pp: 1859–1868, 2018.
46. R. Patel, C. Li, X. Yu, and B. McGrath, "Optimal Automatic Generation Control of an Interconnected Power System Under Network Constraints", *IEEE Transactions on Industrial Electronics*, volume: 65, issue: 9, pp: 7220–7228, 2018.

47. T. Huang, B. Satchidanandan, P.R. Kumar, and L. Xie, "An Online Detection Framework for Cyber Attacks on Automatic Generation Control", *IEEE Transactions on Power Systems*, volume: 33, issue: 6, pp: 6816–6827, 2018.
48. S. Sridhar and M. Govindarasu, "Model-Based Attack Detection and Mitigation for Automatic Generation Control", *IEEE Transactions on Smart Grid*, volume: 5, issue: 2, pp: 580–591, 2014.
49. N. Narang, J.S. Dhillon, and D.P. Kothari, "Multi-objective Short-Term Hydrothermal Generation Scheduling Using Predator–Prey Optimization", *Electric Power Components and Systems*, volume: 40, issue: 15, pp: 1708–1730, 2012.
50. L.D. Arya and A. Koshti, "Modified Shuffled Frog Leaping Optimization Algorithm Based Distributed Generation Rescheduling for Loss Minimization", *Journal of The Institution of Engineers (India): Series B,* volume: 99, issue: 4, pp: 397–405, 2019.

CHAPTER 9 Symmetrical Fault Analysis

9.1 ▶ INTRODUCTION

So far we have dealt with the steady state behaviour of power system under normal operating conditions and its dynamic behaviour under small scale perturbations. This chapter is devoted to abnormal system behaviour under conditions of symmetrical short circuit (symmetrical three-phase fault*). Such conditions are caused in the system accidentally through insulation failure of equipment or flashover of lines initiated by a lightning stroke or through accidental faulty operation. The system must be protected against flow of heavy short circuit currents (which can cause permanent damage to major equipment) by disconnecting the faulty part of the system by means of circuit breakers operated by protective relaying. For proper choice of circuit breakers and protective relaying, we must estimate the magnitude of currents that would flow under short circuit conditions—this is the scope of fault analysis (study).

The majority of system faults are not three-phase faults but faults involving one line to ground or occasionally two lines to ground. These are unsymmetrical faults requiring special tools like symmetrical components and form the subject of study of the next two chapters. Though the symmetrical faults are rare, the symmetrical fault analysis must be carried out, as this type of fault generally leads to most severe fault current flow against which the system must be protected. Symmetrical fault analysis is, of course, simpler to carry out.

A power network comprises synchronous generators, transformers, lines and loads. Though the operating conditions at the time of fault are important, the loads can be neglected during fault, as voltages dip very low so that currents drawn by loads can be neglected in comparison to fault currents.

The synchronous generator during short circuit has a characteristic time-varying behaviour. In the event of a short circuit, the flux per pole undergoes dynamic change with associated transients in damper and field windings. The reactance of the circuit model of the machine changes in the first few cycles from a low subtransient reactance to a higher transient value, finally settling at a still higher synchronous (steady state) value. Depending upon the arc interruption time of circuit breakers, a suitable reactance value is used for the circuit model of synchronous generators for short circuit analysis.

In a modern large interconnected power system, heavy currents flowing during a fault must be interrupted much before the steady state conditions are established. Furthermore, from the considerations of mechanical forces that act on circuit breaker components, the maximum current that a breaker has to carry momentarily must also be determined. For selecting a circuit breaker we must, therefore, determine the initial current that flows on occurrence of a short circuit and also the current in the transient that flows at the time of circuit interruption.

* Symmetrical fault may be a solid three-phase short circuit or may involve arc impedance.

9.2 ▶ TRANSIENT ON A TRANSMISSION LINE

Let us consider the short circuit transient on a transmission line. Certain simplifying assumptions are made at this stage.

1. The line is fed from a constant voltage source (the case when the line is fed from a realistic synchronous machine will be treated in Section 9.3).
2. Short circuit takes place when the line is unloaded (the case of short circuit on a loaded line will be treated later in this chapter).
3. Line capacitance is negligible and the line can be represented by a lumped *RL* series circuit.

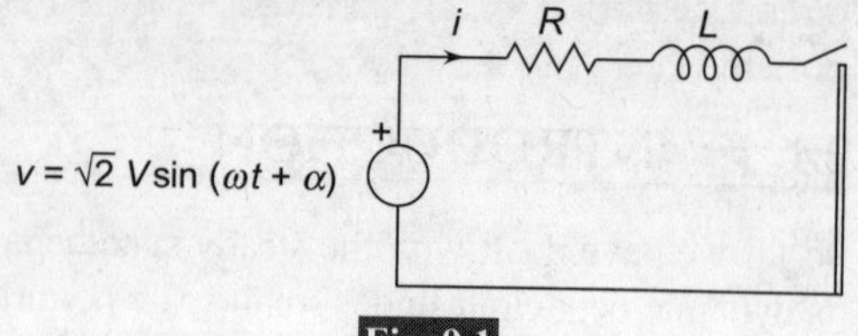

With the above assumptions, the line can be represented by the circuit model of Fig. 9.1. The short circuit is assumed to take place at $t = 0$. The parameter α controls the instant on the voltage wave when short circuit occurs. It is known from circuit theory that the current after short circuit is composed of two parts, i.e.,

$v = \sqrt{2}\, V \sin(\omega t + \alpha)$, i, R, L

Fig. 9.1

$$i = i_s + i_t$$

where

$$i_s = \text{steady state current}$$
$$= \frac{\sqrt{2}V}{|Z|} \sin(\omega t + \alpha - \theta)$$
$$Z = (R^2 + \omega^2 L^2)^{1/2} \angle \left(\theta = \tan^{-1} \frac{\omega L}{R} \right)$$

i_t = transient current [it is such that $i(0) = i_s(0) + i_t(0) = 0$ being an inductive circuit; it decays corresponding to the time constant L/R].

$$= -\, i_s(0) e^{-(R/L)t}$$
$$= \frac{\sqrt{2}V}{|Z|} \sin(\theta - \alpha) e^{-(R/L)t}$$

Thus, short circuit current is given by

$$i = \underbrace{\frac{\sqrt{2}V}{|Z|} \sin(\omega t + \alpha - \theta)}_{\text{Symmetrical short circuit current}} + \underbrace{\frac{\sqrt{2}V}{|Z|} \sin(\theta - \alpha) e^{-(R/L)t}}_{\text{DC off-set current}} \tag{9.1}$$

A plot of i_s, i_t and $i = i_s + i_t$ is shown in Fig. 9.2. In power system terminology, the sinusoidal steady state current is called the *symmetrical short circuit current* and the unidirectional transient component is called the *DC off-set current*, which causes the total short circuit current to be unsymmetrical till the transient decays.

It easily follows from Fig. 9.2 that the *maximum momentary short circuit current* i_{mm} corresponds to the first peak. If the decay of transient current in this short time is neglected,

$$i_{mm} = \frac{\sqrt{2}V}{|Z|} \sin(\theta - \alpha) + \frac{\sqrt{2}V}{|Z|} \tag{9.2}$$

Since transmission line resistance is small, $\theta \simeq 90°$.

$$\therefore \quad i_{mm} = \frac{\sqrt{2}V}{|Z|} \cos\alpha + \frac{\sqrt{2}V}{|Z|} \tag{9.3}$$

This has the maximum possible value for $\alpha = 0$, i.e., short circuit occurring when the voltage wave is going through zero. Thus,

$$i_{mm\ (\text{max possible})} = 2\frac{\sqrt{2}V}{|Z|} \tag{9.4}$$

= twice the maximum of symmetrical short circuit current (*doubling effect*)

For the selection of circuit breakers, momentary short circuit current is taken corresponding to its maximum possible value (a safe choice).

The next question is 'what is the current to be interrupted?' As has been pointed out earlier, modern day circuit breakers are designed to interrupt the current in the first few cycles (five cycles or less). With reference to Fig. 9.2, it means that when the current is interrupted, the DC off-set (i_t) has not yet died out and so contributes to the current to be interrupted. Rather than computing the value of the DC off-set at the time of interruption (this would be highly complex in a network of even moderately large size), the symmetrical short circuit current alone is calculated. This figure is then increased by an empirical multiplying factor to account for the DC off-set current. Details are given in Section 9.5.

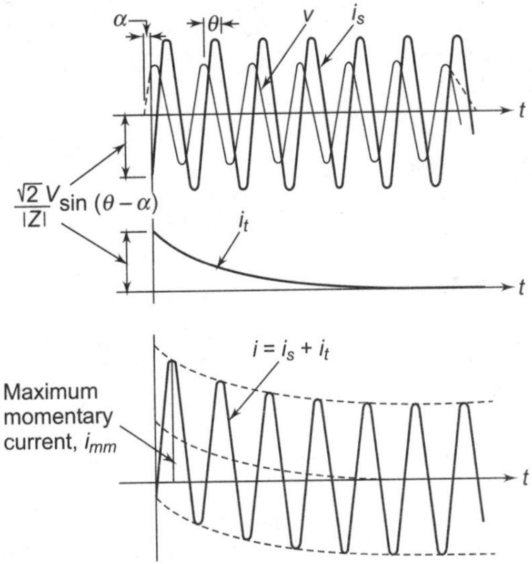

Fig. 9.2 *Waveform of a short circuit current on a transmission line*

9.3 ▶ SHORT CIRCUIT OF A SYNCHRONOUS MACHINE (ON NO LOAD)

Under steady state short circuit conditions, the armature reaction of a synchronous generator produces a demagnetising flux. In terms of a circuit, this effect is modelled as a reactance X_a in series with the induced emf. This reactance when combined with the leakage reactance X_l of the machine is called *synchronous reactance* X_d (direct axis synchronous reactance in the case of salient pole machines). Armature resistance being small can be neglected. The steady state short circuit model of a synchronous machine is shown in Fig. 9.3(a) on per phase basis.

(a) Steady state short circuit model of a synchronous machine

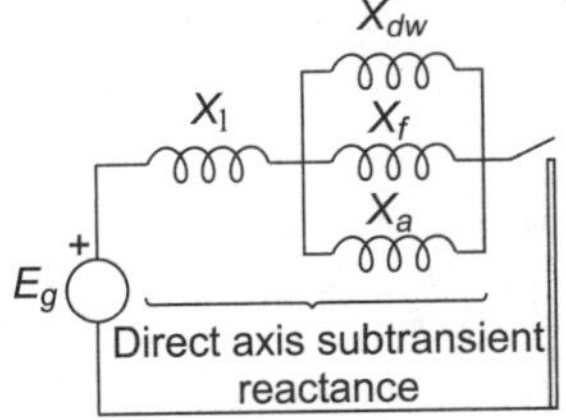

(b) Approximate circuit model during subtransient period of short circuit

(c) Approximate circuit model during transient period of short circuit

Fig. 9.3

Consider now the sudden short circuit (three-phase) of a synchronous generator initially operating under open circuit conditions. The machine undergoes a transient in all the three phases finally ending up in steady state conditions described above. The circuit breaker must, of course, interrupt the current much before steady conditions are reached. Immediately upon short circuit, the DC off-set currents appear in all the three phases, each with a different magnitude since the point on the voltage wave at which short circuit occurs is different for each phase. These DC off-set currents are accounted for separately on an empirical basis and, therefore, for short circuit studies, we need to concentrate our attention on symmetrical (sinusoidal) short circuit current only. Immediately in the event of a short circuit, the symmetrical short circuit current is limited only by the leakage reactance of the machine. Since the air gap flux cannot change instantaneously (*theorem of constant flux linkages*), to counter the demagnetisation of the armature short circuit current, currents appear in the field winding as well as in the damper winding in a direction to help the main flux. These currents decay in accordance with the winding time constants. The time constant of the damper winding which has low leakage inductance is much less than that of the field winding, which has high leakage inductance. Thus, during the initial part of the short circuit, the damper and field windings have transformer currents induced in them so that in the circuit model their reactances—X_f of field winding and X_{dw} of damper winding—appear in parallel* with X_a as shown in Fig. 9.3(b). As the damper winding currents are first to die out, X_{dw} effectively becomes open-circuited and at a later stage X_f becomes open-circuited. The machine reactance, thus changes from the parallel combination of X_a, X_f and X_{dw} during the initial period of the short circuit to X_a and X_f in parallel [Fig. 9.3(c)] in the middle period of the short circuit, and finally to X_a in steady state [Fig. 9.3(a)]. The reactance presented by the machine in the initial period of the short circuit, i.e.,

$$X_l + \frac{1}{(1/X_a + 1/X_f + 1/X_{dw})} = X_d'' \tag{9.5}$$

is called the *subtransient reactance* of the machine, while the reactance effective after the damper winding currents have died out, i.e.,

$$X_d' = X_1 + (X_a \parallel X_f) \tag{9.6}$$

is called the *transient reactance* of the machine. Of course, the reactance under steady conditions is the *synchronous reactance* of the machine. Obviously $X_d'' < X_d' < X_d$. The machine thus offers a time-varying reactance which changes from X_d'' to X_d' and finally to X_d.

If we examine the oscillogram of the short circuit current of a synchronous machine after the DC off-set currents have been removed from it, we will find the current wave shape as given in Fig. 9.4(a). The envelope of the current wave shape is plotted in Fig. 9.4(b). The short circuit current can be divided into three periods—initial subtransient period when the current is large as the machine offers subtransient reactance, the middle transient period where the machine offers transient reactance, and finally the steady state period when the machine offers synchronous reactance.

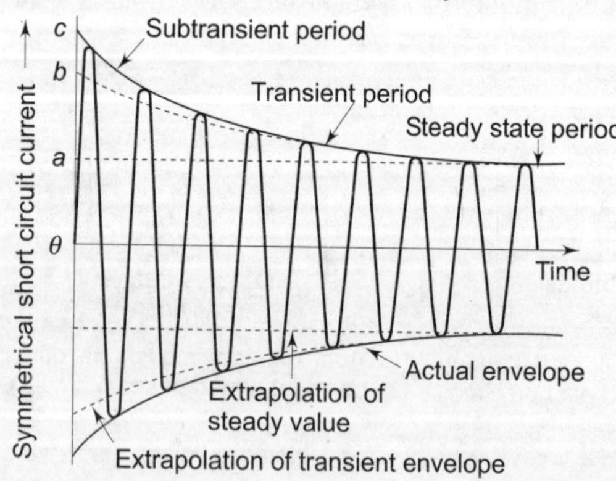

(a) Symmetrical short circuit armature current in synchronous machine

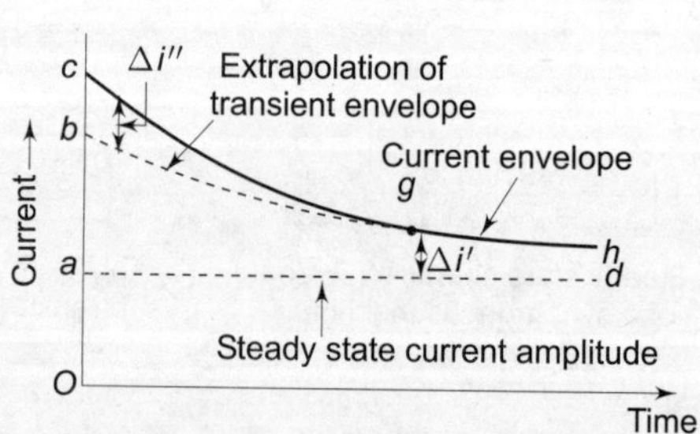

(b) Envelope of synchronous machine symmetrical short circuit current

Fig. 9.4

* Unity turn ratio is assumed here.

If the transient envelope is extrapolated backwards in time, the difference between the transient and subtransient envelopes is the current $\Delta i''$ (corresponding to the damper winding current) which decays fast according to the damper winding time constant. Similarly, the difference $\Delta i'$ between the steady state and transient envelopes decays in accordance with the field time constant.

In terms of the oscillogram, the currents and reactances discussed above, we can write

$$|I| = \frac{Oa}{\sqrt{2}} = \frac{|E_g|}{X_d} \tag{9.7a}$$

$$|I'| = \frac{Ob}{\sqrt{2}} = \frac{|E_g|}{X_d'} \tag{9.7b}$$

$$|I''| = \frac{Oc}{\sqrt{2}} = \frac{|E_g|}{X_d''} \tag{9.7c}$$

where

$|I|$ = steady state current (rms)
$|I'|$ = transient current (rms) excluding DC component
$|I''|$ = subtransient current (rms) excluding DC component
X_d = direct axis synchronous reactance
X_d' = direct axis transient reactance
X_d'' = direct axis subtransient reactance
$|E_g|$ = per phase no load voltage (rms)
Oa, Ob, Oc = intercepts shown in Figs 9.4(a) and (b).

The intercept Ob for finding transient reactance can be determined accurately by means of a logarithmic plot. Both $\Delta i''$ and $\Delta i'$ decay exponentially as

$$\Delta i'' = \Delta i''_0 \exp(-t/\tau_{dw})$$

$$\Delta i' = \Delta i'_0 \exp(-t/\tau_f)$$

where τ_{dw} and τ_f are respectively damper, and field winding time constants with $\tau_{dw} \ll \tau_f$. At time $t \gg \tau_{dw}$, $\Delta i''$ practically dies out and we can write

$$\log(\Delta i'' + \Delta i')\big|_{t \gg \tau_{dw}} \simeq \log \Delta i_0' - t/\tau_f = -\Delta i_0'(-t/\tau_f)$$

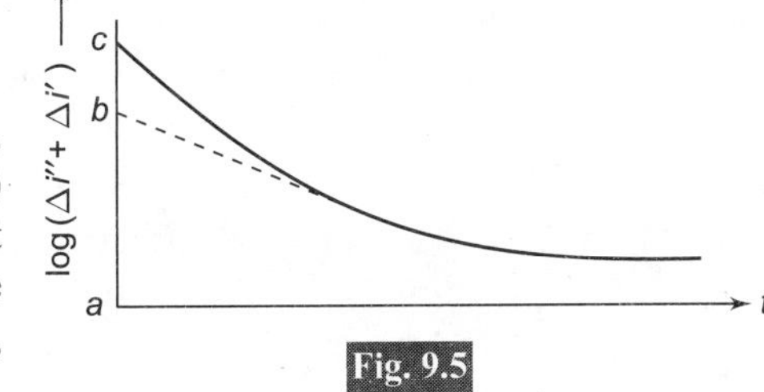

Fig. 9.5

The plot of $\log(\Delta i'' + \Delta i')$ versus time for $t \gg \tau_{dw}$, therefore, becomes a straight line with a slope of $(-1/\tau_f)$ as shown in Fig. 9.5. As the straight line portion of the plot is extrapolated (straight line extrapolation is much more accurate than the exponential extrapolation of Fig. 9.4), taking inverse log of intercept corresponding to $t = 0$ is

$$\log^{-1}(ab) = \Delta i'\big|_{t=0} = \Delta i_0' \exp(-t/\tau_f)\big|_{t=0} = \Delta i_0' = ab$$

Though the machine reactances are dependent upon magnetic saturation (corresponding to excitation), the values of reactances normally lie within certain predictable limits for different types of machines. Table 9.1 gives typical values of machine reactances which can bc uscd in fault calculations and in stability studies.

Normally, both generator and motor subtransient reactances are used to determine the momentary current flowing on occurrence of a short circuit. To decide the interrupting capacity of circuit breakers, except those which open instantaneously, subtransient reactance is used for generators and transient reactance for synchronous motors. As we shall see later the transient reactances are used for stability studies.

The machine model to be employed when the short circuit takes place from loaded conditions will be explained in Section 9.4.

Table 9.1 Typical values of synchronous machine reactances (All values expressed in pu of rated MVA)

Type of machine	*Turbo-alternator (Turbine generator)*	*Salient pole (Hydroelectric)*	*Synchronous compensator (Condenser/ capacitor)*	*Synchronous motors**
X_s (or X_d)	1.00 –2.0	0.6–1.5	1.5–2.5	0.8–1.10
X_q	0.9–1.5	0.4–1.0	0.95–1.5	0.65–0.8
X_d'	0.12–0.35	0.2–0.5	0.3–0.6	0.3–0.35
X_d''	0.1–0.25	0.13–0.35	0.18–0.38	0.18–0.2
X_2	$=X_d''$	$=X_d''$	0.17–0.37	0.19–0.35
X_0	0.04–0.14	0.02–0.2	0.025–0.16	0.05–0.07
r_a	0.003–0.008	0.003–0.015	0.004–0.01	0.003–0.012

r_a = AC resistance of the armature winding per phase.

* High-speed units tend to have low reactance and low-speed units high reactance.

The method of computing short circuit current is illustrated through examples given below.

Example 9.1 For the radial network shown in Fig. 9.6, a three-phase fault occurs at F. Determine the fault current and the line voltage at 11 kV bus under fault conditions.

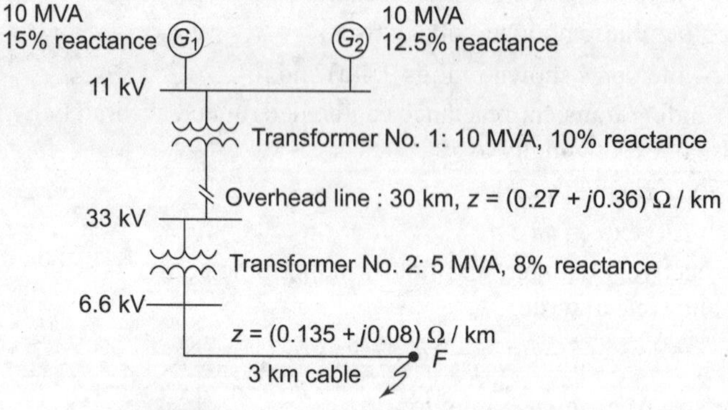

Fig. 9.6 *Radial network for Example 9.1*

Solution Select a system base of 100 MVA.

Voltage bases are: 11 kV in generators, 33 kV for overhead line and 6.6 kV for cable.

$$\text{Reactance of } G_1 = j\frac{0.15 \times 100}{10} = j1.5 \text{ pu}$$

$$\text{Reactance of } G_2 = j\frac{0.125 \times 100}{10} = j1.25 \text{ pu}$$

$$\text{Reactance of } T_1 = j\frac{0.1 \times 100}{10} = j1.0 \text{ pu}$$

$$\text{Reactance of } T_2 = j\frac{0.08 \times 100}{5} = j1.6 \text{ pu}$$

$$\text{Overhead line impedance} = \frac{Z \text{ (in ohms)} \times \text{MVA}_{\text{Base}}}{(\text{kV}_{\text{Base}})^2}$$

$$= \frac{30 \times (0.27 + j0.36) \times 100}{(33)^2}$$
$$= (0.744 + j0.99) \text{ pu}$$

$$\text{Cable impedance} = \frac{3(0.135 + j0.08) \times 100}{(6.6)^2}$$
$$= (0.93 + j0.55) \text{ pu}$$

Circuit model of the system for fault calculations is shown in Fig. 9.7. Since the system is on no load prior to occurrence of the fault, the voltages of the two generators are identical (in phase and magnitude) and are equal to 1 pu. The generator circuit can thus be replaced by a single voltage source in series with the parallel combination of generator reactances as shown.

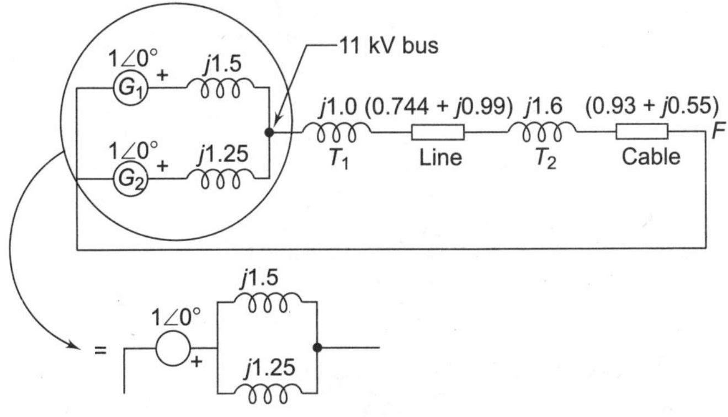

Fig. 9.7

$$\text{Total impedance} = (j1.5 \,||\, j1.25) + (j1.0) + (0.744 + j0.99) + (j1.6) + (0.93 + j0.55)$$
$$= 1.674 + j4.82 = 5.1 \angle 70.8° \text{ pu}$$

$$I_{SC} = \frac{1\angle 0}{5.1\angle 70.8°} = 0.196 \angle -70.8° \text{ pu}$$

$$I_{\text{Base}} = \frac{100 \times 10^3}{\sqrt{3} \times 6.6} = 8750 \text{ A}$$

$\therefore$ $$I_{SC} = 0.196 \times 8750 = 1715 \text{ A}$$

Total impedance between F and 11 kV bus

$$= (0.93 + j0.55) + (j1.6) + (0.744 + j0.99) + (j1.0)$$
$$= 1.674 + j4.14 = 4.43 \angle 76.8° \text{ pu}$$

$$\text{Voltage at 11 kV bus} = 4.43 \angle 67.8° \times 0.196 \angle -70.8°$$
$$= 0.88 \angle -3° \text{ pu} = 0.88 \times 11 = 9.68 \text{ kV}$$

Example 9.2 A 25 MVA, 11 kV generator with $X_d'' = 20\%$ is connected through a transformer, line and a transformer to a bus that supplies three identical motors as shown in Fig. 9.8. Each motor has $X_d'' = 25\%$ and $X_d' = 30\%$ on a base of 5 MVA, 6.6 kV. The three-phase rating of the step-up transformer is 25 MVA, 11/66 kV with a leakage reactance of 10% and that of the step-down transformer is 25 MVA, 66/6.6 kV with a leakage reactance of 10%. The bus voltage at the motors is 6.6 kV when a three-phase fault occurs at the point F. For the specified fault, calculate

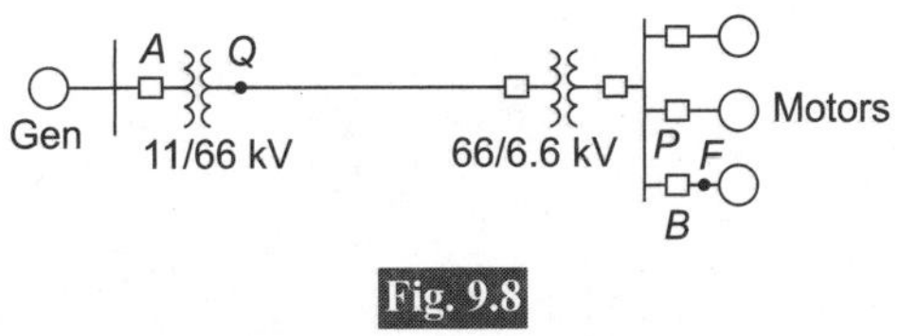

Gen A Q 11/66 kV 66/6.6 kV P F B Motors

Fig. 9.8

(a) the subtransient current in the fault,
(b) the subtransient current in the breaker B,
(c) the momentary current in breaker B, and
(d) the current to be interrupted by breaker B in five cycles.

Given: Reactance of the transmission line = 15% on a base of 25 MVA, 66 kV.

Assume that the system is operating on no load when the fault occurs.

Solution Choose a system base of 25 MVA.

For a generator voltage base of 11 kV, line voltage base is 66 kV and motor voltage base is 6.6 kV.

(a) For each motor

$$X''_{dm} = j0.25 \times \frac{25}{5} = j1.25 \text{ pu}$$

Line, transformers and generator reactances are already given on proper base values.

The circuit model of the system for fault calculations is given in Fig. 9.9(a). The system being initially on no load, the generator and motor induced emfs are identical. The circuit can therefore be reduced to that of Fig. 9.9(b) and then to Fig. 9.9(c). Now

$$I_{SC} = 3 \times \frac{1}{j1.25} + \frac{1}{j0.55} = -j4.22 \text{ pu}$$

$$\text{Base current in 6.6 kV circuit} = \frac{25 \times 1000}{\sqrt{3} \times 6.6} = 2187 \text{ A}$$

$$\therefore \qquad I_{SC} = 4.22 \times 2187 = 9229 \text{ A}$$

(b) From Fig. 9.9(c), current through circuit breaker B is

$$I_{SC}(B) = 2 \times \frac{1}{j1.25} + \frac{1}{j0.55} = -j3.42$$

$$= 3.42 \times 2187 = 7479.5 \text{ A}$$

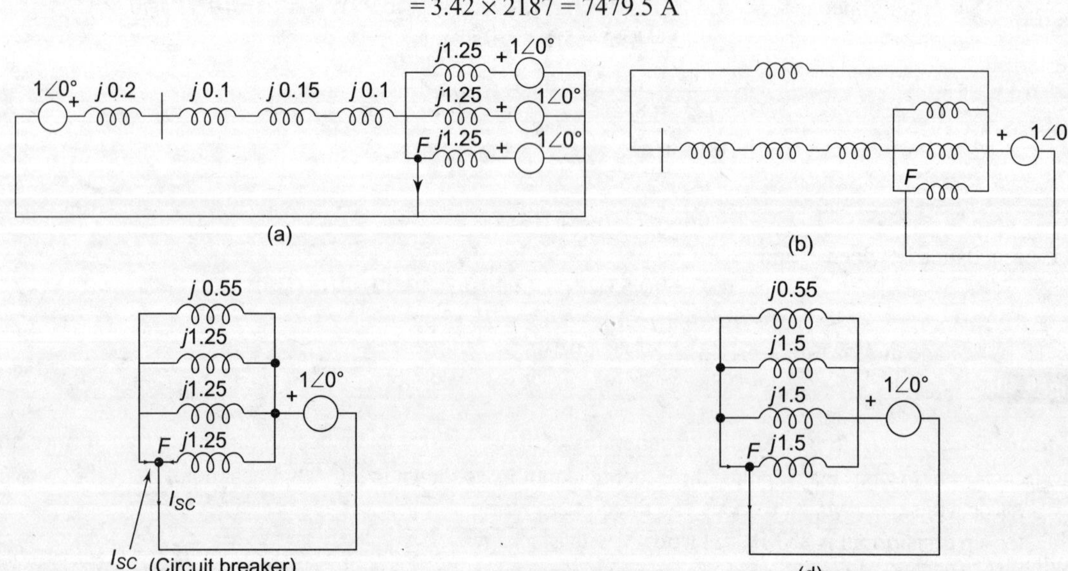

Fig. 9.9

(c) For finding momentary current through the breaker, we must add the DC off-set current to the symmetrical subtransient current obtained in part (b). Rather than calculating the DC off-set current, allowance is made for it on an empirical basis. As explained in Section 9.5,

$$\text{Momentary current through breaker } B = 1.6 \times 7479.5$$
$$= 11967 \text{ A}$$

(d) To compute the current to be interrupted by the breaker, motor subtransient reactance ($X_d'' = j0.25$) is now replaced by transient reactance ($X_d' = j0.30$).

$$X_d'(\text{motor}) = j0.3 \times \frac{25}{5} = j1.5 \text{ pu}$$

The reactances of the circuit of Fig. 9.9(c) now modify to that of Fig. 9.9(d). Current (symmetrical) to be interrupted by the breaker (as shown by arrow)

$$= 2 \times \frac{1}{j1.5} + \frac{1}{j0.55} = 3.1515 \text{ pu}$$

Allowance is made for the DC off-set value by multiplying with a factor of 1.1 (Section 9.5). Therefore, the current to be interrupted is

$$1.1 \times 3.1515 \times 2187 = 7581 \text{ A}$$

9.4 ▶ SHORT CIRCUIT OF A LOADED SYNCHRONOUS MACHINE

In the previous article on the short circuit of a synchronous machine, it was assumed that the machine was operating at no load prior to the occurrence of short circuit. The analysis of short circuit on a loaded synchronous machine is complicated and is beyond the scope of this book. We shall, however, present here the methods of computing short circuit current when short circuit occurs under loaded conditions.

Figure 9.10 shows the circuit model of a synchronous generator operating under steady conditions supplying a load current I^0 to the bus at a terminal voltage of V^0, E_g is the induced emf under loaded condition and X_d is the direct axis synchronous reactance of the machine. When short circuit occurs at the terminals of this machine, the circuit model to be used for computing short circuit current is given in Fig. 9.11(a) for subtransient current, and in Fig. 9.11(b) for transient current. The induced emfs to be used in these models are given by

$$E_g'' = V^0 + jI^0X_d'' \quad (9.8)$$

$$E_g' = V^0 + jI^0X_d' \quad (9.9)$$

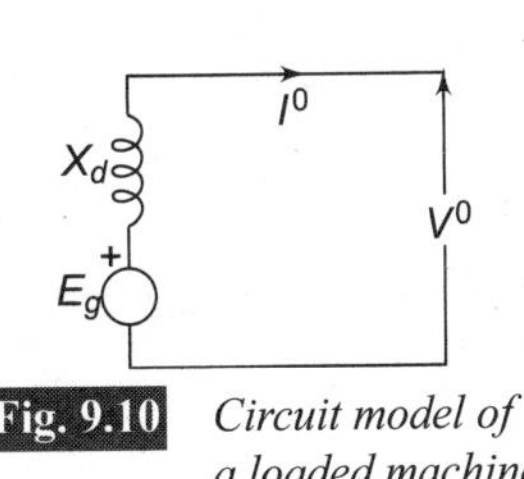

Fig. 9.10 *Circuit model of a loaded machine*

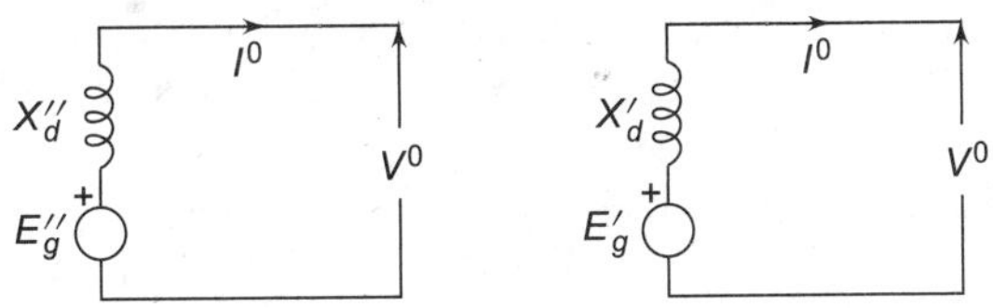

(a) Circuit model for computing subtransient current

(b) Circuit model for computing transient current

Fig. 9.11

The voltage E_g'' is known as the *voltage behind the subtransient reactance* and the voltage E_g' is known as the *voltage behind the transient reactance*. In fact, if I^0 is zero (no load case), $E_g'' = E_g' = E_g$, the no load voltage, in which case the circuit model reduces to that discussed in Section 9.3.

Synchronous motors have internal emfs and reactances similar to that of a generator except that the current direction is reversed. During short circuit conditions, these can be replaced by similar circuit models except that the voltage behind subtransient/transient reactance is given by

$$E''_m = V^0 - jI^0X''_d \tag{9.10}$$

$$E'_m = V^0 - jI^0X'_d \tag{9.11}$$

Whenever we are dealing with short circuit of an interconnected system, the synchronous machines (generators and motors) are replaced by their corresponding circuit models having voltage behind subtransient (transient) reactance in series with subtransient (transient) reactance. The rest of the network being passive remains unchanged.

Example 9.3 A synchronous generator and a synchronous motor each rated 25 MVA, 11 kV having 15% subtransient reactance are connected through transformers and a line as shown in Fig. 9.12(a). The transformers are rated 25 MVA, 11/66 kV and 66/11 kV with leakage reactance of 10% each. The line has a reactance of 10% on a base of 25 MVA, 66 kV. The motor is drawing 15 MW at 0.8 power factor leading and a terminal voltage of 10.6 kV when a symmetrical three-phase fault occurs at the motor terminals. Find the subtransient current in the generator, motor and fault.

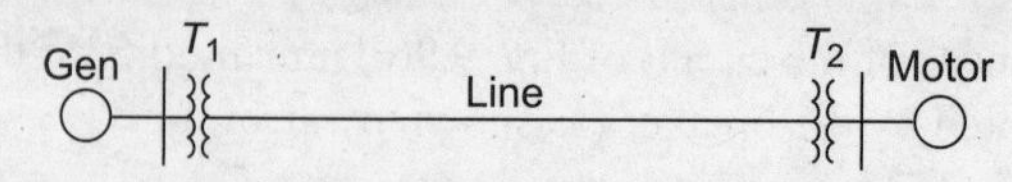

(a) One-line diagram for the system of Example 9.3

(b) Prefault equivalent circuit

(c) Equivalent circuit during fault

Fig. 9.12

Solution All reactances are given on a base of 25 MVA and appropriate voltages.

$$\text{Prefault voltage } V^0 = \frac{10.6}{11} = 0.9636 \angle 0^\circ \text{ pu}$$

$$\text{Load} = 15 \text{ MW, } 0.8 \text{ pf leading}$$

$$= \frac{15}{25} = 0.6 \text{ pu, } 0.8 \text{ pf leading}$$

$$\text{Prefault current } I^0 = \frac{0.6}{0.9636 \times 0.8} \angle 36.9^\circ$$

$$= 0.7783 \angle 36.9^\circ \text{ pu}$$

Voltage behind subtransient reactance (generator)

$$E''_g = 0.9636 \angle 0^\circ + j0.45 \times 0.7783 \angle 36.9^\circ$$

$$= 0.7536 + j0.28 \text{ pu}$$

Voltage behind subtransient reactance (motor)

$$E''_m = 0.9636 \angle 0^\circ - j0.15 \times 0.7783 \angle 36.9^\circ$$

$$= 1.0336 - j0.0933 \text{ pu}$$

The prefault equivalent circuit is shown in Fig. 9.12(b). Under faulted condition [Fig. 9.12(c)],

$$I''_g = \frac{0.7536 + j0.2800}{j0.45} = 0.6226 - j1.6746 \text{ pu}$$

$$I''_m = \frac{1.0336 - j0.0933}{j0.15} = -0.6226 - j6.8906 \text{ pu}$$

$$\text{Current in fault } I^f = I''_g + I''_m = -j8.5653 \text{ pu}$$

$$\text{Base current (gen/motor)} = \frac{25 \times 10^3}{\sqrt{3} \times 11} = 1{,}312.2 \text{ A}$$

Now,

$$I''_g = 1{,}312.2\,(0.6226 - j1.6746) = (816.4 - j2{,}197.4)\text{ A}$$
$$I''_m = 1{,}312.2\,(-\,0.6226 - j6.8906) = (-\,816.2 - j9{,}041.8)\text{ A}$$
$$I^f = -j11{,}239\text{ A}$$

9.4.1 Short Circuit (SC) Current Computation through the Thevenin Theorem

An alternate method of computing short circuit currents is through the application of the Thevenin theorem. This method is faster and easily adopted to systematic computation for large networks. While the method is perfectly general, it is illustrated here through a simple example.

Consider a synchronous generator feeding a synchronous motor over a line. Figure 9.13(a) shows the circuit model of the system under conditions of steady load. Fault computations are to be made for a fault at F, at the motor terminals. As a first step the circuit model is replaced by the one shown in Fig. 9.13(b), wherein the synchronous machines are represented by their transient reactances (or subtransient reactances if subtransient currents are of interest) in series with voltages behind transient reactances. This change does not disturb the prefault current I^0 and prefault voltage V^0 (at F).

As seen from FG the Thevenin equivalent circuit of Fig. 9.13(b) is drawn in Fig. 9.13(c). It comprises prefault voltage V^0 in series with the passive Thevenin impedance network. It is noticed that the prefault current I^0 does not appear in the passive Thevenin impedance network. It is therefore to be remembered that this current must be accounted for by superposition after the SC solution is obtained through use of the Thevenin equivalent.

Consider now a fault at F through an impedance Z^f. Figure 9.13(d) shows the Thevenin equivalent of the system feeding the fault impedance. We can immediately write

$$I^f = \frac{V^0}{jX_{Th} + Z^f} \tag{9.12}$$

Current caused by fault in generator circuit

$$\Delta I_g = \frac{X'_{dm}}{(X'_{dg} + X + X'_{dm})} I^f \tag{9.13}$$

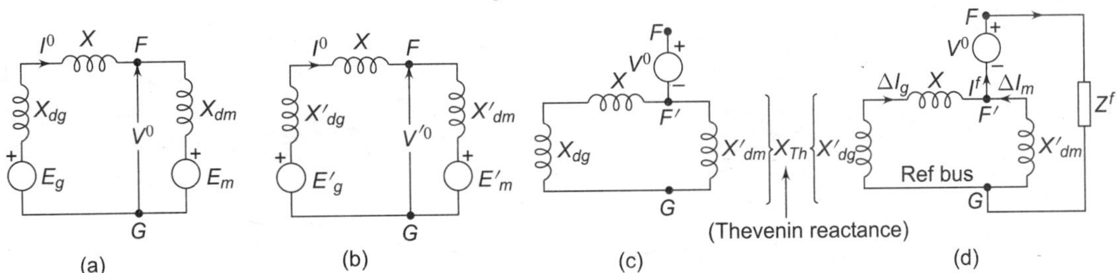

Fig. 9.13 *Computation of SC current by the Thevenin equivalent*

Current caused by fault in motor circuit

$$\Delta I_m = \frac{X'_{dg} + X}{(X'_{dm} + X + X'_{dg})} I^f \tag{9.14}$$

Postfault currents and voltages are obtained as follows by superposition:

$$I^f_g = I^0 + \Delta I_g$$
$$I^f_m = -\,I^0 + \Delta I_m \text{ (in the direction of } \Delta I_m) \tag{9.15}$$

Postfault voltage

$$V^f = V^0 + (-jX_{Th}I^f) = V^0 + \Delta V \tag{9.16}$$

where $\Delta V = -jX_{Th}I^f$ is the voltage of the fault point F' on the Thevenin passive network (with respect to the reference bus G) caused by the flow of fault current I^f.

An observation can be made here. Since the prefault current flowing out of fault point F is always zero, the postfault current out of F is independent of load for a given prefault voltage at F.

The above approach to SC computation is summarised in the following four steps:

Step 1 Obtain steady state solution of loaded system (load flow study).

Step 2 Replace reactances of synchronous machines by their subtransient/transient values. Short circuit all emf sources. The result is the passive Thevenin network.

Step 3 Excite the passive network of step 2 at the fault point by negative of prefault voltage [see Fig. 9.13(d)] in series with the fault impedance. Compute voltages and currents at all points of interest.

Step 4 Postfault currents and voltages are obtained by adding results of steps 1 and 3.

The following assumptions can be safely made in SC computations leading to considerable computational simplification:

Assumption 1: All prefault voltage magnitudes are 1 pu.

Assumption 2: All prefault currents are zero.

The first assumption is quite close to actual conditions as under normal operation all voltages (pu) are nearly unity.

The changes in current caused by short circuit are quite large, of the order of 10–20 pu and are purely reactive; whereas the prefault load currents are almost purely real. Hence, the total postfault current which is the result of the two currents can be taken in magnitude equal to the larger component (caused by the fault). This justifies assumption 2.

Let us illustrate the above method by recalculating the results of Example 9.3.

The circuit model for the system of Example 9.3 for computation of postfault condition is shown in Fig. 9.14.

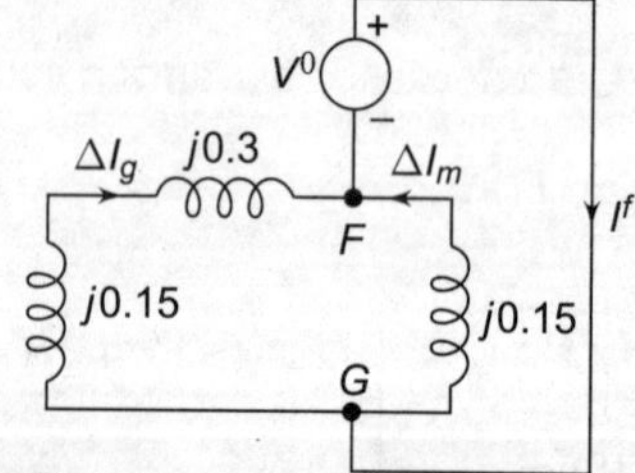

Fig. 9.14 *F is the fault point on the passive Thevenin network*

$$I^f = \frac{V^0}{(j0.15 \,||\, j0.45)} = \frac{0.9636 \times j0.60}{j0.15 \times j0.45} = -j8.565 \text{ pu}$$

Change in generator current due to fault, $\Delta I_g = -j8.565 \times \dfrac{j0.15}{j0.60} = -j2.141$ pu

Change in motor current due to fault, $\Delta I_m = -j8.565 \times \dfrac{j0.45}{j0.60} = -j6.424$ pu

To these changes we add the prefault current to obtain the subtransient current in machines. Thus,

$$I_g'' = I^0 + \Delta I_g = (0.623 - j1.674) \text{ pu}$$
$$I_m'' = -I^0 + \Delta I_m = (-0.623 - j6.891) \text{ pu}$$

which are the same (and should be) as calculated already.

We have thus solved Example 9.3 alternatively through the Thevenin theorem and superposition. This, indeed, is a powerful method for large networks.

9.5 ▶ SELECTION OF CIRCUIT BREAKERS

Two of the circuit breaker ratings which require the computation of SC current are *rated momentary current* and *rated symmetrical interrupting current.* Symmetrical SC current is obtained by using subtransient reactances for synchronous machines. Momentary current (rms) is then calculated by multiplying the symmetrical momentary current by a factor of 1.6 to account for the presence of DC off-set current.

Symmetrical current to be interrupted is computed by using subtransient reactances for synchronous generators and transient reactances for synchronous motors—induction motors are neglected.* The DC off-set value to be added to obtain the current to be interrupted is accounted for by multiplying the symmetrical SC current by a factor as tabulated below:

Circuit Breaker Speed	*Multiplying Factor*
8 cycles or slower	1.0
5 cycles	1.1
3 cycles	1.2
2 cycles	1.4

If SC MVA (explained below) is more than 500, the above multiplying factors are increased by 0.1 each. The multiplying factor for air breakers rated 600 V or lower is 1.25.

The current that a circuit breaker can interrupt is inversely proportional to the operating voltage over a certain range, i.e.,

$$\text{Amperes at operating voltage} = \text{amperes at rated voltage} \times \frac{\text{rated voltage}}{\text{operating voltage}}$$

Of course, operating voltage cannot exceed the maximum design value. Also, no matter how low the voltage is, the rated interrupting current cannot exceed the rated maximum interrupting current. Over this range of voltages, the product of operating voltage and interrupting current is constant. It is therefore logical as well as convenient to express the circuit breaker rating in terms of SC MVA that can be interrupted, defined as

$$\text{Rated interrupting MVA (three-phase) capacity} = \sqrt{3}\,|V(\text{line})|_{\text{rated}} \times |I(\text{line})|_{\text{rated interrupting current}}$$

where V(line) is in kV and I (line) is in kA.

Thus, instead of computing the SC current to be interrupted, we compute three-phase SC MVA to be interrupted, where

$$\text{SC MVA (3-phase)} = \sqrt{3} \times \text{prefault line voltage in kV} \times \text{SC current in kA.}$$

If voltage and current are in per unit values on a three-phase basis

$$\text{SC MVA (3-phase)} = |V|_{\text{prefault}} \times |I|_{SC} \times (\text{MVA})_{\text{Base}} \tag{9.17}$$

Obviously, rated MVA interrupting capacity of a circuit breaker is to be more than (or equal to) the SC MVA required to be interrupted.

For the selection of a circuit breaker for a particular location, we must find the maximum possible SC MVA to be interrupted with respect to type and location of fault and generating capacity (also synchronous motor load) connected to the system. A three-phase fault though rare is generally the one which gives the highest SC MVA and a circuit breaker must be capable of interrupting it. An exception is an LG (line-to-ground) fault close to a synchronous generator.** In a simple system, the fault location which gives the highest SC MVA may be obvious but in a large system various possible locations must be tried out to obtain the highest SC MVA, requiring repeated SC computations. This is illustrated by the examples that follow.

---

* In some recent attempts, currents contributed by induction motors during a short circuit have been accounted for.

** This will be explained in Ch. 11.

Example 9.4 Three 6.6 kV generators A, B and C, each of 10% leakage reactance and MVA ratings 40, 50 and 25, respectively, are interconnected electrically, as shown in Fig. 9.15, by a tie bar through *current limiting reactors*, each of 12% reactance based upon the rating of the machine to which it is connected. A three-phase feeder is supplied from the bus bar of generator A at a line voltage of 6.6 kV. The feeder has a resistance of 0.06 Ω/phase and an inductive reactance of 0.12 Ω/phase. Estimate the maximum MVA that can be fed into a symmetrical short circuit at the far end of the feeder.

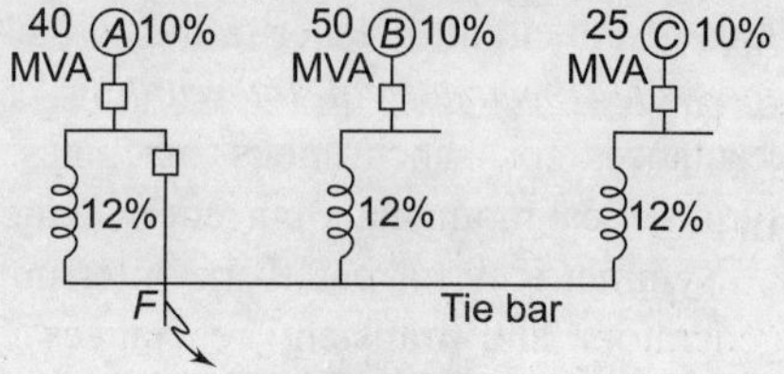

Fig. 9.15

Solution Choose as base 50 MVA, 6.6 kV

$$\text{Feeder impedance} = \frac{(0.06 + j0.12) \times 50}{(6.6)^2} = (0.069 + j0.138) \text{ pu}$$

$$\text{Gen } A \text{ reactance} = \frac{0.1 \times 50}{40} = 0.125 \text{ pu}$$

$$\text{Gen } B \text{ reactance} = 0.1 \text{ pu}$$

$$\text{Gen } C \text{ reactance} = 0.1 \times \frac{50}{25} = 0.2 \text{ pu}$$

$$\text{Reactor } A \text{ reactance} = \frac{0.12 \times 50}{40} = 0.15 \text{ pu}$$

$$\text{Reactor } B \text{ reactance} = 0.12 \text{ pu}$$

$$\text{Reactor } C \text{ reactance} = \frac{0.12 \times 50}{25} = 0.24 \text{ pu}$$

Assume no load prefault conditions, i.e., prefault currents are zero. Postfault currents can then be calculated by the circuit model of Fig. 9.16(a) corresponding to Fig. 9.13(d). The circuit is easily reduced to that of Fig. 9.16(b), where

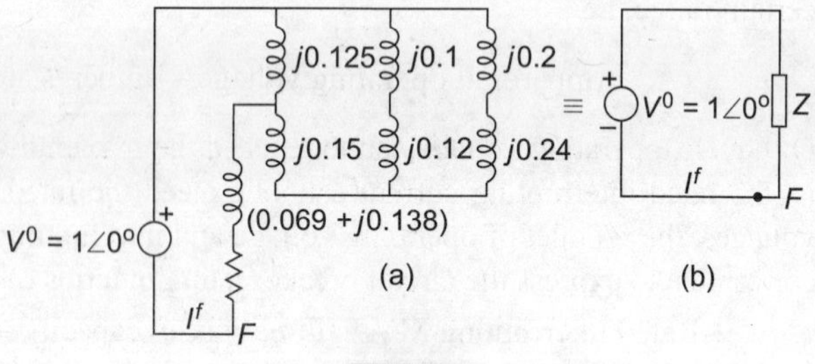

Fig. 9.16

$$Z = (0.069 + j0.138) + j0.125 \,||\, (j0.15 + j0.22 \,||\, j0.44)$$
$$= 0.069 + j0.226 = 0.236\angle 73^\circ$$

$$\text{SC MVA} = V^0 I^f = V^0 \left(\frac{V^0}{Z}\right) = \frac{1}{Z} \text{ pu (since } V^0 = 1 \text{ pu)}$$

$$= \frac{1}{Z} \times (\text{MVA})_{\text{Base}}$$

$$= \frac{50}{0.236} = 212 \text{ MVA}$$

Example 9.5 Consider the four-bus system of Fig. 9.17. Buses 1 and 2 are generator buses and 3 and 4 are load buses. The generators are rated 11 kV, 100 MVA, with transient reactance of 10% each. Both the transformers are 11/110 kV, 100 MVA with a leakage reactance of 5%. The reactances of the lines to a base of 100 MVA, 110 kV are indicated on the figure. Obtain the short circuit solution for a three-phase solid fault on bus 4 (load bus).

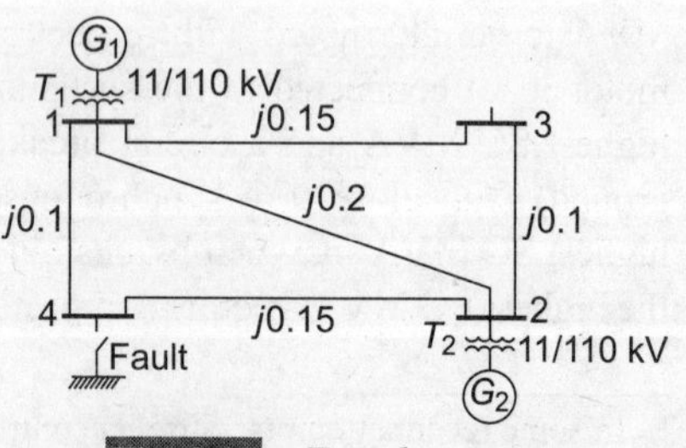

Fig. 9.17 *Four-bus system*

Assume prefault voltages to be 1 pu and prefault currents to be zero.

Solution Changes in voltages and currents caused by a short circuit can be calculated from the circuit model of Fig. 9.18. Fault current I^f is calculated by systematic network reduction as in Fig. 9.19.

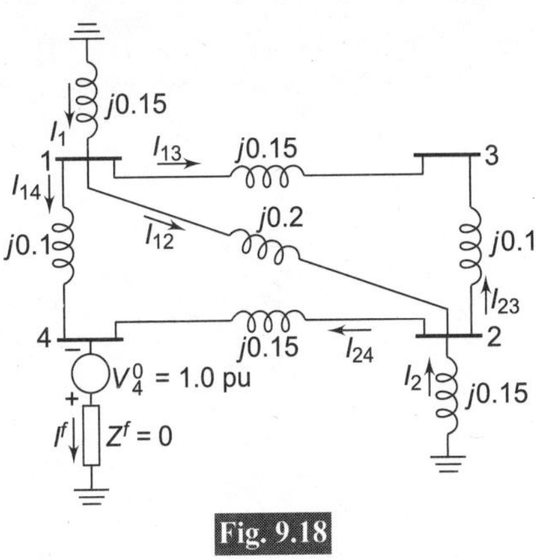

Fig. 9.18

From Fig. 9.19(e), we get directly the fault current as

$$I^f = \frac{1.0}{j0.13560} = -j7.37463 \text{ pu}$$

From Fig. 9.19(d), it is easy to see that

$$I_1 = I^f \times \frac{j0.19583}{j0.37638} = -j3.83701 \text{ pu}$$

$$I_2 = I^f \times \frac{j0.18055}{j0.37638} = -j3.53762 \text{ pu}$$

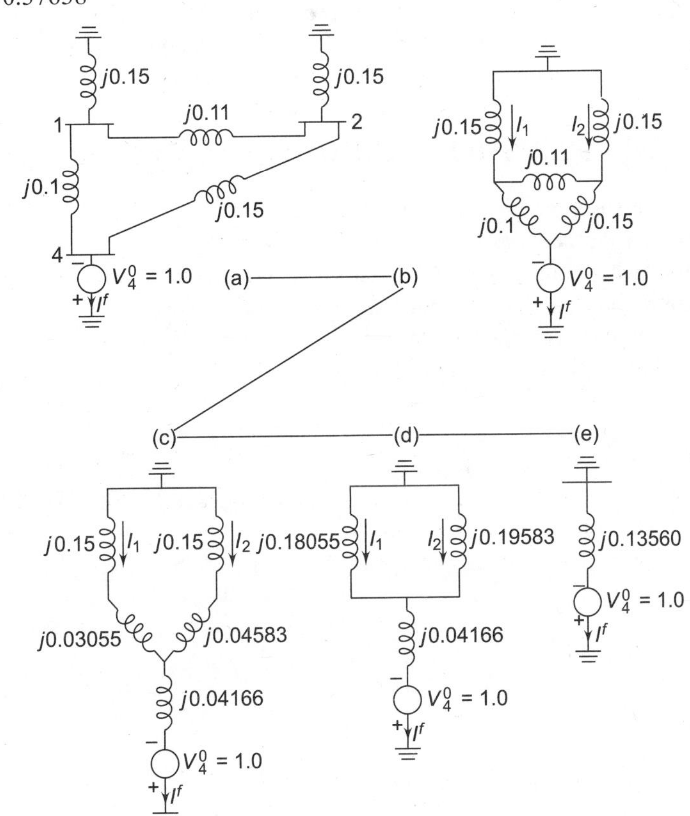

Fig. 9.19 *Systematic reduction of the network of Fig. 9.18*

Let us now compute the voltage changes for buses 1, 2 and 3. From Fig. 9.19(b), we have

$$\Delta V_1 = 0 - (j0.15)(-j3.83701) = -0.57555 \text{ pu}$$

$$\Delta V_2 = 0 - (j0.15)(-j3.53762) = -0.53064 \text{ pu}$$

Now,

$$V_1^f = 1 + \Delta V_1 = 0.42445 \text{ pu}$$

$$V_2^f = 1 + \Delta V_2 = 0.46936 \text{ pu}$$

$$\therefore \quad I_{13} = \frac{V_1^f - V_2^f}{j0.15 + j0.1} = j0.17964 \text{ pu}$$

Now,

$$\Delta V_3 = 0 - [(j0.15)(-j3.83701) + (j0.15)(j0.17964)]$$
$$= -0.54860 \text{ pu}$$

$$\therefore \quad V_3^f = 1 - 0.54860 = 0.4514 \text{ pu}$$

$$V_4^f = 0$$

The determination of currents in the remaining lines is left as an exercise to the reader.

Short circuit study is complete with the computation of SC MVA at bus 4.

$$(\text{SC MVA})_4 = 7.37463 \times 100 = 737.463 \text{ MVA}$$

It is obvious that the heuristic network reduction procedure adopted above is not practical for a real power network of even moderate size. It is, therefore, essential to adopt a suitable algorithm for carrying out short circuit study on a digital computer. This is discussed in Section 9.6.

9.6 ▶ ALGORITHM FOR SHORT CIRCUIT STUDIES

So far we have carried out short circuit calculations for simple systems whose passive networks can be easily reduced. In this section, we extend our study to large systems. In order to apply the four steps of short circuit computation developed earlier to large systems, it is necessary to evolve a systematic general algorithm so that a digital computer can be used.

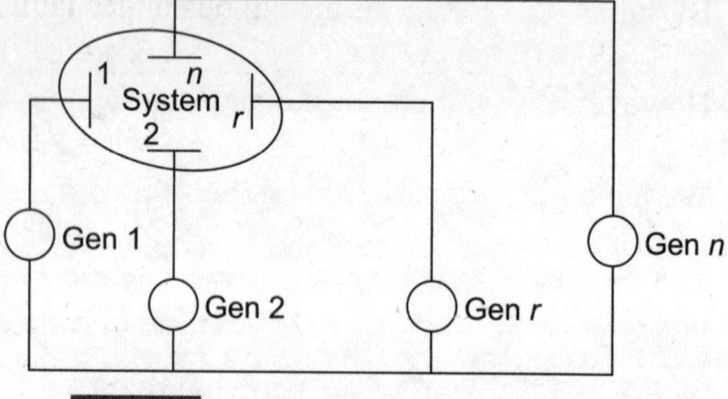

Fig. 9.20 *n-bus system under steady load*

Consider an n-bus system shown schematically in Fig. 9.20 operating at steady load. The first step towards short circuit computation is to obtain prefault voltages at all buses and currents in all lines through a load flow study. Let us indicate the prefault bus voltage vector as

$$V^0_{\text{BUS}} = \begin{bmatrix} V_1^0 \\ V_2^0 \\ \vdots \\ V_n^0 \end{bmatrix} \tag{9.18}$$

Let us assume that the rth bus is faulted through a fault impedance Z^f. The postfault bus voltage vector will be given by

$$V^f_{\text{BUS}} = V^0_{\text{BUS}} + \Delta V \tag{9.19}$$

where ΔV is the vector of changes in bus voltages caused by the fault.

As step 2, we drew the passive Thevenin network of the system with generators replaced by transient/subtransient reactances with their emfs shorted (Fig. 9.21).

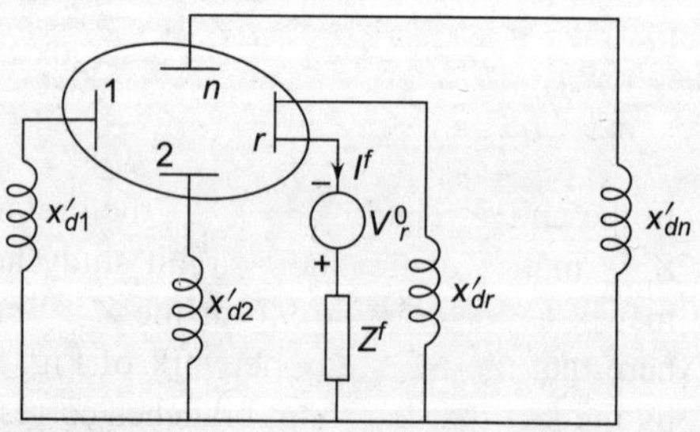

Fig. 9.21 *Network of the system of Fig. 9.20 for computing changes in bus voltages caused by the fault*

As per step 3, we now excite the passive Thevenin network with $-V_r^0$ in series with Z^f as in Fig. 9.21. The vector $\Delta \boldsymbol{V}$ comprises the bus voltages of this network.

Now,

$$\Delta \boldsymbol{V} = \boldsymbol{Z}_{\text{BUS}} \boldsymbol{J}^f \tag{9.20}$$

where

$$\boldsymbol{Z}_{\text{BUS}} = \begin{bmatrix} Z_{11} & \cdots & Z_{1n} \\ \vdots & & \vdots \\ Z_{n1} & \cdots & Z_{nn} \end{bmatrix} = \text{bus impedance matrix of the passive Thevenin network} \tag{9.21}$$

$\boldsymbol{J}^f$ = bus current injection vector

Since the network is injected with current $-I^f$ only at the rth bus, we have

$$J^f = \begin{bmatrix} 0 \\ 0 \\ \vdots \\ I_r^f = -I^f \\ \vdots \\ 0 \end{bmatrix} \tag{9.22}$$

Substituting Eq. (9.22) in Eq. (9.20), we have for the rth bus

$$\Delta V_r = -Z_{rr} I^f$$

By step 4, the voltage at the rth bus under fault is

$$V_r^f = V_r^0 + \Delta V_r^0 = V_r^0 - Z_{rr} I^f \tag{9.23}$$

However, this voltage must equal

$$V_r^f = Z^f I^f \tag{9.24}$$

We have from Eqs. (9.23) and (9.24)

$$Z^f I^f = V_r^0 - Z_{rr} I^f$$

or

$$I^f = \frac{V_r^0}{Z_{rr} + Z^f} \tag{9.25}$$

At the ith bus [from Eqs. (9.20) and (9.22)]

$$\Delta V_i = -Z_{ir} I^f$$

∴

$$V_i^f = V_i^0 - Z_{ir} I^f, \; i = 1, 2, ..., n \tag{9.26}$$

Substituting for I^f from Eq. (9.25), we have

$$V_i^f = V_i^0 - \frac{Z_{ir}}{Z_{rr} + Z^f} V_r^0 \tag{9.27}$$

For $i = r$ in Eq. (9.27)

$$V_r^f = \frac{Z^f}{Z_{rr} + Z^f} V_r^0 \tag{9.28}$$

In the above relationship V_i^0s, the prefault bus voltages are assumed to be known from a load flow study. Z_{BUS} matrix of the short-circuit study network of Fig. 9.21 can be obtained by the inversion of its Y_{BUS} matrix as in Example 9.6 or the Z_{BUS} building algorithm presented in Section 9.7. It should be observed here that the SC study network of Fig. 9.21 is different from the corresponding load flow study network by the fact that the shunt branches corresponding to the generator reactances do not appear in the load flow study network. Further, in formulating the SC study network, the load impedances are ignored, these being very much larger than the impedances of lines and generators. Of course, synchronous motors must be included in Z_{BUS} formulation for the SC study.

Postfault currents in lines are given by

$$I_{ij}^f = Y_{ij}\left(V_i^f - V_j^f\right) \tag{9.29}$$

For calculation of postfault generator current, examine Figs 9.22(a) and (b). From the load flow study (Fig. 9.22(a))

Prefault generator output = $P_{Gi} + jQ_{Gi}$

$$\therefore \quad I_{Gi}^0 = \frac{P_{Gi} - jQ_{Gi}}{V_i^0} \quad \text{(prefault generator output} = P_{Gi} + jQ_{Gi}) \tag{9.30}$$

$$E'_{Gi} = V_i + jX'_{Gi}I_{Gi}^0 \tag{9.31}$$

From the SC study, V_i^f is obtained. It then follows from Fig. 9.22(b) that

$$I_{Gi}^f = \frac{E'_{Gi} - V_i^f}{jX'_{Gi}} \tag{9.32}$$

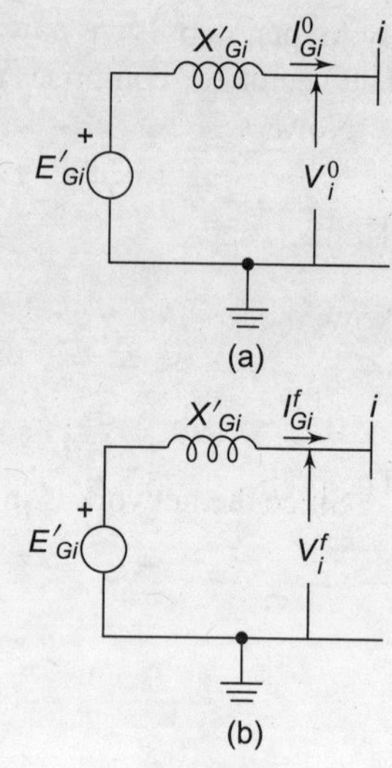

Fig. 9.22

Example 9.6 To illustrate the algorithm discussed above, we shall re-compute the short circuit solution for Example 9.5 which was solved earlier using the network reduction technique.

Solution First of all the bus admittance matrix for the network of Fig. 9.18 is formed as follows:

$$Y_{11} = \frac{1}{j0.15} + \frac{1}{j0.15} + \frac{1}{j0.1} + \frac{1}{j0.2} = -j28.333$$

$$Y_{12} = Y_{21} = \frac{-1}{j0.2} = j5.000$$

$$Y_{13} = Y_{31} = \frac{-1}{j0.15} = j6.667$$

$$Y_{14} = Y_{41} = \frac{-1}{j0.1} = j10.000$$

$$Y_{22} = \frac{1}{j0.15} + \frac{1}{j0.15} + \frac{1}{j0.1} + \frac{1}{j0.2} = -j28.333$$

$$Y_{23} = Y_{32} = \frac{-1}{j0.1} = j10.000$$

$$Y_{24} = Y_{42} = \frac{-1}{j0.15} = j6.667$$

$$Y_{33} = \frac{1}{j0.15} + \frac{1}{j0.1} = -j16.667$$

$$Y_{34} = Y_{43} = 0.000$$

$$Y_{44} = \frac{1}{j0.1} + \frac{1}{j0.15} = -j16.667$$

$$\boldsymbol{Y}_{\text{BUS}} = \begin{bmatrix} -j28.333 & j5.000 & j6.667 & j10.000 \\ j5.000 & -j28.333 & j10.000 & j6.667 \\ j6.667 & j10.000 & -j16.667 & j0.000 \\ j10.000 & j6.667 & j0.000 & -j16.667 \end{bmatrix}$$

By inversion, we get $\boldsymbol{Z}_{\text{BUS}}$ as

$$\boldsymbol{Z}_{\text{BUS}} = \begin{bmatrix} j0.0903 & j0.0597 & j0.0719 & j0.0780 \\ j0.0597 & j0.0903 & j0.0780 & j0.0719 \\ j0.0719 & j0.0780 & j0.1356 & j0.0743 \\ j0.0780 & j0.0719 & j0.0743 & j0.1356 \end{bmatrix}$$

Now, the postfault bus voltages can be obtained using Eq. (9.27) as

$$V_1^f = V_1^0 - \frac{Z_{14}}{Z_{44}} V_4^0$$

The prefault condition being no load, $V_1^0 = V_2^0 = V_3^0 = V_4^0 = 1$ pu

$$V_1^f = 1.0 - \frac{j0.0780}{j0.1356} \times 1.0 = 0.4248 \text{ pu}$$

$$V_2^f = V_2^0 - \frac{Z_{24}}{Z_{44}} V_4^0$$

$$= 1.0 - \frac{j0.0719}{j0.1356} \times 1.0 = 0.4698 \text{ pu}$$

$$V_3^f = V_3^0 - \frac{Z_{34}}{Z_{44}} V_4^0$$

$$= 1.0 - \frac{j0.0743}{j0.1356} 1.0 = 0.4521 \text{ pu}$$

$$V_4^f = 0.0$$

Using Eq. (9.25), we can obtain the fault current as

$$I^f = \frac{1.000}{j0.1356} = -j7.37463 \text{ pu}$$

These values agree with those obtained earlier in Example 9.5. Let us also calculate the short circuit current in lines 1–3, 1–2, 1–4, 2–4 and 2–3.

$$I_{13}^f = \frac{V_1^f - V_3^f}{z_{13}} = \frac{0.4248 - 0.4521}{j0.15} = j0.182 \text{ pu}$$

$$I_{12}^f = \frac{V_1^f - V_2^f}{z_{12}} = \frac{0.4248 - 0.4698}{j0.2} = j0.225 \text{ pu}$$

$$I_{14}^f = \frac{V_1^f - V_4^f}{z_{14}} = \frac{0.4248 - 0}{j0.1} = -j4.248 \text{ pu}$$

$$I_{24}^f = \frac{V_2^f - V_4^f}{z_{24}} = \frac{0.4698 - 0}{j0.15} = -j3.132 \text{ pu}$$

$$I_{23}^f = \frac{V_2^f - V_3^f}{z_{23}} = \frac{0.4698 - 0.4521}{j.01} = -j0.177 \text{ pu}$$

For the example on hand this method may appear more involved compared to the heuristic network reduction method employed in Example 9.5. This, however, is a systematic method and can be easily adopted on the digital computer for practical networks of large size. Further, another important feature of the method is that having computed Z_{BUS}, we can at once obtain all the required short circuit data for a fault on any bus. For example, in this particular system, the fault current for a fault on bus 1 (or bus 2) will be

$$I^f = \frac{1.000}{Z_{11}(\text{or } Z_{22})} = \frac{1.00}{j0.0903} = -j11.074197 \text{ pu}$$

9.7 ► Z_{BUS} FORMULATION

9.7.1 By Inventing Y_{BUS}

$$J_{BUS} = Y_{BUS}\, V_{BUS}$$

or

$$V_{BUS} = [Y_{BUS}]^{-1} J_{BUS} = Z_{BUS}\, J_{BUS} \tag{9.33}$$

or

$$Z_{BUS} = [Y_{BUS}]^{-1}$$

The sparsity of Y_{BUS} may be retained by using an efficient inversion technique [1] and nodal impedance matrix can then be calculated directly from the factorised admittance matrix. This is beyond the scope of this book.

9.7.2 Current Injection Technique

Equation (9.33) can be written in the expanded form

$$\begin{aligned} V_1 &= Z_{11}I_1 + Z_{12}I_2 + \cdots + Z_{1n}I_n \\ V_2 &= Z_{21}I_1 + Z_{22}I_2 + \cdots + Z_{2n}I_n \\ &\cdots\cdots\cdots\cdots\cdots\cdots\cdots\cdots \\ V_n &= Z_{n1}I_1 + Z_{n2}I_2 + \cdots + Z_{nn}I_n \end{aligned} \tag{9.34}$$

It immediately follows from Eq. (9.34) that

$$Z_{ij} = \left.\frac{V_i}{I_j}\right|_{\substack{I_1 = I_2 = \cdots = I_n = 0 \\ I_j \neq 0}} \tag{9.35}$$

Also, $Z_{ij} = Z_{ji}$; (Z_{BUS} is a symmetrical matrix).

As per Eq. (9.35), if a unit current is injected at bus (node) j, while the other buses are kept open circuited, the bus voltages yield the values of the jth column of Z_{BUS}. However, no organised computerisable techniques are possible for finding the bus voltages. The technique had utility in AC Network Analysers where the bus voltages could be read by a voltmeter.

Example 9.7 Consider the network of Fig. 9.23(a) with three buses one of which is a reference. Evaluate Z_{BUS}.

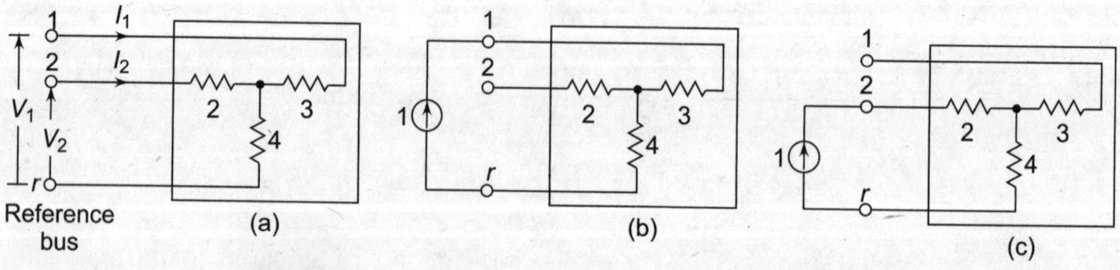

Fig. 9.23 *Current injection method of computing Z_{BUS}*

Solution Inject a unit current at bus 1 keeping bus 2 open circuit, i.e., $I_1 = 1$ and $I_2 = 0$ as in Fig. 9.22(b). Calculating voltages at buses 1 and 2, we have

$$Z_{11} = V_1 = 7$$
$$Z_{21} = V_2 = 4$$

Now, let $I_1 = 0$ and $I_2 = 1$. It similarly follows that

$$Z_{12} = V_1 = 4 = Z_{12}$$
$$Z_{22} = V_2 = 6$$

Collecting the above values

$$Z_{\text{BUS}} = \begin{bmatrix} 7 & 4 \\ 4 & 6 \end{bmatrix}$$

Because of the above computational procedure, the Z_{BUS} matrix is referred to as the 'open-circuit impedance matrix'.

9.7.3 Z_{BUS} Building Algorithm

It is a step-by-step programmable technique which proceeds branch by branch. It has the advantage that any modification of the network does not require complete rebuilding of Z_{BUS}.

Consider that Z_{BUS} has been formulated upto a certain stage and another branch is now added. Then,

$$Z_{\text{BUS}}\,(\text{old}) \xrightarrow{Z_b \,=\, \text{branch impedance}} Z_{\text{BUS}}\,(\text{new})$$

Upon adding a new branch, one of the following situations is presented.

1. Z_b is added from a new bus to the reference bus (i.e., a new branch is added and the dimension of Z_{BUS} goes up by one). This is *type-1 modification.*
2. Z_b is added from a new bus to an old bus (i.e., a new branch is added and the dimension of Z_{BUS} goes up by one). This is *type-2 modification.*
3. Z_b connects an old bus to the reference branch (i.e., a new loop is formed but the dimension of Z_{BUS} does not change). This is *type-3 modification.*
4. Z_b connects two old buses (i.e., new loop is formed but the dimension of Z_{BUS} does not change). This is *type-4 modification.*
5. Z_b connects two new buses (Z_{BUS} remains unaffected in this case). This situation can be avoided by suitable numbering of buses and from now onwards will be ignored.

Notation: i, j— old buses; r— reference bus; k— new bus.

Type-1 Modification Figure 9.24 shows a passive (linear) n-bus network in which branch with impedance Z_b is added to the new bus k and the reference bus r. Now,

$$V_k = Z_b I_k$$

$\therefore$

$$Z_{ki} = Z_{ik} = 0;\ i = 1, 2, \ldots, n$$
$$Z_{kk} = Z_b$$

Hence,

$$Z_{\text{BUS}}\,(\text{new}) = \left[\begin{array}{c|c} Z_{\text{BUS}}(\text{old}) & \begin{matrix} 0 \\ | \\ | \\ | \\ 0 \end{matrix} \\ \hline 0 \;-\;-\;-\; 0 & Z_b \end{array}\right] \tag{9.36}$$

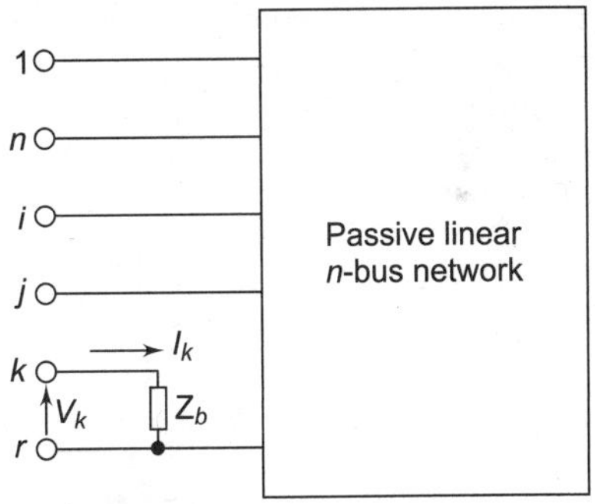

Fig. 9.24 *Type-1 modification*

Type-2 Modification Z_b is added from new bus k to the old bus j as in Fig. 9.25. It follows from this figure that

$$V_k = Z_b I_k + V_j$$
$$= Z_b I_k + Z_{j1} I_1 + Z_{j2} I_2 + \cdots + Z_{jj}(I_j + I_k) + \cdots + Z_{jn} I_n$$

Rearranging,

$$V_k = Z_{j1} I_1 + Z_{j2} I_2 + \cdots + Z_{jj} I_j + \cdots + Z_{jn} I_n + (Z_{jj} + Z_b) I_k$$

Consequently,

$$Z_{\text{BUS}}\text{ (new)} = \left[\begin{array}{c|c} Z_{\text{BUS}}\text{(old)} & \begin{matrix} Z_{1j} \\ Z_{2j} \\ \vdots \\ Z_{nj} \end{matrix} \\ \hline Z_{ji} Z_{j2} \ldots Z_{jn} & Z_{jj} + Z_b \end{array}\right] \tag{9.37}$$

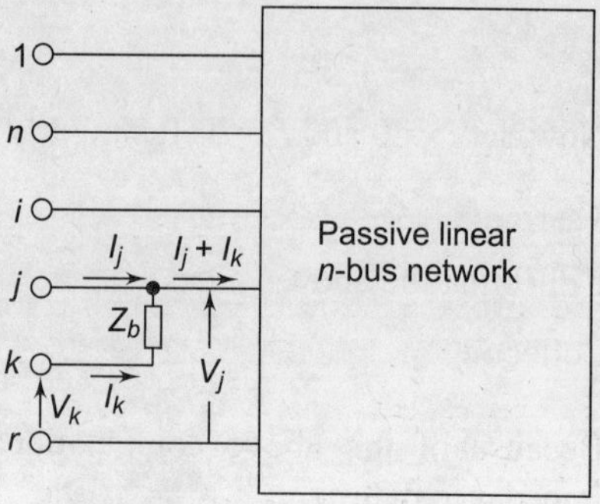

Fig. 9.25 Type-2 modification

Type-3 Modification Z_b connects an old bus (j) to the reference bus (r) as in Fig. 9.26. This case follows from Fig. 9.25 by connecting bus k to the reference bus r, i.e., by setting $V_k = 0$.

Thus,

$$\begin{bmatrix} V_1 \\ V_2 \\ \vdots \\ V_n \\ \hline 0 \end{bmatrix} = \left[\begin{array}{c|c} Z_{\text{BUS}}\text{(old)} & \begin{matrix} Z_{1j} \\ Z_{2j} \\ \vdots \\ Z_{nj} \end{matrix} \\ \hline Z_{j1} Z_{j2} \ldots Z_{jn} & Z_{jj} + Z_b \end{array}\right] \begin{bmatrix} I_1 \\ I_2 \\ \vdots \\ I_n \\ I_k \end{bmatrix} \tag{9.38}$$

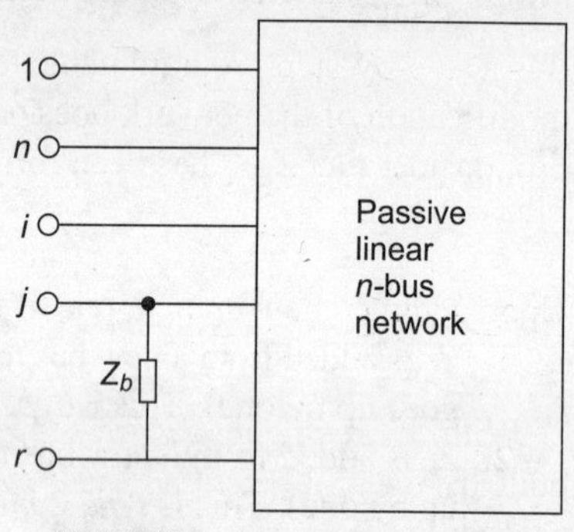

Fig. 9.26 Type-3 modification

Eliminate I_k in the set of equations contained in the matrix operation (9.38),

$$0 = Z_{j1} I_1 + Z_{j2} I_2 + \cdots + Z_{jn} I_n + (Z_{jj} + Z_b) I_k$$

or

$$I_k = -\frac{1}{Z_{jj} + Z_b}(Z_{j1} I_1 + Z_{j2} I_2 + \cdots + Z_{jn} I_n) \tag{9.39}$$

Now,

$$V_i = Z_{i1} I_1 + Z_{i2} I_2 + \cdots + Z_{in} I_n + Z_{ij} I_k \tag{9.40}$$

Substituting Eq. (9.40) in Eq. (9.39)

$$V_i = \left[Z_{i1} - \frac{1}{Z_{jj} + Z_b}(Z_{ij} Z_{j1})\right] I_1 + \left[Z_{i2} - \frac{1}{Z_{jj} + Z_b}(Z_{ij} Z_{j2})\right] I_2 + \cdots + \left[Z_{in} - \frac{1}{Z_{jj} + Z_b}\left(Z_{ij}\ Z_{jn}\right)\right] I_n \tag{9.41}$$

Equation (9.37) can be written in matrix form as

$$Z_{\text{BUS}}\text{ (new)} = Z_{\text{BUS}}\text{ (old} - \frac{1}{Z_{jj} + Z_b}\begin{bmatrix} Z_{1j} \\ \vdots \\ Z_{nj} \end{bmatrix}[Z_{j1} \ldots Z_{jn}] \tag{9.42}$$

Type-4 Modification Z_b connects two old buses as in Fig. 9.27. Equations can be written as follows for all the network buses.

$$V_i = Z_{i1} I_1 + Z_{i2} I_2 + \cdots + Z_{1i}(I_i + I_k) + Z_{ij}(I_j - I_k) + \cdots + Z_{in} I_n \tag{9.43}$$

Similar equations follow for other buses.

The voltages of the buses i and j are, however, constrained by the equation (Fig. 9.27)

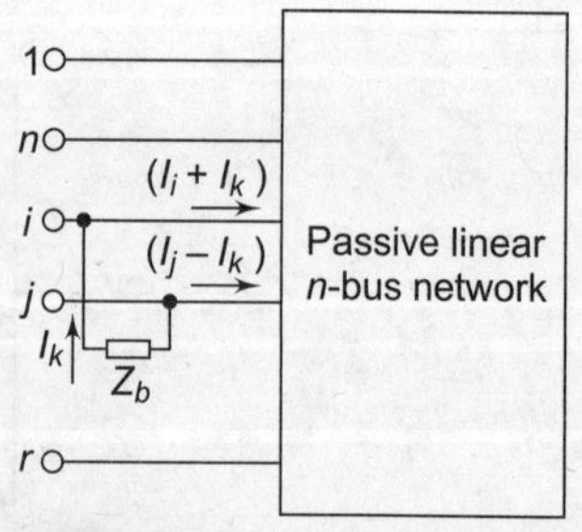

Fig. 9.27 Type-4 modification

$$V_j = Z_b I_k + V_i \tag{9.44}$$

or $\quad Z_{j1}I_1 + Z_{j2}I_2 + \cdots + Z_{ji}(I_i + I_k) + Z_{jj}(I_j - I_k) + \cdots + Z_{jn}I_n$

$$= Z_b I_k + Z_{i1}I_1 + Z_{i2}I_2 + \cdots + Z_{ii}(I_i + I_k) + Z_{ij}(I_j - I_k) + \cdots + Z_{in}I_n$$

Rearranging,

$$0 = (Z_{i1} - Z_{j1})I_1 + \cdots + (Z_{ii} - Z_{ji})I_i + (Z_{ij} - Z_{jj})I_j + \cdots + (Z_{in} - Z_{jn})I_n + (Z_b + Z_{ii} + Z_{jj} - Z_{ij} - Z_{ji})I_k \tag{9.45}$$

Collecting equations similar to Eq. (9.43) and Eq. (9.45), we can write

$$\begin{bmatrix} V_1 \\ V_2 \\ \vdots \\ V_n \\ - \\ 0 \end{bmatrix} = \left[\begin{array}{c|c} & (Z_{1i} - Z_{1j}) \\ & (Z_{2i} - Z_{2j}) \\ Z_{\text{BUS}} & | \\ & (Z_{ni} - Z_{nj}) \\ \hline (Z_{i1} - Z_{j1}) \ldots (Z_{in} - Z_{jn}) & Z_b + Z_{ii} + Z_{jj} - 2Z_{ij} \end{array}\right] \begin{bmatrix} I_1 \\ I_2 \\ \vdots \\ I_n \\ \hline I_j \end{bmatrix} \tag{9.46}$$

Eliminating I_k in Eq. (9.46) on lines similar to what was done in type-2 modification, it follows that

$$Z_{\text{BUS}}(\text{new}) = Z_{\text{BUS}}(\text{old}) - \frac{1}{Z_b + Z_{ii} + Z_{jj} - 2Z_{ij}} \begin{bmatrix} Z_{1i} & - & Z_{1j} \\ & \vdots & \\ Z_{ni} & - & Z_{nj} \end{bmatrix} [Z_{i1} - Z_{j1}] \ldots (Z_{in} - Z_{jn})] \tag{9.47}$$

With the use of four relationships Eqs. (9.36), (9.37), (9.42) and (9.47) bus impedance matrix can be built by a step-by-step procedure (bringing in one branch at a time) as illustrated in Example 9.8. This procedure being a mechanical one can be easily computerised.

When the network undergoes changes, the modification procedures can be employed to revise the bus impedance matrix of the network. The opening of a line (Z_{ij}) is equivalent to adding a branch in parallel to it with impedance $-Z_{ij}$ (see Example 9.8).

Example 9.8 For the three-bus network shown in Fig. 9.28 build Z_{BUS}.

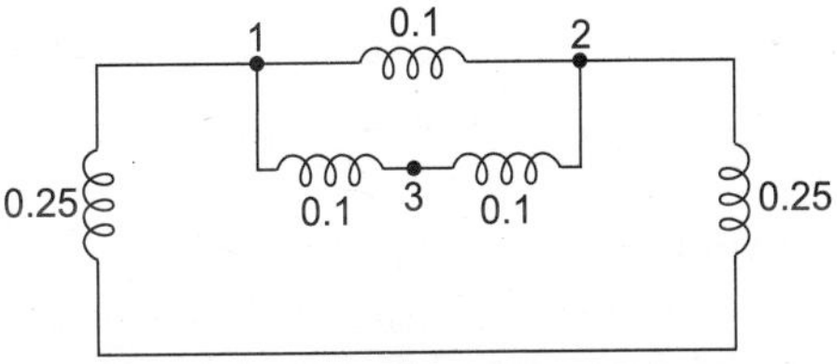

1 0.1 2
0.25 0.1 3 0.1 0.25
Ref bus r

Fig. 9.28

Solution

Step 1 Add branch $z_{1r} = 0.25$ (from bus 1 (new) to bus r)

$$Z_{\text{BUS}} = [0.25] \tag{i}$$

Step 2 Add branch $z_{21} = 0.1$ (from bus 2 (new) to bus 1 (old)); type-2 modification

$$Z_{\text{BUS}} = \begin{matrix} 1 \\ 2 \end{matrix}\begin{bmatrix} 0.25 & 0.25 \\ 0.25 & 0.35 \end{bmatrix} \tag{ii}$$

Step 3 Add branch $z_{13} = 0.1$ (from bus 3 (new) to bus 1 (old)); type-2 modification

$$Z_{\text{BUS}} = \begin{bmatrix} 0.25 & 0.25 & 0.25 \\ 0.25 & 0.35 & 0.25 \\ 0.25 & 0.25 & 0.35 \end{bmatrix} \tag{iii}$$

Step 4 Add branch z_{2r} (from bus 2 (old) to bus r); type-3 modification

$$Z_{\text{BUS}} = \begin{bmatrix} 0.25 & 0.25 & 0.25 \\ 0.25 & 0.35 & 0.25 \\ 0.25 & 0.25 & 0.35 \end{bmatrix} - \frac{1}{0.35 + 0.25}\begin{bmatrix} 0.25 \\ 0.35 \\ 0.25 \end{bmatrix} [0.25\ 0.35\ 0.25]$$

$$= \begin{bmatrix} 0.1458 & 0.1042 & 0.1458 \\ 0.1042 & 0.1458 & 0.1042 \\ 0.1458 & 0.1042 & 0.2458 \end{bmatrix}$$

Step 5 Add branch $z_{23} = 0.1$ (from bus 2 (old) to bus 3 (old)); type-4 modification

$$Z_{\text{BUS}} = \begin{bmatrix} 0.1458 & 0.1042 & 0.1458 \\ 0.1042 & 0.1458 & 0.1042 \\ 0.1458 & 0.1042 & 0.2458 \end{bmatrix} - \frac{1}{0.1 + 0.1458 + 0.2458 - 2 \times 0.1042}$$

$$= \begin{bmatrix} -0.1042 \\ 0.0417 \\ -0.0417 \end{bmatrix} [-0.1042 \quad 0.0417 \quad -0.0417]$$

$$= \begin{bmatrix} 0.1397 & 0.1103 & 0.1250 \\ 0.1103 & 0.1397 & 0.1250 \\ 0.1250 & 0.1250 & 0.1750 \end{bmatrix}$$

Opening a line (line 3-2): This is equivalent to connecting an impedance – 0.1 between bus 3 (old) and bus 2 (old) i.e., type-4 modification.

$$Z_{\text{BUS}} = Z_{\text{BUS}}\,(\text{old}) - \frac{1}{(-0.1) + 0.175 + 0.1397 - 2 \times 0.125} \begin{bmatrix} 0.0147 \\ -0.0147 \\ 0.0500 \end{bmatrix} [0.0147 \; - \; 0.0147 \;\; 0.0500]$$

$$= \begin{bmatrix} 0.1458 & 0.1042 & 0.1458 \\ 0.1042 & 0.1458 & 0.1042 \\ 0.1458 & 0.1042 & 0.2458 \end{bmatrix}; \text{(same as in step 4)}$$

Example 9.9 For the power system shown in Fig. 9.29, the pu reactance is shown therein. For a solid three-phase fault on bus 3, calculate the following

(a) Fault current

(b) V_1^f and V_2^f

(c) I_{12}^f, I_{13}^f and I_{23}^f

(d) I_{G-1}^f, and I_{G2}^f

Assume prefault voltage to be 1 pu.

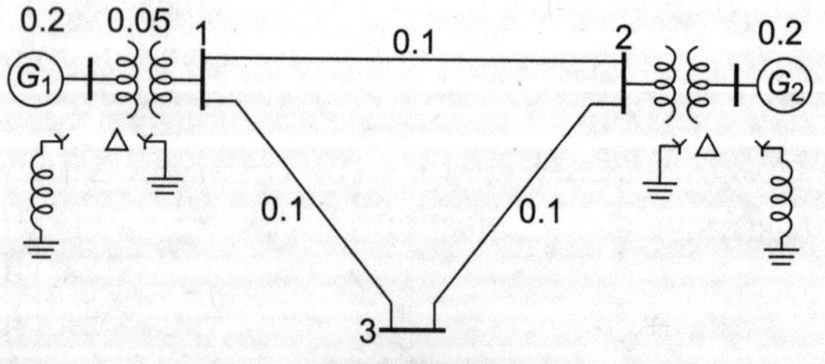

Fig. 9.29

Solution The Thevenin passive network for this system is drawn in Fig. 9.28 with its Z_{BUS} given in Eq. (iv) of Example 9.8.

(a) As per Eq. (9.25),

$$I^f = \frac{V_r^0}{Z_{rr} + Z^f}$$

or
$$I^f = \frac{V_3^0}{Z_{33}} = \frac{1}{j0.175} = -j5.71$$

(b) As per Eq. (9.26),

$$I_i^f = V_i^0 - \frac{Z_{ir}}{Z_{rr} + Z^f} V_r^0$$

Now,
$$V_1^f = \left(1 - \frac{Z_{13}}{Z_{33}}\right) = 1 - \frac{0.125}{0.175}$$

$$= 0.286$$

and
$$V_2^f = \left(1 - \frac{Z_{23}}{Z_{33}}\right) = 0.286$$

The two voltages are equal because of the symmetry of the given power network

(c) From Eq. (9.29),

$$I_{ij}^f = Y_{ij} (V_i^f - V_j^f)$$

$$I_{12}^f = \frac{1}{j0.1}(0.286 - 0.286) = 0$$

and
$$I_{13}^f = I_{31}^f = \frac{1}{j0.1}(0.286 - 0)$$

$$= -j2.86$$

(d) As per Eq. (9.32),

$$I_{G1}^f = \frac{E'_{G1} - V_1^f}{jX'_{iG} + jX_T}$$

But
$$E'_{G1} = 1 \text{ pu (prefault no load)}$$

∴
$$I_{G1}^f = \frac{1 - 0.286}{j0.2 + j0.05} = -j2.86$$

Similarly,

$$I_{G2}^f = j2.86$$

9.8 ▶ SUMMARY

After studying modelling, characteristics and steady-state behaviour of power systems under normal operating conditions, this chapter has discussed abnormal system behaviour under symmetrical three-phase fault. Short circuit of a synchronous machine with and without loading is deliberated. Circuit breaker selection is also dealt with. Finally Z_{BUS} formulation is discussed and algorithm is presented for short circuit studies.

Problems

9.1 A transmission line of inductance 0.1 H and resistance 5 ohms is suddenly short circuited at $t = 0$ at the bar end as shown in Fig. P-9.1. Write the expression for short circuit current $i(t)$. Find approximately the value of the first current maximum (maximum momentary current). [*Hint:* Assume that the first current maximum occurs at the same time as the first current maximum of the symmetrical short circuit current.]

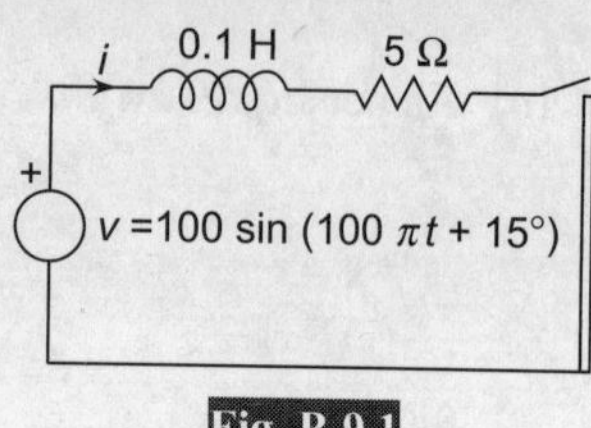

Fig. P-9.1

9.2 (a) What should the instant of short circuit be in Fig. P-9.1 so that the DC off-set current is zero?

(b) What should the instant of short circuit be in Fig. P-9.1 so that the DC off-set current is maximum?

9.3 For the system of Fig. 9.8 (Example 9.2), find the symmetrical currents to be interrupted by circuit breakers A and B for a fault at (i) P and (ii) Q.

9.4 For the system in Fig. P-9.4, the ratings of the various components are

Generator:	25 MVA, 12.4 kV, 10% subtransient reactance
Motor:	20 MVA, 3.8 kV, 15% subtransient reactance
Transformer T_1:	25 MVA, 11/33 kV, 8% reactance
Transformer T_2:	20 MVA, 33/3.3 kV, 10% reactance
Line:	20 ohms reactance

The system is loaded so that the motor is drawing 15 MW at 0.9 leading power factor, the motor terminal voltage being 3.1 kV. Find the subtransient current in generator and motor for a fault at generator bus.

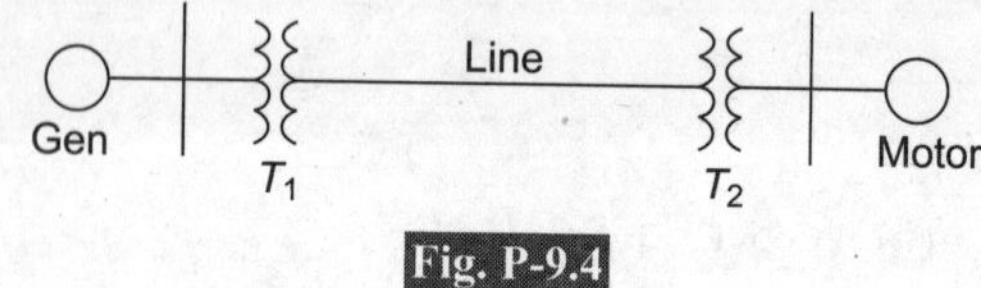

Fig. P-9.4

[*Hint:* Assume a suitable voltage base for the generator. The voltage base for transformers, line and motor would then be given by the transformation ratios. For example, if we choose generator voltage base as 11 kV, the line voltage base is 33 kV and motor voltage base is 3.3 kV. Per unit reactances are calculated accordingly.]

9.5 Two synchronous motors are connected to the bus of a large system through a short transmission line as shown in Fig. P-9.5. The ratings of various components are

Motors (each):	1 MVA, 440 V, 0.1 pu transient reactance
Line:	0.05 ohm reactance
Large system:	Short circuit MVA at its bus at 440 V is 8.

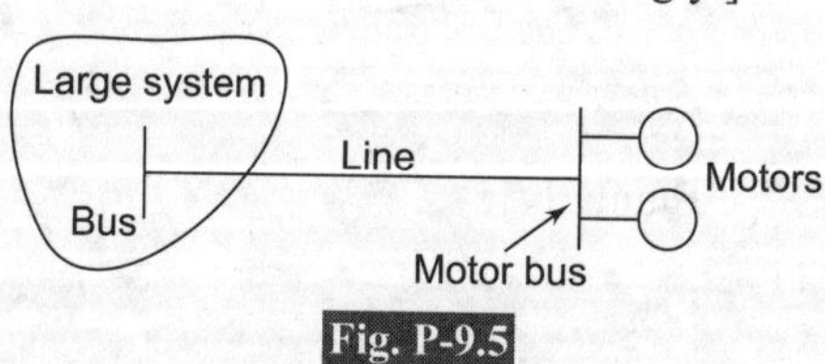

Fig. P-9.5

When the motors are operating at 440 V, calculate the short circuit current (symmetrical) fed into a three-phase fault at motor bus.

9.6 A synchronous generator rated 500 kVA, 440 V, 0.1 pu subtransient reactance is supplying a passive load of 400 kW at 0.8 lagging power factor. Calculate the initial symmetrical rms current for a three-phase fault at generator terminals.

9.7 A generator-transformer unit is connected to a line through a circuit breaker. The unit ratings are

Generator: 10 MVA, 6.6 kV; $X''_d = 0.1$ pu, $X'_d = 0.20$ pu and $X_d = 0.80$ pu

Transformer: 10 MVA, 6.9/33 kV, reactance 0.08 pu

The system is operating no load at a line voltage of 30 kV, when a three-phase fault occurs on the line just beyond the circuit breaker. Find

(a) the initial symmetrical rms current in the breaker,
(b) the maximum possible DC off-set current in the breaker,
(c) the momentary current rating of the breaker,
(d) the current to be interrupted by the breaker and the interrupting kVA, and
(e) the sustained short circuit current in the breaker.

9.8 The system shown in Fig. P-9.8 is delivering 50 MVA at 11 kV, 0.8 lagging power factor into a bus which may be regarded as infinite. Particulars of various system components are

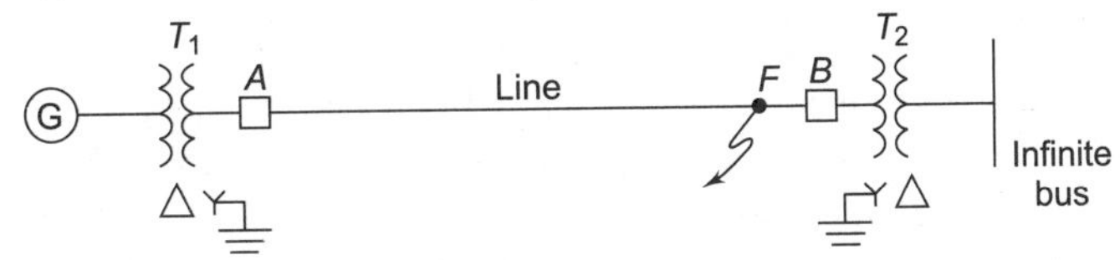

Fig. P-9.8

Generator: 60 MVA, 12 kV, $X'_d = 0.35$ pu

Transformers (each): 80 MVA, 12/66 kV, $X = 0.08$ pu

Line: Reactance 12 ohms, resistance negligible

Calculate the symmetrical current that the circuit breakers *A* and *B* will be called upon to interrupt in the event of a three-phase fault occurring at *F* near the circuit breaker *B*.

9.9 A two-generator station supplies a feeder through a bus as shown in Fig. P-9.9. Additional power is fed to the bus through a transformer from a large system which may be regarded as infinite. A reactor *X* is included between the transformer and the bus to limit the SC rupturing capacity of the feeder circuit breaker *B* to 333 MVA (fault close to breaker). Find the inductive reactance of the reactor required. System data are

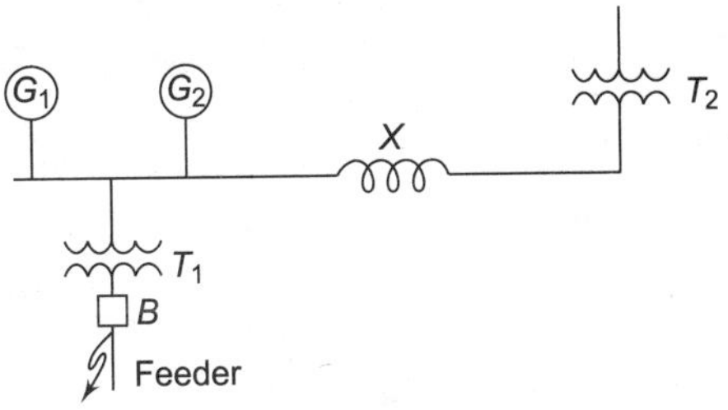

Generator G_1: 25 MVA, 15% reactance

Generator G_2: 50 MVA, 20% reactance

Transformer T_1: 100 MVA; 8% reactance

Transformer T_2: 40 MVA; 10% reactance.

Fig. P-9.9

Assume that all reactances are given on appropriate voltage bases. Choose a base of 100 MVA.

9.10 For the three-phase power network shown in Fig. P-9.10, the ratings of the various components are

Generator G_1: 100 MVA, 0.30 pu reactance

Generator G_2: 60 MVA, 0.18 pu reactance

Transformers (each): 50 MVA, 0.10 pu reactance

Inductive reactor *X*: 0.20 pu on a base of 100 MVA

Lines (each): 80 ohms (reactive); neglect resistance.

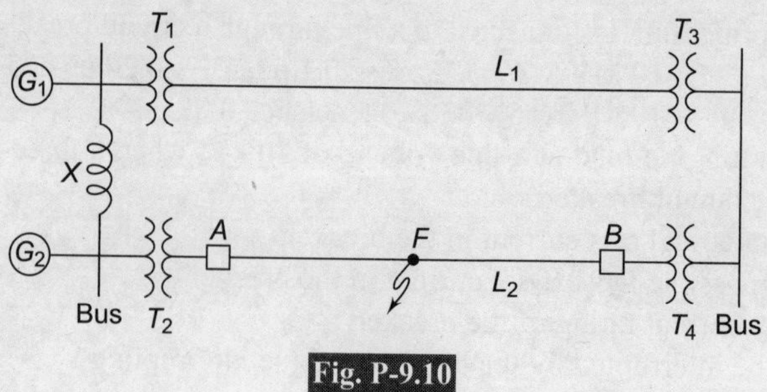

Fig. P-9.10

With the network initially unloaded and a line voltage of 110 kV, a symmetrical short circuit occurs at mid point F of line L_2.

Calculate the short circuit MVA to be interrupted by the circuit breakers A and B at the ends of the line. What would these values be, if the reactor X was eliminated? Comment.

9.11 A synchronous generator feeds bus 1 of a system. A power network feeds bus 2 of the system. Buses 1 and 2 are connected through a transformer and a transmission line. Per unit reactances of the various components are

Generator (connected to bus bar 1):	0.25
Transformer:	0.12
Transmission line:	0.28

The power network can be represented by a generator with a reactance (unknown) in series.

With the generator on no load and with 1.0 pu voltage at each bus under operating condition, a three-phase short circuit occurring on bus 1 causes a current of 5.0 pu to flow into the fault. Determine the equivalent reactance of the power network.

9.12 Consider the three-bus system of Fig. P-9.12. The generators are 100 MVA, with transient reactance 10% each. Both the transformers are 100 MVA with a leakage reactance of 5%. The reactance of each of the lines to a base of 100 MVA, 110 kV is 10%. Obtain the short circuit solution for a three-phase solid short circuit on bus 3.

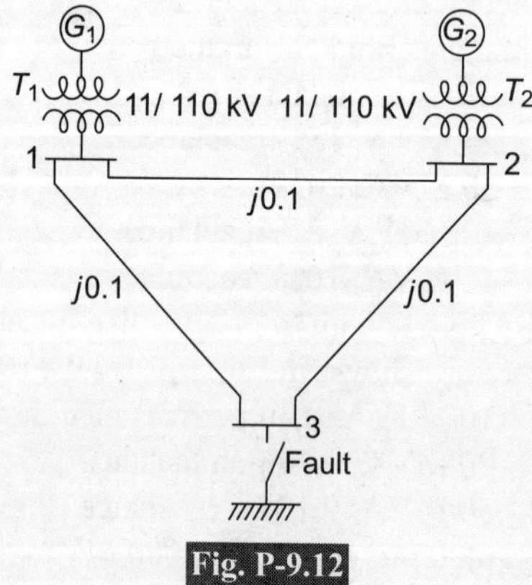

Fig. P-9.12

Assume prefault voltages to be 1 pu and prefault currents to be zero.

9.13 In the system configuration of Fig. P-9.12, the system impedance data are given below:

Transient reactance of each generator = 0.15 pu

Leakage reactance of each transformer = 0.05 pu

$z_{12} = j0.1,\ z_{13} = j0.12,\ z_{23} = j0.08$ pu

For a solid three-phase fault on bus 3, find all bus voltages and short circuit currents in each component.

9.14 For the fault (solid) location shown in Fig. P-9.14. Find the short circuit currents in lines 12 and 13. Prefault system is on no-load with 1 pu voltage and prefault currents are zero. Use Z_{BUS} method and compute its elements by the current injection technique.

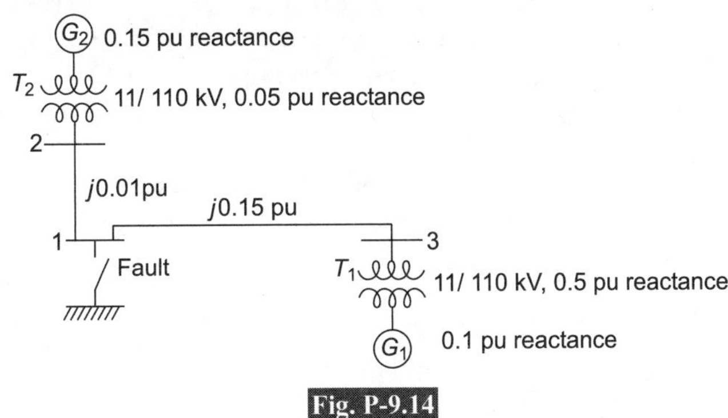

Fig. P-9.14

Multiple Choice Questions

9.1 Transients in electric circuits normally disappear within a time equal to

(a) 4 × time constant (b) 2 × time constant (c) 8 × time constant (d) time constant

9.2 A short circuit occurs in a transmission line (neglect line capacitance) when the voltage wave is going through zero, the maximum possible momentary short circuit current corresponds to

(a) Twice the maximum of symmetrical short circuit current

(b) The maximum of symmetrical short circuit current

(c) Thrice the maximum of symmetrical short circuit current

(d) Four times the maximum of symmetrical short circuit current

9.3 Which one of the following is correct

(a) $X''_d = X'_d = X_d$ (b) $X''_d < X'_d < X_d$ (c) $X''_d = \dfrac{X_d}{2}$ (d) $X''_d = \dfrac{X_d}{2}$

9.4 The pu synchronous reactance X_s (at rated MVA) of a turbo generator comes in the range

(a) 4.00 to 5.00 (b) 0.25 to 0.90 (c) 20 to 30 (d) 1.00 to 2.00

9.5 The three phase SC MVA to be interrupted by a circuit breaker in a power system is given by

(a) $\sqrt{3}$ × post fault line voltage in kV × SC current in kA

(b) 3 × prefault line voltage in kV × SC current in kA

(c) $\sqrt{3}$ × prefault line voltage in kV × SC current in kA

(d) $\dfrac{1}{\sqrt{3}}$ × prefault line voltage in kV × SC current in kA

9.6 Fault level means

(a) Voltage at the point of fault (b) Fault current
(c) Fault power factor (d) Fault MVA

9.7 Fault calculations using computer are usually done by

(a) Y_{bus} Method (b) Z_{bus} Method
(c) None of the above (d) Any of the above

9.8 When a line-to-ground fault occurs, the current in a faulted phase is 100 A. The zero sequence current in this case will be

(a) Zero (b) 33.3 A (b) 66.6 A (d) 100 A

9.9 The rated breaking capacity (MVA) of a circuit breaker is equal to

(a) The product of rate voltage (kV) and rated breaking current (kA)
(b) The product of rated voltage (kV) and rated symmetrical breaking current (kA)
(c) The product of breaking current (kA) and fault voltage (kV)
(d) Twice the value of rated current (kA) and rated voltage (kV)

9.10 The following sequence currents were recorded in a power system under a fault condition

$$I_{\text{positive}} = j\,1.753 \text{ pu}$$

$$I_{\text{negative}} = -j\,0.6 \text{ pu}$$

$$I_{\text{zero}} = -j\,1.153 \text{ pu}$$

The fault is

(a) Line to ground (b) Three phase
(c) Line to line ground (d) Line to line

9.11 The most severe fault in power system is

(a) Single line to ground fault (b) Double line to ground fault
(c) Line to line fault (d) Symmetrical fault

9.12 Which of the following results is related to a symmetrical fault?

(a) Single-phase to earth (b) Phase to phase
(c) All the three phase to earth (d) Two-phase to earth

9.13 The power fed into the system in case of a 3-phase short circuit in a system is

(a) Mostly reactive power (b) Mostly active power
(c) Active and reactive powers (d) Active power only

9.14 The use of high speed circuit breakers

(a) Improves system stability (b) Decreases system stability
(c) Reduces the short circuit current (d) Increases the short circuit current

9.15 A three-phase, 33 kV oil circuit breaker is rated 1200 A, 2000 MVA, 3 secs. The symmetrical breaking current is

(a) 35 kA (b) 45 kA (c) 50 kA (d) 55 kA

9.16 On which among the following factors does the magnitude of the fault current depend?

(a) Total impedance upto the fault.
(b) Voltage at the fault point
(c) Both (a) and (b)
(d) None of these

9.17 Which among the following method is generally used for the calculation of symmetrical faults?

(a) Norton theorem (b) Thevnin's theorem
(c) Kirchhoff's laws (d) Only (b) and (c)

9.18 Which among the following reactances has a greater value in power system?
(a) Sub-transient reactance (b) Synchronous reactance
(c) Transient reactance (d) All of these

9.19 Four identical alternators with ratings of 5 MVA, 11 kV, with 20% reactance are working in parallel. The short circuit level at bus is
(a) 6.25 MVA (b) 20 MVA (c) 25 MVA (d) 100 MVA

9.20 The most serious consequences of a major uncleared short circuit fault can be
(a) Blowing of a fuse (b) Heavy voltage drop
(c) Fire due to high current (d) None of the above

9.21 Possible faults that may occur on a transmission line of a composite power system are
1. 3-phase fault 2. L-L-G fault 3. L-L fault 4. L-G fault
The decreasing order of severity of the fault from the stability point of view is
(a) 1-2-3-4 (b) 2-3-4-1 (c) 3-4-1-2 (d) 4-3-2-1

9.22 In which portion of the transmission system is the occurrence of the fault more common?
(a) Alternators (b) Transmission lines
(c) Transformers (d) Underground cables

9.23 Which portion of the power system is least prone to faults?
(a) Switchgears (b) Transformer
(c) Overhead lines (d) Alternator

9.24 An isolated synchronous generator with transient reactance of 0.1 pu on a 100 MVA base is connected to the high voltage bus through a step up transformer of reactance 0.1 pu on a 100 MVA base. Fault level at the bus is
(a) 1000 MVA (b) 50 MVA (c) 500 MVA (d) 10 MVA

9.25 Circuit breaker usually operates under
(a) Steady state short circuit current
(b) Sub-transient state of short circuit current
(c) Transient state of short circuit current
(d) None of the above

9.26 Which among these is the most commonly occurring fault?
(a) Single line to ground fault.
(b) Double line to ground fault
(c) Line to line fault
(d) Fault due to all the three phases to earth.

9.27 The maximum short circuit current occurs in the case of
(a) Double line to ground fault (b) Line to line fault
(c) Single line to ground fault (d) Three-phase fault

9.28 Which of the following faults results into a three-phase fault?
(a) Single line to ground fault (b) Double line to ground fault
(c) Line to line fault (d) Fault due to all the three phases to earth

9.29 For a fault at the terminals of synchronous generator, the fault current is maximum for
(a) Three-phase fault (b) Three-phase to ground fault
(c) Single line to ground fault (d) Line to line fault

9.30 Fault calculations using computer are usually done by
(a) Y-bus method (b) Z-bus method
(c) both (a) and (b) (d) None of the above

References

Books

1. H.E. Brown, *Solution of Large Network by Matrix Methods*, Wiley, New York, 1975.
2. J.R. Neuenswander, *Modern Power Systems*, International Textbook Company, New York, 1971.
3. G.W. Stagg and A.H. El-Abiad, *Computer Methods in Power Systems Analysis*, McGraw-Hill, New York, 1968.
4. P.M. Anderson, *Analysis of Faulted Power Systems*, Iowa State Press, Ames, Iowa, 1973.
5. E. Clarke, *Circuit Analysis of Alternating Current Power Systems*, volume: 1, Wiley, New York, 1943.
6. W.D. Stevenson Jr, *Elements of Power Systems Analysis*, 4th edn, McGraw-Hill, New York, 1982.
7. J.D. Glover and M.S. Sarma, *Power System Analysis and Design*, 3rd edn, Thomson, Bangalore, 2002.

Paper

8. H.E. Brown, *et al.*, "Digital Calculation of Three-Phase Short Circuits by Matrix Methods", *AIEE Trans.,* volume: 79, issue: 1277, 1960.
9. J.G. Rao and A.K. Pradhan, "Differential Power-Based Symmetrical Fault Detection During Power Swing", *IEEE Transactions on Power Delivery*, volume: 27, issue: 3, pp: 1557–1564, 2012.
10. B. Mahamedi and J.G. Zhu, "A Novel Approach to Detect Symmetrical Faults Occurring During Power Swings by Using Frequency Components of Instantaneous Three-Phase Active Power", *IEEE Transactions on Power Delivery*, volume: 27, issue: 3, pp: 1368–1376, 2012.
11. S. Lotfifard, J. Faiz, and M. Kezunovic, "Detection of Symmetrical Faults by Distance Relays During Power Swings", *IEEE Transactions on Power Delivery*, volume: 25, issue: 1, pp: 81–87, 2010.
12. M. Cuevas, R. Romary, J. Lecointe, F. Morganti, and T. Jacq, "Noninvasive Detection of Winding Short-Circuit Faults in Salient Pole Synchronous Machine with Squirrel-Cage Damper", *IEEE Transactions on Industry Applications*, volume: 54, issue: 6, pp: 5988–5997, 2018.
13. "IEEE Recommended Practice for Conducting Short-Circuit Studies and Analysis of Industrial and Commercial Power Systems", *IEEE Standard 3002.3-2018*, volume: pp: 1–184, 2019.
14. F. Immovilli, C. Bianchini, E. Lorenzani, A. Bellini, and E. Fornasiero, "Evaluation of Combined Reference Frame Transformation for Interturn Fault Detection in Permanent-Magnet Multiphase Machines", *IEEE Transactions on Industrial Electronics*, volume: 62, issue: 3, pp: 1912–1920, 2015.
15. G. Choi and T.M. Jahns, "Investigation of Key Factors Influencing the Response of Permanent Magnet Synchronous Machines to Three-Phase Symmetrical Short-Circuit Faults", *IEEE Transactions on Energy Conversion*, volume: 31, issue: 4, pp: 1488–1497, 2016.
16. C. Pang and M. Kezunovic, "Fast Distance Relay Scheme for Detecting Symmetrical Fault During Power Swing", *IEEE Transactions on Power Delivery*, volume: 25, issue: 4, pp: 2205–2212, 2010.
17. X. Lin, Y. Gao, and P. Liu, "A Novel Scheme to Identify Symmetrical Faults Occurring During Power Swings", *IEEE Transactions on Power Delivery*, volume: 23, issue: 1, pp: 73–78, 2008.
18. Y. Qi, E. Bostanci, V. Gurusamy, and B. Akin, "A Comprehensive Analysis of Short-Circuit Current Behavior in PMSM Interturn Short-Circuit Faults", *IEEE Transactions on Power Electronics*, volume: 33, issue: 12, pp: 10784–10793, 2018.
19. H. Wu, L. Yuan, L. Sun, and X. Li, "Modeling of Current-Limiting Circuit Breakers for the Calculation of Short-Circuit Current", *IEEE Transactions on Power Delivery*, volume: 30, issue: 2, pp: 652–656, 2015.

20. "IEEE Recommended Practice for the Selection, Field Testing, and Life Expectancy of Molded-Case Circuit Breakers for Industrial Applications", *IEEE Standard 1458-2017 (Revision of IEEE Standard 1458-2005)*, pp: 1–89, 2018.
21. C. Jäger, I. Grinbaum, and J. Smajic, "Dynamic Short-Circuit Analysis of Synchronous Machines", *IEEE Transactions on Magnetics*, volume: 53, issue: 6, pp: 1–4, 2017.
22. D. Dufournet and G. Montillet, "Three-Phase Short Circuit Testing of High-Voltage Circuit Breakers Using Synthetic Circuits", *IEEE Transactions on Power Delivery*, volume: 15, issue: 1, pp: 142–147, 2000.
23. Y. Zhang, G. Liu, W. Zhao, H. Zhou, Q. Chen and M. Wei, "Online Diagnosis of Slight Interturn Short-Circuit Fault for a Low-Speed Permanent Magnet Synchronous Motor," *IEEE Transactions on Transportation Electrification*, volume: 7, issue: 1, pp: 104–113, March 2021.

CHAPTER

10 Symmetrical Components

10.1 ▶ INTRODUCTION

In our work so far, we have considered both normal and abnormal (short circuit) operations of power system under completely balanced (symmetrical) conditions. Under such operation, the system impedances in each phase are identical and the three-phase voltages and currents throughout the system are completely balanced, i.e., they have equal magnitudes in each phase and are progressively displaced in time phase by 120° (phase *a* leads/lags phase *b* by 120° and phase *b* leads/lags phase *c* by 120°). In a balanced system, analysis can proceed on a single-phase basis. The knowledge of voltage and current in one phase is sufficient to completely determine voltages and currents in the other two phases. Real and reactive powers are simply three times the corresponding per phase values.

Unbalanced system operation can result in an otherwise balanced system due to unsymmetrical fault, e.g., line-to-ground fault or line-to-line fault. These faults are, in fact, of more common occurrence* than the symmetrical (three-phase) fault. System operation may also become unbalanced when loads are unbalanced as in the presence of large single-phase loads. Analysis under unbalanced conditions has to be carried out on a three-phase basis. Alternatively, a more convenient method of analysing unbalanced operation is through symmetrical components where the three-phase voltages (and currents) which may be unbalanced are transformed into three sets of balanced voltages (and currents) called symmetrical components. Fortunately, in such a transformation the impedances presented by various power system elements (synchronous generators, transformers, lines) to symmetrical components are decoupled from each other resulting in independent system networks for each component (balanced set). This is the basic reason for the simplicity of the symmetrical component method of analysis.

10.2 ▶ SYMMETRICAL COMPONENT TRANSFORMATION

A set of three balanced voltages (phasors) V_a, V_b, V_c is characterised by equal magnitudes and interphase differences of 120°. The set is said to have a phase sequence *abc* (*positive sequence*) if, V_b lags V_a by 120° and V_c lags V_b by 120°. The three phasors can then be expressed in terms of the reference phasor V_a as

$$V_a = V_a,\ V_b = \alpha^2 V_a,\ V_c = \alpha V_a$$

where the complex number operator α is defined as

$$\alpha = e^{j120°}$$

---

* Typical relative frequencies of occurrence of different kinds of faults in a power system (in order of decreasing severity) are

Three-phase (3L) faults	5%
Double line-to-ground (LLG) faults	10%
Double line (LL) faults	15%
Single line-to-ground (LG) faults	70%

It has the following properties:

$$\left.\begin{array}{ll} \alpha^2 = e^{j240°} = e^{-j120°} & = \alpha^* \\ (\alpha^2)^* & = \alpha \\ \alpha^3 & = 1 \\ 1 + \alpha + \alpha^2 & = 0 \end{array}\right\} \quad (10.1)$$

If the phase sequence is *acb* (*negative sequence*), then

$$V_a = V_a,\ V_b = \alpha V_a,\ V_c = \alpha^2 V_a$$

Thus, a set of balanced phasors is fully characterised by its reference phasor (say V_a) and its phase sequence (positive or negative).

Suffix 1 is commonly used to indicate positive sequence. A set of (balanced) positive sequence phasors is written as

$$V_{a1},\ V_{b1} = \alpha^2 V_{a1},\ V_{c1} = \alpha V_{a1} \quad (10.2)$$

Similarly, suffix 2 is used to indicate negative sequence. A set of (balanced) negative sequence phasors is written as

$$V_{a2},\ V_{b2} = \alpha V_{a2},\ V_{c2} = \alpha^2 V_{a2} \quad (10.3)$$

A set of three voltages (phasors) equal in magnitude and having the same phase is said to have zero sequence. Thus, a set of *zero sequence* phasors is written as

$$V_{a0},\ V_{b0} = V_{a0},\ V_{c0} = V_{a0} \quad (10.4)$$

Consider now a set of three voltages (phasors) V_a, V_b, V_c which in general may be unbalanced. According to Fortesque's theorem* the three phasors can be expressed as the sum of positive, negative and zero sequence phasors defined above. Thus,

$$V_a = V_{a1} + V_{a2} + V_{a0} \quad (10.5)$$

$$V_b = V_{b1} + V_{b2} + V_{b0} \quad (10.6)$$

$$V_c = V_{c1} + V_{c2} + V_{c0} \quad (10.7)$$

The three phasor sequences (positive, negative and zero) are called the *symmetrical components* of the original phasor set V_a, V_b, V_c. The addition of symmetrical components as per Eqs. (10.5) to (10.7) to generate V_a, V_b, V_c is indicated by the phasor diagram of Fig. 10.1.

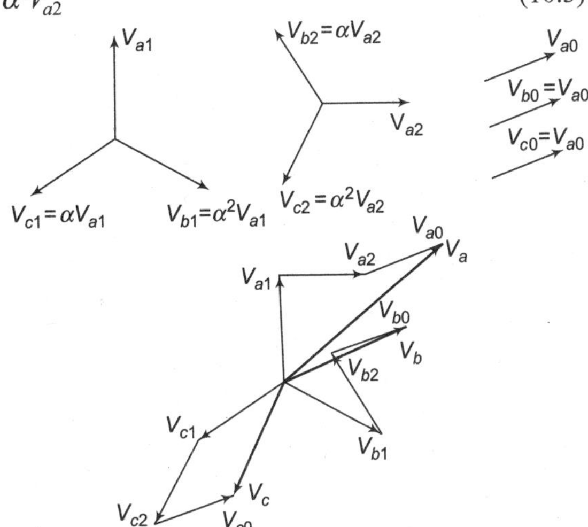

Fig. 10.1 *Graphical addition of the symmetrical components to obtain the set of phasors V_a, V_b, V_c (unbalanced in general)*

Let us now express Eqs. (10.5) to (10.7) in terms of reference phasors V_{a1}, V_{a2} and V_{a0}. Thus,

$$V_a = V_{a1} + V_{a2} + V_{a0} \quad (10.8)$$

$$V_b = \alpha^2 V_{a1} + \alpha V_{a2} + V_{a0} \quad (10.9)$$

$$V_c = \alpha V_{a1} + \alpha^2 V_{a2} + V_{a0} \quad (10.10)$$

These equations can be expressed in the matrix form

$$\begin{bmatrix} V_a \\ V_b \\ V_c \end{bmatrix} = \begin{bmatrix} 1 & 1 & 1 \\ \alpha^2 & \alpha & 1 \\ \alpha & \alpha^2 & 1 \end{bmatrix} \begin{bmatrix} V_{a1} \\ V_{a2} \\ V_{a0} \end{bmatrix} \quad (10.11)$$

* The theorem is a general one and applies to the case of *n* phasors [7].

or

$$\boldsymbol{V_p} = \boldsymbol{A V_s} \tag{10.12}$$

where

$$\boldsymbol{V_p} = \begin{bmatrix} V_a \\ V_b \\ V_c \end{bmatrix} = \text{vector of original phasors}$$

$$\boldsymbol{V_s} = \begin{bmatrix} V_{a1} \\ V_{a2} \\ V_{a0} \end{bmatrix} = \text{vector of symmetrical components}$$

$$\boldsymbol{A} = \begin{bmatrix} 1 & 1 & 1 \\ \alpha^2 & \alpha & 1 \\ \alpha & \alpha^2 & 1 \end{bmatrix} \tag{10.13}$$

We can write Eq. (10.12) as

$$\boldsymbol{V_s} = \boldsymbol{A}^{-1}\boldsymbol{V_p} \tag{10.14}$$

Computing $\boldsymbol{A}^{-1}$ and utilising relations (10.1), we get

$$\boldsymbol{A}^{-1} = \frac{1}{3}\begin{bmatrix} 1 & \alpha & \alpha^2 \\ 1 & \alpha^2 & \alpha \\ 1 & 1 & 1 \end{bmatrix} \tag{10.15}$$

In expanded form, we can write Eq. (10.14) as

$$V_{a1} = \frac{1}{3}\,(V_a + \alpha V_b + \alpha^2 V_c) \tag{10.16}$$

$$V_{a2} = \frac{1}{3}\,(V_a + \alpha^2 V_b + \alpha V_c) \tag{10.17}$$

$$V_{a0} = \frac{1}{3}\,(V_a + V_b + V_c) \tag{10.18}$$

Equations (10.16) to (10.18) give the necessary relationships for obtaining symmetrical components of the original phasors, while Eqs. (10.5) to (10.7) give the relationships for obtaining original phasors from the symmetrical components.

The symmetrical component transformations though given above in terms of voltages hold for any set of phasors and therefore automatically apply for a set of currents. Thus,

$$\boldsymbol{I_p} = \boldsymbol{A I_s} \tag{10.19}$$

and

$$\boldsymbol{I_s} = \boldsymbol{A}^{-1}\boldsymbol{I_p} \tag{10.20}$$

where

$$\boldsymbol{I_p} = \begin{bmatrix} I_a \\ I_b \\ I_c \end{bmatrix} \text{ and } \boldsymbol{I_s} = \begin{bmatrix} I_{a1} \\ I_{a2} \\ I_{a0} \end{bmatrix}$$

Of course $\boldsymbol{A}$ and $\boldsymbol{A}^{-1}$ are the same as given earlier.

In expanded form, the relations (10.19) and (10.20) can be expressed as follows:

(i) Construction of current phasors from their symmetrical components:

$$I_a = I_{a1} + I_{a2} + I_{a0} \tag{10.21}$$

$$I_b = \alpha^2 I_{a1} + \alpha I_{a2} + I_{a0} \tag{10.22}$$

$$I_c = \alpha I_{a1} + \alpha^2 I_{a2} + I_{a0} \tag{10.23}$$

(ii) Obtaining symmetrical components of current phasors:

$$I_{a1} = \frac{1}{3}\,(I_a + \alpha I_b + \alpha^2 I_c) \tag{10.24}$$

$$I_{a2} = \frac{1}{3}\,(I_a + \alpha^2 I_b + \alpha I_c) \tag{10.25}$$

$$I_{a0} = \frac{1}{3}\,(I_a + I_b + I_c) \tag{10.26}$$

Certain observations can now be made regarding a three-phase system with neutral return as shown in Fig. 10.2.

The sum of the three line voltages will always be zero. Therefore, the zero sequence component of line voltages is always zero, i.e.,

$$V_{ab0} = \frac{1}{3}\,(V_{ab} + V_{bc} + V_{ca}) = 0 \tag{10.27}$$

On the other hand, the sum of phase voltages (line to neutral) may not be zero so that their zero sequence component V_{a0} may exist.

Since the sum of the three line currents equals the current in the neutral wire, we have

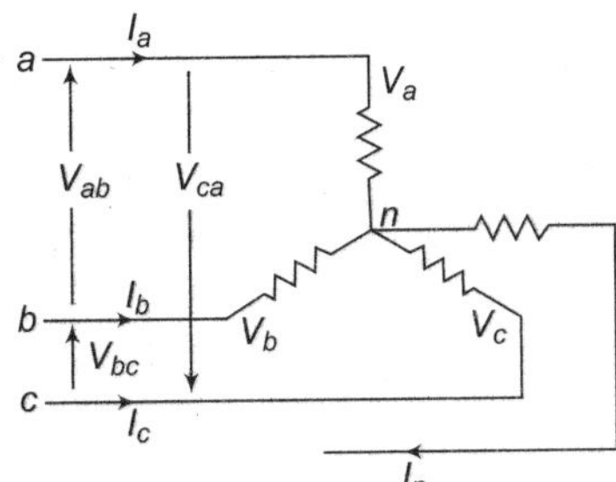

Fig. 10.2 *Three-phase system with neutral return*

$$I_{a0} = \frac{1}{3}\,(I_a + I_b + I_c) = \frac{1}{3}\,I_n \tag{10.28}$$

i.e., the current in the neutral is three times the zero sequence line current. If the neutral connection is severed,

$$I_{a0} = \frac{1}{3}\,I_n = 0 \tag{10.29}$$

i.e., in the absence of a neutral connection the zero sequence line current is always zero.

10.2.1 Power Invariance

We shall now show that the symmetrical component transformation is power invariant, which means that the sum of powers of the three symmetrical components equals the three-phase power.

Total complex power in a three-phase circuit is given by

$$\boldsymbol{S} = \boldsymbol{V}_p^T \boldsymbol{I}_p^* = V_a I_a^* + V_b I_b^* + V_c I_c^* \tag{10.30}$$

or

$$\boldsymbol{S} = [\boldsymbol{A}\boldsymbol{V}_s]^T [\boldsymbol{A}\boldsymbol{I}_s]^*$$

$$= \boldsymbol{V}_s^T \boldsymbol{A}^T \boldsymbol{A}^* \boldsymbol{I}_s^* \tag{10.31}$$

Now,

$$\boldsymbol{A}^T\boldsymbol{A}^* = \begin{bmatrix} 1 & \alpha^2 & \alpha \\ 1 & \alpha & \alpha^2 \\ 1 & 1 & 1 \end{bmatrix} \begin{bmatrix} 1 & 1 & 1 \\ \alpha & \alpha^2 & 1 \\ \alpha^2 & \alpha & 1 \end{bmatrix} = 3 \begin{bmatrix} 1 & 0 & 0 \\ 0 & 1 & 0 \\ 0 & 0 & 1 \end{bmatrix} = 3U \tag{10.32}$$

$$\therefore \quad \boldsymbol{S} = 3\boldsymbol{V}_s^T\boldsymbol{U}\boldsymbol{I}_s^* = 3\boldsymbol{V}_s^T\boldsymbol{I}_s^*$$
$$= 3V_{a1}I^*_{a1} + 3V_{a2}I^*_{a2} + 3V_{a0}I^*_{a0} \qquad (10.33)$$
$$= \text{sum of symmetrical component powers}$$

Example 10.1 A delta connected balanced resistive load is connected across an unbalanced three-phase supply as shown in Fig. 10.3. With currents in lines A and B specified, find the symmetrical components of line currents. Also find the symmetrical components of delta currents. Do you notice any relationship between symmetrical components of line and delta currents? Comment.

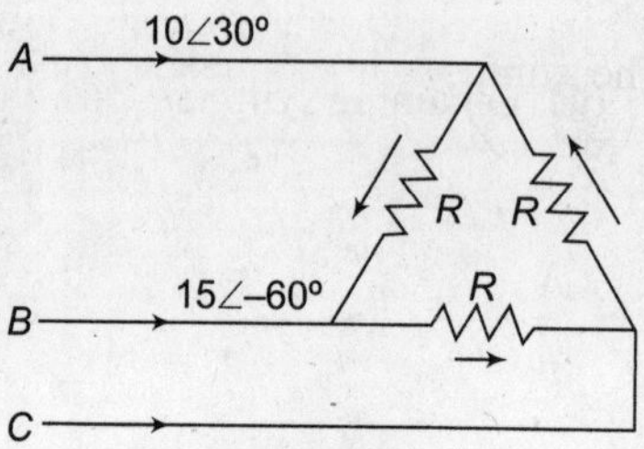

Fig. 10.3

Solution

$$I_A + I_B + I_C = 0$$

or

$$10\angle 30° + 15\angle -60° + I_C = 0$$

$$\therefore \quad I_C = -16.2 + j8.0 = 18\angle 154° \text{ A}$$

From Eqs. (10.24) to (10.26),

$$I_{A1} = \frac{1}{3}(10\angle 30° + 15\angle(-60° + 120°) + 18\angle(154° + 240°))$$
$$= 10.35 + j9.3 = 14\angle 42° \text{ A} \qquad \text{(i)}$$

$$I_{A2} = \frac{1}{3}(10\angle 30° + 15\angle(-60° + 240°) + 18\angle(154° + 120°))$$
$$= -1.7 - j4.3 = 4.65\angle 248° \text{ A} \qquad \text{(ii)}$$

$$I_{A0} = \frac{1}{3}(I_A + I_B + I_C) = 0 \qquad \text{(iii)}$$

From Eq. (10.2),

$$I_{B1} = 14\angle 282° \text{ A} \qquad I_{C1} = 14\angle 162° \text{ A}$$
$$I_{B2} = 4.65\angle 8° \text{ A} \qquad I_{C2} = 4.65\angle 128° \text{ A}$$
$$I_{B0} = 0 \text{ A} \qquad I_{C0} = 0 \text{ A}$$

Check:

$$I_A = I_{A1} + I_{A2} + I_{A0} = 8.65 + j5 = 10\angle 30°$$

Converting delta load into equivalent star, we can redraw Fig. 10.3 as in Fig. 10.4. Delta currents are obtained as follows:

$$V_{AB} = \frac{1}{3}(I_A - I_B)$$

Now,

$$I_{AB} = V_{AB}/R = \frac{1}{3}(I_A - I_B)$$

Similarly,

$$I_{BC} = \frac{1}{3}(I_B - I_C)$$

$$I_{CA} = \frac{1}{3}(I_C - I_A)$$

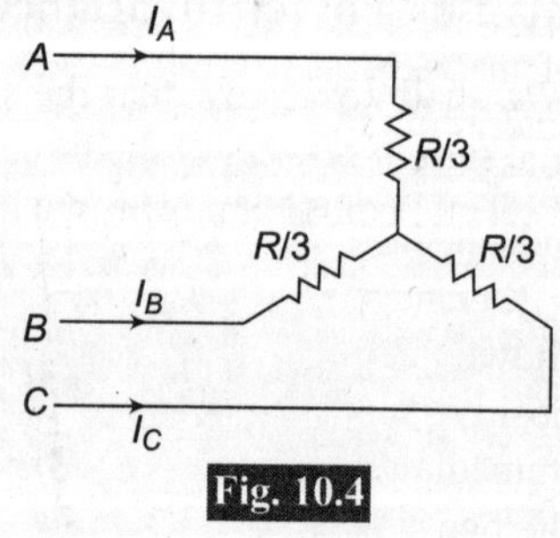

Fig. 10.4

Substituting the values of I_A, I_B and I_C, we have

$$I_{AB} = \frac{1}{3}(10\angle 30° - 15\angle -60°) = 6\angle 86° \text{ A}$$

$$I_{BC} = \frac{1}{3}(15\angle-60^\circ - 18\angle154^\circ) = 10.5\angle-41.5^\circ \text{ A}$$

$$I_{CA} = \frac{1}{3}(18\angle154^\circ - 10\angle30^\circ) = 8.3\angle173^\circ \text{ A}$$

The symmetrical components of delta currents are

$$I_{AB1} = \frac{1}{3}(6\angle86^\circ + 10.5\angle(-41.5^\circ + 120^\circ) + 8.3\angle(173^\circ + 240^\circ)) \quad \text{(iv)}$$

$$= 8\angle72^\circ \text{ A}$$

$$I_{AB2} = \frac{1}{3}(6\angle86^\circ + 10.5\angle(-41.5^\circ + 240^\circ) + 8.3\angle(173^\circ + 120^\circ)) \quad \text{(v)}$$

$$= 2.7\angle218^\circ \text{ A}$$

$$I_{AB0} = 0 \quad \text{(vi)}$$

$I_{BC1}, I_{BC2}, I_{BC0}, I_{CA1}, I_{CA2}$ and I_{CA0} can be found by using Eq. (10.2).

Comparing Eqs. (i) and (iv), and (ii) and (v), the following relationship between symmetrical components of line and delta currents are immediately observed:

$$I_{AB1} = \frac{I_{A1}}{\sqrt{3}}\angle30^\circ \quad \text{(vii)}$$

$$I_{AB2} = \frac{I_{A2}}{\sqrt{3}}\angle-30^\circ \quad \text{(viii)}$$

The reader should verify these by calculating I_{AB1} and I_{AB2} from Eqs. (vii) and (viii) and comparing the results with Eqs. (iv) and (v).

10.3 ▶ PHASE SHIFT IN STAR-DELTA TRANSFORMERS

Positive and negative sequence voltages and currents undergo a phase shift in passing through a star-delta transformer which depends upon the labelling of terminals. Before considering this phase shift, we need to discuss the standard polarity marking of a single-phase transformer as shown in Fig. 10.5. The transformer ends marked with a dot have the same polarity. Therefore, voltage V'_{HH} is in phase with voltage V'_{LL}. Assuming that the small amount of magnetising current can be neglected, the primary current I_1, entering the dotted end cancels the demagnetising ampere-turns of the secondary current I_2 so that I_1 and I_2 with directions of flow as indicated in the diagram are in phase. If the direction of I_2 is reversed, I_1 and I_2 will be in phase opposition.

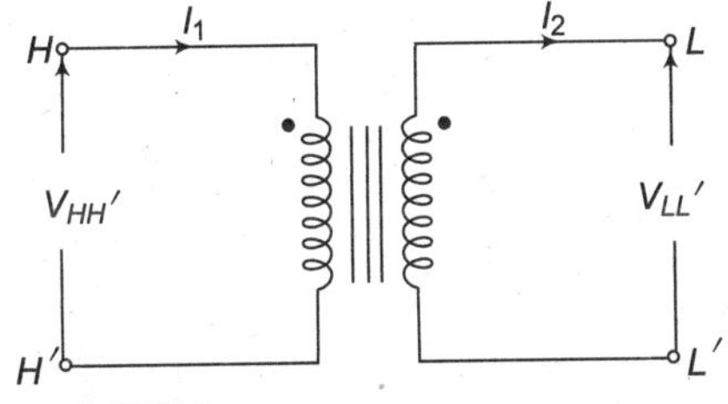

Fig. 10.5 *Polarity marking of a single-phase transformer*

Consider now a star/delta transformer with terminal labelling as indicated in Fig. 10.6(a). Windings shown parallel to each other are magnetically coupled. Assume that the transformer is excited with positive sequence voltages and carries positive sequence currents. With the polarity marks shown, we can immediately draw the phasor diagram of Fig. 10.7. The following interrelationship between the voltages on the two sides of the transformer is immediately observed from the phasor diagram:

$$V_{AB1} = x\, V_{ab1}\angle30^\circ,\ x = \text{phase transformation ratio} \quad (10.34)$$

As per Eq. (10.34), the positive sequence line voltages on star side lead the corresponding voltages on the delta side by 30° (The same result would apply to line-to-neutral voltages on the two sides). The same also applies for line currents.

(a) Star side quantities lead delta side quantities by 30°

(b) Delta side quantities lead star side quantities by 30°

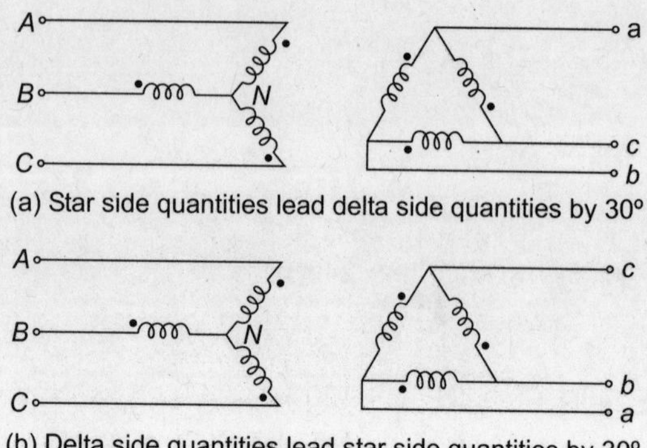

Fig. 10.6 *Labelling of the star/delta transformer*

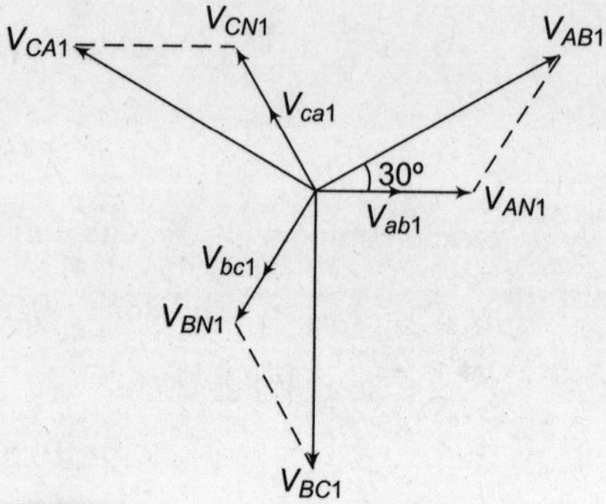

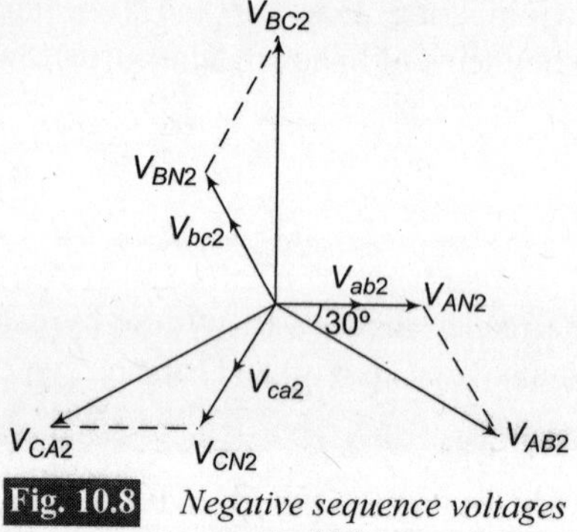

Fig. 10.7 *Positive sequence voltages on a star/delta transformer*

If the delta side is connected as in Fig. 10.6(b), the phase shift reverses (the reader should draw the phasor diagram); the delta side quantities lead the star side quantities by 30°.

Instead, if the transformer of Fig. 10.6(a) is now excited by negative sequence voltages and currents, the voltage phasor diagram will be as in Fig. 10.8. The phase shift in comparison to the positive sequence case now reverses, i.e., the star side quantities lag the delta side quantities by 30°. The result for Fig. 10.6(b) also correspondingly reverses.

It shall from now onwards be assumed that a star/delta transformer is so labelled that the positive sequence quantities on the HV side lead their corresponding positive sequence quantities on the LV side by 30°. The reverse is the case for negative sequence quantities wherein HV quantities lag the corresponding LV quantities by 30°.

Fig. 10.8 *Negative sequence voltages on a star/delta transformer*

10.4 ▶ SEQUENCE IMPEDANCES OF TRANSMISSION LINES

Figure 10.9 shows the circuit of a fully transposed line carrying unbalanced currents. The return path for I_n is sufficiently away for the mutual effect to be ignored. Let

X_s = self reactance of each line

X_m = mutual reactance of any line pair

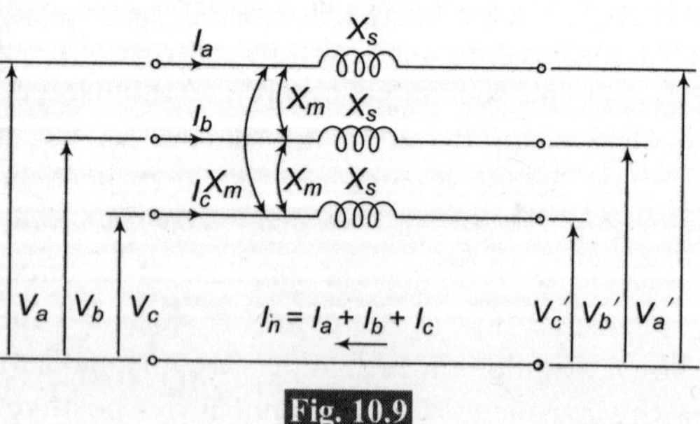

The following KVL equations can be written down from Fig. 10.9.

$$
\begin{aligned}
V_a - V_a' &= jX_sI_a + jX_mI_b + jX_mI_c \\
V_b - V_b' &= jX_mI_a + jX_sI_b + jX_mI_c \\
V_c - V_c' &= jX_mI_a + jX_mI_b + jX_sI_c
\end{aligned}
\tag{10.35}
$$

Fig. 10.9

or in matrix form,

$$
\begin{bmatrix} V_a \\ V_b \\ V_c \end{bmatrix} - \begin{bmatrix} V_a' \\ V_b' \\ V_c' \end{bmatrix} = j \begin{bmatrix} X_s X_m X_m \\ X_m X_s X_m \\ X_m X_m X_s \end{bmatrix} \begin{bmatrix} I_a \\ I_b \\ I_c \end{bmatrix}
\tag{10.36}
$$

or $$V_p - V_p' = ZI_p \tag{10.37}$$
or $$A\,(V_s - V_s') = ZAI_s \tag{10.38}$$
or $$V_s - V_s' = A^{-1}ZAI_s \tag{10.39}$$
Now,

$$A^{-1}ZA = \frac{1}{3}\begin{bmatrix} 1 & \alpha & \alpha^2 \\ 1 & \alpha^2 & \alpha \\ 1 & 1 & 1 \end{bmatrix}\begin{bmatrix} jX_s & jX_m & jX_m \\ jX_m & jX_s & jX_m \\ jX_m & jX_m & jX_s \end{bmatrix}\begin{bmatrix} 1 & 1 & 1 \\ \alpha^2 & \alpha & 1 \\ \alpha & \alpha^2 & 1 \end{bmatrix} \tag{10.40}$$

$$= j\begin{bmatrix} X_s - X_m & 0 & 0 \\ 0 & X_s - X_m & 0 \\ 0 & 0 & X_s + 2X_m \end{bmatrix}$$

Thus, Eq. (10.37) can be written as

$$\begin{bmatrix} V_1 \\ V_2 \\ V_0 \end{bmatrix} - \begin{bmatrix} V_1' \\ V_2' \\ V_0' \end{bmatrix} = j\begin{bmatrix} X_s - X_m & 0 & 0 \\ 0 & X_s - X_m & 0 \\ 0 & 0 & X_s + 2X_m \end{bmatrix}\begin{bmatrix} I_1 \\ I_2 \\ I_0 \end{bmatrix} \tag{10.41}$$

$$= \begin{bmatrix} Z_1 & 0 & 0 \\ 0 & Z_2 & 0 \\ 0 & 0 & Z_0 \end{bmatrix}\begin{bmatrix} I_1 \\ I_2 \\ I_0 \end{bmatrix} \tag{10.42}$$

wherein

$$Z_1 = j(X_s - X_m) = \textit{positive sequence impedance} \tag{10.43}$$
$$Z_2 = j(X_s - X_m) = \textit{negative sequence impedance} \tag{10.44}$$
$$Z_0 = j(X_s + 2X_m) = \textit{zero sequence impedance} \tag{10.45}$$

We conclude that a fully transposed transmission has

1. equal positive and negative sequence impedances.
2. zero sequence impedance much larger than the positive (or negative) sequence impedance (it is approximately 2.5 times).

It is further observed that the sequence circuit equations (10.42) are in *decoupled* form, i.e., there are no mutual sequence inductances. Equation (10.42) can be represented in network form as in Fig. 10.10.

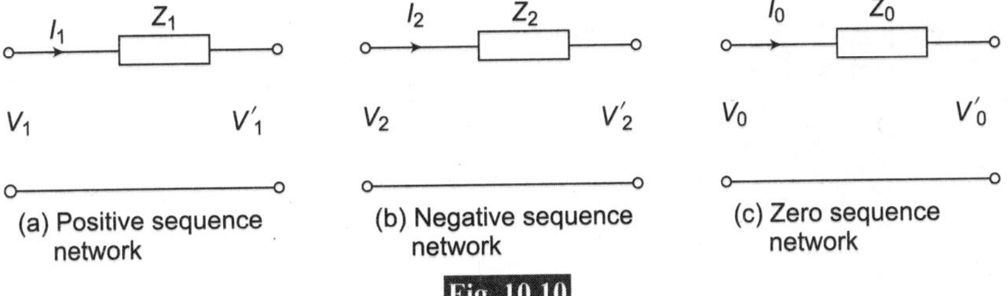

(a) Positive sequence network (b) Negative sequence network (c) Zero sequence network

Fig. 10.10

The decoupling between sequence networks of a fully transposed transmission holds also in three-phase synchronous machines and three-phase transformers. This fact leads to considerable simplifications in the use of symmetrical components method in unsymmetrical fault analysis.

In case of three static unbalanced impedances, coupling appears between sequence networks and the method is no more helpful than a straight forward three-phase analysis.

10.5 ▶ SEQUENCE IMPEDANCES AND SEQUENCE NETWORK OF POWER SYSTEM

Power system elements—transmission lines, transformers and synchronous machines—have a three-phase symmetry because of which when currents of a particular sequence are passed through these elements, voltage drops of the same sequence appear, i.e., the elements possess only self-impedances to sequence currents. Each element can therefore be represented by three decoupled *sequence networks* (on single-phase basis) pertaining to positive, negative and zero sequences, respectively. EMFs are involved only in a positive sequence network of synchronous machines. For finding a particular sequence impedance, the element in question is subjected to currents and voltages of that sequence only. With the element operating under these conditions, the sequence impedance can be determined analytically or through experimental test results.

With the knowledge of sequence networks of elements, complete positive, negative and zero sequence networks of any power system can be assembled. As will be explained in the next chapter, these networks are suitably interconnected to simulate different unsymmetrical faults. The sequence currents and voltages during the fault are then calculated from which actual fault currents and voltages can be found.

10.6 ▶ SEQUENCE IMPEDANCES AND NETWORKS OF SYNCHRONOUS MACHINE

Figure 10.11 depicts an unloaded synchronous machine (generator or motor) grounded through a reactor (impedance Z_n). E_a, E_b and E_c are the induced emfs of the three phases. When a fault (not shown in the figure) takes place at machine terminals, currents I_a, I_b and I_c flow in the lines. Whenever the fault involves ground, current $I_n = I_a + I_b + I_c$ flows to neutral from ground via Z_n. Unbalanced line currents can be resolved into their symmetrical components I_{a1}, I_{a2} and I_{a0}. Before we can proceed with fault analysis (Ch. 11), we must know the equivalent circuits presented by the machine to the flow of positive, negative and zero sequence currents, respectively. Because of winding symmetry currents of a particular sequence produce voltage drops of that sequence only. Therefore, there is no coupling between the equivalent circuits of various sequences*.

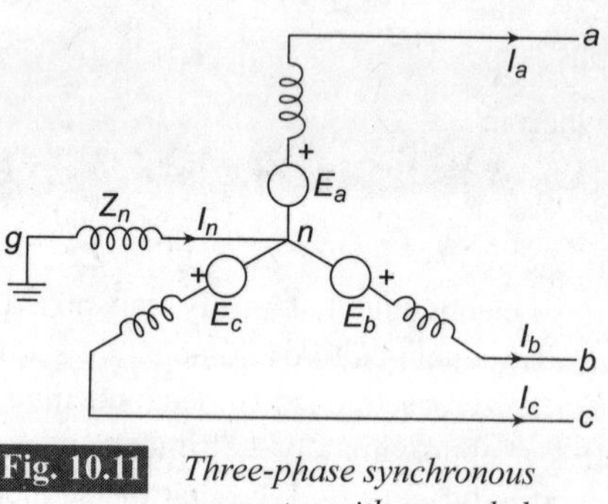

Fig. 10.11 *Three-phase synchronous generator with grounded neutral*

10.6.1 Positive Sequence Impedance and Network

Since a synchronous machine is designed with symmetrical windings, it induces emfs of positive sequence only, i.e., no negative or zero sequence voltages are induced in it. When the machine carries positive sequence currents only, this mode of operation is the balanced mode discussed at length in Ch. 9. The armature reaction field caused by positive sequence currents rotates at synchronous speed in the same direction as the rotor, i.e., it is stationary with respect to field excitation. The machine equivalently offers a direct axis reactance whose value reduces from subtransient reactance (X''_d) to transient reactance (X'_d) and finally to steady state (synchronous) reactance (X_d), as the short circuit transient progresses in time. If armature resistance is assumed negligible, the positive sequence impedance of the machine is

* This can be shown to be so by synchronous machine theory [5].

$$Z_1 = jX_d'' \text{ (if 1 cycle transient is of interest)} \tag{10.46}$$

$$= jX_d' \text{ (if 3 – 4 cycle transient is of interest)} \tag{10.47}$$

$$= jX_d \text{ (if steady state value is of interest)} \tag{10.48}$$

If the machine short circuit takes place from unloaded conditions, the terminal voltage constitutes the positive sequence voltage. On the other hand, if the short circuit occurs from loaded conditions, the voltage behind appropriate reactance (subtransient, transient or synchronous) constitutes the positive sequence voltage.

Figure 10.12(a) shows the three-phase positive sequence network model of a synchronous machine. Z_n does not appear in the model as $I_n = 0$ for positive sequence currents. Since it is a balanced network, it can be represented by the single-phase network model of Fig. 10.12(b) for purposes of analysis. The reference bus for a positive sequence network is at neutral potential. Further, since no current flows from ground to neutral, the neutral is at ground potential.

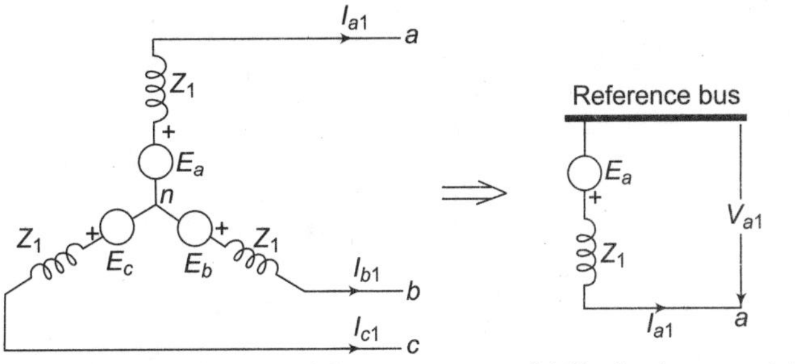

(a) Three-phase model (b) Single-phase model

Fig. 10.12 *Positive sequence network of synchronous machine*

With reference to Fig. 10.12(b), the positive sequence voltage of terminal a with respect to the reference bus is given by

$$V_{a1} = E_a - Z_1 I_{\alpha 1} \tag{10.49}$$

10.6.2 Negative Sequence Impedance and Network

It has already been said that a synchronous machine has zero negative sequence induced voltages. With the flow of negative sequence currents in the stator, a rotating field is created which rotates in the opposite direction to that of the positive sequence field and, therefore, at double synchronous speed with respect to rotor. Currents at double the stator frequency are therefore induced in rotor field and damper winding. In sweeping over the rotor surface, the negative sequence mmf is alternately presented with reluctances of direct and quadrature axes. The negative sequence impedance, presented by the machine with consideration given to the damper windings, is often defined as

$$Z_2 = j\frac{X_q'' + X_d''}{2}; \ |Z_2| < |Z_1| \tag{10.50}$$

Negative sequence network models of a synchronous machine, on a three-phase and single-phase basis, are shown in Figs. 10.13(a) and (b), respectively. The reference bus is of course at neutral potential which is the same as ground potential.

From Fig. 10.13(b), the negative sequence voltage of terminal a with respect to reference bus is

$$V_{a2} = -Z_2 I_{a2} \tag{10.51}$$

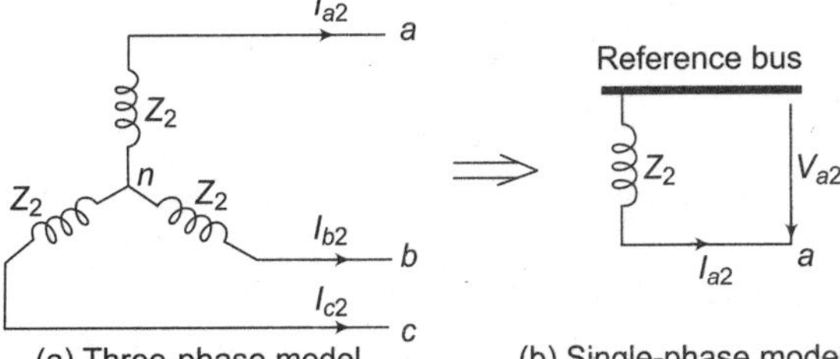

(a) Three-phase model (b) Single-phase model

Fig. 10.13 *Negative sequence network of a synchronous machine*

10.6.3 Zero Sequence Impedance and Network

We state once again that no zero sequence voltages are induced in a synchronous machine. The flow of zero sequence currents create three mmfs which are in time phase but are distributed in space phase by 120°. The resultant air gap field caused by zero sequence currents is therefore zero. Hence, the rotor windings present leakage reactance only to the flow of zero sequence currents ($Z_{0g} < Z_2 < Z_1$).

Zero sequence network models on a three- and single-phase basis are shown in Figs. 10.14(a) and (b). In Fig. 10.14(a), the current flowing in the impedance Z_n between neutral and ground is $I_n = 3I_{a0}$. The zero sequence voltage of terminal *a* with respect to ground, the reference bus, is therefore

$$V_{a0} = -3Z_nI_{a0} - Z_{0g}I_{a0}$$
$$= -(3Z_n + Z_{0g})I_{a0} \quad (10.52)$$

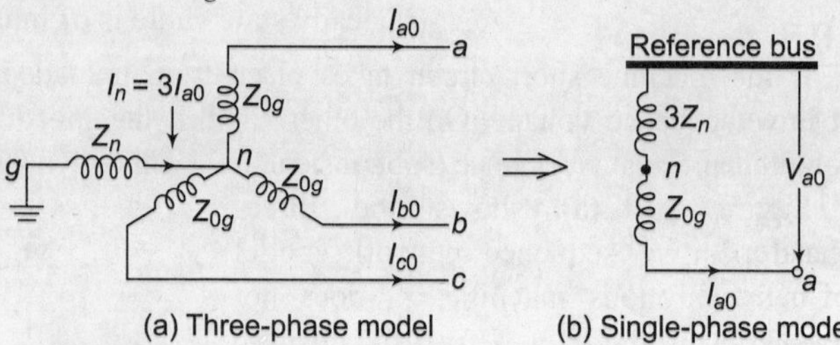

Fig. 10.14 *Zero sequence network of a synchronous machine*

where Z_{0g} is the zero sequence impedance per phase of the machine. Since the single-phase zero sequence network of Fig. 10.14(b) carries only per phase zero sequence current, its total zero sequence impedance must be

$$Z_0 = 3Z_n + Z_{0g} \quad (10.53)$$

in order for it to have the same voltage from *a* to reference bus. The reference bus here is, of course, at ground potential.

From Fig. 10.14(b), zero sequence voltage of point *a* with respect to the reference bus is

$$V_{a0} = -Z_0I_{a0} \quad (10.54)$$

10.6.4 Order of Values of Sequence Impedances of a Synchronous Generator

Typical values of sequence impedances of a turbo-generator rated 5 MVA, 6.6 kV, 3,000 rpm are

$$Z_1 = 12\% \text{ (subtransient)}$$
$$Z_1 = 20\% \text{ (transient)}$$
$$Z_1 = 110\% \text{ (synchronous)}$$
$$Z_2 = 12\%$$
$$Z_0 = 5\%$$

For typical values of positive, negative and zero sequence reactances of a synchronous machine refer to Table 9.1.

10.7 ▶ SEQUENCE IMPEDANCES OF TRANSMISSION LINES

A fully transposed three-phase line is completely symmetrical and therefore the per phase impedance offered by it is independent of the phase sequence of a balanced set of currents. In other words, the impedances offered by it to positive and negative sequence currents are identical. The expression for its per phase inductive reactance accounting for both self and mutual linkages has been derived in Ch. 2.

When only zero sequence currents flow in a transmission line, the currents in each phase are identical in both magnitude and phase angle. Part of these currents return via the ground, while the rest return through the overhead ground wires. The ground wires being grounded at several towers, the return currents in the ground wires are not necessarily uniform along the entire length. The flow of zero sequence currents through the transmission lines, ground wires and ground creates a magnetic field pattern which is very different from that caused by the flow of positive or negative sequence currents where the currents have a phase difference of 120° and the return current is zero. The zero sequence impedance of a transmission line also accounts for the ground impedance ($Z_0 = Z_{l0} + 3Z_{g0}$). Since the ground impedance heavily depends on soil conditions, it is essential to make some simplifying assumptions to obtain analytical results. The zero sequence impedance of transmission lines usually ranges from 2 to 3.5 times the positive sequence impedance*. This ratio is on the higher side for double circuit lines without ground wires.

10.8 ▶ SEQUENCE IMPEDANCES AND NETWORKS OF TRANSFORMERS

It is well known that almost all present-day installations have three-phase transformers since they entail lower initial cost and have smaller space requirements and higher efficiency.

The positive sequence series impedance of a transformer equals its leakage impedance. Since a transformer is a static device, the leakage impedance does not change with alteration of phase sequence of balanced applied voltages. The transformer negative sequence impedance is also therefore equal to its leakage reactance. Thus, for a transformer

$$Z_1 = Z_2 = Z_{\text{leakage}} \tag{10.55}$$

Assuming such transformer connections that zero sequence currents can flow on both sides, a transformer offers a zero sequence impedance which may differ slightly from the corresponding positive and negative sequence values. It is, however, normal practice to assume that the series impedances of all sequences are equal regardless of the type of transformer.

The zero sequence magnetising current is somewhat higher in a core type than in a shell type transformer. This difference does not matter as the magnetising current of a transformer is always neglected in short circuit analysis.

Above a certain rating (1,000 kVA), the reactance and impedance of a transformer are almost equal and are therefore not distinguished.

10.8.1 Zero Sequence Networks of Transformers

Before considering the zero sequence networks of various types of transformer connections, three important observations are made:

1. When magnetising current is neglected, transformer primary would carry current only if there is current flow on the secondary side.
2. Zero sequence currents can flow in the legs of a star connection only if the star point is grounded which provides the necessary return path for zero sequence currents. This fact is illustrated by Figs. 10.15(a) and (b).

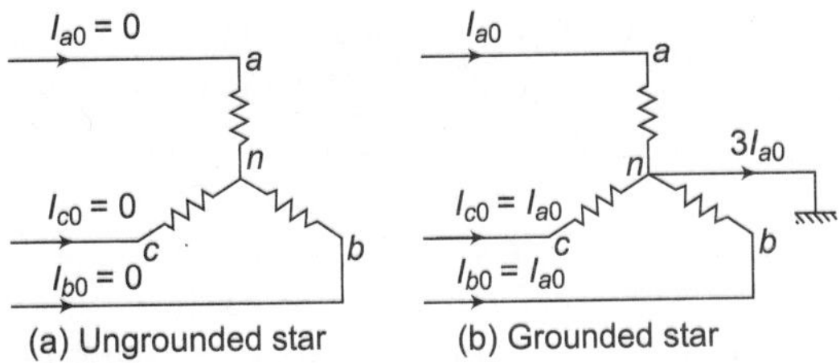

Fig. 10.15 *Flow of zero sequence currents in a star connection*

---

* We can easily compare the forward path positive and zero sequence impedances of a transmission line with ground return path infinitely away. Assume that each line has a self inductance L and mutual inductance M between any two lines (completely symmetrical case). The voltage drop in line a caused by positive sequence currents is

$$V_{Aa1} = \omega L I_{a1} + \omega M I_{b1} + \omega M I_{c1}$$
$$= [\omega L + (\alpha^2 + \alpha)\,\omega M] I_{a1} = \omega(L - M) I_{a1}$$

∴ Positive sequence reactance = $\omega(L - M)$

The voltage drop in line a caused by zero sequence currents is

$$V_{Aa0} = \omega L I_{a0} + \omega M I_{b0} + \omega M I_{c0}$$
$$= \omega(L + 2M) I_{a0}$$

∴ Zero sequence reactance = $\omega(L + 2M)$

Obviously, zero sequence reactance is much more than positive sequence reactance. This result has already been derived in Eq. (10.45).

3. No zero sequence currents can flow in the lines connected to a delta connection as no return path is available for these currents. Zero sequence currents can, however, flow in the legs of a delta—such currents are caused by the presence of zero sequence voltages in the delta connection. This fact is illustrated by Fig. 10.16.

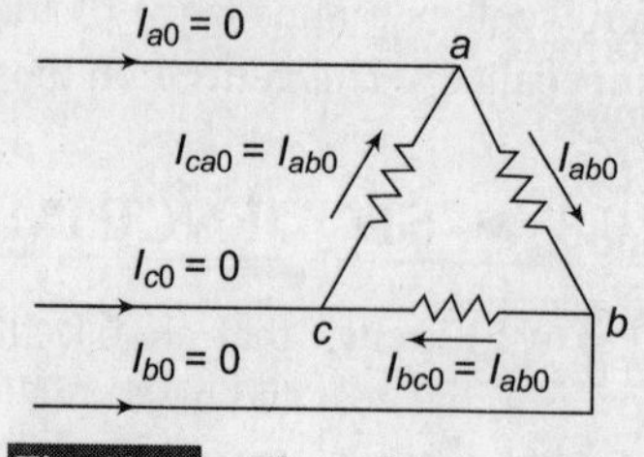

Fig. 10.16 *Flow of zero sequence currents in a delta connection*

Let us now consider various types of transformer connections.

Case 1: Y-Y transformer bank with anyone neutral grounded If anyone of the two neutrals of a Y–Y transformer is ungrounded, zero sequence currents cannot flow in the ungrounded star and consequently, these cannot flow in the grounded star. Hence, an open circuit exists in the zero sequence network between H and L, i.e., between the two parts of the system connected by the transformer as shown in Fig. 10.17.

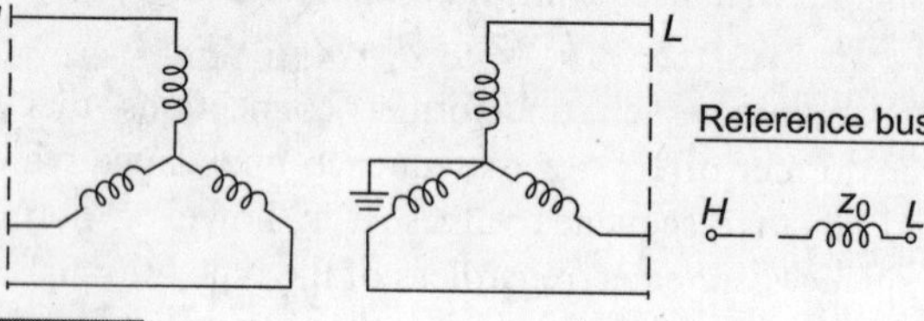

Fig. 10.17 *Y-Y transformer bank with one neutral grounded and its zero sequence network*

Case 2: Y-Y transformer bank both neutrals grounded When both the neutrals of a Y–Y transformer are grounded, a path through the transformer exists for zero sequence currents in both windings via the two grounded neutrals. Hence, in the zero sequence network H and L are connected by the zero sequence impedance of the transformer as shown in Fig. 10.18.

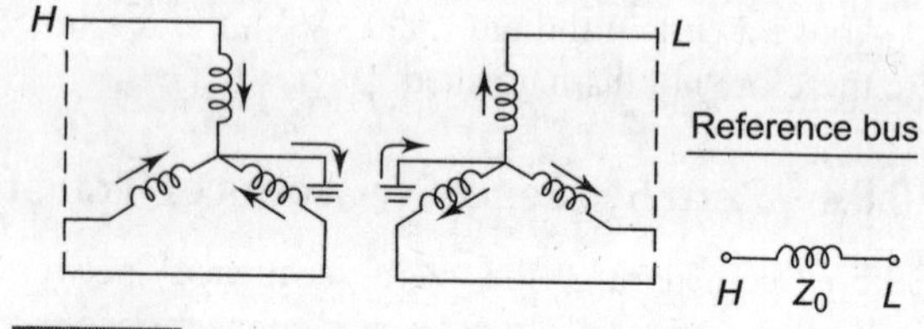

Fig. 10.18 *Y-Y transformer bank with neutrals grounded and its zero sequence network*

Case 3: Y–Δ transformer bank with grounded Y neutral If the neutral of star side is grounded, zero sequence currents can flow in star because a path is available to ground and the balancing zero sequence currents can flow in delta. Of course, no zero sequence currents can flow in the line on the delta side. The zero sequence network must therefore have a path from the line H on the star side through the zero sequence impedance of the transformer to the reference bus, while an open circuit must exist on the line L side of delta (see Fig. 10.19). If the star neutral is grounded through Z_n, an impedance $3Z_n$ appears in series with Z_0 in the sequence network.

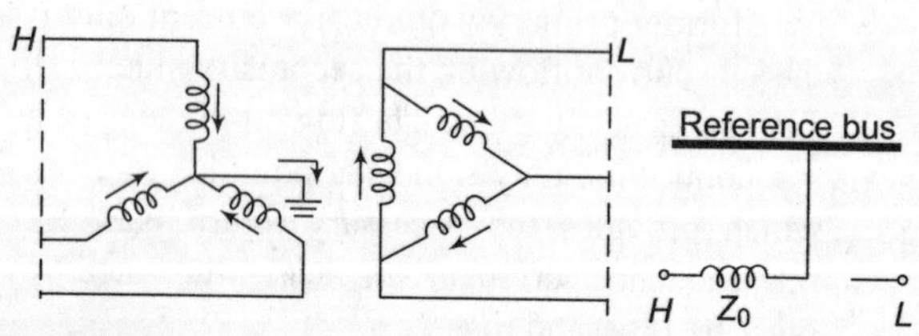

Fig. 10.19 *Y-Δ Transformer bank with grounded y neutral and its zero sequence network*

Case 4: Y-Δ transformer bank with ungrounded star This is the special case of Case 3 where the neutral is grounded through $Z_n = \infty$. Therefore, no zero sequence current can flow in the transformer windings. The zero sequence network then modifies to that shown in Fig. 10.20.

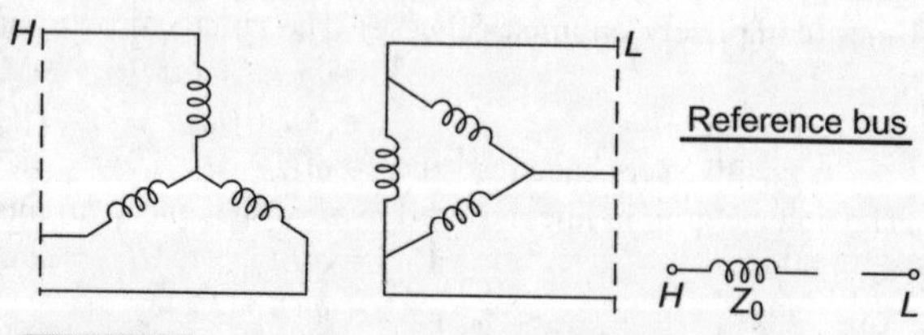

Fig. 10.20 *Y-Δ Transformer bank with ungrounded star and its zero sequence network*

Case 5: Δ-Δ transformer bank Since a delta circuit provides no return path, the zero sequence currents cannot flow in or out of Δ–Δ transformer; however, it can circulate in the delta windings*. Therefore, there is an open circuit between H and L and Z_0 is connected to the reference bus on both ends to account for any circulating zero sequence current in the two deltas (see Fig. 10.21).

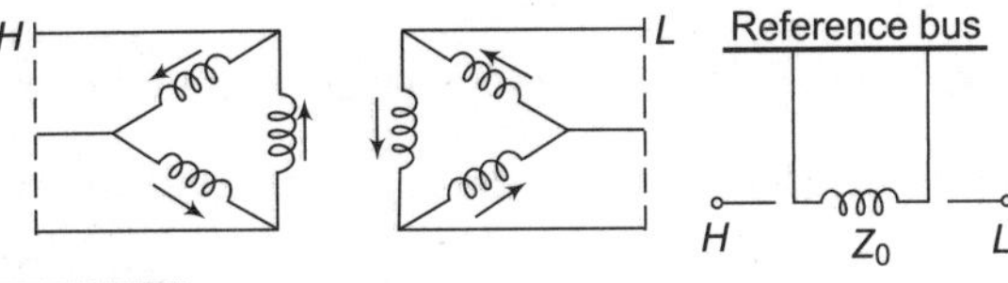

Fig. 10.21 *Δ-Δ Transformer bank and its zero sequence network*

10.9 ▶ CONSTRUCTION OF SEQUENCE NETWORKS OF A POWER SYSTEM

In the previous sections, the sequence networks for various power system elements—synchronous machines, transformers and lines—have been given. Using these, complete sequence networks of a power system can be easily constructed. To start with, the positive sequence network is constructed by examination of the one-line diagram of the system. It is to be noted that positive sequence voltages are present in synchronous machines (generators and motors) only. The transition from positive sequence network to negative sequence network is straightforward. Since the positive and negative sequence impedances are identical for static elements (lines and transformers), the only change necessary in positive sequence network to obtain negative sequence network is in respect of synchronous machines. Each machine is represented by its negative sequence impedance, the negative sequence voltage being zero.

The reference bus for positive and negative sequence networks is the system neutral. Any impedance connected between a neutral and ground is not included in these sequence networks as neither of these sequence currents can flow in such an impedance.

Zero sequence subnetworks for various parts of a system can be easily combined to form complete zero sequence network. No voltage sources are present in the zero sequence network. Any impedance included in generator or transformer neutral becomes three times its value in a zero sequence network. Special care needs to be taken of transformers in respect of zero sequence network. Zero sequence networks of all possible transformer connections have been dealt with in the preceding section.

The procedure for drawing sequence networks is illustrated through the following examples.

Example 10.2 A 25 MVA, 11 kV, three-phase generator has a subtransient reactance of 20%. The generator supplies two motors over a transmission line with transformers at both ends as shown in the one-line diagram of Fig. 10.22. The motors have rated inputs of 15 and 7.5 MVA, both 10 kV with 25% subtransient reactance. The three-phase transformers are both rated 30 MVA, 10.8/121 kV, connection Δ–Y with leakage reactance of 10% each. The series reactance of the line is 100 ohms. Draw the positive and negative sequence networks of the system with reactances marked in per unit. Assume that the negative sequence reactance of each machine is equal to its subtransient reactance. Omit resistances. Select generator rating as base in the generator circuit.

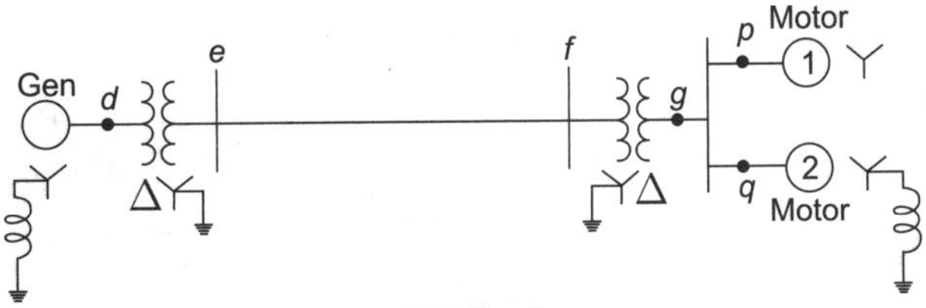

Fig. 10.22

Solution A base of 25 MVgbnA, 11 kV in the generator circuit requires a 25 MVA base in all other circuits and the following voltage bases:

$$\text{Transmission line voltage base} = 11 \times \frac{121}{10.8} = 123.2 \text{ kV}$$

* Such circulating currents would exist only if zero sequence voltages are some how induced in either delta winding.

$$\text{Motor voltage base} = 123.2 \times \frac{10.8}{121} = 11 \text{ kV}$$

The reactances of transformers, line and motors are converted to pu values on appropriate bases as follows:

$$\text{Transformer reactance} = 0.1 \times \frac{25}{30} \times \left(\frac{10.8}{11}\right)^2 = 0.0805 \text{ pu}$$

$$\text{Line reactance} = \frac{100 \times 25}{(123.2)^2} = 0.164 \text{ pu}$$

$$\text{Reactance of motor 1} = 0.25 \times \frac{25}{15} \times \left(\frac{10}{11}\right)^2 = 0.345 \text{ pu}$$

$$\text{Reactance of motor 2} = 0.25 \times \frac{25}{7.5} \times \left(\frac{10}{11}\right)^2 = 0.69 \text{ pu}$$

The required positive sequence network is presented in Fig. 10.23.

Since all the negative sequence reactances of the system are equal to the positive sequence reactances, the negative sequence network is identical to the positive sequence network but for the omission of voltage sources. The negative sequence network is drawn in Fig. 10.24.

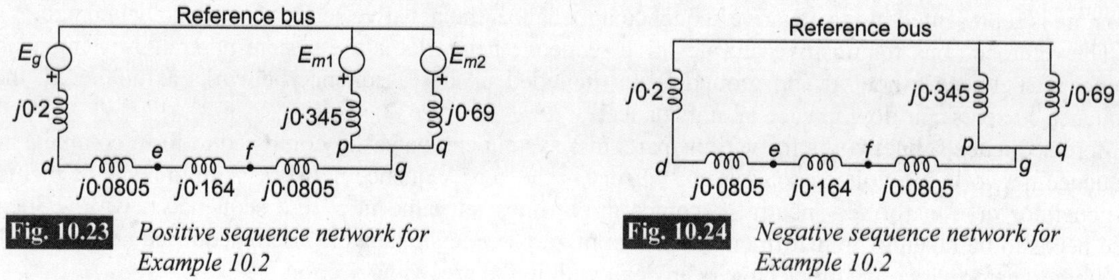

Fig. 10.23 *Positive sequence network for Example 10.2*

Fig. 10.24 *Negative sequence network for Example 10.2*

Example 10.3 For the power system whose one-line diagram is shown in Fig. 10.25, sketch the zero sequence network.

Fig. 10.25

Solution The zero sequence network is drawn in Fig. 10.26.

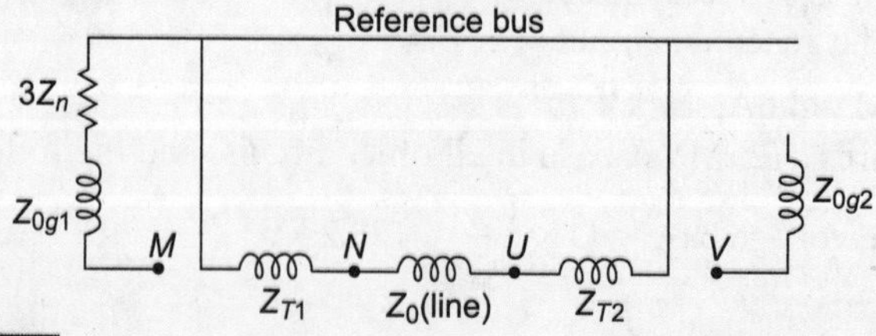

Fig. 10.26 *Zero sequence network of the system presented in Fig. 10.25*

Example 10.4 Draw the zero sequence network for the system described in Example 10.3. Assume zero sequence reactances for the generator and motors of 0.06 per unit. Current limiting reactors of 2.5 ohms each are connected in the neutral of the generator and motor No. 2. The zero sequence reactance of the transmission line is 300 ohms.

Solution The zero sequence reactance of the transformer is equal to its positive sequence reactance. Hence,

Transformer zero sequence reactance = 0.0805 pu

Generator zero sequence reactance = 0.06 pu

$$\text{Zero sequence reactance of motor 1} = 0.06 \times \frac{25}{15} \times \left(\frac{10}{11}\right)^2 = 0.082 \text{ pu}$$

$$\text{Zero sequence reactance of motor 2} = 0.06 \times \frac{25}{7.5} \times \left(\frac{10}{11}\right)^2 = 0.164 \text{ pu}$$

$$\text{Reactance of current limiting reactors} = \frac{2.5 \times 25}{(11)^2} = 0.516 \text{ pu}$$

Reactance of current limiting reactor included in zero sequence network = 3 × 0.516 = 1.548 pu

Zero sequence reactance of transmission line

$$= \frac{300 \times 25}{(123.2)^2} = 0.494 \text{ pu}$$

The zero sequence network is shown in Fig. 10.27.

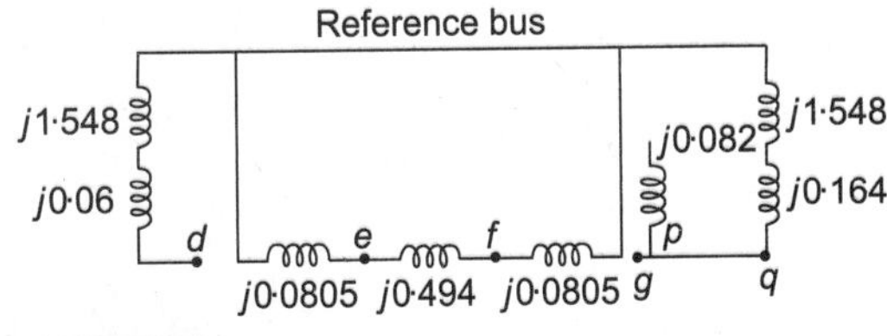

Fig. 10.27 *Zero sequence network of Example 10.4*

10.10 ▶ SUMMARY

For analysing unsymmetrical (unbalanced) faults on power system (Ch. 11), this chapter has presented simple method of analysis called method of symmetrical components given by C.L. Fortescue in 1918 (Ref. 17). How different sequence networks of a power system are constructed is explained.

Problems

10.1 Compute the following in polar form

(i) $\alpha^2 - 1$ (ii) $1 - \alpha - \alpha^2$ (iii) $3\alpha^2 + 4\alpha + 2$ (iv) $j\alpha$

10.2 Three identical resistors are star connected and rated 2,500 V, 750 kVA. This three-phase unit of resistors is connected to the Y side of a Δ-Y transformer. The following are the voltages at the resistor load:

$$|V_{ab}| = 2{,}000 \text{ V}; |V_{bc}| = 2{,}900 \text{ V}; |V_{ca}| = 2{,}500 \text{ V}$$

Choose base as 2,500 V, 750 kVA and determine the line voltages and currents in per unit on the delta side of the transformer. It may be assumed that the load neutral is not connected to the neutral of the transformer secondary.

10.3 Determine the symmetrical components of three voltages

$$V_a = 200\angle 0^\circ,\ V_b = 200\angle 245^\circ \text{ and } V_c = 200\angle 105^\circ \text{ V}$$

10.4 A single-phase resistive load of 100 kVA is connected across lines *bc* of a balanced supply of 3 kV. Compute the symmetrical components of the line currents.

10.5 A delta connected resistive load is connected across a balanced three-phase supply of 400 V as shown in Fig. P-10.5. Find the symmetrical components of line currents and delta currents.

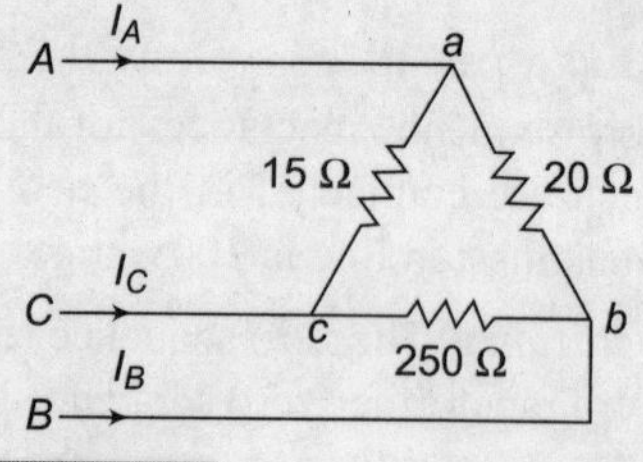

Fig. P-10.5 *Phase sequence ABC*

10.6 Three resistances of 10, 15 and 20 ohms are connected in star across a three-phase supply of 200 V per phase as shown in Fig. P-10.6. The supply neutral is earthed while the load neutral is isolated. Find the currents in each load branch and the voltage of load neutral above earth. Use the method of symmetrical components.

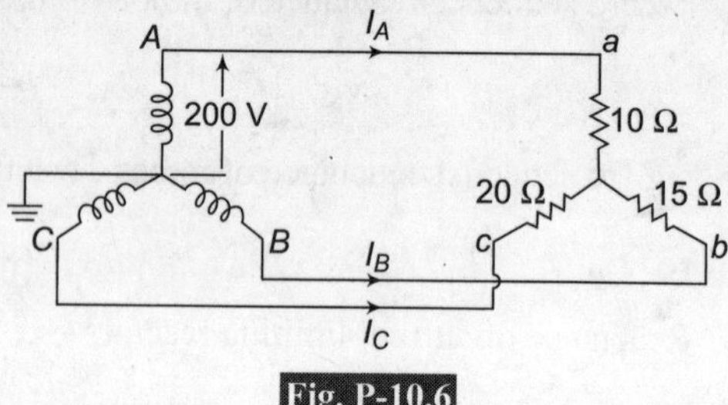

Fig. P-10.6

10.7 The voltages at the terminals of a balanced load consisting of three 20 ohm *Y*-connected resistors are 200 $\angle 0^\circ$, 100 $\angle 255.5^\circ$ and 200 $\angle 151^\circ$ V. Find the line currents from the symmetrical components of the line voltages if the neutral of the load is isolated. What relation exists between the symmetrical components of the line and phase voltages? Find the power expended in three 20 ohm resistors from the symmetrical components of currents and voltages.

10.8 Draw the positive, negative and zero sequence impedance networks for the power system of Fig. P-10.8. Choose a base of 50 MVA, 220 kV in the 50 Ω transmission lines, and mark all reactances in pu. The ratings of the generators and transformers are

Generator 1: 25 MVA, 11 kV, $X'' = 20\%$
Generator 2: 25 MVA, 11 kV, $X'' = 20\%$
Three-phase transformer (each): 20 MVA, 11 *Y*/220 *Y* kV, $X = 15\%$

Fig. P-10.8

The negative sequence reactance of each synchronous machine is equal to its subtransient reactance. The zero sequence reactance of each machine is 8%. Assume that the zero sequence reactances of lines are 250% of their positive sequence reactances.

10.9 For the power system of Fig. P-10.9, draw the positive, negative and zero sequence networks. The generators and transformers are rated as follows:

Generator 1:	25 MVA, 11 kV, $X'' = 0.2$, $X_2 = 0.15$, $X_0 = 0.03$ pu
Generator 2:	15 MVA, 11 kV, $X'' = 0.2$, $X_2 = 0.15$, $X_0 = 0.05$ pu
Synchronous Motor 3:	25 MVA, 11 kV, $X'' = 0.2$, $X_2 = 0.2$, $X_0 = 0.1$ pu
Transformer 1:	25 MVA, 11 Δ/120 *Y* kV, $X = 10\%$
2:	12.5 MVA, 11 Δ/120 *Y* kV, $X = 10\%$
3:	10 MVA, 120 *Y*/11 *Y* kV, $X = 10\%$

Choose a base of 50 MVA, 11 kV in the circuit of generator 1.

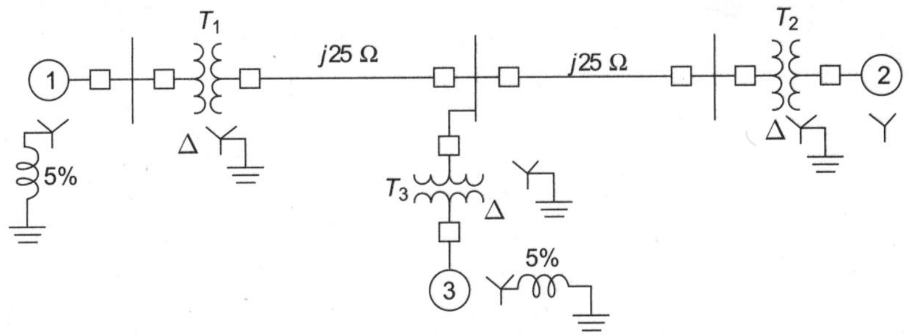

Fig. P-10.9

Note: Zero sequence reactance of each line is 250% of its positive sequence reactance.

10.10 Consider the circuit shown in Fig. P-10.10. Suppose

$V_{an} = 100\ \angle 0^\circ \qquad X_s = 12\ \Omega$

$V_{bn} = 60\ \angle 60^\circ \qquad X_{ab} = X_{bc} = X_{ca} = 5\ \text{W}$

$V_{cn} = 60\ \angle 120^\circ$

(a) Calculate I_a, I_b and I_c without using symmetrical component.

(b) Calculate I_a, I_b and I_c using symmetrical component.

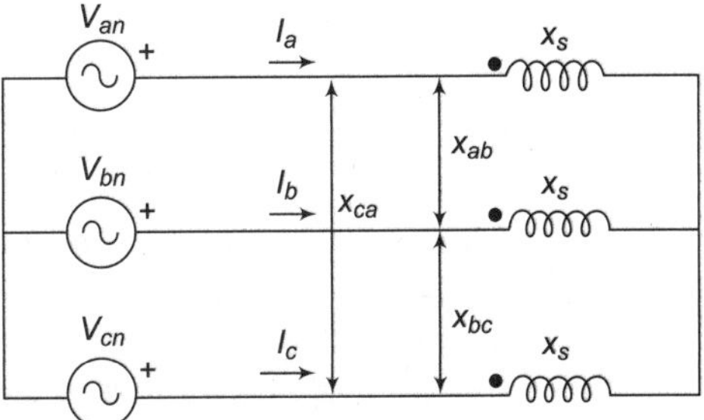

Fig. P-10.10

Multiple Choice Questions

10.1 For the fault analysis in power system, we use symmetrical components because
- (a) The results are required in terms of symmetrical components
- (b) The number of equations becomes smaller
- (c) The sequence network does not have mutual coupling
- (d) All of the above

10.2 For a power transformer
- (a) Positive sequence impedance is more than negative sequence and zero sequence impedances
- (b) Positive, negative and zero sequence impedances are all equal
- (c) Positive and negative sequence impedances are equal
- (d) Positive sequence impedance is less

10.3 For measuring positive, negative and zero sequence voltages in a system, the reference is taken as
- (a) Neutral of the system only
- (b) Ground only
- (c) For zero sequence neutral and for positive and negative the ground
- (d) None of the above

10.4 The positive sequence component of voltage at the point of fault becomes zero when it is a
- (a) Three-phase fault
- (b) Line to line fault
- (c) LLG fault
- (d) Line to ground fault

10.5 Zero sequence currents can flow from a line into a transformer bank if the windings are in

(a) Grounded star-delta (b) Delta-star
(c) Star-grounded star (d) Delta-delta

10.6 Which of the following faults occurs most frequently

(a) Three-phase (3L) faults (b) LLG faults
(c) Double line faults (d) Single line to ground faults

10.7 In the symmetrical component expression of voltages, we have

$$\begin{bmatrix} V_a \\ V_b \\ V_c \end{bmatrix} = [A] \begin{bmatrix} V_{a1} \\ V_{b2} \\ V_{a0} \end{bmatrix}$$

where matrix $[A]$ is

(a) $\begin{bmatrix} 1 & \alpha & 1 \\ \alpha^2 & \alpha & 1 \\ \alpha & \alpha^2 & 1 \end{bmatrix}$ (b) $\begin{bmatrix} 1 & \alpha & \alpha^2 \\ 1 & \alpha^2 & \alpha \\ 1 & \alpha & \alpha^2 \end{bmatrix}$ (c) $\begin{bmatrix} 1 & 1 & 1 \\ \alpha^2 & \alpha & 1 \\ \alpha & \alpha^2 & 1 \end{bmatrix}$ (d) $\begin{bmatrix} 1 & 1 & 1 \\ \alpha & \alpha^2 & 1 \\ \alpha^2 & \alpha & 1 \end{bmatrix}$

10.8 If X_s is self reactance of each line and X_n is mutual reactance of any line pair then positive sequence impedance of the transmission line is equal to

(a) $j(X_s + X_m)$ (b) $j(X_s - X_m)$ (c) jX_s (d) $-jX_m$

10.9 For a fully transposed transmission line

(a) Equal positive and negative sequence impedances
(b) Zero sequence impedance much larger than the positive sequence impedance
(c) Both (a) and (b)
(d) None of the above

10.10 The zero sequence impedance of a 3-ϕ transformer is shown below. The connection of its winding is

(a) Delta-delta
(b) Star-delta
(c) Delta-star with neutral grounded
(d) Star-star with both neutral grounded

Reference bus
H L
Z_0

10.11 A transmission line has self and mutual impedances of 0.8 pu and 0.2 pu. The positive, negative and zero sequence impedances are respectively

(a) 0.6, 0.8 and 1.2 pu (b) 0.8, 0.8 and 1.2 pu
(c) 0.6, 0.6 and 1.2 pu (d) 0.8, 0.6 and 1.2 pu

10.12 Phase shift of symmetrical components happens in which among the following?

(a) Delta-delta (b) Star-delta
(c) Delta-star (d) Both (b) and (c)

10.13 A transmission line has self and mutual impedances are 0.8 and 0 pu, respectively. Find the positive, negative and zero sequence impedances respectively?

(a) 0.6, 0.8 and 1.2 pu (b) 0.8, 0.8 and 0.8 pu
(c) 0.6, 0.6 and 0.6 pu (d) 0.6, 0.6 and 1.2 pu

10.14 Zero sequence currents can flow from a line into a transformer bank if the windings are in

(a) delta/star (b) star/grounded star
(c) ground star/delta (d) delta/delta

10.15 If the positive, negative and zero sequence reactances of an element of a power system are 0.3, 0.3 and 0.8, respectively, then the element would be a

(a) Synchronous generator (b) Synchronous motor
(c) Transmission line (d) Static load

10.16 The positive sequence reactance will be equal to negative sequence if the equipment is

(a) Generator (b) Motor
(c) Transformer and transmission lines (d) None of these

10.17 The symmetrical components are used in the fault analysis because

(a) The number of equations becomes smaller
(b) The sequence networks do not have mutual coupling
(c) The sequence networks are mutually coupled
(d) Results are required in terms of symmetrical components

11.18 For symmetrical network, the neutral current is

(a) Zero (b) Infinity
(c) Maximum (d) None of the above

11.19 The zero sequence component of current in the case of balanced 3-phase current is

(a) Minimum (b) Maximum
(c) Zero (d) None of the above

11.20 What is the value of $(1 + a + a^2)$?

(a) 1 (b) −1 (c) ∞ (d) 0

10.21 The zero sequence currents in a star connected system without neutral grounding are

(a) Zero
(b) Phasor sum of phase current
(c) Same as RMS value of phase current
(d) Same as peak value of phase current

10.22 A balanced three-phase system consists of

(a) Zero sequence current only
(b) Negative sequence current only
(c) Positive sequence current only
(d) Zero, negative and positive sequence current

10.23 Positive sequence current of a transmission line is

(a) Always zero
(b) Equal to negative sequence current
(c) One-third of negative sequence current
(d) Three times the negative sequence current

10.24 The positive, negative and zero sequence impedances of a transmission line are 0.5, 0.5 and 1.1 pu, respectively. The self (Z_s) and mutual (Z_m) impedances of the line will be given by

(a) $Z_s = 0.5$ pu, $Z_m = 0.6$ pu (b) $Z_s = 0.2$ pu, $Z_m = 0.7$ pu
(c) $Z_s = 0.6$ pu, $Z_m = 0.5$ pu (d) $Z_s = 0.7$ pu, $Z_m = 0.2$ pu

10.25 An unbalanced system of three-phase voltage having RYB sequence actually consists of

(a) A positive sequence component
(b) A negative sequence component
(c) A zero sequence component
(d) All of the above

10.26 The positive sequence current is always equal to
(a) Always zero
(b) 1/3 of the negative sequence current
(c) Negative sequence current
(d) 3 times the negative sequence current

10.27 In case of an unbalanced star connected load supplied from an unbalanced 3-phase, 3-wire system, load current will consist of
(a) Positive sequence components
(b) Negative sequence components
(c) Zero sequence components
(d) Only (a) and (b)

10.28 For an unbalanced fault with paths for zero sequence currents at the point of fault
(a) Negative sequence and zero sequence voltages are minimum
(b) Negative sequence and zero sequence voltages are maximum
(c) Negative sequence voltage is minimum and zero sequence voltage is maximum
(d) Negative sequence voltage is maximum and zero sequence voltage is minimum

10.29 What is the value of the zero sequence current?
(a) 3 times the current in the neutral wire
(b) 1/3 times the current in the neutral wire
(c) √3 times the current in the neutral wire
(d) Equal to the current in the neutral wire

10.30 Negative sequence reactance of a transformer is
(a) Equal to the positive sequence reactance
(b) Larger than the positive sequence reactance
(c) Smaller than the positive sequence reactance
(d) Any of the above

References

Books

1. C.F. Wagner and R.D. Evans, *Symmetrical Components,* McGraw-Hill, New York, 1933.
2. E. Clarke, *Circuit Analysis of Alternating Current Power Systems*, volume: 1, Wiley, New York, 1943.
3. S. Austin Stigant, *Master Equations and Tables for Symmetrical Component Fault Studies*, Macdonald, London, 1964.
4. W.D. Stevenson, *Elements of Power System Analysis,* 4th edn, McGraw-Hill, New York, 1982.
5. D.P. Kothari and I.J. Nagrath, *Electric Machines*, 4th edn, Tata McGraw-Hill, New Delhi, 2010.
6. D.P. Kothari and I.J. Nagrath, *Electric Machines*, 2nd edn, Tata McGraw-Hill, Sigma Series, New Delhi, 2006.

Paper

7. C.L. Fortescue, "Method of Symmetrical Coordinates Applied to the Solution of Polyphase Networks", *AIEE*, volume: 37, issue: 1027, 1918.
8. L.A. Pipes, "Transient Analysis of Symmetrical Networks by The Method of Symmetrical Components", *Electrical Engineering*, volume: 59, issue: 8, pp: 457–459, 1940.
9. T.H. Barton and M. Poloujadoff, "A Generalized Symmetrical Component Transformation for Clyindrical Electrical Machines", *IEEE Transactions on Power Apparatus and Systems*, volume: PAS-91, issue: 5, pp: 1781–1786, 1972.

10. G.C. Paap, "Symmetrical Components in the Time Dcmain and Their Application to Power Network Calculations", *IEEE Trans. on Power Systems*, volume: 15, issue: 2, pp: 522–528, 2000.
11. M. Karimi-Ghartemani and H. Karimi, "Processing of Symmetrical Components in Time-Domain", *IEEE Transactions on Power Systems*, volume: 22, issue: 2, pp: 572–579, 2007.
12. G. Chicco, P. Postolache, and C. Toader, "Analysis of Three-Phase Systems with Neutral under Distorted and Unbalanced Conditions in the Symmetrical Component-Based Framework", *IEEE Transactions on Power Delivery*, volume: 22, issue: 1, pp: 674–683, 2007.
13. M.I. Marei, E.F. El-Saadany, and M.M.A. Salama, "A New Approach to Control DVR Based on Symmetrical Components Estimation", *IEEE Transactions on Power Delivery*, volume: 22, issue: 4, pp: 2017–2024, 2007.
14. M.D. Kusljevic, "Symmetrical Components Estimation through Maximum Likelihood Algorithm and Adaptive Filtering", *IEEE Transactions on Instrumentation and Measurement*, volume: 56, issue: 6, pp: 2386–2394, 2007.
15. X.F. St-Onge, J. Cameron, S. Saleh, and E.J. Scheme, "A Symmetrical Component Feature Extraction Method for Fault Detection in Induction Machines", *IEEE Transactions on Industrial Electronics*, volume: 66, issue: 9, pp: 7281–7289, 2019.
16. T. Hao, F. Gao, and T. Xu, "Fast Symmetrical Component Extraction From Unbalanced Three-Phase Signals Using Non-Nominal dq-Transformation", *IEEE Transactions on Power Electronics*, volume: 33, issue: 11, pp: 9134–9141, 2018.
17. L.H.B. Liboni, M.C. de Oliveira, and I.N. d. Silva, "Optimal Kalman Estimation of Symmetrical Sequence Components", *IEEE Transactions on Instrumentation and Measurement*, volume: 69, issue: 11, pp: 8844–8852, 2020.
18. M.B.K. Bouzid and G. Champenois, "New Expressions of Symmetrical Components of the Induction Motor Under Stator Faults", *IEEE Transactions on Industrial Electronics*, volume: 60, issue: 9, pp: 4093–4102, 2013.
19. F. Della Torre, S. Leva, and A.P. Morando, "Symmetrical Components and Space-Vector Transformations for Four-Phase Networks", *IEEE Transactions on Power Delivery*, volume: 23, issue: 4, pp: 2191–2200, 2008.
20. A. Gandelli, S. Leva, and A.P. Morando, "Topological considerations on the symmetrical components transformation", *IEEE Transactions on Circuits and Systems I: Fundamental Theory and Applications*, volume: 47, issue: 8, pp: 1202–1211, 2000.
21. H. Abdollahzadeh and B. Mozafari, "Delayless Extraction of Instantaneous Symmetrical Components in Power System Fault Conditions", *IEEE Transactions on Circuits and Systems II: Express Briefs*, volume: 65, issue: 8, pp: 1064–1068, 2018.
22. P.C. Krause, "The Method of Symmetrical Components Derived by Reference Frame Theory", *IEEE Trans. on Power Apparatus and Systems*, volume: PAS-104, issue: 6, pp: 1492–1499, 1985.
23. A. Camacho, M. Castilla, J. Miret, L.G. de Vicuña, and R. Guzman, "Positive and Negative Sequence Control Strategies to Maximize the Voltage Support in Resistive–Inductive Grids During Grid Faults", *IEEE Transactions on Power Electronics*, volume: 33, issue: 6, pp: 5362–5373, 2018.
24. Z. Emin and D.S. Crisford, "Negative Phase-Sequence Voltages on E&W Transmission System", *IEEE Transactions on Power Delivery*, volume: 21, issue: 3, pp: 1607–1612, 2006.
25. M.K. Enns, "Object-Oriented Sequence-Domain Representation of Transformers for Network Analysis", *IEEE Transactions on Power Systems*, volume: 16, issue: 2, pp: 188–193, 2001.

26. E. Rosolowski and M. Michalik, “Fast Identification of Symmetrical Components by Use of a State Observer”, *IEE Proceedings—Generation, Transmission and Distribution*, volume: 141, issue: 6, pp: 617–622, 1994.
27. A.J. Degens, “Microprocessor-Implemented Digital Filters for the Calculation of Symmetrical Components”, *IEE Proceedings C—Generation, Transmission and Distribution*, volume: 129, issue: 3, pp: 111–118, 1982.
28. V.V. Terzija and D. Markovic, “Symmetrical Components Estimation through Nonrecursive Newton-Type Numerical Algorithm”, *IEEE Transactions on Power Delivery*, volume: 18, issue: 2, pp: 359–363, 2003.

CHAPTER 11

Unsymmetrical Fault Analysis

11.1 ▶ INTRODUCTION

Chapter 9 was devoted to the treatment of symmetrical (three-phase) faults in a power system. Since the system remains balanced during such faults, analysis could conveniently proceed on a single-phase basis. In this chapter, we shall deal with unsymmetrical faults. Various types of unsymmetrical faults that occur in power systems are

Shunt Type Faults

1. Single line-to-ground (LG) fault
2. Line-to-line (LL) fault
3. Double line-to-ground (LLG) fault

Series Type Faults

1. Open conductor (one or two conductors open) fault.

It was stated in Ch. 9 that a three-phase (3L) fault being the most severe must be used to calculate the rupturing capacity of circuit breakers, even though this type of fault has a low frequency of occurrence, when compared to the unsymmetrical faults listed above. There are, however, situations when an LG fault can cause greater fault current than a three-phase fault (this may be so when the fault location is close to large generating units). Apart from this, unsymmetrical fault analysis is important for relay setting, single-phase switching and system stability studies (Ch. 12).

The probability of two or more simultaneous faults (cross-country faults) on a power system is remote and is therefore ignored in system design for abnormal conditions.

The method of symmetrical components presented in Ch. 10 is a powerful tool for study of unsymmetrical faults and will be fully exploited in this chapter.

11.2 ▶ SYMMETRICAL COMPONENT ANALYSIS OF UNSYMMETRICAL FAULTS

Consider a general power network shown in Fig. 11.1. It is assumed that a shunt type fault occurs at point F in the system, as a result of which currents I_a, I_b, I_c flow out of the system, and V_a, V_b, V_c are voltages of lines a, b, c with respect to ground.

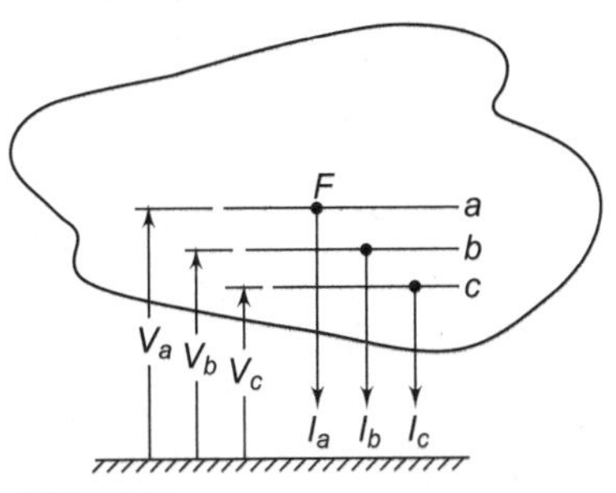

Fig. 11.1 *A general power network*

Let us also assume that the system is operating at no load before the occurrence of a fault. Therefore, the positive sequence voltages of all synchronous machines will be identical and will equal the prefault voltage at F. Let this voltage be labelled as E_a.

As seen from F, the power system will present positive, negative and zero sequence networks, which are schematically represented by Figs. 11.2(a), (b) and (c). The reference bus is indicated by a thick line and the point F is identified on each sequence network. Sequence voltages at F and sequence currents flowing out of the networks at F are also shown on the sequence networks. Figures 11.3(a), (b) and (c), respectively, give the Thevenin equivalents of the three sequence networks.

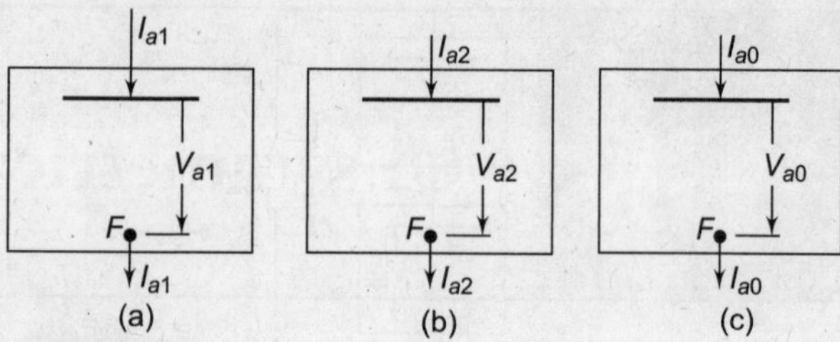

Fig. 11.2 *Sequence networks as seen from the fault point F*

Recognising that voltage E_a is present only in the positive sequence network and that there is no coupling between sequence networks, the sequence voltages at F can be expressed in terms of sequence currents and Thevenin sequence impedances as

$$\begin{bmatrix} V_{a1} \\ V_{a2} \\ V_{a0} \end{bmatrix} = \begin{bmatrix} E_a \\ 0 \\ 0 \end{bmatrix} - \begin{bmatrix} Z_1 & 0 & 0 \\ 0 & Z_2 & 0 \\ 0 & 0 & Z_0 \end{bmatrix} \begin{bmatrix} I_{a1} \\ I_{a2} \\ I_{a0} \end{bmatrix} \tag{11.1}$$

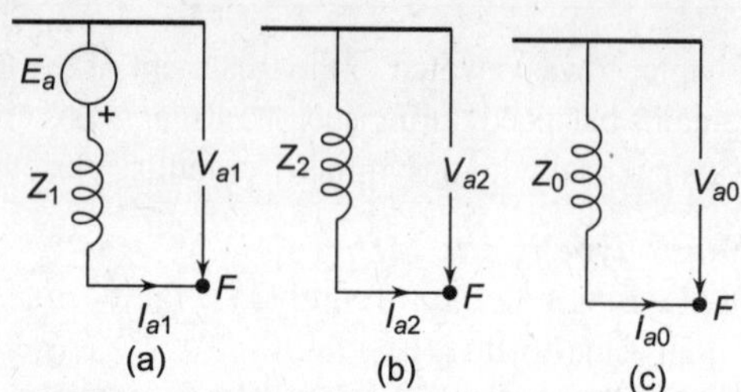

Fig. 11.3 *Thevenin equivalents of the sequence networks as seen from the fault point F*

Depending upon the type of fault, the sequence currents and voltages are constrained, leading to a particular connection of sequence networks. The sequence currents and voltages and fault currents and voltages can then be easily computed. We shall now consider the various types of faults enumerated earlier.

11.3 ▶ SINGLE LINE-TO-GROUND (LG) FAULT

Figure 11.4 shows a line-to-ground fault at F in a power system through a fault impedance Z^f. The phases are so labelled that the fault occurs on phase a.

At the fault point F, the currents out of the power system and the line-to-ground voltages are constrained as follows:

$$I_b = 0 \tag{11.2}$$

$$I_c = 0 \tag{11.3}$$

$$V_a = Z^f I_a \tag{11.4}$$

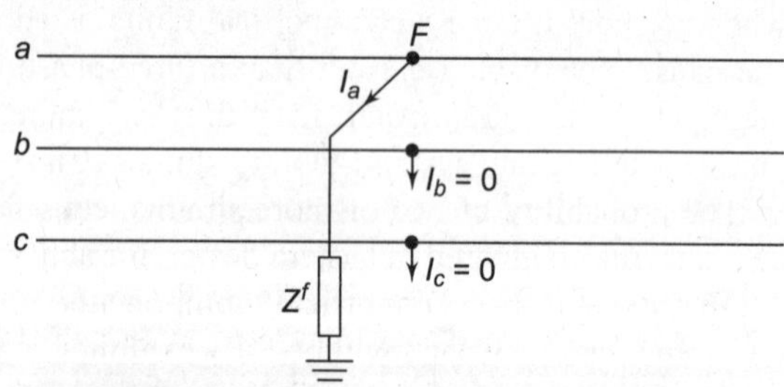

Fig. 11.4 *Single line-to-ground (LG) fault at F*

The symmetrical components of the fault currents are

$$\begin{bmatrix} I_{a1} \\ I_{a2} \\ I_{a0} \end{bmatrix} = \frac{1}{3} \begin{bmatrix} 1 & \alpha & \alpha^2 \\ 1 & \alpha^2 & \alpha \\ 1 & 1 & 1 \end{bmatrix} \begin{bmatrix} I_a \\ 0 \\ 0 \end{bmatrix}$$

from which it is easy to see that

$$I_{a1} = I_{a2} = I_{a0} = \frac{1}{3} I_a \tag{11.5}$$

Expressing Eq. (11.4) in terms of symmetrical components, we have

$$V_{a1} + V_{a2} + V_{a0} = Z^f I_a = 3Z^f I_{a1} \tag{11.6}$$

As per Eqs. (11.5) and (11.6), all sequence currents are equal and the sum of sequence voltages equals $3Z^f I_{a1}$. Therefore, these equations suggest a series connection of sequence networks through an impedance $3Z^f$ as shown in Figs. 11.5(a) and (b).

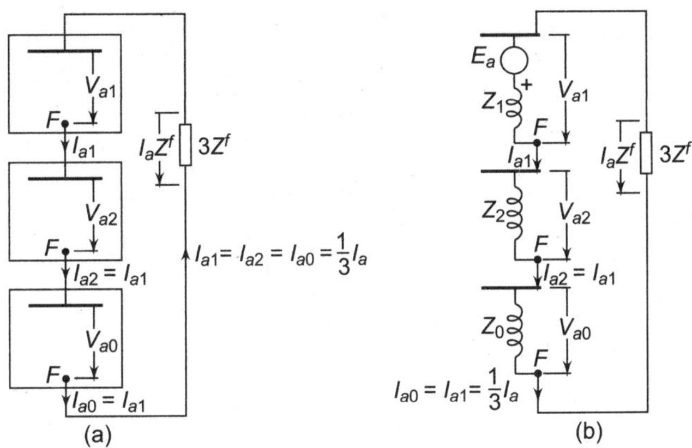

Fig. 11.5 *Connection of sequence network for a single line-to-ground (LG) fault*

In terms of the Thevenin equivalent of sequence networks, we can write from Fig. 11.5(b).

$$I_{a1} = \frac{E_a}{(Z_1 + Z_2 + Z_0) + 3Z^f} \tag{11.7}$$

Fault current I_a is then given by

$$I_a = 3I_{a1} = \frac{3E_a}{(Z_1 + Z_2 + Z_0) + 3Z^f} \tag{11.8}$$

The above results can also be obtained directly from Eqs. (11.5) and (11.6) by using V_{a1}, V_{a2} and V_{a0} from Eq. (11.1). Thus,

$$(E_a - I_{a1}Z_1) + (-I_{a2}Z_2) + (-I_{a0}Z_0) = 3Z^f I_{a1}$$

or

$$[(Z_1 + Z_2 + Z_0) + 3Z^f]I_{a1} = E_a$$

or

$$I_{a1} = \frac{E_a}{(Z_1 + Z_2 + Z_0) + 3Z^f}$$

The voltage of line b to ground under fault condition is

$$V_b = \alpha^2 V_{a1} + \alpha V_{a2} + V_{a0}$$

$$= \alpha^2\left(E_a - Z_1\frac{I_a}{3}\right) + \alpha\left(-Z_2\frac{I_a}{3}\right) + \left(-Z_0\frac{I_a}{3}\right)$$

Substituting for I_a from Eq. (11.8) and reorganising, we get

$$V_b = E_a \frac{3\alpha^2 Z^f + Z_2(\alpha^2 - \alpha) + Z_0(\alpha^2 - 1)}{(Z_1 + Z_2 + Z_0) + 3Z^f} \tag{11.9}$$

The expression for V_c can be similarly obtained.

11.3.1 Fault Occurring Under Loaded Conditions

When a fault occurs under balanced load conditions, positive sequence currents alone flow in a power system before the occurrence of the fault. Therefore, negative and zero sequence networks are the same as without load. The positive sequence network must of course carry the load current. To account for load current, the synchronous machines in the positive sequence network are replaced by subtransient, transient or synchronous reactances (depending upon the time after the occurrence of fault, when currents are to be determined) and voltages behind appropriate reactances. This change does not disturb the flow of prefault positive sequence currents (see Ch. 9). This positive sequence network would then be used in the sequence network connection of Fig. 11.5(a) for computing sequence currents under fault.

In case the positive sequence network is replaced by its Thevenin equivalent as in Fig. 11.5(b), the Thevenin voltage equals the prefault voltage V_f^0 at the fault point F (under loaded conditions). The Thevenin impedance is the impedance between F and the reference bus of the passive positive sequence network (with voltage generators short circuited). This is illustrated by a two-machine system in Fig. 11.6. It is seen from this figure that while the prefault currents flow in the actual positive sequence network of Fig. 11.6(a), the same do not exist in its Thevenin equivalent network of Fig. 11.6(b). Therefore, when the Thevenin equivalent of positive sequence network is used for calculating fault currents, the positive sequence currents within the network are those due to fault alone and we must superimpose on these the prefault currents. Of course, the positive sequence current into the fault is directly the correct answer, the prefault current into the fault being zero.

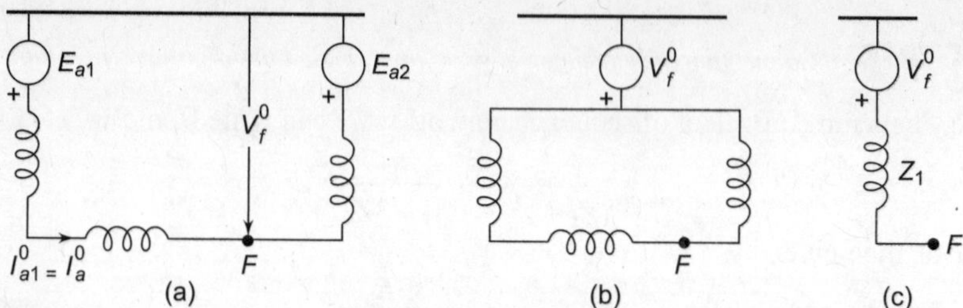

Fig. 11.6 *Positive sequence network and its Thevenin equivalent before occurrence of a fault*

The above remarks are valid for the positive sequence network, independent of the type of fault.

11.4 ▶ LINE-TO-LINE (LL) FAULT

Figure 11.7 shows a line-to-line fault at F in a power system on phases b and c through a fault impedance Z^f. The phases can always be relabelled, such that the fault is on phases b and c.

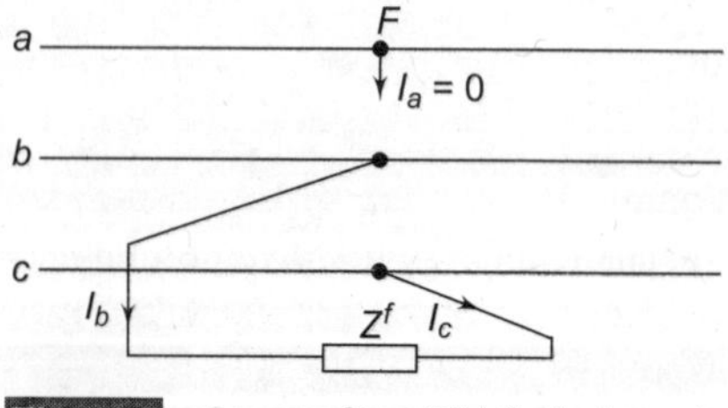

The currents and voltages at the fault can be expressed as

$$I_p = \begin{bmatrix} I_a = 0 \\ I_b \\ I_c = -I_b \end{bmatrix}; \; V_b - V_c = I_b Z^f \qquad (11.10)$$

Fig. 11.7 *Line-to-line (LL) fault through impedance Z^f*

The symmetrical components of the fault currents are

$$\begin{bmatrix} I_{a1} \\ I_{a2} \\ I_{a0} \end{bmatrix} = \frac{1}{3}\begin{bmatrix} 1 & \alpha & \alpha^2 \\ 1 & \alpha^2 & \alpha \\ 1 & 1 & 1 \end{bmatrix}\begin{bmatrix} 0 \\ I_b \\ -I_b \end{bmatrix}$$

from which we get

$$I_{a2} = -I_{a1} \qquad (11.11)$$

$$I_{a0} = 0 \qquad (11.12)$$

The symmetrical components of voltages at F under fault are

$$\begin{bmatrix} V_{a1} \\ V_{a2} \\ V_{a0} \end{bmatrix} = \frac{1}{3}\begin{bmatrix} 1 & \alpha & \alpha^2 \\ 1 & \alpha^2 & \alpha \\ 1 & 1 & 1 \end{bmatrix}\begin{bmatrix} V_a \\ V_b \\ V_b - Z^f I_b \end{bmatrix} \qquad (11.13)$$

Writing the first two equations, we have

$$3V_{a1} = V_a + (\alpha + \alpha^2)\, V_b - \alpha^2 Z^f I_b$$
$$3V_{a2} = V_a + (\alpha + \alpha^2)\, V_b - \alpha Z^f I_b$$

from which we get

$$3(V_{a1} - V_{a2}) = (\alpha - \alpha^2) Z^f I_b = j\sqrt{3}\, Z^f I_b \tag{11.14}$$

Now,

$$I_b = (\alpha^2 - \alpha)\, I_{a1}\ (\because I_{a2} = -I_{a1};\ I_{a0} = 0)$$
$$= -j\sqrt{3} I_{a1} \tag{11.15}$$

Substituting I_b from Eq. (11.15) in Eq. (11.14), we get

$$V_{a1} - V_{a2} = Z^f I_{a1} \tag{11.16}$$

Equations (11.11) and (11.16) suggest parallel connection of positive and negative sequence networks through a series impedance Z^f as shown in Figs. 11.8(a) and (b). Since $I_{a0} = 0$ as per Eq. (11.12), the zero sequence network is unconnected.

In terms of the Thevenin equivalents, we get from Fig. 11.8(b)

$$I_{a1} = \frac{E_a}{Z_1 + Z_2 + Z^f} \tag{11.17}$$

From Eq. (11.15), we get

$$I_b = -I_c = \frac{-j\sqrt{3}E_a}{Z_1 + Z_2 + Z^f} \tag{11.18}$$

Knowing I_{a1}, we can calculate V_{a1} and V_{a2} from which voltages at the fault can be found.

If the fault occurs from loaded conditions, the positive sequence network can be modified on the lines of the later portion of Section 11.3.

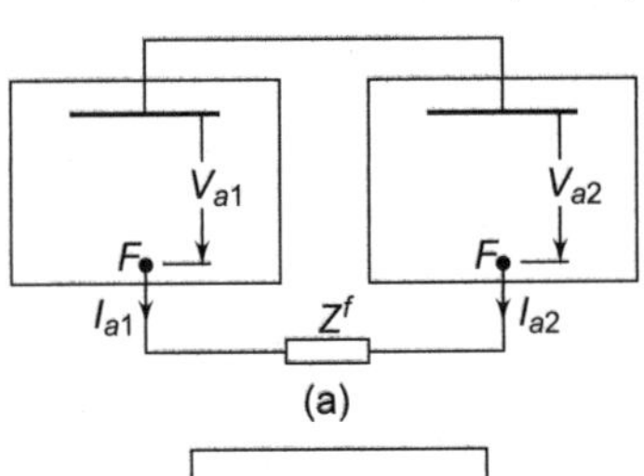

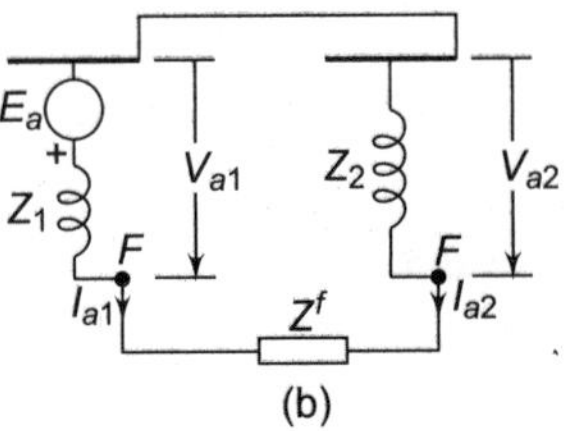

Fig. 11.8 *Connection of sequence networks for a line-to-line (LL) fault*

11.5 ▶ DOUBLE LINE-TO-GROUND (LLG) FAULT

Figure 11.9 shows a double line-to-ground fault at F in a power system. The fault may in general have an impedance Z^f as shown.

The current and voltage (to ground) conditions at the fault are expressed as

$$I_a = 0$$

or

$$\left\{ \begin{matrix} I_a = 0 \\ I_{a1} + I_{a2} + I_{a0} = 0 \end{matrix} \right\} \tag{11.19}$$

$$V_b = V_c = Z^f(I_b + I_c) = 3Z^f I_{a0} \tag{11.20}$$

The symmetrical components of voltages are given by

$$\begin{bmatrix} V_{a1} \\ V_{a2} \\ V_{a0} \end{bmatrix} = \frac{1}{3} \begin{bmatrix} 1 & \alpha & \alpha^2 \\ 1 & \alpha^2 & \alpha \\ 1 & 1 & 1 \end{bmatrix} \begin{bmatrix} V_a \\ V_b \\ V_b \end{bmatrix} \tag{11.21}$$

Fig. 11.9 *Double line-to-ground (LLG) fault through impedance Z^f*

from which it follows that

$$V_{a1} = V_{a2} = \frac{1}{3}[V_a + (\alpha + \alpha^2)V_b] \tag{11.22a}$$

$$V_{a0} = \frac{1}{3}(V_a + 2V_b) \tag{11.22b}$$

From Eqs. 11.22(a) and 11.22(b)

$$V_{a0} - V_{a1} = \frac{1}{3}(2 - \alpha - \alpha^2)\, V_b = V_b = 3Z^f I_{a0}$$

or

$$V_{a0} = V_{a1} + 3Z^f I_{a0} \tag{11.23}$$

From Eqs. (11.19), 11.22(a) and (11.23), we can draw the connection of sequence networks as shown in Figs. 11.10(a) and (b). The reader may verify this by writing mesh and nodal equations for these figures.

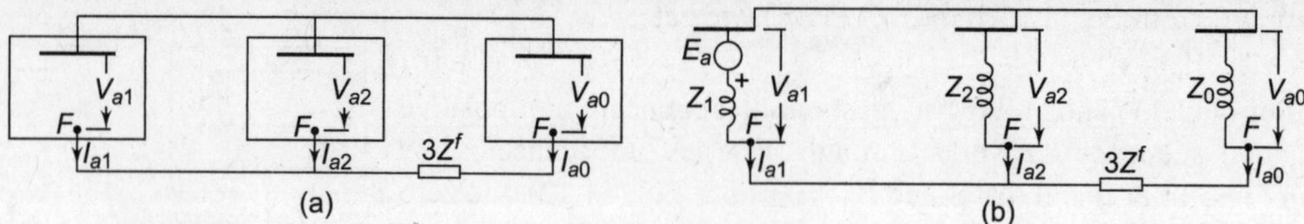

Fig. 11.10 *Connection of sequence networks for a double line-to ground (LLG) fault*

In terms of the Thevenin equivalents, we can write from Fig. 11.10(b)

$$I_{a1} = \frac{E_a}{Z_1 + Z_2 \parallel (Z_0 + 3Z^f)}$$

$$= \frac{E_a}{Z_1 + Z_2(Z_0 + 3Z^f)/(Z_2 + Z_0 + 3Z^f)} \tag{11.24}$$

The above result can be obtained analytically as follows:

Substituting for V_{a1}, V_{a2} and V_{a0} in terms of E_a in Eq. (11.1) and premultiplying both sides by Z^{-1} (inverse of sequence impedance matrix), we get

$$\begin{bmatrix} Z_1^{-1} & 0 & 0 \\ 0 & Z_2^{-1} & 0 \\ 0 & 0 & Z_0^{-1} \end{bmatrix} \begin{bmatrix} E_a - Z_1 I_{a1} \\ E_a - Z_1 I_{a1} \\ E_a - Z_1 I_{a1} + 3Z^f I_{a0} \end{bmatrix}$$

$$= \begin{bmatrix} Z_1^{-1} & 0 & 0 \\ 0 & Z_2^{-1} & 0 \\ 0 & 0 & Z_0^{-1} \end{bmatrix} \begin{bmatrix} E_a \\ 0 \\ 0 \end{bmatrix} - \begin{bmatrix} I_{a1} \\ I_{a2} \\ I_{a0} \end{bmatrix} \tag{11.25a}$$

Premultiplying both sides by row matrix [1 1 1] and using Eqs. (11.19) and (11.20), we get

$$-\frac{3Z^f}{Z_0} I_{a0} + \left(1 + \frac{Z_1}{Z_0} + \frac{Z_1}{Z_2}\right) I_{a1} = \left(\frac{1}{Z_2} + \frac{1}{Z_0}\right) E_a \tag{11.25b}$$

From Eq. 11.22(a), we have

$$E_a - Z_1 I_{a1} = -Z_2 I_{a2}$$

Substituting

$$I_{a2} = -(I_{a1} + I_{a0}) \text{ [see Eq. (11.19)]}$$

$$E_a - Z_1 I_{a1} = Z_2(I_{a1} + I_{a0})$$

or

$$I_{a0} = \frac{E_a}{Z_2} - \left(\frac{Z_1 + Z_2}{Z_2}\right) I_{a1}$$

Substituting this value of I_{a0} in Eq. 11.25(b) and simplifying, we finally get

$$I_{a1} = \frac{E_a}{Z_1 + Z_2(Z_0 + 3Z^f)/(Z_2 + Z_0 + 3Z^f)} \tag{11.26}$$

If the fault takes place from loaded conditions, the positive sequence network will be modified as discussed in Section 11.3.

Example 11.1 Figure 11.11 shows a synchronous generator whose neutral is grounded through a reactance X_n. The generator has balanced emfs and sequence reactances X_1, X_2 and X_0 such that $X_1 = X_2 \gg X_0$.

(a) Draw the sequence networks of the generator as seen from the terminals.

(b) Derive expression for fault current for a solid line-to-ground fault on phase *a*.

(c) Show that, if the neutral is grounded solidly, the LG fault current would be more than the three-phase fault current.

(d) Write expression for neutral grounding reactance, such that the LG fault current is less than the three-phase fault current.

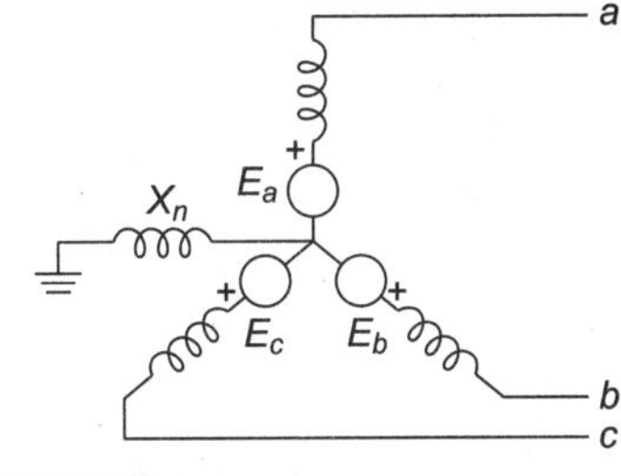

Fig. 11.11 *Synchronous generator grounded through neutral reactance*

Solution

(a) Figure 11.12 gives the sequence networks of the generator. As stated earlier voltage source is included in the positive sequence network only.

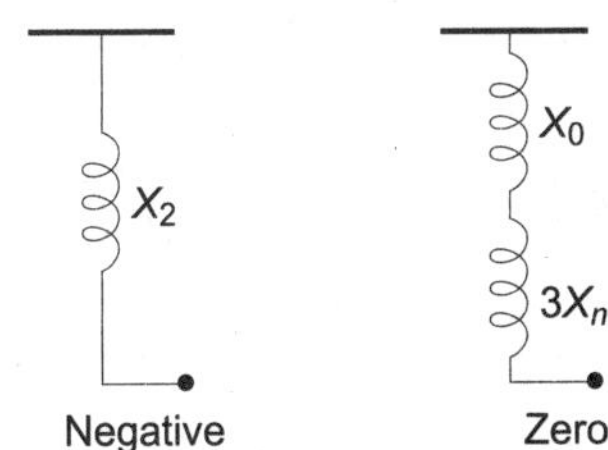

Fig. 11.12 *Sequence networks of synchronous generator grounded through neutral impedance*

(b) Connection of sequence networks for a solid LG fault ($Z^f = 0$) is shown in Fig. 11.13, from which we can write the fault current as

$$|I_a|_{LG} = \frac{3|E_a|}{2X_1 + X_0 + 3X_n} \tag{i}$$

(c) If the neutral is solidly grounded

$$|I_a|_{LG} = \frac{3|E_a|}{2X_1 + X_0} \tag{ii}$$

For a solid three-phase fault (see Fig. 11.14),

$$|I_a|_{3L} = \frac{|E_a|}{X_1} = \frac{3|E_a|}{3X_1} \tag{iii}$$

Comparing (ii) and (iii), it is easy to see that

$$|I_a|_{LG} > |I_a|_{3L}$$

An important observation is made here that, when the generator neutral is solidly grounded, LG fault is more severe than a 3L fault. It is so because $X_0 \ll X_1 = X_2$ in generator. However, for a line $X_0 \gg X_1 = X_2$, so that for a fault on a line sufficiently away from generator, 3L fault will be more severe than an LG fault.

(d) With generator neutral grounded through reactance, comparing Eqs. (i) and (iii), we have for LG fault current to be less than 3L fault

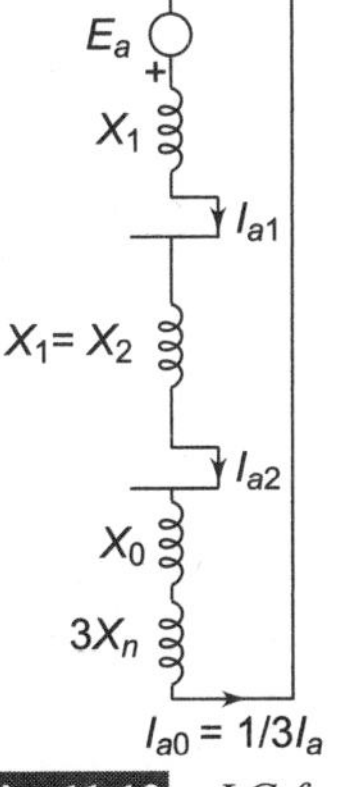

Fig. 11.13 *LG fault*

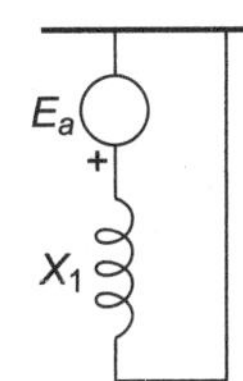

Fig. 11.14 *Three-phase fault*

$$\frac{3|E_a|}{2X_1 + X_0 + 3X_n} < \frac{3|E_a|}{3X_1}$$

or

$$2X_1 + X_0 + 3X_n > 3X_1$$

or

$$X_n > \frac{1}{3}(X_1 - X_0) \tag{iv}$$

Example 11.2 Two 11 kV, 20 MVA, three-phase, star connected generators operate in parallel as shown in Fig. 11.15; the positive, negative and zero sequence reactances of each being, respectively, $j0.18$, $j0.15$, $j0.10$ pu. The star point of one of the generators is isolated and that of the other is earthed through a 2.0 ohm resistor. A single line-to-ground fault occurs at the terminals of one of the generators. Estimate (i) the fault current, (ii) current in grounding resistor and (iii) the voltage across grounding resistor.

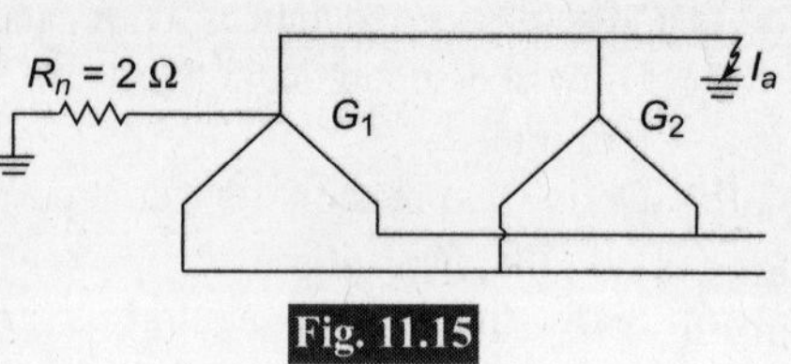

Fig. 11.15

Solution (**Note:** All values are given in per unit.) Since the two identical generators operate in parallel,

$$X_{1eq} = \frac{j0.18}{2} = j\,0.09, X_{2eq} = \frac{j0.15}{2} = j0.075$$

Since the star point of the second generator is isolated, its zero sequence reactance does not come into picture. Therefore,

$$Z_{0eq} = j0.10 + 3R_n = j0.10 + 3 \times \frac{2 \times 20}{(11)^2} = 0.99 + j0.1$$

For an LG fault, using Eq. (11.8), we get

$$I_f \text{(fault current for LG fault)} = I_a = 3I_{a1} = \frac{3E_a}{X_{1eq} + X_{2eq} + Z_{0eq}}$$

(a)

$$I_f = \frac{3 \times 1}{j0.09 + j0.075 + j0.1 + 0.99} = \frac{3}{0.99 + j0.265}$$

$$= 2.827 - j0.756$$

(b) Current in the grounding resistor $= I_f = 2.827 - j0.756$

$$|I_f| = 2.926 \times \frac{20}{\sqrt{3} \times 11} = 3.07 \text{ kA}$$

(c) Voltage across grounding resistor $= \frac{40}{121}(2.827 - j0.756)$

$$= 0.932 - j0.249$$

$$= 0.965 \times \frac{11}{\sqrt{3}} = 6.13 \text{ kV}$$

Example 11.3 For the system of Example 10.3, the one-line diagram is redrawn in Fig. 11.16. On a base of 25 MVA and 11 kV in generator circuit, the positive, negative and zero sequence networks of the system have been drawn already in Figs. 10.23, 10.24 and 10.27. Before the occurrence of a solid LG at bus

g, the motors are loaded to draw 15 and 7.5 MW at 10 kV, 0.8 leading power factor. If prefault current is neglected, calculate the fault current and subtransient current in all parts of the system.

What voltages behind subtransient reactances must be used in a positive sequence network if prefault current is to be accounted for?

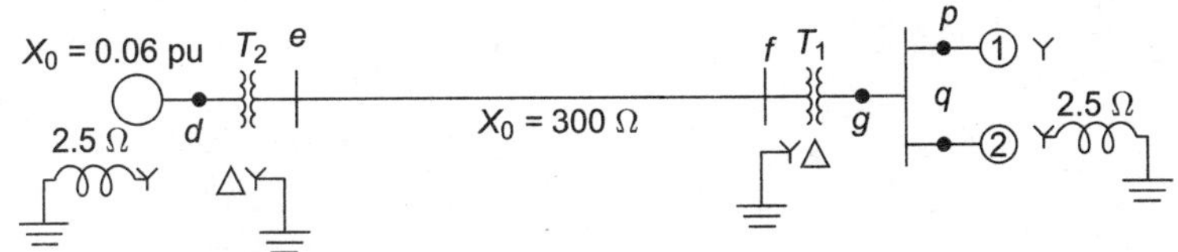

Fig. 11.16 *One-line diagram of the system of Example 11.3*

Solution The sequence networks given in Figs. 10.23, 10.24 and 10.27 are connected in Fig. 11.17 to simulate a solid LG fault at bus g (see Fig. 11.16). If prefault currents are neglected,

$$E''_g = E''_{m1} = E''_{m2} = V_f^0 \text{(prefault voltage at } g)$$

$$= \frac{10}{11} = 0.909 \text{ pu}$$

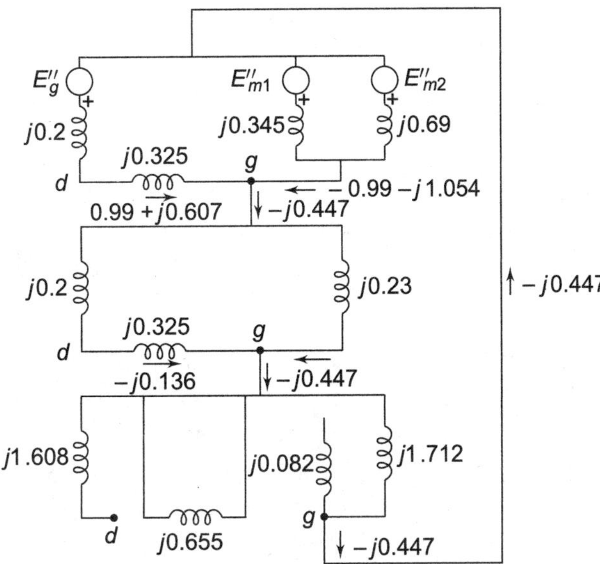

Fig. 11.17 *Connection of the sequence networks of Example 11.3. Subtransient currents are shown on the diagram in pu for a solid line-to-ground fault at g*

The positive sequence network can now be easily replaced by its Thevenin equivalent as shown in Fig. 11.18.

Now,

$$Z_1 = \frac{j0.525 \times j0.23}{j0.755} = j0.16 \text{ pu}$$

$$Z_2 = Z_1 = j0.16 \text{ pu}$$

From the sequence network connection

$$I_{a1} = \frac{V_f^0}{Z_1 + Z_2 + Z_0}$$

$$= \frac{0.909}{j2.032} = -j0.447 \text{ pu}$$

$$I_{a2} = I_{a0} = I_{a1} = -j0.447 \text{ pu}$$

Fault current $= 3I_{a0} = 3 \times (-j0.447) = -j1.341$ pu

The component of I_{a1} flowing towards g from the generator side is

$$-j0.447 \times \frac{j0.23}{j0.755} = -j0.136 \text{ pu}$$

and its component flowing towards g from the motor's side is

$$-j0.447 \times \frac{j0.525}{j0.755} = -j0.311 \text{ pu}$$

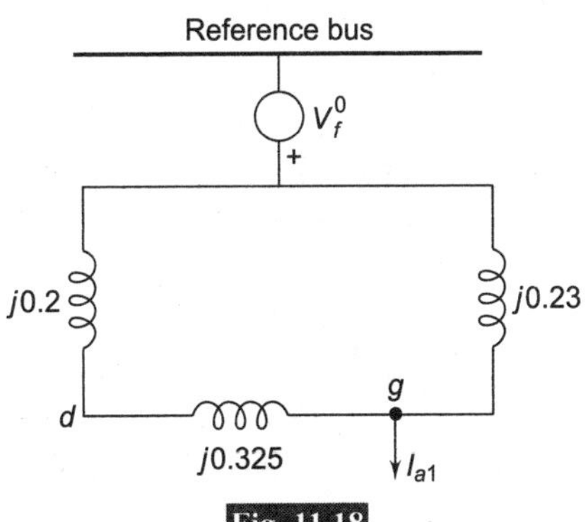

Fig. 11.18

Similarly, the component of I_{a2} from the generator side is $-j0.136$ pu and its component from the motor's side is $-j0.311$. All of I_{a0} flows towards g from motor 2.

Fault currents from the generator towards g are

$$\begin{bmatrix} I_a \\ I_b \\ I_c \end{bmatrix} = \begin{bmatrix} 1 & 1 & 1 \\ \alpha^2 & \alpha & 1 \\ \alpha & \alpha^2 & 1 \end{bmatrix} \begin{bmatrix} -j0.136 \\ -j0.136 \\ 0 \end{bmatrix} = \begin{bmatrix} -j0.272 \\ j0.136 \\ j0.136 \end{bmatrix} \text{ pu}$$

and to g from the motors are

$$\begin{bmatrix} I_a \\ I_b \\ I_c \end{bmatrix} = \begin{bmatrix} 1 & 1 & 1 \\ \alpha^2 & \alpha & 1 \\ \alpha & \alpha^2 & 1 \end{bmatrix} \begin{bmatrix} -j0.311 \\ -j0.311 \\ -j0.447 \end{bmatrix} = \begin{bmatrix} -j1.069 \\ -j0.136 \\ -j0.136 \end{bmatrix} \text{ pu}$$

The positive and negative sequence components of the transmission line currents are shifted –90° and +90°, respectively, from the corresponding components on the generator side to T_2, i.e.,

Positive sequence current $= -j(-j0.136) = -0.136$ pu

Negative sequence current $= j(-j0.136) = 0.136$ pu

Zero sequence current $= 0$ ($\because$ there are no zero sequence currents on the transmission line, see Fig. 11.17)

$\therefore$ Line a current on the transmission line $= -0.136 + 0.136 + 0 = 0$

I_b and I_c can be similarly calculated.

Let us now calculate the voltages behind subtransient reactances to be used if the load currents are accounted for. The per unit motor currents are

$$\text{Motor 1: } \frac{15}{25 \times 0.909 \times 0.8} \angle 36.86^\circ = 0.825 \angle 36.86^\circ = 0.66 + j0.495 \text{ pu}$$

$$\text{Motor 2: } \frac{7.5}{25 \times 0.909 \times 0.8} \angle 36.86^\circ = 0.4125 \angle 36.86^\circ = 0.33 + j0.248 \text{ pu}$$

Total current drawn by both motors $= 0.99 + j0.743$ pu

The voltages behind subtransient reactances are calculated below:

$$\text{Motor 1: } E''_{m1} = 0.909 - j0.345 \times 0.825 \angle 36.86^\circ$$
$$= 1.08 - j0.228 = 1.104 \angle -11.92^\circ \text{ pu}$$

$$\text{Motor 2: } E''_{m2} = 0.909 - j0.69 \times 0.4125 \angle 36.86^\circ$$
$$= 1.08 - j0.228 = 1.104 \angle -11.92^\circ \text{ pu}$$

$$\text{Generator: } E''_g = 0.909 + j0.525 \times 1.2375 \angle 36.86^\circ$$
$$= 0.52 + j0.52 = 0.735 \angle 45^\circ \text{ pu}$$

It may be noted that with these voltages behind subtransient reactances, the Thevenin equivalent circuit will still be the same as that of Fig. 11.18. Therefore, in calculating fault currents taking into account prefault loading condition, we need not calculate E''_{m1}, E''_{m2} and E''_g. Using the Thevenin equivalent approach, we can first calculate currents caused by fault to which the load currents can then be added.

Thus, the actual value of positive sequence current from the generator towards the fault is

$$0.99 + j0.743 - j0.136 = 0.99 + j0.607$$

and the actual value of positive sequence current from the motors to the fault is

$$-0.99 - j0.743 - j0.311 = -0.99 - j1.054$$

In this problem, because of large zero sequence reactance, load current is comparable with (in fact, more than) the fault current. In a large practical system, however, the reverse will be the case, so that it is normal practice to neglect load current without causing an appreciable error.

Example 11.4 For Example 11.2, assume that the grounded generator is solidly grounded. Find the fault current and voltage of the healthy phase for a line-to-line fault on terminals of the generators. Assume solid fault ($Z^f = 0$).

Solution For the LL fault, using Eq. (11.17) and substituting the values of X_{1eq} and X_{2eq} from Example 11.2, we get

$$I_{a1} = \frac{E_a}{X_{1eq} + X_{2eq}} = \frac{1}{j0.09 + j0.075} = -j6.06$$

Using Eq. (11.15), we have

$$I_f(\text{fault current}) = I_b = -j\sqrt{3}I_{a1} = (-j\sqrt{3})(-j6.06) = -10.496$$

Now,

$$V_{a1} = V_{a2} = E_a - I_{a1}X_{1eq} = 1.0 - (-j6.06)\,(j0.09)$$
$$= 0.455$$

$$V_{a0} = -I_{a0}Z_0 = 0 \quad (\because \; I_{a0} = 0)$$

Voltage of the healthy phase,

$$V_a = V_{a1} + V_{a2} + V_{a0} = 0.91$$

Example 11.5 For Example 11.2, assume that the grounded generator is solidly grounded. Find the fault current in each phase and voltage of the healthy phase for a double line-to-ground fault on terminals of the generator. Assume solid fault ($Z^f = 0$).

Solution Using Eq. (11.24) and substituting the values of Z_{1eq}, Z_{2eq} and Z_{0eq} from Example 11.2, we get (note $Z^f = 0$, $Z_{0eq} = j0.1$)

$$I_{a1} = \frac{1 + j0}{j0.09 + \dfrac{j0.075 \times j0.10}{j0.075 + j0.10}} = -j7.53$$

$$V_{a1} = V_{a2} = V_{a0} = E_a - I_{a1}\,Z_{1eq} = 1 - (-j7.53)\,(j0.09)$$
$$= 0.323$$

$$I_{a2} = -\frac{V_{a2}}{Z_{2eq}} = -\frac{0.323}{j0.075} = j4.306$$

$$I_{a0} = -\frac{V_{a0}}{Z_{0eq}} = -\frac{0.323}{j0.10} = j3.23$$

Now,

$$I_b = \alpha^2 I_{a1} + \alpha I_{a2} + I_{a0}$$
$$= (-0.5 - j0.866)\,(-j7.53) + (-0.5 + j0.866)\,(j4.306) + j3.23$$
$$= -10.248 + j4.842 = 11.334\angle 154.74^\circ$$

$$I_c = \alpha I_{a1} + \alpha^2 I_{a2} + I_{a0}$$
$$= (-0.5 + j0.866)\,(-j7.53) + (-0.5 - j0.866)\,(j4.306) + j3.23$$
$$= 10.248 + j4.842 = 11.334\angle 25.28^\circ$$

Voltage of the healthy phase, $V_a = 3V_{a1} = 3 \times 0.323 = 0.969$

11.6 ▶ OPEN CONDUCTOR FAULTS

An open conductor fault is in series with the line. Line currents and series voltages between broken ends of the conductors are required to be determined.

Figure 11.19 shows currents and voltages in an open conductor fault. The ends of the system on the sides of the fault are identified as *F*, *F′*, while the conductor ends are identified as *aa′*, *bb′* and *cc′*. The set of series currents and voltages at the fault are

$$I_p = \begin{bmatrix} I_a \\ I_b \\ I_c \end{bmatrix}; \; V_p = \begin{bmatrix} V_{aa'} \\ V_{bb'} \\ V_{cc'} \end{bmatrix}$$

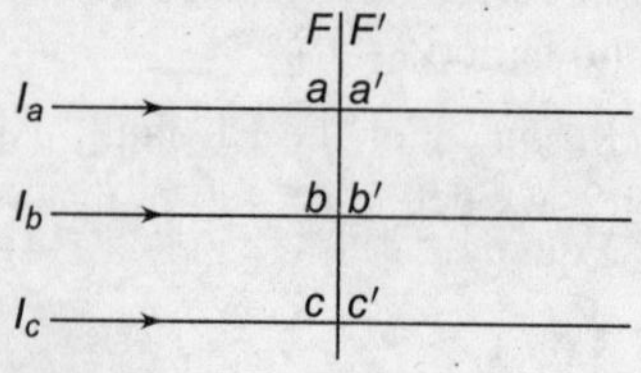

Fig. 11.19 *Currents and voltages in open conductor fault*

The symmetrical components of currents and voltages are

$$I_s = \begin{bmatrix} I_{a1} \\ I_{a2} \\ I_{a0} \end{bmatrix}; \; V_s = \begin{bmatrix} V_{aa'1} \\ V_{aa'2} \\ V_{aa'0} \end{bmatrix}$$

The sequence networks can be drawn for the power system as seen from *FF′* and are schematically shown in Fig. 11.20. These are to be suitably connected depending on the type of fault (one or two conductors open).

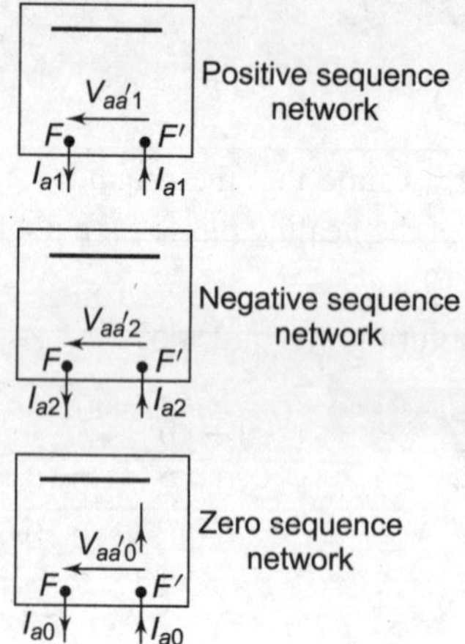

Fig. 11.20 *Sequence networks for open conductor fault at FF′*

11.6.1 Two Conductors Open

Figure 11.21 represents the fault at *FF′* with conductors *b* and *c* open. The currents and voltages due to this fault are expressed as

$$V_{aa'} = 0 \tag{11.27}$$

$$I_b = I_c = 0 \tag{11.28}$$

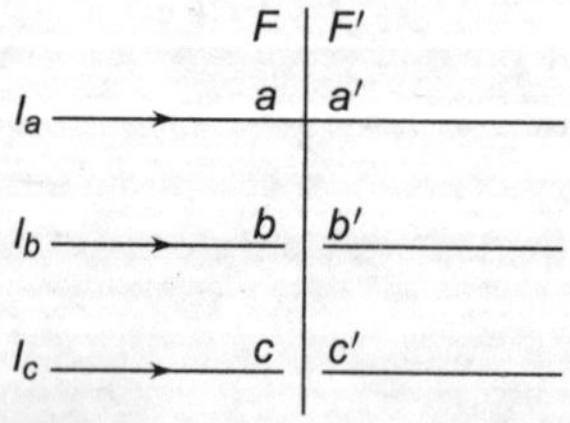

In terms of symmetrical components, we can write

$$V_{aa'1} + V_{aa'2} + V_{aa'0} = 0 \tag{11.29}$$

$$I_{a1} = I_{a2} = I_{a0} = \frac{1}{3} I_a \tag{11.30}$$

Fig. 11.21 *Two conductors open*

Equations (11.29) and (11.30) suggest a series connection of sequence networks as shown in Fig. 11.22. Sequence currents and voltages can now be computed.

11.6.2 One Conductor Open

For one conductor open as in Fig. 11.23, the circuit conditions require

$$V_{bb'} = V_{cc'} = 0 \tag{11.31}$$

$$I_a = 0 \tag{11.32}$$

In terms of symmetrical components these conditions can be expressed as

$$V_{aa'1} = V_{aa'2} = V_{aa'0} = \frac{1}{3} V_{aa'} \tag{11.33}$$

$$I_{a1} + I_{a2} + I_{a0} = 0 \tag{11.34}$$

Equations (11.33) and (11.34) suggest a parallel connection of sequence networks as shown in Fig. 11.24.

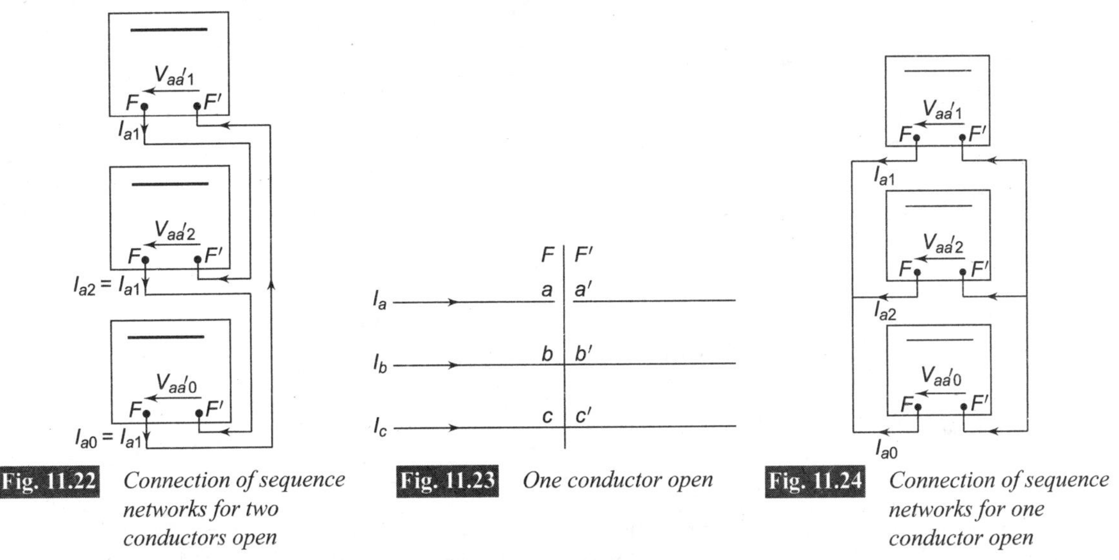

Fig. 11.22 Connection of sequence networks for two conductors open

Fig. 11.23 One conductor open

Fig. 11.24 Connection of sequence networks for one conductor open

11.7 ▶ BUS IMPEDANCE MATRIX METHOD FOR ANALYSIS OF UNSYMMETRICAL SHUNT FAULTS

Bus impedance method of fault analysis, given for symmetrical faults in Ch. 9, can be easily extended to the case of unsymmetrical faults. Consider, for example, an LG fault on the rth bus of an n-bus system. The connection of sequence networks to simulate the fault is shown in Fig. 11.25. The positive sequence network has been replaced here by its Thevenin equivalent, i.e., prefault voltage V^0_{1-r} of bus r in series with the passive positive sequence network (all voltage sources short circuited). Since negative and zero sequence prefault voltages are zero, both these are passive networks only.

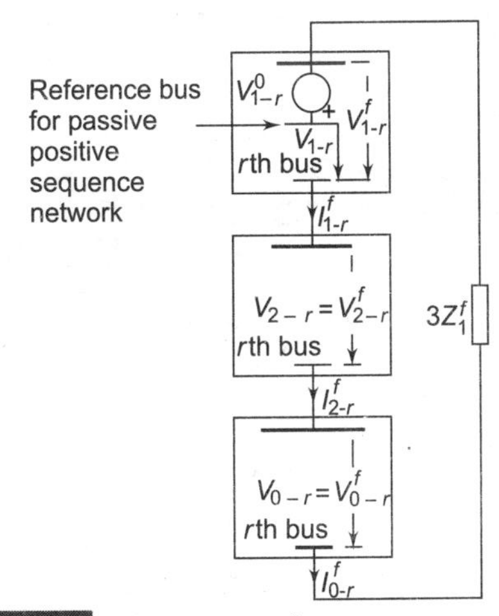

Fig. 11.25 Connection of sequence networks for LG fault on the rth bus (positive sequence network represented by its Thevenin equivalent)

It may be noted that subscript a has been dropped in sequence currents and voltages, while integer subscript is introduced for bus identification. Superscripts 0 and f, respectively, indicate prefault and postfault values.

For the passive positive sequence network

$$\boldsymbol{V}_{1\text{-BUS}} = \boldsymbol{Z}_{1\text{-BUS}} \boldsymbol{J}_{1\text{-BUS}} \tag{11.35}$$

where

$$\boldsymbol{V}_{1\text{-BUS}} = \begin{bmatrix} V_{1-1} \\ V_{1-2} \\ \vdots \\ V_{1-n} \end{bmatrix} = \text{positive sequence bus voltage vector} \tag{11.36}$$

$$\boldsymbol{Z}_{1\text{-BUS}} = \begin{bmatrix} Z_{1-11} & \cdots & Z_{1-1n} \\ \vdots & & \vdots \\ Z_{1-n1} & \cdots & Z_{1-nn} \end{bmatrix} = \text{positive sequence bus impedance matrix} \tag{11.37}$$

and

$$\boldsymbol{J}_{1\text{-BUS}} = \begin{bmatrix} J_{1-1} \\ J_{1-2} \\ \vdots \\ J_{1-n} \end{bmatrix} = \text{positive sequence bus current injection vector} \tag{11.38}$$

As per the sequence network connection, current $-I^f_{1-r}$ is injected only at the faulted rth bus of the positive sequence network, we have therefore

$$\boldsymbol{J}_{1\text{-BUS}} = \begin{bmatrix} 0 \\ 0 \\ \vdots \\ -I^f_{1-r} \\ \vdots \\ 0 \end{bmatrix} \tag{11.39}$$

Substituting Eq. (11.39) in Eq. (11.35), we can write the positive sequence voltage at the rth bus of the passive positive sequence network as

$$\boldsymbol{V}_{1-r} = -\boldsymbol{Z}_{1-rr}\boldsymbol{I}^f_{1-r} \tag{11.40}$$

Thus, the passive positive sequence network presents an impedance $\boldsymbol{Z}_{1-rr}$ to the positive sequence current $\boldsymbol{I}^f_{1-r}$.

For the negative sequence network

$$\boldsymbol{V}_{2-\text{BUS}} = \boldsymbol{Z}_{2-\text{BUS}}\boldsymbol{J}_{2\text{-BUS}} \tag{11.41}$$

The negative sequence network is injected with current $\boldsymbol{I}^f_{2-r}$ at the rth bus only. Therefore,

$$\boldsymbol{J}_{2\text{-BUS}} = \begin{bmatrix} 0 \\ 0 \\ \vdots \\ -I^f_{2-r} \\ \vdots \\ 0 \end{bmatrix} \tag{11.42}$$

The negative sequence voltage at the rth bus is then given by

$$\boldsymbol{V}_{2-r} = -\boldsymbol{Z}_{2-rr}\boldsymbol{I}^f_{2-r} \tag{11.43}$$

Thus, the negative sequence network offers an impedance $\boldsymbol{Z}_{2-rr}$ to the negative sequence current $\boldsymbol{I}^f_{2-r}$

Similarly, for the zero sequence network

$$\boldsymbol{V}_{0\text{-BUS}} = \boldsymbol{Z}_{0\text{-BUS}}\boldsymbol{J}_{0\text{-BUS}} \tag{11.44}$$

$$\boldsymbol{J}_{0\text{-BUS}} = \begin{bmatrix} 0 \\ 0 \\ \vdots \\ -I^f_{0-r} \\ \vdots \\ 0 \end{bmatrix} \tag{11.45}$$

and
$$\boldsymbol{V}_{0-r} = -\boldsymbol{Z}_{0-rr}\boldsymbol{I}^f_{0-rr} \tag{11.46}$$

That is, the zero sequence network offers an impedance $\boldsymbol{Z}_{0-rr}$ to the zero sequence current $\boldsymbol{I}^f_{0-r}$.

From the sequence network connection of Fig. 11.25, we can now write

$$I^f_{1-r} = I^f_{2-r} = I^f_{0-r} = \frac{V^0_{1-r}}{Z_{1-rr} + Z_{2-rr} + Z_{0-rr} + 3Z^f} \tag{11.47}$$

Sequence currents for other types of faults can be similarly computed using Z_{1-rr}, Z_{2-rr} and Z_{0-rr} in place of Z_1, Z_2 and Z_0 in Eqs. (11.7), (11.17) and (11.24) with $E_a = V^0_{1-r}$.

Postfault sequence voltages at any bus can now be computed by superposing on prefault bus voltage, the voltage developed owing to the injection of appropriate sequence current at bus r.

For passive positive sequence network, the voltage developed at bus i owing to the injection of $-I^f_{1-r}$ at bus r is

$$V_{1-i} = -Z_{1-ir}I^f_{1-r} \tag{11.48}$$

Hence, postfault positive sequence voltage at bus i is given by

$$V^f_{1-i} = V^0_{1-i} - Z_{1-ir}I^f_{1-r}; \quad i = 1, 2, ..., n \tag{11.49}$$

where

V^0_{1-i} = prefault positive sequence voltage at bus i

Z_{1-ir} = irth component of $Z_{1\text{-BUS}}$

Since the prefault negative sequence bus voltages are zero, the postfault negative sequence bus voltages are given by

$$\begin{aligned} V^f_{2-i} &= 0 + V_{2-i} \\ &= -Z_{2-ir}I^f_{2-r} \end{aligned} \tag{11.50}$$

where

Z_{2-ir} = irth component of $Z_{2\text{-BUS}}$

Similarly, the postfault zero sequence bus voltages are given by

$$V^f_{0-i} = -Z_{0-ir}I^f_{0-r}; \quad i = 1, 2, ..., n \tag{11.51}$$

where

Z_{0-ir} = irth component of $Z_{0\text{-BUS}}$

With postfault sequence voltages known at the buses, sequence currents in lines can be computed as For line uv, having sequence admittances y_{1-uv}, y_{2-uv} and y_{0-uv}

$$\begin{aligned} I^f_{1-uv} &= y_{1-uv}(V^f_{1-u} - V^f_{1-v}) \\ I^f_{2-uv} &= y_{2-uv}(V^f_{2-u} - V^f_{2-v}) \\ I^f_{0-uv} &= y_{0-uv}(V^f_{0-u} - V^f_{0-v}) \end{aligned} \tag{11.52}$$

Knowing sequence voltages and currents, phase voltages and currents can be easily computed by the use of the symmetrical component transformation

$$V_p = AV_s$$
$$I_p = AI_s$$

It appears at first, as if this method is more labourious than computing fault currents from Thevenin impedances of the sequence networks, as it requires computation of bus impedance matrices of all the three sequence networks. It must, however, be pointed out here that once the bus impedance matrices have been assembled, fault analysis can be conveniently carried out for all the buses, which, in fact, is the aim of a fault study. Moreover, bus impedance matrices can be easily modified to account for changes in power network configuration.

Example 11.6 For Example 10.3, positive, negative and zero sequence networks have been drawn in Figs. 10.23, 10.24 and 10.27. Using the bus impedance method of fault analysis, find fault currents for a solid LG fault at (i) bus *e* and (ii) bus *f*. Also find bus voltages and line currents in case (i). Assume the prefault currents to be zero and the prefault voltages to be 1 pu.

Solution Figure 11.26 shows the connection of the sequence networks of Figs. 10.23, 10.24 and 10.27 for a solid LG fault at bus *e*.

Refer to Fig. 11.26 to find the elements of the bus admittance matrices of the three sequence networks, as follows:

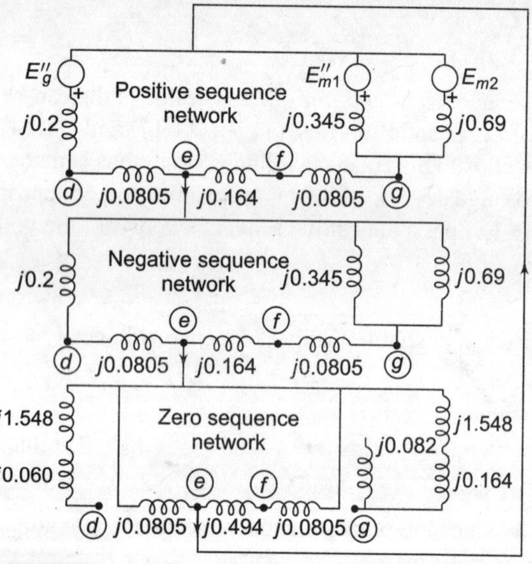

$$Y_{1-dd} = \frac{1}{j0.2} + \frac{1}{j0.0805} = -j17.422$$

$$Y_{1-fg} = Y_{1-de} = \frac{-1}{j0.0805} = j12.422$$

$$Y_{1-ff} = Y_{1-ee} = \frac{1}{j0.0805} + \frac{1}{j0.164} = -j18.519$$

$$Y_{1-ef} = \frac{-1}{j0.164} = j6.097$$

$$Y_{1-gg} = \frac{1}{j0.085} + \frac{1}{j0.345} + \frac{1}{j0.69} = -j16.769$$

Fig. 11.26 *Connection of the sequence networks of Example 11.6 for an LG fault at bus e*

$$Y_{1-\text{BUS}} = Y_{2-\text{BUS}} = j \begin{array}{c} \\ d \\ e \\ f \\ g \end{array} \begin{array}{c} \begin{array}{cccc} d & e & f & g \end{array} \\ \begin{bmatrix} -17.422 & 12.422 & 0 & 0 \\ 12.422 & -18.519 & 6.097 & 0 \\ 0 & 6.097 & -18.519 & 12.422 \\ 0 & 0 & 12.422 & -16.769 \end{bmatrix} \end{array}$$

$$Y_{0-dd} = \frac{1}{j1.608} = -j0.621$$

$$Y_{0-ee} = Y_{0-ff} = \frac{1}{j0.0805} + \frac{1}{j0.494} = -j14.446$$

$$Y_{0-gg} = \frac{1}{j1.712} = -j0.584$$

$$Y_{0-de} = 0.0$$

$$Y_{0-ef} = \frac{-1}{j0.494} = j2.024$$

$$Y_{0-fg} = 0.0$$

$$Y_{0\text{-BUS}} = j\begin{array}{c} \\ d \\ e \\ f \\ g \end{array}\begin{array}{c} \begin{array}{cccc} d & e & f & g \end{array} \\ \begin{bmatrix} -0.621 & 0 & 0 & 0 \\ 0 & -14.446 & 2.024 & 0 \\ 0 & 2.024 & -14.446 & 0 \\ 0 & 0 & 0 & -0.584 \end{bmatrix} \end{array}$$

Inverting the three matrices above renders the following three-bus impedance matrices

$$Z_{1\text{-BUS}} = Z_{2\text{-BUS}} = j\begin{bmatrix} 0.14706 & 0.12575 & 0.08233 & 0.06102 \\ 0.12575 & 0.17636 & 0.11547 & 0.08558 \\ 0.08233 & 0.11547 & 0.18299 & 0.13563 \\ 0.06102 & 0.08558 & 0.13563 & 0.16019 \end{bmatrix}$$

$$Z_{0\text{-BUS}} = j\begin{bmatrix} 1.61031 & 0 & 0 & 0 \\ 0 & 0.07061 & 0.00989 & 0 \\ 0 & 0.00989 & 0.07061 & 0 \\ 0 & 0 & 0 & 1.71233 \end{bmatrix}$$

The fault current with LG fault on bus e is

$$I_e^f = \frac{3\times 1}{j0.17636 + j0.17636 + j0.07061} = -j7.086 \text{ pu} \tag{i}$$

The fault current with LG fault on bus f is

$$I_f^f = \frac{3\times 1}{j0.18299 + j0.18299 + j0.07061} = \frac{3}{j0.43659}$$

$$= -j6.871 \text{ pu} \tag{ii}$$

Bus voltages and line currents in case (i) can easily be computed using Eqs. (11.49) to (11.52). Given below is a sample calculation for computing voltage at bus f and current in line ef.

From Eq. (11.49)

$$V_{1-d}^f = V_{1-d}^0 - Z_{1-de} - I_{1-e}^f$$

$$= 1.0 - j0.12575\left(-j\frac{7.086}{3}\right) = 0.703 \text{ pu}$$

$$V_{1-f}^f = V_{1-f}^0 - Z_{1-fe} - I_{1-e}^f$$

$$= 1.0 - j0.11547\left(-j\frac{7.086}{3}\right) = 0.728 \text{ pu}$$

$$V_{1-e}^f = V_{1-e}^0 - Z_{1-ee} - I_{1-e}^f$$

$$= 1.0 - j0.17638\,(-j2.363) = 0.584 \text{ pu}$$

$$V_{1-g}^f = V_{1-g}^0 - Z_{1-ge} - I_{1-e}^f$$

$$= 1.0 - j0.08558\,(-j2.363) = 0.798 \text{ pu}$$

$$V^f_{2-f} = -Z_{2-fe} I^f_{2-e}$$
$$= -j0.11547 \times (-j2.362) = -0.272 \text{ pu}$$

$$V^f_{0-f} = -Z_{0-fe} I^f_{0-e} = -j0.00989 \times (-j2.362)$$
$$= -0.023 \text{ pu}$$

$$V^f_{2-e} = -Z_{2-ee} I^f_{2-e} = -j0.17636 \times (-j2.362)$$
$$= -0.417 \text{ pu}$$

$$V^f_{0-e} = -Z_{0-ee} I^f_{0-e} = -j0.0706 \times (-j2.362)$$
$$= -0.167 \text{ pu}$$

$$V^f_{2-g} = -Z_{2-ge} I^f_{2-e} = -j0.08558 \times (-j2.362)$$
$$= -0.202 \text{ pu}$$

$$V^f_{0-g} = -Z_{0-ge} I^f_{0-e} = 0$$

Using Eq. (11.52), the currents in various parts of Fig. 11.26 can be computed as follows:

$$I^f_{1-fe} = y_{1-fe}\,(V^f_{1-f} - V^f_{1-fe})$$
$$= -j6.097\,(0.728 - 0.584)$$
$$= -j0.88$$

$$I^f_{1-de} = y_{1-de}\,(V^f_{1-d} - V^f_{1-e})$$
$$= -j12.422\,(0.703 - 0.584) = -j1.482$$

$$\therefore \quad I_{a1} = I^f_{1-fe} + I^f_{1-de} = -j0.88 + (-j1.482)$$
$$= -j2.362$$

which is the same as obtained earlier [see Eq. (i)] where $I^f_e = 3I_{a1}$.

$$I^f_{1-gf} = y_{1-gf}(V^f_{1-g} - V^f_{1-f})$$
$$= j12.422\,(-0.798 - 0.728) = -j0.88$$

Notice that as per Fig. 11.26, it was required to be the same as I^f_{1-fe}.

$$I_{2-fe} = y_{2-fe}\,(V^f_{2-f} - V^f_{2-e})$$
$$= -j6.097\,(-0.272 + 0.417) = -j0.884$$

$$I^f_{0-fe} = y_{0-fe}\,(V^f_{0-f} - V^f_{0-e})$$
$$= -j2.024\,(-0.023 + 0.167) = -j0.291 \text{ pu}$$

$$\therefore \quad I^f_{fe}\,(\text{a}) = I^f_{1-fe} + I^f_{2-fe} + I^f_{0-fe}$$
$$= -j0.88 + (-j0.88) + (-j0.291)$$
$$= -j2.05$$

Similarly, other currents can be computed.

Example 11.7 A single line-to-ground fault (on phase a) occurs on the bus 1 of the system of Fig. 11.27. Find

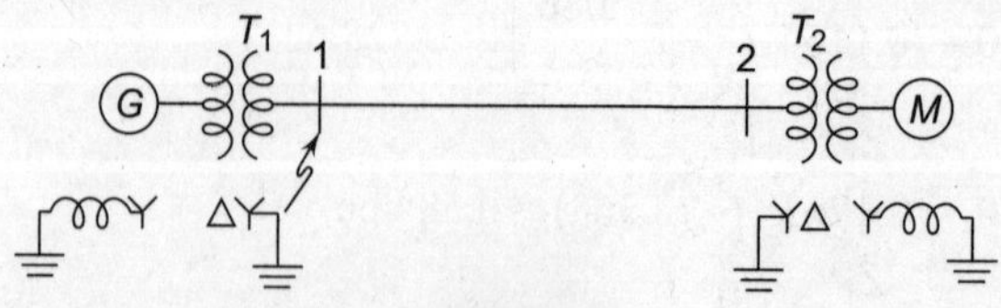

Fig. 11.27

(a) Current in the fault.
(b) SC current on the transmission line in all the three phases.
(c) SC current in phase *a* of the generator.
(d) Voltage of the healthy phases of the bus 1.

Given: Rating of each machine 1200 kVA, 600 V with $X' = X_2 = 10\%$, $X_0 = 5\%$. Each three-phase transformer is rated 1200 kVA, 600 V – Δ/3300 V–*Y* with leakage reactance of 5%. The reactances of the transmission line are $X_1 = X_2 = 20\%$ and $X_0 = 40\%$ on a base of 1200 kVA, 3300 V. The reactances of the neutral grounding reactors are 5% on the kVA and voltage base of the machine.

Note: Use Z_{BUS} method.

Solution Figure 11.28 shows the passive positive sequence network of the system of Fig. 11.27. This also represents the negative sequence network for the system. Bus impedance matrices are computed below:

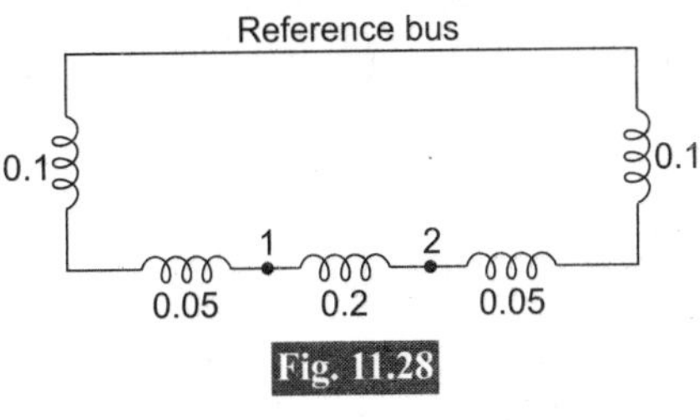

Fig. 11.28

Bus 1 to reference bus

$$Z_{1\text{-BUS}} = j[0.15]$$

Bus 2 to Bus 1

$$Z_{1\text{-BUS}} = j\begin{bmatrix} 0.15 & 0.15 \\ 0.15 & 0.35 \end{bmatrix}$$

Bus 2 to reference bus

$$Z_{1\text{-BUS}} = j\begin{bmatrix} 0.15 & 0.15 \\ 0.15 & 0.35 \end{bmatrix} - \frac{j}{0.35 + 0.15}\begin{bmatrix} 0.15 \\ 0.35 \end{bmatrix}[0.15 \quad 0.35]$$

or

$$Z_{1\text{-BUS}} = j\begin{bmatrix} 0.105 & 0.045 \\ 0.045 & 0.105 \end{bmatrix} = Z_{2\text{-BUS}} \tag{i}$$

Zero sequence network of the system is drawn in Fig. 11.29 and its bus impedance matrix is computed below:

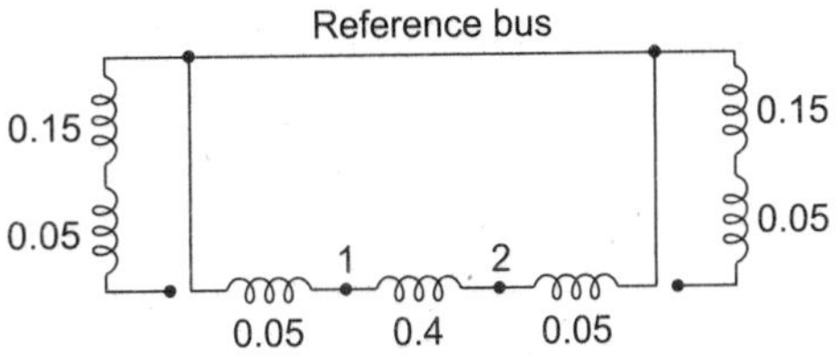

Fig. 11.29

Bus 1 to reference bus

$$Z_{0\text{-BUS}} = j[0.05]$$

Bus 2 to bus 1

$$Z_{0\text{-BUS}} = j\begin{bmatrix} 0.05 & 0.05 \\ 0.05 & 0.45 \end{bmatrix}$$

Bus 2 to reference bus

$$Z_{0\text{-BUS}} = j\begin{bmatrix} 0.05 & 0.05 \\ 0.05 & 0.45 \end{bmatrix} - \frac{j}{0.45 + 0.05}\begin{bmatrix} 0.05 \\ 0.45 \end{bmatrix}[0.05 \quad 0.45]$$

or

$$Z_{0\text{-BUS}} = j\frac{1}{2}\begin{bmatrix} 0.045 & 0.005 \\ 0.005 & 0.045 \end{bmatrix} \tag{ii}$$

As per Eq. (11.47)

$$I_{1-1}^{f} = \frac{V_1^0}{Z_{1-11} + Z_{2-11} + Z_{0-11} + 3Z^f}$$

But,

$$V_1^0 = 1 \text{ pu (system unloaded before fault)}$$

Then,

$$I^f_{1-1} = \frac{-j1.0}{0.105 + 0.105 + 0.045} = -j3.92 \text{ pu}$$

$$I^f_{1-1} = I^f_{2-1} = I^f_{a-1} = -j3.92 \text{ pu}$$

(a) Fault current, $I^f_1 = 3I^f_{1-1} = -j11.7$ pu

(b)

$$V^f_{1-1} = V^0_{1-1} = Z_{1-11} I^f_{1-1}$$
$$= 1.0 - j0.105 \times -j3.92 = 0.588; \; V^0_{1-1} = 1 \text{ pu}$$

$$V^f_{1-2} = V^0_{1-2} - Z_{1-21} I^f_{2-1}; \; V^0_{1-2} = 1.0 \text{ (system unloaded before fault)}$$
$$= 1.0 - j0.045 \times -j3.92 = 0.824$$

$$V^f_{2-1} = -Z_{2-11} I^f_{2-1}$$
$$= -j0.105 \times -j3.92 = 0.412$$

$$V^f_{2-2} = -Z_{2-21} I^f_{2-1}$$
$$= -j0.045 \times -j3.92 = -0.176$$

$$V^f_{0-1} = -Z_{0-11} I^f_{0-1}$$
$$= -j0.045 \times -j3.92 = -0.176$$

$$V^f_{0-2} = -Z_{0-21} I^f_{0-1}$$
$$= -j0.005 \times -j3.92 = -0.02$$

$$I^f_{1-12} = y_{1-12} (V^f_{1-1} - V^f_{1-3})$$
$$= \frac{1}{j0.2} (0.588 - 0.824) = j1.18$$

$$I^f_{2-12} = y_{2-12} (V^f_{2-1} - V^f_{2-2})$$
$$= \frac{1}{j0.2} (-0.412 + 0.176) = j1.18$$

$$I^f_{0-12} = y_{0-12} (V^f_{0-1} - V^f_{0-2})$$
$$= \frac{1}{j0.4} (-0.176 + 0.020) = j0.39$$

$$\begin{bmatrix} I^f_{a-12} \\ I^f_{b-12} \\ I^f_{c-12} \end{bmatrix} = -\begin{bmatrix} 1 & 1 & 1 \\ \alpha^2 & \alpha & 1 \\ \alpha & \alpha^2 & 1 \end{bmatrix} \begin{bmatrix} I^f_{1-12} \\ I^f_{2-12} \\ I^f_{0-12} \end{bmatrix}$$

$$= \begin{bmatrix} 1 & 1 & 1 \\ \alpha^2 & \alpha & 1 \\ \alpha & \alpha^2 & 1 \end{bmatrix} \begin{bmatrix} j1.18 \\ j1.18 \\ j0.39 \end{bmatrix}$$

$$I^f_{a-12} = j1.18 + j1.18 + j0.39 = j2.75$$

$$I^f_{b-12} = j1.18 \angle 240^\circ + j1.18 \angle 120^\circ + j0.39$$
$$= -j079$$

$$I^f_{c-12} = j1.18 \angle 120^\circ + j1.18 \angle 240^\circ + j0.39$$
$$= j0.79$$

(c)

$$I^f_{1-G} = \frac{1}{j0.15} (1 - 0.588) \angle -33^\circ$$
$$= -1.37 - j2.38$$

$$I^f_{2-G} = \frac{1}{j0.15}[0-(0.412)]\angle 30^\circ$$
$$= 1.37 - j2.38$$
$$I^f_{0-G} = 0 \text{ (see Fig. 11.29)}$$
$$\therefore \quad I^f_{a-G} = (-1.37 - j2.38) + (1.37 - j2.38)$$
$$= -j4.76$$

Current in phases b and c of the generator can be similarly calculated.

(d)
$$V^f_{b-1} = V^f_{1-1} + V^f_{2-1} + V^f_{0-1}$$
$$= 0.588\angle 240^\circ - 0.412\angle 120^\circ - 0.176$$
$$= -0.264 - j0.866 = 0.905\angle -107^\circ$$
$$V^f_{c-1} = V^f_{1-1} + V^f_{2-1} + V^f_{0-1}$$
$$= 0.588\angle 120^\circ - 0.412\angle 240^\circ - 0.176$$
$$= -0.264 + j0.866 = 0.905\angle 107^\circ$$

11.8 ▶ SUMMARY

Various types of unsymmetrical fault analysis have been discussed in this chapter. Both shunt and series faults are dealt with. Finally Z_{BUS} method is presented.

Problems

11.1 A 25 MVA, 11 kV generator has a $X''_d = 0.2$ pu. Its negative and zero sequence reactances are respectively 0.3 and 0.1 pu. The neutral of the generator is solidly grounded. Determine the subtransient current in the generator and the line-to-line voltages for subtransient conditions when an LG fault occurs at the generator terminals. Assume that before the occurrence of the fault, the generator is operating at no load at rated voltage. Ignore resistances.

11.2 Repeat Problem 11.1 for (a) an LL fault; and (b) an LLG fault.

11.3 A synchronous generator is rated 25 MVA, 11 kV. It is star-connected with the neutral point solidly grounded. The generator is operating at no load at rated voltage. Its reactances are $X'' = X_2 = 0.20$ and $X_0 = 0.08$ pu. Calculate the symmetrical subtransient line currents for (i) single line-to-ground fault; (ii) double line fault; (iii) double line-to-ground fault; and (iv) symmetrical three-phase fault. Compare these currents and comment.

11.4 For the generator of Problem 11.3, calculate the value of reactance to be included in the generator neutral and ground, so that line-to-ground fault current equals the three-phase fault current. What will be the value of the grounding resistance to achieve the same condition?

With the reactance value (as calculated above) included between neutral and ground, calculate the double line fault current and also double line-to-ground fault current.

11.5 Two 25 MVA, 11 kV synchronous generators are connected to a common bus bar which supplies a feeder. The star point of one of the generators is grounded through a resistance of 1.0 ohm, while that of the other generator is isolated. A line-to-ground fault occurs at the far end of the feeder. Determine: (a) the fault current; (b) the voltage to ground of the sound phases of the feeder at the fault point; and (c) voltage of the star point of the grounded generator with respect to ground.

The impedances to sequence currents of each generator and feeder are given below:

	Generator (per unit)	Feeder (ohms/phase)
Positive sequence	$j0.2$	$j0.4$
Negative sequence	$j0.15$	$j0.4$
Zero sequence	$j0.08$	$j0.8$

11.6 Determine the fault currents in each phase following a double line-to-ground short circuit at the terminals of a star-connected synchronous generator operating initially on an open circuit voltage of 1.0 pu. The positive, negative and zero sequence reactances of the generator are, respectively, $j0.35$, $j0.25$ and $j0.20$, and its star point is isolated from ground.

11.7 A three-phase synchronous generator has positive, negative and zero sequence reactances per phase, respectively, of 1.0, 0.8 and 0.4 Ω. The winding resistances are negligible. The phase sequence of the generator is *RYB* with a no load voltage of 11 kV between lines. A short circuit occurs between lines *Y* and *B* and earth at the generator terminals.

Calculate sequence currents in phase *R* and current in the earth return circuit, (a) if the generator neutral is solidly earthed; and (b) if the generator neutral is isolated.

Use *R* phase voltage as reference.

11.8 A generator supplies a group of identical motors as shown in Fig. P-11.8. The motors are rated 600 V, 90% efficiency at full load unity power factor with sum of their output ratings being 5 MW. The motors are sharing equally a load of 4 MW at rated voltage, 0.8 power factor lagging and 90% efficiency when an LG fault occurs on the low voltage side of the transformer.

Specify completely the sequence networks to simulate the fault so as to include the effect of prefault current. The group of motors can be treated as a single equivalent motor.

Find the subtransient line currents in all parts of the system with prefault current ignored.

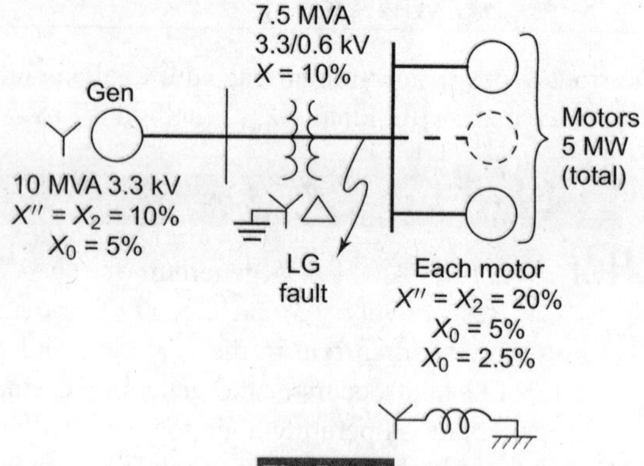

Fig. P-11.8

11.9 A double line-to-ground fault occurs on lines *b* and *c* at point *F* in the system of Fig. P-11.9. Find the subtransient current in phase *c* of machine 1, assuming prefault currents to be zero. Both machines are rated 1,200 kVA, 600 V with reactances of $X'' = X_2 = 10\%$ and $X_0 = 5\%$. Each three-phase transformer is rated 1,200 kVA, 600 V–Δ/3,300 V–*Y* with leakage reactance of 5%. The reactances of the transmission line are $X_1 = X_2 = 20\%$ and $X_0 = 40\%$ on a base of 1,200 kVA, 3,300V. The reactances of the neutral grounding reactors are 5% on the kVA base of the machines.

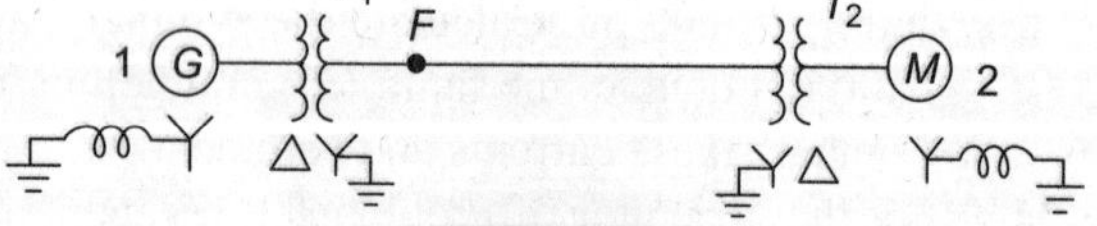

Fig. P-11.9

11.10 A synchronous machine 1 generating 1 pu voltage is connected through a *Y*/*Y* transformer of reactance 0.1 pu to two transmission lines in parallel. The other ends of the lines are connected through a *Y*/*Y* transformer of reactance 0.1 pu to a machine 2 generating 1 pu voltage. For both transformers $X_1 = X_2 = X_0$.

Calculate the current fed into a double line-to-ground fault on the line side terminals of the transformer fed from machine 2. The star points of machine 1 and of the two transformers are solidly grounded. The reactances of the machines and lines referred to a common base are

	X_1	X_2	X_0
Machine 1	0.35	0.25	0.05
Machine 2	0.30	0.20	0.04
Line (each)	0.40	0.40	0.80

11.11 Figure P-11.11 shows a power network with two generators connected in parallel to a transformer feeding a transmission line. The far end of the line is connected to an infinite bus through another transformer. Star point of each transformer, generator 1 and infinite bus are solidly grounded. The positive, negative and zero sequence reactances of various components in per unit on a common base are

Fig. P-11.11

	Positive	Negative	Zero
Generator 1	0.15	0.15	0.08
Generator 2	0.25	0.25	∞ (i.e. neutral isolated)
Each transformer	0.15	0.15	0.15
Infinite bus	0.15	0.15	0.05
Line	0.20	0.20	0.40

(a) Draw the sequence networks of the power system.

(b) With both generators and infinite bus operating at 1.0 pu voltage on no load, a line-to-ground fault occurs at one of the terminals of the star-connected winding of the transformer *A*. Calculate the currents flowing (i) in the fault; and (ii) through the transformer *A*.

11.12 A star-connected synchronous generator feeds bus bar 1 of a power system. Bus bar 1 is connected to bus bar 2 through a star/delta transformer in series with a transmission line. The power network connected to bus bar 2 can be equivalently represented by a star-connected generator with equal positive and negative sequence reactances. All star points are solidly connected to ground. The per unit sequence reactances of various components are given below:

	Positive	Negative	Zero
Generator	0.20	0.15	0.05
Transformer	0.12	0.12	0.12
Transmission Line	0.30	0.30	0.50
Power Network	X	X	0.10

Under no load condition with 1.0 pu voltage at each bus bar, a current of 4.0 pu is fed to a three-phase short circuit on bus bar 2. Determine the positive sequence reactance X of the equivalent generator of the power network.

For the same initial conditions, find the fault current for single line-to-ground fault on bus bar 1.

11.13 The reactance data for the three-phase system of Fig. P-11.13 are

Generator: $X_1 = X_2 = 0.1$ pu; $X_0 = 0.05$ pu

X_g (grounding reactance) = 0.02 pu

Transformer: $X_1 = X_2 = X_0 = 0.1$ pu

X_g (grounding reactance) = 0.04 pu

Form the positive, negative and zero sequence bus impedance matrices. For a solid LG fault at bus 1, calculate the fault current and its contributions from the generator and transformer.

Hint: Notice that the line reactances are not given. Therefore, it is convenient to obtain $Z_{1-\text{BUS}}$ directly rather than by inverting $Y_{1-\text{BUS}}$. Also $Y_{0-\text{BUS}}$ is singular and $Z_{0-\text{BUS}}$ cannot be obtained from it. In such situations, the method of unit current injection outlined below can be used.

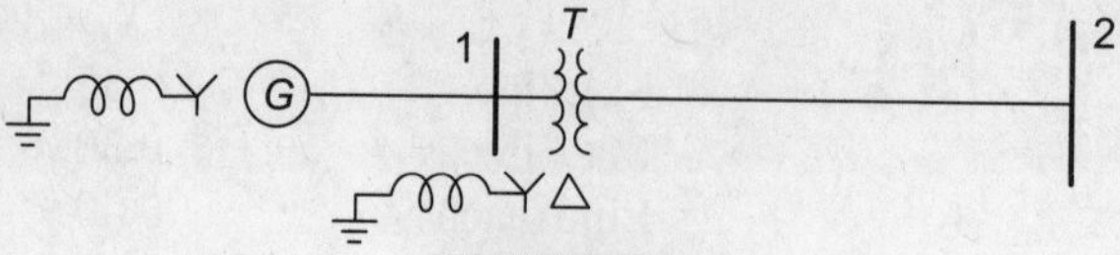

For a two-bus case

$$\begin{bmatrix} V_1 \\ V_2 \end{bmatrix} = \begin{bmatrix} Z_{11} & Z_{12} \\ Z_{21} & Z_{22} \end{bmatrix} \begin{bmatrix} I_1 \\ I_2 \end{bmatrix}$$

Injecting unit current at bus 1 (i.e., $I_1 = 1$, $I_2 = 0$), we get

$$Z_{11} = V_1$$
$$Z_{21} = V_2$$

Similarly, injecting unit current at bus 2 (i.e., $I_1 = 0, I_2 = 1$), we get

$$Z_{12} = V_1$$
$$Z_{22} = V_2$$

Z_{BUS} could thus be directly obtained by this technique.

Fig. P-11.13

11.14 Consider the 2-bus system of Example 11.3. Assume that a solid LL fault occurs on bus *f*. Determine the fault current and voltage (to ground) of the healthy phase.

11.15 Write a computer programme to be employed for studying a solid LG fault on bus 2 of the system shown in Fig. 9.17. Our aim is to find the fault current and all bus voltages and the line currents following the fault. Use the impedance data given in Example 9.5. Assume all transformers to be *Y*/Δ type with their neutrals (on HV side) solidly grounded.

Assume that the positive and negative sequence reactances of the generators are equal, while their zero sequence reactance is one-fourth of their positive sequence reactance. The zero sequence reactances of the lines are to be taken as 2.5 times their positive sequence reactances. Set all prefault voltages = 1 pu.

Multiple Choice Questions

11.1 The most frequently occurring fault in the power system is
(a) Single line to ground fault (b) Line to line (LL) fault
(c) Double line to ground fault (d) Symmetrical fault (3-ϕ fault)

11.2 In which type of faults given below, all the 3 components I_{a0}, I_{a1} and I_{a2} are equal?
(a) Single line to ground fault (b) Line to line (LL) fault
(c) Double line to ground fault (d) None to the above

11.3 In which type of fault listed below, the positive and negative sequence voltages are equal ($V_{a1} = V_{a2}$)?
(a) Line to line (LL) fault (b) Double line to ground fault
(c) Single line to ground fault (d) None of the above

11.4 In a transmission line, there is a flow of zero sequence current when
(a) There is an occurrence of overvoltage on line due to a charged cloud
(b) Line to line fault
(c) 3-phase fault
(d) Double line to ground fault

11.5 Which of the following networks gets affected by the method of neutral grounding?
(a) Zero sequence network (b) Positive sequence network
(c) Negative sequence network (d) All of the above

11.6 During the analysis of a fault, the symmetrical components are used because
(a) The results are required in terms of symmetrical components
(b) The sequence networks do not have any mutual coupling
(c) The number of equations becomes smaller
(d) All of the above

11.7 Choose the correct one from the statement given below

(a) There is a minimum zero sequence voltage and maximum negative sequence voltage at the fault point and increase and decrease, respectively, towards the neutral

(b) The zero and negative sequence voltages are maximum at fault point towards neutral

(c) The zero and negative sequence voltages are minimum at fault point and increases towards neutral

(d) None of the above

11.8 For a single line to ground fault the zero sequence current is given by $j3.0$ pu. The current carried by the neutral during the fault is

(a) $j1.0$ pu (b) $j3.0$ pu (c) $j9.0$ pu (d) $j6.0$ pu

11.9 When a fault occurs in a power system the zero sequence component of current becomes zero. The type of fault is

(a) Three phase to ground fault (b) Double line fault

(c) Double line to ground fault (d) Single line to ground fault

11.10 When a fault occurs in a power system the following sequence currents are recorded.

$$I_{\text{zero}} = -j1.246 \text{ pu}$$

$$I_{\text{positive}} = j1.923 \text{ pu}$$

$$I_{\text{negative}} = -j0.8 \text{ pu}$$

The fault is

(a) Line to ground (b) Line to line

(c) Line to line to ground (d) Three-phase

10.11 A fault occurring at the terminals of an unloaded synchronous generator operating at its rated voltage has resulted in the following values of currents and voltages:

$$I_{R0} = j2.37 \text{ pu}, I_{R1} = -j3.05 \text{ pu}, I_{R2} = j0.68 \text{ pu and } V_{R0} = V_{R1} = V_{R2} = 0.237 \text{ pu}$$

Which of the following faults has occurred?

(a) LL (b) LG (c) LLL (d) LLG

10.12 In an unbalanced three-phase system, phase current $I_{a1} = 1\angle(-90^{\circ})$ pu, negative sequence current $I_{b2} = 4\angle(150^{\circ})$ pu, zero sequence current $I_{c0} = 3\angle 90^{\circ}$ pu. The magnitude of phase current I_b in pu is

(a) 1.00 (b) 7.81 (c) 11.53 (d) 13.00

10.13 The positive, negative and zero sequence impedances of a solidly grounded system under steady-state condition always follow the relations

(a) $Z_1 > Z_2 > Z_0$ (b) $Z_1 < Z_2 < Z_0$ (c) $Z_0 < Z_1 < Z_2$ (d) $Z_1 = Z_2 = Z_0$

10.14 The sequence components of the fault current in a power system are as follows:

$$I_{\text{positive}} = j1.5 \text{ pu}, I_{\text{negative}} = -j0.5 \text{ pu}, I_{\text{zero}} = -j1 \text{ pu}$$

The type of fault in the system is

(a) LG (b) LL (c) LLG (d) LLLG

10.15 The current in a faulted phase is 100A when a line-to-ground fault occurs. The zero sequence current in this case will be

(a) Zero (b) 33.3 A (c) 66.6 A (d) 100 A

10.16 A single line to ground fault occurs on a three-phase isolated neutral system with a line to neutral voltage of V kV. The potentials on the healthy phases rise to a value equal to

(a) $\sqrt{2}$V kV (b) $\sqrt{3}$V kV (c) 3V kV (d) $(1/\sqrt{3})$V kV

10.17 If all the sequence voltages at the fault point in a power system are equal, then the fault is a
(a) Three-phase fault (b) Line to ground fault
(c) Line to line fault (d) Double line to ground fault

10.18 Zero sequence fault currents are absent when the fault is
(a) Single line to ground fault (b) Line to line fault
(c) Double line to ground fault (d) Three phase fault

10.19 What is the value of zero sequence impedance in line to line faults?
(a) $Z_0 = 1$ (b) $Z_0 = \infty$ (c) $Z_0 = 3$ Zn (d) $Z_0 = 0$

10.20 The positive, negative and zero sequence impedances of a three-phase generator are Z_1, Z_2 and Z_0, respectively. For a line-to-line fault with fault impedance Z_f the fault current $If_1 = kI_f$, where I_f is the fault current with zero fault impedance. The relation between Z_f and k is
(a) $Z_f = (z_1 + z_2)(1 - k)/k$ (b) $Z_f = (z_1 + z_2)(1 + k)/k$
(c) $Z_f = (z_1 + z_2)k/(1 - k)$ (d) $Z_f = (z_1 + z_2)\, k/(1 + k)$

References

Books

1. W.D. Stevenson, *Elements of Power System Analysis*, 4th edn, McGraw-Hill, New York, 1982.
2. O.I. Elgerd, *Electric Energy Systems Theory—An Introduction*, 2nd edn, McGraw-Hill, New York, 1982.
3. C.A. Gross, *Power System Analysis*, Wiley, New York, 1979.
4. J.R. Neuenswander, *Modern Power Systems*, International Textbook Co., New York, 1971.
5. P. Anderson, *Analysis of Faulted Power Systems*, IEEE Press, 1995.
6. A.R. Bergan and V. Vittal, *Power System Analysis*, 2nd edn, Pearson Education Asia, Delhi, 2000.
7. S.A. Soman, S.A. Khaparde, and Shubha Pandit, *Computational Methods for Large Sparse Power Systems Analysis*, KAP, Boston, 2002.

Papers

8. H.E. Brown and C.E. Person, "Short Circuit Studies of Large Systems by the Impedance Matrix Method", *Proc. PICA*, p: 335, 1967.
9. D.R. Smith, "Digital Simulation of Simultaneous Unbalances Involving Open and Faulted Conductors", *IEEE Trans,* PAS, p: 1826, 1970.
10. W. Zhou, F. Li, C. Xie, B. Wang, L. Gong, and S. Yang, "Adaptive Auto-Reclosing Scheme for Line-to-Line Non-grounded Faults on Double-Circuit Transmission Lines Based on Phase-to-Phase Reactive Power", *IEEE Access*, volume: 8, pp: 144092–144104, 2020.
11. A.R. Miller and W.S. Weil, "Alternator Short-Circuit Currents Under Unsymmetrical Terminal Conditions", *Electrical Engineering*, volume: 56, issue: 10, pp: 1268–1276, 1937.
12. J. Teng, "Unsymmetrical Short-Circuit Fault Analysis for Weakly Meshed Distribution Systems", *IEEE Transactions on Power Systems*, volume: 25, issue: 1, pp: 96–105, 2010.
13. T.M.M. O'Flaherty and A.S. Aldred, "Synchronous-Machine Stability Under Unsymmetrical Faults", *Proceedings of the IEE—Part A: Power Engineering*, volume: 109, issue: 47, pp: 431–436, 1962.
14. M. Stemmle et al., "Analysis of Unsymmetrical Faults in High Voltage Power Systems With Superconducting Fault Current Limiters", *IEEE Transactions on Applied Superconductivity*, volume: 17, issue: 2, pp: 2347–2350, June 2007.

15. W.H. Kersting and W.H. Phillips, "Modeling and Analysis of Unsymmetrical Transformer Banks Serving Unbalanced Loads", *IEEE Transactions on Industry Applications*, volume: 32, issue: 3, pp: 720–725, 1996.
16. E.H. Badawy, M.K. El-Sherbiny, A.A. Ibrahim, and M.S. Farghaly, "A Method of Analyzing Unsymmetrical Faults on Six-Phase Power Systems", *IEEE Transactions on Power Delivery*, volume: 6, issue: 3, pp: 1139–1145, 1991.
17. A.A. Girgis, C.M. Fallon, and D.L. Lubkeman, "A Fault Location Technique for Rural Distribution Feeders", *IEEE Transactions on Industry Applications*, volume: 29, issue: 6, pp: 1170–1175, 1993.
18. Jen-Hao Teng, "Systematic Short-Circuit-Analysis Method for Unbalanced Distribution Systems", *IEE Proceedings—Generation, Transmission and Distribution*, volume: 152, issue: 4, pp: 549–555, 2005.
19. E. Pillet, M. Poloujadoff, and J.P. Chassande, "Time Constants of Unsymmetrical Short Circuits of Synchronous Machines", *IEEE Transactions on Power Apparatus and Systems*, volume: PAS-98, issue: 6, pp: 2172–2180, 1979.
20. J.B. Smith and C.N. Weygandt, "Double-Line-to-Neutral Short Circuit of an Alternator", *Transactions of the American Institute of Electrical Engineers*, volume: 56, issue: 9, pp: 1149–1155, 1937.
21. M.A. El-kady and G.L. Ford, "An Advanced Probabilistic Short-Circuit Program", *IEEE Transactions on Power Apparatus and Systems*, volume: PAS-102, issue: 5, pp: 1240–1248, 1983.
22. J. Pedra, L. Sainz, F. Corcoles, and L. Guasch, "Symmetrical and Unsymmetrical Voltage Sag Effects on Three-Phase Transformers", *IEEE Transactions on Power Delivery*, volume: 20, issue: 2, pp: 1683–1691, 2005.
23. M. Mirzaei, B. Vahidi, and S.H. Hosseinian, "Accurate Fault Location and Faulted Section Determination Based on Deep Learning for a Parallel-Compensated Three-Terminal Transmission Line", *IET Generation, Transmission & Distribution*, volume: 13, issue: 13, pp: 2770–2778, 2019.
24. L. Guasch, F. Corcoles, and J. Pedra, "Effects of Symmetrical and Unsymmetrical Voltage Sags on Induction Machines", *IEEE Transactions on Power Delivery*, volume: 19, issue: 2, pp: 774–782, 2004.
25. V.C. Strezoski and D.D. Bekut, "A Canonical Model for the Study of Faults in Power Systems", *IEEE Transactions on Power Systems*, volume: 6, issue: 4, pp: 1493–1499, 1991.
26. Yao Zhang, Qingchao Zhang, Wennan Song, Yixin Yu, and Xiao Li, "Transmission Line Fault Location for Double Phase-to-Earth Fault on Non-Direct-Ground Neutral System", *IEEE Transactions on Power Delivery*, volume: 15, issue: 2, pp: 520–524, 2000.
27. Zhang Qingchao, Zhang Yao, Song Wennan, and Fang Dazhong, "Transmission Line Fault Location for Single-Phase-to-Earth Fault on Non-Direct-Ground Neutral System", *IEEE Transactions on Power Delivery*, volume: 13, issue: 4, pp: 1086–1092, 1998.
28. N. Kang and Y. Liao, "Double-Circuit Transmission-Line Fault Location Utilizing Synchronized Current Phasors", *IEEE Transactions on Power Delivery*, volume: 28, issue: 2, pp: 1040–1047, 2013.
29. S. Shimizu, H. Kado, Y. Uriu, and T. Ishigohka, "Single-Line-to-Ground Fault Test of a 3-Phase Superconducting Fault Current Limiting Reactor", *IEEE Transactions on Magnetics*, volume: 28, issue: 1, pp: 442–445, 1992.

CHAPTER 12

Power System Stability

12.1 ▶ INTRODUCTION

Developed societies of today need an ever-increasing supply of electrical power, and the demand has been increasing every year. Very complex power systems have been built to satisfy this increasing demand. The trend in electric power production is toward an interconnected network of transmission lines linking generators and loads into large integrated systems, some of which span entire continents. This vast enterprise of supplying electrical energy presents many engineering problems that provide the engineer with a variety of challenges. The planning, construction and operation of such systems become exceedingly complex. The entire design must be predicated on automatic control and not on the slow response of human operators.

Successful operation of a power system depends largely on the ability to provide reliable and uninterrupted service to the loads. Ideally, the loads must be fed at constant voltage and frequency at all times. In practical terms, this means that both voltage and frequency must be held within close tolerances so that the consumer's equipment may operate satisfactorily. The stability problem is concerned with the behaviour of the synchronous machines after they have been perturbed. If the perturbation does not involve any net change in power, the machines should return to their original state. If an unbalance between the supply and demand is created by a change in load, in generation, or in network conditions, a new operating state is necessary. In any case, *all* interconnected synchronous machines should remain in synchronism if the system if stable, i.e., they should all remain operating in parallel and at the same speed. If the oscillatory response of a power system during the transient period following a disturbance is damped and the system settles in a finite time to a new steady operating condition, we say the system is stable. If the system is not stable, it is considered unstable. This primitive definition of stability requires elaboration depending on the nature of disturbance and the nature of the system response.

12.1.1 Classification of Power System Stability

The problem of defining and classifying power system stability has been addressed by several CIGRE and IEEE Task Force reports. CIGRE Study Committee 38 and the IEEE Power System Dynamic Performance Committee addresses the issue of stability definition and classification in power systems from a fundamental viewpoint and closely examines the practical ramifications. The report aims to define power system stability more precisely, provide a systematic basis for its classification, and discuss linkages to related issues such as power system reliability and security [Kundur P et al., *IEEE Transactions on Power Systems*, Vol 19, No. 2, May 2004]. The task force defines power system stability as

"*Power system stability is the ability of an electric power system, for a given initial operating condition, to regain a state of operating equilibrium after being subjected to a physical disturbance, with most system variables bounded so that practically the entire system remains intact.*"

Figure 12.1 gives the overall picture of the power system stability problem, identifying its categories and subcategories. The following are brief descriptions of the corresponding forms of stability phenomena.

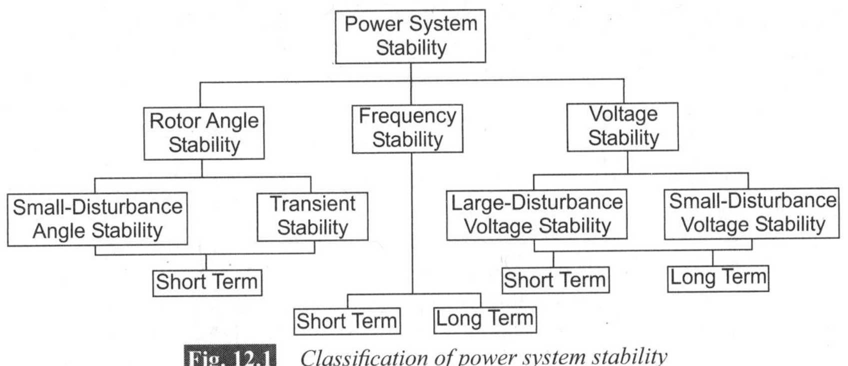

Fig. 12.1 *Classification of power system stability*

Rotor Angle Stability Rotor angle stability refers to the ability of synchronous machines of an interconnected power system to remain in synchronism after being subjected to a disturbance. It depends on the ability to maintain/restore equilibrium between electromagnetic torque and mechanical torque of each synchronous machine in the system. Instability that may result occurs in the form of increasing angular swings of some generators leading to their loss of synchronism with other generators. Basic phenomena associated with angle stability are

1. Imbalance between accelerating and decelerating generator torque.
2. Temporary (negative) surplus energy is stored in the rotating masses.
3. Capture range of synchronising torque is limited by Pull-out torque or power.
4. If the limits exceed, stability/synchronised operating may be lost.

Small-disturbance (or small-signal) rotor angle stability is concerned with the ability of the power system to maintain synchronism under small disturbances. The disturbances are considered to be sufficiently small that linearisation of system equations is permissible for purposes of analysis.

Large-disturbance rotor angle stability or transient stability, as it is commonly referred to, is concerned with the ability of the power system to maintain synchronism when subjected to a severe disturbance, such as a short circuit on a transmission line. The resulting system response involves large excursions of generator rotor angles and is influenced by the nonlinear power-angle relationship.

Transient stability depends on both the initial operating state of the system and the severity of the disturbance. Instability is usually in the form of a periodic angular separation due to insufficient synchronising torque, manifesting as *first swing instability.* However, in large power systems, transient instability may not always occur as first swing instability associated with a single mode; it could be a result of superposition of a slow inter-area swing mode and a local-plant swing mode causing a large excursion of rotor angle beyond the first swing. It could also be a result of nonlinear effects affecting a single mode causing instability beyond the first swing. *The time frame of interest in transient stability studies is usually 3 to 5 seconds following the disturbance. It may extend to 10–20 seconds for very large systems with dominant inter-area swings.*

The term *dynamic stability* also appears in the literature as a class of rotor angle stability. However, it has been used to denote different phenomena by different authors.

Voltage Stability Voltage stability refers to the ability of a power system to maintain steady voltages at all buses in the system after being subjected to a disturbance from a given initial operating condition. It depends on the ability to maintain/restore equilibrium between load demand and load supply from the power system. Instability that may result occurs in the form of a progressive fall or rise of voltages of some buses. A possible outcome of voltage instability is loss of load in an area, or tripping of transmission lines and other elements by their protective systems leading to cascading outages. Loss of synchronism of some generators may result from these outages or from operating conditions that violate field current limit.

Progressive drop in bus voltages can also be associated with rotor angle instability. For example, the loss of synchronism of machines as rotor angles between two groups of machines approach 180 causes rapid drop in voltages at intermediate points in the network close to the electrical centre. Normally, protective systems operate to separate the two groups of machines and the voltages recover to levels depending on the post-separation conditions.

The term *voltage collapse* is also often used. It is the process by which the sequence of events accompanying voltage instability leads to a blackout or abnormally low voltages in a significant part of the power system. Stable (steady) operation at low voltage may continue after transformer tap changers reach their boost limit, with intentional and/or unintentional tripping of some load. A major factor contributing to voltage instability is the voltage drop that occurs when active and reactive power flow through inductive reactances of the transmission network; this limits the capability of the transmission network for power transfer and voltage support. The power transfer and voltage support are further limited when some of the generators hit their field or armature current time-overload capability limits. Voltage stability is threatened when a disturbance increases the reactive power demand beyond the sustainable capacity of the available reactive power resources. Basic phenomenon associated with voltage stability is

1. High (reactive) loading reduces the voltage in an area.
2. Temporary load reduction.
3. Transfer capacity to the area is reduced.
4. Load demand recovers.
5. Voltage is further reduced.
6. If there is no solution to load flow, the voltage collapses.

Large-disturbance voltage stability refers to the system's ability to maintain steady voltages following large disturbances such as system faults, loss of generation or circuit contingencies. This ability is determined by the system and load characteristics, and the interactions of both continuous and discrete controls and protections. Determination of large-disturbance voltage stability requires the examination of the nonlinear response of the power system over a period of time sufficient to capture the performance and interactions of such devices as motors, under-load transformer tap changers and generator field-current limiters. The study period of interest may extend from a few seconds to tens of minutes.

Small-disturbance voltage stability refers to the system's ability to maintain steady voltages when subjected to small perturbations such as incremental changes in system load. This form of stability is influenced by the characteristics of loads, continuous controls and discrete controls at a given instant of time. This concept is useful in determining, at any instant, how the system voltages will respond to small system changes. With appropriate assumptions, system equations can be linearised for analysis thereby allowing computation of valuable sensitivity information useful in identifying factors influencing stability.

The time frame of interest for voltage stability problems may vary from a few seconds to tens of minutes. Therefore, voltage stability may be either a short-term or a long-term phenomenon as identified in Fig. 12.1.

Short-term voltage stability involves dynamics of fast acting load components such as induction motors, electronically controlled loads, and HVDC converters. The study period of interest is in the order of several seconds and analysis requires solution of appropriate system differential equations; this is similar to analysis of rotor angle stability. Dynamic modelling of loads is often essential. In contrast to angle stability, short circuits near loads are important. It is recommended that the term *transient voltage stability* not be used.

Long-term voltage stability involves slower acting equipment such as tap-changing transformers, thermostatically controlled loads and generator current limiters. The study period of interest may extend to several or many minutes, and long-term simulations are required for analysis of system dynamic performance. Stability is usually determined by the resulting outage of equipment, rather than the severity of the initial disturbance. Instability is due to the loss of long-term equilibrium (e.g., when loads try to restore their power beyond the capability of the transmission network and connected generation), post-disturbance steady-state operating point being small-disturbance unstable or a lack of attraction towards the stable post-disturbance equilibrium (e.g., when a remedial action is applied too late).The disturbance could also be a sustained load buildup (e.g., morning load increase).

Frequency Stability refers to the ability of a power system to maintain steady frequency following a severe system upset resulting in a significant imbalance between generation and load. It depends on the ability to maintain/restore equilibrium between system generation and load, with minimum unintentional loss of load. Instability that may result occurs in the form of sustained frequency swings leading to tripping of generating units and/or loads.

Severe system upsets generally result in large excursions of frequency, power flows, voltage and other system variables, thereby invoking the actions of processes, controls and protections that are not modelled in conventional transient stability or voltage stability studies. These processes may be very slow, such as boiler dynamics, or only triggered for extreme system conditions, such as volts/Hertz protection tripping generators. In large interconnected power systems, this type of situation is most commonly associated with conditions following splitting of systems into islands. Stability in this case is a question of whether or not each island will reach a state of operating equilibrium with minimal unintentional loss of load. It is determined by the overall response of the island as evidenced by its mean frequency, rather than relative motion of machines.

Generally, frequency stability problems are associated with inadequacies in equipment responses, poor coordination of control and protection equipment, or insufficient generation reserve. During frequency excursions, the characteristic times of the processes and devices that are activated will range from fraction of seconds, corresponding to the response of devices such as under-frequency load shedding and generator controls and protections, to several minutes, corresponding to the response of devices such as prime mover energy supply systems and load voltage regulators. Therefore, as identified in Fig. 12.1, frequency stability may be a ***short-term*** phenomenon or a ***long-term*** phenomenon. An example of short-term frequency instability is the formation of an under-generated island with insufficient under-frequency load shedding such that frequency decays rapidly causing blackout of the island within a few seconds. On the other hand, more complex situations in which frequency instability is caused by steam turbine over-speed controls or boiler/reactor protection and controls are longer-term phenomena with the time frame of interest ranging from tens of seconds to several minutes.

12.1.2 Relationship between Reliability, Security and Stability

Reliability of a power system refers to the probability of its satisfactory operation over the long run. It denotes the ability to supply adequate electric service on a nearly continuous basis, with few interruptions over an extended time period.

Security of a power system refers to the degree of risk in its ability to survive imminent disturbances (contingencies) without interruption of customer service. It relates to robustness of the system to imminent disturbances and, hence, depends on the system operating condition as well as the contingent probability of disturbances.

Stability of a power system, as discussed earlier, refers to the continuance of intact operation following a disturbance. It depends on the operating condition and the nature of the physical disturbance.

NERC (North American Electric Reliability Council) defines power system reliability as follows:

Reliability, in a bulk power electric system, is the degree to which the performance of the elements of that system results in power being delivered to consumers within accepted standards and in the amount desired. The degree of reliability may be measured by the frequency, duration, and magnitude of adverse effects on consumer service.

Reliability can be addressed by considering two basic functional aspects of the power systems:

Adequacy The ability of the power system to supply the aggregate electric power and energy requirements of the customer at all times, taking into account scheduled and unscheduled outages of system components.

Security The ability of the power system to withstand sudden disturbances such as electric short circuits or non-anticipated loss of system components.

The following are the essential differences among the three aspects of power system performance:

1. Reliability is the overall objective in power system design and operation. To be reliable, the power system must be secure most of the time. To be secure, the system must be stable but must also be secure against other contingencies that would not be classified as stability problems e.g., damage to equipment such as an explosive failure of a cable, fall of transmission towers due to ice loading or sabotage. As well, a system may be stable following a contingency, yet insecure due to post-fault system conditions resulting in equipment overloads or voltage violations.
2. System security may be further distinguished from stability in terms of the resulting consequences. For example, two systems may both be stable with equal stability margins, but one may be relatively more secure because the consequences of instability are less severe.
3. Security and stability are time-varying attributes which can be judged by studying the performance of the power system under a particular set of conditions. Reliability, on the other hand, is a function of the time-average performance of the power system; it can only be judged by consideration of the system's behaviour over an appreciable period of time.

The dynamics of a power system are characterised by its basic features given below:

1. Synchronous tie exhibits the typical behaviour that as power transfer is gradually increased a maximum limit is reached beyond which the system cannot stay in synchronism, i.e., it falls out of step.
2. The system is basically a spring-inertia oscillatory system with inertia on the mechanical side and spring action provided by the synchronous tie wherein power transfer is proportional to sin δ or δ (for small δ, δ being the relative internal angle of machines).
3. Because of power transfer being proportional to sin δ, the equation determining system dynamics is nonlinear for disturbances causing large variations in angle δ. Stability phenomenon peculiar to non-linear systems as distinguished from linear systems is therefore exhibited by power systems (stable up to a certain magnitude of disturbance and unstable for larger disturbances).

Accordingly power system stability problems are classified into three basic types*—steady state, dynamic and transient.

The study of steady state stability is basically concerned with the determination of the upper limit of machine loadings before losing synchronism, provided the loading is increased gradually.

Dynamic instability is more probable than steady state instability. Small disturbances are continually occurring in a power system (variations in loadings, changes in turbine speeds, etc.) which are small enough

* There are no universally accepted precise definitions of this terminology. For a definition of some important terms related to power system stability, refer to IEEE Standard Dictionary of Electrical and Electronic Terms, IEEE, New York, 1972.

not to cause the system to lose synchronism but do excite the system into the state of natural oscillations. The system is said to be dynamically stable if the oscillations do not acquire more than certain amplitude and die out quickly (i.e., the system is well-damped). In a dynamically unstable system, the oscillation amplitude is large and these persist for a long time (i.e., the system is underdamped). This kind of instability behaviour constitutes a serious threat to system security and creates very difficult operating conditions. Dynamic stability can be significantly improved through the use of power system stabilisers. Dynamic system study has to be carried out for 5–10 s and sometimes up to 30 s. Computer simulation is the only effective means of studying dynamic stability problems. The same simulation programmes are, of course, applicable to transient stability studies.

Following a sudden disturbance on a power system rotor speeds, rotor angular differences and power transfer undergo fast changes whose magnitudes are dependent upon the severity of disturbance. For a large disturbance, changes in angular differences may be so large as to cause the machines to fall out of step. This type of instability is known as *transient instability* and is a fast phenomenon usually occurring within 1 s for a generator close to the cause of disturbance. There is a large range of disturbances which may occur on a power system, but a fault on a heavily loaded line which requires opening the line to clear the fault is usually of greatest concern. The tripping of a loaded generator or the abrupt dropping of a large load may also cause instability.

The effect of short circuits (faults), the most severe type of disturbance to which a power system is subjected, must be determined in nearly all stability studies. During a fault, electrical power from nearby generators is reduced drastically, while power from remote generators is scarcely affected. In some cases, the system may be stable even with a sustained fault, whereas other systems will be stable only if the fault is cleared with sufficient rapidity. Whether the system is stable on occurrence of a fault depends not only on the system itself, but also on the type of fault, location of fault, rapidity of clearing and method of clearing, i.e., whether cleared by the sequential opening of two or more breakers or by simultaneous opening and whether or not the faulted line is reclosed. The transient stability limit is almost always lower than the steady state limit, but unlike the latter, it may exhibit different values depending on the nature, location and magnitude of disturbance.

Modern power systems have many interconnected generating stations, each with several generators and many loads. The machines located at anyone point in a system normally act in unison. It is, therefore, common practice in stability studies to consider all the machines at one point as one large machine. Also machines which are not separated by lines of high reactance are lumped together and considered as one equivalent machine. Thus, a multimachine system can often be reduced to an equivalent few machine system. If synchronism is lost, the machines of each group stay together although they go out of step with other groups. Qualitative behaviour of machines in an actual system is usually that of a two-machine system. Because of its simplicity, the two-machine system is extremely useful in describing the general concepts of power system stability and the influence of various factors on stability. It will be seen in this chapter that a two-machine system can be regarded as a single-machine system connected to infinite system.

Stability study of a multimachine system must necessarily be carried out on a digital computer.

12.2 ▶ DYNAMICS OF SYNCHRONOUS MACHINE

The kinetic energy of the rotor at synchronous machine is

$$\text{K.E.} = \frac{1}{2} J\omega^2_{sm} \times 10^{-6} \text{ MJ}$$

where J = rotor moment of inertia in kg-m^2

ω_{sm} = synchronous speed in rad (mech)/s

But $\omega_s = \left(\frac{P}{2}\right) \omega_{sm}$ = rotor speed in rad (elect)/s

where P = number of machine poles

$$\therefore \quad \text{K.E.} = \frac{1}{2}\left(J\left(\frac{2}{P}\right)^2 \omega_s \times 10^{-6}\right)\omega_s$$

$$= \frac{1}{2} M\omega_s$$

where $M = J\left(\frac{2}{P}\right)^2 \omega_s \times 10^{-6}$

= moment of inertia in MJ-s/elect rad

We shall define the inertia constant H such that

$$GH = \text{K.E.} = \frac{1}{2} M\omega_s \text{ MJ}$$

where G = machine rating (base) in MVA (three-phase)

H = *inertia constant* in MJ/MVA or MW-s/MVA

It immediately follows that

$$M = \frac{2GH}{\omega_s} = \frac{GH}{\pi f} \text{ MJ-s/elect rad} \tag{12.1}$$

$$= \frac{GH}{180 f} \text{ MJ-s/elect degree}$$

M is also called the *inertia constant.*

Taking G as base, the inertia constant in pu is

$$M(\text{pu}) = \frac{H}{\pi f} \text{ s}^2\text{/elect rad} \tag{12.2}$$

$$= \frac{H}{180 f} \text{ s}^2\text{/elect degree}$$

The inertia constant H has a characteristic value or a range of values for each class of machines. Table 12.1 lists some typical inertia constants.

Table 12.1 Typical inertia constants of synchronous machines[1]

Type of Machine	*Inertia Constant H Stored Energy in MW-s per MVA*[2]	
Turbine Generator		
Condensing	1,800 rpm	9–6
	3,000 rpm	7–4
Non-Condensing	3,000 rpm	4–3
Waterwheel Generator		
Slow-speed (< 200 rpm)		2–3
High-speed (> 200 rpm)		2–4
Synchronous Condenser[3]		
Large		1.25

(*Contd.*)

Table 12.1 (Contd.)

Type of Machine	*Inertia Constant H Stored Energy in MW-s per MVA*[2]
Small	1.00
Synchronous Motor with load varying from 1.0 to 5.0 and higher for heavy flywheels	2.00

It is observed from Table 12.1 that the value of H is considerably higher for steam turbogenerator than for water wheel generator. Thirty to sixty per cent of the total inertia of a steam turbogenerator unit is that of the primemover, whereas only 4–15% of the inertia of a hydroelectric generating unit is that of the waterwheel, including water.

[1] Reprinted with permission of the Westinghouse Electric Corporation from Electrical Transmission and Distribution Reference Book.

[2] Where range is given, the first figure applies to the smaller MVA sizes.

[3] Hydrogen-cooled, 25 per cent less.

The Swing Equation Figure 12.2 shows the torque, speed and flow of mechanical and electrical powers in a synchronous machine. It is assumed that the windage, friction and iron-loss torque is negligible. The differential equation governing the rotor dynamics can then be written as

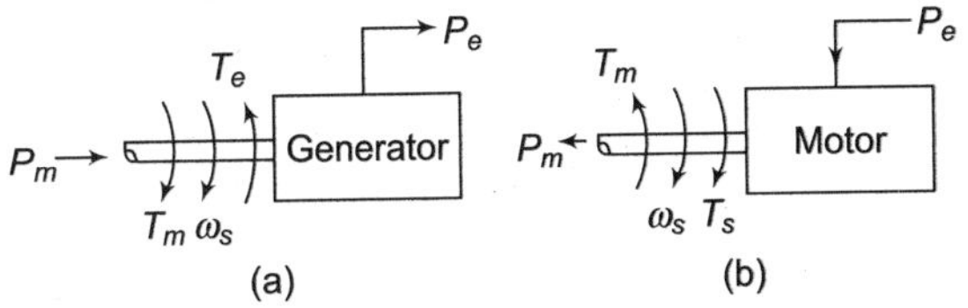

Fig. 12.2 *Flow of mechanical and electrical powers in a synchronous machine*

$$J\frac{d^2\theta_m}{dt^2} = T_m - T_e \text{ Nm} \tag{12.3}$$

where

θ_m = angle in rad (mech)

T_m = turbine torque in Nm; it acquires a negative value for a motoring machine

T_e = electromagnetic torque developed in Nm; it acquires negative value for a motoring machine

While the rotor undergoes dynamics as per Eq. (12.3), the rotor speed changes by insignificant magnitude for the time period of interest (1s) [Section 12.1]. Equation (12.3) can therefore be converted into its more convenient power form by assuming the rotor speed to remain constant at the synchronous speed (ω_{sm}). Multiplying both sides of Eq. (12.3) by ω_{sm} we can write

$$J\omega_{sm}\frac{d^2\theta_m}{dt^2} \times 10^{-6} = P_m - P_e \text{ MW} \tag{12.4}$$

where

P_m = mechanical power input in MW

P_e = electrical power output in MW; stator copper loss is assumed negligible

Rewriting Eq. (12.4)

$$\left(J\left(\frac{2}{P}\right)^2 \omega_s \times 10^{-6}\right)\frac{d^2\theta_e}{dt^2} = P_m - P_e \text{ MW}$$

where θ_e = angle in rad (elect)

or

$$M\frac{d^2\theta_e}{dt^2} = P_m - P_e \tag{12.5}$$

It is more convenient to measure the angular position of the rotor with respect to a synchronously rotating frame of reference. Let

$\delta = \theta_e - \omega_s t$; rotor angular displacement from synchronously rotating reference frame (called *torque angle/power angle*) (12.6)

From Eq. (12.6)

$$\frac{d^2\theta_e}{dt^2} = \frac{d^2\delta}{dt^2} \tag{12.7}$$

Hence, Eq. (12.5) can be written in terms of δ as

$$M\frac{d^2\delta}{dt^2} = P_m - P_e \text{ MW} \tag{12.8}$$

With M as defined in Eq. (12.1), we can write

$$\frac{GH}{\pi f}\frac{d^2\delta}{dt^2} = P_m - P_e \text{ MW} \tag{12.9}$$

Dividing throughout by G, the MVA rating of the machine,

$$M(\text{pu})\frac{d^2\delta}{dt^2} = P_m - P_e;\text{ in pu of machine rating as base} \tag{12.10}$$

where

$$M(\text{pu}) = \frac{H}{\pi f}$$

or

$$\frac{H}{\pi f}\frac{d^2\delta}{dt^2} = P_m - P_e \text{ pu} \tag{12.11}$$

This equation, Eq. (12.10)/Eq. (12.11), is called the *swing equation* and it describes the rotor dynamics for a synchronous machine (generating/motoring). It is a second-order differential equation where the damping term (proportional to $d\delta/dt$) is absent because of the assumption of a lossless machine and the fact that the torque of *damper winding* has been ignored. This assumption leads to pessimistic results in transient stability analysis—damping helps to stabilise the system. Damping must of course be considered in a dynamic stability study. Since the electrical power P_e depends upon the sine of angle δ [see Eq. (12.29)], the *swing equation is a nonlinear second-order differential equation.*

12.2.1 Multimachine System

In a multimachine system, a common system base must be chosen.

Let

$$G_{\text{mach}} = \text{machine rating (base)}$$
$$G_{\text{system}} = \text{system base}$$

Equation (12.11) can then be written as

$$\frac{G_{\text{mach}}}{G_{\text{system}}}\left(\frac{H_{\text{mach}}}{f}\frac{d^2\delta}{dt^2}\right) = (P_m - P_e)\frac{G_{\text{mach}}}{G_{\text{system}}}$$

or

$$\frac{H_{\text{system}}}{\pi f}\frac{d^2\delta}{dt^2} = P_m - P_e \text{ pu in system base} \tag{12.12}$$

where

$$H_{\text{system}} = H_{\text{mach}}\left(\frac{G_{\text{mach}}}{G_{\text{system}}}\right) \tag{12.13}$$

$$= \text{machine inertia constant in system base}$$

12.2.2 Machines Swinging Coherently

Consider the swing equations of two machines on a *common system base*.

$$\frac{H_1}{\pi f}\frac{d^2\delta_1}{dt^2} = P_{m1} - P_{e1} \text{ pu} \tag{12.14}$$

$$\frac{H_2}{\pi f}\frac{d^2\delta_2}{dt^2} = P_{m2} - P_{e2} \text{ pu} \tag{12.15}$$

Since the machine rotors swing together (coherently or in unison)

$$\delta_1 = \delta_2 = \delta$$

Adding Eqs. (12.14) and (12.15),

$$\frac{H_{eq}}{\pi f}\frac{d^2\delta}{dt^2} = P_m - P_e \tag{12.16}$$

where

$$\begin{aligned} P_m &= P_{m1} + P_{m2} \\ P_e &= P_{e1} + P_{e2} \\ H_{eq} &= H_1 + H_2 \end{aligned} \tag{12.17}$$

The two machines swinging coherently are thus reduced to a single machine as in Eq. (12.16). The equivalent inertia in Eq. (12.17) can be written as

$$H_{eq} = H_{1\text{ mach}}\, G_{1\text{ mach}}/G_{\text{system}} + H_{2\text{ mach}}\, G_{2\text{ mach}}/G_{\text{system}} \tag{12.18}$$

The above results are easily extendable to any number of machines swinging coherently.

Example 12.1 A 50 Hz, four-pole turbogenerator rated 100 MVA, 11 kV has an inertia constant of 8.0 MJ/MVA.

(a) Find the stored energy in the rotor at synchronous speed.

(b) If the mechanical input is suddenly raised to 80 MW for an electrical load of 50 MW, find rotor acceleration, neglecting mechanical and electrical losses.

(c) If the acceleration calculated in part (b) is maintained for 10 cycles, find the change in torque angle and rotor speed in revolutions per minute at the end of this period.

Solution

(a) Stored energy = $GH = 100 \times 8 = 800$ MJ

(b) $P_a = 80 - 50 = 30$ $\qquad \text{MW} = \text{M}\,\dfrac{d^2\delta}{dt^2}$

$$M = \frac{GH}{180f} = \frac{800}{180 \times 50} = \frac{4}{45} \text{ MJ-s/elect deg}$$

$\therefore$

$$\frac{4}{45}\frac{d^2d}{dt^2} = 30$$

or

$$\alpha = \frac{d^2\delta}{dt^2} = 337.5 \text{ elect deg/s}^2$$

(c) 10 cycles = 0.2 s

$$\text{Change in } \delta = \frac{1}{2}(337.5) \times (0.2)^2 = 6.75 \text{ elect deg}$$

$$\alpha = 60 \times \frac{337.5}{2 \times 360°} = 28.125 \text{ rpm/s}$$

∴ Rotor speed at the end of 10 cycles

$$= \frac{120 \times 50}{4} + 28.125 \times 0.2$$

$$= 1505.625 \text{ rpm}$$

12.3 ▶ POWER ANGLE EQUATION

In solving the swing equation [Eq. (12.10)], certain simplifying assumptions are usually made. These are

1. Mechanical power input to the machine (P_m) remains constant during the period of electromechanical transient of interest. In other words, it means that the effect of the turbine governing loop is ignored, being much slower than the speed of the transient. This assumption leads to pessimistic result—governing loop helps to stabilise the system.
2. Rotor speed changes are insignificant—these have already been ignored in formulating the swing equation.
3. Effect of voltage regulating loop during the transient is ignored, as a consequence the generated machine emf remains constant. This assumption also leads to pessimistic results—voltage regulator helps to stabilise the system.

Before the swing equation can be solved, it is necessary to determine the dependence of the electrical power output (P_e) upon the rotor angle.

12.3.1 Simplified Machine Model

For a salient pole machine, the per phase induced emf-terminal voltage equation under steady conditions is

$$E = V + jX_d I_d + jX_q I_q;\ X_d > X_q \tag{12.19}$$

where

$$I = I_d + I_q \tag{12.20}$$

and usual symbols are used.

Under transient condition

$$X_d \rightarrow X'_d < X_d$$

but

$$X'_q = X_q \text{ since the main field is on the } d\text{-axis}$$

$$X'_d < X_q \text{; but the difference is small}$$

Equation (12.19) during the transient modifies to

$$E' = V + jX'_d I_d + jX_q I_q \tag{12.21}$$

$$= V + jX_q(I - I_d) + jX'_d I_d$$

$$= (V + jX_q I) + j(X'_d - X_q)I_d \tag{12.22}$$

The phasor diagram corresponding to Eqs. (12.21) and (12.22) is drawn in Fig. 12.3.

Since under transient condition, $X'_d < X_d$ but X_q remains almost unaffected, it is fairly valid to assume that

$$X'_d \approx X_q \tag{12.23}$$

Equation (12.22) now becomes

$$E' = V + jX_q I$$

$$= V + jX'_d I \tag{12.24}$$

The machine model corresponding to Eq. (12.24) is drawn in Fig. 12.4 which also applies to a cylindrical rotor machine where $X'_d = X'_q = X'_s$ (transient synchronous reactance).

The simplified machine model of Fig. 12.4 will be used in all stability studies.

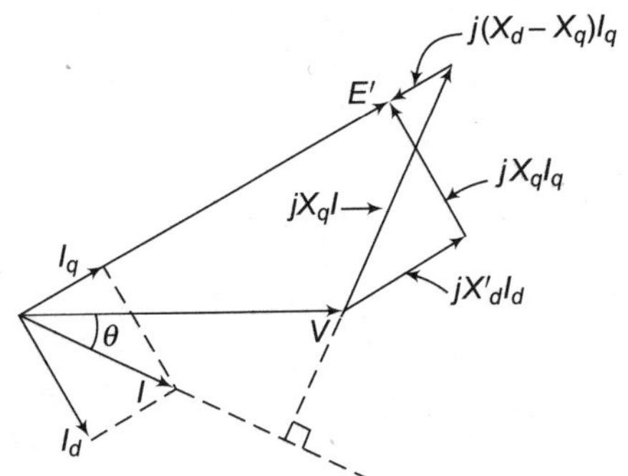

Fig. 12.3 *Phasor diagram—salient pole machine*

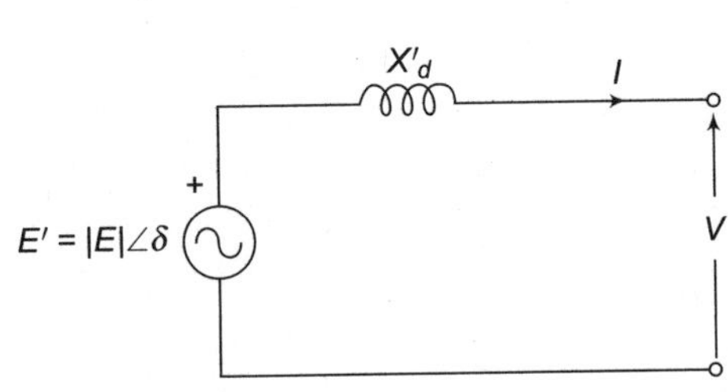

Fig. 12.4 *Simplified machine model*

12.3.2 Power Angle Curve

For the purposes of stability studies $|E'|$, transient emf of generator/motor remains constant or is the independent variable determined by the voltage regulating loop but V, the generator determined terminal voltage is a dependent variable. Therefore, the nodes (buses) of the stability study network pertain to the emf terminal in the machine model as shown in Fig. 12.5, while the machine reactance (X_d') is absorbed in the system network as different from a load flow study. Further, the loads (other than large synchronous motors) will be replaced by equivalent static admittances (connected in shunt between transmission network buses and the reference bus). This is so because load voltages vary during a stability study (in a load flow study, these remain constant within a narrow band).

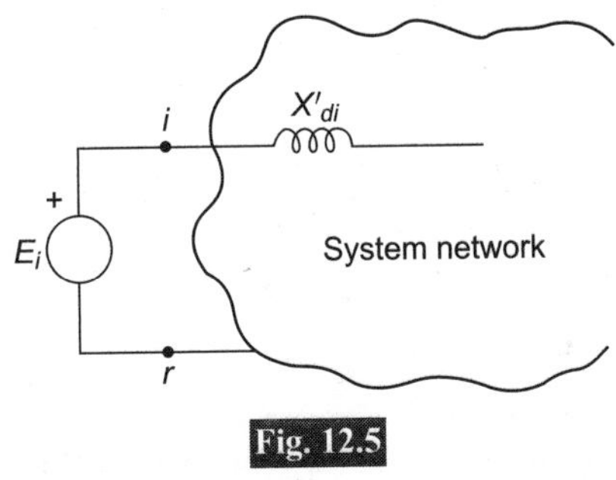

Fig. 12.5

For the two-bus system of Fig. 12.6,

$$\boldsymbol{Y}_{\text{BUS}} = \begin{bmatrix} Y_{11} & Y_{12} \\ Y_{21} & Y_{22} \end{bmatrix}; \; Y_{12} = Y_{21} \qquad (12.25)$$

Complex power into bus is given by

$$P_i + jQ_i = E_i I_i^*$$

At bus 1,

$$P_1 + jQ_1 = E_1'(Y_{11}E_1')^* + E_1\,(Y_{12}E_2')^* \qquad (12.26)$$

But,

$$E_1' = |E_1'| \angle\delta_1; \; E_2' = |E_2'| \angle\delta_2$$

$$Y_{11} = G_{11} + jB_{11}; \; Y_{12} = |Y_{12}| \angle\theta_{12}$$

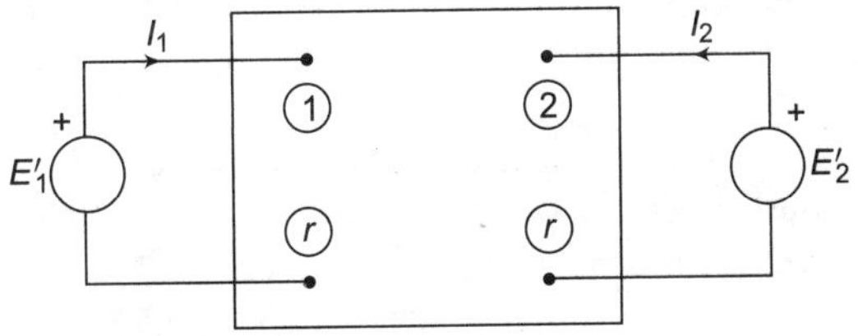

Fig. 12.6 *Two-bus stability study network*

Since in solution of the swing equation only real power is involved, we have from Eq. (12.26)

$$P_1 = |E_1'|^2\, G_{11} + |E_1'|\, |E_2'|\, |Y_{12}| \cos\,(\delta_1 - \delta_2 - \theta_{12}) \qquad (12.27)$$

A similar equation will hold at bus 2.

Let

$$|E_1'|^2 G_{11} = P_c$$

$$|E_1'|\, |E_2'|\, |Y_{12}| = P_{\max}$$

$$\delta_1 - \delta_2 = \delta$$

and

$$\phi_{12} = \pi/2 - \gamma$$

Then Eq. (12.27) can be written as

$$P_1 = P_c + P_{\max} \sin(\delta - \gamma); \textit{ Power Angle Equation} \tag{12.28}$$

For a purely reactive network

$$G_{11} = 0 \; (\therefore \;\; P_c = 0); \text{ lossless network}$$

$$\theta_{12} = \pi/2, \quad \therefore \quad \gamma = 0$$

Hence,

$$P_e = P_{\max} \sin \delta \tag{12.29a}$$

where

$$P_{\max} = \frac{|E_1'||E_2'|}{X}; \text{ simplified power angle equation} \tag{12.29b}$$

where

X = transfer reactance between nodes (i.e., between E_1' and E_2').

The graphical plot of power angle equation [Eq. (12.29)] is shown in Fig. 12.7.

The swing equation [Eq. (12.10)] can now be written as

$$\frac{H}{\pi f} \frac{d^2\delta}{dt^2} = P_m - P_{\max} \sin \delta \text{ pu} \tag{12.30}$$

which, as already stated, is a nonlinear second-order differential equation with no damping.

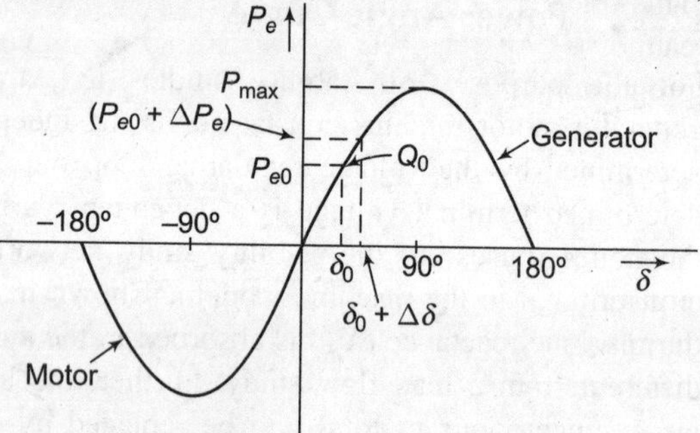

Fig. 12.7 *Power angle curve*

12.4 ▶ NODE ELIMINATION TECHNIQUE

In stability studies, it has been indicated that the buses to be considered are those which are excited by the internal machine voltages (transient emfs) and not the load buses which are excited by the terminal voltages of the generators. Therefore, in Y_{BUS} formulation for the stability study, the load buses must be eliminated. Three methods are available for bus elimination. These are illustrated by the simple system of Fig. 12.8(a) whose reactance diagram is drawn in Fig. 12.8(b). In this simple situation, bus 3 gets easily eliminated by parallel combination of the lines. Thus,

$$X_{12} = 0.25 + 0.1 + \frac{0.5}{2}$$
$$= 0.6$$

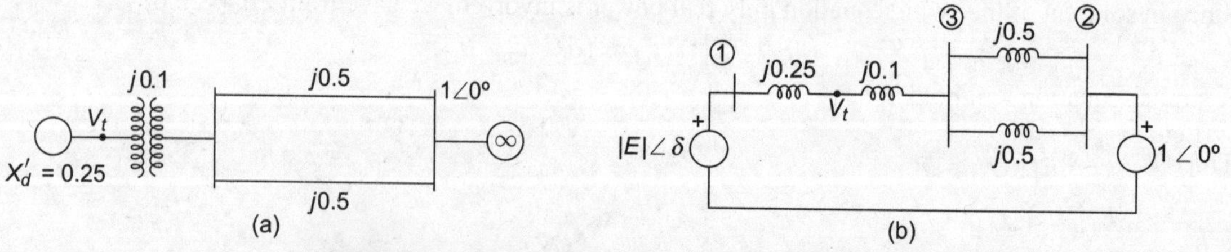

Fig. 12.8 *A simple system with its reactance diagram*

Consider now a more complicated case wherein a three-phase fault occurs at the midpoint of one of the lines in which case the reactance diagram becomes that of Fig. 12.9(a).

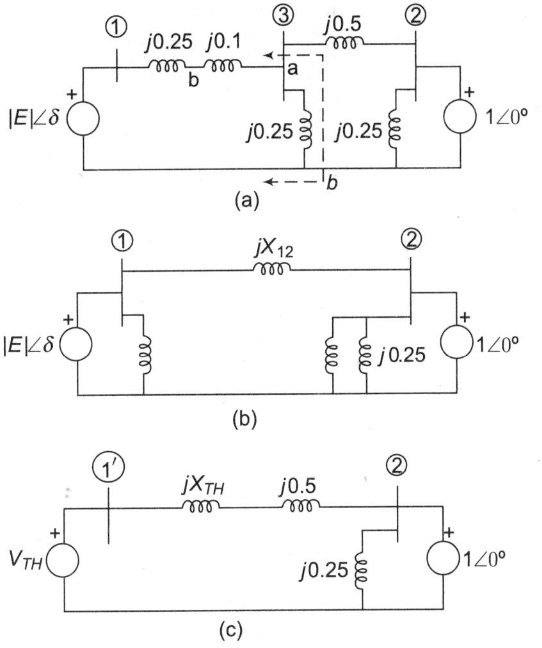

(a)

(b)

(c)

Fig. 12.9

12.4.1 Star-Delta Conversion

Converting the star at the bus 3 to delta, the network transforms to that of Fig. 12.9(b) wherein

$$X_{12} = \frac{0.25 \times 0.35 + 0.35 \times 0.5 + 0.5 \times 0.25}{0.25}$$

$$= 1.55$$

This method for a complex network, however, cannot be mechanised for preparing a computer programme.

12.4.2 Thevenin's Equivalent

With reference to Fig. 12.9(a), the Thevenin's equivalent for the network portion to the left of terminals *ab* as drawn in Fig. 12.9(c) wherein bus 1 has been modified to 1′,

$$V_{TH} = \frac{0.25}{0.25 + 0.35} |E'| \angle\delta$$

$$= 0.417 |E'| \angle\delta$$

$$X_{TH} = \frac{0.35 \times 0.25}{0.35 + 0.25} = 0.146$$

Now,

$$X_{12} = 0.146 + 0.5 = 0.646^*$$

This method obviously is cumbersome to apply for a network of even small complexity and cannot be computerised.

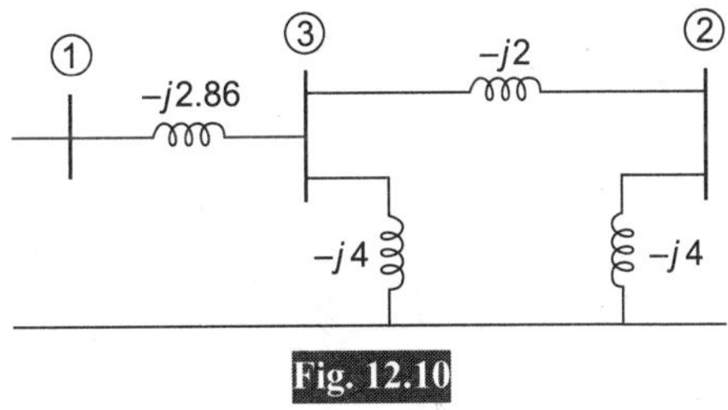

Fig. 12.10

12.4.3 Node Elimination Technique

Formulate the bus admittances for the three-bus system of Fig. 12.9(a). This network is redrawn in Fig. 12.10 wherein instead of reactance branch, admittances are shown. For this network,

$$Y_{BUS} = j \begin{matrix} 1 \\ 2 \\ 3 \end{matrix} \begin{bmatrix} -2.86 & 0 & 2.86 \\ 0 & -6 & 2 \\ 2.86 & 2 & -8.86 \end{bmatrix}$$

The bus 3 is to be eliminated.

* This value is different from that obtained by star delta transformation as V_{TH} is no longer $|E'| \angle\delta$; in fact it is 0.417 $|E'| \angle\delta$.

In general for a three-bus system

$$\begin{bmatrix} I_1 \\ I_2 \\ I_3 \end{bmatrix} = \begin{bmatrix} Y_{11} & Y_{12} & Y_{13} \\ Y_{21} & Y_{22} & Y_{23} \\ Y_{31} & Y_{32} & Y_{33} \end{bmatrix} \begin{bmatrix} V_1 \\ V_2 \\ V_3 \end{bmatrix} \tag{12.31}$$

Since no source is connected at the bus 3,

$$I_3 = 0$$

or

$$Y_{31}V_1 + Y_{32}V_2 + Y_{33}V_3 = 0$$

or

$$V_3 = -\frac{Y_{31}}{Y_{33}}V_1 - \frac{Y_{32}}{Y_{33}}V_2 \tag{12.32}$$

Substituting this value of V_3 in the remaining two equations of Eq. (12.31), thereby eliminating V_3,

$$I_1 = Y_{11}V_1 + Y_{12}V_2 + Y_{13}V_3$$

$$= \left(Y_{11} - \frac{Y_{13}Y_{31}}{Y_{33}}\right)V_1 + \left(Y_{12} - \frac{Y_{13}Y_{32}}{Y_{33}}\right)V_2$$

In compact form

$$\boldsymbol{Y}_{\text{BUS}}\text{ (reduced)} = \begin{bmatrix} Y'_{11} & Y'_{12} \\ Y'_{21} & Y'_{22} \end{bmatrix} \tag{12.33}$$

where

$$Y'_{11} = Y_{11} - \frac{Y_{13}Y_{31}}{Y_{33}} \tag{12.34a}$$

$$Y'_{12} = Y'_{21} = Y_{12} - \frac{Y_{13}Y_{32}}{Y_{33}} \tag{12.34b}$$

$$Y'_{22} = Y_{22} - \frac{Y_{23}Y_{32}}{Y_{33}} \tag{12.34c}$$

In general, in eliminating node n

$$Y_{kj}\text{ (new)} = Y_{kj}\text{ (old)} - \frac{Y_{kn}\text{(old)}Y_{rj}\text{(old)}}{Y_{nn}\text{(old)}} \tag{12.35}$$

Applying Eq. (12.34) to the example in hand

$$\boldsymbol{Y}_{\text{BUS}}\text{ (reduced)} = j\begin{bmatrix} -1.937 & 0.646 \\ 0.646 & -5.549 \end{bmatrix}$$

It then follows that

$$X_{12} = \frac{1}{0.646} = 1.548\ (\approx 1.55)$$

Example 12.2 In the system shown in Fig. 12.11, a three-phase static capacitive reactor of reactance 1 pu per phase is connected through a switch at motor bus bar. Calculate the limit of steady state power with and without reactor switch closed. Recalculate the power limit with capacitive reactor replaced by an inductive reactor of the same value. Assume the internal voltage of the generator to be 1.2 pu and that of the motor to be 1.0 pu.

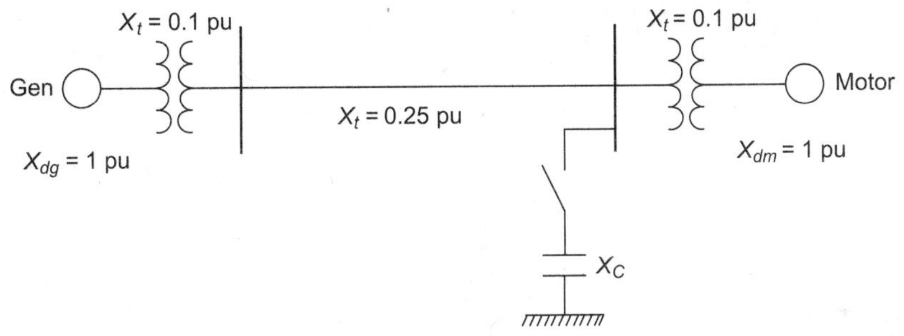

Fig. 12.11

Solution

1. Steady state power limit without reactor

$$= \frac{|E_g||E_m|}{X(\text{total})} = \frac{1.2 \times 1}{1 + 0.1 + 0.25 + 0.1 + 1} = 0.49 \text{ pu}$$

2. Equivalent circuit with capacitive reactor is shown in Fig. 12.12(a).
   Converting star to delta, the network of Fig. 12.12(a) is reduced to that of Fig. 12.12(b) where

$$jX(\text{transfer}) = \frac{j1.35 \times j1.1 + j1.1 \times (-j1.0) + (-j1.0) \times j1.35}{-j1.0}$$

$$= j0.965$$

$$\text{Steady state power limit} = \frac{1.2 \times 1}{0.965} = 1.244 \text{ pu}$$

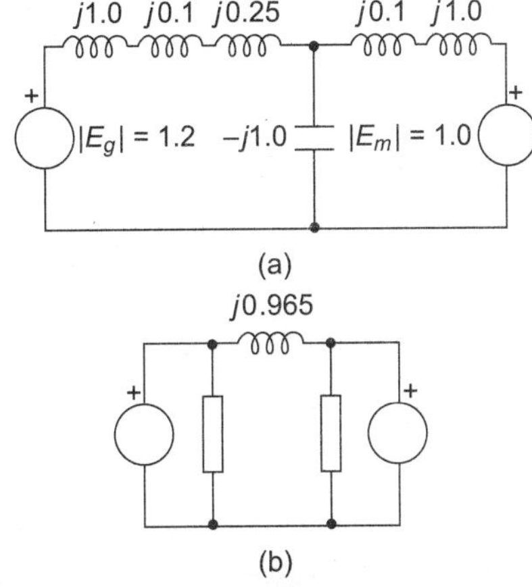

Fig. 12.12

3. With capacitive reactance replaced by inductive reactance, we get the equivalent circuit of Fig. 12.13. Converting star to delta, we have the transfer reactance of

$$jX(\text{transfer}) = \frac{j1.35 \times j1.1 + j1.1 \times j1.0 + j1.0 \times j1.35}{j1.0}$$

$$= j3.935$$

$$\text{Steady state power limit} = \frac{1.2 \times 1}{3.935} = 0.304 \text{ pu}$$

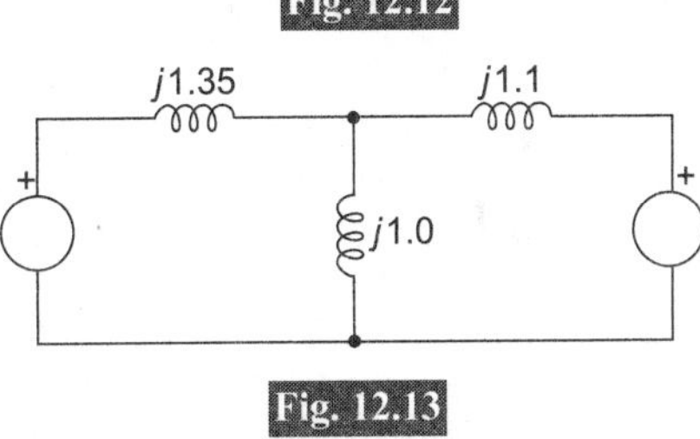

Fig. 12.13

Example 12.3 The generator of Fig. 12.8(a) is delivering 1.0 pu power to the infinite bus ($|V| = 1.0$ pu), with the generator terminal voltage of $|V_i| = 1.0$ pu. Calculate the generator emf behind transient reactance. Find the maximum power that can be transferred under the following conditions:

(a) System healthy
(b) One line shorted (3-phase) in the middle
(c) One line open.

Plot all the three power angle curves.

Solution

Let $$V_t = |V_t| \angle\alpha = 1\angle\alpha$$

From power angle equation

$$\frac{|V_t||V|}{X} \sin\alpha = P_e$$

or $$\left(\frac{1\times 1}{0.25+0.1}\right)\sin\alpha = 1$$

or $$\alpha = 20.5^\circ$$

Current into infinite bus,

$$I = \frac{|V_t|\angle\alpha - |V|\angle 0^\circ}{jX}$$

$$= \frac{1\angle 20.5^\circ - 1\angle 0^\circ}{j0.35}$$

$$= 1 + j0.18 = 1.016\ \angle 10.3^\circ$$

Voltage behind transient reactance,

$$E' = 1\angle 0^\circ + j0.6 \times (1 + j0.18)$$

$$= 0.892 + j0.6 = 1.075\ \angle 33.9^\circ$$

(a) System healthy

$$P_{max} = \frac{|V||E'|}{X_{12}} = \frac{1\times 1.075}{0.6} = 1.79 \text{ pu}$$

$\therefore$ $$P_e = 1.79 \sin\delta \qquad \text{(i)}$$

(b) One line shorted in the middle: As already calculated in this section,

$$X_{12} = 1.55$$

$\therefore$ $$P_{max} = \frac{1\times 1.075}{1.55} = 0.694 \text{ pu}$$

or $$P_e = 0.694 \sin\delta \qquad \text{(ii)}$$

(c) One line open:

It easily follows from Fig. 12.8(b) that

$$X_{12} = 0.25 + 0.1 + 0.5 = 0.85$$

$\therefore$ $$P_{max} = \frac{1\times 1.075}{0.85} = 1.265$$

or $$P_e = 1.265 \sin\delta \qquad \text{(iii)}$$

The plot of the three power angle curves [Eqs. (i), (ii) and (iii)] is drawn in Fig. 12.14. Under healthy condition, the system is operated with $P_m = P_e = 1.0$ pu and $\delta_0 = 33.9^\circ$, i.e., at the point P on the power angle curve 1.79 sin δ. As one line is shorted in the middle, P_m remains fixed at 1.0 pu (governing system acts instantaneously) and is further assumed to remain fixed throughout the transient (governing action is slow), while the operating point instantly shifts to Q on the curve 0.694 sin δ at $\delta = 33.9^\circ$. Notice that because of machine inertia, the rotor angle can not change suddenly.

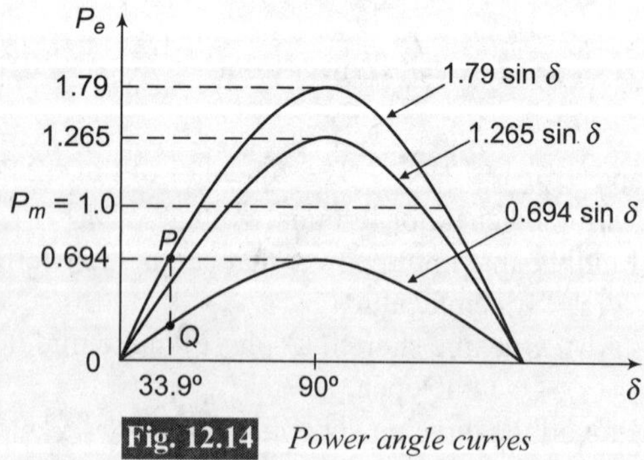

Fig. 12.14 *Power angle curves*

12.5 ▶ SIMPLE SYSTEMS

12.5.1 Machine Connected to Infinite Bus

Figure 12.15 is the circuit model of a single machine connected to infinite bus through a line of reactance X_e. In this simple case

$$X_{\text{transfer}} = X'_d + X_e$$

From Eq. 12.29(b)

$$P_e = \frac{|E'||V|}{X_{\text{transfer}}} \sin \delta = P_{\max} \sin \delta \qquad (12.36)$$

The dynamics of this system are described in Eq. (12.11) as

$$\frac{H}{\pi f}\frac{\mathrm{d}^2\delta}{\mathrm{d}t^2} = P_m - P_e \text{ pu} \qquad (12.37)$$

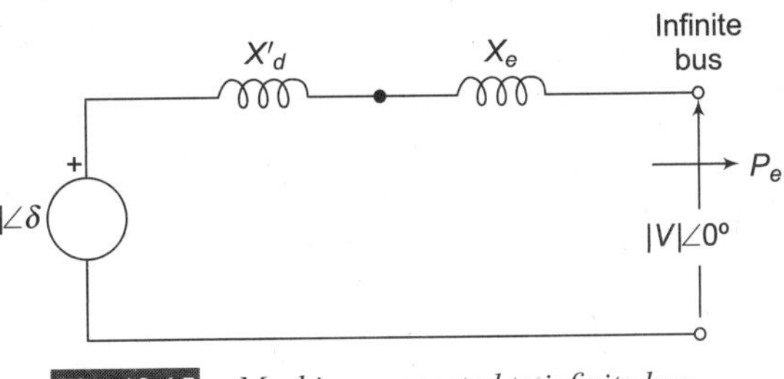

Fig. 12.15 *Machine connected to infinite bus*

12.5.2 Two-Machine System

The case of two finite machines connected through a line (X_e) is illustrated in Fig. 12.16 where one of the machines must be generating and the other must be motoring. Under steady condition, before the system goes into dynamics,

$$P_{m1} = -P_{m2} = P_m \qquad (12.38a)$$

Fig. 12.16 *Two-machine system*

and the mechanical input/output of the two machines is assumed to remain constant at these values throughout the dynamics (governor action assumed slow). During steady state or in dynamic condition, the electrical power output of the generator must be absorbed by the motor (network being lossless). Thus, at all time

$$P_{e1} = -P_{e2} = P_e \qquad (12.38b)$$

The swing equations for the two machines can now be written as

$$\frac{\mathrm{d}^2\delta_1}{\mathrm{d}t^2} = \pi f\left(\frac{P_{m1} - P_{e1}}{H_1}\right) = \pi f\left(\frac{P_m - P_e}{H_1}\right) \qquad (12.39a)$$

and

$$\frac{\mathrm{d}^2\delta_2}{\mathrm{d}t^2} = \pi f\left(\frac{P_{m2} - P_{e2}}{H_2}\right) = \pi f\left(\frac{P_e - P_m}{H_2}\right) \qquad (12.39b)$$

Subtracting Eq. 12.39(b) from Eq. 12.39(a)

$$\frac{\mathrm{d}^2(\delta_1 - \delta_2)}{\mathrm{d}t^2} = \pi f\left(\frac{H_1 + H_2}{H_1H_2}\right)(P_m - P_e) \qquad (12.40)$$

or

$$\frac{H_{eq}}{\pi f}\frac{\mathrm{d}^2\delta}{\mathrm{d}t^2} = P_m - P_e \qquad (12.41)$$

where

$$\delta = \delta_1 - \delta_2 \qquad (12.42)$$

$$H_{eq} = \frac{H_1H_2}{H_1 + H_2} \qquad (12.43)$$

The electrical power interchange is given by expression

$$P_e = \frac{|E_1'||E_2'|}{X_{d1}' + X_e + X_{d2}'} \sin \delta \tag{12.44}$$

The swing equation Eq. (12.41) and the power angle equation Eq. (12.44) have the same form as for a single machine connected to infinite bus. Thus a two-machine system is equivalent to a single machine connected to infinite bus. Because of this, the single-machine (connected to infinite bus) system would be studied extensively in this chapter.

Example 12.4 In the system of Example 12.3, the generator has an inertia constant of 4 MJ/MVA, write the swing equation upon occurrence of the fault. What is the initial angular acceleration? If this acceleration can be assumed to remain constant for $\Delta t = 0.05$ s, find the rotor angle at the end of this time interval and the new acceleration.

Solution Swing equation upon occurrence of fault,

$$\frac{H}{180 f} \frac{d^2\delta}{dt^2} = P_m - P_e$$

$$\frac{4}{180 \times 50} \frac{d^2\delta}{dt^2} = 1 - 0.694 \sin \delta$$

or

$$\frac{d^2\delta}{dt^2} = 2250\,(1 - 0.694 \sin \delta)$$

Initial rotor angle $\delta_0 = 33.9°$ (calculated in Example 12.3)

$$\left.\frac{d^2\delta}{dt^2}\right|_{t=0+} = 2250\,(1 - 0.694 \sin 33.9°)$$

$$= 1379 \text{ elect deg/s}^2$$

$$\left.\frac{d\delta}{dt}\right|_{t=0+} = 0; \text{ rotor speed cannot change suddenly}$$

$$\Delta\delta \,(\text{in } \Delta t = 0.05\,\text{s}) = \frac{1}{2} \times 1379 \times (0.05)^2$$

$$= 1.7°$$

$$\delta_1 = \delta_0 + \Delta\delta = 33.9 + 1.7° = 35.6°$$

$$\left.\frac{d^2\delta}{dt^2}\right|_{t=0.05\,s} = 2250\,(1 - 0.694 \sin 35.6°)$$

$$= 1341 \text{ elect deg/s}^2$$

Observe that as the rotor angle increases, the electrical power output of the generator increases and so the acceleration of the rotor reduces.

12.6 ▶ STEADY STATE STABILITY

The steady state stability limit of a particular circuit of a power system is defined as the maximum power that can be transmitted to the receiving end without loss of synchronism.

Consider the simple system of Fig. 12.15 whose dynamics is described by equations

$$M\frac{d^2\delta}{dt^2} = P_m - P_e \text{ MW; Eq. (12.8)}$$

$$M = \frac{H}{\pi f} \text{ in pu system} \tag{12.45}$$

and

$$P_e = \frac{|E||V|}{X_d} \sin\delta = P_{max} \sin\delta \tag{12.46}$$

For determination of steady state stability, the direct axis reactance (X_d) and voltage behind X_d are used in the above equations.

The plot of Eq. (12.46) is given in Fig. 12.7. Let the system be operating with steady power transfer of $P_{e0} = P_m$ with torque angle δ_0 as indicated in the figure. Assume a small increment ΔP in the electric power with the input from the prime mover remaining fixed at P_m (governor response is slow compared to the speed of energy dynamics), causing the torque angle to change to $(\delta_0 + \Delta\delta)$. Linearising about the operating point Q_0 (P_{e0}, δ_0), we can write

$$\Delta P_e = \left(\frac{\partial P_e}{\partial \delta}\right)_0 \Delta\delta$$

The excursions of $\Delta\delta$ are then described by

$$M\frac{d^2\Delta\delta}{dt^2} = P_m - (P_{e0} + \Delta P_e) = -\Delta P_e$$

or

$$M\frac{d^2\Delta\delta}{dt^2} + \left[\frac{\partial P_e}{\partial \delta}\right]_0 \Delta\delta = 0 \tag{12.47}$$

or

$$\left[Mp^2 + \left(\frac{\partial P_e}{\partial \delta}\right)_0\right]\Delta\delta = 0$$

where $p = \frac{d}{dt}$.

The system stability to small changes is determined from the characteristic equation

$$Mp^2 + \left[\frac{\partial P_e}{\partial \delta}\right]_0 = 0$$

whose two roots are

$$p = \pm\left[\frac{-(\partial P_e/\partial\delta)_0}{M}\right]^{\frac{1}{2}}$$

As long as $(\partial P_e/\partial\delta)_0$ is positive, the roots are purely imaginary and conjugate and the system behaviour is oscillatory about δ_0. Line resistance and damper windings of machine, which have been ignored in the above modelling, cause the system oscillations to decay, the system is therefore stable for a small increment in power as long as

$$(\partial P_e/\partial\delta)_0 > 0 \tag{12.48}$$

When $(\partial P_e/\partial\delta)_0$ is negative, the roots are real, one positive and the other negative but of equal magnitude. The torque angle therefore increases without bound upon occurrence of a small power increment (disturbance) and the synchronism is soon lost. The system is therefore unstable for

$$(\partial P_e/\partial\delta)_0 < 0$$

$\left(\frac{\partial P_e}{\partial \delta}\right)_0$ is known as *synchronising coefficient*. This is also called *stiffness* (electrical) of synchronous machine.

Assuming $|E|$ and $|V|$ to remain constant, the system is unstable, if

$$\frac{|E||V|}{X} \cos \delta_0 < 0$$

or

$$\delta_0 > 90^\circ \tag{12.49}$$

The maximum power that can be transmitted without loss of stability (steady state) occurs for

$$\delta_0 = 90^\circ \tag{12.50}$$

and is given by

$$P_{max} = \frac{|E||V|}{X} \tag{12.51}$$

If the system is operating below the limit of steady stability condition (Eq. 12.48), it may continue to oscillate for a long time if the damping is low. Persistent oscillations are a threat to system security. The study of system damping is the study of dynamical stability.

The above procedure is also applicable for complex systems wherein governor action and excitation control are also accounted for. The describing differential equation is linearised about the operating point. Condition for steady state stability is then determined from the corresponding characteristic equation (which now is of order higher than two).

It was assumed in the above account that the internal machine voltage $|E|$ remains constant (i.e., excitation is held constant). The result is that, as loading increases, the terminal voltage $|V_t|$ dips heavily which cannot be tolerated in practice. Therefore, we must consider the steady state stability limit by assuming that excitation is adjusted for every load increase to keep $|V_t|$ constant. This is how the system will be operated practically. It may be understood that we are still not considering the effect of automatic excitation control.

Steady state stability limit with $|V_t|$ and $|V|$ constant is considered in Example 12.6.

Example 12.5 A synchronous generator of reactance 1.20 pu is connected to an infinite bus bar ($|V| = 1.0$ pu) through transformers and a line of total reactance of 0.60 pu. The generator no load voltage is 1.20 pu and its inertia constant is $H = 4$ MW-s/MVA. The resistance and machine damping may be assumed negligible. The system frequency is 50 Hz.

Calculate the frequency of natural oscillations if the generator is loaded to (i) 50% and (ii) 80% of its maximum power limit.

Solution

(i) For 50% loading

$$\sin \delta_0 = \frac{P_e}{P_{max}} = 0.5 \text{ or } \delta_0 = 30^\circ$$

$$\left[\frac{\partial P_e}{\partial \delta}\right]_{30^\circ} = \frac{1.2 \times 1}{1.8} \cos 30^\circ$$

$$= 0.577 \text{ MW (pu)/elect rad}$$

$$M(\text{pu}) = \frac{H}{\pi \times 50} = \frac{4}{\pi \times 50} \text{ s}^2\text{/elect rad}$$

From characteristic equation

$$p = \pm j\left[\left(\frac{\partial P_e}{\partial \delta}\right)_{30^\circ} \Big/ M\right]^{\frac{1}{2}}$$

$$= \pm j \left(\frac{0.577 \times 50\,\pi}{4} \right)^{\frac{1}{2}} = \pm j4.76$$

Frequency of oscillations $= 4.76$ rad/sec $= \dfrac{4.76}{2\pi} = 0.758$ Hz

(ii) For 80% loading

$$\sin \delta_0 = \frac{P_e}{P_{max}} = 0.8 \text{ or } \delta_0 = 53.1^\circ$$

$$\left(\frac{\partial P_e}{\partial \delta} \right)_{53.1^\circ} = \frac{1.2 \times 1}{1.8} \cos 53.1^\circ$$

$$= 0.4 \text{ MW (pu)/elect rad}$$

$$p = \pm j \left(\frac{0.4 \times 50\,\pi}{4} \right)^{\frac{1}{2}} = \pm j3.96$$

Frequency of oscillations $= 3.96$ rad/sec $= \dfrac{3.96}{2\pi} = 0.63$ Hz

Example 12.6 Find the steady state power limit of a system consisting of a generator equivalent reactance 0.50 pu connected to an infinite bus through a series reactance of 1.0 pu. The terminal voltage of the generator is held at 1.20 pu and the voltage of the infinite bus is 1.0 pu.

Solution The system is shown in Fig. 12.17. Let the voltage of the infinite bus be taken as reference. Then

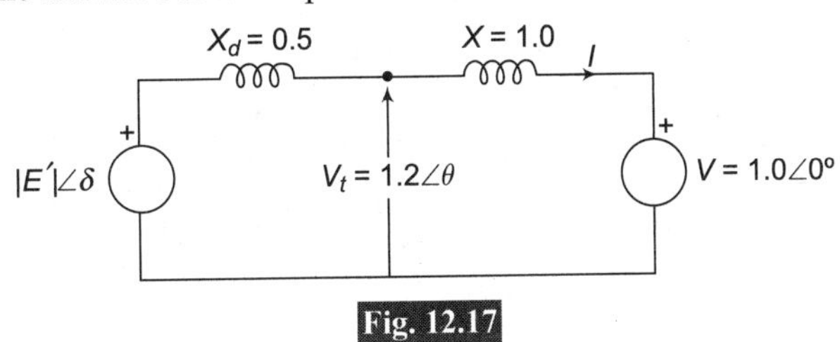

Fig. 12.17

$$V = 1.0 \angle 0^\circ,\ V_t = 1.2 \angle \theta$$

Now, $I = \dfrac{V_t - V}{jX} = \dfrac{1.2 \angle \theta - 1.0}{j1}$

$$E = V_t + jX_d I = 1.2 \angle \theta + j0.5 \left[\frac{1.2 \angle \theta - 1.0}{j1} \right]$$

or

$$E = 1.8 \angle \theta - 0.5 = (1.8 \cos \theta - 0.5) + j1.8 \sin \theta$$

Steady state power limit is reached when E has an angle of $\delta = 90^\circ$, i.e., its real part is zero. Thus,

$$1.8 \cos \theta - 0.5 = 0$$

or

$$\theta = 73.87^\circ$$

Now,

$$V_t = 1.2 \angle 73.87^\circ = 0.332 + j1.152$$

$$I = \frac{0.332 + j1.152 - 1}{j1} = 1.152 + j0.668$$

$$E = 0.332 + j1.152 + j0.5\,(1.152 + j0.668)$$

$$= -0.002 + j1.728 \approx 1.728 \angle 90^\circ$$

Steady state power limit is given by

$$P_{max} = \frac{|E|\,|V|}{X_d + X} = \frac{1.728 \times 1}{1.5} = 1.152 \text{ pu}$$

If instead, the generator emf is held fixed at a value of 1.2 pu, the steady state power limit would be

$$P_{max} = \frac{1.2 \times 1}{1.5} = 0.8 \text{ pu}$$

It is observed that regulating the generator emf to hold the terminal generator voltage at 1.2 pu raises the power limit from 0.8 pu to 1.152 pu; this is how the voltage regulating loop helps in power system stability.

12.6.1 Some Comments on Steady State Stability

A knowledge of steady state stability limit is important for various reasons. A system can be operated above its transient stability limit but not above its steady state limit. Now, with increased fault clearing speeds, it is possible to make the transient limit closely approach the steady state limit.

As is clear from Eq. (12.51), the methods of improving steady state stability limit of a system are to reduce X and increase either or both $|E|$ and $|V|$. If the transmission lines are of sufficiently high reactance, the stability limit can be raised by using two parallel lines which incidentally also increases the reliability of the system. Series capacitors are sometimes employed in lines to get better voltage regulation and to raise the stability limit by decreasing the line reactance. Higher excitation voltages and quick excitation system are also employed to improve the stability limit.

12.7 ▶ TRANSIENT STABILITY

It has been shown in Section 12.4 that the dynamics of a single synchronous machine connected to infinite bus bars is governed by the nonlinear differential equation

$$M \frac{d^2\delta}{dt^2} = P_m - P_e$$

where

$$P_e = P_{max} \sin \delta$$

or

$$M \frac{d^2\delta}{dt^2} = P_m - P_{max} \sin \delta \tag{12.52}$$

As said earlier, this equation is known as the *swing equation*. No closed form solution exists for swing equation except for the simple case $P_m = 0$ (not a practical case) which involves elliptical integrals. For small disturbance (say, gradual loading), the equation can be linearised (see Section 12.6) leading to the concept of steady state stability where a unique criterion of stability ($\partial P_e/\partial\delta > 0$) could be established. No generalised criteria are available* for determining system stability with large disturbances (called transient stability). The practical approach to the transient stability problem is therefore to list all important severe disturbances along with their possible locations to which the system is likely to be subjected according to the experience and judgement of the power system analyst. Numerical solution of the swing equation (or equations for a multimachine case) is then obtained in the presence of such disturbances giving a plot of δ *v.* t called the *swing curve*. If δ starts to decrease after reaching a maximum value, it is normally assumed that the system is stable and the oscillation of δ around the equilibrium point will decay and finally die out. As already pointed out in the introduction, important severe disturbances are a short circuit or a sudden loss of load.

For ease of analysis certain assumptions and simplifications are always made (some of these have already been made in arriving at the swing equation (Eq. (12.52)). All the assumptions are listed below along with their justification and consequences upon accuracy of results.

* Recent literature gives methods of determining transient stability through Liapunov and Popov's stability criteria, but these have not been of practical use so far.

1. Transmission line as well as synchronous machine resistance is ignored. This leads to pessimistic result as resistance introduces damping term in the swing equation which helps stability. In Example 12.11, line resistance has been taken into account.
2. Damping term contributed by synchronous machine damper windings is ignored. This also leads to pessimistic results for the transient stability limit.
3. Rotor speed is assumed to be synchronous. In fact it varies insignificantly during the course of the stability transient.
4. Mechanical input to machine is assumed to remain constant during the transient, i.e., regulating action of the generator loop is ignored. This leads to pessimistic results.
5. Voltage behind transient reactance is assumed to remain constant, i.e., action of voltage regulating loop is ignored. It also leads to pessimistic results.
6. Shunt capacitances are not difficult to account for in a stability study. Where ignored, no greatly significant error is caused.
7. Loads are modelled as constant admittances. This is a reasonably accurate representation.

Note: Since rotor speed and hence frequency vary insignificantly, the network parameters remain fixed during a stability study.

A digital computer programme to compute the transient following sudden disturbance can be suitably modified to include the effect of governor action and excitation control.

Present day power systems are so large that even after lumping of machines [Eq. (12.17)], the system remains a multimachine one. Even then, a simple two-machine system greatly aids the understanding of the transient stability problem. It has been shown in Section 12.4 that an equivalent single-machine infinite bus system can be found for a two-machine system [Eqs. (12.41) to (12.43)].

Upon occurrence of a severe disturbance, say a short circuit, the power transfer between the machines is greatly reduced, causing the machine torque angles to swing relatively. The circuit breakers near the fault disconnect the unhealthy part of the system so that power transfer can be partially restored, improving the chances of the system remaining stable. The shorter the time to breaker operating, called *clearing time*, the higher is the probability of the system being stable. Most of the line faults are transient in nature and get cleared on opening the line. Therefore, it is common practice now to employ *autoreclose breakers* which automatically close rapidly after each of the two sequential openings. If the fault still persists, the circuit breakers open and lock permanently till cleared manually. Since in the majority of faults the first reclosure will be successful, the chances of system stability are greatly enhanced by using autoreclose breakers.

The procedure of determining the stability of a system upon occurrence of a disturbance followed by various switching 'off' and switching 'on' actions is called a *stability study*. Steps to be followed in a stability study are outlined below for a single-machine infinite bus bar system shown in Fig. 12.18. The fault is assumed to be a transient one which is cleared by the time of first reclosure. In the case of a permanent fault, this system completely falls apart. This will not be the case in a multimachine system. The steps listed, in fact, apply to a system of any size.

Fig. 12.18

1. From prefault loading, determine the voltage behind transient reactance and the torque angle δ_0 of the machine with reference to the infinite bus.
2. For the specified fault, determine the power transfer equation $P_e(\delta)$ during fault. In this system $P_e = 0$ for a three-phase fault.

3. From the swing equation starting with δ_0 as obtained in step 1, calculate δ as a function of time using a numerical technique of solving the non-linear differential equation.
4. After clearance of the fault, once again determine $P_e(\delta)$ and solve further for $\delta(t)$. In this case, $P_e(\delta) = 0$ as when the fault is cleared, the system gets disconnected.
5. After the transmission line is switched 'on', again find $P_e(\delta)$ and continue to calculate $\delta(t)$.
6. If $\delta(t)$ goes through a maximum value and starts to reduce, the system is regarded as stable. It is unstable if $\delta(t)$ continues to increase. Calculation is ceased after a suitable length of time.

An important numerical method of calculating $\delta(t)$ from the swing equation will be given in Section 12.9. For the single machine infinite bus bar system, stability can be conveniently determined by the equal area criterion presented in the following section.

12.8 ▶ EQUAL AREA CRITERION

In a system where one machine is swinging with respect to an infinite bus, it is possible to study transient stability by means of a simple criterion, without resorting to the numerical solution of a swing equation.

Consider the swing equation

$$\frac{d^2\delta}{dt^2} = \frac{1}{M}(P_m - P_e) = \frac{P_a}{M}\ ;\ P_a = \text{accelerating power}$$

$$M = \frac{H}{\pi f} \text{ in pu system} \tag{12.53}$$

If the system is unstable δ continues to increase indefinitely with time and the machine loses synchronism. On the other hand, if the system is stable, $\delta(t)$ performs oscillations (nonsinusoidal) whose amplitude decreases in actual practice because of damping terms (not included in the swing equation). These two situations are shown in Fig. 12.19. Since the system is non-linear, the nature of its response $[\delta(t)]$ is not unique and it may exhibit instability in a fashion different from that indicated in Fig. 12.19, depending upon the nature and severity of disturbance. However, experience indicates that the response $\delta(t)$ in a power system generally falls in the two broad categories as shown in the figure. It can easily be visualised now (this has also been stated earlier) that for a stable system, indication of stability will be given by observation of the first swing where δ will go to a maximum and will start to reduce. This fact can be stated as a stability criterion, that the system is stable if at some time

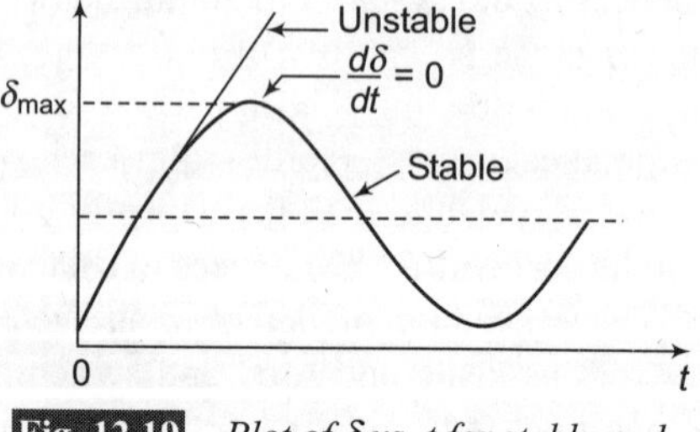

Fig. 12.19 *Plot of δ vs. t for stable and unstable systems*

$$\frac{d\delta}{dt} = 0 \tag{12.54}$$

and is unstable, if

$$\frac{d\delta}{dt} > 0 \tag{12.55}$$

for a sufficiently long time (more than 1 s will generally do).

The stability criterion for power systems stated above can be converted into a simple and easily applicable form for a single-machine infinite bus system. Multiplying both sides of the swing equation by $\left(2\frac{d\delta}{dt}\right)$, we get

$$2\,\frac{d\delta}{dt}\cdot\frac{d^2\delta}{dt^2} = \frac{2P_a}{M}\,\frac{d\delta}{dt}$$

Integrating, we have

$$\left(\frac{d\delta}{dt}\right)^2 = \frac{2}{M}\int_{\delta_0}^{\delta} P_a d\delta$$

or

$$\frac{d\delta}{dt} = \left(\frac{2}{M}\int_{\delta_0}^{\delta} P_a\, d\delta\right)^{\frac{1}{2}} \tag{12.56}$$

where δ_0 is the initial rotor angle before it begins to swing due to disturbance.

From Eqs. (12.55) and (12.56), the condition for stability can be written as

$$\left(\frac{2}{M}\int_{\delta_0}^{\delta} P_a\, d\delta\right)^{\frac{1}{2}} = 0$$

or

$$\int_{\delta_0}^{\delta} P_a\, d\delta = 0 \tag{12.57}$$

The condition of stability can therefore be stated as: the system is stable if the area under P_a (accelerating power) – δ curve reduces to zero at some value of δ. In other words, the positive (accelerating) area under P_a–δ curve must equal the negative (decelerating) area and hence the name 'equal area' criterion of stability.

To illustrate the equal area criterion of stability, we now consider several types of disturbances that may occur in a single-machine infinite bus bar system.

12.8.1 Sudden Change in Mechanical Input

Figure 12.20 shows the transient model of a single machine tied to infinite bus bar. The electrical power transmitted is given by

Fig. 12.20

$$P_e = \frac{|E'|\,|V|}{X'_d + X_e}\sin\delta = P_{max}\sin\delta$$

Under steady operating condition

$$P_{m0} = P_{e0} = P_{max}\sin\delta_0$$

This is indicated by the point a in the P_e – δ diagram of Fig. 12.21.

Let the mechanical input to the rotor be suddenly increase to P_{m1} (by opening the steam valve). The accelerating power $P_a = P_{m1} - P_e$ causes the rotor speed to increase ($\omega > \omega_s$) and so does the rotor angle. At angle δ_1, $P_a = P_{m1} - P_e$ (= P_{max} sin δ_1) = 0 (state point at b) but the rotor angle continues to increase as $\omega > \omega_s$. P_a now becomes negative (decelerating), the rotor speed begins to reduce but the angle continues to

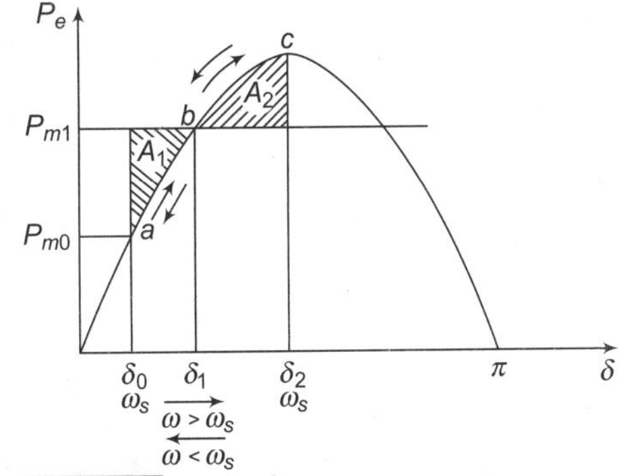

Fig. 12.21 *P_e = δ diagram for sudden increase in mechanical input to generator of Fig. 12.20*

increase till at angle δ_2, $\omega = \omega_s$ once again (state point at c). At c, the decelerating area A_2 equals the accelerating area A_1 (areas are shaded), i.e., $\int_{\delta_0}^{\delta_2} P_a \, d\delta = 0$. Since the rotor is decelerating, the speed reduces below ω_s and the rotor angle begins to reduce. The state point now traverses the P_e–δ curve in the opposite direction as indicated by arrows in Fig. 12.21. It is easily seen that the system oscillates about the new steady state point b ($\delta = \delta_1$) with angle excursion up to δ_0 and δ_2 on the two sides. These oscillations are similar to the simple harmonic motion of an inertia–spring system except that these are not sinusoidal.

As the oscillations decay out because of inherent system damping (not modelled), the system settles to the new steady state where

$$P_{m1} = P_e = P_{\max} \sin \delta_1$$

From Fig. 12.21, areas A_1 and A_2 are given by

$$A_1 = \int_{\delta_0}^{\delta_1} (P_{m1} - P_e) \, d\delta$$

$$A_2 = \int_{\delta_1}^{\delta_2} (P_e - P_{m1}) \, d\delta$$

For the system to be stable, it should be possible to find angle δ_2 such that $A_1 = A_2$. As P_{m1} is increased, a limiting condition is finally reached when A_1 equals the area above the P_{m1} line as shown in Fig. 12.22. Under this condition, δ_2 acquires the maximum value such that

$$\delta_2 = \delta_{\max} = \pi - \delta_1 = \pi - \sin^{-1} \frac{P_{m1}}{P_{\max}} \quad (12.58)$$

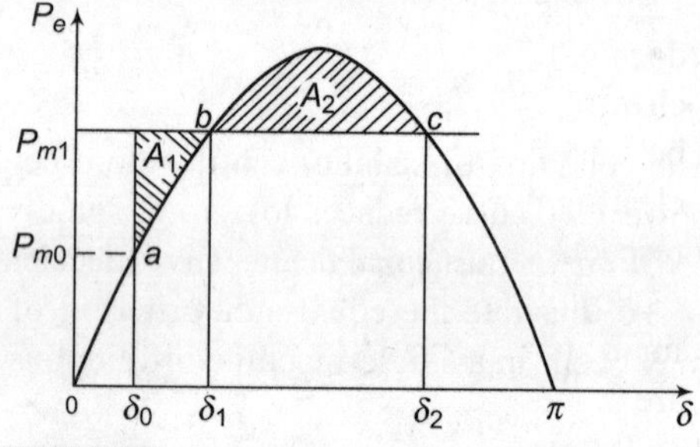

Fig. 12.22 *Limiting case of transient stability with mechanical input suddenly increased*

Any further increase in P_{m1} means that the area available for A_2 is less than A_1, so that the excess kinetic energy causes δ to increase beyond point c and the decelerating power changes over to accelerating power, with the system consequently becoming unstable. It has thus been shown by use of the equal area criterion that there is an upper limit to sudden increase in mechanical input ($P_{m1} - P_{m0}$), for the system in question to remain stable.

It may also be noted from Fig. 12.22 that the system will remain stable even though the rotor may oscillate beyond $\delta = 90°$, so long as the equal area criterion is met. The condition of $\delta = 90°$ is meant for use in steady state stability only and does not apply to the transient stability case.

12.8.2 Effect of Clearing Time on Stability

Let the system of Fig. 12.23 be operating with mechanical input P_m at a steady angle of δ_0 ($P_m = P_e$) as shown by the point a on the P_e–δ diagram of Fig. 12.24. If a three-phase fault occurs at the point P of the outgoing radial line, the electrical output of the generator instantly reduces to zero, i.e., $P_e = 0$ and the state point drops to b. The acceleration area A_1 begins to increase and so does the rotor angle while the state point moves along bc. At time t_c corresponding to angle δ_c the faulted line is cleared by the opening of the line circuit breaker. The values of t_c and δ_c are respectively known as *clearing time* and *clearing angle*. The

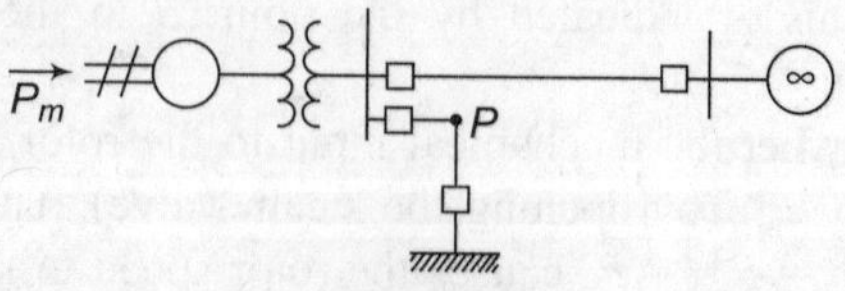

Fig. 12.23

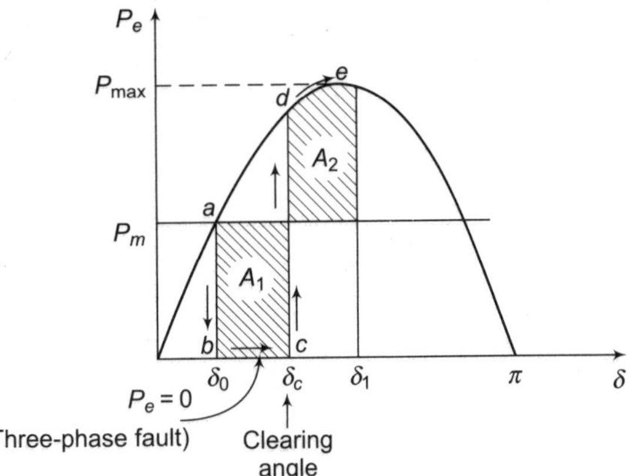

Fig. 12.24

system once again becomes healthy and transmits $P_e = P_{max} \sin \delta$, i.e., the state point shifts to d on the original P_e–δ curve. The rotor now decelerates and the decelerating area A_2 begins while the state point moves along de.

If an angle δ_1 can be found such that $A_2 = A_1$, the system is found to be stable. The system finally settles down to the steady operating point a in an oscillatory manner because of inherent damping.

The value of clearing time corresponding to a clearing angle can be established only by numerical integration except in this simple case. The equal area criterion therefore gives only qualitative answer to system stability as the time when the breaker should be opened is hard to establish.

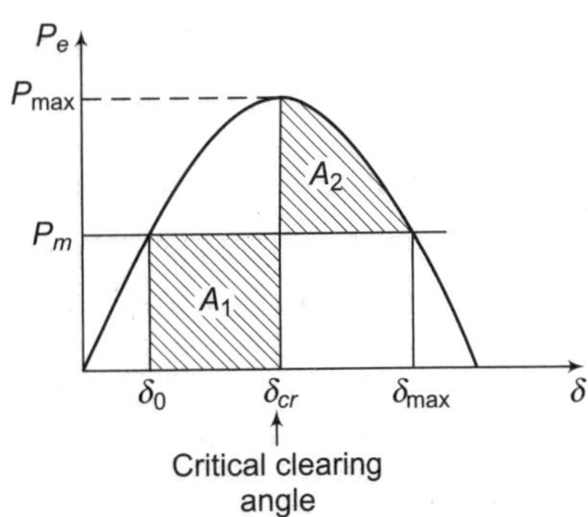

Fig. 12.25 *Critical clearing angle*

As the clearing of the faulty line is delayed, A_1 increases and so does δ_1 to find $A_2 = A_1$ till $\delta_1 = \delta_{max}$ as shown in Fig. 12.25. For a clearing time (or angle) larger than this value, the system would be unstable as $A_2 < A_1$. The maximum allowable value of the clearing time and angle for the system to remain stable are known respectively as *critical clearing time* and *angle*.

For this simple case ($P_e = 0$ during fault), explicit relationships for δ_c (critical) and t_c (critical) are established below. All angles are in radians.

It is easily seen from Fig. 12.25 that

$$\delta_{max} = \pi - \delta_0 \tag{12.59}$$

and

$$P_m = P_{max} \sin \delta_0 \tag{12.60}$$

Now,

$$A_1 = \int_{\delta_0}^{\delta_{cr}} (P_m - 0)\, d\delta = P_m (\delta_{cr} - \delta_0)$$

and

$$A_2 = \int_{\delta_{cr}}^{\delta_{max}} (P_{max} \sin \delta - P_m)\, d\delta$$

$$= P_{max} (\cos \delta_{cr} - \cos \delta_{max}) - P_m (\delta_{max} - \delta_{cr})$$

For the system to be stable, $A_2 = A_1$, which yields

$$\cos \delta_{cr} = \frac{P_m}{P_{max}} (\delta_{max} - \delta_0) + \cos \delta_{max} \tag{12.61}$$

where δ_{cr} = critical clearing angle

Substituting Eqs. (12.59) and (12.60) in Eq. (12.61), we get

$$\delta_{cr} = \cos^{-1} [(\pi - 2\delta_0) \sin \delta_0 - \cos \delta_0] \tag{12.62}$$

During the period the fault is persisting, the swing equation is

$$\frac{d^2\delta}{dt^2} = \frac{\pi f}{H} P_m; \; P_e = 0 \tag{12.63}$$

Integrating twice

$$\delta = \frac{\pi f}{2H} P_m t^2 + \delta_0$$

or

$$\delta_{cr} = \frac{\pi f}{2H} P_m t^2_{cr} + \delta_0 \tag{12.64}$$

where

t_{cr} = critical clearing time
δ_{cr} = critical clearing angle

From Eq. (12.64)

$$t_{cr} = \left(\frac{2H\,(\delta_{cr} - \delta_0)}{\pi f P_m} \right)^{\frac{1}{2}} \tag{12.65}$$

where δ_{cr} is given by the expression of Eq. (12.62)

An explicit relationship for determining t_{cr} is possible in this case as during the faulted condition $P_e = 0$ and so the swing equation can be integrated in closed form. This will not be the case in most other situations.

12.8.3 Sudden Loss of One of Parallel Lines

Consider now a single machine tied to infinite bus through two parallel lines as in Fig. 12.26(a). Circuit model of the system is given in Fig. 12.26(b).

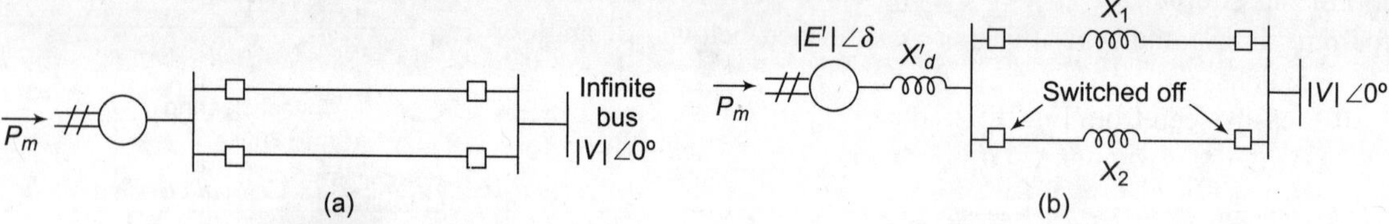

Fig. 12.26 *Single machine tied to infinite bus through two parallel lines*

Let us study the transient stability of the system when one of the lines is suddenly switched off with the system operating at a steady load. Before switching off, power angle curve is given by

$$P_{eI} = \frac{|E'||V|}{X'_d + X_1 \| X_2} \sin\delta = P_{\max I} \sin\delta$$

Immediately on switching off line 2, power angle curve is given by

$$P_{eII} = \frac{|E'||V|}{X'_d + X_1} \sin\delta = P_{\max II} \sin\delta$$

Both these curves are plotted in Fig. 12.27, wherein $P_{\max II} < P_{\max I}$ as $(X'_d + X_1) > (X'_d + X_1 \| X_2)$. The system is operating initially with a steady power transfer $P_d = P_m$ at a torque angle δ_0 on curve I.

Immediately on switching off line 2, the electrical operating point shifts to curve II (point b). Accelerating energy corresponding to area A_1 is put into rotor followed by decelerating energy for $\delta > \delta_1$. Assuming that an area A_2 corresponding to decelerating energy (energy out of rotor) can be found such that $A_1 = A_2$, the system will be stable and will finally operate at c

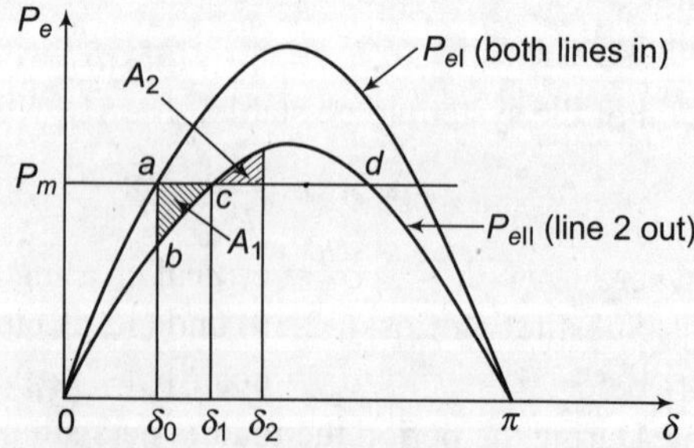

Fig. 12.27 *Equal area criterion applied to the opening of one of the two lines in parallel*

corresponding to a new rotor angle $\delta_1 > \delta_0$. This is so because a single line offers larger reactance and larger rotor angle is needed to transfer the same steady power.

It is also easy to see that if the steady load is increased (line P_m is shifted upwards in Fig. 12.27), a limit is finally reached beyond which decelerating area equal to A_1 cannot be found and, therefore, the system behaves as an unstable one. For the limiting case of stability, δ_1 has a maximum value given by

$$\delta_1 = \delta_{max} = \pi - \delta_c$$

which is the same condition as in the previous example.

12.8.4 Sudden Short Circuit on One of Parallel Lines

Case a Short circuit at one end of line

Let us now assume the disturbance to be a short circuit at the generator end of line 2 of a double circuit line as shown in Fig. 12.28(a). We shall assume the fault to be a three-phase one.

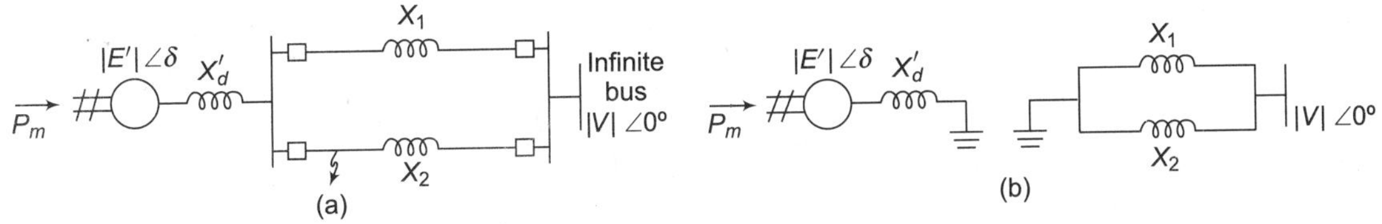

Fig. 12.28 *Short circuit at one end of the line*

Before the occurrence of a fault, the power angle curve is given by

$$P_{eI} = \frac{|E'||V|}{X'_d + X_1 \parallel X_2} \sin\delta = P_{max\,I} \sin\delta$$

which is plotted in Fig. 12.26.

Upon occurrence of a three-phase fault at the generator end of line 2 [see Fig. 12.25(a)], the generator gets isolated from the power system for purposes of power flow as shown by Fig. 12.28(b). Thus during the period the fault lasts,

$$P_{eII} = 0$$

The rotor therefore accelerates and angle δ increases. Synchronism will be lost unless the fault is cleared in time.

The circuit breakers at the two ends of the faulted line open at time t_c (corresponding to angle δ_c), the clearing time, disconnecting the faulted line. The power flow is now restored via the healthy line (through higher line reactance X_2 in place of $X_1 \parallel X_2$), with power angle curve

$$P_{eIII} = \frac{|E'||V|}{X'_d + X_1} \sin\delta = P_{max\,II} \sin\delta$$

Obviously, $P_{max\,II} < P_{max\,I}$. The rotor now starts to decelerate as shown in Fig. 12.29. The system will be stable if a decelerating area A_2 can be found equal to accelerating area A_1 before δ reaches the maximum allowable value δ_{max}. As area A_1 depends upon clearing time t_c (corresponding to clearing angle δ_c), clearing time must be less than a certain value (critical clearing time) for the system to be stable. It is to be observed that the equal area criterion helps to

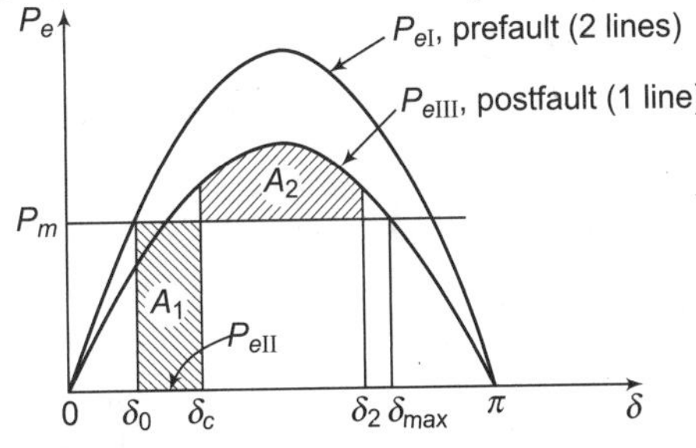

Fig. 12.29 *Equal area criterion applied to the system of Fig. 12.25(a), I—system normal, II—fault applied, III—faulted line isolated*

determine critical clearing angle and not critical clearing time. Critical clearing time can be obtained by numerical solution of the swing equation (discussed in Section 12.8).

It also easily follows that larger initial loading (P_m) increases A_1 for a given clearing angle (and time) and therefore quicker fault clearing would be needed to maintain stable operation.

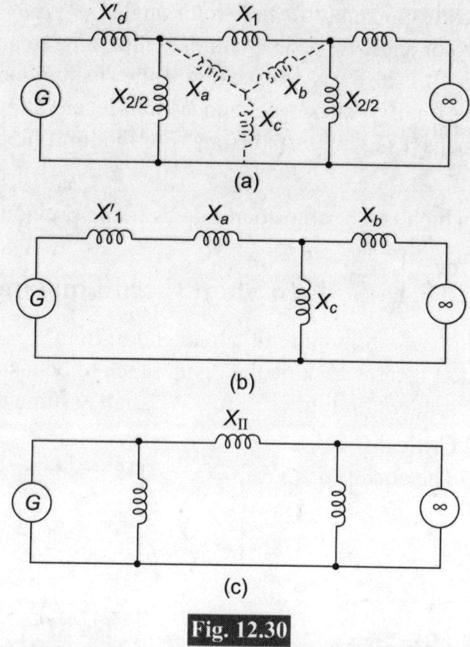

Fig. 12.30

Case b Short circuit away from line ends

When the fault occurs away from line ends (say in the middle of a line), there is some power flow during the fault though considerably reduced, as different from case *a* where $P_{eII} = 0$. Circuit model of the system during fault is now shown in Fig. 12.30(a). This circuit reduces to that of Fig. 12.30(c) through one delta-star and one star-delta conversion. Instead, node elimination technique of Section 12.3 could be employed profitably. The power angle curve during fault is therefore given by

$$P_{eII} = \frac{|E'||V|}{X_{II}} \sin \delta = P_{\max II} \sin \delta$$

P_{eI} and P_{eIII} as in Fig. 12.29 and P_{eII} as obtained above are all plotted in Fig. 12.31. Accelerating area A_1 corresponding to a given clearing angle δ_c is less in this case, than in case *a*, giving a better chance for stable operation. Stable system operation is shown in Fig. 12.31, wherein it is possible to find an area A_2 equal to A_1 for $\delta_2 < \delta_{\max}$. As the clearing angle δ_c is increased, area A_1 increases and to find $A_2 = A_1$, δ_2 increases till it has a value $\delta_{\max}$, the maximum allowable for stability. This case of critical clearing angle is shown in Fig. 12.32.

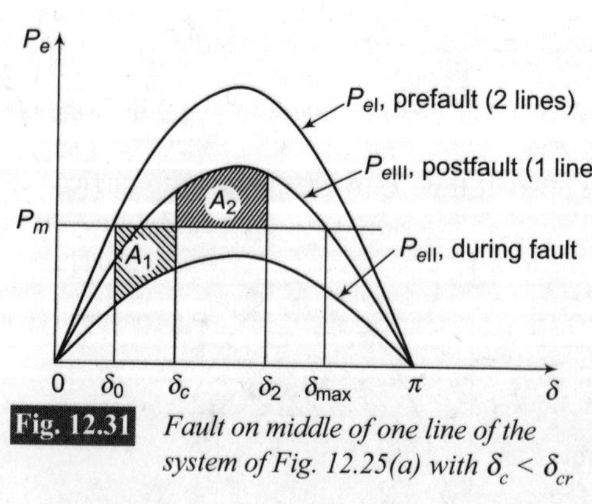

Fig. 12.31 *Fault on middle of one line of the system of Fig. 12.25(a) with $\delta_c < \delta_{cr}$*

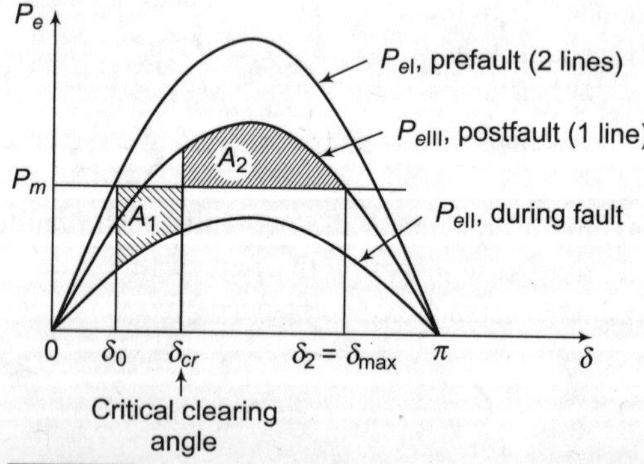

Fig. 12.32 *Fault on middle of one line of the system of Fig. 12.25(a), case of critical clearing angle*

Applying equal area criterion to the case of critical clearing angle of Fig. 12.32, we can write

$$\int_{\delta_0}^{\delta_{cr}} (P_m - P_{\max II} \sin \delta)\, d\delta = \int_{\delta_{cr}}^{\delta_{\max}} (P_{\max III} \sin \delta - P_m)\, d\delta$$

where

$$\delta_{\max} = \pi - \sin^{-1}\left(\frac{P_m}{P_{\max\,III}}\right) \tag{12.66}$$

Integrating, we get

$$(P_m\delta + P_{\max II}\cos\delta)\Big|_{\delta_0}^{\delta_{cr}} + (P_{\max\,III}\cos\delta + P_m\delta)\Big|_{\delta_{cr}}^{\delta_{\max}} = 0$$

or

$$P_m(\delta_{cr} - \delta_0) + P_{\max II}(\cos\delta_{cr} - \cos\delta_0) + P_m(\delta_{\max} - \delta_{cr}) + P_{\max III}(\cos\delta_{\max} - \cos\delta_{cr}) = 0$$

or

$$\cos\delta_{cr} = \frac{P_m(\delta_{\max} - \delta_0) - P_{\max\,II}\cos\delta_0 + P_{\max\,III}\cos\delta_{\max}}{P_{\max\,III} - P_{\max\,II}} \tag{12.67}$$

Critical clearing angle can be calculated from Eq. (12.67) above. The angles in this equation are in radians. The equation modifies as below if the angles are in degrees.

$$\cos\delta_{cr} = \frac{\dfrac{\pi}{180}P_m(\delta_{\max} - \delta_0) - P_{\max\,II}\cos\delta_0 + P_{\max\,III}\cos\delta_{\max}}{P_{\max\,III} - P_{\max\,II}}$$

Case c Reclosure

If the circuit breakers of line 2 are reclosed successfully (i.e., the fault was a transient one and therefore vanished on clearing the faulty line), the power transfer once again becomes

$$P_{eIV} = P_{eI} = P_{\max I}\sin\delta$$

Since reclosure restores power transfer, the chances of stable operation improve. A case of stable operation is indicated by Fig. 12.33.

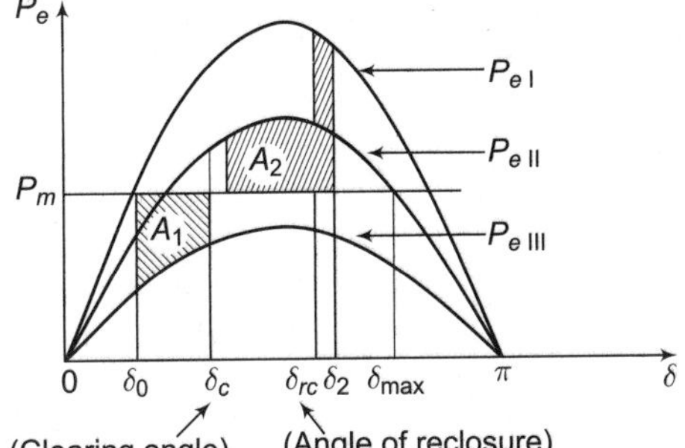

Fig. 12.33 *Fault in middle of a line of the system of Fig. 12.28(a)*

For critical clearing angle,

$$\delta_1 = \delta_{\max} = \pi - \sin^{-1}(P_m/P_{\max I})$$

$$\int_{\delta_0}^{\delta_{cr}}(P_m - P_{\max II}\sin\delta)d\delta = \int_{\delta_{cr}}^{\delta_{rc}}(P_{\max III}\sin\delta - P_m)d\delta + \int_{\delta_{rc}}^{\delta_{\max}}(P_{\max I}\sin\delta - P_m)d\delta$$

where

$$t_{rc} = t_{cr} + \tau;\ \tau = \text{time between clearing and reclosure.}$$

Example 12.7 Given the system of Fig. 12.34 where a three-phase fault is applied at the point P as shown.

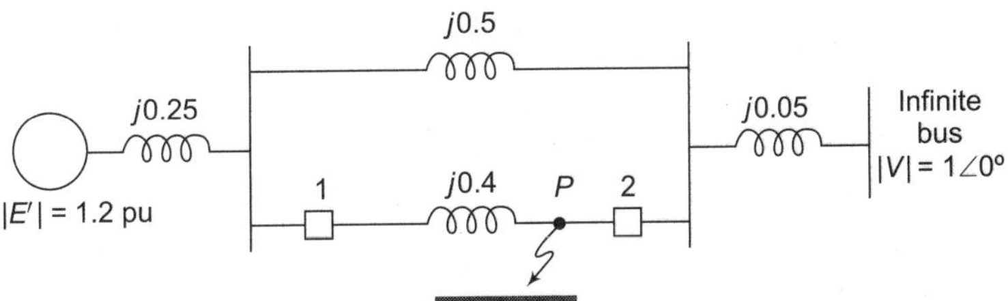

Fig. 12.34

Find the critical clearing angle for clearing the fault with simultaneous opening of the breakers 1 and 2. The reactance values of various components are indicated on the diagram. The generator is delivering 1.0 pu power at the instant preceding the fault.

Solution With reference to Fig. 12.32, three separate power angle curves are involved.

I. Normal operation (prefault)

$$X_{\text{I}} = 0.25 + \frac{0.5 \times 0.4}{0.5 + 0.4} + 0.05$$

$$= 0.522 \text{ pu}$$

$$P_{e\text{I}} = \frac{|E'|\,|V|}{X_I} \sin\delta = \frac{1.2 \times 1}{0.522} \sin\delta$$

$$= 2.3 \sin\delta \qquad \text{(i)}$$

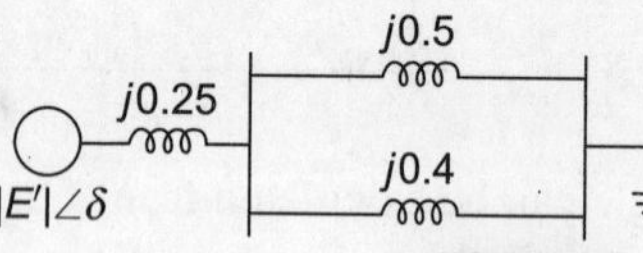

Prefault operating power angle is given by

$$1.0 = 2.3 \sin\delta_0$$

or

$$\delta_0 = 25.8^\circ = 0.45 \text{ radians}$$

Fig. 12.35

II. During fault It is clear from Fig. 12.32 that no power is transferred during fault, i.e.,

$$P_{e\text{II}} = 0$$

III. Post faultoperation (fault cleared by opening the faulted line)

$$X_{\text{III}} = 0.25 + 0.5 + 0.05 = 0.8$$

$$P_{e\text{III}} = \frac{1.2 \times 1.0}{0.8} \sin\delta = 1.5 \sin\delta \qquad \text{(iii)}$$

The maximum permissible angle δ_{max} for area $A_1 = A_2$ (see Fig. 12.36) is given by

$$\delta_{max} = \pi - \sin^{-1}\frac{1}{1.5} = 2.41 \text{ radians}$$

Applying equal area criterion for critical clearing angle δ_c

$$A_1 = P_m(\delta_{cr} - \delta_0)$$

$$= 1.0(\delta_{cr} - 0.45) = \delta_{cr} - 0.45$$

$$A_2 = \int_{\delta_{cr}}^{\delta_{max}} (P_{e\text{III}} - P_m)\, d\delta$$

$$= \int_{\delta_{cr}}^{2.41} (1.5 \sin\delta - 1)\, d\delta$$

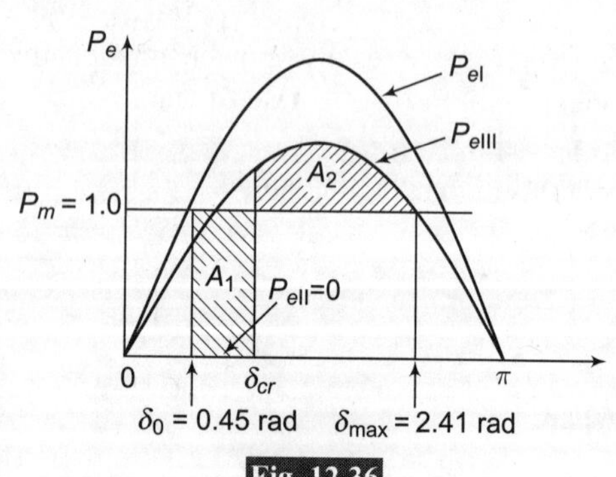

Fig. 12.36

$$= -1.5\cos\delta - \delta \Big|_{\delta_{cr}}^{2.41}$$

$$= -1.5(\cos 2.41 - \cos\delta_{cr}) - (2.41 - \delta_{cr})$$

$$= 1.5 \cos\delta_{cr} + \delta_{cr} - 1.293$$

Setting $A_1 = A_2$ and solving

$$\delta_{cr} - 0.45 = 1.5\cos\delta_{cr} + \delta_{cr} - 1.293$$

or

$$\cos\delta_{cr} = 0.843/1.5 = 0.562$$

or

$$\delta_{cr} = 55.8^\circ$$

The corresponding power angle diagrams are shown in Fig. 12.36.

Example 12.8 Find the critical clearing angle for the system shown in Fig. 12.37 for a three-phase fault at the point P. The generator is delivering 1.0 pu power under prefault conditions.

Solution I. Prefault operation Transfer reactance between generator and infinite bus is

$$X_{\text{I}} = 0.25 + 0.17 + \frac{0.15 + 0.28 + 0.15}{2} = 0.71$$

$$\therefore \quad P_{e\text{I}} = \frac{1.2 \times 1}{0.71} \sin \delta = 1.69 \sin \delta \qquad \text{(i)}$$

Fig. 12.37

The operating power angle is given by

$$1.0 = 1.69 \sin \delta_0$$

or

$$\delta_0 = 0.633 \text{ rad}$$

II. During fault The positive sequence reactance diagram during fault is presented in Fig. 12.38(a).

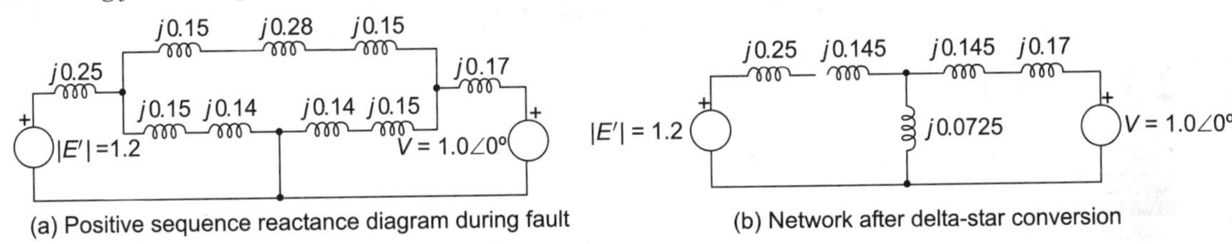

(a) Positive sequence reactance diagram during fault

(b) Network after delta-star conversion

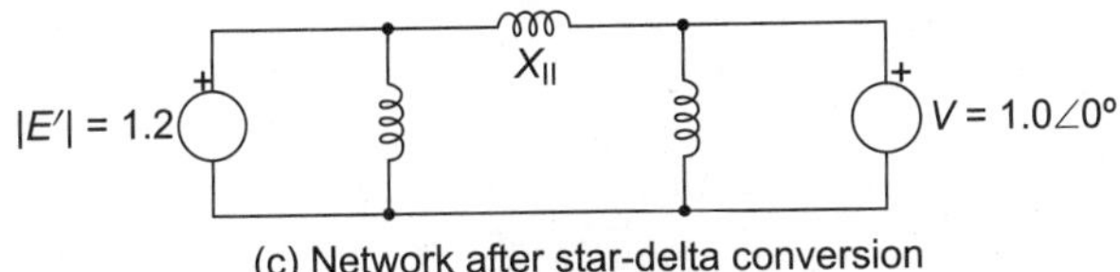

(c) Network after star-delta conversion

Fig. 12.38

Converting delta to star*, the reactance network is changed to that of Fig. 12.38(b). Further, upon converting star to delta, we obtain the reactance network of Fig. 12.38(c). The transfer reactance is given by

$$X_{\text{II}} = \frac{(0.25 + 0.145)\, 0.0725 + (0.145 + 0.17)\, 0.0725 + (0.25 + 0.145)\,(0.145 + 0.17)}{0.075} = 2.424$$

$$\therefore \qquad P_{e\text{II}} = \frac{1.2 \times 1}{2.424} \sin \delta = 0.495 \sin \delta \qquad \text{(ii)}$$

III. Postfault operation (faulty line switched off)

$$X_{\text{III}} = 0.25 + 0.15 + 0.28 + 0.15 + 0.17 = 1.0$$

$$P_{e\text{III}} = \frac{1.2 \times 1}{1} \sin \delta = 1.2 \sin \delta \qquad \text{(iii)}$$

With reference to Fig. 12.31 and Eq. (12.66), we have

$$\delta_{\max} = \pi - \sin^{-1} \frac{1}{1.2} = 2.155 \text{ rad}$$

To find the critical clearing angle, areas A_1 and A_2 are to be equated.

$$A_1 = 1.0\,(\delta_{cr} - 0.633) - \int_{\delta_0}^{\delta_{cr}} 0.495 \sin \delta \, d\delta$$

* Node elimination technique would be used for complex network.

and
$$A_2 = \int_{\delta_{cr}}^{\delta\max} 1.2\sin\delta d\delta - 1.0(2.155 - \delta_c)$$

Now,
$$A_1 = A_2$$

or
$$\delta_{cr} = 0.633 - \int_{0.633}^{\delta_{cr}} 0.495\sin\delta d\delta$$
$$= \int_{\delta_{cr}}^{2.155} 1.2\sin\delta d\delta - 2.155 + \delta_{cr}$$

or
$$-0.633 + 0.495 \cos\delta \Big|_{0.633}^{\delta_{cr}} = -1.2\cos\delta \Big|_{\delta_{cr}}^{2.155} - 2.155$$

or
$$-0.633 + 0.495 \cos\delta_{cr} - 0.399 = 0.661 + 1.2\cos\delta_{cr} - 2.155$$

or $\cos\delta_{cr} = 0.655$

or $\delta_{cr} = 49.1°$

Example 12.9 A generator operating at 50 Hz delivers 1 pu power to an infinite bus through a transmission circuit in which resistance is ignored. A fault takes place reducing the maximum power transferable to 0.5 pu whereas before the fault, this power was 2.0 pu and after the clearance of the fault, it is 1.5 pu. By the use of equal area criterion, determine the critical clearing angle.

Solution All the three power angle curves are shown in Fig. 12.31. Here,

$$P_{\max I} = 2.0 \text{ pu}, P_{\max II} = 0.5 \text{ pu and } P_{\max III} = 1.5 \text{ pu}$$

Initial loading $P_m = 1.0$ pu

$$\delta_0 = \sin^{-1}\left(\frac{P_m}{P_{\max I}}\right) = \sin^{-1}\frac{1}{2} = 0.523 \text{ rad}$$

$$\delta_{\max} = \pi \sin^{-1}\left(\frac{P_m}{P_{\max III}}\right)$$
$$= \pi - \sin^{-1}\frac{1}{1.5} = 2.41 \text{ rad}$$

Applying Eq. (12.67)

$$\cos\delta_{cr} = \frac{1.0(2.41 - 0.523) - 0.5\cos 0.523 + 1.5\cos 2.41}{1.5 - 0.5} = 0.337$$

or $\delta_{cr} = 70.3°$

12.9 ▶ NUMERICAL SOLUTION OF SWING EQUATION

In most practical systems, after machine lumping has been done, there are still more than two machines to be considered from the point of view of system stability. Therefore, there is no choice but to solve the swing equation of each machine by a numerical technique on the digital computer. Even in the case of a single machine tied to infinite bus bar, the critical clearing time cannot be obtained from equal area criterion and we have to make this calculation numerically through swing equation. There are several sophisticated methods now available for the solution of the swing equation including the powerful Runge-Kutta method. Here we shall treat the point-by-point method of solution which is a conventional, approximate method like all numerical methods but a well tried and proven one. We shall illustrate the point-by-point method for one machine tied to infinite bus bar. The procedure is, however, general and can be applied to every machine of a multimachine system.

Consider the swing equation

$$\frac{d^2\delta}{dt^2} = \frac{1}{M}(P_m - P_{\max}\sin\delta) = P_a/M;$$

$$\left(M = \frac{GH}{\pi} \text{ or in pu system } M = \frac{H}{\pi f}\right)$$

The solution $\delta(t)$ is obtained at discrete intervals of time with interval spread of Δt uniform throughout. Accelerating power and change in speed which are continuous functions of time are discretised as below:

1. The accelerating power P_a computed at the beginning of an interval is assumed to remain constant from the middle of the preceding interval to the middle of the interval being considered as shown in Fig. 12.39.
2. The angular rotor velocity $\omega = d\delta/dt$ (over and above synchronous velocity ω_s) is assumed constant throughout any interval, at the value computed for the middle of the interval as shown in Fig. 12.39.

In Fig. 12.39, the numbering on $t/\Delta t$ axis pertains to the end of intervals. At the end of the $(n-1)$th interval, the acceleration power is

$$P_{a(n-1)} = P_m - P_{\max}\sin\delta_{n-1} \tag{12.68}$$

where δ_{n-1} has been previously calculated. The change in velocity ($\omega = d\delta/dt$), caused by the $P_{a(n-1)}$, assumed constant over Δt from $(n - 3/2)$ to $(n - 1/2)$ is

$$\omega_{n-1/2} - \omega_{n-3/2} = (\Delta t/M)\, P_{a(n-1)} \tag{12.69}$$

The change in δ during the $(n-1)$th interval is

$$\Delta\delta_{n-1} = \delta_{n-1} - \delta_{n-2} = \Delta t\,\omega_{n-3/2} \tag{12.70a}$$

and during the nth interval

$$\Delta\delta_n = \delta_n - \delta_{n-1} = \Delta t\,\omega_{n-1/2} \tag{12.70b}$$

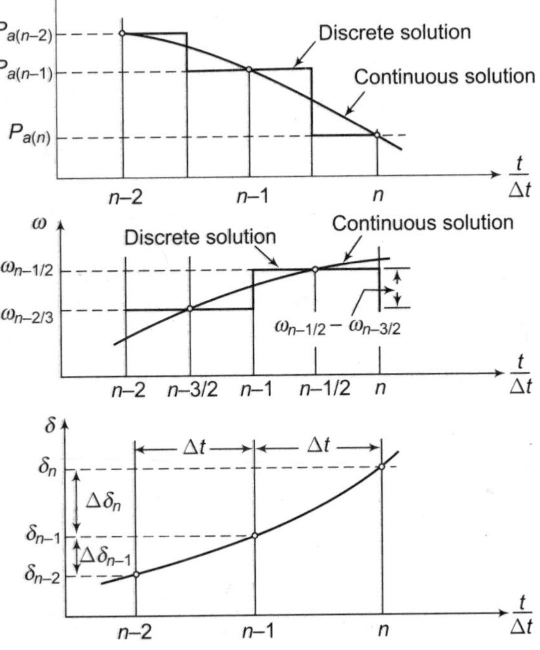

Fig. 12.39 *Point-by-point solution of swing equation*

Subtracting Eq. 12.70(a) from Eq. 12.70(b) and using Eq. (12.69), we get

$$\Delta\delta_n = \Delta\delta_{n-1} + \frac{(\Delta t)^2}{M} P_{a(n-1)} \tag{12.71}$$

Using this, we can write

$$\delta_n = \delta_{n-1} + \Delta\delta_n \tag{12.72}$$

The process of computation is now repeated to obtain $P_{a(n)}$, $\Delta\delta_{n+1}$ and δ_{n+1}. The time solution in discrete form is thus carried out over the desired length of time, normally 0.5 s. Continuous form of solution is obtained by drawing a smooth curve through discrete values as shown in Fig. 12.39. Greater accuracy of solution can be achieved by reducing the time duration of intervals.

The occurrence or removal of a fault or initiation of any switching event causes a discontinuity in accelerating power P_a. If such a discontinuity occurs at the beginning of an interval, then the average of the values of P_a before and after the discontinuity must be used. Thus, in computing the increment of angle occurring during the first interval after a fault is applied at $t = 0$, Eq. (12.71) becomes

$$\Delta\delta_1 = \frac{(\Delta t)^2}{M} + \frac{P_{a0+}}{2}$$

where P_{a0+} is the accelerating power immediately after occurrence of fault. Immediately before the fault the system is in steady state, so that $P_{a0-} = 0$ and δ_0 is a known value. If the fault is cleared at the beginning of the nth interval, in calculation for this interval one should use for $P_{a(n-1)}$ the value $\frac{1}{2}[P_{a(n-1)-} + P_{a(n-1)+}]$, where $P_{a(n-1)-}$ is the accelerating power immediately before clearing and $P_{a(n-1)+}$ is that immediately after clearing the fault. If the discontinuity occurs at the middle of an interval, no special procedure is needed. The increment of angle during such an interval is calculated, as usual, from the value of P_a at the beginning of the interval.

The procedure of calculating solution of swing equation is illustrated in the following example.

Example 12.10 A 20 MVA, 50 Hz generator delivers 18 MW over a double circuit line to an infinite bus. The generator has kinetic energy of 2.52 MJ/MVA at rated speed. The generator transient reactance is $X'_d = 0.35$ pu. Each transmission circuit has $R = 0$ and a reactance of 0.2 pu on a 20 MVA base. $|E'| = 1.1$ pu and infinite bus voltage $V = 1.0\angle 0°$. A three-phase short circuit occurs at the mid point of one of the transmission lines. Plot swing curves with fault cleared by simultaneous opening of breakers at both ends of the line at 2.5 cycles and 6.25 cycles after the occurrence of fault. Also plot the swing curve over the period of 0.5 s if the fault is sustained.

Solution Before we can apply the step-by-step method, we need to calculate the inertia constant M and the power angle equations under prefault and postfault conditions.

$$\text{Base MVA} = 20$$

$$\text{Inertia constant, } M(\text{pu}) = \frac{H}{180\,f} = \frac{1.0 \times 2.52}{180 \times 50}$$
$$= 2.8 \times 10^{-4}\ \text{s}^2/\text{elect degree}$$

I. Prefault

$$X_\text{I} = 0.35 + \frac{0.2}{2} = 0.45$$

$\therefore$
$$P_{e\text{I}} = P_{\max\text{I}} \sin\delta$$
$$= \frac{1.1 \times 1}{0.45}\sin\delta = 2.44\sin\delta \quad \text{(i)}$$

$$\text{Prefault power transfer} = \frac{18}{20} = 0.9\ \text{pu}$$

Initial power angle is given by

$$2.44\sin\delta_0 = 0.9$$

or
$$\delta_0 = 21.64°$$

II. During fault A positive sequence diagram is shown in Fig. 12.40(a). Converting star to delta, we obtain the network of Fig. 12.40(b), in which

$$X_{II} = \frac{0.35 \times 0.1 + 0.2 \times 0.1 + 0.35 \times 0.2}{0.1} = 1.25 \text{ pu}$$

$$\therefore \quad P_{eII} = P_{\max II} \sin \delta$$

$$= \frac{1.1 \times 1}{1.25} \sin \delta = 0.88 \sin \delta \qquad \text{(ii)}$$

III. Postfault With the faulted line switched off,

$$X_{III} = 0.35 + 0.2 = 0.55$$

$$\therefore \quad P_{eIII} = P_{\max III} \sin \delta$$

$$= \frac{1.1 \times 1}{0.55} \sin \delta = 2.0 \sin \delta \qquad \text{(iii)}$$

Let us choose $\Delta t = 0.05$ s.

The recursive relationships for step-by-step swing curve calculation are reproduced below.

$$P_{a(n-1)} = P_m - P_{\max} \sin \delta_{n-1} \qquad \text{(iv)}$$

$$\Delta\delta_n = \Delta\delta_{n-1} + \frac{(\Delta t)^2}{M} P_{a(n-1)} \qquad \text{(v)}$$

$$\delta_n = \delta_{n-1} + \Delta\delta_n \qquad \text{(vi)}$$

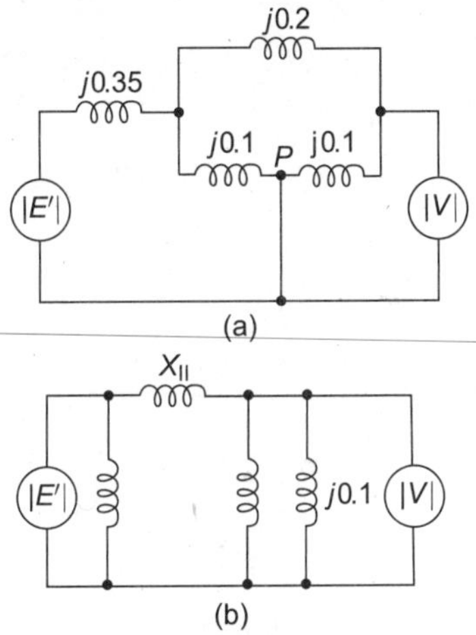

Fig. 12.40

Since there is a discontinuity in P_e and hence in P_a, the average value of P_a must be used for the first interval.

$$P_a(0_-) = 0 \text{ pu and } P_a(0_+) = 0.9 - 0.88 \sin 21.64° = 0.576 \text{ pu}$$

$$P_a(0_{\text{average}}) = \frac{0 + 0.576}{2} = 0.288 \text{ pu}$$

12.9.1 Sustained Fault

Calculations are carried out in Table 12.2 in accordance with the recursive relationship (iv), (v) and (vi) above. The second column of the table shows $P_{\max}$ the maximum power that can be transferred at time t given in the first column. $P_{\max}$ in the case of a sustained fault undergoes a sudden change at $t = 0_+$ and remains constant thereafter. The procedure of calculations is illustrated below by calculating the row corresponding to $t = 0.15$ s.

$$(0.1 \text{ s}) = 31.59°$$

$$P_{\max} = 0.88$$

$$\sin \delta (0.1 \text{ s}) = 0.524$$

$$P_e (0.1 \text{ s}) = P_{\max} \sin \delta (0.1 \text{ s}) = 0.88 \times 0.524 = 0.461$$

$$P_a (0.1 \text{ s}) = 0.9 - 0.461 = 0.439$$

$$\frac{(\Delta t)^2}{M} P_a (0.1 \text{ s}) = 8.929 \times 0.439 = 3.92°$$

$$\delta (0.15 \text{ s}) = \Delta\delta (0.1 \text{ s}) + \frac{(\Delta t)^2}{M} P_a (0.1 \text{ s})$$

$$= 7.38° + 3.92° = 11.33°$$

$$\delta (0.15 \text{ s}) = \delta (0.1 \text{ s}) + \Delta\delta (0.15 \text{ s})$$

$$= 31.59° + 11.30° = 42.89°$$

Table 12.2 Point-by-point computations of swing curve for sustained fault, $\Delta t = 0.05$ s

t	P_{max}	$\sin\delta$	$P_e = P_{max}\sin\delta$	$P_a = 0.9 - P_e$	$\frac{(\Delta t)^2}{M} Pa$	$\Delta\delta$	δ
s	pu		pu	pu	$= 8.929\ P_a$ deg	deg	deg
0_-	2.44	0.368	0.9	0.0	—	—	21.64
0_+	0.88	0.368	0.324	0.576	—	—	21.64
0_{avg}	—	0.368	—	0.288	2.57	2.57	21.64
0.05	0.88	0.41	0.361	0.539	4.81	7.38	24.21
0.10	0.88	0.524	0.461	0.439	3.92	11.30	31.59
0.15	0.88	0.680	0.598	0.301	2.68	13.98	42.89
0.20	0.88	0.837	0.736	0.163	1.45	15.43	56.87
0.25	0.88	0.953	0.838	0.06	0.55	15.98	72.30
0.30	0.88	0.999	0.879	0.021	0.18	16.16	88.28
0.35	0.88	0.968	0.852	0.048	0.426	16.58	104.44
0.40	0.88	0.856	0.754	0.145	1.30	17.88	121.02
0.45	0.88	0.657	0.578	0.321	2.87	20.75	138.90
0.50	0.88	—	—	—	—	—	159.65

$\delta(t)$ for sustained fault as calculated in Table 12.2 is plotted in Fig. 12.41 from which it is obvious that the system is unstable.

Fault Cleared in 2.5 Cycles

$$\text{Time to clear fault} = \frac{2.5}{50} = 0.05 \text{ s}$$

P_{max} suddenly changes from 0.88 at $t = 0.05_-$ to 2.0 at $t = 0.05_+$. Since the discontinuity occurs at the beginning of an interval, the average value of P_a will be assumed to remain constant from 0.025 s to 0.075 s. The rest of the procedure is the same and complete calculations are shown in Table 12.3. The swing curve is plotted in Fig. 12.41 from which we find that the generator undergoes a maximum swing of 37.5° but is stable as δ finally begins to decrease.

Fault Cleared in 6.25 Cycles

$$\text{Time to clear fault} = \frac{6.25}{50} = 0.125 \text{ s}$$

Since the discontinuity now lies in the middle to an interval, no special procedure is necessary, as in deriving Eqs. (iv)–(vi) discontinuity is assumed to occur in the middle of the time interval. The swing curve as calculated in Table 12.4 is also plotted in Fig. 12.41. It is observed that the system is stable with a maximum swing of 52.5° which is much larger than that in the case of 2.5 cycle clearing time.

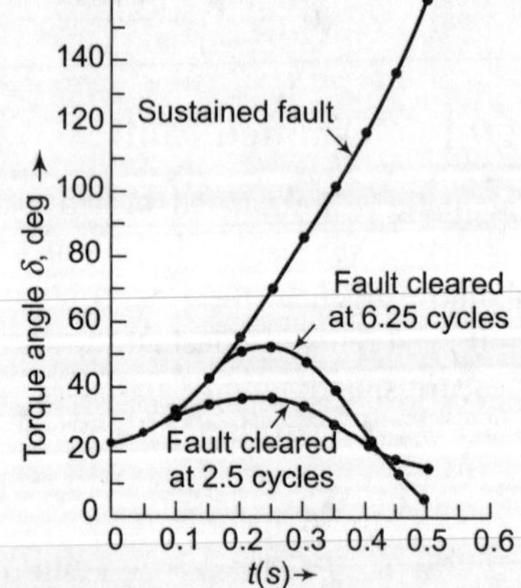

Fig. 12.41 *Swing curves for Example 12.10 for a sustained fault and for clearing in 2.5 and 6.25 cycles*

To find the critical clearing time, swing curves can be obtained, similarly, for progressively greater clearing time till the torque angle δ increases without bound. In this example, however, we can first find the critical clearing angle using Eq. (12.67) and then read the critical clearing time from the swing curve corresponding to the sustained fault case. The values obtained are

Critical clearing angle = 118.62°

Critical clearing time = 0.38 s

Table 12.3 Computations of swing curve for fault cleared at 2.5 cycles (0.05 s), $\Delta t = 0.05$ s

t	P_{max}	$sin\ \delta$	$P_e = P_{max} sin\ \delta$	$P_a = 0.9 - P_e$	$\frac{(\Delta t)^2}{M} Pa$	$\Delta\delta$	δ
s	pu		pu	pu	$= 8.929\ P_a$ deg	deg	deg
0_-	2.44	0.368	0.9	0.0	—	—	21.64
0_+	0.88	0.368	0.324	0.576	—	—	21.64
0_{avg}	—	0.368	—	0.288	2.57	2.57	21.64
0.05_-	0.88	0.41	0.36	0.54	—	—	24.21
0.05_+	2.00	0.41	0.82	0.08	—	—	24.21
0.05_{avg}				0.31	2.767	5.33	24.21
0.10	2.00	0.493	0.986	– 0.086	– 0.767	4.56	29.54
0.15	2.00	0.56	1.12	– 0.22	– 1.96	2.60	34.10
0.20	2.00	0.597	1.19	– 0.29	– 2.58	0.02	36.70
0.25	2.00	0.597	1.19	– 0.29	– 2.58	– 2.56	37.72
0.30	2.00	0.561	1.12	– 0.22	– 1.96	– 4.52	34.16
0.35	2.00	0.494	0.989	– 0.089	– 0.79	– 5.31	29.64
0.40	2.00	0.41	0.82	0.08	0.71	– 4.60	24.33
0.45	2.00	0.337	0.675	0.225	2.0	– 2.6	19.73
0.50							17.13

Table 12.4 Computations of swing curve for fault cleared at 6.25 cycles (0.125 s), $\Delta t = 0.05$ s

t	P_{max}	$sin\ \delta$	$P_e = P_{max} sin\ \delta$	$P_a = 0.9 - P_e$	$\frac{(\Delta t)^2}{M} Pa$	$\Delta\delta$	δ
s	pu		pu	pu	$= 8.929\ P_a$ deg	deg	deg
0_-	2.44	0.368	0.9	0.0	–	–	21.64
0_+	0.88	0.368	0.324	0.576	–	–	21.64
0_{avg}	–	0.368	–	0.288	2.57	2.57	21.64
0.05	0.88	0.41	0.361	0.539	4.81	7.38	24.21
0.10	0.88	0.524	0.461	0.439	3.92	11.30	31.59
0.15	2.00	0.680	1.36	– 4.46	– 4.10	7.20	42.89
0.20	2.00	0.767	1.53	– 0.63	– 5.66	1.54	50.09
0.25	2.00	0.78	1.56	– 0.66	– 5.89	– 4.35	51.63
0.30	2.00	0.734	1.46	– 0.56	– 5.08	– 9.43	47.28
0.35	2.00	0.613	1.22	– 0.327	– 2.92	– 12.35	37.85
0.40	2.00	0.430	0.86	0.04	0.35	– 12.00	25.50
0.45	2.00	0.233	0.466	0.434	3.87	– 8.13	13.50
0.50	2.00						5.37

12.10 ▶ MULTIMACHINES STABILITY

From what has been discussed so far, the following steps easily follow for determining multimachine stability.

1. From the prefault load flow data determine E'_k voltage behind transient reactance for all generators. This establishes generator emf magnitudes $|E_k|$ which remain constant during the study and initial rotor angle $\delta_k^0 = \angle E_k$. Also record prime mover inputs to generators, $P_{mk} = P_{Gk}^0$.
2. Augment the load flow network by the generator transient reactances. Shift network buses behind the transient reactances.
3. Find Y_{BUS} for various network conditions—during fault, postfault (faulted line cleared), after line reclosure.
4. For faulted mode, find generator outputs from power angle equations [generalised forms of Eq. (12.27)] and solve swing equations step by step (point-by-point method).
5. Keep repeating the above step for postfault mode and after line reclosure mode.
6. Examine $\delta(t)$ plots of all generators and establish the answer to the stability question.

The above steps are illustrated in the following example.

Power System Stability Solution of Swing Eq.

Runge–Kutta Order-2 Method: Considering a first-order differential equation such that

$$\frac{dx}{dt} = f(x,t)$$

1. Assume initial solution at t_0 is x_0.
2. Take step size Δt, then solution of given differential equation at $t_1 = t_0 + \Delta t$ is $x_1 = x_0 + \Delta x$.

where
$$\Delta x = \frac{k_1 + k_2}{2}$$

and
$$k_1 = f(x_0, t_0) \cdot \Delta t$$
$$k_2 = f(x_0 + k_1, t_0 + \Delta t) \cdot \Delta t$$

3. Similarly for ith generator

$$k_{1i} = f(x_i, t_i) \,.\, \Delta t$$
$$k_{2i} = f[(x_i + k_{1i}), (t_i + \Delta t)] \cdot \Delta t$$

and solution

$$x_{i+1} = x_i + \left(\frac{k_{1i} + k_{2i}}{2}\right) \quad \text{for } t_{i+1} = t_i + \Delta t$$

Runge–Kutta Order-4 Method: Let a first-order differential equation

$$\frac{dx}{dt} = f(x, t)$$

1. Assume initial solution at t_0 is x_0.
2. Set step size Δt, then solution of given differential equation is given at $t_1 = t_0 + \Delta t$ as

$$x_1 = x_0 + \Delta x$$

where
$$\Delta x = \frac{1}{6}[k_1 + 2k_2 + 2k_3 + k_4]$$

and
$$k_1 = f(x_0, t_0) \cdot \Delta t$$
$$k_2 = f\left(x_0 + \frac{k_1}{2}, t_0 + \frac{\Delta t}{2} \cdot \Delta t\right)$$
$$k_3 = f\left(x_0 + \frac{k_2}{2}, t_0 + \frac{\Delta t}{2} \cdot \Delta t\right)$$
$$k_4 = f(x_0 + k_3, t_0 + \Delta t) \cdot \Delta t$$

3. Similarly for ith generator,

$$k_{1i} = f(x_i, t_i) \,.\, \Delta t$$
$$k_{2i} = f\left(x_i + \frac{k_{1i}}{2},\ t_i + \frac{\Delta t}{2}\right) \cdot \Delta t$$
$$k_{3i} = f\left(x_i + \frac{k_{2i}}{2},\ t_i + \frac{\Delta t}{2}\right) \cdot \Delta t$$
$$k_{4i} = f(x_i + k_{3i}, t_i + \Delta t) \,.\, \Delta t$$

and solution,

$$x_{i+1} = x_i + \frac{1}{6}\left[k_{1i} + 2k_{2i} + 2k_{3i} + k_{4i}\right]$$

Runge–Kutta Method for Swing Equation The swing equation for ith generator is

$$\frac{d^2\delta_i}{\partial t^2} = \frac{\pi f}{H_i}(P_{mi} - P_{ei}\sin\delta_i);\ i = 1, 2, \quad ...m \tag{i}$$

For multimachine system swing equation is written in state variable form.

$$x_{1i} = \delta_i = \angle E'_k$$
$$x_{1i} = \delta_i$$

Then,

$$x_{1i} = x_{2i} = \delta_i = \omega_i = f_1(\delta_i, \omega_i)$$
$$x_{2i} = \frac{\pi f}{H_i}(P_{mi} - P_{ei}\sin\delta_i) = f_2(\delta_i, \omega_i) \tag{ii}$$

⇒ Algorithm for Runge–Kutta Order-2;

1. Carry out the load flow study (before transient) using specified voltage and power.
2. Find the voltage behind transient reactances of generator (E_i°)
3. Compute Y_{BUS} (during fault, postfault, line reclosed)
4. Set time count $\gamma = 0$ and set step-size Δt (for $t^{(0)}, {}_t^{(1)}$ ....)
5. Compute x_{1i} and x_{2i} from equation (ii).
6. Compute the two constants for each differential equation of equation (ii).

$$k_1^r = f_1(\delta_i^r, \omega_i^r) \,.\, \Delta t$$
$$h_1^r = f_2(\delta_i^r, \omega_i^r) \,.\, \Delta t$$
$$k_2^r = f_1(\delta_i^r + k_1^r, \omega_i^r + h_1^r) \cdot \Delta t$$
$$h_2^r = f_2(\delta_i^r + k_1^r, \omega_i^r + h_1^r) \cdot \Delta t$$

7. Compute next state estimation such that

$$\delta_i^{(r+1)} = \delta_i^r + \Delta\delta_i^r$$

where

$$\Delta\delta_i^r = \frac{1}{2}(k_1^r + k_2^r)$$

and

$$\omega_i^{(r+1)} = \omega_i^r + \Delta\omega_i^r$$

where

$$\Delta\omega_i^r = \frac{1}{2}(h_1^r + h_2^r)$$

8. Test for time limit for which swing curve is to be plotted. If $r < r_{\text{final}}$ then $r = r + 1$ and repeat from step 5 above, otherwise print results and stop.
9. Plot the curve between rotor angle (δ) and time (t).

Example 12.11 Solution of problem using Rk-2 method.

Base MVA = 20

$$\text{Inertia constant } M(\text{pu}) = \frac{H}{180 f} = \frac{1.0 \times 2.52}{180 \times 50}$$
$$= 2.8 \times 10^{-4} \text{ s}^2/\text{elect degree}$$

or $\quad 1/(62.30)\ s^2/\text{rad}$

⇒ Pre-fault

$$x_1 = 0.35 + \frac{0.2}{2} = 0.45$$
$$P_{ei} = P_{\max} \sin \delta$$
$$= \frac{1.1 \times 1}{0.45} \sin \delta = 2.44 \sin \delta \tag{i}$$
$$\text{Pre-fault power transfer } P_m = \frac{18}{20} = 0.9 \text{ pu}$$

Initial power angle is given by

$$2.44 \sin \delta_0 = 0.9$$
$$\delta_0 = 21.64°$$

⇒ During fault

$$X_{\text{II}} = \frac{0.35 \times 0.1 + 0.2 \times 0.1 + 0.35 \times 0.2}{0.1} = 1.25 \text{ pu}$$
$$P_{e\text{II}} = P_{\max \text{ II}} \sin \delta$$
$$= \frac{1.1 \times 1}{1.25} \sin \delta = 0.88 \sin \delta_0 \tag{ii}$$

⇒ Postfault with faulted line switched off

$$X_{\text{III}} = 0.35 + 0.2 = 0.55$$
$$P_{e\text{III}} = P_{\max \text{ III}} \sin \delta$$
$$= \frac{1.1 \times 1}{0.55} \sin \delta = 2.0 \sin \delta \tag{iii}$$

Let ω choose $\Delta t = 0.05$ s.

$$\text{And initial rotor angle } \delta_0 = 21.64°$$
$$= 0.377 \text{ rad.}$$
$$\omega_0 = \frac{d\delta_0}{dt} = 0$$
$$f_1(\delta, \omega) = \frac{d\delta}{dt} = \omega \tag{iv}$$
$$f_2(\delta, \omega) = \frac{d^2\delta}{dt} = \frac{\pi f}{H}(P_m - P_e \sin \delta) \tag{v}$$

⇒ Find Runge–Kutta order-2 Method's constants for Eqs. (iv) and (v)

$$k_1 = f_1(\delta_0, \omega_0) \,.\, \Delta t = \omega_0 \times 0.05 = 0$$
$$h_1 = f_2(\delta_0, \omega_0) \,.\, \Delta t = 62.3\,(0.9 - 0.88 \sin \delta_0) \times 0.05 = 1.794$$
$$k_2 = f_1(\delta_0 + k_1, \omega_0 + h_1) \,.\, \Delta t = 0.089$$
$$h_2 = f_2(\delta_0 + k_1, \omega_0 + h_1) \,.\, \Delta t = 1.794$$

Now,

$$\Delta\delta_0 = \frac{1}{2}(k_1 + k_2) = 0.0445 \text{ rad.}$$
$$\Delta\omega_0 = \frac{1}{2}(h_1 + h_2) = 1.794 \text{ rad/sec.}$$

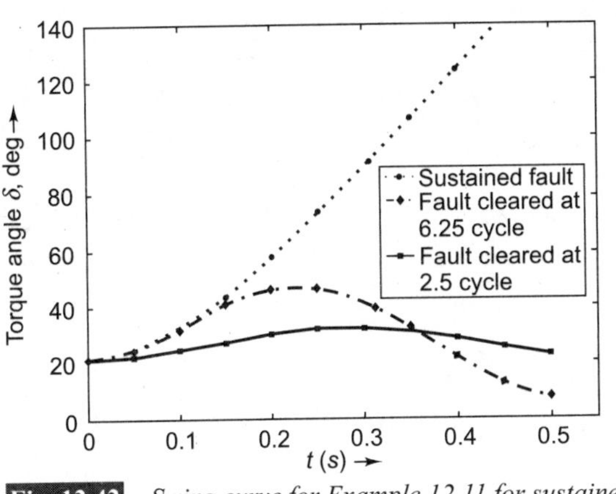

Fig. 12.42 *Swing curve for Example 12.11 for sustained fault and for clearing in 2.5 and 6.25 cycles (RK-2 Method)*

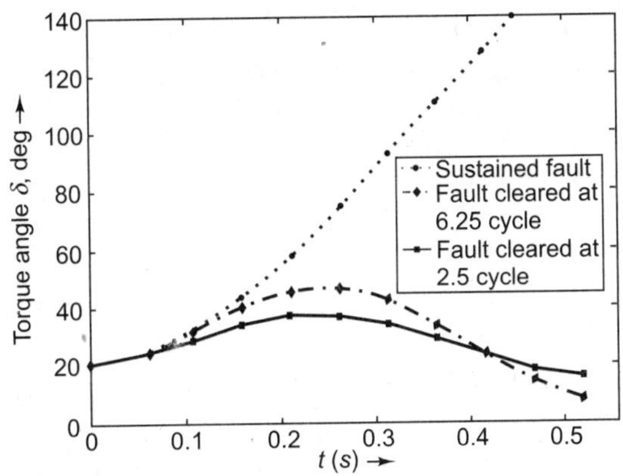

Fig. 12.43 *Swing curve for Example 12.11 for sustained fault and for clearing in 2.5 and 6.25 cycles (RK-4 Method)*

Table 12.5 Swing curve for sustained fault using Runge–Kutta (order-2) method

t	*di*	*wi*	*Pm*	*Pmax*	k_1	*l1*	*k2*	*l2*	*ddi*	*dwi*	*d (i + 1)*
0	*0.3770*	*0*	*0.9000*	*2.4400*	*0*	*0*	*0*	*0*	*0*	*0*	*0*
0.0500	0.4222	1.8097	0.9000	0.8800	0	1.8097	0.0905	1.8097	0.0452	1.8097	24.1927
0.1000	0.5551	3.3926	0.9000	0.8800	0.0905	1.6945	0.1752	1.4712	0.1328	1.5829	31.8043
0.1500	0.7590	4.5751	0.9000	0.8800	0.1696	1.3704	0.2381	0.9947	0.2039	1.1826	43.4862
0.2000	1.0109	5.2974	0.9000	0.8800	0.2288	0.9249	0.2750	0.5196	0.2519	0.7222	57.9178
0.2500	1.2879	5.6310	0.9000	0.8800	0.2649	0.4850	0.2891	0.1823	0.2770	0.3337	73.7884
0.3000	1.5737	5.7488	0.9000	0.8800	0.2816	0.1728	0.2902	0.0628	0.2859	0.1178	90.1676
0.3500	1.8627	5.8695	0.9000	0.8800	0.2874	0.0628	0.2906	0.1786	0.2890	0.1207	106.7268
0.4000	2.1607	6.2210	0.9000	0.8800	0.2935	0.1798	0.3025	0.5232	0.2980	0.3515	123.7994
0.4500	2.4850	7.0416	0.9000	0.8800	0.3111	0.5301	0.3376	1.1110	0.3243	0.8205	142.3806
0.5000	2.8656	8.6108	0.9000	0.8800	0.3521	1.1399	0.4091	1.9986	0.3806	1.5692	164.1861

Table 12.6 Swing curve for fault cleared at 2.5 cycles (0.05 sec.) using Runge–Kutta (order-2) method

t	*di*	*wi*	*Pm*	*Pmax*	*k1*	*l1*	*k2*	*12*	*ddi*	*dwi*	*d(i + 1)*
0	*0.3770*	*0*	*0.9000*	*2.4400*	*0*	*0*	*0*	*0*	*0*	*0*	*0*
0.0500	0.3899	0.5144	0.9000	2.0000	0	0.5144	0.0257	0.5144	0.0129	0.5144	22.3373
0.1000	0.4266	0.8795	0.9000	2.0000	0.0257	0.4395	0.0477	0.2908	0.0367	0.3651	24.4404
0.1500	0.4762	0.9828	0.9000	2.0000	0.0440	0.2278	0.0554	–0.0212	0.0497	0.1033	27.2863
0.2000	0.5241	0.7944	0.9000	2.0000	0.0491	–0.0530	0.0465	–0.3238	0.0478	–0.1884	30.0259
0.2500	0.5559	0.3710	0.9000	2.0000	0.0397	–0.3166	0.0239	–0.5302	0.0318	–0.4234	31.8482
0.3000	0.5622	–0.1662	0.9000	2.0000	0.0186	–0.4880	–0.0059	–0.5865	0.0064	–0.5372	32.2120
0.3500	0.5408	–0.6659	0.9000	2.0000	–0.0083	–0.5218	–0.0344	–0.4775	–0.0214	–0.4997	30.9883
0.4000	0.4974	–0.9829	0.9000	2.0000	–0.0333	–0.4076	–0.0537	–0.2264	–0.0435	–0.3170	28.4969
0.4500	0.4440	–1.0158	0.9000	2.0000	–0.0491	–0.1703	–0.0577	0.1045	–0.0534	–0.0329	25.4370
0.5000	0.3964	–0.7414	0.9000	2.0000	–0.0508	0.1287	–0.0444	0.4202	–0.0476	0.2745	22.7113

Table 12.7 Swing curve for fault cleared at 6.25 cycles (0.125 sec.) using Runge–Kutta (order-2) method

t	*di*	*wi*	*Pm*	*Pmax*	*k1*	*l1*	*k2*	*l2*	*ddi*	*dwi*	*d(i + 1)*
0	*0.3770*	*0*	*0.9000*	*2.4400*	*0*	*0*	*0*	*0*	*0*	*0*	*0*
0.0500	0.4222	1.8097	0.9000	0.8800	0	1.8097	0.0905	1.8097	0.0452	1.8097	24.1927
0.1000	0.5551	3.3926	0.9000	0.8800	0.0905	1.6945	0.1752	1.4712	0.1328	1.5829	31.8043
0.1500	0.7126	2.4817	0.9000	2.0000	0.1696	−0.4839	0.1454	−1.3378	0.1575	−0.9109	40.8300
0.2000	0.8047	0.9226	0.9000	2.0000	0.1241	−1.2806	0.0601	−1.8374	0.0921	−1.5590	46.1052
0.2500	0.8083	−0.8757	0.9000	2.0000	0.0461	−1.7003	−0.0389	−1.8964	0.0036	−1.7984	46.3128
0.3000	0.7216	−2.4946	0.9000	2.0000	−0.0438	−1.7161	−0.1296	−1.5218	−0.0867	−1.6189	41.3460
0.3500	0.5638	−3.5084	0.9000	2.0000	−0.1247	−1.3233	−0.1909	−0.7042	−0.1578	−1.0137	32.3040
0.4000	0.3751	−3.5495	0.9000	2.0000	−0.1754	−0.5304	−0.2019	0.4480	−0.1887	−0.0412	21.4936
0.4500	0.2108	−2.4901	0.9000	2.0000	−0.1775	0.5253	−0.1512	1.5936	−0.1643	1.0594	12.0773
0.5000	0.1241	−0.5907	0.9000	2.0000	−0.1245	1.5128	−0.0489	2.2860	−0.0867	1.8994	7.1106

Table 12.8 Swing curve for sustained fault using Runge–Kutta (order-4) method

t	*di*	*wi*	*Pm*	*Pmax*	*k1*	*l1*	*k2*	*l2*	*ddi*	*dwi*	*d(i + 1)*
0	*0.3770*	*0*	*0.9000*	*2.4400*	*0*	*0*	*0*	*0*	*0*	*0*	*0*
0.0500	0.4218	1.7712	0.9000	0.8800	0	1.8097	0.0452	1.8097	0.0448	1.7712	24.1651
0.1000	0.5504	3.3236	0.9000	0.8800	0.0886	1.6957	0.1310	1.5852	0.1287	1.5525	31.5377
0.1500	0.7477	4.4934	0.9000	0.8800	0.1662	1.3814	0.2007	1.1908	0.1972	1.1697	42.8377
0.2000	0.9923	5.2183	0.9000	0.8800	0.2247	0.9477	0.2484	0.7323	0.2446	0.7250	56.8520
0.2500	1.2630	5.5574	0.9000	0.8800	0.2609	0.5127	0.2737	0.3358	0.2707	0.3391	72.3632
0.3000	1.5441	5.6679	0.9000	0.8800	0.2779	0.1928	0.2827	0.1022	0.2812	0.1105	88.4732
0.3500	1.8294	5.7585	0.9000	0.8800	0.2834	0.0638	0.2850	0.0811	0.2853	0.0906	104.8187
0.4000	2.1234	6.0536	0.9000	0.8800	0.2879	0.1548	0.2918	0.2839	0.2940	0.2951	121.6617
0.4500	2.4421	6.7915	0.9000	0.8800	0.3027	0.4743	0.3145	0.7200	0.3187	0.7379	139.9230
0.5000	2.8145	8.2547	0.9000	0.8800	0.3396	1.0475	0.3658	1.4306	0.3724	1.4633	161.2604

Table 12.9 Swing curve for fault cleared at 2.5 cycles (0.05 sec.) using Runge–Kutta (order-4) method

t	*di*	*wi*	*Pm*	*Pmax*	*k1*	*l1*	*k2*	*l2*	*ddi*	*dwi*	*d(i + 1)*
0	*0.3770*	*0*	*0.9000*	*2.4400*	*0*	*0*	*0*	*0*	*0*	*0*	*0*
0.0500	0.4218	1.7712	0.9000	0.8800	0	1.8097	0.0452	1.8097	0.0448	1.7712	24.1651
0.1000	0.5124	1.7701	0.9000	2.0000	0.0886	0.2553	0.0949	0.0041	0.0906	−0.0011	29.3564
0.1500	0.5907	1.2954	0.9000	2.0000	0.0885	−0.2528	0.0822	−0.4921	0.0783	−0.4747	33.8449
0.2000	0.6362	0.4888	0.9000	2.0000	0.0648	−0.6720	0.0480	−0.8391	0.0455	−0.8066	36.4544
0.2500	0.6375	−0.4393	0.9000	2.0000	0.0244	−0.9059	0.0018	−0.9674	0.0012	−0.9281	36.5257
0.3000	0.5941	−1.2579	0.9000	2.0000	−0.0220	−0.9122	−0.0448	−0.8565	−0.0434	−0.8186	34.0415
0.3500	0.5171	−1.7546	0.9000	2.0000	−0.0629	−0.6898	−0.0801	−0.5244	−0.0770	−0.4967	29.6297
0.4000	0.4266	−1.7827	0.9000	2.0000	−0.0877	−0.2789	−0.0947	−0.0364	−0.0905	−0.0282	24.4446
0.4500	0.3473	−1.3146	0.9000	2.0000	−0.0891	0.2274	−0.0835	0.4848	−0.0793	0.4681	19.9011
0.5000	0.3017	−0.4696	0.9000	2.0000	−0.0657	0.6887	−0.0485	0.8839	−0.0457	0.8450	17.2834

Table 12.10 Swing curve for fault cleared at 6.25 cycles (0.125 sec. using Runge–Kutta (order-4) method

t	*di*	*wi*	*Pm*	*Pmax*	*k1*	*l1*	*k2*	*l2*	*ddi*	*dwi*	*d(i + 1)*
0	*0.3770*	*0*	*0.9000*	*2.4400*	*0*	*0*	*0*	*0*	*0*	*0*	*0*
0.0500	0.4218	1.7712	0.9000	0.8800	0	1.8097	0.0452	1.8097	0.0448	1.7712	24.1651
0.1000	0.5504	3.3236	0.9000	0.8800	0.0886	1.6957	0.1310	1.5852	0.1287	1.5525	31.5377
0.1500	0.6982	2.4633	0.9000	2.0000	0.1662	–0.4590	0.1547	–0.8922	0.1477	–0.8604	40.0020
0.2000	0.7868	1.0164	0.9000	2.0000	0.1232	–1.2115	0.0929	–1.5000	0.0886	–1.4469	45.0810
0.2500	0.7960	–0.6555	0.9000	2.0000	0.0508	–1.6217	0.0103	–1.7330	0.0092	–1.6719	45.6058
0.3000	0.7236	–2.1830	0.9000	2.0000	–0.0328	–1.6622	–0.0743	–1.5895	–0.0723	–1.5274	41.4611
0.3500	0.5862	–3.2001	0.9000	2.0000	–0.1091	–1.3327	–0.1425	–1.0697	–0.1374	–1.0171	33.5890
0.4000	0.4175	–3.3959	0.9000	2.0000	–0.1600	–0.6486	–0.1762	–0.2192	–0.1687	–0.1959	23.9237
0.4500	0.2628	–2.6444	0.9000	2.0000	–0.1698	0.2795	–0.1628	0.7757	–0.1547	0.7516	15.0593
0.5000	0.1665	–1.1162	0.9000	2.0000	–0.1322	1.1949	–0.1023	1.5993	–0.0964	1.5282	9.5377

Example 12.12 A 50 Hz, 220 kV transmission line has two generators and an infinite bus as shown in Fig. 12.44. The transformer and line data are given in Table 12.11. A three-phase fault occurs as shown. The prefault load flow solution is presented in Table 12.12. Find the swing equation for each generator during the fault period.

Data are given below for the two generators on a 100 MVA base.

Generator 1 500 MVA, 25 kV, $X_d' = 0.067$ pu, H = 12 MJ/MVA

Generator 2 300 MVA, 20 kV, $X_d' = 0.10$ pu, H = 9 MJ/MVA

Plot the swing curves for the machines at buses 2 and 3 for the above fault which is cleared by simultaneous opening of the circuit breakers at the ends of the faulted line at (i) 0.275 s and (ii) 0.08 s.

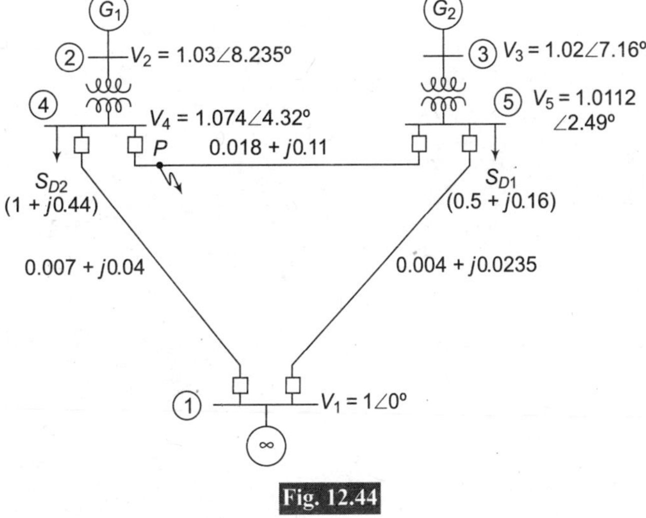

Fig. 12.44

Table 12.11 Line and transformer data for Example 12.12. All values are in pu on 220 kV, 100 MVA base

Bus to bus	*Series Z*		*Half line charging*
	R	*X*	
Line 4–5	0.018	0.11	0.113
Line 5–1	0.004	0.0235	0.098
Line 4–1	0.007	0.04	0.041
Trans: 2–4	—	0.022	—
Trans: 3–5	—	0.04	—

Solution Before determining swing equation, we have to find transient internal voltages.

The current into the network at bus 2 based on the data in Table 12.12 is

$$I_2 = \frac{P_2 - jQ_2}{V_2^*} = \frac{3.25 - j0.6986}{1.03\angle -8.23519^\circ}$$

$$\therefore \quad I_2 X'_{de} = \frac{3.25 - j0.6986}{1.03\angle -8.23519^\circ} \times 0.067\angle 90^\circ$$

$$E'_2 = (1.0194 + j0.1475) + \frac{3.25 - j0.6986}{1.03\angle -8.23519^\circ} \times 0.067\angle 90^\circ$$

$$= 1.0340929 + j0.3632368$$

$$= 1.0960333\angle 19.354398^\circ = 1.0960\angle 0.3377 \text{ rad}$$

$$E'_1 = 1.0\angle 0^\circ \text{ (slack bus)}$$

$$E'_3 = (1.0121 + j0.1271) + \frac{2.1 - j0.311}{1.02\angle -7.15811^\circ} \times 0.1\angle 90^\circ$$

$$= 1.0166979 + j0.335177 = 1.0705\angle 18.2459^\circ$$

$$= 1.071\angle 0.31845 \text{ rad}$$

The loads at buses 4 and 5 are represented by the admittances calculated as follows:

$$Y_{L4} = \frac{1.0 - j0.44}{(1.0174)^2}(0.9661 - j0.4251)$$

$$Y_{L5} = \frac{0.5 - j0.16}{(1.0112)^2}(0.4889 - j0.15647)$$

Table 12.12 Bus data and prefault load-flow values in pu on 220 kV, 100 MVA base

S.No. and Bus No.	Voltage Polar-Form	Bus type	Voltage		Generation		Load	
			Real e	*Imaginary f*	*P*	*Q*	*P*	*Q*
1	$1.0\angle 0^\circ$	Slack	1.00	0.0	– 3.8083	– 0.2799	0	0
2	$1.03\angle 8.35^\circ$	PV	1.0194	0.1475	3.25	0.6986	0	0
3	$1.02\angle 7.16^\circ$	PV	1.0121	0.1271	2.10	0.3110	0	0
4	$1.0174\angle 4.32^\circ$	PQ	1.0146	0.767	0	1.0	1.0	0.44
5	$1.0112\angle 2.69^\circ$	PQ	1.0102	0.0439	0	0	0.5	0.16

12.10.1 Prefault Bus Matrix

Load admittances, along with the transient reactances, are used with the line and transformer admittances to form the prefault augmented bus admittance matrix which contains the transient reactances of the machines. We will, therefore, now designate as buses 2 and 3, the fictitious internal nodes between the internal voltages and the transient reactances of the machines. Thus, we get

$$Y_{22} = \frac{1}{(j0.067 + j0.022)} = -j11.236$$

$$Y_{24} = j11.236 = Y_{42}$$

$$Y_{33} = \frac{1}{j0.04 + j0.1} = -j7.143$$

$Y_{35} = j7.143 = Y_{53}$

$$Y_{44} = Y_{L4} + Y_{41} + Y_{45} + \frac{B_{41}}{2} + \frac{B_{45}}{2} + Y_{24}$$
$$= 0.9660877 - j0.4250785 + 4.245 - j24.2571 + 1.4488 - j8.8538 + j0.041 + j0.113 - j11.2359$$
$$= 6.6598977 - j44.6179$$

$$Y_{55} = Y_{L5} + Y_{54} + Y_{51} + \frac{B_{54}}{2} + \frac{B_{51}}{2} + Y_{35}$$
$$= 0.4889 - j0.1565 + 1.4488 - j8.8538 + 7.0391 - j41.355 + j0.113 + j0.098 - j7.1428$$
$$= 8.976955 - j57.297202$$

The complete augmented prefault Y_{BUS} matrix is shown in Table 12.13.

Table 12.13 The augmented prefault bus admittance matrix for Example 12.12, admittances in pu

Bus	*1*	*2*	*3*	*4*	*5*
1	$11.284 - j65.473$	0	0	$-4.245 + j24.257$	$-7.039 + j41.355$
2	0	$-j11.2359$	0	$j11.2359$	0
3	0	0	$-j7.1428$	0	$j7.1428$
4	$-4.245 + j24.257$	$j11.2359$	0	$6.6598 - j44.617$	$-1.4488 + j8.8538$
5	$-7.039 + j41.355$	0	$0 + j7.1428$	$-1.4488 + j8.8538$	$8.9769 + j57.2972$

12.10.2 During Fault Bus Matrix

Since the fault is near bus 4, it must be short circuited to ground. The Y_{BUS} during the fault conditions would, therefore, be obtained by deleting 4th row and 4th column from the above augmented prefault Y_{BUS} matrix. Reduced fault matrix (to the generator internal nodes) is obtained by eliminating the new 4th row and column (node 5) using the relationship

$$Y_{kj(\text{new})} = Y_{kj(\text{old})} - Y_{kn(\text{old})}\, Y_{nj(\text{old})} / Y_{nn(\text{old})}$$

The reduced faulted matrix (Y_{BUS} during fault) (3 × 3) is given in Table 12.14, which clearly depicts that bus 2 decouples from the other buses during the fault and that bus 3 is directly connected to bus 1, showing that the fault at bus 4 reduces to zero the power pumped into the system from the generator at bus 2 and renders the second generator at bus 3 to give its power radially to bus 1.

Table 12.14 Elements of Y_{BUS} (during fault) and Y_{BUS} (postfault) for Example 12.12, admittances in pu

Reduced during fault Y_{BUS}			
Bus	***1***	***2***	***3***
1	$5.7986 - j35.6301$	0	$-0.0681 + j5.1661$
2	0	$-j11.236$	0
3	$-0.0681 + j5.1661$	0	$0.1362 - j6.2737$
Reduced postfault Y_{BUS}			
1	$1.3932 - j13.8731$	$-0.2214 + j7.6289$	$-0.0901 + j6.0975$
2	$-0.2214 + j7.6289$	$0.5 - j7.7898$	0
3	$-0.0901 + j6.0975$	0	$0.1591 - j6.1168$

12.10.3 Postfault Bus Matrix

Once the fault is cleared by removing the line, simultaneously opening the circuit breakers at the either ends of the line between buses 4 and 5, the prefault Y_{BUS} has to be modified again. This is done by substituting $Y_{45} = Y_{54} = 0$ and subtracting the series admittance of line 4–5 and the capacitive susceptance of half the line from elements Y_{44} and Y_{55}.

$$\begin{aligned} Y_{44(\text{postfault})} &= Y_{44(\text{prefault})} - Y_{45} - B_{45}/2 \\ &= 6.65989 - j44.6179 - 1.448 + j8.853 - j0.113 \\ &= 5.2111 - j35.8771 \end{aligned}$$

Similarly,

$$Y_{55(\text{postfault})} = 7.5281 - j48.5563$$

The reduced postfault Y_{BUS} is shown in the lower half of Table 12.14. It may be noted that 0 element appears in 2nd and 3rd rows. This shows that, physically, the generators 1 and 2 are not interconnected when line 4–5 is removed.

During Fault Power Angle Equation

$$\begin{aligned} P_{e2} &= 0 \\ P_{e3} &= \text{Re}\,[Y_{33}E_3'E_3'^* + E_3'^*\,Y_{31}E_1'], \text{ since } Y_{32} = 0 \\ &= |E_3'|^2\,G_{33} + |E_1'|\,|E_3'|\,|Y_{31}| \cos(\delta_{31} - \theta_{31}) \\ &= (1.071)^2\,(0.1362) + 1 \times 1.071 \times 5.1665 \cos(\delta_3 - 90.755^\circ) \\ P_{e3} &= 0.1561 + 5.531 \sin(\delta_3 - 0.755^\circ) \end{aligned}$$

Postfault Power Angle Equations

$$\begin{aligned} P_{e2} &= |E_2'|^2\,G_{22} + |E_1'|\,|E_2'|\,|Y_{21}| \cos(\delta_{21} - \theta_{21}) \\ &= 1.096^2 \times 0.5005 + 1 \times 1.096 \times 7.6321 \cos(\delta_2 - 91.662^\circ) \\ &= 0.6012 + 8.365 \sin(\delta_2 - 1.662^\circ) \\ P_{e3} &= |E_3'|^2 G_{33} + |E_1'|\,|E_3'|\,|Y_{31}| \cos(\delta_{31} - \theta_{31}) \\ &= 1.071^2 \times 0.1591 + 1 \times 1.071 \times 6.098 \cos(\delta_3 - 90.8466^\circ) \\ &= 0.1823 + 6.5282 \sin(\delta_3 - 0.8466^\circ) \end{aligned}$$

Swing Equations—During Fault

$$\begin{aligned} \frac{d^2\delta_2}{dt^2} &= \frac{180f}{H_2}(P_{m2} - P_{e2}) = \frac{180f}{H_2}P_{a_2} \\ &= \frac{180f}{12}(3.25 - 0) \text{ elect deg/s}^2 \\ \frac{d^2\delta_3}{dt^2} &= \frac{180f}{H_3}(P_{m3} - P_{e3}) \\ &= \frac{180f}{9}[2.1 - \{0.1561 + 5.531 \sin(\delta_3 - 0.755^\circ)\}] \\ &= \frac{180f}{9}[1.9439 - 5.531 \sin(\delta_3 - 0.755^\circ)] \text{ elect deg/s}^2 \end{aligned}$$

Swing Equations—Postfault

$$\begin{aligned} \frac{d^2\delta_2}{dt^2} &= \frac{180f}{11}[3.25 - \{0.6012 + 8.365 \sin(\delta_2 - 1.662^\circ)\}] \text{ elect deg/s}^2 \\ \frac{d^2\delta_3}{dt^2} &= \frac{180f}{9}[2.10 - \{0.1823 + 6.5282 \sin(\delta_3 - 0.8466^\circ)\}] \text{ elect deg/s}^2 \end{aligned}$$

It may be noted that in the above swing equations, P_a may be written in general as follows:

$$P_a = P_m - P_c - P_{max} \sin(\delta - \gamma)$$

12.10.4 Digital Computer Solution of Swing Equation

The above swing equations (during fault followed by postfault) can be solved by the point-by-point method presented earlier or by the Euler's method presented in the later part of this section. The plots of δ_2 and δ_3 are given in Fig. 12.45 for a clearing time of 0.275 s and in Fig. 12.46 for a clearing time of 0.08 s. For the case (i), the machine 2 is unstable, while the machine 3 is stable but it oscillates wherein the oscillations are expected to decay if effect of damper winding is considered. For the case (ii), both machines are stable but the machine 2 has large angular swings.

If the fault is a transient one and the line is reclosed, power angle and swing equations are needed for the period after reclosure. These can be computed from the reduced Y_{BUS} matrix after line reclosure.

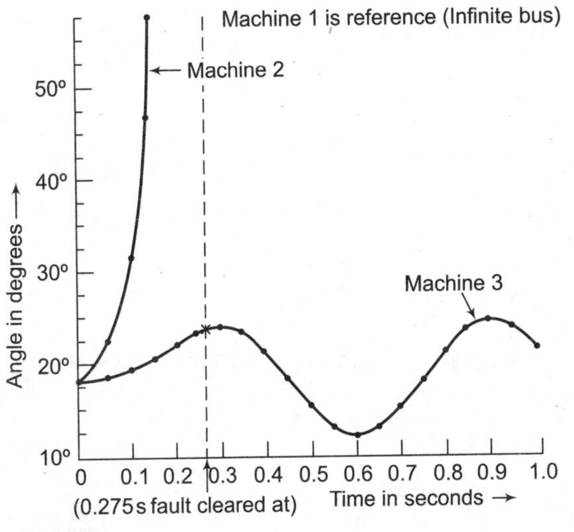

Fig. 12.45 *Swing curves for machines 2 and 3 of Example 12.12 for clearing at 0.275 s*

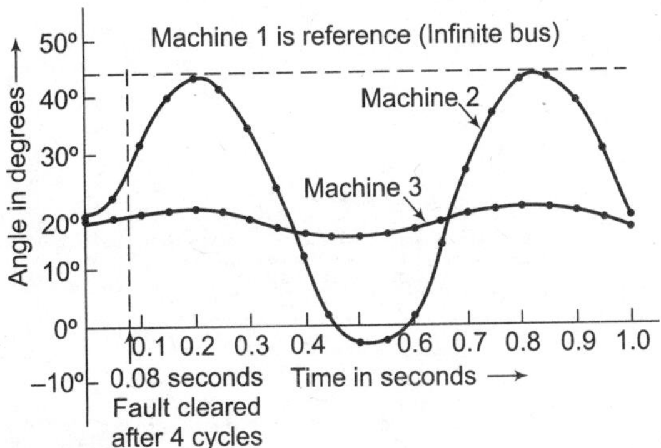

Fig. 12.46 *Swing curves for machines 2 and 3 of Example 12.12 for clearing at 0.08 s*

12.10.5 Consideration of Automatic Voltage Regulator (AVR) and Speed Governor Loops

This requires modelling of these two control loops in the form of differential equations. At the end of every step in the stability algorithm, the programme computes the modified values of E'_k and P_{mk} and then proceeds to compute the next step. This considerably adds to the dimensionality and complexity of stability calculations. To reduce the computational effort, speed control can continue to be ignored without loss of accuracy of results.

12.10.6 State Variable Formulation of Swing Equations

The swing equation for the kth generator is

$$\frac{d^2\delta_k}{dt^2} = \frac{\pi f}{H_k}(P^0_{Gk} - P_{Gk}),\ k = 1, 2, \ldots, m \tag{12.73}$$

For the multimachine case, it is more convenient to organise Eq. (12.73) in state variable form. Define

$$x_{1k} = \delta_k = \angle E_k'$$
$$x_{2k} = \dot{\delta}_k$$

Then,

$$\left\{\begin{aligned} \dot{x}_{1k} &= x_{2k} \\ \dot{x}_{2k} &= \frac{\pi f}{H_k}(P_{Gk}^0 - P_{Gk}),\ k = 1, 2, \ldots, m \end{aligned}\right\} \tag{12.74}$$

Initial state vector (upon occurrence of fault) is

$$x_{1k}^0 = \delta_k^0 = \angle E_k^0$$
$$x_{2k}^0 = 0 \tag{12.75}$$

The state form of swing equation (Eq. (12.74)) can be solved by the many available integration algorithms (modified Euler's method is a convenient choice).

12.10.7 Computational Algorithm for Obtaining Swing Curves Using Modified Euler's Method

1. Carry out a load flow study (prior to disturbance) using specified voltages and powers.
2. Compute voltage behind transient reactances of generators (E_k^0) using Eq. (9.31). This fixes generator emf magnitudes and initial rotor angle (reference slack bus voltage V_1^0).
3. Compute Y_{BUS} (during fault, postfault, line reclosed).
4. Set time count $r = 0$.
5. Compute generator power outputs using appropriate Y_{BUS} with the help of the general form of Eq. (12.27). This gives $P_{Gk}^{(r)}$ for $t = t^{(r)}$.
   Note: After the occurrence of the fault, the period is divided into uniform discrete time intervals (Δt) so that time is counted as $t^{(0)}$, $t^{(1)}$, ... A typical value of Δt is 0.05 s.
6. Compute $[(\dot{x}_{1k}^{(r)}, \dot{x}_{2k}^{(r)}), k = 1, 2, ..., m]$ from Eq. (12.74).
7. Compute the first state estimates for $t = t^{(r+1)}$ as
$$x_{1k}^{(r+1)} = x_{1k}^{(r)} + \dot{x}_{1k}^{(r)}\,\Delta t$$
$$k = 1, 2, ..., m$$
$$x_{2k}^{(r+1)} = x_{2k}^{(r)} + \dot{x}_{2k}^{(r)}\,\Delta t$$
8. Compute the first estimates of $E_k^{(r+1)}$
$$E_k^{(r+1)} = E_k^0\,(\cos x_{1k}^{(r+1)} + j\sin x_{1k}^{(r+1)})$$
9. Compute $P_{Gk}^{(r+1)}$ (appropriate Y_{BUS} and Eq. (12.72)).
10. Compute $[(\dot{x}_{1k}^{(r+1)}, \dot{x}_{2k}^{(r+1)}), k = 1, 2, ..., m]$ from Eq. (12.74).
11. Compute the average values of state derivatives
$$\dot{x}_{1k,\,\text{avg}}^{(r)} = \frac{1}{2}\,[\dot{x}_{1k}^{(r)} + \dot{x}_{1k}^{(r+1)}]$$
$$k = 1, 2, ..., m$$
$$\dot{x}_{2k,\,\text{avg}}^{(r)} = \frac{1}{2}\left[\dot{x}_{2k}^{(r)} + \dot{x}_{2k}^{(r+1)}\right]$$
12. Compute the final state estimates for $t = t^{(r+1)}$.
$$x_{1k}^{(r+1)} = x_{1k}^{(r)} + \dot{x}_{1k,\,\text{avg}}^{(r)}\,\Delta t$$
$$k = 1, 2, \ldots, m$$

$$x_{2k}^{(r+1)} = x_{2k}^{(r)} + \dot{x}_{2k,\,\text{avg}}^{(r)} \Delta t$$

13. Compute the final estimate for E_k at $t = t^{(r+1)}$ using

$$E_k^{(r+1)} = |E_k^0| (\cos x_{1k}^{(r+1)} + j \sin x_{1k}^{(r+1)})$$

14. Print $(x_{1k}^{(r+1)}, x_{2k}^{(r+1)})$; $k = 1, 2, ..., m$
15. Test for time limit (time for which swing curve is to be plotted), i.e., check if $r > r_{\text{final}}$. If not, $r = r + 1$ and repeat from step 5 above. Otherwise print results and stop.

The swing curves of all the machines are plotted. If the rotor angle of a machine (or a group of machines) with respect to other machines increases without bound, such a machine (or group of machines) is unstable and eventually falls out of step.

The computational algorithm given above can be easily modified to include simulation of voltage regulator, field excitation response, saturation of flux paths and governor action.

12.10.8 Stability Study of Large Systems

To limit the computer memory and the time requirements and for the sake of computational efficiency, a large multimachine system is divided into a study subsystem and an external subsystem. The study subsystem is modelled in detail whereas approximate modelling is carried out for the external subsystem. The total study is rendered by the modern technique of dynamic equivalencing. In the external subsystem, the number of machines is drastically reduced using various methods—coherency based methods being most popular and widely used by various power utilities in the world.

12.11 ▶ SOME FACTORS AFFECTING TRANSIENT STABILITY

We have seen in this chapter that the two-machine system can be equivalently reduced to a single machine connected to infinite bus bar. The qualitative conclusions regarding system stability drawn from a two-machine or an equivalent one-machine infinite bus system can be easily extended to a multimachine system. In the last article we have studied the algorithm for determining the stability of a multimachine system.

It has been seen that transient stability is greatly affected by the type and location of a fault, so that a power system analyst must at the very outset of a stability study decide on these two factors. In our examples we have selected a 3-phase fault which is generally more severe from the point of view of power transfer. Given the type of fault and its location, let us now consider other factors which affect transient stability and therefrom draw the conclusions, regarding methods of improving the transient stability limit of a system and making it as close to the steady state limit as possible.

For the case of one machine connected to infinite bus, it is easily seen from Eq. (12.71) that an increase in the inertia constant M of the machine reduces the angle through which it swings in a given time interval offering thereby a method of improving stability but this cannot be employed in practice because of economic reasons and for the reason of slowing down the response of the speed governor loop (which can even become oscillatory) apart from an excessive rotor weight.

With reference to Fig. 12.31, it is easily seen that for a given clearing angle, the accelerating area decreases but the decelerating area increases as the maximum power limit of the various power angle curves is raised, thereby adding to the transient stability limit of the system. The maximum steady power of a system can be increased by raising the voltage profile of the system and by reducing the transfer reactance. These conclusions, along with the various transient stability cases studied, suggest the following method of improving the transient stability limit of a power system.

1. Increase of system voltages, use of AVR.
2. Use of high speed excitation systems.
3. Reduction in system transfer reactance.
4. Use of high speed reclosing breakers (see Fig. 12.33). Modern tendency is to employ single-pole operation of reclosing circuit breakers.

When a fault takes place on a system, the voltages at all buses are reduced. At generator terminals, these are sensed by the automatic voltage regulators which help restore generator terminal voltages by acting within the excitation system. Modern exciter systems having solid state controls quickly respond to bus voltage reduction and can achieve from one-half to one and one-half cycles ($\frac{1}{2}$ to $1\frac{1}{2}$) gain in critical clearing times for three-phase faults on the HT bus of the generator transformer.

Reducing transfer reactance is another important practical method of increasing stability limit. Incidentally this also raises system voltage profile. The reactance of a transmission line can be decreased (i) by reducing the conductor spacing, and (ii) by increasing conductor diameter [see Eq. (2.37)]. Usually, however, the conductor spacing is controlled by other features such as lightning protection and minimum clearance to prevent the arc from one phase moving to another phase. The conductor diameter can be increased by using material of low conductivity or by hollow cores. However, normally, the conductor configuration is fixed by economic considerations quite apart from stability. The use of bundled conductors is, of course, an effective means of reducing series reactance.

Compensation for line reactance by series capacitors is an effective and economical method of increasing stability limit specially for transmission distances of more than 350 km. The degree of series compensation, however, accentuates the problems of protective relaying, normal voltage profiles, and overvoltages during line-to-ground faults. Series compensation becomes more effective and economical if part of it is switched on so as to increase the degree of compensation upon the occurrence of a disturbance likely to cause instability. Switched series capacitors simultaneously decrease fluctuation of load voltages and raise the transient stability limit to a value almost equal to the steady state limit. Switching shunt capacitors on or switching shunt reactors off also raises stability limits (see Example 12.2) but the MVA rating of shunt capacitors required is three to six times the rating of switched series capacitors for the same increase in stability limit. Thus, series capacitors are preferred unless shunt elements are required for other purposes, say, control of voltage profile.

Increasing the number of parallel lines between transmission points is quite often used to reduce transfer reactance. It adds at the same time to reliability of the transmission system. Additional line circuits are not likely to prove economical until after all feasible improvements have been carried out in the first two circuits.

As the majority of faults are transient in nature, rapid switching and isolation of unhealthy lines followed by reclosing have been shown earlier to be a great help in improving the stability margins. The modern circuit breaker technology has now made it possible for line clearing to be done as fast as in two cycles. Further, a great majority of transient faults are line-to-ground in nature. It is natural that methods have been developed for selective single-pole opening and reclosing which further aid the stability limits. With reference to Fig. 12.18, if a transient LG fault is assumed to occur on the generator bus, it is immediately seen that during the fault there will now be a definite amount of power transfer, as different from zero power transfer for the case of a three-phase fault. Also when the circuit breaker pole corresponding to the faulty line is opened, the other two lines (healthy ones) remain intact so that considerable power transfer continues to take place via these lines in comparison to the case of three-pole switching when the power transfer on fault clearing will be reduced to zero. It is, therefore, easy to see why the single-pole switching and reclosing aid in stability problem and is widely adopted. These facts are illustrated by means of Example 12.13. Even when the stability margins are sufficient, single-pole switching is adopted to prevent large swings and consequent voltage dips. Single-pole switching and reclosing is, of course, expensive in terms of relaying and introduces the associated problems of overvoltages caused by single-pole opening owing to line capacitances. Methods are available to nullify these capacitive coupling effects.

12.11.1 Recent Trends

Recent trends in design of large alternators tend towards lower short circuit ratio (SCR = $1/X_d$), which is achieved by reducing machine air gap with consequent savings in machine mmf, size, weight and cost. Reduction in the size of rotor reduces inertia constant, lowering thereby the stability margin. The loss in stability margin is made up by such features as lower reactance lines, faster circuit breakers and faster excitation systems as discussed already, and a faster system valving to be discussed later in this article.

A stage has now been reached in technology whereby the methods of improving stability, discussed above, have been pushed to their limits, e.g., clearing times of circuit breakers have been brought down to virtually irreducible values of the order of two cycles. With the trend to reduce machine inertias there is a constant need to determine availability, feasibility and applicability of new methods for maintaining and/or improving system stability. A brief account of some of the recent methods of maintaining stability is given below:

HVDC Links Increased use of HVDC links employing thyristors would alleviate stability problems. A DC link is asynchronous, i.e., the two AC system at either end do not have to be controlled in phase or even be at exactly the same frequency as they do for an AC link, and the power transmitted can be readily controlled. There is no risk of a fault in one system causing loss of stability in the other system.

Breaking Resistors For improving stability where clearing is delayed or a large load is suddenly lost, a resistive load called a breaking resistor is connected at or near the generator bus. This load compensates for at least some of the reduction of load on the generators and so reduces the acceleration. During a fault, the resistors are applied to the terminals of the generators through circuit breakers by means of an elaborate control scheme. The control scheme determines the amount of resistance to be applied and its duration. The breaking resistors remain on for a matter of cycles both during fault clearing and after system voltage is restored.

Short Circuit Current Limiters These are generally used to limit the short circuit duty of distribution lines. These may also be used in long transmission lines to modify favourably the transfer impedance during fault conditions so that the voltage profile of the system is somewhat improved, thereby raising the system load level during the fault.

Turbine Fast Valving or Bypass Valving The two methods just discussed above are an attempt at replacing the system load so as to increase the electrical output of the generator during fault conditions. Another recent method of improving the stability of a unit is to decrease the mechanical input power to the turbine. This can be accomplished by means of fast valving, where the difference between mechanical input and reduced electrical output of a generator under a fault, as sensed by a control scheme, initiates the closing of a turbine valve to reduce the power input. Briefly, during a fast valving operation, the interceptor valves are rapidly shut (in 0.1 to 0.2 s) and immediately reopened. This procedure increases the critical switching time long enough so that in most cases, the unit will remain stable for faults with stuck-breaker clearing times. The scheme has been put to use in some stations in the USA.

Full Load Rejection Technique Fast valving combined with high-speed clearing time will suffice to maintain stability in most of the cases. However, there are still situations where stability is difficult to maintain. In such cases, the normal procedure is to automatically trip the unit off the line. This, however, causes several hours of delay before the unit can be put back into operation. The loss of a major unit for this length of time can seriously jeopardise the remaining system.

To remedy these situations, a full load rejection scheme could be utilised after the unit is separated from the system. To do this, the unit has to be equipped with a large steam bypass system. After the system has recovered from the shock caused by the fault, the unit could be resynchronised and reloaded. The main disadvantage of this method is the extra cost of a large bypass system.

Example 12.13 The system shown in Fig. 12.47 is loaded to 1 pu. Calculate the swing curve and ascertain system stability for

(i) LG fault three-pole switching followed by reclosure, line found healthy.
(ii) LG fault single-pole switching followed by reclosure, line found healthy.

Switching occurs at 3.75 cycles (0.075 s) and reclosure occurs at 16.25 cycles (0.325 s). All values shown in the figure are in pu.

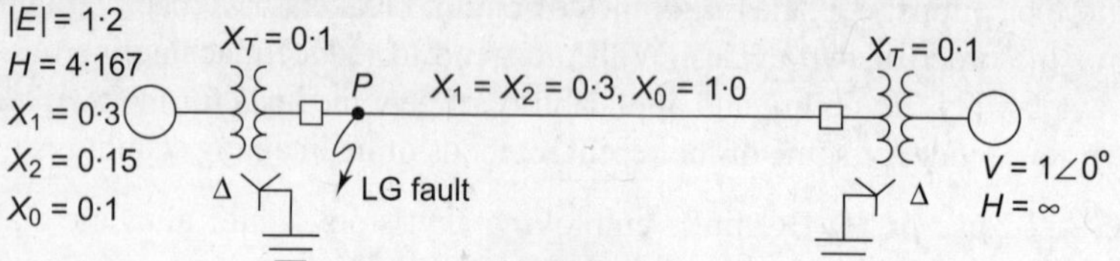

Fig. 12.47

Solution The sequence networks of the system are drawn and suitably reduced in Figs 12.48(a), (b) and (c).

For an LG fault at P the sequence networks will be connected in series as shown in Fig. 12.49. A star-delta transformation reduces Fig. 12.49 to that of Fig. 12.50 from which we have the transfer reactance

$$X_{12}(\text{LG fault}) = 0.4 + 0.4 + \frac{0.4 \times 0.4}{0.246} = 1.45$$

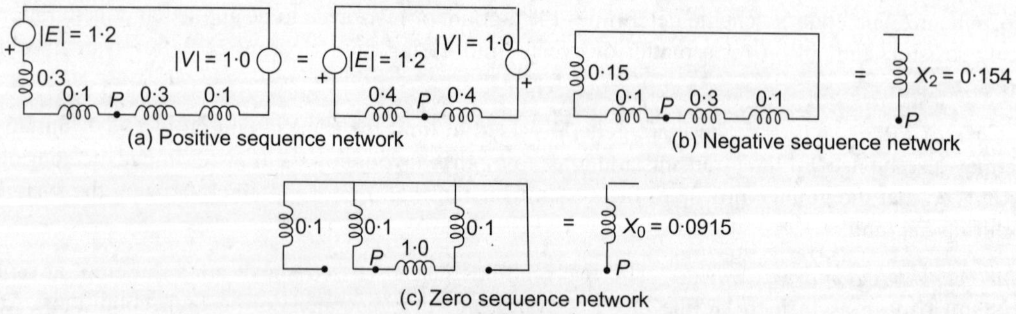

(a) Positive sequence network

(b) Negative sequence network

(c) Zero sequence network

Fig. 12.48

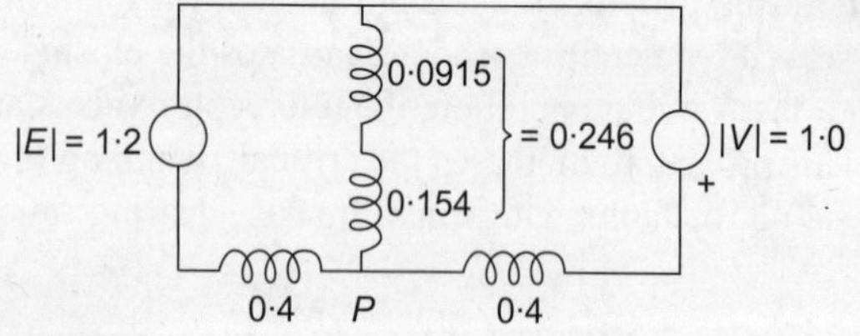

Fig. 12.49 *Connection of sequence networks for an LG fault*

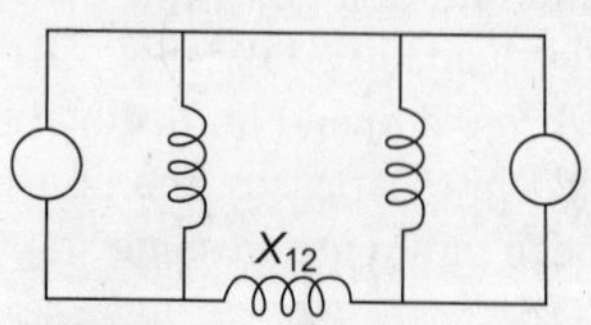

Fig. 12.50 *Transfer impedance for an LG fault*

When the circuit breaker poles corresponding to the faulted line are opened (it corresponds to a single-line open fault) the connection of sequence networks is shown in Fig. 12.51. From the reduced network of Fig. 12.52, the transfer reactance with faulted line switched off is

$$X_{12} \text{ (faulted line open)} = 0.4 + 0.42 + 0.4 = 1.22$$

Under healthy conditions transfer reactance is easily obtained from the positive sequence network of Fig. 12.48(a) as

$$X_{12}\text{(line healthy)} = 0.8$$

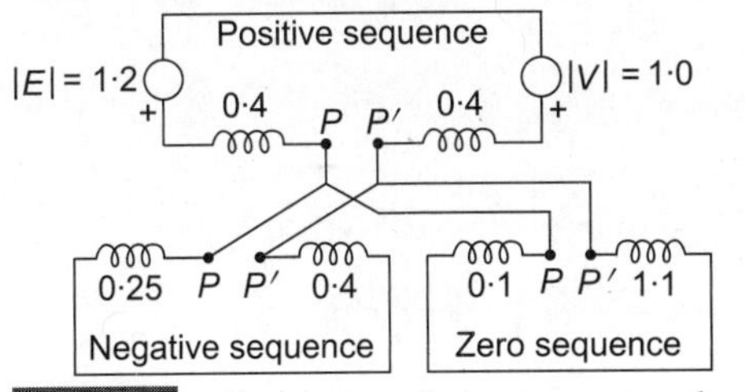

Fig. 12.51 *Connection of sequence networks with faulted line switched off*

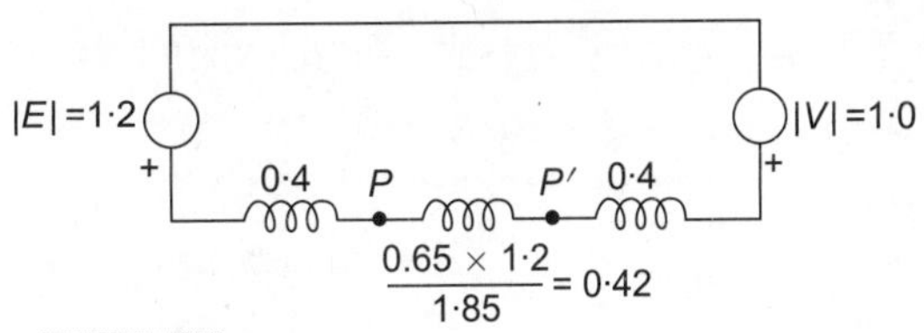

Fig. 12.52 *Reduced network of Fig. 12.51 giving transfer reactance*

Power angle equations

Prefault

$$P_{eI} = \frac{|E||V|}{X_{12}} \sin \delta = \frac{1.2 \times 1}{0.8} \sin \delta = 1.5 \sin \delta$$

$$\text{Initial load} = 1.0 \text{ pu}$$

Initial torque angle is given by

$$1 = 1.5 \sin \delta_0$$

or

$$\delta_0 = 41.8°$$

During fault

$$P_{eII} = \frac{1.2 \times 1}{1.45} \sin \delta = 0.827 \sin \delta$$

During single-pole switching

$$P_{eIII} = \frac{1.2 \times 1}{1.22} \sin \delta = 0.985 \sin \delta$$

During three-pole switching

$$P_{eIII} = 0$$

Postfault

$$P_{eIV} = P_{eI} = 1.5 \sin \delta$$

Now,

$$\Delta\delta_n = \Delta\delta_{n-1} + \frac{(\Delta t)^2}{M} P_{a(n-1)}$$

$$H = 4.167 \text{ MJ/MVA}$$

$$M = \frac{4.167}{180 \times 50} = 4.63 \times 10^{-4} \text{ s}^2\text{/electrical degree}$$

Taking $\Delta t = 0.05$ s

$$\frac{(\Delta t)^2}{M} = \frac{(0.05)^2}{4.63 \times 10^{-4}} = 5.4$$

Time when single-three-pole switching occurs = 0.075 s (during middle of Δt)
Time when reclosing occurs = 0.325 (during middle of Δt)

Table 12.15 Swing curve calculation – three-pole switching

t s	P_{max} (pu)	sin δ	P_e (pu)	P_a (pu)	5.4 P_a elec deg	Δδ elec deg	δ elec deg
0_-	1.5	0.667	1.0	0.0			41.8
0_+	0.827	0.667	0.552	0.448			41.8
0_{avg}				0.224	1.2	1.2	41.8
0.05	0.827	0.682	0.564	0.436	2.4	3.6	43.0
0.075→							
0.10	0.0	0.726	0.0	1.0	5.4	9.0	46.6
0.15	0.0		0.0	1.0	5.4	14.4	55.6
0.20	0.0		0.0	1.0	5.4	19.8	70.0
0.25	0.0		0.0	1.0	5.4	25.2	89.8
0.30	0.0		0.0	1.0	5.4	30.6	115.0
0.325→							
0.35	1.5	0.565	0.85	0.15	0.8	31.4	145.6
0.40	1.5	0.052	0.078	0.922	5.0	36.4	177.0
0.45	1.5	– 0.55	– 0.827	1.827	9.9	46.3	213.4
0.50	1.5	– 0.984	– 1.48	2.48	13.4	59.7	259.7
0.55	1.5	– 0.651	– 0.98	1.98	10.7	70.4	319.4
0.60	1.5	0.497	0.746	0.254	1.4	71.8	389.8
0.65							461.6

The swing curve is plotted in Fig. 12.53 from which it is obvious that the system is unstable.

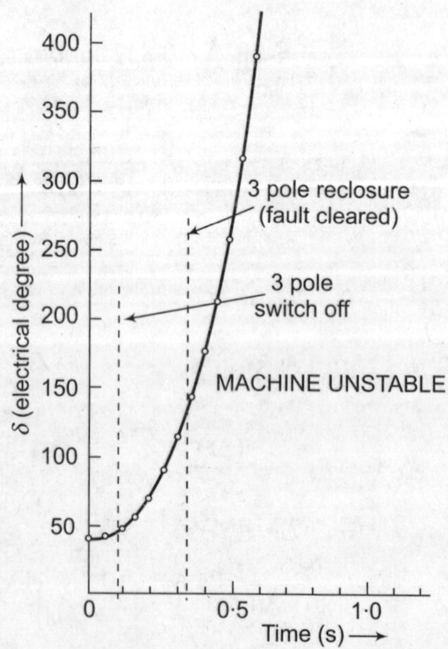

Fig. 12.53 *Swing curve for three-pole switching with reclosure*

Table 12.16 Swing curve calculation – single-pole switching

	t *s*	P_{max} *(pu)*	*sin δ*	P_e *(pu)*	P_a *(pu)*	*5.4* P_a *elec deg*	*Δδ elec deg*	*δ elec deg*
	0_-	1.5	0.667	1.0	0.0			41.80
	0_+	0.827	0.667.	0.552	0.448			41.8
	0_{avg}				0.224	1.2	1.2	41.8
	0.05	0.827	0.682	0.564	0.436	2.4	3.6	43.0
0.075→								
	0.10	0.985	0.726	0.715	0.285	1.5	5.1	46.6
	0.15	0.985	0.784	0.77	0.230	1.2	6.3	51.7
	0.20	0.985	0.848	0.834	0.166	0.9	7.2	58.0
	0.25	0.985	0.908	0.893	0.107	0.6	7.8	65.2
	0.30	0.985	0.956	0.940	0.060	0.3	8.1	73.0
0.325→								
	0.35	1.5	0.988	1.485	– 0.485	– 2.6	5.5	81.1
	0.40	1.5	0.988	1.5	– 0.5	– 2.7	2.8	86.6
	0.45	1.5	1.0	1.5	– 0.5	– 2.7	0.1	89.4
	0.50	1.5	1.0	1.5	– 0.5	– 2.7	– 2.6	89.5
	0.55	1.5	0.9985	1.5	– 0.5	– 2.7	– 5.3	86.9
	0.60	1.5	0.989	1.485	– 0.485	– 2.6	– 7.9	81.6
	0.65	1.5	0.96	1.44	– 0.44	– 2.4	– 10.3	73.7
	0.70	1.5	0.894	1.34	– 0.34	– 1.8	– 12.1	63.4
	0.75	1.5	0.781	1.17	– 0.17	– 0.9	– 13.0	51.3
	0.80	1.5	0.62	0.932	0.068	0.4	– 12.6	38.3
	0.85	1.5	0.433	0.65	0.35	1.9	– 10.7	25.7
	0.90	1.5	0.259	0.39	0.61	3.3	– 7.4	15.0
	0.95	1.5	0.133	0.2	0.8	4.3	– 3.1	7.6
	1.00	1.5	0.079	0.119	0.881	4.8	1.7	4.5
	1.05	1.5	0.107	0.161	0.839	4.5	6.2	6.2
	1.10	1.5	0.214	0.322	0.678	3.7	9.9	12.4
	1.15	1.5	0.38	0.57	0.43	2.3	12.2	22.3
	1.20	1.5	0.566	0.84	0.16	0.9	13.1	34.5
	1.25	1.5	0.738	1.11	– 0.11	– 0.6	12.5	47.6
	1.30	1.5	0.867	1.3	– 0.3	– 1.6	10.9	60.1
	1.35	1.5	0.946	1.42	– 0.42	– 2.3	8.6	71.0
	1.40	1.5	0.983	1.48	– 0.48	– 2.6	6.0	79.6
	1.45	1.5	0.997	1.5	– 0.5	– 2.7	3.3	85.6
	1.50	1.5						88.9

The swing curve is plotted in Fig. 12.54 from which it follows that the system is stable.

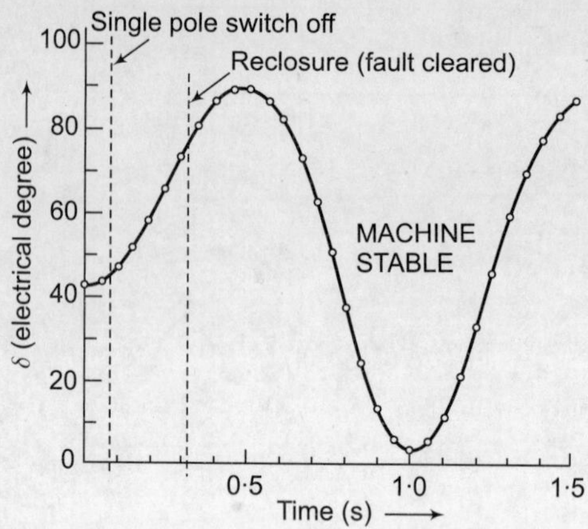

Fig. 12.54 *Swing curve for single-pole switching with reclosure*

12.12 ▶ SUMMARY

This chapter deals with various types of power system stability, gives it dynamics, discusses equal area criterion, swing equation and its numerical solution is presented. Multimachine stability is also considered. Finally, various factors affecting transient stability are highlighted.

Problems

12.1 A two-pole, 50 Hz, 11 kV turboalternator has a rating of 100 MW, power factor 0.85 lagging. The rotor has a moment of inertia of a 10,000 kg-m^2. Calculate H and M.

12.2 Two turboalternators with ratings given below are interconnected via a short transmission line.
Machine 1: 4 pole, 50 Hz, 60 MW, power factor 0.80 lagging, moment of inertia 30,000 kg-m^2
Machine 2: 2 pole, 50 Hz, 80 MW, power factor 0.85 lagging, moment of inertia 10,000 kg-m^2
Calculate the inertia constant of the single equivalent machine on a base of 200 MVA.

12.3 Power station 1 has four identical generator sets each rated 80 MVA and each having an inertia constant 7 MJ/MVA; while power station 2 has three sets each rated 200 MVA, 3 MJ/MVA. The stations are located close together to be regarded as a single equivalent machine for stability studies. Calculate the inertia constant of the equivalent machine on 100 MVA base.

12.4 A 50 Hz transmission line 500 km long with constants given below ties up two large power areas:

$R = 0.11\ \Omega$/km $\qquad L = 1.45$ mH/km

$C = 0.009\ \mu$F/km $\qquad G = 0$

Find the steady state stability limit if $|V_S| = |V_R| = 200$ kV (constant). What will the steady state stability limit be if line capacitance is neglected? What will the steady state stability limit be if line resistance is also neglected? Comment on the results.

12.5 A power deficient area receives 50 MW over a tie line from another area. The maximum steady state capacity of the tie line is 100 MW. Find the allowable sudden load that can be switched on without loss of stability.

12.6 A synchronous motor is drawing 30% of the maximum steady state power from an infinite bus bar. If the load on motor is suddenly increased by 100 per cent, would the synchronism be lost? If not, what is the maximum excursion of torque angle about the new steady state rotor position.

12.7 The transfer reactances between a generator and an infinite bus bar operating at 200 kV under various conditions on the interconnector are

Prefault	150 Ω per phase
During fault	400 Ω per phase
Postfault	200 Ω per phase

If the fault is cleared when the rotor has advanced 60 degrees electrical from its prefault position, determine the maximum load that could be transferred without loss of stability.

12.8 A synchronous generator is feeding 250 MW to a large 50 Hz network over a double circuit transmission line. The maximum steady state power that can be transmitted over the line with both circuits in operation is 500 MW and is 350 MW with anyone of the circuits.

A solid three-phase fault occurring at the network-end of one of the lines causes it to trip. Estimate the critical clearing angle in which the circuit breakers must trip so that synchronism is not lost.

What further information is needed to estimate the critical clearing time?

12.9 A synchronous generator represented by a voltage source of 1.05 pu in series with a transient reactance of $j0.15$ pu and an inertia constant $H = 4.0$ s is connected to an infinite inertia system through a transmission line. The line has a series reactance of $j0.30$ pu, while the infinite inertia system is represented by a voltage source of 1.0 pu in series with a transient reactance of $j0.20$ pu.

The generator is transmitting an active power of 1.0 pu when a three-phase fault occurs at its terminals. If the fault is cleared in 100 millisec, determine if the system will remain stable by calculating the swing curve.

12.10 For Problem 12.9 find the critical clearing time from the swing curve for a sustained fault.

12.11 A synchronous generator represented by a voltage of 1.15 pu in series with a transient reactance is connected to a large power system with voltage 1.0 pu through a power network. The equivalent transient transfer reactance X between voltage sources is $j0.50$ pu.

After the occurrence of a three-phase to ground fault on one of the lines of the power network, two of the line circuit breakers A and B operate sequentially as follows with corresponding transient transfer reactance given therein.

(i) Short circuit occurs at $\delta = 30°$, A opens instantaneously to make $X = 3.0$ pu.

(ii) At $\delta = 60°$, A recloses, $X = 6.0$ pu.

(iii) At $\delta = 75°$, A reopens.

(iv) At $\delta = 90°$, B also opens to clear the fault making $X = 0.60$ pu

Check if the system will operate stably.

12.12 A 50 Hz synchronous generator with inertia constant $H = 2.5$ s and a transient reactance of 0.20 pu feeds 0.80 pu active power into an infinite bus (voltage 1 pu) at 0.8 lagging power factor via a network with an equivalent reactance of 0.25 pu.

A three-phase fault is sustained for 150 millisec across generator terminals. Determine through swing curve calculation the torque angle δ, 250 millisec, after fault initiation.

12.13 A 50 Hz, 500 MVA, 400 kV generator (with transformer) is connected to a 400 kV infinite bus bar through an interconnector. The generator has $H = 2.5$ MJ/MVA, voltage behind transient reactance of 450 kV and is loaded 460 MW. The transfer reactances between generator and bus bar under various conditions are

Prefault	0.5 pu
During fault	1.0 pu
Postfault	0.75 pu

Calculate the swing curve using intervals of 0.05 s and assuming that the fault is cleared at 0.15 s.

12.14 Plot swing curves and check system stability for the fault shown on the system of Example 12.10 for fault clearing by simultaneous opening of breakers at the ends of the faulted line at three cycles and eight cycles after the fault occurs. Also plot the swing curve over a period of 0.6 s if the fault is sustained. For the generator assume $H = 3.5$ pu, $G = 1$ pu and carry out the computations in per unit.

12.15 Solve Example 12.10 for a LLG fault.

Multiple Choice Questions

12.1 The study of steady state stability is concerned with the upper limit of machine loadings before losing synchronism when the load is gradually increased
(a) True (b) False

12.2 When there is a sudden disturbance in the power system, rotor speed, rotor angular difference and power transfer undergo fast changes whose magnitude depends upon the severity of disturbance, it comes under the study of
(a) Dynamic stability (b) Transient stability
(c) Steady state stability (d) None of the above

12.3 When $\left(\frac{\partial P}{\partial \delta}\right)$ synchronising co-efficient is positive, the torque angle increases on small power increment and the synchronism is soon lost
(a) True (b) False

12.4 For transient stability analysis, as long as equal area criterion is satisfied, the maximum angle to which rotor angle can oscillate is
(a) 90° (b) 45° (c) Greater than 90° (d) Less than 90°

12.5 For a turbo alternator of 100 MVA, the inertia constant is 5. The value of H for a alternator of 50 MVA is
(a) 8 (b) 12 (c) 10 (d) 15

12.6 By using the method of equal area criterion, we get the information about
(a) Swing curves (b) Stability region (c) Relative stability (d) Absolute stability

12.7 For a power system we can improve the steady state stability limit by
(a) Single-pole switching (b) Reducing fault clearing time
(c) Using double circuit line instead of single circuit line (d) Decreasing the generator inertia

12.8 For a fault in a power system, the term critical clearing time is related to

(a) Reactive power limit (b) Transient stability limit
(c) Short circuit current limit (d) Steady state stability limit

12.9 A shunt reactor is added at the infinite bus, which is fed by the synchronous generator. The stability limit will

(a) Decrease (b) Increase
(c) Remains the same (d) Any of the above

12.10 For stable operation, the normal value of δ normally lies between

(a) 0 to 30° (b) 0 to 90° (c) 0 to 60° (d) 0 to 180°

12.11 The significance of the steady state stability of a power system is

(a) Maintaining the rated voltage
(b) Maintaining rated frequency
(c) Maintaining a synchronism between machines and tie-lines
(d) All of the mentioned

12.12 The power angle equation of a synchronous machines is

(a) An equation between electrical power generated to the angular displacement of the rotor
(b) An equation between mechanical power generated to the angular displacement of the rotor
(c) An equation between electrical power generated to the angular displacement of stator windings
(d) An equation between mechanical power generated to the angular displacement of stator windings

12.13 The steady state stability of the power system can be improved by

(a) Using machines of high impedance
(b) Connecting transmission line in series
(c) Connecting transmission in parallel
(d) Reducing the excitation of the machines

12.14 The transient stability limit of power system is

(a) The maximum flow of power through a particular point in the power system without loss of stability when small disturbances occur.
(b) The maximum power flow possible through a particular component connected in the power system.
(c) The maximum flow of power through a particular point in the power system without loss of stability when large and sudden disturbances occur
(d) All of these

12.15 The steady state stability limit of power system is

(a) The maximum flow of power through a particular point in the power system without loss of stability when small disturbances occur.
(b) The maximum power flow possible through a particular component connected in the power system.
(c) The maximum flow of power through a particular point in the power system without loss of stability when sudden disturbances occur
(d) All of these

12.16 The measure to improve the transient stability of the power system during the unbalanced or unsymmetrical fault can be taken as

(a) Single-pole switching of CB
(b) Excitation control
(c) Phase-shifting transformer
(d) Increasing turbine valve opening

12.17 The frequency stability of a power system is

(a) To maintain steady frequency following severe disturbance resulting in the imbalance between transformer and load
(b) To maintain steady frequency following severe disturbances resulting in the imbalance between generators and load
(c) To maintain a steady frequency in all the protection components and the transmission lines.
(d) Both (a) and (b)

12.18 Which among the following is a classification of power system stability?

(a) Frequency stability (b) Voltage stability
(c) Rotor angle stability (d) All of these

12.19 The steady state stability of the synchronous generator can be improved for a better performance of the power system

(a) Increasing the excitation (b) Increasing reactance
(c) Decreasing moment of inertia (d) Increasing moment of inertia

12.20 The value of transient stability limit in power system is

(a) Higher than steady state stability limit
(b) Lower than steady state stability limit
(c) Depending upon the severity of load
(d) All of these

12.21 The swing curve provides which of the following information?

(a) Stability of the system (b) Performance of the machine
(c) The rotor performance (d) Reliability of the system

12.22 The critical clearing time of a fault in power system is related to

(a) Reactive power limit (b) Short circuit limit
(c) Steady-state stability limit (d) Transient stability limit

12.23 What kind of differential equation is swing equation?

(a) Linear second order (b) Nonlinear first order
(c) Linear first order (d) Nonlinear second order

12.24 The transient stability limit of a power system can be improved by using which of the following component?

(a) Series resistance (b) Series capacitor
(c) Series inductor (d) Shunt resistance

12.25 The stability of a power system cannot be affected by which of the following parameters?

(a) Generator reactance (b) Line losses
(c) Excitation of generators (d) Line reactance

References

Books

1. W.D. Stevenson, *Elements of Power System Analysis*, 4th edn, McGraw-Hill, New York, 1982.
2. O.I. Elgerd, *Electric Energy Systems Theory: An Introduction*, 2nd edn, McGraw-Hill, New York, 1982.
3. P.M. Anderson and A.A. Fouad, *Power System Control and Stability*, The Iowa State University Press, Ames, Iowa, 1977.
4. G.W. Stagg and A.H. O-Abiad, *Computer Methods in Power System Analysis*, Chaps 9 and 10, McGraw-Hill, New York, 1968.
5. S.B. Crary, *Power System Stability*, volume: I (Steady State Stability), volume: II (Transient Stability), Wiley, New York, 1945–1947.
6. E.W. Kimbark, *Power System Stability*, volumes: 1, 2 and 3, Wiley, New York, 1948.
7. V.A. Venikov, *Transient Phenomena in Electrical Power System* (translated from the Russian), Mir Publishers, Moscow, 1971.
8. R.T. Byerly and E.W. Kimbark (Eds), *Stability of Large Electric Power Systems*, IEEE Press, New York, 1974.
9. J.R. Neuenswander, *Modern Power Systems*, International Text Book Co., New York, 1971.
10. M.A. Pai, *Power System Stability Analysis by the Direct Method of Lyapunov*, North-Holland, System and Control Services, volume: 3, 1981.
11. A.A. Fouad and V. Vittal, *Power System Transient Stability Analysis using the Transient Energy Function Method*, Prentice-Hall, Englewood Cliffs, New Jersey, 1992.
12. P. Kundur, *Power System Stability and Control*, McGraw-Hill, New York, 1994.
13. A. Chakrabarti, D.P. Kothari, A.K. Mukhopadhyay, and A. De, *An Int. to Reactive Power Control and Voltage Stability in Power Transmision Systems*, PHI, New Delhi, 2010.
14. K.R. Padiyar, *Power System Dynamics: Stability and Control*, 2nd edn, B S Publications, Hyderabad, 2002.
15. P.W. Sauer and M.A. Pai, *Power System Dynamics and Stability*, Prentice Hall, New Jersey, 1998.

Papers

16. E.W. Cushing, *et al.*, "Fast Valving as an Aid to Power System Transient Stability and Prompt Resynchronization and Rapid Reload after Full Load Rejection", *IEEE Trans.*, PAS, volume: 91, p: 1624, 1972.
17. E.W. Kimbark, "Improvement of Power System Stability", *IEEE Trans.*, PAS, volume: 88, p: 773, 1969.
18. N.D. Rao, "Routh-Hurwitz Condition and Lyapunov Methods for the Transient Stability Problem", *Proc. IEE*, volume: 116, p: 533, 1969.
19. M.L. Shelton, *et al.*, "BPA 1400 MW Braking Resistor", *IEEE Trans.*, volume: 94, p: 602, 1975.
20. J. Nanda, D.P. Kothari, P.R. Bijwe, and D.L. Shenoy, "A New Approach for Dynamic Equivalents Using Distribution Factors Based on a Moment Concept", *Proc. IEEE Int. Conf. on Computers, Systems and Signal Processing*, Bangalore, Dec. 10–12, 1984.

21. T.S. Dillon, "Dynamic Modelling and Control of Large Scale Systems", *Int. Journal of Electric Power and Energy Systems*, volume: 4, p: 29, Jan. 1982.
22. M.A. Pai, *Energy Function Analysis for Power System Stability*, 0-7923-9035-0.
23. R. Patel, T.S. Bhatti, and D.P. Kothari, "Improvement of Power System Transient Stability using Fast Valving: A Review", *Electric Power Components and Systems*, volume: 29, pp: 927–938, Oct. 2001.
24. R. Patel, T.S. Bhatti, and D.P. Kothari, "MATLAB/Simulink Based Transient Stability Analysis of a Multimachine Power System", *IJEEE*, volume: 39, issue: 4, pp: 339–355, Oct. 2002.
25. R. Patel, T.S. Bhatti, and D.P. Kothari, "A Novel Scheme of Fast Valving Control", *IEEE Power Engineering Review*, pp: 44–46, Oct. 2002.
26. J. Ma, S. Wang, Y. Qiu, Y. Li, Z. Wang, and J.S. Thorp, "Angle Stability Analysis of Power System With Multiple Operating Conditions Considering Cascading Failure", *IEEE Transactions on Power Systems*, volume: 32, issue: 2, pp: 873–882, 2017.
27. S. Bhat, M. Glavic, M. Pavella, T.S. Bhatti, and D.P. Kothari, "A Transient Stability Tool Combining the SIME Method with MATLAB and SIMULINK", *IJEEE*, volume: 43, issue: 2, pp: 119–133, April 2006.
28. L.D. Arya, V.S. Pande, and D.P. Kothari, "A Technique for Load Shedding based on Voltage Stability Considerations", *JEPES*, volume: 27, pp: 506–517, 2005.
29. F. Milano, "On Current and Power Injection Models for Angle and Voltage Stability Analysis of Power Systems", *IEEE Transactions on Power Systems,* volume: 31, issue: 3, pp: 2503–2504, 2016.
30. E. Gholipour and S. Saadate, "Improving of Transient Stability of Power Systems Using UPFC", *IEEE Transactions on Power Delivery*, volume: 20, issue: 2, pp: 1677–1682, 2005.
31. L. Aolaritei, D. Lee, T. L. Vu, and K. Turitsyn, "A Robustness Measure of Transient Stability under Operational Constraints in Power Systems", *IEEE Control Systems Letters*, volume: 2, issue: 4, pp: 803–808, 2018.
32. H. Bosetti and S. Khan, "Transient Stability in Oscillating Multi-Machine Systems Using Lyapunov Vectors", *IEEE Transactions on Power Systems*, volume: 33, issue: 2, pp: 2078–2086, 2018.
33. P. Rastgoufard, A. Yazdankhah, and R. A. Schlueter, "Multi-Machine Equal Area Based Power System Transient Stability Measure", *IEEE Transactions on Power Systems*, volume: 3, issue: 1, pp: 188–196, 1988.
34. Z. Wang and J. Wang, "A Practical Distributed Finite-Time Control Scheme for Power System Transient Stability", *IEEE Transactions on Power Systems*, volume: 35, issue: 5, pp: 3320–3331, 2020.
35. L.S. Titare, P. Singh, and L.D. Arya, "Genetic Algorithm Used for Load Shedding Based On Sensitivity to Enhance Voltage Stability", *Journal of The Institution of Engineers (India)*: Series B, volume: 95, issue: 4, pp: 337–343, 2014.
36. L.S. Titare, P. Singh, L.D. Arya, and S.C. Choube, "Optimal Reactive Power Rescheduling Based on Epsde Algorithm to Enhance Static Voltage Stability", *International Journal of Electrical Power & Energy Systems*, volume: 63, pp: 588–599, 2014.
37. L.D. Arya, S.C. Choube, and R.K. Saket, "Composite System Reliability Evaluation Based on Static Voltage Stability Limit", *Journal of the Institution of Engineers (India)*: Series-B, Springer, volume: 80, pp: 133–140, 2000.

38. W. Du, W. Dong, Y. Wang, and H. Wang, "A Method to Design Power System Stabilizers in a Multi-Machine Power System Based on Single-Machine Infinite-Bus System Model", *IEEE Transactions on Power Systems*, doi: 10.1109/TPWRS.2020.3041037, 2021.
39. W. Du, Q. Fu, and H. F. Wang, "Power System Small-Signal Angular Stability Affected by Virtual Synchronous Generators", *IEEE Transactions on Power Systems*, volume: 34, issue: 4, pp: 3209–3219, 2019.
40. N. Hatziargyriou et al., "Definition and Classification of Power System Stability Revisited & Extended", *IEEE Transactions on Power Systems*, doi: 10.1109/TPWRS.2020.3041774, 2021.

CHAPTER 13 Power System Transients

13.1 ▶ INTRODUCTION

In Chapters 6–8, the types of problems studied can be classified as

1. The power system operating in steady-state, wherein the system models are nonlinear algebraic equations.
2. Small-scale dynamic perturbations around the steady-state operating point, wherein the system models are *linear* differential equations with constant parametric values.

In this chapter we will discuss the abnormal situation, wherein the power system is in dynamic state with large scale perturbation caused by a fault, or opening or closing of a switch, or other large scale disturbances. This is the study of power system transients. Fault currents upon occurrence of a short circuit have already been studied in Chapters 9 and 11.

Transient phenomenon lasts in a power system for a very short period of time, ranging from a few μs upto 1 s. Yet the study and understanding of this phenomenon are extremely important, as during these transients, the system is subjected to the greatest stress from excessive over-currents or voltages which, depending upon their severity, can cause extensive damage. In some extreme cases, there may be a complete shut-down of a plant, or even a black-out of a whole area. Because of this, it is necessary that a power system engineer should have a clear understanding of power system transients, to enable him to find out their impact on the system, to prevent them if possible, or at least control their severity or mitigate the damage caused. This chapter is devoted to the study of power system transients.

13.2 ▶ TYPES OF SYSTEM TRANSIENTS

The main causes of momentary excessive voltages and currents are

(i) Lightning, (ii) switching, (iii) short-circuits and (iv) resonance conditions.

Out of these, lightning and switching are the most common, and usually the most severe causes. Transients caused by short-circuits or resonance conditions usually arise as secondary effects, but may well lead to the plant breakdown in EHV (500–765 kV) systems. Also in EHV systems the voltage transients or surges caused by switching, i.e., opening and closing of circuit breakers, are becoming increasingly important. On cable systems, of course, lightning transients rarely occur and the other causes become more important.

Depending upon the speed of the transients, these can be classified as

1. Surge phenomena (extremely fast transients)
2. Short-circuit phenomena (medium fast transients)
3. Transient stability (slow transients)

13.2.1 Surge Phenomena

This type of transient is caused by lightning (atmospheric discharges on overhead transmission lines) and switching. Physically, such a transient initiates an electromagnetic wave (surge) travelling with almost the speed of light (3×10^8 m/s) on transmission lines. In a 150 km line, the travelling wave completes a round trip in 1 ms. Thus, the transient phenomena associated with these travelling waves occur during the first few milli-seconds after their initiation. The ever-present line losses cause pretty fast attenuation of these waves, which die out after a few reflections.

The reflection of surges at open line ends, or at transformers which present high inductance, leads to multiplicative effect on voltage build-up, which may eventually damage the insulation of high-voltage equipment with consequent short-circuit (medium fast transient). The high inductance of the transformer plays the beneficial role of insulating the generator windings from transmission line surges. The travelling charges in the surges are discharged to ground via *lightning arresters* without the initiation of a line short-circuit, thereby protecting the equipment.

Selection of insulation level of various line equipment and transformers is directly related to the over-voltages caused by surge phenomena. Hence the importance of studying this class of transients.

13.2.2 Short-circuit Phenomena

About more than 50% short-circuits take place on exposed overhead lines, owing to the insulation failure resulting from over-voltages generated by surge phenomena described earlier, birds and other mechanical reasons. Short-circuits result from symmetrical (three-phase) faults, as well as unsymmetrical (LG, LL, LLG) faults. The occurrence of a symmetrical fault brings the power transfer across the line to zero immediately, whereas the impact is only partial in case of unsymmetrical faults. Like surge phenomena, short-circuits are also fully electric in nature. Their speed is determined by the time constants of the generator windings, which vary from a few cycles of 50 Hz wave for the damper windings to around 4 s for the field winding. Therefore, these transients will be sufficiently slower than the surge phenomena. The time range of practical importance to power system analyst is from 10 to 100 ms, i.e., the first few (5–10) cycles of the short-circuit currents.

The short-circuit currents may attain such high values that, if allowed to persist, they may result in *thermal damage* to the equipment. Therefore, the faulty section should be isolated as quickly as possible. Most of the short-circuits do not cause permanent damage. As soon as the fault is cleared, short-circuit path is deionised, and the insulation is restored. Reclosing breakers are, therefore, used in practice which automatically close periodically to find out if the line has recovered. If the fault continues for some time, then, of course, the breaker has to open permanently. This whole operation of successive closing–opening cycle may last for a second or so.

13.2.3 Transient Stability

Whenever a short-circuit takes place at any part of the integrated system, there is an instantaneous total or partial collapse of the bus voltages of the system. This also results in the reduction of the generator power output. Since initially for some instants the input turbine power remains constant, as there is always some time delay before the controllers can initiate corrective actions, each generator is subjected to a positive accelerating torque. This condition, if sustained for some time, can result in the most severe type of transients, namely the mechanical oscillations of the synchronous machine rotors. These *electromechanical* transients may, under extreme conditions, lead to loss of synchronism for some or all of the machines, which implies that the power system has reached its *transient stability limit*. Once this happens, it may take several hours for an electric system engineer to resynchronise such as 'blacked-out' system. Thus, it is quite necessary to simulate this phenomenon on the computers and use the switching and load-management strategies that will avoid, or minimise, the ill effects of short-circuits.

The rotor swings are quite slow, as they are mechanical in nature. A transient stability study, thus, may confine itself for the time period of a few milliseconds to one minute in most of the cases. Power system stability has been the subject matter of Ch. 12.

In this chapter, we address ourselves to the problem of surge phenomena.

13.3 ▶ TRAVELLING WAVES AND PROPAGATION OF SURGES

The mathematical model used here assumes that the line is lossless, i.e., line resistance and shunt conductance are ignored (ωL and $\omega C \gg R$ and G). The resulting equations have analytical solution and the results obtained are safe, i.e., pessimistic. Further, this simplification leads to better understanding of the phenomena involved. For advanced study, the reader may refer to Bewley [1], Greenwood [3] and Bickford *et al.* [2].

As already modelled in Ch. 5, Fig. 13.1 shows the elemental section (length Δx) of a transmission line on per phase basis with R and G ignored.

The series voltage rise over the element in the direction of x is

$$\frac{\partial v}{\partial x}\Delta x = -(L\Delta x)\frac{\partial i}{\partial t}$$

or

$$\frac{\partial v}{\partial x} = -L\frac{\partial i}{\partial t} \qquad (13.1)$$

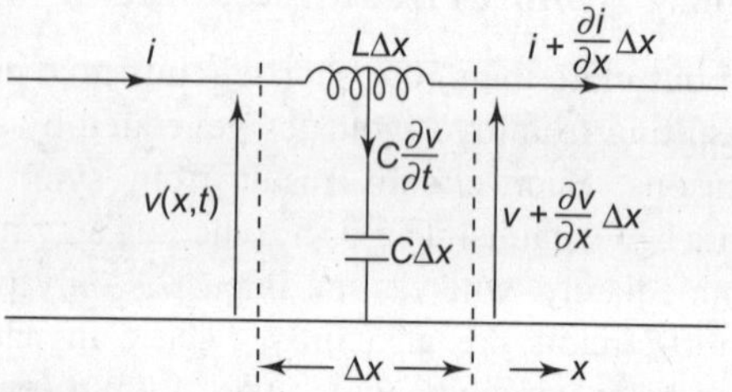

Also, the current, in passing through the element, increases by the negative of the current through shunt capacitance, i.e.,

$$\frac{\partial i}{\partial x}\Delta x = -(C\Delta x)\frac{\partial v}{\partial t}$$

or

$$\frac{\partial i}{\partial x} = -C\frac{\partial v}{\partial t} \qquad (13.2)$$

Fig. 13.1 *Schematic diagram of an elemental section of a transmission line showing one phase and neutral*

Differentiating Eq. (13.1) wrt x and Eq. (13.2) wrt t, and eliminating the term $\partial_i^2/\partial x\ \partial t$ between these, finally yields

$$\frac{\partial^2 v(x,t)}{\partial x^2} = LC\frac{\partial^2 v(x,t)}{\partial t^2} \qquad (13.3)$$

The general solution of this equation is given by

$$v(x, t) = v_f(x - vt) + v_b(x + vt) \qquad (13.4)$$

where $v = \dfrac{1}{\sqrt{LC}}$ = speed of waves in m/s.

By differentiating Eq. (13.4) twice wrt x and t, it can be verified that these satisfy Eq. (13.3).

In Eq. (13.4), v_f is the voltage wave which travels in the forward (positive) direction of x with speed γ, and v_b travels in the backward direction with the same speed. The actual wave shape of these functions is determined by the initial distribution of charges along line and at terminations.

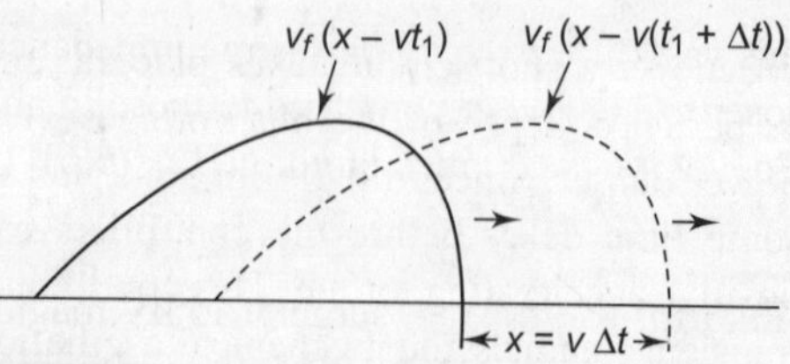

Fig. 13.2 *A forward travelling voltage wave shown for values of time t_1 and $t_1 + \Delta t$*

At $t = t_1$, the forward travelling wave has a distribution $v_f(x - \gamma t_1)$, which bodily (as it is) moves forward by a distance $\Delta x = \gamma \Delta t$ at time $t_1 + \Delta t$ as shown in Fig. 13.2.

13.3.1 Current Solution

The current waves that are implied by the motion of the charges, and which accompany the voltage waves can be found as under:

Differentiating Eq. (13.4) wrt x and using in Eq. (13.1), we have

$$\frac{\partial v}{\partial x} = v_f' + v_b' = -L\frac{\partial i}{\partial t} \tag{13.5}$$

where v_f' and v_b' are derivatives wrt the total variables i.e., $(x - \gamma t)$ and $(x + \gamma t)$.

Integrating Eq. (13.5) wrt t,

$$\int v_f'\, dt + \int v_b'\, dt = -Li(x, t) \tag{13.6}$$

But

$$\int v_f'\, dt = \int \frac{dv_f}{d(x - vt)} dt = \frac{1}{\gamma}\int dv_f = -\frac{1}{\gamma} v_f(x - vt)$$

Similarly,

$$\int v_f'\, dt = \frac{1}{v} v_b\,(x + vt)$$

Hence from Eq. (13.6),

$$-\frac{1}{\gamma} v_f\,(x - vt) + \frac{1}{v} v_b(x + vt) = -Li(x, t)$$

or

$$i(x, t) = \frac{1}{\sqrt{L/C}} v_f\,(x - vt) - \frac{1}{\sqrt{L/C}} v_b(x + vt)$$

$$= \frac{v_f(x - vt)}{Z_c} - \frac{v_b(x + vt)}{Z_c} \tag{13.7a}$$

$$= i_f(x - vt) + i_b(x + vt) \tag{13.7b}$$

where $Z_c = \sqrt{L/C}$ = *characteristic (surge) impedance.*

The surge impedance has the dimensions of resistance for a lossless line. The negative sign in the backward component of current in Eq. 13.7(a) is explained by the fact that current travelling in the backward direction has a negative value (wrt positive direction of x).

Typical values of surge impedance of overhead transmission lines and cables are given below:

$$\left.\begin{aligned} Z_c(\text{TL}) &\approx 400 \\ Z_c(\text{Cable}) &\approx 80 \end{aligned}\right\} \tag{13.8}$$

This vast difference in their surge impedances is because of the fact that in a cable the conductors are much closer to each other compared to those in an overhead transmission line so that it possesses much smaller L [Eq. 2.25(a)] and much larger C [Eq. (3.6)] (per unit length).

Example 13.1 A surge of 15 kV magnitude travels along a cable towards its junction with an overhead transmission line. The inductance and capacitance of the cable and overhead line are 0.3 mH, 0.4 μF and 1.5 mH, 0.012 μF per kilometres, respectively. Find the voltage rise at the junction due to the surge phenomena.

Solution According to problem statement, the surge travels from the cable towards the overhead transmission line and hence there will be positive voltage reflection at the junction.

The natural impedance of the cable and line $Z_c = \sqrt{\dfrac{L}{C}}$

The natural impedance of the cable $= \sqrt{\dfrac{0.3\times10^{-3}}{0.4\times10^{-6}}} = \sqrt{\dfrac{3\times10^{-4}}{0.4\times10^{-6}}} = 27.38\ \Omega$

Similarly,

The natural impedance of the line $= \sqrt{\dfrac{1.5\times10^{-3}}{0.012\times10^{-6}}} = \sqrt{\dfrac{1.5\times10^{-3}}{0.12\times10^{-7}}} = 353\ \Omega$

The voltage rise at the junction is the voltage transmitted into the overhead line as the voltage is zero before the surge reaches the junction.

The refracted voltage wave $E'' = V\cdot\dfrac{2\times Z2}{Z1+Z2}$

$$E'' = \frac{2\times353\times15}{353+27} = \frac{2\times353\times15}{380} = 27.87\ \text{kV}$$

13.3.2 Physical Interpretation of Results

Consider an ideal charge distribution on a transmission line (uniform over 1 km length abruptly reducing to zero on each side). This charge distribution has its associated voltage distribution as shown in Fig. 13.3(a). The voltage distribution is equivalent to two voltage waves v_f and v_b of half the strength, identical in shape and travelling in opposite directions. The current waves associated with these voltage waves have opposite sign and these at this instant ($t = 0$) superimpose to zero resultant current as illustrated. At $t = t_1$ when each of the wave sets (voltage and current) have travelled 1/4 km (say) in opposite directions, the resultant picture is illustrated in Fig. 13.3(b). Again in Fig. 13.3(c) is illustrated the case when the wave sets have travelled so far that no parts of these overlap.

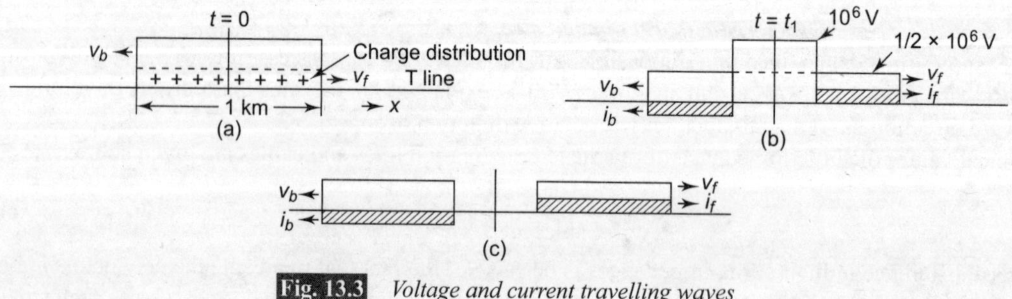

Fig. 13.3 *Voltage and current travelling waves*

13.3.3 Reflection and Refraction of Travelling Waves

When a travelling wave arrives at a discontinuity in a line, where the Z_c of the line changes (abruptly), some adjustment must take place, if the proportionality between voltage and current wave (Z_c) is to be maintained. This adjustment takes the form of the initiation of two new wave pairs. The reflected voltage wave and its companion current wave travel back down the line and are superimposed on the incident (incoming) wave. The *refracted* (continuing or transmitted) wave pair penetrates and travels beyond the discontinuity.

Figure 13.4 shows the junction of two lines (these could also be a line and a cable) with characteristic impedances of Z_{c1} and Z_{c2}. Here,

v_i, i_i = incident wave pair

v_r, i_r = reflected wave pair

v_t, i_t = reflected (transmitted) wave pair

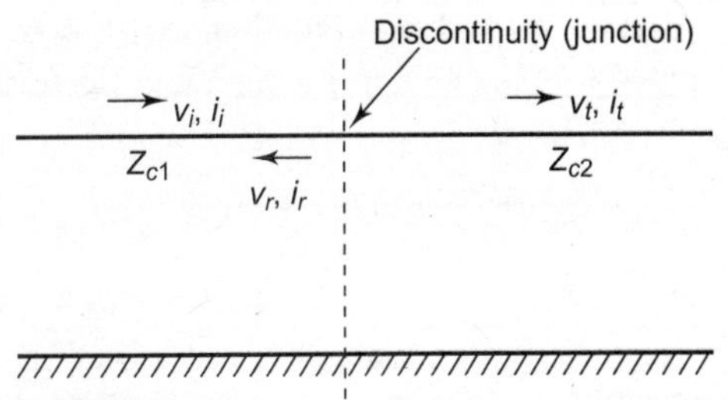

Fig. 13.4 *Reflection and refraction of travelling waves*

Applying the Kirchhoff's voltage and current laws at the junction

$$i_i + i_r = i_t \tag{13.9}$$

$$v_i + v_r = v_t \tag{13.10}$$

Equation (13.9) can be written in terms of voltage waves as

$$\frac{v_i}{Z_{c1}} - \frac{v_r}{Z_{c1}} = \frac{v_t}{Z_{c2}} \tag{13.11}$$

From Eqs. (13.10) and (13.11), we get by elimination

$$v_r = \left(\frac{Z_{c2} - Z_{c1}}{Z_{c2} + Z_{c1}}\right) v_i \tag{13.12}$$

$$= \alpha v_{\mathrm{i}}$$

where $\alpha = \dfrac{Z_{c2} - Z_{c1}}{Z_{c2} + Z_{c1}}$ = reflection coefficient (for voltage)

Also,

$$v_t = \left(\frac{2Z_{c_2}}{Z_{c2} + Z_{c1}}\right) v_i \tag{13.13}$$

$$= \beta v_i$$

where $\beta = \left(\dfrac{2Z_{c_2}}{Z_{c2} + Z_{c1}}\right)$ = refraction (transmission) coefficient (for voltage). It may be easily noted that

$$\beta = 1 + \alpha \tag{13.14}$$

From Eq. (13.12),

$$-\left(-\frac{v_r}{Z_{c1}}\right) = \alpha \frac{v_i}{Z_{c1}}$$

or

$$i_r = -\alpha i_i \tag{13.15}$$

It means that the reflection coefficient for current is negative of the reflection coefficient for voltage.

For three special cases,

1. Open-circuited line: $Z_{c2} = 0$ gives $\alpha = 1$, $\beta = 2$.
2. Short-circuited line: $Z_{c2} = 0$ gives $\alpha = -1$, $\beta = 0$.
3. Line terminated in its characteristic impedance (*matched termination*): $Z_{c2} = Z_{c1}$ gives $\alpha = 0$, $\beta = 1$.

It is seen from above that in the case of *matched termination*, there is no reflection and the line acts as if it is infinitely long. This thought is of importance in communication lines, but not in power lines.

Treatment of lines with lumped discontinuities (series lumped L or shunt lumped C) requires the use of the Laplace transform, and will be taken up at the end of this section.

Open-circuited Line As seen above

$$v_r = \alpha v_i = v_i$$

$$i_r = -\alpha v_i/Z_c = -v_i/Z_c = -i_i$$

Various stages in the process of reflection of a rectangular voltage wave and its associated current at the open-circuited end of a line are illustrated in Fig. 13.5. At $t = t_3$, voltage becomes double and current reduces to zero. At this stage all the energy stored in line inductance has been transferred to line capacitance, i.e.,

$$\frac{1}{2}Li_i^2 = \frac{1}{2}Cv_r^2$$

or

$$v_r = \sqrt{L/C}\; i_i = Z_c\, i_i = v_i$$

which is already indicated by the voltage reflection coefficient of $\alpha = 1$.

At $t = t_5$, it is seen that the voltage and current wave pair has been fully reflected (voltage positively and current negatively) at the open line end and are now travelling in the opposite direction.

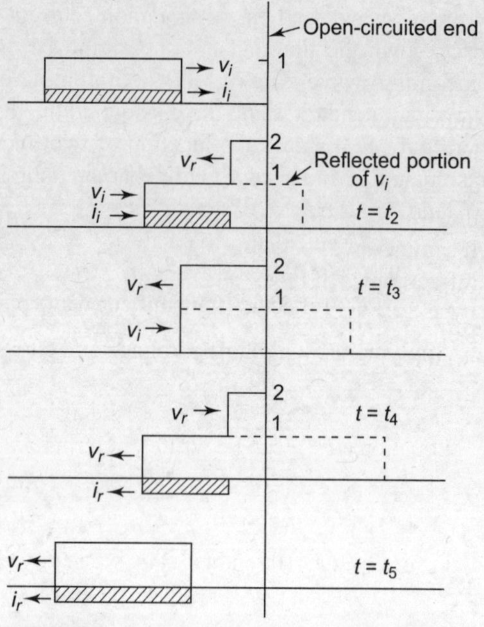

Fig. 13.5 *Reflections of an open-circuited line*

Short-circuited Line At a short-circuited end

$$v_r = \alpha v_i = -v_i$$

$$i_r = -(-v_i/Z_c) = i_i$$

Various stages in the reflection process are now illustrated in Fig. 13.6. At $t = t_3$, line current has doubled, but line voltage has been reduced to zero (all the energy is transformed to electromagnetic form). Finally, at $t = t_5$, the voltage and current waves have been fully reflected and are now travelling in opposite directions (voltage reflected negatively and current positively).

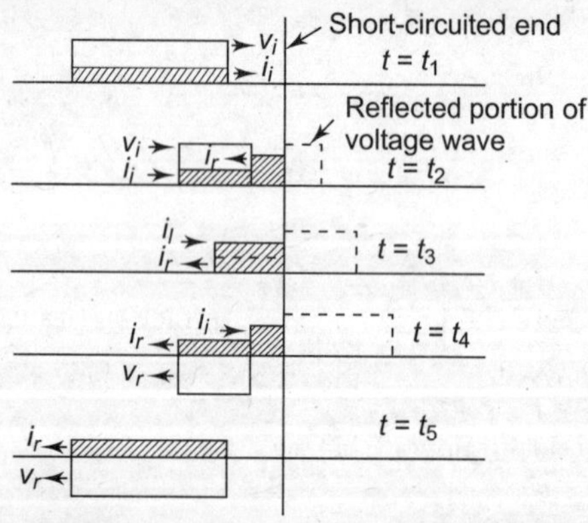

Fig. 13.6 *Reflections at a short-circuited line*

Line Connected to Cable A voltage wave upon entering a cable from a line gets modified as [Eq. (13.13)]

$$v_t = \left(\frac{2Z_2}{Z_2 + Z_1}\right)v_i$$

As for a cable

$$Z_2 < Z_1$$

it follows that

$$v_t < v_i$$

It means that voltage wave travelling along a line reduces in strength upon entering a cable—a beneficial effect of connecting a line to transformer via a cable.

13.3.4 Reflection and Refraction at a T-junction

A travelling wave (E, I) travelling on a line of surge impedance, Z_1 meets a junction with two lines having surge impedances respectively of Z_2 and Z_3 as shown in Fig. 13.8(a). On reaching the junction the wave sees the circuit as shown in Fig. 13.8(b). It immediately follows that the reflection and refraction coefficients for voltage at the junction are

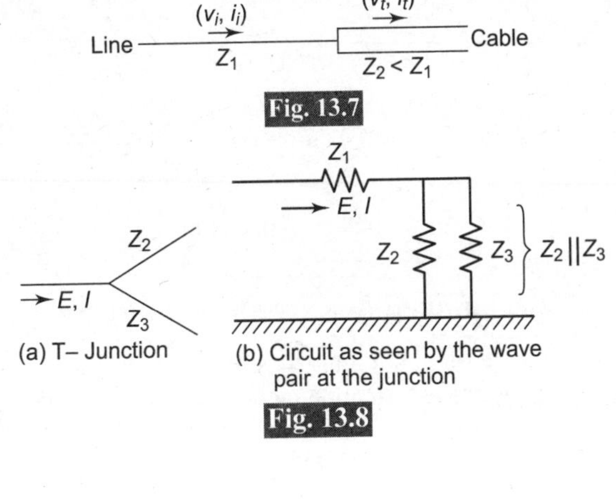

Fig. 13.7

(a) T– Junction

(b) Circuit as seen by the wave pair at the junction

Fig. 13.8

$$\text{Reflection coefficient, } \alpha = \frac{Z_2 || Z_3 - Z_1}{Z_2 || Z_3 + Z_1} = \frac{\frac{1}{Z_1} - \frac{1}{Z_2} - \frac{1}{Z_3}}{\frac{1}{Z_1} + \frac{1}{Z_2} + \frac{1}{Z_3}} \quad (13.16)$$

$$\text{Refraction coefficient, } \beta = 1 + \alpha = \frac{\frac{2}{Z_1}}{\frac{1}{Z_1} + \frac{1}{Z_2} + \frac{1}{Z_3}} \quad (13.17)$$

The wave pictures immediately following the reflection in terms of voltage and current waves are drawn in Fig. 13.9, which is self-explanatory (it is assumed that $\alpha < 0$).

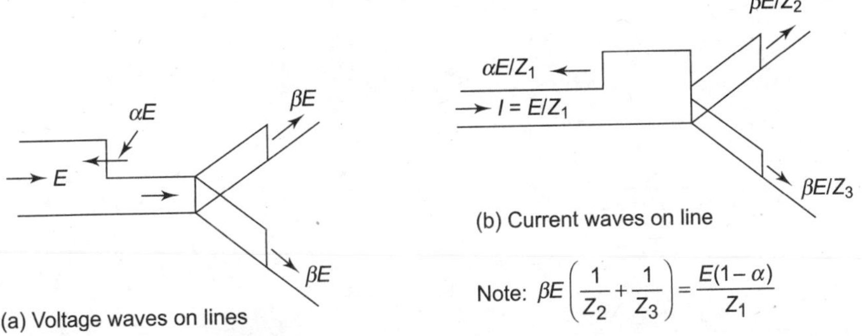

(a) Voltage waves on lines

(b) Current waves on line

Note: $\beta E\left(\frac{1}{Z_2} + \frac{1}{Z_3}\right) = \frac{E(1-\alpha)}{Z_1}$

Fig. 13.9 *Travelling waves on a T-junction*

Example 13.2 A surge of 100 kV travelling in a line of natural impedance 600 Ω arrives at a junction with two lines of impedances 800 Ω and 200 Ω, respectively. Find the surge voltages and currents transmitted into each branch line.

Solution The problem deals with a reflection at a T-joint. The natural impedances are $Z_1 = 600\ \Omega$, $Z_2 = 800\ \Omega$, $Z_3 = 200\ \Omega$. The surge magnitude is 100 kV.

The surge as it reaches the joint suffers reflection and here the two lines are operating in parallel; therefore, the transmitted voltage will have the same magnitude and is given by

$$E'' = \frac{\frac{2E}{Z_1}}{\frac{1}{Z_1} + \frac{1}{Z_2} + \frac{1}{Z_3}} = \frac{2 \times \frac{100}{600}}{\frac{1}{600} + \frac{1}{800} + \frac{1}{200}}$$

$$= \frac{0.333}{(1.67+1.25+5.0)\times 10^{-3}} = \frac{0.333\times 10^{3}}{7.92}$$

$$\frac{33.3}{7.92}\times 10 = 42.04 \text{ kV}$$

The transmitted current in line $Z_2 = \dfrac{42.04\times 1000}{800}$ amps = 52.55 amps

The transmitted current in line $Z_3 = \dfrac{42.04\times 1000}{200}$ amps = 210.2 amps

13.3.5 Lumped Reactive Junctions

When series or shunt lumped reactive elements are present on transmission line, recourse has to be taken to the Laplace transformation technique.

Shunt Capacitance Figure 13.10(a) shows a line with a shunt capacitance and Fig. 13.10(b) is its equivalent circuit as seen by the travelling wave (e, i) as it reaches the junction J. Let the voltage wave be a step wave of strength E_0, i.e.,

$$e(x, t) = E_0\, u(\gamma t - x) \qquad (13.18)$$

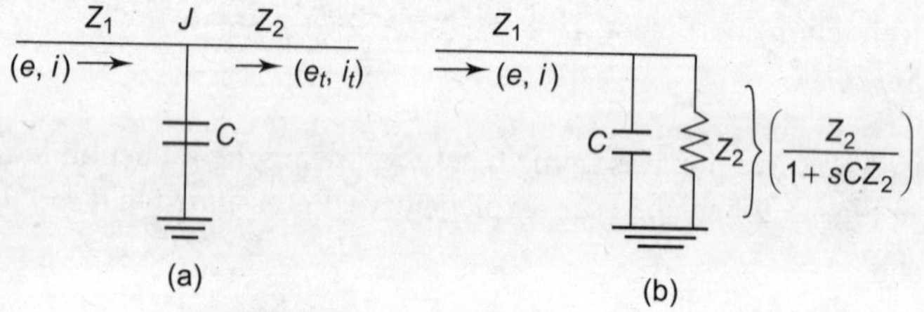

Let $t = 0$ when the wave front reaches the junction. It is observed at the junction as a time function

$$e(t) = E_0\, u(t) \qquad (13.19)$$

Fig. 13.10 *Line with shunt capacitance*

From Eq. (13.13), the junction voltage in the Laplace transform form is given by

$$E_J(s) = \frac{2\left(\dfrac{Z_2}{1+sCZ_2}\right)}{Z_1 + \dfrac{Z_2}{1+sCZ_2}} E(s)$$

$$= \frac{2/Z_1C}{s + 2/Z'C} E(s);\; Z' = \frac{Z_1Z_2}{Z_1+Z_2} \qquad (13.20)$$

For step incoming wave

$$E(s) = E_0/s$$

$$\therefore \quad E_J(s) = \frac{(2/Z_1C)\,E_0}{s\,(s+1/Z'C)} \qquad (13.21)$$

Inverse Laplace transforming, we get

$$e_J(t) = E_{J0}\,(1 - e^{-t/Z'C})\, u(t) \qquad (13.22)$$

where

$$E_{J0} = \left(\frac{2Z_2}{Z_2+Z_1}\right) E_0 \qquad (13.23)$$

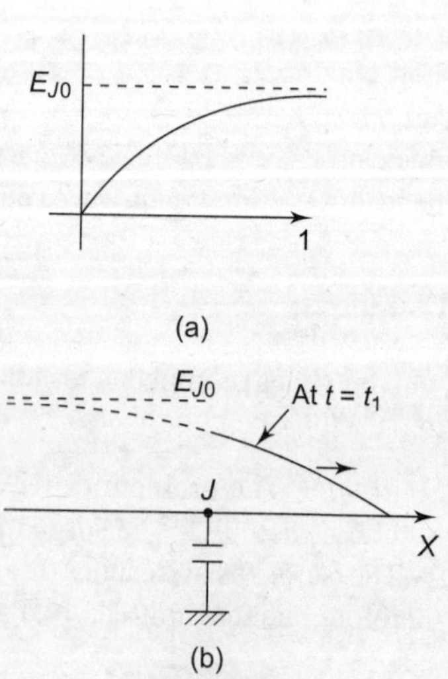

The junction voltage waveform is sketched in Fig. 13.11(a). This wave is injected into the line beyond C as shown in Fig. 13.11(b).

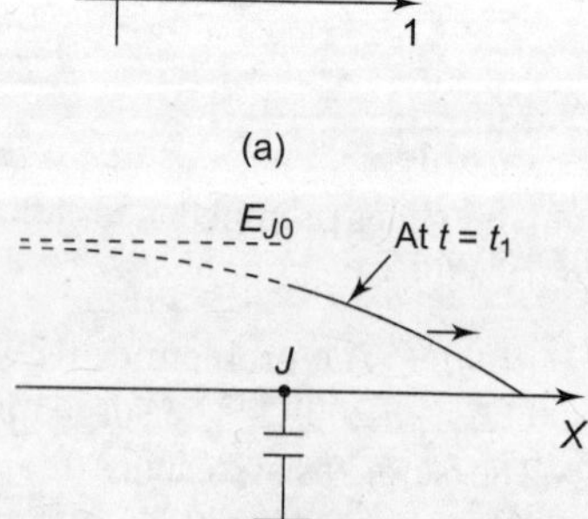

Fig. 13.11

The mathematical form of the onward travelling voltage wave is obtained by replacing

$$t \rightarrow (\gamma t - x)$$

in Eq. (13.21). Thus,

$$e_t(x, t) = E_{J0}\,[1 - E^{-(\gamma t - x)/Z'C}]\; u(\gamma t - x) \tag{13.24}$$

The incoming and outgoing voltage waves are sketched in Fig. 13.12. It is observed from this figure that while the incoming voltage wave rises at infinite rate (step function), the outgoing voltage wave has a much reduced rate of rise. This is the wave front modifying property of a shunt capacitance. The rate of rise of voltage is an important factor in determining insulation failure of the terminal equipment. Thus, a shunt capacitance hanging on a line protects the terminal equipment.

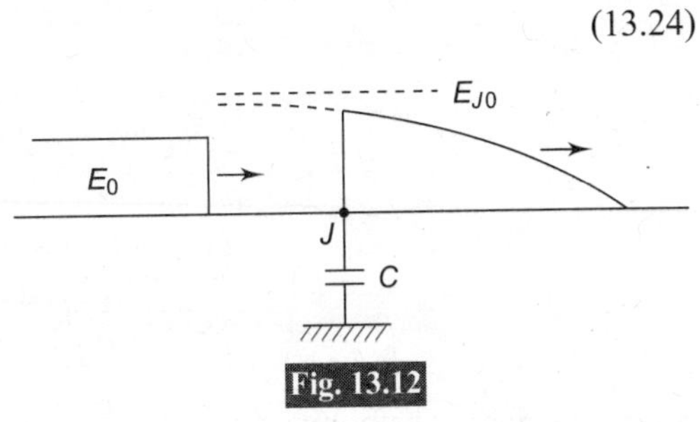

Fig. 13.12

The reflected voltage wave seen as time function at J is

$$e_r(t) = e_J(t) - e(t)$$

$$= E_0\left[\left(\frac{Z_2 - Z_1}{Z_2 + Z_1}\right) - \left(\frac{2Z_2}{Z_2 + Z_1}\right)e^{-t/Z'C}\right]u(t) \tag{13.25}$$

Special Case The results for the case, when the capacitance C is at the termination end of a line, can be obtained by letting $Z_2 = \infty$ in Eqs. (13.22) and (13.25). Thus,

$$e_J(t) = 2E_0\,(1 - e^{-1t/Z_1C})\; u(t) \tag{13.26}$$

and

$$e_r(t) = E_0\,(1 - 2e^{-1t/Z_1C})\; u(t) \tag{13.27}$$

The incoming voltage wave, the reflected voltage wave, the resultant and the corresponding current waves as per the above results are shown in Fig. 13.13 at a particular instant of time. It is confirmed from this figure that the capacitance acts as a short-circuit as the wave just reaches it (voltage becomes zero, current becomes double the incoming current wave), and as time elapses, it acts as an open-circuit (voltage becomes double the incoming voltage wave and current reduces to zero).

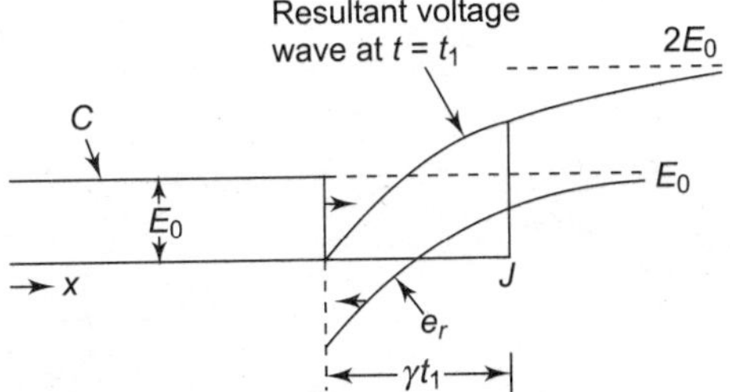

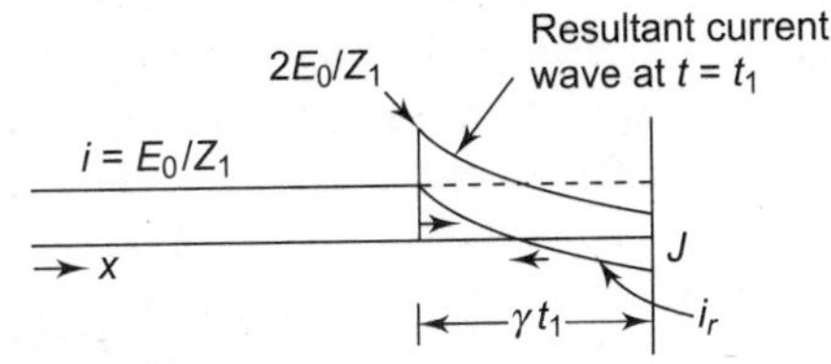

Fig. 13.13 *Voltage and current waves on transmission line terminated in a capacitance*

13.3.6 Series Inductance

Figure 13.14(a) is that of a line with series inductance and Fig. 13.14(b) shows the circuit seen by the incoming wave when it reaches the first junction J_1. The wave is assumed to be a step. [Eqs. (13.18) and (13.19)].

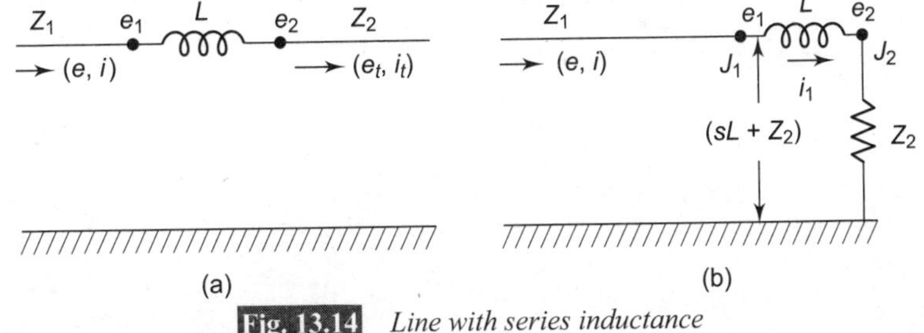

Fig. 13.14 *Line with series inductance*

From Eq. (13.13),

$$E_1(s) = \frac{2(sL+Z_2)}{(sL+Z_2)+Z_1}E(s) \tag{13.28}$$

Therefore,

$$I_1(s) = \frac{E_1(s)}{sL+Z_2} = \frac{2E(s)}{sL+(Z_2+Z_1)} \tag{13.29}$$

and

$$E_2(s) = Z_2 I_1(s)$$

$$= \frac{2Z_2E_0}{s[sL+(Z_2+Z_1)]} = \frac{(2Z_2/L)E_0}{s\left(s+\dfrac{Z_2+Z_1}{L}\right)} \tag{13.30}$$

Inverse Laplace transforming Eq. (13.30),

$$e_2(t) = \left(\frac{2Z_2}{Z_2+Z_1}\right)E_0\left[1-\exp\left(-\frac{Z_2+Z_1}{L}t\right)\right]u(t) \tag{13.31}$$

The time voltage wave of Eq. (13.31) then travels along the line beyond L (with characteristic impedance Z_2). Its mathematical expression is

$$e^t(\gamma t - x) = \left(\frac{2Z_2}{Z_2+Z_1}\right)E_0\left[1-\exp\left\{-\left(\frac{Z_2+Z_1}{L}\right)(\gamma t - x)\right\}\right]u(\gamma t - x) \tag{13.32}$$

The incoming and outgoing voltage waves are sketched in Fig. 13.15. It is again observed that while the rate of rise of incoming wave is infinite (step function), the outgoing wave beyond L rises much more gradually—wave modifier effect of a series inductance. As in the case of a shunt capacitance, it helps to reduce the failure inducing stresses in the insulation of the terminal equipment.

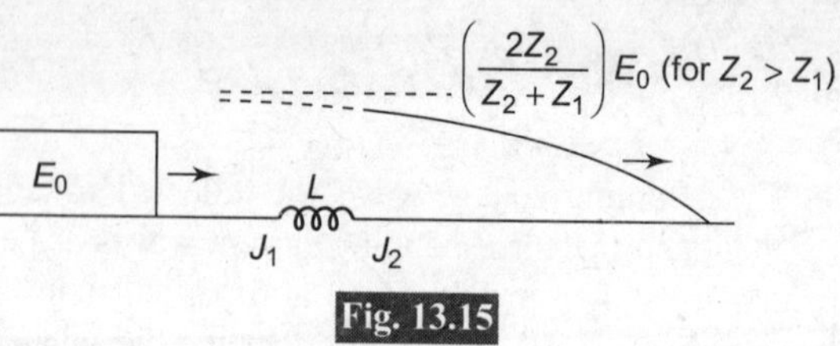

Fig. 13.15

Example 13.3 A 500 kV 2μ sec rectangular surge on a line having a surge impedance of 350 Ω approaches a station at which the concentrated earth capacitance is 3000 pF. Determine the maximum value of the transmitted wave.

Solution The maximum value of voltage is given by the following equation.

$$E'' = 2E\left[1-\exp\left(-\frac{\tau}{ZC}\right)\right]$$

$$= 2\times 500\left[1-\exp\left(-\frac{2\times 10^{-6}\times 10^{12}}{350\times 3000}\right)\right]$$

$$= 2\times 500\left[1-\exp\left(-\frac{2\times 10^{3}}{350\times 3}\right)\right]$$

$$= 2\times 500[1-e^{-1.9}]$$

$$= 2\times 500[1-0.15]$$

$$= 850 \text{ kV}$$

13.3.7 Attenuation and Distortion of Travelling Waves

In this chapter so far lossless simple twin-conductor transmission lines have been considered. But the behaviour of travelling waves on multiconductor transmission lines is extremely complex [3]. Waves travel in more than one mode on multiconductor lines and these different modes may have different velocities.

In this section, we shall briefly deal with attenuation and distortion of travelling waves. Distortion is caused by losses and multiconductor effect. Except in a very special case where $R/L = G/C$, which does not occur in practical power lines, attenuation in travelling waves is accompanied by distortion. Distortionless lines are obviously very desirable in communication circuits and steps are taken to achieve it. But in power transmission lines, it is not a matter of any significance. Here resistive losses are always much greater than those due to leakage. A distortionless condition is hardly an incentive to artificially increase the leakage losses.

Attenuation is mainly caused by series resistance and leakage resistance, and these quantities are considerably larger (about 50 times) for travelling waves than their power frequency values. There are other phenomena that are responsible for attenuation and distortion, of which the most important is *corona*. Voltage surges on lines are unaffected by corona until their potential exceeds the corona threshold. Normally, lines are operated well below the corona threshold, but corona can be observed in wet whether when the corona voltage is lower. Corona reduces the initial peak considerably by the time the wave travels only 1 to 2 km. After that attenuation continues, but at a reduced rate.

Determination of attenuation is normally empirical, and use is made of the expression $v_x = v_i e^{-\alpha x}$, where v_x is the magnitude of the surge at distance x from the point of origination. Considering the power and losses over an incremental length dx of a line of resistance and shunt conductance per unit length of $R\Omega$ and $G\ \Omega$, the power loss

$$dp = i^2 R\, dx + v^2 G\, dx \tag{13.33}$$

Also,

$$p = vi = i^2 Zc;\ dp = -2i\, Z_c\, di \tag{13.34}$$

Here negative sign has been included in dp, as there is reduction in power as the wave travels with time.

From Eqs. (13.33) and (13.34),

$$-2i\, Z_c\, di = (i^2 R + v^2 G)\, dx$$

or

$$\frac{di}{i} = \frac{1}{2}\left(\frac{R + Z_c^2 G}{Z_c}\right) dx$$

yielding

$$i = i_i \exp\left[-0.5\left(\frac{R}{Z_c} + GZ_c\right)x\right] \tag{13.35a}$$

where $i = i_i$ = surge amplitude at $x = 0$

or

$$i = i_i\, e^{-\alpha x} \tag{13.35b}$$

where

$$a = \frac{R + Z_c^2 G}{2Z_c}$$

Similarly it can be proved that

$$v = v_i\, e^{-\alpha x} \tag{13.36}$$

and the power at x

$$p_x = v_i\, i_i \exp\left[-\left(\frac{R}{Z_c} + GZ_c\right)\right]x \tag{13.37}$$

If R and G are correctly found out, including corona effect, attenuation may be accounted for in the travelling wave analysis.

From Eqs. 13.35(b) and (13.36), it is clear that the current and voltage waves get attenuated exponentially as they travel over the line, and the magnitude of attenuation depends on the line parameters. The value of line resistance depends not only on the size of the conductors but also on their shape and the length of waves. An empirical relation due to Foust and Menger relating the original voltage (V_0) to the voltage (V) at any point on the line after attenuation is given below:

$$V = \frac{V_0}{1 + kxV_0} \tag{13.38}$$

where x is the distance travelled in km, and V and V_0 in kV, and the attenuation constant k is given as

$$\begin{aligned} k &= 0.00037 \text{ for chopped waves} \\ &= 0.00019 \text{ for short waves} \\ &= 0.0001 \text{ for long waves} \end{aligned}$$

In the estimation of transmission-line transients, the effects of attenuation and distortion are normally ignored for simplicity and ease of analysis. The results so obtained are pessimistic—voltages computed are higher than those obtained actually.

13.3.8 Determination of System Voltages Produced by Travelling Waves

As already seen in this chapter, switching operations, faults, lightning surges, and other intended or unintended disturbances cause temporary overvoltages and currents in power systems. The system must withstand these overvoltages with a certain probability, or their effects must be reduced and limited with protective devices. The simulation of transient phenomena is, therefore, important for coordination of the insulation, as well as the proper design of protection schemes. Such simulation is also needed to analyse unexpected transient phenomena after their occurrence—such as ferro-resonance and subsynchronous resonance. By nature these phenomena are a combination of travelling wave effects on overhead lines and cables, and of oscillations in lumped-circuits of generators, transformers and other devices. It is practically impossible to study these electromagnetic transients using hand calculations, except for very simple cases. This complexity led to the development of transient network analysers in the late 1930s [4] which are still widely used today.

Travelling waves problems were already studied with graphical methods in the 1920s and 1930s, long before digital computers became available. Basically two techniques became popular, namely, Bewley's lattice diagram technique and Bergeron's method. We will study only the former in detail in this section. Both techniques were later adopted for computer solutions, the lattice diagram technique [8] as well as Bergeron's method [9]. It appears that Bergeron's method is better suited for digital computer solutions, and most existing general-purpose programmes use it. Both these methods are only efficient for lossless, or distortionless, lines. Good accuracy is often obtained by lumping resistance at one or more points along the line. Most general-purpose programmes solve transients problems directly in the time domain. Although many mathematical techniques are available, and in fact used, the one due to Bewley [1] will only be described here as it clearly indicates the physical changes occurring in time.

Bewley Lattice Diagram In order to keep track of the multiplicity of the successive reflections at the discontinuities in the system, Bewley has devised a time-space diagram which shows at a glance the position and direction of motion of every incident, reflected, and refracted wave on the system at every instant of time. The effect of attenuation and wave distortion can be accounted without much problem.

In the lattice diagram two axes are established, a horizontal one scaled in distance along the system, and a vertical one scaled in time. Lines showing the passage of surges are drawn such that their slopes give the time corresponding to distances travelled. At each point of change in impedance, the reflected and transmitted waves are obtained by multiplying the incidence wave magnitude by the proper reflection and refraction coefficients. Lattice diagrams for current may also be drawn. It should, however, be noted that the reflection coefficient for current is always the negative of the reflection coefficient for voltage.

To illustrate the method of constructing the Bewley lattice diagram, consider the simple system of Fig. 13.16, wherein a DC generator of unit voltage is switched 'on' to a lossless (no attenuation) line of characteristic impedance Z_c, with a load resistance R_c at its receiving end. For simplicity, it is assumed that the generator has zero impedance, such that a unit voltage wave is continuously fed to the line after the switching instant. The reflection coefficient at the receiving end is

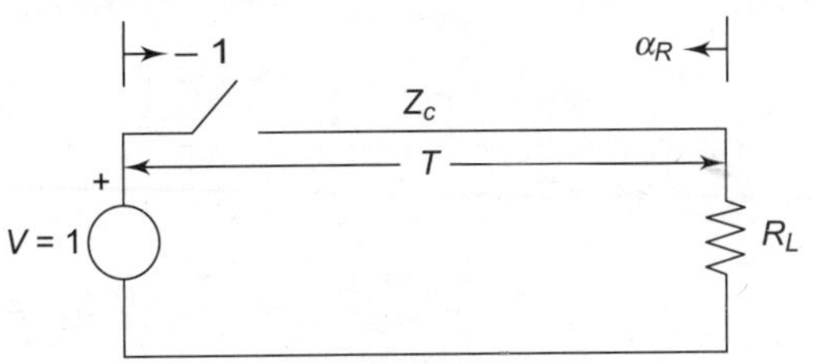

Fig. 13.16

$$\alpha_R = \frac{R_L - Z_c}{R_L + Z_c}$$

and that at the sending end is $\alpha_S = -1$, as the generator acts like a short-circuit with the assumption of zero impedance. Let the time of travel of surge from one end of the line to the other be T.

Immediately upon switching a unit, step voltage surge (infinite length) travels down the line towards the receiving end. This fact is recorded diagrammatically by a line sloping downward (left to right) as shown in Fig. 13.17. When the surge reaches the line end (in T s), a surge of amplitude α_R is originated in the reflection process, which then travels towards the generator end reaching there at $t = 2T$ represented by a sloping line (right to left). The reflection at the generator end causes an outward surge of strength—α_R. This process continues indefinitely, and some of its steps are illustrated in the Bewley lattice diagram of Fig. 13.17.

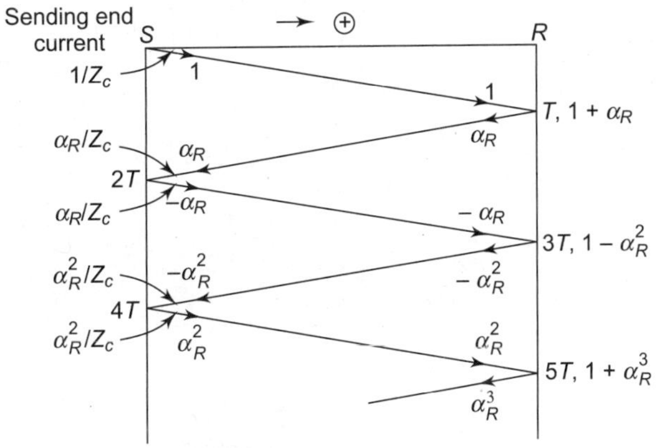

Fig. 13.17 *Bewley lattice diagram*

It is easily observed from the Bewley lattice diagram that, at the receiving-end, the increment of voltage at each reflection is the sum of the incident and reflected waves. The resultant voltages at various instants are written down in the right side of this diagram. In terms of series

$$V_R = (1 + \alpha_R) - (\alpha_R + \alpha_R^2) + (\alpha_R^2 + \alpha_R^3) - \cdots$$
$$= (1 + \alpha_R)\,[(1 + \alpha_R^2 + \alpha_R^4 + \cdots - (\alpha_R + \alpha_R^3 + \alpha_R^5 + \cdots)]$$

After infinite reflections, the voltage becomes

$$V_R = (1 + \alpha_R)\left[\frac{1}{1-\alpha_R^2} - \frac{\alpha_R}{1-\alpha_R^2}\right]$$
$$= 1$$

as it should be in the steady-state.

The receiving-end voltage is plotted against time in Fig. 13.18(a) and (b) for $\alpha_R > 0$ and $\alpha_R < 0$, respectively. In the former case the voltage settles to unit value in an oscillatory manner (square wave oscillations) and the latter case represents an overdamped situation.

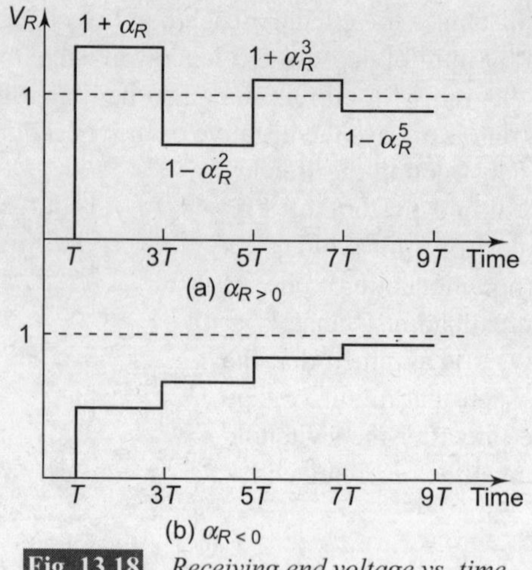

Fig. 13.18 *Receiving end voltage vs. time*

Let us now plot the sending end current. Each out-going surge is accompanied by a current wave of strength (voltage/Z_c) and each incoming wave is accompanied by a current wave (– voltage/Z_c). The plot of sending-end current vs. time is drawn in Fig. 13.19 for $\alpha_R > 0$. The steady value of the sending-end current is given by

$$I_S = \frac{1}{Z_c}\ [1 - 2\alpha_R + \alpha^2_R - 2\alpha^3_R + \cdots]$$

$$= \frac{1}{R_L} \text{ (the reader should prove this)}$$

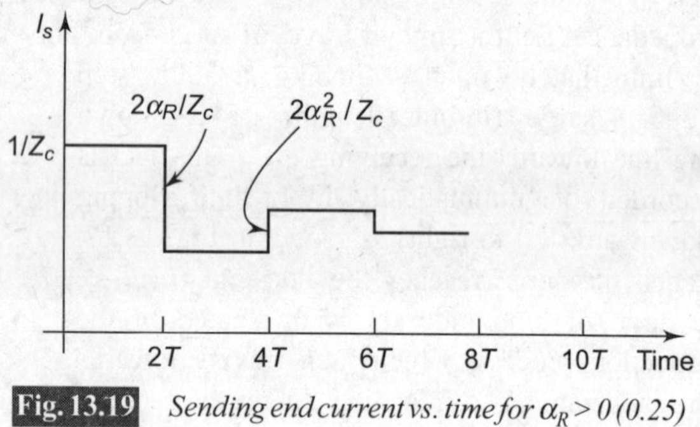

Fig. 13.19 *Sending end current vs. time for $\alpha_R > 0$ (0.25)*

Example 13.4 A unit-step voltage surge is travelling on a long line of surge impedance Z_1. It reaches the junction with a cable of finite length whose far end is open. The cable has a surge impedance of Z_2 and the time of one-way wave travel on it is T. Draw the Bewley lattice diagram and find from it the value of voltage at the junction at time $4T$ after the surge reaches the line-cable junction.

Given: $Z_1/Z_2 = 9$

Solution

Reflection coefficient line to cable, $\alpha_1 = \dfrac{1-9}{1+9} = -0.8$

Reflection coefficient cable to line, $\alpha_2 = \dfrac{9-1}{9+1} = +0.8$

Refraction coefficient line to cable, $\beta_1 = \dfrac{2 \times 1}{1+9} = 0.2$

The Bewley lattice diagram is drawn in Fig. 13.20

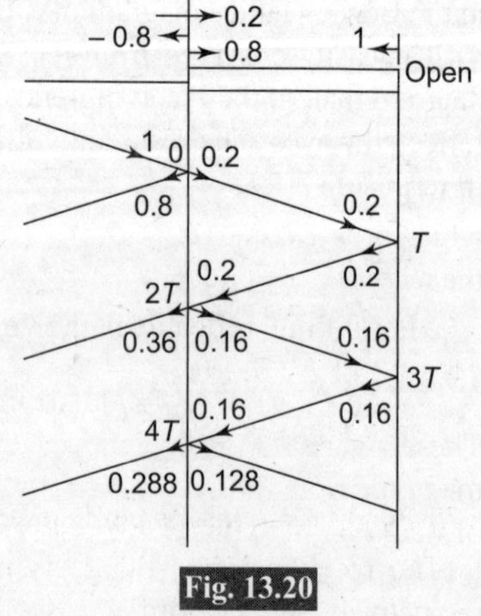

Fig. 13.20

Voltage at junction $4T^+$ (just after reflection has taken place)

$$= 1 - 0.8 + 0.36 + 0.288 = 0.848$$

Case of Finite Generator Impedance With finite generator impedance Z_g, the voltage impressed on the line will be

$$\left(\frac{Z_c}{Z_g + Z_c}\right)V_g \tag{13.39}$$

where V_g is presented with the voltage divider circuit of Fig. 13.21.

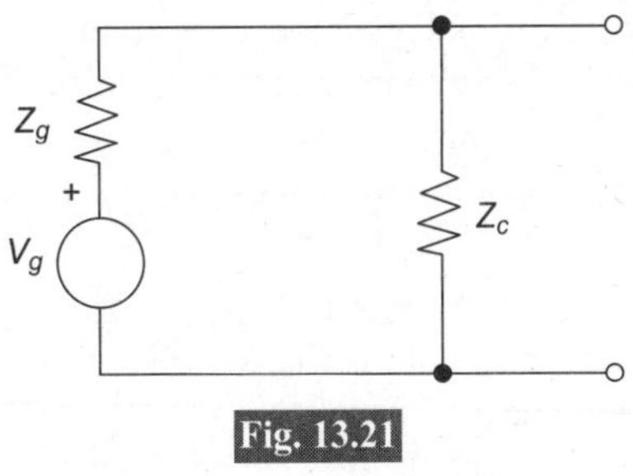

Fig. 13.21

13.4 ▶ GENERATION OF OVERVOLTAGES ON TRANSMISSION LINES

Transmission lines and power apparatus have to be protected from overvoltages. The overvoltages in a power system fall under three categories:

1. Resonance overvoltages
2. Switching overvoltages
3. Lightning overvoltages

Overvoltages due to the latter two causes, though transient in nature, constitute the basis for selection of insulation level of lines and apparatus, and of devices for surge protection. Resonance overvoltages, on the other hand, decide the steady voltage rating of such devices. Resonance and switching overvoltages are directly related to the system operating voltage, but the level of lightning overvoltages caused by the natural phenomenon are independent of it. At transmission line voltages upto around 230 kV, the insulation level is dictated by the requirement of protection against lightning. For voltages from 230 kV to 700 kV, both switching transients and lightning overvoltages must be accounted for in deciding the insulation levels. In EHV (>700 kV), switching surges cause higher overvoltages than lightning, and are therefore mainly responsible for insulation level decision. Fortunately cables are not exposed to lightning, and are automatically immune to the line surges which attenuate upon entering a cable (see Section 13.3). However, lines are preferred to cables for economic and technical reasons.

13.4.1 Resonance Overvoltages

Though it is unlikely that resonance in a supply network be obtained at normal supply frequencies, it is possible to have this condition at harmonic frequencies. Near resonance conditions may occur under certain type of unsymmetrical faults. Temporary overvoltages are also caused by inrush current, when transformers or reactors are energised (ferroresonance). Such overvoltages are important in choosing lightning arresters, which are not supposed to operate at these voltages. Thus, they indirectly determine the insulation level of the network.

13.4.2 Switching Overvoltages

These overvoltages are caused by normal switchgear operation and/or power system faults, and their magnitudes are related to the system operating voltages. Further, these overvoltages have a very wide range of magnitudes and wave shapes and last for durations ranging from a few μs to several seconds. At EHV levels the most important causes of switching overvoltages are classified as

1. Sustained earth fault on phase conductors.
2. Energisation or reclosure of long lines.

3. Load rejection at receiving end.
4. Fault initiation and reclosure.

Switching transients are also classified as single-energy or double-energy transients. In a single-energy transient, energy is redistributed in the circuit inductance or capacitance while in a double-energy transient, one transient is interchanged between system inductance and capacitance, giving rise to natural frequency ($f_n = 1/2\pi\sqrt{L/C}$ with $R = 0$) voltages and currents. Closing a circuit may result in excessive currents, and perhaps voltages also, while its opening normally results only in excessive transient voltages.

Among factors which decide the switching behaviour of power systems are the nature of source, characteristics of the transmission circuit, its length, the termination condition, the characteristic of earthing and shunt compensation. When the terminations are such that the energy is entirely or almost entirely reflected, high surge voltages are likely to build up (see Section 13.2).

The most important switching operations to be considered are line energisation and reclosing. With the improvement of arc restriking performance of circuit breakers, the consequent surges—interruption of line charging current and chopping of magnetising current are no longer of significance.

Attenuation of surges caused by line losses, and corona and reflection at the far end of the line from a loaded transformer help reduce the switching overvoltages, but mutual effects of sequential reclosing of the three phases tend to accentuate these.

The cost of EHV transmission system may be lowered by decreasing the switching overvoltages. This can be achieved by employing a circuit breaker, filled with a closing resistor of the order of the line surge impedance, in series with the breaker and the line which is subsequently short-circuited. The system is energised in two stages, producing two overvoltages, both of which are smaller than the overvoltage produced without the resistor.

13.4.3 Lightning Overvoltages

Lightning is a naturally occurring phenomenon (for theory of lightning consult reference [5]) wherein clouds get charged to several thousand kilovolts, and a discharge (stroke) can occur to high ground objects, or even to the ground. Transmission lines and towers being high objects attract lightning stroke, the underground cables being inherently immune to strokes. Lightning transients to which power system (lines, towers, substations and generating stations) are susceptible may occur on account of

1. Indirect strokes
2. Direct strokes to phase conductors
3. Direct strokes to towers
4. Direct strokes to earth wires

Direct Stroke A direct stroke occurs when a thunder cloud directly discharges on to transmission lines, tower or earth wires. This is the most severe and rarest form of stroke.

Indirect Stroke When a thunder cloud passes over ground objects, it induces a positive charge in them. Over a period of hundreds of seconds, positive charges leak from the tower along the string insulators to the line conductors. This happens due to high field gradients involved. In the event the cloud discharges to some earth object, the line is left with a huge free concentration of positive charge, which cannot leak suddenly, but instead travels in the form of two identical surges in either line direction. This is called an indirect stroke.

Typical lightning voltage surge in waveform and amplitude that may be injected in direct stroke on line conductors in absence of ground wire is shown in Fig. 13.22(a). Typical lightning current on transmission line towers is shown in Fig. 13.22(b). High voltages of the form of Fig. 13.22(a) are known as *impulse voltages*. The standard test impulse voltage will be defined later in this section.

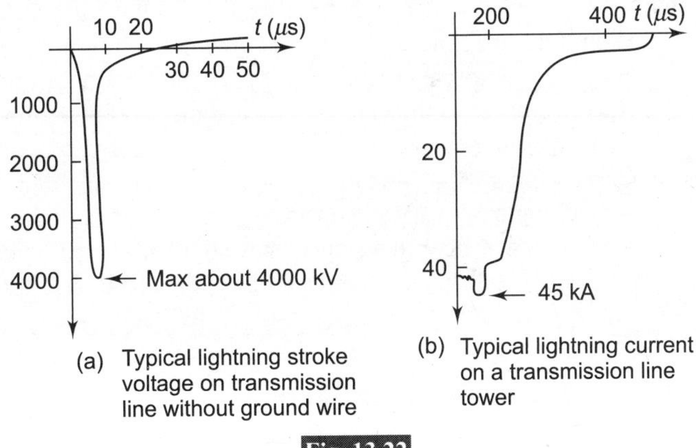

(a) Typical lightning stroke voltage on transmission line without ground wire

(b) Typical lightning current on a transmission line tower

Fig. 13.22

Back Flashover A direct stroke to tower causes a high voltage to be set up across the tower inductance and tower footing resistance by the fast changing lightning current (say 10 kA/μs). This appears as an overvoltage between the tower top and conductors which are at lower voltage and can cause a flashover from tower to line conductor across the line insulator, called back flashover. The voltage wave caused on the line because of back flashover has a very high rate of rise which can cause damage to terminal equipment.

The amplitudes of voltages induced indirectly by lightning strokes to a tower, earth wire or nearby ground object, are normally much less than those caused by direct stroke to a line conductor. This voltage depends upon electrical nature of tower footing resistance and stroke characteristics. They are of significance at lower voltages, such as 33 kV and below, and may even be important above this voltage.

Lightning Performance Parameters Lightning performance is the estimation of the annual number of lightning induced flashovers versus the critical flashover voltage of the line insulators. Indirect lightning strokes are more frequent on distribution lines due to the limited height of distribution lines in the vicinity of tall structures. Direct lightning strikes on transmission lines cause insulation flashover in majority of the cases. An accurate knowledge of the parameters of lightning strokes is essential for prediction of the severity of transient voltages generated by lightning strokes. Lightning being random in nature, its parameters are expressed in probabilistic terms. The significant parameters of a lightning flash are

1. Peak lightning current
2. Waveshape expressed as a double exponential function to represent a transient wave
3. Velocity of return stroke of the lightning
4. Total flash charge

The statistical variation of the random variable 'x' of the lightning stroke parameters is approximated by a lognormal distribution, which follows the statistical Gaussian distribution. The probability density function, $p(x)$, is given by

$$p(x) = \frac{1}{\sqrt{2\pi x \sigma_{\ln x}}} \exp\left[-0.5\left(\frac{\ln x - \ln x_m}{\sigma_{\ln x}}\right)^2\right] \tag{13.40}$$

where $\sigma_{\ln x}$ is the standard deviation of ln$x$, and x_m is the median value of x.

The lightning performance on transmission lines is measured by the flashover rate. Based on measured data, Monte Carlo simulation, a statistical approach is commonly used with a suitable modelling of power system components for calculating lightning overvoltages.

Parametric calculations are very useful to analyse the influence of transmission line and lightning stroke parameters. Sensitivity study is performed to determine the range of values of concern. The median values of the peak current magnitude and the rise time of the return stroke have high influence over the flash rate. The back flashover rate is very sensitive to the coefficient of correlation between the peak current and the rise time. The total flashover rate decreases as the value of correlation coefficient increases.

The effects of lightning strokes on transmission lines are reduced by providing shield wires, line arresters and by the presence of instrumented towers installed in mountains to collect lightning data.

Recently, several new methodologies, such as expert systems, genetic algorithms, artificial neural networks, fuzzy logic and wavelets, have been developed that could lead to accurate and fast diagnostic techniques for analysing power systems transients. The reader is suggested to refer [7] for more information on lightning performance.

13.5 ▶ PROTECTION OF TRANSMISSION LINES AGAINST LIGHTNING

Surges due to lightning are mostly injected into the power system through long cross-country transmission lines. Substation apparatus is always well shielded against direct lightning strokes. The protection of transmission lines against direct strokes requires a shield to prevent lightning from striking the electrical conductors. Adequate drainage facilities and adequate insulation structures must be provided so that the discharge can drain to ground without affecting the conductors. This prevents any arc from line conductor to ground.

13.5.1 Protection Using Shielding Wires or Ground Wires

The ground wire is a conductor run parallel to the main conductors of the transmission line. It is placed higher than the main conductors, is supported on the same towers and is earthed at equally and regularly spaced towers. It acts in two ways to protect the main conductors.

1. The ground wire helps to increase the effective capacitance between the line conductor and ground, such that the voltage appearing between conductor and ground because of static cloud charge is reduced. This is illustrated by the capacitor equivalent of the cloud–conductor system shown in Fig. 13.23.
2. Being higher than the ground wire shields the main conductor against direct strokes, though it increases the probability of a direct stroke to itself (more than what it would be for the main conductor if the ground wire were absent). *The protection* (*or shielding*) angle of a ground wire is found to be 30° for tower heights of 30 m or less. The protection zones of one and two ground wires are shown in Fig. 13.24(a) and (b), while Fig. 13.24(c) shows a double circuit line protected by a single ground wire. The height of the ground wire above the highest line conductor can be easily determined by the protection zone geometry. However, the present trend in fixing tower height and the shielding angle is by considering flashover rates and failure probabilities.

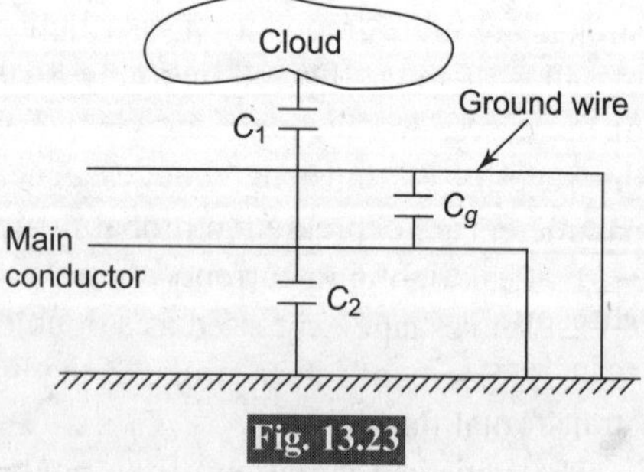

Fig. 13.23

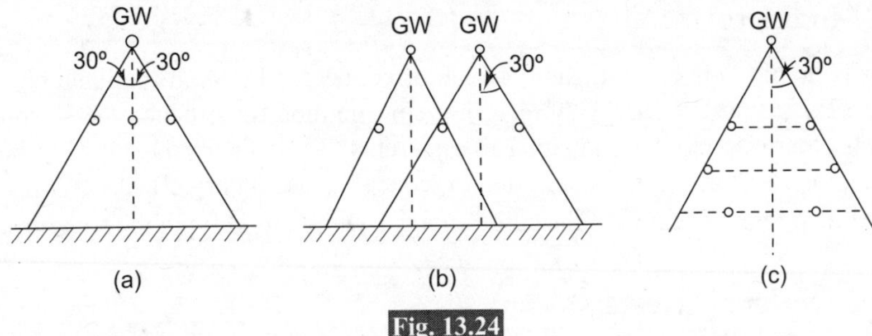

Fig. 13.24

3. The presence of ground wire(s) helps reduce the rise of back flashover in the event of direct stroke to tower, as the instantaneous potential to which the tower top is raised is reduced by the fact that half the surge impedance ($Z_g/2$) of the ground wire appears in parallel to the tower surge impedance (Z_T). It follows from Fig. 13.25 that the tower top voltage is

$$V_T = \left(\frac{Z_T}{1 + \dfrac{2Z_T}{Z_g}} \right) I_i \tag{13.41}$$

where I_i is the impulse current injected into the tower. It is easily seen that Z_g (as low as possible) reduces V_T.

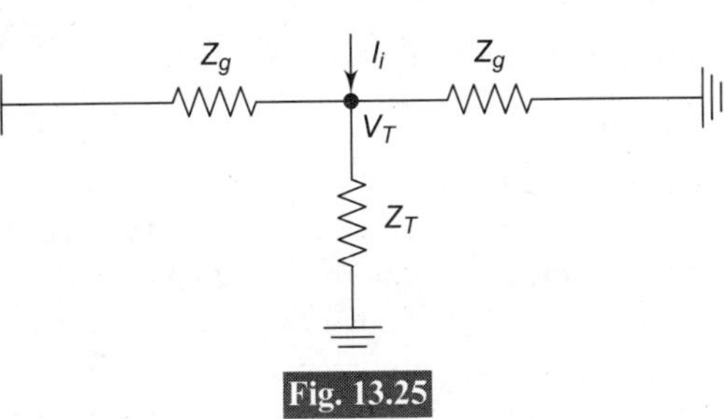

Fig. 13.25

If the surge impedance of the tower which is the effective tower footing resistance is reduced, the tower top surge voltage reduces to a considerable extent. Towers are grounded by providing driven ground rods and counterpoise wires [7] connected to tower legs at its foundations.

The standard value of this resistance is around 10 ohms for 66 kV lines, and increases with the operating voltage. For 400 kV it is approximately 80 ohms. The tower footing resistance is the value of the footing resistance when measured at 50 Hz. It is made as low as economically justifiable.

13.6 ▶ PROTECTION OF POWER SYSTEM APPARATUS AGAINST SURGES

In spite of the protection of transmission lines described earlier, sufficiently intense voltage surges can reach the substation and can damage the apparatus. The apparatus at substation (switchgear and transformer) is very expensive and outages can be prolonged, and must therefore be provided with almost 100% protection against surges. A two-pronged approach is followed in the protective scheme for apparatus. Surges before they reach the substation are modified to reduce the slope of their wave front. Upon reaching the substation, surges above a certain peak value are diverted into a shunt path to discharge their energies. As a result, the surges that finally reach the apparatus are so modified and reduced in strength as to be completely innocuous. The shunt discharge path for the surge must be autoclearing so as not to constitute a fault on the line.

13.6.1 Surge Modifiers

A surge modifier is nothing but a small shunt capacitor connected between the line and earth, or a series air-cored inductor. By temporary energy storage in them, the modifiers reduce the steepness of the surge wave front, which otherwise can be damaging to apparatus. Their theory has already been explained in Section 13.3. Damping resistors may be connected to reduce the oscillatory effects.

Corona on lines also removes some of the surge energy, thereby modifying the wave front.

13.6.2 Surge Diverters (Arresters)

Terminal equipment is protected against surges by surge diverters, also called surge arresters. A diverter is connected in shunt between the line and ground. Ideally it should

1. become conducting at voltage above diverter rating;
2. restrict the voltage across its terminals to the design value;
3. become nonconducting again when the line-to-neutral voltage becomes lower than the design value. In other words it should not permit any *power follow-on current*;
4. not conduct any current at normal or somewhat above normal power frequency voltages.

Three types of surge diverters are described below in principle, construction and application.

Rod Gap This is constituted of a plain air-gap between two square rods (1 cm^2) bent at right angles and connected between the line and earth as shown for the case of a transformer bushing in Fig. 13.26. The gap may also be in the form of horns or arcing rings.

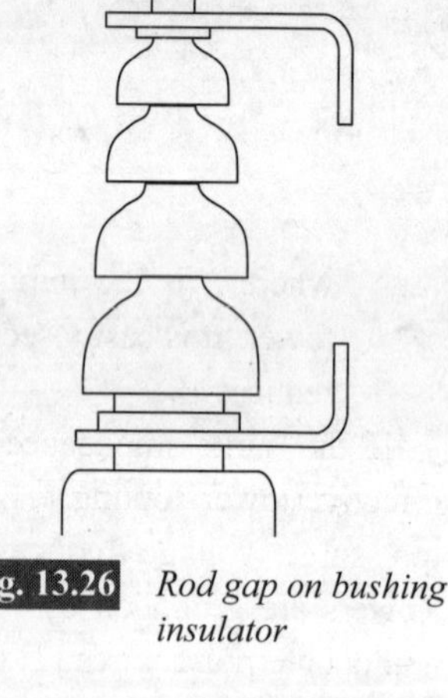

Fig. 13.26 *Rod gap on bushing insulator*

When the surge voltage reaches the design value of the gap, an arc appears in the gap providing an ionised path to ground, essentially a short-circuit. The gap suffers from the defect that after the surge has discharged, power frequency current continues to flow through the ionised path and the arc has to be extinguished by opening of circuit breakers resulting in outage. Rod gap is therefore generally used as back-up protection.

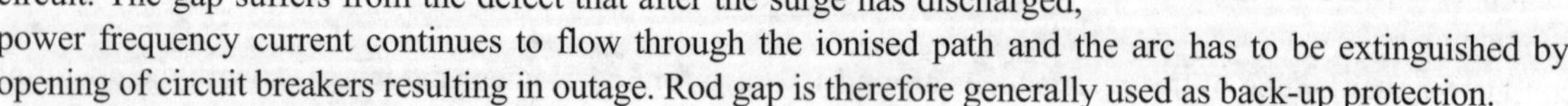

For a given gap the time to breakdown varies inversely with the applied voltage. It is normally recommended that a rod gap should be so set that it breaks down at a voltage no less than 30% below the voltage withstand level of the equipment to be protected.

Expulsion Type of Lightning Arrester (Protector Tube) It is improvement over a rod gap. In Fig. 13.27 the series gap is set to arc over at a specified voltage lower than the withstand voltage of the equipment to be protected. The follow-on current is confined to the space inside the relatively small fibre tube. Part of the tube material vaporises, and the high pressure gases so formed are expelled through the vent at the lower end of the tube, causing the power follow-in arc to be extinguished. The device, therefore, has the desired self-clearing property. Because of the vaporisation of the tube material and weathering

Line
Series (external) gap
Electrode
Fibre tube
Arc chamber
Bottom
Vent for gases

Fig. 13.27 *Expulsion type lightning arrester*

effect, the protector tube requires frequent replacement and lack of proper maintenance may lead to occasional outage. It has not, therefore, found favour in application and is practically out of use now.

Valve Type (Nonlinear) Lightning Arrester (LA) The valve type lightning arrester consists of nonlinear resistors in series with spark-gaps, as shown in Fig. 13.28. The spark-gap assembly acts as a fast switch, which gets ionised (conducting) at specified voltage. The nonlinear resistor elements are stacked, one over the other, in two or three sections. The problem of non-uniform voltage distribution across gap is solved by capacitors and nonlinear resistors connected in parallel across each gap as shown in Fig. 13.29. As a result, the gap assembly has a high degree of consistency of breakdown (flashover) voltage. The entire assembly is placed in porcelain housing, properly sealed to keep out dust and moisture.

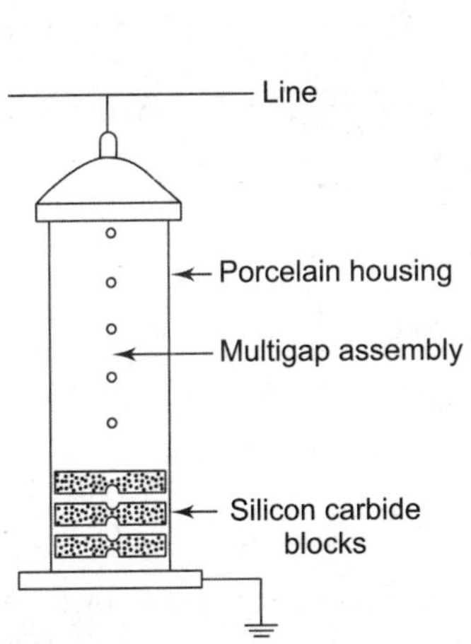

Fig. 13.28 *Valve type lightning arrester (LA)*

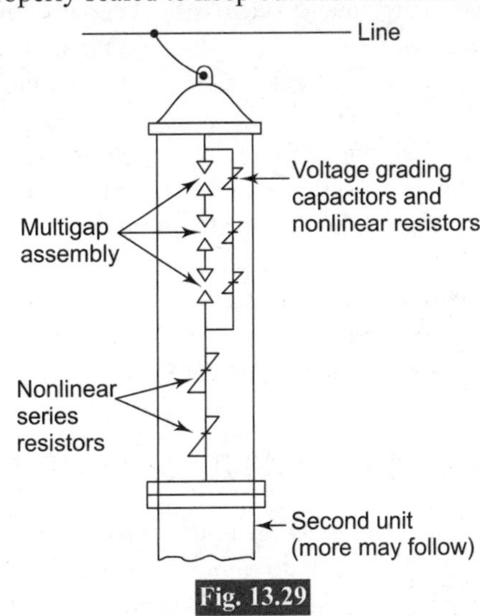

Fig. 13.29

The nonlinear resistors are made of loosely packed *silicon carbide*. The modern trend is to use *zinc oxide*, which gives more desirable characteristics. Because of loose packing of silicon carbide particles, the conduction process through it is mainly by means of short arcs and hence the nonlinear resistor characteristic. The static characteristic is empirically expressed as

$$I = KV^a \tag{13.42}$$

where I = discharge current

v = voltage across the element

a = an exponent more than unity (≈ 4)

K = constant

K and a depend upon the material, packing and dimensions of the element.

Because of the exponent a being close to 4, the current through the element rises more rapidly with the applied voltage than in the linear case which, in other words, means that the element offers a much lower resistance at higher currents. The dynamic characteristic of the diverter (several elements in series) for a surge current (rising and then falling) is shown in Fig. 13.30.

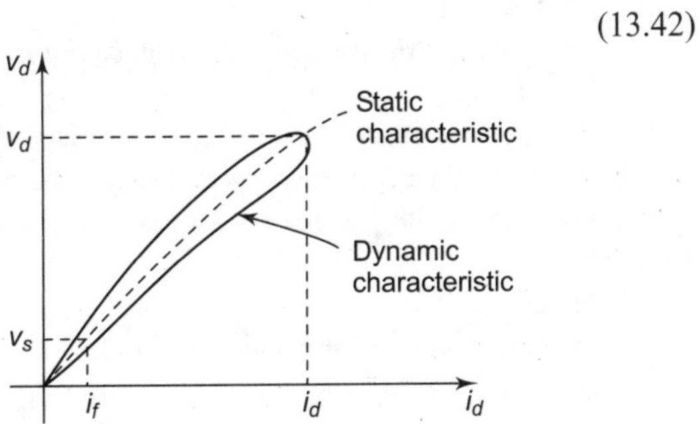

Fig. 13.30 *Dynamic volt–ampere characteristic of surge diverter*

Because of the nonlinear diverter characteristic, the power follow-on current at system voltage is so small that the cooling and deionising effects of gap assembly are able to extinguish the arc. This gives the self-clearing property to the diverter, which is essential to its operation after the surge current has been discharged to ground.

As a voltage surge shown in Fig. 13.31 travelling on the line reaches the surge diverter, it breaks down at a specified voltage v_{bd}. The voltage across the diverter instantly dips and then, as the surge current shown discharges through it, a nearly constant voltage of value v_r, called *residual voltage* is maintained across it. After the surge current has discharged, the power follow-on current is interrupted by the gap assembly. The zinc oxide diverters maintain a practically constant residual voltage over a very wide current range. Further their power follow-on current is so small that it is not essential to use a series air-gap to limit this current.

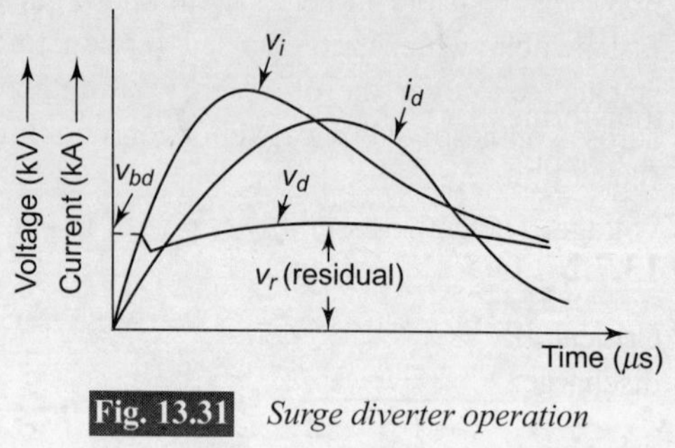

Fig. 13.31 *Surge diverter operation*

The important ratings of a surge diverter are

1. Rated system voltage (it should be able to withstand an overvoltage of 5%)
2. Breakdown voltage
3. Residual voltage
4. Peak discharge current

13.7 ▶ INSULATION CO-ORDINATION

Insulation co-ordination is the correlation of the insulation levels of various equipment of a high-voltage power system so as to minimise damage and loss of supply due to overvoltages. The insulation level of an equipment is defined as the combination of voltages (power-frequency and impulse) that characterise the insulation with regard to its ability to withstand various stresses. A proper insulation co-ordination has to ensure

1. that the system insulation will withstand all normal, and most of the abnormal, stresses;
2. that the overvoltages (generated internally or externally injected) are efficiently discharged to ground; and
3. the external flashovers will protect equipment against failure, such as puncture or breakdown of insulation.

The problem of insulation co-ordination is that of a trade-off between the cost of equipment insulation sufficient to withstand overvoltages that are permitted to reach it by the protective devices (ground wire, LAs), the cost of the protective devices, the probability of equipment damage and the frequency and severity of outages.

The insulation co-ordination in a power system requires

1. the determination of line insulation level;
2. the selection of the basic insulation level (BIL) (defined later) and insulation level of other equipment; and
3. that selection of proper protective devices, such as LAs, so as to provide to the equipment economically justifiable protection.

Before proceeding to tackle the co-ordination problem enunciated above, certain terms used in HV technology must be defined.

13.7.1 Basic Impulse Insulation Level or Basic Insulation Level (BIL)

Basic impulse insulation level or basic insulation level (BIL) is expressed as the impulse crest (peak) voltage of a standard wave not longer than 1.2×50 μs wave (defined later). Apparatus insulation levels as demonstrated by suitable tests should be equal to, or greater than, the BIL.

BIL measures the ability to withstand test voltages without disruptive discharge. For example, a transformer for 400 kV system tested successfully at 900 kV peak is said to have a BIL of $\left(900 \div \frac{400\sqrt{2}}{\sqrt{3}}\right)$ = 2.76 pu.

13.7.2 Critical Flashover (CFO) Voltage

Critical flashover (CFO) voltage is the peak voltage for a 50% probability of flashover or disruptive discharge.

13.7.3 Impulse Ratio

Impulse ratio (for flashover or puncture of insulation) is the impulse peak voltage divided by the peak value of the power frequency voltage to cause flashover or puncture.

Each equipment is normally tested for both the normal AC frequency and impulse strength.

13.7.4 Standard Impulse Test Wave

Impulse tests are generally carried out with typical impulse test wave called '1.2×50 μs standard test wave', which reaches 90% of its peak value in 1.2 μs and falls to half the peak value in 50 μs as shown in Fig. 13.32. This also typifies lightning surges. Mathematically, this wave can be expressed as the difference of two decaying exponentials, i.e.,

$$v = V_0(e^{-\alpha t} - e^{-\beta t}) \tag{13.43}$$

with $\beta > \alpha$.

The standard test wave is obtained from an impulse generator, where capacitors are charged in parallel and discharged in series through resistors.

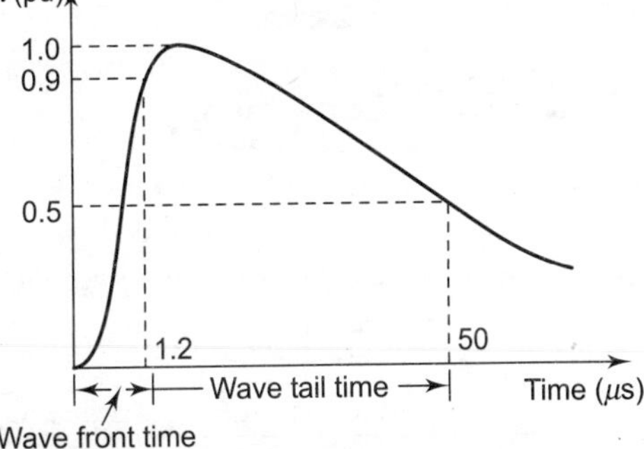

Fig. 13.32 *Standard 1.2×5 μs test wave (time not to scale)*

Switching surges comprise damped oscillatory waves, the frequency of which is given by system configuration and parameters. They are generally of amplitude 2–4 pu (base voltage – peak value of line to earth operating voltage).

13.7.5 Volt-time Characteristic (Curve)

For proper insulation coordination, one needs the understanding of the volt-time characteristic, apart from the meaning of BIL. It is a graphical indication of the relation between the crest flashover voltages and the time to flashover of an equipment for a series of impulse applications of a given wave shape. Figure 13.33 shows that keeping the wave front time as constant and raising in steps the peak voltage from relatively low values, a peak voltage is reached which is the highest at which the test object does not flashover. This peak value is the full wave impulse withstand voltage. If flashover occurs on the front of the wave, the flashover point is taken on the volt-time curve. If the flashover occurs on the tail side of the wave, in this case draw a horizontal line from the peak value of this wave and also draw a vertical line passing through the point where the flashover occurs. The intersection of the horizontal and vertical lines gives the point on volt-time curve.

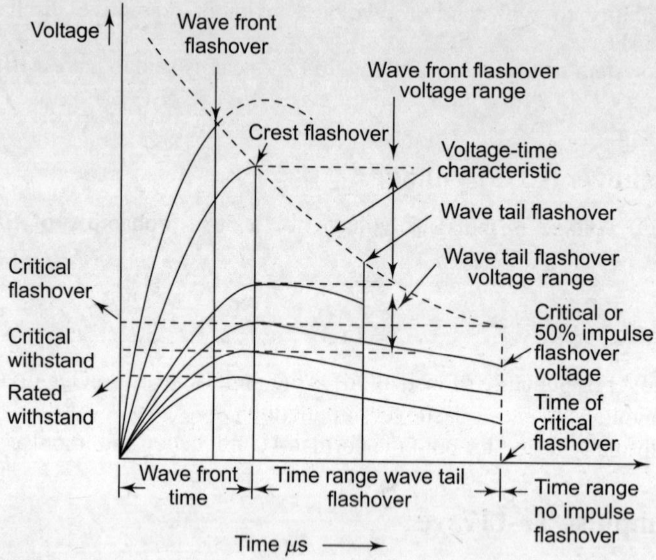

Fig. 13.33 *Voltage–time characteristic of equipment under impulse voltage test*

13.7.6 BIL of Equipment

To help in the process of insulation co-ordination, standard insulation levels are recommended and are summarised in Table 13.1. Reduced basic insulation levels are employed while considering switching surges (see Table 13.1) or for solidly grounded systems.

Table 13.1 Recommended standard BILs at various operating voltages

Reference Class (kV)	*Standard Basic Impulse Level (kV)*	*Reduced BIL (kV)*
23	150	
34.5	200	
46	250	
69	350	
92	450	
115	550	400
138	650	500
161	750	600
196	900	—
230	1050	900
287	1300	1050
345	1550	1300
500	1800	1550

The apparatus to be protected should have a withstand test value not less than the kV magnitude given in second column of Table 13.1 whatever may be the polarity of the wave and irrespective of the type of system grounding. At 345 kV, the switching voltage is considered to be 2.7 pu, i.e., 931.5 kV, which corresponds to the lightning level. At 500 kV, however, a 2.7 pu switching impulse would require 40% more tower insulation than that governed by lightning. The trend is, therefore, for another design of switching impulse level to be forced lower with increasing system operating voltage and controlling the surges by use of resistive switching in the circuit breakers. Thus for 500 kV network the level is 2 pu and, with further increase in system voltage, it is envisaged to decrease the level to 1.5 pu.

13.7.7 Insulation Co-ordination

Proper insulation co-ordination should ensure that the volt-time curve of the weakest piece of equipment in the system will lie above the volt-time curve of the protective device such as lightning arrester, over the whole range of the volt-time curve as shown in Fig. 13.34. This weakest piece is always the transformer, the single most expensive equipment with intricately formed insulation. It is easily seen here that the incoming voltage surge which would have otherwise damaged the transformer insulation is reduced to that of the volt–time curve (residual voltage) of the lightning arrester such that the transformer is fully protected.

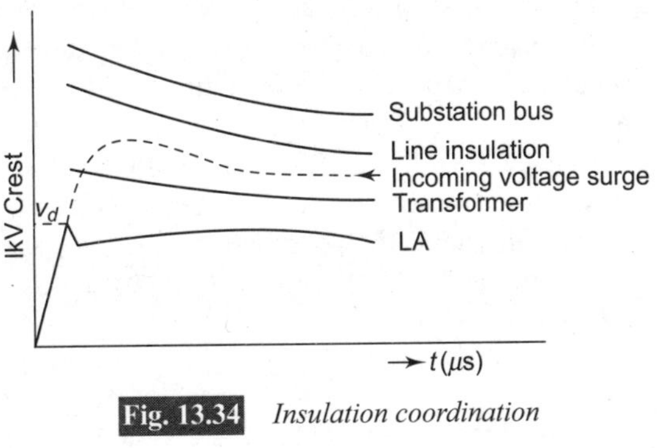

Fig. 13.34 *Insulation coordination*

In order that line insulators do not flashover, their volt-time curve should lie over that of possible strongest surge wave except for rare surges of extreme strength, in which case insulator failure is accepted as an economic design. Thus, the line insulation is sufficient to prevent flashover for power frequency overvoltages and switching surges taking into account all the local unfavourable conditions, such as rain, dust, insulator pollution, which decrease their flashover voltage. The substation bus is always designed to have the highest located volt-time curve such that it can even withstand an occasional direct stroke.

Based on handbook data appropriate safety margins are provided among the various equipment volt-time curves as illustrated in Fig. 13.34. The modern practice, however, is to make use of probability theory and statistical procedures for close adjustment of insulation. These methods are, though tedious, proving useful and economical.

13.7.8 Location of Lightning Arrester Relative to Transformer

Figure 13.35 shows a Lightning Arrester (LA) located at distance L from the transformer it is protecting. The LA modifies the incoming surge to a rising wave front which, after reaching the residual voltage (v_r) of the LA, remains almost flat. This modified wave, as it approaches the transformer, gets positively reflected (transformer can be almost regarded as an open end). The voltage at the transformer, therefore, rises at twice

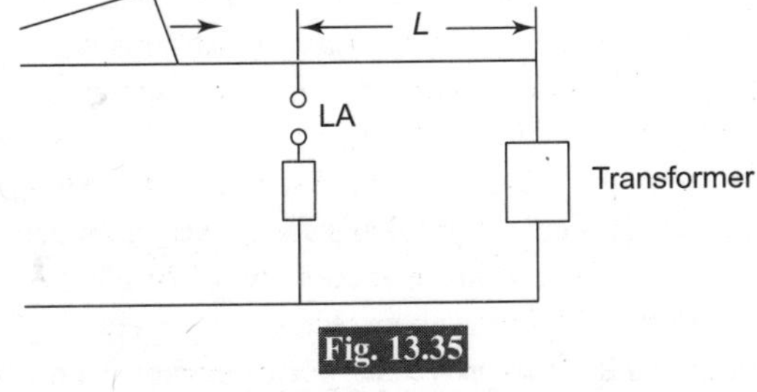

Fig. 13.35

the initial slope of the incoming wave front. The portion of the voltage wave reflected at the transformer gets negatively reflected at the LA which offers a low resistance shunt path. This negative voltage reaching the transformer does not allow the voltage at the transformer to build up to twice that of the incoming wave, as it otherwise would have. To what maximum does the voltage at the transformer build up, depends upon the time of travel or distance between the transformer and LA. The smaller is this distance, the earlier this negatively reflected wave arrives and the smaller is the transformer voltage build up. This voltage is the least when the LA is located on the transformer and would equal the residual voltage of the LA. In conclusion therefore the LA should be located as close to the transformer as is physically possible.

13.7.9 Insulation Co-ordination Based on Waveshape [7]

Switching overvoltages are generally decisive in deciding the insulation design of EHV and UHV transmission system. Insulation co-ordination procedure is based on the insulation strength characteristics. Insulation strength is characterised by a discharge probability function since every applied impulse magnitude is associated with a probability of flashover. Switching transients are random in nature. Therefore, Monte Carlo simulations are run in EMTP programmes to generate sufficient number of overvoltage waveforms. The waveform parameters–V_p, the peak voltage, times to crest of basic and superimposed waveforms are extracted to calculate $U_{50}\%$ and $\sigma/U_{50}\%$.

Gaussian cumulative distribution function, described by its mean value, the 50% breakdown voltage, $U_{50}\%$, is generally used to represent the probability of flashover. The probability of flashover P is given by

$$P(V_p) = \frac{1}{\sqrt{2\pi\sigma}} \int_{-\infty}^{V_p} \left[\exp -\frac{1}{2}\left(\frac{x - U_{50}\%}{\sigma}\right)^2 \right] dx \qquad (13.44)$$

Switching overvoltage waves in real systems have irregular waveshapes. The switching surge overvoltage is thought of two components, one basic wave having low frequency component and the other one is the superimposed wave with rapid variations with time. A new procedure reported in the recent literature considers the effect of waveshape impulses of the air gap strength. The application of this procedure to a 1050 kV transmission system with an inductive source has shown that there has been a 15% reduction in the insulating distance with that calculated with traditional method. The effective insulation co-ordination procedure based on waveshape of switching overvoltages may benefit from smaller transmission line structure and rights of way. The reader is suggested to refer [7] for more details.

13.8 ▶ LIGHTNING PHENOMENA

Lightning has always been attracting mankind since the early times. Franklin in 18th century was the first to initiate research on it. Lightning is a natural electrical phenomenon consisting of a high current, short time discharge that neutralises an accumulation of charge in the atmosphere. The discharge path can be between two different locations in a cloud, two clouds, a cloud and the earth (or any structure connected to the earth). The mechanisms by which such charge accumulations take place is not yet fully known, but is related to the motions of large air masses that come across certain conditions of humidity, temperature and pressure. When the electric fields become excessive a breakdown or lightning flash takes place; this is normally a high current discharge. As explained earlier, lightning strokes that terminate on or near to power lines create problems for power engineers. The real incentive to obtain additional knowledge about lightning came from the necessity of the electrical industry to protect against its effects. It has been proved [3] that lightning is the greatest single cause of outages on transmission sector. A continuous effort has been made to improve the performance of power systems during thunderstorms. This has resulted in the development and application of ground wires, counter-poise, lightning arresters, etc.

Various theories [12] have been advanced explaining the charge formulation, such as Wilson's theory of charge separation and Simpson and Scarse's theory. We shall discuss these briefly below.

13.8.1 Wilson's Theory of Charge Separation

The theory assumes that many ions are present in the atmosphere which get themselves attached to tiny dust and water particles. It further assumes the presence of an electric field in the earths atmosphere during fair weather directed towards the earth [Fig. 13.36(a)]. The field intensity is roughly 1 V/cm at the earth's surface, and progressively decreases with height so that at 10,000 m it is only about 0.02 V/cm.

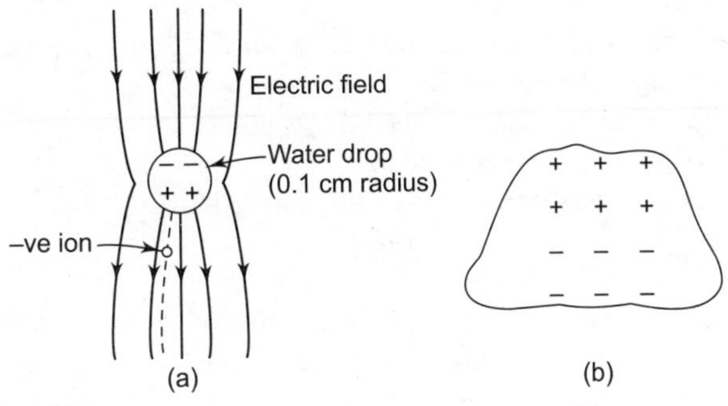

Fig. 13.36 *(a) Capture of negative ions by large falling rains drops; (b) Charge separation in a thunder cloud*

Because of the atmospheric electric field, raindrops become polarised, the upper side gets a negative charge and the lower side a positive charge as shown in Fig. 13.36(a). Later, the lower part of the drops attracts negative ions from the atmosphere, acquiring an overall negative charge while leaving a proponderance of positive charges in the air. The upward motion of air currents takes positively charged air and smaller drops to the top of the cloud. Heavier rain drops settle on the base of the cloud as shown in Fig. 13.36(b). Thus, according to Wilson's theory, a thundercloud is bipolar with positive charges at the top and negative at the bottom, normally separated by several kilometres. When the electric field strength becomes more than the breakdown value, a lightning discharge is commenced.

13.8.2 Simpson and Scarse's Theory

This theory is based on the temperature variations in the various regions of the cloud as shown in Fig. 13.37. In Fig. 13.37, a cloud is shown to be travelling from left to right along with the air currents. When these air currents collide with the water particles in the bottom of the cloud, the water drops are broken and carried upwards, unless they combine and remain in a small pocket of positive charges. With the collision of water drops the air is negatively charged and water particles positively charged. These negative charges in the air are at once absorbed by the cloud particles, which move upward with air currents. Figure 13.37 shows meteorological and electrical conditions within a thundercloud. A positive charge resides in the upper portion of the cloud above a region of separation from the negative charge in which the temperature is between – 10 and –20°C. Thus, a net positive charge will occur above the mid level of the cloud, and the negative charge will be distributed more generally throughout the cloud body. This is how the charge is separated in a thunder cloud. Once this is done, the conditions are set for initiation of a lightning stroke.

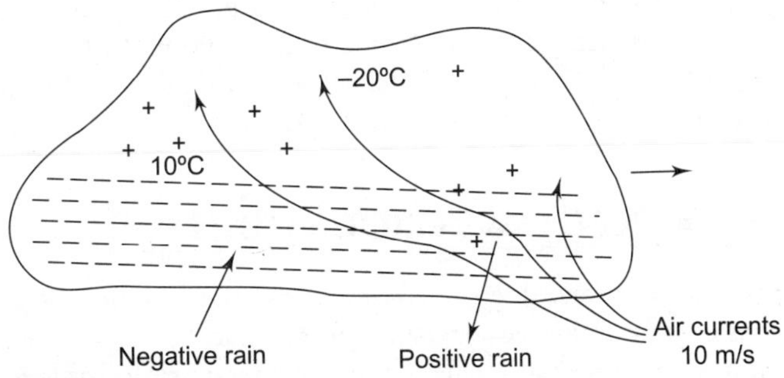

Fig. 13.37 *Charge generation and separation in a thunder cloud as per Simpson's theory*

13.8.3 Mechanism of Lightning Stroke

Lightning is the discharge of the cloud to the ground. The cloud and the ground form two plates of a gigantic capacitor, and the air is the dielectric between them. Since the lower part of the cloud is negatively charged, the earth gets positively charged by induction. Lightning discharge will need the puncture of the air between the cloud and the earth. Because of the high altitude, i.e., lower pressure and moisture, for the breakdown of air the electric field required is only 10 kV/cm.

When the electric field strength becomes more than the breakdown value, a lightning discharge begins. The first discharge travels towards the earth in steps (*stepped leader stroke*) as shown in Fig. 13.38. When near the earth, a much faster and more luminous *return stroke* travels upwards along the initial channel, and several such leaders and return strokes constitute a lightning flash. The ratio of negative to positive strokes is about 5 to 1 in temperature regions. The magnitude of the return stroke can be as high as 240 kA (average value of the order of 25 kA). A second stroke to the earth takes place in the ionised path formed by the original stroke after a very short interval from the initial stroke. Again a return stroke follows. Normally, several such subsequent strokes (called *dart leaders*) take place. The complete sequence is known as a multiple stroke lightning flash and a typical representation of the strokes at various time intervals is shown in Fig. 13.38. Usually, only the large current flowing over the first 50 μs is of significance, and the current-time relationship is generally of the form $i = i_{\max} (e^{-\alpha t} - e^{-\beta t})$ as stated earlier.

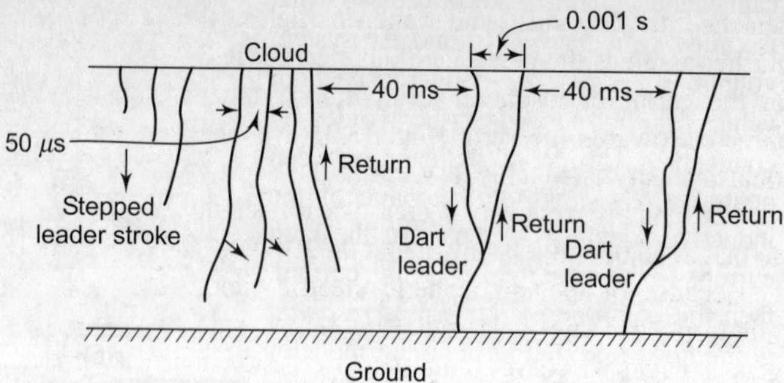

Fig. 13.38 *Sequence of strokes at various time intervals in a multiple lightning stroke*

In conclusion, we can say that thunderstorms appear to follow more or less definite paths as influenced by local terrain, which produces large localised variations in storm and lightning stroke density. Of the several proposed theories of charge formation (only two were discussed here), none explains completely all the factors involved [9]. It is thus clear that though a lot of progress has been made in lightning research, there are still many questions that are left unanswered and these require further investigation.

13.9 ▶ NEUTRAL GROUNDING

From the unbalanced fault analysis, it has been seen that the neutral connections (transformer and generator) considerably influence the fault currents and voltages. Protective relaying and stability analysis are also influenced by neutral grounding. In most modern HV systems, the system neutral is solidly (or effectively) grounded, i.e., connected directly to the ground. Of course the generators are grounded through a resistance to limit the stator fault currents, and also for stability considerations. The advantages of neutral grounding are

1. Voltages to ground are limited to the phase voltages.
2. The high voltages due to arcing faults or transient line to ground faults are eliminated.
3. Sensitive protective relays against line to ground faults can be employed.

The main advantage in operating with an isolated neutral is the possibility of maintaining a supply even with a fault on one line. Also, interference with telephone lines is reduced due to the absence of zero sequence currents.

With normal balanced operation, the neutrals of an ungrounded or isolated system are held at ground voltage because of the system capacitance to earth as in Fig. 13.39(a). The phasor diagram for balanced operation is given in Fig. 13.39(b). For a fault on phase C, the phasor diagram is drawn in Fig. 13.39(c). A charging current thrice that of the per phase value flows. The voltage of healthy phases equals $\sqrt{3}V_{ph}$. The presence of inductance and capacitance in the system leads to what is called *arcing grounds*, and the system voltage may rise to dangerously high values. These voltages can be avoided by connecting a suitable inductor between neutral and ground. If the value of the inductive reactance is such that the fault current I_c balances the charging current, then the grounding is known as *resonant grounding*, and the grounding inductor is known as *ground fault neutraliser* or *Peterson coil*. The reactance of this coil is in the range of 90–110% of the value required to neutralise the capacitive current. The phasor diagram for the resonant grounded system of Fig. 13.40(a) is shown in Fig. 13.40(b).

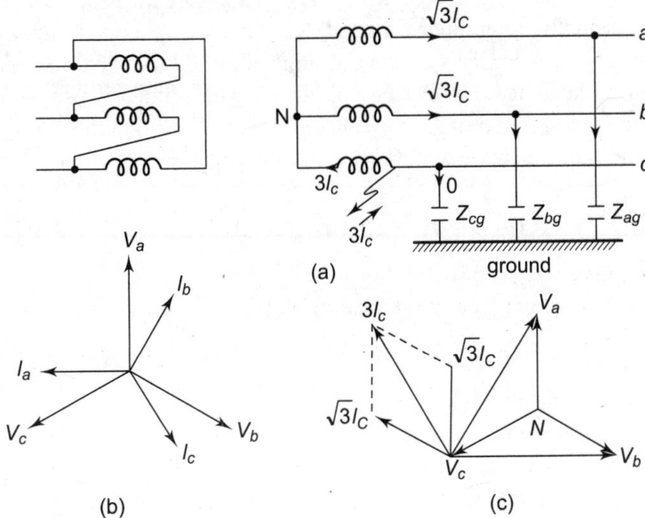

Fig. 13.39 *(a) Isolated neutral system: fault on phase C, (b) Phasor diagram for balanced system, (c) Phasor diagram for fault on phase C*

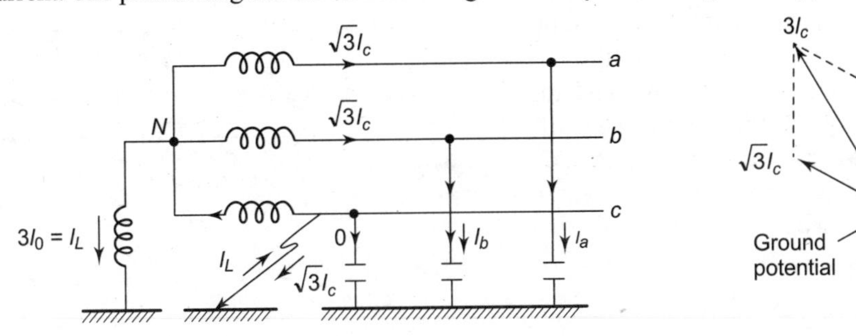

(a) System with Peterson coil; fault on phase C

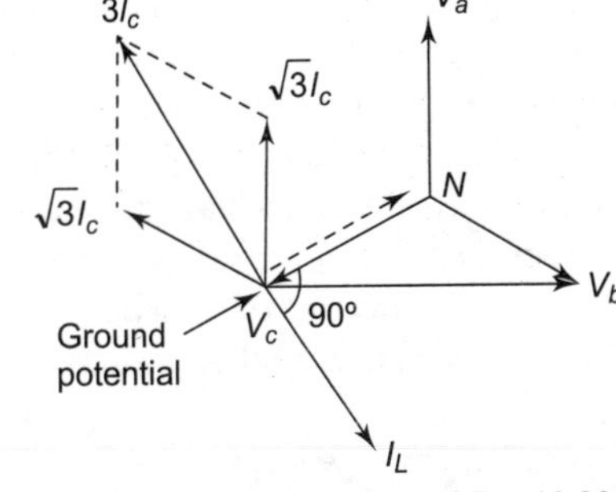

(b) Phasor diagram for the system of Fig. 13.39(a)

Fig. 13.40

If V_{ph} is the line to ground voltage of the system, then voltage of the healthy phases will be $\sqrt{3}V_{ph.}$. If C is the capacitance to ground of each phase, then charging current will be $3V_{ph}\ \omega C$. If L is the inductance of the Peterson coil, then

$$I_L = V_{ph}/\omega L$$

For balance condition,

$$I_L = 3V_{ph}\ \omega C = V_{ph}/\omega L$$

or

$$L = \frac{1}{3\omega^2 C} \tag{13.45}$$

and

$$X_L = \frac{1}{3\omega C} \tag{13.46}$$

This result may also be arrived at by analysing the ground fault with the help of symmetrical components.

Normally, ungrounded neutral systems lead to serious arcing fault voltages if the arc current exceeds the range 5–10 A for the systems operating above 33 kV. Peterson coils should be used for such systems operating with isolated neutrals. Because of the resonant condition, use of Peterson's coil leads to excessive overvoltages (voltage to ground of healthy phases rises to line voltage value) and, therefore, its use is not recommended in modern systems. Most of the systems at normal transmission voltages have grounded neutrals.

13.9.1 Methods of Neutral Grounding

Various methods of neutral grounding are:

1. Solid or effective grounding
2. Resistance grounding
3. Reactance grounding
4. Voltage transformer grounding
5. Zig-zag transformer grounding

Resistance grounding is normally used where the charging current is small, i.e., for low voltage short lines. It facilitates relaying of ground faults. It helps in improving the system stability during ground fault. Whether a system is solidly grounded or reactance grounded depends on the ratio of X_0/X_1. For reactance grounded system $X_0/X_1 > 3.0$, otherwise it is solidly grounded system for $X_0/X_1 < 3.0$. Reactance grounding lies between effective grounding and resonant grounding. This method may be employed for grounding the neutral of synchronous motors and capacitors, and systems having large charging currents.

For delta connection, busbar points, etc., a zig-zag transformer is used for neutral grounding as shown in Fig. 13.41. In the absence of such a transformer, a star-delta transformer can be used without loading the delta side.

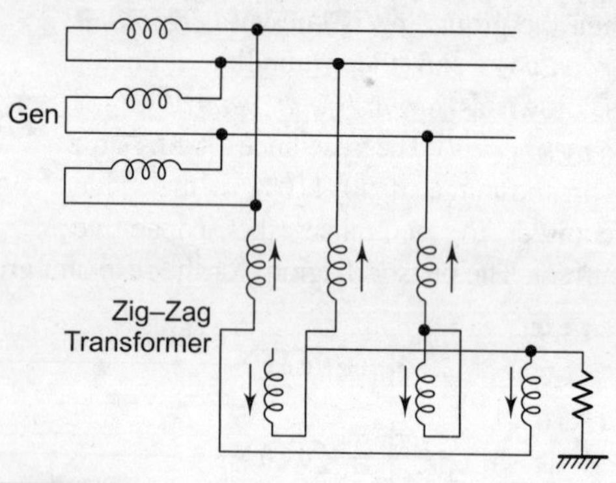

Fig. 13.41 *Zig-zag transformer for neutral grounding*

13.10 ▶ SUMMARY

In this chapter a detailed account on Power System Transients is presented along with insulation coordination, lightning phenomena and neutral grounding.

Problems

13.1 An overhead line, with inductance and capacitance per km of 1.2 mH and 0.9 μF, respectively, is connected in series with an underground cable having inductance and capacitance of 0.16 mH/km and 0.28 μF/km. Calculate the values of transmitted and reflected waves of voltage and current at the junction due to a voltage surge of 110 kV travelling to the junction (i) along the line towards the cable and (ii) along the cable towards the line.

13.2 An overhead line with surge impedance 500 ohm bifurcates into two lines of surge impedance 500 ohm and 50 ohm, respectively. If a surge of 25 kV is incident on the overhead line, determine the magnitudes of voltage and current which enter the bifurcated lines.

13.3 An overhead line is connected to terminal apparatus through a length of single-phase cable, the characteristic impedances being 500 and 25 ohms, respectively. A travelling wave of vertical front and infinite tail of 230 kV magnitude originates in the line and travels towards the junction with the cable. Calculate the energy transmitted into the cable during a period 5 μs after the arrival of the wave at the junction. What voltage is reflected back into the line?

13.4 A DC source of 100 V with negligible resistance is switched 'on' to a lossless line of characteristic impedance $Z_c = 25\ \Omega$ terminated in a resistance of 75 Ω. Plot (i) the receiving-end voltage and (ii) sending end current versus time until $t = 5T$ where T is the time of wave travel on the line. Also find the steady values of the receiving-end voltage and the sending-end current.

13.5 Repeat Problem 13.4, if the receiving-end resistance is reduced to 25/3 Ω.

13.6 Solve Problem 13.4, if a resistance of 45 Ω is in series with the source.

13.7 A unit-step voltage is travelling on a long line of surge impedance Z_1. It reaches the junction with a cable of finite length whose far end is open. The cable has a surge impedance of Z_2, and the time of one-way wave travel on it is T. Draw the Bewley lattice diagram and find from it the value of voltage at the junction at time $4T$.
Given: $Z_1/Z_2 = 9$.

13.8 A DC voltage source of unit voltage is switched on to a lossless transmission line with surge impedance Z_s terminated in the far end by a lumped resistance R; the ratio $R/Z_s = 3$. The line length is 150 km. Draw the Bewley lattice diagram for voltage and current and, therefrom, plot the voltage vs. time at the far end of the line and current vs. time at the sending-end of line.

13.9 In Problem 13.8 plot voltage vs. time and current vs. time at a point one-third the line length from the sending-end.

13.10 A square wave voltage surge of magnitude E_0 and length D is travelling at speed γ on a transmission line of surge impedance Z_s. A capacitor C is connected between line and ground at the midpoint of the line. Derive analytically the expression for the voltage surge that travels along the line beyond the point where the capacitor is connected. Also sketch the voltage waveform.

13.11 A voltage pulse of magnitude E_0 and length D travels on a transmission line of characteristic impedance Z_c at speed γ. In the middle of the line, it meets a series lumped inductance L. Find the expression for the voltage wave as a function of time that will be injected into the line on the other side of the inductance. Also sketch the voltage wave form.

13.12 A unit-step voltage wave is travelling along a line of characteristic impedance Z_c. The line terminates in a shunt inductance L. Derive the expression for the voltage at the line and the inductance junction as a function of time.

13.13 Solve Problem 13.2, if the line terminals in a shunt capacitance C.

Multiple Choice Questions

13.1 Transient phenomenon lasts in a power system for a period ranging from
(a) Few ms to 1 seconds (b) 1 second to 2 seconds
(c) 2 seconds to 3 seconds (d) Greater than 3 seconds

13.2 The main cause of momentary excessive voltages and current are
1. Lightening 2. Switching 3. Short circuit 4. Resonance
Out of these the most common and most severe causes are
(a) 1 and 3 (b) 1 and 2 (c) 4 and 2 (d) 3 and 4

13.3 The reflection of surges at open line ends (transformer ends) leads to voltage build up, which may eventually damage the high voltage equipment.
(a) True (b) False

13.4 A major part of short circuit takes place on exposed overhead lines, due to the insulation failure caused by the surge phenomenon
(a) True (b) False

13.5 Lightening arrester should be located
(a) Near the circuit breaker (b) Away from the circuit breaker
(c) Near the transformer (d) Away from the transformer

13.6 In a power system lightening arresters are used to protect the electrical equipment against
(a) Power frequency of overvoltages (b) Direct strokes of lightening
(c) Overcurrent due to lightening stroke (d) Overvoltages due to indirect lightening stroke

13.7 In an Extra High Voltage overhead transmission line earth wire is provided to protect the line against
(a) Switching surge (b) Lightening surge (c) Corona effect (d) Ensure fault voltages

13.8 During among faults in a power system severe overvoltages are produced with neutral
(a) Solidly earthed (b) Isolated
(c) Earthed through an inductive coil (d) Earthed through a low resistance

13.9 Consider the following statement about ground wires
1. Ground wire helps to increase the effective capacitance between the line conductor and ground
2. It shields the main conductor against direct strokes
3. It is placed higher than the main conductors and supported on the same tower
4. It helps to reduce the risk of back flashover in case of direct strokes

(a) 1 and 2 are correct (b) 2 and 3 are correct
(c) 1, 2 and 4 are correct (d) 1, 2, 3, 4 are correct

13.10 Switching over voltages may be caused by the
1. Sustained earth fault on phase conductors
2. Energisation or reclosure of long lines
3. Load Rejection at the receiving-end
4. Fault initiation and

(a) 1 and 2 (b) 2 and 3 (c) 1, 2 and 3 (d) 1, 2, 3 and 4

13.11 A short length of cable is connected between dead-end tower and sub-station at the end of a transmission line. Which of the following will decrease, when voltage wave is entering from overhead line to cable?
1. Velocity of propagation of voltage wave
2. Steepness of voltage wave
3. Magnitude of voltage wave

Select the correct answer using the codes given below
(a) 1 and 2 (b) 2 and 3 (c) 3 and 1 (d) 1, 2 and 3

13.12 Lightning is a huge spark caused by electric discharge taking place between
(a) Clouds (b) Within the same cloud
(c) Cloud and earth (d) Any of the above

13.13 A short length of cable between the dead end tower and the power transformer
(a) Always reduces the steepness of the incident wave
(b) Reduces the steepness of the wave under certain conditions only
(c) It does not change the steepness
(d) None of the above

13.14 The coefficient of reflection for current for an open ended line is
(a) 1.0 (b) 0.5 (c) –1.0 (d) Zero

13.15 The coefficient of reflection of voltage for a short-circuited line is
(a) 1.0 (b) –1.0 (c) Zero (d) 2.0

13.16 The protection against direct lightning strokes and high voltage steep waves is provided by
(a) Ground wires (b) Lightning arresters
(c) Lightning arresters and ground wires (d) Earthing of neutral

13.17 An overhead line with a surge impedance of 400 Ω is connected to a transformer by a short length of cable of surge impedance 100 Ω. If a rectangular surge wave of 40 kV travels along the line towards the cable, then the voltage of the wave traveling from the junction of the overhead line through the cable towards the transformer would be
(a) 16 kV (b) 32 kV (c) 30 kV (d) 36 kV

13.18 If a traveling-wave travels along a loss-free overhead line does not result in any reflection after it has reached the far end, then the far end of the line is
(a) Open circuited
(b) Short circuited
(c) Terminated into a resistance equal to surge impedance of the line
(d) Terminated into a capacitor

13.19 A traveling wave 400/1/50 means crest value of
(a) 400 V with rise time 1 μs and fall time 50 μs
(b) 400 kV with rise time 1 s and fall time 50 s
(c) 400 kV with rise time 1 μs and fall time 50 μs
(d) 400 V with rise time 1 μs and fall time 50 μs

13.20 Main cause of momentary excessive voltages and current are
1. Lightning 2. Switching
3. Short circuit 4. Resonance
Out of these the most common and most severe causes are
(a) 1 and 3 (b) 1 and 2 (c) 4 and 2 (d) 3 and 4

13.21 Characteristic impedance of transmission line depends upon
(a) Shape of the conductor
(b) Conductivity of the conductor material
(c) Geometrical configuration of the conductor
(d) None of the above

13.22 In case the characteristic impedance of a transmission line is equal to the load impedance
(a) The system will resonate badly
(b) All the energy sent will be absorbed by the load
(c) All the energy sent will pass to the earth
(d) All the energy will be lost in transmission line as transmission losses

13.23 Characteristic impedance of an overhead transmission line is usually in the range of
(a) 100 to 200 Ω (b) 200 to 300 Ω (c) 0 to 100 Ω (d) 400 to 500 Ω

13.24 Surge impedance of a transformer is in the range of
(a) 80 to 100 Ω (b) 400 to 500 Ω (c) 1000 to 2000 Ω (d) None of the above

13.25 The receiving-end voltage of a transmission line will be greater than sending-end voltage if the load is
(a) Greater than surge impedance loading
(b) Less than surge impedance loading
(c) Equal to surge impedance loading
(d) Insufficient data

13.26 The Surge impedance of 400 km long overhead transmission line is 400 Ω. For 200 km length of the same line the surge impedance will be
(a) 200 Ω (b) 800 Ω (c) 400 Ω (d) 100 Ω

13.27 The transmission capacity of a line at 50 Hz as compared to that at 60 Hz is
(a) Lower (b) Higher (c) Same (d) Insufficient data

13.28 When the load on a transmission line is equal to the surge impedance loading
(a) Receiving-end voltage is less than sending-end voltage
(b) Sending-end voltage is less than receiving-end voltage
(c) Receiving-end voltage is equal to the sending-end voltage
(d) None of the above

13.29 Which of the following factors should be considered in the design of transmission lines against lightning with ground wire?
(a) Mechanical strength of ground wire
(b) Clearance between the line conductor and ground wire
(c) Clearance between line conductor and earth
(d) All of the above

13.30 Protection of rotating machines against lightning surges is carried out by
(a) Lightning arresters
(b) Capacitor
(c) Lightning arresters and capacitor both
(d) Lightning conductor in arresters

References

Books

1. L.V. Bewley, *Travelling Waves on Transmission Systems*, Dover Books, New York, 1963 (Reprint of 1951 edn).
2. J.P. Bickford, N. Mullineux, and J.R. Reed, *Computation of Power System Transients*, IEE Monograph, 1976.
3. A. Greenwood, *Electrical Transients in Power Systems*, Wiley Interscience, New York, 1971.
4. H.A. Peterson, *Transients in Power Systems*, Dover Books, New York, 1966 (Reprint of 1951 edn).
5. E.O. Taylor (Ed.), *Power System Transients*, George Newnes, London, 1954.
6. *Transmission Line Reference Book, 345 kV and above*, Electric Power Research Institute, Palo Alto, Ca., 1975.
7. C.S. Indulkar, D.P. Kothari, and K. Ramlingam, *Power System Transients: A Statistical Approach*, 2nd edn, PHI, New Delhi, 2010.
8. H. Cotton and H. Barber, *The Transmission and Distribution of Electrical Energy*, 3rd edn, BI Publishers, New Delhi, 1970.
9. *Electrical T&D Ref Book*, Westinghouse Elect & Manufacturing Co, East Pittsburgh, Penn, 1964.
10. *EHV Transmission Line Reference Book*, Edison Electric Institute, New York, 1968.
11. A.T. Starr, *Generation, Transmission and Utilization of Electric Power*, Pitman, 1962.
12. E.O. Taylor (Ed), *Power System Transients*, George Newnes Ltd, London, 1954.
13. *Transmission Line Reference Book, 345 kV and Above*, Electric Power Research Institute, Palo Alto, Ca., 1975.

Papers

14. M.H.J. Bollen, E. Styvaktakis, and Irene Yu-Hua Gu, "Categorization and Analysis of Power System Transients", *IEEE Transactions on Power Delivery*, volume: 20, issue: 3, pp: 2298–2306, 2005.
15. A.M. Stankovic and A.T. Saric, "Transient Power System Analysis with Measurement-Based Gray Box and Hybrid Dynamic Equivalents", *IEEE Transactions on Power Systems*, volume: 19, issue: 1, pp: 455–462, 2004.
16. J.A. Martinez and D.W. Durbak, "Parameter Determination for Modeling Systems Transients-Part V: Surge Arresters", *IEEE Transactions on Power Delivery*, volume: 20, issue: 3, pp: 2073–2078, 2005.
17. P. Demetriou, M. Asprou, J. Quiros-Tortos, and E. Kyriakides, "Dynamic IEEE Test Systems for Transient Analysis", *IEEE Systems Journal*, volume: 11, volume: 4, pp: 2108–2117, 2017.
18. Y. Shin, E.J. Powers, M. Grady, and A. Arapostathis, "Power Quality Indices for Transient Disturbances", *IEEE Transactions on Power Delivery*, volume: 21, issue: 1, pp: 253–261, 2006.
19. W.A. Wilkinson and M.D. Cox, "Discrete Wavelet Analysis of Power System Transients", *IEEE Transactions on Power Systems*, volume: 11, issue: 4, pp: 2038–2044, 1996
20. T. Imai and Y. Watanabe, "Calculation of Traveling Waves on Single-Conductor Cable Circuit with Cross-Bonding", *IEEE Transactions on Power Apparatus and Systems*, PAS, volume: 87, issue: 6, pp: 1507–1514, 1968.
21. S. Sekioka, K. Aiba, T. Miyazaki, and S. Okabe, "Lightning Overvoltages in Low-Voltage Circuit for Various Lightning Striking Points", *IEEE Transactions on Power Delivery*, volume: 25, issue: 4, pp: 3095–3104, 2010.
22. V. Cooray, "Calculating Lightning-Induced Overvoltages in Power Lines. A Comparison of Two Coupling Models", *IEEE Transactions on Electromagnetic Compatibility*, volume: 36, issue: 3, pp: 179–182, 1994.
23. F.H. Silveira, A. De Conti, and S. Visacro, "Lightning Overvoltage due to First Strokes Considering a Realistic Current Representation", *IEEE Transactions on Electromagnetic Compatibility*, volume: 52, issue: 4, pp: 929–935, 2010.
24. S. Okabe and J. Takami, "Occurrence Probability of Lightning Failure Rates at Substations in Consideration of Lightning Stroke Current Waveforms", *IEEE Transactions on Dielectrics and Electrical Insulation*, volume: 18, issue: 1, pp: 221–231, 2011.
25. J. Takami, S. Okabe, and E. Zaima, "Study of Lightning Surge Overvoltages at Substations Due to Direct Lightning Strokes to Phase Conductors", *IEEE Transactions on Power Delivery*, volume: 25, issue: 1, pp: 425–433, 2010.
26. S. Sekioka, K. Mori, N. Fukazu, K. Aiba, and S. Okabe, "Simulation Model for Lightning Overvoltages in Residences Caused by Lightning Strike to the Ground", *IEEE Transactions on Power Delivery*, volume: 25, issue: 2, pp: 970–978, 2010.
27. M.S. Savic, "Medium Voltage Distribution Systems Lightning Performance Estimation", *IEEE Transactions on Power Delivery*, volume: 18, issue: 3, pp: 910–914, 2003.
28. A. Soares, M.A.O. Schroeder, and S. Visacro, "Transient Voltages in Transmission Lines Caused by Direct Lightning Strikes", *IEEE Transactions on Power Delivery*, volume: 20, issue: 2, pp: 1447–1452, 2005.
29. J.A. Martinez and F. Gonzalez-Molina, "Statistical Evaluation of Lightning Overvoltages on Overhead Distribution Lines Using Neural Networks", *IEEE Transactions on Power Delivery*, volume: 20, issue: 3, pp: 2219–2226, 2005.
30. T. Henriksen, B. Gustavsen, G. Balog, and U. Baur, "Maximum Lightning Overvoltage along a Cable Protected by Surge Arresters", *IEEE Transactions on Power Delivery*, volume: 20, issue: 2, pp: 859–866, 2005.

CHAPTER 14

High Voltage DC (HVDC) Transmission

14.1 ▶ INTRODUCTION

Application of electricity originally started with the use of direct current. The first Central Electric Station was installed by Edison in New York in 1882 supplying power at 110 V DC. The invention of transformer and induction motor and the concept of three-phase AC around 1890 initiated the use of AC. The advantages of three-phase AC almost eliminated the use of DC systems except for some special applications in electrolytic processes and adjustable speed motor drives.

Today DC transmission has staged a comeback in the form of HVDC transmission to supplement the HVAC transmission system. The first commercially used HVDC link (20 MW, 100 kV) in the world was built in 1954 between the Mainland of Sweden and the island of Gotland. This was a monopolar, 100 kV, 20 MW cable system making use of sea return.

Since then the technique of power transmission by HVDC has been continuously developing. In 1970, thyristor valves replaced the valves based on the mercury-arc technique. In 1961, an underwater DC link (cross-channel) of 2000 MW was set up between England and France. This was a bipolar, ±100 kV, 160 MW cable system. Since 1972 all new HVDC systems are using thyristors. To date, the biggest HVDC transmission is ITAIPU in Brazil (two bipoles, 6,300 MW and ±300 kV). DC transmission is an effective means to improve system performance. It is mainly used to complement AC systems rather than to displace these. In India, the first HVDC 810 km long distance OH line is Rihand-Delhi (±500 kV, 1500 MW) for bulk power transmission from Rihand/Singrauli complex to Delhi. The largest device rating is now in the range of 5 kV, 3 kA. The highest transmission voltage reached is ±600 kV. At present, the world has over 60 HVDC schemes in operation for a total capacity of more than 66,000 MW and the growth of DC transmission capacity has reached an overage of 2,500 MW/year. HVDC is also used to interconnect systems of different frequency (e.g., the connection between north and south islands in Japan, which have 50 Hz and 60 Hz, respectively).

14.2 ▶ CONVERTOR BASICS

DC transmission requires a convertor at each end of the line. The sending end convertor acts as a rectifier converting AC to DC and the receiving end converter acts as an inverter converting DC to AC. The rectifier is fed from an AC source through a transformer and the inverter feeds AC load through a transformer. As we shall see later, the role of the converter is easily reversed from rectifier to inverter and vice versa, thereby, reversing the flow of DC power on the line.

Modern industrial converters are thyristor based. Some basic understanding of the thyristor converter—its operation and control—is essential at this stage.

14.2.1 Thyristor (Valve)

It is a three-terminal solid-state device whose symbol is shown in Fig. 14.1(a). The three terminals are Anode, Cathode and Gate. When Anode is connected to positive polarity of a source and Cathode to its negative polarity and a short duration positive pulse is applied at the Gate, the current will be conducted from anode to cathode whose magnitude is dependent on the external circuit. If anode is negative and cathode positive, no current can flow irrespective of the gate pulse.

With proper anode and cathode polarities, the conduction is initiated by the gate pulse after which the gate loses control over conduction.

The device will return to nonconducting state after anode to cathode current becomes zero (naturally or otherwise). It can be pulsed (fired) again to start conduction, if the anode–cathode polarities are right. The two-transistor analogy of a thyristor is shown in Fig. 14.1(b) to understand the operation of SCR.

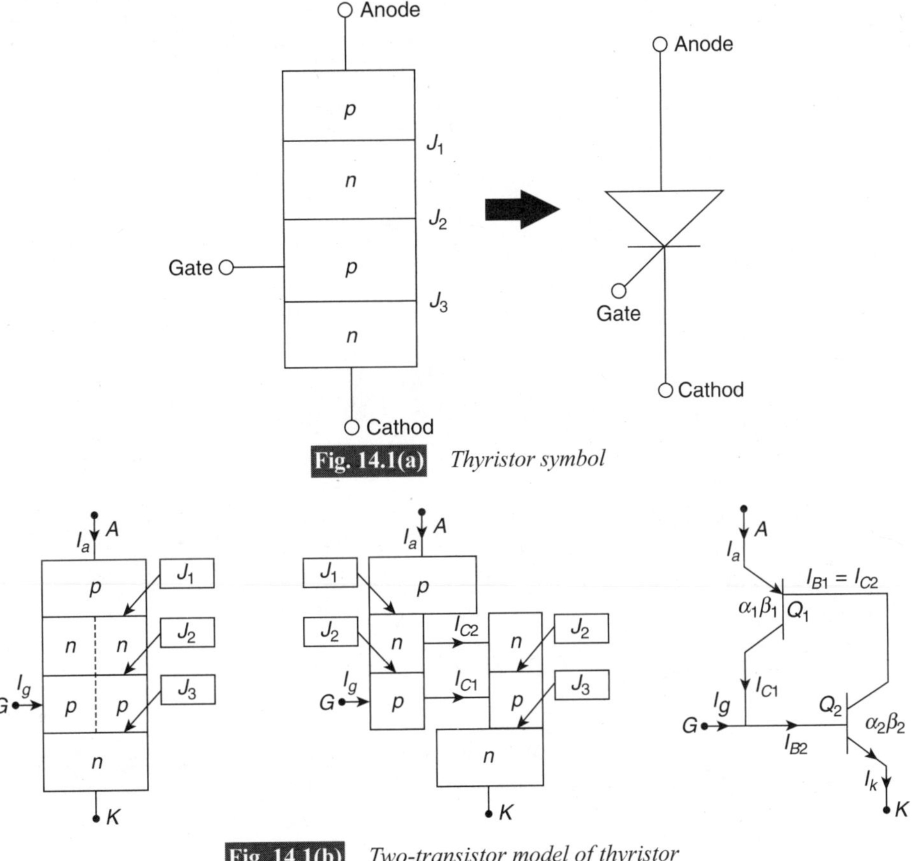

Fig. 14.1(a) *Thyristor symbol*

Fig. 14.1(b) *Two-transistor model of thyristor*

14.2.2 Thyristor Converter

The connection diagram of a thyristor bridge converter is drawn in Fig. 14.2. The six thyristors are connected in three sets of two thyristors each across the DC terminals; in each set (or row) the thyristors have the same conduction direction.

Upon pulsing the gate of Th_1 it begins to conduct and the current which was being conducted by Th_4 shifts (commutes) to Th_1, which then conducts the current for 180°. This process keeps repeating between Th_1 and Th_4 every 180°. The same process occurs between Th_2 and Th_5 displaced by 120° from Th_1 and Th_4 and also between Th_3 and Th_6 displaced another 120°. In all there are 6 pulses per cycle of AC and the pulse rate is 6 times that of AC frequency.

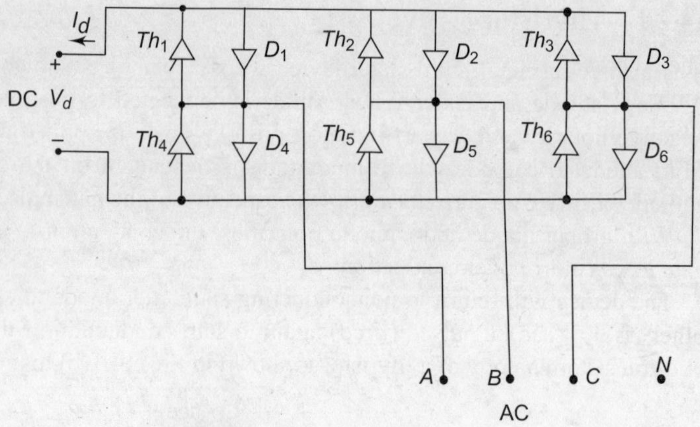

Fig. 14.2 *Thyristor bridge converter*

The basic control over DC voltage magnitude and polarity is achieved by the angle of thyristor firing (α). The waveform of voltage (line) v_{ab} is drawn in Fig. 14.3. This voltage appears across Th_1 and Th_5, where Th_5 is already conducting. Upon firing Th_1 at angle α it will conduct current I_d for 180° (upto $\pi + \alpha$). The average (DC) voltage V_d is positive.

The converter is therefore acting as a *rectifier*. As angle α is increased V_d reduces till at $\alpha = 90°$, $V_d = 0$. Of course from α, the commutation occurs in overlap angle μ and is completed at $\delta = \alpha + \mu$, the extinction angle. This overlap affects (reduces) the value of V_d.

(I_d is flowing out of +ve terminal of V_d)

As angle α is increased beyond 90°, V_d (average voltage) becomes negative while I_d flows in the same direction. The DC power flows into the converter, while AC power flows out of it. The converter is therefore acting as an *inverter*.

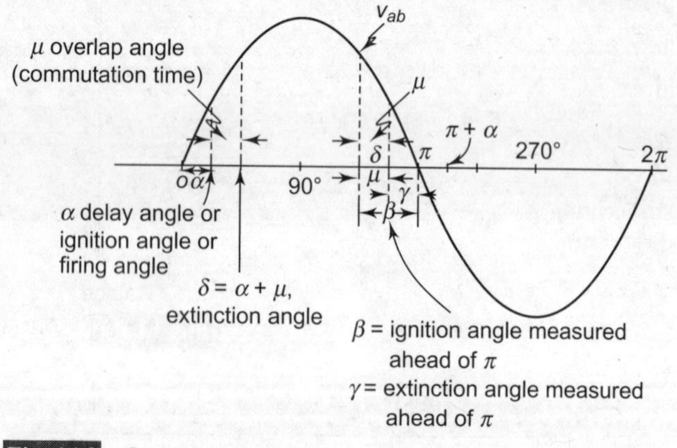

Fig. 14.3 *Important angles for rectifier and inverter operation of a converter*

To summarise:

$$\text{Rectifier } 0 < \alpha < 90°$$
$$\text{Inverter } 90° < \alpha < 180°$$

As from the firing angle onwards, the current flows for 180°, while voltage condition across thyristor changes. This is because the current is out of phase with voltage. So for a part of time, current is conducted by diodes, called free wheeling diodes.

14.2.3 Thyristor Ratings

1. Maximum current carrying capacity.
2. Maximum inverse voltage above which the thyristor breaks down.

At present thyristor are available with current rating of 2.5 kA and voltage rating of 3 kV.

For higher current carrying and higher voltage rating converter, each converter row (branch) is formed by series-parallel combination of thyristors.

The detailed derivation of converter performance equation will be carried out in Section 14.9.

14.2.4 Harmonics

The alternating current waveform injected by the inverter into the AC system has a high harmonic content. The rectifier draws nearly trapezoidal current which contains the fundamental sine wave and also harmonics of order depending upon the number (n) of thyristors (valves). For a six-valve bridge the harmonic order is $6n \pm 1$ i.e., 5, 7, 11, ... 25.

By Fourier series it is found that

$$i = \frac{2\sqrt{3}}{\pi} I_d \left(\cos \omega t + \frac{1}{5} \cos 5\, \omega t - \frac{1}{7} \cos 7\, \omega t - \frac{1}{11} \cos 11\, \omega t\right)$$

The harmonics are affected by the two operating angles of the converters. These are

μ = commutation or overlap angle

α = delay angle

Harmonic magnitude decreases with decrease in μ. However, α for a given μ does cause any significant effect on harmonics. The largest variation in α is between 0 and 10°.

For normal operation α is less than 10° and $-\mu \approx 20°$, resulting in low harmonic content.

During faults, however, α may reach ≈ 90° while μ remains small, resulting in substantial increase in harmonic content.

Pulse Number (p) The number of pulsations (i.e., cycles of ripple) of the direct voltage per cycle of alternating voltage.

Ripple The AC component from DC power supply arising from the conversion processes. It is expressed in peak, peak-to-peak, rms volts, or as % rms of DC voltage. Since HVDC converters have large DC smoothing reactors, approximately 1 H, the resultant DC is practically constant (ripple free). However, the direct voltage on the valve side of the smoothing reactor has ripple.

Ripple Amplitude The maximum value of the instantaneous difference between the average and instantaneous value of a pulsating unidirectional wave.

Smoothing Reactor An inductive reactor between the DC output of the converter and the load. It is used to smooth the ripple in the DC properly, to reduce harmonic voltages and currents in the DC line, and to limit the magnitude of the fault current (reduce the rate of rise of fault current on DC line).

14.3 ► TYPES OF DC LINKS (TRANSMISSION MODES)

The DC links can be classified into the following types:

(a) ***Monopolar Link*** It has only one energised conductor normally of negative polarity and uses ground or sea water as the return path. It may be noted that earth has a much lower resistance to DC as compared to AC. The negative polarity is preferred on overhead lines due to lesser radio interference. Figure 14.4 shows a monopolar link.

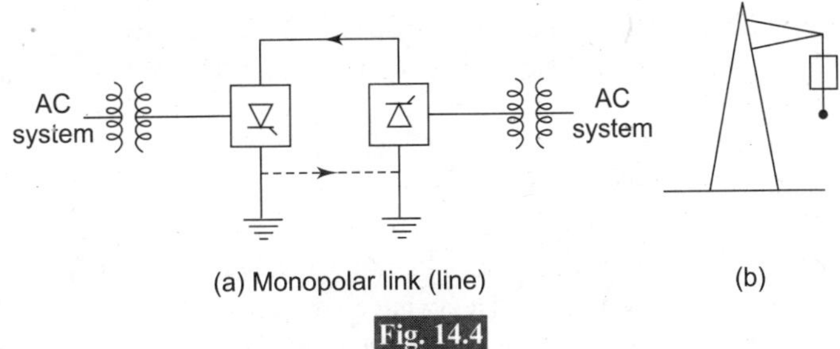

(a) Monopolar link (line) (b)

Fig. 14.4

(b) ***Bipolar Link*** This link has two conductors, one positive and the other negative potential of the same magnitude (e.g., ±650 kV). At each terminal, two converters of equal rated voltages are connected in series on the DC side. The neutral points (i.e., the junctions between converters) are grounded, at one or both ends. If both the neutrals are grounded, the two poles operate independently. If the currents in the two conductors are equal, the ground current is zero. If one conductor has a fault, the other conductor (along with ground return) can supply half the rated load. The rated voltage of bipolar link is given as (say) ±650 kV.

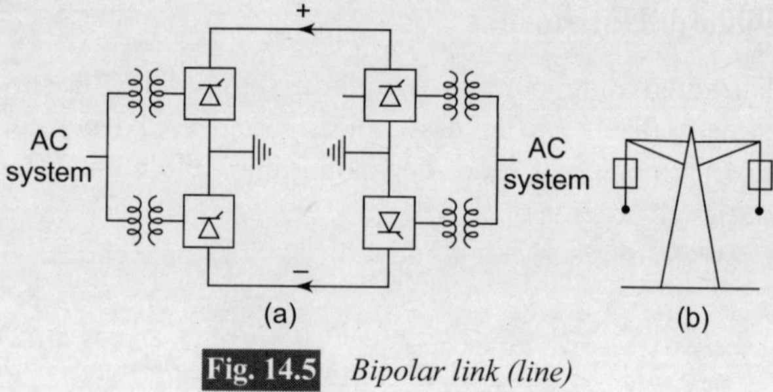

Fig. 14.5 *Bipolar link (line)*

A bipolar transmission has two circuits which are almost independent of each other A bipolar line can be operated as a monopolar line in an emergency.

In some applications continuous current through earth is not permitted, and a bipolar arrangement is the natural solution.

(c) ***Homopolar Link*** A homopolar link shown in Fig. 14.6 has two or more conductors, all having the same polarity (usually negative), as the corona loss and radio interference get reduced, and it always operates with ground as the return. If one of the conductors develops a fault, the converter equipment can be reconnected so that the healthy conductor (with some overload capacity) can supply more than 50% of the rated power.

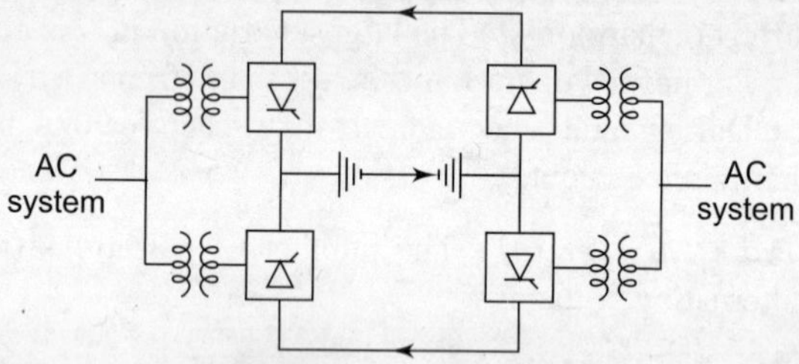

Fig. 14.6 *Homopolar link*

A two-conductor DC line is more reliable than a three-conductor AC line, because in the event of a fault on one conductor, the other conductor can continue to operate with ground return during the fault period. The same is not possible with the AC line.

Furthermore if a two-pole (homopolar) DC line is compared with a double-circuit three-phase AC line, the DC line costs would be about 45% less than the AC line. In general, the cost advantage of the DC line increases at higher voltages.

14.4 ► STRUCTURE OF HVDC TRANSMISSION

HVDC transmission consists of two converter stations which are connected to each other by a DC cable or an overhead DC line. A typical arrangement of main components of an HVDC transmission is shown in Fig. 14.7.

Two series connected 6-pulse converters (12-pulse bridge) consisting of valves and converter transformers are used. The valves convert AC to DC, and the transformers provide a suitable voltage ratio to achieve the desired direct voltage and galvanic separation of the AC and the DC systems. A smoothing reactor in the DC circuit reduces the harmonic currents in the DC line, and possible transient overcurrents. Filters are used to take care of harmonics generated at the conversion. Thus we see that, in an HVDC transmission, power is taken from one point in an AC network, where it is converted to DC in a converter station (rectifier), transmitted to another converter station (inverter) via line or a cable and injected into an AC system.

By varying the firing angle α (point on the voltage wave when the gating pulse is applied and conduction starts), the DC output voltage can be controlled between two limits, +ve and –ve. When α is varied, we get

Maximum DC voltage when $\alpha = 0°$

Rectifier operation when $0 < \alpha < 90°$

Inverter operation when $90° < \alpha < 180°$

While discussing inverter operation, it is common to define extinction (a chance) angle $\gamma = 180° - \alpha$.

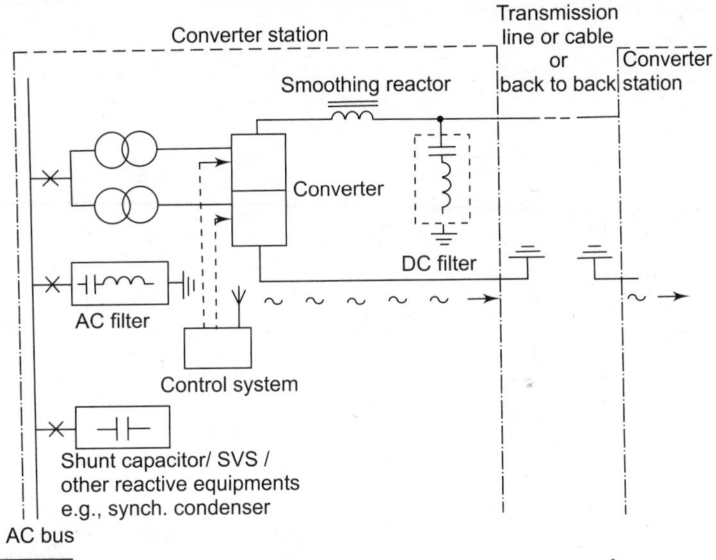

Fig. 14.7 *Main components of an HVDC transmission—a typical arrangement*

14.4.1 Harmonics

The AC/DC converters are sources of harmonics on AC as well as DC sides. The harmful effects of harmonics are the possibility of resonance of the transmission circuit and the high frequency harmonics enhance interference with communication networks. To reduce the harmonic amplitude series and shunt filters are installed on both AC and DC sides as shown in Fig. 14.7. The shunt capacitors of the filter are helpful in supplying reactive power to the converters. A smoothing reactor (choke) is installed on the DC side to limit the harmonics.

14.4.2 Reactive Power Demand

The requirement of reactive power at converter stations is due to

1. The control of HVDC converter (α, γ) which introduces a phase shift between the fundamentals of AC current and voltage.
2. The commutation process, in which the DC current is commutated from one valve to another, and which introduces further phase shift.

In addition to reactive power consumption by converters, converter transformers also consume reactive power. Considering normal values of α (rectifier) or γ (inverter), the reactive power demand usually is in the range of 50–60% of the transmitted active power.

The reactive power may be supplied from

1. AC filters
2. Shunt capacitors (least costly)
3. AC network
4. Static compensators (SVS) (for fast voltage regulation), and
5. Synchronous condensers (if AC network is weak).

While choosing reactive power generation equipment, one must consider both economic and technical aspects.

14.5 ▶ PRINCIPLES OF HVDC CONTROL

One of the most important aspects of HVDC systems is its fast and stable controllability. In DC transmission, the current and power flows from higher voltage (rectifier side) to lower voltage (inverter side) and is proportional to the voltage difference between the two sides as shown in Fig. 14.8. The amount of power transmitted is, therefore, easily controlled by adjusting the two voltages. For reversal of power flow the roles of rectifier and inverter are interchanged by adjusting their firing angles. This automatically causes the reversal of DC polarity.

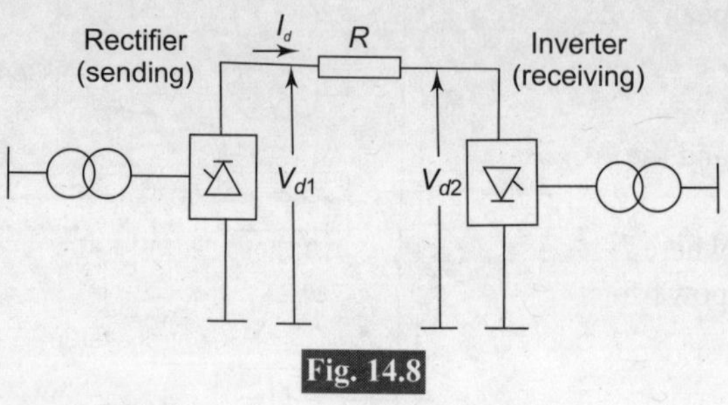

Fig. 14.8

In an HVDC transmission, one of the converter stations, generally the inverter station, is so controlled that the direct voltage of the system is fixed and has a rigid relation to the voltage on the AC side. Tap changers take care of the slow variations on the AC side. The other terminal station (rectifier) adjusts the direct voltage on its terminal so that the current is controlled to the desired transmitted power.

In Fig. 14.8

$$I_d = \frac{V_{d1} - V_{d2}}{R} \tag{14.1}$$

where R is the resistance of link and includes loop transmission resistance (if any), and resistance of smoothing reactors and converter valves. The power received is, therefore, given as

$$P = \left(\frac{V_{d1} - V_{d2}}{R}\right)V_{d2} = I_d V_{d2} \tag{14.2}$$

The rectifier and inverter voltages are given by

$$V_{d1} = n\left(\frac{3\sqrt{2}E_{L-L_r}}{\pi}\cos\alpha - \frac{3X_{cr}}{\pi}.I_d\right) \tag{14.3}$$

$$V_{d2} = n\left(\frac{3\sqrt{2}E_{L-L_i}}{\pi}\cos\gamma - \frac{3X_{ci}}{\pi}I_d\right) \tag{14.4}$$

where n = number of series connected bridges.

E_{L-L_r}, E_{L-L_i} = line to line AC voltages at the rectifier and inverter bridges, respectively

X_{cr}, X_{ci} = commutation reactance at the rectifier and inverter, respectively.

From Eq. (14.2) it is clear that the DC power per pole is controlled by relative control of DC terminal voltages, V_{d1} and V_{d2}. Control on DC, voltage is exercised by the converter control angles α and γ as given by Eqs. (14.3) and (14.4). Normal operating range of control angles is

$$\alpha_{min} = 5°, \alpha_{max} = (15 \pm 3)°, \gamma_{min} = 15°$$

The prime considerations in HVDC transmission are to minimise reactive power requirement at the terminals and to reduce the system losses. For this, DC voltage should be as high as possible and α should be as low as possible.

14.6 ▶ ECONOMIC CONSIDERATIONS

Consider an AC line and a DC line employing the same number of conductors and insulators. Let us compare the power per conductor on the two lines. If in each case the current is limited by temperature rise, the direct current equals the rms alternating current. Assume also that the insulators withstand the same peak voltage to ground in each case. Then the direct voltage is $\sqrt{2}$ times the rms AC voltage

The DC power per conductor is

$$P_{dc} = V_{dc} I_{dc} \tag{14.5}$$

and the AC power per conductor is

$$P_{ac} = V_{ac} I_{ac} \cos \phi \tag{14.6}$$

where I_{dc} and I_{ac} are the currents per conductor, V_{dc} and V_{ac} the conductor-to-ground voltages, and $\cos \phi$ the power factor. Now,

$$\frac{P_{dc}}{P_{ac}} = \frac{V_{dc} I_{dc}}{V_{ac} I_{ac} \cos \phi} = \frac{\sqrt{2}}{\cos \phi} \tag{14.7}$$

taking

$$\cos \phi = 0.945, \; P_{dc}/P_{ac} = 1.5 \tag{14.8}$$

Now compare a three-phase, three-conductor AC line with a bipolar two-conductor DC line. The power capabilities of the respective circuits are

$$P'_{dc} = 2P'_{dc} \text{ and } P'_{ac} = 3P'_{ac} \tag{14.9}$$

$$P'_{dc}/P'_{ac} = \frac{2}{3} \times 1.5 = 1 \tag{14.10}$$

Both lines carry the same power. The DC line, however, is simpler and cheaper, having two conductors instead of three. Further, an overhead line requires only 2/3 as many insulators, and the towers are simpler, cheaper and narrower. A narrower right of way would be required. Both lines have the same power loss per conductor. The percentage loss of the DC line is only two-thirds that of AC line.

If cables are used instead of line, the permissible working stress (voltage per unit thickness of insulation) is higher for DC than for AC, and, further, the power factor for DC is unity and, for AC, considerably lower than that used above. Both changes further favour DC as compared to AC by increasing the ratio of DC power to AC power per conductor. The resulting ratio may be between 5 and 10.

Since the power limit of an overhead AC line is normally fixed by factors other than conductor heating, the ratio of DC power per conductor to AC power per conductor may be as high as 4.

However, the cost of terminal equipment is much more in case of DC (converting stations) than in case of AC (transformer/substations). If we plot the variation of cost of power as a function of transmission distance, it will be as shown in Fig. 14.9. The slope gives cost per unit length of the line and other accessories. The point of intersection P is called a *breakeven* point which shows that if the transmission distance is more than 0_p, is preferable to use DC; otherwise AC should be used.

There is hardly any scope to reduce the cost of AC terminal equipment. But a lot of progress has been made in the development of converting devices, and the breakeven distances are reducing with further development of these devices.

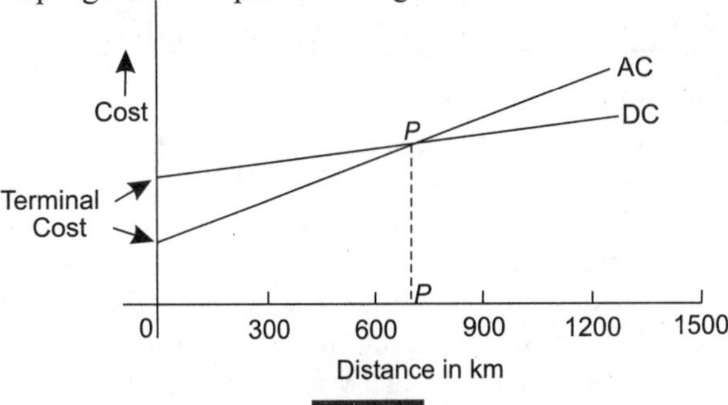

Fig. 14.9

Present day breakeven distance in favour of DC transmission is 7 km for overhead lines. However, the breakeven distance varies with each individual project and should always be checked. The difference installation costs between AC and DC submarine or underground cable is several times as high as the corresponding difference in overhead line costs. This means that the breakeven distance for a cable transmission is much shorter and is of the order of 30–50 km.

14.7 ▶ HVDC APPLICATIONS

The following modes of implanting a DC link in a predominant AC system may be used:

1. ***Interconnection of Systems of the Same Frequency through a Zero Length DC Link (back-to-back connection)*** This does not require any DC transmission line and AC lines terminate on the rectifier and inverter which are connected back-to-back (Fig. 14.10). A typical example is the Eel river scheme in Canada connecting the Québec hydro system with that of New Brunswick. This helps in interconnecting two AC systems without increasing their fault levels. In India a 400 kV, 500 MW Singrauli to Vindhyachal back-to-back link is working at Vindhyachal since 1991 (the breakeven distance concept is meaningless for such schemes).

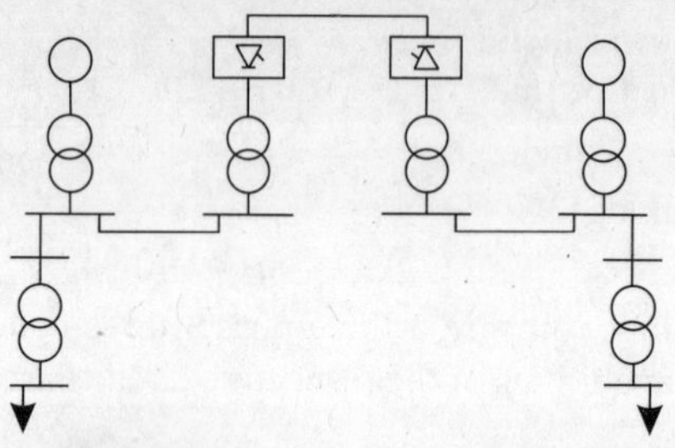

Fig. 14.10 *Back-to-back connection*

2. HVDC links are used to evacuate power from the remote super power stations to the load centres situated several hundred kilometres away. If there are faults in the AC network, this will not trip the units at the power station since the asynchronous DC link insulates the power station from the AC system.

3. ***Interconnection between Power Systems or Pools*** For smooth interchange of power between neighbouring grids irrespective of voltage and frequency fluctuations, such links ensure retention of the tie under the most stringent conditions of the constituent grids.

4. ***High Power Underground (Submarine) Distribution System Feeders*** Here it is found that DC may be cheaper at distances greater than approximately 50 km with a power level of 1000–2000 MW. With AC we need forced cooling due to the higher amount of heat produced. Also there are increased dielectric losses at EHV AC.

5. Stabilising AC system by modulating DC power flow.

14.8 ▶ ADVANTAGES AND DISADVANTAGES OF HVDC SYSTEMS

Advantages

1. These systems are economical for long distance bulk power transmission by overhead lines (reduced tower and cable costs).
2. There is greater power per conductor and simpler line construction.
3. Ground return is possible.
4. There is no charging current and skin effect.
5. The voltage regulation problem is much less serious for DC, since only the IR drop is involved (IX = 0). For the same reason steady-state stability is no longer a major problem.

6. There is easy reversibility and controllability of power flow through a DC link.
7. The DC line is an asynchronous or flexible link (resynchronisation is not required) and it can interconnect two rigid systems operating at different frequencies.
8. For a single DC line between two converter stations, circuit breakers are unnecessary since control of the converters can be used to block current flow during faulted conditions.
9. Each conductor can be operated as an independent circuit.
10. Smaller amount of right of way and narrower towers are required. The distance between two outside conductors of a 400 kV AC line is normally 20 m, whereas the same between a corresponding DC line is roughly half, i.e., 10 m only.
11. There is considerable insulation economy. The peak voltage of the 400 kV AC line is $\sqrt{2} \times 400 = 564$ kV. So the AC line requires more insulation between the tower and conductors, as well as greater clearance above the earth as compared to corresponding 400 kV DC line.
12. There is no technical limit to the distance over which power may be transmitted by lines or underground or undersea cables because of absence of both charging current and stability limitations.
13. Line losses are smaller.
14. It is possible to bring more power into an AC system via a DC link without rising the fault level and circuit breaker ratings.
15. No reactive compensation of DC lines is required.
16. Corona loss, radio interference and audible emissions are less as compared to AC.
17. HVAC line and HVDC link can be used in parallel as an AC–DC system.
18. The contribution of HVDC link to SCC of AC system is considerably less as compared to that of an alternative AC link.
19. DC cables can be worked at higher voltage gradient.
20. Low SC current is required on DC line.
21. Fast control of converters can be used to damp out connected AC system oscillations.

Disadvantages

1. The systems are costly since installation of complicated converters and DC switchgear is expensive.
2. Converters require considerable reactive power.
3. Harmonics are generated which required filters.
4. Converters do not have overload capability.
5. Lack of HVDC circuit breakers hampers multiterminal or network operation. There is no DC device which can perform excellent switching operations and ensure protection. (Simultaneous control at all converters is difficult).
6. There is nothing like DC transformer which can change the voltage level in a simple way. Voltage transformation has to be provided on the AC sides of the system.
7. Reactive power required by the load is to be supplied locally as no reactive power can be transmitted over a DC link.
8. Contamination of insulators is polluted in some areas or along the sea coast. Pollution affects DC more than AC. More frequent cleaning of insulators is required.

14.9 ▶ THREE-PHASE BRIDGE CONVERTER PERFORMANCE

The thyristor based three-phase bridge converter has been discussed in Section 14.2. It has been shown that the converter operates as rectifier for $0 < \alpha < 90°$ and as inverter for $90° < \alpha < 180°$, where α is the firing or delay angle.

The delay angle also controls the voltage magnitude in both type of converter operation. The results derived for converter as rectifier are valid for inverter in the range α as above.

14.10 ▶ RECTIFIER

If the commutation time, i.e., overlap angle (μ) is ignored, the average direct voltage can be found from Fig. 14.2 as

$$V_d = \frac{3\sqrt{3}}{\pi} E_m \cos\alpha \tag{14.11}$$

$$= V_{d0} \cos\alpha \tag{14.12}$$

where $$V_{d0} = \frac{3\sqrt{3}}{\pi} E_m \tag{14.13}$$

E_m = maximum phase to neutral voltage

For $\alpha = 0,\ V_d = V_{d0}$

Equation (14.13) can be written as

$$V_{d0} = \frac{3\sqrt{6}}{\pi} E_{L-N} \text{ (rms)} \tag{14.14}$$

$$= 2.34\ E_{L-N}$$

Also, $$V_{d0} = \frac{3\sqrt{2}}{\pi} E_{L-L} = 1.35\ E_{L-L} \tag{14.15}$$

where

E_{L-N} = rms line-to-neutral alternating voltage

E_{L-L} = rms line-to-line alternating voltage

We can now write $$V_{d0} = \frac{3\sqrt{6}}{\pi} E_{L-N} \cos\alpha \tag{14.16}$$

From Eq. (14.12) it is easy to see that the delay angle α can change the average direct voltage by the factor cos α. Since α can take values from 0 to almost 180°, the average direct voltage can take values from $+V_{d0}$ to $-V_{d0}$. However, the negative direct voltage V_d with positive current I_d causes the power to flow in the opposite direction. Hence, the converter operates as an inverter rather than as a rectifier. It may be noted that since the current can flow from anode to cathode, the direction of current I_d remains the same.

It can be shown that the rms value of the fundamental frequency component of AC is

$$I_{L1} = \frac{\sqrt{6}}{\pi} I_d \tag{14.17}$$

$$= 0.78\ I_d \tag{14.18a}$$

If losses are neglected

$$P_{ac} = P_{dc} \tag{14.18b}$$

where $$P_{ac} = 3E_{L-N} I_{L1} \cos\phi \tag{14.19a}$$

$$P_{dc} = V_d I_d \tag{14.19b}$$

Substituting Eq. (14.17) in Eq. (14.19a),

$$P_{ac} = \frac{3\sqrt{6}}{\pi} E_{L-N}\, I_d \cos\phi \tag{14.20}$$

Substituting Eq. (14.16) into (14.19b)

$$P_{dc} = \frac{3\sqrt{6}}{\pi} E_{L-N} I_d \cos\alpha \tag{14.21}$$

As $P_{ac} = P_{dc}$, we get from Eqs. (14.20) and (14.21) that

$$\cos\phi = \cos\alpha \tag{14.22}$$

or displacement factor (vector pf) = cos (delay angle)

Thus, the converter draws reactive power from the AC system. In the words of Kimbark [3], the rectifier is said to take lagging current from the AC system, and the inverter is said either to deliver leading current to the AC system or draw lagging current from it.

An overlap angle (μ) causes the alternating current in each phase to lag behind its voltage. Hence, the corresponding decrease in direct voltage due to the commutation delay can be written as

$$\Delta V_d = \frac{V_{d0}}{2} [\cos\alpha - \cos(\alpha + \mu)] \tag{14.23}$$

The associated average direct voltage is then expressed as

$$V_d = V_{d0} \cos\alpha - \Delta V_d \tag{14.24}$$

or

$$V_d = \frac{1}{2} V_{d0} [\cos\alpha + \cos l, \delta] \tag{14.25}$$

where extinction angle $\delta = \alpha + \mu$

From the above equations, we get

$$\Delta V_d = \frac{1}{2} V_{d0} (\cos\alpha - \cos\delta) \tag{14.26}$$

and

$$V_d = \frac{1}{2} V_{d0} (\cos\alpha + \cos\delta) \tag{14.27}$$

The overlap angle μ is owing to the fact that the AC supply source has inductance. Therefore, the currents in it cannot change instantaneously. Hence, the current transfer from one phase to another takes a certain time, which is known as the commutation time or overlap time (μ/ω). In normal operation $0° < \mu < 60°$ holds good whereas in the abnormal operation mode $60° < \mu < 120°$. The commutation delay takes place when two phases of the supplying AC source are short circuited. Thus, it can be shown that at the end of the commutation,

$$I_d = I_s [\cos\alpha - \cos\delta] \tag{14.28}$$

but

$$I_s = \frac{\sqrt{3} E_m}{2\omega L_c} \tag{14.29}$$

Substituting Eq. (14.29) into Eq. (14.28),

$$I_d = \frac{\sqrt{3} E_m}{2\omega L_c} [\cos\alpha - \cos\delta] \tag{14.30}$$

where I_s = maximum value of current in line-to-line short circuit on AC source

L_c = series inductance per phase of AC source

Dividing Eq. (14.23) by Eq. (14.28), we get

$$\frac{\Delta V_d}{I_d} = \frac{V_{d0}}{2 I_s} \tag{14.31}$$

$$\therefore \qquad \Delta V_d = \frac{I_d}{2I_s} V_{d0} \tag{14.32}$$

Substituting ΔV_d in Eq. (14.24) gives

$$V_d = V_{d0}\left(\cos\alpha - \frac{I_d}{2I_s}\right)$$

or

$$V_d = V_{d0}\cos\alpha - R_c I_d \tag{14.33}$$

where

R_c = equivalent commutation resistance per phase:

$$= \frac{3}{\pi} X_c \quad \text{or} \quad R_c = \frac{3}{\pi}\omega L_c \tag{14.34}$$

This does not consume any power and represents voltage drop due to commutation.

or

$$R_c = 6fL_c \tag{14.35}$$

Figure 14.11 shows equivalent circuit of a bridge rectifier based on Eq. (14.33). The direct voltage V_d can be controlled by changing the delay angle α or by varying the no-load direct voltage using a transformer tap changer.

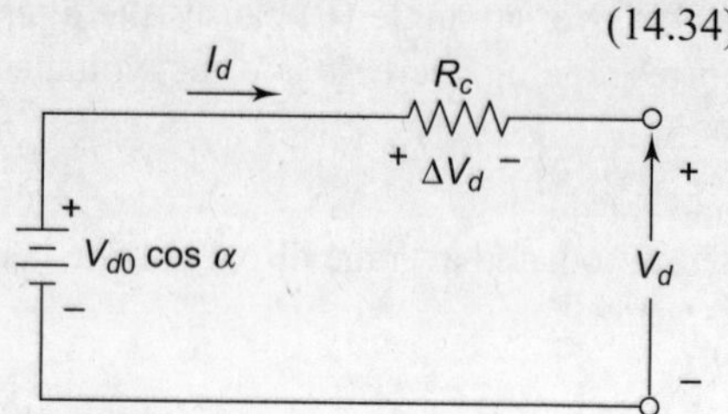

Fig. 14.11 *Equivalent circuit representation of bridge rectifier*

14.11 ► INVERTER

It has already been well explained as to how the converter operation can be changed from rectification to inversion resulting in change in the direction of power flow (DC to AC). The direction of DC current does not change but the DC voltage polarity reverses. It has already been shown that inversion operation results when delay angle α is in the range $90° < \alpha < 180°$.

AC line voltage wave forms and current wave forms for both rectifier and inverter are drawn in Fig. 14.12. Observe that the curvature of the front of a current wave form during commutation is different in rectification and inversion.

References [3] and [7] give the following relationships among various inverter angles are

$\beta = \pi - \alpha$; inverter ignition angle

$\gamma = \pi - \delta$; inverter extinction angle

$u = \delta - \alpha = \beta - \gamma$

To allow for sufficient time for charge carrier to move back, the extinction angle γ should be in the range 1°–10°. In adequate γ can cause *commutation failure*.

The rectifier equations can be employed for describing inverter operation by substituting α and δ by $\pi - \beta$ and $\alpha - \gamma$, respectively. To differentiate the inverter theory from the rectifier theory, it is normal practice to use the subscripts *i* and *r* to identify the inverter and rectifier operations, respectively. Hence, it can be put as

$$I_{di} = I_s(\cos\gamma - \cos\beta) \tag{14.36}$$

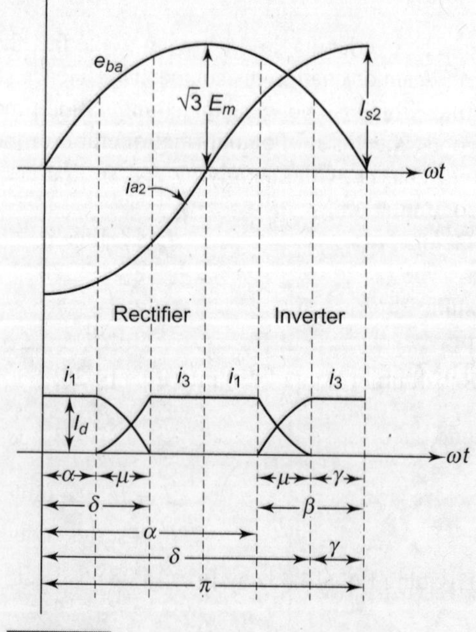

Fig. 14.12 *Relations among angles employed in converter theory [3, 7]*

Substituting the inverter equivalent of Eq. (14.30) into Eq. (14.36)

$$I_{di} = \frac{\sqrt{3}E_m}{2\omega L_c}(\cos\gamma - \cos\beta) \tag{14.37}$$

Correspondingly from Eq. (14.27), the inverter voltage is

$$V_{di} = \frac{1}{2} V_{d0i}(\cos\gamma + \cos\beta) \tag{14.38}$$

Whenever inverter voltage is used along with a rectifier voltage in a given equation, inverter voltage is expressed as negative. When used alone, it is positive.

Also, for inverters with constant-ignition-angle (CIA) control,

$$V_{di} = V_{d0i}\cos\beta + R_c I_d \tag{14.39}$$

or

$$V_{di} = V_{d0i}\cos\beta + \frac{3}{\pi}X_c I_d \tag{14.40}$$

and for inverters with constant-extinction-angle (CEA) control,

$$V_{di} = V_{d0i}\cos\gamma - R_c I_d \tag{14.41}$$

or

$$V_{di} = V_{d0i}\cos\gamma - \frac{3}{\pi}X_c I_d \tag{14.42}$$

It may be noted that it is better to operate inverters with CEA control rather than with CIA control. Figure 14.13 depicts the corresponding equivalent inverter circuits.

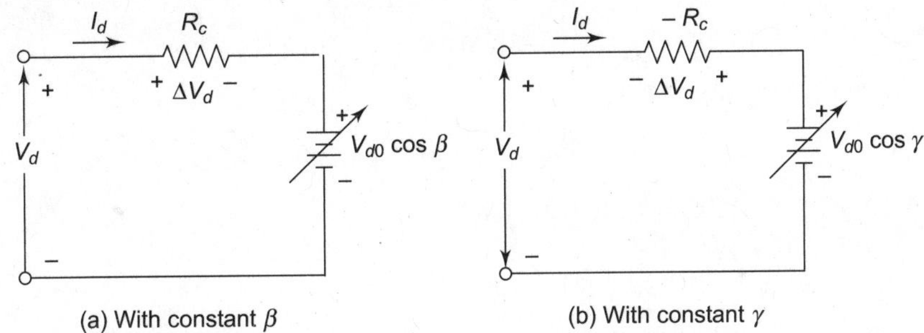

(a) With constant β (b) With constant γ

Fig. 14.13 *Equivalent circuits of inverter (suffix i not used)*

It may be seen that an inverter has a leading power factor, as against rectifier, which has a lagging power factor.

The required additional reactive power by the inverter is provided by the synchronous capacitors or by static shunt capacitors. Also, harmonic filters are required on both AC and DC sides of the converters to prevent the harmonics generated by the rectifier and inverter from entering into the AC and DC systems. The order of harmonics in the direct voltage is given by

$$N = pq \tag{14.43}$$

and the order of harmonics in the alternating current is given by

$$N = pq \pm 1 \tag{14.44}$$

where p = pulse number

q = integer number

Example 14.1 A transformer secondary line voltage to a 3-ϕ bridge converter rectifier is 38 kV (i.e., E_{L-L} = 38 kV).

Calculate the gross voltage O/P, when the overlap and commutation angle is 15° or delay angle is (a) 0°, (b) 15°, (c) 30°, (d) 45°

Solution The average direct voltage V_d is given by

$$V_d = \frac{V_{d0}}{2} \ (\cos\alpha + \cos\delta)\ [\delta = \alpha + \mu]$$

α = delay angle

μ = overlap angle

δ = extinction angle

$$V_{d0} = \frac{3\sqrt{2}}{\pi} \times E_{L-L}$$

$$= \frac{3\sqrt{2}}{\pi} \times 38$$

$$= 51.31 \text{ kV}$$

$$V_d = \frac{V_{d0}}{2} (\cos\alpha + \cos\delta)$$

(a) $\alpha = 0°$, $\delta = 15°$

$$V_{dr} = \frac{81.31}{2} [\cos 0° + \cos 15°]$$

$$V_{dr} = 50.43 \text{ kV}$$

(b) $\alpha = 15°$, $\delta = 30°$

$$V_{dr} = \frac{81.31}{2} [\cos 15° + \cos 30°] = 47 \text{ kV}$$

(c) $\alpha = 30°$, $\delta = 30° + 15° = 45°$

$$V_d = \frac{51.31}{2} [\cos 30° + \cos 45°]$$

$$V_d = 40.35 \text{ kV}$$

(d) $\alpha = 45°$, $\delta = 45° + 15° = 60°$

$$V_{dr} = \frac{51.31}{2} [\cos 45° + \cos 60°]$$

$$V_{dr} = 30.96 \text{ kV}$$

Observe that V_{dr} reduce as α is advanced (increased).

Example 14.2 Assume for a 3-ϕ bridge rectifier the transformer secondary leakage reactance is 0.3 Ω and the line voltage is 440 V if the output current is 220 A. Find the angle of overlap and DC output voltage at a delay angle of 15°?

Solution

$$X_c = 0.3\ \Omega, \quad E_{L-L} = 440 \text{ V}$$

$$I_d = 220 \text{ A}, \quad \alpha = 15°$$

$$V_{d0} = \frac{3\sqrt{2}}{\pi} \quad E_{L-L} = \frac{3\sqrt{2}}{\pi} \times 440 \quad \text{(Eq. (14.20))}$$

$$= 594.2 \text{ V}$$

Equivalent Commutation Resistance $R_c = \dfrac{3X_c}{\pi}$

$$= \frac{3 \times 0.3}{\pi} = 0.286\ \Omega$$

$$I_d = \frac{\sqrt{3}E_m}{2\omega L_c}(\cos\alpha - \cos\delta) \quad \text{Eq. (14.30)}$$

But,

$$V_{d0} = \frac{3\sqrt{3}E_m}{\pi} \text{ and } \omega L_c = \frac{\pi R_c}{3}$$

So,

$$I_d = \frac{V_{d0}}{2R_c}(\cos\alpha - \cos\delta)$$

Substituting the value, we have

$$220 = \frac{594.2}{2 \times 0.286}[\cos 15° - \cos\delta]$$

which gives

$$\cos\delta = 0.7541$$

or

$$\delta = 41.05°$$

Overlap angle $\mu = (\delta - \alpha) = 41.05° - 15°$

or

$$\mu = 26.05°$$

The average direct voltage is given by

$$V_d = \frac{V_{d0}}{2}[\cos\alpha + \cos\delta]; \quad \text{(Eq. (14.27)}$$

or

$$V_d = \frac{594.2}{2}[\cos 15° + \cos 41.05°]$$

We find

$$V_d = 511.02 \text{ V}$$

Example 14.3 A 3-ϕ bridge inverter has commutation reactance of 100 Ω, the current and voltage at the DC side are 950 A and 245 kV, respectively. The AC line voltage is 325 kV. Calculate the extinction angle and the overlap angle.

Solution General converter relationships

$$I_{L1} = \frac{\sqrt{6}}{\pi} I_d;$$

$$V_{d0} = \frac{3\sqrt{2}}{\pi} E_{L-L}$$

$$V_{d0} = \frac{3\sqrt{3}\,E_m}{\pi} = \frac{3\sqrt{2}\,E_{L-L}}{\pi}; \quad \text{Eq. (14.13)}$$

Given:

$$X_{Ci} = 100 \ \Omega$$
$$V_{di} = 245 \text{ kV}$$
$$I_{di} = 950 \text{ A}$$
$$V_{Li} = 325 \text{ kV}$$

For the inverter

$$V_{d0i} = \frac{3\sqrt{2}\,E_{(L-L_i)}}{\pi}$$

$$= \frac{3\sqrt{2}}{\pi} \times 325 = 438.90 \text{ kV}$$

From the equivalent circuit of Fig. 14.8(b)

$$V_{di} = V_{d0i}\cos\gamma - RC_i I_{di}$$

$$245 \times 10^3 = 438.90 \times 10^3 \cos\gamma - \frac{3}{\pi} \times 100 \times 950 = 438.90 \cos\gamma - 907.8$$

Solving, we get

$$\cos\gamma = 0.7649 \quad \text{or} \quad \gamma = 40.1°$$

From Eq. (14.51)

$$V_{di} = \frac{V_{d0i}}{2}(\cos\beta + \cos\gamma)$$

or

$$V_{di} = \frac{V_{d0i}}{2}(\cos(\gamma + \mu) + \cos\gamma)$$

Substituting values

$$245 \times 10^3 = \frac{438.9 \times 10^3}{2}(\cos(\gamma + \mu) + 0.7649)$$

$$\cos(\gamma + \mu) = 0.3515$$

$$\gamma + \mu = 69.4°$$

$$\therefore \quad \mu = 69.4° - 40.1° = 29.3° \text{ (overlap angle)}$$

$$\therefore \quad \mu = 69.4° - 40.10$$

14.12 ► CIRCUIT BREAKING IN HVDC

It is easy to interrupt AC currents because of their natural zeros. Since DC is a steady unidirectional current it does not have a natural zero and therefore it is difficult to interrupt large DC currents at high voltages. The faults on the DC line or in the converters are cleared by using the control grids of the converter valves to stop the DC temporarily.

In DC breakers the direct current is reduced to zero by some auxiliary means. A vacuum interrupter is used for circuit breaking in HVDC systems. The application of DC breakers is required mainly for fault clearing in MTDC systems. However, even for two terminal DC systems, the DC breakers can be useful in several situations e.g. when the converters feed two parallel DC lines; when parallel connected converters feed the same line.

14.12.1 AC–DC Link

At times it is required to put a DC link in parallel with an existing AC link. Such a scheme is employed to reinforce the AC link and to improve its stability. A DC link has an extremely fast speed of response (of the order of 50 ms) and hence, it can change its transmitted power much more rapidly than (say) a turbine-generator can adjust its output. This feature can be used to improve the stability of an existing AC link. Action can be taken to damp the oscillations within a system but inter area oscillations pose more severe problems and in such cases a DC link offers better solution.

The maximum transmitted power capability of an AC link may be set by its steady state-stability limit or transient stability limit. It can be shown that connecting a DC link in parallel with AC link raises the steady-state and transient stability limits of the AC link. The 3100 MW, 1362 km pacific inter tie in USA is a typical example of this application.

14.12.2 Multi-Terminal DC Links

All large AC power systems are effectively of multi-terminal variety. However, most of the DC links are two-terminal links. There is Kingsnorth-London multi-terminal DC link. A multi-terminal DC network has a number of rectifier and inverter stations. We need of course large DC circuit breakers, as mentioned earlier. A three-terminal HVDC link has been set up in Italy-Corsica-Sardina [8]. In the three-terminal HVDC link, two converters can operate as rectifiers and the third as inverter. It can be reversed also, i.e., 2 inverters and 1 rectifier. Thus there is a greater flexibility of operation.

14.13 ▶ RECENT ADVANCES

The basic element in an HVDC converter is thyristor. Thyristors using about 150 mm diameter wafers have been developed. This has reduced the costs of HVDC projects and increased the reliability. Light triggered thyristors are also being developed. Use of digital systems and microprocessors for control, protection and supervision is popular. Now GTOs are being used in some HVDC projects. Active AC and DC filters are also used for tackling harmonics. Finally advanced fully digital control systems are being used with optical fibres. MOS (metal oxide semiconductor) controlled thyristor or MCT (MOS controlled thyristor) appears to be a better technology [9].

14.13.1 Conversion of Existing AC Lines

The constraints on ROW are forcing some companies to look into the option of converting existing AC circuits to DC in order to increase the power transfer limit.

14.13.2 Recent Indian HVDC Projects

HVDC Bipolar Links in India Recent India has the following six operational HVDC links to provide satisfactory and reliable power supply to industrial areas. Rihand–Dadri, Ballia–Bhiwadi, Chandrapur–Padge, Talcher–Kolar, Mundra–Mohindergarh and Biswanath–Agra links are the major HVDC links operating in India. The first HVDC link commissioned in 1991 in India is Rihand–Dadri link. This link connects the thermal power plant Rihand (Eastern part of the Northern Grid) and Dadri (Western part of the Northern Grid). This link has a line length of about 816 km. Each pole of this link has a continuous electric power carrying capacity of 750 MW with about 10% two hours overload and 33% five seconds overload capability. It provides the reverse power flow capability with a converter transformer rating of 6 × 315 MVA at Rihand Terminal and 6 × 305 MVA at Dadri Terminal.

The next Indian HVDC project Chandrapur–Padge HVDC link is connected between Chandrapur (Central India) and Padge (Mumbai) in 1999. This link transmits 1500 MW power over 752 km and helps in stabilising the Maharashtra grid by increasing power flow on the existing 400 KV lines and minimising total line losses. The Talcher–Kolar HVDC link connecting Talcher (Odisha) with Kolar (Karnataka) was completed in June 2003. This link designed for transmission of 2000 MW continuous rating with inherent short-term overload capacity over 1369 km. It is the longest HVDC link with a converter transformer rating of 6 × 398 MVA.

The 780 km HVDC link connecting Ballia (UP) and Bhiwadi (Rajasthan) started in monopolar mode in March 2010 and bipolar mode in March 2011. During inclement weather conditions it operates at 70–80% DC voltage owing to reverse power flow capability with a converter transformer rating of 8 × 498 MVA on both sides. The Mundra–Mohindergarh link has been the most recently commissioned HVDC link connecting the Western region to the Northern region for over 986 km operating at 1500 MW.

The North East Region–Agra HVDC link is the world's first multi-terminal project at ±800 kV, linking rectifier stations at Biswanath–Chariali and Alipurduar with inverter station at Agra. Multi Terminal HVDC (MTDC) systems require complex actions for their operation and control. India's first multi-terminal link is the North East Region (NER)–Agra HVDC link. The link connects terminal stations at

Biswanath–Chariali (BNC) and Alipurduar (APD) to Agra. This link is the world's first ever ±800 kV system using 12-pulse converters. Power Grid Corporation of India announced that Pole-I of 800kV Agra–Bishwanath Chariali HVDC Line has been completed and power flow has commenced. This project is first 800kV HVDC Transmission Line in the country and world's longest multi-terminal HVDC transmission line with line length of approx. 1,750 km and capacity of 6,000 MW HVDC bipolar line from Bishwanath-Chariali (3,000 MW HVDC Station) in Assam to Agra (6,000 MW HVDC Station) in UP via Alipurduar (3,000 MW) in West Bengal. The comprehensive description of HVDC bipolar links of India is given in Table 14.1.

Table 14.1 HVDC Bipolar Links in India

Sr. No.	*Project Name*	*Connecting Region*	*Commissioned on*	*Power Rating*	*AC Voltage*	*DC Voltage*	*Mode of operation*	*No. of Poles/ Blocks*	*Length of Line*
1	Rihand–Dadri	ER-WR	December 1991	1500 MW	400 KV	500 KV	Bipole	2	816 Km
2	Chandrapur–Padge	CR-WR	1999	1500 MW	400 KV	500 KV	Bipole	2	752 Km
3	Talcher–Kolar	ER-SR	June 2003	2000 MW	400 KV	500 KV	Bipole	2	1369 Km
4	Ballia–Bhiwadi	ER-NR	Pole1: March 2010 Pole 2: March 2011	2500 MW	400 KV	500 KV	Bipole	2	780 Km
5	Mundra–Mohindergarh	WR-NR	2012	1500 MW	400 KV	500 KV	Bipole	2	986 Km
6	Bishwanath–Agra	NER-ER	2015	6000 MW	400 KV	800 KV	Multi-Terminal	2	1728 Km

Back-to-Back HVDC Project in India Back-to-back HVDC stations are those where both the converters are housed in the same building and the length of the DC line is kept as short as possible. There are currently four operational back-to-back projects in India namely, Vidhyanchal Back to Back, Chandrapur Back to Back, Sasaram Back to Back and Gazuwaka Back to Back.

The first commercial Back-to-back HVDC project Vindyanchal commissioned in April 1989 distributes power of 2 × 250 MW and connects Vindhyanchal Super Thermal Power Station to Singrauli Super Thermal Power Station. It has the advantage of bidirectional power flow. The plant achieves the load diversity of Northern and Western region of the Indian Grid using a Converter Transformer of 8 × 156 MVA.

Chandrapur back to back was the second such project, commissioned in 1993 connecting Chandrapur Thermal Power Station to Ramagundum Thermal Power Station. It is coupled with the bidirectional power flow capability. It achieves load diversity of Western and Southern Region of the Indian Grid with a Converter Transformer of 12 × 234 MVA.

Sasaram Back to back was commissioned in September 2002 delivering 500 MW having a Converter Transformer rating of 6 × 234 MVA. It connects Pusali (Eastern Region) to Sasaram (Eastern part of Northern grid). The Block 1 of the Gazuwaka back to back HVDC Project was commissioned in 1999 and Block 2 in March 2005. It connects Jeypore to Gazuwaka Thermal Station with a converter transformer rating of 6 × 234 MVA for block 1 and 6 × 201.2 MVA for block 2. It meets the high demand of southern region using the surplus power available. An overview of projects of HVDC back to back in India is given in Table 14.2.

Table 14.2 Back-to-Back HVDC Project in India

Sr. No.	Project Name	Connecting Region	Commissioned on	Power Rating	AC Voltage	DC Voltage	Mode of operation	No. of Poles/ Blocks
1	Vidhyanchal	WR-NR	April 1989	2 × 250 MW	400 KV	70 KV	Back-to-Back	2
2	Chandrapur	WR-SR	December 1997	2 × 500 MW	400 KV	205 KV	Back-to-Back	2
3	Sasaram	ER-SR	September 2002	1 × 500 MW	400 KV	205 KV	Back-to-Back	2
4	Gazuwaka	ER-SR	March 2005	2 × 500 MW	400 KV	Block 1: 205 KV Block 2: 177 KV	Back-to-Back	2

14.13.3 DC Reactor

A DC reactor is connected in series with each pole of a converter station. Inductance is around 0.4 to 1 H. It is used to

1. prevent consequent commutation failures in the inverter,
2. decrease harmonic voltages and currents in the DC line,
3. decrease ripple factor,
4. limit the current in the rectifier when a short circuit occurs on the line.

The value of the inductance should be such that a resonance of the DC circuit does not occur at power frequency.

14.14 ▶ FUTURE TRENDS

Considerable research and development work is under way to provide a better understanding of the performance of HVDC links to achieve more efficient and economic designs of the thyristor valves and related equipment and to justify the use of alternative AC/DC system configurations.

Future power systems would include a transmission mix of AC and DC. Future controllers would be more and more microprocessor based, which can be modified or upgraded without requiring hardware changes, and without bringing the entire system down. While one controller is in action the duplicate controller is there as a 'hot standby' in case of a sudden need.

In the near future, it is expected that fibre optic system would be used to generate firing signal and the direct light fired thyristor would be employed for HVDC converters. Availability of 100 mm thyristors has eliminated the need of paralleling thyristors as these can handle currents of the order of 4 kA.

Although presently HVDC schemes operate perfectly well without the assistance of DC circuit breakers, it is clear that the prospective extension from point to point to other DC power system configurations can gain versatility and operational flexibility with the use of DC circuit breakers. The lack of current zero presents a difficult problem to the opening of DC circuits.

It is by now clear that HVDC transmission is already a reliable, efficient and cost-effective alternative to HVAC for many applications.

Currently a great deal of effort is being devoted to further research and development in solid-state technology due to which one can hope that HVDC converters and multi-terminal DC (MTDC) systems will play an even greater role in the power systems of the 21st century.

14.15 ▶ SUMMARY

In this chapter HVDC transmission, principles of AC/DC conversion and HVDC control, economic considerations applications, transmission modes, principles and working of converters, merits and demerits of HVDC have been fully explained in considerable details. The chapter ends with future trends and recent advances.

Problems

14.1 Calculate the necessary secondary line voltage of the T/F for a 3-ϕ bridge rectifier to provide a voltage of 110 kV. Assume $\alpha = 25°$ $\mu = 12°$. Calculate the effective reactance X_c if the rectifier is delivering a current $I_d = 750$ A.

14.2 The AC line voltage of a 3-ϕ bridge inverter is 140 kV, the extinction angle is 18° and with an overlap angle of 22°.
(i) Calculate the DC voltage at the inverter, (ii) Calculate the necessary extinction angle to maintain the AC line voltage at 140 kV, when DC voltage drops to 170 kV. Assume overlap angle to remain unchanged.

Multiple Choice Questions

14.1 The first commercially used HVDC link was built in
(a) 2006 (b) 1954 (c) 1886 (d) Yet to be built

14.2 Reactive power to HVDC system may be supplied from
(a) AC filters (b) Shunt capacitors (c) SVS (d) All of the above

14.3 Two AC systems can be connected through a zero length DC link
(a) True (b) False

14.4 Such a connection (Question 14.3) is called
(a) Front to front connection (b) Back-to-back connection
(c) Front to back connection (d) Back to front connection

14.5 Normal value of breakeven distance in DC transmission is around
(a) 70 km (b) 700 km (c) 7000 km (d) Any distance

14.6 HVDC transmission lines are more economical for
(a) Short distance transmission (b) Long distance transmission
(c) Any distance transmission (d) Interconnected systems

14.7 As compared to an HVAC line, the corona and radio interference on a HVDC line are
(a) lower (b) more (c) the same (d) none of the above

14.8 In 12-pulse valve group operation, the most troublesome harmonics on AC side are
(a) 24th and 25th (b) 3rd and 5th (c) 11th and 13th (d) none

14.9 Which one of the following is untrue for HVDC transmission?
(a) Corona loss is much more than an HVAC (b) Back-to-back connection is possible
(c) Distance limitation exists (d) Extra reactor power has to be supplied

14.10 In HVDC converter station equipment using thyristors, it is necessary to use a large number of thyristors in series because
(a) Voltage ratings of thyristors are low
(b) Current ratings of thyristors are low
(c) Thyristors always fail to an internal open circuit
(d) None of the above

14.11 Which among the following is a part of the HVDC link?
(a) Two earth electrodes (b) Converter valves
(c) Bipolar DC line (d) All of these

14.12 At what location are the shunt capacitors installed for voltages above 33 kV and above?
(a) Are located near the motors (b) Are installed in distribution substations
(c) Are located near the generators (d) Both (b) and (c)

14.13 The world's and India's first multi-terminal HVDC Project at ±800 kV system using 12-pulse converters is
(a) Rihand–Dadri HVDC link (b) Chandrapur–Padge HVDC link
(c) Biswanath–Agra HVDC link (d) Talcher–Kolar HVDC link

14.14 The HVDC Bipolar Links in India is
(a) Vidhyanchal link (b) Sasaram link
(c) Gazuwaka link (d) Biswanath link

14.15 The following project is not related to back-to-back HVDC Project of India:
(a) Sasaram back to back (b) Gazuwaka back to back
(c) Biswanath back to back (d) Vidhyanchal back to back

15.16 The back-to-back HVDC project in India is
(a) Mundra back to back (b) Vidhyanchal back to back
(c) Bishwanath back to back (d) Rihand back to back

15.17 The highest power rating of the following HVDC project in India is 6000 MW.
(a) Rihand–Dadri HVDC link (b) Chandrapur–Padge HVDC link
(c) Biswanath–Agra HVDC link (d) Talcher–Kolar HVDC link

15.18 The first commercial back-to-back HVDC project commissioned in April 1989 is
(a) Sasaram back to back (b) Gazuwaka back to back
(c) Vidhyanchal back to back (d) Biswanath back to back

15.19 The first HVDC link commissioned in 1991 in India is
(a) Talcher–Kolar HVDC link (b) Rihand–Dadri link
(c) Chandrapur–Padge HVDC link (d) Biswanath–Agra HVDC link

15.20 The Raigarh–Pugalur ultra-high-voltage direct current (UHVDC) system connects Raigarh in Central India to Pugalur in the southern state of Tamil Nadu. The transmission capacity of the UHVDC system is
(a) 765 kV (b) 800 kV (c) 440 kV (d) 132 kV

References

Books

1. C. Adamson and N.G. Hingorani, *High Voltage Direct Current Power Transmission*, Garraway, London, 1960.
2. J. Arrillaga, *High Voltage Direct Current Transmission*, Peter Peregrinus, London, 1983.
3. E.W. Kimbark, *Direct Current Transmission*, volume: 1, Wiley, New York, 1971.
4. J. Nanda and D.P. Kothari, *Recent Trends in Electric Energy Systems*, Prentice-Hall, New Delhi, 1988.
5. K.R. Padiyar, *HVDC Power Transmission Systems*, 2nd edn, New Age Ltd., New Delhi, 2010.
6. E. Ullmann, *Power Transmission by Direct Current*, Springer-Verlag, Berlin, 1975.
7. T. Gönen, *Electric Power Transmission System Engineering*; *Analysis and Design*, John Wiley, NY, 1988.
8. B.R. Gupta, *Power System Analysis and Design*, S. Chand, New Delhi, 2006.

9. D.P. Kothari and I.J. Nagrath, *Electric Machines*, 4th edn, Tata McGraw-Hill, New Delhi, 2010 (Ch. 12).
10. J. Arrillaga, *et al*, *Computer Modelling of Electrical Power Systems*, John Wiley, NY, 1983.
11. D.P. Kothari and I.J. Nagrath, *Power System Engineering*, 2nd edn, Tata McGraw-Hill, New Delhi, 2008.

Papers

12. R. Li and L. Xu, "A Unidirectional Hybrid HVDC Transmission System Based on Diode Rectifier and Full-bridge MMC", *IEEE Journal of Emerging and Selected Topics in Power Electronics*, Early access, 2021.
13. T.H. Nguyen, D. Lee, and C. Kim, "A Series-Connected Topology of a Diode Rectifier and a Voltage-Source Converter for an HVDC Transmission System", *IEEE Transactions on Power Electronics*, volume: 29, issue: 4, pp: 1579–1584, 2014.
14. S. Li, W. Chen, X. Yin, D. Chen, and Y. Teng, "A Novel Integrated Protection for VSC-HVDC Transmission Line Based on Current Limiting Reactor Power", *IEEE Transactions on Power Delivery*, volume: 35, issue: 1, pp: 226–233, 2020.
15. B. Hu, K. Xie, and H. Tai, "Reliability Evaluation and Weak Component Identification of ±500-kV HVDC Transmission Systems With Double-Circuit Lines on the Same Tower", *IEEE Transactions on Power Delivery*, volume: 33, issue: 4, pp: 1716–1726, 2018.
16. K. Xie, B. Hu, and C. Singh, "Reliability Evaluation of Double 12-Pulse Ultra HVDC Transmission Systems", *IEEE Transactions on Power Delivery*, volume: 31, issue: 1, pp: 210–218, 2016.
17. B. Hu, K. Xie, and H. Tai, "Optimal Reliability Allocation of ±800 kV Ultra HVDC Transmission Systems", *IEEE Transactions on Power Delivery*, volume: 33, issue: 3, pp: 1174–1184, 2018.
18. G. Song, T. Wang, and K. S. T. Hussain, "DC Line Fault Identification Based on Pulse Injection from Hybrid HVDC Breaker", *IEEE Transactions on Power Delivery*, volume: 34, issue: 1, pp: 271–280, 2019.
19. G.N. Bathurst, B.C. Smith, N.R. Watson, and J. Arrillaga, "Modelling of HVDC Transmission Systems in the Harmonic Domain", *IEEE Transactions on Power Delivery*, volume: 14, issue: 3, pp: 1075–1080, 1999.
20. C.M. Franck, "HVDC Circuit Breakers: A Review Identifying Future Research Needs", *IEEE Transactions on Power Delivery*, volume: 26, issue: 2, pp: 998–1007, 2011.

CHAPTER

15 Power System Security

15.1 ▶ INTRODUCTION

In Chapter 7, we have been primarily concerned with the economical operation of a power system. An equally important factor in the operation of a power system is the desire to maintain system security. System security involves practices suitably designed to keep the system operating when components fail. Besides economising on fuel cost and minimising emission of gases (CO, CO_2, NO_x, SO_2), the power system should be operationally 'secure'. An operationally 'secure' power system is one with low probability of system black out (collapse) or equipment damage. If the process of cascading failures continues, the system as a whole or its major parts may completely collapse. This is normally referred to as *system blackout.* All these aspects require security constrained power system optimisation (SCO).

Since security and economy normally have conflicting requirements, it is inappropriate to treat them separately. The final aim of economy is the security function of the utility company. The energy management system (EMS) is to operate the system at minimum cost, with the guaranteed alleviation of emergency conditions. The emergency condition will depend on the severity of violations of operating limits (branch flows and bus voltage limits). The most severe violations result from contingencies. An important part of security study, therefore, moves around the power system's ability to withstand the effects of contingencies. A particular system state is said to be secure only with reference to one or more specific contingency cases, and a given set of quantities monitored for violation. Most power systems are operated in such a way that any single contingency will not leave other components heavily overloaded, so that cascading failures are avoided.

Most of the security related functions deal with static 'snapshots' of the power system. They have to be executed at intervals compatible with the rate of change of system state. This quasi-static approach is, to a large extent, the only practical approach at present, since dynamic analysis and optimisation are considerably more difficult and computationally more time consuming.

System security can be said to comprise three major functions that are carried out in an energy control centre: (i) system monitoring, (ii) contingency analysis, and (iii) corrective action analysis.

System monitoring supplies the power system operators or dispatchers with pertinent up-to-date information on the conditions of the power system on real time basis as load and generation change. Telemetry systems measure, monitor and transmit the data, voltages, currents, current flows and the status of circuit breakers and switches in every substation in a transmission network. Further, other critical and important information such as frequency, generator outputs and transformer tap positions can also be telemetered. Digital computers in a control centre then process the telemetered data and place them in a data base form and inform the operators in case of an overload or out of limit voltage. Important data are also displayed on large size monitors. Alarms or warnings may be given if required.

State estimation (Chapter 14) is normally used in such systems to combine telemetered data to give the best estimate (in statistical sense) of the current system condition or 'state'. Such systems often work with supervisory control systems to help operators control circuit breakers and operate switches and taps remotely. These systems together are called SCADA (supervisory control and data acquisition) systems.

The second major security function is contingency analysis. Modern operation computers have contingency analysis programs stored in them. These foresee possible system troubles (outages) before they occur. They study outage events and alert the operators to any potential overloads or serious voltage violations. For example, the simplest form of contingency analysis can be put together with a standard LF program as studied in Chapter 6, along with procedures to set up the load flow data for each outage to be studied by the LF program. This allows the system operators to locate defensive operating states where no single contingency event will generate overloads and/or voltage violations. This analysis thus evolves operating constraints which may be employed in the ED (economic dispatch) and UC (unit commitment) program. Thus contingency analysis carries out emergency identification and 'what if' simulations.

The third major security function, corrective action analysis, permits the operator to change the operation of the power system if a contingency analysis program predicts a serious problem in the event of the occurrence of a certain outage. Thus this provides preventive and post-contingency control. A simple example of corrective action is the shifting of generation from one station to another. This may result in change in power flows and causing a change in loading on overloaded lines.

These three functions together consist of a very complex set of tools that help in the secure operation of a power system.

15.2 ► SYSTEM STATE CLASSIFICATION

A formal classification of power system security levels was first suggested by DyLiacco [14] and further clarified by Fink and Carlsen [24] in order to define relevant EMS (Energy Management System) functions. Stott et al [16] have also presented a more practical static security level diagram (see Fig. 15.1) by incorporating correctively secure (Level 2) and correctable emergency (Level 4) security levels.

In Fig. 15.1, arrowed lines represent involuntary transitions between Levels 1 and 5 due to contingencies. The removal of violations from Level 4 normally requires EMS directed 'corrective rescheduling' or 'remedial action' bringing the system to Level 3, from where it can return to either Level 1 or 2 by further EMS, directed 'preventive rescheduling' depending upon the desired operational security objectives.

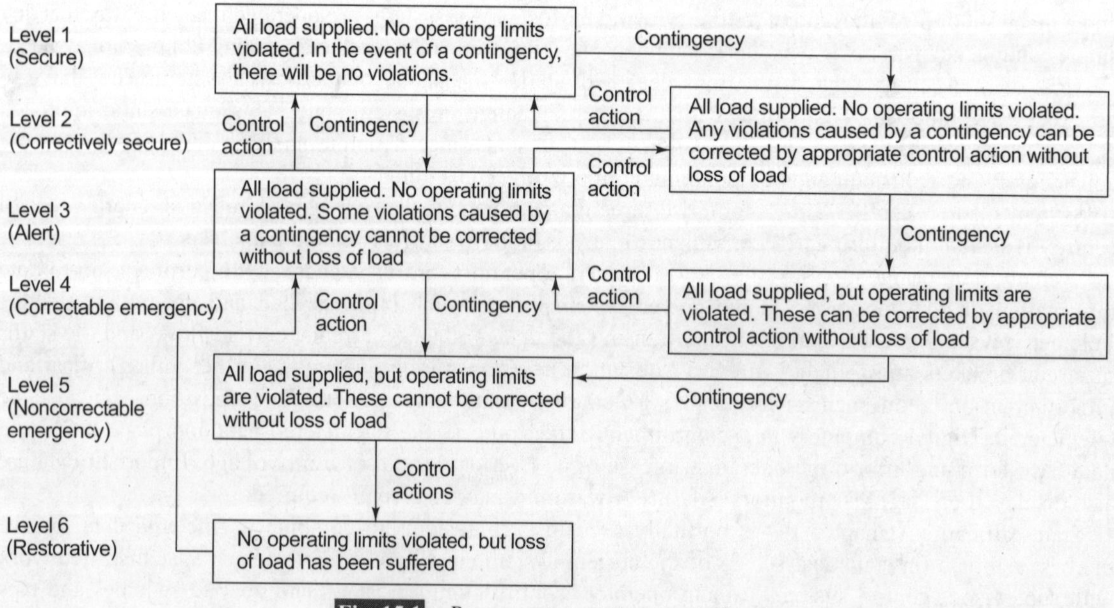

Fig. 15.1 *Power system static security levels*

Levels 1 and 2 represent normal power system operation. Level 1 has the ideal security but is too conservative and costly. The power system survives any of the credible contingencies without relying on any post-contingency corrective action. Level 2 is more economical, but depends on post-contingency corrective rescheduling to alleviate violations without loss of load, within a specified period of time. Post-contingency operating limits might be different from their pre-contingency values.

15.2.1 Power System Operating States

A classification of operating states was first proposed by Fink and Carlsen in 1978 [24]. The system is said to be normal if (i) all the loads are met, (ii) the frequency and bus voltage magnitudes are within the prescribed limits and (iii) no components of power system are overloaded. For more than 99 per cent of the time, a typical power system is found in its normal state. In this state, the frequency and the bus voltages are kept at prescribed values. The 'equality' between generation and demand is a fundamental prerequisite for system 'normalcy' and is indicated by the symbol '*E*' which refers to Equality constraints, i.e., the power balance and flow equations are satisfied and frequency and voltage constancy observed. The second symbol '*I*' indicates that certain 'inequality' must also be observed in the normal state. The symbol '*I*' refers to Inequality constraints and implies that the system is operating within rated limits of the component, i.e., generator and transformer, loads must not exceed the rated values and transmission lines must not be loaded above their thermal or static stability limit. The subscript '*v*' refers to the constraint violation.

If a system suffers from any event, i.e., reduction in the security level (e.g., sudden increase of load), then the system would switch to 'insecure normal' state. The '*E*' and '*I*' would still be satisfied Refs [11, 3, 10] (Elgerd, 1981), (Kundur, 1994), (Momoh, 2001). However, with preventive control strategy, the operator would seek to return the system to its 'normal' state. In the 'insecure normal' state, if some additional disturbance occurs or in 'normal' state a grievous disturbance is encountered (e.g., tripping of tie line or loss of an additional generator), then the system will enter to 'emergency' state. In this state the system remains intact, i.e., '*E*' is still satisfied but '*I*' changes to 'I_v' (e.g., overloads of system components). By means of corrective control (i.e., generator rescheduling) the operator would try to relieve the overload situations. If corrective control is not possible, then emergency control (i.e., generator rescheduling/load shedding) is restored to. If the emergency control fails, then a series of cascading events may lead to the 'cascade (extremis)' state. Typically, the system would breakup into 'islands', each of which would be operating at their own frequencies. Both '*E*' and '*I*' would then change to 'E_v' and 'I_v', respectively, and the system will result in a blackout. A series of resynchronisation controls are required to restart generators and gradually pickup loads. This is a long process and at this stage the system is in the 'restorative' state. The various transitions due to disturbances, as well as various control actions, are shown in Fig. 15.2. In practice, the power system never remains in the normal state due to disturbances, as a result preventive/corrective control actions are required to bring back the system to the normal state.

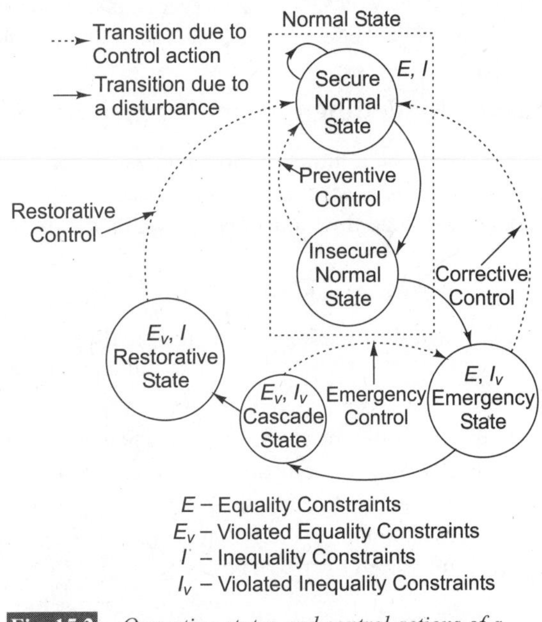

Fig. 15.2 *Operating states and control actions of a power system*

15.3 ▶ SECURITY ANALYSIS

System security can be broken down into two major functions that are carried out in an operations control centre: (i) security assessment and (ii) security control. The former gives the security level of the system operating state. The latter determines the appropriate security constrained scheduling required to optimally attain the target security level.

The security functions in an EMS can be executed in 'real time' and 'study' modes. Real time application functions have a particular need for computing speed and reliability.

The static security level of a power system is characterised by the presence or otherwise of emergency operating conditions (limit violations) in its actual (pre-contingency) or potential (post-contingency) operating states. System security assessment is the process by which any such violations are detected.

System assessment involves two functions (i) system monitoring and (ii) contingency analysis. System monitoring provides the operator of the power system with pertinent up-to-date information on the current conditions of the power system. In its simplest form, this just detects violations in the actual system operating state. Contingency analysis is much more demanding and normally performed in three distinct states, i.e., contingency definition, selection and evaluation. Contingency definition gives the list of contingencies to be processed whose probability of occurrence is high. This list, which is usually large, is in terms of network changes, i.e., branch and/or injection outages. These contingencies are ranked in rough order of severity employing contingency selection algorithms to shorten the list. Limited accuracy results are required, therefore an approximate (linear) system model is utilised for speed. Contingency evaluation is then performed (using AC power flow) on the successive individual cases in decreasing order of severity. The evaluation process is continued up to the point where no post-contingency violations are encountered. Hence, the purpose of contingency analysis is to identify the list of contingencies that, if occur, would create violations in system operating states. They are ranked in order of severity.

The second major security function, security control, allows operating personnel to change the power system operation in the event that a contingency analysis program predicts a serious problem, should a certain outage occur. Normally the security control is achieved through SCO (security constrained optimisation) program.

15.3.1 Modelling for Contingency Analysis

The power system limits of most interest in contingency analysis are those on line flows and bus voltages. Since these are soft limits, limited-accuracy models and solutions are justified. The most fundamental approximate load flow model is the NR model discussed in Chapter 6.

$$\begin{bmatrix} \Delta P \\ \Delta Q \end{bmatrix} = [J] \begin{bmatrix} \Delta \delta \\ \Delta |V| \end{bmatrix} \tag{15.1}$$

The DC load flow model in its incremental version is normally preferred.

$$[\Delta P] = [B'] [\Delta \delta] \tag{15.2}$$

This model assumes voltages to remain constant after contingencies. However, this is not true for weak systems. The utility has to prespecify whether it wants to monitor post-contingency 'steady-state' conditions immediately after the outage (system inertial response) or after the automatic controls* (governor, AGC, ED) have responded. Depending upon this decision, different participation factors are used to allocate the MW generation among the remaining units. The reactive problem tends to be more nonlinear and voltages are also influenced by active power flows.

---

* See Chapter 8 for details about these controls.

FDLF (Chapter 6) is normally the best for this purpose since its Jacobian matrix is constant and single-line outages can be modelled using the matrix inversion lemma.

The model often used is

$$[\Delta Q / |V|] = [B''] [\Delta |V|] \tag{15.3}$$

15.3.2 Contingency Selection

There are two main approaches:

Direct Methods These involve screening and direct ranking of contingency cases. They monitor the appropriate post-contingent quantities (flows, voltages). The severity measure is often a performance index.

Indirect Methods These give the values of the contingency case severity indices for ranking, without calculating the monitored contingent quantities directly.

Simulation of line outage is more complex than a generator outage, since line outage results in a change in system configurations. The inverse matrix modification lemma (IMML) or 'compensation' method is used throughout the contingency analysis field [13]. The IMML helps in calculating the effects of network changes due to contingencies, without reconstructing and refactorising or inverting the base case network matrix. It is also possible to achieve computational economy by getting only local solutions by calculating the inverse elements in the vicinity of the contingencies. The question is how far one should go. Some form of sensitivity analysis may be used.

The problem of studying hundreds of possible outages becomes very difficult to solve if it is desired to present the results quickly so that corrective actions can be taken. One of the simplest ways of obtaining a quick calculation of possible overloads is to use network sensitivity factors. These factors show the approximate change in line flows for changes in generation on the network configuration and are derived from the DC load flow [1]. They are of two types:

1. Generation shift distribution factors
2. Line outage distribution factors

These are discussed in detail in the next section.

In a practical situation when a contingency causing emergency occurs, control action to alleviate limit violations is always taken, if such a capability exists and a protective system [Ref. 1 of Chapter 15] permits time to do so.

The security control function (which is normally achieved by SCO) responds to each insecure contingency case (as obtained by contingency analysis), usually in decreasing order of severity by

1. Rescheduling the precontingency operating state to alleviate the emergency resulting from the contingency, and/or
2. Developing a post-contingency control strategy that will eliminate the emergency, or
3. Taking no action, on the basis that post-contingency emergency is small and/or probability of its occurrence is very low.

A specific security control function, then, is designed to

1. Operate in real time or study mode
2. Schedule active or reactive power controls or both
3. Achieve a defined security level
4. Minimise a defined operational objective.

Only a small proportion of work on optimal power flow (OPF) has taken into account the security constraints. The most successful applications have been to the security constrained MW dispatch OPF sub-problem. The contingency-constrained voltage/var rescheduling problem, as of the writing of this text, still remains to be solved to a satisfactory degree.

The total number of contingency constraints imposed on SCO is enormous. The SCO or contingency constrained OPF problem is solved with or without first optimising with respect to the base case (precontingency) constraints. The general procedure adopted is as follows:

1. Contingency analysis is carried out and cases with violations or near violations are identified.
2. The SCO problem is solved.
3. The rescheduling in Step 1 might have created new violations, and therefore Step 1 should be repeated till no violations exist.

Hence, SCO represents a potentially massive additional computing effort. An excellent comprehensive overview of various available methods is presented by Stott et al [16].

There is still great potential for further improvement in power system security control. Better problem formulations, theory, computer solution methods and implementation techniques are required.

15.4 ► CONTINGENCY ANALYSIS

In the past many widespread blackouts have occurred in interconnected power systems. Therefore, it is necessary to ensure that power systems should be operated most economically such that power is delivered reliably. Reliable operation implies that there is adequate power generation and the same can be transmitted reliably to the loads. Most power systems are designed with enough redundancy so that they can withstand all major failure events. Here we shall study the possible consequences and remedial actions required by two main failure events: line outages and generating unit failures.

To explain the problem briefly, we consider the five-bus system of Reference [10]. The base case load flow results for the example are given in Fig. 15.3 and show a flow of 24.7 MW and 3.6 MVAR on the line from bus 2 to bus 3. Let us assume that at present, we are only interested in the MW loading of the line. Let us examine what will happen if the line from bus 2 to bus 4 were to open*. The resulting line flows and voltages are shown in Fig. 15.4. It may be noted that the flow on the line 2–3 has increased to 37.5 MW and that most of the other line flows are also changed. It may also be noted that bus voltage magnitudes also get affected, particularly at bus 4, the change is almost 2% less from 1.0236 to 1.0068 pu. Suppose the line from bus 2 to bus 5 were to open. Figure 15.5 shows the resulting flows and voltages. Now the maximum change in voltage is at bus 5 which is almost 10% less.

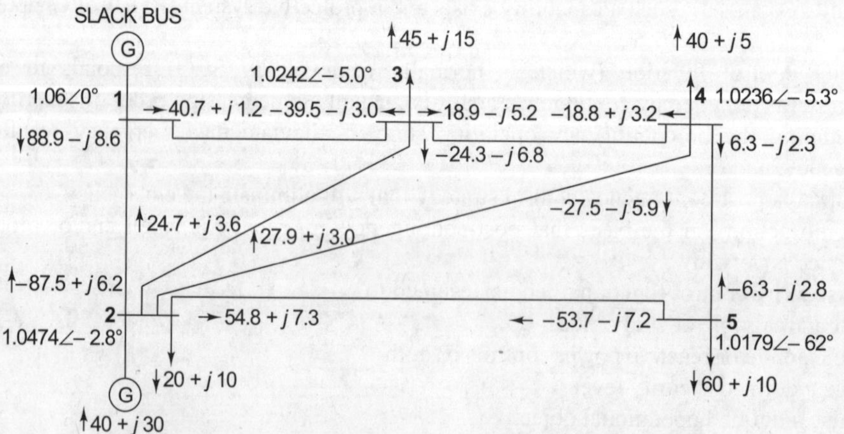

Fig. 15.3 *Base Case AC Line flow for sample 5 bus system*

* Simulation of line outage is more complex than a generator outage, since line outage results in a change in system configurations.

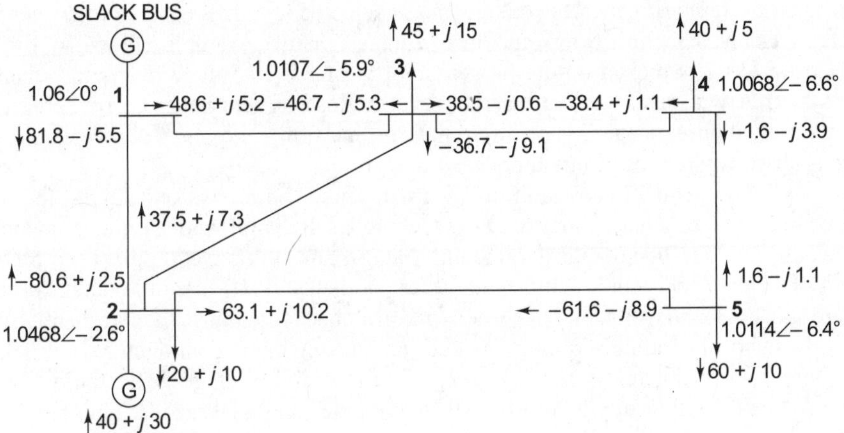

Fig. 15.4 *Post-outage AC Load Flow (Line between 2 and 4 is open)*

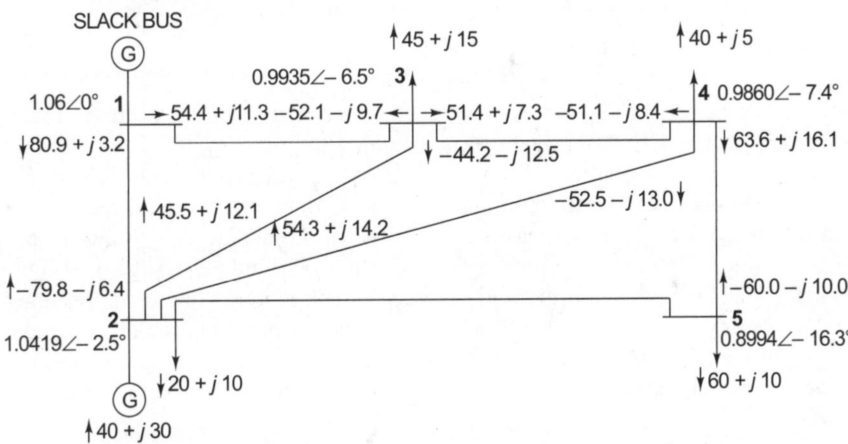

Fig. 15.5 *Post-outage AC Load Flow (Line between 2 and 5 is open)*

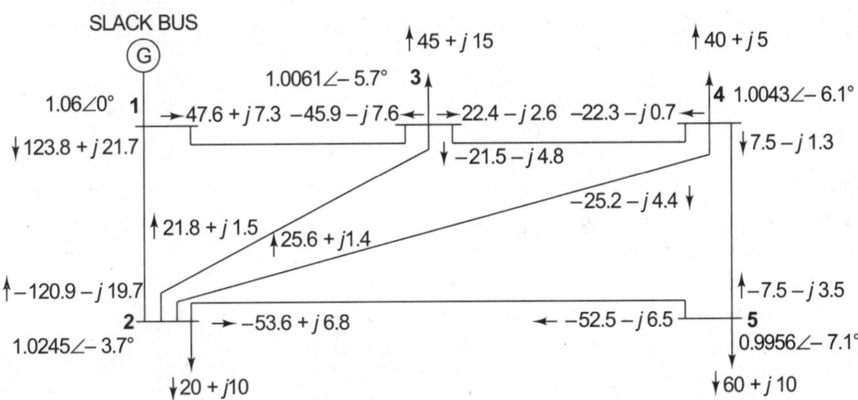

Fig. 15.6 *Post-outage AC Load Flow (Generator 2 outage, lost generation is picked up by generator 1)*

Figure 15.6 is an example of generator outage and is selected to explain the fact that generator outages can also result in changes in line flows and bus voltages. In the example shown in Fig. 15.6 all the generation lost from bus 2 is picked up on the generator at bus 1. Had there been more than 2 generators in the sample system say at bus 3 also, it was possible the loss of generation on bus 2 is made up by an increase in generation at buses 1 and 3. The differences in line flows and bus voltages would show how the lost generation is shared by the remaining units is quite significant.

It is important to know which line or unit outages will render line flows or voltages to cross the limits. To find the effects of outages, contingency analysis techniques are employed. Contingency analysis models single failure events, i.e., one-line outages or one unit outages) or multiple equipment failure events (failure of multiple unit or lines or their combination) one after another until all 'credible outages' are considered. For each outage, all lines and voltages in the network are checked against their respective limits. Figure 15.7 depicts a flow chart illustrating a simple method for carrying out a contingency analysis.

One of the important problems is the selection of 'all credible outages'. Execution time to analyse several thousand outages is typically 1 min based on computer and analytical technology as of 2000. An approximate model such as DC load flow may be used to achieve speedy solution if voltage is also required, then full AC load flow analysis has to be carried out.

15.5 ► SENSITIVITY FACTORS

A security analysis program is run in a load dispatch centre very quickly to help the operators. This can be attempted by carrying out an approximate analysis and using a computer system having multiple processors or vector processors for speedy analysis. The system may be adequately described and an equivalent should be used for neighbours connected through tie-lines. We can eliminate all non-violation cases and run complete exact program for 'critical' cases only. This can be achieved by using techniques such as 'contingency selection' or 'contingency screening', or 'contingency ranking'. Thus, it will be easy to warn the operation staff in advance to enable them to take corrective action if one or more outages will result in serious overloads or any violations. One of the simplest ways to present a quick calculation of possible overloads is to employ network (linear) sensitivity factors. These factors give the approximate change in line flows for changes in generation in the system and can be calculated from the DC load flow. They are mainly of two types:

1. Generation shift factors
2. Line outage distribution factors

Briefly we shall now describe the use of those factors without deriving them. Reference [7] gives their derivation.

The generation shift factors, α_{li} are defined as

$$\alpha_{li} = \frac{\Delta f_l}{\Delta P_{Gi}} \tag{15.4}$$

where

Δf_l = Change in MW power flow on line l when a change in generation, ΔP_{Gi}, takes place at the ith bus.

Here, it is assumed that ΔP_{Gi} is fully compensated by an equal and opposite change in generation at the slack (reference) bus, with all other generators remaining fixed at their original power generations. The factor α_{li} then gives the sensitivity of the lth line flow to a change in generation at ith bus. Let us now study the outage of a large generating unit and assume that all the lost generation (P^0_{Gi}) would be supplied by the slack bus generation. Then,

$$\Delta P_{Gi} = -P^{\circ}_{Gi} \tag{15.5}$$

and the new power flow on each line could be calculated using a precalculated set of 'α' factors as given below.

$$\hat{f}_l = f^{\circ}_l + \alpha_{li}\Delta P_{Gi} \quad \text{for all lines } \forall\, l \tag{15.6}$$

where $\hat{f}_l$ = power flow on lth line after the failure of ith generator

f_l° = power flow on lth line before the failure or precontingency power flow

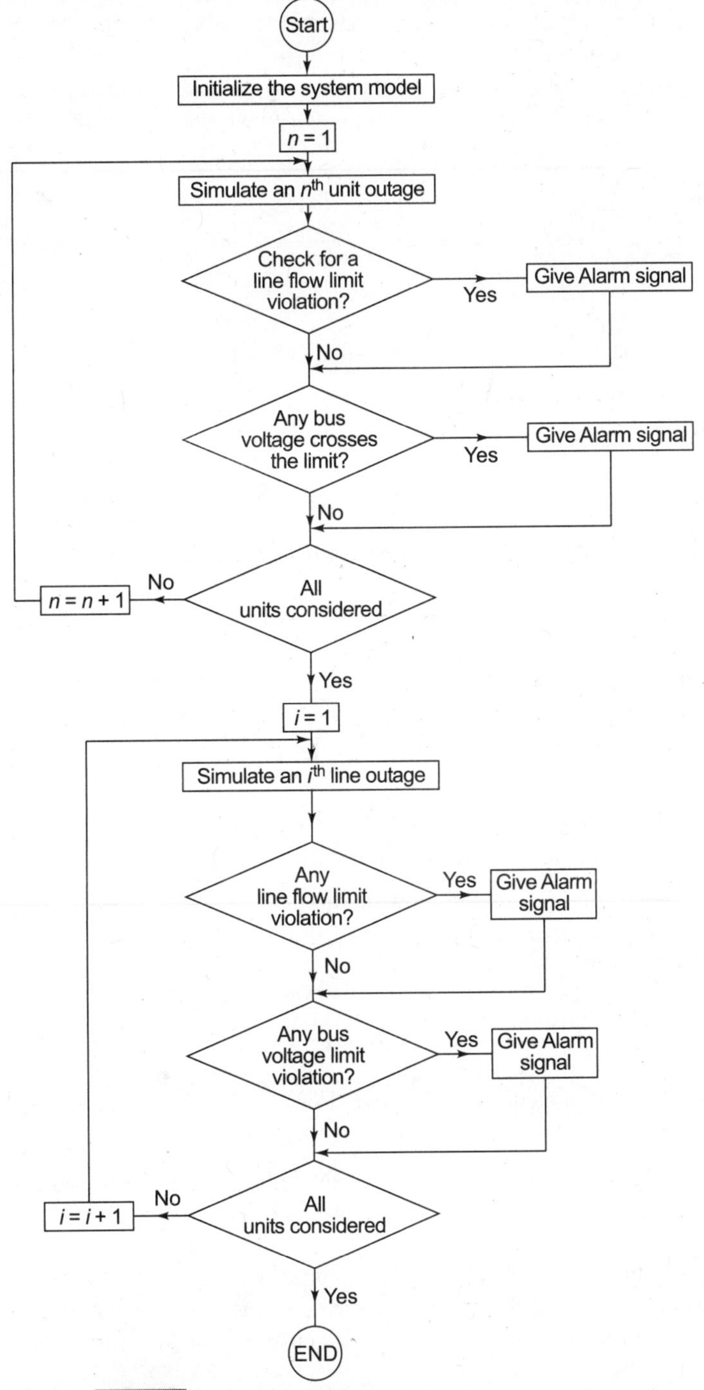

Fig. 15.7 *A simple technique for contingency analysis*

The values of line flows obtained from Eq. (15.6) can be compared to their limits and those violating their limit can be informed to the operator for necessary control action.

The generation shift sensitivity factors are linear estimates of the change in line flow with a change in power at a bus. Thus, the effects of simultaneous changes on a given number of generating buses can be computed using the principle of superposition.

Let us assume that the loss of the ith generator is to be made up by governor action on all generators of the interconnected system and pick up in proportion to their maximum MW ratings. Thus, the proportion of generation pick up from unit k ($k \neq i$) would be

$$\beta_{ki} = \frac{P_{GK_{\max}}}{\sum\limits_{\substack{m \\ m \neq i}} P_{Gm_{\max}}} \tag{15.7}$$

where

$P_{Gm_{\max}}$ = maximum MW rating for mth generator

β_{ki} = proportionality factor for pick up on kth unit when ith unit fails.

Now, for checking the lth line flow, we may write

$$\hat{f}_l = f_l^o + \alpha_{li} \Delta P_{Gi} - \sum_{k \neq i} [\alpha_{lk} \beta_{ki} \Delta P_{Gi}] \tag{15.8}$$

In Eq. (15.8) it is assumed that no unit will violate its maximum limit. For unit limit violation, algorithm can easily be modified.

Similarly, the line outage distribution factors can be used for checking if the line overloads when some of the lines are lost.

The line outage distribution factor is defined as

$$d_{l,i} = \frac{\Delta f_l}{f_i^0} \tag{15.9}$$

where

$d_{l,i}$ = line outage distribution factor when monitoring lth line after an outage of ith line.

Δf_l = change in MW flow on lth line.

f_i^o = precontingency line flow on ith line.

If precontingency line flows on lines l and i, the power flow on line l with line i out can be found out employing 'd' factors.

$$\hat{f}_l = f_l^o + d_{l,i} f_i^o \tag{15.10}$$

Here,

f_l^o and f_i^o = precontingency or preoutage flows on lines l and i respectively

$\hat{f}_l$ = power flow on lth line with ith line out.

Thus one can check quickly by precalculating 'd' factors all the lines for overloading for the outage of a particular line. This can be repeated for the outage of each line one by one and overloads can be found out for corrective action.

It may be noted that a line flow can be positive or negative. Hence, we must check f against $-f_{l\max}$ as well as $f_{l\max}$. Line flows can be found out using telemetry systems or with state estimation techniques. If the network undergoes any significant structural change, the sensitivity factors must be updated.

Example 15.1 Find the generation shift factors and the line outage distribution factors for the five-bus sample network discussed earlier.

Solution Table 15.1 gives the [x] matrix for the five-bus sample system, together with the generation shift distribution factors and the line outage distribution factors are given in Tables 15.2 and 15.3, respectively.

Table 15.1 X Matrix for Five-bus Sample System (Bus 1 as a reference)

0	0	0	0	0
0	0.05057	0.03772	0.04029	0.4714
0	0.03772	0.08914	0.07886	0.05143
0	0.04029	0.07886	0.09514	0.05857
0.	0.04714	0.05143	0.05857	0.13095

Table 15.2 Generation Shift Distribution Factor for Five-bus System

	Bus 1	***Bus 2***
$l = 1$ (line 1-2)	0	–0.8428
$l = 2$ (line 1-3)	0	–0.1572
$l = 3$ (line 2-3)	0	0.0714
$l = 4$ (line 2-4)	0	0.0571
$l = 5$ (line 2-5)	0	0.0286
$l = 6$ (line 3-4)	0	–0.0857
$l = 7$ (line 4-5)	0	–0.0285

Table 15.3 Line Outage Distribution Factors for Five-bus Sample System

	$j = 1$ ***(line 1-2)***	$j = 2$ ***(line 1-3)***	$j = 3$ ***(line 2-3)***	$j = 4$ ***(line 2-4)***	$j = 5$ ***(line 2-5)***	$j = 6$ ***(line 3-4)***	$j = 7$ ***(line 4–5)***
$l = 1$ (line 1-2)	0.0	1.0001	–0.3331	–0.2685	–0.2094	0.3735	0.2091
$l = 2$ (line 1-3)	1.0	0.0	0.3332	0.2686	0.2092	–0.3735	–0.2093
$l = 3$ (line 2-3)	–0.4542	0.4545	0	0.4476	0.3488	–0.6226	–0.3488
$l = 4$ (line 2-4)	–0.3634	0.3636	0.4443	0.0	0.4418	0.6642	–0.4418
$l = 5$ (line 2-5)	–0.1819	0.1818	0.2222	0.2835	0.0	0.3321	1.0
$l = 6$ (line 3-4)	0.5451	–0.5451	–0.6662	0.7161	0.5580	0.0	–0.5580
$l = 7$ (line 4-5)	0.1816	–0.1818	–0.2222	–0.2835	1.0002	–0.3321	0.0

It has been found that if we calculate the line flows by the sensitivity methods, they come out to be reasonably close to the values calculated by the full AC load flows. However, the calculations carried out by sensitivity methods are faster than those made by full AC load flow methods and therefore are used for real time monitoring and control of power systems. However, where reactive power flows are mainly required, a full AC load flow method (NR/FDLF) is preferred for contingency analysis.

The simplest AC security analysis procedure merely needs to run an AC load flow analysis for each possible unit, line and transformer outage. One normally does ranking or shortlisting of most likely bad cases which are likely to result in an overload or voltage limit violation and other cases need not be analysed. Any good *PI* (performance index can be selected) is used for ranking. One such *PI* is

$$PI = \sum_{\forall l} \left(\frac{P_{\text{flow},l}}{P_{l,\max}} \right)^{2n} \tag{15.11}$$

For large *n*, *PI* will be a small number if all line flows are within limit, and will be large if one or more lines are overloaded.

For $n = 1$ exact calculations can be done for *PI*. *PI* table can be ordered from largest value to least. Suitable number of candidates then can be chosen for further analysis [7].

If voltages are to be included, then the following *PI* can be employed.

$$PI = \sum_{\forall l} \left(\frac{P_{\text{flow},l}}{P_{l,\max}} \right)^{2n} + \sum_{\forall i} \left(\frac{\Delta|V_i|}{\Delta|V|_{\max}} \right)^{2m} \tag{15.12}$$

Here, $\Delta|V_i|$ is the difference between the voltage magnitude as obtained at the end of the 1P1Q FDLF algorithm $\Delta|V|_{\max}$ is the value fixed by the utility.

Largest value of *PI* is placed at the top. The security analysis may now be started for the desired number of cases down the ranking list.

Summary and Further Reading: Reference [26] has discussed the concept for screening contingencies. Such contingency selection/screening techniques form the foundation for many realtime computer security analysis algorithms.

Reference [16] gives a broad overview of security assessment and contains an excellent bibliography covering the literature on security assessment up to 1987.

Reference [12] gives an excellent bibliography on voltage stability. This topic is discussed briefly in the next section.

15.6 ▶ POWER SYSTEM VOLTAGE STABILITY

Power transmission capability has traditionally been limited by either rotor angle (synchronous) stability or by thermal loading capabilities. The blackout problem has been linked with transient stability. Luckily this problem is now not that serious because of fast short circuit clearing, powerful excitation systems and other special stability controls. Electric companies are now required to squeeze the maximum possible power through existing networks owing to various constraints in the construction of generation and transmission facilities.

Voltage (load) stability, however, is now a main issue in planning and operating electric power systems and is a factor leading to limit power transfers. Voltage stability is concerned with the ability of a power system to maintain acceptable voltages at all buses in the system under normal conditions and after being subjected to a disturbance. A power system is said to have entered a state of voltage instability when a disturbance results in a progressive and uncontrollable decline in voltage.

Inadequate reactive power support from generators and transmission lines leads to voltage instability or voltage collapse, which has resulted in several major system failures in the world. They are

1. South Florida, USA, system disturbance of 17 May 1985, (transient, 4 sec)
2. French system disturbance of December 19, 1978 and January 12, 1987, (longer term).
3. Swedish system disturbance of December 27, 1983 (longer term, 55 sec)
4. Japanese (Tokyo) system disturbance of July 23, 1987 (longer term, 20 min)
5. NREB grid disturbance in India in 1984 and 1987.
6. Belgium, Aug 4, 1982 (longer term, 4.5 min)
7. Baltimore, Washington DC, USA, 5th July 1990 (longer term, insecure for hours)

Hence, a full understanding of voltage stability phenomena and designing mitigation schemes to prevent voltage instability is of great value to utilities. Consequently over the last ten years, utility engineers, consultants and researchers have thoroughly studies voltage stability.

Voltage stability covers a wide range of phenomena. Because of this, voltage stability means different things to different engineers. Voltage instability and voltage collapse are used somewhat interchangeably by many researchers. Voltage instability or collapse is a faster dynamic process. As opposed to angle stability, the dynamics mainly involves the loads and the means for voltage control. Ref [12] provides a comprehensive list of books, reports, workshops and technical papers related to voltage stability and security.

Definitions [2] A power system at a given operating state is *small-disturbance voltage stable* if, following any small disturbance, voltages near loads are identical or close to the pre-disturbance values. The concept of small-disturbance voltage stability is related to steady-state stability (Chapter 12) and can be analysed using small-signal (linearised) model of the system.

A power system at a given operating state and subject to a given disturbance is *voltage stable* if voltages near loads approach post-disturbance equilibrium values. The concept of voltage stability is related to the transient stability of a power system. The analysis of voltage stability normally requires simulation of the system modelled by nonlinear differential-algebraic equations.

A power system at a given operating state and subject to a given disturbance undergoes *voltage collapse* if post-disturbance equilibrium voltages are below acceptable limits. Voltage collapse may be total (blackout) or partial. The voltage instability and collapse may occur in a time frame of a second. In this case, the term *transient voltage* stability is used. Sometimes, it may take up to tens of minutes in which case the term *long-term voltage stability* is used.

The term *voltage security* means the ability of a system, not only to operate stably, but also to remain stable following any reasonably credible contingency or adverse system change such as load increases [2].

Voltage stability involves dynamics, but load flow based static analysis methods are generally used for quick and approximate analysis.

Figure 15.8 depicts how voltage stability can be classified into transient and long-term time frame [2].

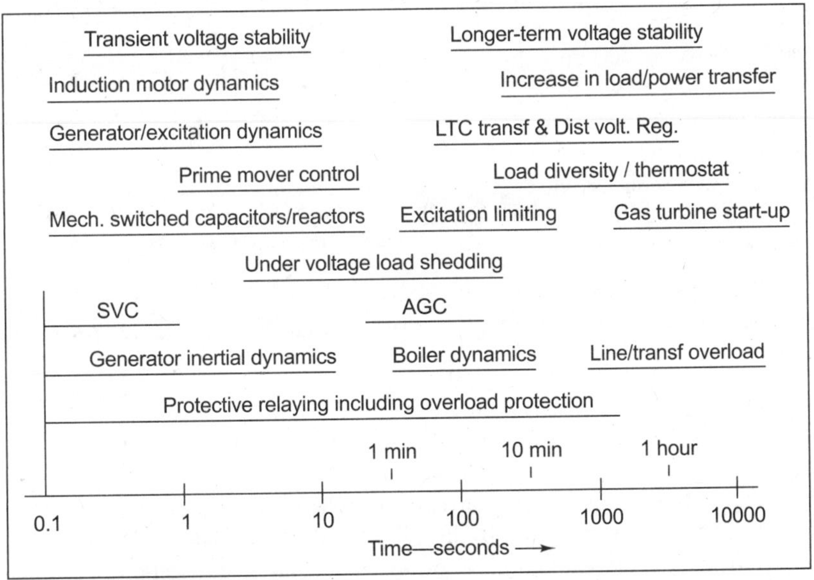

Fig. 15.8 *Voltage stability phenomena and time responses*

Voltage stability problems normally occur in heavily stressed systems. Voltage stability and rotor angle (or synchronous) stability are more or less interlinked. Rotor angle stability, as well as voltage stability, is affected by reactive power control. Voltage stability is concerned with load areas and load characteristics. For rotor angle stability, the main concern is the integration of remote power plants to a large system over long transmission lines. Voltage stability is basically *load stability* and rotor angle stability is basically *generator stability.* In a large inter-connected system, voltage collapse of a load area is possible without loss of synchronism of any generators.

The slower forms of voltage instability are often analysed as steady-state problems. 'Snapshots' in time following an outage or during load buildup are simulated. In addition to post-disturbance load flows, two other load flow based methods are widely used: P-V curves and Q-V curves. PV curves are used for conceptual analysis of voltage stability especially for radial systems.

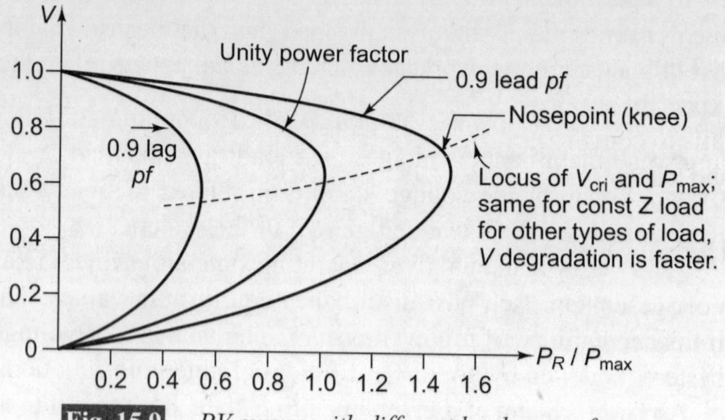

Fig. 15.9 *PV curves with different load power factors*

For carrying out static analysis, PV curves (Fig. 15.9), QV curves (Fig. 15.10), computation of nose point (see Fig. 15.9) and methods to quantify nose point, i.e., proximity indicators are computed. Power flow analysis determines how power system equilibrium point values such as voltages and line flows vary as various system parameters and controls are changed. Two values of load voltage exist for each value of load. The upper one indicates stable voltage whereas lower one is the unacceptable value (multiple load flow). At limiting stage of voltage stability, i.e., at nose point single load flow solution exists. Nearer the nose point, lesser is the stability margin.

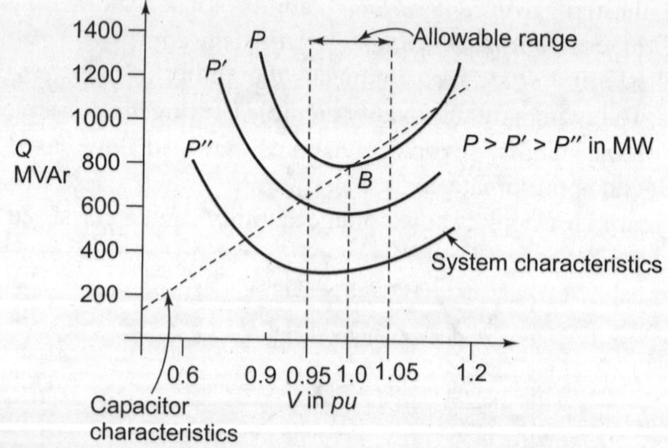

Fig. 15.10 *System and shunt capacitor steady-state Q–V characteristics, capacitor MVAr shown at rated voltage*

15.6.1 Effective Counter Measures to Prevent or Contain Voltage Instability

1. Generator terminal voltage should be raised.
2. Generator transformer tap value may be increased.
3. Q-injection should be carried out at an appropriate location.
4. Load-end OLTC (on-load tap changer) should be suitably used.
5. For under voltage conditions, strategic load shedding should be resorted to.

System reinforcement may be carried out by installing new transmission lines between generation and load centres. Series and shunt compensation may be carried out and SVCs (static var compensation) may be installed. Generation rescheduling and starting-up of gas turbines may be carried out.

Practical aspects of Q-flow problems leading to voltage collapse in EHV lines:

1. For long lines with uncontrolled buses, receiving-end or load voltages increase for light load conditions and decrease for heavy load conditions.
2. For radial transmission lines, if any loss of a line takes place, reactance goes up, I^2X loss increases resulting in increase in voltage drop. This should be suitably compensated by local Q injection. Of course, this involves cost. If there is a shortage of local Q source, then import of Q through long line may have to be resorted to. However, this is not desirable.

Only the operating points above the critical points represent satisfactory operating conditions. At the 'knee' of the V-P curve, the voltage drops rapidly with an increase in load demand. Power-flow solution fails to converge beyond this limit indicating instability. Operation at or near the stability limit is impractical and a satisfactory operating condition is ensured by permitting sufficient 'power margin'.

15.6.2 Voltage Collapse

Voltage collapse is the process by which the sequence of events accompanying voltage instability leads to unacceptable voltage profile in a significant part of the power system. It may be manifested in several different ways. Voltage collapse may be characterised as follows:

1. The initiating event may be due to variety of reasons: Small gradual system changes such as natural increase in system load, or large sudden disturbances such as loss of a generating unit or a heavily loaded line.
2. The crux of the problem is the inability of the system to meet its reactive demands. When transport of reactive power from neighbouring areas is difficult, any change that requires additional reactive power support may eventually lead to voltage collapse.
3. The voltage collapse generally manifests itself as a slow decay of voltage. It is the result of an accumulative process involving the actions and interactions of many devices, controls, and protective systems. The time frame of collapse in such cases would be of the order of several minutes. Voltage collapse is strongly influenced by system conditions and characteristics.
4. Reactive compensation can be made most effective by the judicious choice of a mixture of shunt capacitors, static var system and possibly synchronous condensers.

15.6.3 Methods of Improving Voltage Stability

Voltage stability can be improved by adopting the following means:

1. Enhancing the localised reactive power support (SVC) is more effective and C-banks are more economical. FACTS devices or synchronous condenser may also be used.
2. Compensating the line length reduces net reactance and power flow increases.
3. Additional transmission line may be erected. It also improves reliability.
4. Enhancing excitation of generator, system voltage improves and Q is supplied to the system.
5. HVDC tie may be used between regional grids.
6. By resorting to strategic load shedding, voltage goes up as the reactive burden is reduced.

15.6.4 Future Trends and Challenges

1. Optimal siting of FACTs devices.
2. Better and probabilistic load modelling.
3. Develop techniques and models for study of nonlinear dynamics of large size systems. For example, new methods to obtain network equivalents suitable for voltage stability analysis.
4. Better and fuller representation of AC system in AC-DC system.

5. Post-disturbance MW/MV AR margins should be translated to pre-disturbance operating limits that operators can monitor.
6. Training in voltage stability basis (a training simulator) for control centre and power plant operators should be imparted.

15.7 ▶ SUMMARY

Power system security (including voltage stability) is likely to challenge planners, analysts, researchers and operators for the foreseeable future. As load grows, and as new transmission lines and new generations would be increasingly difficult to build or add, more and more utilities will face the security challenge.

Deregulation and socio-economic trends compounded by technological developments have increased the likelihood of voltage instability.

Luckily many creative persons are working tirelessly to find new methods and innovative solutions to meet this challenge.

Multiple Choice Questions

15.1 An operationally secure power system is one with
(a) Low probability of system blackout (b) Medium probability of system blackout
(c) High probability of system blackout (d) Zero probability of system blackout

15.2 Energy management system ensures
(a) Minimum cost (b) Minimum environmental cost
(c) High security (d) All of the above

15.3 Energy control centre is supposed to perform the following security functions
(a) System monitoring (b) Contingency analysis
(c) Corrective action analysis (d) All of the above

15.4 Contingency analysis provides operating constrains to be employed in
(a) Economic dispatch (b) Unit commitment (c) Emission dispatch (d) (a) and (c)

15.5 Voltage stability problems normally occurs
(a) Heavily stressed system (b) Medium stressed system
(c) Low stressed system (d) None of the above

15.6 Voltage stability is basically
(a) Generator stability (b) Load stability
(c) Transformer stability (d) None of the above

15.7 For prevention/containment of voltage instability are
(a) Generator transformer tap value may be increased
(b) Q injection should be carried out at an appropriate location
(c) Load end OLTC (on-load tap changer) should be suitably used
(d) All of the above

15.8 Voltage stability can be improved
(a) Enhancing the localised reactive power support (SVC)
(b) Compensating line reactance
(c) Enhancing the excitation system of generator
(d) All of the above

15.9 A security analysis program normally uses
(a) DC load flow (b) AC load flow (c) AC–DC load flow (d) Any of the above

15.10 A system blackout means
(a) Total collapse (b) Partial collapse (c) Load shedding (d) System brown out

15.11 A power system is operationally secure means
(a) It is safe from lightning rokes
(b) It is safe against switching surges.
(c) All line flows and load bus voltages are within limit
(d) The operating cost is minimum

15.12 A power system has secure and economic operation implies that
(a) Operating cost is minimum subject emission constraints.
(b) Operating cost is minimum subject to line flow constraints.
(c) Magnitudes of line flows are minimum.
(d) Transmission real power losses are minimum.

15.13 Which one of the indexes will have learnt changes of masking in contingency selection.
(a) $\Sigma\,|f_{ij} / f_{i,\,\text{limit}}|$ (b) $\Sigma\,(f_{ij} / f_{i},\ _{\text{limit}})^2$ (c) $\Sigma\,(f_{ij} / f_{i,\,\text{limit}})^{20}$ (d) $\Sigma\,(f_{i\text{-}j} / f_{i\text{-}j})^{21}$

15.14 A power system operating where by meeting all the loads and equality and inequality constraints are satisfied may have an operating level
(a) Secure (b) Correctively secure
(c) Alert (d) Either (a) or (b) or (c)

15.15 Contingency definition gives the list of component outages
(a) Which includes the contingencies with high probability of occurrence.
(b) Which provides the contingency in decreasing order of severity.
(c) For outage simulation
(d) Any one of the above

15.16 Contingency selection is usually performed using DC power flow model because
(a) Accurate results are required
(b) Limited accuracy results are required
(c) Masking is to be removed
(d) All of the above

15.17 Pre-contingency corrective rescheduling is required for system operation to be
(a) Most economical (b) In security level-I
(c) Incorrective by secure (d) None of the above

15.18 Post-contingency corrective rescheduling is required for
(a) Security level-1 operation (b) Security level-2 operation
(c) System operation in at least leveled (d) None of the above

15.19 Pre-plus post-contingency corrective rescheduling is required at times for
(a) The network corrective capability is limited.
(b) The network operation is required in alert state
(c) The network operation is required in non-corrective emergency
(d) None of the above

15.20 Line outage distribution factors are primarily useful for
(a) System monitoring (b) Contingency definition
(c) Contingency selection (d) Security control.

15.21 Power system security means
(a) Security of power system when load is unbalanced
(b) Practices designed to keep the system operating when the components fail
(c) Secure all the generating stations against the failure
(d) Secure all the transmission lines against the failure

15.22 Three major functions of power system security are
(a) Economical operation, Economical Dispatch, Load scheduling
(b) State Estimation, Economical Dispatch, Generation Scheduling
(c) System Monitoring, Contingency analysis, Security constrained OPF
(d) Both (b) and (c) are correct

15.23 Power system monitoring is usually done by
(a) ETAP (b) SCADA (c) Matlab (d) PSPM

15.24 SCADA means
(a) Supervisory Control and Data Acquisition
(b) System Control and Data Acquisition
(c) Super Control and Data Acquisition
(d) Super Computer and Data Acquisition

15.25 Optimum dispatch is the state that
(a) The power system is in optimum condition
(b) The power system is in prior to any contingency
(c) The power system is in economical mode
(d) Both (a) and (b) are correct

15.26 Secure dispatch is the state of power system where
(a) Contingency outage is always present
(b) Contingency outage is not present
(c) Security is not present
(d) Both (a) and (b) are correct

15.27 The possible way to study thousands of possible outages is
(a) Load flow (b) State estimation
(c) Linear sensitivity factor (d) Numerical approach

15.28 National Load Dispatch Center is run by
(a) Power Grid Corporation of India Limited (PGCIL)
(b) Power System Operation Corporation Limited (POSOCO)
(c) Ministry of Power, Government of India
(d) National Thermal Power Corporation (NTPC)

15.29 National Load Dispatch Centre is situated at
(a) New Delhi (b) Mumbai (c) Kolkata (d) Bangalore

15.30 The worst blackout in recent history occurred in northern India on following two consecutive days.
(a) 30–31 July, 2012 (b) 14–15 October, 2013
(c) 30–31 December, 2013 (d) 12–13 February 2012

References

Books

1. D.P. Kothari and I.J. Nagrath, *Power System Engineering*, 2nd edn, Tata McGraw-Hill, New Delhi, 2008.
2. C.W. Taylor, *Power System Voltage Stability,* McGraw-Hill, New York, 1994.
3. P. Kundur, *Power System Stability and Control,* Sections 2.12, 11.2 and Chapter 14, McGraw-Hill, New York, 1994.
4. T.J.E. Miller, Editor, *Reactive Power Control in Electric Systems,* John Wiley and Sons, New York, 1982.

5. T.V. Cutsem and C. Vournas, *Voltage Stability of Electric Power Systems,* Kluwer Academic Publishers, London, 1998.
6. A.J. Wood and W.F. Wollenberg, *Power Generation, Operation, and Control,* 2nd Edn, John Wiley, New York, 1996.
7. J.J. Grainger and W.D. Stevenson, *Power System Analysis,* McGraw-Hill, New York, 1994.
8. G.L. Kusic, *Computer-Aided Power Systems Analysis,* Prentice-Hall, New Jersey, 1986.
9. G.W. Stagg and A.H. El-Abiad, *Computer Methods in Power System Analysis,* McGraw-Hill, New York, 1968.
10. J.A. Momoh, *Electric Power System Applications of Optimization*, Marcel Dekker, Inc Madison Avenue, New York, 2001.

Papers

11. O.I. Elgerd, "Control of electric power systems", *IEEE Control System Magazine,* volume: 1, issue: 2, pp: 4–16, 1981.
12. V. Ajjarapu and B. Lee, "Bibliography on Voltage Stability", *IEEE Trans. on Power Systems,* volume: 13, issue: 1, pp: 115–125, February 1998.
13. L.D. Arya, "Security Constrained Power System Optimization", PhD thesis, IIT Delhi, 1990.
14. T.E. DyLiacco, "The Adaptive Reliability Control System", *IEEE Trans. on PAS,* volume: PAS-86, pp: 517–531, May 1967.
(This is a key paper on system security and energy control system)
15. A.A. Fouad, "Dynamic Security Assessment Practices in North America", *IEEE Trans on Power Systems,* volume: 3, issue: 3, pp: 1310–1321, 1988.
16. B. Stott, O. Alsac, and A.J. Monticelli, "Security Analysis and Optimization", *Proc IEEE,* volume: 75, issue: 12, pp: 1623–1644, Dec 1987.
17. A.T. Saric and A.M. Stankovic, "Model Uncertainty in Security Assessment of Power Systems", IEEE Transactions on Power Systems, volume: 20, issue: 3, pp: 1398–1407, 2005.
18. P.R. Bijwe, D.P. Kothari, and L.D. Arya, "Alleviation of Line Overloads and Voltage Violations by Corrective Rescheduling", *IEE Proc* C, volume: 140, issue: 4, pp: 249–255, July 1993.
19. P.R. Bijwe, D.P. Kothari, and L.D. Arya, "Overload Ranking of Line Outages with Postoutage Generation Rescheduling", *Electric Machines and Power Systems,* volume: 22, issue: 5, pp: 557–568, 1994.
20. L.D. Arya, D.P. Kothari et al, "Post Contingency Line Switching for Overload Alleviation or Rotation", *International Journal of Electric Power and Energy Systems,* volume: 23, issue: 3, pp: 345–352, 1995.
21. P.R. Bijwe, S.M. Kelapure, D.P. Kothari, and K.K. Saxena, "Oscillatory Stability Limit Enhancement by Adaptive Control Rescheduling", *International Journal of Electric Power and Energy Systems*, volume: 21, issue: 7, pp: 507–514, 1999.
22. L.D. Arya, S.C. Chaube, and D.P. Kothari, "Line Switching for Alleviating Overloads under Line Outage Condition Taking Bus Voltage Limits into Account", *International Journal of Electric Power and Energy Systems,* volume: 22, issue: 3, pp: 213–221, 2000.
23. P.R. Bijwe, D.P. Kothari, and S. Kelapure, "An Effective Approach to Voltage Security and Enhancement", *International Journal of Electric Power and Energy Systems*, volume: 22, issue: 7, pp: 483–486, 2000.
24. L. Fink and K. Carlsen, "Operating under Stress and Strain", *IEEE Spectrum,* pp: 48–50, March 1978.
25. S.M. Kelapure, "Voltage Security Analysis and Enhancement", Ph. D. thesis, IIT Delhi, 2000.

26. G.C. Ejebe, et al, “Fast Contingency Screening and Evaluation for Voltage Security Analysis”, *IEEE Trans. on Power Systems,* volume: 3, issue: 4, pp: 1582–1590, Nov 1988.
27. P.A. Oyewole and D. Jayaweera, “Power System Security with Cyber-Physical Power System Operation”, *IEEE Access*, volume: 8, pp: 179970–179982, 2020.
28. F. Thams, A. Venzke, R. Eriksson, and S. Chatzivasileiadis, “Efficient Database Generation for Data-Driven Security Assessment of Power Systems”, *IEEE Transactions on Power Systems*, volume: 35, issue: 1, pp: 30–41, 2020.
29. G. Wijeweera, U.D. Annakkage, W. Zhang, A. D. Rajapakse, and M. Rheault, “Development of an Equivalent Circuit of a Large Power System for Real-Time Security Assessment”, *IEEE Transactions on Power Systems*, volume: 33, issue: 4, pp: 3490–3499, 2018.
30. R. Billinton and Guangbin Lian, “Composite Power System Health Analysis Using a Security Constrained Adequacy Evaluation Procedure”, *IEEE Transactions on Power Systems*, volume: 9, issue: 2, pp: 936–941, 1994.
31. H. Sun et al., “Automatic Learning of Fine Operating Rules for Online Power System Security Control”, *IEEE Transactions on Neural Networks and Learning Systems*, volume: 27, issue: 8, pp: 1708–1719, 2016.
32. M. Perninge, F. Lindskog, and L. Soder, “Importance Sampling of Injected Powers for Electric Power System Security Analysis”, *IEEE Transactions on Power Systems*, volume: 27, issue: 01, pp: 3–11, 2012.
33. Yong Min, Zifeng Lin, Jiageng Qiao, and Xiaohua Jiang, “On-line Steady State Security Assessment of Power Systems by SMES”, *IEEE Transactions on Applied Superconductivity*, volume: 15, issue: 2, pp: 1923–1926, 2005.
34. C. Ren and Y. Xu, “Transfer Learning-Based Power System Online Dynamic Security Assessment: Using One Model to Assess Many Unlearned Faults”, *IEEE Transactions on Power Systems*, volume: 35, issue: 1, pp: 821–824, 2020.
35. O.A. Alimi, K. Ouahada, and A.M. Abu-Mahfouz, “A Review of Machine Learning Approaches to Power System Security and Stability”, *IEEE Access*, volume: 8, pp: 113512–113531, 2020.

CHAPTER 16

Voltage Stability

16.1 ▶ INTRODUCTION

Voltage control and stability problems are very much familiar to the electric utility industry but are now receiving special attention by every power system analyst and researcher. With growing size along with economic and environmental pressures, the possible threat of voltage instability is becoming increasingly pronounced in power system networks. In recent years, voltage instability has been responsible for several major network collapses in New York, France, Florida, Belgium, Sweden and Japan [4, 5]. Research workers, *R* and *D* organisations and utilities throughout the world, are busy in understanding, analysing and developing newer and newer strategies to cope up with the menace of voltage instability/collapse.

Voltage stability* covers a wide range of phenomena. Because of this, voltage stability means different things to different engineers. Voltage stability is sometimes also called load stability, because the stability problems due to the lower voltages initiate at the load ends. The terms voltage instability and voltage collapse are often used interchangeably. The voltage instability is a dynamic process wherein contrast to rotor angle (synchronous) stability, voltage dynamics mainly involves loads and the means for voltage control. Voltage collapse is also defined as a process by which voltage instability leads to very low voltage profile in a significant part of the system. Voltage instability limit is not directly correlated to the network maximum power transfer limit.

A CIGRE Task Force [25] has proposed the following definitions for voltage stability.

16.1.1 Small-disturbance Voltage Stability

A power system at a given operating state is *small-disturbance voltage stable* if, following any small disturbance, voltages near loads do not change or remain close to the pre-disturbance values. The concept of small-disturbance voltage stability is related to steady-state stability and can be analysed using small-signal (linearised) model of the system.

16.1.2 Voltage Stability

A power system at a given operating state is voltage stable if on being subjected to a certain disturbance, the voltages near loads approach the post-disturbance equilibrium values.

The concept of voltage stability is related to transient stability of a power system. The analysis of voltage stability normally requires simulation of the system modelled by non-linear differential-algebraic equations.

16.1.3 Voltage Collapse

Following voltage instability, a power system undergoes voltage collapse if the post-disturbance equilibrium voltages near loads are below acceptable limits. Voltage collapse may be total (blackout) or partial.

* The problem of voltage stability has already been briefly tackled in Ch. 15. Here it is again discussed in greater detail by devoting a full chapter.

Voltage security is the ability of a system, not only to operate stably, but also to remain stable following credible contingencies or load increases.

Although voltage stability involves dynamics, power flow based static analysis methods often serve the purpose of quick and approximate analysis.

16.2 ▶ COMPARISON OF ANGLE AND VOLTAGE STABILITY

The problem of rotor angle (synchronous) stability (covered in Ch. 12) is well understood and documented [3, 4]. However, with power system becoming overstressed on account of economic and resource constraint on addition of generation, transformers, transmission lines and allied equipment, the voltage instability has become a serious problem. Therefore, voltage stability studies have attracted the attention of researchers and planners worldwide and is an active area of research.

Rotor angle instability is related to the real or active power and causes due to the limitations on the generations. Similarly reactive power is central to voltage instability analyses. It is well known that the reactive power is responsible for maintaining the voltages in the AC power systems. Thus deficit or excess reactive power has direct impact over the voltage profile in the power systems and leads to voltage instability either locally or globally and any increase in loadings may lead to voltage collapse. Other important aspect is the reactive losses in the system, which is growing as quadratic with rise in load. For example, 10% rise in load will increase the losses in the network by nearly 20%. Also the support from the reactive injections like capacitors will reduce the drop in voltages with increase in load. Thus, voltage instability becomes major concern, when the loads are increased. And at threshold of loading and the reactive power losses, the power system reaches voltage instability.

16.2.1 Voltage Stability Studies

The voltage stability can be studied either on static or dynamic considerations. Depending on the nature of disturbance and system/subsystem dynamics, voltage stability may be regarded a slow or fast phenomenon.

16.2.2 Static Voltage Analysis

Load flow analysis reveals as to how system equilibrium values (such as voltage and power flows) with the variation in system parameters and controls. Power flow is a static analysis tool wherein dynamics is not explicitly considered. (Of course, tap changing and the generator limit violations can be considered as dynamics, but not related to the time response.) Many of the indices used to assess voltage stability are related to NR load flow study. Details of static and dynamic voltage stability will be considered further in Section 16.5.

16.2.3 Some Countermeasures

Since the voltage stability is directly linked to the reactive power and specifically the rise in the reactive power losses with increase in load, the countermeasures are normally linked to the support of reactive power or the devices like transformer which has control over the voltages. It is very important to keep in mind that the transformers do not add reactive power to the system to save the system from the voltage instability, but has a impact over the voltage dependent loads. Thus, these control measures are to be used judiciously and could be helpful at some point of time but could deteriorate the condition otherwise.

Certain countermeasures to avoid voltage instability are

1. series compensation–capacitors (TCSC, FACTS, etc.)
2. shunt compensation–reactive power injection at appropriate locations
3. generator terminal voltage increase (only limited control possible)

4. load-end OLTC blocking
5. increase of generator transformer tap
6. strategic load shedding (on occurrence of undervoltage)

Since the voltage instability problems are related to the low voltages near load ends, the countermeasures which are supporting reactive power to the system at load end (or the areas whether the problems are detected) will be more effective. The changes generation controls will be of limited use because the reactive power cannot be transmitted over the long distances.

Series capacitor also has direct impact over the reduction on the system losses and varying appropriately with the loading condition.

Though undesirable, the strategic load shedding will always be helpful and can save the systems from the voltage instabilities in case all other controls are exhausted or are ineffective. This has direct impact on reducing the reactive power losses in the areas of problem (bottlenecks)

Countermeasures to prevent voltage collapse shall be taken up in Section 16.6.

16.3 ▶ REACTIVE POWER FLOW AND VOLTAGE COLLAPSE

Certain situations in power system cause problems in reactive power flow which lead to system voltage collapse. Some of the situations that can occur are listed and explained below:

1. *Long Transmission Lines*: In power systems, long lines with voltage uncontrolled buses at the receiving ends create major voltage problems during light load or heavy load conditions.
2. *Radial Transmission Lines*: In a power system, most of the parallel EHV networks are composed of radial transmission lines. Any loss of an EHV line in the network causes an enhancement in system's effective reactance. Under certain conditions, the increase in reactive power delivered by the line(s) to the load for a given drop in voltage is less than the increase in reactive power required by the load for the same voltage drop. In such a case, a small increase in load causes the system to reach a voltage unstable state.
3. *Shortage of Local Reactive Power*: There may occur a disorganised combination of outage and maintenance schedule that may cause localised reactive power shortage leading to voltage control problems. Any attempt to import reactive power through long EHV lines will not be successful. Under this condition, the bulk system can suffer a considerable voltage drop.

16.4 ▶ MATHEMATICAL FORMULATION OF VOLTAGE STABILITY PROBLEM

The slower forms of voltage instability are normally analysed as steady-state problems using power flow simulation as the primary study method. 'Snapshots' in time following an outage or during load build up are simulated. Besides these post-disturbance power flows, two other power flow based methods are often used; *PV* curves and *VQ* curves (see also Section 13.6). These two methods give steady-state loadability limits which are related to voltage stability. Conventional load flow programs can be used for approximate analysis.

P–V curves are useful for conceptual analysis of voltage stability and for study of radial systems.

The model that will be employed here to judge voltage stability is based on a single line performance. The voltage performance of this simple system is qualitatively similar to that of a practical system with many voltage sources, loads and the network of transmission lines.

Consider the radial two-bus system of Fig. 16.1. This is the same diagram as that of Fig. 5.26 except that symbols are simplified. Here E is V_S and V is V_R and E and V are magnitudes with E leading V by δ. Line angle $\phi = \tan^{-1} X/R$ and $|z| \approx X$.

In terms of P and Q, the system load end voltage can be expressed as [1]:

$$V = \left[-\frac{2QX + E^2}{2} \pm \frac{1}{2}\sqrt{(2QX - E^2)^2 - 4X^2(P^2 + Q^2)} \right]^{1/2} \tag{16.1}$$

It is seen from Eq. (16.1) that V is a double-valued function (i.e., it has two solutions) of P for a particular pf which determines Q in terms of P. The PV curves for various values of pf are plotted in Fig. 16.2. For each value of pf, the higher voltage solution indicates stable voltage case, while the lower voltage lies in the unstable voltage operation zone.

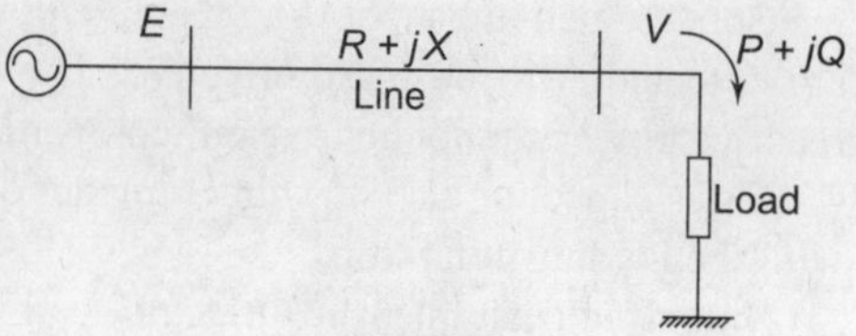

Fig. 16.1

The changeover occurs at V_{cri} (critical) and P_{max}. The locus of V_{cri}–P_{max} points for various pfs is drawn in dotted line in the Fig. 16.2. Any attempt to increase the load above P_{max} causes a reversal of voltage and load. Reducing voltage causes an increasing current to be drawn by the load. In turn the larger reactive line drop causes the voltage to dip further. This being unstable operation causes the system to suffer voltage collapse. This is also brought out by the fact that in upper part of the curve $\frac{dP}{dV} < 0$ and in the lower part (unstable part) $\frac{dP}{dV} > 0$ (reducing load means reducing voltage and vice versa). It may be noted here that the type of load assumed in Fig. 16.2 is constant impedance. In practical systems, the type of loads is mixed or predominantly constant power type such that system voltage degradation is more and voltage instability occurs much prior to the theoretical power limit.

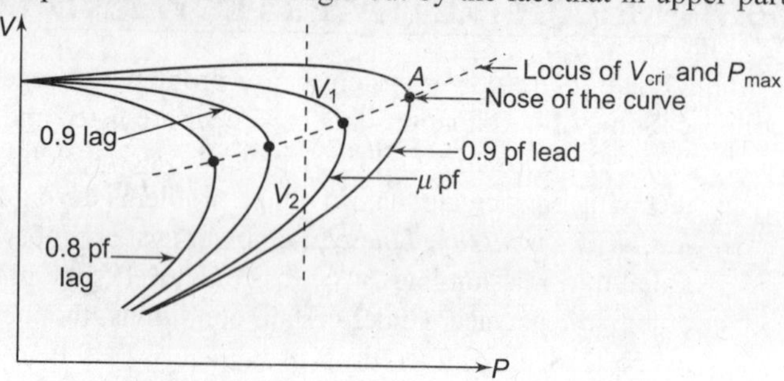

Fig. 16.2 *PV curves for various power factors*

As in the case of single line system, in a general power system, voltage instability occurs above certain bus loading and certain Q injections. This condition is indicated by the singularity of the Jacobian of Load Flow equations and level of voltage instability is assessed by the minimum singular value.

Certain results that are of significance for voltage stability are as under:

1. Voltage stability limit is reached when

$$\left| \frac{S}{Y_{LL}^* V^2} \right| = 1 \tag{16.2}$$

where S = complex power at load bus,
Y_{LL} = load bus admittance,
V = load bus voltage.

Nearer the magnitude in Eq. (16.2) to unity, lesser the stability margin.

2. The loading limit of a transmission line can be determined from

$$|S| = V_{cri}^2 / X_{cri} \tag{16.3}$$

X_{cri} is the critical system reactance beyond which voltage stability is lost. It can be expressed as

$$X_{cri} = \frac{E^2}{2P}(-\tan\phi + \sec\phi) \tag{16.4}$$

We have so far considered how the PV characteristics with constant load power factor affect the voltage that follows stability of a system. A more meaningful characteristic for certain aspects of voltage stability is the QV characteristic, which brings out the sensitivity and variation of bus voltage with respect to reactive power injections (+ve or –ve).

Consider once again the simple radial system of Fig. 16.1. For Q flow it is sufficiently accurate to assume $X \gg R$ i.e., $\phi \approx 90°$.

$$Q = \frac{EV}{X}\cos\delta - \frac{V^2}{X} \tag{16.5}$$

or

$$V^2 - EV\cos\delta + QX = 0 \tag{16.6}$$

Taking derivative wrt V gives

$$\frac{dQ}{dV} = \frac{E\cos\delta - 2V}{X} \tag{16.7}$$

The QV characteristic on normalised basis (Q/P_{max}, V/E) for various values of P/P_{max} are plotted in Fig. 16.3. The system is voltage stable in the region where dQ/dV is positive, while the voltage stability limit is reached at $dQ/dV = 0$ which may also be termed as the critical operating point.

The limiting value of the reactive power transfer at the limiting stage of voltage stability is given by

$$Q_{lim} = \frac{V^2}{X}\cos 2\delta \tag{16.8}$$

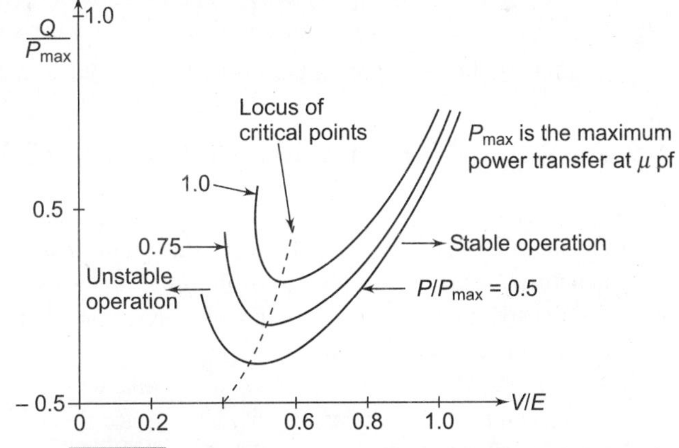

Fig. 16.3 *QV characteristics for the system of Fig. 16.1 for various values of P/P_{max}*

The inferences drawn from the simple radial system qualitatively apply to a practical size system. Other factors that contribute to system voltage collapse are strength of transmission system, power transfer levels, load characteristics, generator reactive power limits and characteristics of reactive power compensating devices.

16.4.1 Other Criteria of Voltage Stability

1. $\frac{dE}{dV}$ criterion: (E = generator voltage; V = load voltage). Using this criterion, the voltage stability limit is reached when

$$\cos\delta\left\{\frac{dQ}{dV} + \frac{2V}{X}\right\} + \sin\delta\,\frac{dP}{dV} - \frac{E}{X} = 0 \tag{16.9}$$

Using the decoupling principle, i.e., $\frac{dP}{dV} = 0$, we get

$$\frac{E}{X} = \cos\delta\left[\frac{dQ}{dV} + \frac{2V}{X}\right]$$

or

$$I_{SC} = \cos\delta\left[\frac{dQ}{dV} + \frac{2V}{X}\right]$$

or

$$EI_{SC} = E\cos\delta\left[\frac{dQ}{dV} + \frac{2V}{X}\right]$$

Voltage stability is achieved when

$$E \cos \delta \left(\frac{dQ}{dV} + \frac{2V}{X} \right) > EI_{SC} \text{ (short circuit MVA of power source)} \tag{16.10}$$

2. $\frac{dZ}{dV}$ criterion

   Voltage instability occurs when the system Z is such that

$$\frac{dV}{dZ} = \infty \text{ or } \frac{dZ}{dV} = 0 \tag{16.11}$$

   Application of this criterion gives value of Z_{cri}.

3. Ratio of source to load reactance is very important and for voltage stability

$$\frac{x_{source}}{x_{load}} < a^2 \tag{16.12}$$

   a indicates the off-nominal tap ratio of the OLTC transformer at the load end.

16.5 ▶ VOLTAGE STABILITY ANALYSIS

The voltage stability analysis for a given system state involves examining following two aspects:

1. *Proximity to voltage instability*: Distance to instability may be measured in terms of physical quantities, such as load level, real power flow through a critical interface, and reactive power reserve. Possible contingencies, such as a line outage, loss of a generating unit or a reactive power source must be given due consideration.
2. *Mechanism of voltage instability*: How and why does voltage instability take place? What are the main factors leading to instability? What are the voltage-weak areas? What are the most effective ways to improve voltage stability?

The static analysis techniques permit examination of a wide range of system conditions and can describe the nature of the problem and give the main contributing factors. Dynamic analysis is useful for detailed study of specific voltage collapse situations, coordination of protection and controls, and testing of remedial measures. Dynamic simulations further tell us whether and how the steady-state equilibrium point will be reached.

16.5.1 Modelling Requirements of various Power System Components

Load Load modelling is very critical in voltage stability analysis. Detailed subtransmission system representation in a voltage-weak area may be required. This may include transformer ULTC action, reactive power compensation and voltage regulators.

It is essential to consider the voltage and frequency dependence of loads. Induction motors should also be modelled.

16.5.2 Generators and their Excitation Controls

It is necessary to consider the droop characteristics of the AVR, load compensation, SVSs (static var system), AGC, protection and controls should also be modelled appropriately [4].

16.5.3 Dynamic Analysis

The general structure of the system model for voltage stability analysis is similar to that for transient stability analysis. Overall system equations may be expressed as

$$\dot{X} = f(X, V) \tag{16.13}$$

and a set of algebraic equations

$$I(X, V) = Y_N V \tag{16.14}$$

with a set of known initial conditions (X_0, V_0).

where X = system state vector
V = bus voltage vector
I = current injection vector
Y_N = network node admittance matrix

Equations (16.13) and (16.14) can be solved in time domain by employing any of the numerical integration methods described in Ch. 12 and power flow analysis methods described in Ch. 6. The study period is of the order of several minutes. As the special models representing the 'slow system dynamics' leading to voltage collapse have been included, the stiffness of the system differential equations is considerably higher than that of transient stability models. Stiffness is also called synchronising coefficient as discussed in Ch. 12.

16.5.4 Static Analysis

The static approach captures *snapshots* of system conditions at various time frames along the time-domain trajectory. At each of these time frames, $\dot{X}$ in Eq. (16.13) is assumed to be zero, and the state variables take on values appropriate to the specific time frame. Thus, the overall system equations reduce to purely algebraic equations allowing the use of static analysis techniques.

In static analysis, voltage stability is determined by computing VP and VQ curves at selected load buses. Special techniques using static analysis have been reported in literature. Methods based on VQ sensitivity such as eigenvalue (or modal) analysis have been devised. These methods give stability-related information from a system-wide perspective and also identify areas of potential problems [13–15].

16.5.5 Proximity to Instability

Proximity to small-disturbance voltage instability is determined by increasing load-generation in steps until the system becomes unstable or the load flow fails to converge. References [16–18] discuss special techniques for determining the point of voltage collapse and proximity to voltage instability.

16.5.6 Voltage Stability Assessment using Modal Analysis

Consider the increment power flow equation as follows:

$$\begin{bmatrix} J_1 & J_2 \\ J_3 & J_4 \end{bmatrix} \begin{bmatrix} \Delta\delta \\ \Delta V \end{bmatrix} = \begin{bmatrix} \Delta P \\ \Delta Q \end{bmatrix} \tag{16.15}$$

Where $J_1 - J_4$ are load flow sub-Jacobians given by

$$[J_1] = (\partial P/\partial \delta],\ [J_2] = [\partial P/\partial V]\ [J_3] = [\partial Q/\partial \delta] \text{ and } [J_4] = [\partial Q/\partial V]$$

Since basically voltage stability problem is related to voltage variation with reactive power variation hence setting $\Delta P = 0$ and following relations are obtained.

$$[J_1]\,[\Delta\delta] + [J_2][\Delta V] = 0$$

$$[\Delta\delta] = -J_1^{-1} J_2\,[\Delta V] \tag{16.16}$$

$$[J_3][\Delta\delta] + [J_4][\Delta V] = \Delta Q \tag{16.17}$$

Putting value of $[\Delta\delta]$ from (16.16) into (16.17) following incremental relation between $[\Delta V]$ and $[\Delta Q]$ is obtained.

$$[J_4 - J_3 J_1^{-1} J_2][\Delta V] = [\Delta Q] \tag{16.18}$$

or

$$[J_R]\,[\Delta V] = [\Delta Q] \tag{16.19}$$

When J_R is known as reduced Jacobian and defined as follows:

$$[J_R] = [J_4] - [J_3][J_1^{-1}]\,[J_2]$$

If $Q - \delta$ and PV coupling is neglected then reduced Jacobian is

$$[J_R] = [J_4]\ [J_R] = [J_4]$$

Modal solution Eq. (16.19) is written as [4]

$$\Delta V = \sum_i \frac{(\eta_i^T \Delta Q)\xi_i}{\lambda_i} \tag{16.20}$$

where λ_i and ξ_i are eigen values and right eigen value of Jacobian $[J_R]$. η_i^T is left eigen value (row) corresponding to λ_i. ΔQ represents reactive power injection at load buses.

Assume that $\Delta Q = \xi_k$, i.e., reactive power variation is along an eigen vector ξ_k corresponding to eigen value λ_k. In this case modal solution for load bus voltage variation is

$$\Delta V^{(k)} = \xi_k/\lambda_i \tag{16.21}$$

Equation (16.21) suggests that for system to be voltage-stable eigen value λ_k should be positive. Otherwise positive (negative) reactive power injection changes with negative (positive) changes in voltage variation. For example, let us assume that lth component of ξ_k is 0.15 and $\lambda_k = 0.95$. Since reactive power variation injection is positive, i.e., 0.15, the change is voltage must be positive or $\Delta V_1 = 0.15/.95 = 0.1578$. And this is required for voltage stable operation. Now suppose that $\lambda_k = -0.95$ and ξ_{k1} is 0.15. In this case $\Delta V_l = -0.15/0.95 = -0.1578$. This amounts that if one injects positive vars, then voltage of that bus decreases. This is voltage unstable operation. Further if $\lambda_k = 0$, then change in bus voltages will be theoretically infinite. This corresponds to a situation at saddle node bifurcation point (SNP) or at collapse point. This amounts that as long as all the eigen values of the load flow Jacobian (J_R) are positive, then system operation is voltage-stable and if any of the eigen values is negative, system voltage is unstable and if any eigen value is zero means the system is at voltage collapse point. This means that minimum eigen value of load flow Jacobian is a proximity indicator which varies from some high value to zero as voltage collapse point is approached. This is represented as follows.

I: Represents with no reactive power limit violation at PV-buses.

II: Represents with limit violation at PV-bus at A, B, C

For any load point if the reactive power limits violation for a generator bus takes place, then that bus becomes P-Q bus and V is left free. Thus, this gives rise to increase in the size of load flow Jacobian by 1. This gives rise to sudden drop in the minimum eigen value of Jacobian. This is happening at A, B and C in Fig. 16.4.

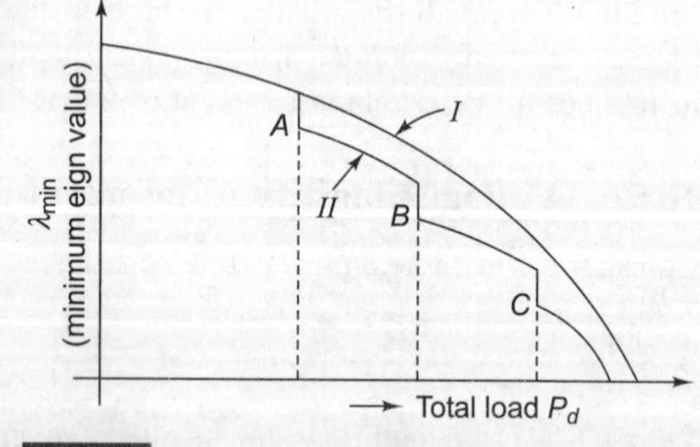

Fig. 16.4 *Variation of minimum eigen value wrt total lead*

Further it is observed from Eq. (16.20) that voltage is modal.

Expanding relation (16.20)

$$\Delta V = (\alpha_1\ \xi_1)/\lambda_1 + (\alpha_2\ \xi_2)/\lambda_2 \ldots + (\alpha_k\ \xi_k)/\lambda_k \tag{16.22}$$

It is observed as the system is stressed one of the eigen values reduces and practically very near to zero at collapse point and that time voltage changes will be dominated by that mode which is having least value. Let us assume that mode is kth. In this situation, if $\alpha_k\ (\eta^T{}_k\ \Delta Q)$ is zero voltage collapse will not occur. But if α_k is finite then voltage collapse will occur if λ_k is practically very near to zero. Hence, it is said that voltage collapse is modal.

Mechanism of voltage collapse: Bus participation factor

Consider Eq. (16.20) and set

$$\Delta Q = \xi_k = [0, 0, \dots 1 \dots 0 \dots 0]$$
$$\downarrow$$
$$k\text{th entry}$$

i.e., the reactive power variation is at kth bus. Then, 'ΔVk' change in kth bus voltage is written as

$$\Delta V_k = \sum_i (\eta_{ik} \cdot \xi_{ki}) / \lambda_i \tag{16.23a}$$

or

$$\Delta V_k = \sum_i p_{ki} / \lambda_i \tag{16.23b}$$

where $p_{ki} = \eta_{ik} \cdot \xi_{ki}$ is known as *bus participation factor*. This exhibits the participation of kth bus to ith mode. It is to be noted further

$$\sum_k p_{ki} = \eta_i^T \xi_i = 1 \tag{16.24}$$

The eigen value having least value is of great significance. The buses which are contributing to this 'worst' mode can be identified from following vector of bus participation factor.

$$[p_{1i}, p_{2i}, \dots p_{ki} \dots p_{krb}]$$

Larger the value of p_{ji} larger will be contribution of jth bus to ith mode. If any component is zero then that bus is not contributing to the 'worst' mode. Based on the magnitude of these factors buses may be selected for compensation and buses may be identified which contribute to voltage instability.

Since J_R is near symmetric matrix $\eta^T_i = \xi^T_i$. In this situation the one may calculate $p_{ki} = \xi_{ik}\, \xi_{ki} = (\xi_{ki})^2$

The mode may be classified in the following two categories.

1. Localised mode: This contains a small number of buses with dominant participation and little participation from remaining buses. This may occur due to load buses at the end of long radial transmission lines. If such localised 'modes' are outside the region of load increase and do not contain reactive sources, they may be of little significance in the stability analysis.
2. Nonlocalised modes: Nonlocalised mode involves a significant portion of the system. If a mode contains a large number of buses the participation for each bus is generally small because the sum of all bus participation is equal to unity.

Branch Participation Factor Let us consider that reactive power variations are made along the eigen vector ξ_i corresponding to λ_i the least eigen value. Change in load bus voltage vector may be

$$[\Delta V]^{(i)} = (1/\lambda_i)\, \xi_i \tag{16.25}$$

Now phase angle changes are calculated using relation [Eq. (16.16)] as follows:

$$[\Delta\delta]^{(i)} = -[J_1]^{-1}\,[J_2][\Delta V]^{(i)} = \{-[J_1]^{-1}[J_2][\xi_i]\}/\lambda_i \tag{16.26}$$

Reactive power loss in a transmission line connected between buses p and q is given as follows:

$$Q_{\text{loss},j} = b_j\,(V_p^2 + V_q^2) - 2_{bj}\, V_p\, V_q \cos(\delta_p - \delta_q) \tag{16.27}$$

Change in reactive power loss ($\Delta\, Q_{\text{loss},j}$) may be calculated as

$$\Delta\, Q_{\text{loss},j} = C_1.\Delta V_p^{(i)} + C_2.\Delta V_q^{(i)} + C_3(\Delta\delta_p - \Delta\delta_q)$$

where

$$C_1 = \partial Q_{\text{loss},j}/\partial V_p$$
$$C_2 = \partial\, Q_{\text{loss},j}/\partial V_q$$

$$C_3 = \partial Q_{\text{loss},j} / \partial V_{pq}$$

C_1, C_2, C_3 are evaluated at current operating point.

The maximum change in reactive power loss and the line 'l' can be identified as

$$\Delta Q_{\text{loss},l} = \text{Max}_j \ \{\Delta Q_{\text{loss},j}\}$$

Now branch participation factor is defined as

$$p_{j\text{-}i} = (\Delta Q_{\text{loss},j}) / \Delta Q_{\text{loss},l}$$

Branch participation factor indicates that for the mode, z, which branches consume the most reactive power in response to an incremental change in reactive load. Lines with high participation are either weak lines or heavily loaded branch participation factors may be useful in identifying lines for series compensation.

Generation Participation Factors Once changes $\Delta V^{(i)}$ or $\Delta\delta^{(i)}$ are obtained changes in reactive power output of each generator can be calculated. Maximum change in generator output is noted in

$$\Delta Q_g,(u) = \text{Max}_k \ \{\Delta Q_g, k\}$$

Then generation participation factor is defined as normalised value.

$$P_{g,k,i} = \Delta Q_{k,i} \ / \ \Delta Q_{g,u}$$

= reactive power change required at k^{th} bus/maximum generation change required at a generation.

Generation participation factor indicates for each mode, which generator supplies the most reactive output in response to an incremental change in system reactive demand. Generators with 'high' $P_{gk\text{-}i}$ are important in maintaining stability with respect to mode, i

ΔQ_{k-i} can be calculated as

$$\Delta Q_{ki} = \Sigma_{li} \ \Delta Q_{l\text{'}i}$$

ΔQ_{l-i} is changes in 'li' line connector to the kth generator. Changes can be calculated using linearised expression for line flows.

For example, if three transmission lines are connected at kth generator bus as shown in Fig. 16.5

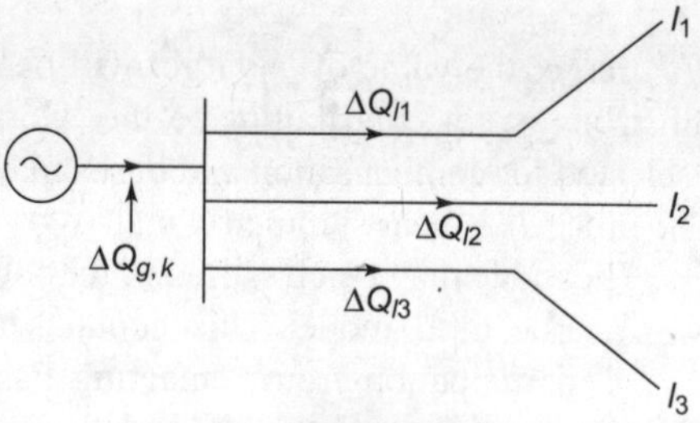

Then,

$$\Delta Q_{g,k} = \Delta Q_{l1} + \Delta Q_{l2} + \Delta Q_{l3}$$

Fig. 16.5

Now,

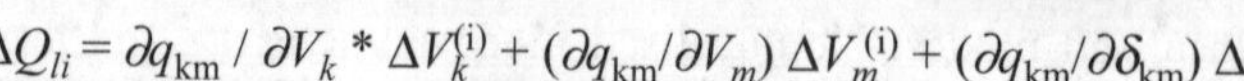

$$\Delta Q_{li} = \partial q_{\text{km}} \ / \ \partial V_k * \Delta V_k^{(i)} + (\partial q_{\text{km}} / \partial V_m) \, \Delta V_m^{(i)} + (\partial q_{\text{km}} / \partial \delta_{\text{km}}) \, \Delta \delta_{\text{km}}$$

where l ith line is connected between k (generator bus) and other bus 'm'. The expression for q_{km}, reactive power flow from kth to mth is written as follows:

$$q_{\text{km}} = b_i^{\ 1} \ V_k^{\ 2} - V_k \ V_m b_i \cos(\delta_k - \delta_m) - V_k V_{mgi} \sin(\delta_k - \delta_m)$$

$$x_i = \text{Reactance of } i\text{th line}$$

$$r_i = \text{Resistance of } i\text{th line}$$

$$b_{sh} = \text{Half line charging admittance}$$

$$b_i = b_i - b_{sh}$$

$$b_i = x_i / (r_i^2 + x_i^2)$$

$$g_i = r_i / r_i^2 + x_i^2)$$

Determination of Minimum Eigen Value of Jacobian Minimum eigen value of reduced load flow Jacobian is a proximity indicator. As load on the system is increased this minimum value decreasing and practically very near to zero at collapse point. Using inverse iteration procedure this value may be obtained. The IIP method gives largest eigen value. So if one wants to obtain minimum eigen value then largest value of J_R^{-1} has to be obtained and then minimum eigen value will be reciprocal of it. Hence, in the following iterative procedure $A = QJ_R^{-1}$

Select a vector $X_0 = [1, 0, 0, ...0]$

As unit vector, obtain $X_1, X_2, ... X_r$ as follows:

$$A X_0 = X_1$$

Then estimate $\lambda est^{(1)} = ||X_1||$

Obtain unit vector

$$X_1 = X_1/||X||$$

Again $AX_1 = X_2$

$$\lambda_{est}^{(2)} = ||X_2||$$

Repeat above iterative process

$$AX_{i-1} = X_i$$

$$\lambda_{est}^{(i)} = ||X_i||$$

If

$$|\lambda_{est}^{(i)} - \lambda^{(i-1)}{}_{est}| \leq \varepsilon$$

Stop, otherwise

$$X_i = X_i/||X_i||$$

Then repeat the iterative procedure.

Then minimum eigen value of J_R is given as

$$\lambda_{min} = 1/\lambda^{(i)}{}_{est}$$

then 'X_i' will be the right eigen vector. ξ_i for this lead eigen value.

Illustration: Assume that minimum eigen value of the following matrix is required

$$B = \begin{bmatrix} 1/3 & -1/6 \\ -1/6 & 1/3 \end{bmatrix}$$

Eigen value of this matrix is obtained as

$$(1/3 - \lambda)^2 - 1/36 = 0$$

$$(1/3) - \lambda = \pm\, 1/6$$

$$\lambda = 1/3 \pm 1/6$$

$$\lambda_1 = 1/2, \quad \lambda_2 = 1/6$$

Thus, minimum eigen value is 1/6

We get max eigen value

$$A = B^{-1} = \begin{bmatrix} 4 & 2 \\ 2 & 4 \end{bmatrix}$$

A has eigen values 2, 6

$$\begin{bmatrix} 4 & 2 \\ 2 & 4 \end{bmatrix}\begin{bmatrix} 1 \\ 0 \end{bmatrix} = \begin{bmatrix} 4 \\ 2 \end{bmatrix}$$

$$\lambda^1{}_{est} = \sqrt{}(16 + 4) = \sqrt{20} = 4.472$$

$$X_1 = \begin{bmatrix} 0.894 \\ 0.447 \end{bmatrix}$$

$$\begin{bmatrix} 4 & 2 \\ 2 & 4 \end{bmatrix}\begin{bmatrix} 0.894 \\ 0.447 \end{bmatrix} = \begin{bmatrix} 4.470 \\ 3.576 \end{bmatrix}$$

$$\lambda^{(2)}{}_{est} = \sqrt{}(19.9809 + 12.7877)$$

$$= 5.724$$

$$X_2 = \begin{bmatrix} 0.7804 \\ 0.6247 \end{bmatrix}$$

$$\begin{bmatrix} 4 & 2 \\ 2 & 4 \end{bmatrix}\begin{bmatrix} 0.7804 \\ 0.6247 \end{bmatrix} = \begin{bmatrix} 4.373 \\ 4.0606 \end{bmatrix}$$

$$\lambda_{\text{est}}^{(3)} = 5.967$$

$$X_3 = \begin{bmatrix} 0.732 \\ 0.6814 \end{bmatrix}$$

$$\begin{bmatrix} 4 & 2 \\ 2 & 4 \end{bmatrix}\begin{bmatrix} 0.732 \\ 0.6814 \end{bmatrix} = \begin{bmatrix} 2.928 + 1.3628 \\ 1.464 + 2.7256 \end{bmatrix}$$

$$= \begin{bmatrix} 4.2908 \\ 4.1896 \end{bmatrix}$$

$$\lambda_{\text{est}}^{(4)} = \sqrt{(17.552 + 18.410)}$$

$$= \sqrt{(35.96)}$$

$$= 5.9969$$

$$\lambda_{\text{est}}^{(4)} - \lambda_{\text{est}}^{(3)} = 0.0294$$

$$X_4 = \begin{bmatrix} 0.715 \\ 0.698 \end{bmatrix}$$

As the solution converges $X_3 \to X_4$
One may further continue for better accuracy.

16.5.7 The Continuation Power-flow Analysis

The Jacobian matrix becomes singular at the voltage stability limit. As a result, conventional load-flow algorithms may have convergence problems at operating conditions near the stability limit. The continuation power-flow analysis overcomes this problem by reformulating the load-flow equations so that they remain well-conditioned at all possible loading conditions. This allows the solution of load-flow problem for both upper and lower portions of the *P-V* curve [17].

The continuation method of power-flow analysis is robust and flexible and suited for solving load-flow problems with convergence difficulties. However, the method is very slow and time-consuming. Hence, the better approach is to use combination of conventional load flow method (NR/FDLF) and continuation method. Starting from the base case, LF is solved using a conventional method to compute power flow solutions for successively increasing load levels until a solution cannot be obtained. Hereafter, the continuation method is resorted to obtain the load-flow solutions. Normally, the continuation method is required only if solutions are required exactly at and past the critical point.

16.5.8 Voltage Stability with HVDC Links

High voltage direct current* (HVDC) links are used for extremely long distance transmission and for asynchronous interconnections. An HVDC link can be either a back-to-back rectifier/inverter link or can include long distance dc transmission. Multi-terminal HVDC links are also feasible.

The technology has come to such a level that HVDC terminals can be connected even at voltage-weak points in power systems. HVDC links may present unfavourable 'load' characteristics to the power system as HVDC converter consumes reactive power equal to 50–60% of the dc power.

* For detailed account of HVDC, the reader may refer to [3].

HVDC-related voltage control (voltage stability and fundamental frequency temporary over voltages) may be studied using a transient stability program. Transient stability is often interrelated with voltage stability. Reference [2] considers this problem in greater detail.

16.6 ▶ PREVENTION OF VOLTAGE COLLAPSE

1. *Application of reactive power-compensating devices*: Adequate stability margins should be ensured by proper selection of compensation schemes in terms of their size, ratings and locations.
2. *Control of network voltage and generator reactive output*: Several utilities in the world, such as EDF (France), ENEL (Italy), are developing special schemes for control of network voltages and reactive power.
3. *Coordination of protections/controls*: Adequate coordination should be ensured between equipment protections/controls based on dynamic simulation studies. Tripping of equipment to avoid an overloaded condition should be the last alternative. Controlled system separation and adaptive or intelligent control could also be used.
4. *Control of transformer tap changers*: Tap changers can be controlled, either locally or centrally, so as to reduce the risk of voltage collapse. Microprocessor-based OLTC controls offer almost unlimited flexibility for implementing ULTC control strategies so as to take advantage of the load characteristics.
5. *Undervoltage load shedding*: For unplanned or extreme situations, it may be necessary to use undervoltage load-shedding schemes. This is similar to under frequency load shedding, which is a common practice to deal with extreme situations resulting from generation deficiency. Strategic load shedding provides cheapest way of preventing widespread voltage collapse. Load shedding schemes should be designed so as to differentiate between faults, transient voltage dips and low voltage conditions leading to voltage collapse.
6. *Operators' role*: Operators must be able to recognise voltage stability-related symptoms and take required remedial actions to prevent voltage collapse. On-line monitoring and analysis to identify potential voltage stability problems and appropriate remedial measures are extremely helpful.

16.7 ▶ STATE-OF-THE-ART, FUTURE TRENDS AND CHALLENGES

The present day transmission networks are getting more and more stressed due to economic and environmental constraints. The trend is to operate the existing networks optimally close to their loadability limit. This consequently means that the system operation is also near voltage stability limit (nose point) and there is increased possibility of voltage instability and even collapse.

Off-line and on-line techniques of determining state of voltage stability and when it enters the unstable state provide the tools for system planning and real time control. Energy management system (EMS) provides a variety of measured and computer processed data. This is helpful to system operators in taking critical decisions *inter alia* reactive power management and control. In this regard automation and specialised software relieve the operator of good part of the burden of system management but it does add to the complexity of the system operation.

Voltage stability analysis and techniques have been pushed forward by several researchers and several of these are in commercial use as outlined in this chapter. As it is still hot topic, considerable research effort is being devoted to it.

Pai *et al.* [8] considered an exponential type voltage dependent load model and a new index called condition number for static voltage stability prediction. Eigen value analyses have been used to find critical group of buses responsible for voltage collapse. Some researchers [26] have also investigated aspects of bifurcations (local, Hopf, global) and chaos and their implications on power system voltage stability. FACTS devices can be effectively used for controlling the occurrence of dynamic bifurcations and chaos by proper choice of error signal and controller gains.

Tokyo Electric Power Co. has developed a JP-based controller for coordinated control of capacitor bank switching and network transformer tap changing. HVDC power control is used to improve stability.

More systematic approach is still required for optimal siting and sizing of FACTS devices. The availability of FACTS controllers allows operation close to the thermal limit of the lines without jeopardising security. The reactive power compensation close to the load centres and at the critical buses is essential for overcoming voltage instability. Better and probabilistic load modelling [11] should be tried. It will be worthwhile developing techniques and models for study of nonlinear dynamics of large size systems. This may require exploring new methods to obtain network equivalents suitable for the voltage stability analysis. AI is another approach to centralised reactive power and voltage control. An expert system [9] could assist operators in applying C-banks so that generators operate near μpf. The design of suitable protective measures in the event of voltage instability is necessary.

So far, computed *PV* curves are the most widely used method of estimating voltage security, providing MW margin type indices. Post-disturbance MW or MVAr margins should be translated to predisturbance operating limits that operators can monitor. Both control centre and power plant operators should be trained in the basics of voltage stability. For operator training simulator [10] a real-time dynamic model of the power system that interfaces with EMS controls such as AGC is of great help.

Voltage stability is likely to challenge utility planners and operators for the foreseeable future. As load grows and as new transmission and load area generation become increasingly difficult to build, more and more utilities will face the voltage stability challenge. Fortunately, many creative researchers and planners are working on new analysis methods and an innovative solutions to the voltage stability challenge.

Voltage stability phenomenon has been illustrated in Fig. 16.6 using *PV* curves for IEEE 30 bus system.

Figure 16.6 shows the *PV* curve for the IEEE 30 bus system. The voltages at bus 2, 3, 17 and 30 are plotted against the loading level. The loading levels are basically the scaling parameter used for changing the basecase load. Bus number 2 is having the generator and thus holding/controlling the voltage at bus number 2 to its capacity. Bus number 3 is electrically near to the bus 2. Bus nos. 17 and 30 are intermediate and far end buses respectively. It can clearly be seen that there is more voltage drops for bus nos. 30 and 17 which are electrically far from generator buses. Generator bus 2 is holding the voltage till the reactive limit is hit. After hitting the limit at around 0.9225 loading level, the *PV* bus is behaving like the load or *PQ* bus with consistently drop in voltage. Since buses 2 and 3 are near to the slack bus, voltages are maintained well at these buses. It can also be observed that at loading level 1.53, voltages are falling dawn rapidly and there is fall in the loading level after that. This is a indication of the voltage instability. Also it is important to observe that the voltages at loadability limit (i.e., the tip of the *PV* curves) for the buses 2, 3, 17 and 30 are 0.9082, 0.8306, 0.6925 and 0.5792, respectively. It can also be mentioned that the slope of the *PV* curves

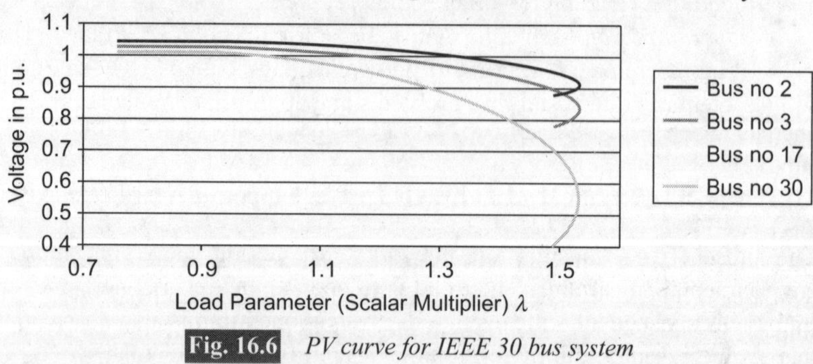

Fig. 16.6 *PV curve for IEEE 30 bus system*

changes on controls hitting limits like generators hitting reactive power limits or the transformers hitting automatic load tap changers limits.

Figures 16.7 and 16.8 illustrate the impact of reactive power injection at bus number 10. Capacitor has been added in two stages, 0.1 p.u. and 0.5 p.u.

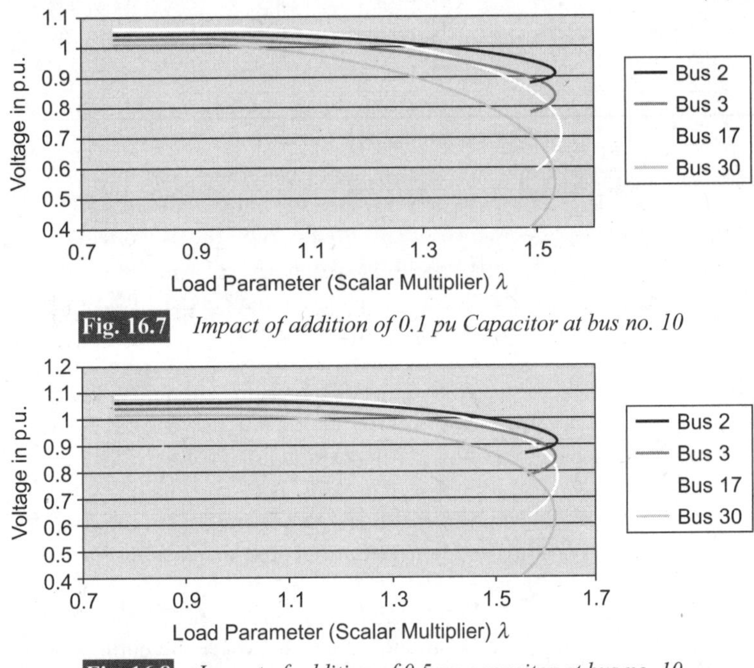

Fig. 16.7 *Impact of addition of 0.1 pu Capacitor at bus no. 10*

Fig. 16.8 *Impact of addition of 0.5 pu capacitor at bus no. 10*

It can clearly be seen that the voltages at the buses 2, 3, 17 and 30 have gone up with the major impact at bus no. 17 which is electrically closest to the bus no. 10. Also it can be observed that the loadability is increasing with insertion of capacitor. The loadability limit without extra capacitor is 1.53, which is gone up to 1.55 and 1.62.

This indicates that the shunt reactive power support increases the loadability with maximum benefit near the reactive support.

Figures 16.9, 16.10 and 16.11 illustrate the impact of branch outages (lines between buses 02–05 and 25–25 and transformer between buses 28–27). The loadability limits have been reduced from 1.53 to 1.13 and 1.25 for line 02–05 and transformer 28–27 outages but line 24–25 has hardly any impact on loadability and is more or less same at 1.53.

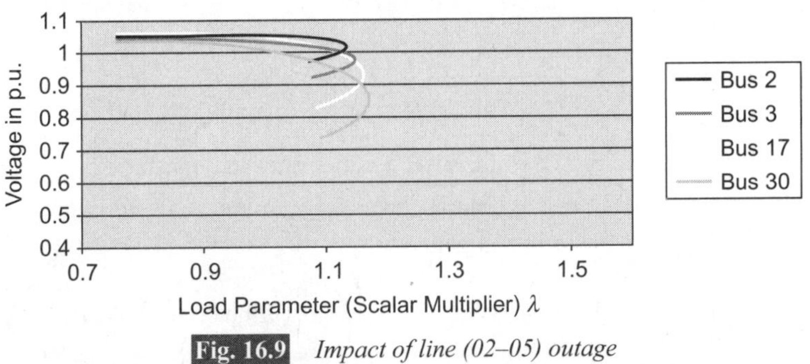

Fig. 16.9 *Impact of line (02–05) outage*

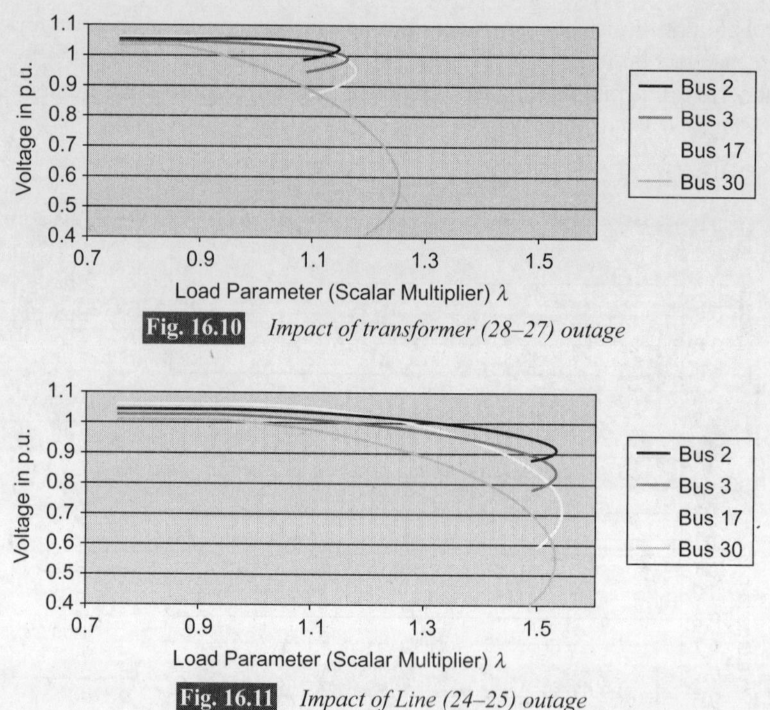

Fig. 16.10 *Impact of transformer (28–27) outage*

Fig. 16.11 *Impact of Line (24–25) outage*

Example 16.1 A load bus is composed of induction motor where the nominal reactive power is 1 pu. The shunt compensation is K_{sh}. Find the reactive power sensitivity at the bus wrt change in voltage.

Solution

$$Q_{load} = Q_{nom} V^2 \text{ [given]}$$

$$Q_{comp} = -K_{sh} V^2 \quad \text{[–ve sign denotes inductive reactive power injection]}$$

$$Q_{net} = Q_{load} + Q_{comp}$$

$\therefore$ Here, $$Q_{net} = V^2 - K_{sh} V^2 \text{ [}Q_{nom} = 1.0 \text{ given]}$$

$$\therefore \quad \frac{dQ_{net}}{dV} = 2V - 2V K_{sh}$$

Sensitivity increases or decreases with K_{sh} as well as the magnitude of the voltage. Say at $V = 1.0$ pu, $K_{sh} = 0.8$

$$\therefore \quad \frac{dQ_{net}}{dV} = 2 - 1.6 = 0.4 \text{ pu.}$$

Example 16.2 Find the capacity of a static VAR compensator to be installed at a bus with ±5% voltage fluctuation. The short circuit capacity is 5000 MVA.

Solution For the switching of static shunt compensator,

Let, ΔV = voltage fluctuation

ΔQ = reactive power variation (i.e., the size of the compensator)

$S_{s/c}$ = system short circuit capacity

Then $\Delta V = \dfrac{\Delta Q}{S_{s/c}}$

$$\Delta Q = \Delta V S_{s/c}$$
$$= \pm (0.05 \times 5000)$$
$$= \pm 250 \text{ MVAR}$$

The capacity of the static VAR compensator is + 250 MVAR.

16.8 ▶ SUMMARY

This chapter deals with yet another important problem of voltage stability, comparing with angle stability (Ch. 12). Finally, state-of-art and future trends along with the challenges are highlighted.

Multiple Choice Questions

16.1 The highest transmission voltage used in India is
(a) 400 kV (b) 765 kV (c) 220 kV (d) 500 kV

16.2 Allowed voltage variation is
(a) ± 10% (b) ± 5% (c) ± 15% (d) any value

16.3 Which of the following leads to voltage instability
(a) Transfer of reactive power (b) Transfer of active power
(c) Transfer of complex power (d) Transfer of apparent power

16.4 The voltage stability in power system is
(a) To maintain steady voltages at all the buses after the occurrence of fault.
(b) To maintain steady voltages at all the buses before the occurrence of fault.
(c) To maintain the system frequency after the severe disturbances
(d) All of these

16.5 The main cause of voltage instability in power system is
(a) Generators (b) Transformers (c) Loads (d) Line losses

16.6 The operation of OLTC improves voltage stability if
(a) The reactive power status at load bus improves
(b) The active power status at load bus improves
(c) The active power status at load bus reduces
(d) None of the above

16.7 Voltage collapse typically occurs in the power system due to
(a) Heavily loaded line (b) Faulted line
(c) Reactive power shortages in line (d) All of the above

16.8 Voltage instability occurs when the system Z is such that
(a) $\dfrac{dv}{dz} = \infty$ (b) $\dfrac{dz}{dv} = 0$ (c) Either (a) or (b) (d) $\dfrac{dv}{dz}$ = any value

16.9 Power system stability means
(a) Power system remains in a state of equilibrium under normal operating condition
(b) To restore an acceptable state of equilibrium after a disturbance
(c) Both (a) and (b)
(d) None of the above

16.10 Effect of HVDC transmission in power system
(a) Improves voltage stability (b) Causes voltage collapse
(c) Has no effect (d) None of the above

16.11 Which of the following is the short-term stability in a generator-driven system?
(a) Rotor-angle stability (b) Short-term voltage stability
(c) Frequency stability (d) Long-term voltage stability

16.12 Which of the following is the long-term stability in a generator-driven system?
(a) Rotor-angle stability (b) Short-term voltage stability
(c) Frequency stability (d) Long-term voltage stability

16.13 Which of the following is the short-term stability in a load-driven system?
(a) Rotor-angle stability (b) Short-term voltage stability
(c) Frequency stability (d) Long-term voltage stability

16.14 Which of the following is the long-term stability in a load-driven system?
(a) Rotor-angle stability (b) Short-term voltage stability
(c) Frequency stability (d) Long-term voltage stability

16.15 What is the result of frequency instability?
(a) Voltage collapse (b) Frequency swings
(c) Tripping of generating units (d) Both b and c

References

Books

1. A. Chakrabarti, D.P. Kothari, and A.K. Mukhopadhyay, *Performance, Operation and Control of EHV Power Transmission Systems*, Wheeler Publishing, New Delhi, 1995.
2. C.W. Taylor, *Power System Voltage Stability*, McGraw-Hill, New York, 1994.
3. I.J. Nagrath and D.P. Kothari, *Power System Engineering,* Tata McGraw-Hill, New Delhi, 1994.
4. P. Kundur, *Power System Stability and Control*, McGraw-Hill, New York, 1994.
5. K.R. Padiyar, *Power System Dynamics: Stability and Control*, John Wiley, Singapore, 1996.
6. T. Van Cutsem and C. Vournas, *Voltage Stability of Electric Power Systems*, Kluwer Int. Series, 1998.

Papers

7. C. Concordia (Ed.), "Special Issue on Voltage Stability and Collapse", *International Journal of Electrical Power and Energy Systems*, volume: 15, issue: 4, August 1993.
8. M.A. Pai and M.G.O. Grady, "Voltage Collapse Analysis with Reactive Generation and Voltage Dependent Constraints", *Elect Machines and Power Systems*, volume: 17, issue: 6, pp: 379–390, 1989.
9. CIGRE Task Force 38–06–01, "Expert Systems Applied to Voltage and Var Control", 1991.
10. "Operator Training Simulator", *EPRI Final Report* EL–7244, May 1991, prepared by EMPROS Systems International.
11. W. Xu and Y. Mansour, "Voltage Stability using Generic Dynamic Load Models", *IEEE, Trans. on Power Systems*, volume: 9, issue: 1, pp: 479–493, Feb 1994.
12. H.K. Verma, L.D. Arya, and D.P. Kothari, "Voltage Stability Enhancement by Reactive Power Loss Minimisation", *JIE (I)*, volume: 76, pp: 44–49, May 1995.

13. IEEE, special Publication 90 TH 0358–2 PWR, "Voltage Stability of Power Systems: Concepts, Analytical Tools, and Industry Experience", 1990.
14. N. Flatabo, R. Ognedal, and T. Carlsen, "Voltage Stability Condition in a Power Transmission System Calculated by Sensitivity Methods", *IEEE Transactions on Power System*, volume: 5, issue: 5, pp: 1286–1293, Nov 1990.
15. B. Gao, G.K. Morison, and P. Kundur, "Voltage Stability Evaluation Using Modal Analysis", *IEEE Transactions on Power System*, volume: 7, issue: 4, pp: 1529–1542, 1992.
16. Cutsem T Van, "A Method to Compute Reactive Power Margins wrt Voltage Collapse", *IEEE Transactions on Power System*, volume: 6, issue: 1, pp: 145–156, 1992.
17. V. Ajjarapu and C. Christy, "The Continuation Power Flow: A Tool for Steady State Voltage Stability Analysis", *IEEE PICA Conf Proc*, pp: 304–311, May 1991.
18. A.P. Löf, T. Sined, G. Anderson, and D.J. Hill, "Fast Calculation of a Voltage Stability Index", *IEEE Transactions on Power System,* volume: 7, issue: 1, pp: 54–64, 1992.
19. L.D. Arya, S.C. Chaube, and D.P. Kothari, "Line Outage Ranking based on Estimated Lower Bound on Minimum Eigen Value of Load Flow Jacobian", *JIE (I)*, volume: 79, pp: 126–129, Dec 1998.
20. P.R. Bijwe, S.M. Kelapure, D.P. Kothari, and K.K. Saxena, "Oscillatory Stability Limit Enhancement by Adaptive Control Rescheduling", *International Journal of Electrical Power and Energy Systems*, volume: 21, issue: 7, pp: 507–514, 1999.
21. L.D. Arya, S.C. Chaube, and D.P. Kothari, "Line Switching for Alleviating Overloads under Line Outage Condition taking Bus Voltage Limits into Account", *International Journal of Electrical Power and Energy Systems*, volume: 22, issue: 3, pp: 213–221, 2000.
22. P.R. Bijwe, D.P. Kothari, and S. Kelapure, "An Efficient Approach to Voltage Security Analysis and Enhancement", *International Journal of Electrical Power and Energy Systems*, volume: 22, issue: 7, pp: 483–486, Oct. 2000.
23. L.D. Arya, S.C. Chaube, and D.P. Kothari, "Reactive Power Optimisation using Static Stability Index (VSI)", *Electric Power Components and Systems*, volume: 29, issue: 7, pp: 615–628, July 2001.
24. L.D. Arya, S.C. Chaube, and D.P. Kothari, "Line Outage Ranking for Voltage Limit Violations with Corrective Rescheduling Avoiding Masking", *International Journal of Electrical Power and Energy Systems*, volume: 23, issue: 8, pp: 837–846, Nov 2001.
25. CIGRE Task Force 38–02–10, "Cigre Technical Brochure: Modelling of Voltage Collapse including Dynamic Phenomena", *Electra*, no. 147, pp: 71–77, April 1993.
26. Mark J. Laufenberg and M.A. Pai, "Hopf bifurcation control in power system with static var compensators", *International Journal of Electrical Power and Energy Systems*, volume: 19, issue: 5, pp: 339–347, 1997.
27. http://www.ee.washington.edu/research/pstca/pt30/ieee30ed.txt)
28. L.D. Arya, L.S. Titare, and D.P. Kothari, "Determination of Probabilistic Risk of Voltage Collapse Using Radial Basis Function (RBF) Network", *Electric Power Systems Research*, volume: 76, pp: 426–434, 2006.
29. L.D. Arya, L.S. Titare, and D.P. Kothari, "Probabilistic Assessment and Preventive Control of Voltage Security Margins Using Artificial Neural Network", *International Journal of Electrical Power and Energy Systems*, volume: 29, pp: 99–105, 2007.

30. L.D. Arya, S.C. Choube, M. Sreevasthav, and D.P. Kothari, "Particles Swarm Optimisation for Determining Shortest Distance to Voltage Collapse", *International Journal of Electrical Power and Energy Systems*, volume: 29, pp: 796–802, 2007.
31. M. Kowsalya, K.K. Ray, and D.P. Kothari, "Voltage Stability Margin Enhancement through Optimal Location of Var Compensation" *Journal of Electrical Engineering*, volume: 9, issue: 2, pp: 11–19, June 2009.
32. L.D. Arya, L.S. Titare, and D.P. Kothari, "An Approach to Mitigate the Risk of Voltage Collapse Accounting Uncertainties Using Improved Particle Swarm Optimization", *Applied Soft Computing*, 9 (2009), pp: 1197–1207.
33. M. Kowsalya, K.K. Ray, and D.P. Kothari, "Loss Optimization for Voltage Stability Enhancement Incorporating UPFC Using Particle Swarm Optimization", *Journal of Electrical Engineering and Technology*, volume: 4, issue: 4, pp: 492–498, 2009.
34. I.J. Raglend, S. Veeravalli, K. Sailaja, B. Sudheera, and D.P. Kothari, "Comparison of AI Techniques to Solve Combined Economic Emission Dispatch Problem with Line Flow Constraints", *International Journal of Electrical Power and Energy Systems,* volume: 32, issue 6, pp: 592–598, July 2010.
35. K.D. Dharmapala, A. Rajapakse, K. Narendra, and Y. Zhang, "Machine Learning Based Real-Time Monitoring of Long-Term Voltage Stability Using Voltage Stability Indices", *IEEE Access*, volume: 8, pp: 222544–222555, 2020.
36. L.S. Titare, P. Singh, and L.D. Arya, "Genetic Algorithm Used for Load Shedding Based on Sensitivity to Enhance Voltage Stability", *Journal of The Institution of Engineers*, volume: 95, issue: 4, pp: 337–343, 2014.
37. L.S. Titare, P. Singh, L.D. Arya, and S.C. Choube, "Optimal Reactive Power Rescheduling Based on EPSDE Algorithm to Enhance Static Voltage Stability", *International Journal of Electrical Power & Energy Systems*, volume: 63, pp: 588–599, 2014.
38. C. Chen, J. Wang, Z. Li, H. Sun, and Z. Wang, "PMU Uncertainty Quantification in Voltage Stability Analysis", *IEEE Transactions on Power Systems*, volume; 30, issue: 4, pp: 2196–2197, 2015.
39. R.K. Saket, R.C. Bansal, and Col. Gurmit Singh, "Reliability Evaluation of Power System Considering Voltage Stability and Continuation Power Flow", *Journal of Electrical Systems*, volume: 3, issue: 2, pp: 48–60, 2007.
40. Y. Song, D.J. Hill, and T. Liu, "Static Voltage Stability Analysis of Distribution Systems Based on Network-Load Admittance Ratio", *IEEE Transactions on Power Systems*, volume: 34, issue: 3, pp: 2270–2280, 2019.
41. L.D. Arya, P. Singh, and L.S. Titare, "Differential Evolution Applied for Anticipatory Load Shedding with Voltage Stability Considerations", *International Journal of Electrical Power & Energy Systems*, volume: 42, issue: 1, pp: 644–652, 2012.
42. H. Ge et al., "An Improved Real-Time Short-Term Voltage Stability Monitoring Method Based on Phase Rectification", *IEEE Transactions on Power Systems*, volume: 33, issue: 1, pp: 1068–1070, 2018.
43. L.D. Arya, A. Koshti, and S.C. Choube, "Distributed Generation Planning Using Differential Evolution Accounting Voltage Stability Consideration", *International Journal of Electrical Power & Energy Systems,* volume: 42, issue: 1, pp: 196–207, 2012.

44. M. Kamel, A. A. Karrar, and A.H. Eltom, "Development and Application of a New Voltage Stability Index for On-Line Monitoring and Shedding", *IEEE Transactions on Power Systems*, volume: 33, issue: 2, pp: 1231–1241, 2018.
45. L.D. Arya, S.C. Choube, and R.K. Saket, "Composite System Reliability Evaluation Based on Static Voltage Stability Limit", *Journal of the Institution of Engineers*, volume: 80, issue: 01, pp: 133–140, 2000.

ANNEXURE 16.1

Data for IEEE 30 Bus System
(Taken from http://www.ee.washington.edu/research/pstca/pf30/ieee30cdf.txt)
08/20/93 UW Archive100.0 1961 W IEEE 30 Bus Test Case
Bus Data Follow 30 Items

1 Glen Lyn	132	1	1	3	1.060	0.0	0.0	0.0	260.2	–16.1	132.0	1.060	0.0	0.0	0.0	0.0	0
2 Claytor	132	1	1	2	1.043	–5.48	21.7	12.7	40.0	50.0	132.0	1.045	50.0	–40.0	0.0	0.0	0
3 Kumis	132	1	1	0	1.021	–7.96	2.4	1.2	0.0	0.0	132.0	0.0	0.0	0.0	0.0	0.0	0
4 Hancock	132	1	1	0	1.012	–9.62	7.6	1.6	0.0	0.0	132.0	0.0	0.0	0.0	0.0	0.0	0
5 Fieldale	132	1	1	2	1.010	–14.37	94.2	19.0	0.0	37.0	132.0	1.010	40.0	–40.0	0.0	0.0	0
6 Roanoke	132	1	1	0	1.010	–11.34	0.0	0.0	0.0	0.0	132.0	0.0	0.0	0.0	0.0	0.0	0
7 Blaine	132	1	1	0	1.002	–13.12	22.8	10.9	0.0	0.0	132.0	0.0	0.0	0.0	0.0	0.0	0
8 Reusens	132	1	1	2	1.010	–12.10	30.0	30.0	0.0	37.3	132.0	1.010	40.0	–10.0	0.0	0.0	0
9 Roanoke	1.0	1	1	0	1.051	–14.38	0.0	0.0	0.0	0.0	1.0	0.0	0.0	0.0	0.0	0.0	0
10 Roanoke	33	1	1	0	1.045	–15.97	5.8	2.0	0.0	0.0	33.0	0.0	0.0	0.0	0.0	0.19	0
11 Roanoke	11	1	1	2	1.082	–14.39	0.0	0.0	0.0	16.2	11.0	1.082	24.0	–6.0	0.0	0.0	0
12 Hancock	33	1	1	0	1.057	–15.24	11.2	7.5	0.0	0.0	33.0	0.0	0.0	0.0	0.0	0.0	0
13 Hancock	11	1	1	2	1.071	–15.24	0.0	0.0	0.0	10.6	11.0	1.071	24.0	–6.0	0.0	0.0	0
14 Bus 14	33	1	1	0	1.042	–16.13	6.2	1.6	0.0	0.0	33.0	0.0	0.0	0.0	0.0	0.0	0
15 Bus 15	33	1	1	0	1.038	–16.22	8.2	2.5	0.0	0.0	33.0	0.0	0.0	0.0	0.0	0.0	0
16 Bus 16	33	1	1	0	1.045	–15.83	3.5	1.8	0.0	0.0	33.0	0.0	0.0	0.0	0.0	0.0	0
17 Bus 17	33	1	1	0	1.040	–16.14	9.0	5.8	0.0	0.0	33.0	0.0	0.0	0.0	0.0	0.0	0
18 Bus 18	33	1	1	0	1.028	–16.82	3.2	0.9	0.0	0.0	33.0	0.0	0.0	0.0	0.0	0.0	0
19 Bus 19	33	1	1	0	1.026	–17.00	9.5	3.4	0.0	0.0	33.0	0.0	0.0	0.0	0.0	0.0	0
20 Bus 20	33	1	1	0	1.030	–16.80	2.2	0.7	0.0	0.0	33.0	0.0	0.0	0.0	0.0	0.0	0
21 Bus 21	33	1	1	0	1.033	–16.42	17.5	11.2	0.0	0.0	33.0	0.0	0.0	0.0	0.0	0.0	0
22 Bus 22	33	1	1	0	1.033	–16.41	0.0	0.0	0.0	0.0	33.0	0.0	0.0	0.0	0.0	0.0	0
23 Bus 23	33	1	1	0	1.027	–16.61	3.2	1.6	0.0	0.0	33.0	0.0	0.0	0.0	0.0	0.0	0
24 Bus 24	33	1	1	0	1.021	–16.78	8.7	6.7	0.0	0.0	33.0	0.0	0.0	0.0	0.0	0.043	0
25 Bus 25	33	1	1	0	1.017	–16.35	0.0	0.0	0.0	0.0	33.0	0.0	0.0	0.0	0.0	0.0	0
26 Bus 26	33	1	1	0	1.000	–16.77	3.5	2.3	0.0	0.0	33.0	0.0	0.0	0.0	0.0	0.0	0
27 Cloverdle	33	1	1	0	1.023	–15.82	0.0	0.0	0.0	0.0	33.0	0.0	0.0	0.0	0.0	0.0	0
28 Cloverdle	132	1	1	0	1.007	–11.97	0.0	0.0	0.0	0.0	132.0	0.0	0.0	0.0	0.0	0.0	0
29 Bus 29	33	1	1	0	1.003	–17.06	2.4	0.9	0.0	0.0	33.0	0.0	0.0	0.0	0.0	0.0	0
30 Bus 30	33	1	1	0	0.992	–17.94	10.6	1.9	0.0	0.0	33.0	0.0	0.0	0.0	0.0	0.0	0
–999																	

Branch Data Follow 41 Items

1	2	1	1	1	0	0.0192	0.0575	0.0528	0	0	0	0.0	0.0	0.0	0.0	0.0	0.0	0.0	0.0
1	3	1	1	1	0	0.0452	0.1652	0.0408	0	0	0	0.0	0.0	0.0	0.0	0.0	0.0	0.0	0.0

(*Contd.*)

2	4	1	1	1	0	0.0570	0.1737	0.0368	0	0	0	0.0	0.0	0.0	0.0	0.0	0.0	0.0	0.0
3	4	1	1	1	0	0.0132	0.0379	0.0084	0	0	0	0.0	0.0	0.0	0.0	0.0	0.0	0.0	0.0
2	5	1	1	1	0	0.0472	0.1983	0.0418	0	0	0	0.0	0.0	0.0	0.0	0.0	0.0	0.0	0.0
2	6	1	1	1	0	0.0581	0.1763	0.0374	0	0	0	0.0	0.0	0.0	0.0	0.0	0.0	0.0	0.0
4	6	1	1	1	0	0.0119	0.0414	0.0090	0	0	0	0.0	0.0	0.0	0.0	0.0	0.0	0.0	0.0
5	7	1	1	1	0	0.0460	0.1160	0.0204	0	0	0	0.0	0.0	0.0	0.0	0.0	0.0	0.0	0.0
6	7	1	1	1	0	0.0267	0.0820	0.0170	0	0	0	0.0	0.0	0.0	0.0	0.0	0.0	0.0	0.0
6	8	1	1	1	0	0.0120	0.0420	0.0090	0	0	0	0.0	0.0	0.0	0.0	0.0	0.0	0.0	0.0
6	9	1	1	1	0	0.0	0.2080	0.0	0	0	0	0.0	0.0978	0.0	0.0	0.0	0.0	0.0	0.0
6	10	1	1	1	0	0.0	0.5560	0.0	0	0	0	0.0	0.969	0.0	0.0	0.0	0.0	0.0	0.0
9	11	1	1	1	0	0.0	0.2080	0.0	0	0	0	0.0	0.0	0.0	0.0	0.0	0.0	0.0	0.0
9	10	1	1	1	0	0.0	0.1100	0.0	0	0	0	0.0	0.0	0.0	0.0	0.0	0.0	0.0	0.0
4	12	1	1	1	0	0.0	0.2560	0.0	0	0	0	0.0	0.932	0.0	0.0	0.0	0.0	0.0	0.0
12	13	1	1	1	0	0.0	0.1400	0.0	0	0	0	0.0	0.0	0.0	0.0	0.0	0.0	0.0	0.0
12	14	1	1	1	0	0.1231	0.2559	0.0	0	0	0	0.0	0.0	0.0	0.0	0.0	0.0	0.0	0.0
12	15	1	1	1	0	0.0662	0.1304	0.0	0	0	0	0.0	0.0	0.0	0.0	0.0	0.0	0.0	0.0
12	16	1	1	1	0	0.0945	0.1987	0.0	0	0	0	0.0	0.0	0.0	0.0	0.0	0.0	0.0	0.0
14	15	1	1	1	0	0.2210	0.1997	0.0	0	0	0	0.0	0.0	0.0	0.0	0.0	0.0	0.0	0.0
16	17	1	1	1	0	0.0524	0.1923	0.0	0	0	0	0.0	0.0	0.0	0.0	0.0	0.0	0.0	0.0
15	18	1	1	1	0	0.1073	0.2185	0.0	0	0	0	0.0	0.0	0.0	0.0	0.0	0.0	0.0	0.0
18	19	1	1	1	0	0.0639	0.1292	0.0	0	0	0	0.0	0.0	0.0	0.0	0.0	0.0	0.0	0.0
19	20	1	1	1	0	0.0340	0.0680	0.0	0	0	0	0.0	0.0	0.0	0.0	0.0	0.0	0.0	0.0
10	20	1	1	1	0	0.0936	0.2090	0.0	0	0	0	0.0	0.0	0.0	0.0	0.0	0.0	0.0	0.0
10	17	1	1	1	0	0.0324	0.0845	0.0	0	0	0	0.0	0.0	0.0	0.0	0.0	0.0	0.0	0.0
10	21	1	1	1	0	0.0348	0.0749	0.0	0	0	0	0.0	0.0	0.0	0.0	0.0	0.0	0.0	0.0
10	22	1	1	1	0	0.0727	0.1499	0.0	0	0	0	0.0	0.0	0.0	0.0	0.0	0.0	0.0	0.0
21	22	1	1	1	0	0.0116	0.0236	0.0	0	0	0	0.0	0.0	0.0	0.0	0.0	0.0	0.0	0.0
15	23	1	1	1	0	0.1000	0.2020	0.0	0	0	0	0.0	0.0	0.0	0.0	0.0	0.0	0.0	0.0
22	24	1	1	1	0	0.1150	0.1790	0.0	0	0	0	0.0	0.0	0.0	0.0	0.0	0.0	0.0	0.0
23	24	1	1	1	0	0.1320	0.2700	0.0	0	0	0	0.0	0.0	0.0	0.0	0.0	0.0	0.0	0.0
24	25	1	1	1	0	0.1885	0.3292	0.0	0	0	0	0.0	0.0	0.0	0.0	0.0	0.0	0.0	0.0
25	26	1	1	1	0	0.2544	0.3800	0.0	0	0	0	0.0	0.0	0.0	0.0	0.0	0.0	0.0	0.0
25	27	1	1	1	0	0.1093	0.2087	0.0	0	0	0	0.0	0.0	0.0	0.0	0.0	0.0	0.0	0.0
28	27	1	1	1	0	0.0	0.3960	0.0	0	0	0	0.0	0.968	0.0	0.0	0.0	0.0	0.0	0.0
27	29	1	1	1	0	0.2198	0.4153	0.0	0	0	0	0.0	0.0	0.0	0.0	0.0	0.0	0.0	0.0
27	30	1	1	1	0	0.3202	0.6027	0.0	0	0	0	0.0	0.0	0.0	0.0	0.0	0.0	0.0	0.0
29	30	1	1	1	0	0.2399	0.4533	0.0	0	0	0	0.0	0.0	0.0	0.0	0.0	0.0	0.0	0.0
8	28	1	1	1	0	0.0636	0.2000	0.0428	0	0	0	0.0	0.0	0.0	0.0	0.0	0.0	0.0	0.0
6	28	1	1	1	0	0.0169	0.0599	0.0130	0	0	0	0.0	0.0	0.0	0.0	0.0	0.0	0.0	0.0
–999																			

Loss Zones Follows Items

1 IEEE 30 Bus

–99

Interchange Data Follows 1 Items

–9

1 2 Claytor 132 0.0 999.99 IEEE 30 IEEE 30 Bus Test Case

Tie Lines Follows 0 Items

–999

End of Data

THREE WINDING TRANSFORMER EQUIVALENTS
HANCOCK
ROANOKE
CLOVERDALE
33 kV
132 kV
GLEN LYN
KUMIS
HANCOCK
ROANOKE
No.1
No.2
REUSENS
BLAINE
CLAYTOR
FIELDALE
Ⓖ GENERATORS
Ⓒ SYNCHRONOUS CONDENSORS

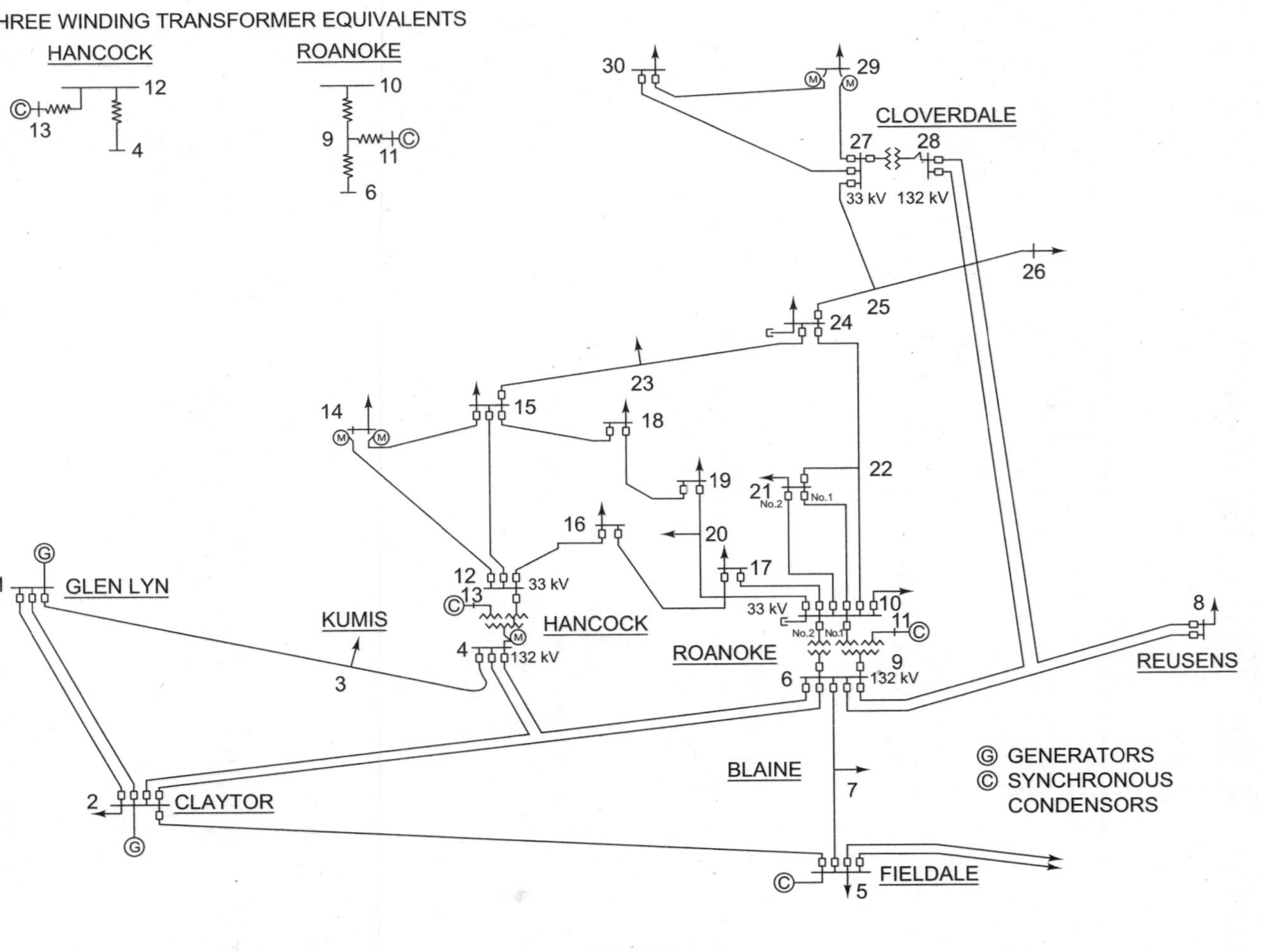

Fig. 16.12

CHAPTER

17 State Estimation of Power Systems

17.1 ► INTRODUCTION

State estimation plays a very important role in the monitoring and control of modern power systems. As in case of load flow analysis, the aim of state estimation is to obtain the best possible values of the bus voltage magnitudes and angles by processing the available network data. Two modifications are, however, introduced now in order to achieve a higher degree of accuracy of the solution at the cost of some additional computations. First, it is recognised that the numerical values of the data to be processed for the state estimation are generally noisy due to the errors present. Second, it is noted that there are a larger number of variables in the system (e.g., P, Q line flows) which can be measured but are not utilised in the load flow analysis. Thus, the process involves imperfect measurements that are redundant and the process of estimating the system states is based on a statistical criterion that estimates the true value of the state variables to minimise or maximise the selected criterion. A well known and commonly used criterion is that of minimising the sum of the squares of the differences between the estimated and 'true' (i.e., measured) values of a function.

Most state estimation programs in practical use are formulated as overdetermined systems of nonlinear equations and solved as weighted least-squares (WLS) problems.

State estimators may be both static and dynamic. Both have been developed for power systems. This chapter will introduce the basic principles of a static-state estimator.

In a power system, the state variables are the voltage magnitudes and phase angles at the buses. The inputs to an estimator are imperfect (noisy) power system measurements. The estimator is designed to give the 'best estimate' of the system voltage and phase angles keeping in mind that there are errors in the measured quantities and that there may be redundant measurements. The output data are then used at the energy control centres for carrying out several real-time or on-line system studies such as economic dispatch (Chapter 7), security analysis (Chapter 13).

17.2 ► LEAST SQUARES ESTIMATION: BASIC SOLUTION [7]–[9]

As will be seen later in Section 17.3, the problem of power system state estimation is a special case of the more general problem of estimation of a random vector x from the numerical values of another related random vector y with relatively little statistical information being available for both x and y. In such cases, the method of least-squared-error estimation may be utilised with good results and has accordingly been widely employed.

Assume that x is a vector of n random variables $x_1, x_2, ..., x_n$, that y is another vector of m ($> n$) random variables $y_1, y_2, ... y_m$ and both are related as

$$\boldsymbol{y} = \boldsymbol{Hx} + \boldsymbol{r} \tag{17.1}$$

where $\boldsymbol{H}$ is a known matrix of dimension $m \times n$ and r is a zero mean random variable of the same dimension as y. The vector x represents the variables to be estimated, while the vector y represents the variables whose numerical values are available. Equation (17.1) suggests that the measurement vector y is linearly related to the unknown vector x and in addition is corrupted by the vector r (error vector).

The problem is basically to obtain the best possible value of the vector x from the given values of the vector y. Since the variable r is assumed to be zero mean, one may take the expectation of Eq. (17.1) and get the relation

$$\bar{y} = H\bar{x} \tag{17.2}$$

where $\bar{x}, \bar{y}$ = expected value of x and y, respectively.

This shows that the load flow methods of Chapter 6 could be used to estimate the mean values of the bus voltages. However, one would like to estimate the actual values of bus voltages rather than their averages.

One possible way of obtaining of least possible estimate of the vector x from y lies in the use of the method of least square estimation (LSE). To develop this method, assume that $\hat{\mathbf{x}}$ represents the desired estimate of x so that $\hat{\mathbf{y}}$ is given by the equation

$$\hat{\mathbf{y}} = H\hat{\mathbf{x}} \tag{17.3}$$

represents the estimate of the vector y. The error $\tilde{y}$ of the estimation of y is then given by

$$\tilde{y} = y - \hat{y} \tag{17.4}$$

The estimate $\hat{\mathbf{x}}$ is defined to be the LSE if it is computed by minimising the estimation index J given by

$$J = \tilde{y}'\tilde{y} \tag{17.5}$$

From Eqs. (17.31) and (17.4), one gets the following expression for the index:

$$J = y'y - y'H\hat{\mathbf{x}} - \hat{\mathbf{x}}'H'y + \hat{\mathbf{x}}'H'H\hat{\mathbf{x}} \tag{17.6}$$

For minimising $J = f_{(\hat{\mathbf{x}})}$, we must satisfy the following condition.

$$\text{grad}_{(\hat{\mathbf{x}})}J = 0 \tag{17.7}$$

It is easy to check (see, e.g. [1]) that Eq. (17.7) leads to the following result.

$$H'H\hat{\mathbf{x}} - H'y = 0 \tag{17.8}$$

This equation is called the 'normal equation' and may be solved explicitly for the LSE of the vector $\hat{\mathbf{x}}$ as

$$\hat{\mathbf{x}} = (H'H)^{-1} H'y \tag{17.9}$$

Example 17.1 In order to illustrate the method of LSE, let us consider the simple problem of estimating two random variables x_1 and x_2 by using the data for a three-dimensional vector y.

Solution

Assume
$$H = \begin{bmatrix} 1 & 0 \\ 0 & 1 \\ 1 & 1 \end{bmatrix}$$

The matrix $H'H$ is then given by

$$H'H = \begin{bmatrix} 2 & 1 \\ 1 & 2 \end{bmatrix}$$ and its inverse is

$$(H'H)^{-1} = \begin{bmatrix} 2/3 & -1/3 \\ -1/3 & 2/3 \end{bmatrix}$$

It is easy to form the vector $H'y$ and combining this with the inverse of $(H'H)$, the following estimate of x is obtained.

$$\hat{\mathbf{x}} = \begin{bmatrix} (2/3)y_1 - (1/3)(y_2 - y_3) \\ -(1/3)y_1 + (2/3)y_2 + (1/3)y_3 \end{bmatrix}$$

17.2.1 Weighted LSE

The estimate given in Eq. (17.9) is often referred to as the 'ordinary' least-squares estimate and is obtained by minimising the index function that puts equal weightage to the errors of estimation of all components of the vector y. It is often desirable to put different weightages on the different components of y since some of the measurements may be more reliable and accurate than the others and these should be given more importance. To achieve this, we define the estimation index as

$$J = \tilde{y}' W \tilde{y} \tag{17.10}$$

where W is a real symmetric weighting matrix of dimension $m \times m$. This is often chosen as a diagonal matrix for simplicity.

It is relatively straightforward to extend the method of LSE to the weighted form of J and to derive the following form of the normal equation.

$$H'WH\hat{\mathbf{x}} - H'Wy = 0 \tag{17.11a}$$

This leads to the desired weighted least squares estimate (WLSE)

$$\hat{\mathbf{x}} = (H'WH)^{-1} H'Wy \tag{17.11b}$$

This pertains to minimisation as the hessian $2H'WH$ is a non-negative definite.

Some Properties:

Rewriting Eq. (17.11b) as

$$\hat{\mathbf{x}} = k\, y \tag{17.12a}$$

where

$$\mathbf{k} = (H'WH)^{-1} H'W. \tag{17.12b}$$

Here the matrix k depends on the value of H and the choice of W.

Using Eqs. (17.1) and (17.12b) it is easy to get t[illegible]e relation as follows.

$$\hat{\mathbf{x}} = KHx + [illegible]$$

$$= (H'WH[illegible]^{-1} (H'WH)\, x + \mathbf{kr}$$

or

$$\hat{\mathbf{x}} = x + kr \tag{17.13}$$

and

$$[illegible]\{\hat{\mathbf{x}}\} = E\{x\} \tag{17.14}$$

In Eq. (17.14) it is assumed th[illegible] e error r is statistically independent of columns of H and the vector $\mathbf{r}$ has a zero mean. An estimate that satisfied Eq. (17.14) is called an unbiased estimate. This implies that the estimation error is zero on an average.

$$\tilde{x} = \mathbf{kr} \tag{17.15a}$$

The covariance of the error of estimation is therefore given by

$$P_x = KRK' \tag{17.15b}$$

where R is the covariance of the error vector r. Note that the covariance P_x is a measure of the accuracy of the estimation and a smaller trace of this matrix indicates a better estimate. Equation (17.15b) suggests that the best possible choice of the weighting matrix is to set $W = R^{-1}$. The optimum value of the error covariance matrix is then given by

$$P_x = (H'R^{-1} H)^{-1} \tag{17.15c}$$

Example 17.2 Assume that in the Example 17.1, we want to [illegible]tain the WLSE of the variable x by choosing the following weighting matrix

$$W = \begin{bmatrix} 0.1 & & \\ & 1 & \\ & & 0.1 \end{bmatrix}$$

Solution

The matrix $H'WH$ is

$$H'WH = \begin{bmatrix} 0.2 & 0.1 \\ 0.1 & 1.1 \end{bmatrix}$$

and the matrix $H'W$ is obtained as

$$H'W = \begin{bmatrix} 0.1 & 0 & 0.1 \\ 0 & 1 & 0.1 \end{bmatrix}$$

The weighted least squares estimate of the vector **x** is then obtained as [from Eq. (17.11b)]

$$\hat{\mathbf{x}} = \begin{bmatrix} (11/21)y_1 & -(10/21)y_2 & (10/21)y_3 \\ -(1/21)y_1 & (20/21)y_2 & (1/21)y_3 \end{bmatrix}$$

If this result is compared with the result in Example 17.1, the effect of introducing the weighting on the estimate is apparent. Note that the choice of W in this case suggests the data for y_2 is considered more valuable and this results in the components of x being more heavily dependent on y_2.

The matrix k is in this case found to be [Eq. (17.12b)]

$$K = \begin{bmatrix} 11/21 & -10/21 & 10/21 \\ -1/21 & 20/21 & 1/21 \end{bmatrix}$$

If the covariance of the measurement error is assumed to be $R = I$, the covariance of the estimation error is obtained as [Ref. Eq. (17.15c)]

$$P_x = (1/147)\begin{bmatrix} 107 & -67 \\ -67 & 134 \end{bmatrix}$$

The choice of W above yields unacceptably large estimation error variances.

Let us now choose the weighting matrix $W = I$. The matrix K is then obtained as

$$K = \begin{bmatrix} 2/3 & -1/3 & 1/3 \\ -1/3 & 2/3 & 1/3 \end{bmatrix}$$

The error covariance matrix is then given by

$$P_x = (1/9)\begin{bmatrix} 6 & -3 \\ -3 & 6 \end{bmatrix}$$

The error variances are now seen to be much smaller as is to be expected.

17.2.2 Nonlinear Measurements

The case of special interest to the power system state estimation problem corresponds to the nonlinear measurement model.

$$y = h(x) + r \tag{17.16}$$

where $h(x)$ represents an m dimensional vector of nonlinear functions of the variable x. It is assumed that the components of the vector $h(x)$ are continuous in their arguments and therefore may be differentiated with respect to the components of x. The problem is to extend the method of least squares in order to estimate the vector x from the data for the vector y with these two variables being related through Eq. (17.16)

To mimic our treatment of the linear measurement case, assume that $\hat{\mathbf{x}}$ represents the desired estimate so that the estimate of the measurement y could be obtained using the relation

$$\hat{\mathbf{y}} = h(\hat{\mathbf{x}}) \tag{17.17a}$$

This yields the error of estimation of the vector y

$$\tilde{y} = y - h(\hat{\mathbf{x}}) \tag{17.17b}$$

In order to obtain the WLSE of x, we must choose the index of estimation J as follows.

$$J = [y - h(\hat{\mathbf{x}})]' \, W \, [y - h(\hat{\mathbf{x}})] \tag{17.18}$$

The necessary condition for the index J to have a minimum at x, is given by Eq. (17.19).

$$[y - h(\hat{\mathbf{x}})] \, H(\hat{\mathbf{x}}) = 0 \tag{17.19}$$

where $H(\hat{\mathbf{x}})$ is the Jacobian of $h(x)$ evaluated at $\hat{\mathbf{x}}$. In general this nonlinear equation can not be solved for the desired estimate $\hat{\mathbf{x}}$. A way out of this difficulty is to make use of the linearisation technique. Let us assume that an *a priori* estimate x_0 of the vector x is available (say from the load flow solution).

Using Taylor series approximation, we get

$$y = h(x_0) + H_0 (x - x_0) + r \tag{17.20}$$

where H_0 stands for the Jacobian evaluated at $x = x_0$ and the noise term r is now assumed to include the effects of the higher order terms in the Taylor series. Equation (17.20) can be rewritten as

$$\Delta y = y - h(x_0) = H_0 \, \Delta x + r \tag{17.21}$$

where Δy is the perturbed measurement and Δx is the perturbed value of the vector x. An WLSE of x is then easily obtained as discussed earlier and this leads to the desired expression for the linearised solution of the nonlinear estimation problem.

$$\hat{x} = x_0 + [H_0' W H_0]^{-1} H_0' W \{y - h(x_0)\} \tag{17.22}$$

It is not likely that the estimate $\hat{x}$ obtained from Eq. (17.22) is going to be of much use since, in general, the *a priori* estimate x_0 may not be close to the optimal value of the vector $\mathbf{x}$. However, Eq. (17.22) provides us with a very useful result in the sense that it shows a mechanism for improving on the initial estimate by making use of the available measurements. Having obtained new estimate $\hat{x}$, the process of linearisation is repeated as many times as desired and this leads to the following iterative form of the solution of the nonlinear estimation problem.

$$\hat{x}(l+1) = \hat{x}(l) + K(l) \, [y - h[\hat{x}(l)]\} \tag{17.23}$$

where the matrix $K(l)$ is defined as

$$K(l) = [H_l' W H_l]^{-1} H_l' W \tag{17.24}$$

The index l represents the iteration number and H_l represents the value of the Jacobian evaluated at $x = \hat{x}(l)$. Usually the iterative process is terminated whenever the norm of the difference of two successive values of the estimate $\hat{x}(l+1) - \hat{x}(l)$ reaches a pre-selected threshold level.

A flow chart for implementing the iterative algorithm is shown in Fig. 17.1. A major source of computation in the algorithm lies in the need to update the Jacobian at every stage of iteration. As discussed earlier in Chap. 6 [see Eqs. (6.86) and (6.87)] it is often possible to reduce the computations by holding the value of H a constant, possibly after l exceeds 2 or 3. This is, in general, permissible in view of the fact that the change in estimate tends to be rather small after a couple of iterations.

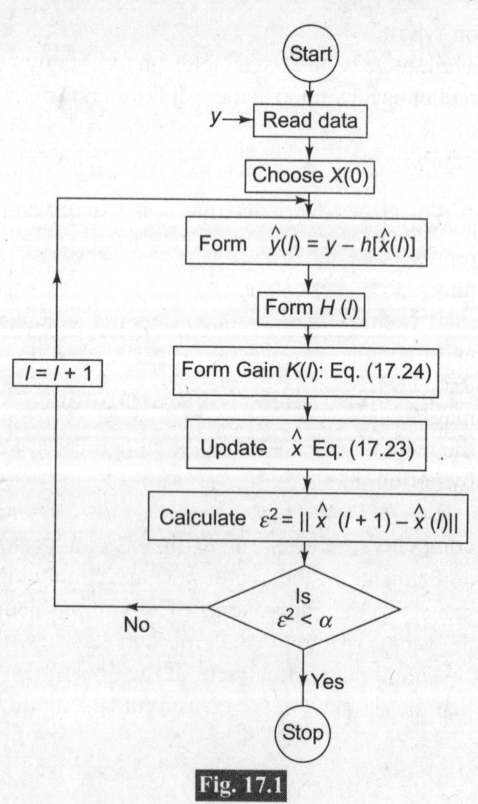

Fig. 17.1

Example 17.3 Consider the simple case of a scalar variable x and assume that the relationship between the measurement y and the variable x is given by

$$y = x^3 + r$$

Solution The Jacobian H_j is easily obtained in this case and the iterative algorithm takes the explicit form

$$\hat{x}(l+1) = \hat{x}(l) + [3\hat{x}(l)]^{-2}\{y - [\hat{x}(l)]^3\}$$

where we have used $W = 1$.

Let the correct value of x' be equal to 2 and assume that due to the effect of r the measured value of y is found to be 8.5. Also, assume that the initial estimate $x(0)$ is taken to be equal to 1. The table below gives the results of the first few iterations.

1	$\hat{x}(l)$
0	1.0
1	3.5
2	2.56
3	2.16

It is apparent that the algorithm would yield the correct solution after several iterations.

17.3 ▶ STATIC STATE ESTIMATION OF POWER SYSTEMS [10]–[12]

As noted earlier, for a system with N buses, the state vector x may be defined as the $2N - 1$ vector of the $N - 1$ voltage angles $\delta_2, \ldots, \delta_N$ and the N voltage magnitudes $V_1, V_2, \ldots, V_N$. The load flow data, depending on type of bus, are generally corrupted by noise and the problem is that of processing an adequate set of available data in order to estimate the state vector. The readily available data may not provide enough redundancy (the large geographical area over which the system is spread often prohibits the telemetering of all the available measurements to the central computing station). The redundancy factor, defined as the ratio m/n should have a value in the range 1.5 to 2.8 in order that the computed value of the state may have the desired accuracy. It may be necessary to include the data for the power flows in both the directions of some of the tie lines in order to increase the redundancy factor. In fact, some 'pseudo measurements' which represent the computed values of such quantities as the active and reactive injections at some remote buses may also be included in the vector $y(k)$.

It is thus apparent that the problem of estimation of the power system state is a non-linear problem and may be solved using either the batch processing or sequential processing formula [see Section 3.3 of Ref. 1]. Also, if the system is assumed to have reached a steady-state condition, the voltage angles and magnitudes would remain more or less constant. The state estimation problem is then a static problem and the methods of Section 17.2 may be used, if so desired. To develop explicit solutions, it is necessary to start by noting the exact forms of the model equations for the components of the vector $y(k)$.

Let P_i and Q_i denote the active and reactive power injections of ith bus. These are related to the components of the state vector through the following equations:

$$P_i = \sum_{j=1}^{N} |V_i||V_j||Y_{ij}|\cos(-\delta_i + \delta_j + \theta_{ij}) \tag{17.25}$$

$$Q_i = -\sum_{j=1}^{N} |V_i||V_j||Y_{ij}|\sin(-\delta_i + \delta_j + \theta_{ij}) \tag{17.26}$$

where $|Y_{ij}|$ represents the magnitude and θ_{ij} represents the angle of the admittance of the line connecting the ith and jth buses. The active and reactive components of the power flow from the ith to the jth bus, on the other hand, are given by the following relations:

$$P_{ij} = |V_i|\,|V_j|\,|Y_{ij}| \cos(\delta_i - \delta_j + \theta_{ij}) - |V_i|^2\,|Y_{ij}| \cos\theta_{ij} \tag{17.27}$$

$$Q_{ij} = |V_i|\,|V_j|\,|Y_{ij}| \sin(\delta_i - \delta_j + \theta_{ij}) - |V_i|^2\,|Y_{ij}| \sin\theta_{ij} \tag{17.28}$$

Let us assume that the vector y has the general form

$$y = [P_1 \ldots P_N\, Q_1 \ldots Q_N\, P_{12} \ldots P_{N-1,\,N}\, Q_{12} \ldots Q_{N-1,\,N},\, \delta_2 \ldots \delta_N\, |V_1|, \ldots, |V_N|]' \tag{17.29}$$

The Jacobian H will then have the form

$$H = \begin{bmatrix} H_1 & H_2 \\ H_3 & H_4 \\ H_5 & H_6 \\ H_7 & H_8 \\ \cdots & \cdots \\ I_{N-1} & 0 \\ 0 & I_N \end{bmatrix} \tag{17.30}$$

where I_N is the identity matrix of dimension N, H_1 is the $N \times (N-1)$ submatrix of the partial derivatives of the active power injections wrt δ's, H_2 is the $N \times N$ submatrix of the partial-derivatives of the active power injections wrt $|V|^s$ and so on. Jacobian H will also be a sparse matrix since Y is a sparse matrix.

Two special cases of interest are those corresponding to the use of only the active and reactive injections and the use of only the active and reactive line flows in the vector y. In the first case, there are a total of $2N$ components of y compared to the $2N - 1$ components of the state x. There is thus almost no redundancy of measurements. However, this case is very close to the case of load flow analysis and therefore provides a good measure of the relative strengths of the methods of load flow and state estimation. In the second case, it is possible to ensure a good enough redundancy if there are enough tie lines in the system. One can obtain two measurements using two separate meters at the two ends of a single tie-line. Since these two data should have equal magnitudes but opposite signs, this arrangement also provides with a ready check of meter malfunctioning. There are other advantages of this arrangement as will be discussed later.

17.3.1 The Injections Only Algorithm

In this case, the model equation has the form

$$y = h[x] + r \tag{17.31}$$

with the components of the nonlinear function given by

$$h_i[x] = \sum_{j=1}^{N} |V_i|\,|V_j|\,|Y_{ij}| \cos(\delta_i - \delta_j + \theta_{ij}),\ i = 1, \ldots N \tag{17.32a}$$

$$= \sum_{j=1}^{N} |V_{N-i}|\,|V_j|\,|Y_{N-i,j}| \sin(\delta_i - \delta_j + \theta_{ij}),\ i = N+1, N+2 \ldots 2N \tag{17.32b}$$

The elements of the submatrices H_1, H_2, H_3 and H_4 are then determined easily as follows:

$$H_1(i, j) = |V_i|\,|V_j|\,|Y_{ij}| \sin(\delta_i - \delta_j + \delta_{ij}), \quad i = 1, 2, \ldots, N,\ j = 1, 2, \ldots, N-1$$

$$H_2(i, j) = |V_i|\,|Y_{ij}| \cos(\delta_i - \delta_j + \theta_{ij}) \quad i = 1, 2, \ldots, N,\ j = 1, 2, \ldots, N.$$

$$H_3(i, j) = -|V_i|\,|V_j|\,|Y_{ij}| \cos(\delta_i - \delta_j + \theta_{ij}) \quad i = 1, 2, \ldots, N,\ j = 1, 2, \ldots, N-1$$

$$H_4(i, j) = |V_i|\,|Y_{ij}| \sin(\delta_i - \delta_j + \theta_{ij}) \quad i = 1, 2, \ldots, N,\ j = 1, 2, \ldots, N. \tag{17.33}$$

Equation (17.33) may be used to determine the Jacobian at any specified value of the system state vector. The injections only state estimation algorithm is then obtained directly from the results of Section 17.2. Since the problem is nonlinear it is convenient to employ the iterative algorithm given in Eq. (17.22).

Applying the principle of decoupling, the submatrices H_2 and H_3 become null with the result that the linearised model equation may be approximated as:

$$\Delta y = \begin{bmatrix} H_1 & 0 \\ 0 & H_4 \end{bmatrix} \Delta x + r \tag{17.34}$$

If we partition the vectors y, x and r as

$$\Delta y = \begin{bmatrix} \Delta y_p \\ \Delta y_q \end{bmatrix}; x = \begin{bmatrix} \Delta y_\delta \\ \Delta x_v \end{bmatrix}; r = \begin{bmatrix} r_p \\ r_q \end{bmatrix}$$

then, Eq. (17.34) may be rewritten in the decoupled form as the following two separate equations for the two partitioned components of the state vector

$$\Delta y_p = H_1 \, \Delta x_\delta + r_p \tag{17.35}$$

$$\Delta y_q = H_4 \, \Delta x_v + r_q \tag{17.36}$$

Based on these two equations, we obtain the following nearly decoupled state estimation algorithms.

$$\hat{x}_\delta(j+1) = x_\delta(j) + [H_1'(j)\, W_p\, H_1(j)]^{-1}\, H_1(j)\, \{y_p - h_p[\hat{x}(j)]\}\; j = 0, 1, 2, \ldots \tag{17.37}$$

$$\hat{x}_v(j+1) = \hat{x}_v(j) + [H_4'(j)\, W_q\, H_4(j)]^{-1}\, H_4'(j)\, W_q\, \{y_q - h_q[\hat{x}(j)]\}\; j = 0, 1, 2, \ldots \tag{17.38}$$

where the subscripts p and q are used to indicate the partitions of the weighing matrix W and the nonlinear function $h(.)$ which correspond to the vectors y_p and y_q, respectively. As mentioned earlier, if the covariances R_p and R_q of the errors r_p and r_q are assumed known, one should select $W_p = R_p^{-1}$ and $W_q = R_q^{-1}$.

Note that Eqs. (17.37) and (17.38) are not truly decoupled because the partitions of the nonlinear function depend on the estimate of the entire state vector. It may be possible to assume that $v_i(j) = 1$ for all i and j while Eq. (17.37) is being used in order to estimate the angle part of the state vector. Similarly one may assume $\delta_i(j) = 0°$ for all i and j while using Eq. (17.38) in order to estimate the voltage part of the state vector. Such approximations allow the two equations to be completely decoupled but may not yield very good solutions. A better way to decouple the two equations would be to use the load flow solutions for x_v and x_δ as their supposedly constant values in Eq. (17.37) and Eq. (17.38), respectively. There are several forms of fast decoupled estimation algorithms based on such considerations (see e.g., [13], [14]). A flow chart for one scheme of fast decoupled state estimation is shown in Fig. 17.2.

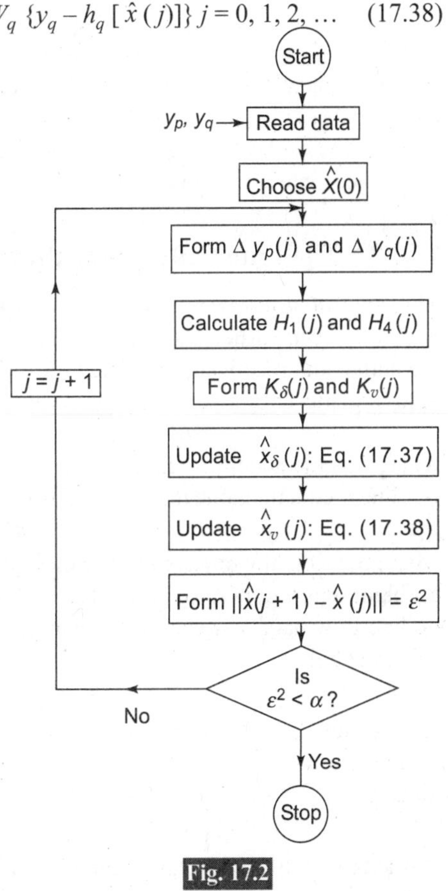

Fig. 17.2

Example 17.4 In order to illustrate an application of the injections only algorithm, consider the simple 2-bus system shown in Fig. 17.3.

Solution Assuming lossless line $\theta_{ij} = 90°$. Also let $Y_{11} = Y_{22} = 2$ and $Y_{12} = Y_{21} = 1$. The power relations in this case would be

$$P_1 = -|V_1|\,|V_2|\,|Y_{12}| \sin \delta_2$$
$$P_2 = |V_1|\,|V_2|\,|Y_{12}| \sin \delta_2$$
$$Q_1 = |Y_{11}|\,|V_1|^2 - |Y_{12}|\,|V_1|\,|V_2| \cos \delta_2$$
$$Q_2 = |Y_{22}|\,|V_2|^2 - |Y_{12}|\,|V_1|\,|V_2| \cos \delta_2$$

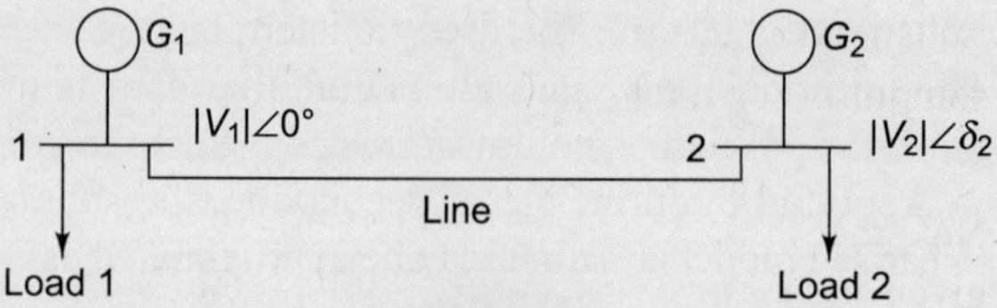

Fig. 17.3

If we choose the initial values $|V_1^o| = V_2^o| = 1$, $\delta_2^o = 0°$, the corresponding power values are $P_1^o = P_2^o = 0$, $Q_1^o = Q_2^o = 1$. The value of the Jacobian matrix evaluated at the above nominal values of the variables turns out to be

$$H_0 = \begin{bmatrix} -1 & 0 & 0 \\ 1 & 0 & 0 \\ 0 & 3 & -1 \\ 0 & -1 & 3 \end{bmatrix}$$

Application of the LSE then yields the following expressions for the estimates of the perturbations in the three state variables around their chosen initial values:

$$\Delta\hat{\delta}_2 = \Delta P_2 - \Delta P_1$$
$$\Delta\hat{V}_1 = 0.78\,\Delta Q_2 - 0.26\,\Delta Q_1$$
$$\Delta\hat{V}_2 = 0.38\,\Delta Q_2 + 0.14\,\Delta Q_1$$

These equations should be used in order to translate the measured values of the perturbations in the active and reactive power injections into the estimates of the perturbations of the state variables.

It is interesting to note that for the simple example, partitions H_2 and H_3 are null matrices so that the decoupled state estimators are the same as those given above.

17.3.2 The Line Only Algorithm

This algorithm has been developed in order to avoid the need for solving a nonlinear estimation problem, which, as seen earlier, requires some approximation or other. In the line flow only algorithm, the data for the active and reactive tie line flows are processed in order to generate the vector of the voltage difference across the tie-lines. Let z denote this vector. A model equation for this vector may be expressed as

$$z = Bx + r_z \tag{17.39}$$

where B is the node-element incidence matrix and r_z is the vector of the errors in the voltage data. Since this is a linear equation, one may use the WLSE technique to generate the estimate as

$$\hat{\mathbf{x}} = [B' WB]^{-1} B' Wz \tag{17.40}$$

where the weighing matrix may be set equal to the inverse of the covariance of r_z if this is known. The main problem with Eq. (17.40) is that the vector z is not directly measurable but needs to be generated from the tie line flow data. V_{ij} denotes the voltage across the line connecting the ith and the jth buses, the following relation holds.

$$V_{ij} = Z_{ij}\,[(P_{ij} - j\,Q_{ij})/V_j^* - V_j\,Y_{ij}] \tag{17.41}$$

Here Z_{ij} stands for the impedance of the line.

This shows that the vector z is related to the vectors $\mathbf{x}$ and $\mathbf{y}$ in a nonlinear fashion and one may use the notation

$$z = g(\mathbf{x}, \mathbf{y}) \tag{17.42}$$

In view of this nonlinear relation, Eq. (17.40) may be expressed in the form

$$\hat{x} = [B' WB]^{-1} B' W g(\hat{x}, y) \tag{17.43}$$

This, being a nonlinear relationship, cannot be solved except through a numerical approach (iterative solution). The iterative form of Eq. (17.43) is

$$\hat{x}(j+1) = [B' WB]^{-1} B' W g[\hat{x}(j), y],\ j = 0, 1, 2, \ldots \tag{17.44}$$

Note that the original problem of estimation of x from the data for z is a linear problem so that the solution given by Eq. (17.40) is the optimal solution. However, the data for z need to be generated using the nonlinear transformation in Eq. (17.42), which in turn has necessitated the use of iterative Eq. (17.44). Compared to the injections only iterative algorithm, the present algorithm has the advantage of a constant gain matrix $[B' W B]^{-1} B' W$. This results in a considerable computational simplification. The concept of decoupled estimation is easily extended to the case of the line flows [15].

17.4 ▶ TRACKING STATE ESTIMATION OF POWER SYSTEMS [16]

Tracking the state estimation of a given power system is important for real time monitoring of the system. As is well known, the voltages of all real system vary randomly with time and should therefore be considered to be stochastic processes. It is thus necessary to make use of the sequential estimation techniques of Ref. [1] in order to obtain the state estimate at any given time point. The power relations in Eqs. (17.25) and (17.26) are still valid but must be rewritten after indicating that the voltage magnitudes and angles are new functions of the discrete time index k.

17.5 ▶ SOME COMPUTATIONAL CONSIDERATIONS

Both the static and the tracking estimation algorithms presented in the preceding sections are computationally intensive, particularly for large power networks which may have more than 200 important buses. It is, therefore, very important to pay attention to such computational issues as illconditioning, computer storage and time requirements. However, we need to first consider the question of existence of a solution of the state estimation problem.

17.5.1 Network Observability [17]

Consider the static WLSE formula [Eq. (17.11b)] which serves as the starting point for all the algorithms. Inverse of information matrix $M_{n \times n} = H' WH$ should exist otherwise there is no state estimate. This will happen if rank of H is equal to n (no. of state variables). Since one can always choose a nonsingular W, so if H has a rank n, the power network is said to be *observable*.

17.5.2 Problem of Ill-conditioning

Even if the given power system is an observable system in terms of the measurements selected for the state estimation purposes, there is no guarantee that the required inversion of the information matrix will exist. During multiplications of the matrices, there is some small but definite error introduced due to the finite word length and quantisation. Whether or not these errors create ill-conditioning of the information matrix may be determined from a knowledge of the condition number of the matrix. This number is defined as the ratio of the largest and the smallest eigen values of the information matrix. The matrix M becomes more and more ill-conditioned as its condition number increases in magnitude. Some detailed results on power system state estimation using Cholesky factorisation techniques may be found in [18]. Factorisation helps to reduce ill-conditioning but may not reduce the computational burden. A technique to reduce computational burden is described in Ref. [19].

17.6 ▶ EXTERNAL SYSTEM EQUIVALENCING [20]

One of the widely practiced methods used for computational simplification is to divide the given system into three subsystems as shown in Fig. 17.4. One of these is referred to as the 'internal' subsystem and consists of those buses in which we are really interested. The second subsystem consists of those buses which are not of direct interest to us and is referred to as the 'external' subsystem. Finally, the buses which provide links between these internal and external subsystems constitute the third subsystem referred to as the 'boundary' subsystem. For any given power network, the identification of the three subsystems may be done either in a natural or in an artificial way.

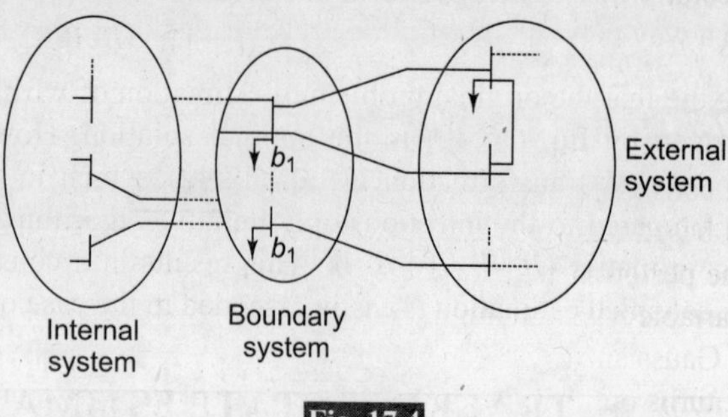

Fig. 17.4

To illustrate the simplification of the state estimation algorithm, consider the linearised measurement equation for the injections only case. Since the system is partitioned into three subsystems, this equation may be written as

$$\begin{bmatrix} \Delta y_i \\ \Delta y_b \\ \Delta y_e \end{bmatrix} = \begin{bmatrix} H_{ii} & H_{ib} & 0 \\ H_{bi} & H_{bb} & H_{be} \\ 0 & H_{eb} & H_{ee} \end{bmatrix} \begin{bmatrix} \Delta x_i \\ \Delta x_b \\ \Delta x_e \end{bmatrix} + \begin{bmatrix} r_i \\ r_b \\ r_e \end{bmatrix} \tag{17.45}$$

It may be noted that the internal measurement vector Δy_t is not completely independent of the external subsystem state Δx_e since Δy_i depends on the boundary subsystem state Δx_b and Δx_b depends on Δx_e.

$$\Delta y_b = \Delta y_{bi} + \Delta y_{bb} + \Delta y_{be} + r_b \tag{17.46}$$

where Δy_{be} represents the injections into the boundary buses from the external buses, Δy_{bb} is the injection from the boundary buses and Δy_{bi} is the injection from the internal buses. It is assumed that the term, Δy_{be} ($= H_{be}\,\Delta x_e$), may be approximated as $\hat{H}\,\Delta x_b$ where $\hat{H}$ is estimated from the relation

$$\hat{H} = \Delta y_{be}, / \Delta x_b \tag{17.47}$$

The component Δy_{be} may be estimated if the terms Δy_{bi} and Δy_{bb} are computed as $H_{bi}\,\Delta x_i$ and $H_{bb}\,\Delta x_b$ and then subtracted from the measured value of Δy_b. This would result in part of Eq. (17.45) to be rewritten as

$$\begin{bmatrix} \Delta y_i \\ \Delta y_b \end{bmatrix} = \begin{bmatrix} H_{ii} & H_{ib} \\ H_{bi} & H^*_{bb} \end{bmatrix} \begin{bmatrix} \Delta x_i \\ \Delta x_b \end{bmatrix} + \begin{bmatrix} r_i \\ r_b \end{bmatrix} \tag{17.48}$$

where $H^*_{bb} = H_{bb} + \hat{H}$ represents the effective Jacobian if the boundary subsystem that accounts for the effects of the external subsystem on the boundary subsystem. Equation (17.48) has a lower dimension than the original measurement equation and would therefore involve less computations. The concept of external system equivalencing may be employed with the line or mixed data situations also.

17.7 ▶ TREATMENT OF BAD DATA [21, 22]

The ability to detect and identify bad measurements is extremely valuable to a load dispatch centre. One or more of the data may be affected by malfunctioning of either the measuring instruments or the data transmission system or both. Transducers may have been wired incorrectly or the transducer itself may be malfunctioning so that it simply no longer gives accurate readings.

If such faulty data are included in the vector $\Delta \mathbf{y}$, the estimation algorithm will yield unreliable estimates of the state. It is therefore important to develop techniques for detecting the presence of faulty data in the measurement vector at any given point of time, to identify the faulty data and eliminate these from the vector y before it is processed for state estimation. It is also important to modify the estimation algorithms in a way that will permit more reliable state estimation in the presence of bad data.

17.7.1 Bad Data Detection [23]

A convenient tool for detecting the presence of one or more bad data in the vector y at any given point of time is based on the 'Chi Square Test'. To appreciate this, first note that the method of least square ensures that the performance index $J(x) = [y - h(x)]' W [y - h(x)] = r'Wr$ has its minimum value when $x = \hat{x}$. Since the variable r is random, the minimum value $J_{\min}$ is also a random quantity. Quite often, r may be assumed to be a Gaussian variable and then $J_{\min}$ would follow a chi square distribution with $L = m - n$ degrees of freedom. It turns out that the mean of $J_{\min}$ is equal to L and its variance is equal to $2L$. This implies that if all the data processed for state estimation are reliable, then the computed value of $J_{\min}$ should be close to the average value (= L). On the other hand, if one or more of the data for y are unreliable, then the assumptions of the least squares estimation are violated and the computed value of $J_{\min}$ will deviate significantly from L.

It is thus possible to develop a reliable scheme for the detection of bad data in y by computing the value of $[y - h(\hat{x})]' W [y - h(\hat{x})]$, $\hat{x}$ being the estimate obtained on the basis of the concerned y. If the scalar so obtained exceeds some threshold $T_j = cL$, c being a suitable number, we conclude that the vector $\mathbf{y}$ includes some bad data. (Note that the data for the component y_i, $i = 1, 2, \ldots, m$ will be considered bad if it deviates from the mean of y_i by more than $\pm 3\sigma_i$, where σ_i is the standard deviation of r_i). Care must be exercised while choosing the value of threshold parameter c. If it is close to 1, the test may produce many 'false alarms' and if it is too large, the test would fail to detect many bad data.

To select an appropriate value of c, we may start by choosing the significance level d of the test by the relation.

$$P\{J(x) > cL/J(x) \text{ follows chi square distribution}\} = d$$

We may select, for example, $d = 0.05$ which corresponds to a 5% false alarm situation. It is then possible to find the value of c by making use of the table $\chi(L)$. Once the value of c is determined, it is simple to carry out the test whether or not $J(x)$ exceeds cL.

17.7.2 Identification of Bad Data [23]

Once the presence of bad data is detected, it is imperative that these be identified so that they could be removed from the vector of measurements before it is processed. One way of doing this is to evaluate the components of the measurement residual $\tilde{y}_i = y_i - h_i(x)$, $i = 1, 2, \ldots, m$. If we assume that the residuals have the Gaussian distribution with zero mean and the variance σ_i^2, then the magnitude of the residual y_i should lie in the range $-3\sigma_i < y_i < 3\sigma_i$ with 95% confidence level. Thus, if any one of the computed residual turns out to be significantly larger in magnitude than three times its standard deviation, then corresponding data is taken to be a bad data. If this happens for more than one component of y, then the component having the largest residual is assumed to be the bad data and is removed from y. The estimation algorithm is re-run with the remaining data and the bad data detection and identification tests are performed again to find out if there are additional bad data in the measurement set. As we will see later bad measurement data are detected, eliminated and replaced by pseudo or calculated values.

17.7.3 Suppression of Bad Data [24]

The procedures described so far in this section are quite tedious and time consuming and may not be utilised to remove all the bad data which may be present in the vector y at a given point of time. It may often be desirable on the other hand to modify the estimation algorithms in a way that will minimise the influence of the bad data on the estimates of the state vector. This would be possible if the estimation index $J(x)$ is chosen to be a nonquadratic function. The reason that the LSE algorithm does not perform very well in the presence of bad data is the fact that because of the quadratic nature of $J(x)$, the index assumes a large value for a data that is too far removed from its expected value. To avoid this overemphasis on the erroneous data and at the same time to retain the analytical tractability of the quadratic performance index, let us choose

$$J(\hat{x}) = g'(\tilde{y})\, W\, g(\tilde{y}) \tag{17.49a}$$

where $g(\tilde{y})$ is a nonlinear function of the residual $\tilde{y}$. There may be several possible choices for this function. A convenient form is the so-called 'quadratic flat' form. In this case, the components of the function $g(y)$ are defined by the following relation.

$$\begin{aligned} g_i(\tilde{y}) &= \tilde{y}_i, \quad \text{for } \tilde{y}_i/\sigma_i \le a_i \\ &= a_i, \quad \text{for } \tilde{y}_i/\sigma_i > a_i \end{aligned} \tag{17.49b}$$

where a_i is a pre-selected constant threshold level. Obviously, the performance index $J(x)$ may be expressed as

$$J(\hat{x}) = \sum_{i=1}^{m} J_i(\hat{x}) \tag{17.50}$$

and each component has a quadratic nature for small values of the residual but has a constant magnitude for residual magnitudes in excess of the threshold. Figure 17.5 shows a typical variation of $J_i(x)$ for the quadratic and the nonquadratic choices.

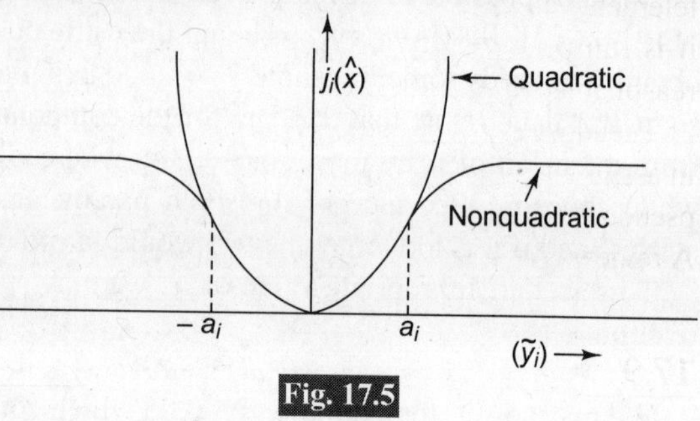

Fig. 17.5

The main advantage of the choice of the form (17.49) for the estimation index is that it is still a quadratic in the function $g(\tilde{y})$ and so the LSE theory may be mimicked in order to derive the following iterative formula for the state estimate.

$$\hat{x}(l+1) = \hat{x}(l) + [H'(l)\, C'\, WCH(l)]\, H'(l)\, WCg\,[\tilde{y}(l)] \tag{17.51a}$$

where the matrix C is diagonal and its elements are computed as

$$\begin{aligned} C_i &= 1, \quad \text{for } \tilde{y}_i/\sigma_i \le a_i \\ &= 0, \quad \text{for } \tilde{y}_i/\sigma_i > a_i \end{aligned} \tag{17.51b}$$

Comparing this solution with that given in Eq. (17.22), it is seen that the main effect of the particular choice of the estimation index in Eq. (17.49) is to ensure that the data producing residuals in excess of the threshold level will not change the estimate. This is achieved by the production of a null value for the matrix C for large values of the residual.

17.8 ▶ NETWORK OBSERVABILITY AND PSEUDO MEASUREMENTS

A minimum amount of data is necessary for State Estimation (SE) to be effective. A more analytical way of determining whether a given data are enough for SE is called observability analysis. It forms an integral part of any real time state estimator. The ability to perform state estimation depends on whether sufficient measurements are well distributed throughout the system. When sufficient measurements are available SE can obtain the state vector of the whole system. In this case the network is observable. As explained earlier in Section 17.5 this is true when the rank of measurement Jacobian matrix is equal to the number of unknown state variables. The rank of the measurement Jacobian matrix is dependent on the locations and types of available measurements as well as on the network topology.

An auxiliary problem in state estimation is where to add additional data or pseudo measurements to a power system in order to improve the accuracy of the calculated state, i.e., to improve observability. The additional measurements represent a cost for the physical transducers, remote terminal or telemetry system, and software data processing in the central computer. Selection of pseudo measurements, filling of missing data, providing appropriate weightage are the functions of the observability analysis algorithm.

Observability can be checked during factorisation. If any pivot becomes very small or zero during factorisation, the gain matrix may be singular, and the system may not be observable.

To find the value of an injection without measuring it, we must know the power system beyond the measurements currently being made. For example, we normally know the generated MWs and MVARs at generators through telemetry channels (i.e., these measurements would generally be known to the state estimator). If these channels are out, we can perhaps communicate with the operators in the plant control room by telephone and ask for these values and enter them manually. Similarly, if we require a load-bus MW and MVAR for a pseudo measurement, we could use past records that show the relationship between an individual load and the total system load. We can estimate the total system load quite accurately by finding the total power being generated and estimating the line losses. Further, if we have just had a telemetry failure, we could use the most recently estimated values from the estimator (assuming that it is run periodically) as pseudo measurements. Thus, if required, we can give the state estimator with a reasonable value to use as a pseudo measurement at any bus in the system.

Pseudo measurements increase the data redundancy of SE. If this approach is adapted, care must be taken in assigning weights to various types of measurements. Techniques that can be used to determine the meter or pseudo measurement locations for obtaining a complete observability of the system are available in Ref. [25]. A review of the principal observability analysis and meter placement algorithms is available in Ref. [26].

17.9 ▶ APPLICATION OF POWER SYSTEM STATE ESTIMATION

In real-time environment the state estimator consists of different modules such as network topology processor, observability analysis, state estimation and bad data processing. The network topology processor is required for all power system analysis. A conventional network topology program uses circuit breaker status information and network connectivity data to determine the connectivity of the network.

Figure 17.6 is a schematic diagram showing the information flow between the various functions to be performed in an operations control centre computer system. The system gets information from remote terminal unit (RTU) that encodes measurement transducer outputs and opened/closed status information into digital signals which are sent to the operation centre over communications circuits. Control centre can also transmit commands such as raise/lower to generators and open/close to circuit breakers and switches. The analog measurements of generator output would be directly used by the AGC program (Chap. 8). However, rest of the data will be processed by the state estimator before being used for other functions such as OLF (Optimal Load Flow) etc.

Before running the SE, we must know how the transmission lines are connected to the load and generator buses, i.e., network topology. This keeps on changing and hence the current telemetered breaker/switch status must be used to restructure the electrical system model. This is called the *network topology program* or *system status processor* or *network configurator.*

The output of the state estimator, i.e., $|V|$, δ, P_{ij}, Q_{ij} together with latest model form the basis for the economic dispatch (ED) or minimum emission dispatch (MED), contingency analysis program, etc.

Further Reading The weighted least-squares approach to problems of static state estimation in power systems was introduced by Schweppe [1969–74]. It was earlier originated in the aerospace industry.

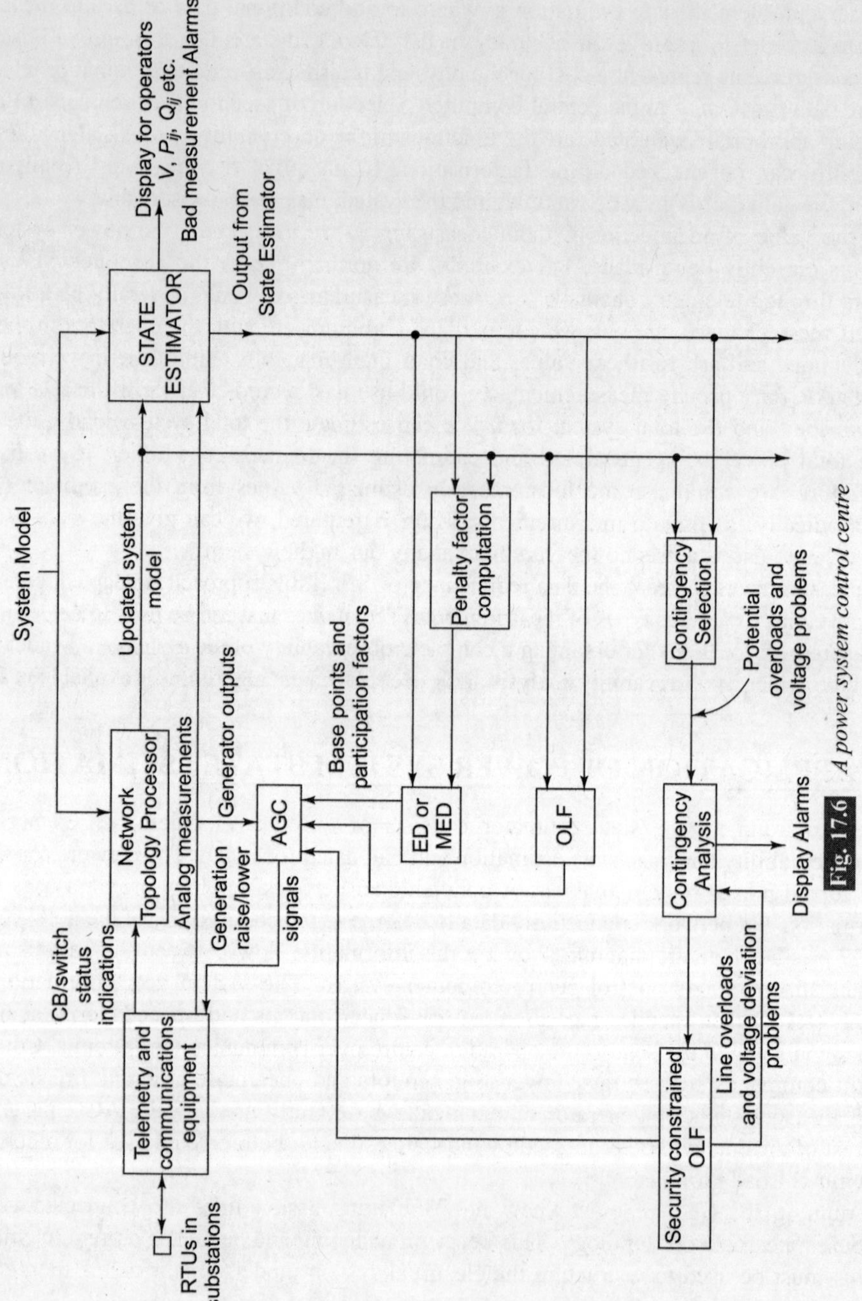

Fig. 17.6 *A power system control centre*

Since 1970s, state estimators have been installed on a regular basis in new energy (power system or load dispatch) control centres and have proved quite helpful. Reviews of the state of the art in state estimation algorithms based on this modelling approach were published by Bose and Clements [27] and Wu [28]. Reviews of external system modelling are available in [29]. A generalised state estimator with integrated state, status and parameter estimation capabilities has been proposed by Alsac et al [30]. The new role of state estimation and other advanced analytical functions in competitive energy markets was discussed in Ref. [31]. A comprehensive bibliography on SE from 1968–89 is available in Ref. [32].

17.10 ▶ SUMMARY

This chapter presents an introduction to state estimation of the power system. The modern technological aspects, comprehensive descriptions, state estimation aspects, state of the arts, present challenges, research illustrations and future trends are highlighted.

Problems

17.1 For Ex. 6.6 if the power injected at buses are given as $S_1 = 1.031 - j0.791$, $S_2 = 0.5 + j1.0$ and $S_3 = -1.5 - j0.15$ pu. Consider $W_1 = W_2 = W_3 = 1$. Bus 1 is a reference bus. Using flat start, find the estimates of $|V_i|$ and δ_i. Tolerance = 0.0001.

17.2 For sample system shown in Fig. P-17.2, assume that the three meters have the following characteristics.

Meter	*Full scale (MW)*	*Accuracy (MW)*	*σ (pu)*
M_{12}	100	± 8	0.02
M_{13}	100	± 4	0.01
M_{32}	100	± 0.8	0.002

Calculate the best estimate for the phase angles δ_1 and δ_2 given the following measurements:

Meter	*Measured value (MW)*
M_{12}	70.0
M_{13}	4.0
M_{32}	30.5

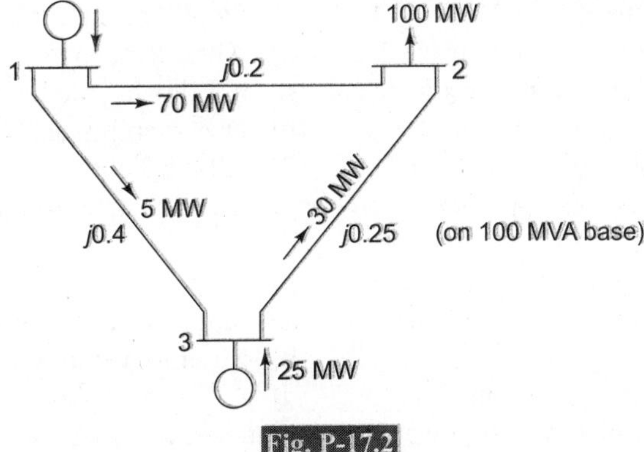

Fig. P-17.2

17.3 Given a single line as shown in Fig. P-17.3, two measurements are available. Using DC load flow, calculate the best estimate of the power flowing through the line.

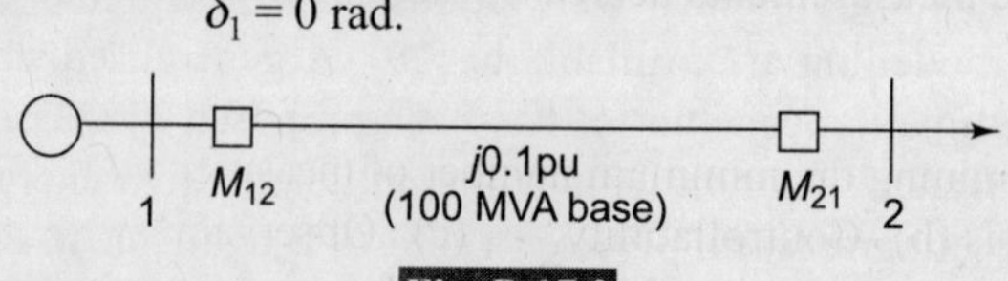

Fig. P-17.3

Meter	*Full scale (MW)*	*Meter standard deviation (σ) in full scale*	*Meter reading (MW)*
M_{12}	100	1	32
M_{21}	100	4	– 26

Multiple Choice Questions

17.1 State estimation and load flow problems are
(a) Similar (b) SE is more accurate
(c) LF is more accurate (d) None of the above

17.2 State estimation may be
(a) Static (b) Dynamic
(c) Either (a) or (b) (d) None of the above

17.3 One estimator is designed to give for $ IVI and phase angles
(a) Best estimate (b) Least estimate
(c) Maximum estimate (d) Random estimate

17.4 The redundancy factor, defined as *m/n*, should have a value in the range of
(a) 0 – 3 (b) 1.5 to 2.8 (c) 0 – 00 (d) Any value is OK

17.5 Power system state estimation is normally a
(a) Nonlinear (b) Linear problem (c) Quadratic problem (d) None of the above

17.6 Factorisation helps to reduce
(a) Computational burden (b) Ill-conditioning
(c) Nonlinearity (d) All of the above

17.7 'Equivalencing' is used to simplify the following:
(a) Load flow problem (b) Stability problem
(c) PS state estimation problem (d) All of the above

17.8 In real-time environment the state estimate consists of following modules:
(a) Network topology processor (b) Observability analysis
(c) Bad data processing (d) All the 3 above

17.9 The weighted least-squares approach to problems of static state estimation in power system was introduced by
(a) Dy-liacco (b) Tinney et al (c) Carpentier (d) Schweppe

17.10 The output of the state estimator together with latest model forms the basis for
(a) ED (b) Minimum emission dispatch (MED)
(c) Contingency analysis program (d) All of the 3 above

17.11 One of the important objectives of power system state estimator is
(a) Monitoring of power system (b) Contingency selection
(c) Security control (d) None of the above

17.12 Usually voltage and current measurements are not used in online state estimation programs because
(a) There measurements do not have phase angle information
(b) Inclusion of these measurements decreases rate of convergence
(c) Both (a) and (b)
(d) None of the above

17.13 The problem of determining the minimum number of measurements for state estimation is known as
(a) Load flow analysis (b) Controllability (c) Observability (d) All of the above

17.14 In an on-line power state, state estimation additional measurements are added to
(a) Attain controllability (b) Obtain a better load flow solution
(c) Improve accuracy (d) Both (a) and (b)

17.15 Usually probability density function of normalised measurement is
(a) exponential (b) Gaussian (c) Uniform (d) Erlang

17.16 Bad data detection is related to
(a) Detect gross errors in the measurements
(b) Outage studies
(c) Determination of residue value of the performance index
(d) Contingency analysis

17.17 Usually the residual of the performance index is evaluated once per minute is related to
(a) Detect topology changes (b) Detect gross errors in measurements
(c) Observability (d) Controllability

17.18 State estimation under noisy measurements is necessary as to account
(a) Uncertainty in the error (b) Outage statistics
(c) Short circuit statistics (d) All of the above

17.19 Line flow state estimator has following limitation
(a) It does not give accurate results
(b) It does not readily accept different ranges and accuracies at single point
(c) It incorporates voltage and current measurements
(d) None of the above

17.20 Weighted least square state estimator is used in on-line state estimator to account
(a) Uncertainties in the measured quantities (b) Voltage and currents measurement
(c) Topology changes (d) All of the above

17.21 The objective of state estimation is to obtain the best possible value of
(a) Bus voltage magnitude and angle
(b) Bus active power
(c) Bus reactive power
(d) Bus apparent power

17.22 The most applicable state estimation algorithm in power system is
(a) Load flow (b) Optimum load flow
(c) Weighted least square (d) None of the above

17.23 The output of state estimation is used in
(a) Economical dispatch and security studies
(b) Load flow
(c) Analysis of fault
(d) Stability study

17.24 Which estimation method is best suitable for state estimation in a power system?
(a) Least-square estimation
(b) Equal weighted least-square estimation
(c) Weighted least-square estimation
(d) Fast decoupled

17.25 State estimation of power system by only active and reactive power injection is same as
(a) Load flow study
(b) Optimum power flow analysis
(c) Economical dispatch
(d) Load forecasting

References

Books

1. A.K. Mahalanabis, D.P. Kothari, and S.I. Ahson, *Computer Aided Power System Analysis and Control*, Tata McGraw-Hill, New Delhi, 1988.
2. D.P. Kothari and I.J. Nagrath, *Power System Engineering*, 2nd edn, Tata McGraw-Hill, New Delhi, 2008.
3. A. Monticelli, *State Estimation in Electric Power Systems, A Generalised Approach*, Kluwer Academic Publishers, Boston, 1999.
4. G.L. Kusic, *Computer-Aided Power Systems Analysis*, Prentice-Hall, NJ 1986.
5. A.J. Wood and B.F. Wollenberg, *Power Generation, Operation and Control*, 2nd edn, John Wiley, NY, 1996.
6. J.J. Grainger and W.D. Stevenson, *Power System Analysis*, McGraw-Hill, NY, 1994.
7. R. Deautsch, *Estimation Theory*, Prentice-Hall Inc, NJ, 1965.
8. C.L. Lawson and R.J. Hanson, *Solving Least Squares Problems*, Prentice-Hall, Inc, NJ, 1974.
9. H.W. Sorenson, *Parameter Estimation*, Mercel Dekker, NY, 1980.

Papers

10. F.C. Schweppe, J. Wildes, D. Rom, "Power System Static State Estimation, Parts I, II and III", *IEEE Trans*, volume: PAS-89, pp: 120–135, 1970.
11. R.E. Larson, *et al*, "State Estimation in Power Systems", Parts I and II, *IEEE Trans*, volume: PAS 89, pp: 345–359, 1970.
12. F.C. Schweppe and E.J. Handschin, "Static State Estimation in Electric Power System", *Proc. of the IEEE*, volume: 62, pp: 972–982, 1975.
13. H.P. Horisberger, J.C. Richard, and C. Rossier, "A Fast Decoupled Static State Estimator for Electric Power Systems", *IEEE Trans*, volume: PAS-95, pp: 208–215, Jan/Feb 1976.
14. A. Monticelli and A. Garcia, "Fast Decoupled Estimators", *IEEE Trans Power Syst*, volume: 5, pp: 556–564, May 1990.
15. J.F. Dopazo, *et al*, "State Calculation of Power Systems from Line Flow Measurements, Parts I and II", *IEEE Trans*, 89, pp: l698–1708, 91, 1972, pp: 145–151.
16. A.S. Debs and R.E. Larson, "A Dynamic Estimator for Tracking the State of a Power System", *IEEE Trans*, volume: 89, pp: 1670–1678, 1970.
17. G.R. Krumpholz, *et al*, "Power System Observability: A Practical Algorithm Using Network Topology", *IEEE Trans*, volume: 99, pp: 1534–1542, 1980.
18. A. Simoes-Costa and V.H. Quintana, "A Robust Numerical Technique for Power System State Estimation," *IEEE Trans*, volume: 100, pp: 691–698, 1981.

19. A. Simoes-Costa and V.H. Quintana, "An Orthogonal Row Processing Algorithm for Power System Sequential State Estimation", *IEEE Trans*, volume: 100, pp: 3791–3799, 1981.
20. A.S. Debs, "Estimation of External Network Equivalents from Internal System Data", *IEEE Trans*, volume: 94, pp: 1260–1268, 1974.
21. A. Garcia, A. Monticelli, and P. Abreu, "Fast Decoupled State Estimation and Bad Data Processing", *IEEE Trans* PAS-98, pp: 1645–1652, Sept/Oct 1979.
22. E. Handschin, *et al*, "Bad Data Analysis for Power System State Estimation", *IEEE Trans*, PAS-94, pp: 329–337, 1975.
23. H.J. Koglin, *et al*, "Bad Data Detection and Identification", *Int J Elec Power*, volume: 12, issue: 2, pp: 94–103, April 1990.
24. H.M. Merril and F.C. Schweppe, "Bad Data Suppression in Power System State Estimation", *IEEE Trans*, volume: PAS-90, pp: 2718–2725, 1971.
25. F. Mafaakher, *et al*, "Optimum Metering Design Using Fast Decoupled Estimator", *IEEE Trans*, volume: PAS-98, pp: 62–68, 1979.
26. K.A. Clements, "Observability Methods and Optimal Meter Placement", *Int. J Elec. Power*, volume: 12, issue: 2, pp: 89–93, April 1990.
27. A. Bose and K.A. Clements, "Real-time Modelling of Power Networks", *IEEE Proc., Special Issue on Computers in Power System Operations*, volume: 75, issue: 12, pp: 1607–1622, Dec 1987.
28. F.F. Wu, "Power System State Estimation: A Survey", *Int. J Elec. Power and Energy Syst.*, volume: 12, pp: 80–87, Jan 1990.
29. F.F. Wu and A. Monticelli, "A Critical Review on External Network Medelling for on-line Security Analysis", *Int. J Elec. Power and Energy Syst.*, volume: 5, pp: 222–235, Oct 1983.
30. O. Alsac, *et al*, "Generalized State Estimation", *IEEE Trans. on Power Systems*, volume: 13, issue: 3, pp: 1069–1075, Aug. 1998.
31. D. Shirmohammadi, *et al*, "Transmission Dispatch and Congestion Management in the Emerging Energy Market Structures", *IEEE Trans. Power System.*, volume: 13, issue: 4, pp: 1466–1474, Nov 1998.
32. M.B. Coutto, *et al*, "Bibliography on Power System State Estimation (1968–1989)", *IEEE Trans. Power Syst.*, volume: 7, issue: 3, pp: 950–961, Aug. 1990.
33. J. Zhao et al., "Power System Dynamic State Estimation: Motivations, Definitions, Methodologies, and Future Work", *IEEE Transactions on Power Systems*, volume: 34, issue: 4, pp: 3188–3198, 2019.
34. E. Ghahremani and I. Kamwa, "Local and Wide-Area PMU-Based Decentralized Dynamic State Estimation in Multi-Machine Power Systems", *IEEE Transactions on Power Systems*, volume: 31, issue: 1, pp: 547–562, 2016.
35. Y. Chen, F. Liu, S. Mei, and J. Ma, "A Robust WLAV State Estimation Using Optimal Transformations", *IEEE Transactions on Power Systems*, volume: 30, issue: 4, pp: 2190–2191, 2015.
36. H. Sun, F. Gao, K. Strunz, B. Zhang, and Q. Li, "Analog-Digital Power System State Estimation Based on Information Theory—Part II: Implementation and Application", *IEEE Transactions on Smart Grid*, volume: 4, issue: 3, pp: 1647–1655, 2013.
37. Y. Yu, Z. Wang, and C. Lu, "A Joint Filter Approach for Reliable Power System State Estimation", IEEE Transactions on Instrumentation and Measurement, volume: 68, issue: 1, pp: 87–94, 2019.

38. B. Uzunoğlu and M.A. Ülker, "Maximum Likelihood Ensemble Filter State Estimation for Power Systems", *IEEE Transactions on Instrumentation and Measurement*, volume: 67, issue: 9, pp: 2097–2106, 2018.
39. S.A. Nugroho, A.F. Taha, and J. Qi, "Robust Dynamic State Estimation of Synchronous Machines with Asymptotic State Estimation Error Performance Guarantees", *IEEE Transactions on Power Systems*, volume: 35, issue: 3, pp: 1923–1935, 2020.
40. Y. Zhang and J. Wang, "Towards Highly Efficient State Estimation with Nonlinear Measurements in Distribution Systems", *IEEE Transactions on Power Systems*, volume: 35, issue: 3, pp: 2471–2474, 2020.

CHAPTER 18 Compensation in Power Systems

18.1 ▶ INTRODUCTION

For reduction of cost and improved reliability, most of the world's electric power systems continue to be interconnected. Interconnections take advantage of diversity of loads, availability of sources and fuel price for supplying power to loads at minimum cost and pollution with a required reliability. In a deregulated electric service environment, an effective electric grid is essential to the competitive environment of reliable electric service.

Now-a-days, greater demands have been placed on the transmission network, and these demands will continue to rise because of the increasing number of nonutility generators and greater competition among utilities themselves. It is not easy to acquire new rights of way. Increased demands on transmission, absence of long-term planning and the need to provide open access to generating companies and customers have resulted in less security and reduced quality of supply.

Compensation in power systems is, therefore, essential to alleviate some of these problems. Series/shunt compensation has been in use for past many years to achieve this objective.

In a power system, given the insignificant electrical storage, the power generation and load must balance at all times. To some extent, the electrical system is self-regulating. If generation is less than load, voltage and frequency drop, and thereby reducing the load. However, there is only a few percent margin for such self-regulation. If voltage is propped up with reactive power support, then load increase with consequent drop in frequency may result in system collapse. Alternatively, if there is inadequate reactive power, the system may have voltage collapse.

This chapter is devoted to the study of various methods of compensating power systems and various types of compensating devices, called compensators, to alleviate the problems of power system outlined above. These compensators can be connected in the system in two ways, in series and in shunt at the line ends (or even in the midpoint).

18.2 ▶ LOADING CAPABILITY

Before studying different forms of compensations, certain limitations of transmission system have to be addressed. There are three kinds of limitations for loading capacity of transmission system: (i) Thermal (ii) Dielectric (iii) Stability.

Thermal capability of an overhead line is a function of the ambient temperature, wind conditions, conditions of the conductor and ground clearance.

There is a possibility of converting a single-circuit to a double-circuit line to increase the loading capability.

Dielectric limitations: From insulation point of view, many lines are designed very conservatively. For a given nominal voltage rating it is often possible to increase normal operating voltages by 10% (i.e.,

400 kV – 440 kV). One should, however, ensure that dynamic and transient overvoltages are within limits [see Chap. 13 of Ref. 7].

Stability issues: There are certain stability issues that limit the transmission capability. These include steady-state stability, transient stability, dynamic stability, frequency collapse, voltage collapse and subsynchronous resonance.

Several good books [1, 2, 6, 7, 8] are available on these topics. The load and line compensation can certainly be used to overcome any of the stability limits, in which case the final limits would be thermal and dielectric.

18.2.1 Load Compensation

Load compensation is the management of reactive power to improve power quality, i.e., V profile and pf. Here the reactive power flow is controlled by installing shunt compensating devices (capacitors/reactors) at the load end bringing about proper balance between generated and consumed reactive power. This is most effective in improving the power transfer capability of the system and its voltage stability. It is desirable both economically and technically to operate the system near unity power factor. This is why some utilities impose a penalty on low pf loads. Yet another way of improving the system performance is to operate it under near balanced conditions so as to reduce the flow of negative sequence currents thereby increasing the system's load capability and reducing power loss.

A transmission line has three critical loadings: (i) natural loading (ii) steady-state stability limit and (iii) thermal limit loading. For a compensated line, the natural loading is the lowest and before the thermal loading limit is reached, steady-state stability limit is arrived.

18.2.2 Line Compensation

Ideal voltage profile for a transmission line is flat, which can only be achieved by loading the line with its surge impedance loading while this may not be achievable, the characteristics of the line can be modified by line compensators so that

1. Ferranti effect is minimised.
2. Underexcited operation of synchronous generators is not required.
3. The power transfer capability of the line is enhanced. Modifying the characteristics of a line(s) is known as *line compensation.*

Various compensating devices are

1. Capacitors
2. Capacitors and inductors
3. Active voltage source (synchronous generator)

When a number of capacitors are connected in parallel to get the desired capacitance, it is known as a bank of capacitors, similarly, a bank of inductors. A bank of capacitors and/or inductors can be adjusted in steps by switching (mechanical).

Capacitors and inductors as such are passive line compensators, while synchronous generator is an active compensator. When solid-state devices are used for switching off capacitors and inductors, this is regarded as active compensation.

Before proceeding to give a detailed account of line compensator, we shall briefly discuss both shunt and series compensation.

Shunt compensation is more or less like load compensation with all the advantages associated with it as discussed in Section 18.2.1. It needs to be pointed out here that shunt capacitors/inductors cannot be distributed uniformally along the line. These are normally connected at the end of the line and/or at midpoint of the line.

Shunt capacitors raise the load pf, which greatly increases the power transmitted over the line as it is not required to carry the reactive power. There is a limit to which transmitted power can be increased by shunt compensation as it would require very large size capacitor bank, which would be impractical. For increasing power transmitted over the line, other and better means can be adopted. For example, series compensation, higher transmission voltage, HVDC, etc.

When switched capacitors are employed for compensation, these should be disconnected immediately under light load conditions to avoid excessive voltage rise and ferroresonance in presence of transformers.

The purpose of series compensation is to cancel part of the series inductive reactance of the line using series capacitors. This helps in (i) increase of maximum power transfer (ii) reduction in power angle for a given amount of power transfer (iii) increased loading. From practical point of view, it is desirable not to exceed series compensation beyond 80%. If the line is 100% compensated, it will behave as a purely resistive element and would cause series resonance even at fundamental frequency. The location of series capacitors is decided by economical factors and severity of fault currents. Series capacitor reduces line reactance thereby level of fault currents.

A detailed discussion on various issues involved in series and shunt compensators now follows.

18.3 ▶ COMPENSATION

As discussed in Chapter 5, Section 5.9, power flow in the transmission line is controlled by

1. Controlling the sending and receiving end voltages V_s and V_r (through voltage regulations at the respective buses).
2. Controlling the angle between V_s and V_r (the maximum angle is selected depending upon the stability margins).
3. Controlling the series reactance (series connected capacitors increase the maximum power transfer capacity). These 3 parameters are controlled by connecting series and shunt compensation in the transmission system.

18.3.1 Series Compensation

A capacitor in series with a line gives control over the effective reactance between line ends. This effective reactance is given by

$$X_l' = X - X_c$$

$$X = \text{Total series reactance} = X_l + X_{\text{gen}} + X_{\text{trans}}$$

where

X_l = line reactance

X_c = capacitor reactance

It is easy to see that capacitor reduces the effective line reactance*. This results in improvement in performance of the system as below.

1. Voltage drop in the line reduces (gets compensated), i.e., minimisation of end-voltage variations.
2. Prevents voltage collapse.

---

* Reactive voltage drops of a series reactance added in a line is I^2X. It is positive if X is inductive and negative if X is capacitive. So a series capacitive reactance reduces the reactance voltage drop of the line, which is an alternative way of saying that

$$X_l' = X_l - X_c.$$

3. Steady-state power transfer increases; it is inversely proportional to X'_l.
4. As a result of 2 transient stability limit increases.

The benefits of the series capacitor compensator are associated with a problem. The capacitive reactance X_C forms a series resonant circuit with the total series reactance X.

The natural frequency of oscillation of this circuit is given by

$$f_C = \frac{1}{2\pi\sqrt{LC}}$$

$$= \frac{1}{2\pi\sqrt{\dfrac{X}{2\pi f}\dfrac{2\pi fC}{2\pi f}}} = f\sqrt{\frac{X_C}{X}}$$

where f = system frequency

$$\frac{X_C}{X} = \text{degree of compensation}$$

$$= 25 \text{ to } 75\% \text{ (recommended)}$$

For this degree of compensation

$$f_C < f$$

which is subharmonic oscillation.

Even though series compensation has often been found to be cost-effective compared to shunt compensation, but sustained oscillations below the fundamental system frequency can cause the phenomenon, referred to as subsynchronous resonance (SSR) first observed in 1937, but got world-wide attention only in the 1970s, after two turbine-generator shaft failures occurred at the Mojave Generating Station in Southern Nevada. Theoretical studies pointed out that interaction between a series capacitor-compensated line, oscillating at subharmonic frequency, and torsional mechanical oscillation of turbine-generator set can result in negative damping with consequent mutual reinforcement of the two oscillations. Subsynchronous resonance is often not a major problem, and low cost countermeasures and protective measures can be applied. Some of the corrective measures are

1. Detecting the low levels of subharmonic currents on the line by use of sensitive relays, which at a certain level of currents triggers the action to bypass the series capacitors.
2. Modulation of generator field current to provide increased positive damping at subharmonic frequency.

Series inductors are needed for line compensation under light load conditions to counter the excessive voltage rise (Ferranti effect).

As the line load and in particular the reactive power flow over the line varies, there is need to vary the compensation for an acceptable voltage profile. The mechanical switching arrangement for adjusting the capacitance of the capacitor bank in series with the line is shown in Fig. 18.1. Capacitance is varied by opening the switches of individual capacitances with the capacitance C_1, being started by a bypass switch. This is a step-wise arrangement. The whole bank can also be bypassed by the starting switch under any emergent conditions on the line. As the switches in series with capacitor are current carrying suitable circuit breaking arrangements are necessary. However, breaker switched capacitors in series are generally avoided these days the capacitor is either fixed or thyristor switched.

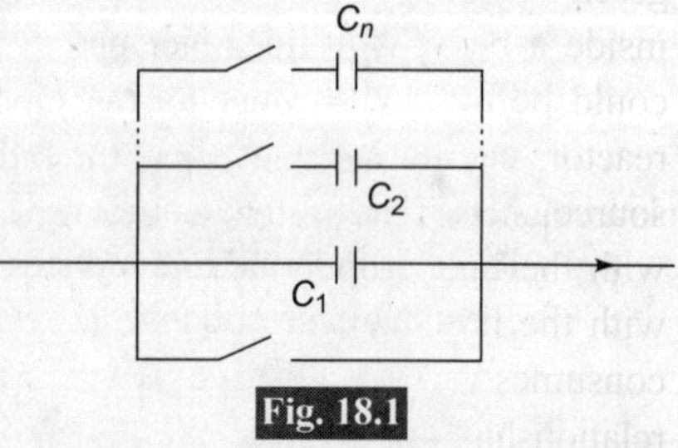

Fig. 18.1

18.3.2 Shunt Compensators

As already explained in Section 18.2.2 and in Chapter 5 (Section 5.10), shunt compensators are connected in shunt at various system nodes (major substations) and sometimes at mid-point of lines. These serve the purposes of voltage control and load stabilisation. As a result of installation of shunt compensators in the system, the nearby generators operate at near unity pf and voltage emergencies mostly do not arise.

18.4 ▶ FLEXIBLE AC TRANSMISSION SYSTEMS (FACTS)

The rapid development of power electronics technology provides exciting opportunities to develop new power system equipment for better utilisation of existing systems. Since 1990, a number of control devices under the term FACTS technology have been proposed and implemented. FACTS devices can be effectively used for power flow control, load sharing among parallel corridors, voltage regulation, enhancement of transient stability and mitigation of system oscillations. By giving additional flexibility, FACTS controllers can enable a line to carry power closer to its thermal rating. Mechanical switching has to be supplemented by rapid response power electronics. It may be noted that FACTS is an enabling technology, and not a one-on-one substitute for mechanical switches.

FACTS employs high speed thyristors for switching in or out transmission line components such as capacitors, reactors or phase shifting transformer for some desirable performance of the systems. The FACTS technology is not a single high-power controller, but rather a collection of controllers, which can be applied individually or in coordination with others to control one or more of the system parameters.

The development of FACTS controllers has followed two different approaches. The first approach employs reactive impedances or a tap changing transformer with thyristor switches as controlled elements. The second approach employs self-commutated static converters as controlled voltage sources.

In general, FACTS controllers can be divided into four categories: (i) series (ii) shunt (iii) combined series-series and (iv) combined series-shunt controllers.

The general symbol for a FACTS controller is given in Fig. 18.2(a), which shows a thyristor arrow inside a box. The *series controller* of Fig. 18.2(b) could be a variable impedance, such as capacitor, reactor, etc. or a power electronics based variable source. All series controllers inject voltage in series with the line. If the voltage is in phase quadrature with the line, the series controller only supplies or consumes variable reactive power. Any other phase relationship will involve real power also.

The *shunt controllers* of Fig. 18.2(c) may be variable impedance, variable source or a combination of these. All shunt controllers inject current into the system at the point of connection.

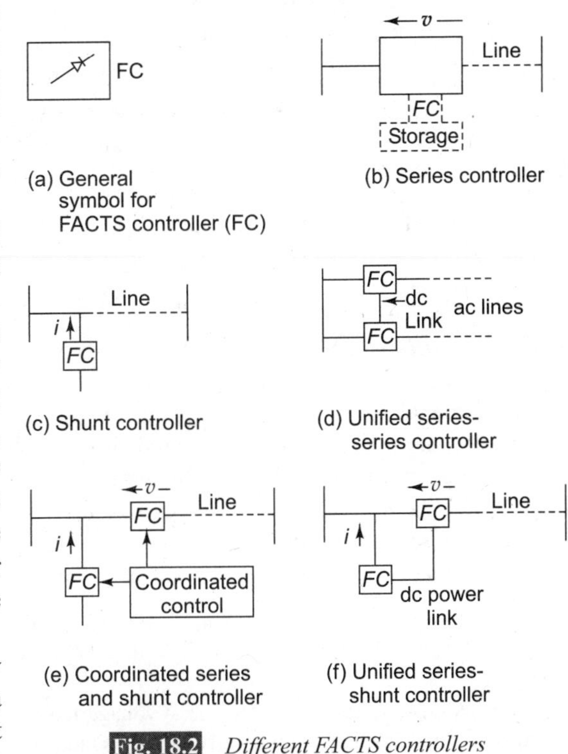

Fig. 18.2 *Different FACTS controllers*

Combined series-series controllers of Fig. 18.2(d) could be a combination of separate series controllers, which are controlled in a coordinated manner or it could be a unified controller.

Combined series-shunt controllers are either controlled in a coordinated manner as in Fig. 18.2(e) or a unified Power Flow Controller with series and shunt elements as in Fig. 18.2(f). For unified controller, there can be a real power exchange between the series and shunt controllers via the dc power link.

Storage source such as a capacitor, battery, superconducting magnet, or any other source of energy can be added in parallel through an electronic interface to replenish the converter's dc storage as shown dotted in Fig. 18.2(b). A controller with storage is much more effective for controlling the system dynamics than the corresponding controller without storage.

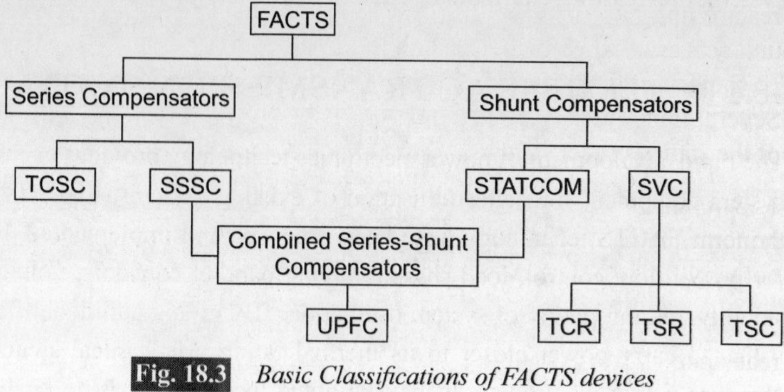

Fig. 18.3 *Basic Classifications of FACTS devices*

Figure 18.3 shows the various types of FACTS devices classified on the basis of connections. The basic classifications of FACTS devices are described as follows. Detailed descriptions are given in sections from 18.4.1 to 18.4.5.

(a) Shunt Compensator

1. Static VAR Compensator (SVC)
2. Static Synchronous Compensator (STATCOM)

(b) Series Compensator

1. Thyristor Controlled Series Compensator (TCSC)
2. Static Synchronous Series Compensator (SSSC)

(c) Combined Series-Shunt Compensator

1. Unified Power Flow Controller (UPFC)

18.4.1 Static VAR Compensator (SVC)

IEEE Definition A shunt connected static VAR generator or absorber whose output is adjusted to exchange capacitive or inductive current so as to maintain or control specific parameters of the electrical power system [2, 9, 16, 17, 18].

These comprise capacitor bank fixed or switched (controlled) or fixed capacitor bank and switched reactor bank in parallel. These compensators draw reactive (leading or lagging) power* from the line thereby regulating voltage, improve stability (steady-state and dynamic), control overvoltage and reduce voltage flicker. These also reduce voltage and current unbalances. In HVDC application these compensators provide the required reactive power and damp out subharmonic oscillations.

* A reactance connected in shunt to line at voltage V draws reactive power V^2/X. It is negative (leading) if reactance is capacitive and positive (lagging) if reactance is inductive.[5]

Since static var compensators use switching for var control. These are also called static var switches or systems. It means that terminology wise

$$SVC = SVS$$

and we will use these interchangeably.

Basic SVC Configurations (or Designs) Thyristors in antiparallel can be used to switch on a capacitor/reactor unit in stepwise control. When the circuitry is designed to adjust the firing angle, capacitor/reactor unit acts as continuously variable in the power circuit.

Capacitor or capacitor and inductor bank can be varied stepwise or continuously by thyristor control. Several important SVS configurations have been devised and are applied in shunt line compensation. Some of the static compensators schemes are discussed in what follows:

1. *Saturated reactor* This is a multi-core reactor with the phase windings so arranged as to cancel the principal harmonics. It is considered as a constant voltage reactive source. It is almost maintenance free but not very flexible with respect to operating characteristics.

2. *Thyristor-controlled reactor (TCR)* A shunt-connected, thyristor-controlled inductor whose effective reactance is varied in a continuous manner by partial-conduction control of the thyristor valve. A thyristor-controlled-reactor (Fig. 18.4) compensator consists of a combination of six-pulse or twelve-pulse thyristor-controlled reactors with a fixed shunt capacitor bank. The reactive power is changed by adjusting the thyristor firing angle. TCRs are characterised by continuous control, no transients and generation of harmonics*. The control system consists of voltage (and current) measuring devices, a controller for error-signal conditioning, a linearising circuit and one or more synchronising circuits.

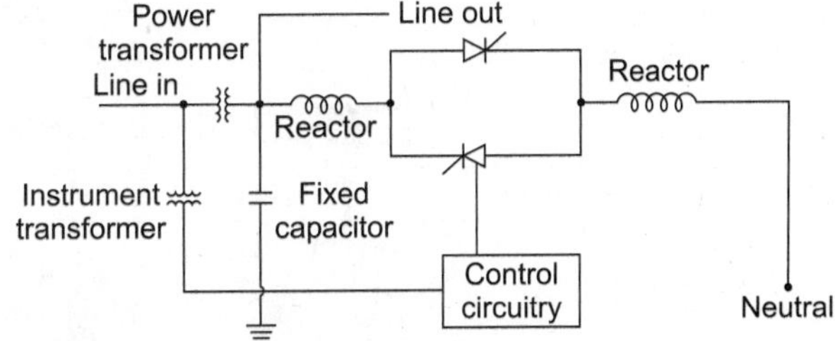

Fig. 18.4 *Thyristor-controlled reactor (TCR) with fixed capacitor*

3. *Thyristor-switched capacitor (TSC)* A shunt-connected, thyristor-switched capacitor whose effective reactance is varied in a stepwise manner by full- or zero-conduction operation of the thyristor valve. It consists of only a thyristor-switched capacitor bank which is split into a number of units of equal ratings to achieve a stepwise control (Fig. 18.5).

As such they are applied as a discretely variable reactive power source, where this type of voltage support is deemed adequate. All switching takes place when the voltage across the thyristor valve is zero, thus providing almost transient free switching.

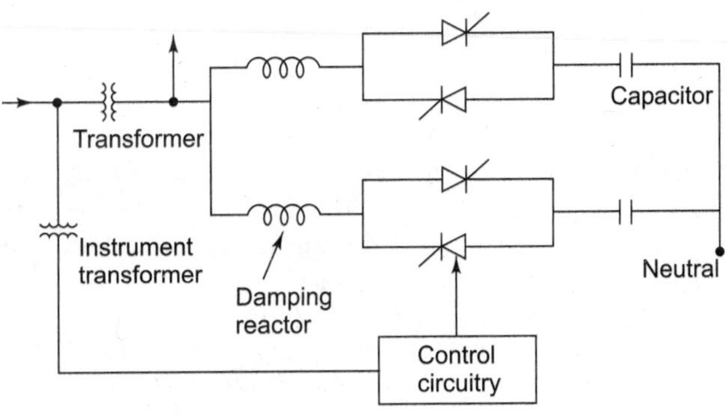

Fig. 18.5 *Thyristor-switched capacitor (TSC)*

* Though λ-connected TCR's are used here, it is better to use Δ-connected TCR's since it is better configuration.

Disconnection is affected by suppressing the firing plus to the thyristors, which will block when the current reaches zero. TSCs are characterised by step-wise control, no transients, very low hormonics, low losses, redundancy and flexibility.

4. *Combined TCR and TSC Compensator* A combined TSC and TCR (Fig. 18.6) is the optimum solution in majority of cases. With this, continuous variable reactive power is obtained throughout the complete control range. Furthermore, full control of both inductive and capacitive parts of the compensator is obtained. This is a very advantageous feature permitting optimum performance during large disturbances in the power system (e.g., line faults, load rejection, etc.) TSC/TCR combinations are characterised by continuous control, no transients, low generations of harmonics, low losses, redundancy, flexible control and operation.

The basic characteristics of the main static var generator schemes are given in Table 18.1.

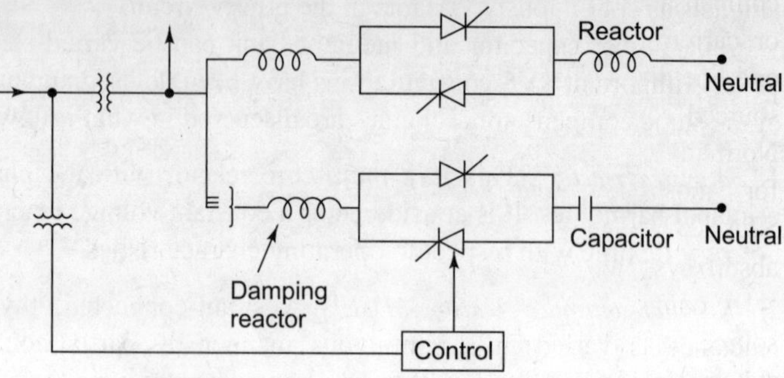

Fig. 18.6 *A combined TCR/TSC compensator*

Table 18.1 Comparison of Static Var Generators

Type of Var Generator	*TCR-FC (1)*	*TSC-(TSR) (2)*	*TCR-TSC (3)*
VI and VQ characteristics	Max comp. current is proportional to system voltage. Max cap. var output decreases with the square of the voltage decrease.	Max. comp. current is proportional to system voltage. Max. cap. var output decreases with the square of the voltage decrease.	Same as in (1) or (2)
Loss Vs var output	High losses at zero output. Losses decrease smoothly with cap. output, increase with inductive output	Low losses at zero ouput. Losses increase step-like with cap. output	Low losses at zero output. Losses increase step-like with cap. output, smoothly with ind. output
Harmonic generation	Internally high (large pu TCR) Requires significant filtering	Internally very low Resonance may necessitate tuning reactors	Internally low (small pu TCR) Filtering required
Max. theoret. delay	1/2 cycle	1 cycle	1 cycle
Transient behaviour under system voltage disturbances	Poor (FC causes transient over-voltages in response to step disturbances)	Can be neutral. (Capacitors can be switched out to minimise transient over-voltages)	Same as in (2)

18.4.2 Static Synchronous Compensator (STATCOM)

IEEE Definition A static synchronous generator operated as a shunt connected static VAR compensator whose Capacitive or Inductive output current can be controlled independent of the ac system voltage [2, 9, 16–18].

STATCOM is a static synchronous generator operated as a shunt-connected static var compensator whose capacitive or inductive output current can be controlled independent of the ac system voltage. The STATCOM, like its conventional counterpart, the SVC, controls transmission voltage by reactive shunt compensation. It can be based on a voltage-sourced or current-sourced converter. Figure 18.7 shows a one-line diagram of STATCOM based on a voltage-sourced converter and a current sourced converter. Normally a voltage-source converter is preferred for most converter-based FACTS controllers. STATCOM can be designed to be an active filter to absorb system harmonics.

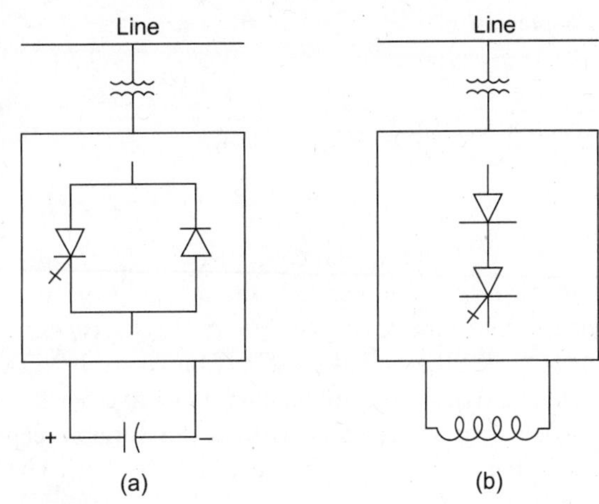

Fig. 18.7 *(a) STATCOM based on voltage-sourced and (b) current-sourced converters*

A combination of STATCOM and any energy source to supply or absorb power is called static synchronous generator (SSG). Energy source may be a battery, flywheel, superconducting magnet, large dc storage capacitor, another rectifier/inverter etc.

18.4.3 Thyristor Controlled Series Compensator (TCSC)

IEEE Definition A capacitive reactance compensator which consists of a series capacitor bank shunted by a thyristor-controlled reactor in order to provide a smoothly variable series capacitive reactance [2, 9, 16–18].

With fast advancement in thyristor devices and associated switching control technology, the capacitance of the series capacitance bank can be controlled much more effectively; both stepwise and smooth control. This is demonstrated by the schematic diagram of Fig. 18.8 wherein the capacitor is shunted by two thyristors in antiparallel. Upon firing the thyristors alternately one carries current in positive half cycle and the other in negative half cycle.

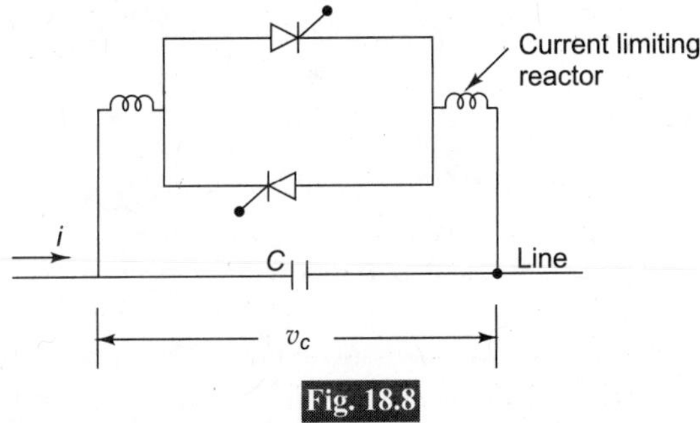

Fig. 18.8

In each half cycle when the thyristor is fired (at an adjustable angle), it conducts current for the rest of the half cycle till natural current zero. During the off-time of the thyristor current is conducted by the capacitor and capacitor voltage is v_c. During on-time of the thyristor capacitor is short circuited, i.e., $v_c = 0$ and current is conducted by the thyristor. The same process is repeated in the other half cycle. This means that v_c can be controlled for any given i, which is equivalent of reducing the capacitance as $C = v_c/i$. By this scheme capacitance can be controlled smoothly by adjusting the firing angle.

Thyristors are now available to carry large current and to withstand (during off-time) large voltage encountered in power systems. The latest device called a Gate Turn Off (GTO) thyristor has the capability that by suitable firing circuit, angle (time) at which it goes on and off can both be controlled.

This means wider range and finer control over capacitance. Similarly control is possible over series reactor in the line.

TCR reactance,

$$X_L(\alpha) = X_L \frac{\pi}{\pi - 2\alpha - \sin 2\alpha} \quad (18.1)$$

Capacitor reactance,

$$X_C = -\frac{1}{2\pi fC} \quad (18.2)$$

Figure 18.9 shows the concept of TCSC model. A TCR is connected in parallel with a fixed capacitor so that to control the reactance by varying thyristor firing angle α. For the variation of α from 0 to 90°, TCR reactance $X_L(\alpha)$ varies from actual inductive reactance (X_L) to infinity. This controlled reactor is connected across the series capacitor, so that the variable capacitive reactance is possible across the TCSC which modify the transmission line reactance. Effective TCSC reactance X_{TCSC} with respect to alpha (α) can be given as [9, 19, 20]

TCSC ⇨ Fixed Capacitor ⇔ Parallel ⇔ TCR

Fig. 18.9 *A structural definition of TCSE devices*

TCSC reactance,

$$X_{\text{TCSC}}(\alpha) = -X_C + a_1(2(\pi - \alpha) + \sin(2(\pi - \alpha))) - a_2 \cos^2(\pi - \alpha)(\omega \tan(\omega(\pi - \alpha)) - \tan(\pi - \alpha)) \quad (18.3)$$

where,

$$a_1 = \frac{X_C + \left(\dfrac{X_C X_L}{X_C - X_L}\right)}{\pi} \quad (18.4)$$

$$a_2 = 4\frac{1}{X_L \pi}\left(\frac{X_C X_L}{X_C - X_L}\right)^2 \quad (18.5)$$

$$\omega = \sqrt{\frac{X_C}{X_L}} \quad (18.6)$$

Figure 18.10 shows the Reactance characteristics curve of TCSC device drawn with respect to firing angle α. The reactance characteristic is divided into three different regions such as Inductive region, Capacitive region and Resonance region. Inductive and capacitive regions are the TCSC working regions and resonance region occurs between these two regions where TCSC should not be operated [19]. Nearer to resonance region, there is large change in reactance for a small change in firing angle. Recently, research works are going on to micro tune the reactance with the concept of split TCSC [20].

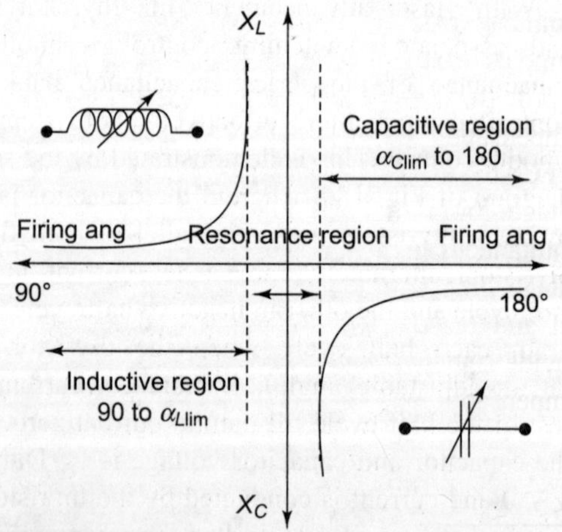

Fig. 18.10 *Reactance Vs firing angle characteristic curve*

Range of firing angle (α)	**Region**
$90 \le \alpha \le \alpha_{Llim}$	Inductive region
$\alpha_{\text{Clim}} \le \alpha \le 180$	Capacitive region
$\alpha_{\text{Llim}} \le \alpha \le \alpha_{\text{Clim}}$	Resonance region

18.4.4 Static Synchronous Series Compensator (SSSC)

IEEE Definition A static synchronous generator operated without an external electric energy source as a series compensator whose output voltage is in quadrature with, and controllable independently of, the line current for the purpose of increasing or decreasing the overall reactive voltage drops across the line and thereby controlling the transmitted electric power [2, 9, 16–18].

It is a series connected controller. Though it is like STATCOM, but its output voltage is in series with the line. It thus controls the voltage across the line and hence its impedance.

This scheme is known as static synchronous series compensator (SSSC). SSSC has the capability to induce both capacitive and inductive voltage in series with line, thereby widening the operating region of the scheme. It can be used for power flow control both increasing or decreasing reactive flow on the line. Further this scheme gives better stability and is more effective in damping out electromechanical oscillations.

18.4.5 Unified Power Flow Controller (UPFC)

IEEE Definition A combination of static synchronous compensator (STATCOM) and a static series compensator (SSSC) which are coupled via a common dc link, to allow bidirectional flow of real power between the series output terminals of the SSSC and the shunt output terminals of the STATCOM, and are controlled to provide concurrent real and reactive series line compensation without an external electrical energy source. The UPFC, by means of angularly unconstrained series voltage injection, is able or, alternatively, the real and reactive power flow in the line. The UPFC may also provide independently controllable shunt reactive compensation [2, 9, 16–18].

This controller is connected as shown in Fig. 18.11. It is a combination of STATCOM and SSSC which are coupled via a common dc link to allow bi-directional flow of real power between the series output terminals of the SSSC and the shunt output terminals of the STATCOM. These are controlled to provide concurrent real and reactive series line compensation without an external energy source. The UPFC, by means of angularly unconstrained series voltage injection, is able to control, concurrently/simultaneously or selectively, the transmission line voltage, impedance, and angle or, alternatively, the real and reactive line flows. The UPFC may also provide independently controllable shunt reactive compensation.

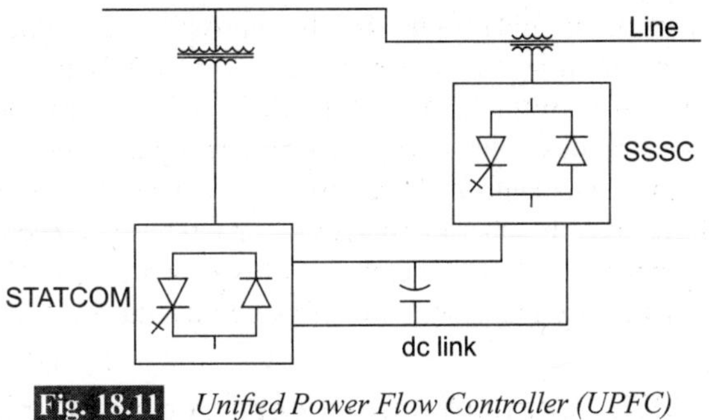

Fig. 18.11 *Unified Power Flow Controller (UPFC)*

18.5 ▶ OTHER FACTS DEVICES

Some other important FACTS devices are [2, 9, 16–18]

Interline Power Flow Controller (IPFC) This is a recently introduced controller [2, 3]. It is a combination of two or more static synchronous series compensators which are coupled via a common dc link to facilitate bi-directional flow of real power between the ac terminals of the SSSCs, and are controlled to provide independent reactive series compensation for the control of real power flow in each line and maintain the desired distribution of reactive power flow among the lines. Thus, it manages a comprehensive overall real and reactive power management for a multi-line mission system.

Thyristor-Controlled Phase-Shifting Transformer (TCPST) This controller is also called Thyristor-Controlled Phase Angle Regulator (TCPAR). A phase shifting transformer controlled by thyristor switches to give a rapidly variable phase angle.

Thyristor-Controlled Voltage Regulator (TCVR) A thyristor controlled transformer which can provide variable in-phase voltage with continuous control.

Interphase Power Controller (IPC) A series-connected controller of active and reactive power consisting, in each phase, of inductive and capacitive branches subjected to separately phase-shifted voltages. The active and reactive power can be set independently by adjusting the phase shifts and/or the branch impedances, using mechanical or electronic switches.

Thyristor-Controlled Braking Resistor (TCBR) It is a shunt-connected thyristor-switched resistor, which is controlled to aid stabilisation of a power system or to minimise power acceleration of a generating unit during a disturbance.

Thyristor-Controlled Voltage Limiter (TCVL) A thyristor-switched metal-oxide varistor (MOV) used to limit the voltage across its terminals during transient conditions.

Battery-Energy-Storage System (BESS) A chemical-based energy-storage system using shunt-connected switching converters to supply or absorb energy to or from an ac system which can be adjusted rapidly.

Static Condenser (STATCON) This term is deprecated in favour of the static synchronous compensator (SSC or STATCOM).

18.6 ► COMPARISON BETWEEN STATCOM AND SVC

It may be noted that in the normal linear operating range, the V-I characteristic and functional compensation capability of the STATCOM and the SVC are similar [2]. However, the basic operating principles of the STATCOM, which, with a converter based var generator, functions as a shunt-connected synchronous voltage source, are basically different from those of the SVC, since SVC functions as a shunt-connected, controlled reactive admittance. This basic operational difference renders the STATCOM to have overall superior functional characteristics, better performance, and greater application flexibility as compared to SVC. The ability of the STATCOM to maintain full capacitive output current at low system voltage also makes it more effective than the SVC in improving the transient (first swing) stability.

18.6.1 Comparison Between Series and Shunt Compensation

Advantages of series compensation

1. Series capacitors are inherently self regulating and a control system is not required.
2. For the same performance, series capacitors are often less costly than SVCs and losses are very low.
3. For voltage stability, series capacitors lower the critical or collapse voltage.
4. Series capacitors possess adequate time-overload capability.
5. Series capacitors and switched series capacitors can be used to control loading of paralleled lines to minimise active and reactive losses.

Disadvantages of series compensation

1. Series capacitors are line connected and compensation is removed for outages and capacitors in parallel lines may be overloaded.
2. During heavy loading, the voltage on one side of the series capacitor may be out-of-range.

3. Shunt reactors may be needed for light load compensation.
4. Subsynchronous resonance may call for expensive countermeasures.

Advantages of SVC

1. SVCs control voltage directly.
2. SVCs control temporary overvoltages rapidly.

Disadvantages of SVC

1. SVCs have limited overload capability.
2. SVCs are expensive.

The best design perhaps is a combination of series and shunt compensation. Because of higher initial and operating costs, synchronous condensers are normally not competitive with SVCs. Technically, synchronous condensers are better than SVCs in voltage-weak networks. Following a drop in network voltage, the increase in condenser reactive power output is instantaneous. Most synchronous condenser applications are now associated with HVDC installations.

18.7 ▶ PERFORMANCE OF FACTS DEVICES

A comparative performance of major FACTS devices in AC system is given in Table 18.2.

Table 18.2 A comparative performance of major FACTS controller

Controller	*Voltage Control*	*Transient Stability*	*Damping-Power Oscillations*	*Reactive-Power Compensation*	*Power-Flow Control*	*SSR Mitigation*
BESS	X		X			
SMES		X	X			
SSSC	X	X	X	X	X	X
STATCOM	X	X	X	X		
SVC	X	X	X	X		
TCPST		X	X		X	X
TCSC	X	X	X		X	X
TSBR		X	X			X
TSSC	X	X	X		X	
UPFC	X	X	X	X	X	X

18.8 ▶ COST COMPARISON BETWEEN UPFC AND SVC

Based on the Siemens AG Database, the cost functions for UPFC, TCSC and SVC are developed [21].

The cost function for UPFC is

$$C_{UPFC} = 0.0003S^2 - 0.2691S + 188.22 \text{ (US\$/kVar)} \tag{18.7}$$

For TCSC:

$$C_{TCSC} = 0.0015S^2 - 0.7130S + 153.75 \text{ (US\$/kVar)} \tag{18.8}$$

For SVC:

$$C_{SVC} = 0.0003S^2 - 0.3051S + 127.38 \text{ (US\$/kVar)} \tag{18.9}$$

Where C_{UPFC}, C_{TCSC} and C_{SVC} are in US\$/kVar and S is the operating range of the FACTS devices in kVar [21].

The cost function for UPFC, TCSC and SVC are shown in Fig. 18.12.

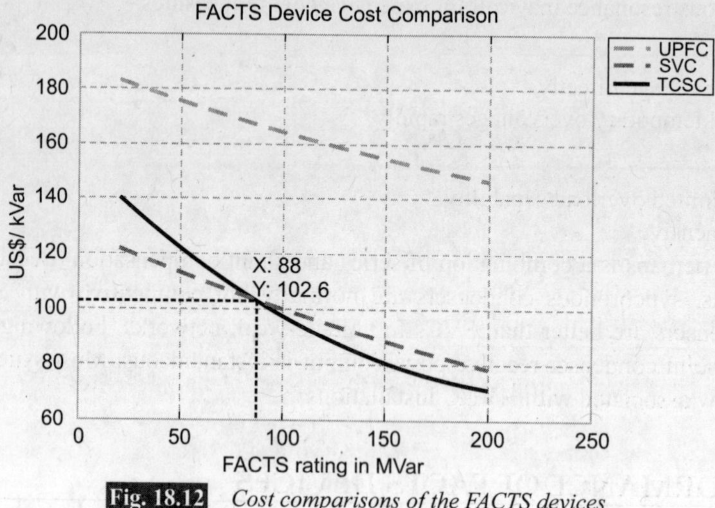

Fig. 18.12 *Cost comparisons of the FACTS devices*

Comparing with SVC and UPFC, initial investment cost for TCSC device is less when TCSC's rating is above 88 MVar. TCSC device MVar ratings are calculated from

$$S_{\text{TCSC}} = I_{\text{Line}}^2 X_{\text{TCSC}} = \frac{V_{\text{TCSC}}^2}{X_{\text{TCSC}}} \tag{18.10}$$

where

S_{TCSC} is MVar rating of TCSC
I_{Line} is Line current in amps
V_{TCSC} is Capacitor Voltage in volts
X_{TCSC} is Reactance compensation in ohms

18.9 ▶ EQUIVALENT CIRCUIT FOR FACTS CONTROLLER

The UPFC is the most versatile FACTS controller with three control variables. The magnitude and phase angle of the series injected voltage in addition to the reactive current drawn by the shunt connected VSC are the three control variables. The equivalent circuit is shown in Fig. 18.13.

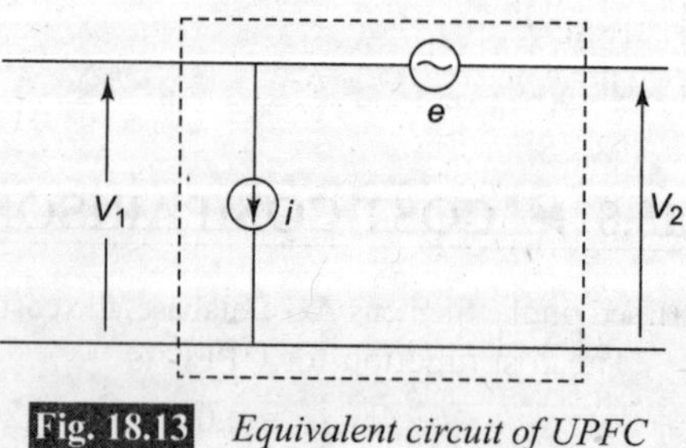

Fig. 18.13 *Equivalent circuit of UPFC*

The shunt current '*I*' has real (I_p) and reactive (I_r) components. Similarly, the series injected voltage *V* has real V_p and reactive (V_r) components. The positive values of I_r and V_r indicate reactive power drawn by the shunt converter and supplied by the series converter. Reglecting losses in a UPFC, the constant equation is

$$V_1 I_p = I_2 V_p$$

The remaining shunt and series connected FACTS controllers are special cases of UPFC. For example, in a STATCOM,

$$V_p = 0, \;\; V_r = 0, \;\; I_p = 0 \text{ and } I_r \text{ is +ve.}$$

In a SSSC, $I_p = 0, J_r = 0, V_p = 0$ and V_r is +ve.

In a SVC, $V_p = 0, V_r = 0, I_p = 0$ and $I_r = -V_i . B_{SVC}$, where B_{SVC} is the control variable in a SVC.

18.10 ▶ BENEFITS AND APPLICATIONS

The power electronic controller acts quite fast and hence regulates voltage and power flow during steady-state and dynamic conditions. The application of FACTS controller include

1. Voltage support at critical buses with shunt connected controllers.
2. Regulate power flow in critical lines with series connected controllers.
3. Both voltage and power flow are controlled using UPFC.

The benefits of FACTs controllers are listed below:

1. The system operation is improved by improving the voltage profile and reducing power losses.
2. The power carrying capacity of lines can be increased upto the thermal limits.
3. The transient stability limit is enhanced by improving dynamic security of the system.
4. TCSC can counter the problem of subsynchronous resonance (SSR) experienced with fixed series capacitors.
5. The voltage fluctuations can be overcome by STATCOM control.
6. Steady-state stability limit is enhanced by providing auxiliary stability controllers to damp low frequency oscillations.

18.10.1 Application of FACTS Controllers for Power Quality Improvement in Distribution System

The concept of FACTS was developed for the transmission network, it has been extended for power quality (PQ) improvement in the distribution system operating at lower voltages. The proliferation in the use of computers, microprocessors and power electronic system has resulted in power quality issues which include deviations in magnitude, frequency and wave form distortion.

PQ problem is defined as any problem manifested in voltage, current or frequency deviation that results in failure or misoperation of customer equipment. The PQ problems are categorised as

1. Transients
   (a) Impulsive
   (b) Oscillatory
2. Short-duration and long-duration variations.
   (a) Sag
   (b) Swell
   (c) Interruptions
3. Voltage unbalance
4. Waveform distortion
   (a) dc offset
   (b) Harmonics
   (c) Interharmonics
   (d) Notching
   (e) Noise
5. Voltage flicker
6. Power frequency variations

1. ***Transients*** The transients decay with time and hence not a steady-state problem. It is also called as 'surge'. An impulsive transient has rise and decay times. It is due to lightning discharge and during operation of circuit breakers of transmission (distribution liner). An oscillator transient has non-power frequency change.

2. ***Long-duration voltage variation*** Long-duration voltage variations are the deviations in RMS voltage which last longer than one minute. They can be either over voltages (> 1.1 pu) or under voltages (less than 0.9 pu). The voltage variations are generally due to switching of capacitor bombs. When the supply voltage has been zero for a period of time greater than one minute, it is called as sustained interruption.

3. ***Short-duration voltage variation*** The short-duration voltage variations are caused by (i) energisation of large induction motors (ii) fault in the lines, etc. and they exist for few cycles or a maximum of one minute. The voltage variations can be temporary voltage disp (sugs) or voltage rises (swell) or a complete loss of voltage (interruptions).

4. ***Voltage unbalance*** The main source of voltage unbalances are single-phase loads on a three-phase circuit resulting in load imbalance.

Wave form distortion Wave form distortion is a steady-state deviation from an ideal sine wave of power frequency. The presence of dc voltage or current is termed as dc offset. The dc current flow in a transformer causes magnetic saturation, at increased losses.

Nonlinear loads and power electronic controllers are the primary source of harmonics. Total harmonics distortion (THD) is the most commonly used measure for harmonics. THD in current is defined as

$$\text{THD} = \frac{\sum_{4=i}^{\alpha} I_h}{I_1}$$

where I_h is the harmonic current of h order and I_1 is the fundamental component.

Major problems due to harmonic distortion are:

1. Additional losses add heating in machines, capacitors, etc.
2. Over voltages due to resonance in the system
3. Telephone interference
4. Over loading of power factor correction capacitors.

Voltages or currents having frequency components that are not integer multiples of the supply frequency are called interharmonics. The main sources of interharmonics are static frequency convertors, cycloconvertors and back to back HVDC links. Interharmonics can affect power line carrier signalling and cause visual flicker in display devices.

Notching is a periodic disturbance in the voltage wave form introduced by power converters when current is commutated from one phase to another.

Noise can be defined as unwanted electrical signals with broadband spectral content less than 200 kHz. It is caused by power converters, arcing equipment or switched mode power supplies. Noise affects electronic devices such as microcomputer and programmable controllers.

5. ***Voltage flicker*** Voltage fluctuations are systematic variations of the voltage envelope or a series of random changes in the voltage magnitude (which lies in the range 0.9 to 1.1 pu). The major causes for flickering are high power loads which draw fluctuating current such as large motor drives and are furnaces. The typical frequency spectrum of a voltage flicker lies in the range from 1 Hz to 30 Hz.

6. ***Power frequency variations*** Power frequency variations are the deviations of the system fundamental frequency from its specified value of 50 or 60 Hz. The control characteristics of the generators affect the shift in the frequency. In an interconnected power system economic incentives are provided to increase the

load when the frequency is high. Similarly, availability based tariff (ABT) that charges for the tie line flows according to the system frequency is considered as a solution to the large frequency variations.

18.10.2 Power Factor (PF) and THD

In a nonlinear load connected to a single-phase ac power supply, the active power drawn is

$$P = V I_{s1} \cos \phi$$

where I_{s1} is the fundamental component of the current drawn from the supply and $\cos \phi$ is the phase angle between the I_{s1} and V_s.

The voltage, (V_s), the current (I_s) and the fundamental current, I_{s1}, are shown in Fig. 18.14.

Power factor is defined as the ratio of active power with the product of voltage and total current.

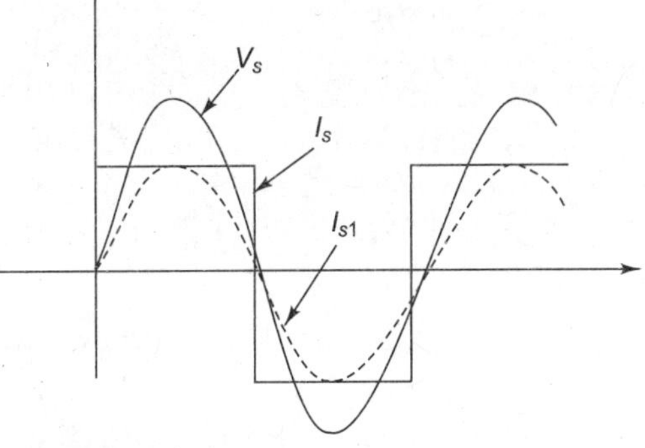

Fig. 18.14 *Current drawn by a nonlinear load*

$$\therefore \qquad \text{PF} = \frac{V_s I_{s1} \cos\phi}{V_s I_s}$$

$$= \frac{I_{s1}}{I_s} \cdot \cos\phi$$

$$= \text{PF}. \cos \phi$$

where PF is called the distribution factor which is the ratio between I_{s1} and I_s.

The relation between THD and PF is as below.

$$\text{PF} = \frac{1}{\sqrt{1+\text{THD}^2}}$$

18.11 ▶ SUMMARY

Since the 1970s, energy cost, environmental restrictions, right-of-way difficulties, along with other legislative social and cost problems have postponed the construction of both new generation and transmission systems in India as well as most of other countries. Recently, because of adoption of power reforms or restructuring or deregulation, competitive electric energy markets are being developed by mandating open access transmission services.

In the late 1980s, the vision of FACTS was formulated. In this, various power electronics based controllers (compensators) regulate power flow and transmission voltage and through fast control action, mitigate dynamic disturbances. Due to FACTS, transmission line capacity was enhanced. Two types of FACTS controllers were developed. One employed conventional thyristor-switched capacitors and reactors, and quadrature tap-changing transformers such as SVC and TCSC. The second category was of self-commutated switching converters as synchronous voltage sources, e.g., STATCOM, SSSC, UPFC and IPFC. The two groups of FACTS controllers have quite different operating and performance characteristics. The second group uses self-commutated dc to ac converter. The converter, supported by a dc power supply or energy storage device can also exchange real power with the ac system besides controlling reactive power independently.

The increasing use of FACTS controllers in future is guaranteed. What benefits are required for a given system would be a principal justification for the choice of a FACTS controller. Its final form and operation will, of course, depend not only on the successful development of the necessary control and communication technologies and protocols, but also on the final structure of the evolving newly restructured power systems.

Note: For numerical problem, refer Example 5.1 in Chap. 5.

Multiple Choice Questions

18.1 An overhead line with series compensation is protected using
(a) Impedance relay (b) Reactance relay
(c) Mho relay (d) None of the above

18.2 Shunt compensation in an EHV is resorted to
(a) Improve the stability
(b) Reduce the fault level
(c) Improve the voltage profile
(d) As a substitute for synchronous phase modifier

18.3 For stability and economic reasons we operate the transmission line with power angle in the range:
(a) 10° to 25° (b) 30° to 45° (c) 60° to 75° (d) 65° to 80°

18.4 Series compensation on EHV lines is resorted to
(a) Improve the stability
(b) Reduce the fault level
(c) Improve the voltage profile
(d) As a substitute for synchronous phase modifier

18.5 The voltage of a particular bus can be controlled by controlling the
(a) Phase angle (b) Reactive power of the bus
(c) Active power of the bus (d) Phase angle and reactive power

18.6 With the help of a reactive compensator it is possible to have
(a) Constant voltage operation only (b) Unity pf operation only
(c) Both constant voltage and unity pf (d) Either constant voltage or unity pf

18.7 For a long uncompensated line the limit to the line loading is governed by
(a) Thermal limit (b) Voltage drop (c) Stability limit (d) Corona loss

18.8 With 100% series compensation of lines
(a) The circuit is series resonant at power frequency
(b) Low transient voltage
(c) High transient current
(d) Both (a) and (c)

18.9 The effect of increasing gating angle in a thyristorised controlled reactor is
(a) To increase the effective inductance of the reactor
(b) To reduce the effective reactive power
(c) Both (a) and (b)
(d) None of the above

18.10 The effect of increasing gating angle in a thyristorised controlled reactor is
(a) To decrease power loss in thyristor controller
(b) To decrease power loss in the reactor
(c) To make current wave form less sinusoidal
(d) All of the above

18.11 The effect of series capacitance compensation is
(a) To decrease the virtual surge impedance
(b) To decrease the effective length of the line
(c) To increase virtual surge impedance loading
(d) All of the above

18.12 For any fixed degree of series compensation additional capacitive shunt compensation
(a) Increases the effective length of line
(b) Increases virtual surge of line
(c) Decreases virtual surge impedance of line
(d) Both (b) and (c)

18.13 For any fixed degree of inductive shunt compensation, additional series capacitive compensation
(a) Increases the effective length of line
(b) Increases virtual surge impedance of line
(c) Decreases virtual surge impedance loading of the line
(d) None of the above

18.14 With 100% inductive shunt compensation the voltage profile is flat for
(a) 100% load of line (b) 50% loading of line (c) Zero loading of line (d) None of the above

18.15 Shunt compensation in an EHV line is used to
(a) Improve stability
(b) Reduce fault level
(c) Improve the voltage profile
(d) Substitute for synchronous phase modifier

18.16 Normally Z_{BUS} matrix is a
(a) Null matrix (b) Sparse matrix (c) Full matrix (d) Unity matrix

18.17 FACTS devices are used in
(a) Generation (b) AC transmission (c) DC transmission (d) Distribution

18.18 Shunt compensation device is
(a) TCSC (b) SSSC (c) UPFC (d) SVC

18.19 Unified Power Flow Controller (UPFC) is combination of
(a) STATCOM and TCSC (b) SSSC and TSC
(c) STATCOM and SSSC (d) TSSC and TCR

18.20 Basic types of FACTS controller are
(a) Series controllers and shunt controllers (b) Combined series-series controllers
(c) Combined series-shunt controllers (d) All of the above

18.21 SSSC is a
(a) Series compensation device (b) Shunt compensation device
(c) Combined compensator (d) Loss reduction device

18.22 The main objective of series compensation is to
(a) Improve the power factor
(b) Reduce the fault currents
(c) Reduce the voltage drop over long distance
(d) Improve the loadability of power system

18.23 SVC stands for
(a) Static VAR compensator (b) Static voltage controller
(c) Synchronous VAR compensator (d) Synchronous voltage controller

18.24 Full form of UPFC is
(a) Unified Power Flow Controller (b) Unified Power Factor Controller
(c) Unified Power Flow Compensator (d) Unique Power Flow Controller

18.25 Which of the following is 3rd generation FACTs device?
(a) UPFC (b) STATCOM (c) SSSC (d) SVC

References

Books

1. A. Chakrabarti, D.P. Kothari, A.K. Mukhopadhyay and A De *Reactive Power Control and Voltage Stability in Power Transmission Systems*, PHI, New Delhi, 2011.
2. N.G. Hingorani and L. Gyugyi, *Understanding FACTS,* IEEE Press, New York, 2000.
3. Y.H. Song and A.T. Johns, *Flexible AC Transmission Systems*, IEE, London, 1999.
4. T.J.E. Miller, *Reactive Power Control in Electric Systems*, John Wiley and Sons, N Y, 1982.
5. D.P. Kothari and I.J. Nagrath, *Electric Machines,* 4th edn, Tata McGRaw-Hill, New Delhi, 2010.
6. C.W. Taylor, *Power System Voltage Stability,* McGraw-Hill, Singapore, 1994.
7. D.P. Kothari and I.J. Nagrath, *Power System Engineering*, 2nd edn, Tata McGraw-Hill, New Delhi, 2008.
8. C.S. Indulkar, D.P. Kothari, and K. Ramalingam, *Power System Transients A Statistical Approach*, 2nd edn, Prentice-Hall of India, New Delhi, 2011.
9. R.M. Mathur and R.K. Verma, *Thyristor-Based FACTS Controllers for Electrical Transmission Systems*, John Wiley, New York, 2002.

Papers

10. A. Edris, "FACTS Technology Development: An Update", *IEEE Power Engineering Review,* volume: 20, pp: 4–9, March 2000.
11. F. Iliceto and E. Cinieri, "Comparative Analysis of Series and Shunt Compensation Schemes for AC Transmission Systems", *IEEE Trans*, volume: PAS 96, issue: 6, pp: 1819–1830, 1977.
12. E.W. Kimbark, "How to Improve System Stability without Risking Subsynchronous Resonance", *IEEE Trans*, volume: PAS, 96, issue: 5, pp: 1608–1619, Sept/Oct 1977.
13. CIGRE, "WG 38–01, *Static Var Compensators,* CIGRE", Paris, 1986.
14. D. Povh, "Use of HVDC and FACTS", *IEEE Proceedings,* volume: 88, issue: 2, pp: 235–245, Feb. 2000.
15. E.W. Kimbark, "A New Look At Shunt Compensation", *IEEE Trans,* volume: PAS-102, issue: 1, pp: 212–218, Jan 1983.
16. A.A. Edris, et al., "Proposed Terms and Definitions for Flexible AC Transmission System (FACTS)", *IEEE Transaction*, volume: 12, issue: 4, pp: 1848–1853, Oct. 1997.
17. IEEE Power Engineering Society/CIGRE, FACTS Overview, Publication 95TP108, IEEE Press, New York, 1995.
18. IEEE Power Engineering Society, FACTS Applications, Publication 96TP116-0, IEEE Press, New York, 1996.
19. S. Meikandasivam, R.K. Nema, and S.K. Jain, "Behavioral Study of TCSC Device – A MATLAB/Simulink Implementation", *International Journal of Electrical Power and Energy Systems Engineering (IJPESE)*-WASET, pp: 102–107, Spring 2008.
20. S. Meikandasivam, R.K. Nema, and S.K. Jain, "Investigation on Thyristor Controlled Series Compensator in Power System Network", PhD Dissertation, MANIT, Bhopal, July, 2010.
21. L.J. Cai, I. Erlich, and G. Stamtsis, "Optimal Choice and Allocation of FACTS Devices in Deregulated Electricity Market using Genetic Algorithms", *Power Systems Conference, IEEE,* volume: 1, pp: 201–207, 2004.
22. M. Kowsalya, K.K. Ray, and D.P. Kothari, "Voltage Stability Margin Enhancement through Optimal Location of Var Compensator", presented at the ICSET 2008–IEEE International Conference, Singapore, November 24–27, 2008.

23. B. Singh, P. Jayaprakash, T.R. Somayajulu, and D.P. Kothari, "Reduced Rating VSC with a Zig-Zag Transformer for Current Compensation in a Three-Phase Four-Wire Distribution System", *IEEE Transactions on Power Delivery*, volume: 24, issue: 1, pp: 249–259, January 2009.
24. A. Chaudhary, V.C. Niraj, S.P. Karthikeyan, R. Nagaraja, I.J. Raglend, and D.P. Kothari, "Dynamic Compensation Requirement Analysis for an Indian Utility in ARPN", *Journal of Engineering and Applied Sciences*, volume: 4, issue: 2, pp: 19–23, April 2009.
25. S. Ziaeinejad and A. Mehrizi-Sani, "Design Tradeoffs in Selection of the DC-Side Voltage for a D-STATCOM", *IEEE Transactions on Power Delivery*, volume: 33, issue: 6, pp: 3230–3232, 2018.
26. L. Wang, C. Lam, and M. Wong, "A Hybrid-STATCOM with Wide Compensation Range and Low DC-Link Voltage", *IEEE Transactions on Industrial Electronics*, volume: 63, issue: 6, pp: 3333–3343, 2016.
27. E. Ghahremani and I. Kamwa, "Optimal Placement of Multiple-Type FACTS Devices to Maximize Power System Loadability Using a Generic Graphical User Interface", *IEEE Transactions on Power Systems*, volume: 28, issue: 2, pp: 764–778, 2013.
28. M.G. Ahsaee and J. Sadeh, "A Novel Fault-Location Algorithm for Long Transmission Lines Compensated by Series FACTS Devices", *IEEE Transactions on Power Delivery*, volume: 26, issue: 4, pp: 2299–2308, 2011.
29. M. A. Chitsazan, M. S. Fadali, and A. M. Trzynadlowski, "State Estimation for Large-Scale Power Systems and FACTS Devices Based on Spanning Tree Maximum Exponential Absolute Value", *IEEE Transactions on Power Systems*, volume: 35, issue: 1, pp: 238–248, 2020.
30. Bhim Singh, P. Jayaprakash, D.P. Kothari, A. Chandra, and K. Al Haddad, "Comprehensive Study of DSTATCOM Configurations", *IEEE Transactions on Industrial Informatics*, volume: 10, issue: 2, pp: 854–870, 2014.
31. B. Singh, P. Jayaprakash, S. Kumar, and D.P. Kothari, "Implementation of Neural-Network-Controlled Three-Leg VSC and a Transformer as Three-Phase Four-Wire DSTATCOM", *IEEE Transactions on Industry Applications*, volume: 47, issue: 4, pp: 1892–1901, 2011.
32. A. Panwar, G. Sharma, I. Nasiruddin, and R.C. Bansal, "Frequency Stabilization of Hydro–Hydro Power System Using Hybrid Bacteria Foraging PSO with UPFC and HAE", *Electric Power Systems Research*, volume: 161, pp: 74–85, 2018.
33. S.P. Karthikeyan, I.J. Raglend, and D.P. Kothari, "Impact of FACTS Devices on Exercising Market Power in Deregulated Electricity Market", *Frontiers in Energy*, Springer Berlin Heidelberg, volume: 7, issue: 4, pp: 448–455, 2013.
34. R. Thirumalaivasan, N. Prabhu, M. Janaki, and D.P. Kothari, "Analysis of Subsynchronous Resonance with Generalized Unified Power Flow Controller", *International Journal of Electrical Power and Energy Systems*, Elsevier, volume: 53, pp: 623–631, 2013.
35. K. Sarita, S. Kumar, A.S.S. Vardhan, R.M. Elavarasan, R.K. Saket, G.M. Shafiullah, and E. Hossain, "Power Enhancement with Grid Stabilization of Renewable Energy-Based Generation System Using UPQC-FLC-EVA Technique", *IEEE Access (USA)*, volume: 8, pp: 207443–207464, 2021.

CHAPTER 19 Load Forecasting Technique

19.1 ▶ INTRODUCTION

Load forecasting plays an important role in power system planning, operation and control. Forecasting means estimating active load at various load buses ahead of actual load occurrence. Planning and operational applications of load forecasting require a certain 'lead time' also called forecasting intervals. Nature of forecasts, lead times and applications are summarised in Table 19.1.

Table 19.1

Nature of forecast	*Lead time*	*Application*
Very short term	A few seconds to several minutes	Generation, distribution schedules, contingency analysis for system security
Short term	Half an hour to a few hours	Allocation of spinning reserve; operational planning and unit commitment; maintenance scheduling
Medium term	A few days to a few weeks	Planning for seasonal peak-winter, summer
Long term	A few months to a few years	Planning generation growth

A good forecast reflecting current and future trends, tempered with good judgement, is the key to all planning, indeed to financial success. The accuracy of a forecast is crucial to any electric utility, since it determines the timing and characteristics of major system additions. A forecast that is too low can result in low revenue from sales to neighbouring utilities or even in load curtailment. Forecasts that are too high can result in severe financial problems due to excessive investment in a plant that is not fully utilised or operated at low capacity factors. No forecast obtained from analytical procedures can be strictly relied upon the judgement of the forecaster, which plays a crucial role in arriving at an acceptable forecast.

Choosing a forecasting technique for use in establishing future load requirements is a nontrivial task in itself. Depending on nature of load variations, one particular method may be superior to another.

The two approaches to load forecasting namely total load approach and component approach have their own merits and demerits. Total load approach has the merit that it is much smoother and indicative of overall growth trends and easy to apply. On the other hand, the merit of the component approach is that abnormal conditions in growth trends of a certain component can be detected, thus preventing misleading forecast conclusions. There is a continuing need, however, to improve the methodology for forecasting power demand more accurately.

The aim of the present chapter is to give brief expositions of some of the techniques that have been developed in order to deal with the various load forecasting problems. All of these are based on the assumption that the actual load supplied by a given system matches the demands at all points of time (i.e., there has not been any outages or any deliberate shedding of load). It is then possible to make a statistical analysis of previous load data in order to set up a suitable model of the demand pattern. Once this has been done, it is generally possible to utilise the identified load model for making a prediction of the estimated demand for the selected lead time. A major part of the forecasting task is thus concerned with that of identifying the best possible model for the past load behaviour. This is best achieved by decomposing the load demand at any given point of time into a number of distinct components. The load is dependent on the industrial, commercial and agricultural activities as well as the weather condition of the system/area. The weather sensitive component depends on temperature, cloudiness, wind velocity, visibility and precipitation. Recall the brief discussions in Ch. 1 regarding the nature of the daily load curve which has been shown to have a constant part corresponding to the base load and other variable parts. For the sake of load forecasting, a simple decomposition may serve as a convenient starting point. Let $y(k)$ represent the total load demand (either for the whole or a part of the system) at the discrete time $k = 1, 2, 3, ...$ It is generally possible to decompose $y(k)$ into two parts of the form

$$y(k) = y_d(k) + y_s(k) \tag{19.1}$$

where the subscript d indicates the deterministic part and the subscript s indicates the stochastic part of the demand. If k is considered to be the present time, then $y(k + j), j > 0$ would represent a future load demand with the index j being the lead time. For a chosen value of the index j, the forecasting problem is then the same as the problem of estimating the value of $y(k + j)$ by processing adequate data for the past load demand.

19.2 ▶ FORECASTING METHODOLOGY

Forecasting techniques may be divided into three broad classes. Techniques may be based on extrapolation or on correlation or on a combination of both. Techniques may be further classified as either deterministic, probabilistic or stochastic.

Extrapolation Extrapolation techniques involve fitting trend curves to basic historical data adjusted to reflect the growth trend itself. With a trend curve the forecast is obtained by evaluating the trend curve function at the desired future point. Although a very simple procedure, it produces reasonable results in some instances. Such a techniqué is called a deterministic extrapolation since random errors in the data or in analytical model are not accounted for standard analytical functions used in trend curve fitting are [3]

1. Straight line $\quad y = a + bx$
2. Parabola $\quad y = a + bx + cx^2$
3. S-curve $\quad y = a + bx + cx^2 + dx^3$
4. Exponential $\quad y = ce^{dx}$
5. Gempertz $\quad y = ln^{-1}\,(a + ce^{dx})$

The most common curve-fitting technique for fitting coefficients and exponents (a–d) of a function in a given forecast is the method of least squares. If the uncertainty of extrapolated results is to be quantified using statistical entities such as mean and variance, the basic technique becomes probabilistic extrapolation. With regression analysis the best estimate of the model describing the trend can be obtained and used to forecast the trend.

Correlation Correlation techniques of forecasting relate system loads to various demographic and economic factors. This approach is advantageous in forcing the forecaster to understand clearly the interrelationship between load growth patterns and other measurable factors. The disadvantage is the need to forecast demographic and economic factors, which can be more difficult than forecasting system load. Typically, such factors as population, employment, building permits, business, weather data and the like are used in correlation techniques.

No one forecasting method is effective in all situations. Forecasting techniques must be used as tools to aid the planner; good judgement and experience can never be completely replaced.

19.3 ▶ ESTIMATION OF AVERAGE AND TREND TERMS

The simplest possible form of the deterministic part of $y(k)$ is given by

$$y_d(k) = \bar{y}_d + bk + e(k) \tag{19.2}$$

where $\bar{y}_d$ represents the average or the mean value of $y_d(k)$, bk represents the 'trend' term that grows linearly with k and $e(k)$ represents the error of modelling the complete load using the average and the trend terms only. The question is one of estimating the values of the two unknown model parameters $\bar{y}_d$ and b to ensure a good model. As seen in Ch. 14, when little or no statistical information is available regarding the error term, the method of LSE is helpful. If this method is to be used for estimating $\bar{y}_d$ and b, the estimation index J is defined using the relation

$$J = E\{e^2(k)\} \tag{19.3}$$

where $E(\cdot)$ represents the expectation operation. Substituting for $e(k)$ from Eq. (19.2) and making use of the first order necessary conditions for the index J to have its minimum value with respect to y_d and b, it is found that the following conditions must be satisfied [2].

$$E\{\bar{y}_d - y_d(k) + bk\} = 0 \tag{19.4a}$$

$$E\{bk^2 - y_d(k)k + \bar{y}_d k\} = 0 \tag{19.4b}$$

Since the expectation operation does not affect the constant quantities, it is easy to solve these two equations in order to get the desired relations.

$$\bar{y}_d = E\{y_d(k)\} - b\{E(k)\} \tag{19.5a}$$

$$b = [E\{y_d(k)k\} - \bar{y}_d\ E\{k\}]/E\{k^2\} \tag{19.5b}$$

If $y(k)$ is assumed to be stationary (statistics are not time dependent) one may involve the ergodic hypothesis and replace the expectation operation by the time averaging formula. Thus, if a total of N data are assumed to be available for determining the time averages, the two relations may be equivalently expressed as follows:

$$\bar{y}_d = \left(\frac{1}{N}\right)\left[\sum_{k=1}^{N} y_d(k) - b\sum_{k=1}^{N} k\right] \tag{19.6a}$$

$$b = \frac{N\left[\sum_{k=1}^{N} y_d(k)k\right] - \left[\sum_{k=1}^{N} k\right]\left[\sum_{k=1}^{N} y_d(k)\right]}{N\sum_{k=1}^{N} k^2 - \left[\sum_{k=1}^{N} k\right]^2} \tag{19.6b}$$

These two relations may be fruitfully employed in order to estimate the average and the trend coefficient for any given load data.

Note that Eqs. (19.6a) and (19.6b) are not very accurate in case the load data behave as a nonstationary process since the ergodic hypothesis does not hold for such cases. It may still be possible to assume that the data over a finite window are stationary and the entire set of data may then be considered as the juxtaposition of a number of stationary blocks, each having slightly different statistics. Equations (19.6a) and (19.6b) may then be repeated over the different blocks in order to compute the average and the trend coefficient for each window of data.

Example 19.1 In order to illustrate the nature of results obtainable from Eqs. (19.6a) and (19.6b), consider the data shown in the graphs of Fig. 19.1 which give the population in millions. The cash values of the agricultural and the industrial outputs are in millions of rupees and the amount of electrical energy consumption (load demand) in MWs in Punjab over a period of seven years starting from 1968. A total of 85 data have been generated from the graphs by sampling the graphs at intervals of 30 days. These have been substituted in Eqs. (19.6a) and (19.6b) in order to compute the average and the trend coefficients of the four variables. The results are given in Table 19.2

Table 19.2

Variable	*Average*	*Trend Coefficient*
Population	13 million	0.2
Industrial output	Rs 397 million	0.54
Agricultural output	Rs 420.9 million	0.78
Load demand	855.8 MW	1.34

Caution The 85 data, used in Example 19.1, are generally not adequate for making statistical calculations so that the values given above may not be entirely adequate. In addition, the statistical characteristics of the set of variables concerned may have changed (i.e., the data may in fact be non-stationary) and this also may introduce some error in the results. Finally, the graphs in Fig. 19.1 are actually based on half yearly data obtained from the Planning Commission document and an interpolation process has been employed in order to generate the monthly data. This may add some unspecified errors to the data which will also affect the accuracy of the estimates.

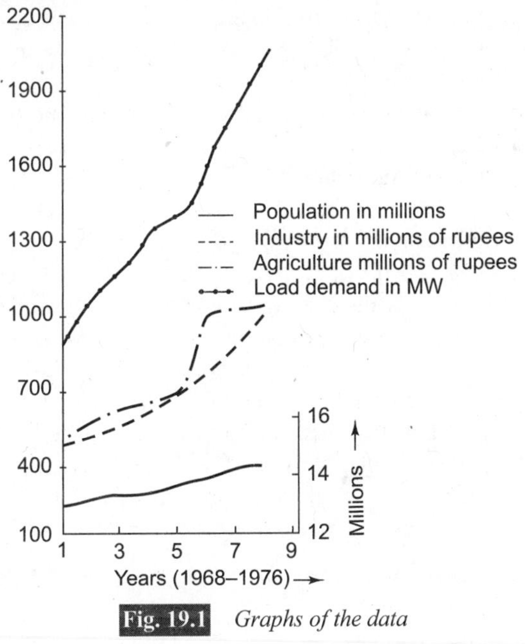

Fig. 19.1 *Graphs of the data*

Prediction of y_d (k + j) Once the model for the deterministic component of the load has been determined, it is simple to make the prediction of its future value. For the simple model in Eq. (19.2), the desired prediction is computed using the relation

$$y_d(k+J) = \bar{y}_d + b(k+j) \tag{19.7}$$

19.3.1 More General Forms of Models

Before leaving this section, it may be pointed out that the load model may be generalised by including second and higher order terms on the right hand side of Eq. (19.2) in order to represent more complex load behaviour. For example, the load model may be assumed to be

$$y(k) = \sum_{i=1}^{L} b_i k_i + e(k) \tag{19.8a}$$

where the coefficient b_i need to be estimated from the past load data. The load model above is obviously a nonlinear function of the time index k and would need L coefficients to be estimated. A much simpler approach to nonlinear modelling of the load is to introduce an exponential form

$$y(k) = c \exp [bk] + e(k) \tag{19.8b}$$

which involves only two unknown coefficients. Besides reducing the number of unknowns, the exponential model has the additional advantage of being readily transformed into a linear form. All that is required is to take the natural log of the given data. In either case, the method of LSE is easily extended to estimate the model parameters from the given historical data.

19.4 ▶ ESTIMATION OF PERIODIC COMPONENTS

The deterministic part of the load may contain some periodic components in addition to the average and the polynomial terms. Consider for example the curve shown in Fig. 19.2 which gives the variation of the active power supplied by a power utility over a period of two weeks. It is observed that the daily load variations are repetitive from day to day except for some random fluctuations. It is also seen that the curve for Sundays differs significantly from those of the week days in view that Sundays are holidays. It turns out that the curve for the entire weekly period starting from, say, the mid-night of one Sunday till the mid-night of the next Sunday behaves as a distinctly periodic waveform with superposed random variations.

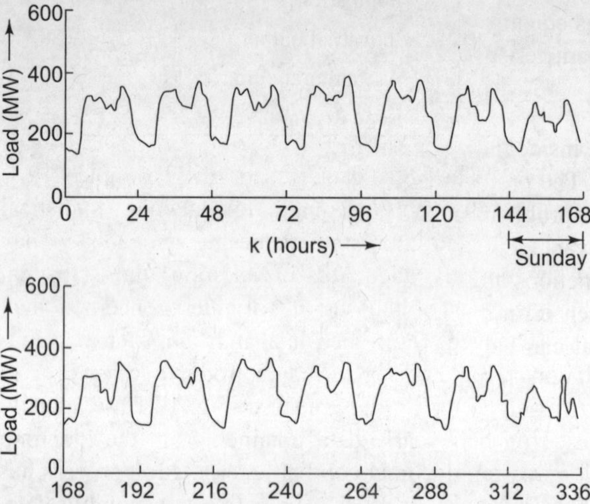

Fig. 19.2 *Hourly load behaviour of Delhi over two consecutive weeks*

If it is assumed that the load data are being sampled at an hourly interval, then there are a total of 168 load data in one period so that the load pattern may be expressed in terms of a Fourier series with the fundamental frequency ω being equal to $2\pi/168$ rads. A suitable model for the load $y(k)$ is then given by

$$y(k) = y + \sum_{i=1}^{L}[a_i \sin i\omega k + b_i \cos i\omega k] + e(k) \tag{19.9}$$

where L represents the total number of harmonics present and a_i and b_i are the amplitudes of respectively the sinusoidal and the cosinusoidal components. Only dominant harmonics need to be included in the model.

Once the harmonic load model is identified, it is simple to make a prediction of the future load $y_d(k + j)$ using the relation

$$\hat{y}_d(k+j) = h'(k+j)\hat{x}(k) \tag{19.10}$$

19.5 ▶ ESTIMATION OF $y_S(k)$: TIME SERIES APPROACH

If $y_d(k)$ is subtracted from the sequence $y(k)$, the result would be a sequence of data for the stochastic part of the load. We have to identify the model for $y_s(k)$ and then use it to make the prediction $y_s(k + j)$. A convenient method for this is based on the use of the stochastic time series models. The simplest form of such a model is the so-called auto-regressive model which has been widely used to represent the behaviour of a zero mean stationary stochastic sequence. The method proposed for the generation of data for $y_s(k)$ ensures that the sequence $y_s(k)$ will have a zero mean. If it is also assumed to be stationary, it may be possible to identify a suitable autoregressive model for this sequence.

19.5.1 Auto-Regressive Models

The sequence $y_s(k)$ is said to satisfy an AR model of order n, i.e., it is [AR(n)], if it can be expressed as

$$y_s(k) = \sum_{i=1}^{n} a_i y_s(k-i) + w(k) \tag{19.11}$$

where a_i are the model parameters and $w(k)$ is a zero mean white sequence. In order that the solution of this equation may represent a stationary process, it is required that the coefficients a_i make the roots of the characteristics equation

$$1 - a_1 z^{-1} - a_2 z^{-2} - \cdots - a_n z^{-n} = 0$$

lie inside the unit circle in the z-plane.

The problem in estimating the value of n is referred to as the *problem of structural identification,* while the problem of estimation of the parameters a_i is referred to as the *problem of parameter estimation.* An advantage of the AR model is that both these problems are solved relatively easily if the autocorrelation functions are first computed using the given data. Once the model order n and the parameter vector a have been estimated, the next problem is that of estimating the statistics of the noise process $w(k)$. The best that can be done is based on the assumption that an estimate of $w(k)$ is provided by the residual $e(k) = y_s(k) - \hat{y}_s(k)$, the estimate $\hat{y}_s(k)$ having been determined from

$$\hat{y}_s(k) = -\sum_{i=1}^{n} a_i y_s(k-i) \tag{19.12}$$

The variance σ^2 of $w(k)$ is then estimated using the relation

$$\sigma^2 = (1/N)\sum_{k=1}^{n} e^2(k) \tag{19.13}$$

19.5.2 Auto-Regressive Moving-Average Models

In some cases, the AR model may not be adequate to represent the observed load behaviour unless the order n of the model is made very high. In such a case ARMA (n, m) model is used.

$$y_s(k) = -\sum_{i=1}^{n} a_i y_s(k-i) + \sum_{j=1}^{m} b_j w(k-j) + w(k) \tag{19.14}$$

Estimation of two structural parameters n and m as well as model parameters a_i, b_j and the variance σ^2 of the noise term $w(k)$ is required. More complex behaviour can be represented. The identification problem is solved off-line. The acceptable load model is then utilised on-line for obtaining on-line load forecasts. ARMA model can easily be modified to incorporate the temperature, rainfall, wind velocity and humidity data [2]. In some cases, it is desirable to show the dependence of the load demand on the weather variables in an explicit manner. The time series models are easily generalised in order to reflect the dependence of the load demand on one or more of the weather variables.

19.6 ▶ ESTIMATION OF STOCHASTIC COMPONENT: KALMAN FILTERING APPROACH

The time series approach has been widely employed in dealing with the load forecasting problem in view of the relative simplicity of the model forms. However, this method tends to ignore the statistical information about the load data which may often be available and may lead to improved load forecasts if utilised properly. In ARMA model, the model identification problem is not that simple. These difficulties may be avoided in some situations if the Kalman filtering techniques are utilised.

19.6.1 Application to Short-term Forecasting

An application of the Kalman filtering algorithm to the load forecasting problem has been first suggested by Toyada et al. [11] for the very short-term and short-term situations. For the latter case, for example, it is possible to make use of intuitive reasonings to suggest that an acceptable model for load demand would have the form

$$y_s(k) = y_t(k) + v(k) \tag{19.15}$$

where $y_s(k)$ is the observed value of the stochastic load at time k, $y_t(k)$ is the true value of this load and $v(k)$ is the error in the observed load. In addition, the dynamics of the true load may be expressed as

$$y_t(k+1) = y_t(k) + z(k) + u_1(k) \tag{19.16}$$

where $z(k)$ represents the increment of the load demand at time k and $u_1(k)$ represents a disturbance term which accounts for the stochastic perturbations in $y_t(k)$. The incremental load itself is assumed to remain constant on an average at every time point and is modelled by the equation

$$z(k+1) = z(k) + u_2(k) \tag{19.17}$$

where the term $u_2(k)$ represents a stochastic disturbance term.

In order to make use of the Kalman filtering techniques, the noise terms $u_1(k)$, $u_2(k)$ and $v(k)$ are assumed to be zero mean independent white Gaussian sequences. Also, the model equations are rewritten in the form

$$\mathbf{x}(k+1) = F\mathbf{x}(k) + G\mathbf{u}(k) \tag{19.18a}$$

$$y_s(k) = h'\,\mathbf{x}(k) + \mathbf{v}(k) \tag{19.18b}$$

where the vectors $\mathbf{x}(k)$ and $\mathbf{u}(k)$ are defined as

$$x(k) = [y_t(k) \neq (k)]^T \text{ and } u(k) = [u_1(k)\ u_2(k)]^T$$

The matrices F, G and h' are then obtained from Eqs. (19.15) to (19.17) easily and have the following values:

$$F = \begin{bmatrix} 1 & 1 \\ 0 & 1 \end{bmatrix}, G = \begin{bmatrix} 1 & 0 \\ 0 & 1 \end{bmatrix}, h = \begin{bmatrix} 1 \\ 0 \end{bmatrix}$$

Based on model (19.18), it is possible to make use of the Kalman filtering algorithm to obtain the minimum variance estimate of the vector $\mathbf{x}(k)$ based on the data $y_s(k)$: $\{y_s(1), y_s(2) \ldots y_s(k)\}$. This algorithm consists of the following equations:

$$\hat{x}(k/k) = \hat{x}(k/k-1) + K_x(k)[y_s(k) - h'\,\hat{x}(k/k-1)] \tag{19.19a}$$

$$\hat{x}(k/k-1) = F\ \hat{x}((k-1)/(k-1)) \tag{19.19b}$$

$$K_x(k) = P_x(k/k-1)\,h[h'\,P_x(k/k-1)h + R(k)]^{-1} \tag{19.19c}$$

$$P_x(k/k) = [I - K_x(k)\,h']\,P_x(k/k-1) \tag{19.19d}$$

$$P_x(k/k-1) = FP_x(k-1/k-1)F' + GQ(k-1)G' \tag{19.19e}$$

where

$Q(k)$ = covariance of $u(k)$

$R(k)$ = covariance of $v(k)$

$\hat{x}(k/k)$ = filtered estimate of $x(k)$

$\hat{x}(k/k-1)$ = single step prediction of $x(k)$

$K_x(k)$ = filter gain vector of same dimension as $x(k)$

$P_x(k/k)$ = filtering error covariance

$P_x(k/k-1)$ = prediction error covariance

From Eq. (19.18b) obtain the prediction $\hat{x}((k+1)/k)$

From this the one step ahead load forecast is obtained as

$$\hat{y}_s(k+1) = h'\,\hat{x}((k+1)/k) \tag{19.19f}$$

It may be noted that filtering implies removal of disturbance or stochastic term with zero mean.

It is also possible to obtain a multi-step ahead prediction of the load from the multi-step ahead prediction of the vector $\mathbf{x}(k)$. For example, if the prediction $x(k+d)$ by processing the data set $Y_s(k)$ is required for any $d > 1$, it is possible to use the solution of Eq. (19.18a) for the vector $\mathbf{x}(k+d)$ to get the result

$$\hat{x}(k+d) = F^d\hat{x}(k/k) \tag{19.19g}$$

In order to be able to make use of this algorithm for generating the forecast of the load $y_s(k+d)$, it is necessary that the noise statistics and some other information be available. The value of $R(k)$ may often be estimated from a knowledge of the accuracy of the meters employed. However, it is very unlikely that the value of the covariance $Q(k)$ will be known to start with and will, therefore, have to be obtained by some means. An adaptive version of the Kalman filtering algorithm may be utilised in order to estimate the noise statistics along with the state vector $\mathbf{x}(k)$ [2]. Now let it be assumed that both $R(k)$ and $Q(k)$ are known quantities. Let it also be assumed that the initial estimate $\hat{\mathbf{x}}(0/0)$ and the covariance $P_x(0/0)$ are known. Based on these *a priori* information, it is possible to utilise Eq. (19.19a) to (19.19c) recursively to process the data for $y_s(1), y_s(2), ..., y_s(k)$ to generate the filtered estimate $\hat{x}(k/k)$. Once this is available, Eq. (19.19g) may be utilised to generate the desired load forecast.

Example 19.2 To illustrate the nature of the results obtainable through the algorithm just discussed, the data for the short term load behaviour for Delhi have been processed. A total of 1030 data collected at the interval of 15 minutes have been processed. It has been assumed that, in view of the short time interval over which the total data set lies, the deterministic part of the load may be assumed to be a constant mean term. Using the sample average Formula (19.7) (with $b = 0$), we get $\bar{y} = 220$ MW. The data for $y_s(k)$ have then been generated by subtracting the mean value from the measured load data.

Solution To process these stochastic data, the following *a priori* information have been used:

$$R(k) = 3.74, \qquad Q(k) = \begin{bmatrix} 20 & 0 \\ 0 & 0.386 \end{bmatrix}$$

$$\hat{x}(0/0) = \begin{bmatrix} 0 \\ 0 \end{bmatrix} \qquad P_x(0/0) = \begin{bmatrix} 0.1 & 0 \\ 0 & 0.01 \end{bmatrix}$$

The results of application of the prediction Algorithm (19.19) are shown in Fig. 19.3. It is noted that the error of 15 minutes ahead load prediction is around 8 MW which is about 3% of the average load and less than 2% of the daily maximum load.

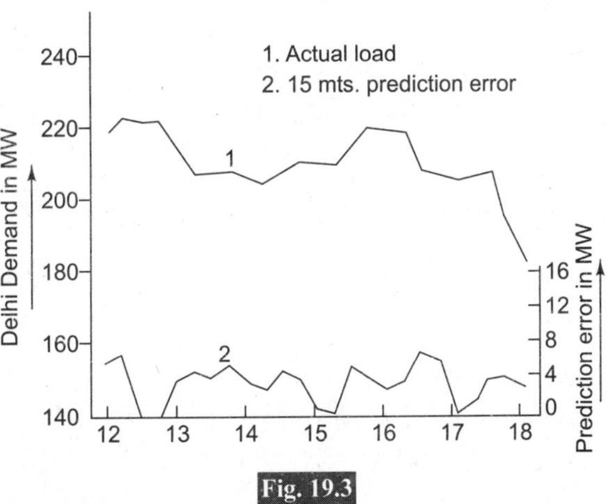

Fig. 19.3

Comment Application of Kalman filtering and prediction techniques is often hampered by the non-availability of the required state variable model of the concerned load data. For the few cases discussed in this section, a part of the model has been obtainable from physical considerations. The part that has not been available includes the state and output noise variances and the data for the initial state estimate and the corresponding covariance. In a general load forecasting situation, none of the model parameters may be available to start with and it would be necessary to make use of system identification techniques in order to obtain the required state model. It has been shown that the Gauss-Markov model described by Eq. (19.18) in over-parameterised from the model identification point of view in the sense that the data for $y_s(k)$ do not permit the estimation of all the parameters of this model. It has been shown in Ref. [12] that a suitable model that is identifiable and is equivalent to the Gauss-Markov model for state estimation purposes is the innovation model used for estimation of the stochastic component.

19.6.2 On-line Techniques for Non-stationary Load Prediction

Most practical load data behave as nonstationary and it is therefore important to consider the question of adapting the techniques discussed so far to the nonstationary situation. Reference [2] has discussed the three models for this purpose, viz., (i) ARIMA Models, (ii) Time varying model and (iii) Nondynamic models.

19.7 ▶ LONG-TERM LOAD PREDICTIONS USING ECONOMETRIC MODELS

If the load forecasts are required for planning purposes, it is necessary to select the lead time to lie in the range of a few months to a few years. In such cases, the load demand should be decomposed in a manner that reflects the dependence of the load on the various segments of the economy of the concerned region. For example, the total load demand $y(k)$ may be decomposed as

$$y(k) = \sum_{i=1}^{M} a_i y_i(k) + e(k) \tag{19.20a}$$

where a_i are the regression coefficients, $y_i(k)$ are the chosen economic variables and $e(k)$ represents the error of modelling. A relatively simple procedure is to rewrite the model equation in the familiar vector notation

$$y(k) = h'(k)x + e(k) \tag{19.20b}$$

where $h'(k) = [y_1(k)\ y_2(k)\ \dots\ y_M(k)]$ and $x = [a_1\ a_2\ \dots\ a_M]$.

The regression coefficients may then be estimated using the convenient least-squares algorithm. The load forecasts are then possible through the simple relation

$$\hat{y}(k+1) = \hat{x}'(k)\ \hat{h}(k+1/k) \tag{19.21}$$

where $\hat{x}(k)$ is the estimate of the coefficient vector based on the data available till the kth sampling point and $\hat{h}(k+1/k)$ is the one-step-ahead prediction of the regression vector $h(k)$.

19.8 ▶ REACTIVE LOAD FORECAST

Reactive loads are not easy to forecast as compared to active loads, since reactive loads are made up of not only reactive components of loads, but also of transmission and distribution networks and compensating VAR devices such as SVC, FACTS, etc. Therefore, past data may not yield the correct forecast as reactive load varies with variations in network configuration during varying operating conditions. Use of active load forecast with power factor prediction may result in somewhat satisfactory results. Of course, here also, only very recent past data (few minutes/hours) may be used, thus assuming steady-state network configuration. Forecasted reactive loads are adapted with current reactive requirements of network including VAR compensation devices. Such forecasts are needed for security analysis, voltage/reactive power scheduling, etc. If control action is insufficient, structural modifications have to be carried out, i.e., new generating units, new lines or new VAR compensating devices normally have to be installed.

19.9 ▶ FUTURE TRENDS

Forecasting electricity loads had reached a comfortable state of performance in the years preceding the recent waves of industry restructuring. As discussed in this chapter adaptive time-series techniques based on ARMA, Kalman Filtering, or spectral methods are sufficiently accurate in the short term for operational purposes, achieving errors of 1–2%. However, the arrival of competitive markets has been associated with the expectation of greater consumer participation. Overall we can identify the following trends.

1. Forecast errors have significant implications for profits, market shares, and ultimately shareholder value.
2. Day ahead, weather-based, forecasting is becoming the most crucial activity in a deregulated market.
3. Information is becoming commercially sensitive and increasingly trade secret.
4. Distributed, embedded and dispersed generation may increase.

A recent paper [7] takes a selective look at some of the forecasting issues which are now associated with decision-making in a competitive market. Forecasting loads and prices in the wholesale markets are mutually intertwined activities. Models based on simulated artificial agents may eventually become as important on supply side as artificial neural networks have already become important for demand prediction. These would, however, need further research and integration with conventional time-series methods in order to provide a more precise forecasting.

19.10 ▶ SUMMARY

Load forecasting is the basic step in power system planning. A reasonably self-contained account of the various techniques for the load prediction of a modern power system has been given in this chapter with an emphasis on the short-term prediction problems. Applications of time series. Gauss-Markov and innovation models in setting up a suitable dynamic model for the stochastic part of the load data have been discussed. The time series model identification problem has also been dealt with through the least-squares estimation techniques developed in Chap. 17.

In an interconnected power system, load forecasts are usually needed at all the important load buses. A great deal of attention has in recent years been given to the question of setting up the demand models for the individual appliances and their impact on the aggregated demand. It may often be necessary to make use of non-linear forms of load models and the question of identification of the nonlinear models of different forms is an important issue.

Finally, a point may be made that no particular method or approach will work for all utilities. All methods are strung on a common thread, and that is the judgement of the forecaster. In no way the material presented here is exhaustive. The intent has been to introduce some ideas currently used in forecasting system load requirements.

Review Questions

19.1 Which method of load forecasting would you suggest for long term and why?
19.2 Which method of load forecasting would you suggest for very short term and why?
19.3 What purpose does medium term forecasting serve?

19.4 How is the forecaster's knowledge and intuition considered superior to any load forecasting method? Should a forecaster intervene to modify a forecast, when, why and how?

19.5 Why and what are the nonstationary components of load changes during very short, short, medium and long terms?

Multiple Choice Questions

19.1 Load forecasting is a prerequisite for the following:
(a) Unit commitment (b) Economic dispatch
(c) Load flow (d) All of the above

19.2 Forecasting techniques may be based on
(a) Extra polation (b) Correlation
(c) Deterministic (d) Probabilistic (or) stochastic
(e) All of the above

19.3 Reactive load forecasting is needed for
(a) Security analysis (b) Voltage profile analysis
(c) Reactive power scheduling (d) All of the above

19.4 For long term load forecasting the techniques used are
(a) Extrapolation (b) Sophisticated probability
(c) Interpolation (d) All of the above

19.5 The following are on-line techniques for nonstationary load prediction:
(a) ARMA Models (b) Time varying models
(c) Nondynamic models (d) All of the above

19.6 The main load forecasting approaches are
(a) Total load approach (b) Component approach
(c) Both (a) and (b) (d) None of the above

19.7 Very short term load forecasting is required with load time of
(a) 1 hour (b) 1 day
(c) 1 month (d) Few seconds to several minutes

19.8 For fitting straight line curve, the equation is
(a) $y = a + bx + cx^2$ (b) $y = c + edx$ (c) $y = ax + b$ (d) y – ln-1 $(a + cedx)$

19.9 The load is dependent on
(a) Industrial (b) Commercial (c) Agricultural (d) Weather condition
(e) All of the above

19.10 The permissible error for short term load forecasting technique is
(a) 10% (b) 5 – 10% (c) 50% (d) 1 – 2%

19.11 Short term load forecasting is for
(a) Allocation for spinning reserve (b) Contingency analysis
(c) State estimation (d) Planning generation growth

19.12 Load forecasting for load time which ranges from few seconds to 5 minutes is required for
(a) State estimation (b) Planning for generation growth
(c) Unit commitments (d) Contingency analysis

19.13 Auto-Regressive Models (AR Models) are not adequate to represent observed load behaviour when
(a) Order 'n' of the model is large (b) order 'n' of model is small
(c) None of the above (d) All of the above

19.14 Extrapolation technique does not account
(a) Random errors in the data
(b) Deterministic extrapolation
(c) For short term load variation
(d) None of the above

19.15 Harmonic load model is required for
(a) Separation of periodic components of load variation
(b) Obtaining load duration curve
(c) Determination of load factor
(d) Determination of demand factor

19.16 Kalman filtering technique is used for load forecasting since
(a) Time series approach tends to ignore statistical information
(b) It does account voltage variation
(c) It is useful for state estimation
(d) All of the above

19.17 Reactive load forecast is difficult than active power load forecast because
(a) Part data are not available
(b) Of the presence of VAR devices
(c) Voltage stability margin is not known a prior
(d) Active power load forecast is not of much use

19.18 For obtaining anticipatory reactive power control strategy load forecasting
(a) For load period of 1 hr is required
(b) Load period for a few hours is required
(c) Load period for 24 hrs is required
(d) None of the above

19.19 Low revenue from sales to neighbouring may result due to
(a) Too high load forecast
(b) Too low load forecast
(c) Both (a) and (b)
(d) None of the above

19.20 Too high load forecasts may result in
(a) Excessive investments
(b) Loss of revenue
(c) Load curtailment
(d) Excessive corrective rescheduling
(e) (a) and (d) depend on load time

19.21 Which of the following approaches is utilised to overcome the limitation of Kalman and prediction method?
(a) Time series
(b) Average and tread term
(c) Innovation model
(d) None of the above

19.22 Limitation of Kalman and prediction techniques
(a) Requires large time to estimate
(b) Depends on availability of required state variable model of the load data which is not available at starting
(c) Requires more space to data storage
(d) All of the above

19.23 What is the limitation of estimation of average and trend term of deterministic part of load.
(a) Requires more space in computer
(b) Requires fast computer
(c) Data processed may not be adequate for statistics calculation.
(d) All of the above

19.24 Which of the following methods is generally adapted for curve fitting
(a) Weighted least square
(b) Extrapolation least square
(c) Least square
(d) None of the above

References

Books

1. D.P. Kothari and I.J. Nagrath, *Power System Engineering*, 2nd edn, Tata McGraw-Hill, New Delhi, 2008.
2. A.K. Mahalanabis, D.P. Kothari, and S.I. Ahson, *Computer Aided Power System Analysis and Control*, Tata McGraw-Hill, New Delhi, 1988.
3. R.L. Sullivan, *Power System Planning*, McGraw-Hill Book Co, New York, 1977.
4. A.S. Pabla, *Electrical Power Systems Planning*, Macmillan India Ltd, NewDelhi, 1998.
5. A.S. Pabla, *Electric Power Distribution*, 4th edn, Tata McGraw-Hill, New Delhi, 1997.
6. X. Wang and J.R. McDonald (Eds), *Modern Power System Planning*, McGraw-Hill, Singapore, 1994.

Papers

7. D.W. Bunn, "Forecasting Loads and Prices in Competitive Power Markets", *Proc of the IEEE*, volume: 88, issue: 2, pp: 163–169, Feb 2000.
8. P.K. Dash, *et al*, "Fuzzy Neural Network and Fuzzy Expert System for Load Forecasting", *Proc IEE*, volume: 143, issue: 1, pp: 106–114, 1996.
9. R. Ramanathan, *et al*, "Short-run Forecasts of Electricity Loads and Peaks", *Int J of Forecasting*, volume: 13, pp: 161–174, 1997.
10. A. Mohammed *et al*, "Short-term Load Demand Modelling and Forecasting A Review", *IEEE Trans SMC*, volume: SMC-12, issue: 3, pp: 370–382, 1982.
11. J. Tyoda, *et al*, "An Application of State Estimation to Short-term Load Forecasting", *IEEE Trans*, volume: PAS-89, pp: 1678–1688, 1970.
12. R.K. Mehra, "On-line Identification of Linear Dynamic Systems with Application to Kalmann Filtering", *IEEE Trans*, volume: AC-16, pp: 12–21, 1971.
13. Y. Wang, Q. Chen, N. Zhang, and Y. Wang, "Conditional Residual Modeling for Probabilistic Load Forecasting", *IEEE Transactions on Power Systems*, volume: 33, issue: 6, pp: 7327–7330, 2018.
14. W. Kong, Z.Y. Dong, D.J. Hill, F. Luo, and Y. Xu, "Short-Term Residential Load Forecasting Based on Resident Behaviour Learning", *IEEE Transactions on Power Systems*, volume: 33, issue: 1, pp: 1087–1088, 2018.
15. B. Liu, J. Nowotarski, T. Hong, and R. Weron, "Probabilistic Load Forecasting via Quantile Regression Averaging on Sister Forecasts", *IEEE Transactions on Smart Grid*, volume: 8, issue: 2, pp: 730–737, 2017.
16. J. Xie, T. Hong, and J. Stroud, "Long-Term Retail Energy Forecasting with Consideration of Residential Customer Attrition", *IEEE Transactions on Smart Grid*, volume: 6, issue: 5, pp: 2245–2252, 2015.
17. Y. Wang, Q. Xia, and C. Kang, "Secondary Forecasting Based on Deviation Analysis for Short-Term Load Forecasting", *IEEE Transactions on Power Systems*, volume: 26, issue: 2, pp: 500–507, 2011.
18. C. Feng, M. Sun, and J. Zhang, "Reinforced Deterministic and Probabilistic Load Forecasting via Q-Learning Dynamic Model Selection", *IEEE Transactions on Smart Grid*, volume: 11, issue: 2, pp: 1377–1386, 2020.
19. M.R. Haq and Z. Ni, "A New Hybrid Model for Short-Term Electricity Load Forecasting", *IEEE Access*, volume: 7, pp: 125413–125423, 2019.

20. Y. Hong, Y. Zhou, Q. Li, W. Xu, and X. Zheng, "A Deep Learning Method for Short-Term Residential Load Forecasting in Smart Grid", *IEEE Access*, volume: 8, pp: 55785–55797, 2020.
21. K. Chen, K. Chen, Q. Wang, Z. He, J. Hu, and J. He, "Short Term Load Forecasting with Deep Residual Networks", *IEEE Transactions on Smart Grid*, volume: 10, issue: 4, pp: 3943–3952, 2019.
22. Y. Wang, N. Zhang, Y. Tan, T. Hong, D.S. Kirschen, and C. Kang, "Combining Probabilistic Load Forecasts", *IEEE Transactions on Smart Grid*, volume: 10, issue: 4, pp: 3664–3674, 2019.
23. T. Li, Y. Wang, and N. Zhang, "Combining Probability Density Forecasts for Power Electrical Loads", *IEEE Transactions on Smart Grid*, volume: 11, issue: 2, pp: 1679–1690, 2020.
24. A.A. Mamun, M. Sohel, N. Mohammad, M.S. Haque Sunny, D.R. Dipta, and E. Hossain, "A Comprehensive Review of the Load Forecasting Techniques Using Single and Hybrid Predictive Models", *IEEE Access*, volume: 8, pp: 134911–134939, 2020.
25. T. Hong, J. Wilson, and J. Xie, "Long Term Probabilistic Load Forecasting and Normalization with Hourly Information", *IEEE Transactions on Smart Grid*, volume: 5, issue: 1, pp: 456–462, 2014.
26. Y. Wang, Q. Chen, N. Zhang, and Y. Wang, "Conditional Residual Modeling for Probabilistic Load Forecasting," *IEEE Transactions on Power Systems*, volume: 33, issue: 6, pp: 7327–7330, 2018.
27. W. Kong, Z.Y. Dong, D.J. Hill, F. Luo, and Y. Xu, "Short-Term Residential Load Forecasting Based on Resident Behavior Learning," *IEEE Transactions on Power Systems*, volume: 33, issue: 1, pp: 1087–1088, 2018.
28. C. Zhang and R. Li, "A Novel Closed-Loop Clustering Algorithm for Hierarchical Load Forecasting," *IEEE Transactions on Smart Grid*, volume: 12, issue: 1, pp: 432–441, 2021.
29. R. Bo and F. Li, "Probabilistic LMP Forecasting Considering Load Uncertainty," *IEEE Transactions on Power Systems*, volume: 24, issue: 3, pp: 1279–1289, 2009.
30. M.R. Haq and Z. Ni, "A New Hybrid Model for Short-Term Electricity Load Forecasting," *IEEE Access*, volume: 7, pp: 125413–125423, 2019.

CHAPTER 20

Modern Aspects of Future Grid

20.1 ▶ INTRODUCTION

20.1.1 Some Aspects of Future Grid

In the present era, due to increased power demand, the shortfalls in power generation must be resolved between supply and demand, which can be accomplished through the development of national grid-connected systems. Where all the national power generation sources are connected to the national grid and based on the zonal requirement, energy management is implemented. An 'electricity grid' is not a single entity but an aggregate of multiple networks and multiple power generation companies. Numerous operators employ varying communication and coordination levels, mostly controlled manually.

With this concept, the earlier power shortage has been equated and can control the transmission losses and improve transmission efficiency to some extent. It contrasts with 60% efficiency for grids based on the latest technology, which may solve the above problem. A smart grid is referred to by other names, including 'Smart Electric Grid', 'Smart Power Grid', 'Intelligrid' and 'Future Grid'.

To systematically implement the energy requirement for different zones, it necessarily requires a strategic distribution of energy. Supervisory Control and Data Acquisition (SCADA) and other continuously monitoring systems though in vogue but for quick effective and efficient distribution of energy needs, a smart system which can take into account the requirements of the zones and the availability of energy from the different sources in the zones is required without human interference. Smart grids increase the connectivity, automation and coordination between these suppliers, consumers and networks that perform either long-distance transmission or local distribution tasks.

A smart grid is an umbrella term that covers the modernisation of both the transmission and distribution grids. A smart grid concept is a 'digital upgrade' of distribution and long-distance transmission grids to optimise current operations by reducing the losses and opening up new markets for alternative energy production.

Some of the benefits of such a modernised electricity network include the ability to reduce power consumption at the consumer side during peak hours, called demand side management (DSM); enabling grid connection of distributed generated power (with photovoltaic arrays, small wind turbines, micro-hydro or even combined heat power generators in buildings); incorporating grid energy storage for distributed generation load balancing and eliminating failures such as widespread power grid cascading failures. The smart grid's increased efficiency and reliability are expected to save consumers money and help reduce CO_2 emissions. Governments increasingly focus on energy security, investing in the smart grid could be used to reduce dependence on nondomestic energy sources. It could also make the grid more resistant to military or terrorist attacks by physical or digital means.

20.1.2 What Is a Smart Grid?

A smart grid's idea joins a few advances, end-user arrangements and addresses numerous strategy and regulatory drivers. It does not have a solitary clear definition. The European Technology Platform defines the smart grid as a power network that can astutely incorporate all users' activities associated with it – generators, purchasers and those that do both – to convey manageable, economical and secure power supplies efficiently.

As per the US Department of Energy:

> A shrewd matrix utilises advanced innovation to improve unwavering quality, security, and efficiency (both financial and energy) of the electric framework from huge generation, through the conveyance systems to power purchasers and a developing number of appropriated generation and storage assets.

In smarter grids: The opportunity, the smart grid is defined as:

> A smart grid utilises detecting, installed preparing, and computerised interchanges to empower the power network to be discernible (ready to be estimated and pictured), controllable (ready to controlled and upgraded), mechanised (ready to adjust and self-recuperate), completely coordinated (completely interoperable with existing frameworks and with the ability to consolidate a different arrangement of energy sources).

The literature recommends the accompanying credits of the smart grid:

- It empowers demand reaction and DSM by coordinating smart energy metres, brilliant machines and purchaser loads, generation in the microgrid, power stockpiling (electric vehicles) and giving clients data about energy use and costs. It is foreseen that clients will be furnished with data and impetuses to alter their utilisation structures to conquer a portion of the power framework's limitations.
- It obliges and encourages all renewable energy sources (RES), distributed generation, private micro-generation of houses and societies and capacity choices (storage), hence decreasing the entire power area's ecological effect and gives methods for collection. It will provide simplified interconnection like 'plug-and-play'.
- It upgrades and works efficiently by the delivery framework's intellectual activity (rerouting power, working self-governing) and performing efficient resource management and operation. It incorporates using affirms, contingent upon what is required and when it is required.
- It guarantees and improves unwavering quality and the security of supply by being robust to aggravations, assaults and cataclysmic events, envisioning and reacting to unsettling influences (preventive and predictive maintenance and self-mending), and reinforcing supply through upgraded transfer capacities.
- It keeps up the power supply's quality to oblige sensitive equipment that increments the advanced economy.
- It opens admittance to the business sectors through expanded transmission ways, amassed supply, demand response activities and auxiliary help arrangements.

20.1.3 Why Smart/Future Grid is a Need?

The aging effect of electrical assets and deficiency of circuit capacity are the major factors that lead to the smart grid. As the load demand increases regularly, the transmission lines, transformers and others have been degraded in their load handling capacity. The thermal limits of existing distribution and transmission lines must be monitored to transfer the power within their capability. Further, voltage and frequency are the two crucial factors needed to be maintained for a system's stable operation. Overvoltage leads to the electrical equipment's insulation breakdown, while undervoltage forces the system to operate beyond its thermal limits.

However, frequency deviation from 50/60 Hz occurs rarely; the system operator has to maintain it regularly for the system's stable operation. The smart grid requirement also ensures a reliable electrical power supply by continuously monitoring the post and pre-fault conditions in the power system. Several countries, including China, Japan, the United Kingdom and the United States, have already initiated their smart grid objectives. So, the time has come where countries must focus on smart grid initiatives. Several initiatives, including an active distribution network, virtual power plant and many others, have been incorporated for smart grid.

Example 20.1 **What are the different objectives of smart grid?**

Answer: Smart grids are designed to fulfil the following objectives:

- Reduce the electricity demand of loads on the utility grid during the daily peak demand period.
- Utilise the electricity generated from renewable energy sources, including wind farms and solar photovoltaic.
- For remote areas, the electricity generation is made independent of the utility grids.

20.2 ▶ SMART GRID – A ROADMAP

20.2.1 Aims of the Smart Grids – The Vision

Smart grid technology is not a single concept; it involves various essential aspects of generation, distribution and utilisation. The following are the aims of the smart grids:

- Provide a user-centric approach and allow new services to enter the market.
- Establish innovation as an economic driver for electricity network renewal.
- Maintain security of supply, ensure integration and interoperability.
- Provide accessibility to a liberalised market and foster competition.
- Enable distributed generation and utilisation of renewable energy sources.
- Ensure the best use of the central generation.
- Consider the impact of environmental limitations appropriately.
- Enable demand side participation (DSR, DSM).
- Inform the political and regulatory aspects.
- Consider the societal aspects.

20.2.2 Pathways to a Smart Grid

Movement from static infrastructure to a flexible power grid with enhanced observability, controllability and process efficiency is described in Table 20.1.

Table 20.1 Movement from static infrastructure to a flexible power grid

From	*To*
Manual reaction to critical network situations. Primary equipment condition not well-known limited control of power flow	**Blackout prevention** by increasing situational awareness and automated countermeasures **Condition monitoring** for a controlled overload of bottlenecks and reliability-centred asset management
Centralised generation, decentralised consumption	**Power flow control** and transmission capacity increase by using power electronic components
Unmanaged, not transparent consumption	Integration of **distributed generation and storage** by virtual power plants **Smart metering** and load management

Example 20.2 **Give information of severe power blackout in India if any.**

Answer: Two severe power blackouts affected most of northern and eastern India on 30 and 31 July 2012.

20.3 ▶ SMART GRID - COMPONENTS AND MODEL

20.3.1 Components of Smart Grid

The various smart grid components have been illustrated in Fig. 20.1. The critical challenges for smart grids:

- Fortifying the grid system – guaranteeing that there is sufficient bandwidth to interconnect energy assets, generally sustainable energy resources.
- Moving seaward – building up the most efficient associations for seaward wind ranches and other marine innovations.
- Creating decentralised structures – empowering more limited size power supply systems to work amicably with the complete system.
- Interchanges conveying the correspondences system to permit conceivably a huge number of gatherings to work and exchange the single market.
- The active or dynamic consumer side empowers all buyers, with or without their power generation, to assume a functioning part in the system's activity.
- Incorporating irregular power generation – finding the ideal methods of coordinating discontinuous generation, including private microgeneration.
- Improved knowledge of generation and load request.
- Getting ready for electric vehicles, while smart grids should oblige buyers' requirements. Electric vehicles are especially underlined because of their versatile and profoundly scattered character and conceivable massive deployment before long, which would yield a significant test for the future power networks.

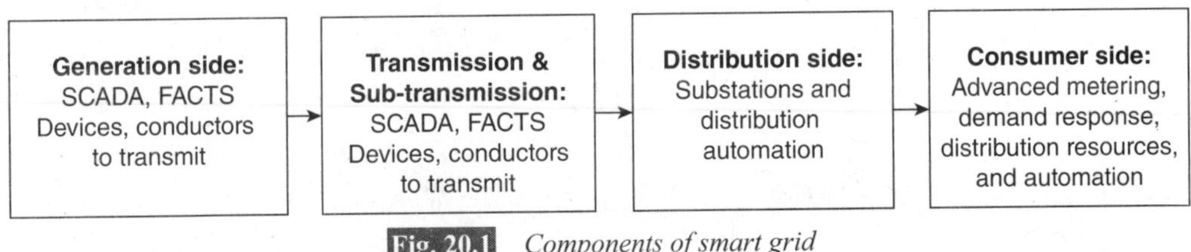

Fig. 20.1 *Components of smart grid*

The earliest and still largest example of a smart grid is the Italian system installed by Enel SpA of Italy. The project was completed in 2005. The Telegestore project was highly unusual in the utility world because the company had designed and manufactured their metres, acted as their system integrator and developed their system software. The Telegestore project is widely regarded as the first commercial-scale use of smart grid technology to the home.

20.3.2 A Model Set Up

A smart grid network is shown in Fig. 20.2, which shows that the power system operates under the smart grid structure. For the smart grid's vision to become a reality, a plan of action is needed to allow the many facets of technical, regulatory, environmental and cultural issues to be addressed in an optimised manner.

It will provide a coherent deployment of research and development results, integrated with existing infrastructure and technology, delivering early benefits, while maintaining steady progress and evolution towards the main goals.

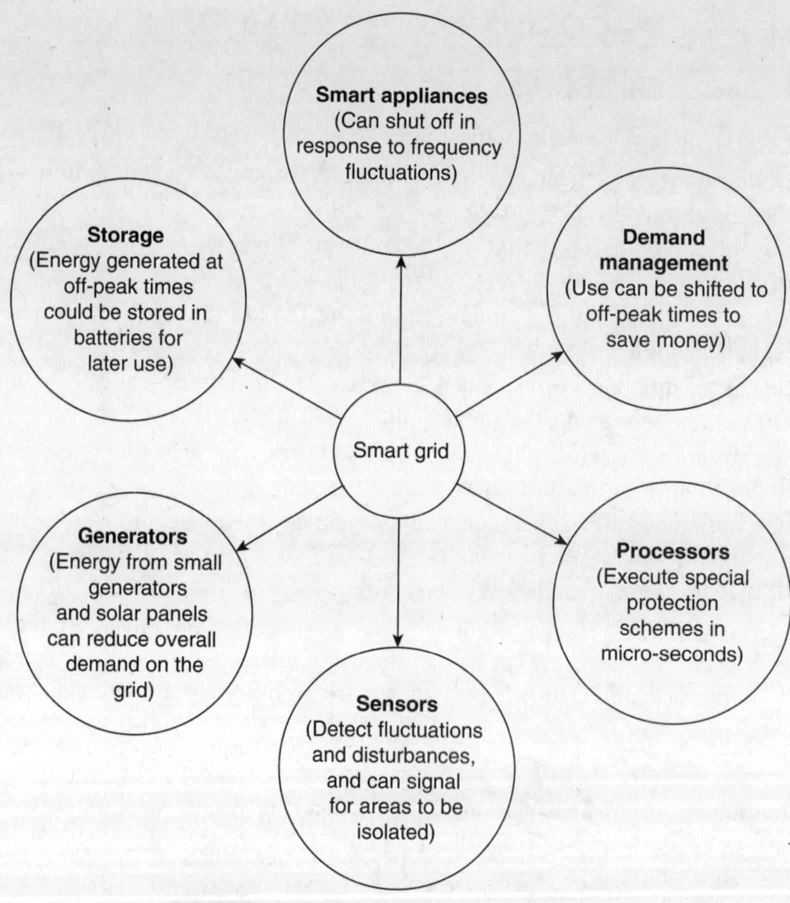

Fig. 20.2 *A model set up of smart grid network*

20.3.3 Conceptual Smart House

The smart home is becoming a reality in the developed world with energy efficiency and reduction in carbon footprints riding high on most governments and states' agendas. The technological advances in smart metres, Internet communication and smart appliances have made it achievable and sustainable. The list of smart devices includes:

1. Electricity smart metre
2. Gas smart metre (more likely to communicate via smart electricity metre)
3. Water smart metre (more likely to communicate via smart electricity metre)
4. Home automation gateway (more likely to communicate via the Internet and radio)

5. Home smart appliances, including the following (more likely to communicate over radio).
   - Heating, ventilation and air-conditioning
   - Fridge
   - Washing machine
   - Audio and video
   - Lightning
   - Robotics

Smart grid is crucial as it will take us towards energy independence and environmentally sustainable economic growth. A smart home model has been illustrated in Fig. 20.3. This chapter briefly talks about the evolution of smart power grid system development. It is still in its nascent stage. The whole power community is busy now understanding and developing a smart power grid system that is no longer a future theme. The growth of smart power grid in India will slowly but surely take us towards fulfilling the dreams of former President of India Dr. APJ Abdul Kalam, 'Energy for all and energy forever' and achieving the ultimate goal of making a 'National Grid' a reality.

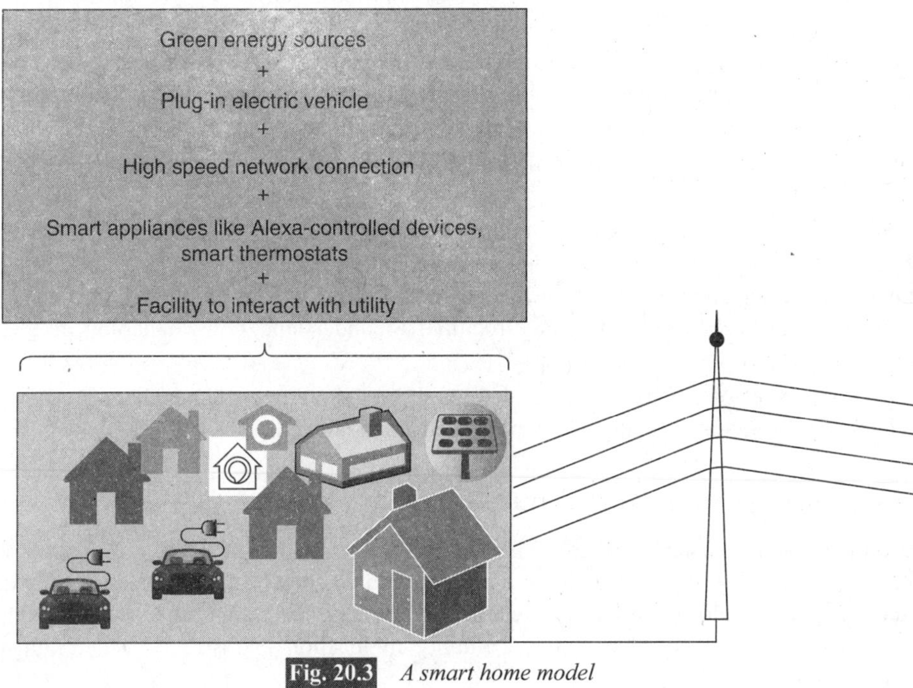

Fig. 20.3 *A smart home model*

Example 20.3 **What is a smart home?**

Answer: A smart home automate and connect household appliances, thermostats and in-home control devices, giving more control than ever before. The saving of electricity bill is also expected to be an essential aspect of a smart home using green power sources.

20.4 ▶ SMART GRID OPTIMISATION

20.4.1 Optimising Grid Operation and Use

The existing transmission and distribution networks require improved integration and coordination to manage the ever-increasing demands for energy trading and security of supply. To control electric power flows across state borders, advanced applications and tools that are already available today should be deployed to manage the complex interaction of operational security and trading and provide active prevention and remedy disturbances.

Key elements and priority components are as follows:

- Wide area monitoring (WAM) and wide area control (WAC) systems with the regulation of static var compensators, optionally in a closed-loop, to maximise the use of available transmission capacity while reducing the likelihood of disturbances.
- Distributed state estimators for large synchronous areas with real-time power system security assessment and optimised dispatching with dynamic constraints.
- System operators' staff training is covering legal issues (e.g., power system control) and emerging issues (e.g., electricity market and regulation).
- Coordinated ancillary services, including balancing markets and coordination of reserves throughout the grids/control areas – the integration of balancing markets is of particular importance both for enhanced power system security and improved market liquidity.
- Steady-state and dynamic (transient) simulators with modelling of renewable energy sources and nonlinear devices.
- Coordinated operation of power flow control systems (Flexible AC Transmission System [FACTS], phase shifters, etc.) with devices for automatic countermeasures/system defence. These applications exist in the component form today, but not many more will be deployed in a short time unless encouraged. Further work is urgently required to understand how to deploy and validate these solutions in closed-loop operation.
- Regulatory issues of relevance for the defined targets should be re-considered to ensure innovative technological solutions are adequately promoted and deployed.

20.4.2 Optimising Grid Infrastructure

New and efficient asset management solutions for the transmission and distribution grids are required, coordinated and coherent grid infrastructure planning should be done. Rather than being only deterministic, coordinated planning should be based on scenarios and include the necessary risk management elements to cope with the increased volatility and uncertainty in location and size of generation and growing intermittent generation.

Key elements and priority components are as follows:

- Expanding the grids (notably transmission) with new infrastructure (e.g., HVDC) will depend on accelerating permitting procedures and making them much more efficient than today.
- New overhead line configurations to increase capacity and reduce electromagnetic fields are required.
- Refurbishment/enforcement of the existing high-voltage lines by creative network assets, including superconductivity technology.
- New asset management and grid planning methods for transmission and distribution.
- Development of systems and components to maintain power quality at acceptable levels while encouraging new types of generators.

Example 20.4 **What is meant by grid optimisation?**

Answer: This is a new term that is known after renewable energy sources' connection with the grid utility. Grid optimisation is a broad area that includes the three major components: demand response, management of renewable energy sources and the implementation of non-wire alternative programs.

20.5 ▶ INTEGRATION OF RENEWABLES

20.5.1 Integrating Large-Scale Intermittent Generation

Large-scale forms of generation, for example, wind farms and the future (concentrated) solar thermal generation require networks to enable efficient collection of the power generated and enable system balancing, either by energy storage, conventional generation or by demand-side participation. Offshore wind energy needs marine power collection networks and reinforcement of the terrestrial networks. This deployment priority is also about promoting and fostering the large-scale integration of renewable energy resources to meet the requirements of grid security while considering economic efficiency.

Key elements and priority components are as follows:

- Technically viable and commercially affordable solutions for offshore networks for collection of wind power.
- Grid connections from offshore networks should consider security and quality of supply, economy and environmental sustainability.
- Transnational and cross-border grid re-enforcements should be considered. The present long-licensing procedures should be shortened.
- Solutions should be developed to allow for efficient and secure system operation of future grids with significant intermittent generation, heavy bulk power and/or not easily dispatchable.

20.5.2 Energy Storage System in Smart Grid

Several energy storage system (ESS) schemes based on different technologies have been implemented for electricity storage, which is illustrated as follows:

- Flywheel
- Supercapacitor
- Lead-acid battery
- Superconducting magnetic storage
- NaS battery
- Flow battery

ESS includes the following uses:

(i) **Power quality:**
ESS is utilised in uninterruptible power supplies to relieve the transient loss of power and power fluctuations. An ESS can likewise be used to alleviate voltage fluctuations and improve other power quality issues, for example, harmonics. In contrast to ESS for power quality applications, the option is to make the highly sensitive equipment's control frameworks more vigorous.

(ii) **Service arrangement to renewable generation:**
Irregular supply and absence of controllability are natural qualities of sustainable power generation. It is a test for the safe activity of the power framework. ESS upholds both the power framework and environmentally friendly power sources by smoothing their yield, coordinating agreement positions (or empowering scheduled dispatch) and moving the produced energy as expected.

Example 20.5 **Why is ESS needed in renewable energy sources-based generation system?**

Answer: In renewable energy-based grids, the most challenging tasks are to achieve uninterrupted, reliable and continuous power supply from these grids. The problems in these grids and their associated solutions are (a) discrepancy between generation and demand: this is resolved by hybrid solar–wind ESS, (b) requirement of improved efficiency and reliability: this is achieved by the use of state-of-the-art controllers and innovative switching systems, (c) analysis of dynamic systems, optimisation and control: for these, mathematical modelling of systems is prepared, which is a challenging task as solar, wind and battery system contain nonlinear parameters.

20.6 ► INFORMATION COMMUNICATION TECHNOLOGY IN SMART GRID

20.6.1 Data Communication

Data transfer is an important way of communication in smart grid. Data communication is possible through intelligent electronic device (IED), which transfers data to a human–machine interface (HMI) for display. Some of the power system devices have been mentioned in Table 20.2, which are necessary for a communication system. Simultaneously, Table 20.3 illustrates the data communication requirement for several power system applications.

Table 20.2 Power system devices for the communication system

Component	*Device*
Communication channel	Local area network (LAN) Ethernet
Destination	HMI with visual display, IED for protection and control
Receiver	Network interfaced card
Source	Voltage and current transformers
Transmitter	Remote terminal unit (RTU)

Table 20.3 Data communication requirement for several power system applications

Application	*Time to response (ms)*	*Network topology and communication technology*
Transmission circuit's protection	<20	Point-to-point links are dedicated
Distribution circuit's protection	<100	Circuit and packet switching

As seen in Fig. 20.4, CT is used for analogue measurements. The extracted data are then digitised by using an encoder, which is situated inside the IED.

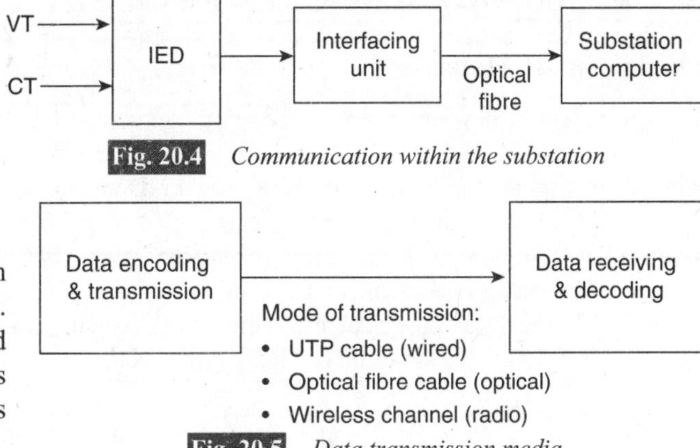

Fig. 20.4 *Communication within the substation*

20.6.2 Communication Channels

The channels can be wired or wireless, such as optical fibre, copper cable and radio link. These channels are further divided as guided and unguided mediums. Fig. 20.5 illustrates the data communication media such as wired, optical and radio.

Fig. 20.5 *Data transmission media*

Power line carrier (PLC) utilises the electrical cable as an actual correspondence media could likewise be viewed as an open-wire communication system. It offers the chance of sending information all the while with power over a similar medium. PLC utilises a line matching unit to infuse signals into a high-voltage transmission or conveyance line, as shown in Fig. 20.6. The infused signal is kept from spreading to different pieces of the power network by line traps. A portion of the smart grid's correspondence innovations is as per the following, which should be made sure about through the cryptography method.

- IEEE 802 series
- Mobile communications
- Multi-protocol label switching
- Power line communication

Example 20.6 **What is IoT? What are the main components of IoT systems?**

Answer: The Internet of Things (IoT) is a network used to communicate from one place to another using Internet. The IoT system consists of three main components: sensors, network connectivity and data storage applications.

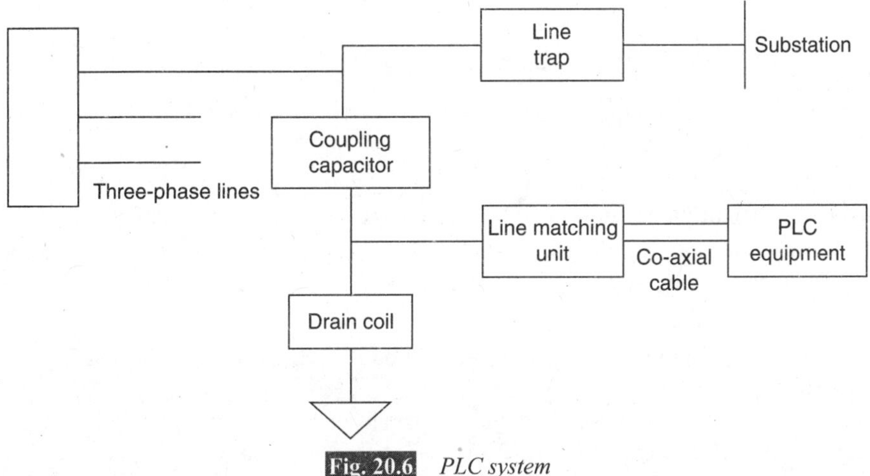

Fig. 20.6 *PLC system*

20.7 ▶ SENSING, MEASUREMENT AND AUTOMATION

20.7.1 Smart Metering

The integration of new energy resources in the existing electrical grid compensated for the increased load demands. Therefore, demand-side programs have been introduced widely to better use the existing power supply infrastructure and control demand growth. Demand-side integration (DSI) refers to the relationships between the electric power system, the energy supply and the end-user load. DSI needs an effective advanced ICT of system loads. Smart metering refers to techniques that measure, collect, analyse and manage energy use using advanced ICT.

Fig. 20.7 illustrates electrical metering development, from necessary electro-mechanical aggregation metering to cutting edge smart metering.

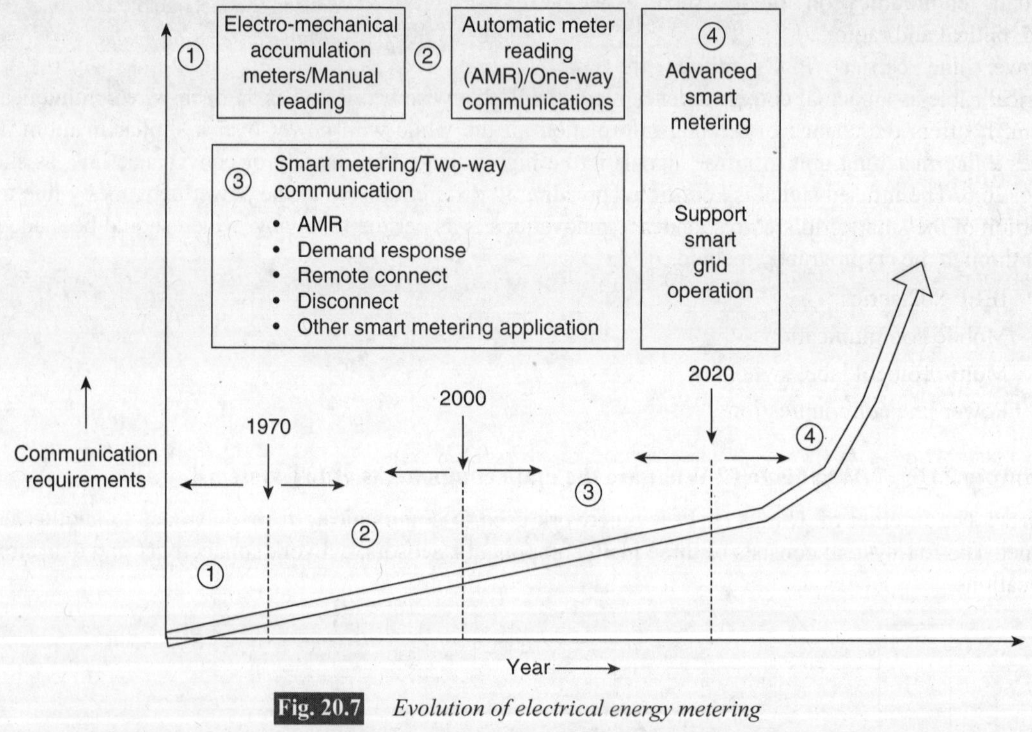

Fig. 20.7 *Evolution of electrical energy metering*

Example 20.7 A smart metre shows current harmonic estimations up to the fifth harmonic part. What ought to be the base inspecting sampling frequency utilised in the signal moulding or conditioning stage? Accept that the frequency of the power supply is 50 Hz.

Answer: The frequency of the fifth harmonic part = 5 × 50 Hz = 250 Hz.

To catch up to the fifth component, the signal should be filtered by an anti-aliasing filter with a cut-off frequency = 250 Hz.

As per the Nyquist criteria, the base sampling frequency or the minimum sampling frequency should then be 2 × 250 Hz = 500 Hz, as shown in Fig. 20.8.

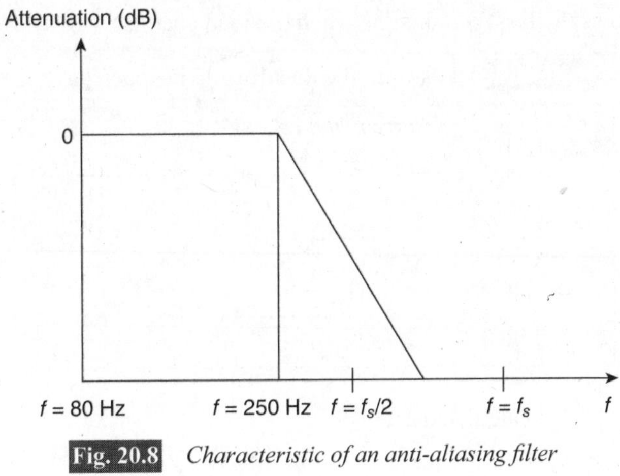

Fig. 20.8 *Characteristic of an anti-aliasing filter*

Example 20.8 Consider the circuit that appeared in Fig. 20.9. The 33/11 kV transformer has an on-load tap changer transformer, which keeps up the load voltage at 11 kV. Compute the rate decrease in energy loss in the 33 kV line if load moving appeared in Fig. 20.10 is managed. Disregard the 33/11 kV transformer losses.

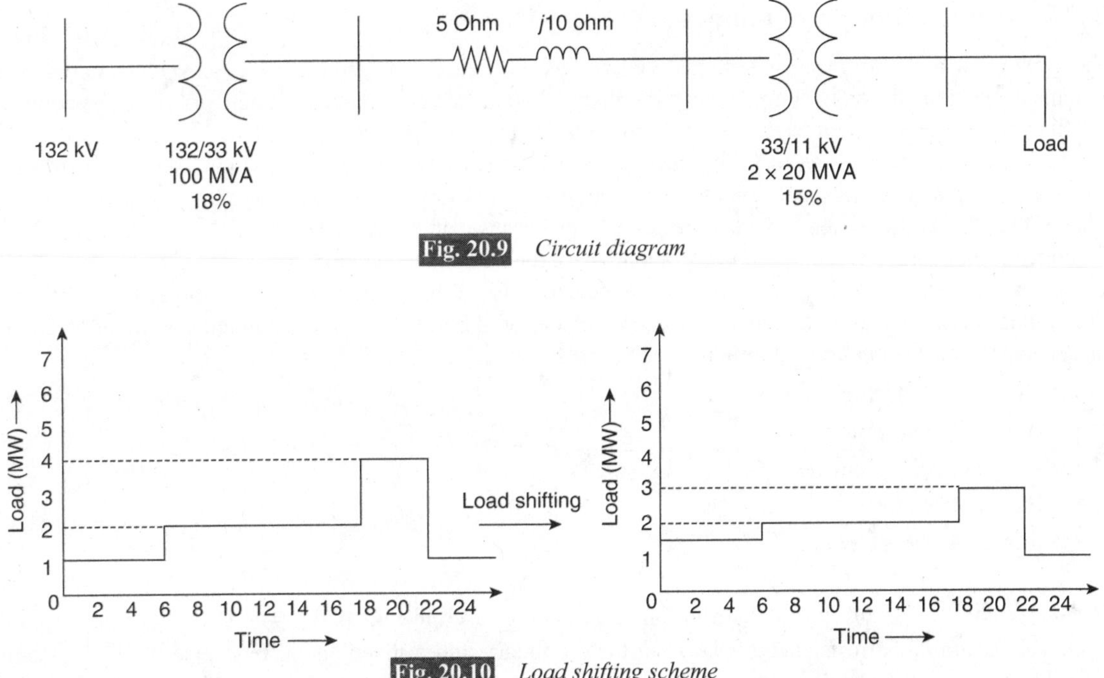

Fig. 20.9 *Circuit diagram*

Fig. 20.10 *Load shifting scheme*

Solution Table 20.4 shows the losses in the line when the load changes.

Table 20.4 Losses in the line during the load change

Load (MW)	*Current in the 33 kV line (A)*	*Losses (kW)*
1	17.5	1.53
1.5	26.3	3.45
2	35.0	6.13
3	52.5	13.78
4	70.0	24.50

Loss of energy without DSI is calculated as:

$$8 \times 1.53 + 12 \times 6.13 + 4 \times 24.5 = 183.8 \text{ kWh}$$

(Note that for 8 hours for each day, the load was 1 MW, for 12 hours for every day, it was 2 MW and for 4 hours, it was 4 MW.)

Then, the loss of energy with DSI is calculated as:

$$8 \times 3.45 + 12 \times 6.13 + 4 \times 13.78 = 156.3 \text{ kWh}$$

Hence, rate decrease = $[(183.8 - 156.3)/183.8] \times 100 = 15\%$

20.7.2 Automation Technologies

The generation and transmission systems' activity is checked and constrained by SCADA systems. The systems connect the different components through correspondence communication networks (e.g., microwave and fibre optic circuits) and interface the transmission substations and generators to a monitored control centre that keeps up system security and encourages coordinated activity. The mechanisation (automation) in the distributed system has expanded to improve supply and coordinate more distributed generation. Network voltage changes and deficiency levels are ascending because of the association of distributed generation. Without the network's dynamic administration, the expenses of association of distributed generation will increment, and extra distributed generation association might be restricted. The relationship of sizeable discontinuous energy sources and module electric vehicles will build DSI and distribution system automation.

The substation automation equipment is as follows:

- Voltage transformer
- Current transformer
- Intelligent electronic devices
- Bay controller
- Remote terminal units

Example 20.9 A piece of a distribution circuit is appeared in Fig. 20.11. The CT utilised is a 10 VA Class 10P20 and has a resistance of 0.6 Ω in the secondary and a magnetising reactance of $j15$ Ω. Using the CT's equivalent circuit, get the percentage current magnitude error and phase displacement error at the rated current and at the accuracy limit when the load connected in the secondary side is rated value.

Solution The rated burden is given as 10 volt-ampere, the corresponding secondary resistance can be calculated as:

$$R_{\text{burden}} = \frac{10}{5^2} = 0.4\ \Omega$$

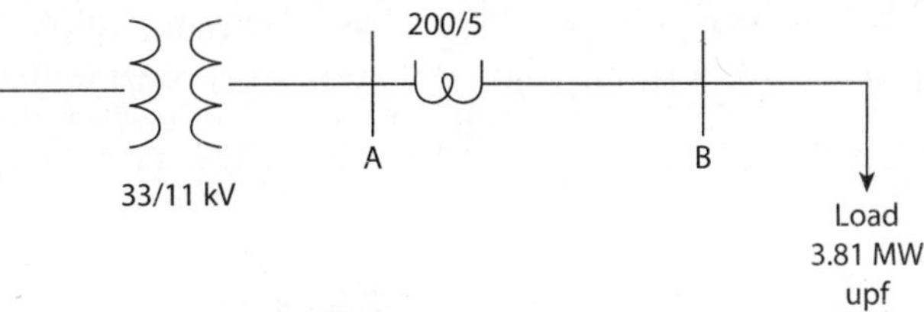

Fig. 20.11 *Circuit diagram*

The CT's equivalent circuit (per phase) with the rated current is shown in Fig. 20.12.

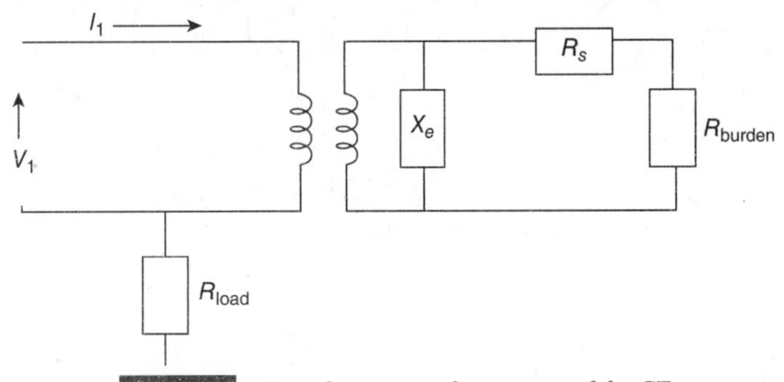

Fig. 20.12 *Per-phase equivalent circuit of the CT*

$$V_1 = 11000/\sqrt{3} = 6350.9\ \text{V}$$

$$R_{\text{load}} = 3 \times (6350.9)23.81 \times 106 = 31.75$$

On transforming the values of primary quantities into secondary (by multiplying the voltage by the turns ratio 40, and primary resistance by the square of 40), the following circuit is obtained, as shown in Fig. 20.13.

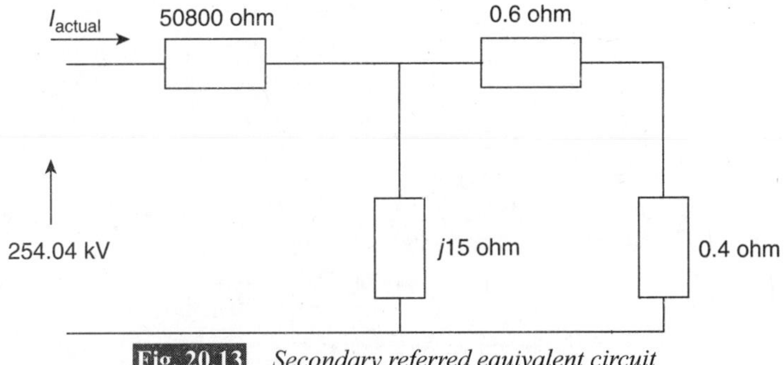

Fig. 20.13 *Secondary referred equivalent circuit*

$$\text{The current in the secondary circuit} = \frac{2.54 \times 10^5}{50.8 \times 10^3 + [j15 \times 1/(1 + j15)]}$$

$$= 5.0007\angle 0^\circ$$

$$\text{Therefore, the percentage current magnitude error} = \frac{(5.0007 - 5)}{5} \times 100 = 0.014\%$$

Phase angle error is 0°.

When the current is at the accuracy limit, 4×10^3 A is flowing in the primary, instead of the resistive load in the equivalent circuit, fault resistance appears in the transformer primary.

$$R_{\text{fault}} = \frac{6.35\times 10^3}{4\times 10^3} = 1.5875\ \Omega$$

$$\text{New actual current in the secondary circuit} = \frac{2.54\times 10^5}{1.59\times 40^2 + [j15\times 1/(1+j15)]} = 99.8194\angle -0.0015°$$

$$\text{Therefore, the percentage current magnitude error} = \frac{99.8194-(5\times 20)}{5\times 20}\times 100 = -0.18\%$$

The phase angle error is 0.0015°.

20.7.3 Distribution Management System

A DMS includes several applications that use modelling and analysis tools and data sources and interfaces to external systems, as shown in Fig. 20.14. The modelling and analysis tools are pieces of software that support one or more applications.

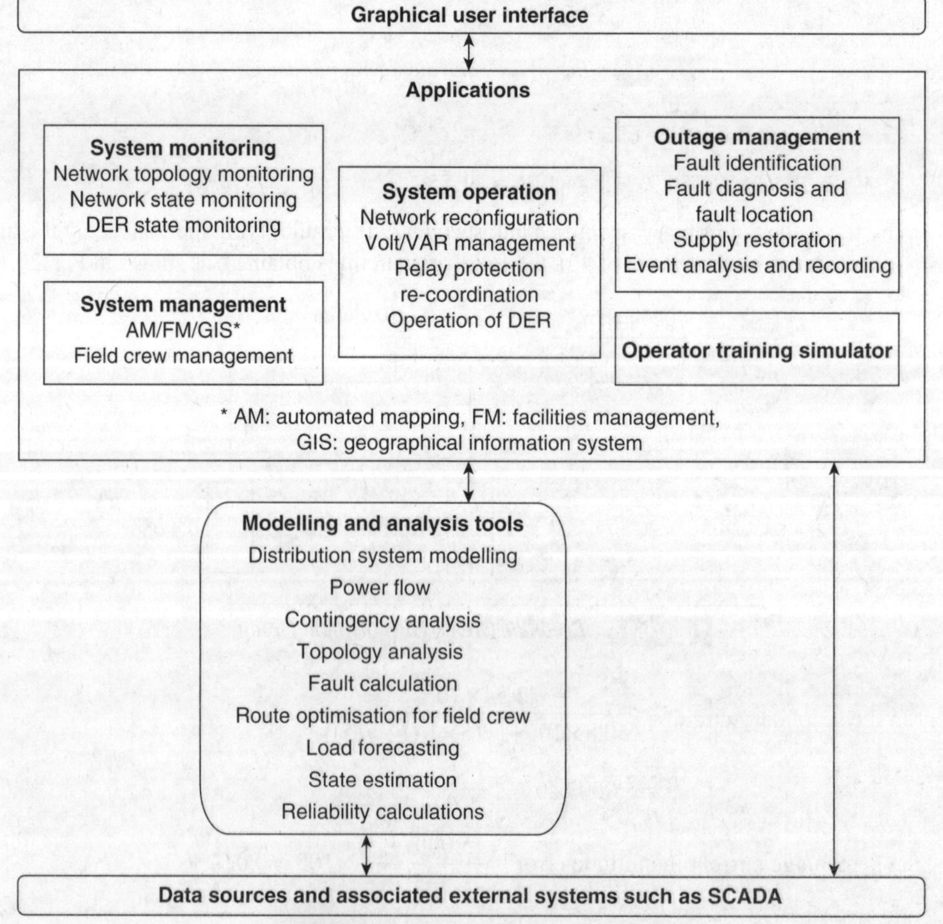

Fig. 20.14 *Main components of a DMS*

DMS applications can be considered as per the following attributes.

- For system operation, monitoring and management. These are the applications liable for the everyday running of the network with the essential object of keeping up the supply's congruity.
- To help deal with the utility's resources, for example, inventory control, development, plant records, drawings and planning. These incorporate the computerised planning framework, the management system for facilities and the geographical data framework.
- Related with the plan and getting ready for network extensions. These applications are utilised for framework activity reviews to decide momentary arrangements and ideal development to accomplish framework support at least expense.

Each of these applications requires demonstrating and investigating devices for which network parameters, client data and network data status are utilised as information sources. A portion of the displaying and examination tools used for modelling and analysis are as per the following requirements.

- Distribution system modelling
- Load forecasting
- Power flow analysis
- Fault calculations
- State estimation

20.7.4 Transmission System

The transmission system faces unpredictable changes in operating conditions with the increasing integration of RESs. The power flow in lines and bus voltage must be within limits for the system to be stable. Therefore, it is required to aid the transmission system operators (TSOs) to monitor and control transmission systems' operation. The TSOs use a suite of applications collected into an energy management system (EMS). The systems are also referred to as EMS/SCADA, as SCADA often provides the EMS monitoring and control functions. The EMS is arranged in the System Control Center, and the continuous checking and controller are accessible between the Control Center and the generating stations and transmission substations.

It is expected from phasor measurement units (PMUs) that, later on, PMU estimations will be incorporated with EMS. Be that as it may, as of now, PMUs are mostly integrated into discrete wide area applications. It is seen that EMS and wide area applications coincide independently for quite a while. Fig. 20.15 shows how unique information sources feed into applications.

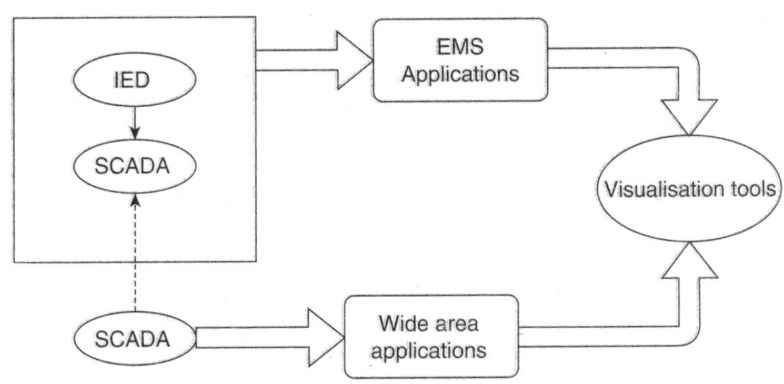

Fig. 20.15 *EMS/SCADA and wide area applications*

Example 20.10 The power flow on the transmission line in Fig. 20.16 is 5 pu, and the voltage at both busbars is 1.0 pu. The system frequency is 50 Hz. The power flow is estimated using the phase difference between busbars 1 and 2, using $\varphi_1 - \varphi_2$. The measurement of the phase angle φ_1 has a timestamp error of 0.1 ms, and that of the phase angle φ_2 is zero. Find the error in the estimated power flow.

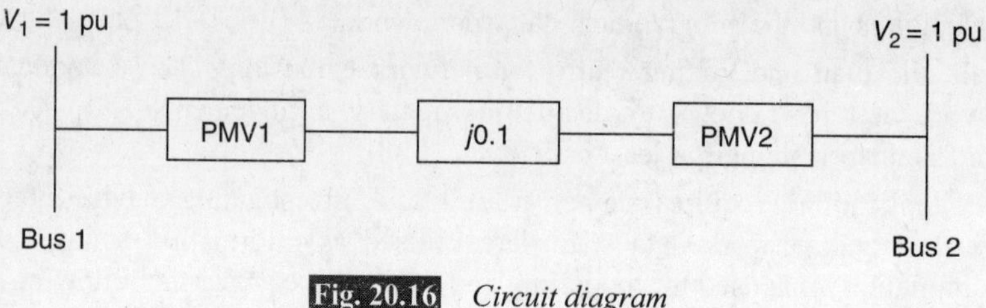

Fig. 20.16 *Circuit diagram*

Solution The phase angle error $\Delta\varphi$ is derived from the time stamp error of 0.1 ms and is given by:

$$\Delta\varphi = \frac{0.1}{20} \times 2\pi = \sim 0.0314 \text{ rad}$$

The phase angle difference $\varphi_1 - \varphi_2$ is calculated in the following way:

$$P = \frac{V_1 V_2}{x} \sin(\varphi_1 - \varphi_2) = 5 \text{ pu}$$

Therefore, $\varphi_1 - \varphi_2 = \pi/6$

The estimated power flow error ΔP is shown in Fig. 20.17 and is given by:

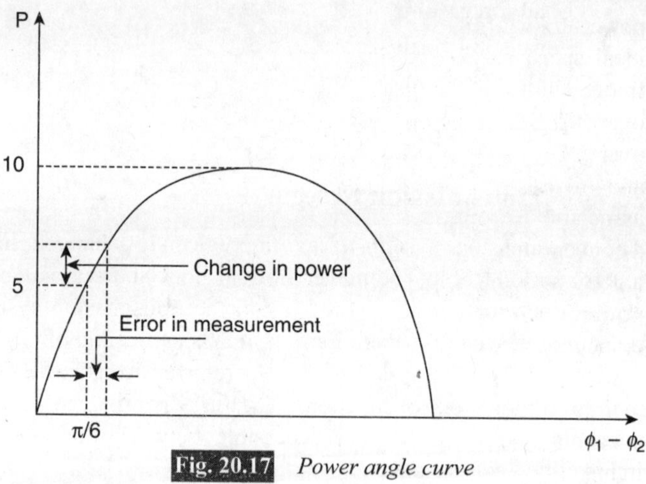

Fig. 20.17 *Power angle curve*

$$\Delta P = \frac{V_1 V_2}{x} \sin(\varphi_1 - \varphi_2 + \Delta\varphi) - \frac{V_1 V_2}{x} \sin(\varphi_1 - \varphi_2) = 0.272 \text{ pu}$$

20.8 ▶ POWER ELECTRONICS IN SMART GRID

Power electronics (PE) mainly includes FACTS and converters in the power system. The FACTS devices have some typical applications, which are illustrated as follows:

- Damping oscillations
- Transient and dynamic stability
- Voltage stability

FACTS devices with their applications have been described in Table 20.5.

Table 20.5 FACTS devices with their applications

Type	*FACTS devices*	*Switches*	*Applications*
Shunt	SVC, STATCOM	Thyristor, IGBT, IGCT	Voltage control, VAR compensation
Series	TCSC, TSSC	Thyristor	Power flow control
Shunt and Series	IPFC, UPFC	IGBT, IGCT	Active and reactive power control

Further, the integration of RESs such as wind, solar, biomass and many others reduces CO_2 emission and ensures sustainable electrical energy. However, RESs integration shows some variations in system's parameters, which can be avoided by integrating the power electronics devices.

The variable-speed turbines related to distributed generations, such as wind, small hydro and tidal, mostly use AC–DC–AC power transformation. The turbine is arranged to turn at the ideal speed to get the maximum power possible. The variable frequency power output from the generator is first changed over to DC. A subsequent converter is utilised to change over DC into 50/60 Hz AC. The output of a PV panel is DC, and in this manner, a DC–AC converter is essential for grid association. Biomass advances utilise a steam or gas turbine and a conventional generator. The power electronic interface between a RES and the grid can be utilised to control reactive output power. Consequently, the network voltage and real output power empower the generator to react to the grid's prerequisites.

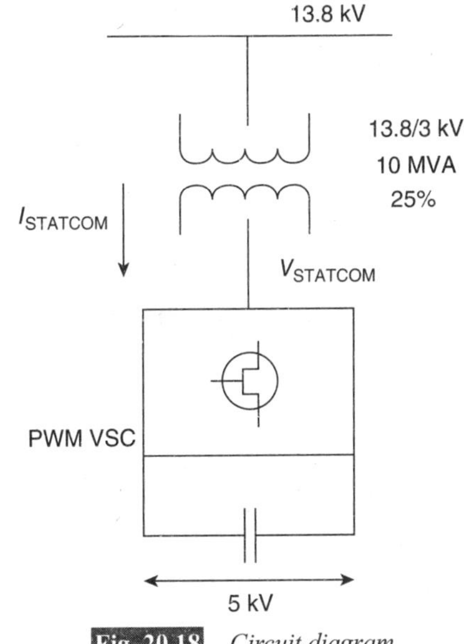

Fig. 20.18 *Circuit diagram*

Example 20.11 Consider the D-STATCOM as reflected in Fig. 20.18. Assume that a six-pulse VSC operating on sinusoidal PWM is utilised for the D-STATCOM. Find the modulation index required to: (1) generate 5 MVar of reactive power and (2) absorb 5 MVar of reactive power.

Given: For a six-pulse VSC operating on sinusoidal PWM $V_{LL} = 0.612 \times m_a \times V_{DC}$ where V_{LL} is the line to line voltage at D-STATCOM terminals, m_a is the modulation index, and V_{DC} is the DC capacitor voltage.

Solution Assuming the base MVA is 10 MVA, the transformer's base primary voltage is 13.8 kV, and the base secondary voltage is 3 kV.

The transformer leakage reactance = 0.25 pu.

D-STATCOM terminal voltage $= 0.612 \times m_a \times 5/3 = 1.02 \times m_a$ pu

The pu equivalent circuit is shown in Fig. 20.19.

1. When D-STATCOM is generating 5 MVar, in pu $Q = +0.5$ pu

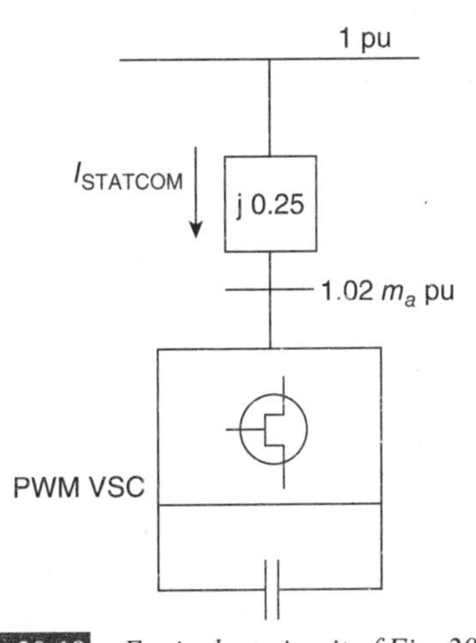

Fig. 20.19 *Equivalent circuit of Fig. 20.18*

Then from the pu equivalent circuit:

$$Q = 0.5 = \frac{1.02m_a - 1}{0.25}$$

Therefore, $m_a = 1.1$.

When $m_a > 1$, the PWM-VSC operates in the over-modulation region, and the linear relationship between m_a and STATCOM terminal voltage is no longer valid. m_a should be greater than 1.1 to generate 5 MVar of reactive power. The exact value of m_a needs a more precise calculation of the PWM output voltage.

2. D-STATCOM absorbs 5 MVar, in pu $Q = -0.5$ pu

Then from the pu equivalent circuit:

$$Q = -0.5 = \frac{1.02m_a - 1}{0.25}$$

Therefore, $m_a = 0.86$.

Example 20.12 A PV system is shown in Fig. 20.20 has two series-connected PV modules. The V–I characteristic is given in Fig. 20.21. The one-phase inverter operates with sinusoidal pulse width modulation, and it is connected directly to the 230 V mains. The solar irradiance on the module is assumed as 1000 W/m^2.

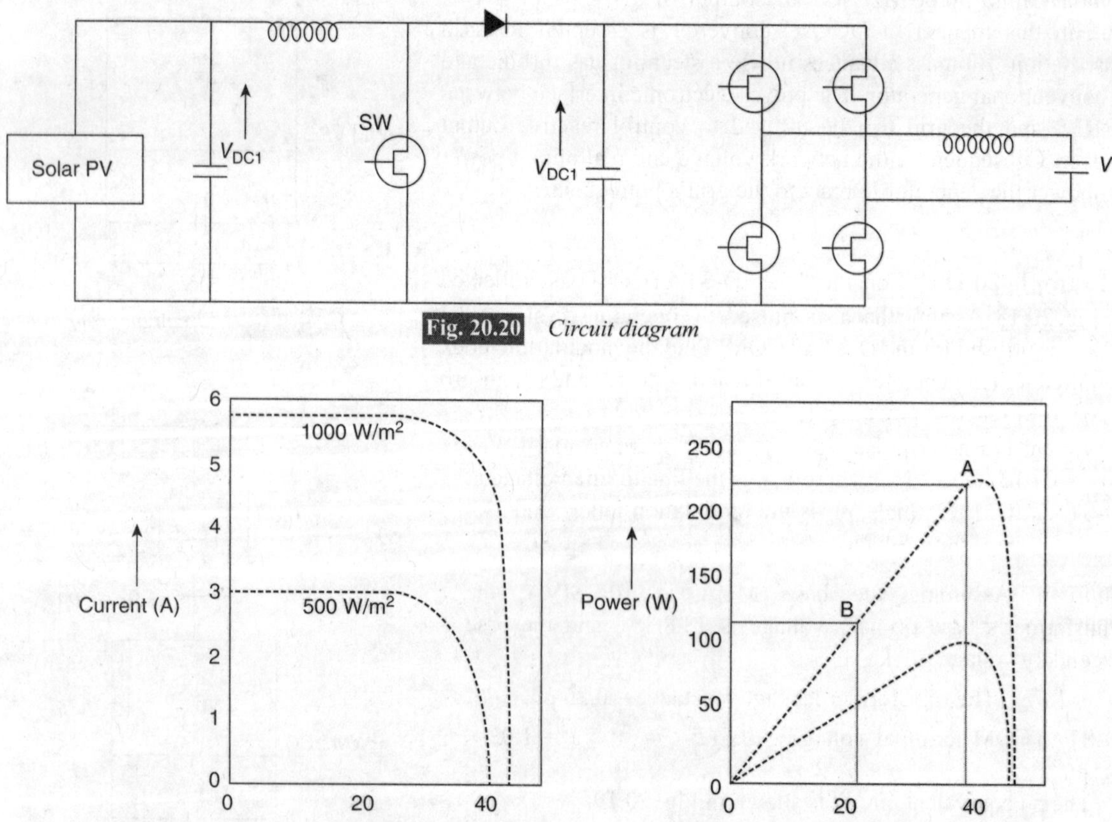

Fig. 20.20 *Circuit diagram*

Fig. 20.21 *Typical current–voltage and power–voltage characteristics of a PV module for irradiance of 1000 W/m^2 and 500 W/m^2*

1. Suggest a possible control strategy that could be used.
2. Determine the amplitude modulation index of the inverter to maintain V_{DC2} at 350 V?
3. Calculate the duty ratio of the switch SW that is required to extract maximum power.
4. If, due to the local power network constraints, the output of the PV system was reduced by 50%, calculate the new duty ratio required for switch SW.

Data: For the boost converter: $V_{DC2} = (1/(1 - D)) \times V_{DC1}$ where D is the switch SW's duty ratio.

For a single-phase inverter operating with sinusoidal PWM $V_1 = m_a \times V_{DC2}$ where V_1 is the peak value of fundamental of the inverter output voltage, m_a is the modulation index.

Solution (1) V_{DC2} is always maintained at a reference value by changing the inverter's modulation index. When the MPPT algorithm detects that V_{DC1} should be increased, the duty ratio (D) is reduced. On the other hand, when the MPPT algorithm detects that V_{DC1} should be decreased, the duty ratio increases.

(2) V_1 is $230 \times \sqrt{2} = 325$ V. Hence from $V_1 = m_a \times V_{DC2}$, to maintain V_{DC2} at 350 V:

$$m_a = 325/350 = 0.93.$$

(3) Voltage V_{DC1} should be maintained at 80 V (voltage across each series modules should be maintained approximately at 40 V as shown in point A in Fig. 21) to extract peak power.

Then, $$350 = 1/(1 - D) \times 80$$

Therefore, $D = 0.77$.

(4) If the PV system's power output needs to be reduced by 50%, as the irradiance is not changed, V_{DC1} should be changed to 40 V (see point B in Fig. 21).

Then: $350 = 1/(1 - D) \times 40$

Therefore, $D = 0.89$.

20.9 ► SMART MICROGRID

Volatile and rising energy prices are forcing organisations to rethink their energy consumption patterns. Sustainability goals, budget pressures and expanding regulations continue to impose new objectives on facilities management, such as reducing energy use or deployment of renewable energy. There is a common refrain to do more with less and identify ways to cut costs. Facilities and energy managers struggle under these requirements and need the tools to implement a new energy strategy.

A smart microgrid includes intelligent management and optimisation of production, storage and energy consumption needed to achieve these objectives. A smart microgrid can reduce costs and help maximise your return on investment from your energy assets while achieving sustainability goals.

Conceptually, a microgrid is easy. Local generation (combined heat and power), distribution and energy consumption across a campus or commercial facility is a basic microgrid. Rudimentary microgrids are not an unusual part of a corporate energy strategy. But, a basic microgrid approach is passive with little-to-no opportunity for:

- Real-time management and optimisation of energy usage.
- Maximising cost savings and carbon emissions reductions against priorities of reliability and comfort.
- Monitoring and control of disparate building management systems and sources of distributed energy.
- Intelligence to identify energy efficiency opportunities.
- Forecasting to improve the attainment of targets.
- Reporting and billing on energy, environmental and financial results.

Components of a smart microgrid are:

The key components to a smart microgrid are the integration following four components into a centrally managed, campus-based energy infrastructure:

- Supply: storage and distributed generation (renewable and non-renewable sources).
- Demand: energy consumption devices across the entire organisation, including but not limited to lightning, HVAC and IT equipment.
- Energy management platform: intelligent system to optimise energy supply and demand based on management objectives and conditioning factors.
- Environmental factors: variables external to the management system that will influence energy use, such as weather, pricing and comfort.

Intelligent energy management solutions are the brains and nervous system of a campus smart microgrid. The lack of this critical component has kept facilities managers from broadly and efficiently implementing smart microgrids. This platform must cover four essential tasks of management:

- Collect and analyse data.
- Identify opportunities for managers and administrators to take action on information or automatically execute actions.
- Provide powerful communication tools on objectives and progress through real-time dashboards.
- Provide optimisation tools and interface with different automation management systems to increase personnel and asset.

Example 20.13 A 400 kV transmission line has a reactance of 0.05 pu on a 100 MVA base. The sending end's voltage is $1.02\angle 2°$, and that of the receiving end is $1.0\angle 0°$. What voltage should be injected in quadrature with the sending end voltage to increase the power transfer across the line by 20%?

Solution The power transfer through the lines is:

$$P = \frac{V_1 V_2}{x}\sin(\delta_s - \delta_r) = 0.71 \text{ pu}$$

If the power transfer is increased by 20%, P = 0.85 pu. Assuming that the sending voltage phasor is constant, from new power transfer:

$$0.85 = \frac{1.02 \times 1}{0.05}\sin(2^0 - \delta_r)$$

Therefore, $\delta_R = -0.4°$.

From the phasor diagram of Fig. 20.22, we get

Injected voltage = V_S tan (2.4°) = 1.02 tan (2.4°) = 0.04 pu.

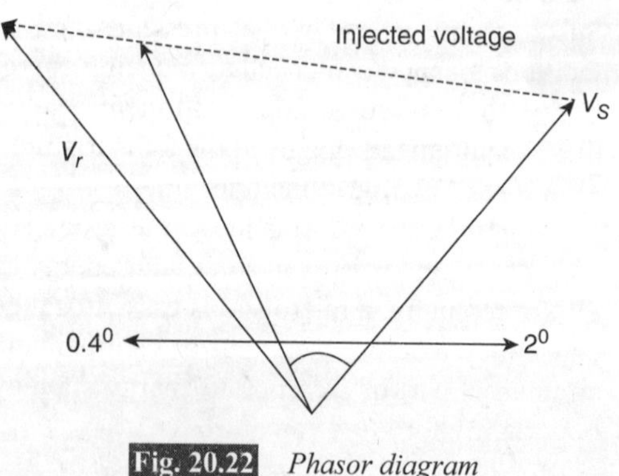

Fig. 20.22 *Phasor diagram*

20.10 ▶ SUMMARY

In this chapter, modern technological aspects and future smart grid considerations are described in detail as a future grid. It is explained that a smart grid is referred to by other names, including 'Smart Electric Grid', 'Smart Power Grid', 'Intelligrid' and 'Future Grid'. Brief illustrations on the importance of power electronics devices are described in this chapter.

Problems

20.1 Consider the microgrid given in Fig. P-20.1 with the following data:

I. Transformer rated at 440 V/11 kV, with the reactance of 0.16 Ω and resistance of 0.02 Ω, and rated at 60 kVA.

II. A three-phase, eight-pole induction machine rated at 440 V, 60 Hz and 50 kVA, 440 V, 60 Hz, with stator resistance of 0.2 Ω/phase, rotor referred resistance in the stator side of 0.2 Ω/phase, stator reactance of 1.6 Ω/phase, and rotor referred reactance of 0.8 Ω/phase. The generator speed is 1200 rpm. Perform the following:

(i) Give the per unit (pu) model of the system.

(ii) Compute the power delivered to the local power grid.

(iii) Compute the reactive power flow between the grid and the induction generator. Assume base values equal to the rating of the induction machine.

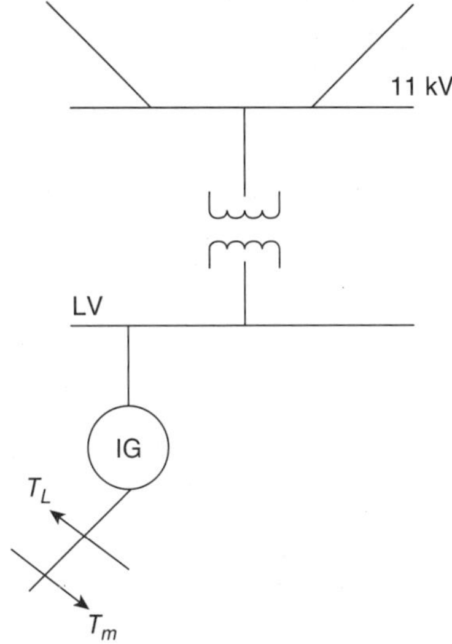

Fig. P-20.1 *The microgrid connected to a local power grid*

20.2 The microgrid of Fig. P-20.2 is supplied by an induction generator. The system has a local load rated 100 kVA at a power factor rated 0.8 lagging. The three-phase transformer is rated at 11/0.44 kV, 300 kVA and reactance of 6%. A three-phase, eight-pole induction machine rated at 440 V, 60 Hz and 500 kVA, 440 V, 60 Hz, with stator resistance of 0.1 Ω/phase, rotor referred resistance in the stator side of 0.1 Ω/phase, stator reactance of 0.8 Ω/phase and rotor referred reactance of 0.4 Ω/phase. Compute the following:

(i) The per unit power flow model and short-circuit model are based on a base of 500 kVA and 440 V.

(ii) If the induction generator's speed is 1000 rpm, what is the rotor frequency?

20.3 In a parallel LC circuit, the PLC equipment uses a carrier frequency of 100 kHz. If the inductance value in the line trap is 0.25 mH, what is the value of the capacitance required?

20.4 The rated current and power dissipation of a smart metre are 100 A and 3 W, respectively. The metre works with a current-sensing resistor of 200 μΩ. When the load current is at the smart metre's rated current value, then calculate the following.

a. The power dissipation in all the other components of the smart metre.

b. The voltage across the current-sensing resistor.

c. The gain of the Programmable Gain Amplifier to match with an analogue to digital converter (ADC) having a full scale of 5 V.

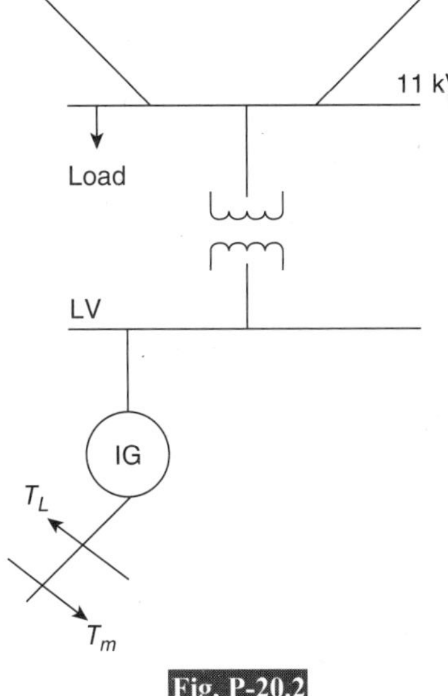

Fig. P-20.2

20.5 A smart metre uses the same 16-bit analogue to digital converter for current and voltage measurements. It uses a 100:5 A current transformer for current measurements and a 415: 10 V potential divider for voltage measurements. When the metre shows a current measurement of 50 A and a voltage measurement of 400 V, what is the maximum possible error in the apparent power reading because of the quantisation of voltage and current signals?

20.6 A 50 MW wind farm is connected to the distribution system. Due to the blades passing the towers, it was observed that the power generated by the wind farm is given by 40 + 4 sin(10t) MW. Calculate the current that should be injected by the Voltage Source Converters with Energy Storage (VSC-ES) to compensate for the power's blade-passing frequency. For simplified calculations, assume that reactive power at the point of connection is zero. Further, believe that with the VSC-ES, the voltage at the point of contact is constant at 33 kV.

Multiple Choice Questions

20.1 Which among the following is a renewable energy source?
(a) Heating oil (b) Hydropower
(c) Natural gas (d) Hydrocarbon gas liquids

20.2 Which of the following is not the example of renewable energy form?
(a) Geothermal energy (b) Natural gas
(c) Hydropower energy (d) Biogas

20.3 Which of the following is a disadvantage of renewable energy?
(a) High pollution (b) Available only in few places
(c) High running cost (d) Unreliable supply

20.4 A solar is an electrical device that converts the energy of light directly into electricity by the
(a) Photovoltaic effect (b) Chemical effect
(c) Atmospheric effect (d) Physical effect

20.5 The world's first 100% solar-powered airport is located at
(a) Cochin, Kerala (b) Bengaluru, Karnataka
(c) Chennai, Tamil Nadu (d) Mumbai, Maharashtra

20.6 Geothermal energy is an alternative source of energy. For this energy, the most feasible regions are those that:
(a) Are near the coastal regions (b) Have coal mines
(c) Have thermal power plants (d) Are over hot spots in the crust

20.7 Nuclear energy cannot be counted under renewable energy sources due to:
(i) Presence of uranium deposits
(ii) Presence of nuclear waste
(iii) Presence of nuclear pollutants due to nuclear waste
Which one is the correct answer?
(a) Both (i) and (ii) are correct (b) Both (ii) and (iii) are correct
(c) Both (i) and (iii) are correct (d) All (i), (ii) and (iii) are correct

20.8 The group of solar cells joined together in a definite pattern is called a:
(a) Battery (b) Solar heater
(c) Solar cooker (d) Solar cell panel

20.9 For a standard PV panel, the maximum sunlight conversion to electricity will be around:
(a) 75% (b) 20% (c) 42% (d) 5%

20.10 Sunlight completely falls with 25% efficiency on a solar cell having an area of 4 m^2 at an angle of incidence of 60° to the cell. Find the output power of the cell.

(a) 150 W (b) 350 W (c) 500 W (d) 650 W

20.11 The surface temperature and emissive power of a grey opaque surface is 60°C and 800 W/m^2, respectively. What will be the surface's radiosity when solar radiation having 1000 W/m^2 falls perpendicular on it with emissivity 0.5.

(a) 700 W/m^2 (b) 1000 W/m^2 (c) 1100 W/m^2 (d) 1300 W/m^2

20.12 The maximum achievable efficiency of the wind turbine as per Betz limit is:

(a) 75.7% (b) 59.3% (c) 45.5% (d) 60%

20.13 The commercially available biomass fuel is not:

(a) Straw (b) Wood chips (c) Pellets (d) Husk

20.14 In a typical flat-plate solar collector, for absorbing more heat, which among the following is used?

(a) Glazing covers (b) Absorber plates
(c) Insulation layers (d) Recuperating tubes

20.15 The purpose of concentric glass cover in focusing type solar collector is to:

(i) Reduce fluid losses
(ii) Reduce convective losses
(iii) Reduce radiative losses

Which is the correct answer?

(a) Both (i) and (ii) are the correct answer
(b) Both (ii) and (iii) are the correct answer
(c) Both (i) and (iii) are the correct answer
(d) Only (iii) is correct

20.16 The Energy Park Scheme in 1998–99 promoted by the Ministry of New and Renewable Energy Sources was to:

(a) Promote fixed and portable type of Chulhas in household
(b) Promote solar water heating systems in offices
(c) Promote students and teachers to understand the working of renewable energy systems
(d) Promote shopkeepers to sell renewable energy systems

20.17 Under the four levels of energy audit analysis, which level describes the assessment of building energy efficiency?

(a) Level 0 (b) Level 1 (c) Level 2 (d) Level 3

20.18 Choose the incorrect statement regarding wind power:

(a) It is expected to harness wind power to a minimum in open space.
(b) The potential energy content of wind blowing at high altitudes is the source of wind power.
(c) Wind hitting at the blades of a windmill causes them to rotate. The rotation thus achieved can be utilised further.
(d) One possible method of utilising the energy of rotational motion of the blades of a windmill is to run the turbine of an electric generator.

20.19 Smart metre is an essential element in building the smart grid. These advanced metres

(a) Measure electricity usage in real time
(b) Can send data to and from electric companies and their customers
(c) Allows computers to give consumers more information about their electricity usage and communicate current electricity prices
(d) All of the above

20.20 Smart grid technologies are aimed at improvement of
(a) Only Power Transmission System
(b) Only Power Distribution System
(c) Both Power Transmission and Distribution System
(d) Neither Power Transmission nor Power Distribution System

20.21 Which is not the key driver of smart grids?
(a) Reduction of T&D losses in all utilities as well as improved collection efficiency
(b) Peak load management
(c) Financial sound utilities
(d) Timely completion of projects

20.22 What is the full form of DR in the context of smart grids?
(a) Delivery rate (b) Divide and rule
(c) Demand response (d) Dangerous regions

20.23 Is dynamic programming part of an optimisation technique used in smart grids?
(a) Yes (b) No

20.24 Sensors cannot be used for the following purposes in smart grids:
(a) Detect mechanical failures; the tower collapses, extreme mechanical conditions
(b) Real-time mechanical and electrical conditions of power lines
(c) Diagnose imminent as well as permanent faults
(d) Maintains balanced load in industrial areas

20.25 Which is not used to manage the demand on a smart grid network?
(a) Shifting demand to another time or day
(b) Use of excessive energy
(c) Rescheduling usage
(d) Reducing consumption

20.26 Which layer is not related to smart grid communication?
(a) Application layer (b) Communication layer
(c) Cross-platform layer (d) Power layer
(e) Control and Security layers

20.27 Which is not used in wireless technologies?
(a) Powerline communication (b) Cellular
(c) Cognitive radio (d) Satellite

20.28 The long-term benefits of demand response are given below.
(i) Reduce peak demand (ii) Increase network life
(iii) Increase reliability (iv) Postpone upgrades
Which is the correct answer?
(a) Only (i), (ii) and (iii) are correct.
(b) Only (ii), (iii) and (iv) are correct
(c) Only (ii) and (iii) are correct
(d) All are correct

20.29 A localised grouping of electricity generations, energy storages and loads is termed as:
(a) Virtual power plant (b) Macro grid
(c) Microgrid (d) Traditional grid

20.30 Which is not the communication dimensions for a smart grid.
(a) Reliability and stability (b) Understandability and clarity
(c) Measurability and stability (d) Availability and flexibility

References

Papers

1. M. Rizwan, M. Jamil, and D.P. Kothari, "Generalized Neural Network Approach for Global Solar Energy Estimation in India", *IEEE Transactions on Sustainable Energy*, volume: 3, issue: 3, pp: 576–584, 2012.
2. S. Morozumi, S. Kikuchi, Y. Chiba, et al., "Distribution Technology Development and Demonstration Projects in Japan", *2008 IEEE Power and Energy Society General Meeting - Conversion and Delivery of Electrical Energy in the 21st Century*, July 20–24, 2008.
3. S. Kasa, P. Ramanathan, S. Ramasamy, and D.P. Kothari, "Effective Grid Interfaced Renewable Sources With Power Quality Improvement Using Dynamic Active Power Filter", *International Journal of Electrical Power & Energy Systems*, volume: 82, pp: 150–160, 2016.
4. N. Hatziargyriou, H. Asano, R. Iravani, and C. Marnay, "Microgrids", *IEEE Power and Energy Magazine*, volume: 5, issue: 4, pp: 78–94, July–Aug 2007.
5. B. Singh, P. Jayaprakash, S. Kumar, and D.P. Kothari, "Implementation of Neural-Network-Controlled Three-Leg VSC and a Transformer as Three-Phase Four-Wire DSTATCOM", *IEEE Transactions on Industry Applications*, volume: 47, issue: 4, pp: a1892–1901, 2011.
6. M. Begoviae, A. Pregelj, A. Rohatgi, et al., "Impact of Renewable Distributed Generation on Power Systems", in Proceeding of the 34th Hawaii International Conference on System Sciences, 2001.
7. European Commission (2006), "European Smart Grids Technology Platform: Vision and Strategy for Europe's Electricity", Available at: http://ec.europa.eu/research/energy/pdf/smartgrids_en.pdf (Accessed on 4 August 2011).
8. "U.S. Department of Energy, Smart Grid System Report", July 2009, Available at: http://www.oe.energy.gov/sites/prod/files/oeprod/DocumentsandMedia/SGSRMain_090707_lowres.pdf (Accessed on 4 August 2011).
9. "Department of Energy and Climate Change", UK, Smarter Grids: The Opportunity, December 2009, Available at: http://www.decc.gov.uk/assets/decc/what%20we%20do/uk%20energy 20 supply/futureelectricitynetworks/1_20091203163757_e_@@_smartergridsopportunity.pdf (Accessed on 4 August 2011).
10. "A Compendium of Modern Grid Technologies", July 2009, Available at: http://www.netl.doe.gov/smartgrid/referenceshelf/whitepapers/Compendium_of_Technologies_APPROVED_2009_08_18.pdf (Accessed on 4 August 2011).
11. "European Commission, ICT for a Low Carbon Economy: Smart Electricity Distribution Networks", July 2009, Available at: http://ec.europa.eu/information_society/activities/sustainable_growth/docs/sb_publications/pub_smart_edn_web.pdf (Accessed on 4 August 2011)
12. World Economic Forum (2009), "Accelerating Smart Grid Investments", Available at: http://www.weforum.org/pdf/SlimCity/SmartGrid2009.pdf (Accessed on 4 August 2011).
13. Y. Kojima, M. Koshio, S. Nakamura, et al., "A Demonstration Project in Hachinohe: Microgrid With Private Distribution Line", IEEE International Conference on SoSE '07, pp: 1–6, April 16–18, 2007.
14. IEEE Standard for Interconnecting Distributed Resources With Electric Power Systems, IEEE Standard, 1547, 2003.
15. R.H. Lasseter, "The Role of Distributed Energy Resources in Future Electric Power Systems", Energy Systems Seminar, March, 2006.
16. R. Aggarwal and P. Moore, "Digital communications for protection", *Power Engineering Journal*, volume: 7, issue: 6, pp: 281–287, 1993.

17. N. Jenkins, J.B. Ekanayake, and G. Strbac (2010), "Distributed Generation", IET, London.
18. P. Djapic, C. Ramsay, D. Pudjianto, et al, "Taking an Active Approach", *IEEE Power and Energy Magazine*, volume: 5, issue: 4, pp: 68–77, 2007.
19. D. Debnath, A. De, A. Chakrabarti, and D.P. Kothari, "Studies on the Impact of Capacitor Bank Switching on Grid Connected Transformers", *International Journal of Electrical Power & Energy Systems*, volume: 43, issue: 1, pp: 126–130, 2012.
20. S.P. Bihari, P.K. Sadhu, Kumari Sarita, B. Khan, L.D. Arya, R.K. Saket, D.P. Kothari, "A Comprehensive Review of Microgrid Control Mechanism and Impact Assessment for Hybrid Renewable Energy Integration," *IEEE Access*, volume: 9, pp. 88942–88958, 2021.
21. K. Palanisamy, D.P. Kothari, M.K. Mishra, S. Meikandashivam, and I.J. Raglend, "Effective Utilization of Unified Power Quality Conditioner for Interconnecting PV Modules With Grid Using Power Angle Control Method", *International Journal of Electrical Power & Energy Systems*, volume: 48, pp: 131–138, 2013.
22. S. Kumari, S. Kumar, and R.K. Saket, "Open-Circuit Fault Diagnosis of Multilevel Converter Using Entropy Features-Based SVM Technique Along With Two-Samples Based Detection Algorithm", *Computers & Electrical Engineering*, Early Access, 2021.
23. P. Jayaprakash, B. Singh, D.P. Kothari, A. Chandra, and K. Al-Haddad, "Control of Reduced-Rating Dynamic Voltage Restorer With a Battery Energy Storage System", *IEEE Transactions on Industry Applications*, volume: 50, issue: 2, pp: 1295–1303, 2013.
24. S. Kumar, S. Kumari, A.S.S. Vardhan, R. Elavarasan, R.K. Saket, and N. Das, "Reliability Assessment of Wind-Solar PV Integrated Distribution System Using Electrical Loss Minimization Technique", *Energies*, volume: 13, issue: 21, pp: 5631, 2020.
25. S. Upadhyay, D.P. Kothari, and U. Shanker, "Renewable Energy Technologies for Cooking: Transforming Rural Lives", *IEEE Technology and Society Magazine*, volume: 32, issue: 3, pp: 65–72, 2013.
26. B. Singh, P. Jayaprakash, D.P. Kothari, A. Chandra, and K. Al Haddad, "Comprehensive Study of DSTATCOM Configurations", *IEEE Transactions on Industrial Informatics*, volume: 10, issue: 2, pp: 854–870, 2014.
27. Sachin Kumar, R.K. Saket, D.K. Dheer, P. Sanjeevikumar, and F. Blaabjerg, "Layout Optimization Algorithms and Reliability Assessment of Wind Farm for Microgrid Integration: A Comprehensive Review", *IET Renewable Power Generation*, volume: 15, issue: 10, pp: 2063–2084, 2021.
28. M. Rizwan, M. Jamil, S. Kirmani, and D.P. Kothari, "Fuzzy Logic Based Modeling and Estimation of Global Solar Energy Using Meteorological Parameters", *Energy*, volume: 70, pp: 685–691, 2014.
29. S. Kumar, R.K. Saket, D.K. Dheer, J.B. Holm-Nielsen, and P. Sanjeevikumar, "Reliability Enhancement of Electrical Power System Including Impacts of Renewable Energy Sources: A Comprehensive Review", *IET Generation, Transmission & Distribution*, volume: 14, issue: 10, pp: 1799–1815, 2020.
30. S. Mishra, C.K. Panigrahi, and D.P. Kothari, "Design and Simulation of a Solar–Wind–Biogas Hybrid System Architecture Using HOMER in India", *International Journal of Ambient Energy*, volume: 37, issue: 2, pp: 184–191, 2016.
31. S. Kumari, S. Kumar, A. Singh, S. Vardhan, R.M. Elavarasan, R.K. Saket, G.M. Shafiullah, and E. Hossain. "Power Enhancement With Grid Stabilization of Renewable Energy-Based Generation System Using UPQC-FLC-EVA Technique", *IEEE Access*, volume: 8, pp: 207443–207464, 2020.

CHAPTER

21 Power System Reliability

21.1 ▶ INTRODUCTION

Reliability is an old concept and a new discipline of engineering and technology. Things, systems and people have been called reliable for ages if they have lived up to certain expectations and unreliable otherwise. A reliable person would never fail to deliver what he had promised. The types of expectations to judge reliability by having all been related to some function or duty performance. A device's reliability has been considered high if it had repeatedly performed its functions with success and low if it had tended to fail in repeated trials. Experience has helped to form advance estimates as to the degree of trust that one could place in success, or extend that one had to fear failure.

Reliability theory as an extension of probability theory was first applied in electronics, nuclear and space industries after the Second World War, where high reliability was a requirement from these increasingly complex systems. The reliability theory developed was mainly applicable to these specific fields. Since the first failure is most important in such an application, the theory idea of reliability was mainly developed for non-repairable systems. The development of reliability analysis methods for the repairable system was at a slow pace. Concurrently with the development of reliability aspects, an enormous amount of component failure data was collected, analysed and published in the field of electronics engineering. Nowadays, reliability studies are performed in almost all engineering branches. Such studies evolve applications for both repairable and non-repairable systems in all areas.

The beginning of the reliability theory developments can be traced back to the days of the Second World War. The first formal reliability evaluation was reported to occur when an explanation was sought for the poor performance of the German V-1 and V-2 missiles. These were constructed of a large number of components considered highly reliable. The main problems related to reliability evaluation of component or system are lack of data, limitation of computational resources, lack of realistic reliability techniques, aversion to probabilistic approaches and misunderstanding of the significance and meaning of probabilistic criteria and risk indices. These reasons are not valid today since most utilities have useful and applicable data, reliability evaluation techniques are very developed and most engineers have a working understanding of probabilistic approaches. Our intention in this chapter is to illustrate the development of reliability evaluation techniques suitable for power system applications and to explain the significance of the various reliability indices that can be evaluated.

Whenever the reliability of a component, device and system affects human life, the reliability problem usually becomes part of a large issue known as safety considerations. The reliability considerations are essential factors in any engineering design. Such concerns evaluate system usefulness or goodness, accounting the required constraints imposed on the system, one of the important constraints as the system's cost. This might be the operating cost or planning cost, including initial investment.

The reliability analysis must also include the operating environment, time of operation and quality of service rendered by the system. Naturally, under these considerations, the utility or goodness of the system must be judged not quantitatively but by a numerical measure based on probability theory and known as reliability index since any qualitative judgement is meaningless for any engineer who is designing or planning a system. The operating environment must get due consideration. This environment will affect the failure rate of the system. For example, a transmission line installed in coastal areas and those in the region having fair weather conditions will have different failure and repair rates; hence, it will have a different probability of success and failure. Therefore, any reliability modelling must account for the operating environment.

Naturally, the time of operation of a repairable or non-repairable component is of significant concern. The probability of a system's successful operation decreases for an increase in the intended time of operation of a system. Quality of service requires special attention because it may assist, but it may not satisfy the consumer. For example, electricity supply may be available at some consumer's premises, but supply voltage and frequency may be too low to use it effectively in a production process. Hence, the classical definition of reliability may be stated as the probability of a component performing its required function adequately for the intended period of operation under a given operating environment.

21.2 ▶ CONCEPT OF RELIABILITY

Reliability engineering is the study of the longevity and the failure of equipment. The principle of science and mathematics is applied to the investigation of how devices age and fail. The intent is that a better understanding of device failure will help identify ways in which product designs can be improved to increase life length and limit the adverse consequences of failure. The key point here is that the focus is on design. New product and system designs must be safe and reliable before their fabrication and use. Nowadays, reliability studies are performed in almost all engineering branches. Such studies evolve applications for both repairable and non-repairable systems in all areas.

Electric power systems are prime examples of a system where a very high degree of reliability is expected. The reliability is usually divided into adequacy and security. Adequacy relates to the existence of sufficient facilities within the system to satisfy the customer load demand. These include the facilities necessary to generate adequate energy and the associated transmission and distribution facilities required to transport the energy to the actual customer load points. Adequacy assessment usually required probabilistic models for different parts of the power system, such as load and generation. Security relates to the ability of the system to respond to disturbances arising within that system.

In engineering applications, concepts must have numerical measures; that is, procedures must be available. Various magnitudes of each are correlated with a number scale. Thus, by which their actual amounts can be measured. Therefore, before reliability is transplanted into engineering applications, it must be converted into one or several measurable quantities by suitable definitions. Reliability is the probability of a device or system performing its function adequately for the period intended, under the operating conditions intended. The reliability is defined through the mathematical concept of probability. The expected performance can be very different in different applications. Electric power systems are prime examples of the system where a very high degree of reliability is expected. In many power systems, the average duration of interruptions that a customer an experience is a total of 2–3 hr/yr, and can be much less than that in some areas. A high degree of reliability is also essential for some industrial customers. For this reason, reliability is and always has been one of the major factors in the planning, design, operation and maintenance of electric power systems. The formal concepts and reliability theory methods have been applied to almost every aspect of power system reliability evaluations.

The reliability of an electric power supply system has been defined as the probability of providing the users with continuous service of satisfactory quality. The quality constraint refers to the requirement that the frequency and the voltage of the power supply should remain within prescribed tolerances. The actual degree of reliability experienced by a customer will, of course, vary from location to location. In addition, different parts of the power network, such as the generation, transmission and distribution system, will exhibit different reliabilities. It is easy to see that achieve the degree of reliability quoted above at the customer level; each of these systems must provide an even higher degree of reliability.

The concept of adequacy is generally considered to be the existence of sufficient facilities within the system to satisfy consumer demand. These facilities include those necessary to generate adequate energy and the associated transmission and distribution networks required to transport the energy to the actual consumer load points. Adequacy is therefore considered to be related to static conditions which do not include system disturbances. On the other hand, security is considered to connect to the system's ability to respond to disruptions arising within that system. Security is therefore associated with the response of the system to whatever disturbances they are subjected. These are considered to include conditions causing local and widespread effects and the loss of significant generation and transmission facilities.

The most convenient approach for dividing the system is to use its main functional zones. These are generation systems, composite generation and transmission (or bulk power) systems, and distribution systems. These primary functional zones can be sub-divided to study a subset of the problem. Particular sub-zones include individual generating stations, substations and protection systems. The determination of the required amount of system generating capacity to ensure an adequate supply is an essential aspect of power system planning and operation.

The total problem can be divided into 2 conceptually different areas designated as static and operating capacity requirements. The static capacity area relates to the long-term evaluation of this overall system requirement. The operating capacity area relates to the short-term assessment of the actual capacity required to meet a given load level. Both areas must be examined at the planning level in evaluating alternative facilities; however, once the decision has been made, the short-term requirement becomes a functional problem. The fundamental generating unit parameter used in the static capacity evaluation is the probability of finding the unit on the forced outage at some distant time in the future. The probability was defined in engineering systems as the unit unavailability, and historically in power system applications, it is known as the unit forced outage rate.

21.2.1 Life Distribution of Power Components: An Overview

In principle, any distribution may be used to model equipment longevity. In practice, distribution functions having monotonic hazard functions seem most realistic, and within that class, there are a few that are generally thought to provide the most reasonable models of device reliability. The most common choices of life distribution models are given below.

Binomial Distribution Consider a trial in which there are only 2 possible outcomes, say, success or failure. Let p be the probability of success, and $(1 - p) = q$ is the failure in any one experiment. Consider X is the random variable that equals the number of success in n trials. Then the probability getting x success is $b(x, n, p) = {}^nC_x p^x q^{n-x}$, where $x = 0, 1, 2, \ldots, n$ and combinatorial quantities ${}^nC_x = \dfrac{n!}{(n-x)!x!}$ are referred to as binomial coefficients. This distribution is called a binomial distribution.

Corollary: The sum of the probabilities

$$\sum_{x=0}^{n} f(x) = \sum_{x=0}^{n} {}^nC_x p^x q^{n-x} = q^n + {}^nC_1 p^1 q^{n-1} + \cdots + p^n + (q+p)^n = 1 \tag{21.1}$$

The applications of the binomial distribution are the evaluation of the number of rounds fired from a gun hitting a target, radar detection in military support systems, calculation of numbers of defectives in a sample from the production line and estimation of reliability of interconnected bulk power system.

Exponential Distribution The most widely used distribution function for modelling reliability is the exponential distribution. It is such a popular device reliability model because it is algebraically simple and thus tractable and is considered representative of the device life cycle's functional life interval. The device is expected to be absolute before reaching the wear-out period, so an appropriate device reliability model is one having constant hazard.

Definition: A continuous random variable X assuming non-negative values is said to have an exponential distribution with parameter $\alpha > 0$ if its PDF is given by

$$f(x) = \begin{cases} \alpha e^{-\alpha x}, & x \geq 0 \\ 0, & \text{otherwise} \end{cases}$$

The distribution function $\{F(x)\}$ is given by

$$F(x) = \int_0^x \alpha e^{-\alpha x} dx. \tag{21.2}$$

Poisson Distribution The Poisson variants' probability density function can be obtained as a limiting case of the binomial probability density function when $p \to 0$ and $n \to \infty$. Thus Poisson distribution is the distribution of a variable x with relative frequency.

$$f(x,m) = \frac{e^{-m} m^x}{x!} \quad \text{and} \quad \sum_{x=0}^{\infty} f(x,m) = \sum_{x=0}^{\infty} \frac{e^{-m} m^x}{x!} = e^{-m} \sum_{x=0}^{\infty} \frac{m^x}{x!} = e^{-m} e^m = 1. \tag{21.3}$$

It is an exponential probability distribution with only one parameter, 'm'.

The applications of Poisson distribution are the evaluation of the spatial distribution of bomb hits, estimation of several fragments from a shell hitting a target, evaluation of arrival pattern of defective vehicles in an engineering workshop, demand pattern for certain spare parts, and reliability evaluation of power components.

Example 21.1 A manufacturer of capacitors knows that 5% of his product is defective. Suppose he sells capacitors in boxes of 100 and guarantees that not more than 10 capacitors will be faulty. What is the approximate probability that a box will fail to meet the guaranteed quality?

Solution Given $n = 100$

Let p = probability of a defective capacitors = 5% = 0.05

$\therefore$ m = mean number of defective capacitors in a box of 100 = np = 100 × 0.05 = 5.

Since p is small, we can use Poisson distribution. Probability of x defective capacitors in a box of 100 is

$$P(X = x) = \frac{e - mmx}{x!} = \frac{e - 55x}{x!}, x = 0, 1, 2, \ldots$$

The probability that a box will fail to meet the guaranteed quality is,

$$P(X > 10) = 1 - P(X \leq 10) = 1 - \sum_{x=0}^{10} \frac{e^{-5} 5^x}{x!} = 1 - e^{-5} \sum_{x=0}^{10} \frac{e^{-5} 5^x}{x!} = 1 - e^{-5} \sum_{x=0}^{\infty} \frac{5^x}{x!}$$

$$\Rightarrow [1 - P(X \leq 10)] = 1 - e^{-5} \left[\frac{5^0}{0!} + \frac{5^1}{1!} + \frac{5^2}{2!} + \frac{5^3}{3!} \cdots \frac{5^{10}}{10!} \right]$$

$\Rightarrow [1 - P(X \le 10)] = 1 - e^{-5} [1 + 5 + 12.5 + 20.8333 + 26.0417 + 26.0417 + 21.7014 + 15.5001 + 9.6881 + 5.3823 + 2.6911]$

$\Rightarrow [1 - P(X \le 10)] = 1 - e^{-5} [146.3797] = 1 - 0.00673 \times 146.3797 = (1 - 0.985135) = 0.0148646$

Geometric Distribution Suppose in an experiment, the number of trials n is not fixed. If the first success is to come on the Xth trial, it has to be preceded by $(x - 1)$ failures, and if the probability of success is p, the probability of $(x - 1)$ failures in $(x - 1)$ trials is $(1 - p)x - 1$.

Definition: A random variable X is said to have a geometric distribution if it assumes only non-negative values and its probability mass function is given by

$$P(X = x) = \begin{cases} pq^{x-1}, & x = 1, 2, 3, \ldots, 0 < p \le 1, q = 1 - p \\ 0, & \text{otherwise.} \end{cases} \tag{21.4}$$

This probability distribution is called the geometric distribution.

Example 21.2 A circuit breaker is operating in a composite power system independently. The probability that the circuit breaker works successfully during any 1 fault is 0.7.

(i) What is the probability that the protection would be an attempt on the 10th attempt?
(ii) What is the probability that it takes less than 4 attempts?
(iii) What is the probability that it takes an even number of attempts?

Solution Here $p = 0.7$ then $q = (1 - p) = 0.3$

(i) The probability that the target would be attempt on 10th attempt = $(0.7)\,(0.3)^{10-1} = (0.7)\,(0.3)^9 = 0.000014$.
(ii) The probability that it takes less than 4 attempts is

$$P(X < 4) = \sum_{n=1}^{4-1} pq^{n-1} = \sum_{n=1}^{3} (0.7)(0.3)^{n-1}$$
$$= (0.7)[(0.3)^0 + (0.3)^1 + (0.3)^2] = (0.7)[1 + 0.3 + 0.09]$$
$$= (0.7)(1.39) = 0.973.$$

(iii) The probability that it has taken an even number of attempts.

$$\sum_{n=1}^{\infty} (0.7)(0.3)^{2n-1} = (0.7)(0.3)\sum_{n=1}^{\infty} (0.3)^{2n-2} = (0.7)(0.3)\frac{1}{1-(0.3)^2} = 0.23$$

Normal Distribution Definition: A continuous X is said to follow a normal distribution or Gaussian distribution with parameters μ and σ if its probability density function is given by

$$f(x) = \frac{1}{\sigma\sqrt{2\pi}} e^{-\frac{1}{2}\left(\frac{x-\mu}{\sigma}\right)^2}; \quad -\infty < x < \infty \tag{21.5}$$

Symbolically, X follows $N(\mu, \sigma)$, Here mean of $X = \mu$ and standard deviation $= \sigma$.

The total area bounded by the normal curve and the X-axis is 1. The area under the curve between 2 ordinates $X = a$ and $X = b$ (where $a < b$) represents the probability that X lies between a and b. This probability is denoted by $P[a < X < b]$.

Suppose the variable X is expressed in terms of standard units $[Z = (X - \mu)/\sigma]$, equation (21.5) is replaced as $\phi(Z) = \frac{1}{\sqrt{2\pi}} e^{-\frac{z^2}{2}}$, $-\infty < Z < \infty$ and is called standard normal distribution. This is obtained by putting $\mu = 0$ and $\sigma = 1$ and by changing x into Z, i.e., if X has the distribution.

$$N(\mu, \sigma) \text{ then } Z = \left(\frac{X-\mu}{\sigma}\right) \text{ has the distribution } N(0, 1).$$

Some properties of the normal distribution given by equation (21.5) are listed below:

Mean = μ, Variance = σ^2, standard deviation = σ

$$\text{Mean deviation about the mean} = \int_{-\infty}^{\infty} |x-\mu| f(x)dx = \sqrt{\frac{2}{\pi}}\sigma = \frac{4}{5}\sigma \text{ (approx.)}$$

$$\text{Quartile deviation} = \frac{2}{3}\sigma$$

Moment generating function of $N(\mu, \sigma)$

$$M_x(t) = M_{\sigma Z+\mu}(t) \qquad \left(\because Z = \frac{X-\mu}{\sigma}\right)$$

$$= e^{\mu t} M_z(\sigma t)$$

$$= e^{\mu t} \cdot e^{\sigma 2t2/2} \qquad (\text{since } Mz(t) = e^{t^2/2} \text{ verify it})$$

$$= e^{t\left(\mu+\frac{\sigma^2 t}{2}\right)} = 1 + \frac{t}{1!}\left(\mu+\frac{\sigma^2 t}{2}\right) + \frac{t^2}{2!}\left(\mu+\frac{\sigma^2 t}{2}\right)^2 + \cdots \qquad (21.6)$$

$\therefore E(X) = \mu;\ E(X^2) = \sigma^2 + \mu^2, \ldots$

Thus, we get $\mu_1 = 0$, $\mu_2 = \sigma^2$, $\mu_3 = 0$; $\mu_4 = 3\sigma^4$ etc.

The standard distribution approach applications are the computation of hit probability of a shot, estimation of statistical inference in almost every branch of science and technology, calculation of errors made by chance in experimental measurements and reliability evaluation of composite power systems.

Example 21.3 The lifetime of specific electronics devices has a mean of 300 hours and a standard deviation of 25 hours. Assuming that these lifetimes' distribution is measured to the nearest hour can be approximated closely with a standard curve. Find the probability that any electronic device will have a lifetime of more than 35 hours.

(i) What percentage will have lifetimes of 300 hours or less?

(ii) What percentage will have lifetimes from 220 or 260 hours?

Solution Here X follows $N(\mu = 300, \sigma = 25)$

(i) $$P(X > 350) = \left[\frac{X-300}{25} > \frac{350-300}{25}\right]$$

$$= \phi[Z > 2] = 1 - \phi(Z \le 2)$$

$$= 1 - 0.9772 = 0.0228$$

$$P(X = 300) = \left[\frac{X-300}{25} > \frac{300-300}{25}\right]$$

$$= \phi(Z = 0) = 0.5000$$

$\therefore$ The required percentage = $0.5 \times 100 = 50\%$

(ii) $$P(220 \le X \le 260) = \phi(-3.2 \le Z \le -1.6)$$

$$= \phi(-1.6) - \phi(-3.2)$$

$$= [1 - \phi(1.6)] - [1 - \phi(3.2)]$$

$$= [1 - 0.9452] - [1 - 0.9903]$$

$$= 0.0548 - 0.0007 = 0.0541$$

∴ The required percentage = 0.0541 × 100 = 5.41%

Gamma Distribution Definition: Continuous random variables X, which is distributed accordingly to the probability law.

$$f(x) = \begin{cases} \dfrac{e^{-x}x^{\alpha-1}}{\Gamma(\alpha)} & \alpha > 0, 0 < x < \infty \\ 0, & \text{otherwise} \end{cases} \tag{21.7}$$

It is known as a Gamma variable with parameter α and referred to as $\Gamma(\alpha)$ variant and its distribution is called the Gamma distribution.

Remarks: The function $f(x)$ defined above represents a probability function, since

$$\int_0^\infty f(x)dx = \frac{1}{\Gamma(\alpha)}; \int_0^\infty e^{-x}x^{\alpha-1}dx = 1 \tag{21.8}$$

A continuous random variable having the following PDF is said to have a gamma distribution with parameter α, u

$$f(x) = \begin{cases} \dfrac{\alpha^u}{\Gamma(u)} e^{-ax}x^{u-1}; & \alpha, u > 0, 0 < x < \infty \\ 0, & \text{otherwise} \end{cases} \tag{21.9}$$

21.3 ▶ BASIC CONCEPTS OF SYSTEM RELIABILITY

The main attributes of reliability are probability, adequate function, a period and the operating condition of the system. The reliability of a system or a component will often depend on the length of time it has been in service. Thus, of fundamental importance in reliability studies is the failure-time distribution that is the distribution of the time to failure of a component under given environmental conditions. The power system component may be repairable or non-repairable.

A component will be termed repairable if it can be restored to its original condition after it has failed, without affecting system operation. Availability, maintainability, mean time to failure (MTTF), mean time to repair (MTTR), mean uptime (MUT), mean downtime (MDT), mean time between failure (MTBF) and loss of load probability (LOLP) are the main keywords of the power system reliability. A useful way to characterise this distribution is by utilising its associated instantaneous failure rate.

21.3.1 Reliability Functions

Let a component is put into operation at some specified time, say $t = 0$, and let $f(t)$ be the probability density of the time to failure of a given component. The probability that the component will fail between times to failure of a given component is the probability that the component will fail between t and $t + \Delta t$ is given by $f(t)\Delta t$. Then the probability that the component will fail on the inter from 0 to t is provided by the cumulative distribution function of $t, F(t) = \int_0^t f(x)dx$ and the reliability function, expressing the probability that it survives to time t, is given by $R(t) = 1 - F(t)$.

The probability of success, thus the probability that the component will fail in the interval from t to $t + \Delta t$ is $F(t + \Delta t) - F(t)$, and the conditional probability of failure in this interval, given that the component survived to time t, is expressed by

$$\frac{F(t+\Delta t)-F(t)}{Rt} \tag{21.10}$$

Dividing by Δt, we find that the average rate of failure in the interval from t to $t + \Delta t$, given that the component survived to time t, is

$$\frac{F(t+\Delta t)-F(t)}{\Delta t}\cdot\frac{1}{R(t)} \tag{21.11}$$

Taking the limit as $\Delta t \to 0$, we then get the instantaneous failure rate, or simply the failure rate

$$Z(t)=\frac{F'(t)}{R(t)}=\frac{1}{R(t)}\frac{dF}{dt}(t). \tag{21.12}$$

Finally, observing that the PDF $= f(t) = \dfrac{dF(t)}{dt}$, we get the relation $Z(t) = \dfrac{f(t)}{1-F(t)}$ (21.13)

Let us now derive an important relationship expressing the failure – time density in terms of the failure rate function. Making use of the fact that the reliability function $R(t) = 1 - F(t)$ and hence, that $F'(t) = -R'(t)$, $Z(t)$ can be written as

$$Z(t)=-\frac{R'(t)}{R(t)} \tag{21.14}$$

Solving this differential equation for $R(t)$, we obtain

$$\log R(t) = -\int_0^t Z(x)ax$$

$$\Rightarrow \quad R(t) = e^{\int_0^t z(x)ax} \tag{21.15}$$

And, making use of the relation $f(t) = Z(t)\,R(t)$,

Finally we get $f(t) = Z(t)\exp\left[-\int_0^t Z(x)ax\right]$. This equation is called general equation for failure – time distribution. Relation between reliability functions are illustrated in following Table 21.1.

Table 21.1 Relation between probabilistic functions

–	**F(t)**	**f(t)**	**R(t)**	**h(t)**
$F(t)$	–	$\int_0^t f(t)\,dt$	$1 - R(t)$	$1-e^{-\int_0^t h(t)dt}$
$f(t)$	$\dfrac{dF(t)}{dt}$	–	$-\dfrac{dR(t)}{dt}$	$h(t)e^{-\int_0^t h(t)dt}$
$R(t)$	$1 - F(t)$	$\int_0^\infty f(t)dt$	–	$e^{-\int_0^t h(t)dt}$
$h(t)$	$\dfrac{dF(t)}{dt}\Big/[1-F(t)]$	$\dfrac{f(t)}{\int_0^\infty f(t)dt}$	$-\dfrac{d}{dt}\log R(t)$	–

For a constant failure rate, the following relations are given for reliability assessment of the power components.

(1) Reliability function $R(t) = e^{-\int_0^t h(t)dt}$
put $h(t) = \lambda$ = constant failure rate of the components
$R(t) = e^{-\int_0^\infty \lambda dt}$
$R(t) = e^{-\lambda t}$
$R(t) = (1 - P_f)$
The failure probability of power component $P_f = [1 - R(t)] = (1 - e^{-\lambda t})$

(2) The failure density facture (PDF) of power component $f(t) = \dfrac{-dR(t)}{dt}$
$f(t) = \lambda e^{-\lambda t}$

(3) The mean time to failure (MTTF) $= \int_0^\infty R(t)dt$

$\text{MTTF} = \int_0^\infty e^{-\lambda t} dt$

$\text{MTTF} = \dfrac{1}{\lambda}$

$R(t) = e^{-\lambda t}$

21.3.2 Mean Time to Failure (MTTF) of Component

We are often interested in knowing the MTTF of the component rather than the complete failure details. The parameter is assumed to be identical for all the same design components and operate under similar conditions. If we have life tests information on a population of N items with failure time $t_1, t_2, \ldots, t_n$, then the MTTF is defined as:

$$\text{MTTF} = \frac{1}{N}\sum_{i=1}^{n} t_i \tag{21.16}$$

However, suppose its reliability function describes a component. In that case, the MTTF is given by the mathematical expectation of the random variable T describing the time to failure of the component. Therefore,

$$\text{MTTF} = E[T] = \int_0^\infty tf(t)\,dt \tag{21.17}$$

But $f(t)\dfrac{dF(t)}{dt} = -\dfrac{dR(t)}{dt}$. Hence

$$\text{MTTF} = -\int_0^\infty tdR(t)dt = -[tR(t)]_0^\infty + \int_0^\infty R(t)dt$$

$$= \int_0^\infty R(t)dt \qquad (\because R(\infty) = 0)$$

$$\text{MTTF} = \int_0^\infty R(t)dt \tag{21.18}$$

The MTTF can also be computed using the Laplace transform of $R(t)$,

i.e., $$\text{MTTF} = \int_0^\infty R(t)dt \; \underset{t\to\infty}{Lt} \int_0^\infty R(t)dt$$

However, $\underset{t\to\infty}{Lt}\int_0^t R(x)dx = \underset{s\to 0}{Lt}\ R(s)$,

Thus,
$$\text{MTTF} = \underset{s\to 0}{Lt}\ R(s) \tag{21.19}$$

Remark: Var $(T) = E\,[T - E\,(T)]^2 = E[T^2] - [E(T)]^2 \int_0^t t^2 f(t)dt - (\text{MTTF})2$

21.4 ▶ RELIABILITY ANALYSIS OF POWER SYSTEM STRUCTURES

Among reliability specialists, it is generally accepted that there are 3 generic types of structural relationships between a device and its components. These are series, parallel and series-parallel (k-out-of-n systems). This section shall discuss the system reliability for these simple but relatively essential cases. All models are based on the assumptions that the components fall independently of each other, i.e., the failure of 1 component does not change the failure of other components.

21.4.1 Reliability Estimation of Series Systems

The simplest and most commonly encountered configuration of components is the series system. The formal definition of a series system is: a series system is one in which all components must function properly for the system to work correctly. Series or non-redundant system is one in which the components of the system are connected. Consider a system having a total of n components for reliability estimation.

In a series configuration, all the components must function for the system to function. In other words, the failure of any component causes system failure. Several complex systems are reduced to such a simple structure.

Let E_i denotes that the component i is good (i.e., functions satisfactorily) and E_i the event that the component i is bad. The event representing system success is then the intersection of $E_1, E_2,\ldots, E_n$. Let $R_i(t)$ be the reliability of the ith component in the series, i.e., $R_i(t) = P_r(E_i)$. Then the reliability of the system is the probability of this event and is given by

$$R_s = P_r(E_1 \cap E_2 \cap \ldots \cap E_n)$$

$$P_r(E_1)P_r(E_2)\ldots\ldots P_r(E_n) \qquad \text{(since components are independent)}$$

This can be evaluated using failure events E_i also. In this case, $R_s = 1 -$ (probability of the system failure). The system fails if any of the components fail, and therefore $R_s = 1 - P_r\,(E_1 \cup E_2 \cup \ldots \cup E_n)$. The time-dependent reliability function is $R_s(t) = p_1(t)p_2(t)\ldots p_n(t)$.

Where $p_i(t)$ is the probability that the component i is good at time t. If time to failure of components are exponentially distributed, then, in this case, $p_i(t) = e^{-\lambda_i t}$.

and
$$R_s(t) = e^{-\lambda_1 t}\cdot e^{-\lambda_2 t}\cdots e^{-\lambda_n t} = e^{-t\sum_{i=1}^{n}\lambda_i} \tag{21.20}$$

The mean time to failure of the system is given by

$$\text{MTTF} = \int_0^\infty R_s(t)dt = \int_0^\infty e^{-t\sum_{i=1}^{n}\lambda_i}dt = \frac{1}{\sum_{i=1}^{n}\lambda_i} = \frac{1}{\sum_{i=1}^{n}\frac{1}{T_i}} \tag{21.21}$$

Where T_i is the mean life of component i

For any general hazard model

$$R(t) = \exp\left[-\int_0^t \sum_{i=1}^{n} Z_i(x)dx\right] \tag{21.22}$$

In most series systems, the components are independent of their probabilities of proper function. The system reliability function is an increasing function of the component reliability values and decreases the number of components.

Example 21.4 The reliability scheme of a composite power system consists of 5 independent components in series, each having reliability of 0.970. What is the reliability of the series system?

Solution The reliability of the 5 components series system is

$$R\,(t) = (0.970) \times (0.970) \times (0.970) \times (0.970) \times (0.970) = (0.970)^5 = 0.859$$

Example 21.5 A power system component has a 99% reliability with a constant failure rate. Determine the maximum number of components that can be connected in series to maintain 95% system reliability?

Solution The system reliability is $(0.99)^n = 0.95$.

$\Rightarrow n \log(0.99) = \log(0.95)$

$\Rightarrow n = 5$

21.4.2 Parallel Systems

The second type of structure is the parallel structure. The conceptual analogue is the electrical circuit, and the definition is: a parallel system is one in which the proper function of any one component implies system function. One example of a parallel system is the set of 2 engines on a 2-engine airplane. As long as at least one engine functions, the flight is sustained. However, this example implies that simply maintaining flight corresponds to proper operation. Another more appealing example is that the communication satellites presently in use have triple redundancy for each communication channel. Their copies of each set of transmitting components are installed in the satellite and arranged in parallel to assure the channel's continued operation.

It is appropriate to mention that the parallel arrangement of components is often referred to as redundancy. It is because the proper function of any of the parallel components implies the proper function of the structure. Thus, the additional components are redundant until a component fails. Often but not always, the parallel components are identical. A distinction is made between redundancy obtained using a parallel structure. All components functioned simultaneously and are obtained using parallel components of which one functions and the others wait as standby units until the functioning unit's failure. In parallel configurations of the systems, the following aspects are possible.

(1) If all the components have the same reliability, then $R(t) = 1 - [1 - p(t)]^n$

(2) In the case of constant failure rates $R(t) = 1 - [1 - e^{-\lambda t}]^m$

(3) The mean time to failure of the system is $\text{MTTF} = \int_0^\infty \left\{1 - \left[1 - e^{-\lambda t}\right]^n\right\} dt$

Putting $(1 - e^{-\lambda t}) = x$, we get $= \dfrac{1}{\lambda}\displaystyle\int_0^1 \left[\frac{1 - x^n}{1 - x}\right] dx = \frac{1}{\lambda}\int_0^1 (1 + x + x^2 + \cdots + x^{n-1})\, dx$

$$= \frac{1}{\lambda}\int_0^1 \left(1 + \frac{1}{2} + \frac{1}{3} + \cdots + \frac{1}{n}\right) = \frac{1}{\lambda}\sum_{i=1}^{n} \frac{1}{i}$$

When the unit reliabilities are unequal, then

$$\text{MTTF} = \int_0^{\infty}\left[1-\left\{\left(1-e^{-\lambda_1 t}\right)\left(1-e^{-\lambda_2 t}\right)\cdots\left(1-e^{-\lambda_n t}\right)\right\}\right]dt$$

Simplifying, we get

$$= \sum_i \frac{1}{\lambda_i} - \sum_{i<j}\frac{1}{\lambda_i+\lambda_j} + \sum_{i<j<k}\frac{1}{\lambda_i+\lambda_j+\lambda_k} - \cdots + (-1)^{m-1}\frac{1}{\lambda_1+\lambda_2+\cdots+\lambda_n} \tag{21.23}$$

The system reliability function for a parallel system increases both the component reliability values and the number of components.

Example 21.6 A power system component has 95% reliability for a period of operation. Determine the minimum number of components connected in the parallel so that the combination reliability remains at least 99%?

Solution Reliability of parallel combination is $R_p = [1 - (1 - r)^n]$.

$\Rightarrow 0.99 = [1 - (1 - 0.95)^n]$

$\Rightarrow n = 2$

21.4.3 Series–Parallel (k-out-of-n) Systems

The third type of system structure is the k-out-of-n structure. There is no apparent conceptual analogue for this structure. A formal definition of it is: a k-out-of-n system is one in which the proper function of any k of the n components that comprise the system implies adequate system function. A system in which k-subsystems are connected in parallel where each subsystem has n-components connected in series. An example of a k-out-of-n system is the rear axle of a large tractor-trailer on which the functioning of any 3 out of the 4 wheels is sufficient to assure mobility. Another example is that some (1-k) electronic memory arrays are configured so that any 126 of the 128 memory address corresponds to satisfactory operation.

Assuming the resistibility of the subsystem $S_i = P_i$ and the reliability of the path $i = R_i$,

$$R_1 = p_1p_2;\ R_2 = p_3p_4;\ R_3 = p_5p_6$$

Then the resistibility of the entire structure is: $R = [1 - \{(1 - R_1)(1 - R_2)(1 - R_3)\ldots\}]$.

In general, $R = [1 - \{(1 - R_1)(1 - R_2)(1 - R_3)\ldots(1 - R_k)\}]$

Following 2 configurations of this system are possible in the electrical power system.

(i) A group contains n components in parallel, then $R_p = [1 - (1 - r)^n]$. If N such groups are connected in series, then combination reliability becomes

$$R_p = [1 - (1 - r)^n]^N \tag{21.24a}$$

(ii) A group contains n components in series, then $R_s = [1 - (1 - r)^n]$. If N such groups are connected in parallel, then combination reliability

$$R_s = [1 - \{(1 - r)^n\}^N] \tag{21.24b}$$

21.5 ▶ FAILURE DISTRIBUTION FUNCTIONS FOR RELIABILITY EVALUATION

In principle, any distribution function may be used to model equipment longevity. In practice, distribution functions having monotonic hazard functions seem most realistic. Within that class, a few are generally thought to provide the most reasonable models of device reliability. The most common choices of life distribution models have been described as follows:

21.5.1 Reliability Evaluation Based on Exponential Distribution

The most widely used distribution function for modelling reliability is the exponential distribution. It is algebraically simple and, thus, tractable and is considered representative of the device life cycle's functional life interval. Suppose we make the exponential assumption about the distribution of failure times. In that case, some beneficial results can be derived connecting the mean time between the failures (MTBF), the mean time between the failure of series and parallel systems. We shall first have to obtain a relation expressing the reliability of a component in terms of its service time *T*. Making use of the fact that

$$R(t) = 1 - F(t) = 1 - \int_0^t f(x)\,dx \qquad \left(\because f(t) = \frac{dF(t)}{dt}\right)$$

If the time to failure *T* follows an exponential distribution with parameter α, then its PDF is given by $f(t) = \alpha e^{\alpha t}$, $t \geq 0$.

Then,

$$R(t) = 1 - \int_0^t \alpha e^{-\alpha x}\,dx = 1 - \alpha\left[\frac{e^{-\alpha x}}{-\alpha}\right]_0^t = 1 + [e^{-\alpha t} - 1] = e^{-\alpha t} \tag{21.25a}$$

Conversely, when $Z(t) = \dfrac{f(t)}{R(t)} = \dfrac{\alpha e^{\alpha t}}{e^{-\alpha t}} = \alpha, \text{constant},$

We get, from (6), $f(t) = \alpha e^{\int_0^t \alpha\,dx}$

$$\Rightarrow f(t) = \alpha e^{-\alpha t},\ t \geq 0. \tag{21.25b}$$

Due to this property, the exponential distribution is often referred to as constant failure rate distribution in reliability contexts.

Therefore,
$$\text{MTTF} = E(T) = \frac{1}{\alpha} \tag{21.26a}$$

And
$$\text{var}\ (T) = \sigma_T^2 = \frac{1}{\alpha^2}$$

Also
$$R(t/T_0) = \frac{R(T_0 + t)}{R(T_0)} = \frac{e^{-\alpha(T_0+t)}}{e^{-\alpha T_0}} = e^{\alpha t}. \tag{21.26b}$$

It means that the time to failure of a component is not dependent on how long the component has been functioning. In other words, the reliability of the component for the net 1000 hours, say, is the same regardless of whether the component is brand new or has been operating for several hours. This property is known as the memoryless property of the constant failure rate distribution.

Example 21.7 A power system component has MTBF = 100 hours and MTTR = 20 hours with both failure and repair distributions exponential. Find the availability and unavailability of the component after a long time.

Solution Given $\text{MTBF} = \dfrac{1}{\lambda} = 100 \quad \Rightarrow \lambda = 0.01$

$$\text{MTTR} = \frac{1}{\mu} = 20 \quad \Rightarrow \mu = 0.05$$

∴ The component availability

$$A(\infty) = \frac{\text{MTBF}}{\text{MTBF} + \text{MTTR}} = \frac{\frac{1}{\lambda}}{\frac{1}{\lambda} + \frac{1}{\mu}} = \frac{100}{100 + 20} = 0.83$$

The component unavailability

$$\overline{A}(\infty) = \frac{\lambda}{\lambda + \mu} = \frac{0.01}{0.01 + 0.05} = \frac{0.01}{0.06} = 0.1666.$$

21.5.2 Reliability Evaluation Based on the Normal Distribution

The normal distribution provides another popular model of device life length. It is a very appropriate model for the reliability evaluation of structural components of the power system. If the time to failure T follows a normal distribution $N(\mu, \sigma)$ its PDF is given by,

$$f(t) = \frac{1}{\sigma\sqrt{2\pi}} \exp\left[\frac{-(t-\mu)^2}{2\sigma^2}\right], -\infty < t < \infty. \tag{21.27a}$$

In this case, MTTF = $E(T) = \mu$ and
Var $(T) = \sigma_T^2 = \sigma^2$.

$R(t) = \int_t^\infty f(t)dt$ is found out by expressing the integral in terms of the standard normal integral and using the normal tables.

Then $\lambda(t) = \frac{f(t)}{R(t)}$ is called the instantaneous failure rate or hazard function of the component, and the conditional reliability is

$$R(t/T_0) = P\left\{T > \frac{T_0 + t}{T} > T_0\right\} = e^{-\int_{T_0}^{T_0} \lambda(t)dt} \tag{21.27b}$$

21.6 ▶ RELIABILITY AND MTBF EVALUATION USING EXPONENTIAL MODEL

The most widely used distribution function for modelling reliability is the exponential distribution. Reliability and MTBF of series and parallel connected systems can be evaluated using the exponential model as follows.

21.6.1 Series-Connected Components

Suppose now that a system consists of n components connected in series and that these components have the respective failure rates $\alpha_1, \alpha_2, \ldots \alpha_n$. The product law of reliabilities can be written as follows.

$$R_s(t) = e^{-t\sum_{i=1}^{n} \alpha_i} \tag{21.28}$$

The mean time between failures (MTBF) of a series system is,

$$\mu_s = \frac{1}{\frac{1}{\mu_1} + \frac{1}{\mu_2} + \cdots + \frac{1}{\mu_n}} \tag{21.29}$$

Where μ_i is MTBF of ith component. In the special case where all n components have the same failure rate α and hence the same MTBF μ, the system failure rate is $n\alpha$, and the system MTBF is $\frac{1}{\mu\alpha} = \frac{\mu}{n}$.

21.6.2 Parallel-Connected Components

The mean time to failure of a parallel system is also difficult to obtain in general, but in the special case where all components have the same failure rate α, an interesting and useful result is obtained. In this special case, the system reliability function becomes

$$R_p(t) = 1-(1-e^{-\alpha t})^n = \binom{n}{1}e^{-\alpha t} - \binom{n}{2}e^{-2\alpha t} + \cdots + (-1)^{n-1}e^{-n\alpha t}$$

Then, making use of the fact that $f_p(t) = R_p'(t)$,

$$f_p(t) = \alpha\binom{n}{1}e^{-\alpha t} - 2\alpha\binom{n}{2}e^{-2\alpha t} + \cdots + (-1)^{n-1}n\alpha e^{-n\alpha t}$$

We obtain

$$\mu_p = \int_0^\infty t\cdot f_p(t)dt$$

and the mean of the failure-time distribution is given by

$$= \alpha\binom{n}{1}\int_0^\infty te^{-\alpha t}dt - 2\alpha\binom{n}{2}\int_0^\infty te^{-2\alpha t}dt + \cdots + (-1)^{n-1}n\alpha\int_0^\infty te^{-n\alpha t}dt$$

$$= \frac{1}{\alpha}\binom{n}{1} - \frac{1}{2\alpha}\binom{n}{2} + \cdots + (-1)^{n-1}\frac{1}{n\alpha} \tag{21.30}$$

Then the mean time between failures (MTBF) in the parallel system is $\mu_p = \frac{1}{\alpha}\left(1+\frac{1}{2}+\cdots+\frac{1}{n}\right)$. The MTBF of the system consists of n components having the identical failure rate α provided each defective component is replaced whenever the whole parallel system fails. Thus, if we use 2 parallel components rather than one, the mean time to failure of the pair exceeds that of the single component by 50%, rather than doubling it.

21.7 ▶ POWER SYSTEM RELIABILITY: AN OVERVIEW

The reliability evaluation of a bulk interconnected combined generation, transmission and distribution power system is a significant concern in power system planning. Generating stations, transmission lines and distribution systems are the main components of an electrical power system. Generating stations and a distribution system are interconnected through transmission lines, connecting one power system to another. For economical and technological reasons, individual power systems are interconnected to form a national grid. Under conditions of a sudden increase in loads or loss of generation in one area, it is immediately possible to borrow power from an adjoining interconnected area. Interconnection of bulk power systems causes a larger current to flow in a transmission line under faulty conditions or under overloaded conditions. Such a heavy current can damage the power system. For the planning of operation, improvement and expansion of the bulk power system, a power system engineer needs reliability evaluation of overloaded electrical power system. The adequacy of the generating capacity in a power system is generally improved by interconnecting the system to another power system. Each interconnected system can operate at a given risk level with a lower reserve than required without the interconnection. This condition is brought about by the diversity in the probabilistic occurrence of load and capacity outages in the different systems. The actual interconnection benefits depend on the installed capacity in each system, the total tie capacity, the forced outage rates of the tie lines, the load levels and their residual uncertainties in each system and the type of agreement between the systems. One of the essential elements in power system planning is determining how much generation capacity must give a reasonable assurance of satisfying the load requirements. In this case, the concern is to determine whether there is sufficient capacity to generate the required energy to meet the system load.

A second but equally important element in the planning process is developing a suitable transmission network to convey the customer load points' energy. The transmission network can be divided into 2 general areas of bulk transmission and distribution facilities. The distinction between these 2 areas cannot be made strictly on a voltage basis but must include the facility's function within the system. Bulk transmission facilities must be matched with the generation to permit energy movement from these sources to determine where the distribution or sub-transmission facilities can provide a direct and often radial path to the customer. Distribution design, in many systems, is almost entirely decoupled from the transmission system development process. Given the terminal station's location and size emanating from the bulk transmission system, distribution system design becomes a separate and independent process. Coupling between the 2 systems in reliability evaluation can be accommodated using the load point indices evaluated for the bulk transmission system as the distribution system's input reliability indices.

A power system engineer is very concerned about the problems associated with modern large interconnected power systems. These problems may be related to generation, transmission, distribution and load management. Again it may be thought that the nature of the issues may be steady-state analysis, or transient analysis, or dynamic control of the system. The steady-state analysis of the power system mainly concerns the control variables' base point setting to have dependent variables within limits (these may include line flows, load bus voltages and reactive generation). The solution to such problems assures the power network's secure operation under the power system's static operation. The analysis and performance optimisation under such a situation requires and involves the solution of non-linear algebraic equations. Security assessment, security-constrained power system optimisation, state estimation, environmentally constrained secure economic dispatch, unit commitment and static voltage stability assessment and control are examples of the problems which fall in such category. The earlier studies in power system reliability were confined to generating reserve capacity evaluations. Simultaneously, the need for such studies, which is based on a probabilistic approach, was recognised in several publications in the 1930s. The probability mathematics used in these papers was comparatively simple. The results were summarised in an AIEE Committee report. Simultaneously, efforts were made to extend the investigations to transmission and distribution systems, employing more complex analytical techniques, such as modelling the Markov processes' power system.

Power system reliability studies received a new impetus in North America after the power failure in November 1965 when large parts of the North-East United States and of Eastern Canada were left without supply for several hours. As a direct consequence of this incident, utility groups with interconnected systems formed 9 coordinating agencies that include the National Electric Reliability Council. In the last 10 years, the investigations have branched out almost every aspect of power system reliability. Even the methods for generating reserve capacity evaluations have significantly been refined. The development in power system reliability methods and techniques has been documented in an ever-increasing number of publications. The basic terms used in power system reliability evaluation are given below.

(i) **Component:** A piece of equipment, a line, a section of the line, or a group of items that are viewed as an entity for reporting, analysing and predicting outages.

(ii) **System:** A group of components connected or associated in a fixed configuration to perform a specified function.

(iii) **Outage:** Describes the state of a component when it is not available to perform its intended function due to some event directly associated with that component. An outage may or may not cause an interruption of service to consumers depending on system configuration.

(a) **Forced outage:** An outage that results from emergency conditions directly associated with a component requiring that it be taken out of service immediately, either automatically or as soon as switching operations can be performed, or an outage caused by improper operation of equipment or human error.

(b) **Scheduled outage:** An outage that results when a component is deliberately taken out of service at a selected time, usually for purposes of construction, preventive maintenance or repair.

(c) **Transient forced outage:** An outage whose cause is immediately self-clearing so that the affected component can be restored to service either automatically or as soon as a switch or circuit breaker can be reclosed or a fuse replaced. An example of a transient forced outage is a lightning flashover, which does not permanently disable the flashed component.

(d) **Permanent forced outage:** An outage whose cause is not immediately self-clearing but must be corrected by eliminating the hazard or repairing or replacing the component before it can be returned to service. An example of a permanently forced outage is a lightning flashover that shatters an insulator, thereby disabling the component until repair or replacement can occur.

(iv) **Exposure time:** The time during which a component is performing its intended function and is subject to an outage.

(v) **Outage rate:** For a particular classification of outage and type of component, the mean number of outages per unit exposure time per component.

(a) Adverse weather permanent forced outage rate (AWPFOR): For a particular type of component, the mean number of outages per unit of adverse weather exposure time per component.

(b) Normal weather permanent forced outage rate (NWPFOR): For a particular type of component, the mean number of outages per unit of normal weather exposure time per component.

(vi) **Outage duration:** The period from the initiation of an outage until the affected component or its replacement once again becomes available to perform its intended function.

(a) Permanent forced outage duration (PFOD): The period from the outage initiation until the component is replaced or repaired.

(b) Transient forced outage duration (TFOD): The period from the outage initiation until the component is restored to service by switching or fuse replacement.

(c) Scheduled outage duration (SOD): The period from the outage initiation until construction, preventive maintenance or repair work is completed.

(vii) **Switching time:** The period from the time a switching operation is required due to a forced outage until that switching operation is performed.

(viii) **Interruption:** The loss of service to one or more consumers. An interruption is the result of one or more component outages.

(a) Scheduled interruption (SCI): An interruption caused by a scheduled outage.

(b) Forced interruption (FI): An interruption caused by a forced outage.

(ix) **Interruption duration:** The period from the initiation of an interruption to a consumer until service has been restored to that consumer.

(a) Momentary interruption (MI): An interruption of duration limited to the period required to restore service by automatic or supervisory controlled switching operations or by manual switching at locations where an operator is immediately available.

(b) Sustained interruption (SUI): A sustained interruption is any interruption not classified as a momentary interruption.

(x) **Redundancy:** Redundancy in the generating system means installing more generating capacity than normally required; this excess capacity is then a reserve needed only in emergencies. Redundancy in the transmission system means ties between stations stronger than required by normal loads or links where none are necessary for the basic design. However, the extra transmission capacity may be needed to avoid (i) overloading and/or (ii) voltage-VAR related problem under unusual operating conditions. Sufficient redundancy must be available at both generation and transmission levels. So as this is required to have adequate supply to the distribution network under emergency conditions. In the power system, the concepts of reliability and reserves are near bound together, and in turn, reliability and costs of installing additional components and operating the system increase together. For economic reasons, some of the generating units are kept as a cold reserve and sometimes are needed before such units can be put in service, while other units are kept as spinning reserve. Since in an emergency, there is not always enough time available for them to put into service.

21.8 ▶ RELIABILITY MODELS OF POWER SYSTEM

The power system has 3 basic components, namely, generation, transmission and distribution subsystems. The ultimate goal of reliability studies is to evaluate the reliability indices of the overall system. This requires involved modelling and analytical tools. A literature trend is used to evaluate the indices simultaneously for composite transmission and generation systems and separate studies for distribution systems. An independent reliability study ensures more flexibility in selecting failure criteria and making appropriate assumptions. Long-term reliability evaluations may be performed to assist in long-range system planning, while short-term reliability predictions may be sought to assist in day-to-day operating decisions. In such studies, assessment of system security (voltage and line flow constraints) is included. If an improvement in system reliability is required, it can be affected by using either better components or a system design incorporating redundancy.

21.8.1 Markov Model

Simulation methods estimate the reliability indices by simulating the actual process and random behaviour of the system. The technique, therefore, treats the problem as a series of real experiments. The techniques can theoretically take into account virtually all aspects and contingencies inherent in the planning, design and operation of a power system. These include random events such as outages and repairs of elements represented by general probability distributions, dependent events and component behaviour, queuing of failed components, load variations, the variation of energy input/such as that occurring in hydrogenation and all different types of operating policies. Suppose the operating life of the system is simulated over a long period. In that case, it is possible to study the system's behaviour and obtain a clear picture of the type of deficiencies that the system may suffer. This recorded information permits the expected values of reliability indices together with their frequency distributions to be evaluated. This comprehensive information gives a very detailed description, and hence understanding, of the system's reliability. Power systems are repairable, i.e., they consist of repairable components. In the repairable system, the failure state and up states are of prime importance as, in turn, these states or a combination of these states will decide the success or failure probability of the system. Weather conditions are illustrated below.

(a) Normal weather condition (NWC): Includes all-weather not designated as an adverse or major disaster.

(b) Adverse weather condition (AWC): Designates weather conditions which cause an abnormally high rate of forced outages for exposed components while such conditions persist but do not qualify as major storm disasters. Adverse weather conditions can be defined for a particular system by selecting the proper values and combinations of conditions reported by the weather bureau: thunderstorms, tornadoes, wind velocities, precipitation, temperature, etc.

(c) Major storm disaster condition (MSDC): Designates weather that exceeds plant design limits. The MSDC satisfies the conditions: the extensive mechanical damage to the plant; more than a specified percentage of customers out of service; and service restoration times longer than a specified time.

Availability and Unavailability Functions The failure and repair rate of an alternator or transmission line is assumed to be constant. It amounts that failure and repair both have distribution law as exponential. Such a transition process is represented by the memoryless process known as the Markov process. In a Markov process, the random variable's probabilities at time t_n depend on the random variable's value at t_{n-1} but not on the realisation of the process prior to t_{n-1}. Loosely speaking, the state probabilities at a future instant, given the present state of the process, do not depend on the states occupies in the past.

Consider a Markov process $X(t)$ with a continuous-time parameter 't'.

Define, $t_{n-1} = t$, and $t_n = (t + h)$

The conditional probability relation simplifies to $P\,[x(t + h) = j/X(t) = i] = p_{ij}(t, h)$

These conditional probabilities are known as transition probabilities. If p_{ij} depends on h (time difference) only, the Markov process is called homogenous. For small $h = \Delta t$ values, the Markov process becomes

$$P\,[X(t + \Delta t) = j/X(t) = i] = p_{ij}\,\Delta t \cong q_{ij}\,\Delta t$$

and

$$P\,[X(t + \Delta t) = i/X(t) = i] = p_{ij}\,\Delta t \cong (1 - q_{ij}\,\Delta t)$$

where

q_{ij} = transition state from ith to jth state.

$p_{ij}\,\Delta t$ = the probability that no change in state will occur in a time interval of length Δt given that process is in state 'i' at the beginning of the interval.

q_i = the total rate of departure from state 'i'

The transition rates are constant in a homogenous Markov process.

State space equations can be written from state transition diagram representing Markov process as follows:

$$P^T(t) = p^T(t) \cdot A \tag{21.31}$$

where

$P(t)$ = is the state probability vector.

The element of matrix A is written as follows:

$$a_{ii} = -q_i \text{ (Negative of the total rate of departure from state } i\text{)}$$

where $a_{ij} = q_{ij}$ = Total rate of departure from state i to state j.

The general solution to state equations is written as follows:

$$P^T(t) = p^T(o)e^{AT} \tag{21.32}$$

The steady-state solution of equation (3.1) is obtained by solving the following set of equations:

$$P^T A = 0 \quad \text{and} \quad \Sigma P_i = 1 \tag{21.33}$$

This solution is utilised for short-term planning, whereas steady-state solution (3.3) is used for long-term planning, where one can neglect the transient exponentially decaying term tending to zero for a large time of reliability study. One can partition the state diagram into 2 portions based on system success criteria. One portion consists of system states, which give system success, and the other portion consists of system failure states. The 2 sets can be designated as W and F.

The availability function $A(t)$ and unavailability function $\overline{A}(t)$ are given as

$$A(t) = \sum_{i \in W} p_i \tag{21.34}$$

and

$$\bar{A}(t) = \sum_{j \in f} p_j = [1 - A(t)] \tag{21.35}$$

Consider a generator has λ and μ as failure and repair rate respectively and it has 2 states 'Up' and 'Down' states. These state equations are given as follows:

$$\begin{bmatrix} \dot{p}_{up^{*}} & \dot{p}_{dn} \end{bmatrix} = \begin{bmatrix} p_{up} & p_{dn} \end{bmatrix} \begin{pmatrix} -\lambda & \lambda \\ \mu & -\mu \end{pmatrix} \tag{21.36}$$

General solution to eqn. (3.6) can be written as follows:

$$p_{up}(t) = A(t) = \frac{\mu}{\lambda+\mu} + \frac{\lambda}{\lambda+\mu} e^{-(\lambda+\mu)t} \tag{21.37}$$

$$p_{dn}(t) = \bar{A}(t) = \frac{\lambda}{\lambda+\mu} - \frac{\lambda}{\lambda+\mu} e^{-(\lambda+\mu)t} \tag{21.38}$$

where

$p_{up}(t)$ – Probability that the generator is working.

$p_{dn}(t)$ – Probability that the generator has failed.

The steady-state probabilities are written as $t \to \infty$ as follows:

$$p_{up}, \text{ss} = \mu/(\lambda + \mu) \tag{21.39}$$

$$p_{dn}, \text{ss} = \lambda/(\lambda + \mu) \tag{21.40}$$

After Markov process next section discusses generation models of the composite power system.

Two-Weather Markov Model In this model, the fluctuating weather environment is represented by a 2-state Markov model. Assuming exponential distributions for the normal and severe weather conditions, the transmission rates in this model are

$$\lambda_N = \frac{1}{T_N} \quad \text{and} \quad \lambda_w = \frac{1}{T_w}$$

This weather model is combined with the system model assuming that the weather cycles are independent of component failures and repairs. The 4-state models can describe a single component placed into a 2-weather environment. The steady-state probabilities are given as follows for the above 4-state model.

$$P_N = \frac{\lambda w \cdot D}{\lambda_N(A+C)+\lambda_w(B+D)} \tag{21.41}$$

$$p'_N = p_n \frac{\lambda_N}{\lambda_w} \frac{A}{D}$$

$$p_F = p_N \frac{B}{D}, p'_F = p_N \frac{\lambda_N}{\lambda_w} \frac{C}{D}$$

where

$$A = \mu\lambda_w + \mu'(\lambda + \lambda_N + \mu)$$

$$B = \lambda'\lambda_N + \lambda(\lambda' + \lambda_w + \mu')$$

$$C = \lambda\lambda_w + \lambda'(\lambda + \lambda_N + \mu)$$

$$D = \mu'\lambda_N + \mu(\lambda' + \lambda_W + \mu')$$

The states are clearly defined as follows:

N: Normal state of component in normal weather.

N': Normal state of component in severe weather.

F: Failed state of component in normal weather.

F': Failed state of component in severe weather.

Based on these probabilities availability, unavailability and frequencies can be calculated

$$A = p_N + p'_N$$

$$\bar{A} = (1 - A) = p_F + p'_F$$

Frequency is given by the following relation using the boundary wall concept.

$$f = p_N \lambda + p'_N \cdot \lambda' \tag{21.42}$$

Mean up time (MUT) is given as MUT = A/f, and mean downtime (MDT) is given as MDT = $\bar{A}/f$.

21.8.2 Power Generation Model

A 2-state representation of the generator is adequate most of the time. This modelling, as expressed in the earlier section, requires failure rate λ and repair rate μ to obtain availability (Success probability) and unavailability (failure probability) as expressed in the power system. At times the generating unit may operate at the partial output, resulting in derated states. In such a situation, the multi-state model will result. Such models are usually used in operational reserve planning.

A traditional term for the unit unavailability is defined as FOR (forced outage rate).

$$\text{FOR} = \frac{\text{Forced outage hours}}{\text{In-service hours} + \text{forced outage hours}}$$

It is stressed here that if FOR is computed over a long period, it is equal to the unavailability index. Partial outages are accounted for (derated operating state) by increasing forced outage hours by an appropriate amount of time called equivalent forced outage hours. Based on this equivalent FOR (EFOR) is defined as follows:

$$\text{EFOR} = \frac{\text{Forced outage hours} + \text{Equivalent forced outage hours}}{\text{In-service hours} + \text{Forced outage hours}}$$

Where the in-service hours include the actual partial outage time as well. Equivalent forced outage hours are obtained by actual partial outage hours are multiplied by the corresponding fractional capacity reduction and then summing these products. In summing in most of generating capacity reliability studies, generating a 2-state model represents units. The failure probability of a generating unit is given by its unavailability, which is calculated from the previous equation or provided by an appropriate FOR value taken from data collections. If partial outages are also considered, then EFOR is computed from the collected or published data. After the unit representation, the system model is depicted in the form of a capacity outage probability table, as discussed below.

Capacity Outage Probability The generation model required in the loss of load approach is sometimes known as a capacity outage probability table. As the name suggests, it is a simple array of capacity levels and the associated probabilities of existence. If all the system units are identical, the capacity outage probability table can be easily obtained using the binomial distribution. The capacity outage probability table tabulates states, their probabilities and corresponding capacity available or/and out. Suppose all units in the system are identical. In that case, the capacity outage probability table can be constructed using Binomial expansion and unavailability of 'r' out of total 'n' units are given as follows:

$$P(x_r) = \left[{}^{n}C_r \bar{A}^r (1-\bar{A})^{n-r} \right] \tag{21.43}$$

where

$P(x_r)$ shows rth states in (corresponding to an outage of r units) capacity outage probability table. The above expression gives the probability of each state, and capacity out and available are given as follows:

$$\text{Capacity out} = r \times C_g$$
$$\text{Capacity available} = (n - r)\, C_g$$

If all units are not similar, then the capacity outage probability table for each similar group is prepared as explained above. Then these tables are merged to obtain a combined capacity outage table. Assume that there are 2 groups (group may constitute one unit ever) of similar units having states and capacities as follows:

$X_0, X_1, X_2, \ldots, X_u$ – X-group.

and $Y_0, Y_1, Y_2, \ldots, Y_v$ – Y-group.

Each state in each group will have associated capacity available/out combined probability table can be obtained as follows:

$$(X_0 + X_1 + X_2 + \cdots + X_p)\,(Y_0 + Y_1 + Y_2 + Y_3 + \cdots + Y_q)$$

Equivalent states will be written as,

$$\begin{array}{llll}
X_0\,Y_0, & X_0\,Y_1, & X_0\,Y_2, \ldots, & X_0\,Y_v, \\
X_1\,Y_0, & X_1\,Y_1, & X_1\,Y_2, \ldots, & X_1\,Y_v, \\
X_2\,Y_0, & X_2\,Y_1, & X_2\,Y_2, \ldots, & X_2\,Y_v, \\
\vdots & \vdots & \vdots & \vdots \\
\vdots & \vdots & \vdots & \vdots \\
X_u\,Y_0, & X_u\,Y_1, & X_u\,Y_2, \ldots, & X_u\,Y_v,
\end{array}$$

Since the failure probability of each unit is assumed to be independent, the probability of each event (State) in the combined table,

$$P\,(z_i) = p\,(X_r Y_s) = p\,(X_r),\, p\,(X_s)$$

And the capacity available/out in the merged table will be the sum of capacity available or out as follows.

$$CZ_i = CX_r + CY_s$$

where

Z_i Combined state $(X_r.\ Y_s)$
CZ_i capacity available for ith state in the combined table
CX_r capacity of rth state in X group
CY_s capacity of sth state in Y group

In summary, if we are merging 2 capacity outage probability tables, take the combination of all events in 2 tables, multiplying the probabilities, and adding each individual table's capacity. The sequentially third group can be merged into this table, and this way, one can combine any number of separate tables. Total events, in combination, will be (UxV). Total events can be represented in matrix form as follows:

$$[Z] = X_L Y_L \begin{bmatrix} X_0\,Y_0 & X_0\,Y_1 & X_0\,Y_2 & \ldots & X_0\,Y_v \\ X_1\,Y_0 & X_1\,Y_1 & X_1\,Y_2 & \ldots & X_1\,Y_v \\ X_2\,Y_0 & X_2\,Y_1 & X_2\,Y_2 & \ldots & X_2\,Y_v \\ \vdots & \vdots & \vdots & & \vdots \\ X_L Y_0 & X_L Y_1 & X_L Y_2 & & X_L Y_v \\ \vdots & \vdots & \vdots & & \vdots \\ X_u Y_0 & X_u Y_1 & X_u Y_2 & \ldots & X_u\,Y_v \end{bmatrix} \tag{21.44a}$$

$[Z]$ matrix represents the states of the merged table. The probability of each event in the above state matrix is given by multiplying the probabilities of the respective event and given by

$$p(Z) = \begin{bmatrix} p(X_0)\,p(Y_0) & p(X_0)\,p(Y_1) & p(X_0)\,p(Y_2) & \ldots & p(X_0)\,p(Y_v) \\ p(X_1)\,p(Y_0) & p(X_1)\,p(Y_1) & p(X_1)\,p(Y_2) & \ldots & p(X_1)\,p(Y_v) \\ p(X_2)\,p(Y_0) & p(X_2)\,p(Y_1) & p(X_2)\,p(Y_2) & \ldots & p(X_2)\,p(Y_v) \\ \vdots & \vdots & \vdots & & \vdots \\ p(X_L)\,p(Y_0) & p(X_L)\,p(Y_1) & p(X_L)\,p(Y_2) & \ldots & p(X_L)\,p(Y_v) \\ \vdots & \vdots & \vdots & & \vdots \\ p(X_u)\,p(Y_0) & p(X_u)\,p(Y_1) & p(X_u)\,p(Y_2) & \ldots & p(X_u)\,p(Y_v) \end{bmatrix} \tag{21.44b}$$

The following equation gives the capacity of each combined state:

$$[C] = \begin{bmatrix} C(X_0)+C(Y_0) & C(X_0)+C(Y_1) & C(X_0)+C(Y_2) & \ldots & C(X_0)+C(Y_v) \\ C(X_1)+C(Y_0) & C(X_1)+C(Y_1) & C(X_1)+C(Y_2) & \ldots & C(X_1)+C(Y_v) \\ C(X_2)+C(Y_0) & C(X_2)+C(Y_1) & C(X_2)+C(Y_2) & \ldots & C(X_2)+C(Y_v) \\ \vdots & \vdots & \vdots & & \vdots \\ C(X_L)+C(Y_L) & C(X_L)+C(Y_1) & C(X_L)+C(Y_2) & \ldots & C(X_L)+C(Y_v) \\ \vdots & \vdots & \vdots & & \vdots \\ C(X_u)+C(Y_0) & C(X_u)+C(Y_1) & C(X_u)+C(Y_2) & \ldots & C(X_u)+C(Y_v) \end{bmatrix} \tag{21.44c}$$

From the matrices $[Z]$, $[p(Z)]$ and $[C]$ the capacity outage probability can be tabulated. It also amounts that capacity distribution is assumed to be continuous rather than discrete. It is further justified because each unit may derate capacity states depending on the partial failure of auxiliary units. Hence, the overall capacity available may be treated as a continuous random variable.

Loss of Load Expectation (LOLE) Several probabilistic methods are available at present, which provides a quantitative reliability assessment of interconnected system generation facilities. The loss of load expectation (LOLE) approach is the most widely used technique due to its flexibility and application simplicity. Two different approaches are presented in this chapter for calculating the LOLE indices in interconnected systems. They are the probability array method and the equivalent assisting unit method. In the first approach, a capacity model is developed for each system, and an array of simultaneous capacity outage existence probabilities is then obtained from the individual models.

The second method models the assisting system as an equivalent assisting unit that can be moved through the tie lines and added into the assisted system's existing capacity model. The computation of the risk in the assisted system proceeds as in a normal single-system study. The individual daily peak loads can be used in conjunction with the capacity outage probability table to obtain the expected number of days in the specified period. The daily peak load will exceed the available capacity. The index, in this case, is designated as the LOLE.

$$\text{LOLE} = \sum\nolimits_{i=1}^{n} P(Ci - Li) \text{ days/period}$$

Where

C_i = available capacity on the day i.

L_i = forecast peak load on the day i.

$P_i(C_i - L_i)$ = probability of loss of loads on day i. This value is obtained directly from the capacity outage cumulative probability table.

The same LOLE index can also be obtained using the daily peak load variation curve. A particular capacity outage will contribute to the system LOLE by an amount equal to the product of the probability of the existence of the particular outage the number of time units in the study interval that loss of load would occur if such a capacity outage was to exist. Capacity outage less than the reserve will not contribute to the system LOLE. Outages of capacity over the reserve will result in varying numbers of time units during which loss of load could occur. Expressed mathematically, the contribution to the system LOLE made by capacity outage O is p time units where p is the individual probability of the capacity outage O. The total LOLE for the study interval is $\text{LOLE} = \sum\nolimits_{k=1}^{n} Pk \cdot Tk$ (in time units).

The p_k values in the equation are the individual probabilities associated with the capacity outage states. The equation can be modified to use the cumulative state probabilities. In this case,

$$\text{LOLE} = \sum\nolimits_{k=1}^{n} (tk - Tk - 1)P_k$$

Note: P_k = cumulative outage probability for capacity state O_k.

The annual LOLE_a can be obtained by dividing the year into periods and calculating LOLE values using the modified capacity model and the appropriate period load model.

$$\text{LOLE} = \sum\nolimits_{p=1}^{n} \text{LOLE}_p$$

The modified capacity model can be obtained by creating a new capacity outage probability table for each capacity condition. The total installed capacity may also increase during the year due to the commissioning of a new unit. If the new unit's actual in-service date is uncertain, it can be represented by a probability distribution and incorporated periodically using the following equation.

$$\text{LOLE}_p = (\text{LOLE}_{pa})\, a + (\text{LOLE}_{pu})\, u$$

where

LOLE$_p$ = period LOLE value

LOLE$_{pa}$ = period LOLE value including the unit

LOLE$_{pu}$ = period LOLE value without the unit

a = probability of the unit coming into service

u = probability of the unit not coming into service

The unit still has the opportunity to fail, given that it comes into service. It is included in the LOLE$_{pa}$ value.

Loss of load Probability (LOLP) The loss of load probability (LOLP) evaluation of the power system is given below. The $P[L > C]$ is the probability of load exceeds the generating capacity at power plant and is described below.

$$\Rightarrow \quad [L > C] = (L > C)\,x_1 + [L > C]\,x_2 + [L > C]\,x_3 + \cdots + (L > C)\,x_n$$

$$\Rightarrow \quad P[L > C] = \Sigma P[(L > C)x_i]$$

$$\Rightarrow \quad P[L > C] = \text{LOLP} = \sum_{i=1}^{n} \left\{ P\left[\frac{(L > C)}{xi}\right] \cdot P(xi) \right\}$$

$$\Rightarrow \quad \text{LOLP} = P[L > C] = \sum_{i=1}^{n} \left[\left[P\left\{\frac{(L > C)}{xi}\right\}\right] \cdot P\{xi\} \right]$$

The expected loss of load of the system is given by $E(L_i - C_i) = \sum_{i=1}^{n} (Li - Ci) \cdot f(xi)\,\text{MW}$.

Example 21.8 Four identical generators with 50 MW individual generation capacity are working in parallel at a super thermal power plant. The total generation capacity of the plant is 200 MW with a constant load of 100 MW. The failure probability of identical generators is 0.05. Make a capacity outage probability table of the plant. Evaluate loss of load expectation and loss of load probability.

Solution The failure probability of generator = P_f = 5%, the success probability = p_s = 95%, and total constant load on plant = 100 MW. The plant follows the conditions $(L_i - C_i) = 0$, if $L_i = C_i$ and no loss of load if $(C_i > L_i)$. The LOLE and LOLP are evaluated using the Pascal triangle and Binomial distribution approach (Table 21.2).

Table 21.2 Capacity outage probability table

Sr. No.	*State (x_i)*	*Available capacity (C_i)*	*Capacity out*	$(L_i - C_i)$	$p(x_i)$	$E(L_i - C_i)\,p(x_i)$	$p[(L > C)/x_i]$	$p[(L > C)/x_i][p(x_i)]$
1	All generators working	200 MW	0 MW	0	$(0.95)^4 \times (0.05)^0$	0	0	0
2	One generator out	150 MW	50 MW	0	$4 \times (0.95)^4 \times 0.05$	0	0	0
3	Two generator out	100 MW	100 MW	0	$6 \times (0.95)^2 \times (0.05)^2$	0	0	0
4	Three generator out	50 MW	150 MW	50	$4 \times (0.95) \times (0.05)^3$	$50 \times 4 \times (0.95) \times (0.05)^3$	1	$1 \times 4 \times (0.95) \times (0.05)^3$
5	All generator out	0 MW	200 MW	100	$(0.95)^0 \times (0.05)^4$	$100 \times (0.95)^0 \times (0.05)^4$	1	$1 \times (0.95)^0 \times (0.05)^4$
					$(p + q)^4$	Σ = LOLE	-	Σ = LOLP

(i) Evaluation of expected loss of load (ELOL) or loss of load expectation (LOLE)

ELOL = LOLE = $50 \times 4 \times (0.95) \times (0.05)^3 + 100 \times (0.95)^0 \times (0.05)^4 = (0.02375 + 0.000625) = 0.024375 = 2.4375 \times 10^{-2}$

(ii) Evaluation of loss of load probability (LOLP)

LOLP = $1 \times 4 \times (0.95) \times (0.05)^3 + 1 \times (0.95)^0 \times (0.05)^4 = (0.000475 + 0.00000625) = 0.00048125 = 4.8125 \times 10^{-4}$

21.8.3 Load Model

As pointed earlier, the capacity and load models are essentially merged using a suitable analytical technique to obtain a generation-transmission system reliability index. The brief discussion on load models tried in reliability evaluation is given below.

Constant Load This indicates that load remains constant throughout the study. It is a simplified model of load, which is not valid, especially for modern large power networks, interconnected and posse's much-diversified loads.

Load Having Normal Distribution Variations around the constant mean of distribution can model the load. Applicability of such loads can be where an isolated system is needed a specific or non-diversified load pattern. The load distribution function is written as follows:

$$f(L) = \frac{1}{\sigma_L \sqrt{2\pi}} e^{-0.5\left(\frac{L-\bar{L}}{\sigma_L}\right)^2} \tag{21.45}$$

where L = total load in MW.

$\bar{L}$ = mean load.

σ_L = standard deviation of the load.

$F(L)$, as given above, is the normal distribution.

Load Duration Curve This is one of the most practical load models used in practice to evaluate the loss of load probability index (LOLP). It is constructed from a chronological daily load curve. A typical load duration curve is shown in previous chapters. This curve shows that at any duration, 't' (in per unit of total time 1) load is greater than $L(t)$. As a function relationship, it can be expressed as $L = L(t)\ 0 < t < 1$. Where 't' denotes the specified duration from zero onwards.

Two-Level Representation of Daily Load In the load duration curve, which is a cumulative curve of daily peak loads, the variation of load within a day is not recognised in it. Hence, LOLP is a crude approximation of system failure probability, and, therefore, system failure frequency is not calculated using the load duration curve. For system failure frequency calculations, a 2-level load representation is used, and Markov modelling is used to represent the transition of the load from load level to another. A 2-level load representation may be the true chronological load curve and the approximated model as 2 levels. It is assumed that low load is always the same every day and designated as L_o. L_i's peak load varies daily and may occur in a random sequence with a relative frequency of occurrence. The mean duration t_i of the peak is described by the exposure factor $e = t_i/d_o$. Where d_o is the length of the load cycle typically may be 24 hours. The factor 'e' is considered the same every day; its magnitude lies between 0 and 1. No rule can be specified on how to choose 'e'. It has been observed that results are not much sensitive to the value of 'e'.

If we assume that the total number of days is 'n' and peak level L_i occurs for n_i days, then the relative frequency of occurrence of this peak level is written as

$$\alpha_i = \frac{n_i}{n} \tag{21.46a}$$

Moreover, note that,

$$\sum_i \alpha_i = 1 \tag{21.46b}$$

Now it is observed that at any instant of time, the load will be in any of the states represented by levels L_o, $L_1, L_2, L_3 \ldots L_i$ and as state transition diagram. Using Markov modelling, the probabilities of each state rate of transitions can be put on the diagram.

Total duration of study = $n \cdot d_o$

Duration of load level $L_0 = (1 - e)\, d_o \cdot n$

Hence, P_{Lo} = Probabilities of load level L_o

$$P_{Lo} = \frac{(1-e)d_o \cdot n}{n \cdot d_o} = (1-e) \tag{21.47}$$

Duration of load level $L_i = n_i e d_o$

Hence P_{Li} probability of load level

L_i state is given as:

$$P_{Li} = \frac{n_i \cdot e \cdot d_o}{n \cdot d_o} = \alpha_i e \tag{21.48}$$

Further, it is pointed out that transition from L_o to any higher level L_i state will take place at a rate

$$(\lambda + i) = [L_i /(1 - e)\, d_o] \tag{21.49}$$

Transition from higher level L_i will take place to L_o only with transition rate

$$(\lambda + i) = 1/ed_o \tag{21.50}$$

These way relations and steady-state probabilities specify the complete Markov modelling of 2-level representation of the daily load. This type of load modelling is a part of frequency and duration calculation.

21.8.4 Transmission Line Model

The failure rate of the transmission line depends largely on weather conditions. Under normal weather conditions, the failure rate is quite low. Under severe weather conditions, it may quite high. The simple way of accounting for the effects of changing weather is to use modified failure and repair rates for the transmission line. These modified rates are weighted averages of the corresponding normal and severe weather rates. Assume λ and μ are failure and repair rates under normal conditions and λ' and μ' are failure and repair rates under severe conditions. If T_N and T_w are mean durations for normal and severe weather conditions, then the modified failure rate is given as follows:

$$\lambda_t = \left(\frac{T_N}{T_N + T_W}\right)\lambda + \left(\frac{T_W}{T_N + T_W}\right)\lambda' \tag{21.51}$$

Assume that repair mean time under normal and severe weather conditions are given as T_r and T_r'

$$\mu_r = \frac{1}{T_r} \quad \text{and} \quad \mu_r' = \frac{1}{T_r'}$$

Weighted mean repair time can be given as

$$T_r = \frac{\lambda T_N T_r + \lambda' T_W T_r'}{\lambda T_N + \lambda' T_W}$$

Or modified repair rates μ_t is given as follows:

$$\mu_t = \frac{\lambda T_N + \lambda' T_W}{\lambda T_N T_r + \lambda' T_W \cdot T_r}$$

$$\Rightarrow \qquad \mu_t = \frac{\lambda T_N + \lambda T_W}{\frac{\lambda}{\mu} T_N + \frac{\lambda'}{\mu'} T_W} \tag{21.52}$$

These relations are used to calculate the availability and unavailability of a transmission line. The representation through weighted averages has limited applications. It can be used to evaluate single failures; multiple failures can be evaluated by this approach only if the lines involved are exposed to weather conditions that are independent of each other. Line in the same region and subjected to the same weather fluctuations cannot be considered in this method because the results for double and higher order failures would become grossly inaccurate.

21.9 ▶ GENERATION CAPACITY RELIABILITY EVALUATION

Loss of load probability (LOLP) is one of the most commonly used indexes for planning generating capacity. This index is generally obtained by convolving the generation model with a load model. The generation system model used is known as the capacity outage probability table. The traditional and well-accepted algorithms for generation system modelling based on recursive procedures are discussed in this section. Such methods are theoretically accurate for calculating the discrete probability distribution of the generation capacity outages. These discrete probability distributions resulted from failure, repair density functions and derived availability and unavailability functions.

Moreover, in such modelling, each unit's failure and repair distribution functions are assumed to be independent. Hence, for identical units, the binomial distribution is adopted. Recently many researchers have used continuous probability distribution as an approximation for capacity outage probability distribution. Many of them have utilised normal distribution. Some approaches are based on Laguerre polynomials, which used Gamma distribution as the basic building blocks. A generalised approach is presented to the use of continuous distribution approximation for generating capacity reliability evaluation. Gram-Charlier's expression is shown to have a special of this formulation. This method's potential lies in the fact that any continuous distribution function can be examined for its suitability for modelling generation systems or any discrete distribution function. LOLP distribution is based on 2 and 3 parameters Gamma distribution functions. Loss of load expression in days per year has been calculated based on daily peaks.

A methodology for evaluating the probability of failure based on continuous load and generation model at safety factor considerations. It is based on generation system reliability evaluation using probability theory. In this method, methodologies have been introduced to evaluate generating system reliability using different load and generation models. The evaluation of loss and load probabilities has been based on load generation models. The assessment also accounts for the various load models as load duration curve, normal load distribution with constant mean. A frequency and duration approach for generation reliability evaluation has used methods of stages. Their approach postulates multi-parameter distribution for the probability and frequency of generating capacity outages. Then, parameters of these distributions are obtained from the generating unit parameters by using the moment matching techniques. The technique used is the frequency and duration approach, coupled with the equivalent load duration curve (ELDC) method. This chapter presents the methodologies for evaluating the probability of failure based on the continuous load and generation model and safety factor considerations.

21.9.1 Probabilistic Methods for Reliability Evaluation

Reliability of a system is the probability of a system performing its function adequately for a period intended under the operating conditions intended. According to this statement, success probability, adequate function, period and operating condition are the system's primary attributes. Reliability indices and success and failure probabilities have been evaluated using the Gaussian distribution approach (GDA), peak load consideration (PLC), and safety factor concept (SFC) and Simpson 1/3 rule successfully.

Gaussian Distribution Approach (GDA) The load model is Gaussian distributed for a specified time interval.

$$f(P_d) = \frac{1}{\sigma_d\sqrt{2\pi}} e^{-0.5\left(\frac{P_d - \overline{P}_d}{\sigma_d}\right)^2} \tag{21.53}$$

where

P_d = Demand at the generating stations.

$\overline{P}_d$ = Average or mean load at the plant.

σ_d = Standard deviation of demand.

The aggregate generation capacity model is Gaussian distributed system.

$$f(C) = \frac{1}{\sigma_c\sqrt{2\pi}} e^{-0.5\left(\frac{C - \overline{C}}{\sigma_c}\right)^2} \tag{21.54}$$

Where C = capacity of the generating station, $\overline{C}$ = mean capacity of the plant, σ_c = Standard deviation of capacity.

The failure probability (P_F) for the above generation and load models of the developed system is described as follows:

$$P_F = (1 - P_s) \tag{21.55}$$

The success probability (P_s) of the developed power system using GDA can be expressed as follows.

$$P_s = \int_{-\infty}^{\infty}\int_{-\infty}^{C} \frac{1}{2\pi\sigma_c\sigma_d} e^{-0.5\left[\frac{C-\overline{C}}{\sigma_c}\right]^2} e^{-0.5\left[\frac{P_d - \overline{P}_d}{\sigma_d}\right]^2} dc \cdot dP_d \tag{21.56}$$

where

P_F = probability of failure of generating power station.

P_S = probability of success of generating power station.

C = generating capacity of the power plant.

$\overline{C}$ = mean generating capacity available of the power plant.

Putting, $x = \dfrac{C-\overline{C}}{\sigma_c}$ and $y = \dfrac{P_d - \overline{P}_d}{\sigma_d}$

The above equation can be written as follows after simplification according to substitution conditions.

$$P_s = \int_{-\infty}^{\infty}\left[\int_{-\infty}^{z} e^{-0.5(x^2+y^2)}dy\right]dx \tag{21.57}$$

$$\text{where, } Z = \frac{\sigma_c x + \overline{C} - \overline{P}_d}{\sigma_d}$$

Further making substitution as follows, consider

$$x' = x\cos\theta + y\sin\theta$$

$$y' = -x\sin\theta + y\cos\theta$$

Above transformation corresponds to a rotation of axis by θ angle. Following substitutions have been made in equation (5).

Let $\sin\theta = \dfrac{\sigma_c}{\sqrt{P_d^2+\sigma_C^2}}$ and $\cos\theta = \dfrac{\sigma_d}{\sqrt{P_d^2+\sigma_C^2}}$

Because of the above substitution, the success probability of the MHPP is given written as follows:

$$P_s = \int_{-\infty}^{\infty}\int_{-\infty}^{\beta}\frac{1}{2\pi}e^{-0.5(x'^2+y'^2)}dy'dx' \tag{21.58}$$

where $\beta = \dfrac{\overline{C}-\overline{P}_d}{\sqrt{\sigma_d^2+\sigma_c^2}}$

The limit β comes out to be independent of x'. The above equation is further simplified as follows.

$$P_s = \int_{-\infty}^{\beta}\left[\int_{-\infty}^{\infty}\frac{1}{\sqrt{2\pi}}e^{-0.5(x'^2)}dx'\right]e^{-0.5(y'^2)}dy'$$

$$P_s = \int_{-\infty}^{+\beta}\frac{1}{\sqrt{2\pi}}e^{-0.5(y'^2)}dy' = \varphi(\beta) \tag{21.59}$$

The numerical value of φ (β) is the area under the normal distribution curve having mean = 0 and standard deviation $\int_{-\infty}^{\beta}$ [N(0,1)] = 1, and this value can be conveniently obtained from the standard normal distribution table. Failure probability v/s generating capacity curves have been plotted for different values of the capacity and load models.

Daily variation in the load can be accounted for by predicting the various load levels P_{di}. The relative frequency of occurrence of these levels is assumed to be L_o, L_1, L_2 …, L_i, and frequency of occurrences $\alpha_0\ \alpha_1\ \alpha_2$, …, α_I. For each load level, probability of failure can be calculated, and the overall probability of failure is given as follows:

$$P_F = \sum_i \alpha_i P_{fi} \tag{21.60}$$

where

α_I = Relative frequency of occurrence.

P_{fi} = Failure probability for L_ith load level.

From eqn. (4.7) it follows that

$$P_{fi} = 1 - \Phi(\beta_i) \tag{21.61}$$

Hence, overall failure probability is given as follows

$$P_F = \sum_i \alpha_i [1 - \phi(\beta_i)] \tag{21.62}$$

The above expression can be used to calculate failure probabilities. It is obvious that failure probability dependent on α_i, and β_i, i.e., on the relative frequency of occurrence of various load levels and β_i as given below:

$$\alpha_i = n_i n$$

$$\beta_i = \frac{\overline{C}_i - \overline{L}_i}{\sigma_{d_i}^2 + \sigma_{C_i}^2} \tag{21.63}$$

where

n = Total duration of the study.

N_i = Duration for which L_ith load level occurs.

C_i = Average generation capacity is available for L_ith load level.

L_i = Mean L_ith load level.

Reliability Evaluation Based on Peak Load Consideration (PLC) and Safety Factor Concept (SFC) The probability distribution function of generation capacity is obtained as Gaussian. Peak loading of the system dominates over low-level loading, whereas failure under low load level is negligible. If P_{dmax} is the peak load on the system, the safety factor 'S' is defined as follows:

$$S = C/P_{\text{dmax}} \tag{21.64}$$

The generating capacity 'C' is normally distributed, and S is a random variable. At constant P_{dmax} the distribution of the safety factor 'S' will also be normally distributed. The safety factor function is given as follows:

$$f_s = \frac{P_{d\max}}{\sqrt{2\pi\sigma_c}} e^{-0.5\left(\frac{P_{d\max} S - \overline{C}}{\sigma_c}\right)} \tag{21.65}$$

Safety factor S has a Gaussian distribution with mean.

$$\overline{S} = \frac{C}{P_{d\max}} \quad \text{and} \quad \sigma_s = \frac{\sigma_c}{P_{d\max}} \tag{21.66}$$

The probability of failure of the system is given as follows:

$$P_F = \int_{-\infty}^{1} \frac{P_{d\max}}{\sqrt{2\pi\sigma_s}} e^{-0.5\left(\frac{s - \overline{c}/Pd\max}{\sigma_s}\right)^2} ds = \varphi\left[\frac{1 - \dfrac{\overline{C}}{P_{d\max}}}{\dfrac{\sigma_c}{P_{d\max}}}\right] \tag{21.67}$$

The system's failure probability has obtained using the above equation at different generation capacity and peak loads. P_F v/s $\dfrac{\overline{C}}{P_{d\max}}$ curve is plotted for reliability evaluation of the system using the safety factor concept. These curves can be used as a standard curve for evaluating the generating capacity's failure probability using the above equation.

LOLP Evaluation Using Simpson 1/3 Rule The failure probability is evaluated with a more realistic model as the load duration curve in this section. The individual daily peak loads can be arranged in descending order to form a cumulative load model, which is known as the daily peak load variation curve (DPLVC). The resultant model is known as the load duration curve (LDC) when the individual hourly load variance is used. The generation model adopted in this system has a Normal distribution function. The reliability evaluation is based on the maximum average generation capacity available.

The probability of load exceeding the generation capacity is called the loss of load probability (LOLP). A 'loss of load' will occur only when the system load level exceeds the generation capacity's capability remaining in service. The LDC is divided into a number of steps to produce the multi-step model. The amount of approximation can be reduced by increasing the number of steps in this approximation. Maximum 100 steps of the SLDC are considered for evaluation of the LOLP of the composite power system. Various steps of the stepped load duration curve (SLDC) indicate variation in load during the power system's 24 hours operation. The following approximation is based on Simpson's 1/3 rule for evaluation of the reliability index: LOLP. The LOLP of the power system using SLDC is written as follows:

$$\text{LOLP} = \int_0^{100} \frac{t}{100}\left[\int_{-\infty}^{P_d(t)} \frac{1}{\sqrt{2\pi}\sigma_c} e^{-0.5\left(\frac{C-\overline{C}}{\sigma_c}\right)^2} dc\right] dt \tag{21.68}$$

Putting, $\dfrac{C-\overline{C}}{\sigma_c} = Z$

The LOLP expression for 100 steps of the SLDC using the above equation is expressed as follows:

$$\text{LOLP} = \int_0^{100} \frac{t}{100}\left[\int_{-\infty}^{P_d(t)} \frac{1}{\sqrt{2\pi}\sigma_c} e^{-0.5(Z)^2} dz\right] dt \tag{21.69}$$

$$\text{LOLP} = \int_0^{100} \frac{t}{100}\varphi\left[\frac{P_d(t)-\overline{C}}{\sigma_c}\right] dt \tag{21.70}$$

The inner integral represents the area under the [N (0,1)] curve for the various values of 't' and, hence, replaced by the $\phi\dfrac{[P_d(t)-\overline{C}]}{\sigma_c}$ function. Thus the expression (4.15) can be evaluated by any one of the methods of area evaluation. The LOLP based on the SLDC of a power system is evaluated by Simpson's 1/3 rule for reliability approximation. LOLP of the system is evaluated considering LDC as SLDC with a maximum of 100 steps. This may be possible if the daily load duration curve can be approximated as a multilevel representation, as in the case with Markov modelling of load in frequency and duration calculations. Generally, load varies every moment during the 24-hour operation of the system. Load varies many times in steps daily. The SLDC of the power system is an important keyword for power system planning and reliability evaluation of the system. The reliability evaluation of an interconnected power system using the above methodologies is explained in the following numerical example.

Example 21.9 An interconnected composite power system contains the following generation capacity:

(1) $2 \times 200 = 400$ MW Nuclear power plant
(2) $10 \times 50 = 500$ MW Thermal power plant
(3) $3 \times 100 = 300$ MW Hydropower plant

The annual daily peak load variation is from 300 MW to 1000 MW.

(a) Prepare the generation capacity state table, including the standard deviation data for graphical illustration and reliability evaluation of the power system.
(b) Calculate the failure probabilities for (i) constant mean load of 480 MW, (ii) constant generation capacity of 500 MW and (iii) provide a graphical illustration of the power system using Gaussian distribution approach.
(c) Calculate the failure probabilities of power system considering safety factor concept and peak load consideration for (i) constant load of P_d = 480 MW, (ii) peak load variation from P_{dmax} = 480 MW to P_{dmax} = 510 MW and (iii) provide the graphical illustration for reliability analysis of power system.
(d) Evaluate the LOLP of the system for P_{dmax} = 1000 MW and P_{dmin} = 300 MW for 10 steps of the stepped load duration curve and draw the LOLP v/s generation capacity curves for analysis of the power system.

Solution **(a)** The generation capacity state data and standard deviation data of power stations are given in the following table. The subscript 0, 1, 2, 3, 4, etc., present the generation unit availability in the power system due to nuclear (X), thermal (Y) and hydro (Z) power plants (Table 21.3).

Table 21.3 The generation capacity state data and standard deviation data of power stations

Sr. no.	*Capacity state*	*Availability of generation capacity in MW*	$\sigma_c = 5\%$	$\sigma_c = 10\%$	$\sigma_c = 15\%$	$\sigma_c = 20\%$	$\sigma_c = 25\%$
1	$X_1Y_0Z_0$	200	10	20	30	40	50
2	$X_2Y_0Z_0$	400	20	40	60	80	100
3	$X_1Y_1Z_0$	450	22.5	45	67.5	90	112.5
4	$X_1Y_2Z_0$	500	25	50	75	100	125
5	$X_1Y_3Z_0$	550	27.5	55	82.5	110	137.5
6	$X_1Y_4Z_0$	600	30	60	90	120	150
7	$X_1Y_5Z_0$	650	32.5	65	97.5	130	162.5
8	$X_1Y_6Z_0$	700	35	70	105	140	175
9	$X_1Y_7Z_0$	750	37.5	75	112.2	150	187.5
10	$X_1Y_8Z_0$	800	40	80	120	160	200
11	$X_1Y_9Z_0$	850	42.5	85	127.5	170	212.5
12	$X_1Y_{10}Z_0$	900	45	90	135	180	225
13	$X_1Y_{10}Z_1$	1000	50	100	150	200	250
14	$X_1Y_{10}Z_2$	1100	55	110	165	220	275
15	$X_1Y_{10}Z_3$	1200	60	120	180	240	300

(b) Failure probability evaluation using Gaussian distribution approach

(i) Failure probability evaluation at a constant mean load of 480 MW

The failure probability is evaluated, keeping the mean load constant at 480 W using the GDA equation and standard deviation data table. The standard deviations for generating capacity and mean load have assumed 10% of the generating capacity and mean load. The probability of failure for generation capacity C = 490 MW is $P_f = 0.3853$. Similarly, using this equation, the failure probability can be calculated considering available generating capacity states at a fixed value of the mean load at 480 MW.

Various plots of failure probability versus generating capacity are shown in Fig. 21.1 with different values of standard deviations. The failure probabilities are illustrated in curve: A (σ_c = 5% of capacity and σ_d = 5% of load), curve: B (σ_c = 5% of capacity and σ_d = 15% of load), curve: C (σ_c = 15% of capacity and σ_d = 5% of load) and curve: D (σ_c = 15% of capacity and σ_d = 15% of load). The various curves are labelled for various combinations of σ_c and σ_d. It is observed from A and B that for the same generating capacity of the system, the probability of failure with B is more than A. It is because of the large uncertainty involved in generating capacity distribution function.

Similarly, by observing the curve A and C for the same generating capacity, the probability of B's failure is more than C and so on. From the curve D, the failure probability for any generating capacity is more than from other curves. In summary, the probability of failure increases with either increase of σ_c or an increase of σ_d or both.

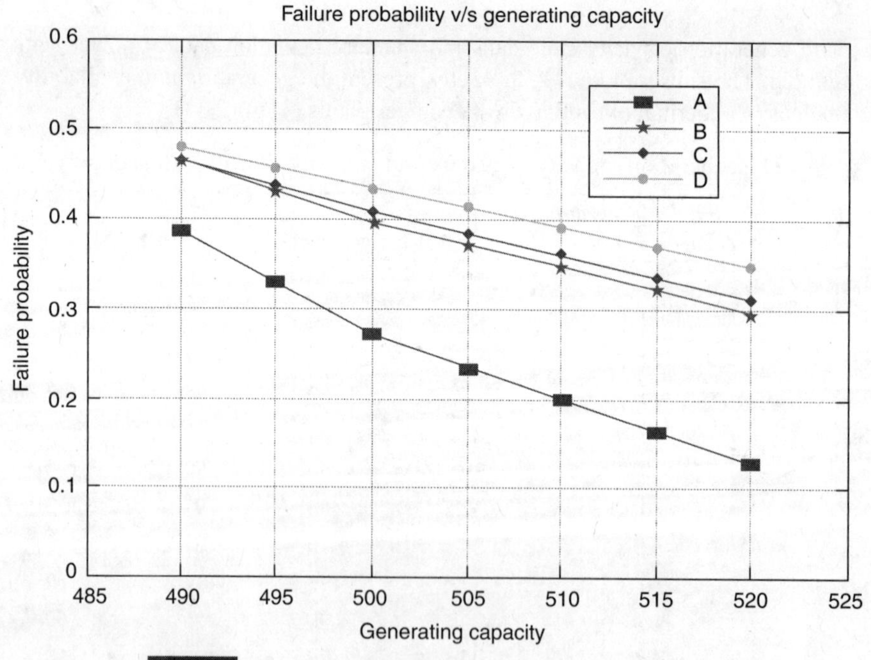

Fig. 21.1 P_F v/s C of the developed system at constant load

(ii) Failure probability evaluation at constant generation capacity

The failure probability of at constant generation capacity (500 MW) is evaluated using GDA in this section. The standard deviations for both generating capacity and mean load have been assumed 5% of the generating capacity and mean load, respectively. The probability of failure for generation capacity C = 500 MW as $P_f = 0.4432$. Now the load is increased in step of 5 MW at the fixed value of the mean capacity of 500 MW, and the probability of failure is calculated. Various plots of failure probability versus generating capacity are shown in the following figure, selecting the different values of the standard deviations.

The failure probabilities are illustrated in curve: A (σ_c = 10% of capacity and σ_d = 10% of load), curve: B (σ_c = 10% of capacity and σ_d = 20% of load), curve: C (σ_c = 20% of capacity and σ_d = 10% of load) and curve: D (σ_c = 20% of capacity and σ_d = 20% of load). If the mean load and generating capacity are equal, then the probability of failure and success probability is exactly equal to 50%. It is the same in all cases independent of standard deviations, as shown in Fig. 21.2. Below the intersection point, the probability of failure increases as the variations σ_c and σ_d increases, and above the intersection point, it varies oppositely. The P_F has been evaluated for σ_d = 10% of $\bar{L}$ and σ_C = 10% of $\bar{C}$ using the GDA equation, and the overall failure probability is evaluated as $P_F = 0.0594$. If the values of standard deviations σ_C and σ_1 are increased from 10% to 20%, the overall failure probability is increased by the same values of generating capacity and load levels at a fixed frequency of occurrence. At the value of σ_C = 20% of $\bar{C}$ and σ_d = 20% of $\bar{L}$, the failure probability P_F is 0.0986.

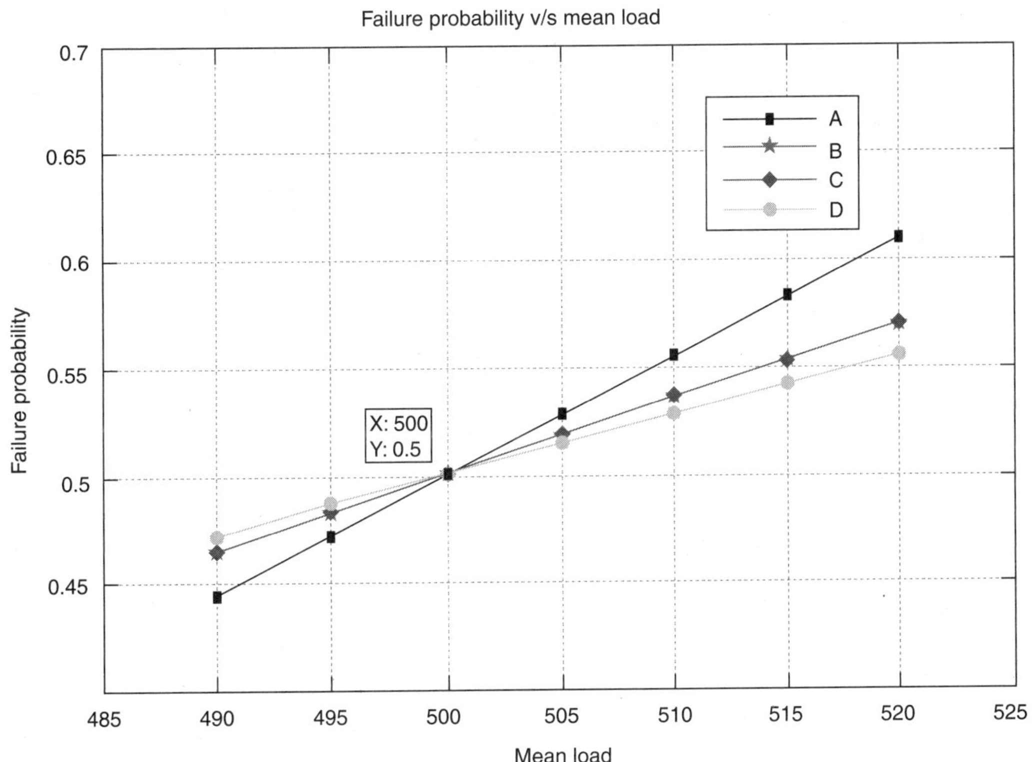

Fig. 21.2 *P_F v/s generating capacity at constant capacity*

(c) Failure probability evaluation using SFC and PLC (Table 21.4).

Table 21.4 Load levels and corresponding mean capacity

$\overline{L_i}$	1000 MW	1200 MW	1500 MW	1800 MW	2000 MW
$\overline{C_i}$	1250 MW	1500 MW	1875 MW	2250 MW	2500 MW
α_i	0.1	0.2	0.4	0.2	0.1

(i) Failure probability evaluation at constant load

This section discusses generating capacity adequacy evaluation based on safety factors and worst-case loading conditions, assuming maximum loading P_{dmax} = 480 MW on the system. The curves have been plotted between the probability of failure and safety factor (C/P_{dmax}) for different value of standard deviations considering the approximations: curve: *A* for σ_c = 10% of *C*, curve *B* for σ_c = 12% of *C*, curve *C* for σ_c = 15% of *C* and curve *D* for σ_c = 18% of *C*. It is observed from curves *A* and *B*, the probability of failure with σ_c = 12% of *C* is more than σ_c = 10% of *C* for the same generating capacity or safety factor of the system, Now if σ_c increased for same values of generation capacity and safety factor of the system, the P_f is increased.

Failure probability of system decreased with increasing the safety factor for all values of the generation capacity. For any value of generation capacity's safety factor, failure probability rises with an increase in its standard deviation. The Fig. 21.3 presents failure probability v/s safety factor approximation at constant load and variable generation capacity. For the 10.5% safety factor, failure probability increases with increasing values of the generation capacity's standard deviation.

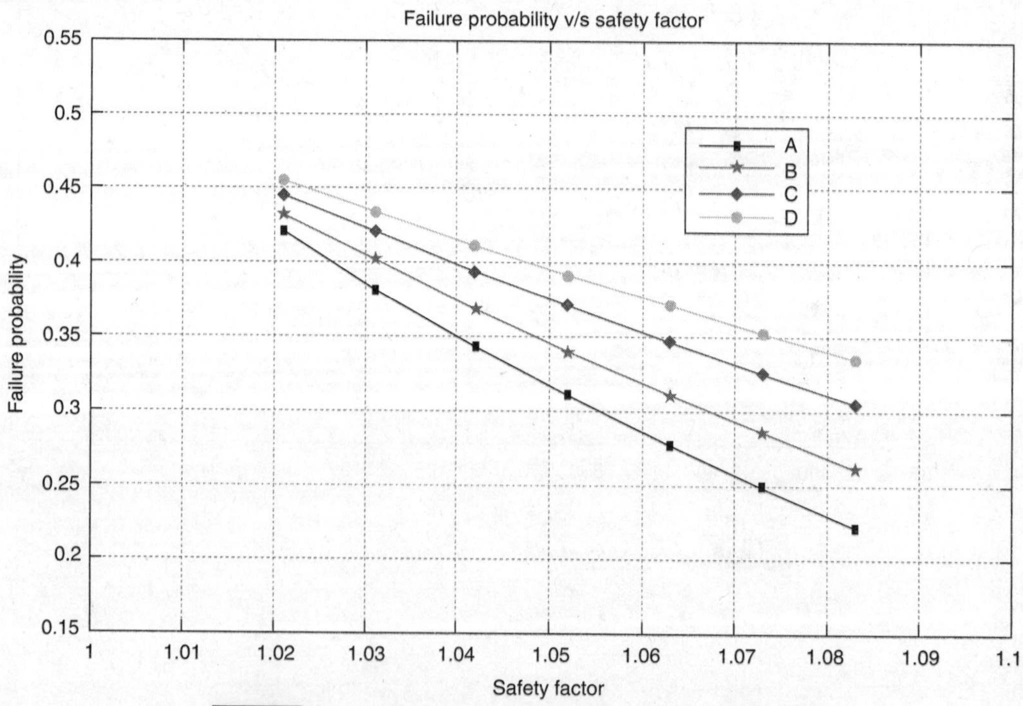

Fig. 21.3 *Failure probability v/s safety factor at constant load*

(ii) Failure probability evaluation at variable load

If the maximum loading increased from $P_{dmax} = 480$ MW to 510 MW, for the same value of safety factor $(\bar{C}/P_{dmax})$ the various curves are shown in the following figure for the curve: A for $\sigma_c = 10\%$ of C, curve B for $\sigma_c = 12\%$ of C, curve C for $\sigma_c = 15\%$ of C and curve D for $\sigma_c = 18\%$ of C. The P_F increases with an increase of σ_C for the same values of generation capacity. It is because of the considerable uncertainty involved in the generating capacity distribution factor.

The generation system's failure probability is constant and equal to 50% for all curves at variable load if the safety factor is one. If the safety factor is below one, then the failure probability for $\sigma_c = 10\%$ of C is more than $\sigma_c = 12\%$ of C. If it is more significant than one, the failure probability is simply varied oppositely. The safety factor is the ratio of the generation capacity and peak load demand. The safety factor is one at equal values of the generation capacity and peak load. At this instant, failure and success probability both are 50%, as shown in Fig. 21.4. Suppose the generation capacity is higher than the load. In that case, curve A's failure probability is higher than curves B, C and D. Similarly, if the load is higher than the generation capacity, the failure probability of curve A is less than the B and vice versa.

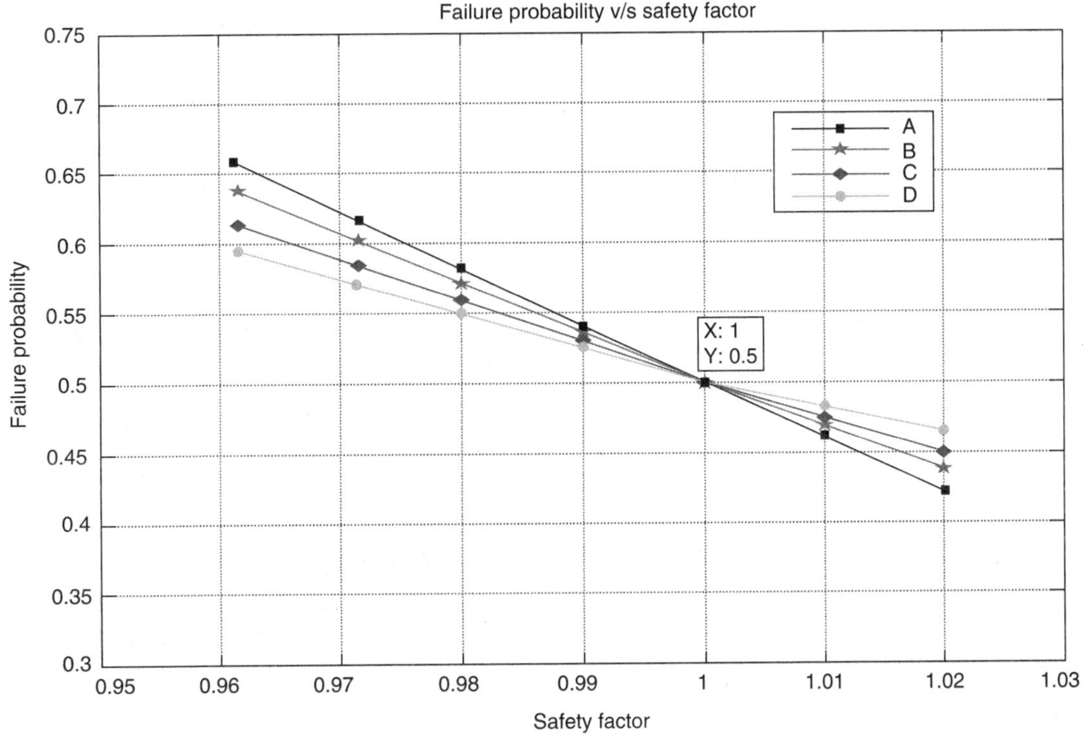

Fig. 21.4 *Failure probability v/s safety factor at variable load*

(d) LOLP evaluation using Simpson 1/3 rule

The LDC is a straight line with $P_{dmax} = 1000$ MW and $P_{dmin} = 300$ MW for reliability evaluation of the system using Simpson 1/3 rule. Simpson 1/3 rule approximation is used for a maximum of 100 steps of the SLDC in the example. As discussed earlier, systems load varies in many steps during 24 hours operation of the power system. The following figure represents the relation between LOLP and various generating capacity available for 10 steps of SLDC with effects of different σ_C. The curves A, B, C and D in Fig. 21.5 show the relations of LOLP and generating capacity at σ_C = 10%, 15%, 20% and 25% of generating capacity, respectively, for 10 steps of the SLDC. The LOLP of the system increases with increments in σ_C due to the considerable uncertainty involved in the generating capacity distribution function. For a particular value of the generation capacity, the LOLP of the system increases with standard deviation. Considered 10 steps of the SLDC indicate 10 variations in load during the developed system's 24-hour operation.

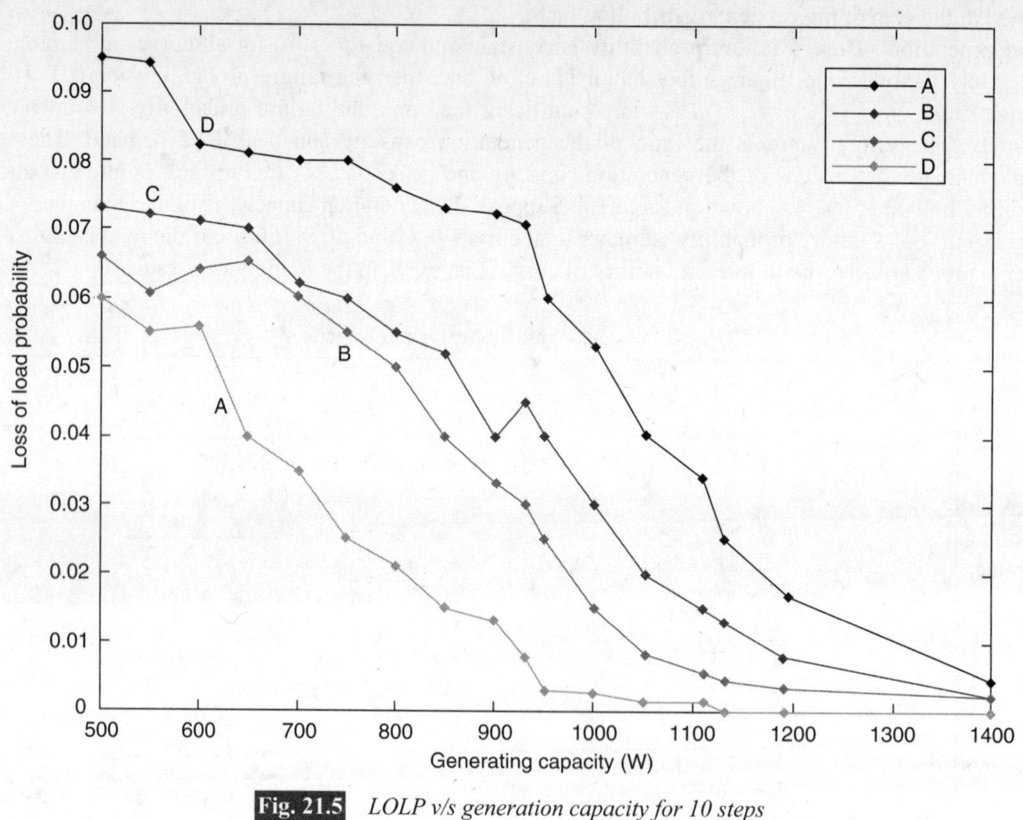

Fig. 21.5 *LOLP v/s generation capacity for 10 steps*

21.9.2 Frequency and Duration Method for Failure Probability Calculations

This approach load model used is 2 levels or multilevel Markov model and merged with the states of the capacity outage probability table. Halperin and Adler first introduced a frequency and duration approach to capacity evaluation in 1958. There are increasingly many attempts to incorporate the generation and major transmission elements into an overall or composite system evaluation procedure, providing both load point and overall system adequacy indices.

Frequency and duration are the most useful indices for customer or load point evaluation. Therefore, creating similar indices for capacity assessment appears to offer increased compatibility in the overall assessment. The frequency and duration (F&D) method requires additional system data to use basic probabilistic methods to illustrate the fundamental 2-state model for a baseload generating unit. The LOLE or LOEE methods utilise steady-state availability A and the unavailability U parameters for this model. The combined state diagram is partitioned into 2 sets; one is with positive margin states called 'W' sets (having $C_k - L_k$ positive). The other sets with negative margin (having $C_k - L_k$ negative) called failed set 'F'. The probability of each combined state is the product of the corresponding load state and generation state probabilities. Then expression for failure frequency is given as follows:

$$f = \sum_{i \varepsilon w} p_i \sum_{j \varepsilon f} q_{ij} \quad \text{or} \quad f = \sum_{j \varepsilon f} p_j \sum_{j e f} q_{ji} \tag{21.71}$$

where

p_i and p_j are the probabilities of the combined generation and load system.

q_{ij} is the transition rate from ith state to jth state.

Failure probability is given as follows:

$$P_F = \sum_{j \varepsilon f} p_i$$

And success probability is given as follow:

$$P_W = \sum_{j \varepsilon w} p_i$$

Expressions for mean uptime (MUT) and mean downtime (MDT) are given as follows:

$$\text{MUT} = P_W/f \quad \text{and} \quad \text{MDT} = P_F/f \tag{21.72}$$

The generation system model gives the probability and frequency of having a given level of capacity forced out of service and the complementary level of capacity in use. This generation system model can be modified to provide cumulative probabilities and frequencies rather than values corresponding to a specific capacity level. The cumulative values give the probability and frequency of having that capacity or more forced out of service at any given capacity level. The capacity model developed using the frequency and duration approach can be reduced considerably by truncating the table for cumulative probabilities less than a pre-specified magnitude. It is the most significant reduction factor in a large system study.

21.10 ► COMPOSITE GENERATION AND TRANSMISSION SYSTEM RELIABILITY

Reliability evaluation of the combined generation–transmission (bulk power system as shown in Fig. 21.6) has been a significant concern in power system planning. Such a composite system can be divided into many operating states in terms of the capacity available to fulfil demand subject to the satisfaction and security limits (line flows and voltage limit). Hence, the evaluation of a reliability index for a composite system is very computationally demanding. Power system reliability is usually categorised into the regions of adequacy and security. System adequacy is defined as the system's ability to supply its load accounting line flow constraints and accounting outages of generators and branches. System security (dynamic) is defined as the power system's ability to withstand disturbances arising from faults or unscheduled removal of bulk power supply equipment. It means adequacy assessment is the steady-state post outage analysis of the composite power system, while security assessment (in reliability evaluation aspect) involves dynamic condition analysis.

This chapter focuses attention on adequacy assessment. Many researchers have developed reliability evaluation methodologies based on linear programming model accounting voltage and line flow constraints used for adequacy assessment of bulk power system, a reliability evaluation methodology for a composite system based on Monte-Carlo sampling with a variance reduction scheme which permits the incorporation of planner's experience or of analytical models as 'Regression' variables, and an efficient new approach for power system reliability evaluation using the decomposition simulation approach. The interconnected systems have been modelled by a probabilistic flow network with capacitated areas. A node in the network denotes each area. Additional nodes represent source and load.

Reliability evaluation of generation and transmission systems is computationally very demanding due to large system size and a large number of system states that must be assessed and complexities in failure effect analysis (FEA) necessary to assess each state. Computational efficiency can be achieved by a suitable choice of load flow technique and truncation of state space. In composite system reliability evaluation, D.C. power flow or compensation injection-based power flow can be used to reduce computational time in FEA. An efficient continuation power flow technique can be used. Most of composite system reliability evaluation considers only single- and double-line failures. Typically 5-fold failure states are investigated for a combined generation – transmission reliability evaluation. The truncated state space is limit to the state where $(l + g) \leq 5$ and $l \leq 3$, where 'l' and 'g' denote the number of line and generator failures, respectively.

A major difficulty in adequacy evaluation of composite generation and transmission of bulk power systems is the computation time required when the power system is large and high-outage levels are investigated. A technique for adequacy estimation of a selected area in a power system network is used in which the remaining network is modelled as an adequacy equivalent. This approach can be useful in large power networks, where it is necessary to perform detailed adequacy evaluation of selected specific areas in the overall network. The equivalent approval may also not be possible when the entire composite power system network is considered. The basic concepts are illustrated using a simple radial power system. The proposed method's advantages are described by presenting system study results for the IEEE 2-area reliability test system. Electric power systems can be generally categorised into 3 segments or functional zones of generation, transmission and distribution. Reliability evaluation is usually conducted separately in these 3 zones and is not typically applied directly to the entire system due to the enormity of the problems.

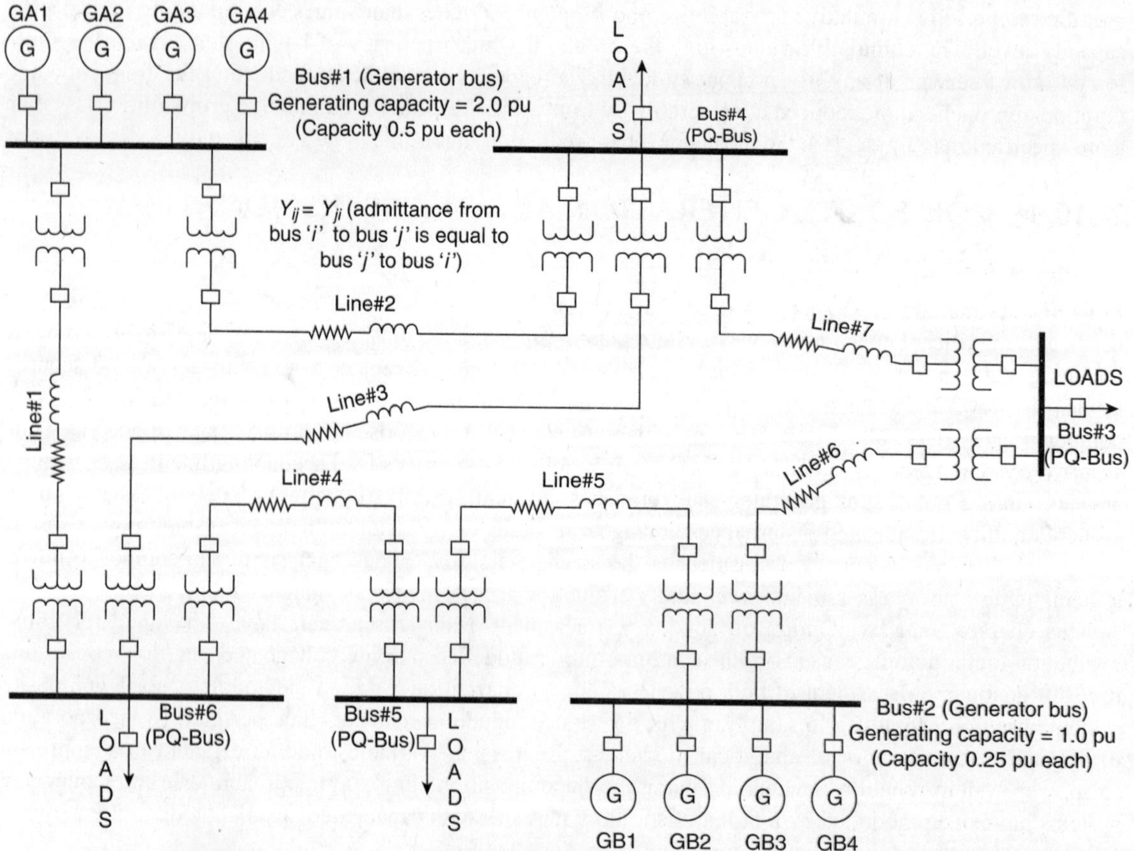

Fig. 21.6 *One line diagram of 6-bus 7-line interconnected composite power system*

The methodology for evaluating a composite system's reliability based on peak load considerations is illustrated in this section, which considers the steady-state voltage stability limit. The voltage stability limit is obtained for the probable outage of transmission lines and removal of generating equipment along with the combined state probabilities. The loss of load probability index (LOLP) is evaluated by merging the capacity probability list with the load model. The state spaces are truncated by assuming the limit on the total number of outages. A predictor-corrector technique is used along with a one-dimensional search method to optimise the stability limit for each outage state. The algorithm has been implemented on the following 6-bus test system. A methodology has been developed for calculating the failure probability of composite generation and transmission systems based on voltage stability consideration. This chapter's main objective is to evaluate the reliability of a bulk power system considering voltage stability at various outages of generators and transmission lines and overloaded conditions of the interconnected composite electrical power system. Six-bus system data are given in Tables 21.5–21.9.

Table 21.5 System data

No. of bus	*No. of shunt*	*No. of lines*	$\in$
6	2	7	0.000

Table 21.6 Line data

Line no.	*Bus no.*		*Resistance in PU*	*Reactance in PU*	B_{line} *in PU*	*Tap*
	From	*To*				
1	1	6	0.1230	0.5180	0.0000	1.0000
2	1	4	0.0800	0.3700	0.0000	1.0000
3	4	6	0.0970	0.4070	0.0000	1.0000
4	6	5	0.0000	0.3000	0.0000	1.0000
5	5	2	0.2820	0.6400	0.0000	1.0000
6	2	3	0.7230	1.0500	0.0000	1.0000
7	4	3	0.0000	0.1330	0.0000	1.0000

Table 21.7 Bus data

Bus	*Voltage* $\|V\|$	$\angle\delta$	P_G	Q_G	P_L	Q_L
1 (Slack)	1.1500	0.0000	0.0000	0.0000	0.0000	0.0000
2 (PV)	1.1500	0.0000	0.5000	0.0000	0.0000	0.0000
3 (PQ)	1.0000	0.0000	0.0000	0.0000	0.2750	0.0650
4 (PQ)	1.0000	0.0000	0.0000	0.0000	0.0000	0.0000
5 (PQ)	1.0000	0.0000	0.0000	0.0000	0.1500	0.0900
6 (PQ)	1.0000	0.0000	0.0000	0.0000	0.2500	0.0250

Table 21.8 Shunt data

Bus	1	2	3	4	5	6
Shunt	0.0000	0.0000	0.0000	0.0500	0.0500	0.0000

Table 21.9 Maximum reactive generation

Bus	1	2	3	4	5	6
Q_{limit}	2.0000	1.5000	0.0000	0.0000	0.0000	0.0000

The interconnection assistance between power systems in a function of many variables such as the system installed capacity, generation dispatch, forced and scheduled outages of generating units, load duration characteristics, the accuracy of load forecast, load diversity, the capability of the interconnections and the operating limits imposed on the transmission network due to thermal voltage and stability considerations. This chapter describes a probabilistic approach for evaluating the IA that a system can provide at any selected location without affecting its reliability level. The method calculates the expected value and the probability distribution of IA of each type. The reliability evaluation of a composite power system using the predictor-corrector technique is based on the Newton-Raphson algorithm. This methodology is combined with outages screening for composite system reliability evaluation based on Monte-Carlo simulation. In this approach, an acceleration table is formed according to the screening of single and double outages. While performing the simulation, all the outages are considered and evaluated using the acceleration table, which is discussed in the next example. The heuristics algorithm is adopted to reduce computational quality.

The effects of voltage collapse in the reliability evaluation of the composite system and an approach to calculate the voltage collapse related to bulk reliability indices as well as their impact on the adequacy reliability indices are described. In this approach, the adequacy analysis of each selected system state carries out in 2 steps. A system state transition sequence is utilised to calculate the frequency index. Topological analysis is used for the state enumeration approach to evaluate the bulk power system reliability. System frequency, duration and availability indices are obtained using topological enumeration. This methodology discusses the reliability assessment at a restructured power system using reliability network equivalent techniques. The main objective of power system restructuring and deregulation is to introduce competition in the power industry and to allow customers to select their suppliers based on price and reliability. The methodology is based on a non-sequential Monte-Carlo simulation combined with a linear optimisation model. The load at every bus is represented by 2 components: a firm and non-firm portion. Expected values of not served energy (EENS), not served demand (E PNS) and LOLP are computed for the whole system.

Unreliability cost evaluation of an entire power system provides a set of indexes that a system planner can use to balance the investments in different segments of the system to provide acceptable load point reliability. None of the references cited above accounted for the effects of voltage stability-related problems in the composite system's reliability evaluation. Nowadays, voltage stability is a severe problem that power utilities usually explore in the planning stage. The combined generation and transmission systems' capacity state must be evaluated based on the static voltage stability limit. It has become important because this limit in the power network is approaching much earlier than the thermal or angle stability constrained limit due to network limitations or reactive power deficiency. The voltage stability indicator is calculated for all possible system contingencies. In this chapter, a methodology is illustrated to evaluate the probability of failure based on peak load for the composite system accounting for voltage stability considerations. The steady-state voltage stability limit for possible line outages and generation outages is calculated along with the combined (generation–transmission) state probabilities. Thus, the capacity probability list may be merged with a suitable load model (peak load/load duration curve) to evaluate the load probability index's loss. State-space is truncated by assuming the limits on the total number of components (generation + transmission line) failure. A predictor-corrector technique is used along with a one-dimensional search method to get an optimised stability limit. Safe operating capacity in each combined state has been assumed to be 80% of maximum loadability.

21.10.1 Predictor-Corrector Technique for Steady-State Voltage Stability Limit

The predictor-corrector technique overcomes the non-convergence of the conventional N-R method of load flow analysis near the voltage stability limit. This technique used an iterative process involving predictor and corrector steps. A new solution is predicted for a specified pattern or load increases by using a known initial solution and the tangent vector. The corrector step converges to the exact solution point by using these estimated solutions. Continuation power flow equations are similar to those of conventional power flow analysis except that the increase in total load is added as a parameter t. The general form of equations results as follows:

$$F(V, \delta, t, k, \beta, \alpha) = 0 \tag{21.73}$$

Where t is a load parameter, δ is a vector of bus voltage angles, V is a vector of bus voltage magnitudes, k, α vector of generation participation and load participation factor, respectively, β is the vector of tan θ_p, and θ_p power factor angle at pth bus.

Predictor Step It is assumed that an initial load flow solution is available. For predicting the next step, solution tangent vector is obtained by setting differential of equation (21.73) equals to zero as follows:

$$[F_\delta \quad F_v \quad F_t]\begin{bmatrix} d\delta \\ dv \\ dt \end{bmatrix} = 0 \tag{21.74}$$

Where $$F_\delta = \frac{\partial F}{\partial \delta}, F_v = \frac{\partial F}{\partial v}, F_t = \frac{\partial F}{\partial t}$$

The appearance of the load variation parameter 't' adds one more equation. To solve equation (21.74), one of the tangent vector components is set +1 or −1. It also removes ill-conditioning of the equations. This component is called the continuation parameter. Now equation (21.74) is written as follows:

$$\begin{bmatrix} F_\delta & F_v & F_t \\ e_k^T & 0 & 0 \end{bmatrix}\begin{bmatrix} d\delta \\ dv \\ dt \end{bmatrix} = \begin{bmatrix} 0 \\ \pm 1 \end{bmatrix} \tag{21.75}$$

Where e_k^T is a row vector with all elements equal to zero except the kth element corresponding to the continuation parameter being equal to one. Initially, the load parameter is chosen as the continuation parameter, and the corresponding component of the tangent vector is set to +1. When the system is heavily stressed, then the continuation parameter is chosen to be the state variable. The most significant rate of change near the given solution and sign of its slope determines the sign of the corresponding component of the tangent vector. After solving for tangent vector, the prediction for the next solution is given by the following equation.

$$\begin{bmatrix} \delta \\ v \\ t \end{bmatrix} = \begin{bmatrix} \delta^0 \\ v^0 \\ t^0 \end{bmatrix} + \sigma \begin{bmatrix} d\delta \\ dv \\ dt \end{bmatrix} \tag{21.76}$$

$\{\delta^0, v^0, t^0\}$ is the initial solution vector. The corrector step solution's convergence will mainly depend on the step size σ; if convergence is not obtained in the corrector step, that predicted solution should be obtained newly, using equation (21.76) with the reduced value of step size σ and again corrector step is repeated with a new expected solution.

Corrector Step In the corrector step, the continuation power equation is augmented by one more equation that specifies the continuation parameter as follows:

$$\begin{bmatrix} F(v, \delta, t, k, \alpha, \beta) \\ (X_k - \eta) \end{bmatrix} = 0 \tag{21.77}$$

X_k is the continuation variable, and η its predicted value. Equation (21.77) is solved by the N-R method using the initial condition. The introduction of one additional equation specifying X_k models the Jacobian on N-R method, non-singular even at collapse point. Thus, it is possible to obtain a steady-state voltage stability limit.

21.10.2 Optimisation of Steady-State Voltage Stability Limit

For each generating capacity state, the objective is to obtain the maximum static voltage stability limit accounting for the real and reactive power generation limits. The complete formulation is written as follows:

$$J = \text{Max}\{P_d^{\text{limit}}\} \tag{21.78}$$

Subject to following constraints,

$$U_p^{\min} \le U_p \le U_p^{\max}, \quad p = 1, NC \tag{21.79}$$

$$Q_p^{\min} \le Q_p \le Q_p^{\max}, \quad p = 1, NC \tag{21.80}$$

$$P_i^{\min} \le P_i \le P_i^{\max}, \quad i = 1, NC \tag{21.81}$$

$$V_i^{\min} \le V_i \le V_i^{\max}, \quad i = 1, NC \tag{21.82}$$

$$f_i \le f_i^{\text{limit}} \tag{21.83}$$

where

P_d^{limit} = static voltage stability limit
NC = total number of reactive power control variables
U_p = Pth reactive power control variables
$U_p^{\min}$, U_p^{Max} = lower and upper limits on pth reactive power control variables
$Q_p^{\min}$, Q_p^{Max} = lower and upper limits on reactive power generation limits at pth bus
$P_i^{\min}$, P_i^{Max} = lower and upper limits on real power generation at ith bus
$V_i^{\min}$, V_i^{Max} = lower and upper limits on ith bus voltage
f_i = ith line MW flow
f_i^{limit} = line flow limit

The methodology used in optimising the objective function of equation (21.77) is a local variation r direct search method. Each iteration, one control variable is varied, and by using the continuation power flow algorithm, the maximum of equation (21.77) is obtained. It is repeated for all control variables within limits till no change in the objective function is observed. In iterations, it is also observed that the control is varied until no violation of the operating constraint occurs. These constraints are represented in relations given in equations (21.78)–(21.82). The computational steps are shown in the flowchart of Fig. 21.7. Starting point of the algorithm initial load flow solution and initial maximum load ability limit [dp lim(0)] and specified operating constraints in all the 2 iteration loops. Inner iteration loop from blocks 4 to 9 obtain maximum load ability limit by varying individual control variables U_p, for p = 1, NC in sequence. Such sequence is repeated by the outer iteration loop in blocks (3–11). This outer loop is repeated till there is no change in the static voltage stability limit. ΔU_p denotes the change in pth control variables in kth iteration. It is worth mentioning at this stage that in block 6, for determining the static voltage stability limit, the load is increased in the specified direction at each bus till there is no violation in operating constraints like line flow limits and bus voltages. In block number 8, the initial load ability limit is modified and changed to an increased value in iterations.

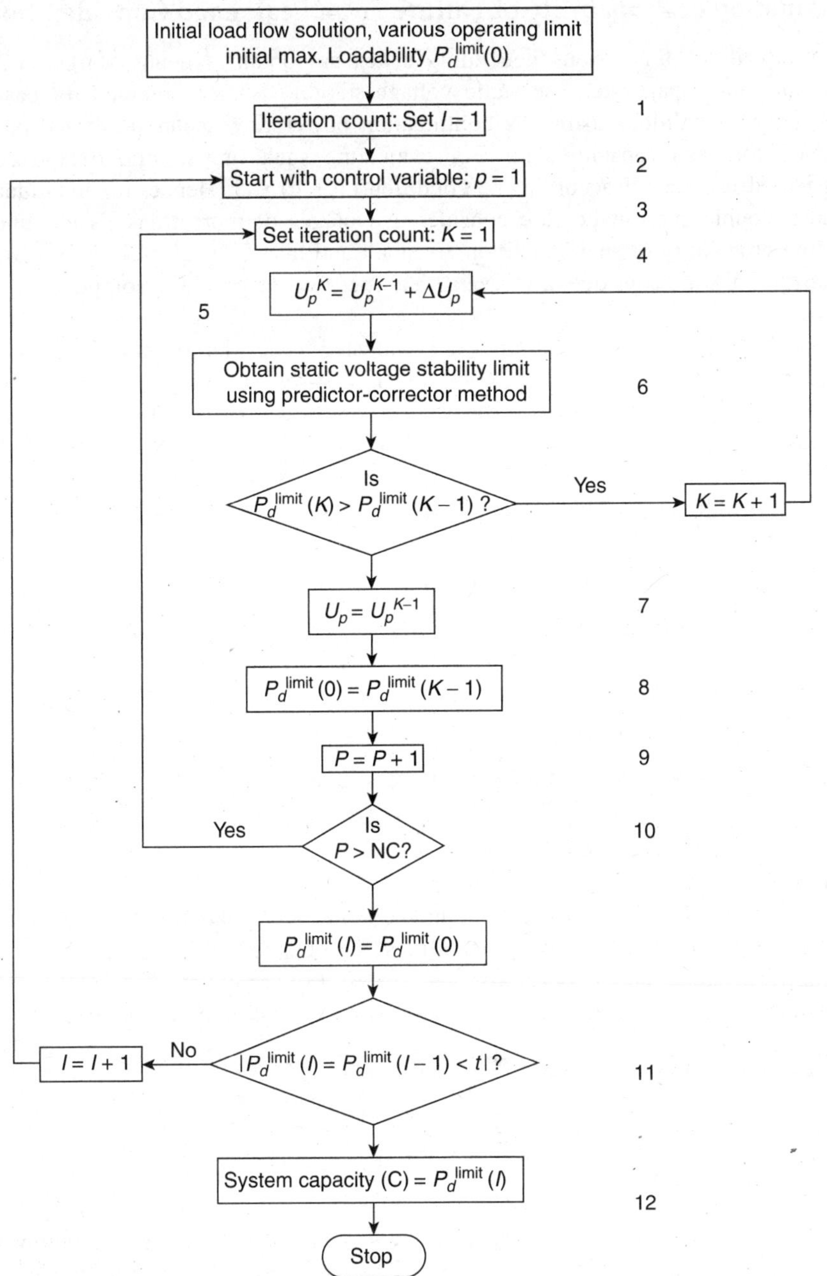

Fig. 21.7 *Flowchart for obtaining maximum load ability using method of local variation (MLV) and predictor-corrector method*

21.10.3 Evaluation of Probability of Failure From Peak Load Consideration

The discrete probabilities for various generating states are obtained using Markov modelling based on constant failure and repair rate. The static voltage stability is then obtained for base case and for different line outages conditions using the continuation power flow technique based on the predictor-corrector method for each capacity state. For evaluating such limits, total outage components are normally considered less than 5 according to condition $(1 + g) \leq 5$. Hence, for individual line outages and at the most, double-line outages are considered. Outages of more transmission lines may not be significant as the probability of such conditions is small and may be neglected. It is again stressed here that static security limits are considered. It means that after the outage of the components, synchronism is maintained.

The probabilities of line outage states are again evaluated using Markov modelling as availability and unavailability functions. Generation and transmission line states are merged and corresponding to each combined state (capacity associated with) probabilities. States can be partitioned, and the probability of success and failure, i.e., availability and unavailability of bulk power systems, are evaluated. The steps are shown in the flowchart (21.74) of Fig. 21.8. In blocks 2 and 3, generation and transmission models are calculated. Specifically using failure (λ) and repair (μ) rate, the availability and unavailability of each generating unit are calculated as

$$A_i = \frac{\mu_i}{(\lambda_i + \mu_i)} \tag{21.84}$$

$$A_i = \frac{\lambda_i}{(\lambda_i + \mu_i)} \tag{21.85}$$

State probabilities $p(X_i)$ is calculated as follows:

$$P(X_i) = \prod_k A_k \prod_n \overline{A_i} \tag{21.86}$$

Where k lies in the sets of generation available and n lies in sets of alternator not available in ith state. Hence, generation capacity and capacity probabilities are obtained as x_i, C_i and $p\ (x_i)$. Similarly, the transmission network state Y_i and associated probabilities $p\ (Y_i)$ are obtained in block 3. Combined state space is obtained by merging the generation and transmission system as follows in block 4.

$$Z_k = (X_i, Y_j) \tag{21.87}$$

And

$$p\ (Z_k) = p\ (X_i), p\ (Y_j) \tag{21.88}$$

The capacity corresponding to each combined state is obtained by solving the optimisation problem in block 5. Composite system capacity and probabilities $C(z_i)$ and $p(z_i)$ and load models are merged to evaluate success and failure probability in block 6.

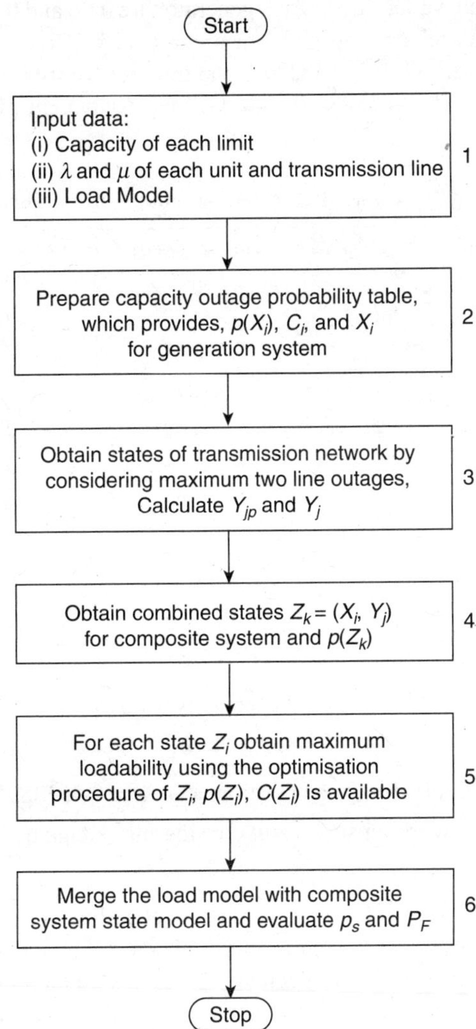

Fig. 21.8 *Flowchart for evaluating failure and success probability of composite power system*

Example 21.10 Draw the one-line diagram and develop the algorithm for 6-bus 7-line IEEE test system considering bus 1 and bus 2 are the generator buses. The generator bus 1 is connected with 4 generators having a real power generation capacity of 0.5 pu, and the reactive power limit of each generator is 0.5 pu. Similarly, generator bus 2 is connected with 4 generators having 0.25 pu real power generation capacity, and a reactive power limit of each generator is 0.25 pu. Shunts are provided at load bus 4 and bus 5 of magnitude 0.05 pu each. The failure and repair rates of each generator are 0.4/year and 9.6/year, respectively. Similarly, each transmission line's failure and repair rates are 0.02/year and 0.25/year, respectively. Draw the capacity outage probability table and evaluate probability states, success probability, loadability and failure probability of interconnected composite power system at peak loads.

Solution The availability and unavailability of each generator are 0.96 and 0.04, respectively. Similarly, the availability and unavailability of each transmission line are as 0.9259 and 0.074074. Whenever the lines are working, the probability of an event is $A^7 = 0.583376$, and the probability of an event for one line is faulty, and all others are working is $\bar{A}A^7 = 0.04607884$. Similarly, we can calculate all possible states of the system, as shown in Tables 21.10–21.12.

Table 21.10 Generation capacity outage probability table

State x_i	Capacity at state 1 (pu)	Capacity at state 2 (pu)	Total capacity C_i (pu)	Probability state $p(x_i)$	State (x_i)
1	2.00	1.00	3.00	0.721389579	$X_0\,Y_0$
2	2.00	0.75	2.75	0.030057899	$X_0\,Y_1$
3	2.00	0.50	2.50	0.0012541246	$X_0\,Y_2$
4	1.50	1.00	2.50	0.030057899	$X_1\,Y_0$
5	1.50	0.75	2.25	0.0012541296	$X_1\,Y_1$
6	1.50	0.50	2.00	0.521838×10^{-4}	$X_1\,Y_2$
7	1.00	1.00	2.00	0.12524×10^{-2}	$X_2\,Y_0$
8	1.00	0.75	1.75	0.521838×10^{-4}	$X_2\,Y_1$
9	1.00	0.50	1.50	0.21743×10^{-5}	$X_2\,Y_2$

The probability of 2 lines faulty and 5 lines working is given by $\bar{A}^2 A^5 = 3.7338083 \times 10^{-3}$

The probability of working all generators at power station 1 or station 2 is $A^4 = 0.8493465$

The probability of failing one generator at each station is $\bar{A}^1 A^3 = 0.0353894$

The probability of 2 generators working successful considering outage of 2 generators at either station is given as $\bar{A}^2 A^2 = 1.47456 \times 10^{-3}$

The outage of 2 generators at each bus is considered for reliability evaluation. Similarly, the outage of a maximum of 2 transmission lines is considered in this evaluation. The combined data are included in the generating capacity outage probability table. In this table, X and Y are notations for generator buses 1 and 2, respectively. The subscript indicates the number of unavailability of the generator at that bus as given below:

0 = all generators are available at a specified bus.

1 = one generator is unavailable at a specified bus.

2 = 2 generators are unavailable at a specified bus.

For each capacity state of the above table, the continuation power flow solution is made, and overall composite static voltage stability limits were evaluated in base case conditions and single- and double-line outage conditions. For the safe limit operation, the actual working limit has been assumed to be 80% of critical loading points in each case. The probability of each transmission network is also evaluated, and peak loadability with all possible capacity and probability states of the composite electrical power system is given. The combined states (transmission and generation) and corresponding capacity (reduced to 80%) are obtained. The system availability and unavailability are calculated for different values of peak loads. The probability and capacity for composite system state were arranged in descending order of loadability. From the following table for different peak load considerations, success and failure probabilities are obtained. The graphical plot of success and failure probability against peak load may be drawn.

21.11 ▶ DISTRIBUTION SYSTEM RELIABILITY

The reliability indices that have been evaluated using classical concepts are the 3 primary ones of average failure rate, average outage duration and average annual unavailability or average annual outage time. These indices are generally referred to as failure rate, outage duration and annual outage time. However, it should be noted that they are not deterministic values but are the expected or average values of an underlying probability distribution and hence only represent the long-run average values. Similarly, the word 'average' or 'expected' will be generally omitted from all other indices to be described. Still, it should be noted that this adjective is always implicit in using these terms.

Although the 3 primary indices are fundamentally important, they do not always give a complete representation of the system's behaviour and response. For instance, the same indices would be evaluated irrespective of whether one customer or 100 customers were connected to the load point or whether the average load at a load point was 10 kW or 100 MW. Additional reliability indices can be and frequently evaluated to reflect the severity or significance of a system outage. The other indices that are most commonly used for distribution system reliability evaluation are defined in the following sections.

21.11.1 Customer-Orientated Indices

(i) System Average Interruption Frequency Index (SAIFI)

$$\text{SAIFI} = \frac{\text{Total number of customer interruptions}}{\text{Total number of customers served}} = \frac{\Sigma \lambda_i N_i}{\Sigma N_i}$$

Where λ_i is the failure rate and N_i, is the number of customers of load point *i*.

(ii) Customer Average Interruption Frequency Index (CAIFI)

$$\text{CAIFI} = \frac{\text{Total number of customer interruptions}}{\text{Total number of customers affected}}$$

This index differs from SAIFT only in the value of the denominator. It is advantageous when a given calendar year 1s compared with other calendar years. Not all customers will be affected in any given calendar year, and many will experience complete continuity of supply. Therefore, the value of CAIF is beneficial in recognising chronological trends in the reliability of a particular distribution system. In applying this index, the customers affected should be counted only once, regardless of the number of interruptions they may have experienced in the year.

(iii) System Average Interruption Duration Index (SAIDI)

$$\text{SAIDI} = \frac{\text{Sum of customer interruption durations}}{\text{Total number of customer}} = \frac{\Sigma U_i N_i}{\Sigma N_i}$$

U_i is the annual outage time, and N_i, which is the number of customers of load point *i*.

(iv) Customer Average Interruption Duration Index (CAIDI)

$$\text{CAIDI} = \frac{\text{Sun or customer interruption durations}}{\text{Total number of customer interruptions}} = \frac{\Sigma U_i N_i}{\Sigma \lambda_i N_i}$$

Where λ_i is the failure rate, U_i is the annual outage time, and N_i is the number of customers of load point *i*.

(v) Average Service Availability (Unavailability) Index (ASAI and ASUI)

$$\text{ASAI} = \frac{\text{Customer hours of available service}}{\text{Customer hours demanded}} = \frac{\sum N_i \times 8760 - \sum U_i N_i}{\sum N_i \times 8760}$$

$$\text{ASUI} = (1 - \text{ASAI}) = \frac{\text{Customer hours of unavailable service}}{\text{Customer hours demanded}} = \frac{\sum U_i N_i}{\sum N_i \times 8760}$$

Where 8760 is the number of hours in a calendar year.

21.11.2 Load and Energy-Orientated Indices

One of the essential parameters required to evaluate load-orientated and energy-orientated indices is the average load at each load-point bus bar. The average load L, is given by

(a) $L_a = L_p f$

Where L_p = peak load demand, f = load factor

(b) $L_a = \dfrac{\text{Total energy demanded in period of interest}}{\text{Period of interest}} = \dfrac{Ed}{t}$

Where E_d and t are associated with load-duration curve and t is normally one calendar year.

(i) Energy Not Supplied Index (ENSI)

ENSI = Total energy not supplied by the system = $\sum L_{a\,(i)} U_i$

Where $L_{a\,(i)}$ is the average load connected to load point i.

(ii) Average Energy Not Supplied (AENS) or Average System Curtailment Index (ASCI)

$$\text{AENS} = \frac{\text{Total energy not supplied}}{\text{Total no. of customers served}} = \frac{\sum L_a(i) U_i}{\sum N_i}$$

(iii) Average Customer Curtailment Index (ACCI)

$$\text{ACCI} = \frac{\text{Total energy not supplied}}{\text{Total no. of customer affected}}$$

This index differs from AENS in the same way that CAIFI differs from SAIP. Therefore, it is a useful index for monitoring the changes in average energy not supplied between one calendar year and another.

The customer- and load-orientated indices described are very useful for assessing the severity of system failures in future reliability prediction analysis. However, they can also be used as a means of evaluating the past performance of a system. In fact, at present, they are probably more widely used in this respect than as measures of future performance. Assessment of system performance is a valuable procedure for 3 fundamental reasons:

(a) It establishes the chronological changes in system performance and helps identify weak areas and the need for reinforcement.

(b) It establishes existing indices that serve as a guide for acceptable values in future reliability assessments.

(c) It enables previous predictions to be compared with actual operating experience.

Example 21.11 The number of customers and the average load connected to bus bars are given in the following table. Assume that 4 system failures occur in one given calendar year of interest having the interruption effects. Illustrate system performance indices' evaluation by considering a portion of a distribution system having 6-load point bus bars.

Solution The load-orientated indices are evaluated and included in Tables 21.11–21.12.

$$\text{SAIFI} = \frac{\Sigma N_c}{\Sigma N} = \frac{3100}{4000} = 0.775 \text{ interruptions/customer}$$

$$\text{CAIFI} = \frac{\Sigma N_c}{N_a} = \frac{3100}{4200} = 1.409 \text{ interruptions/customer affected}$$

Table 21.11 Details of the distribution system

Load point	*No. of the customer, N*	*The average load connected, L_a (kW)*
1	1000	5000
2	800	3600
3	600	2800
4	800	4300
5	500	2400
6	300	1800
Total	**4000**	**19,000**

Table 21.12 Interruption effects in a given calendar year

Interruption case	*Load point affected*	*Number of customers disconnected*	*Load curtailed, L_c (kW)*	*Duration of interruption, d (hr)*	*Customer hours curtailed, $N_c d$*	*Energy not supplied $L_c d$ (kWh)*
1	2	800	3600	3	2400	10,800
	3	600	1800	3	1800	8400
2	6	300	1800	2	600	3600
3	3	600	2800	1	600	2800
4	5	500	2400	1.5	750	3600
	6	300	1800	1.5	450	2700
Total		**3100**	**15,200**		**6600**	**31,900**

No. of customer affected = 800 + 600 + 300 + 500 = 2200 = N_a.

$$\text{SAIDI} = \frac{\Sigma N_c d}{\Sigma N} = \frac{6600}{3100} = 1.65 \text{ hours/customer}$$

$$= 99.0 \text{ min/customer}$$

$$\text{CAIDI} = \frac{\Sigma N_c d}{\Sigma N_c} = \frac{6600}{3100} = 2.13 \text{ hours/customer interruption}$$

$$= 127.7 \text{ hours/customer interruption}$$

$$\text{ASAI} = \frac{\Sigma N \times 8760 - \Sigma N_c d}{\Sigma N \times 8760} = \frac{4000 \times 8760 - 6600}{4000 \times 8760}$$

$$= 0.999812$$

$$\text{ASUI} = 1 - 0.999812 = 0.000188$$

$$\text{ENS} = \sum L_c d = 31{,}900 \text{ kWh/customer}$$

$$\text{AENS} = \frac{\text{ENS}}{\Sigma N} = \frac{31{,}900}{4000} = 7.98 \text{ kWh/customer}$$

$$\text{ACCI} = \frac{\text{ENS}}{N_a} = \frac{31{,}900}{2200} = 14.5 \text{ kWh/customer affected}$$

Additional Solved Examples

Example 21.12 A power component has an MTTF = 34 hours and an MTTR = 2.5 hours. What is the steady-state availability? If the MTTR is reduced to 1.5 hours, what MTTF can be tolerated without decreasing the power component's steady-state availability?

Solution Steady-state availability $= \dfrac{\text{MTTF}}{\text{MTTF} + \text{MTTR}} = \dfrac{34}{34 + 2.5} = 0.931$

MTTR is reduced to 1.5 hours.

Now, $\dfrac{\text{MTTF}}{\text{MTTF} + 1.5} = 0.931$

$\Rightarrow$ MTTF = 0.931 (MTTF + 1.5)

$\Rightarrow$ (1 – 0.931) MTTF = 0.931 × 1.5

$\Rightarrow$ $\text{MTTF} = \dfrac{0.931 \times 1.5}{1 - 0.931} = 20.239$ hours.

Example 21.13 The power transmission system possesses 5 serial segments in the protection scheme. If each part includes a constant failure rate of 0.23 failures per year, segment failures are independent, find the system's reliability function and MTTF.

Solution The failure rate is constant, and the failure-time distribution is exponential with parameter $\lambda = 0.23$.

$\therefore$ $R_1(t) = e^{-(0.23)t}$ for Onesegment

Here 5 segments are in series.

Since the segment failures being independent, reliability for the system is

$$R(t) = R_1(t) \cdot R_2(t) \cdot R_3(t) \cdot R_4(t) \cdot R_5(t)$$

$$= e^{-(0.23)t} \times e^{(0.23)t} \times e^{-(0.23)t} \times e^{-(0.23)t} \times e^{-(0.23)t} = e^{-(1.15)t}$$

$$\text{MTTF} = \int_0^\infty R(t)dt = \int_0^\infty e^{-(1.15)}dt = \left[\frac{e^{-(1.15)t}}{-1.15}\right] = 0.8696$$

21.12 ▶ SUMMARY

The analysis presented in this chapter provides a means for relating power system reliability to component reliability for many equipment designs. The system configurations based on binary component states and independent components are sufficient to permit a reductionist approach to reliability analysis. Reliability should be studied at the component level because the dependence of system reliability on component reliability is well defined. For composite power system designs, focusing independently on individual component reliability performance is essential to achieving high-reliability levels. Examples of applications of the methods are given to illustrate the advantages and limitations of the different techniques, together with case studies drawn from the author's experience of academia, research and consultancy. The comprehensive coverage of the basic concepts of probability theory, redundant system for reliability improvement and power component structures with reliability evaluations has been performed. Hazard model for failure analysis of component, various probability distributions related to reliability illustrations and solved as well as unsolved numerical examples in each section and sub-sections are described in this chapter.

Problems

21.1 In a distribution transformer factory, machines *A*, *B* and *C* manufacture respectively 25%, 35% and 40% of the total. Of their output 5%, 4% and 2% are defective distribution transformers. A transformer is drawn at random from the product and is found to be faulty. What are the probabilities that it was manufactured by machines *A*, *B* and *C*?

21.2 Four techniques regularly make repairs when breakdowns occur on an automated production line. *A*, who services 20% of the breakdowns, makes an incomplete repair 1 time in 20; *B*, who services 60% of the breakdowns, makes an incomplete repair 1 time in 10; *C*, who services 15% breakdowns, makes an incomplete repair 1 time in 10 and *D*, who services 5% of breakdowns, makes an incomplete repair 1 time in 20. For the next problem with the production line diagnosed as being due to an initial repair that was incomplete, what is the probability that this initial repair was made by *A*?

21.3 Three machines M_1, M_2 and M_3 produce identical induction motors. Of their respective output, 5%, 4% and 3% of items are faulty. On a certain day, M_1 has produced 25% of the total output, M_2 has produced 30% and M_3 the remainder. An induction motor is selected at random is found to be faulty. What are the chances that the machine produced it with the highest output?

21.4 The time to failure in operating hours of a critical solid-state power unit of the high voltage transmission system has hazard rate function

$$\lambda(t) = 0.003\left(\frac{t}{500}\right)^{0.5}, \text{ for } t \geq 0.$$

(i) What is the reliability of the power unit that must operate continuously for 50 hours?
(ii) Determine the design life is the reliability of 0.90 is desired.
(iii) Compute MTTF.
(iv) Given that the unit has operated for 50 hours, what is the probability that it will survive a second 50 hours of operation?

21.5 A bulk power system consisting of several identical components connected in parallel is to have a failure rate of at most 4×10^{-4} per hour. What is the least number of components that must be used if each has a constant failure rate of 9×10^{-4}.

21.6 Five components are connected in series in the power transmission system. *N* such groups are connected in parallel for reliability improvements of the system. Identical components have 95% reliability. Determine the minimum number (*N*) of series groups connected in parallel so that combination reliability remains at least 99.99%

21.7 A power controller device consists of 5 components with a series combination. The arrangement has a Weibull failure distribution with a shape parameter of 1.5. Their characteristics live in operating cycles are 3600, 7200, 5850, 4780 and 9300. Find the reliability function of the controller device and the MTTF.

21.8 A lathe cutting tool used in an electric machine manufacturing company has a lifetime that is usually distributed with an S.D. of 12.0 cutting hours. If the reliability of 0.99 is desired over 100 hours of use, find the corresponding MTTF. If the reliability has to life (0.8, 0.9), find the range within which the tool has to be used?

21.9 A power system component has a constant failure rate of 0.02 per thousand hours.
(i) What is the probability that it will operate satisfactorily for at least 20,000 hours?
(ii) What is the 5000-hour reliability of a component consisting of 4 such components connected in series?

21.10 An electric billing office maintains an online electric bill system with a standby computer available if the primary fails. The on-line system fails at the constant rate of once per day while the standby fails (only when online) at a constant rate of twice per day. If the primary unit may be repaired at a constant rate with an MTTR of 0.5 of a day, what is the single day reliability?

21.11 An electric switch wears out with a time to failure that is normally distributed. It is known that about 34.5% of the switches fail before 9 working days, and about 78.8% fail before 12 working days.
(i) Compute MTTF.
(ii) Determine its design life for a reliability of 0.99.
(iii) Determine the probability that the switch will last 1 more day given that it has been in use for 5 days.

21.12 A power system contains the following generating capacities.
(a) 3×40 MW hydro units FOR = 0.005
(b) 1×50 MW thermal unit FOR = 0.02
(c) 1×60 MW thermal unit FOR = 0.02
A straight line gives the annual daily peak load variation curve from 100% to 40%. Calculate the loss of load expectation for the following peak load values.
(i) 150 MW (ii) 160 MW (iii) 170 MW (iv) 180 MW
(v) 190 MW (vi) 200 MW

Multiple Choice Questions

21.1 Following method is related to reliability evaluation of an interconnected composite power system based on peak load consideration and continuation power flow.
(a) Weibull distribution approach (b) Gaussian distribution approach
(c) Predictor-corrector technique (d) Trapezoidal method

21.2 The attributes of the engineering system reliability evaluation are:
(a) Success probability and system performance
(b) Operating conditions and adequate function
(c) System stability and risk analysis
(d) System safety and operating cost

21.3 Following aspects illustrate the power system reliability evaluation.

(a) Probability of components and operating time
(b) Operating time and system performance
(c) System performance and operating cost
(d) Operating cost and risk improvement

21.4 Three machines are producing 10,000, 20,000 and 30,000 MOSFETs for power system applications. These machines are known to produce 1%, 2% and 1% defectives. One MOSFET is taken at random on a day's production of 3 machines that are found to be defective. What is the probability that this component is produced by a third machine?

(a) 2/8 (b) 3/8 (c) 7/8 (d) 1/4

21.5 A power system component has 99% reliability with a constant failure rate. How many components should be connected in series to maintain 95% system reliability?

(a) 1 (b) 10 (c) 5 (d) 7

21.6. A power component has 95% reliability for a period of operation. How many components should be connected in parallel to maintain 99% combination reliability?

(a) 11 (b) 2 (c) 8 (d) 6

21.7 Five electrical components are connected in series in an interconnected power system for reliability enhancement. N such groups are connected in parallel for reliability improvement of the system. Identical components have 95% reliability. Determine the minimum number of series groups (N) connected in parallel so that combinations reliability remains at least 99.99%.

(a) 2 (b) 13 (c) 11 (d) 7

21.8 Following index is related to the combined generation–transmission system reliability evaluation.

(a) SAIFI (b) CAIFI (c) ACCI (d) LOLP

21.9 The power transmission system possesses 5 serial segments in the protection scheme. If each segment possesses a constant failure rate of 0.23 failures per year, segment failures being independent, the MTTF for the system is:

(a) 0.5279 (b) 0.8696 (c) 0.7638 (d) 0.9825

21.10 An interconnected power system component has a constant failure rate of 0.02 per thousand hours. What is the probability that it will operate satisfactorily for at least 20,000 hours?

(a) 98.45% (b) 84.94% (c) 67.03% (d) 59.57%

21.11 Which one of the following statements is true about bathtub curve?

(a) The early phase shows a decreasing failure rate
(b) The middle phase shows a decreasing failure rate
(c) The middle phase shows an increasing failure rate
(d) The early phase represents wear-out failures

21.12 How does quality engineering different from reliability engineering function?

(a) Quality is a static measure of product meeting its specification, whereas reliability is a dynamic measure of product performance.
(b) Poor quality system can have better reliability and a good quality system can have poor reliability.
(c) The difference between quality and reliability is that quality shows how well an object performs its proper function, while reliability shows how well this object maintains its original level of quality over time, through various conditions.
(d) All of the above are correct

21.13 What are the main components of a reliability statement?

(a) Probability, quality, test parameters, environmental aspects
(b) Probability, adequate function, period of time, operating condition

(c) Failure rate, MTTF, MTBF, adequate function, environment
(d) Failure rate, useful life, operating condition

21.14 What should be the role of reliability engineering in product development?
(a) Providing the design team with information on competitors models
(b) Providing reliability estimates to the design team from the earliest design stages
(c) Testing and analysing the reliability of units as they leave the production process
(d) Testing of reliability during component operation

21.15 What refers to wear-out failure?
(a) Increasing failure rate (b) Deceasing failure rate
(c) Maintenance requirement (d) Failure assessment

21.16 Which of the following power system distribution gives the greater reliability?
(a) Radial system of the distribution
(b) Ring system of the distribution
(c) D.C. 3-wire system of the distribution
(d) A.C. 3-phase 4-wire system

21.17 Following 2 statements related to reliability, stability and security of a power system are given.
(i) Security and stability are time-varying attributes which can be judged by studying the performance of the power system under a particular set of conditions.
(ii) Reliability is a function of the time-average performance of the power system; it can only be judged by consideration of the system's behaviour over an appreciable period of time.
Select the correct answer
(a) Only (i) is correct (b) Only (ii) is correct
(c) Both (i) and (ii) are correct (d) Neither (i) nor (ii) is correct

21.18 The bathtub curve of an electric power component provides the following information.
(a) The early region of bathtub curve shows a constant failure rate
(b) The middle region of bathtub curve gives variable failure rate
(c) The middle region of bathtub curve presents a constant failure rate
(d) The early region represents wear-out failures and dynamic reliability

21.19 What would happen, if an equipment possesses reliability and maintainability to the maximum extent in accordance to MTTR?
(a) Failure rate is higher and downtime is longer
(b) Failure rate is lower and downtime is longer
(c) Failure rate is higher and downtime is shorter
(d) Failure rate is lower and downtime is shorter

21.20 According to exponential law of reliability, the relationship between the reliability and the system failure due to consistency in occurrence of failure rate can be generally expressed as ______
(a) $R = \lambda t$ (b) $R = -\lambda t$ (c) $R = e^{\lambda t}$ (d) $R = e^{-\lambda t}$

References

Books

1. R. Billinton and R.N. Allan, Reliability Evaluation of Power System, Springer.

Papers

1. R.C. Bansal, T.S. Bhatti, and D.P. Kothari, Discussion of "Bibliography on the Application of Probability Methods in Power System Reliability Evaluation", *IEEE Transaction on Power System*, volume: 17, issue: 3, 2002.

2. R. Billinton and A. Jonnavithula, “Composite System Adequacy Assessment Using Sequential Monte Carlo Simulation With Variance Reduction Techniques”, *IEEE Proceedings Generation, Transmission and Distribution*, volume: 144, issue: 1, pp: 1–6. 1997.
3. L.D. Arya, S.C. Choube, and R.K. Saket, “Generation System Adequacy Evaluation Using Probability Theory”, *Journal of the Institution of Engineers (India): Series-B*, volume: 81, pp: 170–174, 2001.
4. W. Zhang and R. Billinton, “Application of an Adequacy Equivalent Method in Bulk Power System Reliability Evaluation”, *IEEE Transactions on Power Systems*, volume: 13, issue: 2, pp: 661–666, 1998.
5. L.D. Arya, S.C. Choube, and R.K. Saket, “Composite System Reliability Evaluation Based on Static Voltage Stability Limit”, *Journal of the Institution of Engineers (India): Series-B*, volume: 80, pp: 133–140, 2000.
6. R. Billinton and W. Zhang, “Algorithm for Failure Frequency and Duration Assessment of Composite Power Systems”, *IEEE Proceedings: Generation, Transmission and Distribution*, volume: 145, issue: 2, pp: 117–122, 1998.
7. S. Kumar, R.K. Saket, D.K. Dheer, J.B. Holm-Nielsen, and P. Sanjeevikumar, “Reliability Enhancement of Electrical Power System Including Impacts of Renewable Energy Sources: A Comprehensive Review”, *IET Generation, Transmission & Distribution*, volume: 14, issue: 10, pp: 1799–1815, 2020.
8. R. Billinton and W. Zhang, “Adequacy Equivalent Development of Composite Generation and Transmission Systems Using a DC Load Flow”, *Reliability Engineering and System Safety*, volume: 65, issue: 3, pp: 295–305, 1999.
9. S. Kumar, S. Kumar, K.S.A. Kumar, O.P. Bharti, L. Varshney, R.K. Saket, and D.N. Vishwakarma, “Probabilistic Evaluation and Design Aspects for Reliability Enhancement of Induction Motor”, *International Journal of Reliability and Safety*, volume: 13, issue: 4, pp: 267–290, 2019.
10. R. Billinton and P. Wang, “Reliability Network Equivalent Approach to Distribution System Reliability Evaluation”, *IEEE Proceedings: Generation, Transmission and Distribution*, volume: 145, issue: 2, pp: 149–153, 1998.
11. O.P. Bharti, R.K. Saket, and S.K. Nagar, “Reliability Assessment and Performance Analysis of DFIG Based WT for Wind Energy Conversion System”, *International Journal of Reliability and Safety*, volume: 13, issue: 04, pp: 235–266, 2019.
12. R. Billinton and P. Wang, “Deregulated Power System Planning Using a Reliability Network Equivalent Technique”, *IEEE Proceedings Generation, Transmission and Distribution*, volume: 146, issue: 1, pp: 25–30, 1999.
13. L. Varshney and R.K. Saket, “Reliability Evaluation of SEIG Rotor Core Magnetization With Minimum Capacitive Excitation for Unregulated Renewable Energy Applications in Remote Areas”, *Ain Shams Engineering Journal*, volume: 5, issue: 3, pp: 751–757, 2014.
14. P. Wang and R. Billinton, “Optimum Load-Schedding Techniques to Reduce the Total Customer Interruption Cost in Distribution System”, *IEEE Proceedings Generation, Transmission and Distribution*, volume: 147, pp: 51–56, 2000.
15. R.K. Saket, “Design Aspects and Probabilistic Approach for Generation Reliability Evaluation of MWW Based Micro-hydro Power Plant”, *Renewable and Sustainable Energy Reviews*, volume: 28, pp: 917–929, 2013.
16. R. Billinton and J. Pan, “Application of Monte-Carlo Simulation to Optimal Maintenance Scheduling in Parallel-Redundant System”, *IEEE Proceedings Generation, Transmission and Distribution*, volume: 147, pp: 274–278, 2000.

17. R.K. Saket, R.C. Bansal, and G. Singh, "Power Systems Component Modelling and Reliability Evaluation of Generation Capacity", *International Journal of Reliability and Safety*, volume: 03, issue: 04, pp: 427–441, 2009.
18. R. Billinton and P. Wang, "Teaching Distribution System Reliability Evaluation Using Monte Carlo Simulation", *IEEE Transactions on Power Systems*, volume: 14, issue: 2, pp: 397–403, 1999.
19. R.K. Saket, R.C. Bansal, and G. Singh, "Reliability Evaluation of Power System Considering Voltage Stability and Continuation Power Flow", *Journal of Electrical Systems, Engineering and Scientific Research Groups*, volume: 3, issue: 2, pp: 48–60, 2007.
20. R. Bilinton and S. Aboreshaid, "Voltage Stability Consideration in Composite Power System Reliability Evaluation", *IEEE Transactions on Power Systems*, volume: 13, issue: 2, pp: 655–660, 1998.
21. R.K. Saket, R.C. Bansal, and G. Singh, "Generation Capacity Adequacy Evaluation Based on Peak Load Considerations", *The South Pacific International Journal on Natural Sciences*, volume: 24, pp: 38–44, 2006.
22. Lokesh Varshney, Aanchal Singh S. Vardhan, Akanksha Singh S. Vardhan, Sachin Kumar, R.K. Saket, and S. Padmanaban, "Performance Characteristics and Reliability Assessment of Self-Excited Induction Generator for Wind Power Generation", *IET Renewable Power Generation*, volume: 15, issue: 9, pp: 1927–1942, 2021.
23. R. Arya, S.C. Choube, and L.D. Arya, "Reliability Evaluation and Enhancement of Distribution Systems in the Presence of Distributed Generation Based on Standby Mode", *International Journal of Electrical Power and Energy Systems*, volume: 43, issue: 1, pp: 607–616, 2012.
24. Sachin Kumar, Kumari Sarita, R.K. Saket, D.K. Dheer, R.C. Bansal, and Saad Mekhilef, "Reliability Assessment for DFIG-based WECS Considering the Impact of 3-phase Fault and Lightning Impulse Voltage", *International Transactions on Electrical Energy Systems*, e12952, pp: 1–19, May 2021.
25. R. Arya, A. Tiwary, S.C. Choube, and L.D. Arya, "A Smooth Bootstrapping Based Technique for Evaluating Distribution System Reliability Indices Neglecting Random Interruption Duration", *International Journal of Electrical Power and Energy Systems*, volume: 51, pp: 307–310, 2013.
26. Sachin Kumar, R.K. Saket, D.K. Dheer, P. Sanjeevikumar, and F. Blaabjerg, "Layout Optimization Algorithms and Reliability Assessment of Wind Farm for Microgrid Integration: A Comprehensive Review", *IET Renewable Power Generation*, volume: 15, issue: 10, pp: 2063–2084, 2021.
27. L.D. Arya, S.C. Choube, R. Arya, and A. Tiwary, "Evaluation of Reliability Indices Accounting Omission of Random Repair Time for Distribution Systems Using Monte Carlo Simulation", *International Journal of Electrical Power and Energy Systems*, volume: 42, issue: 1, pp: 533–541, 2012.
28. R. Arya, S.C. Choube, L.D. Arya, and D.P. Kothari, "Reliability Enhancement of a Radial Distribution System Using Coordinated Aggregation Based Particle Swarm Optimization Considering Customer and Energy Based Indices", *Applied Soft Computing*, volume: 12, issue: 11, pp: 3325–3331, 2012.
29. L.D. Arya, L.S. Titare, and D.P. Kothari, "Distribution System Adequacy Assessment Accounting Customer Controlled Generator Sets", *International Journal of Electrical Power and Energy Systems*, volume: 33, issue: 5, pp: 1161–1164, 2011.
30. L.D. Arya, S.C. Choube, and R. Arya, "Probabilistic Reliability Indices Evaluation of Electrical Distribution System Accounting Outage Due to Overloading and Repair Time Omission", *International Journal of Electrical Power and Energy Systems*, volume: 33, issue: 2, pp: 296–302, 2011.
31. L.D. Arya, S.C. Choube, and R. Arya, "Differential Evolution Applied for Reliability Optimization of Radial Distribution Systems", *International Journal of Electrical Power and Energy Systems*, volume: 33, issue: 2, pp: 271–277, 2011.

APPENDIX

A Generalised Circuit Constants

We can represent, as we saw in Ch. 5, a three-phase transmission line* by a circuit with two input terminals (sending-end, where power enters) and two output terminals (receiving-end, where power exits). This two-terminal pair circuit is *passive* (since it does not contain any electric energy sources), *linear* (impedances of its elements are independent of the amount of current flowing through them), and *bilateral* (impedances being independent of direction of current flowing). It can be shown that such a two-terminal pair network can be represented by an equivalent *T*- or π-network.

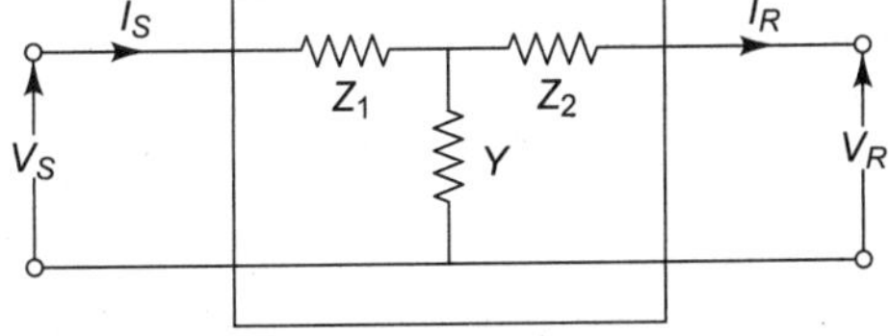

Fig. A-1 *Unsymmetrical T-circuit equivalent to a general two-terminal pair network*

Consider the unsymmetrical *T*-network of Fig. A-1, which is equivalent to the general two-terminal pair network.

For Fig. A-1, the following circuit equations can be written

$$I_S = I_R + Y(V_R + I_R Z_2) \tag{A-1}$$

or

$$I_S = YV_R + (1 + YZ_2)I_R$$

$$V_S = V_R + I_R Z_2 + I_S Z_1$$

$$= V_R + I_R Z_2 + Z_1 Y V_R + I_R Z_1 + I_R Y Z_1 Z_2$$

or

$$V_S = (1 + YZ_1)\, V_R + (Z_1 + Z_2 + YZ_1 Z_2)I_R \tag{A-2}$$

Equations (A-1) and (A-2) can be simplified by letting

$$A = 1 + YZ_1 \quad B = Z_1 + Z_2 + YZ_1Z_2 \tag{A-3}$$

$$C = Y \qquad D = 1 + YZ_2$$

Using these, Eqs. (A-1) and (A-2) can be written in matrix form as

$$\begin{bmatrix} V_S \\ I_S \end{bmatrix} = \begin{bmatrix} A & B \\ C & D \end{bmatrix} \begin{bmatrix} V_R \\ I_R \end{bmatrix} \tag{A-4}$$

This equation is the same as Eq. (A-1) and is valid for any linear, passive and bilateral two-terminal pair network. The constants *A*, *B*, *C* and *D* are called the *generalised circuit constants* or the *ABCD* constants of the network, and they can be calculated for any such two-terminal pair network.

It may be noted that *ABCD* constants of a two-terminal pair network are complex numbers in general, and always satisfy the following relationship:

---

* A transformer is similarly represented by a circuit with two input and two output terminals.

$$AD - BC = 1 \qquad \text{(A-5)}$$

Also, for any symmetrical network the constants A and D are equal. From Eq. (A-4) it is clear that A and D are dimensionless, while B has the dimensions of impedance (ohms) and C has the dimensions of admittance (mhos).

The *ABCD* constants are extensively used in power system analysis. A general two-terminal pair network is often represented as in Fig. A-2.

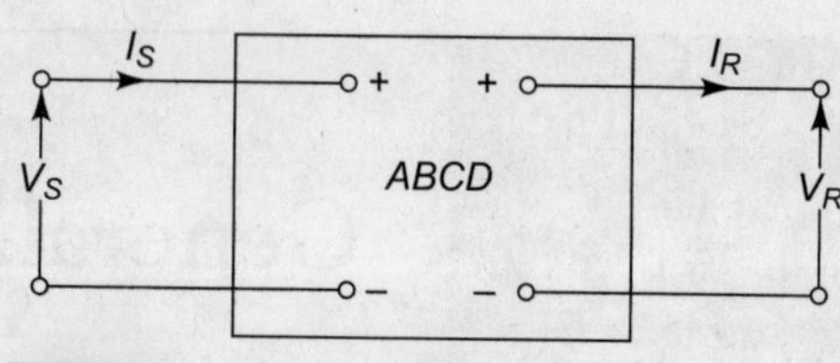

Fig. A-2 *Schematic representation of a two-terminal pair network using ABCD constants*

ABCD CONSTANTS FOR VARIOUS SIMPLE NETWORKS

We have already obtained the *ABCD* constants of an unsymmetrical *T*-network. The *ABCD* constants of unsymmetrical π-network shown in Fig. A-3 may be obtained in a similar manner and are given below:

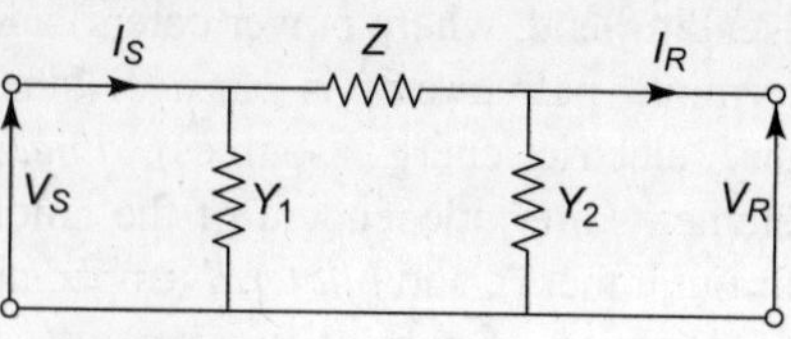

Fig. A-3 *Unsymmetrical π-circuit*

$$\begin{aligned} A &= 1 + Y_2 Z \\ B &= Z \\ C &= Y_1 + Y_2 + Z Y_1 Y_2 \qquad \text{(A-6)} \\ D &= 1 + Y_1 Z \end{aligned}$$

A series impedance often represents short transmission lines and transformers. The *ABCD* constants for such a circuit (as shown in Fig. A-4) can immediately be determined by inspection of Eqs. (A-1) and (A-2), as follows:

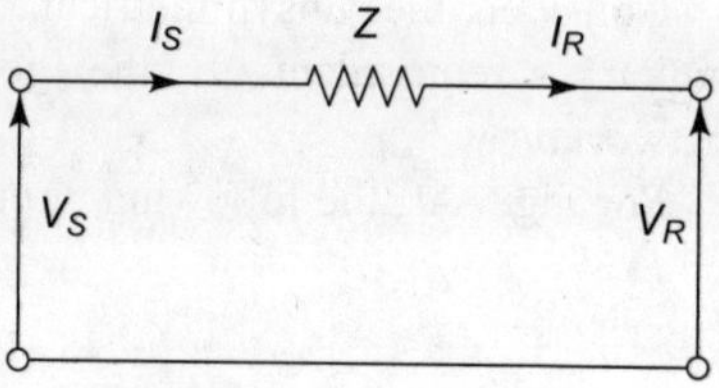

$$\begin{aligned} A &= 1 \\ B &= Z \qquad \text{(A-7)} \\ C &= 0 \\ D &= 1 \end{aligned}$$

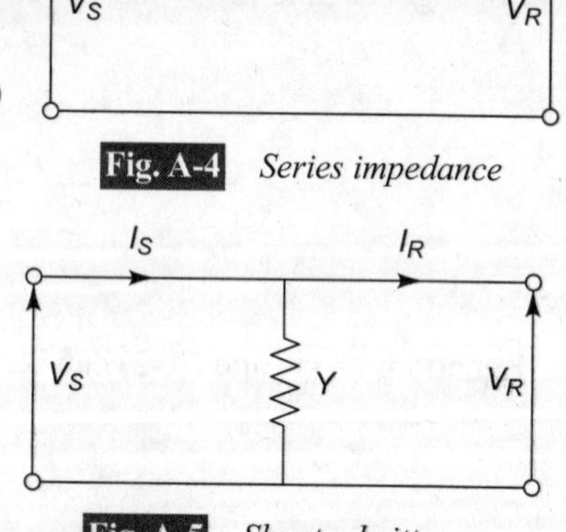

Fig. A-4 *Series impedance*

Another simple circuit of Fig. A-5 consisting of simple shunt admittance can be shown to possess the following *ABCD* constants:

$$\begin{aligned} A &= 1 \\ B &= 0 \qquad \text{(A-8)} \\ C &= Y \\ D &= 1 \end{aligned}$$

Fig. A-5 *Shunt admittance*

It may be noted that whenever *ABCD* constants are computed, it should be checked that the relation $AD–BC = 1$ is satisfied. For example, using Eq. (A-8) we get

$$AD - BC = 1 \times 1 - 0 \times Y = 1$$

If *ABCD* constants of a circuit are given, its equivalent *T*- or π-circuit can be determined by solving Eq. (A-3) or (A-6), respectively, for the values of series and shunt branches. For the equivalent π-circuit of Fig. A-3, we have

$$\begin{aligned} Z &= B \\ Y_1 &= \frac{D-1}{B} \qquad \text{(A-9)} \\ Y_2 &= \frac{A-1}{B} \end{aligned}$$

ABCD Constants of Networks in Series and Parallel

Whenever a power system consists of series and parallel combinations of networks, whose *ABCD* constants are known, the overall *ABCD* constants for the system may be determined to analyse the overall operation of the system.

Consider the two networks in series, as shown in Fig. A-6. This combination can be reduced to a single equivalent network as follows:

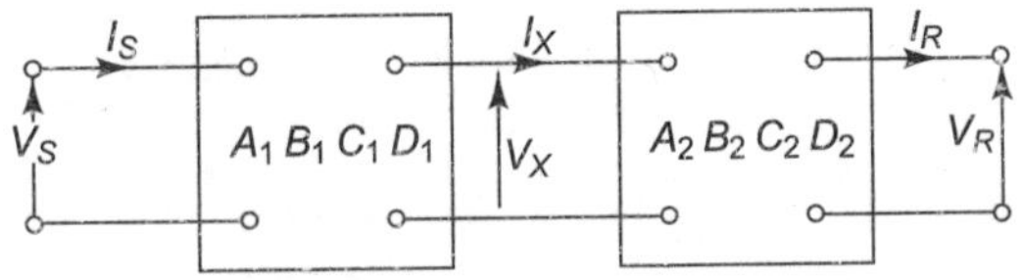

For the first network, we have

$$\begin{bmatrix} V_S \\ I_S \end{bmatrix} = \begin{bmatrix} A_1 & B_1 \\ C_1 & D_1 \end{bmatrix} \begin{bmatrix} V_X \\ I_X \end{bmatrix} \quad \text{(A-10)}$$

Fig. A-6 *Networks in series*

For the second network, we can write

$$\begin{bmatrix} V_X \\ I_X \end{bmatrix} = \begin{bmatrix} A_2 & B_2 \\ C_2 & D_2 \end{bmatrix} \begin{bmatrix} V_R \\ I_R \end{bmatrix} \quad \text{(A-11)}$$

From Eqs. (A-10) and (A-11), we can write

$$\begin{bmatrix} V_S \\ I_S \end{bmatrix} = \begin{bmatrix} A_1 & B_1 \\ C_1 & D_1 \end{bmatrix} \begin{bmatrix} A_2 & B_2 \\ C_2 & D_2 \end{bmatrix} \begin{bmatrix} V_R \\ I_R \end{bmatrix}$$

$$= \begin{bmatrix} A_1A_2 + B_1C_2 & A_1B_2 + B_1D_2 \\ C_1A_2 + D_1C_2 & C_1B_2 + D_1D_2 \end{bmatrix} \begin{bmatrix} V_R \\ I_R \end{bmatrix} \quad \text{(A-12)}$$

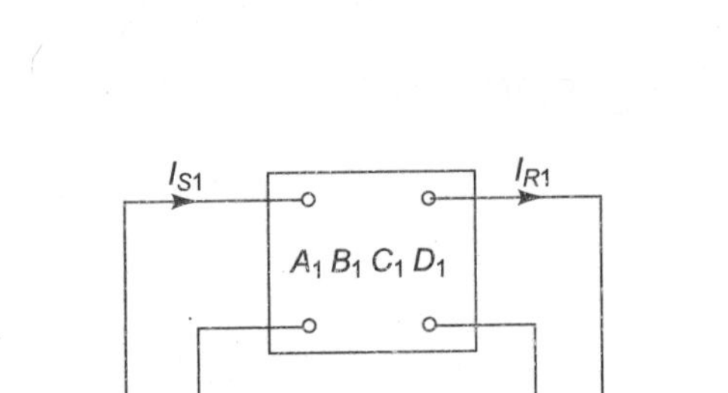

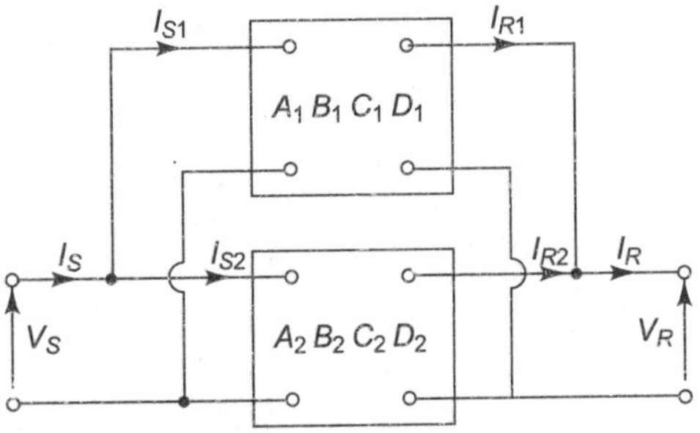

Fig. A-7 *Networks in parallel*

If two networks are connected in parallel as shown in Fig. A-7, the *ABCD* constants of the combined network can be found out similarly with some simple manipulations of matrix algebra. The results are presented below:

$$\begin{aligned} A &= (A_1B_2 + A_2B_1)/(B_1 + B_2) \\ B &= B_1B_2/(B_1 + B_2) \\ C &= (C_1 + C_2) + (A_1 - A_2)(D_2 - D_1)/(B_1 + B_2) \\ D &= (B_2D_1 + B_1D_2)/(B_1 + B_2) \end{aligned} \quad \text{(A-13)}$$

"T-network" (Matrix Method)

$$\begin{bmatrix} V_S \\ I_S \end{bmatrix} = \begin{bmatrix} 1 & Z/2 \\ 0 & 1 \end{bmatrix} \begin{bmatrix} 1 & 0 \\ Y & 1 \end{bmatrix} \begin{bmatrix} 1 & Z/2 \\ 0 & 1 \end{bmatrix} \begin{bmatrix} V_r \\ I_r \end{bmatrix}$$

$$\begin{bmatrix} V_S \\ I_S \end{bmatrix} = \begin{bmatrix} 1+\dfrac{YZ}{2} & Z/2 \\ Y & 1 \end{bmatrix} \begin{bmatrix} 1 & Z/2 \\ 0 & 1 \end{bmatrix} \begin{bmatrix} V_r \\ I_r \end{bmatrix}$$

$$\begin{bmatrix} V_S \\ I_S \end{bmatrix} = \begin{bmatrix} (1+YZ/2 & \dfrac{YZ}{2} \\ Y & (1+YZ/2) \end{bmatrix} \begin{bmatrix} V_r \\ I_r \end{bmatrix}$$

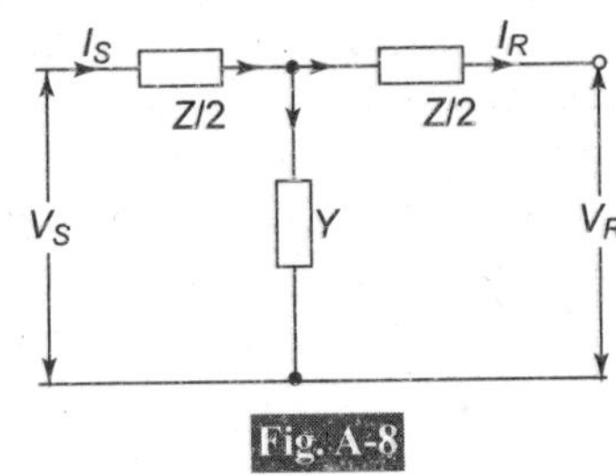

Fig. A-8

$$\therefore \quad A = D = \left(1 + \frac{YZ}{2}\right)$$

$$B = Z\left(1 + \frac{YZ}{4}\right) \text{ and } C = Y$$

Ideal Transformer

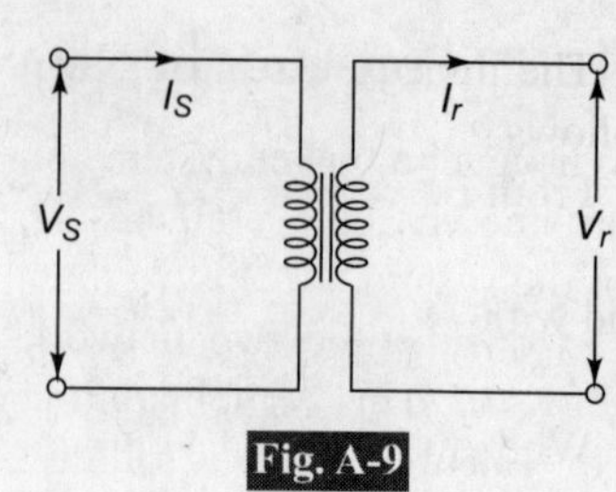

Fig. A-9

$$V_S = nV_r. \text{ (where, } n \text{ is the turns ratio)}$$

$$I_S = \frac{1}{n} I_r.$$

$$\begin{bmatrix} V_S \\ I_S \end{bmatrix} = \begin{bmatrix} n & 0 \\ 0 & \frac{1}{n} \end{bmatrix} \begin{bmatrix} V_r \\ I_r \end{bmatrix};$$

$$\therefore \quad A = n;\ D = \frac{1}{n};$$

$$B = C = 0$$

Actual Transformer

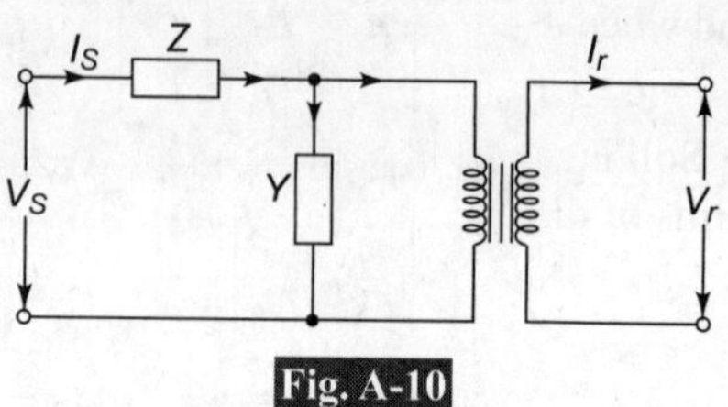

Fig. A-10

$$\begin{bmatrix} V_S \\ I_S \end{bmatrix} = \begin{bmatrix} 1 & Z \\ 0 & 1 \end{bmatrix} \begin{bmatrix} 1 & 0 \\ Y & 1 \end{bmatrix} \begin{bmatrix} n & 0 \\ 0 & \frac{1}{n} \end{bmatrix} \begin{bmatrix} V_r \\ I_r \end{bmatrix}$$

$$\begin{bmatrix} V_S \\ I_S \end{bmatrix} = \begin{bmatrix} (1+YZ) & Z \\ Y & 1 \end{bmatrix} \begin{bmatrix} n & 0 \\ Y & \frac{1}{n} \end{bmatrix} \begin{bmatrix} V_r \\ I_r \end{bmatrix}$$

$$\begin{bmatrix} V_S \\ I_S \end{bmatrix} = \begin{bmatrix} n(1+YZ) & Z/n \\ Y.n & 1/n \end{bmatrix} \begin{bmatrix} V_r \\ I_r \end{bmatrix}$$

$$\therefore \quad A = n\,(1 + YZ)\ ;\ B = Z/n$$

$$C = Y.n \quad \text{and} \quad D = \frac{1}{n}.$$

Measurement of *ABCD* Constants

The generalised circuit constants may be computed for a transmission line which is being designed from a knowledge of the system impedance/admittance parameters using expressions such as those developed above. If the line is already built, the generalised circuit constants can be measured by making a few ordinary tests on the line. Using Eq. (A-4), these constants can easily be shown to be ratios of either voltage or current at the sending-end to voltage or current at the receiving-end of the network with the receiving-end open or short-circuited. When the network is a transformer, generator, or circuit having lumped parameters, voltage and current measurements at both ends of the line can be made, and the phase angles between the sending and receiving-end quantities can be found out. Thus, the *ABCD* constants can be determined.

It is possible, also, to measure the magnitudes of the required voltages and currents simultaneously at both ends of a transmission line, but there is no simple method to find the difference in phase angle between the quantities at the two ends of the line. Phase difference is necessary because the *ABCD* constants are complex. By measuring two impedances at each end of a transmission line, however, the generalised circuit constants can be computed.

The following impedances are to be measured:

Z_{SO} = sending-end impedance with receiving-end open-circuited
Z_{SS} = sending-end impedance with receiving-end short circuited
Z_{RO} = receiving-end impedance with sending-end open-circuited
Z_{RS} = receiving-end impedance with sending-end short-circuited

The impedances measured from the sending-end can be determined in terms of the *ABCD* constants as follows:

From Eq. (A-4), with $I_R = 0$,

$$Z_{SO} = V_S/I_S = A/C \tag{A-14}$$

and with $V_R = 0$,

$$Z_{SS} = V_S/I_S = B/D \tag{A-15}$$

When the impedances are measured from the receiving-end, the direction of current flow is reversed and hence the signs of all current terms in Eq. (5.25). We can therefore rewrite this equation as

$$V_R = DV_S + BI_S \tag{A-16}$$

$$I_R = CV_S + AI_S$$

From Eq. (A-16), with $I_S = 0$,

$$Z_{RO} = V_R/I_R = D/C \tag{A-17}$$

and when $V_S = 0$,

$$Z_{RS} = V_R/I_R = B/A \tag{A-18}$$

Solving Eqs. (A-14), (A-15), (A-17) and (A-18) we can obtain the values of the *ABCD* constants in terms of the measured impedances as follows:

$$Z_{RO} - Z_{RS} = \frac{AD - BC}{AC} = \frac{1}{AC} \quad \text{[using Eq. (A-5)]}$$

$$\frac{Z_{RO} - Z_{RS}}{Z_{SO}} = \frac{1}{AC} \cdot \frac{C}{A} = \frac{1}{A^2}$$

$$\therefore \quad A = \left(\frac{Z_{SO}}{Z_{RO} - Z_{RS}} \right)^{1/2} \tag{A-19}$$

By substituting this value of A in Eqs. (A-14) and (A-18) and substituting the value of C so obtained in Eq. (A-17), we get

$$B = Z_{RS} \left(\frac{Z_{SO}}{Z_{RO} - Z_{RS}} \right)^{1/2} \tag{A-20}$$

$$C = \frac{1}{(Z_{RO}(Z_{SO} - Z_{RS}))^{1/2}} \tag{A-21}$$

$$D = \frac{Z_{RO}}{(Z_{SO}(Z_{RO} - Z_{RS}))^{1/2}} \tag{A-22}$$

References

1. H. Cotton and H. Barber, *The Transmission and Distribution of Electrical Energy*, 3rd edn, BI Publishers, New Delhi, 1970.
2. L. Cai, Z.H. Jiang, and W. Hong, "Broadband Measurement of Substrate Complex Permittivity Using Optimized ABCD Matrix", *IEEE Access*, volume: 8, pp: 224513–224521, 2020.
3. M. Sahoo, P. Ghosal, and H. Rahaman, "Modeling and Analysis of Crosstalk Induced Effects in Multiwalled Carbon Nanotube Bundle Interconnects: An ABCD Parameter-Based Approach", *IEEE Transactions on Nanotechnology*, volume: 14, issue: 2, pp: 259–274, 2015.

4. D. A. Frickey, "Conversions between S, Z, Y, H, ABCD, and T Parameters Which Are Valid for Complex Source and Load Impedances," *IEEE Transactions on Microwave Theory and Techniques*, volume: 42, issue: 2, pp: 205–211, 1994.
5. J. Cho et al., "Mixed-Mode ABCD Parameters: Theory and Application to Signal Integrity Analysis of PCB-Level Differential Interconnects", *IEEE Transactions on Electromagnetic Compatibility*, volume: 53, issue: 3, pp: 814–822, 2011.

APPENDIX B

Elements of Power System Jacobian Matrix

Expressions to be used in evaluating the elements of the Jacobian matrix of a power system are derived below:

From Eq. (6.25b)

$$P_i - jQ_i = V_i^* \sum_{k=1}^{n} Y_{ik} V_k$$
$$= |V_i| \exp(-j\delta_i) \sum_{k=1}^{n} |Y_{ik}| \exp(j\theta_{ik}) |V_k| \exp(j\delta_k) \tag{B-1}$$

Differentiating partially with respect to δ_m $(m \neq i)$

$$\frac{\partial P_i}{\partial \delta_m} - j\frac{\partial Q_i}{\partial \delta_m} = j|V_i| \exp(-j\delta_i) (|Y_{im}| \exp(j\theta_{im}) |V_m| \exp(j\delta_m))$$
$$= j(e_i - jf_i)(a_m + jb_m) \tag{B-2}$$

where

$$Y_{im} = G_{im} + jB_{im}$$
$$V_i = e_i + jf_i$$
$$(a_m + jb_m) = (G_{im} + jB_{im})(e_m + jf_m)$$

Although the polar form of the NR method is being used, rectangular complex arithmetic is employed for numerical evaluation as it is faster.

From Eq. (B-2), we can write

$$\frac{\partial P_i}{\partial \delta_m} = (a_m f_i - b_m e_i) = H_{im}$$
$$\frac{\partial Q_i}{\partial \delta_m} = -(a_m e_i + b_m f_i) = J_{im}$$

For the case of $m = i$, we have

$$\frac{\partial P_i}{\partial \delta_i} - j\frac{\partial Q_i}{\partial \delta_i} = -j|V_i| \exp(-j\delta_i) \sum_{k=1}^{n} |Y_{ik}| \exp(j\theta_{ik}) |V_k| \exp(j\delta_k)$$
$$+ j|V_i| \exp(-j\delta_i) (|Y_{ii}| \exp(j\theta_{ii}) |V_i| \exp(j\delta_i))$$
$$= -j(P_i - jQ_i) + j|V_i|^2 (G_{ii} + jB_{ii}) \tag{B-3}$$

From Eq. (B-3), we can write

$$\frac{\partial P_i}{\partial \delta_i} = -Q_i - B_{ii}|V_i|^2 = H_{ii}$$
$$\frac{\partial Q_i}{\partial \delta_i} = P_i - G_{ii}|V_i|^2 = J_{ii}$$

Now differentiate Eq. (B-1) partially with respect to $|V_m|$ $(m \neq i)$. We have

$$\frac{\partial P_i}{\partial |V_m|} - j\frac{\partial Q_i}{\partial |V_m|} = |V_i| \exp(-j\delta_i)\,(|Y_{im}| \exp(j\theta_{im}) \exp(j\delta_m))$$

Multiplying by $|V_m|$ on both sides,

$$\frac{\partial P_i}{\partial |V_m|}|V_m| - j\frac{\partial Q_i}{\partial |V_m|}|V_m| = |V_i| \exp(-j\delta_i)\,|Y_{im}| \exp(j\theta_{im})\,|V_m| \exp(j\delta_m)$$

$$= (e_i - jf_i)\,(a_m + jb_m) \tag{B-4}$$

It follows from Eq. (B-4) that

$$\frac{\partial P_i}{\partial |V_m|}|V_m| = a_m e_i + b_m f_i = N_{im}$$

$$\frac{\partial Q_i}{\partial |V_m|}|V_m| = a_m f_i - b_m e_i = L_{im}$$

Now for the case of $m = i$, we have

$$\frac{\partial P_i}{\partial |V_i|} - j\frac{\partial Q_i}{\partial |V_i|} = \exp(-j\delta_i) \sum_{k=1}^{n} |Y_{ik}| \exp(j\theta_{ik})\,|V_k| \exp(j\delta_k) + |V_i| \exp(-j\delta_i)\,|Y_{ii}| \exp(j\theta_{ii}) \exp(j\delta_i)$$

Multiplying by $|V_i|$ on both sides

$$\frac{\partial P_i}{\partial |V_i|}|V_i| - j\frac{\partial Q_i}{\partial |V_i|}|V_i| = |V_i| \exp(-j\delta_i) \sum_{k=1}^{n} |y_{ik}| \exp(j\theta_{ik})\,|V_k| \exp(j\delta_k) + |V_i|^2\,|Y_{ii}| \exp(j\theta_{ii})$$

$$= (P_i - jQ_i) + |V_i|^2\,(G_{ii} + jB_{ii}) \tag{B-5}$$

It follows from Eq. (B-5) that

$$\frac{\partial P_i}{\partial |V_i|}|V_i| = P_i + G_{ii}|V_i|^2 = N_{ii}$$

$$\frac{\partial Q_i}{\partial |V_i|}|V_i| = Q_i - B_{ii}|V_i|^2 = L_{ii}$$

The above results are summarised below:

Case 1

$$m \neq i$$

$$H_{im} = L_{im} = a_m f_i - b_m e_i$$

$$N_{im} = -J_{im} = a_m e_i + b_m f_i \tag{B-6}$$

where,

$$Y_{im} = G_{im} + jB_{im}$$

$$V_i = e_i + jf_i \tag{B-7}$$

$$(a_m + jb_m) = (G_{im} + jB_{im})\,(e_m + jf_m)$$

Case 2

$$m = i$$

$$H_{ii} = -Q_i - B_{ii}|V_i|^2$$

$$N_{ii} = P_i + G_{ii}|V_i|^2 \tag{B-8}$$

$$J_{ii} = P_i - G_{ii}|V_i|^2$$

$$L_{ii} = Q_i - B_{ii}|V_i|^2$$

References

1. Y.C. Chen, J. Wang, A.D. Domínguez-García, and P.W. Sauer, "Measurement-Based Estimation of the Power Flow Jacobian Matrix", *IEEE Transactions on Smart Grid*, volume: 7, issue: 5, pp: 2507–2515, 2016.
2. X. Wang, J.W. Bialek, and K. Turitsyn, "PMU-Based Estimation of Dynamic State Jacobian Matrix and Dynamic System State Matrix in Ambient Conditions", *IEEE Transactions on Power Systems*, volume: 33, issue: 1, pp: 681–690, 2018.

APPENDIX C

Convergence of Load Flow Methods

GAUSS–SIEDEL METHOD

The general form of Gauss–Siedel method involves the solution of n non-linear equations in n unknowns. The n equations in matrix form are given as

$$f(x) = 0 \tag{C-1}$$

where

$$f = (f_1(x) \ldots f_n(x))^T$$
$$x = (x_1 \ldots x_n)^T$$

The convergence property of GS method can be understood by considering the single variable problem

$$f(x) = 0 \tag{C-2}$$

Equation (I-2) is written in the form

$$x = g(x) \tag{C-3}$$

assuming that the initial approximate value of x, i.e., x_0 of Eq. (C-2) converges to the exact value after performing GS iteration on Eq. (C-3). Thus, the values of x at various iterations are given by

$$\begin{aligned} x_1 &= g(x_0) \\ x_2 &= g(x_1) \\ x_n &= g(x_n - 1) \end{aligned} \tag{C-4}$$

The iteration is continued till

$$x_n \cong \zeta = g(\zeta) \tag{C-5}$$

Figure (C-1) shows the graph of $g(x)$. In Fig. (C-1) ε_n and ε_{n+1} are the errors in the nth and $(n + 1)$th iteration.

Thus,

$$x_n = \zeta + \varepsilon_n \tag{C-6a}$$
$$x_{n+1} = \zeta + \varepsilon_{n+1} \tag{C-6b}$$

Also,

$$x_{n+1} = g(x_n) \tag{C-6c}$$

Substituting Eq. (C-6a) in Eq. (C-6c),

$$x_{n+1} = g(\zeta + \varepsilon_n)$$

Expanding by Taylor's series about ζ, we get

$$x_{n+1} = \zeta + \varepsilon_{n+1} = g(\zeta) + \varepsilon_n g'(\zeta) + \frac{\varepsilon_n^2}{2} g''(\zeta) + \ldots$$

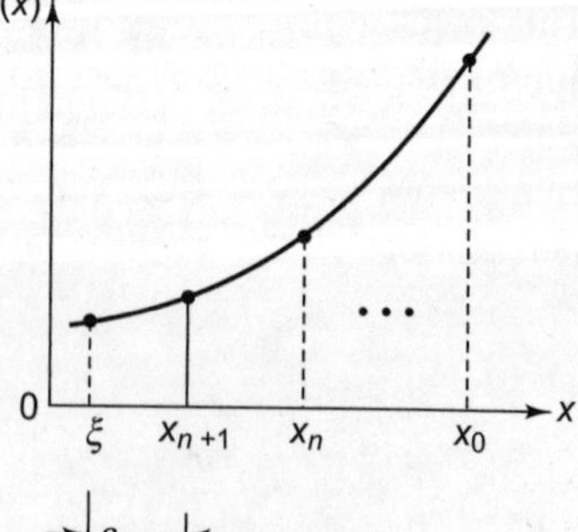

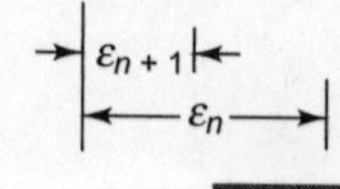

Fig. C-1

Neglecting higher-order terms and substituting the value of $g(\zeta)$ from Eq. (C-5), we get

$$\zeta + \varepsilon_{n+1} = \zeta + \varepsilon_n g'(\zeta)$$

or

$$\varepsilon_{n+1} = g'(\zeta)\varepsilon_n \tag{C-7}$$

Since $g'(\zeta)$ is a constant, the error in the $(n + 1)$th iteration is proportional to the previous error, i.e., in the nth iteration. Hence, the convergence of GS method is linear. Depending on the value of $g'(\zeta)$, the GS method may or may not converge. Thus, we must have

$$g'(\zeta) < 1 \tag{C-8}$$

for convergence, near $x = \zeta$.

Newton–Raphson Method

The Newton–Raphson method involves the solution of n equations (in general nonlinear) in n unknowns, written in the matrix form as,

$$f(x) = 0 \tag{C-9}$$

where

$$f = (f_1(x)\, f_2(x) \ldots f_n(x))^T$$

and

$$x = (x_1\, x_2 \ldots x_n)^T$$

To understand the convergence properties of NR method we consider a single variable problem, such as $f(x) = 0$ where $f(x)$ can be an algebraic or transcendental function.

If we represent $y = f(x)$ graphically (Fig. C-2) the problem can be formulated so that we are looking for the intersection between the curve and the x-axis. We intend to start with a trivial value x_0, then construct better and better approximations of x such as $x_1, x_2, \ldots, x_n$, so that x_n is close to the actual value ζ for which $f(\zeta) = 0$.

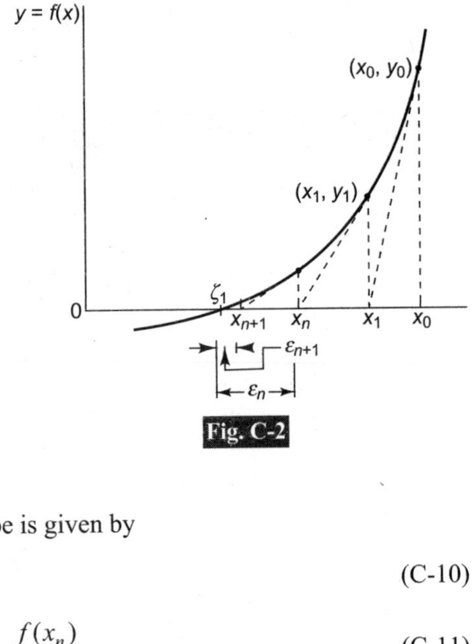

The basic idea is now to replace the curve by a suitable straight line, at the approximate point on the curve whose intersection with the x-axis can be easily computed. The direction of the line passing through the approximate point can be chosen in many ways. In NR method, the line passing through the point (x_n, y_n) has the slope given by $K = f'(x_n)$. The intersection of this line with the x-axis gives the new approximate value of $x = x_{n+1}$ as shown in Fig. C-2. The slope K is not constant, and is a function of the point x_n. Hence the NR method uses the variable tangent method (slope varies at each approximation). From Fig. (C-2), the slope is given by

Fig. C-2

$$f'(x_n) = \frac{y_n}{x_n - x_{n+1}} \quad (\neq 0) \tag{C-10}$$

$$x_{n+1} = x_n - \frac{y_n}{f'(x_n)} = x_n - \frac{f(x_n)}{f'(x_n)} \tag{C-11}$$

From the figure,

$$x_{n+1} = \zeta + \varepsilon_{n+1} \tag{C-12}$$
$$x_n = \zeta + \varepsilon_n$$

where ε_n, ε_{n+1} are the errors

$$\zeta + \varepsilon_{n+1} = \zeta + \varepsilon_n - \frac{f(\zeta + \varepsilon_n)}{f'(\zeta + \varepsilon_n)}$$

$$\varepsilon_{n+1} = \frac{\varepsilon_n f'(\zeta+\varepsilon_n) - f(\zeta+\varepsilon_n)}{f'(\zeta+\varepsilon_n)}$$

$$= \frac{\varepsilon_n (f'(\zeta) + \varepsilon_n f''(\zeta) + \ldots) - (f(\zeta) + \varepsilon_n f(\zeta) + \varepsilon_{n/2}^2 f''(\zeta) + \ldots)}{f'(\zeta+\varepsilon_n)}$$

Considering only the significant terms,

$$\varepsilon_{n+1} = \frac{\varepsilon(f'(\zeta) + \varepsilon_n f''(\zeta)) - (\varepsilon_n f'(\zeta) + \varepsilon_{n/2}^2 f''(\zeta))}{f'(\zeta+\varepsilon_n)} \quad (\text{as } f(\zeta) = 0)$$

or

$$\varepsilon_{n+1} \cong \frac{f''(\zeta)}{2f'(\zeta+\varepsilon_n)}\varepsilon_n^2 \tag{C-13}$$

If x_n is sufficiently close to ζ and $f(x)$ is continuous at $x = \zeta$, we have

$$f'(\zeta+\varepsilon_n) \cong f'(\zeta)$$

Therefore,

$$\varepsilon_{n+1} \cong \frac{f''(\zeta)}{2f'(\zeta)}\varepsilon_n^2 \tag{C-14}$$

Thus, the error $C_{n+1} = (\zeta - x_{n+1})$ is proportional to the square of the previous error $\varepsilon_n^2 = (\zeta - x_n)^2$. This type of convergence is said to be quadratic. It is clear that $f''(\zeta)/2f'(\zeta)$ should not be large for fast convergence. For the cases, where this term is low, the convergence is very fast if $|\varepsilon_n| < 1$.

References

1. H. Le Nguyen, "Newton-Raphson Method in Complex form [power system load flow analysis", *IEEE Transactions on Power Systems*, volume: 12, issue: 3, pp: 1355–1359, 1997.
2. M. Bazrafshan and N. Gatsis, "Convergence of the Z-Bus Method for Three-Phase Distribution Load-Flow with ZIP Loads", *IEEE Transactions on Power Systems*, volume: 33, issue: 1, pp: 153–165, 2018.
3. F. Milano, "Analogy and Convergence of Levenberg's and Lyapunov-Based Methods for Power Flow Analysis", *IEEE Transactions on Power Systems*, volume: 31, issue: 2, pp: 1663–1664, 2016.
4. R. Jean-Jumeau and H. Chiang, "Parameterizations of the Load-Flow Equations for Eliminating Ill-Conditioning Load Flow Solutions", *IEEE Transactions on Power Systems*, volume: 8, issue: 3, pp: 1004–1012, 1993.
5. A. Garces, "On the Convergence of Newton's Method in Power Flow Studies for DC Microgrids", *IEEE Transactions on Power Systems*, volume: 33, issue: 5, pp: 5770–5777, 2018.

APPENDIX D

Power Quality: An Overview

INTRODUCTION

Earlier times, the main concern of consumers of electricity was continuity of supply. But now, the consumers demand quality too. Even though power generation and transmission are reliable, the distribution is not so, even in most advanced countries. The electric power quality is also very important these days, because some of the consumer loads are sensitive to power quality and any outage or trip of the system may lead to huge financial loss. In a broader way, any deviation from the normal condition of the voltage and current is referred to as a power quality issue. Power quality means maintaining the voltage at its rated r.m.s value with negligible amount of harmonics and maintaining frequency within statutory limit and least amount of interruption [1]. A broad classification of power quality problem is as follows:

1. Transient change in voltage (impulsive or oscillatory)
2. Short duration voltage variation (sag, swell or interruption)
3. Long duration voltage variation (Under, Over, sustained interruption)
4. Voltage flicker (due to lightning, etc.)
5. Voltage imbalance (due to single phase loads)
6. Waveform distortion and bad power factor (harmonics, notching, DC offset).

POWER QUALITY TERMS AND DEFINITIONS

1. *Voltage sag*: A momentary voltage dip, lasting for a few seconds. Dips with duration of less than half a cycle are regarded as transients.
2. *Voltage swells*: A momentary voltage rise which lasts for a few seconds.
3. *Over voltage*: A steady state voltage rise lasting for several seconds. Sustained over voltage lasting for few hours may cause damage to appliances.
4. *Under voltage*: A steady state voltage dip lasting for several seconds.
5. *Outage*: A complete loss of voltage for a few seconds to several hours. The voltage sag, voltage swell, outage are as shown in Fig. D-1(a).

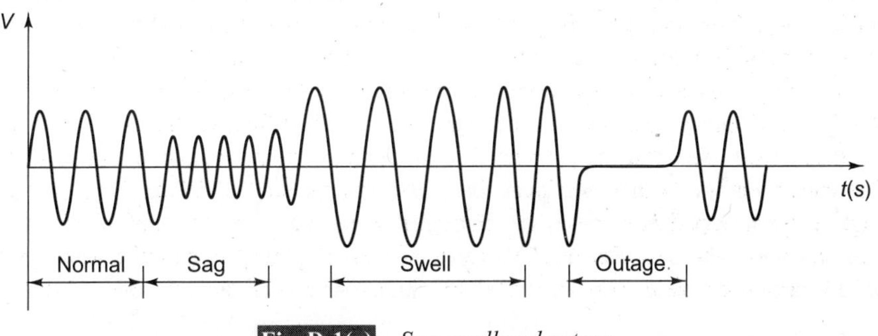

Fig. D-1(a) *Sag, swell and outage*

6. *Transients*: They are of high magnitude for extremely short duration as compared to voltage sag and swell. The transient behaviour is shown in Fig. D-1(b).
7. *Flicker*: Fluctuations in the system voltage can cause perceptible (low frequency) change in lamp output.
8. *Harmonics*: The nonfundamental frequency components of a distorted power frequency waveform. THD (Total Harmonic Distortion) is the measure of harmonics in a system. The wave form distortion is shown in Fig. D-1(c).

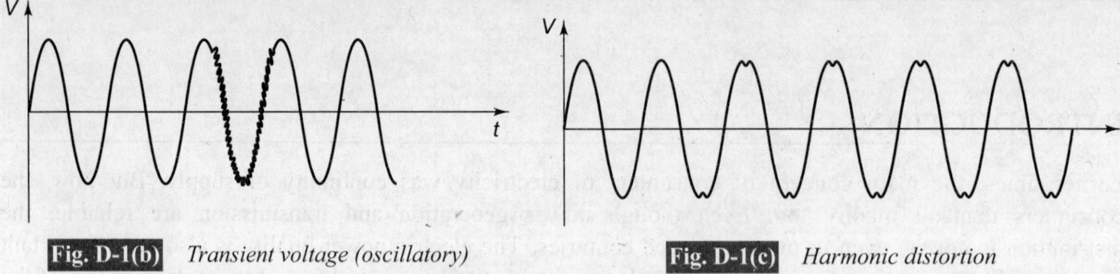

Fig. D-1(b) *Transient voltage (oscillatory)* **Fig. D-1(c)** *Harmonic distortion*

9. *Voltage imbalance*: If the voltage magnitude is unequal in a three-phase voltage sources or the phase difference between them is not equal to 120 electrical degrees or both, the situation is described as unbalanced. The transient behaviour is shown in Fig. D-1(d).

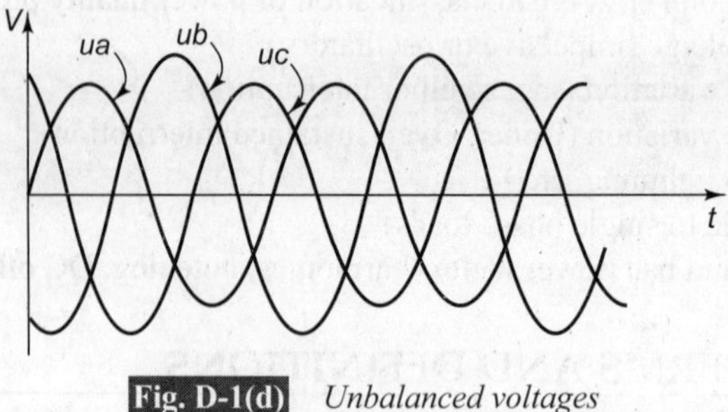

Fig. D-1(d) *Unbalanced voltages*

CAUSES FOR POWER QUALITY (PQ) PROBLEMS

There are various causes for different power quality problem and some of them are capacitor switching, single line to ground fault, switching ON and OFF of loads, single phase loads, power electronic converters, etc. But the main reason for wave form distortion is the nonlinear load in the system. For example, in a power electronic controlled load, the current drawn from the system is not sinusoidal as shown in Fig. D-2.

It can be observed that the load current draws harmonic currents along with the fundamental component. This poor quality of current pollutes the voltage at the point where it is connected. So the individual customers are responsible for the poor quality of power. Hence, the situation is severe as almost all loads are controlled by power electronic converters. Also, single-phase loads cause unbalance in the system. And interestingly, these power electronic converters are mainly affected due to the poor power quality resulted from other power electronic equipment. The harmonics are the integer multiple of the fundamental frequency. The current drawn by any nonlinear load is nonsinusoidal in nature. This nonsinusoidal current flowing through network impedance causes the voltage also become nonsinusoidal, thus leading to a voltage distortion in the network. The 3rd, 5th and 7th harmonics are the most common harmonics that pollute the network. The 3rd harmonics are usually generated by single-phase loads and the other harmonics by 3-phase load. Even harmonics cancel out and are negligible. A common PC generates 4 A/kW of 3rd harmonic and a discharge lamp will produce 1 A/kW 3rd harmonic. The sequence generated by harmonics and their effects are given in Table D-1.

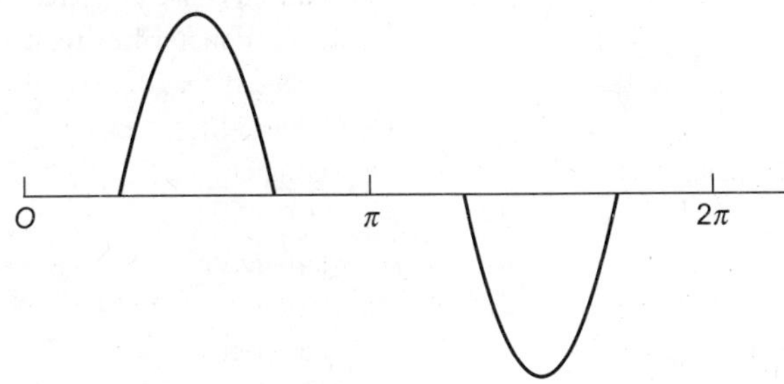

Current wave of switch mode power supply

Spectrum of Typical Switch Mode Power Supply

Harmonic	*Magnitude*	*Harmonic*	*Magnitude*
1	1.000	9	0.157
3	0.810	11	0.024
5	0.605	13	0.063
7	0.370	15	0.079

Fig. D-2 *Typical current wave form of a power electronic converter and harmonic contents*

Table D-1 Harmonics in power system

Sequence	*Harmonics*	*Direction of rotation*	*Effects*
+ ve	7th, 13th	Forward	Heating
– ve	5th, 11th	Backward	Heating and vibration in motors
zero	3rd	Insignificant	Over heating of neutral conductor due to accumulation

POWER QUALITY STANDARDS

There are international standards for the power quality. The Institute of Electrical and Electronics Engineers (IEEE) and International Electrotechnical Commission (IEC) have proposed power quality standards which are followed world over. An example is given below:

IEEE 519: Harmonic standards.

IEC 6100: Classification of power quality. Transients etc.

EFFECTS OF PQ PROBLEMS

The poor power quality affects the whole equipment connected to the electric power system adversely. Some of the cases are mentioned below:

Table D-2 Detrimental effect of harmonics in power system

Equipments	***Effects***
Transformers	Reduced capacity, increased loss
Motors	Reduced motor life, reduced rating, increased loss
Conductors	Increased heating
Capacitors	Reduced life
Power electronic equipment	Malfunction
Meters	Malfunction
Relays	Malfunction
Digital equipment	Malfunction
Telephone/communication equipment	Interference
Lamps	Reduced life

REMEDIES FOR PQ PROBLEMS

There are two kinds of remedies for the PQ problems. One is through introducing devices with power quality that meet the standards and the other is to use the power conditioners which improve the power quality at the point of interconnection with the system.

Improved Power Quality Converters (IPQC)

These are the modifications proposed in the converters so that they draw current with minimum PQ problems. There are a number of converters developed based on this concept and one example with circuit diagram and waveforms showing power factor correction is given in Fig. D-3.

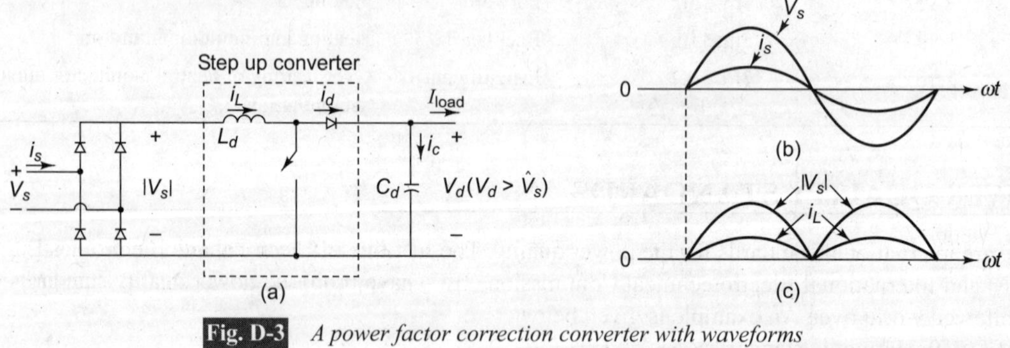

Fig. D-3 *A power factor correction converter with waveforms*

Retrofit Solutions

The harmonic currents can be prevented from entering into the utility system by means of filters. For the distribution systems, the harmonics and reactive power demand can be compensated using series or shunt filters. There are active and passive filters. Hybrid filters are also proposed which can perform both the shunt and series compensation. Another set of devices applied to the distribution system to enhance the quality and reliability of power supplied to customers are called custom power device. These devices are used for active filtering, load balancing, power factor correction and voltage regulation.

Custom Power Devices

The custom power devices are of three types based on the mode of connection with the system. The shunt connected device is DSTATCOM (distribution static compensator), the series connected device is DVR (Dynamic voltage restorer) and UPQC (unified power quality conditioner) has both shunt and series connection.

DSTATCOM (Distribution Static Compensator)

The instantaneous correction of harmonics is proposed in the VSI (Voltage source inverter) based DSTATCOM (Fig. D-4). This device compensates bad power factor, unbalance and voltage regulation along with harmonic compensation. It has a shunt connected structure which is able to inject an unbalanced and harmonically distorted current to eliminate unbalance or distortions in the load.

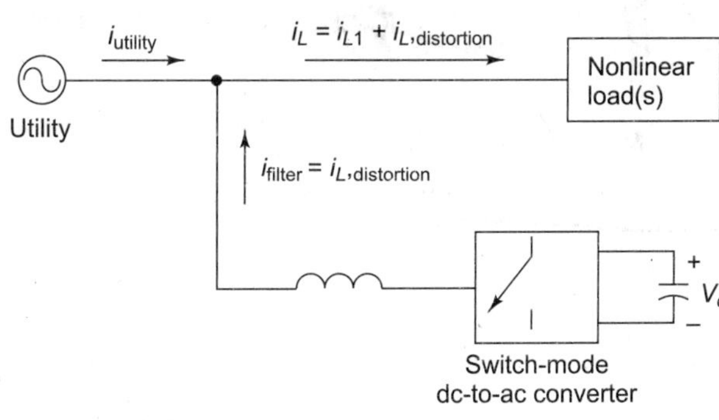

Fig. D-4 *One line diagram of a DSTATCOM*

DVR (Dynamic Voltage Restorer)

This is a series connected device and its main purpose is to protect sensitive loads from sag/swell and interruptions in the supply side. These devices have a VSI (Voltage source inverter) with PWM switching connected in series with the load voltage and inject a distorted voltage to counteract with the harmonic voltage. Also, the voltage unbalance is reduced by injecting unbalanced voltages.

UPQC (Unified Power Quality Conditioner)

This is a versatile device that can inject current in shunt and voltage in series simultaneously in a dual control mode. It must inject unbalanced and distorted voltages and currents to counteract harmonic current and harmonic voltage.

Custom Power Park The concept is a park which supplies power of different power quality levels. High quality power can be supplied using the various custom power devices in a custom power park. Such a park gets its supply from two different feeders that are coupled together. There can be DSTATCOM, DVR or even a UPQC depending upon the grade of the customer. The higher grade customers are supplied power through a diesel-generator set when both incoming feeders are lost.

DISTRIBUTED POWER GENERATION

A trend is emerging currently, in which significantly smaller sized generating units are being connected at the distribution level (Refer Chapter 1 for more details). Some of the factors that contribute to this trend are:

1. Renewable energy sources based smaller sized generating units are supported world-wide due to green house gas issues and aim for sustainable energy supply. The solar, wind, fuel cells and micro turbine-based power generation is increasing.
2. Co-generation is becoming more attractive in medium sized industrial plants. This effectively utilises the byproduct, resulting in higher energy efficiency.
3. Power quality enhancement and reduction in distribution loss.

HARMONIC INDICES AND SOME EXAMPLES

The amplitude of current or voltage is characterised by the THD (Total Harmonic Distortion). It is defined as

$$\text{THD} = \frac{\sqrt{\sum_{2}^{\infty} V_n^2}}{V_1} \tag{D-1}$$

where V_1 is the rms value of fundamental voltage, V_n is the rms harmonic voltage of nth harmonics. If V_s is the rms value of distorted voltage,

$$\text{THD} = \sqrt{\frac{V_s^2 - V_1^2}{V_1^2}} \tag{D-2}$$

In a similar way, for the current drawn,

$$\text{THD} = \sqrt{\frac{I_s^2 - I_1^2}{I_1^2}} \tag{D-3}$$

In the case of linear load, where there is no distortion in the current waveform, the power factor is

$$\text{PF} = \frac{\text{Real Power}}{V_s I_s} = \cos\phi \tag{D-4}$$

where V_s, I_s are the rms value of voltage and current and is the phase angle between voltage and current phasor.

In the presence of distortion in the current, the definition of power factor remains same. But here we take the real power as the power due to the fundamental frequency component only. Then,

$$\text{PF} = \frac{V_s I_1 \cos\phi}{V_s I_s}$$

$$= \frac{I_1}{I_s}\cos\phi \tag{D-5}$$

The ratio $\frac{I_1}{I_s}$ is defined as distortion factor (DF).

$$\text{DF} = \frac{I_1}{I_s} \tag{D-6}$$

Equation (D-5) shows that high distortion in the waveform leads to a low power factor. In terms of THD, Eq. (D-3), DF can be expressed as

$$\text{DF} = \frac{1}{\sqrt{1+\text{THD}^2}} \tag{D-7}$$

Therefore, Eq. (D-5) becomes

$$\text{PF} = \frac{1}{\sqrt{1+\text{THD}^2}}\cos\phi \tag{D-8}$$

Example D.1 The current drawn by an AC-DC converter is shown in Fig. D-5. Calculate the THD and power factor of the load.

Solution

Using the Fourier analysis, the current is

$$i_s(t) = \frac{4I_a}{\pi}\left(\frac{\sin\omega t}{1} + \frac{\sin 3\omega t}{3} + \frac{\sin 5\omega t}{5} + \cdots\right)$$

The rms value of the fundamental component is

$$I_1 = \frac{4I_a}{\pi\sqrt{2}} = 0.9\, I_a$$

The rms value of the input current is

$$I_s = \frac{4I_a}{\pi\sqrt{2}}\left(\frac{1}{1}+\frac{1}{3^2}+\frac{1}{5^2}\cdots\right)^{1/2} = I_a$$

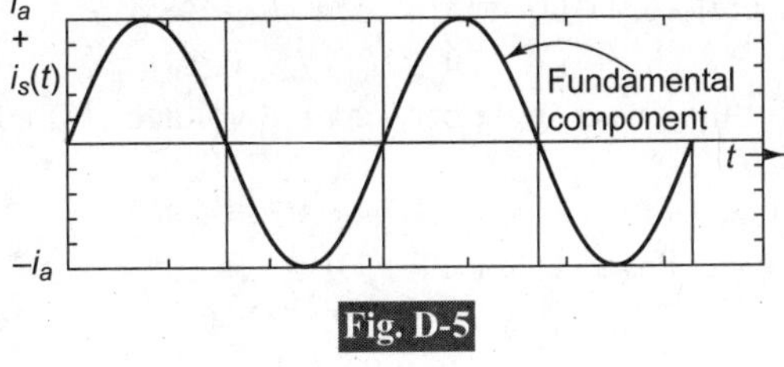

Fig. D-5

The total harmonic distortion (THD) is

$$\text{THD} = \sqrt{\left(\left(\frac{I_s}{I_1}\right)^2 - 1\right)} = \sqrt{\left(\left(\frac{1}{0.9}\right)^2 - 1\right)} = 0.484 \text{ or } 48.4\%$$

The displacement angle, which is the phase angle between the fundamental component of the current with the voltage is, $\Phi = 0$ and hence

$$\cos \Phi = 1.0$$

The power factor (PF) is

$$\text{PF} = \frac{I_1}{I_s} * 1.0 = 0.9\ (lagging)$$

Note: The power factor is not unity because of the distortion in the current waveform.

Numerical Example:

Example D.2 In a single-phase diode rectifier connected to a motor load, the current is 100 A. Find the THD and PF?

Solution The voltage and current wave forms are as shown in Fig. D-5. The dc current Id = 100 A. By applying basic definition, the rms total current is

$$I_s = I_d = 100 \text{ A}$$

By applying fourier analysis, the fundamental compound of current is

$$I_{s1} = 0.9 \quad I_d = 90 \text{ A}$$

$$\text{THD} = \Sigma I_{sh} / I_{s1} = \sqrt{(I_s^2 - I_{s1}^2)} / I_{s1}$$
$$= \sqrt{(100^2 - 90^2)} / 100$$
$$= 0.484$$
$$= 48.4\%$$

The distortion factor, DF $= I_{s1} / I_s = 90 / 100 = 0.9$

The power factor, PF.DF* cos φ

But cos $\varphi = 1$ (as per Fig. D-5)

Therefore PF = 0.9 * 1 = 0.9

Note: In a nonlinear load connected to supply the power factor is 0.9, even though the phase Shift between voltage V_s and current I_{s1} is zero (i.e., cos $\varphi = 1$)

Example D.3 In example 1, if the motor is connected to a thyristor based single phase rectifier, calculate the PF and THD?

Given: Firing (α) = 30° for the thyristor.

Solution The voltage and current wave form for the load are as shown below (Fig. D-6):

It can be observed from the waveform that:

$$I_s = I_d = 100 \text{ A}$$
$$I_{s1} = 0.9 \quad I_d = 90 \text{ A}$$

Therefore, THD = $\sqrt{(I_s^2 - I_{s1}^2)} / I_{s1} = 48.4\%$

$\text{DF} = I_{s1} / I_s = 0.9$

But the phase angle between the voltage (V_s) and the I_{s1} is $\alpha = 30°$

Therefore, $\cos \alpha = \cos 30° = 0.866$

Hence, Power factor, PF = DF * cos 30°

= 0.9 * 0.866

= 0.7794

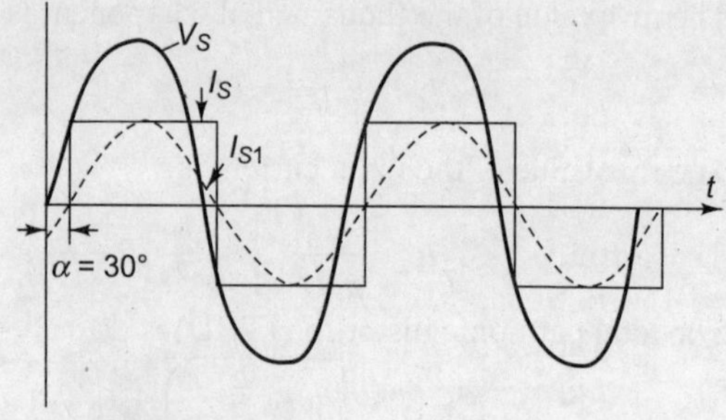

Fig. D-6 *Voltage and current waveform*

SUMMARY

There are real costs from power quality. The sensitive loads like hospitals, semiconductor industries, etc., require high quality power. So, the power quality conditioners are getting more and more importance. The expansion of distributed generation has the potential to significantly change the nature of the distribution system and the associated power quality issues. The future of energy delivery will be an integrated system of multiple sources where power quality as well as energy delivery is addressed.

References

1. A. Ghosh and G. Ledwich, *Power Quality Enhancement Using Custom Power Devices*, Kluwer Academics, 2002.
2. D.T. Heydt, *Electric Power Quality*, Stars in a Circle Publications, 1991.
3. J. Arrillaga, N.R. Wattson, and S. Chen, *Power System Quality Assessment*, John Wiley, 2000.
4. Ned Mohan, *First Course on Power System*, MNPERE, USA, 2006 edition.
5. N.G. Hingorani, Introducing Custom Power, *IEEE Spectrum*, volume: 32, issue: 6, pp: 41–48, June 1995.
6. B. Singh, B.N. Singh, A. Chandra, K. Al-Haddad, A. Pandey, and D.P. Kothari, "A Review of Single-Phase Improved Power Quality AC-DC Converters", *IEEE Transactions on Industrial Electronics*, volume: 50, issue: 5, pp: 962–981, Oct. 2003.
7. B. Singh, B.N. Singh, A. Chandra, K. Al-Haddad, A. Pandey, and D.P. Kothari, "A Review of Three-Phase Improved Power Quality AC-DC Converters", *IEEE Transactions on Industrial Electronics*, volume: 51, issue: 3, pp: 641–660, June 2004.
8. B. Singh, K. Al-Haddad, and A. Chandra, "A Review of Active Filters for Power Quality Improvement", *IEEE Transactions on Industrial Electronics*, volume: 46, issue: 5, pp: 960–971, Oct. 1999.
9. B. Singh, V. Verma, A. Chandra, and K. Al-Haddad, "Hybrid Filters for Power Quality Improvement", *IEE Proceedings Generation, Transmission and Distribution,* volume: 152, issue: 3, pp: 365–378, 6 May 2005.
10. A. Ghosh and G. Ledwich, "Load Compensating DSTATCOM in Weak AC Systems", *IEEE Transactions on Power Delivery*, volume: 18, issue: 4, pp: 1302–1309, Oct. 2003.
11. Muhammad H. Rashid, *Power Electronics Circuits, Drives and Applications*, 2nd edn, Prentice Hall, April 1999.
12. B. Singh, P. Iayaprakash, R. Somayajulu, and D.P. Kothari, "Reduced Rating VSC with a Zig-Zag Transformer for Power Quality Improvement in Three-Phase Four-Wire Distribution System', *IEEE Trans. Power Delivery*, volume: 24, issue: 1, pp: 249–259, January 2009.
13. B. Singh, P. Jayaprakash, and D.P. Kothari, "Star/Hexagon Transformer Based Three-Phase Four-Wire DSTATCOM for Power Quality Improvement", *International Journal of Emerging Electric Power Systems*, December 2008.

14. B. Singh, P. Jayaprakash, and D.P. Kothari, "A T-connected Transformer and Three-Leg VSC based DSTATCOM for Power Quality Improvement", *IEEE Transaction Power Electronics*, volume: 23, pp: 2710–2718, November 2008.
15. B. Singh, P. Jayaprakash, D.P. Kothari, A. Chandra, and K. Al-Haddad, "Comprehensive Study of DSTATCOM Configurations", *IEEE Transactions on Industrial Informatics*, volume: 10, issue: 2, pp: 854–870, 2014.
16. B. Singh, P. Jayaprakash, S. Kumar, and D.P. Kothari, "Implementation of Neural-Network-Controlled Three-Leg VSC and a Transformer as Three-Phase Four-Wire DSTATCOM", *IEEE Transactions on Industry Applications*, volume: 47, issue: 4, pp: 1892–1901, 2011.

APPENDIX E

Restructured and Deregulated Power System

INTRODUCTION

The electric power industry has over the years been dominated by large utilities that had as overall authority over all activities in generation, transmission and distribution of power within its domain of operation. Such utilities have often referred to as vertically integrated utilities.

One of the first steps in the restructuring process of the power industry has been the separation of the transmission activities from the electricity generation activities. The subsequent step was to introduce competition in generation activities, either through creation of power pools, provision for direct bilateral transactions or bidding in the spot markets.

The restructuring processes in all countries are not uniform. While in many instances, it started with the breaking up of a large vertically integrated utility. A system operator was appointed for the whole system and it was entrusted with the responsibility of keeping the system in balance, i.e., to ensure that the production and imports continuously matched the consumption and exports.

Important Terms in Deregulated Electricity Markets

Generation Companies (Gencos) The generators produce and sell electricity. This may refer either to individual generation units or more often to a group of generating units within a single company ownership structure.

Transmission Companies (Transcos) The companies are those entities which own and operate the transmission wires. Their prime responsibility is to transport the electricity from the generators to the customer.

Distribution Companies (Discos) Those companies owning and operating the local distribution network in an area buy whole sale electricity either through spot-markets or through direct contracts with gencos and supply electricity to the end-use customers.

Customers A customer is an entity consuming electricity. In deregulated markets, the customer has several options for buying electricity.

Market Operator The market operator is an entity responsible for the operation of the electricity market trading. It receives bid offer from market participants and determines the market price based on certain in accordance with the market structure.

Benefits of a Competitive Electricity Market

Competitive markets provide the driving force for generators to innovate and operate in the most efficient and economic manner in order to remain in the business and recover their costs.

1. Cheaper electricity: Cheap electrical energy increases the attractiveness of a region as a site for new industry and business opportunities. Lowering production costs for energy intensive customers will allow them to re-invest more profits back into their businesses.

2. Efficient capacity expansion planning
3. Pricing is cost reflective than a set tariff
4. Cost minimisation
5. Better service and employment opportunities with more choices

Effects of Deregulation The deregulation process is still under transition and a clear picture of the structure has not yet emerged in many countries. As of now, Swedish deregulation is just about six years old now and hence drawing conclusive view. The price variation during a year reveals that the summer prices in Sweden are drastically low compared to winter prices.

Independent System Operator (ISO) The ISO is the central entity to have emerged in all deregulated markets with the responsibility of ensuring system security and reliability, fair and equitable transmission tariffs and providing for other system services. It is an independent authority and does not participate in the electricity market traders.

The first and more common one is the pool structure in which the ISO is responsible for both market settlement and security aspects, e.g., UK, Australia, Latin America.

The other structure is that of open access, one dominated by bilateral contracts and can be found in Nordic countries.

In this system, bulk of the energy transactions are directly organised between the generator and the customer.

Unit Commitment in Deregulated Environment In a competitive environment, the genco in principle has no other objective but to produce electricity and sell it with maximum profit.

As long as the objective is profit, the Unit Commitment scheduling can be done as if all generation after fulfilling the bilateral contracts is sold in the spot market. The scheduling is sold in the spot market. The scheduling models are generally based on a price-taking assumption, which means that no participation can influence the spot market price single-handedly. This is an ideal condition and the market in such a case is known as a *perfectly competitive market*. The usually large number of market participants makes a pricing reasonable.

Objective

Profit = (Revenue – Cost)

The various constraints are

1. Demand–Supply balance
2. Limit on Power Selling/sale
3. Ramp rate constraints
4. Up/down time
5. Must run units

Competitive Bidding In a competitive electricity market, the sellers and buyers submit bids for energy buy and sell. The bids are generally in the form of price and quantity quotations and specify how much the seller or buyer is willing to sell or buy and at what price. After the bids are available to the market operator, the latter settle the market based on criterion.

The various parameters affecting bidding strategies are

1. Technical constraints on unit operation.
2. Bilateral contracts.
3. Market clearing prices of the previous day or in the recent few days.
4. Hydro energy availability for the next day.
5. Load and weather forecast for the next day.

Transmission Open Access and Price Issues The basic parameters that characterise the electric power transmission sector are

1. Large sunk and lumped investments.
2. Need for redundancies to meet security requirements.
3. Economics or scale in the construction cost in terms of the capacity of the transmission line.
4. Economics of scope given by the interconnection of electric systems.

In order to prevent the Transco from over changing for the service there is a need for the transmission systems to be regulated.

The need for regulation is all the more important when the transmission grid is the nucleus of competition among geographically dispersed generators. The trend of establishing new legal and regulatory frameworks offering third parties open access to the transmission network may be seen as a logical outcome.

Power Wheeling Exchange of power between utilities has been practices even before the term wheeling came into existence. With the increase in the amount of energy transaction the transmission capacity used for the same is an important problem for the system operation.

Wheeling transactions have been categorised into four types:

1. Bulk power wheeling
2. Customer wheeling
3. Supplier wheeling
4. Supplier to customer wheeling

Transmission Open Access Wheeling is thought of as a one time isolated service for delivering power between two parties by a third party. On the other hand, transmission open access and provision of related services is a business in itself, providing and facilitating electricity market competition.

The basic categories into which transmission services can be classified are

1. Point to point services, and
2. Network services.

The point to point service is further classified as

1. Firm transactions
2. Nonfirm Transaction

Cost Component

1. *Operating Cost* These costs are incurred by a Transco in carrying out the transactions generally relating to the cost of rescheduling.
2. *Opportunity Cost* These costs are associated with the benefits which the Transco has to forgo in order to provide a transmission service.
3. *Reinforcement Cost* This is the capital cost of new transmission facilities needed to accommodate transmission transaction.
4. *Existing Cost* This is the cost of existing facility available in the system.

Security Management in Deregulated Environment The ISO is faced with the difficult task of providing security constituent transmission services in an open market environment that is fair and equitable. In this environment of free markets, the transmission network is liable to be heavily stressed due to the various trades and transactions. It is also to be noted that these networks were originally designed to accommodate transactions following only certain load/generation patterns at best. In deregulation, the generation pattern results from the traditional one, possibly worsening the security margins.

The basic problem therefore that has emerged from deregulation is that to maintain system security at a desired level, how the ISO can evaluate the transactions that do not violate system security. The biggest challenge is that to some extent, every transaction has an effect on all other transactions. For example, by changing one particular transaction, some other transactions may also have to be modified in order to meet the power balance, generation limits and security requirements.

Congestion Management in Deregulation In the vertically integrated utility structure, all entities such as generation transmission and distribution are within the domain of a central energy management system. Generation is dispatched in order to achieve the system least cost operation. In such system, congestion management is usually taken care of by determining the optimal dispatch solution using a model similar to the optimal power flow or the security constrained economic dispatch problem.

This effectively means that a generation pattern is determined such that the power flow limits on the transmission lines are not exceeded. The presence of transmission line capacity constraints in these scheduling. Programs lead to higher marginal cost and reduced revenue for the utility, that in turn acts as a signal to the utility. A persistent congestion problem is an indication to install new generation capacity or to build additional transmission facilities.

Apart from alleviating transmission congestion through the dispatch and scheduling process, other methods such as operation of transformer taps, outage of the congested line and operation of FACTS devices, etc., also available with the ISO.

Ancillary Services Management The function of an electric utility is not limited to power generation, transmission and its distribution to customers. It also has to ensure the required degree of quality and safety. Undertake preventive measures to ward off contingencies and perform several other functions.

Ancillary services are defined as all those activities in the interconnected grid, that are necessity to support the transmission of power while maintaining reliable operation and ensuring the required degree or quality and safety.

Ancillary services would thus include

1. Regulation of frequency and tie line power flows
2. Voltage and reactive power control
3. Ensuring system stability
4. Maintenance of generation and transmission reserves

In deregulated environment, the power industry with generation and transmission becoming separate business, the system operator often has no direct control over individual power stations and has to purchase ancillary services from ancillary service providers. In such an environment, issues pertaining to pricing mechanisms for such services are extremely important for the proper functioning of the system. There are several operator activities and services. The designation of some services and distinctions between some of them are often unclear.

1. *Open Access* Open access is the nondiscriminatory provision for the use of transmission lines or distribution system or associated facilities with such lines or system by any licensee or consumer or a person engaged in generation in accordance with the regulations specified by the appropriate commission. It will promote competition and, in turn, lead to availability of cheaper power.

2. *Wheeling* Wheeling is the operation whereby the distribution system and associated facilities of a transmission or distribution licensee are used by another person for the conveyance of electricity on payment of charges to be determined by appropriate commission.

3. *Energy Banking* Energy banking is a process under which the captive power plant (CPP) or a co-generator supplies power to the grid not with the intention of selling it to either a third party or to a licensee, but with the intention of exercising his eligibility to draw back this power from the grid at a prescribed time during next financial year, after deduction of banking charges.

4. *Unbundling / Corporatisation* Many state electricity boards have either been unbundled or corporatised. Distribution business is privatised in some states such as Delhi and Orissa.

DISTRIBUTED AND DISPERSED GENERATION

Reforms in the Developing World – The Example of India

In developing countries such as India and others in SAARC, Latin America and Africa, the pre-reform scenario is characterised by state-owned power utilities with a vertically integrated and monopolised business comprising generation, transmission, distribution and customer services. Such a monopoly has shown to suffer severe technical and nontechnical efficiency losses. Some of the chief drivers of electricity reform in the developing world have hence been identified as

1. Inherent weakness in the state-run electricity sector in terms of unmet financial targets and inadequate or unreliable service provision.
2. Paucity of funds to meet infrastructure and maintenance requirements, and excess expenditure on subsidies.
3. Rural electrification in developing countries has also suffered due to financial constraints.

Generally the responsibility of the government and the public utilities is to extend the grid to rural areas without having tariff structures or collection ability to recover service costs. This results in urban consumers or national funds subsidising rural access. In poorer countries, the physical factors make the fixed cost of transmission and distribution (T&D) particularly high for grid extension to a rural population. Since the population density and demand are typically low, the average cost is higher; since the fixed costs are divided between fewer people and fewer units.

With strong support from multilateral development agencies such as the World Bank, the traditional model of state-owned power utilities in some developing countries has given way to *restructuring*, and in some cases, market competition for electricity. In India, electricity sector *reforms* are underway primarily to restore efficiency and financial health in the sector. Plagued by inefficient technical and managerial practices, the vertically integrated state electricity boards (SEBs) are unable to meet growing demand and provide quality service. Further, cross-subsidies allowing for almost zero-cost electricity to certain end users, high T&D losses due to theft, and other drains have severely constrained the financial resources of the sector.

After a failed attempt in the early 1990s to invite private participation in electricity generation, various states in India have begun to follow a largely common pattern of reforms, spearheaded by the 'World Bank-supported Orissa' model in the mid-nineties. State-level reforms in India are hence marked by some or all of the following measures:

1. Unbundling into three separate sectors of generation, transmission, and distribution,
2. Corporatisation of the units,
3. Private sector participation in generation and distribution,
4. Tariff and subsidy restructuring, and
5. Establishment of an independent state electricity regulatory commission (SERC).

Added financial impetus to the *reforms* process came in the form of the renamed Accelerated Power Development and Reform Program (APDRP), in which states willing to undertake *distribution reforms* are eligible for drawing funds. It is not immediately apparent how these elements could affect rural access, although literature reveals mainly that rural access through the grid may face more barriers under reforms (6, 10).

Reforms in India aims to refocus subsidies and rationalise tariffs, it is likely that rural customers will have to pay more for services. Secondly, with 'return on investments' becoming a critical evaluation parameter for electrification projects under reforms, addressing the sheer magnitude of rural electricity deprivation may in fact become increasingly expensive. The poorest and most underprivileged sections of rural society may be entirely excluded from electrification plans, since an electricity industry that is attempting to increase its financial viability (as is the case in India) may tend to be biased towards urban areas (they are more profitable in the short run).

Regulation would be required to ensure that access is increased and the rural poor segment of society is not shut out of the market. For rural areas, it would be worthwhile to look at *alternative technology* options such as *distributed generation* and supply based on *renewable sources* of energy.

Due to a number of government initiatives, *distributed generation* and supply using *renewable sources* may be increasingly favoured in India. For example, the Electricity Bill 2001, passed by the Standing Committee on Energy, is the first to make specific reference to renewable energy in the national electricity mix; off-grid systems for rural electrification; and the obligation to extend supply to rural areas. While clause 6 supports complete rural electrification by increasing the involvement of local stakeholders (co-operatives, village panchayats, etc.) in the management of distribution, clause 4 speaks of the formulation of a policy 'permitting stand alone systems including those based on renewable sources of energy (and other nonconventional sources of energy) for rural areas'. Funding opportunities have been announced at the national level. For example, direct funds are now available both for grid extension and standalone power plants under the Prime Minister's Minimum Needs Program—PMGY (Pradhan Mantri Gramodaya Yojana), IREDA (Indian Renewable Energy Development Agency) and MNES' (Ministry of Non-conventional Energy Sources) financing arm continue to provide subsidised interest rates and long repayment schedules to buyers of renewable energy devices. Subsidies, however, have gradually been decreasing due to a shift from direct financial incentives (i.e., subsidies) to indirect fiscal incentives (i.e., interest subsidies). In any case, such funds by themselves may not be effective unless accompanied by a clear strategy for implementation.

Due to 'economy of scale' the power generating stations were large and the capacity was in the range of 150 MW to 1000 MW. For such large power systems require high capital cost, large facilities, including land and personnel need to operate. Moreover, since these big power stations cannot be constructed near the load centre due to safety consideration and many constraints like availability of raw materials, there was a need for High Voltage transmission lines which in turn need an ample amount of money for construction, maintenance and operation. The lengthy structures are vulnerable to natural hazards, which in case become a major reason for partial or full black out. By considering the above factors, one of the best alternatives is to introduce the *distributed generation*, which is located near an electric load.

Deregulation of Electric Generation

One of the biggest and most difficult infrastructure challenges in developing countries lies in their power sector, for which scant solutions are in sight. The transition from large-scale, centralised power generation to small, distributed power generation plants is reported to arise from the *deregulation of electric generation*. Experience has shown that the demand for electricity imposes excessive peaks for short periods of time. On a yearly basis, these 'needle peaks' could be in the order of 200 hours cumulatively, in many developing countries. However, meeting them has produced excessively high costs of electric energy or rolling blackouts when the additional energy was not available. A viable alternative to this excessive cost or blackout is the use of installed emergency and standby capacity (*Distributed Generation*) for these short intervals of time.

Due to inherent resource constraints and increasing government incentives, the future of Power Sector is bound to increasingly find DG being installed to operate in parallel with the distribution system. This also brings about several potential technical conflicts such as over-current protection, instantaneous recluse, ferro-resonance, reduced insulation, transformer connections and ground faults, etc., that need to be addressed.

Distributed Generation (DG) entails using many small generators of 2–50 MW output, installed at various strategic points throughout the area, so that each provides power to a small number of consumers like supplying to single home, business or industrial facility.

The utility may install such generation to provide additional feeder or substation capacity. To achieve additional feeder capacity, the generation must often be installed some distance away from the substation, and the best location may be at a customer's site. One issue that arises is the question of ownership of the generation. Some utilities that are chartered as regulated 'wires' companies may be prohibited from owning any generation, but might benefit from some distributed generation being on the feeder. Service agreements can be structured to provide incentives for customers or independent power producers to install DG so that it can be operated to the benefit of the power delivery system.

Distributed generation is installation and operation of compact, clean and small size electric power generating unit connected directly to the distribution network. Distributed generation is the concept which provides the electric power in the heart of the power system. It is also referred as on-site generation, and decentralised generation.

According to electrical applications and load requirements, the distributed generators are classified into standby units which supplies power to sensitive loads, standalone systems as a power provider instead of connecting to the grid, peak load sharing systems used for supplying peak demand, providing combined heat and power and base load as a part of main required power and helps in improving voltage profile. Green power is the clean power obtained from renewable sources which is possible by distributed generation.

There are different kinds of distributed generation available like traditional generators and nontraditional generators.

Traditional generators consist of wind turbine units, small combined cycle plants, highly efficient gas turbines, micro-turbine, which can operate using natural gas, propane and fuel oils. Nontraditional system comprises electrochemical devices, storage devices and *Renewable devices* such as solar, photovoltaic cells, mini/micro hydro units.

Renewable Energy

It is widely accepted that renewable energy, as a distributed generation option, has a crucial role to play in achieving the objectives of the 'Village Electrification Programme' for remote inaccessible villages, and the objectives like 'Power for All' in developing countries; as a typical relevance and great potential areas of this can be seen in SAARC countries. However, there are unresolved issues pertaining to

1. The extent to which renewable energy can fill the demand-supply gap that is created by the limitations of grid extension, and
2. The facilitating mechanisms that are required to bring renewable based distributed generation and supply of electricity into the mainstream of rural electrification planning.

Broadly, these issues can be categorised under

1. Technology options and their techno-commercial viability.
2. Management and community involvement in planning and implementation.
3. Institutional requirements, including those embedded in regulatory and policy frameworks.

The advantage of distributed system is classified into three main categories like *economical, technical* and *environmental advantages*.

Economical advantage is reduction in fuel cost, saving transmission and distribution cost, reduced health care costs due to improved environment and reducing the electricity price. The environmental advantage is that low emission and less noise. Technical advantage is reduced line losses, improve voltage profile, overall energy efficiency is increased, reduced reserve requirements, improves security for critical loads and improves power quality.

Dispersed Generation

Dispersed generation refers to use of still smaller generating units, of less than 500 kW output and often sized to serve individual homes or businesses. Micro gas turbines, fuel cells, diesel, and small wind and solar PC generators make up this category. The beauty in these are modular and reloadable power generating technologies.

Dispersed generation has been used for decades as an emergency backup power source. Most of these units are used only for reliability reinforcement. Nowadays inverters are being increasingly used in domestic sector as an emergency supply during black outs. The distributed/dispersed generators can be standalone/autonomous or grid connected depending upon the requirement.

At the time of writing this (2011), there still is and will probably always be some economy of scale favouring large generators. But the margin of economy decreased considerably in last 10 years [1]. Even if the power itself costs a bit more than central station power, there is no need of transmission lines and perhaps a reduced need for distribution equipment as well. Another major advantage of dispersed generation is its modularity, portability and relocatability. Dispersed generators also include two new types of fossil fuel units—fuel cells and microgas turbines. The main challenge today is to upgrade the existing technologies and to promote development, demonstration, scaling up and commercialisation of new and emerging technologies for widespread adaptation. In the rural sector, main thrust areas are biomass briquetting, biomass-based cogeneration, etc. In solar PV (Photovoltaic), large size solar cells/modules based on crystalline silicon thin films need to be developed. Solar cells efficiency is to be improved to 15% to be of use at commercial level. Other areas are development of high efficiency inverters. Urban and industrial wastes are used for various energy applications including power generation which was around 79 MW in 2010.

However, recently there has been a considerable revival in connecting generation to the distribution network and this has come to be known as embedded or dispersed generation. The term 'embedded generation' comes from the concept of generation embedded in the distribution network while 'dispersed generation' is used to distinguish it from central generation. The two terms can be used interchangeably.

There are already 35 million improved chulhas. If growing energy needs in the rural areas are met by decentralised and hybrid energy systems (distributed/dispersed generation), this can stem growing migration of rural population to urban areas in search of better living conditions. Thus, India will be able to achieve a smooth transition from fossil fuel economy and bring 'Energy for all' and 'Energy for ever' era for equitable, environment-friendly, and sustainable development.

References

1. H.L. Philipson and L. Willis, *Understanding Electric Utilities and De-Regulation,* Marcel Dekker Pub., 1998.
2. S. Stoft, *Power System Economics: Designing Markets for Electricity,* John Wiley and Sons, 2002.
3. K. Bhattacharya, J.E Daadler, and M.H.J. Boolen, *Operation of Restructured Power System,* Kluwer Academic Pub., 2001.
4. Mohammad Shahidehpour and Muwaffaq Alomoush, *Restructured Electrical Power Systems: Operation, Trading and Volatility,* Marcel Dekker Pub., 2001.
5. Q. Zhao, P. Wang, L. Goel, and Y. Ding, "Impacts of Contingency Reserve on Nodal Price and Nodal Reliability Risk in Deregulated Power Systems", *IEEE Transactions on Power Systems*, volume: 28, issue: 3, pp: 2497–2506, 2013.
6. D.P. Kothari, R. Ranjan, and K.C. Singhal, *Renewable Energy Sources and Technology,* 2nd edition, 2010.
7. T.C. Kandpal and H.P. Garg, *Financial Evaluation of Renewable Technologies,* Macmillian India Ltd, New Delhi, 2003.
8. J.W. Twidell and A.D. Weir, *Renewable Energy Resources,* Taylor and Francis, London, 2nd edition, 2006.
9. Peng Wang and R. Billinton, "Reliability Assessment of a Restructured Power System Considering the Reserve Agreements", *IEEE Transactions on Power Systems*, volume: 19, issue: 2, pp: 972–978, 2004.
10. D.P. Kothari and I.J. Nagrath, *Power System Engineering*, Tata McGraw-Hill, New Delhi, 2nd edition, 2008.

APPENDIX

F Generator Maintenance Scheduling

INTRODUCTION

In order to avoid premature aging and failure of generators in a power system which may cause unplanned and costly power outages, it is important to carry out preventive maintenance of the generating units at regular intervals. Effective maintenance scheduling of power system generators is very important as it not only reduces the overall energy cost (economical) but also increases the system reliability by reducing Forced Outage Rates (FOR), thus ensuring economical and reliable operation of a power system. So, generator maintenance scheduling (GMS) plays a very important role in power system cost and risk management. It involves scheduling and executing the actual maintenance works of generators.

GENERATOR MAINTENANCE SCHEDULING PROBLEM

The Generator Maintenance Scheduling Problem (GMSP) can be described as determining the optimal starting time for each preventive maintenance outage of unit in a weekly period for 1 year in advance, while satisfying the system constraints and maintaining system reliability. The problem is vital to solve for the planning of the secure and reliable operation of a power system, primarily because other short- and long-term planning activities, such as unit commitment, generation dispatch, import/export of power and generation expansion planning are directly affected by such decisions. In modern power systems, the demand for electricity has greatly increased with related expansions in power system size, which has resulted in higher numbers of generators and lower reserve margins, making the GMS problem more complicated. The goal of GMS is to allocate a maintenance timetable for generators in order to maintain high system reliability, reduce total operating costs, and extend generator life time, while still satisfying constraints on the individual generators and the power system as a whole. Due to the nature of the problem formulation, high dimensionality and complexity characterise the GMS problem.

GMS is done for time horizons of different durations. Short-term maintenance scheduling for one hour to one day ahead is important for day-to-day operations, unit commitment and operation planning of power generation facilities. Medium-term scheduling for one day up to a year ahead is essential for resource management. Long-term scheduling of a year to two years ahead is important for future planning. This represents a tough scheduling problem which continues to present a challenge for efficient optimisation solution techniques.

Major objective functions of generator maintenance scheduling are

- Minimise total operating cost (production and maintenance) of the generating unit.
- Minimise outage of unit.
- Levelize reserve and risk.

while system energy supply requirement is satisfied for all the time horizon.

The maintenance scheduling of the generating units in a power system is of great concern in system design, planning and operation management. MSP (Maintenance Scheduling Problem) is a constrained optimization problem. The job of GMS (Generator Maintenance Scheduling) involves arranging periodically units for preventive maintenance at desired security (reliability) level, so that the costs involved are minimized and the system constraints are fulfilled.

On the whole, a good maintenance schedule is expected to achieve the following goals:

I. Increase the reliability and the economic benefits of power system.
II. Extend the generator lifetime.
III. Reduce installations of the new units.

PROBLEM FORMULATION

As mentioned earlier, the GMS problem is to determine the period for which generating units of an electric power utility should be taken off line for planned preventive maintenance over the course of a one- or two-year planning horizon in order to minimise the total operating cost while system energy supply requirement and a number of other constraints are satisfied. There are generally two categories for criteria for GMS problem; based on economic cost and reliability. The most common economic objective is to minimise the total operating cost, which includes the costs of energy production and maintenance. If outage durations are allowed to vary, this results in a trade-off between the energy production cost and the maintenance cost. Shorter outage durations lead to higher maintenance costs but reduce the load of expensive generation and possible energy purchases, resulting in lower energy production costs. However, the operating cost is an insensitive criterion for maintenance schedule plan and as such it requires many approximations. The integrated mathematical formulation of the GMS problem can be expressed as under:

$$\text{Min} \sum_t \left(\sum_i c_{it}(P_{it})(1 - y_{it}) \right) + \sum_i C_{it} \cdot y_{it} \qquad (1)$$

Subject to:

$$y_{it} = 1 \text{ for } xi \le t \le xi + d \text{ or '0' otherwise} \qquad (2)$$

$$\sum_i y_{it} = nc \quad \text{for all } t \qquad (3)$$

$$\sum_t y_{it} = 1 \quad \text{for all } i \qquad (4)$$

$$P_i^{\min} \le P_{it} \le P_i^{\max} \text{ for all } i, t \qquad (5)$$

$$\sum_i P_{it}(1 - y_{it}) = Di \text{ for all } t \qquad (6)$$

Its decomposed model is comprised of two interrelated subproblems described as follows:

(a) ***The maintenance scheduling problem:***

$$\text{Min} \sum_t \left(\sum_i C_{it} \cdot y_{it} \right) \qquad (7)$$

Subject to:

$$y_{it} = 1 \text{ for } xi \le t \le xi + d \text{ or '0' otherwise} \qquad (8)$$

$$\sum_i y_{it} = nc \quad \text{for all } t \qquad (9)$$

$$\sum_t y_{it} = 1 \quad \text{for all } i \qquad (10)$$

(b) ***The power system subproblem:***

$$\text{Min} \sum_{t}\left(\sum_{i} c_{it} \cdot (P_{it})(1 - y_{it})\right) \tag{11}$$

Subject to:

$$P_i^{min} \le P_{it} \le P_i^{max} \qquad \text{for all } i, t \tag{12}$$

$$\sum_{i} P_{it}(1 - y_{it}) = Di \qquad \text{for all } t \tag{13}$$

where

c_{it} = production cost of unit i at time t.
C_{it} = maintenance cost for unit i at time period t (amount per week).
y_{it} = 1, if unit i on maintenance time period t (weeks) and zero otherwise.
nc = number available crew teams for generator maintenance.
xi = starting time of maintenance for unit i.
di = duration of maintenance for unit.
P_{it} = output power from generating unit i at time period i.
P^{max} = maximum output power from unit i.
P^{min} = minimum output power from unit i.
Dt = demand at time t.

The objective function Eq. (7) is the generator maintenance cost. For the same unit, the cost can vary from 1 week to another depending on the available resources, the weather conditions and maintenance crew availability. The objective function Eq. (11) represents the production cost. The production cost for a unit is considered a quadratic function of the output. The maintenance subproblem has integer variables and the power system subproblem variables are continuous.

The maintenance scheduling constraints are

1. Constraint (2) represents the generation maintenance window, where the maintenance window for a unit is set to 1 year.
2. Constraint (3) is the generation crew constraint assigns one unit to one crew at a time.
3. Constraint (4) limits the number of outages for the same unit to one time during the maintenance horizon.

The power system constraints are

1. Constraint (5) is introduced to make sure that a unit is working at or below its maximum output.
2. Constraint (6) is to guarantee the on line units to meet the system demand

SOLUTION TECHNIQUES

A variety of exact mathematical optimisation methods and heuristic techniques have been used to solve the GMS problem. Mathematical methods are mainly based on linear programming, integer programming, dynamic programming, branch-and-bound technique. The main problem with the exact mathematical methods is that the number of combinations of states that must be searched increases exponentially with the size of problem and becomes computationally prohibitive. Also, it may lead to a local optimum solution. Furthermore, these techniques are generally unsuitable for the nonlinear objectives and constraints in their standard form and several assumptions are required to make the problem solvable using reasonable computational resources. The heuristic-based techniques use a specialised method to evaluate the objective function in the time interval under examination. Modern methods of metaheuristic and soft computing based approaches like simulated annealing, fuzzy set theory, expert systems, genetic algorithms, evolutionary programming, etc. have been used to solve the problem and take care of limitations in the classical methods. The modern approaches have been applied to solve a range of optimisation problems in power systems with encouraging results. It has been demonstrated that the performance of genetic algorithm can be improved by combining it with other techniques like hybrid genetic algorithm and simulating annealing, tabu search technique coupled with genetic algorithm and simulating annealing. The hybridisation improves the convergence of the algorithms. Most of these applications formulated the problems using the economic objective with typical problem constraints and a binary string representation to encode a candidate solution. The composition of GMS problem has many features of other optimisation problems posed in power systems. The examples include unit commitment, economic dispatch, generation planning and VAR dispatch. Solving these scheduling problems is important for the economic and reliable operation of the entire power sector. In recent years, researchers have focused much attention on hybrid solution techniques combining exact, heuristic and metaheuristic techniques.

FEW RECENT TRENDS

(a) Unified Generation and Transmission Maintenance Scheduling

Generating units are distributed in different regions and interconnected by transmission lines. This may lead to different composite reliability levels for a given amount of maintenance capacity outage. In addition, generating unit maintenance should consider transmission forced and planned outages. Excluding planned outages of transmission lines for preventive maintenance might produce optimistic results for the GMS problem. On the other hand, due to line loadability limits, a critical loading problem could take place if certain lines and/or generator were removed from the system at the same time for maintenance. In this case, the optimal resulting maintenance schedule may not be suitable for the system at all times. When transmission maintenance and other network constraints are included, the problem becomes considerably more complex and will be referred to as an integrated maintenance scheduler (IMS) which represents a network constrained generation and transmission maintenance scheduling problem. However, it is the only way to assure the applicability of the obtained maintenance schedule.

Coupling Constraints The first IMS requirement is that units and transmission lines be overhauled regularly. This is necessary to keep their efficiency at a reasonable level, keep the incidence of forced outage low, and prolong the life of units and lines. This procedure is incorporated periodically by specifying min/max times that a generating unit may run without maintenance. The time required for overhaul is generally known and hence the number of weks that a unit is 'down' is predetermined. Furthermore, only a limited number of units may be serviced at once due to limited manpower. The available crews can be split into geographical and organisational types. The number of crews in each type required at each stage of overhaul of each unit or line maintenance is specified.

Decoupling Constraints Network constraints in each time period are considered as decoupling; the network can be modelled as either the transportation model or a liberalised power flow model. Transportation model is used to represent system operation limits, peak load balance equation, generating and line capacity limits. In order to avoid over-optimistic planning, generation and transmission outages should also be taken into account for composite reliability evaluation.

Solution Methods Problem can be solved employing the Benders decomposition technique. The problem is decomposed into a master problem and operation sub-problems. The master problem is the minimisation of maintenance cost subject to maintenance constraints as well as feasibility and infeasibility cuts from the operation sub-problems. It is an integer programming problem and solved to generate a trial solution for maintenance schedule decision variables. The master problem is relaxation of the original problem in this it contains only a subset of constraints. Its optimal value is a lower bound on the optimal value of original problem. Once the unit maintenance status and number of lines are fixed, the resulting operation sub-problem can be treated as a set of independent sub-problems, one for each time period. In the operational sub-problem, operation cost is the direct cost associated with load supply. The scheduling must ensure that sufficient reserve exists to provide a secure supply while minimising the cost of operation. The set of operation sub-problems are then solved using the fixed maintenance schedule obtained from the solution of the master problem.

Evolutionary programming (EP) based solution technique can also be employed for solving unified generation and transmission maintenance scheduling problem. EP and the feasibility check of the Hill-climbing technique (HCT) to solve the two interrelated maintenance sub-problems was motivated by the search ability of the former to find a near optimal solution of combinatorial problems and the ability to the latter to move an infeasible solution into feasible region.

(b) Distributed Generator Maintenance Scheduling

Electricity sector has undergone a number of changes that all point in the direction of liberalisation and decentralisation of control. A compelling example that sees increasing interest is the distributed generation of electric power Small rooftop photovoltaic arrays or fuel cells ranging from several to a few hundred kW can be installed at or near the consumer's site. Thus, the customers can also supply power back to the grid, possibly decreasing bottlenecks and costs and increasing fault tolerance and overall efficiency of the system as a whole. The regulatory bodies that oversee the functioning of the power sector have widely begun to believe that new orientations, towards market-based systems with many smaller players are more desirable, and adapt their policies accordingly. Consequently, many aspects of the industry are changing, including its infrastructure and operation. Important shifts in the number and ownership of power production facilities, the volume of power generation and capacity have taken place in the past decade. The diversification and multiplication of the actors of the power sector require new tools and methodologies that are able to deal with these problems in a distributed fashion. For this, distributed constraint satisfaction/optimisation framework (DCOP) is an efficient and competitive tool that has the potential to find wide applicability in power systems related coordination tasks in maintenance scheduling. In the distributed optimisation, each variable and constraint is owned by an agent and an agent can own multiple variables and constraints. The constraints are represented as tables, values and their associated cost. They can express a wide range of functions not restricted to the linear constraints.

(c) Generator Maintenance Scheduling Considering Reserve Margin

In order to make-up the generation capacity due to unexpected outage of units in a power system without rescheduling the demand, sufficient amount of reserve generation capacity is required to be maintained. To factor into above aspect in the generator maintenance scheduling, a number of reliability definitions such as expected lack of peak net reserve, expected energy not supplied, loss of load probability, etc., can be used as reliability criteria for the formulation of GMS objective function. For example, the quality of reserve is considered, whereby the risk of exceeding the available capacity is leveled over the entire period by using the equivalent load carrying for each unit and an equivalent load for each interval. Minimising the sum of the individual loss of load probabilities for each interval can also be a reliability objective under the conditions of load uncertainty and random forced outages of units. The leveling of the reserve generation over the entire operational planning period is the most common reliability criterion. The problem can be solved using genetic algorithm (GA), combined genetic and simulating annealing (GA/SA) technique, hybrid GA/SA/heuristic approaches.

References

1. W.R. Christiaanse and A.H. Palmer, "A Technique for the Automated Scheduling of the Maintenance of Generating Facilities", *IEEE Trans. on Power Apparatus and Systems*, volume PAS-91, issue: 1, pp: 137–144, 1972.
2. H.H. Zurn and V.H. Quintana, "Generator Maintenance Scheduling via Successive Approximation Dynamic Programming", *IEEE Trans. on Power Apparatus and Systems*, volume: PAS-94, issue: 1 pp: 665–671, 1975.
3. G.T. Egan, T.S. Dillon, and K. Morsztyn, "An Experimental Method of Determination of Optimal Maintenance Schedules in Power System using the Branch and Bound Techniques", *IEEE Trans. on Man and Cybernetics*, volume: SMC-6, issue: 8, pp: 538–547, 1976.
4. R. Mukerji, H.M. Merrill, B.W. Erickson, J.H. Parker, and R.E. Friedman, "Power Plant Maintenance Scheduling: Optimising Economics and Reliability", *IEEE Trans. on Power Systems*, volume: 6 pp: 476–483, 1991.
5. M. Marwali and M. Shahidehpour, "A Probabilistic Approach to Generation Maintenance Schedule with Network Constraints", *Electric Power and Energy Systems*, volume: 21, pp: 533–545, 1999.
6. K.P. Dahal, G.M. Burt, J.R. McDonals, and S.J. Galloway, "GA/SA-Based Hybrid Techniques for the Scheduling of Generator Maintenance in Power Systems", *Proc. of IEEE Congress on Evolutionary Computation*, pp: 567–574, Diego, 2000.
7. K.P. Dahal and N. Chhakpitak, "Generator Maintenance Scheduling in Power System using Metaheuristic-Based Hybrid Approaches", *Electric Power System Research*, 2006.
8. H. Kim, Y. Hayashi, and K. Nara, "An Algorithm for Thermal Maintenance Scheduling Through Combined Use of GA, SA and TS", *IEEE Trans. on Power*, volume: 12, pp: 329–335, 1997.
9. Y. Wang and E. Handschin, "A New Genetic Algorithm for Preventive Unit Maintenance Scheduling of Power Systems", *Electric Power and Energy Systems*, volume: 22, pp: 343–348, 2000.
10. M.K.C. Marwali and S.M. Shahidehpour, "Integrated Generation and Transmission Maintenance Scheduling with Network Constraints", *IEEE Trans. on Power Systems*, volume: 13, pp: 1063-1068, 1998.
11. M.Y. El-Sharkh and A.A. El-Keib, "An Evolutionary Programming-based Solution Methodology for Power Generation and Transmission Maintenance Scheduling", *Electric Power System Research*, volume: 65, pp: 35–40, 2003.
12. Aijaz Ahmad and D.P. Kothari, "A Review of Recent Advances in Generator Maintenance Scheduling", *Electric Machines and Power Systems*, volume: 26, issue: 4, pp. 373–387, 1998.
13. D.P. Kothari and J.S. Dhillion, "Power System Optimization", 2nd edition, PHI, 2010.

ANNEXURE

1.1

CARBON CREDIT

A **carbon credit** is a generic term for any tradable certificate or permit representing the right to emit one tonne of carbon dioxide or carbon dioxide equivalent (CO_2-e). The carbon credit system was ratified in conjunction with the Kyoto Protocol. Its goal is to stop the increase of carbon dioxide emissions [1]. Certified Emission Reduction (CER) or in common parlance 'Carbon credit', CRE are issued based on the global warming potential (GWP) of 6 main greenhouse gases namely CO_2, CH_4, Nitrous oxide, HFCs, PFCs and Sulphur Hexafluoride (SF_6).

What Does Carbon Credit Mean?

A permit that allows the holder to emit one tonne of carbon dioxide. Credits are awarded to countries or groups that have reduced their greenhouse gases below their emission quota. For example, if an environmentalist group plants enough trees to reduce emissions by one tonne the group will be awarded a credit. The carbon credit system looks to reduce emissions by having countries honour their emission quotas and offer incentives for being below them.

Carbon credits and carbon markets are a component of national and international attempts to mitigate the growth in concentrations of greenhouse gases (GHGs). Carbon trading is an application of an emissions trading approach. Greenhouse gas emissions are capped and then markets are used to allocate the emissions among the group of regulated sources. The goal is to allow market mechanisms to drive industrial and commercial processes in the direction of low emissions or less carbon intensive approaches than those used when there is no cost to emitting carbon dioxide and other GHGs into the atmosphere. Since GHG mitigation projects generate credits, this approach can be used to finance carbon reduction schemes between trading partners and around the world.

There are also many companies that sell carbon credits to commercial and individual customers who are interested in lowering their carbon footprint on a voluntary basis. These carbon offsetters purchase the credits from an investment fund or a carbon development company that has aggregated the credits from individual projects. The quality of the credits is based in part on the validation process and sophistication of the fund or development company that acted as the sponsor to the carbon project. This is reflected in their price; voluntary units typically have less value than the units sold through the rigorously validated Clean Development Mechanism [2].

The concept of carbon credits came into existence as a result of increasing awareness of the need for controlling emissions. The mechanism was formalised in the Kyoto Protocol, an international agreement between more than 170 countries, and the market mechanisms were agreed through the subsequent Marrakech Accords. The mechanism adopted was similar to the successful US Acid Rain Program to reduce some industrial pollutants.

Emission Allowances

Under the Kyoto Protocol, the 'caps' or quotas for Greenhouse gases for the developed countries are known as **Assigned Amounts** are listed. The quantity of the initial assigned amount is denominated in individual units, called assigned amount units (AAUs), each of which represents an allowance to emit one metric tonne of carbon dioxide equivalent, and these are entered into the country's national registry [3].

In turn, these countries set quotas on the emissions of installations run by local business and other organisations, generically termed 'operators'. Countries manage this through their national registries, which are required to be validated and monitored for compliance by the UNFCCC [4]. Each operator has an allowance of credits, where each unit gives the owner the right to emit one metric tonne of carbon dioxide or other equivalent greenhouse gas. Operators that have not used up their quotas can sell their unused allowances as carbon credits, while businesses that are about to exceed their quotas can buy the extra allowances as credits, privately or on the open market. As demand for energy grows over time, the total emissions must still stay within the cap, but it allows industry some flexibility and predictability in its planning to accommodate this.

By permitting allowances to be bought and sold, an operator can seek out the most cost-effective way of reducing its emissions, either by investing in 'cleaner' machinery and practices or by purchasing emissions from another operator who already has excess 'capacity'.

Emission Markets

For trading purposes, one allowance or CER is considered equivalent to one metric tonne of CO_2 emissions. These allowances can be sold privately or in the international market at the prevailing market price. These trade and settle internationally and hence allow allowances to be transferred between countries. Each international transfer is validated by the UNFCCC. Each transfer of ownership within the European Union is additionally validated by the European Commission.

Currently, there are five exchanges trading in carbon allowances: the Chicago Climate Exchange, European Climate Exchange, Nord Pool, Power Next and the European Energy Exchange. Recently, Nord Pool listed a contract to trade offsets generated by a CDM carbon project called Certified Emission Reductions (CERs). Many companies now engage in emissions abatement, offsetting, and sequestration programs to generate credits that can be sold on one of the exchanges. At least one private electronic market has been established in 2008: CantorCO_2e.[11] Louis Redshaw, head of environmental markets at Barclays Capital predicts that "Carbon will be the world's biggest commodity market, and it could become the world's biggest market overall [5]".

Credits Versus Taxes Carbon credits and carbon taxes each have their advantages and disadvantages. Credits were chosen by the signatories to the Kyoto Protocol as an alternative to Carbon taxes. A criticism of tax-raising schemes is that they are frequently not hypothecated, and so some or all. By treating emissions as a market commodity some proponents insist it becomes easier for businesses to understand and manage their activities, while economists and traders can attempt to predict future pricing using market theories. Thus the main advantages of a tradable carbon credit over a carbon tax are argued to be:

1. The price may be more likely to be perceived as fair by those paying it [6]. Investors in credits may have more control over their own costs.
2. The flexible mechanisms of the Kyoto Protocol help to ensure that all investment goes into genuine sustainable carbon reduction schemes through an internationally agreed validation process.

3. Some proponents state that if correctly implemented a target level of emission reductions may somehow be achieved with more certainty, while under a tax the actual emissions might vary over time.
4. It may provide a framework for rewarding people or companies who plant trees or otherwise meet standards exclusively recognised as 'green'.

The advantages of a carbon tax are argued to be:

1. Possibly less complex, expensive and time-consuming to implement. This advantage is especially great when applied to markets like gasoline or home heating oil.
2. Perhaps some reduced risk of certain types of cheating, though under both credits and taxes, emissions must be verified.
3. Reduced incentives for companies to delay efficiency improvements prior to the establishment of the baseline if credits are distributed in proportion to past emissions.
4. When credits are grandfathered, this puts new or growing companies at a disadvantage relative to more established companies.
5. Allows for more centralised handling of acquired gains.
6. Worth of carbon is stabilised by government regulation rather than market fluctuations. Poor market conditions and weak investor interest have a lessened impact on taxation as opposed to carbon trading.

Creating Real Carbon Credits The first step in determining whether or not a carbon project has legitimately led to the reduction of real, measurable, permanent emissions is understanding the CDM methodology process. This is the process by which project sponsors submit, through a Designated Operational Entity (DOE), their concepts for emissions reduction creation. The CDM Executive Board, with the CDM Methodology Panel and their expert advisors, review each project and decide how and if they do indeed result in reductions that are additional [7].

Additionality and its Importance It is also important for any carbon credit (offset) to prove a concept called *additionality*. The concept of additionality addresses the question of whether the project would have happened anyway, even in the absence of revenue from carbon credits. Only carbon credits from projects that are 'additional to' the business-as-usual scenario represent a net environmental benefit. Carbon projects that yield strong financial returns even in the absence of revenue from carbon credits; or that are compelled by regulations; or that represent common practice in an industry are usually not considered additional, although a full determination of additionality requires specialist review. Additionality is thus critical to the success and integrity of GHG programs that recognise project-based GHG reductions.

Conclusion

Carbon credits are a key component of national and international emissions trading schemes that have been implemented to mitigate global warming. They provide a way to reduce greenhouse effect emissions on an industrial scale by capping total annual emissions and letting the market assign a monetary value to any shortfall through trading. Many developing nations want the opportunity to earn credits by preventing deforestations [8]. The Kyoto Protocol allows for carbon credits to be earned for sequestration projects, such as the planting of trees. For example, forestry companies that replant deforested areas could potentially earn offset credits, as forests absorb carbon dioxide as they grow. A key issue in this area is that the projects must represent an actual reduction of emissions compared to 'business as usual'. In this case, investors would hope to earn carbon credits that can then be applied against their own emissions to help them meet their targets.

References

1. D.P. Kothari, Rakesh Ranjan, and K.C. Singhal, *Renewable Energy Sources and Technology*, 2nd ed. Prentice Hall, New Delhi, 2011.
2. X. Zhao, Y. Bai, L. Ding, and L. Wang, "Tripartite Evolutionary Game Theory Approach for Low-Carbon Power Grid Technology Cooperation with Government Intervention", *IEEE Access*, volume: 8, pp: 47357–47369, 2020.
3. S. Lou, S. Lu, Y. Wu, and D.S. Kirschen, "Optimizing Spinning Reserve Requirement of Power System with Carbon Capture Plants", *IEEE Transactions on Power Systems*, volume: 30, issue: 2, pp: 1056–1063, 2015.
4. M.J. Ashley and M.S. Johnson, "Establishing a Secure, Transparent, and Autonomous Blockchain of Custody for Renewable Energy Credits and Carbon Credits", *IEEE Engineering Management Review*, volume: 46, issue: 4, pp: 100–102, 2018.
5. G. Lakshmi and G. Thiyagarajan, "Decentralized Energy to Power Rural Homes Through Smart Contracts and Carbon Credit", *7th International Conference on Electrical Energy Systems (ICEES)*, pp: 280–283, 2021.
6. A.K. Dash, S. Agarwal, S. Gairola, and A. Banshwar, "A Cumulative Study of Different Power Output and Carbon Credit Earned in Roof Integrated Photovoltaic Thermal (BIPVT) System," *2nd International Conference on Power Energy, Environment and Intelligent Control (PEEIC)*, pp: 224–228, 2019.
7. Q. Hou, Y. Guan, and S. Yu, "Stochastic Differential Game Model Analysis of Emission-Reduction Technology Under Cost-Sharing Contracts in the Carbon Trading Market," *IEEE Access*, volume: 8, pp: 167328–167340, 2020.
8. M. Zhang, B. Li, and S. Yin, "Is Technological Innovation Effective for Energy Saving and Carbon Emissions Reduction? Evidence from China", *IEEE Access*, volume: 8, pp: 83524–83537, 2020.
9. E. Denny and M. O'Malley, "Wind Generation, Power System Operation, and Emissions Reduction", *IEEE Transactions on Power Systems*, volume: 21, issue: 1, pp: 341–347, Feb. 2006.
10. A.S. Algarni, S. Suryanarayanan, H.J. Siegel, and A.A. Maciejewski, "Combined Impact of Demand Response Aggregators and Carbon Taxation on Emissions Reduction in Electric Power Systems," *IEEE Transactions on Smart Grid*, volume: 12, issue: 2, pp: 1825-1827, 2021.

Answers to Problems

CHAPTER 1

1.1 3360 MWh, 280 MW, 80 MW, 6720 MW, 96000 MW, 0.7142

1.2 (a) Rs 1400, Rs 2.8/kWh,
(b) Rs 1616.66, Rs 2.6944/kWh
(c) Rs 1277.6, Rs 2.552/kWh

CHAPTER 2

2.1 $L_{int} = \frac{1}{2} \times 10^{-7} \times \frac{1}{(r_2^2 - r_1^2)^2}\left[(r_2^4 - r_1^4) - 4r_1^2(r_2^2 - r_1^2) + 4r_1^4 \ln \frac{r_2}{r_1}\right]$

2.2 0.658 ohm/km

2.3 $L = \frac{\mu}{2\pi} \ln (R/r)$ H/m

2.4 260.3 V/km

2.5 $H_P = \frac{-I}{3\pi d}$ AT/m^2 (directed upwards)

2.6 $X = \left[\frac{(X_1 - X_{12})(X_2 - X_{12})}{X_1 + X_2 - 2X_{12}}\right]$

2.7 0.00067 mH/km, 0.0314 V/km

2.8 0.0044 $\angle 140°$ mH/km, 0.553 $\angle 140°$ V/km

2.9 0.346 ohm/km

2.10 1.48 m

2.11 0.191 ohm/km/phase

2.12 0.455 mH/km/phase

2.13 2.38 m

2.14 (a) 0.557 $d^{1/2} A^{1/4}$
(b) 0.633 $d^{2/3} A^{1/6}$
(c) 0.746 $d^{3/4} A^{1/8}$

CHAPTER 3

3.1 $$q_a = \frac{2\pi k\,|V|\left[\ln\frac{r}{2D}\angle 30^\circ - \ln\frac{D}{2r}\angle -30^\circ\right]}{2\ln\left(\frac{D}{r}\right)\ln\left(\frac{r}{2D}\right) - \ln\left(\frac{2D}{r}\right)\ln\left(\frac{D}{2r}\right)}\ \text{F/m}$$

$I_a = 2\pi f q_a \angle 90^\circ$ A

3.2 0.0204 μF/km
3.3 0.0096 μF/km
3.4 0.0103 μF/km to neutral
3.5 3.08×10^{-5} Coulomb/km
3.6 5.53×10^{-6} mho/km
3.7 8.54×10^{3} ohm/km
3.8 8.72×10^{-3} μF/km
3.9 71.24 kV

CHAPTER 4

4.1 12 kV

CHAPTER 5

5.1 (a) 992.75 kW (b) No solution possible
5.2 $A' = 0.9\angle 1.5^\circ$, $B' = 239.9\angle 66.3^\circ$, $C' = 0.001\angle 102.6^\circ$ $D' = 0.85\angle 1.96^\circ$
5.3 (a) $0.978\angle 0.5^\circ$, $86.4\angle 68.6^\circ$, $0.00056\angle 90.2^\circ$, $0.978\angle 0.5^\circ$
(b) 165.44 kV, $0.244\angle{-28.3^\circ}$ kA, 0.808 lagging, 56.49 MW
(c) 70.8%
(d) 28.15%
5.4 (a) 273.5 MVA
(b) 1174 A
(c) 467.7 MVA
5.5 133.92 kV, 23.12 MW
5.6 202.2 kV
5.7 At $x = 0$; $i_{x1} = 0.314\cos(\omega t - 21.7^\circ)$, $i_{x_2} = 0.117\cos(\omega t + 109^\circ)$
At $x = 200$ km; $i_{x_1} = 0.327\cos(\omega t - 9.3^\circ)$. $i_{x_2} = 0.112\cos(\omega t + 96.6^\circ)$
5.8 $135.8\angle 7.8^\circ$ kV, $0.138\angle 15.6^\circ$ kA, 0.99 leading 55.66 MW, 89.8%, $373.1\angle{-1.5^\circ}$. 3338 km, 166900 km/s
5.9 $Z' = 128.3\angle 72.6^\circ$, $Y'/2 = 0.00051\angle 89.5^\circ$
5.10 7.12°, $\text{pf}_1 = 0.7$ lagging, $\text{pf}_2 = 0.74$ lagging
5.11 47.56 MVAR lagging
5.12 10.97 kV, 0.98 leading, – 0.27%, 86.2%
5.13 51.16 kV, 38.87 MVAR leading, 40 MW

5.14 238.5 kV, $P_s + j\,Q_s = 53 - j10$, pf = 0.983 leading
5.15 17.39 MVAR leading, 3.54 MW

CHAPTER 6

6.1 For this network tree is shown in Fig. 6.9; A is given by equation (6.20). The matrix is not unique. It depends upon the orientation of the elements.
6.2 $V_2^1 = 0.972 \angle{-8.15°}$
6.3 $V_2^1 = 1.26 \angle{-74.66°}$
6.4 (a)

e \ bus	1	2	3	4
1	1	0	0	0
2	0	1	0	0
3	0	0	1	0
4	0	0	0	1
A = —	—	—	—	—
5	0	0	1	–1
6	–1	0	0	1
7				
8	0	–1	0	1
9	–1	0	1	0

Note: Elements joining each bus to the ground node from the tree

(b)

$$Y = \begin{bmatrix} j\,0.3049 & & & & & & & & \\ & j\,0.1694 & & & & & & & \\ & & j\,0.1948 & & & & & & \\ & & & j\,0.3134 & & & & & \\ & & & & 0.807 - j\,5.65 & & & & \\ & & & & & 0.645 - j\,4.517 & & & \\ & & & & & & 0.968 - j\,6.776 & & \\ & & & & & & & 0.968 - j\,6.776 & \\ & & & & & & & & 0.88 - j\,6.16 \end{bmatrix}$$

(c)

$$\begin{bmatrix} 2.493 - j\,17.148 & | - 0.968 + j\,6.776 | & - 0.880 + j\,6.610 & | - 0.645 + j\,4.517 | \\ 0.968 + j\,6.776 & |1.936 - j\,13.3831 & 0 & | - 0.968 + j\,6.776 \\ -0.880 + j\,6.160 & 0 & 1.687 - j\,11.615 & - 0.807 + j\,5.650 \\ -0.645 + j\,4.517 & | - 0.968 + j\,6.776 | & - 0.807 + j\,5.650 & | - 2.420 - j\,16.630 \end{bmatrix}$$

6.5 $P_{12} = -0.598$ pu; $P_{13} = 0.2$ pu; $= P_{23} = 0.796$ pu
$Q_{12} = Q_{21} = 0.036$ pu; $Q_{13} = Q_{31} = 0.004$ pu;
$Q_{23} = Q_{32} = 0.064$ pu

6.6 (a) $P_{12} = -0.58$ pu; $P_{13} = 0.214$ pu; $P_{23} = 0.792$ pu
$Q_{12} = -0.165$ pu; $Q_{21} = 0.243$ pu; $Q_{13} = 0.204$ pu
$Q_{31} = -0.188$ pu; $Q_{23} = 0.479$ pu; $Q_{32} = -0.321$ pu
(b) $P_{12} = -0.333$ pu; $P_{23} = 0.664$ pu; $P_{31} = -0.333$ pu
$Q_{12} = Q_{21} = 0.011$ pu; $Q_{13} = Q_{31} = 0.011$ pu;
$Q_{23} = Q_{32} = 0.044$ pu

6.7 (a) (i) $\begin{bmatrix} -j10.1015 & j5.0505 & j5 \\ j5.0505 & -j10 & j5 \\ j5 & j5 & -j10 \end{bmatrix}$

(ii) $\begin{bmatrix} -j10 & 5\angle 93^\circ & j5 \\ 5\angle 87^\circ & -j10 & j5 \\ j5 & j5 & -j10 \end{bmatrix}$

(b) (i) $P_{12} = 0.600$ pu; $P_{13} = 0.202$ pu; $P_{23} = 0.794$ pu
$Q_{12} = 0.087$ pu; $Q_{21} = -0.0141$ pu
$Q_{13} = Q_{31} = 0.004$ pu; $Q_{23} = Q_{32} = 0.064$ pu
(ii) $P_{12} = -0.685$ pu; $P_{13} = 0.287$ pu; $P_{23} = 0.711$ pu
$Q_{12} = 0.047$ pu; $Q_{13} = 0.008$ pu; $Q_{23} = 0.051$ pu

6.8 $V_3' = 1.025 - j\,0.095 = 1.029 \angle -53^\circ$ pu

CHAPTER 7

7.1 Rs 22.5/hr

7.2 (a) $P_{G1} = 140.9$ MW, $P_{G2} = 159.1$ MW
(b) Net Saving = Rs 218.16/day

7.3 (i) Generator *A* will share more load than Generator *B*
(ii) Generator *A* and Generator *B* will share load of P_G, and
(iii) Generator *B* will share more load than Generator *A*

7.4 $P_{G1} = 148$ MW. $P_{G2} = 142.9$ MW, $P_{G3} = 109.1$ MW

7.5 $(dC/dP_G) = 0.175\,P_G + 23$

7.6 (a) $P_{G1} = 138.89$ MW. $P_{G2} = 150$ MW. $P_D = 269.6$ MW
(b) $P_{G1} = 310.8$ MW, $P_{G2} = 55.4$ MW
(c) part (a): $C_T =$ Rs 6465.14/hr
(d) part (a): $C_T =$ Rs 7708.15/hr

7.7 $B_{11} = 0.03387$ pu or 0.03387×10^{-2} MW^{-1}
$B_{12} = 9.6073 \times 10^{-5}$ pu or 9.6073×10^{-7} MW^{-1}
$B_{22} = 0.02370$ pu or 0.02370×10^{-2} MW^{-1}

7.8 Economically optimum uc

Time	Load (MW)	Unit Number			
		1	2	3	4
0–4	20	1	1	1	1
4–8	14	1	1	1	0
8–12	6	1	1	0	0
12–16	14	1	1	1	0
16–20	4	1	0	0	0
20–24	10	1	1	0	0

7.9 Total operating cost (both units in service for 24 hrs) = Rs 1,47.960
Total operating cost (unit 1 put off in light-load period) = Rs 1,45,840

7.10 $P_{G1} = 168.495$ MW
$P_{G2} = 46.96$ MW

CHAPTER 8

8.1 Load on G_1 = 123 MW, Load on G_2 = 277 MW, 50.77 Hz, $f_{10} = 51\frac{1}{3}$ Hz, $f_{20} = 51\frac{2}{3}$ Hz

8.2 $\Delta f(t) = -0.029 - 0.04e^{-0.58t} \cos(1.254t + 137.8°)$

8.3 $1/(50K_i)$ sec

8.4 $$\Delta P_{\text{tie, 1}} = \frac{(1/K_{ps1} + K_{i1}b_1 + 1/R_1) - (1/K_{ps2} + K_{i2}b_2 + 1/R_2)}{a_{12}(K_{i2} + 1)(1/K_{ps1} + K_{i1}b_1 + 1/R_1) + (K_{i1} + 1)(1/K_{ps2} + K_{i2}b_2 + 1/R_2)}$$

8.5 $$\Delta P_{\text{tie, 1}}(s) = -\frac{100(0.2s^2 + 0.9s + 1)}{80s^5 + 364s^4 + 458s^3 + 866s^2 + 1050s + 85}$$

System is found to be unstable.

CHAPTER 9

9.1 $i_t = 3.14 \sin(314\,t - 66°) + 2.87e^{-50t}$, $i_{mm} = 5$ A

9.2 (a) 81°
(b) –9°

9.3 (i) $I_A = 2.386$ kA
$I_B = 1.75$ kA
(ii) $I_A = 4.373$ kA
$I_B = 1.75$ kA

9.4 8.87 kA, 4.93 kA

9.5 26.96 kA

9.6 6.97 kA

9.7 (a) 0.9277 kA
(b) 1.312 kA
(c) 1.4843 kA
(d) 1.0205 kA, 53.03 MVA
(e) 0.1959 kA

9.8 8.319 kA

9.9 2.39 pu

9.10 132.1, 47.9
136.9, 45.6

9.11 0.6 pu

9.12 $I^f = -j\,8.006$ pu
$I^f_{13} = -j\,4.004$ pu

CHAPTER 10

10.1 (i) $1.732\angle 210°$
(ii) $2\angle 0°$
(iii) $1.732\angle 150°$
(iv) $1\angle 210°$

10.2 $I_A = j1.16$ pu; $V_{AB} = 1.17\angle 109.5°$ pu;
$V_{BC} = 0.953\angle -65.4°$ pu; $V_{CA} = 0.955\angle -113.1°$ pu.

10.3 $V_{a1} = 197.8\angle -3.3°$ V
$V_{a2} = 20.2\angle 158.1°$ V
$V_{a0} = 21.61\angle 10.63°$ V

10.4 $I_{a1} = 19.23\angle -30°$ A
$I_{a2} = 19.23\angle 150°$ A
$I_{a0} = 0$ A

10.5 $I_{A1} = 27.87\angle -30°$ A
$I_{A2} = 13\angle -44.93°$ A
$I_{A0} = 0$
$I_{ab1} = 16.1$; $I_{ab2} = 7.5\angle -75°$; $I_{ab0} = 7.5\angle 75°$ A

10.6 $I_a = 16.16 + j1.335$ A
$I_b = -9.24 - j10.66$ A
$I_c = -6.93 + j9.32$ A
$|V_{n0}| = |V_{a0}| = 40.75$ V

10.7 1500.2 W

CHAPTER 11

11.1 $-j6.56$ kA,
$|V_{bc}| = 12.83$ kV, $|V_{ab}| = 6.61$ kV, $|V_{ca}| = 6.61$ kV

11.2 (a) $V_{ab} = V_{ac} = 1.8$ pu, $I_b = I_c = -2\sqrt{3}$ pu
(b) $V_{ab} = V_{ac} = 0.816$ pu, $|I_b| = 5.69$ pu

11.3 (i) $-j6.25$ (ii) -4.33 (iii) 6.01 (iv) $-j5$ pu
In order of decreasing magnitude of line currents the faults can be listed as
(a) LG (b) LLG (c) 3-phase (d) LL

11.4 0.1936 ohm, 0.581 ohm, -4.33 pu, $j5$ pu

11.5 (a) 3.51 pu (b) $V_b = 1.19\angle -159.5°$ pu, $V_c = 1.68\angle 129.8°$ pu (c) 0.726 pu

11.6 $I_b = -I_G = -2.887$ pu

11.7 (a) $I_Y = -5.79 + j5.01$ kA, $I_B = 5.79 + j5.01$ kA, $I_G = j10.02$ kA
(b) $I_B = -I_Y = -6.111$ kA, $I_G = 0$

11.8 $I_{ag} = 0$ $\quad I_{am} = -j3.51$ pu
$I_{bg} = -j2.08$ pu $\quad I_{bm} = -j1.2$ pu
$I_{cg} = j2.08$ pu $\quad I_{cm} = -j1.2$ pu

11.9 5,266 A

11.10 $j2.0$ pu

11.11 $I^f = -j6.732$ pu, I_a (A) $= -j4.779$ pu,
I_b (A) $= -j0.255$ pu, I_c (A) $= -j0.255$ pu

11.12 0.42 pu, $-j9.256$ pu

11.13 $-j11.152$ pu, $-j2.478$ pu, $-j1.239$ pu

11.14 4.737 pu, 1 pu

11.15 $I_2 f = -j12.547$ pu, $I_{12} f$ (b) $= -j0.0962$ pu

CHAPTER 12

12.1 4.19 MJ/MVA, 0.0547 MJ-s/elect deg

12.2 4.315 MJ/MVA

12.3 40.4 MJ/MVA

12.4 140.1 MW, 130.63 MW, 175.67 MW

12.5 72.54 MW

12.6 $\delta_3 = 58°$

12.7 127.3 MW

12.8 53°. We need to know the inertia constant M to determine t_c.

12.9 The system is unstable

12.10 70.54°, 0.1725 s

12.11 The system is unstable

12.12 63.36°

12.13 The system is stable

12.14 The system is stable

12.15 The system is unstable for both three pole and single pole switching

CHAPTER 13

13.1 (i) $V_j = -72.3$ kV v_t, $= 37.77$ kV
$j_r = 0.626$ kA
(ii) $V_r = 72.3$ kV $v_t = 182.3$ kV
$I_r = -3.03$ kV

13.2 $V_2 = V_3 = 4.17$ kV
$j_2 = 8.34$ A, 83.4 A
13.3 Energy transmitted = 88.2 J
$V_r = -199$ kV
13.4 (i) $\alpha_R = 0.5$ (ii) $\alpha_s = -1$
$V_R = 100$ V, $I_s = 1.33$ A
13.5 $\alpha_R = 0$
$V_R = 100$ V, $I_s = 4$ A
13.6 $\alpha_R = 0.5$, $\alpha_s = 0.286$
$V_R = 62.5$ V, $I_s = 0.83$ A
13.7 Junction voltage at 4 $T = 0.848$

CHAPTER 14

14.1 $E_{\text{line - line}} = 95.54$ kV
$X_{cr} = 9.7\ \Omega$
14.2 162.32 kV, 12.63°

CHAPTER 17

17.1 $V_1^1 = \angle 0°$, $V_2^1 = 1.04223\ \angle 0.4297°$, $V_3^1 = 0.99824\ \angle -2.1864°$;
Final values: $V_1 = 1.04\ \angle 0°$, $V_2 = 1.080215\ \angle -1.356°$, $V_3 = 1.03831\ \angle -3.736°$
17.3 $\delta_2 = -0.0316$ rad, $P = 31.64$ MW

CHAPTER 20

20.1 (a) By selecting the induction machine's rating as a base,

$$S_b = 50 \text{ kVA}$$

$$V_b = 440 \text{ V}$$

The base impedance of system is

$$Z_b = \frac{V_b^2}{S_b} = 3.872$$

The pu value of transformer resistance is

$$R_{tran,pu} = \frac{R_{tran}}{Z_b} = \frac{0.02}{3.872} = 0.005$$

The pu value of transformer reactance is

$$X_{tran,pu} = \frac{X_{tran}}{Z_b} = \frac{0.16}{3.872} = 0.04$$

The pu value of stator resistance is

$$R_{s,pu} = \frac{0.2}{3.872} = 0.052$$

The pu value of stator reactance is

$$X_{s,pu} = \frac{1.6}{3.872} = 0.413$$

The pu value of rotor resistance referred to primary is $\frac{0.8}{3.872} = 0.207$

(b) Synchronous speed is

$$N_s = \frac{120f}{P} = 900 \text{ rpm}$$

$$\text{slip} = s = \frac{900-1200}{900} = -0.333$$

Rotor voltage frequency $= f_r = sf_s = 0.333 \times 60 = 20$ Hz

Supply voltage= 440 V = 1 pu

Base current is $I_b = \frac{VA_b}{\sqrt{3}V_b} = \frac{50 \times 10^3}{\sqrt{3} \times 440} = 65.61$ A

$$\therefore Z_{pu} = \sqrt{\left(R_{s,pu} + R_{tran,pu} + \frac{R'_{r,pu}}{s}\right)^2 + \left(X_{s,pu} + X_{tran,pu} + X'_{r,pu}\right)^2} = 0.667$$

The power factor angle is

$$\tan^{-1}\left(\frac{X_{s,pu} + X_{tran,pu} + X'_{r,pu}}{R_{s,pu} + R_{tran,pu} + \frac{R'_{r,pu}}{s}}\right) = 98.54°$$

Hence,

$Z_{pu} = 0.667\angle 98.54°$

The pu stator current in the motor convention is

$$I_{pu} = \frac{V_b}{Z_{pu}} = 1.499\angle -98.54°$$

The actual value of current in the motor convention is

$I_m = I_b \times I_{pu} = 98.35\angle -98.54°$ A

Because this angle is more than 90 degree, the power flow is from the induction generator to the local power grid.

The current in generator convention is

$I_G = 98.35\angle 180 - 98.54° = 98.35\angle 81.46°$ A

$P_{grid} = \sqrt{3}V_{grid}I_G\cos(\theta) = 11130$ W

$P_{loss} = 3I_G^2 R_{tran} = 580$ W

$\therefore P = P_{grid} + P_{loss} = 11710$ W

$Q_{grid} = \sqrt{3}V_{grid}I_G\sin\theta = 74121$ W

$Q_{loss} = 3I_G^2 X_{tran} = 4355$ W

$\therefore Q = Q_{grid} - Q_{loss} = 69766$ W

20.2 (a)

$$KVA_b = 500, V_b = 440 \text{ V}$$

For transformer, $X_{old} = 0.06$ pu

$$X_{new} = 0.06 \times \frac{500}{300} = 0.1 \text{ pu}$$

For IM,

$$Z = 0.2 + j1.6\,\Omega$$

$$Z_{pu} = (0.2 + j1.6) \times \frac{0.5}{0.440^2} = 0.516 + j4.13 \text{ pu}$$

(b) Speed of IG = 1000 rpm = N_r

$$N_s = \frac{120 \times 60}{8} = 900 \text{ rpm}$$

$$s = \frac{900 - 1000}{900} = -\frac{1}{9}$$

$$\therefore f_r = sf = \frac{60}{9} = 6.67 \text{ Hz}$$

20.3 Impedance, Z is given as:

$$Z = \frac{j\omega L \times \dfrac{1}{j\omega C}}{j\omega L + \dfrac{1}{j\omega C}} = \frac{\dfrac{L}{C}}{j\left(\omega L - \dfrac{1}{\omega C}\right)}$$

At parallel resonance,

$$\omega L = \frac{1}{\omega C}$$

$$Z \to \infty$$

$$f = \frac{1}{2\pi\sqrt{LC}}$$

$$\therefore C = \frac{1}{(2\pi \times 100 \times 10^3)^2 \times 0.25 \times 10^{-3}} = 10 \text{ nF}$$

20.4 (a) Power dissipated in the current sensing resistor is

$$P_R = I^2 R = 2 \text{ W}$$

Power consumed by the other components is

$$P_{remaining} = 3 - 2 = 1 \text{ W}$$

(b) $IR = 0.02$ V

(c) Gain of the PGA $= \frac{5}{0.02} = 250$

20.5 Current range= 0 to 5 A (to the ADC)

Then, ADC resolution $= \frac{5}{2^{16}} = 76\ \mu\text{A}$

Which is the maximum quantization error of the current.

50 A through the CT primary, so ADC reads $50 \times \frac{5}{100} = 2.5$ A

Voltage range= 0 to 10 V (to the ADC)

Then, ADC resolution = $\frac{10}{2^{16}} = 152\ \mu\text{V}$

Which is the maximum quantization error of the voltage

Voltage divider reads =400 V, so ADC reads $400 \times \frac{10}{415} = 9.64$ V

$\therefore$ Apparent power = $(V + \Delta V)(I + \Delta I) = VI + V\Delta I + I\Delta V + \Delta V \Delta I \cong VI + V\Delta I + I\Delta V$

Above equation gives the maximum possible error in the apparent power reading due to the quantization = $V\Delta I + I\Delta V = 1.11$ mVA

20.6

$$\vec{I} = \frac{P - j}{\overrightarrow{V_R}^*} \quad (1)$$

$$\frac{\overrightarrow{V_s} - \overrightarrow{V_R}}{R + jX} + I_C = I$$

$$V_R = V_s - (I - I_c)(R + jX) \quad (2)$$

From equation 1 and 2, in order to remove the oscillations in the voltage at the connection point, the VSC-ES must inject a time-varying component of the power. The current corresponding to the time varying component of the power = $\vec{I}$

$$\vec{I} = \frac{4 \times 10^6 \times \sin(10t)}{\frac{33 \times 10^3}{\sqrt{3}}} = 210 \sin(10t) \text{ A}$$

If the VSC-ES injects same amount of time-varying current, then the voltage at the connection point will be constant.

So,

$\vec{I} = 210 \sin(10t)$ A

CHAPTER 21

21.1 25/69, 28/69, 16/69

21.2 0.114

21.3 0.355

21.4 (i) $R(50) = 0.9689$], (ii) $t = 111.54$ hours, (iii) 451.65 hours, (iv) $P = 0.9439$

21.5 $n = 5$, failure rate = 3.94×10^{-4}

21.6 11 groups

21.7 $R(t) = e^{-(t/184.7)1.5}$, MTTF = 1664.5 cycles

21.8 128 years, 112.6 years, 117.9 years

21.9 (i) 0.6703, (ii) 0.6703

21.10 0.7125

21.11 (i) $\mu = 10$, $\sigma = 2.5$, MTTF = 10 days, (ii) $T = 4.2$ days, (iii) $R = 0.9672$

21.12 (i) 0.085719 (d/yr), (ii) 0.120551 (d/yr), (iii) 0.151276 (d/yr), (iv) 0.830924 (d/yr), (v) 2.057559 (d/yr), (vi) 3.595240 (d/yr)

Answers to MCQs

CHAPTER 1

1.1 (b)	**1.2** (c)	**1.3** (c)	**1.4** (b)	**1.5** (d)
1.6 (c)	**1.7** (a)	**1.8** (c)	**1.9** (b)	**1.10** (d)
1.11 (b)	**1.12** (a)	**1.13** (a)	**1.14** (d)	**1.15** (d)
1.16 (b)	**1.17** (a)	**1.18** (c)	**1.19** (d)	**1.20** (b)
1.21 (c)	**1.22** (c)	**1.23** (d)	**1.24** (d)	**1.25** (d)
1.26 (a)	**1.27** (c)	**1.28** (b)	**1.29** (a)	**1.30** (d)

CHAPTER 2

2.1 (a)	**2.2** (c)	**2.3** (c)	**2.4** (d)	**2.5** (c)
2.6 (d)	**2.7** (c)	**2.8** (d)	**2.9** (d)	**2.10** (b)
2.11 (d)	**2.12** (c)	**2.13** (a)	**2.14** (b)	**2.15** (c)
2.16 (a)	**2.17** (b)	**2.18** (a)	**2.19** (a)	**2.20** (b)
2.21 (b)	**2.22** (a)	**2.23** (a)	**2.24** (c)	**2.25** (a)
2.26 (a)	**2.27** (b)	**2.28** (d)	**2.29** (c)	**2.30** (c)
2.31 (c)	**2.32** (a)	**2.33** (b)	**2.34** (c)	**2.35** (d)

CHAPTER 3

3.1 (a)	**3.2** (b)	**3.3** (c)	**3.4** (a)	**3.5** (b)
3.6 (a)	**3.7** (d)	**3.8** (c)	**3.9** (b)	**3.10** (c)
3.11 (a)	**3.12** (c)	**3.13** (b)	**3.14** (d)	**3.15** (b)
3.16 (b)	**3.17** (b)	**3.18** (c)	**3.19** (a)	**3.20** (a)
3.21 (d)	**3.22** (b)	**3.23** (d)	**3.24** (a)	**3.25** (b)

CHAPTER 4

4.1 (b)	**4.2** (b)	**4.3** (c)	**4.4** (d)	**4.5** (c)
4.6 (c)	**4.7** (b)	**4.8** (c)	**4.9** (b)	**4.10** (b)
4.11 (b)	**4.12** (c)	**4.13** (a)	**4.14** (a)	**4.15** (c)
4.16 (a)	**4.17** (b)	**4.18** (b)	**4.19** (a)	**4.20** (b)
4.21 (d)	**4.22** (a)	**4.23** (b)	**4.24** (d)	**4.25** (c)
4.26 (c)	**4.27** (a)	**4.28** (c)	**4.29** (d)	**4.30** (c)
4.31 (c)	**4.32** (a)	**4.33** (b)	**4.34** (d)	**4.35** (a)
4.36 (c)	**4.37** (c)	**4.38** (d)	**4.39** (d)	**4.40** (d)

CHAPTER 5

5.1 (a)	**5.2** (b)	**5.3** (a)	**5.4** (d)	**5.5** (b)
5.6 (c)	**5.7** (d)	**5.8** (b)	**5.9** (a)	**5.10** (d)
5.11 (c)	**5.12** (d)	**5.13** (c)	**5.14** (d)	**5.15** (d)
5.16 (b)	**5.17** (b)	**5.18** (d)	**5.19** (d)	**5.20** (b)
5.21 (c)	**5.22** (d)	**5.23** (a)	**5.24** (c)	**5.25** (b)
5.26 (c)	**5.27** (d)	**5.28** (a)	**5.29** (b)	**5.30** (a)
5.31 (a)	**5.32** (d)	**5.33** (d)	**5.34** (a)	**5.35** (b)
5.36 (d)	**5.37** (b)	**5.38** (b)	**5.39** (d)	**5.40** (d)

CHAPTER 6

6.1 (b)	**6.2** (b)	**6.3** (a)	**6.4** (a)	**6.5** (c)
6.6 (b)	**6.7** (b)	**6.8** (b)	**6.9** (c)	**6.10** (a)
6.11 (d)	**6.12** (d)	**6.13** (d)	**6.14** (a)	**6.15** (b)
6.16 (d)	**6.17** (b)	**6.18** (b)	**6.19** (d)	**6.20** (d)
6.21 (a)	**6.22** (d)	**6.23** (c)	**6.24** (b)	**6.25** (c)

CHAPTER 7

7.1 (b)	**7.2** (c)	**7.3** (a)	**7.4** (d)	**7.5** (a)
7.6 (d)	**7.7** (c)	**7.8** (b)	**7.9** (a)	**7.10** (b)
7.11 (d)	**7.12** (c)	**7.13** (d)	**7.14** (d)	**7.15** (b)
7.16 (c)	**7.17** (b)	**7.18** (a)	**7.19** (c)	**7.20** (c)

CHAPTER 8

8.1 (a)	**8.2** (d)	**8.3** (a)	**8.4** (b)	**8.5** (c)
8.6 (a)	**8.7** (a)	**8.8** (a)	**8.9** (a)	**8.10** (b)
8.11 (d)	**8.12** (c)	**8.13** (d)	**8.14** (c)	**8.15** (d)
8.16 (c)	**8.17** (b)	**8.18** (c)	**8.19** (d)	**8.20** (a)
8.21 (b)	**8.22** (d)	**8.23** (d)	**8.24** (b)	**8.25** (c)
8.26 (b)	**8.27** (d)	**8.28** (c)	**8.29** (d)	**8.30** (d)

CHAPTER 9

9.1 (a)	**9.2** (a)	**9.3** (b)	**9.4** (d)	**9.5** (c)
9.6 (d)	**9.7** (b)	**9.8** (b)	**9.9** (b)	**9.10** (c)
9.11 (d)	**9.12** (c)	**9.13** (a)	**9.14** (a)	**9.15** (a)
9.16 (c)	**9.17** (d)	**9.18** (b)	**9.19** (d)	**9.20** (c)
9.21 (c)	**9.22** (b)	**9.23** (d)	**9.24** (c)	**9.25** (c)
9.26 (a)	**9.27** (d)	**9.28** (d)	**9.29** (c)	**9.30** (b)

CHAPTER 10

10.1 (c)	**10.2** (b)	**10.3** (d)	**10.4** (a)	**10.5** (a)
10.6 (d)	**10.7** (c)	**10.8** (b)	**10.9** (c)	**10.10** (c)
10.11 (c)	**10.12** (d)	**10.13** (b)	**10.14** (c)	**10.15** (c)
10.16 (c)	**10.17** (b)	**10.18** (a)	**10.19** (a)	**10.20** (d)
10.21 (a)	**10.22** (c)	**10.23** (b)	**10.24** (d)	**10.25** (d)
10.26 (c)	**10.27** (d)	**10.28** (b)	**10.29** (b)	**10.30** (a)

CHAPTER 11

11.1 (a)	**11.2** (a)	**11.3** (b)	**11.4** (d)	**11.5** (a)
11.6 (b)	**11.7** (b)	**11.8** (c)	**11.9** (b)	**11.10** (c)
11.11 (d)	**11.12** (c)	**11.13** (a)	**11.14** (c)	**11.15** (b)
11.16 (b)	**11.17** (d)	**11.18** (b)	**11.19** (d)	**11.20** (a)

CHAPTER 12

12.1 (a)	**12.2** (b)	**12.3** (b)	**12.4** (c)	**12.5** (c)
12.6 (d)	**12.7** (c)	**12.8** (b)	**12.9** (c)	**12.10** (a)
12.11 (c)	**12.12** (a)	**12.13** (c)	**12.14** (c)	**12.15** (a)
12.16 (a)	**12.17** (b)	**12.18** (d)	**12.19** (a)	**12.20** (b)
12.21 (a)	**12.22** (d)	**12.23** (d)	**12.24** (b)	**12.25** (b)

CHAPTER 13

13.1 (a)	**13.2** (b)	**13.3** (a)	**13.4** (a)	**13.5** (c)
13.6 (d)	**13.7** (b)	**13.8** (b)	**13.9** (d)	**13.10** (d)
13.11 (d)	**13.12** (d)	**13.13** (a)	**13.14** (c)	**13.15** (b)
13.16 (c)	**13.17** (a)	**13.18** (c)	**13.19** (c)	**13.20** (b)
13.21 (c)	**13.22** (b)	**13.23** (d)	**13.24** (c)	**13.25** (b)
13.26 (c)	**13.27** (b)	**13.28** (c)	**13.29** (d)	**13.30** (c)

CHAPTER 14

14.1 (b)	**14.2** (d)	**14.3** (a)	**14.4** (b)	**14.5** (b)
14.6 (b)	**14.7** (a)	**14.8** (c)	**14.9** (a)	**14.10** (a)
14.11 (d)	**14.12** (b)	**14.13** (c)	**14.14** (d)	**14.15** (c)
14.16 (b)	**14.17** (c)	**14.18** (c)	**14.19** (b)	**14.20** (b)

CHAPTER 15

15.1 (a)	**15.2** (d)	**15.3** (d)	**15.4** (a)	**15.5** (a)
15.6 (b)	**15.7** (d)	**15.8** (d)	**15.9** (d)	**15.10** (c)
15.11 (c)	**15.12** (b)	**15.13** (d)	**15.14** (d)	**15.15** (a)
15.16 (a)	**15.17** (b)	**15.18** (b)	**15.19** (a)	**15.20** (c)
15.21 (b)	**15.22** (c)	**15.23** (b)	**15.24** (a)	**15.25** (b)
15.26 (b)	**15.27** (c)	**15.28** (b)	**15.29** (a)	**15.30** (a)

CHAPTER 16

16.1 (b)	**16.2** (b)	**16.3** (a)	**16.4** (a)	**16.5** (c)
16.6 (a)	**16.7** (d)	**16.8** (c)	**16.9** (c)	**16.10** (a)
16.11 (a)	**16.12** (c)	**16.13** (b)	**16.14** (d)	**16.15** (d)

CHAPTER 17

17.1 (b)	**17.2** (c)	**17.3** (a)	**17.4** (b)	**17.5** (a)
17.6 (b)	**17.7** (d)	**17.8** (d)	**17.9** (d)	**17.10** (d)
17.11 (a)	**17.12** (c)	**17.13** (c)	**17.14** (c)	**17.15** (b)
17.16 (a)	**17.17** (a)	**17.18** (a)	**17.19** (b)	**17.20** (a)
17.21 (a)	**17.22** (c)	**17.23** (a)	**17.24** (c)	**17.25** (a)

CHAPTER 18

18.1 (c)	**18.2** (c)	**18.3** (c)	**18.4** (a)	**18.5** (b)
18.6 (d)	**18.7** (c)	**18.8** (a)	**18.9** (d)	**18.10** (c)
18.11 (d)	**18.12** (a)	**18.13** (d)	**18.14** (c)	**18.15** (c)
18.16 (c)	**18.17** (b)	**18.18** (d)	**18.19** (c)	**18.20** (d)
18.21 (a)	**18.22** (c)	**18.23** (a)	**18.24** (a)	**18.25** (a)

CHAPTER 19

19.1 (d)	**19.2** (e)	**19.3** (d)	**19.4** (a)	**19.5** (d)
19.6 (c)	**19.7** (d)	**19.8** (c)	**19.9** (e)	**19.10** (d)
19.11 (a)	**19.12** (d)	**19.13** (a)	**19.14** (a)	**19.15** (a)
19.16 (a)	**19.17** (b)	**19.18** (a)	**19.19** (b)	**19.20** (a)
19.21 (c)	**19.22** (b)	**19.23** (c)	**19.24** (c)	

CHAPTER 20

20.1 (b)	**20.2** (b)	**20.3** (d)	**20.4** (a)	**20.5** (a)
20.6 (d)	**20.7** (d)	**20.8** (d)	**20.9** (b)	**20.10** (c)
20.11 (b)	**20.12** (b)	**20.13** (d)	**20.14** (b)	**20.15** (b)
20.16 (c)	**20.17** (b)	**20.18** (b)	**20.19** (d)	**20.20** (c)
20.21 (d)	**20.22** (c)	**20.23** (a)	**20.24** (d)	**20.25** (b)
20.26 (c)	**20.27** (a)	**20.28** (d)	**20.29** (c)	**20.30** (b)

CHAPTER 21

21.1 (c)	**21.2** (b)	**21.3** (a)	**21.4** (b)	**21.5** (c)
21.6 (b)	**21.7** (c)	**21.8** (d)	**21.9** (b)	**21.10** (c)
21.11 (a)	**21.12** (d)	**21.13** (b)	**21.14** (b)	**21.15** (a)
21.16 (b)	**21.17** (c)	**21.18** (c)	**21.19** (d)	**21.20** (d)

Index

A

B

D

E

H

I

J

K

L

M

N

O

P

Q

R

S

T

U

V

W

Y

Z